1981 ARTIST'S MARKET®

WHERE TO SELL YOUR COMMERCIAL ART

Edited by Lynne Lapin

Writer's Digest Books

International Standard Serial Number 0161-0546
International Standard Book Number 0-89879-029-8

Preface

Aside from walking the pavement and knocking on doors, the commercial artist has few avenues for finding buyers for his/her work. That's why we publish *Artist's Market* for the commercial art world. It is our way of bringing together the people who buy and commission artwork with the artists who create it.

The main thrust of this publication is to show where to market your work. We realize that knowing where the outlets lie isn't enough to make your endeavors professional and productive, so we've also included articles on *how* to sell.

The listings themselves go far beyond the usual directory-like compilation of addresses and phone numbers of agencies, publications and businesses. *Artist's Market* gets to the heart of what is needed to sell to art outlets—how and whom to contact, what they pay, what their terms are and so forth. To produce a sourcebook of serious buyers, we survey thousands of prospective art buyers each year. We ask questions about their marketing methods and even the type of material they like to keep on artists in their files.

This book is a tool for all commercial artists. It is geared to the cartoonist and illustrator as well as to the graphic designer and textile artist.

This is not a book you will leaf through then shelve. It is a valuable reference tool to be consulted as you develop additional ideas, find a need for more outlets, or simply want to know what the market is demanding and paying. It is an avenue for selling your work to the many commercial art markets in the US and Canada.

—Lynne Lapin

Contents

THE Profession

Using Your Artist's Market

Making enough sales to freelance successfully is a tough road to travel. But many artists dream of making the journey. How can you compete?

One of the surest paths to success is to present yourself as a professional. Close attention to the directions given in the market listings and the articles will ensure a polished image.

To best use your *Artist's Market*, start by reading the articles in the front of the book. These include information on how to submit your work, how to price your work, and how to prepare your portfolio. Freelancing is a big business and the more you know about it, the more successful you'll be.

Then move on to the table of contents to see which categories of markets best suit your skills and needs. While all the markets listed are open to freelance artists, most want freelancers who are particularly experienced in a certain art skill.

There are two basic ways to contact the markets listed in *Artist's Market*:

1. Send them actual work they could use. If the market states in its listing that it is willing to receive unsolicited work and you feel that you know the market well enough to perform such work, you can send in material for review. If the market accepts, you get paid; if not, you don't.

2. You show your portfolio of past work for review—either by mail or in person.

Except for the buyers in the periodicals section of *Artist's Market*, the latter method is by far the most preferred.

Each listing states the way it wants to be contacted by freelance artists. You will waste your time and the buyer's time if material is not submitted in the proper way.

Don't treat any of the information in the listings lightly; all of it is there for a reason. Look for the subtle clues.

For example, consider that new companies may not yet have established all their contacts—thus they're usually more open to freelance work. On the other hand, older firms may be more stable, well-established, and have plenty of contacts already. In the magazine section, the format of the publication conveys a sense of the type of publication you'll be dealing with—a Sunday School bulletin or a "slick." The frequency of the publication offers a clue to the deadlines they must keep.

Keep in mind that all price figures are estimates. A market that reports they pay \$5-10 per illustration may be eager to pay \$35 for one that especially catches their eye. Many buyers are willing to negotiate price.

If you run across an unfamiliar term, check the glossary. (For example, SASE means self-addressed stamped envelope—the lack of one with a submission is a sure sign of an amateur.)

Study the market thoroughly before submitting. The more you're familiar with a buyer, the better your chances of success. Send for sample copies (for publications) or catalogs (for other sections) when the listing indicates their availability.

Information in the market listings is as current as possible, but art directors come and go, companies and publications move, and art needs change between the publication of *Artist's Market* and when you buy it. Drop us a note if you have any new information about a market; we research, review and update all listings annually.

When looking for a specific market, check the index. A market might not be listed for one of these reasons:

1. It doesn't need freelance art.
2. It has gone out of business.
3. It doesn't pay for art.
4. It has failed to verify or update its listing that appeared in the last edition.
5. It requests to not be listed.
6. We have received complaints about it and it hasn't answered *Artist's Market* inquiries satisfactorily.

In summary, the key to using your *Artist's Market* is to use it professionally. Freelancing can be a rewarding adventure if approached with the right tools, the right attitude, and the right information. *Artist's Market* provides the information. The rest is up to you.

State Abbreviations

Each listing in this book uses the following US Postal Service's two letter state abbreviations in the address line.

AK	Alaska	LA	Louisiana	OK	Oklahoma
AL	Alabama	MA	Massachusetts	OR	Oregon
AR	Arkansas	MD	Maryland	PA	Pennsylvania
AZ	Arizona	ME	Maine	PR	Puerto Rico
CA	California	MI	Michigan	RI	Rhode Island
CO	Colorado	MN	Minnesota	SC	South Carolina
CT	Connecticut	MO	Missouri	SD	South Dakota
DC	District of Columbia	MS	Mississippi	TN	Tennessee
DE	Delaware	MT	Montana	TX	Texas
FL	Florida	NC	North Carolina	UT	Utah
GA	Georgia	ND	North Dakota	VA	Virginia
HI	Hawaii	NE	Nebraska	VI	Virgin Islands
IA	Iowa	NH	New Hampshire	VT	Vermont
ID	Idaho	NJ	New Jersey	WA	Washington
IL	Illinois	NM	New Mexico	WI	Wisconsin
IN	Indiana	NV	Nevada	WV	West Virginia
KS	Kansas	NY	New York	WY	Wyoming
KY	Kentucky	OH	Ohio		

Art Market Today

BY LYNNE LAPIN

There's good news and bad news for today's artist. The bad news is that a generally slow economy has resulted in fewer artists on company payrolls. The good news, however, is this same phenomenon has made the market for freelance artists better today than ever. Being caught up in this greater supply of artists than demand for them, you must follow this simple rule: Don't allow yourself to use your talent copying the work of others.

There are few art directors who specify they work only with experienced artists. Quite to the contrary, they want to see new styles. The right mixture of individuality and talent is the artist's best opportunity to get a foot in the door. Experiment with styles until you fine-tune one that is distinctively yours and is commercially acceptable.

When Sam Viviano, a successful New York City illustrator went to New York, fresh from a Midwest school, he felt capable of doing a little of everything.

Viviano told art directors he could do it all. Since no art director was looking for "all," Viviano developed a style for caricature art and now has work in major markets. "You need to find what you do best, like best and what will sell best, and reach a compromise," Viviano said. "That should be your specialty."

Choose your specialty, based on your own best judgment of your strengths and shortcomings. Avoid confusing what you do best with what you like doing the most. Take every opportunity to show your work to other artists in different art disciplines to get their evaluations of your weak and strong points.

While it's sometimes easy to assess your talents, a tougher challenge is to determine what kind of artwork sells best—and will continue to sell well in the future.

For example, Nathan Gluck, director of the American Institute of Graphic Arts (AIGA), reviews thousands of artistic works annually for that organization's shows. Books, communication graphics, posters, packaging, covers and illustrations are all submitted from across the country.

His observation is that there is a lull in the graphic arts area, with nothing sensational happening. "There is good work, but nothing sensational."

The only clear trend he has noticed is that a large number of artists are working in a nostalgic vein.

So, a key is to develop your own unique style—remembering not to make your work so outrageous that no one will find a use for it. Next, study the markets in several steps: 1) what markets are there, 2) what new markets are developing, 3) what do the various markets pay, 4) what is the future of the different markets?

"How to Become a Successful Professional" gives sound advice on determining what markets are available, and finding those that are best for you.

A good source for finding out more about each of the various types of markets (advertising, book publishing, businesses, magazines, etc.) is to read. First, start with this book and find out what payment rates are quoted. You should try to read a few of the trade publications listed at the end of each section introduction in this book.

When reading trade publications, pay particular attention to developments and try to predict how these changes will affect the freelance artist. For example, if you read that a shortage of paper is causing magazines to cut back on pages, you might predict there will be less of a need for artwork in this field. Or, if you learn that more and more video is being purchased for use as an advertising tool, you may decide it is time to move from print media to more animation work.

How to Become a Successful Professional

BY CAROLE HOLMAN

Becoming a successful freelancer in a highly competitive world is "the goal" of most artists. Too often it is only a dream. But, by following some basic rules, you can come closer to that goal.

First of all, a quick personal inventory is needed. Forcing yourself to answer questions about your limitations will let you know who you are and where you want to go. What are you trying to accomplish? What do you do well? What don't you do well? What are your career goals? To make a great deal of money? To gain national and international recognition in your field? Do your goals include travel? How important is artistic freedom to you?

What kind of circumstances do you work best in?

- How do you function under pressure?
- Do you meet deadlines?
- Do you prefer full-time jobs or freelance jobs?
- Do you like short projects or long projects?
- Do you enjoy a team approach to creative problem-solving or do you work best alone?
- Do you relate well to non-creative business people? Can you transfer their thoughts into images? *Or*, do you work best taking instructions from an Art Director?
- Can you take projects start-to-finish including production?

Now you have a better idea of who you are. The next step is determining where your particular work sells best. How do you do this? Begin by getting a broad range of advice from those who are familiar with the marketplace. Talk to art professors. Chat with art directors. Ask other artists, too. In areas where art directors' and illustrators' clubs are active, members share information with one another. Attend design and illustration workshops. Ask questions about which clients pay on a timely basis and which companies are currently hiring freelancers. Talk to high school or college placement directors. Employment agencies that specialize in your field may be helpful. Ask if they are free, or do they charge you for their services.

Start to identify possible clients for your work. First, list as many general sources as possible. To help begin your list, consider the following areas:

- Advertising agencies
- Direct mail advertising agencies
- Retail advertising agencies
- Hardbound book publishers
- Paperback book publishers
- Magazine publishers
- Newspapers
- Public relations firms
- Design studios
- Retail stores
- Greeting card companies
- Motion picture studios
- Animation studios
- Educational materials companies
- Printers
- Newsletter publishers
- Sign companies
- Clip art companies
- Hospitals
- Universities
- Corporations
- Architectural firms

Carole Holman *is President of Graphic Arts Agency (a nationwide employment and search firm specializing in design, advertising and marketing). She has seen over 20,000 portfolios, lectures and conducts workshops on portfolio and resume preparation, successful interviewing techniques, salesmanship, and how to find the "perfect" job.*

- Toy companies
- Cosmetic companies
- Record companies
- Display firms
- Sales promotion companies
- Paper products companies

Read trade publications for leads. Note which large accounts are changing agencies or design firms. The new agency may need additional freelancers. Check classified ads in other city newspapers. Think about where your work has sold in the past.

Look through the *Yellow Pages* for ideas. It's also important to read non-trade publications. Read business newspapers and magazines. Find out what "big business" is currently involved with and where.

1981 Artist's Market lists over 2,500 places to sell your work. It will save you hundreds of hours of research because it also tells you what kinds of companies are buying what kinds of work, their pay scale, and even preferred methods of submitting your work to each client.

At this point, you are ready to plan a marketing program.

After compiling a general list, select 10 areas you believe would be most suitable for you. Within those 10 areas, write down the names, addresses and phone numbers of the best prospects in each area. (10-30 names should be sufficient.) We'll call this list your "A" prospect list. It is a list of potential clients that *best* fit your needs. Choose 10-30 more clients, put them on a "B" prospect list. This is your second-choice client list. You may be surprised. Sometimes a second choice will, upon further investigation, become a first choice. Organize your leads using a card system. Complete a 3x5 index card with information on each company. Include name, address, phone number, name of person to contact, how that company wants to be contacted, materials necessary for presentation, and any other information you've gathered regarding the client. Then make notes. Keep track of the date you initially made contact, the name of the person you spoke with, and the outcome of the telephone call.

The telephone can be your quickest marketing aid. Be brief and succinct in your calling. Be pleasant. State your name and why you're calling. You might follow up your call with a brief letter, including a copy of your resume. Don't send form letters. Type each letter separately, being sure you have spelled the addressee and company name correctly.

Every business person needs to have a resume to show that he or she has worked successfully, either on a freelance or permanent basis. A resume lends credibility to your portfolio and increases your stature as a business person (particularly when it comes time to negotiate for freelance fees or for a salary).

A resume should be kept to one page if possible—two if absolutely necessary. It should reflect your ability and personality, be easy to read, concise and informative. Most important, it should be designed to catch the employer's attention. Many employers receive up to 200 resumes and self-promotional mailers each week and most are tossed. So catch the reader's attention through your approach, background, education and special skills.

Here are some basic guidelines for writing your resume:

1. Always type your resume using a clear, easy-to-read typeface.
2. Use lots of white space, making your resume easy on the eyes.
3. Do not abbreviate or use slang.
4. Select high-quality paper stock.
5. Place your name, mailing address, telephone number and message telephone number at the top of the resume.
6. State your job objective in specific terms. For example, "Freelance Book Designer."
7. If you are available for both full-time and freelance work, state that clearly.
8. Have your resume proofread by others for content and possible errors.
9. Make high-quality copies of your resume or have them printed by a low-cost "instant print" shop.
10. List your highest level of educational achievement first. Include the name of your school, its location, date of graduation, and your degree and major, plus any courses you may have taken that might be relevant to the position you want.

11. Mention your grades only if they were outstanding, especially if you received honors or scholarships. This is also the place for the recent graduate to mention special abilities—foreign languages, leadership positions, unique art training, etc.
12. If you are a veteran, include you military status, rank, special training, or commendations.
13. The work experience section of your resume starts with your *most recent* position. It should include the names and locations of your previous employers, dates of employment, your job titles, and specific details of your job responsibilities. Don't be shy about listing your accomplishments. Also, briefly describe freelance assignments you may have had, the names of your clients, and scope of the assignment. Emphasize nationally recognized clients.
14. Under Outside Activities and Interests list anything that might be considered an asset to a prospective employer. Omit anything political or ideological.
15. Recent graduates should include all jobs, even if they weren't in the creative field.
16. If your resume still looks bare, mention any art-related experiences you've had—redesigning the school newspaper, illustrating theater posters for the school play, etc. Also mention your strengths that apply to the business world, such as being well-organized.

A well written resume may fail if it's not accompanied by a well written cover letter. Make your letter to-the-point and direct it specifically to the market you are writing to if you expect to get an interview.

Before proceeding to the personal interview, review your portfolio. Ideally, it should:

- Include 14-20 samples of original, current, imaginative, and representative work.
- Show only your best work.
- Be mounted on dark grey (neutral) boards. (I always suggest dark grey because
- it doesn't detract from your work.)
- Show published work, if you have it. (Many listings in *Artist's Market* specify they
- want to see the original art or roughs in addition to the published piece.)
- Show samples that are relevant in style and content to your potential client.
- Tailor your presentation to the client in question.
- Include samples that are impeccably clean.
- Include mechanicals if you have them.
- Include your name, address and phone number on the outside of your portfolio *and* on the inside.

Wherever possible, make an appointment to meet with a prospective client. Be certain to get specific directions to the client's office. (Avoid dropping by without an appointment.) Always be on time, even though the interviewer or client may make you wait. Be *prepared* to wait. Keep your sense of humor. Be courteous to the receptionist and to those around you. Don't smoke or chew gum. Look professional.

Look well-groomed which means clean and neatly-combed hair, clean, manicured nails, shoes shined, and clean, pressed clothes. Dress appropriately—no jeans or sweat shirts. Women should wear skirts or dresses, not pants. And, women should wear nylons. Men should wear jackets, slacks and ties. Dress conservatively. Remember, it's that *first* impression that counts. Have portfolio and resume in hand. Follow instructions. Read through an annual report or company brochure on each prospective client so that you will be thoroughly familiar with the company and their products during an interview. Remember, a flexible attitude can make the difference between getting that job or not.

Achieving your goal as a freelancer will also require other preparations. Design business cards, stationery and envelopes, and invoice forms for yourself. (Remember to put your name, address and phone number on the invoice forms.) Printed forms and stationery systems help convey the image of being professional.

When contacting clients, your positive personality and salesmanship skills will be critical. Think *beyond* design and illustration. Concentrate on how your product will

ACCOUNT NO.

CHARGE FORM

B. Dalton
America's Favorite Bookseller
P.O. Box 1152
Minneapolis, MN 55440

BILL TO: 762 742 092

STREET TIMOTHY A SAXUM

CITY STATE ZIP

PURCHASE ORDER # 1168082

QTY.	DESCRIPTION	AMOUNT
1	Book	11.95
		TX .48
		12.43
	B DALTON	#386
		1#
	TOTAL	12.43
	CHARGE	12.43
	192393860101088I	

TOTAL INCLUDING TAX (If applicable)

X Timothy Saxum
CUSTOMER SIGNATURE

DATE 11/8/81

SALES PERSON: 5411

STORE # 386

MAIL ORDER | CHARGE TAKE | CHARGE SEND | TELEPHONE ORDER

MAIL TO:

STREET

CITY STATE ZIP

4. CUSTOMER COPY

ORIGINAL INVOICE

60535 (Rev. 3/77)

relate to your client's success. How will your efforts directly increase the client's sales? Then, in writing, or verbally, present your case.

For a mail presentation, be sure to adhere *exactly* to the client's guidelines. Wherever possible, send out work that can be kept by the client. Send duplicate slides. It's helpful to present them in a plastic slide sheet that holds 20 slides since many clients do not have light tables or projectors in their offices. Type a separate written slide description to accompany the slides.

Put your name, address and phone number on each slide. A rubber stamp will help with this chore. Avoid glass mounts. They're costly to mail and inevitably arrive broken. Pack your materials carefully to avoid torn envelopes, bent slides and damaged samples. Always provide an appropriate sized, self-addressed, stamped envelope (SASE) for the return of your work.

Unless you hand-deliver and pick up your slides, there is that chance that they could get lost in the mail. So, again—be sure you're sending out duplicates.

Some private delivery services and the United States Post Office's Express Mail guarantee next day delivery and provide insurance for your work. Or, consider sending your work via certified or registered mail. If you request a return-receipt, both certified and registered mail require a signature upon delivery and will assure that your work has arrived at the client's office. But clients may not always have the time or facilities to return your slides by the same method. Certified mail does *not* provide for insurance. Do the best you can to ensure a timely and safe delivery of your work.

Pricing

When pricing your work, take into consideration:

- What the market will bear.
- What the employer's budget is.
- The complexity of the assignment.
- The degree of exposure the assignment will have (i.e., will it appear nationally or
- locally? Will it appear on a somewhat long term basis?).
- The size and geographic location of the client (big cities typically pay more).
- The ratio of the supply and demand of good freelancers in the area.
- Your reputation in the field.
- Your salesmanship skills.
- Where the actual work is being done. Their office or yours?
- Whose materials you will be using.
- Whether you or the client will be paying for type and printing.
- When the assignment is due.
- Payment arrangements—are you being paid any amount in advance? Will you be
- paid by the hour? Or per assignment? Will there be royalties? "Kill Fee?"
- How revisions are to be handled.
- How much it helps your portfolio, your image, or your need to be challenged.
- How much you want the job.

Terms

Many times a client will complain that the freelancer did not complete the assignment as requested. In some cases, this means the freelancer will not get paid. In other cases, he may get a "kill fee," or a portion of the fee. Or, he may have the opportunity to try again.

To insure that both you and client clearly understand the assignment, outline your discussion in a simple, brief letter to the client. It is not necessary for the client to sign and return a copy of such a letter since he will be tacitly agreeing to it unless he does respond. The letter should include a brief description of the assignment, when it is due, what you are to be paid and when and anything else pertinent to the job.

Listed below are suggested ways of receiving payment that help you get paid on time.

1. Ask for ⅓ of the total payment upon presentation of your sketches or roughs, ⅓

at the approval stage, and ⅓ when you complete the project.

2. Ask for ½ payment before beginning the project, and ½ upon delivery.
3. Ask for total payment upon completion of the job.
4. Ask for total payment within 10-30 days of the completion of the job.

Obviously, the first two suggestions are the preferred methods. However, not all of your clients will be willing to work this way. Many want to work on a "gentlemen's agreement" basis only. It will be your decision on how to handle the project, and how to educate your clients as to your own way of working with them.

Remember that the best negotiations in the world can and will fall apart if you miss deadlines. Be sure to organize your time. Only accept work you know you can deliver *on time*. Don't make up excuses for why you're late. No one cares.

Seek the advice of a competent accountant. It's important to be aware of state and federal tax regulations. You need to know the answers to such questions as: What business licenses do you need, what your tax liabilities will be, will you have to file estimated taxes, what will you be able to deduct, what records does a self-employed person have to maintain, etc.

An attorney can help you write contract agreements, settle disputes, and while he can't go with you to small claims court, he can give you relevant information to help your case.

Now you know *who* you are, *what* you want in the marketplace, *where* your top prospects are located, and *when* and *how* you'll contact the prospective clients. The rest is up to you. Good luck!

Markets

Advertising, Public Relations and Audiovisual Firms

This section of *Artist's Market* is an old gal with new makeup. The 1980 edition of *Artist's Market* has separate Advertising, Public Relations and Audiovisual categories. This year you'll find this trio rolled into one combined section.

Why the merge? The answer is that most of these agencies and firms work with the freelance artist in a similar way.

Advertising/PR and Audiovisual markets are among the most lucrative for the artist. They are also among the most difficult to break into. Inevitably, higher payment for jobs creates more competition.

Working with the markets in this section is different from working with most other markets because you have to please not only the agency you are working for, but his clients as well. Also, your payment won't be based on the agency's budget, but largely on the client's. Fortunately you shouldn't find yourself faltering between the whims of an agency and its client. Your liaison will be the agency art director. It is up to him to understand the client's needs and convey them to you.

You'll find new information in almost all the listings here. We asked these assignment-oriented markets whether or not they maintain a file on artists for future assignments. Well, sure enough, they do. So, we've not only included that fact, but the type of material they want to keep in those files as well. Notice in the write-ups, though, they may want you to make initial contact in one way, but then go on to add that they also want material of another sort for their assignment files. Follow these instructions closely. Not following directions is a sure way to get started on the wrong foot—in fact maybe even no start at all.

Various reference and reading materials are available in the advertising and audiovisual fields. A few you might want to familiarize yourself with include *Standard Directory of Advertising Agencies* (National Register Publishing Co.), *O'Dwyer's Directory of Public Relations Firms* (J.R. O'Dwyer Co., Inc.), *Audiovisual Marketplace* (R.R. Bowker) *Audio-Visual Communications* magazine (United Business Publications, Inc.) and Peter Glenn's *Madison Avenue Handbook*.

A&A ACCREDITED ADVERTISING, Division of Sound Advertising, 1 Ocean Ave., Massapequa NY 11758. Art Director: S. Chinkes. Clients: foods and electronics firms. Annual billing: $200,000.
Needs: Uses artists for layout, illustration, type spec, retouching and paste-up for newspapers, magazines, collateral, direct mail and POP.
First Contact & Terms: Local artists only; call for interview. Pays $25, layout; $5/hour, paste-up.

A.V. MEDIA CRAFTSMAN INC., 110 E. 23rd St., New York NY 10010. (212)228-6644. President: Eph Glasser. Vice President: Carolyn Clark. AV firm. Clients: public relations firms, ad agencies, educational publishers and internal corporate communications departments. Produces filmstrips, multiscreen slide shows, multimedia kits, overhead transparencies, cassettes, soundslide sets and videotapes. Assigns approximately 20 jobs/year.
Needs: Works with 1 illustrator and 1 designer.
First Contact & Terms: Local artists only. Provide resumes and tearsheets to be kept on file for future assignments. Arrange interview; do not mail art. Buys all rights. Payment by hour: $4 minimum, charts/graphs; $4-8, mechanicals and type spec. Pays $10-35/frame.

SOL ABRAMS ASSOCIATES INC., 331 Webster Dr., New Milford NJ 07646. (201)262-4111. Contact: Sol Abrams. Public relations firm. Annual billing: "under 1 million in public relations, not including ads." Clients: real estate, food, fashion, beauty pageants, entertainment (theatrical, television) agricultural, animals and pets, automotive, government, politics, publishers, travel, etc. Media used include billboards, consumer magazines, trade magazines, direct mail, newspapers, P-O-P displays, radio and TV.
Needs: "We work with film, TV video producers and syndicates for theater or broadcast productions."
First Contact & Terms: Send contact sheets or prints and resume with SASE. Negotiates payment based on client's budget.

ACADEMY FILM PRODUCTIONS INC., 3918 W. Estes Ave., Lincolnwood IL 60645. (312)674-2132. President: Bernard Howard. Motion pict/AV producer. Produces motion pictures, filmstrips and slides.
Needs: Uses artists occasionally for animation, technical charts/illustrations, slide and filmstrip art work.
First Contact & Terms: Local artists only; query or call for interview. Buys all rights. Provide tearsheets and samples of work to be kept on file for future assignments. Pays by job.

ACKERMAN ADVERTISING COMMUNICATIONS INC., 55 Northern Blvd., Greenvale NY 11548. (516)484-5150. Creative Director: Skip Ackerman. Art Director: Maxine Brenner. Clients: foods, shopping centers, furniture, banks, automotive and schools. Annual billing: $3,500,000.
Needs: Works with 4 illustrators and 1 designer/month. Uses artists for layout, paste-up, illustration and retouching for newspapers, TV, magazines, transit signage, billboards, collateral, direct mail and POP displays.
First Contact & Terms: Local artists only; arrange interview. No originals returned.

ACTIVITY RECORDS INC., 3355 Bay Front Dr., Baldwin NY 11510. President: Norma Harris. Audiovisuals producer. Clients: educational. Produces filmstrips and multimedia kits. Assigns 20 jobs/year.
Needs: Works with 5 illustrators. Uses artists for album covers, books and filmstrips.
First Contact & Terms: Query with resume and photocopied samples. Reports in 3 weeks. Provide brochures/flyers, resumes, tearsheets and photocopies of work to be kept on file for future assignment. No originals returned to artist at job's completion. Pays $20/frame, filmstrips; $20/page, books.

ADLER, SCHWARTZ INC., 140 Sylvan Ave., Englewood Cliffs NJ 07632. Creative Director: Peter Adler. Ad agency. Clients: automotive, office equipment and building/construction equipment firms. Annual billing: $3,000,000. Buys 50 illustrations/year.
Needs: Works with 2 illustrators. Uses artists for billboards, POP displays, filmstrips, consumer magazines, stationery design, direct mail, slide sets, brochures/flyers, trade magazines, newspapers. Also uses artists for layout, lettering, color separations, paste-up, retouching and type spec for brochures, annual reports, print ads, letterheads, packaging, posters and trademarks. Especially needs line drawings and washes of people, cars and interiors.
First Contact & Terms: Query with samples, tearsheets or call for interview. SASE. Reports in 2 weeks. Provide business cards or tearsheets to be kept on file for future assignment.

AD/MAN, 400 Executive Bldg., Cincinnati OH 45202. (513)651-3220. Art/Creative Director: Don Dickman. Clients: retail and industrial manufacturers. Annual billing: $1,000,000.
First Contact & Terms: Uses mostly local artists. Query with samples. SASE. Contacts artists as needs arise. Pays $15/hour for cartoons and architectural renderings. Pays promised fee for unused assigned work.

ADMASTER INC., 95 Madison Ave., New York NY 10016. (212)679-1134. Art Director: Jack Lazza. Clients: businesses. Produces filmstrips, motion pictures, multimedia kits, overhead tran-

sparencies and slide sets. Assigns 20 jobs/year.
Needs: Works with 10 illustrators and 3 designers/month. Uses artists for filmstrips, motion pictures and slides.
First Contact & Terms: Local artists only. Query and arrange interview. SASE. Reports in 1 week. Provide materials to be kept on file for future assignment. No originals returned to artist at job's completion. Buys all rights. Pays $6-10/hour, charts/graphs and technical art; $6-15/hour, illustrations; $6-7/hour, mechanicals; on acceptance.

THE ADVERTISING CENTRE, Press Bldg., 19 Chenango St., Binghamton NY 13901. Contact: Donna McCue. Ad/PR firm. Clients: retailers, nonprofit and industrial.
Needs: Uses artists for direct mail, television, brochures/flyers, trade magazines, newspapers and mechanicals.
First Contact & Terms: Query with resume and samples. Artists with at least 2 professional assignments only. SASE. Reports in 3-4 weeks. Provide brochures, flyers, business cards, resumes, tearsheets to be kept on file for future assignment. No originals returned to artist at job's completion. Negotiates pay.

ADVISION COMMUNICATIONS LTD., 10012 105 St., Edmonton, Alberta, Canada T5J 1C4. (403)423-1318. Vice President: Arnie Saringer. TV/Animation/AV/Radio (including jingles) producer. Clients: ad agency, corporation, government departments, retail and recording studios.
Needs: Works with about 2 illustrators and 2 animators/month. Uses artists for filmstrips and storyboards.
First Contact & Terms: Write for interview to show portfolio (demo tapes and/or any original work) and send resume. Works on assignment only. Samples returned and reports back on future assignment possibilities. Provide calling card and resume to be kept on file for future assignments. Pay determined by complexity of job.

AERO PRODUCTS RESEARCH INC., 11201 Hindry Ave., Los Angeles CA 90045. Director of Public Relations: J. Parr. Aviation training materials producer. Produces filmstrips, multimedia kits, overhead transparencies, slides and study prints.
Needs: Works with about 2 illustrators/month. Uses artists for brochures, album covers, books, catalogs, filmstrips, advertisements, graphs and illustrations.
First Contact & Terms: Prefers local artists; artist "must be an experienced, rated pilot, and have excellent knowledge of the Federal Aviation Regulations." Query with resume. Provide brochures/flyers, resumes, and tearsheets to be kept on file for future assignment. No originals returned to artist at job's completion. Negotiates pay according to experience and project.

AGRI-EDUCATION INC., Rte. 2, Stratford IA 50249. (515)838-2785. President: Keith Carlson. Estab. 1968. Produces instructional charts, slides and transparencies for high schools and young farmers. Buys 10-20 designs/year. Mail 8x10 pencil or ink sketches. SASE. Reports in 2 weeks. Material copyrighted. Free catalog.
Needs: Uses artists for multimedia kits. Pays $20-100, cover; $10-15, overhead transparency. Farm background with knowledge of animals and machinery is helpful.

AHREND ASSOCIATES INC., 79 Madison Ave., New York NY 10003. (212)533-1640. Vice Pres./Production: Judith Helf. Ad agency. Clients: publishers, industrial, direct response and mail order firms, financial institutions and nonprofit organizations.
Needs: Works with a few illustrators and 3-5 designers/month. Uses designers for consumer magazines, stationery design, direct mail, brochures/flyers, trade magazines and newspapers. Also uses artists for layout, design, lettering, paste-up, retouching and type spec for annual reports, catalogs and letterheads.
First Contact & Terms: Works with local illustrators and designers only. Query or write for interview. Reports in 1 week. Provide business cards, resumes, or tearsheets to be kept on file for future assignments. No originals returned to artist at job's completion. "In each instance, cost is agreed upon (specifically or within a range) before work is assigned." No payment for unsatisfactory assigned work; "if because of client's change of mind, full payment."
Tips: "Should have advertising, preferably direct response, experience. Must know basic requirements for submission to printers, platemakers, and others involved in production of promotional material (except for illustrations or spots which will be used as elements of a mechanical and are not the mechanicals themselves)."

AIE STUDIOS INC., 3905 Braxton, Houston TX 77063. (713)781-2110. Contact: Jack Long, producer. AV/TV/film producer. Clients: industrial and corporate. Produces filmstrips, motion pictures, slide sets, sound-slide sets and videotapes.

Needs: Uses artists for motion picture illustrations, slide, filmstrip or videotape presentations, and some storyboards and proposal illustrations. Uses 8-10 illustrators/year.
First Contact & Terms: Query with resume and samples for files. SASE. Reports in 1 week. Provide samples and resume to be kept on file for future assignments. Pays $20-30/hour.

AITKIN-KYNETT CO., 4 Penn Center Plaza, Philadelphia PA 19103. (215)568-6700. Vice President, Creative Department: Ed Bates. Ad agency. Clients: industrial and consumer.
Needs: Works with 10-15 freelance illustrators. Uses freelancers for consumer and trade magazines, and collateral material.
First Contact & Terms: Call for appointment to show portfolio. Negotiates payment based on where work will appear.
Portfolio Tips: Include samples of previous work, tear sheets and reproductions.

ALAMO AD CENTER INC., 217 Arden Grove, San Antonio TX 78215. (512)225-6294. Art Director: Elias San Miguel. Ad/PR firm. Annual billing: $2,800,000.
Needs: Works with 6 illustrators and 4 designers/month. Uses artists for work in consumer magazines, brochures/flyers, trade magazines, album covers and architectural renderings and "overflow work."
First Contact & Terms: Local artists only. Arrange interview to show portfolio of tearsheets. Provide brochures, flyers, business cards, resumes and tearsheets to be kept on file for future assignments. SASE. Reports in 4 weeks. No originals returned to artist at job's completion. Pays $5-20/hour.

DOM ALBI PRODUCTIONS INC., 183 Madison Ave., New York NY 10016. (212)679-0979. President: Dom Albi. AV/TV/film producer. Clients: industrial and ad agencies. Produces filmstrips, motion pictures, multimedia kits, overhead transparencies, slide sets, sound-slide sets and videotapes.
Needs: Works with 3 illustrators and 3 designers/month. Uses artists for slides, POP displays, brochures and collateral.
First Contact & Terms: Local artists only. Arrange interview to show portfolio. SASE. Reports in 2 weeks. Provide brochures/flyers, resumes and tearsheets to be kept on file for future assignments. No originals returned to artist at job's completion. Negotiates pay.

ALL PRODUCTIONS, Box 19207, San Diego CA 92119. Contact: Steve All. TV/film producer. Clients: educational, military, corporate and industrial. Produces filmstrips, motion pictures, sound-slide sets and videotapes. Assigns 4-6 jobs/year.
Needs: Works with 1-2 illustrators/month. Uses artists for illustrations for children's TV program graphics.
First Contact & Terms: Prefers local artists. Query with samples (tearsheets) and "suggested use." SASE. Reports in 3-4 weeks. No file kept on artists. Pays $7-10 min./hour; $25 max./art card.

ALLEN & DORWARD, INC., 747 Front St., San Francisco CA 94111. (415)956-7470. Contact: Art Director. Ad agency. Clients: retail, industrial, agricultural, food, beverage, etc.
Needs: Works with "quite a few" illustrators/month and seldom works with designers. Uses artists for billboards, P-O-P displays, consumer and trade magazines, direct mail, TV, brochures/flyers and newspapers. Especially needs traditional method illustrators at a reasonable price and marine illustrators.
First Contact & Terms: Call for appointment to show portfolio. Payment negotiable.

ALLVINE ADVERTISING ASSOCIATES, Suite 516, Security National Bank Bldg., Kansas City KS 66101. Contact: Jon Phelps, president. Advertising/public relations firm. Estab. 1964. Clients: Financial, industrial and retail. Annual billing: $400,000. Buys 100 illustrations/year; local artists only. Query with resume and samples; then arrange interview. Contacts artists as needs arise.
Needs: Uses artists for "everything from rough layouts to complete illustrations." Pays $25/hour.

ALLY & GARGANO, INC., 437 Madison Ave., New York NY 10022. (212)688-5300. Art Director: Steve Juliuson. Ad agency. Clients: mostly service accounts, also automobile and fashion.
Needs: Sometimes works with illustrators.
First Contact & Terms: Call for appointment to show portfolio. Negotiates pay based on client's budget and where work will appear.

ALOYSIUS BUTLER & CLARK, 1211 French St., Wilmington DE 19801. Art/Creative Director: Ken Wiggins. Ad agency. Clients: hotels, motels, insurance, banking and construction. Annual billing: $1,000,000.

Needs: Works with 2-3 illustrators and 2-3 designers/month. Uses artists for layout, illustration and paste-up for newspapers, TV, transit, magazines, billboards, collateral, direct mail and POP.
First Contact & Terms: Local artists only. Call for interview. Provide business cards, resumes or tearsheets to be kept on file for future assignments. Originals may be returned to artist at job's completion. Pays $3 min./hour for layout/paste-up.

AMERICAN ADVERTISING SERVICE, 121 Chestnut, Philadelphia PA 19106. Creative Director: Joseph Ball. Prefers personal contact, but mailed art or photocopies OK. Not responsible for art after submission.
Needs: Advertising, billboards, package design, graphic design, commercials, cover design, exhibits and art renderings.

AMERICAN CABLE NETWORK, 701 Airport Rd., Traverse City MI 49684. General Manager: Ross Biederman. Supplier of program material to cable TV systems. Query. Buys all rights.
Needs: Uses artists to prepare documentaries and industrial films. Pay determined by job.

AMERICAN MEDIA ADVERTISING INC., 29 Park Ave., Rutherford NJ 07070. (201)438-3055. Creative Art Directors: Gina Palazzo and Chip Miller. Ad agency/AV producer. Annual billing: $1,978,000. Clients: pharmaceutical, medical, industrial, chemical, land development, consumer and entertainment.
Needs: Works with 3 illustrators and 6 designers/month. Uses artists for POP displays, stationery design, multimedia kits, television, brochures/flyers, album covers and books.
First Contact & Terms: Local artists only. Query with samples or arrange interview to show portfolio of photocopies. Provide tearsheets, resumes, business cards or slides to be kept on file for future assignments. Must have experience working with similar firms. SASE. Reports in 3 weeks. Pays $50-300/job, illustrations; $15-25/hour, designs; $8-15/hour, mechanicals; $20-30/hour, retouching.

AMVID COMMUNICATION SERVICES, INC., 2100 Sepulveda Blvd., Manhattan Beach CA 90266. (213)545-6691. President: James R. Spencer. AV firm. Clients: hospitals, restaurants and corporations.
Needs: Works with 3 illustrators and 2 animators/month. Uses artists for filmstrips, storyboards, packaging and print ads.
First Contact & Terms: Call for appointment to show portfolio. Works on assignment only. Provide resume, calling card, letter of inquiry and brochures/flyers to be kept on file for future assignments. Samples returned by SASE; reports back on future assignment possibilities. Pays $20-50/frame and through negotiation.

ANIMATION ARTS ASSOCIATES INC., 2225 Spring Garden St., Philadelphia PA 19130. (215)563-2520. President: Harry E. Ziegler. AV/motion picture/TV producer. Clients: government, industry, education and TV. Audience: engineers, doctors, military, general public. Produces 35/16mm films, sound/slide programs and filmstrips.
Needs: Works with designers and illustrators. Uses artists for filmstrips, motion pictures and animation.
First Contact & Terms: Call for interview. Provide resumes to be kept on file for future assignments. No work returned at job's completion. Pays $5-10/hour, cartoon and technical animation.

ANIMATION FILMAKERS CORP., 7000 Romaine St., Hollywood CA 90038. (213)851-5526. Production Manager: Paul Backer. Motion picture/TV producer. Clients: businesses, ad agencies and government offices. Produces live and animated commercials, series and features.
Needs: Works with 2 illustrators and 2 animators/month. Uses artists for "illustration of all types: animation, background, layout, ink and paint and storyboards."
First Contact & Terms: Prefers local artists. Query with resume. SASE. Reports in 2 weeks. Provide brochures/flyers, resumes or tearsheets to be kept on file for future assignments. No originals returned to artist at job's completion. Pays $8-15/hour.

APPLE DESIGN, 4800 Rainbow, Shawnee Mission KS 66205. Creative Director: Mike Broadway. Estab. 1976. Clients: Printers and small businesses. Assigns 6 jobs/year; local artists only. Query. SASE. Reports in 1 month.
Needs: Uses artists for illustration and design. Pays $6-8/hour.

APPLIED COMMUNICATIONS INC., 50 Commerce Park Dr., Dayton OH 45404. (513)233-0070. President: George Wisler. AV/TV/film producer. Clients: business and sales training. Produces filmstrips, motion pictures, multimedia kits, slide sets and sound-slide sets. Assigns 25-30 jobs/year.

Needs: Works with about 50 illustrators and 15 designers/year. Uses artists for animation, catalogs, charts/graphs, advertising, direct mail brochures, illustrations, mechanicals, retouching and technical art.
First Contact & Terms: Query with samples or previously published work, or arrange interview. SASE. Reports in 1 week. Pays on publication. Provide material to be kept on file for future assignments. Negotiates pay.

WARD ARCHER & ASSOCIATES, INC., 2996 Directors Row, Memphis TN 38131 or Box 30012, Memphis TN 38130. (901)396-8700. Ad agency/PR firm. Annual billing: approximately $5 million. Clients: industrial, consumer goods. Media used include billboards, consumer magazines, trade magazines, direct mail, newspapers, P-O-P displays and TV.
Needs: Works with 4 illustrators and 2 animators/month. May be assigned as many as 4 jobs in 1 month. Uses artists for POP displays, stationery design, direct mail and brochures/flyers.
First Contact & Terms: Write with resume requesting an interview to show portfolio. Provide card and brochure to be kept on file for future assignments. Negotiates payment based on client's budget, amount of creativity required and artist's experience/reputation.
Portfolio Tips: "Twenty samples are usually sufficient, unless there are some pieces involving experimental processes. I like to see versatility in subject matter. I look for style and techniques, then determine which is best for the particular job at hand. Then, time factors and cost become important to whom I may use."

ARH ADVERTISING, 8686 W. 96th St., Overland Park KS 66212. (913)381-5727. Art Director: Joe Stites. Advertising/design firm. Clients: food, auto and shopping centers.
Needs: Uses artists for "overload of work mostly." Buys 10-12 illustrations/year.
First Contact & Terms: Local artists only. Call to arrange interview to show samples. Reports in 1-2 days.

ARNOLD & CO. INC., 949 Brighton Ave., Portland ME 04102. (207)773-7233. Executive Vice President of Creative Services: Stavros Cosmopulos. Creative Director: Lenny Karsadov. Ad agency. Clients: shoe stores, banks, food, retail stores, clothing stores, muffler shops, fast food outlets, gummed label manufacturers and radio stations.
Needs: Works with 6 illustrators and 1 animator/month. Uses artists for billboards, POP displays, filmstrips, consumer magazines, stationery design, multimedia kits, direct mail, television, slide sets, brochures/flyers, trade magazines and newspapers.
First Contact & Terms: Make an appointment to show portfolio. Provide business cards, flyers or examples of work to be kept on file for future assignments. No originals returned to artist at job's completion. Pays by the job for illustration.

ARNOLD, HOFF AND ASSOCIATES, 2355 S. Arlington Heights Rd., Arlington Heights IL 60005. Art/Creative Director: John F. Perkins. Ad agency. Annual billing: $3,000,000. Clients: health care, financial and insurance.
Needs: Uses 1 illustrator/month. Buys about 15 illustrations/year for filmstrips, multimedia kits, direct mail, brochures/flyers and trade magazines.
First Contact & Terms: Uses mostly local artists. Query with samples (tearsheets or photocopies). Provide brochures, business cards or tearsheets to be kept on file for future assignments. No work samples or assigned work returned. Pays $30-500/job for illustrations and brochures. Pays promised fee for unused assigned work.

ASH/LEDONNE INC., 1500 Broadway, New York NY 10036. (212)221-0140. Exec. Art Director: Don Gordon. Clients: Broadway theatre, motion picture producers and entertainment arenas (Madison Square Gardens). Annual billing: $20,000,000.
Needs: Uses artists for posters, TV, letterheads, newspapers, trademarks, lettering and comps. Especially needs poster and graphic illustrators and "super fast" mechanicals people.
First Contact & Terms: Local artists only. Mail samples and submissions, and arrange interview. No work returned. Reports in 1 week. Pays $12-15/hour, layout; $12/hour, paste-up and mechanicals.

ASSOCIATED AUDIO-VISUAL CORP., 2821 Central St., Evanston IL 60201. Vice President: Don Ivener. AV/TV/film producer. Clients: educational, industrial and corporate. Produces filmstrips, motion pictures, multimedia kits, slide sets, sound-slide sets, videotapes, and visualized sales and business meetings.
Needs: Works with 3-4 illustrators and 1-2 animators/month. Uses artists for motion picture work, filmstrip animation and slide illustration.
First Contact & Terms: Query with resume and samples. SASE. Reports in 2-3 weeks. Provide

resume and samples of work to be kept on file for future assignments. No originals returned to artist at job's completion. Pays $10-40/hour or $10-50/illustration.

AUDIO VISTAS, 200 W. 57th St.; New York NY 10022. (212)688-1569. President: Charles Wantman. AV producer. Clients: educational and industrial. Produces filmstrips, sound-slide sets and videotapes. Assigns 10 jobs/year.
Needs: Works with 1 illustrator and 1 designer/month. Uses artists "to create storyboards and graphics for slide/tape presentations and brochures. These include illustrations and copy slides and some layout work as well."
First Contact & Terms: Local artists with previous AV experience only. Query with resume and samples (slides). SASE. Reports in 4 weeks. Provide brochures/flyers to be kept on file for future assignments. No originals returned to artist at job's completion. Negotiates pay.

AUDITIONS BY SOUNDMASTERS, Box 8135, Chicago IL 60680. (312)787-8220. Executive Vice President: R.C. Hillsman. Produces radio/TV programs, commercials, jingles and records.
Needs: Buys 125-300 designs/year. Uses artists for animation, catalog covers/illustrations, layout, paste-up, multimedia kits and record album design.
First Contact & Terms: Mail 8x10 art. SASE. Reports in 3 weeks. Material copyrighted. Pays $500 minimum, animation; $100-350, record jackets; $50-225, layout; $35-165, paste-up.

AURELIO AND FRIENDS, 11110 SW 128th Ave., Miami FL 33186. President: Aurelio Sica. Vice President: Nancy Sica. Ad agency. Clients: retailers, restaurants, hotels, shopping centers, radio stations and medical facilities.
Needs: Works with 2-3 illustrators and 3-4 designers/month. Uses artists for magazines, billboards, direct mail, brochures/flyers and stationery design.
First Contact & Terms: Provide tearsheets or samples of work to be kept on file for future assignments. No originals returned to artist at job's completion.

AVRETT, FREE AND FISCHER INC., 800 3rd Ave., New York NY 10022. (212)832-3800. Art/Creative Director: Frank C. Ginsberg. Estab. 1971. Clients: Pet foods, personal products, food, proprietary drugs, banks and perfume. Annual billing: $24,000,000. Assigns 10 jobs and buys 20 illustrations/year. Mail art or previously published work. SASE. Reports in 2 weeks.
Needs: Uses artists for storyboards, concept, animation, illustrations and print ads. Pays $150-200.

AVS INC, 97 Compark Rd., Centerville (Dayton) OH 45459. (513)434-3974. President: Dale R. Mercer. AV/Brochure/catalog producer. Clients: business, industrial and institutional.
Needs: Works with illustrators and animators on regular basis as needs arise. Uses artists for filmstrips, multimedia kits, storyboards, charts/graphs and slides.
First Contact & Terms: Call for appointment to show portfolio (lay out, mechanical art, finished slides, brochures, etc.). Works on assignment only. Samples returned by SASE; reports back on future assignment possibilities. Notes from interview and portfolio review kept on file for future assignments. "All payment is determined in advance and is based on assignment type, amount of creativity required and project budget."

N.W. AYER ABH INTERNATIONAL, 111 E. Wacker Dr., Chicago IL 60601. (312)645-8800. Art Buyer: Pam Larson. Ad agency. "We cover very wide range of clients."
First Contact & Terms: Call for personal appointment to show portfolio. Negotiates payment based on client's budget and the amount of creativity required from artist.
Portfolio Tips: Portfolio should consist of past work used by ad agencies and commercial art.

AYER, JORGENSEN, MACDONALD, (Division of N.W. Ayer ABH International, Inc.), 707 Wilshire Blvd, Los Angeles CA 90017. (213)621-1400 or 621-1497. Graphics Supervisor: Art Sherman. Ad agency.
Needs: Uses 1-2 illustrators/month. Uses artists for billboards, POP displays, filmstrips, consumer magazines, direct mail, television, slide sets, brochures/flyers, trade magazines, album covers and newspapers.
First Contact & Terms: Call for personal appointment to show portfolio. "People interested should research what type of clients Ayer, Jorgensen, MacDonald has in such references as Advertising Agency Register and in the Red Book." Provide tearsheets, original art or photocopies to be kept on file for future assignments. Negotiates payment based on client's budget and amount of creativity required from artist. No originals returned to artist at job's completion.

AYER PRITKIN GIBBONS, 27 Maiden Ln., San Francisco CA 94108. (415)391-0650. Contact: Jim Temple. Ad agency. Clients: industry, finance, entertainment, and others.

Needs: Works with 5-10 illustrators, fewer designers/month. Uses talents of both for work with billboards, consumer magazines, direct mail, P-O-P displays, stationery design, and storyboards for TV.
First Contact & Terms: Call for appointment to show portfolio. Selects freelancers from people they come in contact with. Negotiates payment based on client's budget.
Portfolio Tips: Interested in seeing whatever freelancers have.

BACHNER PRODUCTIONS INC., 45 W. 45th St., New York NY 10036. (212)354-8760. Producer/Director: A. Bachner. TV/motion picture producer. Produces TV commercials. Buys 3-5 designs/year; New York artists only.
Needs: Works with 1 illustrator and 4 designers/month. Uses illustrators/designers for motion picture work. Also uses artists for animation, storyboards, title design, graphics, films and videotapes.
First Contact & Terms: New York artists only. Query or write for interview. Reports in 4 weeks. Originals returned to artist after publication. Buys all rights on a work-for-hire basis. Pays $15 min./frame, storyboards; $200-1,000, title layout design.

BAILEY, ORNER, MAKSTALLER INC., 2354 Kemper Lane, Cincinnati OH 45206. (513)281-1338. Contact: Jim Makstaller. Estab. 1972. Clients: Car dealers, insurance firms, restaurants, investment counselors, retail and industry. Query with samples.

BAKER PRODUCTIONS INC., 1503 Walnut St., Philadelphia PA 19102. (215)568-4134. President: Alan Baker. Produces TV film & videotape commercials, documentaries and industrial films.
Needs: Buys approximately 100 designs/year. Uses artists for logo designs for TV commercials, storyboards, title cards and titles.
First Contact & Terms: Local artists only. Prefers artists with broadcast art or ad agency experience. Write for interview. Reports in 1 week "if prospect is pending." Buys all rights. Pays $6/panel, storyboards; $10/title card, titles.

BANNING CO., 11818 Wilshire Blvd., Los Angeles CA 90025. (213)477-8517. Art Director: Orlando Lucia. Ad agency. Clients: mostly print. Annual billing: $750,000.
Needs: Works with 3-4 illustrators and 2-3 designers per month. Buys 25 illustrations/year. Uses illustrators/designers for P-O-P displays, consumer and trade magazines, stationery design, direct mail, brochures/flyers and newspapers.
First Contact & Terms: Prefers "westside" artists. Call for interview. Reports in 1-2 weeks. Provide samples, business card to be kept on file for future assignments. No originals returned at job's completion. Pays original fee for unused assigned illustrations.

BARICKMAN ADVERTISING, Greenwood Plaza, Box 9569, Denver CO 80209. (303)770-4500. Executive Art Director: Todd Ballard. Annual billing: $5 million.
First Contact & Terms: Call for personal appointment to show portfolio. Estimates payment by job. Works with artist according to usage (whether local or national).
Portfolio Tips: Interested in seeing "past work used by other agencies including experimental things artist or photographer may be doing."

BARKIN, HERMAN, SOLOCHECK & PAULSEN, INC., 777 E. Wisconsin Ave., Milwaukee WI 53202. (414)271-7434. Contact: Account Executive. PR firm. Clients: educational organization, financial, manufacturing, hospital, insurance and brewery.
Needs: Firm has 10 account executives and each works with freelance illustrators and designers according to individual needs. Uses artists for all communications media.
First Contact & Terms: Call an account executive for appointment to show portfolio. Negotiates payment depending on job requirements.

TED BARKUS CO. INC., 225 S. 15th St., Philadelphia PA 19102. President/Creative Director: Ted Barkus. Ad/PR firm. Clients: Consumer and industrial.
Needs: Works with 2 illustrators and 1 designer/month. Uses designers for billboards, P-O-P displays, consumer and trade magazines, stationery design, multimedia kits, direct mail, TV, slide sets and newspapers. Uses illustrators for brochures/flyers.
First Contact & Terms: Local artists with experience working with similar firms only. Send materials to be kept on file for future assignments. No original work returned after job completed.

BARLOW/JOHNSON INC., 117 Highbridge St., Fayetteville NY 13066. Art Administrator: John M. Wright. Clients: Dairy and farm products, trucks, pharmaceuticals, banks, paper mak-

ing, hospitals, heavy machinery, clothing, bicycles, machine tools and housing. Annual billing: $8,000,000. Mail samples.
Needs: Uses artists for illustration, commercials and retouching for newspapers, TV, magazines, billboards, direct mail, transit and POP.

BARR FILMS, 3490 E. Foothill Blvd., Pasadena CA 91107. (213)793-6153. Marketing Coordinator: Cathy Braun. Film/AV producer. Clients: schools, libraries, universities, colleges and businesses.
Needs: Works with 1 illustrator/month. Uses artists for filmstrips, print ads, ad flyers (conception and execution).
First Contact & Terms: Call for appointment to show portfolio of published work. Works on assignment only. Samples returned by SASE; reports back on future assignment possibilities. Provide resume, flyer and samples of work to be kept on file for future assignments. Negotiates payment based on client's budget and amount of creativity required.

R. REECE BARRETT ASSOCIATES INC., The Quadrangle, Village of Cross Keys, Baltimore MD 21210. (301)323-1661. Creative Director: Harry Sprow. Ad agency.
Needs: Uses artists for ads, sales promotion and catalogs for business/trade publications.
First Contact & Terms: Submit tearsheets or photocopies of published work. Reports in 1 week. Negotiates payment. Originals returned at job's completion. Pays on acceptance.

BARRETT-YEHLE, 2727 Main, Kansas City MO 64108. Creative Director: Dick Hopkins. Advertising/public relations firm. Estab. 1961. Clients: Retail, industrial and consumer. Annual billing: $5,000,000. Assigns 30-50 jobs/year. Query with samples. SASE. Reports in 3-4 weeks.
Needs: Uses artists for newspaper, magazine and TV illustration. Negotiates pay.

BARRON, HILLMAN & MELLNICK ADVERTISING INC., Boston MA 02110. (617)227-8230. President: Ray Barron. Ad agency. Annual billing: $2,000,000+.
First Contact & Terms: Local artists only. Query with samples. SASE. Provide business card and resume to be kept on file for future assignments. No originals returned to artist at job's completion. No original work returned at job's completion. Pays $25-100, spot illustrations; $10/hour, mechanicals; pays by job for signage.
Needs: Works with 1 illustrator and 1 designer/month. Uses artists for direct mail, slide sets and brochures/flyers.

GENE BARTCZAK ASSOCIATES INC., Box E, North Bellmore NY 11710. (516)781-6230. Manager: Gordon Willson. PR firm. Clients: technical industrial companies and related organizations. Buys 10-15 illustrations/year.
Needs: Works with 1-2 illustrators/month. Uses artists for P-O-P displays, direct mail, brochures/flyers; and design and mechanicals for ads and catalogs. Pays $20/page, design/layout and mechanical paste-up.
First Contact & Terms: Query. SASE. Reports in 2 weeks. No original work returned at job's completion. Pays promised fee for unused assigned work.

TED BATES & CO. INC., 1515 Broadway, New York NY 10036. Senior Vice President/Executive Creative Director: Irving Sonn.

ROBERT BATOR AND ASSOCIATES, 40 Marion St., Chicopee MA 01013. Art Director: Robert Bator. Ad agency. Clients: newspapers, restaurants, small businesses and recording companies.
Needs: Uses artists for illustration, lettering, record jacket design, books, brochures/flyers, album covers, fashions—women's garments, casual and bathing wear—and photography and art okay.
First Contact & Terms: Mail photos or photocopies for files. Provide brochures, flyers, business cards, resumes and tearsheets to be kept on file for future assignments. No originals returned to artist at job's completion. Pays $100-250, comprehensive layout; $8-12/hour, lettering.

BATTEN, BARTON, DURSTINE, & OSBORN, INC., 1640 Northwestern Bank Bldg., Minneapolis MN 55402. (612)338-8401. Creative Coordinator: Sandra Vandervaart. Ad agency. Clients: industrial, food, financial.
Needs: Works with 5 illustrators/month. Uses artists for billboards, consumer and trade magazines, brochures/flyers and newspapers.
First Contact & Terms: Call for personal appointment to show portfolio. Provide flyers to be kept on file for future assignments. No originals returned at job's completion. Negotiates payment based on time involved and sometimes where the work will appear. Also asks for estimates and

reviews them with client's budget in mind.
Portfolio Tips: Portfolio should contain past work used by other agencies and slides.

BATTEN, BARTON, DURSTINE, & OSBORN INC., 383 Madison Ave., New York NY 10017. Contact: Creative Director.

BAUERLEIN, INC., 812 Gravier St., New Orleans LA 70112. (504)522-5461.
Needs: Uses mechanical illustrators occasionally when their workload is too heavy. Uses artists for P-O-P displays, consumer and trade magazines, brochures/flyers and newspapers.
First Contact & Terms: Freelancers can either call an art director and then send resume or send resume followed up with call.
Portfolio Tip: Wants to see variety of illustrator's work. It is helpful if samples can be kept on file for future assignments.

BBDO/WEST, (formerly Hall, Butler & Blathwick), 10960 Wilshire Blvd., Los Angeles CA 90024. (213)879-1673. Creative Director: Bob Kuperman. Clients: packaged goods firms, fast food enterprises, automotive companies, computer manufacturers, airlines, real estate firms, and newspapers. Annual billing: $25 million.
Needs: Works with 5 illustrators and 3-5 designers/month. Uses artists for finished illustrations and storyboards.
First Contact & Terms: Local artists only. Call to arrange interview.Originals returned. Negotiates pay.

BB&W ADVERTISING, 1106 W. State St., Boise ID 83702. (208)343-2572. Art Director: Warren Lassen. Clients: financial, food processors, auto dealers, real estate developers and agricultural. Buys 5 illustrations/year.
Needs: Works with 2-5 illustrators and 2-5 designers/year. Uses designers for direct mail and brochures/flyers. Also uses artists for billboards, catalogs and newspaper ads and illustrations of people for billboards.
First Contact & Terms: Mail art. SASE. Provide brochures, business card and resume to be kept on file for future assignments. No originals returned to artist at job's completion. Reports in 1 week. Pays $50 minimum. Pays promised fee for unused assigned illustrations where layout is followed and/or roughs are approved.

BEAR ADVERTISING, 1424 N. Highland, Hollywood CA 90028. (213)466-6464. Vice-President: Bruce Bear. Clients: fast food enterprises, sporting goods firms and industrial. Annual billing: $3.5 million. Assigns 50-100 jobs/year.
Needs: Works with 1-2 illustrators and 2 designers/month. Illustrations for annual reports, design of direct mail brochures, mechanicals and sign design.
First Contact & Terms: Local artists only. Call for interview. No originals returned. Negotiates pay.

BELL PUBLICOM INC., 1406 Third National Bldg., Dayton OH 45402. Art Director: Bill J. Evans. Association management firm.
Needs: Works with 1 illustrator and 2 designers/month. Uses artists for slide sets, brochures, direct mail brochures, annual reports, newsletters, trade magazines and bulletin graphics. No originals returned to artist at job's completion. Pays $5-10 minimum, keyline/mechanical art.
First Contact & Terms: Local artists only. Mail resume and published samples. Provide resume and representative copies of work to be kept on file for future assignments.

BENAUL ASSOCIATES ADVERTISING, 101 W. 23rd St., New York NY 10011. Art/Creative Director: Bernard Hoffman. Clients: Fashion accessories, real estate, publishing and soft and hard goods. Call for interview.
Needs: Layout, illustration, technical art, paste-up and retouching for newspapers, collateral, direct mail and POP material.

BENEFICIAL STANDARD LIFE INSURANCE CO., (formerly Direct Marketing Corporation of America), 3700 Wilshire Blvd., Los Angeles CA 90010. Art Director: Mary Fretz.
Needs: Works with 2 designers/month. Uses artists for consumer and trade magazines, stationery design, direct mail, slide sets, brochures/flyers, trade magazines and newspapers.
First Contact & Terms: Prefers Los Angeles, Santa Monica, Malibu, Beverly Hills and West Los Angeles artists. Query with resume, minimum rate schedule and printed samples. No originals returned to artist at job's completion.

HERBERT S. BENJAMIN ASSOCIATES, 2736 Florida St., Box 2151. Baton Rouge LA 70821. (504)387-0611. Contact: Mr. Aubrey Shamburger. Clients: dairies, industrial, etc.
Needs: Works with 2-3 illustrators/month. Uses artists for industrial trade and business journals; TV; and brochures/flyers.
First Contact & Terms: Call for appointment to show portfolio. Especially needs a good retail illustrator who can do a great job in retail advertising areas such as furniture, fashion, etc. Negotiates pay based on client's budget and amount of creativity required. Illustrators must conform to rates in their area (as opposed to an area like NY where rates are higher).

BENNETT STUDIOS, 310 Edgewood St., Bridgeville DE 19933. Av producer.
Needs: Works with 1 illustrator and 1 designer/month. Uses artists for filmstrips, slide sets, trade magazine and newspapers. Also uses artists for print finishing, color negative retouching and airbrush work.
First Contact & Terms: Write. No file kept on artists. No originals returned to artist at job's completion. Pays $25/hour.

BENTON & BOWLES INC., 909 3rd Ave., New York NY 10022. Executive Vice President/ Director, Creative Services: Alvin Hampel.

BENTON & BOWLES LTD., 1235 Bay St., Toronto, Ontario Canada M5R 3K4. (416)922-2211. Art Director: Herb Proske. Ad agency. Clients: industrial and packaged goods.
Needs: Works with 2-3 illustrators/month. Uses artists for consumer and trade magazines, TV and newspapers. Especially needs good illustrators who can show variety.
First Contact & Terms: Call for appointment to show portfolio. Negotiates pay based on quotes from freelancers.

BERGER NECHAMKIN & KENT INC., 800 2nd Ave., New York NY 10017. (212)986-1233. Art/Creative Director: Art Nechamkin. Estab. 1973. Clients: Sports, lighting and technical manufacturers. Annual billing: $1,000,000+. Assigns 50 jobs and buys 100 illustrations/year. Query with samples or arrange interview. SASE.
Needs: Payment by job: $100-2,500, annual reports and magazines; $100-2,000, catalogs and posters; $100-1,000, packaging and POP displays; $100-250, letterheads; $100-300, trademarks; $150-1,000, retouching; $100-1,000, lettering. Also needs technical and editorial illustrations. Payment by hour: $8-15, paste-up.

JACK D. BERMAN CO., 50 E. 8th St., New York NY 10003. Contact: Jack D. Berman. Advertising/public relations firm. Estab. 1965. Annual billing: $2,000,000. Assigns 100+ jobs and buys 50+ illustrations/year. Query with resume and nonreturnable samples. SASE.

ALAN BERNI CORP., 666 Steamboat Rd., Greenwich CT 06830. (203)661-4747. Vice President: Stuart Berni. Estab. 1937. Clients: Manufacturers and retailers of consumer products. Buys 25 illustrations/year. Write or call for interview; local professionals only.
Needs: Uses artists for illustration, layout, lettering, paste-up, retouching and type spec for annual reports, catalogs, letterheads, POP displays, packaging, design, production and trademarks. Pays $10-25. Pays promised fee for unused assigned work.

RONALD A. BERNSTEIN AND ASSOCIATES INC., (formerly Perkins, Bernstein Inc.), 875 N. Michigan Ave., Chicago IL 60611. (312)440-3700. Contact: Dave Smith, senior art director. Ad agency. Estab. 1976. Clients: Sports, direct mail and "party plans." Assigns 20-30 jobs/year; prefers local artists. Arrange interview to show portfolio. SASE. Reports in 3-4 weeks.
Needs: Works with 3-4 illustrators and 2 designers/month. Uses artists for layout, illustration, renderings, comps and assembly. Pays by job.

BETZER PRODUCTIONS INC., 450 E. Ohio St., Chicago IL 60611. President: Joseph G. Betzer. Produces slide films and motion pictures.
Needs: Uses artists for motion picture animation and slide film art.
First Contact & Terms: Query with resume.

BILINGUAL EDUCATIONAL SERVICES INC., 1607 Hope St., South Pasadena CA 91030. (213)682-3456. General Manager: Joann N. Baker. Clients: educational, preschool-college. "We specialize in bilingual materials and our filmstrips are developed with the Chicano market in mind." Produces filmstrips, motion pictures and multimedia kits.
Needs: Assigns 6-8 jobs/year. Uses artists for slide illustrations, advertising and catalogs.
First Contact & Terms: Prefers local artists. Query. Reports in 4 weeks. Pays by job.

RALPH BING ADVERTISING CO., 16109 Selva Dr., San Diego CA 92128. Contact: Ralph S. Bing, president. Ad agency. Annual billing: $1,000,000. Clients: industrial (metals, steel warehousing, mechanical devices, glass, packaging, stamping tags and labels), political, automotive, food and entertainment.
Needs: Uses artists for consumer and trade magazines, brochures, layouts, keylines, illustrations and finished art for newspapers, magazines, direct mail and TV.
First Contact & Terms: Local artists only. Arrange interview to show portfolio. "Provide portfolio (of photocopies and tearsheets) and client reference as evidence of quality and/or versatility." Reports promptly. No original work returned to artist at job's completion. Pays $5-50/hour.

THOMAS H. BIRCH ADVERTISING, 4221 Hamilton Ave., Cincinnati OH 45223. (513)541-1441. Contact: Thomas H. Birch. Clients: Industrial, mail order and soft drink firms.
Needs: Buys 10 illustrations/year. Illustrations, layout, lettering, paste-up, retouching, type spec and color separations for ads, letterheads, packaging, POP displays, TV, trademarks and catalogs.
First Contact & Terms: Local artists only. Call for interview. Minimum payment: $15/hour, illustration; $10/hour, layout; $6/hour, paste-up. Pays promised fee for unused assigned work.

BISCH/FARBER/LEVINE, 228 Main St., Venice CA 90291. (213)399-3242. Contact: M. Farber. Graphics/advertising/industrial design collaborative group. Estab. 1978.
Needs: Works with 10 or less illustrators/year. Assigns 75+ jobs and buys 25 illustrations/year. Uses artists for illustration and design of collateral material, ads, brochures and annual reports.
First Contact & Terms: Local artists only. Query with resume. SASE. Negotiates pay.

DAVID H. BLOCK ADVERTISING, INC., 48 Farrand St., Bloomfield NJ 07003. (201)748-0090. Contact: Perri Dromsky or Karen Deluca. Clients: financial, industrial and consumer. Annual billing: $5,000,000. Buys 20-30 illustrations/year.
Needs: Works with 3 illustrators and 1 designer/month. Uses artists for illustrations, layout, lettering, type spec, mechanicals and retouching for ads, annual reports, billboards, catalogs, letterheads, brochures and trademarks.
First Contact & Terms: Prefers to work with "artists with at least 3-5 years experience in paste-up and "on premises" work for mechanicals and design only." Arrange interview. SASE. Reports in 2 weeks. No originals returned to artist at job's completion. Pays $25-250, retouching; $50-100, spot illustration; $10-20/hour, comps/layout; $8-15/hour, paste-up. Full pay for unused assigned work.

BILL BOAL PRODUCTIONS INC., 43 5th Ave., New York NY 10003. (212)924-5040. Contact: Helene Berger. Produces sound filmstrips for elementary and junior high schools. Arrange to show work. Buys all rights.
Needs: Pays $15-25, drawings.

JOHN BORDEN & ASSOCIATES, 5841 73rd Ave. N., Minneapolis MN 55429. (612)566-4515. Contact: John Borden. Ad agency. Clients: business, industrial, agricultural and advertising. Specialists in recruitment advertising and PR. Annual billing: $100,000. Assigns 15 jobs and buys 50 illustrations/year.
Needs: Works with 4 illustrators/month. Uses artists for layouts, finished art, type spec, consumer and trade magazines, stationery design, direct mail, brochures/flyers and newspapers.
First Contact & Terms: Local professionals only. Query with samples or call to arrange interview to show portfolio. SASE. Provide brochures, flyers, business card, resume, (tearsheets, etc.) to be kept on file for future assignments. Originals become client's property at job's completion. Reports in 2 weeks. Pays $12-30/hour.

ROBERT E. BORDEN & ASSOCIATES, 6030 N. Sheridan Rd., Suite 1901, Chicago IL 60660. (312)271-8620. Contact: Robert E. Borden. PR firm with some advertising. Annual billing: $40,000. Clients: banks, savings & loans, designers, manufacturing, hospitals, real estate, development, and building.
Needs: Works with 1-2 freelance illustrators/year. Uses artists for filmstrips, multimedia kits, direct mail, slide sets and brochures/flyers.
First Contact & Terms: Call or write and request personal appointment to show portfolio. No originals returned at job's completion. Negotiates payment based on hourly rate or project basis.

BOTSFORD KETCHUM INC., 55 Union St., San Francisco CA 94111. (415)781-9480. Contact: Art Director. Ad agency. Clients: all types.
Needs: Uses freelancers for consumer and trade magazines, newspapers, print ads and TV.
First Contact & Terms: Call for appointment to show portfolio. Selection based on portfolio

review, mailers from freelancers and contact by reps. Negotiates payment based on client's budget, amount of creativity required from artist and where work will appear.
Portfolio Tips: Wants to see whatever best illustrates freelancer's style. Include past work used by other ad agencies and tear sheets of published art.

BOZELL & JACOBS INTERNATIONAL, INC., 4590 MacArthur Blvd., Newport Beach CA 92660 (714)833-0888. Art Director: Tom McBride. Ad agency. Clients: heavy industrial and real estate. Media used include billboards (rarely), consumer and trade magazines, direct mail, newspapers, radio and TV (rarely).
First Contact & Terms: Call for personal appointment to show portfolio. Negotiates payment based on client's budget.
Portfolio Tips: Show current work; prefers transparencies to printed pieces.

BOZELL & JACOBS INTERNATIONAL, 2440 Embarcadero Way, Palo Alto CA 94303. (415)856-9000. Art Director: Wanda Hartman. Ad agency. Clients: wide range of consumer and industrial, including a vineyard account, realty and computer system account.
Needs: Works with 2-3 freelance illustrators/month. Uses freelancers for consumer and trade magazines, direct mail, brochures/flyers, newspapers and P-O-P displays.
First Contact & Terms: Call for appointment to show portfolio. Negotiates payment based on client's budget, amount of creativity required from artist and where work will appear.
Portfolio Tips: Wants to see whatever shows what individual can do. Include past work used by ad agencies and tear sheets of published art.

BOZELL & JACOBS, 400 Colony Square, Suite 1833, Atlanta GA 30361. (404)892-2221. Contact: Ed Martel, Carey Earle, or Linda Rothwell. Ad agency. Clients: financial and consumer.
Needs: Works with 4-5 freelancers/month; designers work in house. Needs freelancers to work with: consumer magazines, television, brochures/flyers, trade magazines and newspapers.
First Contact & Terms: Write requesting interview to show portfolio to Ed Martel, Carey Earle, or Linda Rothwell. Pays set fee which differs with each job.
Portfolio Tips: Prefers piece itself and reproduced piece. Illustrators should go by Art Director's rough directional.

BOZELL & JACOBS INTERNATIONAL, INC., 444 N. Michigan Ave., Chicago IL 60611. (312)644-9800. Senior Vice President: Ray Scheller. Ad Agency. Clients: industrial, fashion, financial, and entertainment. Media used includes billboards (rarely), consumer and trade magazines, direct mail, newspapers, P-O-P displays, radio, and TV.
First Contact & Terms: Call for personal appointment to show portfolio. Negotiates payment based on client's budget.
Portfolio Tips: Prefers to see past work used by ad agencies, commercial art, and tear sheets of published art.

BOZELL & JACOBS INTERNATIONAL, INC., 100 N. 6th St., Minneapolis MN 55403. (612)371-7500. Creative Secretary: Diane Buttshaw. Ad agency. Clients: industrial, loan company, foods, hotel chain, car dealer, and several volunteer agencies.
Needs: Works with 3 illustrators and 4 designers/month. Uses artists for billboards, P-O-P displays, filmstrips, consumer and trade magazines, direct mail, TV, slide sets, brochures/flyers and newspapers.
First Contact & Terms: Call for personal appointment to show portfolio (tearsheets). "If in Minneapolis area, drop off portfolio so it can be looked at by an art director. Can be picked up ½ or 1 day later. Portfolio can be mailed in if freelancer is from out of town." Provide brochures and flyers to be kept on file for future assignments. Negotiates payment based on client's budget.
Portfolio Tips: "Use example of best work."

BOZELL & JACOBS INTERNATIONAL, Bozell & Jacobs Plaza, Regency Circle, Omaha NE 68114. (402)397-8660. Creative Director: Dick Sullivan. Ad agency. Clients: insurance, transportation, food, services, utilities and financial.
Needs: Works with 1-2 freelance illustrators/month. Uses freelancers for billboards, consumer and trade magazines, direct mail, brochures/flyers, newspapers, P-O-P displays, stationery design and TV.
First Contact & Terms: Send samples of work.

BOZELL & JACOBS INTERNATIONAL, 1 Dag Hammarskjold Plaza, New York NY 10017. (212)644-1835. Vice President/Creative Director: Marion Korman. Ad agency. Annual billing: $350 million. Clients: industrial and packaged goods.

Needs: Works with illustrators on regular basis as needs arise. Uses artists for consumer magazines, newspapers and brochures/flyers.
First Contact & Terms: Make contact only through artist's rep. Works on assignment only. Provide brochures, resume and business card to be kept on file for future assignments. Negotiates payment based on client's budget.

BOZELL & JACOBS INTERNATIONAL, INC., 735 N. Water St., Milwaukee WI 53202. (414)276-2760. Contact: Mr. Terry Finkbeiner. Ad agency. Annual billing: Milwaukee office, $17½ million; Corporatation, approximately $340 million. Clients: industrial (60%), consumer (30%), direct mail and P-O-P (10%). Media used include billboards, consumer and trade magazines, direct mail, newspapers, P-O-P displays, radio, and TV.
First Contact & Terms: Call for personal appointment to show portfolio, contact art director, or send slides. Pays according to previous experience and along general guidelines competitive with other agencies. If a freelancer is very specialized and well-known internationally, this person is in a better position for freer negotiation.
Portfolio Tips: Portfolio should be "stripped down to best work." Wants to see "past work used by ad agencies; and commercial illustrations." Wants to see quality material.

BOZELL & JACOBS/PACIFIC, 10850 Wilshire Blvd., Los Angeles CA 90024. (213)879-1800. Executive Art Director: Mr. Laury Wolfe. Ad Agency. Clients: financial, food, and realty. Media used include consumer magazines (15%), trade magazines (25%), direct mail (2%), newspapers (23%), and radio and TV (35%).
First Contact & Terms: Call for personal appointment to show portfolio. Negotiates payment based on client's budget.
Portfolio Tips: Portfolio should include past work used by ad agencies, commercial art, and tear sheets of published art.

ROBERT J. BRADY CO., Rts. 450 and 197, Bowie MD 20715. (301)262-6300. Art Director: Don Sellers. AV producer/medical textbook publisher. Audience: educational, industrial and institutional; medical, paramedical and firefighters. Produces filmstrips, motion pictures, multimedia kits, overhead transparencies, slide sets, sound-slide sets and videotapes. Buys 500+ illustrations/year.
Needs: Uses illustrators for books, filmstrips and motion pictures. Also uses artists for rough and final filmstrip art, storyboards and overhead transparency art.
First Contact & Terms: Query with resume and samples (original art and/or photocopies) or arrange interview to show portfolio. Reports in 2 weeks. Provide resume to be kept on file for future assignments. Originals become the property of the company. Pays $5-8/hour or $45-65/job.

BRAMAN/DOREMUS & COMPANY, 650 Baker Bldg., Minneapolis MN 55402. (612)339-7123. Contact: Christopher Miller. Ad/PR agency. Clients: arts and entertainment, corporations, financial, industrial, social services, and government.
Needs: Works with 2-5 illustrators, 2-5 designers/month. Uses talents of both for work with direct mail, brochures/flyers, P-O-P displays, and stationery design.
First Contact & Terms: Call for appointment to show portfolio. Negotiates payment based on available budget.
Portfolio Tips: Looks for people who take art direction well. Illustrators: wants to see not only illustrations, but publications and brochures, etc. that the work has appeared in.

JOHN BRANSBY PRODUCTIONS, LTD., 47 W. 57th St., New York NY 10019. Vice President: W. Comcowich. TV/motion picture producer. Clients: "federal government and *Fortune 500*; we concentrate in the fields of science, medicine and technology." Produces filmstrips, motion pictures, multimedia kits, slide sets, sound-slide sets and print materials. Assigns 40 jobs/year.
Needs: Works with 2-3 illustrators and 1-2 designers/month. Uses artists for motion pictures and professional myrographs. Also uses artists for 16mm film animation design and graphics, 35mm slide illustration and graphics, and medical illustrations. Negotiates pay.
First Contact & Terms: Query with resume and samples (no originals). SASE. Reports in 4 weeks. Provide brochures/flyers and resume to be kept on file for future assignments.

BRAUN ADVERTISING INC., 26 W. 43rd St., New York NY 10036. (212)354-8747. Contact: I. Braun. Clients: photographic, industrial, consumer electronic and medical. Annual billing: $500,000.

Needs: Assigns 100 jobs and buys 30 illustrations/year. Uses artists for instructional and technical layout and illustration.
First Contact & Terms: Local artists only. Query with previously published work and arrange interview to show portfolio. SASE.

R.C. BRETH INC., Box 929, Green Bay WI 54305. Ad agency. Clients: industry, publishers, farm and direct mail. Annual billing: $303,000.
Needs: Assigns 25 jobs/year. Uses artists for animation, annual reports, billboards, catalogs, magazines, packaging, POP displays, posters, direct mail, brochures/flyers, TV, newspapers and layout.
First Contact & Terms: Query with resume. Send business card to be kept on file for future reference. Pays promised fee for unused assigned illustrations. SASE. No originals returned to artist after job's completion.

BREWER ADVERTISING INC., Div. of Young & Rubicam, 3 Crown Center, 2440 Pershing Rd., Kansas City MO 64108. (816)471-4610. Manager/Creative Services: Gary Mowry. Ad agency. Clients: auto accessory retail, small appliance manufacturing, auto rental, financial, agricultural and aviation.
Needs: Works with varied number (up to 10) freelance illustrators/month. Uses freelancers for consumer and trade magazines, direct mail, brochures/flyers, TV and some newspapers and P-O-P displays.
First Contact & Terms: Prefers artist to send portfolio for review; illustrator can also call for appointment to show portfolio or make contact through artist's rep. Selection is based on review of portfolios from local freelancers, calls from reps, and studios. Negotiates payment based on client's budget, amount of creativity required from artist, where work will appear and artist's previous experience/reputation.
Portfolio Tips: Illustrators should show style and scope, line work, full color, etc.—whatever things they do best.

ANITA HELEN BROOKS ASSOCIATES PUBLIC RELATIONS, 155 E. 55th St., New York NY 10022. (212)755-4498. President: Anita Helen Brooks. PR firm. Clients: fashion, books, "Society," travel, restaurants, charity balls and art exhibits.
Needs: Uses artists for fashion sketches, "Society" personality sketches, books, TV, newspapers and magazines.
First Contact & Terms: Local artists only. Query with resume. SASE. Reports in 3-4 weeks. No file kept on artists. Negotiates pay.

BROOKS-WESLEY ADVERTISING, Box 299, Topeka KS 66601. Art Director: F.L. Wielandy. Clients: Manufacturers, publishers and insurance firms. Mail samples.
Needs: Uses artists for layout, illustration, paste-up and retouching for newspapers, magazines and direct mail. Pays $15-100, layout; $5-20/hour, paste-up.

E.H. BROWN ADVERTISING AGENCY, 20 N. Wacker Dr., Chicago IL 60606. (312)372-9494. Contact: Art Director. Ad agency. Clients: industrial, financial, consumer products (primarily).
Needs: Works with 1-2 freelance illustrators/month. Uses freelancers for consumer and trade magazines.
First Contact & Terms: Call for appointment to show portfolio. Negotiates payment based on bids and daily rates.

BRYAN DONALD ADVERTISING, 2345 Grand, Suite 2712, Kansas City MO 64108. (816)471-4866. President/Creative Director: Don Funk. Annual billing: $2,000,000.
First Contact & Terms: Local artists only. Call to arrange interview. No originals returned to artist at job's completion. Negotiates pay.
Needs: Works with 2-3 illustrators/month and 2 designers/year. Uses artists to do complete layouts "from start to finish."

BRYANT ADVERTISING & MARKETING, 4735 Belleview, Kansas City MO 64112. (816)931-2701. Art Director: Terry Pritchett. Ad agency. Clients: agricultural and veterinary.
Needs: Uses artists for illustration and production, including keyline and paste-up, consumer and trade magazines and brochures/flyers.
First Contact & Terms: Local artists only. Query by phone. Send business card and resume to be kept on file for future assignments. Negotiates pay. No originals returned to artist at job's completion.

BURDETTE ADVERTISING INC., Box 1667, Fort Myers FL 33902. (813)334-0757. Vice President/Creative Director: Fred Robinson. Ad/PR firm. Clients: financial, retail, residential construction, condominium firms and manufacturers. Annual billing: $1,650,000. Especially needs illustrations of products or people for print and collateral.
Needs: Buys 15-20 illustrations/year. Payment by job: $50-200, annual reports and residential renderings; $50-150, consumer magazines; $35-75, P-O-P displays; $25-50, posters; $25-75, trade magazines. Payment by hour: $10-25, layout and lettering; $15-35, retouching; $10 minimum, mechanicals. Negotiates payment for unused assigned illustrations.
First Contact & Terms: Query with samples. SASE. Reports in 1 week.

DAVID K. BURNAP ADVERTISING, 3480 Office Park Dr., Dayton OH 45439. (513)298-7380. Ad agency. Variety of clients. Buys 100 illustrations/year.
Needs: Uses 5 freelance illustrators/month for work with billboards, P-O-P displays, filmstrips, annual reports, consumer and trade magazines, stationery design, direct mail, TV, brochures/flyers and newspapers.
First Contact & Terms: Query with samples of original art. Provide materials to be kept on file for later assignments. No samples or work returned to artist at job's completion. Reports in 4 weeks. Pays promised fee for unused assigned work.

ED BURNETT, CONSULTANTS INC., 2 Park Ave., New York NY 10016. (212)679-0630 or (800)223-7777, toll-free outside N.Y.C. Contact: Stuart David. Submit samples; local artists only.
Needs: Direct mail promotion, advertising, catalog and convention exhibits. Most projects related to direct mail advertising.

LEO BURNETT CO. LTD., 118-4400 Dominion St., Burnaby, B.C., Canada (604)438-7121. Contact: Don Brown. Clients: primarily automotive.
Needs: Works with about 2 illustrators and 6 designers/month. Uses artists for billboards, P-O-P displays, direct mail, TV, brochures/flyers and occasionally newspapers.
First Contact & Terms: Call for appointment to show portfolio. Negotiates pay depending on job requirements.
Portfolio Tip: Wants to see expertise in automotive field.

LEO BURNETT CO. INC., Prudential Plaza, Chicago IL 60601. Adminstrative Manager/Creative Services Division: M.A. Hiller.

LEO BURNETT COMPANY, INC., 26555 Evergreen Rd., Detroit MI 48076. (313)355-1900. Senior Art Director: Mr. Rickey. Ad agency. Clients: primarily industrial.
Needs: Buys very little art; usually uses studios. Uses talents of illustrators and designers for work with consumer and trade magazines, direct mail, brochures/flyers, newspapers, stationery design (sometimes), and TV.
First Contact & Terms: Call for appointment to show portfolio. Payment depends on where ad runs, (pays more for ad run nationally than one run locally).
Portfolio Tips: Interested in seeing work along the lines they need only. No food, for instance, as they don't have this type of account.

ERIK L. BURRO, THE MARKETING & COMMUNICATIONS GROUP, Box 477, Willingboro NJ 08046. (609)877-3704. President: Erik L. Burro. Ad agency. Clients: companies and organizations in the construction industry. Annual billing: $225,000.
Needs: Works with 2-3 illustrators/month. Uses artists for layout, color separations, lettering, paste-up, retouching and type spec for ads, stationery design, direct mail, brochures/flyers, trade magazines, annual reports, letterheads and trademarks. Especially needs construction-oriented ad illustrations and audiovisuals.
First Contact & Terms: Prefers Philadelphia and New Jersey artists. Query with resume and samples. SASE. Contacts artists as needs arise. Provide business card and/or resume to be kept on file for future assignments. "We return art only if we have purchased 'use rights'. We pay prevailing market price for work." Pays promised fee for unused assigned work.

BUTLER-TURNER ADVERTISING, 2001 9th Ave., Vero Beach FL 32960. Vice President/Art Direction: Karen Manning. Ad agency. Clients: real estate, bank, savings and loan, insurance, packaging, citrus product firm, hospital and chamber of commerce.
Needs: Works with 2 illustrators/month, plus some animators. Uses illustrators for brochures/flyers and newspapers; animators for TV work. "We use pen and ink architectural delineations for newspaper reproduction and full color illustrations for magazines." Additional needs include work on layout, illustration, technical art, type spec, paste-up and lettering for newspapers, radio,

magazines, billboards and direct mail.
First Contact & Terms: Local artists only. Arrange interview. Provide brochures/flyers and sample illustrations to be kept on file for future assignments.

BUTTERFIELD COMMUNICATIONS GROUP, 87 Blanchard Rd., Cambridge MA 02138. Contact: Patricia Butterfield. Estab. 1975. Clients: Membership organizations, service firms, colleges and businesses. Annual billing: $100,000. Assigns 20 jobs/year; local artists only. Query with samples. SASE. Reports in 2 weeks.
Needs: Pays $10-20/hour, annual reports, catalogs, posters, letterheads, trademarks, newspapers, layout and lettering; $10/hour, mechanicals.

HAROLD CABOT & CO., INC., 10 High St., Boston MA. (617)426-7600. Head Art Director: Robert Curry. Ad agency. Clients: 90% consumer and 10% industrial.
Needs: Works with 50 illustrators/month. Uses artists for billboards, consumer and trade magazines, TV, brochures/flyers and newspapers.
First Contact & Terms: Send resume and samples. Negotiates pay based on client's budget, amount of creativity required and where work will appear.
Portfolio Tips: Art directors don't encourage portfolio review—they don't discourage it either, but prefer not to.

CAL-AD CO., 915 N. Hollywood Way, Burbank CA 91505. (213)849-7777. Art/Creative Director: Claude Lagardere. Ad agency/printing firm. Annual billing: $1 million. Clients: arts and crafts, paneling and home hobby manufacturers. Assigns 1,000 jobs and buys 100 illustrations/year.
Needs: Works with 1 designer per month for brochures/flyers and billboards.
First Contact & Terms: Query with samples (tearsheets, original art, photocopies, etc.) or arrange interview. SASE. Reports in 2 weeks. Provides brochures, flyers, business card, resume and tearsheets to be kept on file for future assignments. Returns originals to artist at job's completion if requested. Pays $35 min./hour, annual reports, layout, type spec, mechanicals and paste-up; $25-200/job, magazines and newspapers; $35-2,500/job, catalogs; $25-500/job, packaging; $35-3,000/job, P-O-P displays; $35-1,500/job, letterheads; $35-1,000/job, trademarks.

CALIFORNIA COMMUNICATIONS, 6900 Santa Monica Blvd., Los Angeles CA 90038. (213)466-8511. Editorial Director: Nancy Meyer. President: Bill Muster. Film/AV producer. Clients: financial service company, industrial and charity. Audiences: inside personnel, sales people, retail employees and some public. Produces filmstrips, motion pictures, multimedia, story boards, charts/graphs, slide sets, sound-slide sets and videotapes. Assigns 10-20 jobs/year.
Needs: Works with 2-3 illustrators and occasionally 1 animator/month. Uses artists for filmstrips, motion pictures, titles for video, slides and charts." Also uses artists for titles and illustrations for multi image.
First Contact & Terms: Local artists only. Call for appointment to show portfolio or send resume. SASE. Works on assignment only. Samples returned by SASE except "unsolicited resumes may not elicit a response." Reports in 1 week. Provide tearsheets and resume to be kept on file for future assignments. No originals returned to artist at job's completion. Pays $15/hour minimum, market price or flat bid for slide making, artwork and illustrations.

CAMPBELL AND CO., ADVERTISING AGENCY, 214 N. 8th St., Allentown PA 18102. (215)435-2110. Public Relations Director: Robert O. Campbell. Query with published samples.
Needs: Illustrations for direct mail brochures, annual reports, billboards, public service TV spots, print ads and collateral.

CANON & SHEA ASSOCIATES, INC., 31 E. 28th St., New York NY 10016. (212)682-1812. Art/Creative Director: John E. Shea. Ad/PR firm. Clients: Industrial, consumer and publishing firms.
Needs: Assigns 20-40 jobs and buys 10-20 illustrations/year.
First Contact & Terms: Mostly local artists. Query with non-returnable samples. Payment by hour: $20-35, animation, annual reports, catalogs and consumer magazines; $25-50, packaging; $10-50, corporate identification/graphics; $8-10, layout, lettering and paste-up.
Tips: "Artists should have industrial or consumer materials as samples and should understand the marketplace."

CARGILL, WILSON & ACREE INC., 1150 Tower Place, Atlanta GA 30326. (404)261-8700. Managing Art Director: Alex Wilson. Estab. 1950. Clients: Furniture, lawn care, movies, utilities, real estate, dairy, groceries, transportation, construction, banking, fast foods, mineral and heavy

duty equipment. Annual billing: $24,000,000. Assigns 300 jobs and buys 150 illustrations/year. Arrange interview to show portfolio; local professional artists only. SASE.
Needs: Pays $15-25/hour, comps and mechanicals; $25-35/hour, design; $75-3,000, illustrations for ads.

CARLOCKE/LANGDEN INC., 4122 Main St., Dallas TX 75226. President: Betty Whitlock. Creative Director: Margaret F. Murrell. AV producer. Produces documentary/sales/industrial/motion picture films, public relations TV commercials, filmstrips and slide films. Audience: employees—training and motivational.
Needs: Works with 1 illustrator/month. Uses filmstrip animation.
First Contact & Terms: Query with resume. Provide brochure, flyer and or tearsheets to be kept on file for future assignments. No originals returned at job's completion.

CARTER ADVERTISING INC., 810 Elizabeth Ave., Shreveport LA 71101. (318)227-1920. Contact: Bill Carter. Ad agency. Clients: industrial, interior design, jewelers, plumbers, hotels, oil, automobile dealer, bank, helicopter charter, telephone company and trailer manufacturer. Annual billing: $500,000. Assigns 500 jobs and buys 50 illustrations/year.
Needs: Works with 10-12 illustrators and 10-11 designers/month. Uses artists for billboards, P-O-P displays, filmstrips, consumer magazines, stationery design, multimedia kits, direct mail, television, slide sets, brochures/flyers, trade magazines, album covers, newspapers, books and mechanicals.
First Contact & Terms: Prefers local artists. "Must have heavy production experience." Query with resume or arrange interview to show portfolio. SASE. Reports in 1 month. Provide brochures, flyers, business cards, resumes, tearsheets, etc., to be kept on file for future assignments. No originals returned at job's completion. Pays $15 min./hour.

CASE & McGRATH, 445 Park Ave., New York NY 10022. (212)832-1800. Contact: Vince Ansaldi. Annual billing: $40,000,000. Clients: toiletries and drugs manufacturers, food companies, food product firms, liquor and wine, hosiery, insurance, bank and theater flooring companies. Assigns 50 jobs/year.
Needs: Works with 3 illustrators/month. Uses artists for billboards, consumer magazines and TV storyboards.
First Contact & Terms: Arrange interview. Provide example of artist work along with name, phone number, etc. to be kept on file for future assignments. Originals returned only upon request. Pays $35 max./frame, animation; $100-2,000/job, posters; $20 min., TV; and $10/hour min., mechanicals. No payment for unsatisfactory assigned work; negotiates payment if unused but not artist's fault.

CHAMPION ADVERTISING AGENCY, 62-10 Northern Blvd., Woodside NY 11377. (212)335-2008. Art/Creative Director: Jerry Hahn. Clients: Jewelers. Annual billing: $700,000.
Needs: Assigns 100-150 jobs/year. Need for freelance illustrators varies and uses 2 design studios for needed work—rarely uses freelancer. Uses artists for catalogs; especially needs line art and retouching.
First Contact & Terms: Query in person with samples or previously published work. Originals are returned "only if negotiated on that basis."
Tips: "My agency is a prospect for photographers, retouchers and scratchboard or line artists with jewelry or cosmetic experience, but hourly rates vary and are confidential."

CHANNEL ONE INC., 1727 Clifton Rd., Atlanta GA 30329. Contact: W. Horlock. AV producer. Clients: educational, non-profit, religious.
Needs: Works with 3-4 illustrators/month. Uses artists for album covers, motion pictures and graphic and set design.
First Contact & Terms: Provide materials to be kept on file for future assignments. Originals returned to artist at job's completion if part of job contract.

CHARLES AGENCY, 2530 N. Calvert St., Baltimore MD 21218. (301)467-5200. Contact: Art Director. Ad agency. Clients: automotive aftermarket, vacation camps, kitchen designers, fundraising companies, psychotherapy clinics, model schools and retailers. Annual billing: $2,000,000.
Needs: Works with 4-5 illustrators and 3 designers/month. Uses illustrations, layout, lettering, paste-up, color separations, retouching and type spec for catalogs, print ads, letterheads, packaging, POP displays, posters, TV ads, trademarks and collateral.
First Contact & Terms: Query or arrange interview. SASE. Reports in 1 week. Originals returned to artist at job's completion. Pays $25-600, promised fee for unused assigned work.

THE CHARTMAKERS INC., 25 W. 45th St., New York NY 10036. Vice President/Creative Director: Joseph O'Hehir. Query with resume and samples. Prefers local artists with previous experience with firms of this type.
Needs: Uses artists for multimedia and single-screen slide presentations, including concepting and storyboards. Also uses designers for brochures and print material. Negotiates pay.

THE CHERENSON GROUP, Box 508, Livingston NJ 07039. Senior Art Director: John F. Keller Jr. Clients: Housing developers, financial institutions, sports facilities, real estate firms and retailers. Annual billing: $2,500,000. Buys 100 illustrations/year; local artists only. Query with samples. SASE. Reports in 1 week.
Needs: Illustrations, color separations, layout, lettering, paste-up, type spec and design for annual reports, billboards, catalogs, letterheads, print ads, POP displays, posters and trademarks. Pays $10-40/hour, design; $8-12/hour, mechanicals; $8-25/hour, illustrations. Pays promised fee for unused assigned work.

THE CHERENSON GROUP, Box 535, Livingston NJ 07039. Public Contact: Art Director.
Needs: "We use artists for graphic design, advertising layout, mechanicals, illustration of all types and photography."
First Contact & Terms: Send resume and samples. Price per project quote.

CHIAT/DAY ADVERTISING, 517 S. Olive, Los Angeles CA 90013. (213)622-7454. Senior Art Director: Lee Clow. Estab. 1961. Clients: Stereo equipment firms, home loan companies, Biltmore Hotel, life insurance firms, yogurt and ice cream companies, Yamaha, Fotomat, and beer manufacturers. Annual billing: $35 million. Arrange interview to show portfolio; local artists only.
Needs: Illustration and design work. Negotiates pay.

THE CHICAGO GROUP INC., Division of Resources for Marketing, 744 Well St., Chicago IL 60610. (312)751-0303. Contact: Lester Teichner. Clients: electrical, chemical, machinery, architectural and construction producers. Annual billing: $2,000,000.
Needs: Assigns 10-15 jobs/year. Uses artists for illustrations, layout, lettering, paste-up and type spec for annual reports, catalogs, letterheads, packaging, P-O-P displays, posters, trade magazine ads and trademarks.
First Contact & Terms: Local artists only. Write for interview. No samples returned. Reports in 2 weeks. Pays $100 minimum, illustrations/layouts. Pays original fee for unused assigned work.

CHITTICK EGAN ADVERTISING, 111 Presidential Blvd., Bala Cynwyd PA 19004. (215)667-9600. Creative Director: Robert Zemon. Clients: varied. Annual billing: $3.5 million.
Needs: Works with 1 illustrator and 1 designer/month. Uses artists for TV storyboards, ads, brochures, direct-marketing packages, billboards, etc.
First Contact & Terms: Query with photocopies and follow with a phone call. SASE. Reports in 1 week. Whether originals are returned at job's completion is determined by job. Pays by job on illustrations and photography, $7-10/hour for mechanicals.

CHRISTENSON-BARCLAY & SHAW INC., 3130 Broadway, Kansas City MO 64111. (816)756-0030. Contact: Art Department. Advertising/public relations/marketing firm. Estab. 1955. Clients: Industrial. Assigns 5-6 jobs/year. Arrange interview to show portfolio; local artists only.
Needs: Uses artists for illustration, but "if we are overloaded with work, a freelancer may do anything from layouts to keyline." Negotiates pay.

CHURCHILL FILMS, INC., 151 E. 50th St., New York NY 10022. Contact: Arnie Levey. Motion picture/TV producer. Clients: ad agencies. Produces live action and animation films.
Needs: Works with 1 designer/month. Uses artists for motion pictures.
First Contact & Terms: Arrange interview. No file kept on artists. No original art returned at job's completion.

CINEMA ASSOCIATES INC., Box 9237, Seattle WA 98109. (206)622-7378. Director of Production: Joe Agostino. AV/TV/film producer. Clients: educational, industrial, TV and theatrical. Produces motion pictures, slide sets, sound-slide sets and printed ads.
Needs: Works with 2 illustrators/month. Uses artists for work on motion pictures, slide illustrations, catalog design and advertising art. Assigns 100 jobs/year.
First Contact & Terms: Query with resume and samples (tearsheets). Reports in 2 weeks. Provide resumes and tearsheets. No originals returned at job's completion. Pays $25+/hour for slide

illustrations, film artwork, catalog design and ad illustrations.

CINEMAKERS INC., 200 W. 57th St., New York NY 10019. (212)765-1168. Contact: Carol Hale or Ed Schultz. AV/TV/film producer. Clients: business firms and nonprofit organizations. Produces filmstrips, motion pictures, multimedia kits, sound-slide sets and TV spots.
Needs: Works with approximately 1 illustrator/month. Uses artists on filmstrips.
First Contact & Terms: Local artists only. Arrange interview. SASE. Reports in 1 week. Provide resumes and tearsheets. No originals returned at job's completion. Buys all rights. Pays $25-60/frame for graphics and lettering, illustrations and cartoons for filmstrips. Pays on acceptance.

CINE-PIC HAWAII CORP., 1847 Pacific Heights Rd., Honolulu HI 96813. (808)533-2677. Producer: George Tahara. Motion picture producer. Clients: ad agencies, film production companies, and private and government institutions.
Needs: Works with 6 illustrators and 4 designers/year.
First Contact & Terms: Query with samples. SASE. Provide samples of work and sketches to be kept on file for future assignments. Reports in 3 weeks. Pays on acceptance.

CIRCLE FILMS OF CALIFORNIA, 431 Bryant St., San Francisco CA 94107. Contact: Gaylynn Villines, executive producer. Animation/audiovisuals/TV/film producer. Estab. 1978. Produces filmstrips, motion pictures, slide sets, sound-slide sets and videotapes. Assigns 4 jobs/year. Prefers experienced film and TV personnel. Query with resume and samples or previously used work. SASE. Reports in 4-6 weeks.
Needs: Uses artists for slide illustrations, storyboards, mat work and film titles. Pays by job.

GEORGE P. CLARKE ADVERTISING INC., 420 Madison Ave., New York NY 10017. Creative Director: George P. Clarke. Clients: Automotive aftermarket, financial sporting goods, consumer and trade. Query with resume; prefers local artists.
Needs: Uses artists for layout, illustration and paste-up for newspapers, TV, radio, magazines and direct mail.

CLASSIFIED INTERNATIONAL ADVERTISING SERVICES INC., 1345 E. 10th Ave., Hialeah FL 33010. Art & Research Director: Kevin Greene. Senior Artist: Claudia Cruz. Clients: Auto dealers, real estate agencies and newspapers. Mail samples or call for interview.
Needs: B&w line drawings, cartoons and spot color.

CLASSROOM WORLD PRODUCTIONS, Box 28166, Raleigh NC 27611. Vice President: Van Carter. AV producer. Clients: educational, industrial, governmental and religious. Produces filmstrips, multimedia kits and sound-slide sets.
Needs: Works with 1 designer/month. Uses artists for filmstrip animation, slide illustrations and catalog design.
First Contact & Terms: Query with resume and samples. Reports in 1-4 weeks. Provide brochures, flyers, resume and samples to be kept on file for future assignments. Negotiates pay; sometimes pays royalties.

CLEVELAND & ASSOCIATES, INC., 1008 James St., Seattle WA 98104. (206)624-2710. Ad agency. Annual billing: $2 million. Clients: industrial, fashion retail, financial, general, distributors, Media used include billboards, consumer and trade magazines, direct mail, newspapers, P-O-P, and TV.
First Contact & Terms: Call for personal appointment to show portfolio or send resume. Negotiates payment based on client's budget and amount of creativity required from artist.

COADCO, 1412 Knox, Kansas City MO 64116. Art Director: Bill Harkrider. Estab. 1913. Clients: Resin and paint plants. Assigns 12 jobs/year. Query; local artists only. "Do not send artwork—only a letter telling what kind of artwork you do."
Needs: Uses artists for brochures and newspaper illustrations. Negotiates pay.

COLOSSAL PICTURES, 1338 Mission, San Francisco CA 94115. (415)922-0333. Animation Director: Gary Gutierrez. Animation/TV/film producer. Produces motion pictures and videotapes for TV, theatrical features and exhibition films.
First Contact & Terms: Local artists only. Animation experience preferred. Query with resume and samples. SASE. Reports in 2 weeks. Provide resume to be kept on file for future assignments. Pays $40-100/day.
Needs: Works with 1 illustrator and 1 designer/month. Uses artists for art production, collage

cutouts, storyboard illustrations, background illustrations and designs.

COMMAND PRODUCTIONS INC., 99 Lafayette Ave., White Plains NY 10603. (914)948-6868. Executive Producer: G. Stromberg. AV producer. Clients: industrial and corporate. Produces filmstrips, multimedia kits, slide sets, sound-slide sets, videotapes and print materials.
Needs: Assigns 15 jobs/year. Uses artists for filmstrip and slide graphics, catalogs, filmstrips, slide shows, layouts and mechanicals.
First Contact & Terms: Local artists only. "Send note on availability and previous work." SASE. Reports in 2 weeks. Provide materials to be kept on file for future assignments. No originals returned at job's completion. Pays $7-12/hour.

COMMUNICATION CORPORATION INC., 711 4th St. NW, Washington DC 20001. (202)638-6550. Director of Multimedia: Willie Heinz. TV/Film/Animation/AV producer. Clients: corporate, federal agency, school, industrial and broadcasting.
Needs: Works with 1 illustrator/month. Uses artists for filmstrips, motion pictures and multimedia kits.
First Contact & Terms: Send resume. SASE. Works on assignment only. Samples returned by SASE. Keeps resumes on file for future assignments. Negotiates pay based on client's budget, amount of creativity required and artist's previous experience/reputation.

THE COMMUNICATORS INC., Box 216, Pomfret Center CT 06259. (203)928-7766. Vice President: Marcia A. Ryan. Motion picture/AV producer. Clients: educational markets, including industrial education. Produces advertising, point of sales, brochures, motion pictures, captioned and/or sound filmstrips, and multiscreen slide presentations.
Needs: Works with 12 illustrators and 12 designers/month.
First Contact & Terms: Query with samples. SASE. Reports in 2 weeks. Provide resume, prices and samples of artwork to be kept on file for future assignments. Buys all rights. Pays $35-60/frame on acceptance. Free catalog.
Tips: "We look for talent in illustrating items including nature, people, etc. accurately."

COMMUNICO, 1315 North Highway Dr., Fenton MO 63026. (314)225-6000. General Manager/Graphics: Dan King. Film/AV/Multimedia producer. Clients: association and corporate.
Needs: Uses artists for filmstrips, motion pictures, multimedia kits and print ads.
First Contact & Terms: Call for appointment to show portfolio (drawings or illustrations and design of published work). Works on assignment only. Samples returned by SASE; reports back on future assignment possibilities. Provide resume to be kept on file for future assignments.

COMMUNITY RELATIONS CONSULTANTS, 204 B. Bellevue Ave., Upper Montclair NJ 07043. (201)783-5777. Contact: Nancy Knoerzer. PR firm. Clients: retail merchants, restaurants and service industries. Annual billing: $35,000.
Needs: Works with 3 illustrators and 1 designer/month. Uses artists for consumer magazines, direct mail, brochures/flyers and newspapers. Also for ad layout, signs, maps and charts.
First Contact & Terms: "Most of my art needs are currently met by local artists. However, they are constantly changing and I am often willing to try a new approach." Query with samples or arrange interview to show portfolio. SASE. Reports in 1 month. Provide brochures, illustrations and/or tearsheets to be kept on file for future assignments. Pays $10/ad illustration, $25/publication illustration group, $150/map.

COMPTON ADVERTISING INC., 625 Madison Ave., New York NY 10022. Executive Art Director: Rupert Witalis. Ad agency.
Needs: Works with 4 or 5 illustrators/month. Uses artists for advertising illustration, cartoons and TV storyboards.
First Contact & Terms: "Local artists only except for some extraordinary talent." Call Terry De Marco for list of clients and contact each individually. Pays $200-4,000.

COMPUTER IMAGE CORP, 2475 W. 2nd Ave., Suite 4, Denver CO 80223. (303)934-5801. Art Director: John Wood. Animation producer. Clients: TV and radio stations, financial, retail department store, children's shows and industrial.
Needs: Works with 1-2 illustrators and 1-2 animators/month. Special needs: 1 storyboard designer/illustrator, 1 graphic designer and 1 camera person. Uses artists for storyboards, background illustration and print ads.
First Contact & Terms: Send resume and samples (animated graphics or characters, background illustration, storyboards, graphic design and mechanicals).

CONTACT! VISUAL COMMUNICATIONS, 1726½ Sherman Ave., Evanston IL 60201. (312)475-4656. President: Sidney H. Mayer Jr. AV/motion picture/TV producer/multi-image/live staging (industrial theatre).
Needs: Works with up to 5 illustrators and very few designers/month. Uses artists for animation art, documentaries, slides, industrial films, motion pictures, graphic/set design and some print media illustration.
First Contact & Terms: Call to arrange interview to show portfolio. Provide resume and some indication of style(s) and techniques to be kept on file for future assignments. No originals returned at job's completion. Pays $15-5,500, depending on job.

CONTEMPORARY DRAMA SERVICE, Box 457, Downers Grove IL 60515. Contact: Arthur Zapel. Produces silent and sound filmstrips, 16mm motion pictures, multimedia kits and slides. "We provide educational resource kits for churches and schools. Our primary interest is currently the high school level. Most of our emphasis is on the communications arts–drama, literature, music and language arts."
Needs: Works with various illustrators. Uses artists for books and filmstrips. Uses artists with ad agency and studio (commercial) experience in the applied arts. "We like work with a sense of humor." Needs illustration and filmstrips.
First Contact & Terms: Query with nonreturn samples. SASE. Provide resume and tearsheets. No originals returned to artists at job's completion. Catalog 50¢. Fees negotiable with royalties from 5-10%. Pays $25-45/frame; up to $2,000, projects.

DAVID C. COOK PUBLISHING CO., 850 N. Grove, Elgin IL 60210. (312)741-2400. Art Director: Ed Elsner. Publisher. Produces filmstrips, multimedia kits and books. Clients: churches.
Needs: Works with 20 illustrators and 5 designers/month. Uses illustrators for work on books.
First Contact & Terms: Query by letter (or phone) with samples or previously published work. Prefers artists with previous experience with publishers. SASE. Reports in 2 weeks. Provide tearsheets or material that can be photocopied for our files to be kept on file for future assignments. No originals returned to artist at job's completion. Buys all rights. Most work on assignment only. Payment by job: $40-250 illustrations; on acceptance.

COPY GROUP ADVERTISING, Box 315, Encino CA 91316. Contact: Len Miller. Clients: Resorts, travel spots, vacation areas and direct mail. Reports in 3 days.
Needs: Uses artists for cartoons, illustrations, spot drawings and humorous sketches. "Artists with experience in book publishing, advertising and greeting cards would probably have the skills we're looking for."

FRANK J. CORBETT, INC., 430 N. Michigan Ave., Chicago IL 60611. (312)664-5310. Art Director: Bill Reinwald. Ad agency. Clients: medical and pharmaceutical.
Needs: Works with 2-3 freelance illustrators/month. Uses freelancers primarily for direct mail and some trade magazines.
First Contact & Terms: Call for appointment to show portfolio or make contact through artist's agent. Selection based on portfolio review. Negotiates payment based on client's budget.
Portfolio Tips: Wants to see best of work including that used by ad agencies, and tear sheets of published art. Especially interested in good medical illustrators.

CORNHUSKER FILMS, 1817 Vinton St., Omaha NE 68108. (402)341-4290. Contact: Ernest Jones. Motion picture producer.
Needs: Works with 1 freelance illustrator/year. Uses artists for industrial films and documentaries.
First Contact & Terms: Query with resume.

CORPORATE RESOURCES FOR MARKETING, 31 E. 28 St., New York NY 10016. Contact: John Shea. Estab. 1972. Industrial clients. Buys up to 25 illustrations/year. Send industrial samples.
Needs: Uses artists for layout, lettering, paste-up, retouching, illustrations and type spec for annual reports, catalogs, letterheads, packaging, print ads, trademarks and POP displays. Pays $8-18/hour, mechanicals. Pays promised fee for unused assigned illustrations.

THE CRAMER-KRASSELT CO., 733 N. Van Buren, Milwaukee WI 53202. (414)276-3500. Contact: Bob Hagen. Ad agency. Clients: consumer, financial and service account.
Needs: Works with 5-7 illustrators and 2-3 designers/month. Uses artists for consumer and trade magazines and newspapers.
First Contact & Terms: Call B. Hagen who will supply names of individual art directors to

contact. Sometimes shows are set up for portfolio review by all art directors and interested persons. Negotiates payment based on quotes from freelancers and available budget.
Portfolio Tips: Likes to see artist's best work in color.

CREAMER/FSR, 410 N. Michigan Ave., Chicago IL 60611. (312)467-6800. Estab. 1917. Clients: Agricultural, industrial and heavy consumer. Annual billing: $6,500,000. Query with samples.
Needs: Illustrations, layout, lettering, paste-up and retouching for annual reports, billboards, catalogs, print ads, posters and trademarks. Pay varies.

CREAMER, INC., 1633 Broadway, New York NY 10019. (212)887-8078. Contact: Sandra Camishion. Ad agency. Clients: fashion, industrial and sales promotion.
Needs: Uses artists for P-O-P displays, consumer and trade magazines, brochures/flyers and newspapers.
First Contact & Terms: Call for appointment to show portfolio.

CREATIVE CONCEPTS, 105 Havens Mill Rd., Freehold NJ 07728. Ad agency.
Needs: Works with 6-10 illustrators and 2-4 designers/month. Uses artists for P-O-P displays, consumer magazines, direct mail, brochures/flyers and trade magazines. Also uses artists for realistic and fantasized illustrations for toys, games and general product advertising. "Package designers are also needed."
First Contact & Terms: Mail samples (tearsheets). SASE if samples are to be returned. Reports in 3 weeks. Provide brochures, business cards and tearsheets to be kept on file for future assignments.

THE CREATIVE ESTABLISHMENT, 740 N. Rush St., Chicago IL 60611. President: Joan Beugen. AV/Motion Picture Producer. Clients: Fortune 500 and similar types of businesses as well as a few medical and educational clients. Audience: managers, salesmen, distributors and/or suppliers of the specific client. "We produce slides, films and multimedia presentations primarily for industry but also do some educational and government work in all areas of materials. Our specialty is large sales and management meetings, using multiscreen slide projection. The slides we use range over every conceivable type and format, since we produce in the neighborhood of 4,000 slides a month."
Needs: Works with 1-3 illustrators and 1-3 designers/month. Uses artists for filmstrips, motion pictures and slides. "We use illustrators, cartoonists, designers, costume and set designers, sculptors, model-makers . . . you name it."
First Contact & Terms: I am most interested in hearing from artists and art directors who have experience in slides as opposed to print work. However, we do use illustrators occasionally and show them how to prepare their work for reproduction into slides." Local artists only. Provide resume, tearsheets and sample slides to be kept on file for future assignments. Originals returned to artist at job's completion if special arrangements are made.

CREATIVE HOUSE ADVERTISING INC., 24370 Northwestern Hwy., Southfield MI 48075. (313)355-3344. Creative Director: Robert G. Washburn. Advertising/graphics/display/art firm. Clients: consumer retail, commercial and industrial. Annual billing: $1,400,000. Assigns 20-30 jobs and buys 10-20 illustrations/year.
Needs: Works with 3 illustrators and 2 designers/month. Uses artists for filmstrips, consumer magazines, multimedia kits, direct mail, television, slide sets, brochures/flyers, trade magazines and newspapers. Also uses artists for illustration, design and comp layouts of ads, brochures, catalogs, annual reports and displays.
First Contact & Terms: Local artists only. Query with resume and samples and arrange interview to show portfolio. SASE. Reports in 2 weeks. Provide review and presentation of samples, business card and resume to be kept on file for future assignments. No originals returned to artist at job's completion. Pays $10-50/hour.

CREATIVE MEDIA, 7271 Garden Grove Blvd., Suite E, Garden Grove CA 92641. (714)892-9469. Contact: Tim Keenan, manager. TV/AV/educational video producer. Clients: ad agencies, industrial and medical. Audience: employee/trainees and general public. Produces multimedia kits, slide sets, sound-slide sets and videotapes.
Needs: Works with 1-3 illustrators/month. Uses artists for video (logos/line drawings/illustrations/titles, etc.).
First Contact & Terms: Local artists only. Arrange interview to show portfolio. SASE. Reports in 1 week. Provide brochures/flyers and resume. No originals returned to artist at job's completion. Pays $20-50 minimum for slide and video illustrations, titles and graphics.

CREATIVE PRODUCTIONS INC., 221 N. LaSalle St., Chicago IL 60601. Contact: Leo Cummins. AV producer. Clients: manufacturers and associations.
Needs: Works with 4 illustrators and 4 designers/month. Uses artists for animation, slides, graphics, exhibits and set design.
First Contact & Terms: Provide samples of work to be kept on file for future assignments. Pays $20-50/frame for finished pencil art and uncolored inks on cells.

CREATIVE PROFESSIONAL SERVICES INC., 232 W. Cummings Park, Woburn MA 01801. (617)935-5007. President: John Bell. Query with resume and request interview; local artists only. SASE. Reports in 2 weeks. Needs art for direct mail promotion.

CREATIVE RESOURCES INC., 2000 S. Dixie Hwy., Miami FL 33133. (305)856-3474. President: Mac Seligman. Ad/PR firm. Clients: travel, hotels, airlines and resorts. Annual billing: $760,000.
Needs: Works with 6 illustrators/designers/year. Uses artists for layout, type spec and design for brochures, ads, posters and renderings.
First Contact & Terms: Local artists only. Query or arrange interview to show portfolio. No file kept on artists. Originals work returned after completion of job. Pays $20-30/hour or negotiates pay by job.

CROCUS PRODUCTIONS, 161 E. Grand Ave., Chicago IL 60611. Contact: Tedd Determan. Produces industrial films, slides, filmstrips, and multi-media presentations. Specializes in stop-motion animation.
Needs: Works with 12 illustrators and 20 designers/month. Uses artists for filmstrips and motion pictures. Also uses artists for animation and graphics.
First Contact & Terms: Provide brochures/flyers and resume to be kept on file for future assignments. No originals returned to artist at job's completion.

JOHN CROWE ADVERTISING AGENCY, 1104 S. 2nd St., Springfield IL 62704. (217)528-1076. Contact: John Crowe. Ad/art agency. Annual billing: $100,000. Clients: industries, manufacturers, retailers, banks, publishers, insurance firms, packaging firms, state agencies, aviation and law enforcement agencies.
Needs: Buys 3,000 illustrations/year. Works with 4 illustrators and 3 designers/month. Uses artists for color separations, animation, lettering, paste-up and type spec for work with consumer magazines, stationery design, direct mail, slide sets, brochures/flyers, trade magazines and newspapers. Especially needs layouts, camera-ready art and photo retouching.
First Contact & Terms: Mail art samples (tearsheets, original art, photocopies, etc.). SASE. Provide brochures, business card, resume and/or tearsheets to be kept on file for future assignments. Reports in 5 days. Pays $15/hour illustration/camera-ready art; $4-10 per sketch. No originals returned to artist at job's completion. No payment for unused assigned illustrations.

CRUNCH BIRD STUDIOS INC., 20169 James Couzens, Detroit MI 48235. Contact: Ted Petok. Motion picture/TV producer.
Needs: Works with 2-3 illustrators and designers/month. Uses artists for animation.
First Contact & Terms: Arrange interview. Provide tearsheets and samples to be kept on file for future assignments.

CRYSTAL PICTURES INC., 1560 Broadway, New York NY 10036. (212)757-5130. Contact: S. Tager. Motion picture/TV producer/distributor. General audience.
Needs: Works with 1 illustrator/month. Uses artists for film posters, press books, motion pictures, catalogs, paste-ups and mechanicals.
First Contact & Terms: New York City artists only. Send nonreturnable samples (non-returnable copies) and describe skills relevant to requirements. No file kept on artists. No originals returned to artist at job's completion.

CUMMINGS AND HESTER ADVERTISING AGENCY INC., 3630 Wakeforest, Houston TX 77098. (713)528-5335. Production Manager: Elle Rogers. Clients: industrial, financial, retail, chemical and agricultural. Buys 150 illustrations/year.
Needs: Works with 3 artists/month (includes illustrators, designers touch-up). Uses artists for illustrations, lettering, retouching and design for annual reports, billboards, catalogs, print ads, letterheads, direct mail, posters, full color comps/layout designs and trademarks.
First Contact & Terms: Local artists only. Query or arrange interview. SASE. Reports in 2 weeks. No originals returned to artist at job's completion. Pays $10-30/hour, design; $75-200, 8½x11 line drawing; $25-75, small cartoons.

CUNDALL/WHITEHEAD/ADVERTISING INC., 3000 Bridgeway, Sausalito CA 94965. (415)332-3625. Contact: Alan Cundall. Ad agency. Clients: advertisers and ad agencies.
Needs: Works with 2 illustrators and 6 designers/month. Uses billboards, P-O-P displays, filmstrips, consumer magazines, stationery design, direct mail, television, slide sets, brochures/flyers, trade magazines and newspapers. Also uses artists for layout, lettering, paste-up and type spec. Especially needs spot drawings for collateral.
First Contact & Terms: "We prefer to work face-to-face, but we have gone to Los Angeles for cartoons." Call for appointment. Reports in 1 day. Seldom requests samples. Provide brochures, flyers, business card and resume to be kept on file for future assignments. No originals returned to artist at job's completion. Pays $10/hour or $300, brochure mechanicals; $50 each, spot drawings for brochure; $100, rough layout of magazine ad. Pays original fee as agreed for unused assigned illustrations.
Tips: "Seek the counsel of an agency art director as to the merits of your portfolio before seeing other agencies."

CUNNINGHAM & WALSH, 1 Century Plaza, Century City, Los Angeles CA 90067. (213)556-1600. Art Director: Alex Mendoza. Ad agency. Clients: travel, real estate and entertainment.
Needs: Works with varying number of freelance illustrators depending on assignments. Uses freelancers for final product work.
First Contact & Terms: Call for appointment to show portfolio. Selection based on portfolio review, experience and quality of work. Negotiates payment based on client's budget.
Portfolio Tips: Wants to see individual style; will review work used by other agencies and tear sheets of published art.

CUNNINGHAM & WALSH, 500 Sansome St., San Francisco CA 94111. (415)981-7850. Contact: Art Director. Ad agency. Clients: commercial, industrial, fashion, insurance, consumer foods, cruise line and resort.
Needs: There are 5 art directors in this firm; each one works with about 6 freelance illustrators/year. Uses freelancers for billboards, consumer and trade magazines, direct mail, brochures/flyers, P-O-P displays and TV.
First Contact & Terms: Call for appointment to show portfolio. Selection based on portfolio review. Negotiates payment based on client's budget, amount of creativity required from artist and where work will appear.
Portfolio Tips: Wants to see individual style and previous work used by other ad agencies.

CUNNINGHAM & WALSH INC., 260 Madison Ave., New York NY 10016. Art Buyer: Harry Samalot. Ad agency.
Needs: Works with about 10 illustrators and designers/year. Uses artists for storyboards and illustrations.
First Contact & Terms: Prefers local artists. Call for appointment. Returns original artwork to artist if possible.

AARON D. CUSHMAN AND ASSOCIATES, INC., 200 S. Hanley, Suite 616, St. Louis MO 63105. (314)725-6400. Contact: Ann Tretter. PR firm. Estab. 1978. Clients: real estate, cable television, manufacturing, and travel and tourism.
Needs: Works with about 4 designers/month.
First Contact & Terms: Call for appointment to show portfolio. Negotiates pay based on project and market rates.

KENNETH D, 211 W. Fort St., Detroit MI 48226. (313)961-5296. PR firm. Annual billing: under $500,000. Clients: industrial, financial, hospitals, architectural, insurance, building management, construction, industrial design. Media used includes consumer and trade magazines, direct mail, and newspapers.
Needs: Works with 6 illustrators and 4 designers/month. Uses artists for filmstrips, consumer and trade magazines, stationery design, multimedia kits, direct mail, TV, slide sets, brochures/flyers, album covers, newspapers and books.
First Contact & Terms: Send resume and materials to be kept on file for future assignments. Negotiates payment based on client's budget.

DAILEY & ASSOCIATES, 3055 Wilshire Blvd., Los Angeles CA 90010. (213)386-7823. Contact: Art Secretary. Estab. 1968. Clients: Banks, audio firms, media, restaurants, travel companies, airlines, savings and loan firms, food companies, life insurance companies and fashion enter-

prises. Assigns 20-30 jobs/year. Call to arrange interview; local artists only. Reports same day.
local artists only. Reports same day.
Needs: Illustration. Negotiates pay.

DAILEY & ASSOCIATES, 574 Pacific, San Francisco CA 94133. (415)981-2250. Contact: Art Director. Ad agency. Clients: primarily travel, 1 fashion.
Needs: Works with 6-7 freelance illustrators and 3 freelance designers/month. Uses freelancers for billboards, consumer and trade magazines, direct mail, brochures/flyers, newspapers, P-O-P displays, stationery design and TV.
First Contact & Terms: Call for appointment to show portfolio. Selection based on past association and review of portfolios. Negotiates payment based on usage and where work will appear.
Portfolio Tips: Wants to see features that demonstrate freelancers originality and competency.

DAN ADVERTISING AGENCY, 408 W. Bute St., Norfolk VA 23510. (804)625-2518. Vice President: Bob Gabriel. Ad/PR firm. Annual billing: $2,000,000.
First Contact & Terms: Query with samples of previously published work. SASE. Reports in 3-4 weeks "if interested." Provide brochures, flyers, resume, tearsheets, samples and 3/4 in. video tape when possible to be kept on file for future assignments. Originals returned to artist at completion on some jobs.
Needs: Works with 5-10 illustrators and 2 designers/month. Buys 30+ illustrations/year. Uses artists for work in building and mechanical renderings, air brushing, animation, TV animation, TV/film production, POP displays, filmstrips, consumer magazines, multimedia kits, slide sets, brochures/flyers and finished work. Negotiates pay.

DANCER-FITZGERALD-SAMPLE INC., 405 Lexington Ave., New York NY 10017. Vice President/Director of Art Services: Warren C. Krey. Ad agency. Clients: food, drug, hosiery, candy, beer and automobile firms.
Needs: Works with 25 illustrators and 3 designers/month. Uses artists for billboards, P-O-P displays, filmstrips, consumer and trade magazines, TV, slide sets, brochures/flyers and newspapers. Also uses artists for layout, retouching and lettering.
First Contact & Terms: Mail samples (originals). Provide flyers to be kept on file for future assignments. No originals returned to artist at job's completion. Pays $100-5,000, depending upon use and degree of difficulty.

DANIEL & CHARLES ASSOCIATES, LTD., 261 Madison Ave., New York NY 10016. Creative Director: Brett Shevack. Ad agency. Clients: fashion, liquor, public service, insurance, frozen foods and manufacturers of package goods, fragrances and hard goods. Annual billing: $69,000,000.
Needs: Works with 4-5 illustrators and 1 or less designer/month. Uses artists for animation, billboards, magazines, packaging, posters and newspapers. "We are in constant need of fast, talented sketch people to do storyboard renderings. Finished ad illustration is also greatly needed."
First Contact & Terms: Query with samples (original art or photocopies). Provide brochures, flyers and/or business card to be kept on file for futuue assignments. No originals returned to artist at job's completion. Pays $10-20/hour, lettering and storyboard illustration.
To Break In: "Storyboard artists should be fast, cooperative and be able to give a feeling of environment and action with a nice loose style."

D'ARCY-MacMANUS & MASIUS INC., 1801 Century Park East, Suite 1500, Los Angeles CA 90067. (213)277-2888. Contact: Creative Secretary. Ad agency. Clients: consumer electronics, airline and industrial.
Needs: Works with 10 freelance illustrators/mechanical production artists/month. Works with 1-2 designers/month. Uses freelancers for billboards, consumer and trade magazines, brochures/flyers, newspapers, P-O-P displays and TV.
First Contact & Terms: Call Creative Secretary who will set up appointment with art directors. Selection based on art directors continual review of portfolios. Negotiates payment based on client's budget, use, and amount of money available for job.
Portfolio Tips: Wants to see "best work"—if it's not the very best, don't show it. If freelancer has wide range of styles and techniques, they should be included. Doesn't want freelancers to limit portfolios to just the features they think this agency will want to see because of type of clients. Eyes are open to future needs of new clients. Especially interested in scratch board artists for dealer support materials.

D'ARCY-MacMANUS & MASIUS INC., 433 California St., San Francisco CA 94104. (415)391-2750. Contact: Art Director. Ad agency. Clients: very large and conservative–financial, consumer foods and chemicals, steamship line, newspaper, and consumer and growers association.

Needs: Works with a variable number of freelance illustrators/month. Uses freelancers for consumer and trade magazines, direct mail, brochures/flyers, newspapers, P-O-P displays and especially storyboards and unfinished art. Separate department for graphics–for collateral uses people for graphs and scales.

First Contact & Terms: Call an art director for appointment to show portfolio; or send samples. Negotiates payment based on client's budget and competitive prices. Storyboard frames average $35-50.

Portfolio Tips: Each art director has individual specifications but always looking for "good storyboard art and good comps."

D'ARCY-MacMANUS & MASIUS INC., Box 811, Woodward & Long Lake. Bloomfield Hills MI 48013. (313)646-1000. Contact: Art Director (can send for list of art directors). Ad agency.

Needs: Uses freelancers for consumer and trade magazines, brochures/flyers and newspapers.

First Contact & Terms: Call Art Director for appointment to show portfolio.

Portfolio Tips: Each Art Director has individual specifications.

D'ARCY-MacMANUS & MASIUS INC., Gateway Tower, 1 Memorial Dr., St. Louis MO 63102. (314)342-8600. Vice President/Director of Creative Services: Carl Klinghammer. Ad agency. Clients: all types including brewery.

Needs: Works with 20-30 freelance illustrators and 10 freelance designers/month. Uses freelancers for billboards, consumer and trade magazines, direct mail, brochures/flyers, newspapers, P-O-P displays, stationery design and TV.

First Contact & Terms: Call for appointment to show portfolio. Negotiates payment based on client's budget, amount of creativity required from artist and where work will appear.

Portfolio Tips: Likes to see latest styles and techniques (anything from realism to abstract).

D' ARCY-MacMANUS & MASIUS INC., 437 Madison Ave., New York NY 10022. Contact: Elaine Baumgartner, Creative Director. Uses artist for ad illustrations.

DARINO FILMS, 222 Park Ave. S, New York NY 10003 (212)228-4024. Mailing Address: Box 5173, New York NY 10017. Creative Director: Ed Darino. Film/Animation producer. Clients: educational, some industrial, TV station and corporate.

Needs: Works with 3-5 illustrators and 2-3 animators/month. Also works with freelance designers. Uses artists for motion pictures.

First Contact & Terms: "No visits and no calls." Works on assignment only. Provide calling card, brochure/flyer to be kept on file for future assignments. Reports back on future assignment possibilities. Payment to illustrators by illustration or by week; animators, minimum union salary; background artist, per background only (minimum union). 3-6 month internship program.

R.I. DAVID & CO., 645 N. Michigan Ave., Chicago IL 60614. (312)944-1634. Art/Creative Director: Alicia Ann Adams. Estab. 1950. Clients: Trades. Query with resume or arrange interview; local artists only.

Needs: Uses artists for illustrations (color or line), color separations, layout, lettering, paste-up, retouching, type spec and mechanicals.

DAVIS, JOHNSON, MOGUL & COLOMBATTO INC., 3435 Wilshire Blvd., Los Angeles CA 90010. (213)383-3332. Art Director: Bob Langstaff. Ad agency. Estab. 1861. Clients: Fast food, financial and automotive companies and music parks. Annual billing: $23 million. Query with previously published work; local artists only. No originals returned.

Needs: Works with 5-8 illustrators/month. Finished art. Negotiates pay.

DE MARTINI ASSOCIATES, 414 4th Ave., Haddon Heights NJ 08035. (609)547-2800. Creative Director: Alfred De Martini. Art studio/AV producer. Clients: industrial corporations, universities, marine service organizations, frozen and fast-food firms and plastic eating utensil companies. Annual billing: $750,000.

Needs: Works with 3 illustrators and 3 designers/month. Uses artists for audiovisual, filmstrips and slide programs as well as humorous illustration for newspapers, TV, billboards, direct mail, catalogs, and magazines.

First Contact & Terms: Mail samples. Artist should be versed in contemporary layout and humorous illustrations. Prefers to work by mail, rather than in person. Provide brochures/flyers, resume and tearsheets to be kept on file for future assignments. No originals returned to artist at job's completion. Pays $15-50/hour, layout; $10/hour, paste-up; $100/job, graphic design; $50, layout conceptuals; and $25, spot illustration.

DEFENSE PRODUCTS CO., Audiovisual Division, 645 Azalea Dr., Rockville MD 20850. (301)279-0608. Manager: Harry A. Carragher. AV producer. Clients: industrial, theatrical and government. Produces audiovisuals, distribution and laboratory services.
Needs: Works with 2 illustrators and 1 designer/month. Uses artists for ad illustration, animation, design, filmstrips, dioramas, direct mail brochures, layout, magazine ads, models, multimedia kits, motion picture production and TV spots.
First Contact & Terms: Call or write for interview. SASE. Reports in 2 weeks. Provide brochures/flyers, resume and tearsheets to be kept on file for future assignments. Originals returned to artist at job's completion. Pays $50/hour.

DELTA DESIGN GROUP INC., 518 Central Ave., Box 112, Greenville MS 38701. President: Noel Workman. Ad agency. Annual billing: $600,000. Clients: financial, agricultural, retail, auto, marine, dental and architectural.
Needs: Works with 2 illustrators and 2 designers/month. Uses artists for billboards, P-O-P displays, filmstrips, stationery design, multimedia kits, direct mail, slide sets, brochures/flyers, trade magazines and newspapers.
First Contact & Terms: Query with resume and samples (photocopies). SASE. Provide brochures/flyers, business card and/or resume to be kept on file for future assignments. No originals returned to artist at job's completion. Reports in 2 weeks. Pays $100-300.

DESIGN IN MOTION, 535 N. Michigan, Chicago IL 60611. (312)943-6533. Art Director/Animator: Art Springer. Estab. 1964. Audiovisual/TV/film producer. Clients: Advertising agencies. Produces filmstrips, motion pictures, multimedia kits, slide sets, sound-slide sets and videotapes. Assigns 40-50 jobs/year; local artists only. Pays on production. Buys all rights. Call for interview. SASE. Reports in 1 week.
Needs: Minimum payment by job: $200, animation; $25, charts/graphs; $15, lettering; $50, technical art and illustrations; $30, retouching. Pays $4 min./hour, animation cel inking and painting.

DEUTSCH, SHEA & EVANS, INC., 49 E. 53rd St., New York NY 10022. (212)688-0500. Contact: Daniel Kreischer. Ad agency. Clients: industrial.
Needs: Works with 3-4 illustrators and 1 designer/month. Uses artists for consumer and trade magazines and newspapers. Especially needs realistic work.
First Contact & Terms: Call for appointment to show portfolio. Negotiates pay based on client's budget.

D4 FILM STUDIOS INC., 109 Highland Ave., Needham Heights MA 02194. (617)444-0226. President: Stephen Dephoure. Motion picture producer. Clients: businesses, education, government and hospitals. Produces 16mm motion pictures and complete post-production services. Buys 6 designs/year.
Needs: Uses artists for animation, titles and lettering for logos.
First Contact & Terms: Query. Reports in 1 week. Provide resume to be kept on file for future assignments. No originals returned to artist at job's completion. "We pay $25 to several hundred dollars, depending on job."

NORMAN DIEGNAN & ASSOCIATES, Rt. 2, Lebanon NJ 08833. (201)832-7951. Art/Creative Director: Norman Diegnan. Ad/PR firm. Annual billing: $100,000.
Needs: Buys 6 illustrations/year.
First Contact & Terms: Arrange interview. SASE. Reports in 1 week. Negotiates pay for design, illustration and lettering.

DIENER/HAUSER/BATES CO. INC., 116 N. Robertson Blvd., Los Angeles CA 90048. (213)855-1900. Art Director: Vincent J. Aniano. Ad/art agency. Clients: Paramount and other movie studios. Annual billing: $12 million.
Needs: Uses illustrators for movie promotions and posters, designers for layouts, and production and paste-up artists.
First Contact & Terms: Call or write to arrange to show portfolio, or just send portfolio. Also a good idea to send resume. Provide brochure to be kept on file for future assignments. Originals returned to artist at job's completion. Negotiates payment.

Portfolio Tips: "Showing work accepted by other agencies is best; however, no rules at all governing portfolios."

HERB DIETZ ENTERPRISES INC., 3000 Holiday Dr., Ft. Lauderdale FL 33316. (305)463-1270. President: Herb Dietz. Produces motion pictures, TV spots, AV presentations and filmstrips.
Needs: Buys 10 designs/year. Uses artists for animation, multimedia kits and technical charts/illustrations.
First Contact & Terms: Query. SASE. Reports in 3 weeks. Buys all rights. Pays $200-6,500, animation; $15-100/job, charts/illustrations.

DIRECT MAIL/MARKETING ASSOCIATES, 6 E. 43rd St., New York NY 10017. Contact: Ruth C. Troiani. Trade association.
First Contact & Terms: Query with resume or call for interview; New York City area artists only. No originals returned to artist at job's completion.
Needs: Uses artists for direct mail promotion.

DISCOVERY PRODUCTIONS, 151 E. 50th St., New York NY 10022. (212)752-7575. Contact: David Epstein. Audiovisual/TV/film producer. Clients: educational institutions. Produces filmstrips, motion pictures and videotapes. Assigns 3 jobs/year.
First Contact & Terms: Query with resume. Reports in 2 weeks. Negotiates rights purchased. Provide materials to be kept on file for future assignments. Originals returned to artist at job's completion. Pays $100-5,000 on acceptance.
Needs: Works with as many as 1 illustrator/month. Uses artists for animation, titles and flyers.

DJC & ASSOCIATES, 6117 Florin Rd., Sacramento CA 95823. (916)421-6310. Contact: Donna Cicogni. Ad agency. Annual billing: $250,000. Assigns 120 jobs/year.
Needs: Works with 1 illustrator/month. Uses artists for consumer and trade magazines, stationery design, direct mail, TV, brochures/flyers and newspapers.
First Contact & Terms: Local artists only. Query with samples or arrange interview to show portfolio. SASE. Provide material to be kept on file for future assignments. No originals returned to artist at job's completion. Negotiates pay.

DOE-ANDERSON ADVERTISING AGENCY INC., 223 E. Broadway, Louisville KY 40202. Senior Art Director: Dan Hogan. Ad agency. Clients: financial, heating/air conditioning/ventilating, shipping, retailers, packaging systems, manufacturing, insurance, newspaper, TV, radio, marine, sporting goods and liquor firms.
Needs: Works with 10-20 illustrators and 10-20 designers/year. Uses artists for advertising, architectural renderings, catalog illustrations/covers, graphic design, letterheads, retouching and technical illustration.
First Contact & Terms: No originals returned to artist at job's completion.

DOLPHIN PRODUCTIONS, 140 E. 80th St., New York NY 10021. (212)628-5930. Contact: Allan Stanley. TV producers. Submit 16mm film or cassette (video). Uses artists for animation and graphic design. Provide resume to be kept on file for future assignments.

RALPH L. DOMBROWER CO. INC., Box 1, Richmond VA 23201. (804)643-1113. Art/Creative Director: John Kessler. Advertising/PR Agency. Annual billing: $3,000,000. Assigns 60-70 jobs and buys 25-30 illustrations/year. Send photographs of work and tearsheets. Original art work returned to artist after job is completed. SASE. Reports in 2 weeks. Negotiates pay.
Needs: Works with about 20 illustrators and designers per year. Uses artists for packaging and POP displays. Negotiates pay.

DONARS PRODUCTIONS, Box 24, Loveland CO 80537. (303)669-0586. Manager: Octavio Noda. AV producer. Produces educational slide sets, filmstrips and single slides. Provide resume and photographs of work to be kept on file for future assignments.
Needs: Uses artists for catalog covers/illustrations, direct mail brochures, layout, magazine ads, multimedia kits and technical charts/illustrations.

W.B. DONER & CO., 2305 N. Charles, Baltimore MD 21218. (301)338-1600. Contact: Art Buyer or Art Director. Ad agency. Clients: consumer products.
Needs: Works with 10-30 illustrators/month. Uses artists for all media. Especially needs storyboard illustrators.
First Contact & Terms: Call for appointment. Negotiates payment based on client's budget,

amount of creativity required and where work will appear.

W.B. DONER & CO., 26711 Northwestern Hwy., Southfield MI 48034. (313)354-9700. Creative Director: Steve LaGattuta. Estab. 1937. Clients: Food companies, appliance and department stores, liquor companies, banks and supermarkets. Annual billing: $57,000,000. Buys 75-100 illustrations/year. Query with samples. SASE.
Needs: Animation, paste-up and retouching for TV and print ads. Pays original fee as agreed for unused assigned illustrations.

W.B. DONER & CO., 2777 Allen Parkway, Houston TX. (713)526-1544. Creative Director: Roy Conrad. Ad agency. Clients: retail.
Needs: Uses artists for TV commercials.
First Contact & Terms: Provide business card and samples to be kept on file for future assignments.
Tips: Wants to see actual ads illustrator has done.

JODY DONOHUE ASSOC., INC., 32 E. 57th St., New York NY 10022. (212)688-8653. Contact: Interview, Review Portfolios Department. PR firm. Clients: fashion and beauty. Media used includes direct mail and P-O-P displays.
Needs: Works with 1-5 illustrators and 1-5 designers/month. Uses artists for P-O-P displays, stationery design, multimedia kits, direct mail, slide sets and brochures/flyers.
First Contact & Terms: Call for personal appointment to show portfolio. Provide brochures and flyers to be kept on file for future assignments. No originals returned to artist at job's completion. Negotiates payment based on client's budget, amount of creativity required from artist, and where work will appear.
Portfolio Tips: Wants to see recent work that has been used (printed piece, etc.) and strength in an area (i.e., still life, children, etc.).

DOREMUS & COMPANY, 690 Market St., San Francisco CA 94104. (415)981-4020. Creative Director: Bill McKee. Ad agency. Clients: industrial, financial, cosmetics, food, electronics, banks, and hotel.
Needs: Works with 2 illustrators/month. Uses talents for work with brochures/flyers, annual reports and printed matter.
First Contact & Terms: Call for appointment to show portfolio tearsheets. Negotiates payment based on client's budget.
Portfolio Tips: Illustrators: "things that show style of artist. Tear sheets and past work used by ad agencies OK." Wants to see freelancers' ability to interpret what has to be done. Technical ability important but ability to interpret more important.

DOREMUS & COMPANY, 535 Boylston St., Boston MA 02116. (617)226-2600. Creative Director: Bob Jaczko. Ad agency. Clients: industrial and financial. Media used includes mainly business magazines.
Needs: Works with 1 illustrator/month. Uses artists for P-O-P displays, multimedia kits, direct mail, brochures/flyers and newspapers.
First Contact & Terms: Call for personal appointment to show portfolio (tearsheets) through art director. Provide business cards, resume, brochures and flyers to be kept on file for future assignments. No originals returned to artist at job's completion. Negotiates payment based on client's budget.
Tips: Wants to see past works used by other ad agencies, commercial art, and very interested in seeing published work.

DOREMUS & COMPANY, 120 Broadway, New York NY 10005. (212)964-0700. Art Buyer: Barb Pfaff. Ad agency.
First Contact & Terms: Call for personal appointment to show portfolio or send portfolio for review. "Prefer freelancer make pick up and delivery." Payment is negotiated and depends on job.

DALLAS C. DORT & CO., 811 Citizens Bank Bldg., Flint MI 48502. (313)238-4677. Contact: Lucinda Cooke Ad Agency. Annual billing: $1,000,000. Clients: food processing, building supply, retail and travel services firms.
First Contact & Terms: Mail art (photocopies). SASE. Provide samples of work, business card and resume to be kept on file for future assignments. Originals returned to artist at job's completion. Pays original fee as agreed for unused assigned illustrations.

Needs: Works with 2 illustrators, 2 designers/month. Uses artists for retouching, paste-up and type spec for print ads, billboards, direct mail, catalogs, letterheads, consumer/trade magazines, packaging, POP displays, posters, TV ads and trademarks. Especially needs newspaper layout.

DOYLE DANE BERNBACH INC., 437 Madison Ave., New York NY 10022. Executive Vice President/Art Director: Robert Gage. Ad agency. Provide materials to be kept on file for future assignments.

DOYLE DANE BERNBACH ADV. LTD., 2 Bloor St. W., Toronto, Ontario Canada M4W 1G4. (416)925-8911. Contact: Mr. Ogland or Nick Melton. Ad agency.
Needs: Use of freelance designers varies. Works with artists in all media.
First Contact & Terms: Call for appointment to show portfolio. Negotiates pay based on client's budget, amount of creativity required and where work will appear.

DROZDA-BURCHELL ADVERTISING ASSOCIATES, 216 N. 4th, Lafayette IN 47901. (317)423-1605. Creative Director: W. R. Burchell. Advertising/graphics firm. Ad agency. Clients: foods, retail, hotel, agri-business, industrial and banks. Annual billing: $120,000+.
First Contact & Terms: Query with samples (originals, tearsheets). SASE. Reports in 2 weeks. Provide resume/slides to be kept on file for future assignments. No originals returned to artist at job's completion. Pays $10/hour maximum; provides materials.
Needs: Works with 2 illustrators, 2 designers/month. Uses artists for billboards, stationery design, direct mail, television, brochures/flyers, trade magazines, newspapers, books, mechanicals and engineering graphics.

DRAPER DANIELS, INC., 875 N. Michigan, Chicago IL 60611. (312)751-2244. Executive Art Director: Greg Gwynne. Ad agency. Clients: beauty product, financial, etc.
Needs: Works with 6-7 illustrators and 3-4 designers/year. Uses artists for TV (80%), consumer and trade magazines and newspapers.
First Contact & Terms: Call for appointment to show portfolio (finished work and samples of technique). Payment based on creative ability.

MARK DRUCK PRODUCTIONS, 300 E. 40th St., New York NY 10016. (212)682-5980. President: Mark Druck. Motion picture producer. Produces films and videotapes.
First Contact & Terms: Mail resume. Prefers to work "face to face" with artists. Provide animation and slides to be kept on file for future use. Pays on a per-slide basis.
Needs: Uses artists for animation, technical charts/illustrations and film and videotape production art.

DYKEMAN ASSOCIATES, 1 Lemmon Park N., 3737 Noble, Suite 240, Dallas TX 75204. (214)528-2991. Contact: Alice Dykeman or Diana Pollak. PR firm. Clients: business, industry, sports, environmental, professional association, health and data processing. Assigns 150 jobs/year.
First Contact & Terms: Local artists only. Arrange interview to show portfolio. Provide business card and brochures. No originals returned to artist at job's completion. Pays by job; "artist makes an estimate; we approve or negotiate."
Needs: Works with 5 illustrators/designers per month. "We prefer artists who can do both (design and illustrate)." Uses artists for design of brochures, exhibits, corporate identification, logos, signs, posters, ads, title slides, slide artwork and all design and finished artwork for graphics and printed materials.

DYNACOM COMMUNICATIONS, Box 702, Snowdon Station, Montreal, Quebec, Canada H3X 3X8. (514)342-5200. Director: David P. Leonard. Audiovisual/TV/film producer. Clients: Large industries, government, education and health institutions. Produces motion pictures, multimedia kits, overhead transparencies, slide sets, sound-slide sets, color videotapes and multiscreen mixed media "for training, motivation, sales, orientation and entertainment." Uses artists for album covers.
First Contact & Terms: Query with resume. Reports "only if we have a requirement." Buys all rights. Negotiates time of payment. Pays $20-40/frame, animated cartoons; $15-60, charts/graphs and technical art. Payment by hour: $5-15, advertising and illustrations; $5-10, lettering and mechanicals.

EATOUGH ASSOCIATES ADVERTISING, 4700 Belleview, Kansas City MO 64112. Production Director: Chet Wertz. Ad agency. Clients: retail, industrial and food.

Needs: Works with 2 illustrators/month. Uses illustrators for work on billboards and brochures/flyers.
First Contact & Terms: Local artists only. Arrange interview to show portfolio (original art or photocopies). Provide business card to be kept on file for future assignments. No originals returned after job's completion. Pays $15-35/hour.

DANIEL J. EDELMAN, INC., 1730 Pennsylvania Ave. NW, Washington DC 20006. (202)393-1300. Office Manager: Robin McHugh. PR firm. Clients: trade association and foreign government.
Needs: Works with about 3 illustrators and designers/month. Uses artists for stationery design, brochures and press kit covers.
First Contact & Terms: Call for appointment to show portfolio. Negotiates pay based on freelancer's rate and client's budget.
Tips: Wants to see work already done for trade associations.

DANIEL J. EDELMAN, INC., 221 N. LaSalle St., Chicago IL 60601. (312)368-0400. AV Manager: Mia Christopherson. PR firm.
Needs: Works with 1 illustrator/month. Uses artists for local projects including daily newspapers and trade publications.
First Contact & Terms: Call for appointment to show portfolio.

EDELSTEIN/OKERWALL ADVERTISING AGENCY, (formerly Edelstein-Nelson Advertising Agency), 2711 Crawford, Evanston IL 60201. (312)869-4411. Art Director: Conrad Okerwall. Annual billing: $1,000,000. Clients: industrial.
Needs: Assigns 20 jobs/year. Uses artists for cartoons, design, illustrations, retouching, mechanicals and paste-up for catalogs, brochures, packaging and technical materials. Pays by hour.
First Contact & Terms: Local artists only. Query with resume. SASE. Reports in 2 weeks. Pays by hour.

EDGECOMBE MARKETING INC., Box 1406, Tarboro NC 27886. (919)823-1177. Art Director: Bill Stavro. Ad agency. Annual billing: $800,000. Clients: agricultural, construction equipment.
Needs: Limited freelance needs. Uses illustrators for consumer magazines, brochures/flyers and trade magazines also uses artists for layout, technical art, type spec, paste-up and retouching.
First Contact & Terms: Query with samples of original art. No originals returned to artist at job's completion.

EDUCATIONAL DEVELOPMENT CORP., 4235 S. Memorial Dr., Tulsa OK 74145. (918)622-4522. Art Director: Carol Schaefer. AV producer. Produces educational materials.
Needs: Works with 1 illustrator approximately every 2 months. Uses artists for catalog covers/illustrations, direct mail brochures and technical charts/illustrations.
First Contact & Terms: Local artists only. Arrange interview. Reports in 2 weeks. Free catalog. Provide photocopies to be kept on file for future assignments. Pays $50 minimum, ink illustration; $100 minimum, 4-color illustration.

EDUCATIONAL DIMENSIONS GROUP, Box 126, Stamford CT 06904. (203)327-4612. Visual Editor: Marguerite Mead. AV producer. Audience: schools and libraries. Produces filmstrips, motion pictures, slide sets and videotapes.
Needs: Works with illustrators and designers. Uses catalogs, filmstrips, direct mail flyers and brochures, etc. (designers and mechanical artists)
First Contact & Terms: Query with resume and photocopied samples. Reports in 1-2 weeks. Provide resume to be kept on file for future assignments.Originals only returned at job's completion when return has been negotiated earlier. Pays by job for filmstrip, slide and film illustrations, charts, graphics and diagrams.

EDUCATIONAL MATERIALS AND EQUIPMENT CO., Box 17, Pelham NY 10803. (914)576-1121. Contact: Thomas J. McMahon. AV producer. Produces science materials for elementary, secondary and college students. Clients: education and industry.
Needs: Works with up to 2 illustrators/month. Uses artists for filmstrip assignments.
First Contact & Terms: Submit typewritten frame descriptions and film commentary in conjunction with art submissions. Provide brochures/flyers. Originals returned to artist at job's completion. Buys all rights.

EISAMAN, JOHNS & LAWS ADVERTISING INC., 6255 Sunset Blvd., Los Angeles CA 90028. (213)469-1234. Art Director: Jim Benson. Estab. 1948. Clients: Industrial, fashion and finance

companies. Annual billing: $50,000,000. Call to arrange interview. No originals returned.
Needs: Illustration. Negotiates pay.

ALAN G. EISEN CO. INC., 1188 Round Swamp Rd., Old Bethpage NY 11804. President: Alan G. Eisen. PR firm. Clients: school districts, insurance companies, luggage manufacturers, electronic firms, pharmaceutical companies, restaurants, real estate and financial firms.
Needs: Works with 2-3 illustrators/month. Uses illustrators for jobs dealing with consumer magazines, direct mail, brochures/flyers, trade magazines and newspapers.
First Contact & Terms: Local artists only. Query with resume.

EISNER & ASSOCIATES INC., 14 W. Madison St., Baltimore MD 21201. Associate Creative Director: Ron Carmel. Ad agency. Annual billing: $5,000,000. Clients: fashion, real estate, entertainment, trade associations and banks. Assigns 25-35 jobs/year.
Needs: Works with 3-5 illustrators/month. Uses illustrators for billboards, direct mail, trade magazines and newspapers.
First Contact & Terms: Query with samples (tearsheets or photocopies) or arrange interview to show portfolio. SASE. Provide brochure to be kept on file for future assignments.

JOHN EMMERLING INC., 135 E. 55th St., New York NY 10022. (212)751-7460. Executive Art Director: Art Gilmore. Ad agency. Clients: food, beer, publishers and aviation industry. Annual billing: $4,200,000. Assigns 100+ jobs/year.
Needs: Uses illustrators for billboards, consumer magazines, television, trade magazines and newspapers.
First Contact & Terms: Arrange interview to show portfolio. Provide business card, brochures and flyers to be kept on file for future assignments. Return of originals "depends on price and agreement beforehand."

MOREY ENGLE PRODUCTIONS, 2085 S. Hudson St., Denver CO 80222. (303)758-4436. Contact: Morey Engle. Audiovisuals/TV/film producer. Clients: Industrial, engineering and medical. Produces filmstrips, motion pictures, multimedia kits, slide sets and sound-slide sets. Assigns 7-12 jobs/year. Query. SASE. Reports in 3 weeks.
Needs: Uses artists for slides, titles and animation. Pays $500+.

ERIC ERICSON & ASSOCIATES, 2416 Hillsboro Rd., Nashville TN 37212. (615)385-1050. Contact: Creative Director. Ad firm. Clients: music, food, insurance, banks, home furnishings, manufacturers and air conditioning.
Needs: Works with about 7 illustrators and 1 designer/month. Uses artists for animation, annual reports, billboards, catalogs, consumer magazines, letterheads and newspapers. Especially needs illustrations with cartoon techniques and realism.
First Contact & Terms: Buys 150 illustrations/year. Query with samples. Buys a great deal of "name" art. SASE. Reports in 1-2 weeks. Buys outright. Does not return original artwork to artist after jobs' completion. Pays $20-50/hour, layout; $15-25/hour, paste-up; negotiates fee for lettering. Pays $50-12,000/illustration, depending on complexity of assignment and skill required.

WILLIAM ESTY CO. INC., 100 E. 42nd St., New York NY 10017. Senior Vice President/Executive Art Director: Tony Zamora. Ad agency.
Needs: Works with about 1 illustrator/month. Uses artists for illustration, layout, retouching and lettering for newspapers, TV, transit, billboards and magazines.

EVANS & BARTHOLOMEW, INC., 1430 Larimer Sq., Suite 309, Denver CO 80202. (303)534-2343. Contact: George Pollack. Ad agency. Annual billing: over $50 million (nationally). Clients: consumer, public service, institutional and financial.
Needs: Works with about 6 freelance illustrators/month. Uses freelancers for consumer and trade magazines, brochures/flyers, newspapers and TV.
First Contact & Terms: Call for appointment to show portfolio. Negotiates payment based on client's budget and where work will appear.
Portfolio Tips: Wants to see "great illustrations," past work used by other ad agencies and tear sheets of published art.

DAVID W. EVANS, 1 Oliver Plaza, Pittsburgh PA 15222. (412)232-0067. Vice President/Regional Manager: Dan Huch. Advertising Agency. Estab. 1944. Annual billing: 55 million agency wide. Clients: heavy industry, consumer goods. Media used include magazines, radio, TV and billboards.
Needs: Usually works with local freelancers.

First Contact & Terms: Send portfolio for review. Negotiates payment based on client's budget.
Portfolio Tips: The portfolio should include "4 printed pages, past work used by ad agencies, commerical art, and tear sheet of art work published."

DAVID W. EVANS INC., 110 Social Hall Ave., Salt Lake City UT 84111. (801)364-7452. President/Manager: Burk Divine. Clients: industrial, fashion, and entertainment.
Needs: Works with 2-3 illustrators/month. Uses illustrators for paste-up and multi-media slide show animation.
First Contact & Terms: Call for appointment to show portfolio. Negotiates payment based on client's budget.
Portfolio Tips: Wants to see wide assortment–mattes, mask-up–precision work. Especially interested in food and industrial illustrations.

EVANS/LOWE & STEVENS, INC., 550 Pharr Rd., NE, Atlanta GA 30305. (404)261-6055. Creative Director: Ron Seichrist. Ad agency. Clients: all types but primarily industrial and consumer.
Needs: Works with 4-5 freelance illustrators/month. Uses freelancers for billboards, consumer and trade magazines, direct mail, brochures/flyers, newspapers, P-O-P displays, stationery design and TV.
First Contact & Terms: Send brochure or folder that includes samples of work printed on it. Negotiates payment based on individual needs of job.
Portfolio Tips: Especially interested in realistic illustrators.

EVANS/PACIFIC INC., 190 Queen Anne Bldg., Seattle WA 98109. (206)284-8383. Art Director: Alan Kawashima. Advertising/public relations firm. Estab. 1948. Clients: Food, stereo, food service, fast food, stereo, and bank. Annual billing: $73,000,000. Assigns 500 jobs and buys 100 illustrations/year. Query with samples. Artist should have strong ad agency relationships. Reports in 2 weeks.
Needs: Uses artists for electronic technical illustrations, direct mail brochures, POP displays and ads. Pays $125-1,000 or $25-30/hour.

EVANS WYATT ADVERTISING, 3833 S. Staples, Suite 27, Corpus Christi Texas. (512)854-1661. Contact: Mr. E. Wyatt. Ad/exhibit/display/sign producer. Assigns 225 freelance illustrations/year. Query with samples, query with previously published work or arrange interview to show portfolio.

FAHLGREN & FERRISS, INC., Box 2128, 152 N. Summit, Toledo OH 43603. (419)241-5201. Art Director: Bob Cairl. Ad agency. Clients: industrial and financial.
Needs: Works with 5-6 freelance illustrators/month. Uses freelancers for consumer and trade magazines, direct mail, brochures/flyers, newspapers and P-O-P displays.
First Contact & Terms: Call for appointment to show portfolio or make contact through artist's rep. Selection is usually based on reviewing portfolios through reps, but will see individual freelancers. Negotiates payment based on client's budget, amount of creativity required from artist and where work will appear.
Portfolio Tips: Pieces that are produced are best. "Printed pieces have a lot more credibility."

FAHLGREN FERRIS ADVERTISING INC., 120 E. 4th St., Cincinnati OH 45202. (513)241-9200. Ad agency. Clients: consumer and industrial.
Needs: Works with 1-2 illustrators/month. Uses artists for billboards, consumer and trade magazines, direct mail, newspapers, P-O-P displays and brochures/flyers.
First Contact & Terms: Call for appointment to show portfolio (illustrations, designs and photography). Works on assignment only. Provide sample folders, brochures, etc. small enough to be kept on file for future assignments. Negotiates pay based on client's budget and amount of creativity required from artist/photographer.

MICHAEL FAIN ADVERTISING, 156 5th Ave., New York NY 10010. (212)243-6825. Art/Creative Director: Mike Fain. Ad agency. Clients: industrial and surgical firms.
Needs: Uses designers for P-O-P displays, consumer magazines, direct mail, brochures/flyers, trade magazines and newspapers. Also uses artists for layout, paste-up and retouching.
First Contact & Terms: Local artists only. Call for interview. Provide business card or resume to be kept on file for future assignments. Original artwork not returned if client has not paid for the art.
Tips: "One of the many qualities required of professional artists with whom we deal is a good understanding of copyfitting. An artist designs a layout and indicates space for text. Some artists

are inclined to 'fake' it—instead of actually making sure the required type will fit the space."

RICHARD FALK ASSOC., 1472 Broadway, New York NY 10036. (212)221-0043. PR firm. Annual billing: 500,000. Clients: industry, entertainment.
Needs: Uses 1 artist every 3 months. Uses artists for consumer magazines, brochures/flyers and newspapers.
First Contact & Terms: Send resume. Provide flyers and business card to be kept on file for future assignments. No originals returned to artist at job's completion. Negotiates payment based on client's budget.

FARRAGHER MARKETING SERVICE INC., 7 Court St., Canfield OH 44406. (216)533-3347. Creative Director: A.E. Canon. Marketing service firm. Clients: industrial, scientific and financial. Assigns 20+ jobs/year.
Needs: Uses artists for P-O-P displays, stationery design, direct mail, brochures/flyers and trade magazines. Also uses artists for annual reports, catalogs, brochures, corporate identity, newsletters and promotional materials.
First Contact & Terms: Query with resume and samples. SASE. Provide resume and business card to be kept on file for future assignments. Originals returned to artist at job's completion if requested. Negotiates pay.

FD PRODUCTIONS, 3416 Main St., Dallas TX 75226. (214)742-3170. Contact: Zack Burkett. AV/motion picture producer. Clients: political and industrial. Produces motion pictures and videotapes.
Needs: Assigns 10 jobs and buys 25 illustrations/year. Uses artists for slide titles, illustrations and cartoons for slide shows.
First Contact & Terms: Query with resume and samples (slides). SASE. Reports in 1-2 weeks. Provide name, address and description of type of work capable of to be kept on file for future assignments. Some originals returned to artist at job's completion. Pays $10-100/illustration.

GEORGE FELDMAN ADVERTISING, 15 W. 38th St., New York NY 10018. (212)840-2423. Contact: George Feldman. Call for interview; no mailed samples. Uses art for direct mail promotion.

FILLMAN ADVERTISING INC., 304 W. Hill St., Champaign IL 61820. (217)352-0002. Art/Creative Director: Mary Auth. Ad agency. Clients: equipment manufacturers and real estate development firms. Assigns 40 jobs and buys 10 illustrations/year.
Needs: Works with 1-2 illustrators and 2-3 designers/month. Uses artists for P-O-P displays, stationery design, direct mail, brochures/flyers, trade magazines and newspapers.
First Contact & Terms: Uses mostly local artists. Query with samples (tearsheets). SASE. Reports in 2 weeks. Provide brochure, business card and resume. No originals returned to artist at job's completion. Payment by hour: $15-25, trade magazines, letterheads, newspapers, signage and layout; $25-40, trademarks. Pays promised fee for unused assigned illustrations.

FILM COMMUNICATORS, 11136 Weddington St., North Hollywood CA 91601. Contact: Personnel. Produces educational and training motion pictures, slides, study prints, brochures, mailing pieces and advertisements.
Needs: Ad illustrations, brochures, catalogs, forms.
First Contact & Terms: Send resume in care of advertising department or call same department to set up appointment. Prefers local artists with at least 2 years experience in putting together brochures and ads. Pays by the job.

THE FILM HOUSE INC., 6058 Montgomery Rd., Cincinnati OH 45213. (513)631-0035. President: Ken Williamson. TV/film producer. Clients: industrial and corporate. Produces filmstrips, motion pictures, sound-slide sets and videotapes.
Needs: Assigns 30 jobs/year. Uses artists for filmstrip animation and ad illustrations.
First Contact & Terms: Query with resume. Reports in 3 weeks. Negotiates pay.
Tips: "Maintain continuous contact every 30 or 45 days."

FILMART PRODUCTIONS INC., 199 E. Annapolis St., St. Paul MN 55118. (612)291-2563. Associate Director: Nadia Nowytski. TV/film producer. Clients: educational and corporate. Produces and distributes motion pictures and sound-slide sets.
Needs: Buys 6 illustrations/year. Uses artists for storyboards, brochure and catalog design and ad illustrations.

First Contact & Terms: Local artists only. Query with resume and samples. SASE. Reports in 2 weeks. Negotiates pay.

FILMS FIVE INC., 42 Overlook Rd., Great Neck NY 10020. (516)487-5865. Contact: Walter Bergman. Query with resume.
Needs: Uses artists for documentaries and industrial films.

FILMS FOR CHRIST ASSOCIATION, N. Eden Rd., Rte. 2, Elmwood IL 61529. Contact: Paul S. Taylor. Motion picture producer. Audience: educational, religious and media. Produces filmstrips, motion pictures, slide sets and sound-slide sets.
Needs: Works with 1 illustrator/month. Uses artists for books, catalogs, filmstrips and motion pictures. Also uses artists for filmstrip animation, slide illustrations and ads.
First Contact & Terms: Query with resume and samples (photocopies, tearsheets or snapshots). Reports in 3-4 weeks. Provide brochure/flyers, resume and tearsheets to be kept on file for future assignments. No originals returned to artist at job's completion.

FILMSMITHS INTERNATIONAL, 1814 Bellevue Ave., Seattle WA 98122. (206)324-9755, work; 725-1030, home. Contact: Secretary. Animation/audiovisuals/TV/film producer. Clients: industrial. Produces motion pictures.
Needs: Works with about 7 freelance illustrators/year. Uses artists for illustrations.
First Contact & Terms: Local artists usually. Arrange interview to show portfolio. SASE. Reports in 1 week. Provide resume and portfolio to be kept on file for future assignments. Pays $20-2,000.

FLAX ADVERTISING, 1500 Broadway, New York NY 10036. (212)355-0700. Contact: Elliot Flax. Clients: women's fashions, children's wear, menswear and fabrics. Assigns 100 jobs and buys 100-200 illlustrations/year.
Needs: Uses artists for mechanicals, illustrations, technical art, retouching and lettering for newspapers, magazines, fashion illustration, P-O-P displays, some cartooning and direct mail.
First Contact & Terms: Local artists only. Arrange interview to show portfolio. Reports in 1 week. Provide materials to be kept on file for future assignments. No originals returned to artist at job's completion. Pays $10-15/hour for mechanicals.

FLEISHMAN-HILLARD, INC., 1 Memorial Dr., St. Louis, MO 63102. (314)231-1733. Contact Mr. Beisman. PR firm. Clients: industrial.
Needs: Works with 8-10 illustrators/month. Uses artists for annual reports, folders and brochures.
First Contact & Terms: Call for appointment to show portfolio or send portfolio for review. Negotiates pay based on going rate.

FLETCHER MAYO ASSOCIATES, John Glenn Rd., St. Joseph MO 64505. (816)233-8261. Advertising agency. Clients: industrial, agricultural, consumer and trade. Media used include billboards, consumer magazines, trade magazines, direct mail, newspapers, P-O-P displays, radio and TV.
Needs: Uses 2-12 freelancers/month.
First Contact & Terms: Write and request personal interview to show portfolio, send portfolio for review or send actual photos that might be suited for our clients. Negotiates payment based on client's budget.

FLETCHER TELEVISION INC., (formerly Fletcher-Rollins Television Inc.), 43 Thorncliffe Park Dr., Suite 214, Toronto, Ontario, Canada M4H 1J4. Contact: Howard D. Fletcher. Motion picture producer.
Needs: Uses artists for feature film titles and credits.
First Contact & Terms: Query with resume.

FOCAL POINT STUDIOS, Box 387A, Lansing IL 60438. (312)895-5120. Contact: Brain Pieron. AV producer. Clients: commercial and industrial. Produces filmstrips, motion pictures, multimedia kits, slide sets and sound-slide sets.
Needs: Works with 2-3 illustrators/month. Uses artists for animation, illustration and design.
First Contact & Terms: Local artists only. Arrange interview. SASE. Reports in 2 weeks. Buys all rights. Pays on production.

FOLEY ADVERTISING INC., 75 E. Wacker Dr., Chicago IL 60601. (312)782-1791. Ad agency. President: J.E. Foley. Clients: industrial. Assigns 200 jobs/year.
Needs: Works with 3 designers/month. Uses artists for layout and mechanicals.
First Contact & Terms: Local artists only. Query with samples and arrange interview to show

portfolio. Provides materials to be kept on file for future assignments.

FOOTE, CONE & BELDING ADV. LTD., 1405 Rue Peel, Montreal, Quebec, Canada H3A 1S5. (514)845-0253. Contact: Mr. Dorget. Ad agency. Clients: national advertisers.
Needs: Works with 1 illustrator and 1 designer/month. Uses artists for billboards, P-O-P displays, consumer and trade magazines, TV, brochures/flyers and newspapers.
First Contact & Terms: Call for appointment to show portfolio. Wants to see previous experience and individual style and personality. Interested in rendition type techniques.

FOOTE, CONE & BELDING COMMUNICATIONS INC., 200 Park Ave., New York NY 10017. (212)880-9000. Graphics Director: Hector Robledo. Clients: food, fashion/beauty, travel/airlines, tobacco, industrial, newsweekly, savings bank, consumer products. Media used includes billboards, consumer and trade magazines, direct mail, newspapers, P-O-P displays, radio and TV.
Needs: Uses artists for illustration and paste-up for TV, radio, newspapers, transit, billboards, magazines, direct mail, POP displays and collateral.
First Contact & Terms: Send portfolio for review. Selects freelancers "from files of mailers left after portfolios are screened." Negotiates payment based on client's budget or where the work will appear.
Portfolio Tips: Include "10-15 chromes of experimental and/or job-related work, tearsheets if they're good."

FOOTE, CONE, & BELDING/HONIG, 2727 W. 6th St., Los Angeles CA 90057. (213)736-8500. Creative Director: Mike Wagman. Ad agency. Clients: automotive, supermarket, Ramada Inn, bank, Public Service, ReddiWhip and a food chain.
Needs: Works with 15 freelance illustrators and 6 designers/month. Uses talents for billboards, consumer magazines, direct mail, brochures/flyers, newspaper, P-O-P displays, stationery design, TV, trade magazines, books, multimedia kits and album covers.
First Contact & Terms: Send resume and letter. Provide brochures, flyers, business card, resume and tearsheets to be kept on file for future assignments. Originals returned to artist at job's completion if requested.
Portfolio Tips: Wants to see print-ads, headlines, body copy, tear sheets of art published, and past work used by ad agencies.

FOOTE, CONE, & BELDING/HONIG, 55 Francisco St., San Francisco CA 94119. (415)398-5200. Contact: Susan Larsen. Ad agency. Clients: apparel, food, Levi Strauss, C&H Sugar, Dole, Pacific Telephone, Clorox.
Needs: Works with 15 freelance illustrators and 7 designers/month. Uses talents of illustrators for newspapers and trade magazines, possibly direct mail. Designers needed for consumer and trade magazines, possibly direct mail.
First Contact & Terms: Send samples of work (slides) and follow up by phone. Negotiates payment based on client's budget. No originals returned at job's completion.

FORAY ASSOCIATES, Division of IMC Magnetics Corp., 570 Main St., Westbury NY 11590. (516)334-7195. In-house advertising agency. Advertising Manager: Don Cronan. Clients: Electromechanical. Annual billing: $100,000.
Needs: Uses artists for ads and annual reports.
First Contact & Terms: Query with previously published work. Reports in 2 weeks. Originals not returned. Pays $35 minimum, spot drawings.

FORDHAM EQUIPMENT & PUBLISHING CO., 3308 Edson Ave., Bronx NY 10469. (212)379-7300. President: Al Robbins. AV producer. Clients: schools. Produces filmstrips, multimedia kits, overhead transparencies and children's books.
Needs: Uses artists for filmstrip animation and children's book illustrations.
First Contact & Terms: Arrange interview to show portfolio. Reports in "several" weeks. Provides resume to be kept on file for future assignments. Pays by job.

MARTIN G. FOWLER, 3709 Cedar Lake Rd., Minneapolis MN 55416. Office: (612)872-1200 Evenings: (612)927-5765. Freelance creative advertising/publicity services. Annual billing: $250,000. Clients: food, fashion, government, financial, fairs and expositions. Media used include billboards, consumer magazines, newspapers, P-O-P displays, radio, TV, and public relations.
First Contact & Terms: Call for personal appointment to show portfolio. Negotiates payment based on client's budget and amount of creativity required from artist.

Portfolio Tips: Wants portfolio to show preliminary sketches, finished work and final printed sample.

FOXWORTHY-STEVENS & ASSOCIATES INC., 4407 W. Tradewinds Ave., Lauderdale by the Sea FL 33308. Contact: Donna Foxworthy or Anne Stevens. Clients: land developers, shopping centers, retailers and industries.
Needs: Uses artists for ads, direct mail brochures and annual reports.
First Contact & Terms: Local artists only. Submit samples and resume. Pays $25 minimum.

ANTHONY M. FRANCO, INC., 28 W. Adams Ave., Detroit MI 48226. (313)962-4510. Contact: Biruta Mednis. PR firm. Clients: marketing, corporate, financial, association and political PR.
Needs: Works with 2-3 designers/month. Uses artists for annual reports, brochures, catalogs, posters, AV presentations and newsletters.
First Contact & Terms: Call for appointment to show portfolio. Negotiates pay based on client's budget and needs.
Tips: Wants to see work that has been printed—"a designed and finished product."

ALAN FRANK & ASSOCIATES INC., 1524 S. 11th E., Salt Lake City UT 84105. (801)486-7455. Contact: Kazuo Shiotani. Estab. 1955. Clients: Fast food companies, resorts, commodities and entertainment. Annual billing: $4,000,000. Mail art. SASE. Reports in 2 weeks.
Needs: Illustrations, animation and retouching for annual reports, billboards, ads, letterheads, TV and packaging. Minimum payment: $500, animation; $100, illustrations; $200, brochure layout.

ALBERT FRANK-GUNTHER LAW, INC., 61 Broadway, New York NY 10006. (212)248-5200. Contact: Art Directors. Ad agency. Clients: financial.
Needs: Works with varying number of illustrators and designers/month. Uses artists primarily for trade papers and magazines.
First Contact & Terms: Call for appointment to show portfolio.

CLINTON E. FRANK INC., ADVERTISING, 120 S. Riverside Plaza, Chicago IL 60606. Senior Vice President/Director, Creative Services: Thomas W. Laughlin, Sr.

ALEX T. FRANZ INC., 35 E. Wacker Dr., Chicago IL 60601. (312)782-9090. Vice-President/Art Director: William M. Shanahan. Clients: consumer and industrial products and services.
Needs: Uses artists for print advertising, collateral and product and situation illustration.
First Contact & Terms: Local artists only. Arrange interview to show portfolio. Pays by job "and as budget permits."

LARRY FREDERICKS ASSOCIATES, 845 3rd Ave., 15th Floor, New York NY 10022. Contact: Larry Fredericks. Clients: book publishers, firms with quarterly house organs and retailers.
Needs: Uses artists for layout, illustration, type spec, paste-up and retouching for consumer and trade magazines.
First Contact & Terms: Prefers local artists. Call for interview.

F. WILLIAM FREE & COMPANY, 400 Park Ave., New York NY 10022. (212)754-9696. Contact: Art Director. Ad agency. Clients: all consumer goods.
Needs: Works with 2 illustrators/month and occasionally designers. Uses artists for all consumer broadcast and print.
First Contact & Terms: Call for appointment to show portfolio. Negotiates pay based on client's budget and where work will appear.
Tips: Wants to see best work and past work used by other ad agencies. Also interested in art published.

FRIEDENTAG PHOTOGRAPHICS, 356 Grape St., Denver CO 80220. (303)333-7096. Manager: Harvey Friedentag. Audiovisuals/TV/film producer. Clients: Educational, industrial, corporate and governmental. Produces filmstrips, motion pictures, overhead transparencies, slide sets, sound-slide sets, videotapes and photos.
First Contact and Terms: Prefers local artists. Query with resume and samples. SASE. Reports in 4 weeks. Provide stack of work to be kept on file for future assignments. Negotiates pay.
Needs: Works with about 24 freelance illustrators/year. Uses artists for retouching (especially airbrush artists), cartoons, illustrations, paste-up and preparing camera-ready work.

FULLER PRODUCTION SERVICES, 1102 Lake Otis Dr., Winter Haven FL 33880. (813)294-8911. Production Manager: Sara Fuller. TV/film producer. Clients: ad agencies, TV/

film producers and magazines. Audience: general public. Produces motion pictures, videotapes and still photos.
Needs: Uses 4 artists/year. Uses illustrators for storyboards for commercials.
First Contact & Terms: Query with samples (photocopies and/or tearsheets). SASE. Reports in 2 weeks. Provide brochures/flyers, resume, tearsheets and a copy of work to be kept on file for future assignments. No original returned at job's completion. Buys all rights. Pays on acceptance.

FURMAN FILMS, 3466 21st St., San Francisco CA 94110. President: Will Furman. Motion picture/TV producer. Produces documentaries, industrial films and TV commercials. Clients: ad agencies and corporations. Arrange interview. Provides brochures/flyer, resume and tearsheets to be kept on file for future assignments.
Needs: Works with 2 designers/year. Uses artists for work on motion pictures.

G.M.A. AUDIO-VISUAL, Box 1006, St. Charles IL 60174. (312)317-0004. General Manager: Bruce Meisner. Clients: business and industry. Produces filmstrips, multimedia kits, overhead transparencies, slide sets and sound-slide sets.
Needs: Assigns 6-10 jobs/year.
First Contact & Terms: Query with resume. SASE. Reports in 3 weeks. Buys all rights. Minimum payment by hour: $6.50, charts/graphs; $12, cartoons; $15, illustrations. Pays on production.

THE GABLE AGENCY, INC.,, 409 Camino del Rio S., Suite 305, San Diego, CA 92108. (714)294-9160. Contact: Media director. Ad/PR firm. Clients: hotels, department stores, restaurants, radio stations, professional associations and manufacturers.
Needs: Assigns 40-50 jobs and buys 20-25 illustrations/year. Uses artists for design and production. Also uses artists for menu illustration, brochure design and illustration, advertising, mechanicals and production work.
First Contact & Terms: Local artists only. Query with resume or arrange interview to show portfolio. SASE. Reports in 2 weeks. Pays $200, ¼-page ad; $350, 4-page newsletter; $500, billboard; $250, 1-page flyer.

GALLERYWEST, LTD. MOTION PICTURE PRODUCTIONS, 630 Oakwood Ave., West Hartford CT 06110. (203)246-7231. Producer: Robert J. Hurrie. Director: Paul J. Gregory. TV/Film/Animation/AV producer. Clients: "all varieties of business and industrial clientele. Primarily, we produce on order, sales and market a/vs; training films, corporate image films, slide presentations for business, financial, manufacturing and some high technology."
Needs: Works with 2 illustrators/month. "Graphic as well as illustrative artists are used for slide projects frequently. Animation is often required in our TV commercial productions." Also uses artists for filmstrips, storyboards and packaging.
First Contact & Terms: "Send small, non-returnable sample of style with resume or business card. We like to see published work indicating type of clientele artist has worked with; but any good sample in the commercial art area will give us an idea of individual style for our information. We will not take responsibility for materials sent and can't guarantee their return." Works on assignment only. Reports back on future assignment possibilities. "We try very hard to be courteous and accurate in follow-up." Negotiates payment based on number of slides, length of film, complexity of subject and deadline."

GARDNER ADVERTISING, 10 S. Broadway, St. Louis MO 63102. (314)444-2000. Creative Director: Larry Pfisterer. Ad agency. Clients: Primarily consumer food and dog food; also industrial and financial.
Needs: Works with about 15 illustrators/month and occasionally uses designers for packaging. Uses artists for consumer print and TV.
First Contact & Terms: Call for appointment to show portfolio or make contact through artist's rep. Negotiates pay based on budget and where work will appear as well as color, b&w, etc.

RALPH D. GARDNER ADVERTISING, 745 5th Ave., New York NY 10022. Art/Creative Director: I.W. Wallack. Clients: Art, gifts, typewriters, paint, foreign cars, engineering, foods, liquors, tea, candy, bakery goods, displays and exhibits. Usually gives assignments to those who have previously worked with them. "Artists should not waste time calling. Send a brochure, card, or even a memo stating what you do. A list of credits is not essential, but is helpful. It shows that others have used your work."
Needs: Uses artists for lettering for newspapers, TV, magazines, radio and billboards.

GASKILL-OERTEL ADVERTISING INC., Box 206, Boynton Beach FL 33435. (305)732-9433. President: Alice Gaskill. Ad agency. Annual billing: $150,000. Clients: light industrial.

Needs: Assigns 10-12 jobs/year. Works with 1 or 2 illustrators/month. Uses illustrators for brochures/flyers and trade magazines.
First Contact & Terms: Local artists only. Arrange interview to show portfolio. SASE. Contacts artists as needs arise. Negotiates pay.

GEER, DUBOIS, INC., 1 Dag Hammarskjold Plaza, New York NY 10017. (212)758-6500. Contact: Art Director. Ad agency. Clients; financial, industrial, fashion and packaged goods.
Needs: Works with 2-3 illustrators/month. Uses artists primarily for newspapers and consumer and trade magazines.
First Contact & Terms: Call for appointment to show portfolio, make contact through artist's rep or mail samples. Negotiates pay based on difficulty of job.

GEER-MURRAY INC., 417 N. Sawyer, Oshkosh WI 54901. (414)231-9550. Art/Creative Director: Vern Weber. Estab. 1919. Clients: Manufacturers. Assigns "hundreds" of jobs and buys "hundreds" of illustrations/year. Query. SASE.
Needs: Uses artists for layout and illustration.

ABNER J. GELULA & ASSOCIATES, INC., 4829 Atlantic Ave., Atlantic City NJ 08404. (609)348-3116. Ad agency and public relations firm. Annual billing: $2,900,000. Clients: cities, hotels and travel. Media uses include billboards, consumer magazines, trade magazines, direct mail, newspapers, P-O-P displays, radio and TV.
First Contact & Terms: Call for personal appointment to show portfolio. Negotiates payment based on client's budget.

GENERAL EDUCATIONAL MEDIA INC., 701 Beaver Valley Road, Wilmington, DE 19803. (302)478-1994. President: David Engler. Clients: publishers, businesses and industry. Produces filmstrips, multimedia kits, overhead transparencies, slide sets and sound-slide sets.
Needs: Works with 1 or 2 illustrators/month. Uses illustrators for filmstrips, slides, booklets, manuals, worksheets, etc.
First Contact & Terms: Query. "We will request samples when we are ready to assign a job." SASE. Reports in 3 weeks. Buys all rights. Provide brochures/flyers, resumes and tearsheets to be kept on file for future assignments. No originals returned to artist at job's completion. Pays $15-50/frame, on acceptance.

GERO & BIERSTEIN INC., 190 Moore St., Hackensack NJ 07601. Art/Creative Director: Stephanie Grimaldi. Ad agency. Clients: real estate/land development, automobiles, banks, restaurants, electronics, consumer and furniture.
First Contact & Terms: Prefers local artists. Call for interview. Provide flyers, business cards and resumes to be kept on file for future assignments. No originals returned to artist at job's completion.
Needs: Works with 3 illustrators/month. Uses illustrators for direct mail, brochures/flyers, trade magazines and newspapers. Also uses artists for paste-up, retouching and architectural illustration (interior-exterior).

GILBERT, WHITNEY & JOHNS, 44 Dumont Place, Morristown NJ 07960. (201)538-7766. Executive Art Director: Stan Suhar. Ad agency. Annual billing: $9,500,000. Clients: industrial and consumer. Assigns 30-40 jobs/year.
Needs: Assigns 75-100 jobs/year. Uses artists for P-O-P displays, consumer magazines, multimedia kits, television, slide sets, brochures/flyers, trade magazines and newspapers.
First Contact & Terms: Call and send previously published work. Reports in 1 week. Provide brochures, resumes and tearsheets to be kept on file for future assignments. Pays by job.

GLENN, BOZELL & JACOBS, Box 61200, Dallas-Ft. Worth Airport, Dallas TX 75261. (214)556-1100. Contact: Art Director. Ad agency. Clients: all types.
Needs: Works with 4-5 freelance illustrators/month. Uses freelancers for billboards, newspapers, P-O-P displays, TV, and trade magazines.
First Contact & Terms: Call for appointment to show portfolio. Payment is negotiated.
Portfolio Tips: Wants to see a wide variety including past work used by ad agencies and tear sheets of published art.

GLENN, BOZELL & JACOBS/PR, 2000 Two Allen Center, Houston TX 77002. (713)651-3114. Creative Director: Jim Killinger. Ad Agency. Clients: industry, packaged goods. Media used include consumer magazines, brochures/flyers, newspapers, trade magazines and TV.
First Contact & Terms: Call for an appointment to show portfolio. Negotiates payment based on the going rate.

Portfolio Tips: Interested in "all types of illustrations including: air brush, realistic and far-out." Also interested in corporate-type design and collateral-type design.

IRVING H. GLICK ADVERTISING, 432 Park Ave. S., New York NY 10016. (212)838-8250. Contact: Irving H. Glick, art/creative director. Clients: Toys, insurance, soft goods and packaging. Buys 100+ illustrations/year. Query with samples. SASE. No originals returned.
Needs: Uses artists for all types of artwork. Pays $20-30/hour.

MICHAEL GLICK ADVERTISING, 25152 Lathrup Blvd., Southfield MI 48075. Art/Creative Director: Robert Plonka. Clients: Building products firms, electronics, clothing, toys, children's furniture, tools, realty, builders, gauge companies and sign manufacturers. Call for appointment; Detroit area artists only.
Needs: Illustrations, layout and retouching for newspapers, magazines, direct mail, billboards, TV and POP displays.

GLOBE ADVERTISING, 35075 Automation, Mt. Clemens MI 48043. (313)791-2801. Contact: Craig Tarbeck. Annual billing: $1,000,000. Clients: mail order.
Needs: Buys "several hundred" illustrations/year. Uses artists for color separations, retouching and type spec. Especially needs layout, catalog and magazine illustration and lettering.
First Contact & Terms: Local artists preferred. Query or write for interview. SASE. Reports in 1 week. Minimum payment: $10, layout; $5, illustration. Pays promised fee for unused assigned work.

GOLDEN STATE NEWS BUREAU-CREATIVE ARTISTS, MODELS, & PRESS ACADEMY, 7557 Hampton, West Hollywood CA 90046. (213)874-0301. Contact: Ray Engel.
Needs: Works with 2 illustrators and 2 animators/month. Uses artists for advertising, party invitations, artwork for concerts, movie premieres, fashion and trade shows, dances, beauty pageants, special events, PR receptions, grand openings, house parties, application forms, self-mailers, posters and monthly newsletters. Seeking new animators, artists and illustrators every month for unique party invitations.
First Contact & Terms: Arrange interview by phone or mail samples (tearsheets or originals). Provide brochures, flyers, business cards, resumes, tearsheets, logo samples, stationery samples, etc. to be kept on file for future assignments. No originals returned to artist at job's completion.

GOLDSHOLL ASSOCIATES, 420 Frontage Rd., Northfield IL 60093. Contact: Morton Goldsholl. Clients: corporations. Produces TV commercials, documentaries, industrial films, slides and multimedia productions. "Our film work is quite broad—commercials as well as industrial and cultural films."
Needs: Works with 3-4 illustrators/month. Uses artists for design and animation.
First Contact & Terms: Query by letter or phone with resume. Provide material showing your best work to be kept on file for future assignments. Negotiates pay.

GOODCHILD & EIDSON ADVERTISING INC., 1812 Industrial Bank Bldg., Providence RI 02903. (401)831-7484. Art Director: Algis Jaras. Ad/PR/graphics firm. Clients: foods, hotels, industrial and hardware. Annual billing: $3,000,000.
Needs: Works with 5 illustrators and 2-3 designers/month. Also uses artists for design of ads and collateral.
First Contact & Terms: Query with samples, (promotional pieces) and fees. SASE. Reports in 2-3 weeks. Buys work outright. No originals returned to artist at job's completion. Pays $20/hour, mechanicals; $150/figure, b&w line drawings; $250/figure, color illustrations.

GOODWIN, DANNENBAUM, LITTMAN & WINGFIELD, INC., 7676 Woodway, Houston TX 77063. (713)977-7676. Ad/PR firm. Clients: consumer and trade magazine, newspaper, radio and TV station, packaging, real estate, jewelry, food manufacturers and food chains.
Needs: Works with freelance illustrators and designers. Uses artists for billboards, consumer and trade magazines, direct mail, newspapers, P-O-P displays, radio and TV.
First Contact & Terms: Call for appointment to show portfolio or make contact through artist's rep. Negotiates pay based on client's budget and artist's previous experience/reputation.

FELTON GORDON ASSOCIATES, 3384 Peachtree Rd. NE, Suite 875, Atlanta GA 30326. Public Relations Director: Felton H. Gordon. Public relations counseling firm. Query with resume; prefers local artists.
Needs: Uses artists for direct mail brochures, annual reports and public service TV spots.

CHESTER GORE COMPANY, INC., 515 Madison Ave., New York NY 10022. (212)759-6600. Senior Art Director: Jeff Litson. Ad agency. Clients: liquor and sporting goods.
Needs: Works with 2-3 illustrators/month. Uses artists for consumer and trade magazines, primarily print media. Work such as in fashion field is usually easy to find, but since much of their work is in the sporting goods field, they find that shots and illustrations of such things as golf clubs and tennis rackets are more difficult to find.
First Contact & Terms: Call for appointment to show portfolio or make contact through artist's rep.

THE GRAPHIC EXPERIENCE INC., 341 Madison Ave., New York NY 10022. Contact: Production Manager. Ad agency/direct marketing firm. Clients: national corporations. Annual billing: $900,000. Assigns 800 jobs/year.
Needs: Uses 3-4 illustrators and 6-10 designers/month. Uses artists for consumer magazines, direct mail and brochures/flyers. Also uses artists for annual reports, catalogs, direct mail brochures, packaging, POP displays and print media advertising.
First Contact & Terms: Query with nonreturnable samples or arrange interview. No work returned. Provide brochures/flyers and business cards to be kept on file for future assignments. Original returned to artist at job's completion "only if a prior agreement has been made. If not, all art becomes property of agency." Pays $7-15/hour, mechanicals. Negotiates payment by job for color separations, design, illustrations, layout, paste-up, retouching, lettering and type spec.

GRAY & KILGORE, 2211 E. Jefferson St., Detroit MI 48207. (313)393-1500. Creative Director: Don Newell. Ad agency. Clients: mainly industrial manufacturing and some consumer.
Needs: Works with 6-9 freelance illustrators/year. 5% of freelancers used are illustrators—but need for illustrators is rising. Uses freelancers for trade magazines and newspapers.
First Contact & Terms: Call for appointment to show portfolio or send printed samples. Negotiates payment based on client's budget and experience of artist, i.e., his ability to produce what is needed on the first time around. (Less experienced person likely to need more time to do the job).
Portfolio Tips: Likes to see different styles of approach and types of graphic treatment as opposed to media of any sort.

GRAY & ROGERS, INC., PUBLIC RELATIONS, 1234 Market St. E, Philadelphia PA 19107. (215)864-6800. PR firm. Clients: home furnishings, automotive, utilities, industrial.
Needs: Works with about 6 illustrators/month and occasionally works with designers. Uses artists for "collateral material—never advertising material." Especially needs *good* illustrators in pure b&w pen and ink or brush and ink (not wash drawing) and *good* color retouchers in color photography.
First Contact & Terms: Call Art Director for appointment to show portfolio. Wants to see display of talent, professionalism, uniqueness and contemporary designs. Negotiates pay based on client's budget.

RUSSELL T. GRAY INC., 233 N. Michigan, Chicago IL 60601. Vice President/Art Director: J. Stephen Pribula. Clients: Metrology, earthmoving, chemical/food processing and humidification systems. Call for interview; prefers local artists.
Needs: Uses artists for illustration, technical art and retouching for trade magazines, direct mail and technical catalogs/bulletins.

GREAT AMERICAN CINEMA CO., 10711 Wellworth Ave., Los Angeles CA 90024. (213)475-0937. Animation/audiovisuals/TV/film producer. Estab. 1974. Clients: Advertising agencies, public relations firms, corporations. Produces television commercials, motion pictures, multimedia kits, slide sets, and videotapes. Assigns 1-2 jobs/year; local artists only. Query with resume and samples. SASE. Reports in 2 weeks.
Needs: Uses artists for titles and ads.

GREAT AMERICAN FILM FACTORY, Box 16028, Sacramento CA 95817. Production Director: Robert Williams. Estab. 1972. Clients: Schools. Produces filmstrips. Assigns 20-40 jobs/year. Query with samples or previously published work. SASE. Reports in 3-4 weeks. Buys all rights. Pays on acceptance. Free catalog.
Needs: Uses artists for filmstrips for schools. Payment by job: $5-2,000.

FINLEY GREENE ADVERTISING, 370 Franklin St., Buffalo NY 14202. Art Director: Robert Neiler. Clients: industry, retailers and banks.
Needs: Assigns 30-50 jobs/year. Uses artists for display booth, catalog and brochure design, bank services illustrations and technical industrial illustrations.

First Contact & Terms: Local artists with at least 2 years agency experience only. Query with samples and arrange interview to show portfolio. SASE. Reports in 1 month. Pays $15-25/hour.

MARTIN GREENFIELD ASSOCIATES INC., 525 Northern Blvd., Great Neck NY 11021. (516)487-3700. Vice President: Pamela Fischer. Estab. 1960.
Needs: Uses artists for layout, illustration, paste-up and retouching for newspapers, transit, radio, magazines, billboards, collateral, direct mail and POP displays.

GREY ADVERTISING INC., 3435 Wilshire Blvd., Los Angeles CA 90010. (213)380-0530. Contact: Art Director. Ad agency. Clients: financial, food, cruise line and stereo equipment.
Needs: A total of 10 art directors work with freelance illustrators according to their individual needs. Freelancers used in all media.
First Contact & Terms: Call for appointment to show portfolio or make contact through artist's rep. Some art directors prefer to use reps and others look at freelancer's portfolios. Negotiates payment based on combination of client's budget, amount of creativity required from artists and where work will appear.
Portfolio Tips: Wants to see anything that illustrates individual style.

GREY ADVERTISING INC., 601 California St., San Francisco CA 94108. (415)362-0393. Creative Coordinator: Claudia Ebert. Ad agency. Clients: food, beverage and financial.
Needs: Works with about 5 freelance illustrators/month. Uses freelancers for consumer and trade magazines, newspapers and P-O-P displays.
First Contact & Terms: Call for appointment to show portfolio. Selection based on portfolio review. Negotiates payment based on client's budget and amount of creativity required from artist.
Portfolio Tips: No specific guidelines. Interested in anything that illustrates individual style.

GREY ADVERTISING LTD., 2 Bloor St. W, Suite 2600, Toronto, Ontario Canada M4W 3G1. (416)967-0600. Senior Vice President/Creative Director: Terrence Hill. Ad agency. Clients: consumer foods, watch manufacturer, automotive, consumer magazine, financial and industrial.
Needs: Occasionally uses freelance illustrators and designers for P-O-P displays, consumer and trade magazine, TV, radio, print, brochures/flyers and newspapers.
First Contact & Terms: Provide letter of introduction and resume to T. Hill.
Tips: Wants to see as much variety of capabilities as possible—anything from fruit bowl still life to animation, if possible.

GREY ADVERTISING, Midwest Plaza Bldg. East, Minneapolis MN 55402. (612)341-2701. Art Director: Dan Freiberg. Ad agency. Annual billing: $5-6 million. Clients: retail, bookseller, bedding, WTCN-TV, exercise computer.
Needs: Works with 3-10 freelance illustrators/month. Seldom uses designers; averages 1/month. "Don't buy a lot of out-of-town freelance illustrations." Uses talents of both for work with billboards, consumer and trade magazines, brochures/flyers, newspapers, P-O-P displays, and TV.
First Contact & Terms: Call for appointment or write requesting interview to show portfolio. Negotiates payment based on client's budget.
Portfolio Tips: Wants to see illustrator's best work. Past work used by ad agencies and tear sheets of art published is fine to show if it's good work. Selects freelancers by reputation and reference.

GREY ADVERTISING INC., 777 3rd Ave., New York NY 10017. Executive Vice President/Creative Services: Joel R. Wayne. Needs ad illustrations. Local artists only. Call for an appointment. Negotiates pay.

GREY-NORTH INC., Merchandise Mart, Chicago IL 60654. (312)527-5030. Contact: Art Director. Ad agency. Clients: financial, appliance manufacturing, electronic organs and government (public information campaigns).
Needs: Works occasionally with freelance illustrators. Uses freelancers for consumer and trade magazines, newspapers and for TV storyboards and animatics.
First Contact & Terms: To determine needs, freelancers should talk with telephone operator who has list of art directors. Selection based on portfolio review. Negotiates payment based on client's budget, amount of creativity required from artist and where work will appear.
Portfolio Tips: Likes to see actual work done for someone else. Include step-by-step procedures in accordance with art director's instructions and needs, and final product.

GREYHOUND EXPO, 4829 S. Kedzie Ave., Chicago IL 60632. (312)376-9310. Animation/AV producer. AV Director: Mandy Bayro. Clients: industrial and corporate. Produces filmstrips, motion pictures, mutimedia kits, overhead transparencies, slide sets, sound-slide sets and videotapes.
Needs: Works with 6 illustrators and designers/year. Uses artists for slide layouts and illustrations.
First Contact & Terms: Query with resume; follow up with phone call. Reports in "several" weeks. Pays $5 min./hour.

GARY GRIFFIN PRODUCTIONS, 12667 Memorial Dr., Houston TX 77024. (713)465-9017. Contact: G. Griffin. AV/motion pictures/TV producer. Estab. 1978. Clients: corporate, industrial, ad agencies and private individuals. Produces motion pictures, national AV presentation, TV commercials and live entertainment.
Needs: Assigns 150 jobs/year. Uses artists for filmstrip animation, film-related artwork and ad illustrations.
First Contact & Terms: Query with resume and samples (tearsheets and photocopies of design work). SASE. Reports in 3 weeks. Provide brochures/flyers and tearsheets to be kept on file for future assignments. Pays $100 min./job; $15/hour for small job.

GRIFFITH & SOMERS ADVERTISING AGENCY, 330 Frances Bldg., Sioux City IA 51101. (712)277-3343. President: Margaret Holtze. Ad agency. Clients: industrial, financial, agricultural and business. Annual billing: $500,000.
Needs: Works with 1 illustrator/month. Uses artists for illustrations, cartoons, multi-media kits, brochures, direct mail, catalogs and multipage flyers.
First Contact & Terms: Query with samples (tearsheets). Artist should have previous agency experience. Reports in 3 weeks. Provide brochures and resumes to be kept on file for future assignments. No originals returned to artist at job's completion. Pays $7-20/hour.

GROVES & ASSOCIATES INC., 105 Ridge Rd., Muncie IN 47304. Art Directors: Ron Groves, Ray Decker and Cindy Norrick. Ad agency. Clients: industrial, banks, food chains and religious publishers.
Needs: Works with 2 illustrators/month. Uses illustrators for consumer magazines, direct mail, television, brochures/flyers, trade magazines and newspapers.
First Contact & Terms: Provide brochure and/or resume to be kept on file for future assignments. No originals returned to artist at job's completion.

GRUBB, GRAHAM & WILDER INC., Century 21 Plaza, Champaign IL 61820. Contact: Art Director. Ad agency. Clients: industrial and agricultural producers of wire, seedcorn and food.
Needs: Works with 2 illustrators and 5 designers/month. Uses artists for billboards, filmstrips, direct mail, television, slide sets, brochures/flyers, trade magazines and newspapers. Also uses artists for layout, illustration, technical art and retouching for newspapers, TV, radio, magazines, billboards and direct mail.
First Contact & Terms: Mail samples (original art or photocopies). Provide brochures, business cards and resumes to be kept on file for future assignments. No originals returned to artist at job's completion.

GUMPERTZ/BENTLEY/FRIED, 5900 Wilshire Blvd., Los Angeles CA 90036. (213)931-6301. Art Directors: Darryl Shimazu and Newell Nesheim. Creative Directors: Bernie Rowe and Dale Richards. Ad agency. Clients: Stockbrokers, banks, food companies, visitors' bureaus and tape recorder manufacturers. Annual billing: $8,000,000. Arrange interview to show portfolio.
Needs: Works with 3-4 illustrators/month; 2-3 designers/year. Illustration and paste-up. Negotiates pay.

GUTMAN ADVERTISING AGENCY, Peoples Federal Bldg., Wheeling WV 26003. (304)233-4700. Ad agency. Clients: financial, industrial, TV stations, meat packers, building products (concrete, machine, tool, glassware, paint) and medical firms.
Needs: Works with 3-4 illustrators/month. Uses artists for billboards, stationery design, television, brochures/flyers, trade magazines and newspapers. Also uses artists for retouching work.
First Contact & Terms: Local artists only. Call for interview. Provide materials to be kept on file for future assignments. No originals returned to artist at job's completion.

HANDLEY & MILLER, INC., 1732 N. Meridian, Indianapolis IN 46202. (317)924-5171. Art Director/Vice President: Irvin Showalter. Ad agency. Clients: industrial and consumer food.
Needs: Works with 2 freelance illustrators/month. Uses freelancers for consumer and trade

magazines, brochures/flyers, newspapers and P-O-P displays.
First Contact & Terms: Call I. Showalter for appointment to show portfolio. Selection based on portfolio review. Pays standard day rate.
Portfolio Tips: Likes to see a variety of techniques.

HANNA-BARBERA PRODUCTIONS INC., 3400 Cahuenga Blvd., Hollywood CA 90068. (213)851-5000. Harry Love, supervisor. TV/motion picture producer. Clients: TV networks. Produces animation and motion pictures.
Needs: Works with designers and illustrators on motion pictures. Also uses artists for animation and related artwork.
First Contact & Terms: Uses mostly local artists. Query and arrange interview to show portfolio. Reports "as soon as possible." Provide resume to be kept on file for future assignments. No originals returned to artist at job's completion. Negotiates pay.

CHARLES HANS FILM PRODUCTIONS INC., 228 E. 45th St., New York NY 10017. (212)867-1107. Art Director: Evelyn Simon. AV producer. Clients: industrial and corporate. Produces filmstrips, motion pictures, multimedia kits, overhead transparencies, slide sets, sound-slide sets and videotapes.
Needs: Works with 10-15 illustrators/year. Uses artists for "all phases of artwork," including chart work, paste-ups, mechanicals and some illustration and design as in animation or spot illustrations. The majority of the work is for slides.
First Contact & Terms: Arrange interview to show portfolio. SASE. Reports in 1 week. Provide samples to be kept on file for future assignments. Pays $8-10/hour.

HARMON TRUE PRUITT, 4220 Johnson Dr., Shawnee Mission KS 66205. (913)362-5566. Art Directors: Debra Alt-Turpin and Mike Teterson. Ad/PR firm. Clients: banks, fashion department store, lab equipment, pro football team, outdoor theatre and restaurants.
Needs: Works with 3 illustrators/month. Uses artists for illustration.
First Contact & Terms: Local artists only. Arrange interview to show portfolio. SASE. "Letter kept on file; will call artist if needed." No originals returned to artist at job's completion. Negotiates pay by job.

HARPER & ROW, PUBLISHERS INC., 10 E. 53rd St., New York NY 10022. Associate Producer: Linda Calabro. AV producer. Audience: college students and those involved in adult education. Produces audio cassettes, sound filmstrips, 16mm motion pictures and slides for college and police science markets.
Needs: Works with 2 illustrators and 2 designers/month. Uses artists for books, filmstrips and motion pictures.
First Contact & Terms: Mail art or arrange interview. SASE. Reports in 4 weeks. Provide resumes and brochures/flyers (if available) to be kept on file for future assignments. Originals returned to artist at job's completion. Free catalog.

JOHN AND MARY HARRELL, Box 9006, Berkeley CA 94709. (415)525-7167. Contact: John or Mary Harrell. AV producer. Clients: Protestant and Roman Catholic churches. Produces filmstrips and multimedia kits. Assigns 1 job and buys 50-100 illustrations/year.
Needs: Works with 1 illustrator/month. Uses artists for filmstrip, packaging and advertising art. "We are not interested in usual commercial or 'religious' art."
First Contact & Terms: Local artists only. "A fine arts background is necessary." Query and arrange interview to show portfolio. SASE. Reports in 1 week. "A resume for our files is helpful. A phone conversation, for which I make notes, is very helpful, too." No originals returned to artist at job's completion. "Because filmstrip masters deteriorate in time, we need the original art for remastering." Pays $50 average/piece of art (50-100 pieces) usually amounting to $5,000/job.

HARRIS & ASSOCIATES, 2801 Wayzata Blvd., Minneapolis MN 55405. Creative Director: Bill Rooks. Art/Production Director: Susan Palmer. Clients: Industrial, retail, farm and electronics.
Needs: Illustration, technical art and lettering for magazines, direct mail, POP displays and collateral.

HARSHE-ROTMAN & DRUCK, INC., 3345 Wilshire Blvd., Los Angeles CA 90010. (213)385-5271.
Needs: Work with freelance illustrators/designers varies depending on accounts. Uses artists for annual reports, catalogs, packaging, trademarks, posters, letterheads, layout, lettering, paste-up, type spec and mechanicals, retouching and illustrations.

First Contact & Terms: Send samples of work to the attention of office manager. Reports when interested in material submitted.

HARSHE-ROTMAN & DRUCK INC., 444 N. Michigan Ave., Chicago IL 60611. Director of Design: Don Levy. Estab. 1936. Clients: Insurance, cosmetics, chemicals, carpeting, industrial and entertainment. Assigns 50-100 jobs and buys 5 illustrations/year; local artists only. Query with resume. SASE. Reports in 1 week.
Needs: Pays $7.50-12.50/hour, annual reports, catalogs, packaging, trademarks, posters, letterheads, layout, lettering, paste-up, type spec and mechanicals; $15-250/job, retouching; $25-2,500, illustration. Pays promised fee for unused assigned work.

JAMES NEAL HARVEY, INC., 477 Madison Ave., New York NY 10022. (212)759-2800. Contact: Art Director. Ad agency. Clients: primarily automotive, beauty, pharmaceutical, and paper products.
Needs: Works with about 2 illustrators/year. Uses artists for consumer magazines and newspapers.
First Contact & Terms: Call for appointment or make contact through artist's rep. Negotiates pay based on client's budget and where work will appear. Sometimes buys out work and uses where and when at will.
Tips: Wants to see product illustrations, line drawing and b&w work.

HARWYN MEDICAL PHOTOGRAPHERS, 1001 City Ave., Suite 918 WB, Philadelphia PA 19151. Sales Manager: B. Steinsnyder. Estab. 1950. Clients: Colleges, schools and hospitals. Produces microfilms. Assigns 10 jobs/year; prefers artists with previous experience with firms of this type. Query. SASE. Reports in 4 weeks. Buys one-time rights. Pays on acceptance. Free catalog.
Needs: Pays $20 min./hour, illustrations; can negotiate.

HAYCOX PHOTORAMIC INC., Box 12190, Norfolk VA 23502. (804)855-1911. Art Director: Betty Credle. Animation/AV/TV/film producer. Produces filmstrips, motion pictures, overhead transparencies, slide sets, sound-slide sets and videotapes.
Needs: Assigns 20+ jobs and buys 500+ illustrations/year. Uses artists for slide illustrations, displays, mechanicals and schematics.
First Contact & Terms: Prefers local artists. Query with resume and arrange interview to show portfolio. SASE. Reports in 2 weeks. Provide AV materials and graphic designs to be kept on file for future assignments. Pays $5-7.50/hour.

PAUL HAYES PRODUCTIONS, 2406 S. MacDill Ave., Tampa FL 33609. (813)837-6384. Contact: Paul Hayes. Audiovisuals/TV/film producer. Estab. 1959. Produces filmstrips, motion pictures, multimedia kits, slide sets, sound-slide sets and videotapes. Assigns 3-12 jobs/year. Query with resume. SASE. Reports in 1 week.
Needs: Uses artists for slide films.

HAYES PUBLISHING CO. INC., 6304 Hamilton Ave., Cincinnati OH 45224. (513)681-7559. Office Manager: Mary Schneller. AV producer/book publisher. Produces educational books, brochures and audiovisuals on human sexuality and abortion.
Needs: Uses artists for direct mail brochures and books.
First Contact & Terms: Mail samples. SASE. Reports in 4 weeks. Material copyrighted. Pays by job. Free catalog.

HELITZER ADVERTISING INC., 485 Madison Ave., New York NY 10022. Art Director: Craig Manders. Creative Director: Art Sasso. Estab. 1952. Clients: Toys, games, children's stores, department stores and chemical corporations. Annual billing: $10,000,000. Assigns 50-100 jobs and buys 50-100 illustrations/year. Query with samples; local artists experienced in agency work only. SASE. Contacts artists as needs arise.
Needs: Payment by hour: $15 minimum, layout; $15-25, retouching; $10 minimum, mechanicals. Especially needs freelancers willing to work in-house.

HEPWORTH ADVERTISING CO., 3403 McKinney Ave., Dallas TX 75204. (214)525-7785. Manager: S.W. Hepworth. Ad agency. Clients: financial, food, machinery and insurance.
Needs: Works with 2 illustrators and 2 designers/month. Uses artists for billboards, consumer magazines, direct mail, slide sets, brochures/flyers and trade magazines.
First Contact & Terms: Local artists only. Query with samples (tearsheets). Provide materials to be kept on file for future assignments. No originals returned to artist at job's completion.

HERMAN & ASSOCIATES INC., 488 Madison Ave., New York NY 10022. Vice President: Paula Herman. Clients: Travel, consumer and industrial. Mail samples or write for interview; prefers local artists who have worked on at least 2-3 professional assignments previously.
Needs: Uses artists for mechanicals, illustrations, paste-up and retouching for newspapers, magazines and direct mail.

STUART HERSH PRODUCTIONS, 250 W. 57th St., New York NY 10019. (212)397-9103. Contact: Stuart Hersh. AV/TV/film producer. Produces filmstrips, motion pictures, multimedia kits, slide sets, sound-slide sets and videotapes.
Needs: Assigns 2-3 jobs/year. Uses artists for slide, motion picture and TV illustration.
First Contact & Terms: Local artists only. Query with resume and samples. SASE. Reports in 2 weeks. Negotiates pay.

HILL AND KNOWLTON, INC., 5900 Wilshire Blvd., Los Angeles CA 90036. (213)937-7460. Account Executive/Graphics: Carol Scott. PR firm. Clients: corporations.
Needs: Works with 3-4 illustrators/year; more often with designers. Uses artists for annual reports, brochures, catalogs, press photos, press kits, etc.
First Contact & Terms: Call for appointment to show portfolio.
Tips: Wants to see best work and work that shows individual style.

HILL AND KNOWLTON, INC., 1 Illinois Center, 111 E. Wacker Dr., Chicago IL 60601. (312)565-1200. Contact: Jacquelin Kohn, Virginia Gohagan. PR firm. Clients: retail goods, manufacturing, consumer products, medical, pharmaceutical and public utilities.
Needs: Works with 1-2 illustrators and 2 designers/month. Uses artists for annual reports, brochures, PR releases, all associated print and collateral, corporate collateral, internal publications and more.
First Contact & Terms: Call for appointment to show portfolio. Negotiates pay based on quality of work, client's budget, their own assessment of job needs, on previous work done, etc.
Tips: Has very broad needs. Will discuss these and particular needs during initial call.

HILL AND KNOWLTON, INC., 2500 One Dallas Centre, Dallas TX 75201. (214)651-1761. Contact: Tim Searson. PR firm. Clients: corporate.
Needs: Works with 1 illustrator/month. Uses artists for annual reports.
First Contact & Terms: Call for appointment to show portfolio. Negotiates pay based on client's budget.

BERNARD HODES ADVERTISING, INC., 15760 Ventura Blvd. Ste. A28, Encino CA 91436. (213)501-4613. Creative Director: Daniel Sima. Ad Agency. Clients: Hughes Aircraft, Rockwell. Media used includes brochures/flyers, newspapers and trade magazines.
Needs: Works with 10-12 illustrators and 2-3 designers/month. Uses artists for billboards, P-O-P displays, consumer magazines, stationery design, multimedia kits, direct mail, brochures/flyers, trade magazines and newspapers.
First Contact & Terms: Call for an appointment to show portfolio. No originals returned to artist at job's completion. Negotiates payment based on client's budget.
Portfolio Tips: Interested in illustrations for fashion, technical, drafting, etc. Also interested in designs for album covers, ads, and other products.

BERNARD HODES ADVERTISING, INC., 1101 Embarcadero Rd., Palo Alto CA 94303. (415)856-1000. Art Director: Steve Mitchell. Ad agency. Clients: personnel department and technological company.
Needs: Work with 1-2 freelance illustrators, 1-2 designers/month. Uses talents of both for work with brochures/flyers, newspapers, and trade magazines; also uses designers for TV work.
First Contact & Terms: Send promo piece to Steve Mitchell. Negotiates payment based on client's budget.

BERNARD HODES ADVERTISING, INC., 116 E. Brook Hollow, Santa Ana CA 92707. (714)549-7181. Creative Director: Daniel Sima. Ad agency. Clients: Hughes Aircraft, Rockwell. Media used include brochures/flyers, newspapers and trade magazines.
Needs: Works with 12+ illustrators and 2-3 designers/month. Uses artists for billboards, P-O-P displays, consumer magazines, stationery design, multimedia kits, direct mail, brochures/flyers, trade magazines and newspapers.
First Contact & Terms: Call for an appointment to show portfolio of original art. Provide business cards, resumes and tearsheets to be kept on file for future assignments. No originals returned to artist at job's completion. Negotiates payment based on client's budget.

Portfolio Tips: Interested in illustrations for fashion, technical, drafting, etc. Also interested in designs for album covers, ads, and other products.

BERNARD HODES ADVERTISING, INC., Box 9569, Denver CO 80209. (303)779-1333. Contact: Art Director. Ad agency. Clients: industry.
Needs: Uses 3-4 illustrators/month. "Barrickman art directors are used for all projects. They choose the freelancers." Uses illustrators for consumer magazines, brochures/flyers, trade magazines and newspapers. Uses designers for TV.
First Contact & Terms: Call for an appointment to show portfolio. Negotiates payment, 90% based on client's budget.
Portfolio Tips: Portfolio should show "how problems are approached through illustrations. It should show how well artist can follow art director's instructions."

HOEFER/AMIDEI ASSOCIATES, 426 Pacific Ave., San Francisco CA 94133. President: Neal Amidei. PR firm.
Needs: Works with as many as 3 illustrators and 2 designers/month. Uses artists for billboards, P-O-P displays and brochures/flyers.
First Contact & Terms: Submit resume and samples. Provide business cards, brochures and flyers to be kept on file for future assignments. Originals returned to artist at job's completion.

HOFFMAN YORK, INC., 2300 N. Mayfair Rd., Milwaukee WI 53226. (414)259-2000. Contact: Art Director. Ad agency. Annual billing: $35 million. Clients: typical consumer clients such as washing machine manufacturers and airlines. Also business-to-business type clients (who sell to industry).
Needs: Works with "many" freelance illustrators/month. Needs vary. Uses freelancers for all print media.
First Contact & Terms: Call for appointment to show portfolio.
Portfolio Tips: Wants to see best work. Will probably use freelancer's area of specialty.

HOOD LIGHT & GEISE, 129 State St., Harrisburg PA 17101. (717)234-8091. Contact: Paul Gallo, art director. Advertising/public relations firm. Estab. 1935. Clients: Medical, industrial, banks and tourism. Annual billing: $2,000,000. Query with samples; local artists only. SASE. Reports in 1 week.
Needs: Uses artists for illustrations and brochure paste-up. Pays $3-6/hour, paste-up; pays by job for illustrations.

HENRY HOOK ADVERTISING, 38 W. Bethune, Detroit MI 48202. (313)871-5333. Art/Creative Director: Henry Hook. Ad agency. Clients: premium manufacturers.
Needs: Works with 1 illustrator and 1 designer/month. Uses artists for direct mail, brochures/flyers and trade magazines and cartoons on energy use and conservation.
First Contact & Terms: Mail art (photocopies). SASE. Reports in 2 weeks.

L. P. HORIST AND ASSOCIATES, 2709 Simpson St., Evanston IL 60201. (312)475-4300. President: Karen Horist. Clients: political candidates, industry and fashion.
Needs: Works with 2-3 illustrators; assigns 4-5 jobs/month. Uses artists for P-O-P displays, filmstrips, consumer magazines, stationery design, multimedia kits, direct mail, television, slide sets, brochures/flyers, trade magazines and newspapers.
First Contact & Terms: Query with samples (tearsheets and/or photocopies). No work returned. Reports in 1 month. Provide brochures, flyers, business cards, resumes, tearsheets, etc. to be kept on file for future assignments. No originals returned to artist at job's completion.

THE HORIZON GROUP INC., 2212 Victory Pkwy., Cincinnati OH 45206. (513)281-1888. Creative Director: Douglas E. Smith. Ad/PR firm. Annual billing: $250,000. Clients: industry. Assigns 250-300 jobs/year.
Needs: Works with 3 illustrators and 3 designers/month. Uses artists for stationery design, direct mail, brochures/flyers and trade magazines. Also uses artists for annual reports, catalogs, POP displays, posters, newspapers, trademarks, layout, lettering, paste-up, retouching, type spec and mechanicals. Pays promised fee for unused assigned illustrations.
First Contact & Terms: Uses mostly local artists. Query with samples (photocopies). SASE. Provide individual brochures, tearsheets, and/or individual spec sheets to be kept on file for future assignments. No originals returned to artist at job's completion.

HOUSTON/RITZ & ASSOCIATES, (formerly Houston/Ritz/Cohen/Jagoda), 3603 N. Hall, Dallas TX 75219. Art/Creative Director: Wayne Houston. Clients: Magazines, savings and loan, hotel, fashion and dish manufacturers.

Needs: Magazine editorial illustration (b&w and full color), technical art, paste-up, retouching and lettering for newspapers, TV, magazines, billboards and direct mail.

LLOYD S. HOWARD ASSOCIATES INC., Box N, Millwood NY 10546. Art/Creative Director: L. Howard. Ad agency. Clients: industrial, home furnishing, lighting and swimming pool firms.
Needs: Works with 2 illustrators and 5 designers/month. Uses artists for consumer magazines, direct mail, brochures/flyers, trade magazines and newspapers. Also uses artists for mechanicals and finished art for newspapers, magazines, catalogs and direct mail.
First Contact & Terms: Local or New York City artists only. Call for interview. Provide materials to be kept on file for future assignments. No originals returned to artist at job's completion.

HUGHES DESIGNGROUP, (formerly Thompson-Hughes & Associates), 331 Hemsted Dr., Redding CA 96001. (916)244-3706. President: J.G. Hughes. Ad/PR firm. Estab. 1978. Clients: cosmetic and electronics manufacturers, and automotive dealers. Annual billing: $2,000,000.
Needs: Works with 2-3 illustrators/month. Uses artists for ad, filmstrips, multimedia kits, annual report, direct mail and catalog illustration.
First Contact & Terms: Query with resume and samples. Reports in 4 weeks. Provide brochures, flyers, business cards, resumes, tearsheets, etc. to be kept on file for future assignments. Originals may be returned at job's completion. Negotiates pay.
Tips: "Simple subject matter draws the best response."

HUGHES, MARTINDALE & ASSOCIATES, INC., 1831 Hicks Rd., Rolling Meadows IL 60008. (312)934-4464. President: R. Martindale. Communications consultants. Annual billing: $1¼ million. Clients: financial. Media used includes billboards, consumer and trade magazines, direct mail, newspapers, radio, and TV.
Needs: "Work load varies, usually our extra assignments (beyond what our regular staff can service efficiently) bunch up in active months such as January, May, September, and October. Those extra assignments might be 5 or 6 newspaper ad layouts, 2 or 3 brochures, and maybe a special design assignment." Uses artists for work in direct mail, brochures/flyers and newspapers.
First Contact & Terms: Write and request personal interview to show portfolio. Provide resume to be kept on file for future assignments. Negotiates payment based on client's budget. Uses set fee/job.
Portfolio Tips: "We prefer to let the individual decide what he or she wants to show. If they can't show a strong portfolio, we can't expect them to be strong enough for our purposes."

I.E. INCORPORATED, 736 S. Eddy St., South Bend IN 46615. Contact: Jim Baxter. AV producer. Clients: heavy industry. Audience: Salespeople and distributors, blue collar workers and consumers of industrial products. Produces motion picture documentaries, sound/slide presentations, filmstrips and industrial films.
Needs: Works with 4 illustrators/month. Uses artists for catalogs, filmstrips, motion pictures and 35mm slides.
First Contact & Terms: Arrange interview. Provide materials to be kept on file for future assignments. No originals returned at job's completion. Pays $40/frame, filmstrip art.

I.F. STUDIOS INC., 328 E. 44th St., New York NY 10017. President: Ed Tricomi. Secretary/Treasurer: Lewis Cohen. Motion picture producer. Clients: ad agencies and TV stations. Produces titles, industrial films, documentaries, slides and exhibits.
Needs: Uses 1-2 artists/month for work on motion pictures.
First Contact & Terms: Arrange interview. Provide brochure, resume and tearsheet to be kept on file for future assignments. No originals returned at job's completion.

IMAGE INC., Box 113, Casper WY 82601. Art/Creative Director: Sylvia Arkebauer. Clients: Consumer product firms, manufacturers, services and associations. Mail samples.
Needs: Uses artists for layout, illustration, technical art, type spec, paste-up, retouching and lettering for newspapers, TV, magazines, billboards, radio and direct mail.

IMAGE INNOVATIONS, INC., 14 Buttonwood Dr., Somerset NJ 08873. President: Mark Else. Film/multi-image/video producer. Clients: school, association, corporate and governmental.
Needs: Uses artists for filmstrips, motion picture, multi-image multimedia kits, storyboards, packaging, books and brochures.
First Contact & Terms: Write for interview to show portfolio or send resume. Works on assignment only. Samples returned by SASE. Provide resume, letter of inquiry and/or flyer to be kept on file for future assignments. Negotiates pay based on client's budget, amount of creativity

required, where work is to appear and artist's previous experience/reputation.

IMAGE MEDIA INC., 3532 Humboldt Ave. S., Minneapolis MN 55408. (612)827-6500. President: Michael Rifkin. AV/TV/film producer. Clients: ad agencies, industrial and educational.
Needs: Works with 6 freelance illustrators and 1-3 designers/year. Uses artists for filmstrips, motion pictures, storyboards, print ads, slide illustrations, animation and titles.
First Contact & Terms: Send resume. SASE. Works on assignment only. Samples returned by SASE; reports back on future assignment possibilities. Provide resume and some samples of materials to be kept on file for future assignments. Negotiates pay based on client's budget and amount of creativity required.

IMAGINE THAT!, 500 N. Michigan Ave., Suite 2000, Chicago IL 60611. (312)266-9102. President: John Beele. Clients: broadcast, insurance firm and University of Illinois sports program.
Needs: Assigns 50-100 jobs and buys 20 illustrations/year. Uses artists for layout, illustration, mechanicals and cartoons.
First Contact & Terms: Arrange interview to show portfolio. Pays $50, spot; $2,000, illustration.

IMARC CORP., Box H, Newtown Square PA 19073. (215)356-2000. Manager, Graphics Department: Sheryl Balmas. AV/TV/film producer. Clients: industry, commercial businesses and museums. Produces filmstrips, motion pictures and slide sets. Assigns 100 jobs/year.
Needs: Works with about 4 illustrators and 8-10 designers/year.
First Contact & Terms: Query with resume, mail art and arrange interview. SASE. Reports in 1 week. Provide resume, brochure and tearsheet to be kept on file for future assignments. Buys all rights. Pays on production. Minimum payment by hour: $5, charts/graphs and mechanicals; $10, technical art and type spec; $15, illustrations.

IMPACT PROMOTIONS OF THE SOUTHWEST INC., Box 225975, Dallas TX 75265. (214)638-8190. Project Director/Senior Art Director: David S. Harper. Sales promotion agency. Clients: package goods producers, food producers, petroleum/oil/lubricants producer, sit down and fast food chains and homebuilders. Annual billing: $1,300,000. Assigns 25-35 jobs and buys 75-100 illustrations/year.
Needs: Works with 2-3 illustrators and 1 designer/month.
First Contact & Terms: Uses mostly local artists. Query with resume and samples (work done for other ad agencies). SASE. Reports in 2 weeks. No originals returned at job's completion. Payment by job: $50-250, POP design; $50-4,000, illustrations (from b&w product illustration to multi-piece projects); $50-350, retouching. Payment by hour: $10, layout, paste-up and mechanicals; $10-15, lettering. Pays originally agreed payment for unused assigned illustrations.
Tips: "We prefer experienced freelancers used to high-pressure situations. We do not object to working by mail, but deadlines could make it difficult to impossible, depending on the project."

IMPRESSIONS UNLIMITED INC., 214 Brazilian Ave., Palm Beach FL 33480. (305)659-4011. Creative Services Director: A. Gleimer. Ad/PR/AV/art firm. Clients: theatrical companies, charities, retailers and wholesalers. Assigns 30-40 jobs/year.
Needs: Works with 5 illustrators and 2 designers/month. Uses artists for TV, slide sets, direct mail, brochures/flyers, newspapers and POP displays.
First Contact & Terms: Southern Florida artists only. Query with samples (photocopies) by mail. Prefers professionals with commercial art experience. SASE. Reports in 2 months. Provide as much material as possible to be kept on file for future assignments. No originals returned to artist at job's completion. Pays $100-1,000/job.

INDIANA CABLEVISION CORP., 16830 Edison Rd., Mishawaka IN 46544. Contact: Gary L. Stephenson. TV producer.
Needs: Works with 2 illustrators/year. Uses artists for video presentations.

GEORGE C. INNES & ASSOCIATES, 517 Broad St., Elyria OH 44035. (216)323-4526. President: George C. Innes. Ad/art agency. Clients: industrial and travel trailer industries. Assigns 25-50 jobs/year.
Needs: Works with 3-4 illustrators/month. Uses illustrators for filmstrips, stationery design, multimedia kits, direct mail, slide sets, brochures/flyers, trade magazines, newspapers and books. Also uses artists for layout and design for reports, catalogs, print ads, direct mail/publicity, brochures, displays, employee handbooks, exhibits, products, technical charts/illustrations, trademarks, logos and company publications.
First Contact & Terms: Query with examples (photocopies/tearsheets) of work. SASE required for sample return. Reports in 2 weeks. Provide brochures, flyers, business card, resume and

tearsheet to be kept on file for future assignments. No originals returned to artist at job's completion. Pays $4-10/hour, keyline/line illustrations; $4-12/hour, continuous-tone illustrations; $8-250, paintings.

THE INNOVATION ORGANIZATION, 6684 Charing St., Simi Valley CA 93063. (213)882-0177. Producer: Ron Lewis. Publicity firm.
Needs: Works with 2-3 illustrators and 2-3 designers/month. Uses artists for billboards, POP displays, consumer magazines, mutimedia kits, direct mail, TV, brochure/flyer, trade magazines, album covers and newspaper.
First Contact & Terms: Provide business card, resume and tearsheet to be kept on file for future assignments. No originals returned to artists at job's completion. Negotiates pay. Local artists only. Query with resume and samples. SASE. Reports in 2-4 weeks.

IN-PERSPECTIVE COMMUNICATIONS INC., 205 Lexington Ave., New York NY 10016. (212)889-2111. President: Sheppard Kerman. AV producer. Clients: corporations and on- and off-Broadway shows. Produces multiscreen slide presentations.
Needs: Works with 30 illustrators and designers/year. Storyboards for slide presentation shows, films (16mm) designers.
First Contact & Terms: Local artists only. Send resume or call. "Do not send work." Payment by hour: $5-15, charts/graphs; $4-10, mechanicals. Pays on production. Provide resume to be kept on file for future assignments.

INSGROUP INC., 16052 Beach Blvd., Huntington Beach CA 92647. Contact: Wayne Ingram. AV producer. Clients: educational, industrial and military. Produces charts, film loops, sound filmstrips, multimedia kits, overhead transparencies, slides and illustrated syllabi.
Needs: Works with a varying number of illustrators and designers. Uses artists for catalogs and filmstrips.
First Contact & Terms: Mail resume. Will contact artists as assignments arise. Credentials must include "5 years of documented, cost-effective productivity; local artists only." Material usually copyrighted. Provide brochure and resume to be kept on file for future assignments. Originals sometimes returned at job's completion. Prefers paying royalties. Pay determined by task, complexity and turnaround.

INSTRUCTIONAL DYNAMICS INC., 666 N. Lake Shore Dr., Suite 924, Chicago IL 60611. (312)943-1200. Director, Multimedia Production and Marketing: Linda Thomas-Phillips. AV producer. Clients: educational publishers, national organizations, government and military, school and corporate. Audience: students, business and government personnel. Produces instructional and training filmstrips, multimedia kits, overhead transparencies, slide sets and sound-slide sets. Assigns 50 jobs/year; mainly local artists.
Needs: Has irregular art needs. Uses artists for album covers, books, catalogs and filmstrips. Also uses artists for charts/graphs, filmstrips, multimedia kits, storyboards, packaging and print ads.
First Contact & Terms: Query with resume and previously published work. "Samples will be requested subsequently and returned." Reports in 1 week. Provide resume, brochure and tearsheets to be kept on file for future assignments. Buys all rights. Client retains original after job. Pays on acceptance.

INSTRUCTIONAL MEDIA CENTER (IMC), University of Nebraska-Lincoln, 421 Nebraska Hall, Lincoln NE 68588. (402)472-1900. Contact: Director. Audiovisual center. Produces filmstrips, motion pictures, multimedia kits, overhead transparencies, slide sets and sound-slide sets. Assigns 3-10 jobs/year.
Needs: Works with 1 illustrator/month. Uses illustrations for filmstrips.
First Contact & Terms: Query with resume. SASE. Reports in 2 weeks. Provide brochures/flyers and resume to be kept on file for future assignments. No originals returned to artist at job's completion. Pay determined by job. Pays on production.

INTERNATIONAL PUBLIC RELATIONS GROUP OF COMPANIES, INC., Box 4034, Honolulu HI 96813. (808)536-7677. Public relations firm. Annual billing: $29,583,965. Clients: "Our offices represent all activities." Media used include trade magazines, direct mail, and newspapers.
First Contact & Terms: "Keep the Central Office informed of availability of talent." Negotiates payment based on client's budget.

INTRAMED COMMUNICATIONS, 130 E. 59th St., New York NY 10022. (212)751-0160. Contact: Creative Supervisor. AV/TV/film producers. Clients: corporations and advertising agencies. Produces filmstrips, motion pictures, multimedia kits, slide sets, sound-slide sets and videotapes.

First Contact & Terms: Arrange interview to show portfolio. "We see most freelancers who call." Reports in 1 week. Provide samples and brochure to be kept on file for future assignments.

SAMUEL IRVING ADVERTISING ART & DESIGN, 1719 Walnut St., Philadelphia PA 19103. (215)563-7800. Art/Creative Director: Samuel Irving. Clients: real estate, industrial, government, beverage manufacturers, fundraising groups, mall and apartment developers, publishing, food distributors and art galleries.
Needs: Works with 1 illustrator/month. Uses artist for illustrations, animation, paste-up and retouching for billboards, ads, packaging and POP displays.
First Contact & Terms: Query with samples (tearsheets, roughs, work done for other ad agencies or anything indicating what the artist can do) or call for interview. SASE. Reports in 1 week. Original work not returned unless specifically requested of their client. Pays promised fee for unused assigned work.

ISKER & ADAJIAN INC., 435 N. Michigan Ave., Chicago IL 60611. (312)222-1646. Contact: A. Adajian. Ad agency/PR firm/art agency/AV producer/art studio. Assigns 100 jobs/year.
Needs: Works with artists on billboards, POP displays, filmstrips, consumer, stationery design, multimedia kits, direct mail, TV, slide sets, brochures/flyers, trade magazines, album covers, newspapers and books. Also uses artists for layout, illustration, retouching and mechanicals.
First Contact & Terms: Query with resume and samples (or originals) or arrange interview to show portfolio. SASE. Reports in 2 weeks. Provide business card, resume, brochures/flyers and tearsheet to be kept on file for future assignments. No originals returned to artist at job's completion. Pays "going rates."

J.C. PRODUCTIONS INC., 16 W. 46th St., New York NY 10036. (212)575-9611. Contact: Walter Horn or Joe Conforti. TV producer (producing many test commercials and animatics).
Needs: Works with about 4 illustrators during "heavy" periods and about 1-2 during slow times. Uses artists for animation.
First Contact & Terms: Arrange interview. Provide brochures with samples of style to be kept on file for future assignments. Pays $600-800/spot.

JACOBY & CO., 155 W. Congress St., Detroit MI 48226 and 505 S. Grand, Leland MI 49654. President: Albert K. Jacoby. Ad/PR agency. Clients: manufacturers, services, publishers, sports (racing), auction services, education, marine products, construction, banking and real estate.
Needs: Works with 3 illustrators and 6 designers/month. Uses artists for layout, illustration, technical art, type spec, paste-up, retouching and lettering for newspapers, magazines, TV, billboards, sales meetings, conventions and seminars.
First Contact & Terms: Arrange appointment or mail samples (tearsheets and photocopies). Provide materials to be kept on file for future assignments. No originals returned to artist at job's completion.

JACOBY/STORM PRODUCTIONS INC., 101 Post Rd. E., Westport CT 06880. (203)227-2220. Vice President: Doris Storm. AV/TV/film producer. Clients: schools, corporations and publishers. Produces filmstrips, motion pictures, slide sets, sound-slide sets and videotapes. Pays $5-20/frame, lettering; $20-50/frame, illustrations of educational filmstrip scripts. Also uses artists to design slide show graphics.
Needs: Assigns 10-12 jobs/year. Uses artists for lettering, illustrations for filmstrips and to design slide show graphics.
First Contact & Terms: Prefers local artists with educational filmstrip experience. Query with resume and arrange interview. SASE. Reports in 2 weeks. Usually buys all rights. Pays on acceptance.

JEAN-GUY JACQUE ET COMPAGNIE, 1463 Tamarind Ave., Hollywood CA 90028. (213)462-6474. Contact: J.G. Jacque. TV/film producer. Clients: advertising agencies. Produces motion pictures.
Needs: Assigns 10-20 jobs/year. Uses artists for motion picture animation and illustrations.
First Contact & Terms: Query with resume and photocopied samples. SASE. Reports in 1 week. Buys all rights. Pays on production. Provide brochures/flyers to be kept on file for future assignments. Pays $2,000-3,000, animation; $500-1,000, illustrations.

T.S. JENKINS & ASSOCIATES INC., 140 E. 2nd St., 1 Capitol Court, Flint MI 48502. (313)235-5654. Ad agency. Clients: Bank, educational, retail, promotional and automobile dealers.
Needs: Buys 4-5 illustrations/year. Uses designers and illustrators for billboards, P-O-P displays,

filmstrips, consumer and trade magazines, stationery design, multimedia kits, direct mail, TV, slide sets, brochures/flyers and newspapers. Also uses artists for illustrations, layout, lettering, paste-up, retouching and type spec for annual reports, catalogs, ads, letterheads, packaging, posters, and trademarks.
First Contact & Terms: Call for interview. Have samples in the form of tearsheets and original art. Provide resume to be kept on file for future assignments. Pays $5 min./hour, keyline/paste-up; $5/hour, layout.

JENNINGS & THOMPSON/FCB, 3003 N. Central Ave., Phoenix AZ 85012. (602)263-8588. Contact: Linda Amburgey or Executive Creative Director. Ad agency. Clients: all types.
Needs: Works with varying number of freelance illustrators/month. Uses freelancers for billboards, consumer and trade magazines, brochures/flyers, newspapers, stationery design and TV.
First Contact & Terms: Call L. Amburgey or Exec. Creative Director for appointment. Negotiates payment based on client's budget.
Portfolio Tips: Wants to see background work.

JEPPESEN SANDERSON, 55 Inverness Dr. E., Englewood CO 80112. (303)779-5757. Audiovisual Manager: Ron Jones. AV producer. Produces film loops, sound filmstrips, videotapes, motion pictures and slides on aviation, scuba and skin diving and weather.
Needs: Works with 1-2 illustrators/month.
First Contact & Terms: Prefers local artists. Query with samples. Provide brochures (if available) to be kept on file for future assignments.

ELVING JOHNSON ADVERTISING INC., 7800 W. College Dr., Palos Heights IL 60463. (312)361-2850. Art/Creative Director: Michael McNicholas. Ad agency. Clients: industrial and consumer. Annual billing: $750,000.
Needs: Works with 2 illustrators/month. Uses artists for direct mail, brochures/flyers, trade magazines and newspapers. Also uses artists for layout, illustration, technical art, paste-up and retouching.
First Contact & Terms: Local artists only. Call for interview.

GEORGE JOHNSON, ADVERTISING, 755 New Ballas Rd. S., St. Louis MO 63141. (314)569-3440. Art Director: Fred Chase. Clients: real estate, fast food, savings and loan, community development, automotive, opticians, supermarket labeling systems and computer terminals.
Needs: Works with 4-5 illustrators and 2-3 designers/month. Uses artists for illustrations, animation, layout, lettering, paste-up, retouching, type spec and design for annual reports, billboards, catalogs, print ads, letterheads, packaging, P-O-P displays, posters, TV and trademarks. Pays $15-50/hour.
First Contact & Terms: Local artists only. Write or call for appointment to show agency samples of work (tearsheets, roughs and work done for other ad agencies). SASE. Reports in 1 week. Originals returned to artist at job's completion.

WALTER L. JOHNSON ADVERTISING INC., 9233 Ward Parkway Extension, Suite 290, Kansas City MO 64114. Clients: Industrial and consumer. Mail samples or call for interview; local artists only.
Needs: Uses artists for layout, illustration, technical art and retouching for newspapers, radio, TV, magazines, billboards and direct mail.

JIM JOHNSTON ADVERTISING INC., 551 5th Ave., New York NY 10017. (212)986-1191. Art/Creative Directors: Jim Johnston, Mark Hogan. Clients: "a general list including the media, wine and beer, paper, two-way radio manufacturer, stock brokerage and a symphony orchestra." Annual billing: $10,000,000.
First Contact and Terms: Query with previously published work or samples, or arrange interview. SASE. Reports in 2 weeks. Provide tearsheets to be kept on file for possible future assignments. No originals returned to artist at job's completion. Payment by job: $250-6,500, annual reports; $250-2,000, billboards; $125-2,500, consumer magazines; $150-5,000, packaging; $250-1,000, POP displays; $150-1,500, posters; $125-600, trade magazines; $100-1,000, letterheads; $200-1,500, trademarks; $300-2,500, newspapers. Payment by hour: $20 minimum, catalogs; $5-20, paste-up. Pays 25% of promised fee for unused assigned illustrations.
Needs: Works with 3-4 illustrators/month. Uses artists for consumer magazines, trade magazines and newspapers.

THE GILBERT JONAS CO., INC., 150 E. 58th St., New York NY 10022. (212)421-2120. President: Gilbert Jonas. Vice-President: Terry Monness. PR/fundraising firm. Clients: public

interest causes and charities. Annual billing: $300,000.
Needs: Works with 5-6 artists/year. Uses artists primarily for "design of direct mail brochures and mechanicals; occasionally for other printed materials, such as brochures, booklets, etc."
First Contact & Terms: Uses local freelance artists. Query with resume. Provide brochures/flyers to be kept on file for future assignments. No originals returned to artist at job's completion. Pays $200-400 plus type charges for basic direct mail brochure.

JONES, ANASTASI & MITCHELL, INC., 3715 Poplar, Erie PA 16508. Ad agency. Annual billing: $2,500,000. Clients: financial, commercial, and food. Media used include: billboards, consumer and trade magazines, direct mail, newpapers, P-O-P displays, radio, and TV.
First Contact & Terms: Call or write and request personal appointment to show portfolio.

JONETHIS/LARSON ADVERTISING INC., 310 Fairmount Ave., Box 189, Jamestown NY 14701. Personnel Director: Terry N. Jonethis. Ad agency. Industrial clients.
Needs: Layout and paste-up for newspapers and trade magazines.
First Contact & Terms: Mail samples (original art or photocopies). Provide brochures/flyers and/or business card to be kept on file for future assignments. No originals returned to artist at job's completion.

DAVID KALLAHER INC., Suite 801, 602 Main St., Cincinnati OH 45202. (513)621-6007. Contact: David Kallaher. Art studio/animation/TV/film/special effects producer. Clients: advertising agencies and industry. Produces motion pictures and videotapes.
First Contact & Terms: Query with resume and samples or arrange interview to show portfolio. SASE. Reports in 1-2 weeks. Pays by job. Provide resume along with roughs, sketchbooks and finished art to be kept on file for future assignments. No originals returned to artist at job's completion.
Needs: Works with 1-2 illustrators and 1-2 designers/month. Assigns 50-100 jobs/year. Uses artists for animation, in between work, painting, background and illustrations.

ROBERT FRANCIS KANE, 12 E. 41st St., New York NY 10017. (212)688-6320. Public relations firm. Clients: industrial, financial, corporate, and new products. Media used include: trade magazines and newspapers.
First Contact & Terms: Call or write and request personal interview to show portfolio. Negotiates payment based on client's budget, amount of creativity required from artist, and where work will appear.

KAPCO COMMUNICATIONS, 5221 N. Elston Ave., Chicago IL 60630. Vice President: Karen Dace. Audiovisuals/TV/film producer. Clients: industrial, business and entertainment. Produces motion pictures, multimedia kits, sound-slide sets and videotapes; "the majority of work produced by our business is industrial video."
Needs: Assigns 35 jobs/year. Uses artists for illustrations for videotapes, instructional support texts and audiovisual projects.
First Contact & Terms: Query. SASE. Reports in 3-4 weeks. Provide photocopied samples to be kept on file for future assignments. Originals returned to artist at job's completion. Pays $25-75, illustration; $100-750, audiovisual project.

PAUL S. KARR PRODUCTIONS, Box 11711, 2949 W. Indian School Rd., Phoenix AZ 85017. (602)266-4198. Contact: Paul Karr. Utah Division: Box 1254, 1024 N. 250 East., Orem, UT 84057. (801)225-8485. Contact: Micheal Karr. Film producer. Clients: industrial, business and educational.
Needs: Occasionally works with freelance animators in motion picture projects.
First Contact & Terms: Advise of experience and abilities and whether a sample reel of work is available. Works on assignment only. "Occasionally a gifted person in the motion picture area will come along who has an extra something that he can offer. That's about the scope of what would be of interest to us." Pay depends on "scope, ability and budget available."

KAUFMAN SPICER/MARKETEC, 227 Shelard Plaza, Minneapolis MN 55426. (612)544-2234. Executive Art Director, Jim Kanters. Ad/PR/graphics/display firm. Annual billing: $7,000,000.
Needs: Works with 2 illustrators/month. Uses illustrators for billboards, consumer and trade magazines, brochures/flyers and newspapers. Especially uses artists for "styles we can't handle in-house."
First Contact & Terms: Arrange interview to show portfolio. SASE. Reports in 2 weeks. Provide business card and sample to be kept on file for future assignments. No originals returned to artist at job's completion. Pays $500-2,000.

KAVIC HOUSE INC., Box 308, Wellesley Hills MA 02181. Contact: Syd Green. Produces educational film loops, motion pictures, overhead transparencies and multimedia kits.
First Contact & Terms: Prefers artists with previous professional experience. Query with resume, samples and portfolio or description of project. Negotiates royalties.

KCBN INC. ADVERTISING & PUBLIC RELATIONS, 3434 Fairmont, Dallas TX 75219. (214)521-6400. Contact: Barbara Harwell, Judy Whalen, Logan Broussard, Peggy Cox or Gae Benson. Ad/PR firm. Annual billing: $9 million. Clients: consumer food, communications, industrial, home products, and utility. Media used includes: billboards, consumer and trade magazines, direct mail, newspapers, P-O-P displays, radio, and TV.
Needs: Uses approximately 15-20 freelancers/month on an average of 2-3 jobs/month. Uses 3 illustrators and 3 designers/month. Uses artists for billboards, P-O-P displays, consumer and trade magazines, stationery design, multimedia kits, direct mail, TV, slide sets, brochures/flyers and newspapers.
First Contact & Terms: Call for personal appointment to show portfolio (including tearsheets and original work) or send portfolio for review. Provide brochures/flyers and business card to be kept on file for future assignments. No originals returned to artist at job's completion. Negotiates payment based on client's budget, amount of creativity required from artist, and artist's previous experience/reputation.
Portfolio Tips: "Want to see best work whether varied or not, i.e., if good in color and just adequate in b&w, then we would not be interested in b&w work."

KCFW-TV, Box 857, Kalispell MT 59901. Contact: Mike Stocklin. Query.
Needs: Uses artists for animation and graphic/set design. Pays by job.

KECI-TV, Box 5268, Missoula MT 59807. Contact: Director of Production or Promotion. Query with resume.
Needs: Uses artists for animation, graphic/exhibit/design, ad illustrations and station promotion. Pays $25 minimum.

KECK ADVERTISING INC., Box 207, Oconomowoc WI 53066. (414)567-4467. Contact: Dick Keck. Estab. 1945. Clients: Cheesemaking and food industry equipment, foods, dairy and brewing chemical manufacturers. Buys 10-20 illustrations/year; local artists only. Query or call for interview. Reports in 1 week.
Needs: Illustrations, color separations, layout, paste-up and retouching for catalogs, print ads, letterheads, packaging, POP displays and TV. Pays $7-15, mechanicals; $10-20, layouts. Pays promised fee or 75% of agreed pay for unused assigned work.

KELLY, LEED & RIES INC., 801 Provident Bank Bldg., Cincinnati OH 45202. (513)621-1140. Art Director: Paula Kern. Advertising/public relations firm. Estab. 1967. Clients: Industrial and commercial. Buys 25 illustrations/year. Arrange interview to show portfolio.
Needs: Uses artists for illustrations, technical cutaways, brochure covers, product illustration, 3-dimensional illustration from blueprints, and renderings. Pays $3,000, technical renderings; $150, b&w illustration; $360, color illustration.

KELLY, NASON, INC., 300 E. 42nd St., New York NY 10017. (212)986-4200. Senior Art Director: John Benetos. Ad agency. Clients: consumer foods, pharmaceutical and beauty aid.
Needs: Works with 4 illustrators/year. Uses artists for consumer and trade magazines and newspapers.
First Contact & Terms: Call for appointment to show portfolio or make contact through artist's rep. Negotiates pay based on client's budget.
Tips: What he wants to see largely depends on what he needs at the moment such as food, people, still life, etc. If food illustration "make it look delicious."

KENNEDY ADVERTISING INC., 233 N. Michigan, Chicago IL 60601. (312)565-1440. Estab. 1947. Clients: Industrial. Annual billing: $1,700,000. Assigns 30 jobs/year; local artists only. Query with previously published work or arrange interview to show portfolio. SASE.
Needs: Uses artists for illustration, brochure and ad design. Pays $30-40/hour.
To Break In: "Artist should have Loop location or be willing to make calls in the Loop."

KENRICK ADVERTISING INC., 7711 Carondelet, St. Louis MO 63105. (314)726-6020. Contact: C. Galli, J. Coleman or Terri Meyer. Ad/PR firm. Annual billing: $8.5 million. Clients: agricultural, chemical, food and decorative.
First Contact & Terms: Local artists only. Query with samples (tearsheets or photocopies) and

arrange interview to show portfolio. Reports in 4 weeks. Provide business card and tearsheets to be kept on file for future assignments. Returns original artwork only when "arrangements have been made prior to assignment." Pays $25/hour.
Needs: Works with 3 illustrators and 3 designers/month. Uses illustrators and designers for ad design layout, direct mail brochures, signs, sets, slide shows, P-O-P displays and packages, billboards, filmstrips, letterhead, TV, newspapers, books, flipcharts, illustrative lettering and retouching.

KENYON & ECKHARDT, INCORPORATED, 111 Pine St., San Francisco CA 94111. (415)981-7270. Creative Director: Sam Gaylord. Art Director: Andy Wong. Ad agency. Clients: Chrysler, Plymouth, Dodge is only account.
Needs: Works with at most 1 freelance illustrator/month. Uses talents for work with TV and newspapers (pick up art, camera ready).
First Contact & Terms: Call for appointment to show portfolio. Negotiates payment based on client's budget.
Portfolio Tips: This firm works only with Chrysler, Dodge, and Plymouth so is interested mainly in style.

KENYON & ECKHARDT, INCORPORATED, 10 South Riverside Plaza, Chicago IL 60606. (312)346-4020. Contact: Mr. Tita Horst. Ad agency. Clients: fashion and packaged goods.
Needs: Works with about 6 freelance illustrators and 1-2 freelance designers/month. Uses freelancers for billboards, consumer and trade magazines, direct mail, brochures/flyers, newspapers and P-O-P displays.
First Contact & Terms: Call for appointment to show portfolio. Selection usually based on portfolio review. Negotiates payment based on client's budget, amount of creativity required from artist and where work will appear.
Portfolio Tips: Wants to see best work in all fields.

KENYON & ECKHARDT ADVERTISING INC., 200 Park Ave., New York NY 10017. Automotive Creative Director: William Suchmann. Ad agency.
Needs: Works with 2 illustrators/month and 2 designers/year. Uses artists for billboards, P-O-P displays, filmstrips, consumer and trade magazines, stationery design, multimedia kits, direct mail, TV, slide sets, brochures/flyers and newspapers.
First Contact & Terms: Provide visual samples of work to be kept on file for future assignments.. Particularly interested in seeing tearsheets (shows professional experience) and photocopies (shows originality and style). No originals returned to artist at job's completion.

DUKE KERSTEIN ADVERTISING AGENCY, 1316 Alvarado Dr. NE, Albuquerque NM 87110. Art/Creative Director: H. Duke Kerstein.
Needs: Uses artists for layout and retouching for newspapers, TV, radio, magazines, billboards and direct mail.
First Contact & Terms: Prefers local artists. Call for interview.

J. M. KESSLINGER & ASSOCIATES, 37 Saybrook Place, Newark NJ 07102. (201)623-0007. Art Director: Robert Fischer. Estab. 1929. Clients: Industrial and chemical. Annual billing: $1,500,000. Phone; prefers local artists.
Needs: Uses artists for illustrations and mechanicals. Negotiates pay.

KETCHUM, MacLEOD & GROVE, 1900 W. Loop South, StE 1300, Houston TX 77098. (713)961-0998. Vice President/Executive Art Director: Dick Baker. Ad/PR agency. Clients: financial, entertainment, oil, jewelry, automotive, railroad equipment.
Needs: Works with 5-10 illustrators and 2-3 designers/month. Uses artists for billboards, consumer and trade magazines, direct mail, brochures/flyers, newspapers; also uses designers for stationery design.
First Contact & Terms: Local freelancers, call for appointment to show portfolio and those out-of-town can call or send portfolio or samples for review. Pays on 30 day basis.
Portfolio Tips: Interested in anything showing ability. Past work from other ad agencies is acceptable and also interested in tear sheets of art published.

KEYE/DONNA/PEARLSTEIN, 9440 Santa Monica Blvd., Los Angeles CA 90210. (213)273-9920. Creative Director: Mel Sant. Estab. 1968. Clients: Financial, fashion, electronics, wine and food companies. Annual billing: $9,000,000. Call to arrange interview.
Needs: Illustration. Negotiates pay by job.

KEYES, MARTIN & COMPANY, 841 Mountain Ave., Springfield NJ 07081. (201)376-7300. Ad agency. Annual billing: $27+ million. Clients: consumer, corporate, financial, and industrial. Media used include: billboards, consumer and trade magazines, direct mail, newspapers, P-O-P displays, radio, and TV.
First Contact & Terms: Send resume and portfolio for review. Negotiates payment based on client's budget and artist's rate.

N.C. KINDLUND & ASSOC., 860 Livingston Ave., Syracuse NY 13210. (315)472-1668. Art Director: Nancy Peck. Film/animation/AV producer. Clients: school, association and corporation.
Needs: Works with 4 illustrators and 2 animators/month. Uses artists for filmstrips, multimedia kits, storyboards and overhead transparencies.
First Contact & Terms: Send resume, mail portfolio or write for interview to show portfolio. SASE. File on freelancers kept for future assignments. Works on assignment only. Samples returned by SASE; reports back on future assignment possibilities. Pay determined on where work is to appear.

KINSLEY ADVERTISING INC., Box 31, Worthington OH 43085. (614)885-8170. Art/Creative Director: Gilman Calkins. Ad/PR firm. Clients: Farm equipment distributors, seed growers, livestock growers and marketers, farm finance brokers and equipment expositions. Annual billing: $75,000.
Needs: Works with 3-4 illustrators/year. Uses artists for brochures/trade magazines, newspapers and possibly direct mail.
First Contact & Terms: Uses mostly local artists. Query with resume. SASE.
Needs: Uses artists for animation and graphic/set design. Provide resume to be kept on file for future assignments. Originals returned to artist at job's completion "unless agreed the product is to be created for us or client." Payment by job: $40-110, posters; $15-90, trade magazines; $20-100, layout; $10-75, paste-up; $5-30, retouching; $30-225, mechanicals.
Tips: "Make up samples of uniquely illustrated syndicated sales house organ for the farm-oriented clients we serve."

KINZIE & GREEN INC., 128 Grand Ave., Wausau WI 54401. Executive Art Director: Bill Miller. Clients: heavy industry and housing. Mail samples.
Needs: Illustration for newspapers, TV, magazines and direct mail.

KIRCHER, HELTON & COLLETT INC., 40 W. 4th St., Dayton OH 45402. Art Director: Walter Strubczewski. Ad agency. Clients: banks, savings and loans, paper manufacturers, TV station, caulking, paints, builders, wicker furniture, general housewares and wines.
Needs: Works with 2 designers and 2 illustrators/month. Uses artists for billboards, stationery design, multimedia kits, direct mail and newspapers. Also uses artists for layout, paste-up, retouching and lettering.
First Contact & Terms: Mail samples or call for interview. Provide brochures to be kept on file for future assignments. No originals returned to artist at job's completion.

KLEIN ADVERTISING, INC., 9024 Olympic Blvd., Beverly Hills CA 90211. (213)278-8081. Ad agency. Clients: consumer and general.
First Contact & Terms: Call for personal appointment to show portfolio. Negotiates payment based on client's budget, where and how long work will appear, and artist's previous experience/reputation.
Portfolio Tips: Portfolio "has to be excellent. Show up with really good work. I like to see the best of what they have done. Everyone has done mediocre work."

KLEMTNER ADVERTISING INC., 1185 Ave. of the Americas, New York NY 10036. (212)869-8200. Art Buyer: Ellen Tannenbaum. Ad agency. Clients: pharmaceutical advertising agency.
Needs: Uses variable number of illustrators and designers depending on client's needs. Works with artists on direct mail, brochures/flyers and trade magazines.
First Contact & Terms: Call for appointment to show portfolio of medical work. Negotiates pay based on client's budget.

KNIGHT GOODMAN INC., 520 CG&E Bldg., Middletown OH 45042. Art Director: Herb Goodman. Ad/PR firm. Clients: light industry and fundraising.
Needs: Uses artists for billboards, consumer magazines, direct mail, brochures/flyers and newspapers. Also uses artists for mechanicals and charts.

First Contact & Terms: Local artists only. Arrange interview to show portfolio. SASE. Provide brochures/flyers, business card and resume to be kept on file for future assignments. No originals returned to artist at job's completion. Contacts artists as needs arise. Pays $60 minimum/job.

KNOX PUBLIC RELATIONS, Suite 1011, First National Bank Bldg., Longview TX 75601. (214)758-6439. President: Donna Mayo Knox. PR firm. Clients: civic, social organizations, private schools, dancers, musicians, actors and businesses.
Needs: Works with 2 illustrators/month. Uses artists for billboards, stationery design, multimedia kits, direct mail and brochures/flyers.
First Contact & Terms: Query. SASE. Reports in 3 weeks. Provide resume and portfolio to be kept on file for future assignments. Originals returned to artist at job's completion. Pays by the hour.

KOEHLER COUNSELORS ADVERTISING, 1119 Xenia Ave., Yellow Springs OH 45387. Contact: Karl Koehler.
Needs: Uses artists for magazine/newspaper ad illustrations. Also interested in cartoons.
First Contact & Terms: Query with samples.

JOHN W. KOEHN CO., Box 687, Adrian MI 49221. Contact: James W. Koehn. Clients: Banks, savings and loans, fast food stores, malls, retail apparel and variety/specialty stores. Mail samples.
Needs: Illustration, technical art and retouching for newspapers, TV, radio, consumer magazines, billboards, direct mail and POP displays.

KOLO-TV, Box 10000, Reno NV 89510. (702)786-8880. Creative Director: Hope Schenk. Estab. 1953. Produces commercials. Assigns approximately 50 jobs/year; local artists only. Mail art or samples. SASE. Contacts artists as needs arise. Pays on production.
Needs: Minimum payment by job: $50, charts/graphs, advertising and illustrations; $25, lettering.

J.M. KORN & SON, INC., 3 Parkway, Philadelphia PA 19102. (215)241-7676. Contact: Ed Keane. Ad agency. Clients: mainly food and 1 fashion.
Needs: Works with about 6 freelance illustrators/month. Uses freelancers for consumer and trade magazines, brochures/flyers and P-O-P displays.
First Contact & Terms: Call for appointment to show portfolio or mail sample sheets. Selection based on previous work and portfolio review. Negotiates payment based on client's budget, amount of creativity required from artist and where work will appear.
Portfolio Tips: Wants to see whatever shows individual's style including past work used by other ad agencies.

KREX-TV, Box 789, Grand Junction CO 81501. Production Director: Harley Terrill. Submit slides. SASE.
Needs: Uses artists for set design, audiovisuals, film titles and TV commercials.

LADDIN & CO. INC., 2 Park Ave., New York NY 10016. Executive Art Director: Richard Traeger. Clients: Industrial and marine chemicals, banks, cosmetics, environmental systems, foods and fashion. Send samples (not returnable) and letter. Published samples preferred. Negotiates pay.
Needs: Illustration, technical art and lettering.

SCOTT LANCASTER MILLS ATHA, 2049 Century Park E., Suite 860, Los Angeles CA 90067. (213)552-6050. Art Director: Conrad Bowen. Creative Director: Peggy Lancaster. Ad agency. Estab. 1976. Clients: Toys, stoneware and publishing. Assigns 250 jobs and buys 40 illustrations/year. Query with samples or arrange interview. SASE. Reports in 1 week.
Needs: Uses artists for animation, catalogs, magazines, packaging, POP displays, posters, TV, newspapers, color separations, layout, mechanicals, lettering and retouching. Especially needs spot illustrations.

LANE & LESLIE ADVERTISING AGENCY INC., Petroleum Bldg., P.O. Box 578, Wichita KS 67201. President: David W. Lane. Ad agency. Clients: banks, savings and loans, consumer products and farm product manufacturers.
Needs: Works with 1 illustrator and 6 designers/month. Uses artists for billboards, P-O-P displays, filmstrips, multimedia kits, direct mail, slide sets, brochures/flyers, trade magazines and newspapers. Also uses artists for photography and retouching.
First Contact & Terms: Provide business cards, brochures and resumes to be kept on file for future assignments. No originals returned to artist at job's completion. "We prefer to buy all rights."

DON LANE PICTURES INC., 35 W. 45th St., New York NY 10036. (212)840-6355. Producer/Director: John Armstrong. Motion picture producer. Clients: marketing managers for agricultural, animal health and medical products. Audiences: farmers, veterinarian, doctors and graphics usually with some technical contact. Produces filmstrips, motion pictures, slide sets, sound-slide sets and videotapes. Assigns 10 jobs/year.
Needs: Works with 1-2 illustrators and 1 designer/month. Uses artists for filmstrips, motion pictures and videotapes. Also uses artists for motion picture titles and animation, technical illustrations, video graphics, slide illustrations and booklet design and layout.
First Contact & Terms: Local artists only. Query with previously used work. SASE. Reports in 3-4 weeks. Provide resumes and prints of artwork to be kept on file for future assignments. Artists usually do not request originals to be returned at job's completion. Negotiates pay; $7 min./hour.

LANG ADVERTISING ASSOCIATES INC., 108 S. East Ave., Vineland NJ 08360. President: Fred Lang. Ad agency. Clients: agricultural and industrial equipment manufacturers, educational institutions and industrial parks.
Needs: Uses illustrators and designers for P-O-P displays, direct mail, slide sets, brochures/flyers and trade magazines. Also uses artists for layout, illustration and retouching for trade magazines, direct mail and billboards. "We're moving strongly in the direction of illustration, particularly four-color, using less photography."
First Contact & Terms: Local artists only. Provide photocopies to be kept on file for future assignments. No samples returned. "All rights to design and/or illustration are property of agency or client." Call for interview.

RAYMOND I. LANG ADVERTISING INC., 110 Sutter St., Suite 51, San Francisco CA 94104. (415)982-5028. Art/Creative Director: Signe Drury. Ad/PR firm. Clients: printing and packaging firm, real estate, travel agency, cooking equipment and wallcoverings. Annual billing: $600,000. Assigns 12 jobs/year.
Needs: Works with 1 illustrator/month. Uses artists for brochures/flyers and trade magazines.
First Contact & Terms: No originals returned to artist at job's completion. No file kept on artists. Pays $12-25/hour for layout, paste-up and illustration.

ED LANG INC., 73 Westpark Rd., Dayton OH 46459. (513)433-3133. Contact: Edward R. Lang. Arrange interview.
Needs: Uses artists for animation and graphic/set design.

LARUE COMMUNICATIONS INC., 708 N. Dearborn St., Chicago IL 60610. Art Director: Debra Ustanik. Motion picture/AV producer. Medical clients/audience. Produces educational films, filmstrips, slide programs and printed support material. Assigns 50 jobs/year.
Needs: Works with 5-8 illustrators and 3-5 designers/month. Uses artists for catalogs.
First Contact & Terms: Send resume to be kept on file for future assignments. Also would like to see portfolio. No originals returned to artist at job's completion. Negotiates payment.

LAUER ADVERTISING INC., 303 E. Washington Blvd., Ft. Wayne IN 46807. (219)422-9537. Art Director: Burl Seslar. Estab. 1934. Clients: Food, industrial, moving van lines and auto parts. Annual billing: $4,000,000. Assigns 20 jobs/year. Query with samples or arrange interview to show portfolio. Reports in 2 weeks.
Needs: Uses artists for realistic and abstract brochure, newspaper and logo illustrations. Pays $500, full-color; $100, 1-color ink.

LAUNEY, HACHMANN & HARRIS, 137 E. 52nd St., New York NY 10022. (212)355-4100. Contact: Michele Dexter. Ad agency. Annual billing: $7 million. Clients: general consumer and fashion.
Needs: "In an average month we will hire 2-3 illustrators." Uses artists for brochures/flyers and newspapers.
First Contact & Terms: Call for personal appointment to show portfolio. "When an assignment comes up I will either select an artist I know of whose style is suited for the job, or I will review portfolios of other freelancers I am interested in using. I keep a file of calling cards, samples, etc. to refer to." Negotiates payment based on client's budget, amount of creativity required from artist, where work will appear, and artist's previous experience/reputation. Portfolio should include "15-20 samples."

LAYMAN ASSOCIATES, INC., 709 Statler Bldg., Boston MA 02116. (617)542-8968. President: L.A. Layman. Ad agency. Annual billing: $300,000. Clients: industrial, commercial and services, especially capital equipment manufacturers.

Needs: Works with 2 designers/month. Uses designers for direct mail, slide sets and trade magazines. Also needs artists for technical illustration, type spec, layouts, retouching, paste-up and lettering for newspapers, trade magazines, direct mail, POP displays, collateral and exhibits.
First Contact & Terms: Prefers local artists. Arrange interview or mail art. Provide materials to be kept on file for future assignments. No originals returned to artist at job's completion. Pays $25-50, layout; $7.50-10/hour, paste-up.

LDA INC., Box 645, Woodbury CT 06798. General Manager: Dorothea Witherspoon. AV producer. Clients: business, industrial, educational and professional. Audiences: student, business, medical and industrial. Produces filmstrips, motion pictures, multimedia kits, overhead transparencies, slide sets, sound-slide sets and videotapes.
Needs: Assigns 15-30 jobs/year. Works with 1-2 illustrators/month. Uses artists for filmstrips and motion pictures.
First Contact & Terms: Query. SASE. Reports in 2 weeks. Provide brochures, resumes and tearsheets. No originals returned to artist at job's completion. Buys all rights. Pays on production. Pays $15 min./job, illustrations.

LE JAN ADVERTISING AGENCY, 1888 Century Park E., Suite 1015, Los Angeles CA 90067. Contact: M. Mikolai. Ad agency. Clients: gambling industry.
Needs: Assigns 10-15 jobs and buys 100-150 illustrations/year. Uses artists for consumer magazines, multimedia kits, direct mail, brochures/flyers, trade magazines, newspapers and books.
First Contact & Terms: Mail art or samples. SASE. Reports in 2 weeks. Provide materials to be kept on file for future assignments. Pays $800-1,500, consumer magazines.

AL PAUL LEFTON COMPANY, INC., 71 Vanderbilt Ave., New York NY 10017. (212)867-5100. Director of Graphics: Joe Frazier. Ad/PR agency. Clients: varied.
Needs: Works with 2 or more illustrators and designers/month. Uses artists for consumer magazines, direct mail, television, brochures/flyers, trade magazines and newspapers.
First Contact & Terms: Call for personal appointment to show portfolio. "Most freelancers are referred to us by our friends." Provide business cards or whatever you can supply to be kept on file for future assignments. No originals returned to artist at job's completion. Negotiates payment based on client's budget, amount of creativity required from artist, where work will appear, and artist's previous experience/reputation. "We prefer to find out how much a freelancer will charge for a job and then determine on the basis of all of these whether or not we will hire him."
Tips: "Would like to see whatever they do best. We use just about all types of work."

LENHART ADVERTISING, USA, 22 Chambers St., Princeton NJ 08540. (609)921-8888. Clients: Restaurants, country clubs and large manufacturers. Send samples.
Needs: Illustration, technical art and retouching for newspapers, magazines, billboards and direct mail.

S.R. LEON COMPANY, INC., 515 Madison Ave., New York NY 10022. (212)752-8200. Contact: Max Fiertog. Ad agency. Clients: industrial, drug products, automotive products, dairy products, etc.
Needs: Works with 2-3 illustrators/month and occasionally works with freelance designers. Also uses freelance art directors. Uses artists for consumer and trade magazines, billboards, P-O-P displays, TV, brochures/flyers and newspapers.
First Contact & Terms: Call for appointment to show portfolio. Negotiates pay based on client's budget, amount of creativity required and where work will appear.
Tips: Wants to see general sampling of freelancers work. Past experience important.

LESKO INC., 3 Gateway Center, Pittsburgh PA 15222. (412)566-1680. Art Director: Donald R. Jones. Estab. 1968. Assigns 12 jobs/year. Query with resume.
Needs: Uses artists for design, illustration, displays and signs. Pays $25-40/hour, production; $25-50/hour, other artwork.

MERVIN N. LEVEY CO., 706 Madison Ave., Toledo OH 43624. (419)255-6313 or 536-8186. President: M.N. Levey. Advertising agency. Clients: Manufacturers, distributors, land developers, real estate, insurance, machinery, foods, baked goods, floor coverings, foods, automotive, pet foods, employment services and educational facilities.
Needs: Original art, layout and paste-up for newspapers, magazines, TV, direct mail and POP.

LEVINE, HUNTLEY, SCHMIDT, PLAPLER AND BEAVER, 250 Park Ave., New York NY 10022. (212)557-0900. Contact: Art Director. Ad agency. Clients: book and magazine publishers,

perfume manufacturer, automobile manufacturer, brewery, camera manufacturer, bubble gum manufacturer, crystal manufacturer and champagne distributor.
Needs: Works with 4-10 illustrators/month. Uses artists for billboards, P-O-P displays, consumer and trade magazines, direct mail, TV, brochures/flyers and newspapers.
First Contact & Terms: Call for appointment to show portfolio or send preliminary mailing piece of samples of work. Negotiates pay based on client's budget, amount of creativity required and where work will appear.
Tips: Wants to see freelancer's command of medium, technique and how well he can design and conceptualize.

J.H. LEWIS ADVERTISING AGENCY INC., Box 2024, Mobile AL 36601. (205)438-2507. Contact: John Lewis. Ad agency. Clients: retail, manufacturers, agricultural equipment and direct mail. Annual billing: $5,000,000. Buys 15 illustrations/year.
Needs: Works with illustrators and designers. Uses artists for mechanicals and layout for ads, annual reports, billboards, catalogs, letterheads, packaging, POP displays, posters, TV and trademarks.
First Contact & Terms: Prefers Southern artists. Query. SASE. Reports in 5 days. No originals returned to artist at job's completion. Payment by hour: $40-80, layout; $30-50, mechanicals. Pays promised fee for unused assigned work.

LEWIS BROADCASTING CORP., Box 13646, Savannah GA 31406. Public Relations Director: C.A. Barbieri. TV producer.
Needs: Uses artists for direct mail brochures, billboards, posters, public service TV spots and motion picture work.
First Contact & Terms: Query with resume and printed photocopied samples. Provide materials to be kept on file for future assignments. Originals returned to artist at job's completion.

LIAISON AGENCY INC., 150 E. 58th St., New York NY 10022. (212)888-7272. Production Manager: L. Bridgman. Public relations firm. Clients: industry, fashion and cosmetics.
Needs: Uses artists for stationery design, multimedia kits, direct mail, television, newspapers and books. Also uses artists for illustration and design of annual reports and brochures.
First Contact & Terms: Local artists only. Arrange interview to show portfolio. SASE. Provide business cards, resumes and tearsheets to be kept on file for future assignments. Originals returned to artist at job's completion.

LIBRARY FILMSTRIP CENTER, 3033 Aloma, Wichita KS 67211. (316)682-5925. Contact: Violet Priestley. AV firm. Clients: schools.
Needs: Works with 1 illustrator and 1 animator/month. Uses artists for filmstrips.
First Contact & Terms: Provide resume to be kept on file for futre assignments. Negotiates pay based on amount of creativity required.

LINDBERG PRODUCTIONS INC., 49 W. 46th St., New York NY 10036. (212)582-9060. President: Larry Lindberg. TV/film producer. Clients: CBS, ABC, NBC and PBS. Produces motion pictures and videotapes.
Needs: Works with 1-2 illustrators/year.
First Contact & Terms: Query with samples. SASE. Reports in 1 week. Provide materials to be kept on file for future assignments. Buys all rights. Pays on production. Pays $20/hour for animation and presentations.

LINEAL ASSOCIATES INC., 175 Great Neck Rd., Great Neck NY 11021. (516)482-1880. Art/Creative Director: Leonard Markman. Clients: Educational, industrial and trade. Call for interview; local artists only.
Needs: Uses artists for layout, illustration, technical art, paste-up, lettering and retouching for trade magazines and direct mail.

J.B. LIPPINCOTT CO., MEDIA DEVELOPMENT/DIVISION OF HIGHER EDUCATION, E. Washington Square, Philadelphia PA 19105. (215)574-4235. Managing Editor: H. Michael Eisler. AV producer. Audiences: health and medical professions. Produces self-instructional and other educational multi-frame audiovisual presentations in the health sciences.
Needs: Works with 2 illustrators/month for filmstrips and motion pictures.
First Contact & Terms: Artists should have previous experience with slides, filmstrips and motion pictures and with anatomy, biology and medical illustration. Prefers local artists. Query. SASE. Material copyrighted. Free catalog. Provide brochures/flyers and resumes to be kept on file for future assignments. No originals returned to artist at job's completion. Pays $10-30/frame; negotiable.

LIVING ARTS, 425 E. 79th St., New York NY 10021. Director: Peter Klein. Theatrical agency. Clients: musicians and dance groups. Buys 10-15 illustrations/year.
Needs: Uses artists for catalog layouts, stationery design, posters and publicity brochures.
First Contact & Terms: Query. SASE. Reports in 2 weeks. Provide brochures/flyers and tearsheets to be kept on file for future assignments. Originals returned to artist at job's completion. Minimum payment: $1,000, brochure design; $500, poster design.

CHARLES A. LOONEY ADVERTISING, 710 Patterson Bldg., Fresno CA 93721. Art Director: Dave Mendoza. Advertising/graphics firm. Estab. 1960. Clients: Retail men's fashions, irrigation equipment, outdoor/backpacking goods, agricultural products and construction. Annual billing: $850,000. Assigns 30 jobs/year. Query with resume. Reports in 2 weeks.
Needs: Pays $7/hour, layout design and mechanicals; $25/job, fashion illustrations.

LORI PRODUCTIONS INC., 6430 Sunset Blvd., Hollywood CA 90028. (213)466-7567. Vice President: Emmy Cresciman. TV/film producer. Clients: industrial. Produces filmstrips, motion pictures, multimedia kits, slide sets and sound-slide sets.
Needs: Works with approximately 2 illustrators/year. Uses artists for 16mm animation.
First Contact & Terms: Local artists only. Query with resume and samples. SASE. Reports in 2 weeks. Provide brochures, flyer and/or resume to be kept on file for future assignments. Pays by job.

LOWE & HALL ADVERTISING INC., 1912-B Augusta Rd., Drawer 9098, Greenville SC 29604. Art Director: Tom Hall.
Needs: Uses artists for billboards, direct mail, letterhead design, magazine layout and retouching.
First Contact & Terms: Send samples and resume.

WALTER P. LUEDKE & ASSOCIATES, 814 N. Main St., Rockford IL 61103. Ad/art agency. Clients: recreation vehicle components, restaurant equipment, tension control devices, hydraulic, cylinders, measuring and weighing, switches, timers, counters and motors firms.
Needs: Works with 2 illustrators/month. Uses artists for layout, illustration, technical art, paste-up, exploded views and retouching for newspapers, TV, magazines, billboards, direct mail and P-O-P display.
First Contact & Terms: Provide brochures and business cards to be kept on file for future assignments. No originals returned to artist at job's completion.

LYONS STUDIOS, INC., 200 W. 9th St., Wilmington DE 19801. (302)654-6146. Creative Director: Ben Lisenby. AV/video/literature/display design producer. Clients: corporation and industrial.
Needs: Works with 2 illustrators/month. Also has need for storyboard artists and multi-image designers. Uses artists for multimedia presentations, storyboards, literature and display.
First Contact & Terms: Call for appointment to show portfolio (storyboards and/or finished multi-image and video samples. Screening facilities available.) or send resume. SASE. Provide resume, calling card and flyer to be kept on file for future assignments. Works on assignment only. Samples returned by SASE; reports back on future assignment possibilities. Negotiates pay based on client's budget and amount of creativity required. Contact Mike Keel for information.

M.C. PRODUCTIONS, 900 W. 190th St., New York NY 10040. President: Martin Mauer. Estab. 1968. TV/film producer. Clients: Advertising agencies and feature film distributors. Produces motion pictures, trailer and videotapes. Assigns 6 jobs/year. Query. SASE. Reports in 4 weeks. Pays on acceptance.
Needs: Uses artists for titles and charts. Pays by job.

McANDREW ADVERTISING, 2125 St. Raymond Ave., Bronx NY 10462. (212)892-8660. Art/Creative Director: Robert McAndrew. Ad agency. Annual billing: $200,000. Clients: industrial and technical firms. Assigns 200 jobs and buys 120 illustrations/year.
Needs: Works with 2 illustrators and 4 designers/month. Uses artists for stationery design, direct mail, brochures/flyers and trade magazines.
First Contact & Terms: Uses mostly local artists. Query with resume. Never send work to be returned. Reports in 1 week. Provide business cards to be kept on file for future assignments. No originals returned to artist at job's completion. Pays $20-40/hour for annual reports, catalogs, trade magazines, letterheads, trademarks, layout and paste-up.

McCAFFREY AND McCALL, INC., 575 Lexington Ave., New York NY 10022. (212)421-7500. Ad agency. Annual billing: $115,000,000. Clients: variety.

Needs: Uses freelance illustrators on an as-needed basis. Uses artists for newspapers and magazines.
First Contact & Terms: Send for list of Art Directors and then contact individual director for appointment. Negotiates pay.

McCANN-ERICKSON WORLDWIDE, 44 Montgomery St., San Francisco CA 94104. (415)981-2262. Contact: Art Director. Ad agency. Clients: food, chemical, agricultural, industrial and financial.
Needs: 15 Art Directors work with varying number of freelance illustrators/month. Uses freelancers for all media.
First Contact & Terms: Call for appointment to show portfolio. Selection based on portfolio review. Negotiates payment based on client's budget and by requesting bids.
Portfolio Tips: Interested in seeing wide variety.

McCANN-ERICKSON WORLDWIDE, 10 S. Riverside Plaza, Chicago IL 60606. (312)454-7700. Contact: Art Director. Ad agency. Clients: all types including industrial and financial.
Needs: Works with about 2 freelance illustrators/month. Uses freelancers for consumer and trade magazines, direct mail, brochures/flyers, newspapers, stationery design and TV.
First Contact & Terms: Call for appointment to show portfolio. Selection based on portfolio review.
Portfolio Tips: Art Directors have individual and specific needs which vary from time to time. Request information when calling for appointment.

McCANN-ERICKSON WORLDWIDE, 485 Lexington Ave., New York NY 10017. Chairman/Chief Executive Officer: Eugene H. Kummel.

McCANN-ERICKSON WORLDWIDE, Briar Hollow Bldg., 520 S. Post Oak Rd., Houston TX 77056. (713)965-0303. Contact: Art Director. Ad agency. Clients: all types including industrial, fashion, financial, entertainment.
Needs: Works with about 20 freelance illustrators/month. Uses freelancers in all media.
First Contact & Terms: Call for appointment to show portfolio. Selection based on portfolio review. Negotiates payment based on client's budget and where work will appear.
Portfolio Tips: Wants to see full range of work including past work used by other ad agencies and tear sheets of published art.

McFRANK & WILLIAMS ADVERTISING AGENCY INC., 1501 Broadway, New York NY 10036. President: Michael Bruce.
Needs: Uses artists for layout, illustration, type spec and lettering for newspaper recruitment ads.
First Contact & Terms: Prefers local or Houston, Texas artists. Call for appointment.

REGIS McKENNA ADVERTISING, 348 Waverley St., Palo Alto CA 94301. (415)329-0810. Contact: Rob Janoff, art director. Estab. 1972. Clients: Electronic, athletic, and institutional food services. Annual billing: $10,000,000. Assigns 75-100 jobs and buys 50-75 illustrations/year. Arrange interview to show portfolio. SASE.
Needs: Pays $200-2,000 for advertising and brochure illustrations.

McKINNEY INC., Independence Mall West, Philadelphia PA 19106. (215)922-2635. Creative Director: Jonathan Brand. Ad agency. Annual billing: Philadelphia Office, $10 million; Corporation, $25 million. Clients: industrial.
Needs: Works with 10-15 illustrators/month. Uses artists for P-O-P displays, consumer magazines, multimedia kits, direct mail, brochures/flyers, trade magazines and newspapers. 75% of work is done in magazines. Also does some audiovisual.
First Contact & Terms: Call for appointment to show portfolio. Provide brochures, flyers, business cards, resumes, tearsheets, etc. to be kept on file for future assignments. Mainly selects freelancers by seeing their portfolios but sometimes through reps. Pays according to client's budget, by day rate, and gets estimates on jobs.
Tips: Wants whatever represents artist's style, including past work used by other agencies and tear sheets of art published. Is especially interested in realistic illustrators.

McKINNEY/NEW ENGLAND, 58 Commercial Wharf, Boston MA 02110. (617)227-5090. Senior Art Director: Carol Ross. Ad agency. Clients: industrial (70%) and consumer (30%).
Needs: Uses freelancers for print collateral–ads and brochures.
First Contact & Terms: Usually works by recommendation but does occasionally set up appointments by phone to review portfolio. Negotiates payment based on client's budget, amount of

creativity required from artist, where work will appear and freelancer's expertise in area.
Portfolio Tips: Wants to see illustrator's best work and "a lot of it." Work must be professional, with style, even if it's just a simple line drawing.

MacLAREN ADVERTISING LTD., 415 Yonge St., Toronto, Ontario, Canada M5B 2E6. Vice President/Manager, Creative Department: David Harrison.

THE McMANUS COMPANY, Box 446, Greens Farms, CT 06436. (203)255-3301. President: John F. McManus. AV firm. Clients: corporations, trade associations and charitable funds.
Needs: Works with 4 illustrators/month. Uses artists for art direction (TV commercials), graphic design (print ads and collateral pieces), illustration, publications, filmstrips, multimedia kits, storyboards and packaging.
First Contact & Terms: Send resume (to be kept on file for future assignments) and/or write for interview to show portfolio. Works on assignment only. Samples returned by SASE; reports back on future assignment possibilities. "Payment is determined on use of creative work, whether it will appear in national or regional media."

McMULLEN ADVERTISING, 15305 S. Normandie Ave., Gardena CA 90247. (213)515-1701. Contact: Douglas Magill, art director. Estab. 1960. Clients: Auto aftermarket, motorcycles and boats. Annual billing: $1,000,000+. Assigns 10 jobs and buys 5 illustrations/year; local artists only. Call and send resume and samples. SASE. Reports in 2 weeks.
Needs: Uses artists for ads and brochures. Negotiates pay.

MAHAN & ASSOCIATES INC., 1122 N. Grant, Odessa TX 79761. (915)332-1132. President: Richard L. Mahan. Art studio/ad agency/AV/motion picture/TV producer. Clients: petroleum-related business and industry. Produces filmstrips, motion pictures, multimedia kits, overhead transparencies, slide sets, sound-slide sets, videotapes and print materials. Assigns 20 jobs/year.
First Contact & Terms: Query with resume and samples consisting of tearsheets and/or 35mm slides. SASE. Reports in 2 weeks. Provide resume and tearsheet to be kept on file for future assignments. No originals returned after job's completion.
Needs: Works with 2-3 freelance illustrators and 2-3 freelance designers/month. Uses artists for filmstrips, stationery designs, multimedia kits, slide sets, brochures/flyers, trade magazines and newspapers. Pays $30/hour average. Also uses artists for animation, retouching, catalog design and ad illustrations. Pays $30 minimum/hour; "most jobs are bought on a quotation basis."

MAIL MARKETING SERVICES, 2442 Mary St., East St. Louis IL 62206. General Manager: Troy Atwood. Clients: Manufacturing, industrial, business, direct mail, mail order promotion, publishing and information service firms. Query with resume or mail 4x5 or 8½x11 tearsheets or b&w copies. SASE. Reports in 4-6 weeks. Buys all rights. Pays on acceptance.
Needs: Uses artists in all phases of direct mail/mail order promotion, including catalog and technical illustration.

MAJEGA PRODUCTIONS, 240 E. Radcliffe Dr., Claremont CA 91711. (714)624-0677. President: Gary K. Buckley. AV producer.
Needs: Uses artists for album covers, filmstrips, slide/sound sync programs and multi media productions.
First Contact & Terms: Query with resume and samples. SASE. Reports in 4 weeks. Provide tearsheets (varied styles), brochures or flyers to be kept on file for future assignments. No originals returned to artist at job's completion. Negotiates pay.

MANDEBACH & SIMS, 20 N. Wacker Dr., Suite 3620, Chicago IL 60606. (312)236-5333. Contact: Art Director. Ad agency. Clients: food services, financial, and graphic arts.
Needs: Works with 5-10 freelance illustrators/month. Uses freelancers for billboards, print advertising and collateral material.
First Contact & Terms: Negotiates payment based on client's budget.
Portfolio Tips: Wants to see work relating to their client's needs.

MANGAN RAINS GINNAVEN ASSOCIATES, 911 Savers Federal Bldg., Little Rock AR 72201. Contact: Steve Mangan. Ad agency. Annual billing: $4,000,000.
Needs: Works with 5 designers and 5 illustrators/month. Assigns 50 jobs and buys 50 illustrators/year. Uses artists for consumer magazines, stationery design, direct mail, brochures/flyers, trade magazines and newspapers. Also uses artists for illustrations for print materials.
First Contact & Terms: Query with samples. SASE. Reports in 2 weeks. Provide brochures, flyers and business cards to be kept on file for future assignments. No originals returned to artist at job's completion. Negotiates pay.

MANNING, SELVAGE & LEE INC., 333 N. Michigan Ave., Suite 310, Chicago IL 60601. (312)726-7890. PR firm. Account Executive: Nancy B. Newman. Annual billing: $225,000. Clients: industry, food, travel and corporate. Assigns 8-10 jobs/year.
Needs: Works with 1-2 designers/month. Uses artists for direct mail, brochures/flyers and annual reports.
First Contact & Terms: Local artists only. Query with samples (include prices on samples) and arrange interview to show portfolio. Reports in 1 week. No file kept on artists. Pays $500-5,000; "we ask for estimate in advance."

MANNING, SELVAGE & LEE INC., 99 Park Ave., New York NY 10016. Executive Vice President: Lloyd N. Newman. Public relations firm. Clients: financial, corporate, associations, government, industrial, consumer product and service.
Needs: Assigns 50-100 jobs/year. Works with 2-5 designers/month. Uses designers for filmstrips, consumer magazines, stationery design, multimedia kits, direct mail, slide sets, brochures/flyers and books.
First Contact & Terms: Arrange interview. SASE. Reports in 2 weeks. No file kept on artist. No original work returned at job's completion. Negotiates pay.

MANOFF-GEERS AND GRASS, 845 3rd Ave., New York NY 10022. (212)350-9200. Creative Director: Paul Jervis. Ad agency. Annual billing: $36,000,000. Clients: liquor distributor, car rental, camera and film manufacturer, consumer foods and small appliance.
Needs: Works with 4 illustrators/year. Uses artists for TV storyboards and some print.
First Contact & Terms: Drop off portfolio or call for appointment to show portfolio.

LLOYD MANSFIELD CO. INC., Marine Trust Bldg., Buffalo NY 14202. (716)854-2762. Executive Art Director: Buz Miranda. Ad/PR firm. Annual billing: $4,000,000. Clients: industrial, consumer and utilities.
First Contact & Terms: Local artists only. Query with resume and arrange interview to show portfolio. SASE. Reports in 3 weeks. Pays $7-30/hour.
Needs: Assigns a minimum of 3 jobs and buys 25 illustrations/year. Uses artists for illustrations, mechanicals, layout and retouching.

ROBERT B. MANSOUR, LTD., 2250 Midland Ave., Unit #9, Scarborough, Ontario, Canada. (416)291-2680. President: R.B. Mansour. AV producers. Produces educational filmstrips and filmstrip/cassette combinations.
Needs: Works with 6 illustrators and 3-4 designers/year. Uses artists for animation, multimedia kits and technical charts/illustrations.
First Contact & Terms: Mail samples. SASE. Reports in 1-2 months. Provide resume and samples to be kept on file for future assignments. Free catalog. Pays by job or advance and royalties.

MARKETAIDE, Box 1645, Salina KS 67401. (913)825-7161. Art Director: Peter Pratte. Clients: Midwestern agricultural/industrial advertisers and financial institutions. Query with samples.
Needs: Sales literature, in-house publications, catalog covers/illustrations, exhibit designs and trade publication advertising. Negotiates pay.

MARKETING SUPPORT INC., 233 N. Michigan Ave., Chicago IL 60601. Executive Art Director: Robert Becker.Annual billing: $7,500,000. Clients: hobby tools, plumbing, heating/cooling equipment, chemicals, paints, hardware and electronics.
Needs: Assigns 300 jobs/year. Works with 2-3 illustrators/month. Uses artists for filmstrips, slide sets, brochures/flyers and trade magazines. Also uses artists for layout, illustration, lettering, type spec, paste-up and retouching for trade magazines and direct mail.
First Contact & Terms: Local artists only. Arrange interview to show portfolio. Provide business cards to be kept on file for future assignments. No originals returned to artist at job's completion.

THE MARSCHALK COMPANY, 601 Rockwell Ave., Cleveland OH 44114. (216)687-8800. Senior Art Director: Len Blasko. Ad Agency.
Needs: Works with 6 illustrators/month. Uses artists for consumer and trade magazines and newspapers.
First Contact & Terms: Call for appointment to show portfolio. Negotiates pay based on job complexity.
Tips: Wants to see current work and "imaginative ideas, either published or unpublished."

MARSTELLER INC., 3600 Wilshire Blvd., Los Angeles CA 90009. (213)386-8600. Art Director/Production Manager: Jose Opablaza. Ad agency. Clients: mostly industrial.

Needs: Works with less than 1 illustrator/month. Uses freelancers for billboards and newspapers.
First Contact & Terms: Call for appointment to show portfolio. Selection based on portfolio review. Negotiates payment based on client's budget and where work will appear.
Portfolio Tips: Wants to see past work used by ad agencies and tear sheets of published art. Will also view illustrator's portfolio on transparencies.

CHARLES MARTIGNETTE ASSOCIATES, Box 9295, John Fitzgerald Kennedy Station, Government Center, Boston MA 02114. (617)734-5400. Ad agency/PR firm/AV producer. Art Director: Dudley Winchester. Clients: corporations, businesses and private individuals.
Needs: Works with 5-10 illustrators and 2-5 designers/month. Uses artists for catalogs, consumer magazines, slide sets, album covers, newspapers, books, direct mail brochures, exhibits, flyers, packaging, P-O-P displays, print media and TV advertising.
First Contact & Terms: Mail art or query with samples. SASE. Provide brochures, flyers, business cards, resumes and tearsheets to be kept on file for future assignments. No originals returned to artist at job's completion.

PETER MARTIN ASSOCIATES, 770 Lexington Ave., New York NY 10021. Contact: Jacalyn Pollingher, art director. Estab. 1972. Advertising/public relations firm. Clients: Tourism, airlines and women's products. Annual billing: $1,500,000+. Buys "lots" of illustrations/year; local artists only. Query with samples and arrange interview to show portfolio. SASE. Reports in 2 weeks.
Needs: Uses artists for illustration, technical art, paste-up and retouching for trade magazines and direct mail.

A. MARVIN PRODUCTIONS INC., 1224 N. Dearborn Pkwy., Chicago IL 60610. (312)649-0944. President: Marvin A. Gleicher. Estab. 1972. Clients: Educational, commercial and record industry. Produces videotapes and films. Buys 20 designs/year. Write for interview. SASE. Reports in 10 days. Some material copyrighted.
Needs: Uses artists for animation, catalog covers/illustrations, multimedia kits, record album design and technical services. Pays $75-2,000.

ED MARZOLA & ASSOCIATES, 8831 Sunset Blvd., Suite 408, Hollywood CA 90069. (213)652-7481. Vice President/Creative Director: William Case. AV/TV/film producer. Clients: ad agencies, consumer product firms and TV stations. Audiences: general public and sales people. Produces filmstrips, audiovisuals, slides, motion pictures and videotapes. Assigns 72 jobs/year.
Needs: Works with 3-4 illustrators and designers/month. Uses artists for album covers, catalogs, filmstrips and motion pictures.
First Contact & Terms: Arrange interview. SASE. Reports in 2 weeks. Provide any or all brochures/flyers, resumes or tearsheets to be kept on file for future assignments. No originals returned to artist at job's completion. Negotiates rights. Pays 1/3½ on acceptance. Minimum payment by hour: $10, charts/graphs, direct mail brochures and mechanicals; $15, catalogs and advertising; $20, animation. Negotiates payment for lettering, illustrations, retouching, technical art and type spec.

MAXFILMS INC., 2525 Hyperion Ave., Los Angeles CA 90027. (213)662-3285. Vice President: Mr. Glenar. TV/film producer. Clients: industrial, educational, media and corporate. Produces filmstrips, motion pictures, multimedia kits, slide sets, sound-slide sets and videotapes. Assigns 20-30 jobs and buys 50-100 illustrations/year.
Needs: Works with 2-4 illustrators and 1-2 designers/month. Uses artists for animation, filmstrips, motion pictures, backgrounds, titles, filmstrip charts and illustrations, storyboards, ads and catalog design.
First Contact & Terms: Local artists only. Query with resume and samples (tearsheets). SASE. Reports in 3 weeks. Provide materials to be kept on file for future assignments. No originals returned to artist at job's completion. Pays $15-250 per illustration; $5-25 per storyboard panel; other fees based on job.

CHARLES MAYER STUDIOS INC., 168 E. Market St., Akron OH 44308. (216)535-6121. President: C.W. Mayer, Jr. AV producer. Clients: mostly industrial. Produces film and manufactures visual aids for trade show exhibits.
Needs: Works with 1-2 illustrators/month. Uses illustrators for catalogs, filmstrips, brochures and slides. Also uses artists for brochures/layout, photo retouching and cartooning for charts/visuals.
First Contact & Terms: Send samples (originals) or arrange interview to show portfolio. SASE. Reports in 1 week. Provide resumes and/or tearsheet to be kept on file for future assignments. Originals returned to artist at job's completion. Negotiates pay.

MAYSLES FILMS INC., 250 W. 54th St., New York NY 10019. Contact: Albert or David Maysles. Motion picture/TV producer. Specializes in documentaries; also produces features and commercials.
Needs: Works with 1 illustrator/month.

MAZIN-WYCKOFF CO. INC., 2 W. 46th St., New York NY 10036. (212)586-2226. Art Director: Norman Mazin. Clients: businesses. Produces filmstrips, motion pictures, multimedia kits, slide sets, sound-slide sets and videotapes.
First Contact & Terms: Local artists only. Query with samples. SASE. Pays on acceptance.

MBM PRODUCTIONS INC., 1909 Abrams Rd., Dallas TX 75214. (214)823-7130. President: Bernie Michaels. AV producer. Clients: corporate and industrial. Produces filmstrips, motion pictures, multimedia kits, slide sets, sound-slide sets and videotapes.
Needs: Assigns 15-20 jobs/year. Works with 2 illustrators/month. Uses artists to create storyboards, slide illustrations, videotape and motion picture titles and "leave-behind" brochures. "We're looking for artists who are good at conceptualizing."
First Contact & Terms: Local artists only. Arrange interview to show portfolio. Reports as soon as possible. Provide samples of work if possible and resume to be kept on file for future assignments. Originals returned to artist at job's completion. Pays $25-75/cel, slides; $15-35, mechanicals.

MEDIA FOUR PRODUCTIONS, 6519 Fountain Ave., Hollywood CA 90028. (213)466-2266. Producer: Charles Finance. TV/film producer. Clients: educational, industrial and governmental. Produces filmstrips and motion pictures.
Needs: Works with 1-2 illustrators/year. Uses artists for motion picture animation and graphics.
First Contact & Terms: Local artists only. Query with resume and samples. SASE. Reports in 1-2 weeks. Provide resume and/or other materials to be kept on file for future assignments. Pays by job.

MEDIACOM, INC., 2049 Century Park East, Suite 2020, Los Angeles CA 90067. (213)552-9988. Vice President/Program Development: Stephen R. Strosser. TV/film/AV firm. Also produces print material to support A/V. Estab. 1978. Clients: corporations and associations.
Needs: Works with 3-4 illustrators and 1 animator/month. Uses artists for filmstrips, motion pictures, multimedia kits, storyboards, charts/graphs, packaging and print ads.
First Contact & Terms: Call or write for appointment to show portfolio, send resume and/or brochure/flyer. SASE. Provide resume, calling card, letter of inquiry, brochure/flyer or tearsheets to be kept on file for future assignments. Works on assignment only. Samples returned by SASE; reports back on future assignment possibilities. Pay based on "quality fee for quality work. However, negotiable on a per project basis." Also considers client's budget and amount of creativity required.

MEDIAMAKERS INC., P.O. Box 1264, San Luis Obispo CA 93406. (805)528-4200. Media Coordinator: Patty Hodgin. Produces vocational audiovisual materials–sound filmstrips, sound slide sets, stock captioned slides, overhead transparencies and collateral materials–geared to specific age/acceptance levels: junior high school through college and trade-technical schools.
Needs: Works with about 6-8 freelance illustrators/year. Uses artists for audiovisual art work, animation type (cartoon style) illustrations and graphic designs.
First Contact & Terms: Query with letter, business card, prices or rates (if available) and samples (slides, tearsheets and/or photocopies). SASE for return of requested items. Reports in 1-4 weeks. Provide duplicate slides (in a filing folder) to be kept on file for future assignments. Art work payment is negotiated and based on ability of a project in a timely manner. Contracts up to $1500.
Tips: "We believe double-digit inflation has affected both freelancers and producers dramatically. Since it often takes up to 8 grand + to produce a quality AV project, we're finding it easier to arrange payment of a basic 'up front' fee plus a royalty agreement. This makes it less difficult to 'buy' a freelancer's work and 'sell' the producer's end product in these inflationary times."

MEDICAL MULTIMEDIA CORP., 211 E. 43rd St., New York NY 10017. (212)986-0180. AV/motion picture/TV producer. Clients: manufacturers of diagnostic equipment (e.g. x-ray, ultrasound, ct scanning, nuclear imaging). Audiences: health care industry–sellers and/or users. Produces educational programs in health sciences. Buys 150-200 designs/year.
Needs: Works with 1-2 illustrators/month and infrequently with designers. Uses artists for album covers, books, catalogs, filmstrips and motion pictures. Also uses artists for layout, multimedia kits, paste-up, technical charts and medical illustrations.
First Contact & Terms: New York artists only. Call for interview. Provide brochures/flyers, resumes and tearsheets to be kept on file for future assignments. No originals returned to artist at

job's completion. Buys all rights. Pays $7-12/hour, mechanicals; $20-30/hour, design.

MELDRUM AND FEWSMITH, INC., 1220 Huron Rd., Cleveland OH 44115. (216)241-2141. Vice President/Creative Director: Chris N. Perry. Ad agency. Annual billing: $45 million. Clients: industrial, financial, consumer package goods, retail. Media used includes billboards, consumer and trade magazines, direct mail, newspapers, P-O-P displays, radio, and TV.
Needs: Works with 1-3 illustrators and 1-3 designers/month. Uses artists for consumer magazines, direct mail, brochures/flyers, newspapers, P-O-P displays and trade magazines.
First Contact & Terms: Call for personal appointment to show portfolio. Works on assignment only. No file kept on artists. Negotiates payment based on client's budget and artist's previous experience/reputation.
Tips: Want to see a representative sample of best work—more than ten pieces.

MELTZER, ARON & LEMEN, INC., Stewart Tower, 1 Market Plaza, San Francisco CA 94105. (415)543-0850. Art Director: Richard Wickstrom. Ad agency. Clients: entertainment and electronics.
Needs: Works with 5-6 freelance illustrators/month. Uses freelancers for billboards, consumer and trade magazines, direct mail, brochures/flyers, newspapers, P-O-P displays, stationery design and TV.
First Contact & Terms: Call for appointment to show portfolio. Selection based on portfolio review. Negotiates payment based on client's budget and media used.
Portfolio Tips: Wants to see 12 or more samples of work including that used by other ad agencies and tear sheets of published art. Especially interested in technical illustrators.

MERCHANDISING FACTORY, 222 Front St., San Francisco CA 94111. (415)956-4990. Production Manager: Bonnie Ellison. Marketing and sales promotion agency. Clients: real estate, airlines, restaurants, banks, sporting goods, retail paper products, food services and grocery store products. Annual billing: $5,000,000. Assigns over 100 jobs/year.
Needs: Works with 2 illustrators and 2 designers/month. Uses P-O-P displays, filmstrips, slide sets and brochures/flyers. Also uses artists for color separations, layout, lettering, paste-up, retouching and comps.
First Contact & Terms: Mostly local artists. Query with samples (tearsheets, photocopies) or arrange interview. SASE. Reports in 1 week. Provide business cards and tearsheets to be kept on file for future assignments. No originals returned to artist at job's completion.

MEREDITH & BROTHERS INC., 4819 NW Coves Dr., Kansas City MO 64151. (816)741-6400. Art Director: Dick Halstead. Ad agency. Clients: industrial and retail. Assigns 12 jobs/year.
Needs: Works with 1 illustrator/year. Uses artists for direct mail and trade magazines.
First Contact & Terms: Local artists only. Arrange interview to show portfolio. Contacts artists as needs arise. Pays "usually whatever the artist asks for, if it is reasonable."

ARTHUR MERIWETHER INC., Box 457, 921 Curtiss St., Downers Grove IL 60515. Creative Director: Art Zapel. AV producer. Produces educational (training) audiovisual projects.
Needs: Buys 75 designs/year. Uses artists for filmstrips, books, story illustration, multi-media kits and technical charts/illustrations.
First Contact & Terms: Local artists only; must have some professional experience. Query with small samples. Royalty arrangement on filmstrip art. SASE. Reports in 3 weeks. Provide resume and tearsheets to be kept on file for future assignments. Buys all rights. Catalog 50¢. Pays $75-200, posters; $35-65/frame, filmstrip art; $35-75, charts; $20-150, line art illustrations.

THE MERRILL ANDERSON CO. INC., 55 Post Rd. W., Westport CT 06880. (203)226-7921. Art Director: Louise Cuddihy. Clients: financial.
Needs: Works with 2 illustrators/month. Uses artists for direct mail and brochures/flyers. Also uses artists for cartoons and realistic illustrations. Assigns 25 illustrations/year.
First Contact & Terms: Arrange interview to show portfolio. Provide brochures and business cards to be kept on file for future assignments. No originals returned to artist at job's completion. Pays 50+/job.

META-4 PRODUCTIONS INC., 8727 W. 3rd St., Suite 203, Los Angeles CA 90048. Producer: LaVerne Watson. AV producer. Clients: governmental, industrial and corporate. Produces filmstrips, motion pictures, multimedia kits, overhead transparencies, slide sets, sound-slide sets and videotapes. Assigns 10 jobs and buys 50 illustrations/year.
Needs: Works with 1 illustrator/month. Uses artists for titles for films, filmstrips and slides.
First Contact & Terms: Local artists only. Query with resume and samples (original art, photos of

art, tearsheets). SASE. Reports in 2 weeks. Provide resume to be kept on file for future assignments. No originals returned to artist at job's completion. Negotiates pay.

METCALFE FILMS, 3709 Locksley Dr., Birmingham AL 35223. Contact: Charles Metcalfe. AV producer. Produces documentaries, industrial films and slides.
Needs: Works with 1 illustrator/month.
First Contact & Terms: Query.

ARTHUR MEYERHOFF ASSOCIATES, INC., 410 N. Michigan Ave., Chicago IL 60611. (312)337-7860. Executive Art Director: Zinnie Boecher. Ad Agency. Media used includes 80% TV.
First Contact & Terms: Prefers a resume first, accompanied by a self-addressed post card listing days of the week with boxes to check as to the preferred day of appointment. Negotiates payment based on type of work wanted; keeps client's budget in mind.
Portfolio Tips: Interested in seeing past work used by ad agencies and tear sheet of art published. "Likes to see roughs, and examples of how far worker can carry layout comprehensives."

MICHAEL-SELLERS ADVERTISING, 760 Market St., Suite 600, San Francisco CA 94102. (415)781-7200. Contact: Art Director. Ad agency. Clients: full spectrum including financial, food and music.
Needs: Works with about 10 freelance illustrators/month. Uses freelancers for consumer and trade magazines, direct mail, brochures/flyers and newspapers.
First Contact & Terms: Call for appointment to show portfolio or make contact through artist's rep. Selection based on portfolio review. Negotiates payment based on client's budget; and time and planning involved.
Portfolio Tips: Interested in seeing wide variety of work.

MICHAELJAY COMMUNICATIONS, INC., 802 Wabash Ave., Chesterton IN 46304. (219)926-7615. Art Director: Fred Tokarchuck. AV producer. Clients: business and industrial.
Needs: Use of illustrators and designers varies according to client's needs. "A broad spectrum of applications for a wide variety of clients." Uses artists for filmstrips, motion pictures, multimedia kits, storyboards, charts/graphs, overhead transparencies, print ads, collateral materials, brochures, P-O-P displays, etc.
First Contact & Terms: Call for appointment to show portfolio and/or send resume. SASE. Works on assignment only. Samples returned by SASE; reports back on future assignment possibilities. Provide resume and/or flyer/brochure to be kept on file for future assignments. Negotiates pay based on client's budget, amount of creativity required and artist's previous experience/reputation.

MIDTOWN VIDEO, 130 W. 5th Ave., Denver CO 80204. (303)778-1687. Production Director: K.J. Miller. TV/film producer. Clients: corporations, ad agencies, industry and media. Produces videotapes.
Needs: Works with 12 freelance illustrators and designers/year. Uses artists for TV graphics.
First Contact & Terms: Local artists only. Arrange interview to show portfolio. Provide samples (can be photocopies) of work to be kept on file for future assignments. Pays $12-25/hour.

MILICI/VALENTI ADVERTISING INC., 700 Bishop St., Amfac Bldg., Honolulu HI 96813. (808)536-0881. Senior Art Director: Tony Kenyon. Ad agency. Clients: financial institutions, destination advertisers, packaged goods firms, development firms, corporations, steamship lines, insurance, Blue Cross, hotels and resorts.
Needs: Works with 3-4 illustrators/month. Uses artists for illustration, retouching and lettering for newspapers, multimedia kits, magazines, radio, TV and direct mail.
First Contact & Terms: Artists must be familiar with advertising demands; used to working long distance through the mail; and be familiar with Hawaii. Mail samples. SASE. Provide brochures, flyers and tearsheets to be kept on file for future assignments. No originals returned to artist at job's completion. Pays $200-2,000.

MILLER, ADDISON, STEELE ADVERTISING, 5 E. 57th St., New York NY 10022. Art/Creative Director: James Schaus. Estab. 1968. Clients: Industrial, real estate, travel and consumer. Assigns 15-20 jobs and buys 15-20 illustrations/year; local artists only. Query with previously published work. SASE. Reports in 2 weeks.
Needs: Uses artists for spot illustrations, comp renderings and mechanicals.

N.H. MILLER & CO. INC., 1127 Park Square Bldg., Boston MA 02116. Clients: Eyeglass frame, leather, Early American furniture, plastic molding and housewares firms. Call for interview; local artists only.
Needs: Uses artists for layout, illustration and paste-up for newspapers, trade magazines and direct mail.

MILLER ASSOCIATES, RFD #2, Box 38, De Kalb Junction NY 13630. (315)347-3414. Public relations firm. Clients: industrial, high technology, academic and fashion. Media used includes consumer and trade magazines, direct mail, newspapers, P-O-P displays, radio and TV.
First Contact & Terms: Write and request personal interview to show portfolio. Negotiates payment based on client's budget and amount of creativity required from artist. Pays $100-500/job plus out-of-pocket; "usually books for full day, unlimited coverage in b&w and color."
Portfolio Tips: "Portfolio should be aimed at the particular assignment and these are apt to be highly varied. We usually base selection on known agents who maintain high standards in their clients."

MILLER-BRODY PRODUCTIONS INC., (division of Randon House School Division), 342 Madison Ave., New York NY 10017. (212)661-7166. Contact: Rosemary Killen. AV (filmstrip) producer. Audience: schools and libraries.
Needs: Works with 25 illustrators/month and 5-10 designers/month. Uses artists for album covers, catalogs and filmstrips. Assigns 25 jobs and buys 5,000 illustrations/year.
First Contact & Terms: Arrange interview to show portfolio. SASE. Reports in 3 weeks. Provide brochures/flyers to be kept on file for future assignments. No originals returned to artist at job's completion. Pays $35 per illustration.

MILLS, FIFE & MACDONALD, INC., 2340 River Rd., Des Plaines IL 60018. (312)297-5255. Creative Art Director: W.C. Strausser. Ad/PR marketing support firm. Annual billing: 7,000,000 with capitalized fees. Clients: industrial, commercial (food service).
Needs: Works with 3 illustrators/month and 1 designer/month. Uses artists for filmstrips, stationery design, direct mail, brochures/flyers, trade magazines and newspapers.
First Contact & Terms: Call for personal appointment to show portfolio. Provide flyers, tearsheets, or photocopies of work and/or samples produced for publication—especially work showing technique. Material will be on file for future assignments. No originals returned to artist at job's completion. Negotiates payment based on client's budget.
Tips: Would like to see "just a representation of talent and experience. Concentration on good draftsmanship given priority."

BENNETT J. MINTZ/PUBLIC RELATIONS ADVERTISING, 16200 Ventura Blvd., Encino CA 91436. (213)783-5436. Ad agency/PR firm. Annual billing: $150,000. Clients: non-profit agencies, fly fishing products, retail. Media used includes consumer magazines, trade magazines, newspapers and POP.
Needs: Uses 1-2 illustrators and 2-3 designers/month. "Sometimes we get into doing a number of brochures/flyers or other materials for fund-raising campaigns; other times we might go 2 months with little or nothing." Uses freelancers for brochures, newspapers, magazine ads, flip chart presentations, various brochures, folders, direct mail and annual reports.
First Contact & Terms: Call or write for personal appointment to show portfolio. No originals returned to artist at job's completion. Negotiates payment based on client's budget, amount of creativity required from artist, where the work will appear, and artist's previous experience/reputation.
Portfolio Tips: Would like to see "8-12 illustrations showing imagination." Selects freelancer from outline of work done, price, availability, proximity and budget.

THE MISERY LOVES COMPANY, 1416 N. State Pkwy., Chicago IL 60610. Contact: Robert A. Levin. Mail resume. Uses artists for set design.

HOWARD E. MITCHELL, JR., ADVERTISING, 301 S. Blanchard St., Findlay OH 45840. (419)423-0252. Creative Director: Howard E. Mitchell, Jr. Clients: Automotive, agricultural, industrial, financial, broadcast, publishing and consumer. Annual billing: $750,000. Call or write for appointment. "Must be close by or willing to come to us for assignments."
Needs: Uses artists for illustration, technical art, paste-up and retouching for newspapers, magazines, TV, radio, billboards, direct mail and POP displays. Pays $15/hour, layouts; $12/hour, paste-up.

CAROL MOBERG COMMUNICATIONS, 43 W. 61st St., New York NY 10023. Contact: Jamie Laughridge. Uses New York area artists for consumer booklets and brochures, educational filmstrips and related materials.

MOHAWK ADVERTISING CO., 149 4th St. SW, Mason City IA 50401. (515)423-1354. Vice President: Jim Clark. Ad agency. Clients: financial, industrial and agricultural companies, insurance companies and fast-food restaurants.
Needs: Limited art requirements. Uses artists for filmstrips, multimedia kits, slide sets and brochure/flyers.
First Contact & Terms: Provide brochures, flyers and samples to be kept on file for future assignments. Any samples provided should be color copies. No originals returned to artist at job's completion.

MOLNER & CO., ADVERTISING, 13815 W. Eight Mile Rd., Detroit MI 48235. (313)342-9944. President: Monroe "Bob" Molner. Annual billing: $750,000. Clients: clothing and furniture retailers, car dealers, financial firms and industrial companies.
Needs: Buys 100-150 illustrations/year. Uses artists for print ads, TV storyboards, layouts, and fashion and furniture illustrations.
First Contact & Terms: Local artists only. Query. SASE. Reports in 1 week. Pays $10-50, fashion or furniture illustration; $5-15/hour, layout. Pays original fee as agreed for unused assigned illustrations. No originals returned to artist at job's completion.

ARTHUR MONKS ASSOCIATES INC., 350 Randolph Ave., Milton MA 02186. (617)698-0903. Ad agency and public relations firm. Annual billing: $400,000. Clients: real estate, computer manufacturing, ice cream manufacturing. Media used include billboards, consumer and trade magazines, direct mail, newspapers and radio.
First Contact & Terms: Call for personal appointment to show portfolio. Artists chosen "on the basis of special needs. For instance, architectural renderings. We select those we think have some experience and talent. For ordinary work, we stick with a few we use very often." Negotiates payment based on client's budget, amount of creativity required from artist, artist's previous experience/reputation, and the going rates locally. Pays news shots on a per-photo basis; Pays $300-600/day rate.
Portfolio Tips: "On call, we will describe what kind of service we need, and would expect to be shown relevant samples only."

MONTAGE COMMUNICATIONS, 1556 N. Fairfax Ave., Los Angeles CA 90046. (213)851-8010. Executive Producer: Stan Ono. Film/animation/AV producer. Clients: corporations.
Needs: Works with 1 illustrator and 1 animator/month. Also has need for production artists (contact: Sumie Mishima (213)851-6688). Uses artists for filmstrips, motion pictures, multimedia kits, storyboards and charts/graphs.
First Contact & Terms: Call for appointment to show portfolio (advertising layout, corporate communications and training). SASE. Provide resume, calling card and brochure to be kept on file for future assignments. Works on assignment only. Samples returned by SASE; reports back on future assignment possibilities. Pays $10-15/hour per piece for production and illustration. Also negotiates payment based on client's budget, amount of creativity required, where work is to appear and artist's previous experience/reputation.

DICK MOORE AND ASSOCIATES INC., 850 7th Ave., New York NY 10019. Contact: Dorothy Spears, associate. Estab. 1966. Clients: "Primarily performers' unions for which we produce brochures and pamphlets and edit their official publications." Assigns 30 jobs/year; local artists only. Arrange interview to show portfolio.
Needs: Uses artists for publication cover designs, brochure concepts and designs, line drawings, type spec and mechanicals. Negotiates pay.

FORREST W. MOORE, INC., 9330 Amberton, Suite 146, Dallas TX 75243. (214)690-0701. PR firm. Clients: finance, real estate, community institutions. Media used includes consumer and trade magazines, direct mail, newspapers and A/V presentations.
Needs: Works with 2-3 illustrators and 2-3 designers/month. Uses artists for billboards, consumer magazines, stationery design, direct mail, slide sets, brochures/flyers, trade magazines and newspapers.
First Contact & Terms: Send resume. Provide brochure, flyers, business card and/or resume to be kept on file for future assignments. No originals returned to artist at job's completion. Negotiates payment based on client's budget and amount of creativity required from artist.

BENJAMIN MORSE INC., 16 Aberdeen St., Boston MA 02215. (617)262-1550. Production Manager: Richard Mooney. AV/graphics/paste-up/layout firm. Clients: "Practically all types–varied."
Needs: Works with 1-6 illustrators/month. Uses artists for filmstrips, storyboards, overhead transparencies and especially charts/graphs. Also needs freelancers for paste-up and layout of line graphs, bar charts, simple type pieces, illustrations, etc. (contact R. Mooney).
First Contact & Terms: Call for appointment to show portfolio ("anything recently done relating to my above needs") or send resume. SASE. Provide resume, calling card, letter of inquiry, brochure/flyer, tearsheets, etc. to be kept on file for future assignments. Samples returned by SASE; reports back on future assignment possibilities. Pays "$6/hour for basic paste-up/type spec." Contact R. Mooney or Nat Morse for information regarding internship program.

MORRIS COMMUNICATIONS CORP., 234 Valentine Lane, Yonkers NY 10705. Art/Creative Director: Rudy Michael. Estab. 1974. Clients: Recreation equipment, pharmaceuticals, film distribution and industrial. Annual billing: $500,000. Call for interview; local artists only.
Needs: Uses artists for layout, illustration, type spec, paste-up and retouching for magazines, newspapers, radio, TV, transit, collateral, direct mail and POP displays.

TOM MORRIS INC., 621 Devon, Park Ridge IL 60068. Contact: Tom Morris. AV producer/art studio. Clients: religious, commercial and industrial. Produces print media, charts, filmstrips, motion pictures and slides.
Needs: Works with 10 freelance illustrators and 12 designers/year.
First Contact & Terms: Submit slides and resume.

RUTH MORRISON ASSOC., 509 Madison Ave., New York NY 10022. (212)838-9221. PR firm. Clients: food, home furnishing, liquor and energy. Media include trade magazines, direct mail, newspapers and P-O-P.
Needs: Works with 2-3 illustrators and 2-3 designers/year. Uses artists for brochures/flyers, POP displays, stationery design and trade magazines.
First Contact & Terms: Send a note and photocopies of samples with SASE. Provide flyers and tearsheet to be kept on file for future assignments. No originals returned to artist at job's completion. Negotiates payment based on client's budget and amount of creativity required from artist.

MORVAY ADVERTISING AGENCY, 177 Valley St., South Orange NJ 07079. (201)762-3331. Art Director: Mrs. Tobia L. Meyers. Ad agency. Clients: electronic, food, clothing, florist and interior decorator.
Needs: Assigns 10 jobs/year. Uses artists for catalog covers, photo retouching and paste-up.
First Contact & Terms: Prefers local artists. Query with samples. SASE. Reports in 2 weeks. Provide business card and resume to be kept on file for future assignments. Pays $10 minimum.

MARTIN S. MOSKOF & ASSOCIATES INC., 159 W. 53rd St., New York NY 10019. (212)765-4810. Art Director: Martin Moskof. Clients: museums, foundations, art organizations, publishers, banks, financial firms and film companies.
Needs: Works with 3 designers and 2 illustrators/month. Uses artists for billboards, POP displays, filmstrips, consumer magazines, stationery design, multimedia kits, direct mail, TV, slide sets, brochures/flyers, trade magazines, album covers and books. Also uses artists for layout, lettering, paste-up and retouching. Especially needs book cover illustrations.
First Contact & Terms: Prefers local artists. Query or call for interview. SASE. Reports in 1 week. Provide brochures, resume and tearsheet. No originals returned to artist at job's completion. Pays $100 minimum. Pays kill fee (negotiated) or full payment for unused assigned illustrations.

MOSS COMMUNICATIONS INC., 160 E. 38th St., Suite 6A, New York NY 10016. (212)687-8640. President: Jack Moss. AV/TV/film producer. Estab. 1966. Clients: *Fortune 500*. Produces filmstrips, motion pictures, slide sets, sound-slide sets, videotapes and printed materials.
Needs: Works with 2 illustrators and designers/month. Assigns 10-15 jobs/year. Also uses artists for mechanicals.
First Contact & Terms: Local artists only. Query with resume. Buys all rights. Pays on acceptance. Provide resume and copy of samples to be kept on file for future assignments. Payment by frame: $25-30, filmstrips; $10, type kodaliths. Pays $25-75/drawing for illustrations.

MOTIVATION MEDIA INC., 1245 Milwaukee Ave., Glenview IL 60025. (312)297-4740. Art Director: Don Celing. Clients: industrial. Produces multi-image slide programs, filmstrips, motion pictures, slide sets and sound-slide sets.
First Contact & Terms: Local artists only. Query with resume. SASE. Reports in 2 weeks. Provide

resume to be kept on file for future assignments. Pays $5-15/hour, animation, charts/graphs and advertising; $8-30/hour, illustrations; $8/hour, lettering; on production.
Needs: Works with 10 illustrators and 5 designers/month. Uses artists for multi-image slide programs. Assigns 36 jobs/year.

MRC FILMS, Division of McLaughlin Research Corp., 71 W. 23rd St., New York NY 10010. Contact: Larry Mollot. "Our market is a wide spectrum. Our audience may be business executives, white and blue collar workers, military personnel, children, general TV audiences, etc." Produces motion pictures, sound filmstrips and slides. Write for interview. Pays by job.

PAUL MUCHNICK CO., 5818 Venice Blvd., Los Angeles CA 90019. (213)934-7986. Art/Creative Director: Paul Muchnick. Ad agency. Clients: general consumer and mail order firms handling gifts, housewares, gadgets, household products, baby photos, fire alarms, restaurant supplies, drafting equipment and services.
Needs: Uses artists for layout, paste-up, brochures/flyers and retouching for newspapers, magazines and direct mail.
First Contact & Terms: Local artists only. Call for interview. No originals returned to artist at job's completion.

MULTI IMAGE PRODUCTIONS INC., (Subsidiary of Fotomat Corp.), 8849 Complex Dr., San Diego CA 92123. (714)560-8383. Contact: Debbie Williger. AV producer. Clients: airlines, industrial and fast food. Produces materials pertaining to training, convention attendees and salesmen.
Needs: Works with 1 designer and 1 illustrator/month. Uses artists for tapes/slides, multimedia and set design.
First Contact & Terms: Query with resume. Buys all rights. Provide brochures/flyers and resume to be kept on file for future assignments. No originals returned to artist at job's completion. Pays $100-250/day for crew members; $100-4,000, finished work.

MULTI-MEDIA PRODUCTIONS INC., 1393 S. Inca St., Denver CO 80223. (303)722-2891. President: John T. Kelly. Art Director: Mark Hess. AV/motion picture/TV producer. Clients: business and government. Produces filmstrips, motion pictures, multimedia kits, slide sets and sound-slide sets. Assigns 20 jobs/year
Needs: Works with 2 freelance illustrators/month. Uses artists for graphics, technical art and cartoons.
First Contact & Terms: Local artists only. Query with resume and arrange interview. SASE. Reports in 2 weeks. Buys all rights. Provide slides, brochure/flyer, resume to be kept on file for future assignments.

MULTI-MEDIA WORKS, (formerly Ganung Inc.), 6061 W. 3rd St., Los Angeles CA 90036. (213)939-1185. Art Director: Doug Henry. AV producer. Clients: industrial. Audience: salespeople. Produces filmstrips, multimedia kits, slide sets and sound-slide sets.
Needs: Works with 1 illustrator and 1 designer/month for filmstrips. Also uses artists for slide illustration, paste-up and assembly.
First Contact & Terms: Local artists only. Arrange interview to show portfolio. SASE. Reports in 1 week. Provide resume and tearsheet. No originals returned after job's completion. Pays $8-12/hour.

STANLEY H. MURRAY & ASSOCIATES INC., 19E Elm St., Greenwich CT 06830. (203)869-8803. Contact: Stan Murray. Ad agency/PR firm. Annual billing: $1,700,000. Assigns 250 jobs/year.
First Contact & Terms: Query with resume and samples or arrange interview to show portfolio. SASE. Reports in 1 week. Provide materials to be kept on file for future assignments. No originals returned to artist at job's completion. Pays $30/hour.
Needs: Works with 10 illustrators and 10 designers/month. Uses artists for billboards, POP displays, filmstrips, consumer magazines, stationery design, multimedia kits, direct mail, slide sets, brochures/flyers, trade magazines and newspapers.

MURRAY & CHANEY ADVERTISING, 55 Atterbury Blvd., Hudson OH 44236. Contact: E.A. Schroeder. Clients: rubber, truck, retail food and restaurant outlets.
Needs: Buys 12-24 illustrations/year. Uses technical drawings, animation, design, retouching, layout and paste-up for catalogs, posters, TV and print ads.
First Contact & Terms: Arrange interview or write and send samples of work. SASE. Reports in 1 week. Pays $200-2,500 depending on use, space cost and budget.

MYRICK-NEWMAN-DAHLBERG INC., 5207 McKinney Ave., Dallas TX 75205. Public Relations Director: Walter G. Dahlberg. Architecture/landscaping/planning firm.
First Contact & Terms: Query with published samples. Provide brochure, business card and resume to be kept on file for future assignments. Original art returned to artist at job's completion.
Needs: Works with 1-2 illustrators and 2-4 designers/month. Uses artists for multimedia kits, direct mail, slide sets, brochures, trade magazines, album covers, newspapers and books.

NATIONAL ADVERTISING AND MARKETING ENTERPRISES (N.A.M.E.), 1352 S. Flower St., Los Angeles CA 90015. Contact: J. A. Gatlin.
First Contact & Terms: Submit samples. Sometimes buys previously published work.
Needs: Uses artists for graphic design, letterheads and direct mail brochures.

NATIONAL PAGEANT ASSOCIATION INC., 6036 Metcalf, Overland Park KS 66202. (913)262-2624. President: Bob Myers. Promotion firm. Clients: producers of pageants and shows. Assigns 12 jobs/year.
First Contact & Terms: Query with samples of original art or arrange interview to show portfolio. Provide business card, resume, brochures and tearsheets to be kept on file for future assignments. Contacts artists as needs arise. No originals returned to artist at job's completion. Pays an agreed contract price for each job.
Needs: Uses artists for illustration, paste-up and "all areas really, depending on the job being done." Work is done in the areas of direct mail and slide sets.

NATIONAL PLAZA AGENCY, Box 3329, Tulsa OK 74101. Contact: Margaret Butler, advertising manager. Estab. 1965. Clients: Trucking. Assigns 3 jobs/year; local artists only. Query with samples. SASE. Reports in 2 weeks.
Needs: Uses artists for calendar cover designs and illustrations, "preferably of trucks hauling mobile homes, or recreational vehicles. We prefer pen and inks, but like other types too." Pays by job.

NATIONAL TEACHING AIDS INC., 120 Fulton Ave., Garden City Park NY 11040. (516)248-5590. Contact: Aaron Becker. Publisher. Produces educational silent filmstrips, models and slides.
Needs: Uses books and catalogs. Also uses artists for technical illustration.
First Contact & Terms: Local artists only. Arrange interview. Provide brochures/flyers to be kept on file for future assignments. No originals returned to artist at job's completion. Negotiates pay.

NBC TV NETWORK, 30 Rockefeller Plaza, New York NY 10020. Contact: Charles Blake. Clients: businesses and ad agencies.
Needs: Works with 5-15 freelance illustrators and 5-6 designers/year. Uses artists for audiovisual and graphic design projects. Payments generally above average. Ability to meet short deadlines essential.
First Contact & Terms: Arrange interview. Provide brochure and flyer to keep on file for future assignments. Payments generally above average.

NATIONWIDE ADVERTISING, INC., Euclid Ave. at E. 12th St., Cleveland OH 44115. (216)579-0300. Ad agency. Annual billing: $70,000,000. Clients: "This is a recruitment agency which is utilized by a wide variety of clientele, really indiscriminate."
Needs: Works with 1-2 illustrators/month. Uses artists for trade magazines and newspapers.
First Contact & Terms: Send samples–don't send actual portfolio. "Interested in how easily accessible (freelancers) are and the characteristics of their work." No file kept on artists. No originals returned to artist. Negotiates payment based on client's budget. Offers "no set fee, each job is negotiated."

NEALE ADVERTISING ASSOCIATION, 7060 Hollywood Blvd., Suite 1204, Los Angeles CA 90028. (213)464-4184. President: Ted Neale. Ad agency. Annual billing: $800,000. Clients: financial, manufacturing and mail order retail.
Needs: Works with 2 illustrators, 1 designer/month. Uses artists for billboards, P-O-P displays, consumer magazines, stationery design, direct mail, television, brochures/flyers and newspapers.
First Contact & Terms: Local artists only. Call to arrange interview. No originals returned to artist at job's completion. Negotiates pay.

NEEDHAM & GROHMANN, INC., 30 Rockefeller Plaza, New York NY 10020. (212)245-6200. Ad agency. Annual billing: $7,234,675. Clients: travel and resorts (exclusively).
Needs: Works with 1-2 illustrators and 1-2 designers/month. Uses artists for consumer and trade

magazines, direct mail, brochures/flyers and newspapers.
First Contact & Terms: Call for appointment to show portfolio or make contact through artist's rep. Prefers to see past work used by other ad agencies as opposed to nothing but samples. Negotiates pay based on client's budget, amount of creativity required and where work will appear.

NEEDHAM, HARPER & STEERS, INC., 10889 Wilshire Blvd., Los Angeles CA 90024. (213)478-6525. Contact: Art Secretary. Ad agency. Clients: all types.
Needs: Works with about 6 freelance illustrators/month. Uses freelancers for all media.
First Contact & Terms: Call Art Secretary for appointment to show portfolio. Selection based on portfolio review. Negotiates payment.
Portfolio Tips: Wants to see variety of techniques.

NEEDHAM, HARPER & STEERS, INC., 303 E. Wacker Dr., Chicago IL 60601. (312)861-0200. Art Buyer: Pam Sweeney. Ad agency. Clients: food only.
Needs: Works with 2-3 freelance illustrators/month. Uses freelancers for direct mail, brochures/flyers, newspapers, P-O-P displays, trade magazines and storyboards for TV.
First Contact & Terms: Call for appointment to show portfolio. Selection based on portfolio review. Negotiates payment based on client's budget.
Portfolio Tips: Wants to see general work geared toward food.

NEEDHAM, HARPER & STEERS, INC., Suite 2100, Winters Bank Tower, Dayton OH 45423. (513)226-1515. Creative Director: Robert Graves. Ad agency. Clients: bank, industrial, home building, and appliances.
Needs: Works with 5 freelance illustrators, 4-5 designers/month. Uses talents of both for work with all media.
First Contact & Terms: Call for appointment to show portfolio or make contact through artist's rep. Usually gets freelancers through reps; however, some freelancers make appointment to show own portfolios. Negotiates payment based on client's budget but sometimes shows job and gets 3 estimates.
Portfolio Tips: Wants well-rounded portfolio showing freelancer's style. Past work used by other ad agencies OK.

NELSON PRODUCTIONS INC., 3929 N. Humboldt Blvd., Milwaukee WI 53212. (414)962-4445. Contact: Dave Nelson, president. Film producer/TV/audiovisuals/animation. Clients: educational, industrial and corporate. Produces filmstrips, motion pictures, multimedia.
Needs: Works with 4-6 freelance illustrators/year.
First Contact & Terms: Call or write. Reports in 2 weeks. Provide resume and photocopies of work to be kept on file for future assignments. Pays by job.

NEW ORIENT MEDIA, Communications Building, Second & Main Sts., Dundee IL 60118. (312)428-6000. Producer/Art Director: Darlene Anderson. AV. Clients: corporate, educational and industrial. Produces filmstrips, multimedia kits, sound-slide sets and computer slides.
Needs: Assigns 200 jobs/year. Uses artists for realistic illustrations, cartoon characters, b&w line art and paste-up.
First Contact & Terms: Prefers Chicago area artists. Query with previously used work and arrange interview to show portfolio. SASE. Reports in 1-2 weeks. Negotiates pay.

NEW YORK COMMUNICATIONS, INC., 207 S. State Rd., Upper Darby PA 19082. (215)352-7472. President: Michael Davis. Motion picture/TV/marketing consulting firm. Clients: radio & TV stations. Audiences: all types.
Needs: Uses artists for motion pictures and storyboards.
First Contact & Terms: Works with 2 illustrators and 1 designer/month. Query with resume. Provide resume and sample storyboards to be kept on file for future assignments. No originals returned to artist at job's completion.

RICHARD NEWMAN ASSOCIATES INC., 702 Bloomington Rd., Champaign IL 61820. Art/Creative Director: Dale A. Calvert. Ad agency. Clients: banks, resorts, tourism, attractions and national associations.
Needs: Works with 2 illustrators/month.
First Contact & Terms: Query with samples. SASE. Reports in 3 weeks. Provide artist for whatever samples best portray the abilities of the artist to be kept on file for future assignments. Originals only returned if arranged in advance.

NEWMARK'S ADVERTISING AGENCY INC., 183 Madison Ave., New York NY 10016. Art/Creative Director: Al Wasserman. Art/ad agency. Annual billing: $2,000,000. Clients: manufacturing, industrial, banking and construction firms.
Needs: Works with 1 designer/month. Uses artists for billboards , P-O-P displays, consumer magazines, slide sets, brochures/flyers and trade magazines. Also uses artists for cartoons, technical art, paste-up and retouching.
First Contact & Terms: Provide stat samples to be kept on file for future assignments. No originals returned to artist at job's completion. Pays $8-15/hour, paste-up and $75-3,000/job.

B.C. NEWTON MARKETING & ADVERTISING, 1111 Broad and Locust Bldg., Philadelphia PA 19102. Art/Creative Director: B.C. Newton. Ad agency. Clients: retail, consumer and industrial.
Needs: Buys 200 illustrations/year. Uses artists for billboards, consumer magazines, stationery design, direct mail, television, slide sets, brochures/flyers, trade magazines, newspapers and books. Uses artists for lettering, layout, paste-up and mechanicals. Especially needs layout, paste-up, type spec and illustration.
First Contact & Terms: Local artists only. Provide business card, flyers and brochures. No originals returned to artist at job's completion. Pays$5-10/hour for layout, paste-up and mechanicals.

NEXUS CORP., 4051 Broadway, Suite 206, Kansas City MO 64111. Contact: Nexus Corp. Ad/PR. Clients: food, housing, government and commercial. Annual billing: $500,000.
Needs: Assigns 3 jobs/year. Uses artists for "paste-up and keyline and everything in between."
First Contact & Terms: Local artists only. Arrange interview to show portfolio. SASE. Contacts artists as needs arise. Negotiates pay.

NORMAN, CRAIG & KUMMEL INC., 919 3rd Ave., New York NY 10022. Contact: Creative Director. Send descriptive material on work done for national advertisers. Local representation preferred, but not necessary. Uses artists for spot illustrations. Payment open.

NORTHEAST ADVERTISING INC., 6 Benson Rd., Oxford CT 06483. Advertising/Sales Promotion Manager: Don Feuerstein. Ad agency. Specializes in safety advertising and products including highway emergency and first aid kits.
Needs: Works with 1 illustrator/year. Uses artists for safety calendar illustrations.
First Contact & Terms: Query with samples. Provide materials to be kept on file for future assignments.

NORTHERN LIGHTS CABLE CORP., Box 224, Presque Isle WI 54557. Contact: Thomas J. Forster. Query with samples. Buys all rights.
Needs: Uses artists for animation, graphics and set design. Especially needs educational TV layouts.

THE NOTEWORTHY CO., 100 Church St., Amsterdam NY 12010. (518)842-2660. Contact: Tom Constantino. Advertising specialty manufacturer. Annual billing: $2,000,000. Clients: advertising specialty jobbers with clients in real estate, banks, chain stores, state parks and community service groups. Buys 20 illustrations/year.
Needs: Uses artists for catalogs, packaging and litterbags.
First Contact & Terms: Query with samples. SASE. Reports in 2 weeks. Provide resume and brochures to be kept on file for future assignments. No originals returned to artist at job's completion. Pays $25 minimum, litterbag design.

OGILVY & MATHER, INC., 120 Green St., San Francisco CA 94111. (415)981-0950. Contact: Joey Andelin. Ad agency. Clients: financial, entertainment, outdoor apparel and consumer products.
Needs: Works with 5-6 freelance illustrators/month. Uses freelancers in all media.
First Contact & Terms: Call one of the art directors for appointment to show portfolio. Selection based on portfolio review. Negotiates payment based on client's budget, amount of creativity required from artist and where work will appear.
Portfolio Tips: Wants to see a comprehensive rundown on what a person does best—"what he's selling"—and enough variety to illustrate freelancer's individual style(s).

OGILVY & MATHER, INC., 200 E. Randolph Dr., Chicago IL 60601. (312)861-1166. Contact: Art Director. Ad agency. Clients: all types.
Needs: Works with about 1 freelance illustrator every two months. Uses freelancers for TV storyboards and commercial animatics.

First Contact & Terms: Call art director for appointment to show portfolio. Selection based on portfolio review. Negiotates payment based on client's budget, amount of creativity required from artist and where work will appear.
Portfolio Tips: Wants to see past work used by ad agencies and tear sheets of published art but also interested in less finished work. Especially interested in cartoon styles. This company needs and is actively looking for people who do good work in this field at a more competitive price than the big names.

OGILVY & MATHER INC., 2 E. 48th St., New York NY 10017. (212)688-6100. Contact: West Emmart. Ad agency. Clients: All types.
Needs: Selection of freelancers based on personality and drawing ability. Wants artists to be able to emote with people. "The artist has to be like an actor himself." His personality should spill over into his work. Especially interested in "people artists" particularly pretty girls. Also good people who can draw fashion line for storyboards.
First Contact & Terms: Call W. Emmart for appointment to show portfolio. Wants to see illustrations–no "shorthand stuff"–work on expressions. Looking strictly for the sketch artist, "magic marker renderings" for storyboards and comps. Payment varies. $45/frame minimum for storyboards.

OGILVY & MATHER INC., Place du Canada, Montreal, Quebec Canada H3B 2P6. (514)866-6961. Art Director: Patrick Farei. Ad agency. Clients: packaged goods, liquor, tobacco, etc.
Needs: Number of illustrators and designers used varies with work. Uses artists for all media.
First Contact & Terms: Call art director for appointment to show portfolio. Negotiates pay based on client's budget.

O'HARA HANNIGAN REID, ABH INTERNATIONAL, 920 Yonge St., Toronto, Ontario Canada M4W 3C7. (416)961-9331. Contact: Ms. Vinnie Staffiere. Ad agency. Clients: diamond company.
Needs: Works with 2-3 illustrators and designers/month. Uses artists for P-O-P displays, consumer and trade magazines and brochures.
First Contact & Terms: Call for appointment to show portfolio.
Tips: Since main account is diamonds, wants to see lots of detail. Negotiates pay based on client's budget.

OMNICOM PRODUCTIONS, 3315 S. Pennsylvania, Lansing MI 48910. (517)393-7800. Vice President: Ken Kortge. AV/film producer. Clients: industrial, state governmental and ad agencies. Produces filmstrips, motion pictures, slide sets and sound-slide sets.
Needs: Works with 1 illustrator/month. Uses artists for industrial animation for motion pictures, and cartoons and illustrations for slides and filmstrips. Negotiates pay.
First Contact & Terms: Query with resume and samples and "submit a sample of the end product of anything the artist considers typical." SASE. Reports in 1-2 months. Provide tearsheets (end products preferred–prints of film). Originals "considered client property," not returned to artist. Negotiates pay.

OUR SUNDAY VISITOR INC., Audiovisual Dept., 200 Noll Plaza, Huntington IN 46750. Contact: Rick Hawthorne. AV producer. Religious education audience. Produces sound filmstrips, overhead transparencies and slides. Send samples or call to make appointment to show samples. Prefers artists "as close as possible for personal delivery. I prefer not to send original artwork through the mail or other delivery system." Query. Provide resume, tearsheets and brochures/flyers. No originals returned to artist at job's completion. Pays $35-50 for full-color, comprehensive (often multicharacter) filmstrip art using acrylics, felt tip marker, painted cel or designer colors.
Needs: Works with 2-3 illustrators/month. Uses illustrators and designers for album covers and filmstrips. Subjects range from the miracles and parables of Jesus to modern church history, liturgy, stories and doctrine.

OUTDOOR PICTURES, Box 277, Anacortes WA 98221. (206)293-3200. President: Ernest S. Booth. Clients: schools and libraries. Produces filmstrips, motion pictures, slide sets, sound-slide sets and animal specimens.
First Contact & Terms: Query with samples. SASE. Reports in 1 week. Buys one-time rights. Pays 10% royalties on acceptance.
Needs: Assigns 20-50 jobs/year. Uses artists for filmstrip illustration.

OVATION FILMS INC., 33 W. 46th St., New York NY 10036. (212)581-4406. Contact: Art Petricone. Arrange interview.
Needs: Uses artists for exhibit/set design and animation.

PAIDEIA, 3107 Santa Monica Blvd., Suite F, Santa Monica CA 90404. Contact: John Lord. Clients: educational publishers. Produces filmstrips, motion pictures and multimedia kits. Assigns "a couple" of jobs/year.
Needs: Uses illustrators for filmstrips, motion pictures and multimedia markets.
First Contact & Terms: Local artists only. Query; do not send art. Reports in 2 weeks. Buys all rights. Pays on acceptance. No originals returned to artist at job's completion. Pays $5-12/hour or "thousands" of dollars/job for animation; $10-50/frame, filmstrip illustrations; $10.50 min./hour, mechanicals.

CHARLES PALM & CO. INC., 800 Cottage Grove Rd., Bloomfield CT 06002. (203)242-6258. (Branch office located in Chicago, Illinois.) Art Directors: John Vann and Jeffrey Abbott. Assistant Art Director: Priscilla Janssen. Ad agency. Clients: consumer and industrial products and services.
Needs: Works with 2-3 illustrators/month. Uses illustrators for consumer magazines, trade magazines and technical illustration. Also uses artists for layout, illustration, technical art, paste-up, retouching, lettering and storyboards for TV, newspapers, magazines, radio, billboards, direct mail and collateral.
First Contact & Terms: Submit samples or call for interview. Provide business cards, resumes and samples of work to be kept on file for future assignments. No originals returned to artist at job's completion.

PANORAMIC STUDIOS, 2243 W. Allegheny Ave., Philadelphia PA 19132. (215)228-2113. Contact: Leonard N. Abrams. Model maker. Produces dioramas, models and exhibits. Assigns 10 jobs/year.
Needs: Uses artists for dioramas, models, cartography and technical charts/illustrations.
First Contact & Terms: Query. Reports in 3 weeks. Material copyrighted. Pays $5/hour.

PARAGON PRODUCTIONS AGENCY, Box 52444, Florida National Bank Bldg., Jacksonville FL 32205. (904)353-9322. President: John Mullis. Ad/PR/trade show productions and services firm. Annual billing: $300,000. Clients: associations, trade groups, marketing, public relations and promotion.
Needs: Uses artists for slide sets, brochures, flyers and newspaper work.
First Contact & Terms: Local artists only. Query. SASE. No file kept on artists. No originals returned for refused work. Negotiates pay.

PARKER, WILLOX, FAIRCHILD & CAMPBELL ADVERTISING INC., 808 N. Michigan, Saginaw MI 48602. (517)755-8171. Executive Art Director: Bob Lauka. Art Director: Ron Davis. Annual billing: $5,000,000. Clients: consumer and industrial.
Needs: Buys 25 full-color illustrations/year. Uses artists for illustrations, color separations, layout, lettering, paste-up, retouching and type spec for ads, annual reports, billboards, catalogs, letterheads, packaging, POP displays, posters, TV and trademarks.
First Contact & Terms: Mail printed samples. SASE. Reports in 2 weeks. Artist quotes his price. Agency pays for unused completed work ("assignments usually approved or disapproved at tissue stage").

PASTARNACK ASSOCIATES INC., 231 E. 51st St., New York NY 10022. (212)421-0142. President, Art/Creative Director: Irving J. Pastarnack. Ad agency. Clients: photography, industrial, travel, resort and school.
Needs: Works with 3 illustrators/month. Uses artists for consumer magazines, stationery design, direct mail, brochures/flyers, trade magazines and newspapers.
First Contact & Terms: Prefers local artists. Call for interview. Provide materials to be kept on file for future assignments. No originals returned to artist at job's completion. "If I pay for it, I own it."

BERNARD K. PAWLUS ASSOCIATES, 1306 Tri-State Bldg., Cincinnati OH 45202. (513)621-4030. Contact: Bernard Pawlus. Estab. 1968. Clients: Drug, housewares and furniture producers. Annual billing: $600,000. Buys 20 illustrations/year; local artists only. Write for interview. Reports in 1 week.
Needs: Uses freelancers occasionally—about 3/year. Layout and design for annual reports, catalogs, consumer magazine ads, packaging and TV. Minimum payment: $10/hour, rough layouts; $15/hour or on assignment, design.

PAUL PEASE ADVERTISING INC., 151 University Ave., Palo Alto CA 94301. (415)327-4112. Creative Director: John Johnson. Clients: Instrumentation, high technology and real estate firms. Call for interview; local artists only.
Needs: Design, comps, illustration, paste-up and retouching for newspapers, magazines and direct mail.

PEDERSON HERZOG & NEE INC., 532 Midland Bank Bldg., Minneapolis MN 55401. (612)333-1234. Art Director: Bruce Harrington. Ag agency. Clients: agricultural and industrial. Annual billing: $3,800,000. Assigns 12 illustrations/year.
Needs: Works with 2 illustrators and 2 designers/month. Uses artists for billboards, P-O-P displays, consumer magazines, television, trade magazines, newspapers, and brochures.
First Contact & Terms: Local artists only. Query with samples to be kept on file for future assignments. No originals returned to artist at job's completion. Pays $50-1,500/job.

PENNY/OHLMANN/NEIMAN INC., 1605 N. Main St., Dayton OH 45408. (513)278-0681. Contact: Ralph Neiman. Ad agency.
Needs: Works with 3 illustrators and 3 designers/month. Uses artists for P-O-P displays, album covers, TV, renderings of building interiors, audiovisuals, billboards, calligraphy, cartoons, catalog illustrations/covers, convention exhibits, magazine editorial decorative spots, direct mail brochures, letterheads, layout, posters and trademarks.
First Contact & Terms: "Only pros who have had work published. Proximity is important." Call or write for interview. Provide a brochure and/or business card to be kept on file for future assignments. No originals returned to artist at job's completion. Pays $25-60.

PERKINS, BERNSTEIN INC., 875 N. Michigan Ave., Chicago IL 60611. (312)440-3700. Contact: Barry Parks, senior art director. Estab. 1976. Clients: Sports, direct mail and "party plans." Assigns 20-30 jobs/year; prefers local artists. Arrange interview to show portfolio. SASE. Reports in 3-4 weeks.
Needs: Uses artists for layout, illustration, renderings, comps and assembly. Pays by job.

PERPETUAL MOTION PICTURES INC., 11 E. 44th St., New York NY 10017. (212)953-9110. Producer: Hal Hoffer. Animation/TV/film producer. Clients: industrial, corporate, ad agencies and TV networks.
Needs: Buys 100 designs/year. Uses artists for comps and animatics. Also uses artists for animation design.
First Contact & Terms: Local artists only. Query with resume and samples. SASE. Reports in 2 weeks. Pays $30-100/panel or going rate by day. Pays $150 minimum.

WILLIAM C. PFLAUM CO. INC., Reston International Center, Reston VA 22091. (703)620-3773. PR/AV firm.
Needs: Works with 2 illustrators and 3-4 designers/month. Uses artists for consumer magazines, stationery design, direct mail, television, slide sets, brochures/flyers, trade magazines and newspapers.
First Contact & Terms: Local artists only. Query with samples. No originals returned to artist at job's completion.

PHOENIX FILMS INC., 470 Park Ave. S., New York NY 10016. (212)684-5910. President: Heinz Gelles. Vice President: Barbara Bryant. Clients: libraries, museums, religious institutions, U.S. government, schools, universities, film societies and businesses. Produces and distributes motion pictures. Assigns 20-30 jobs/year.
Needs: Uses artists for motion pictures, catalog sheets, direct mail brochures, posters and study guides.
First Contact & Terms: Local artists only. Query with samples (tearsheets and photocopies). SASE. Reports in 3 weeks. Buys all rights. Provide brochures/flyers, resumes and tearsheets to be kept on file for future assignments. Originals returned to artist at job's request. Pays on production. Free catalog.

PHOTOGRAPHERS' COLOR SERVICE, 22 Surrey Lane, Shrewsbury MA 01545. (617)752-1921. President: M. Richmond. Photographic studio. Clients: educational, industrial and business. Produces filmstrips, slide sets and color prints.
Needs: Assigns 30 jobs/year. Uses artists for slide and ad illustrations.
First Contact & Terms: Query with resume and samples. Reports in 2 weeks. Negotiates pay.

PHOTO-SYNTHESIS INC., 450 Lincoln St., Denver CO 80203. (303)777-1300. Art Director: Richard Kaylin. Av producer. Clients: mostly corporate. Produces slide sets and audiovisual shows. Assigns 6 jobs/year minimum.
Needs: Works with 2-4 illustrators in the fall, usually about October. Uses artists for slide illustrations.
First Contact & Terms: Local artists only. Query with resume and samples and arrange interview to show portfolio. SASE. Reports in 2 weeks. Provide portfolio with resume, tearsheet, brochure and/or flyers to be kept on file for future assignments. Negotiates pay.

BURTON PINCUS, CONSULTANT, Box 194, Linwood NJ 08221. Art Buyer: Burton Pincus. Specializes in direct mail. Uses artists for advertising art/design and direct mail brochures.

PITTARO PRODUCTIONS, Old Castle Point Rd., Wappinger Falls NY 12590. Contact: Ernest M. Pittaro. AV/motion picture producer. Audience: elementary and secondary schools.
Needs: Works with 3-4 illustrators/year. Uses illustrators for slides, filmstrips and motion picturs. Also uses artists for animation, special effects, trick cinematography and construction of special props and models.
First Contact & Terms: Artists must have previous experience with films, filmstrips or slides. Query with resume. Provide resumes only to be kept on file for future assignments. "If job comes up for discussion, we will look at sample portfolio." "We buy all rights–artwork (originals) becomes our property." Pay is "negotiable according to job. Each job is budgeted and artist is given figure in advance on a per foot, per scene, per frame or per job basis. No haggling–artist takes or leaves job on basis of initial negotiation and is paid upon acceptance."

THE POLY COM GROUP INC., 4 E. Huron St., Chicago IL 60611. (312)337-2040. Production Manager: Mr. Carmen V. Trombetta. Vieotape teleproducer. Clients: major Chicago advertising and PR firms and educational/industrial and corporate enterprises. Produces filmstrips, motion pictures, multimedia kits, overhead transparencies, slide sets, sound-slide sets and videotapes.
Needs: Works with 2-3 illustrators/month. Assigns 150-200 jobs/year. Uses artists for motion pictures, videotape teleproduction, television copy art and storyboard animation.
First Contact & Terms: Query with resume and samples. SASE. Reports in 2-3 weeks. Provide resumes and samples to be kept on file for future assignments. Original art returned to artist at job's completion. Negotiates pay by project.
Tips: "Artists must be familiar with film and videotape. Find an idea that is unique to Poly Com, e.g., corporate design, and send periodic examples."

PORETZ & JAFFE, INC., 935 National Press Bldg., Washington DC 20045. (202)783-4848. Contact: Douglas Poretz. PR firm. Estab. 1979. Clients: commercial real estate, banks, national associations, unions, architectural and engineering, economic development. Does not place advertising.
Needs: Works with 1 illustrator and 1 designer/month. Uses artists for stationery design, multimedia kits, direct mail, television, slide sets and brochures/flyers.
First Contact & Terms: Send resume and portfolio for review. "For freelance writers, p.r. people: samples of actual published articles and/or evidence of detailed p.r. campaigns conducted. Freelancers are employed on basis of past experience, personal knowledge, or special expertise." Provide brochures, flyers, business cards, resumes and tearsheets to be kept on file for future assignments. Originals returned to artist only if prearranged. Negotiates payment based on client's budget, amount of creativity required from artist, and artist's previous experience/reputation.
Portfolio Tips: "Interested in samples of produced work and details regarding availability and ability to produce work on short time schedules."

PETER POTTER'S ARTEL STUDIO, 239 Dolan Ave., Gulfport MS 39501. (601)896-8186. Creative Director: Peter Potter. Art agency/AV producer. Clients: manufacturers, graphic arts houses, newspapers, advertising agencies and ad specialty houses. Assigns 20-30 jobs/year.
Needs: Works with 1-3 illustrators/month. Uses artists for billboards, P-O-P displays, filmstrips, stationery design, direct mail, TV, slide sets and brochures/flyers. Also uses artists for paste-up and mechanicals.
First Contact & Terms: Query (with 8x10 b&w samples), *don't* send artwork, slides, etc. "Without return postage and insurance we do not reply." Reports in 2 weeks. Provide printed samples, photocopies of artwork, and name and address to be kept on file for future assignments. "We like full info as to what the artist actually did–not just a printed piece thrown in as a sample." No originals returned to artist at job's completion. Pays $25-50, spot illustration; $25 minimum, mechanicals.

Tips: "Some folks apparently can't/don't read. We throw queries away when they come in without SASE, return postage or insurance. We don't think anyone who would send it that way would do a job right, or on time, or worse, do it his way instead of following instructions!"

PKG CUNNINGHAM & WALSH, INC., (formerly Post Keyes Gardner, Inc.), 875 N. Michigan Ave., Chicago IL 60611. Manager of Creative Services: Charles C. Hatcher. Ad agency. Needs vary.
First Contact & Terms: Provide general resume with experience most helpful; occasionally have received samples to be kept on file for future assignments. In some cases originals may be returned to artist at job's completion.

PRAIRIE PUBLIC TV, (formerly kfme channel thirteen), 4500 S. University Dr., Fargo ND 58103. Contact: Dan Hart. TV broadcaster.
Needs: Uses artists and designers for animation, print ads, posters and graphic/set design.
First Contact & Terms: Arrange interview to show samples (tearsheets, photocopies and printed pieces). Provide brochures/flyers, resumes and tearsheets to kept on file for future assignments. Originals returned to artist after job's completion only if requested.

PRAXIS CREATIVE PUBLIC RELATIONS, 5117 Greensboro Ln., Anaheim CA 92807. (714)637-5709. PR/consulting firm. Clients: "realty, travel agencies, retail shopping, construction, etc. Some non-profit. In general, any individual or firm with a public relations problem." Media used includes: trade magazines, direct mail, newspapers, radio, and TV.
Needs: Works with 1-3 illustrators/month. Uses illustrators for consumer magazines, direct mail and brochures/flyers.
First Contact & Terms: Send resume. Provide brochures to be kept on file for future assignments. Originals returned to artist at job's completion. Negotiates payment based on client's budget and amount of creativity required from artist.

PRICE/McNABB, 400 Northwestern Bank Bldg., Asheville NC 28801. Contact: Ken Fulford. Estab. 1967. Clients: Industrial manufacturers, resorts and tobacco processors. Annual billing: $3,000,000. Assigns 20 jobs/year. Query with samples.
Needs: Uses artists for illustration, retouching, paste-up and design for newspapers, TV, radio, magazines, billboards, direct mail, POP displays and collateral. Pays a negotiated price per assignment. Prefers artists with previous agency experience.

PRO/CREATIVES CO., 25 W. Burda, Spring Valley NY 10977. Contact: David Rapp. Sales promotion/advertising firm. Clients: package goods, publications, sports, entertainment and businesses.
Needs: Works with 3-4 illustrators/month. Uses artists for P-O-P displays, consumer magazines, television, brochures/flyers and newspapers. Also uses artists for layout.
First Contact & Terms: Query with resume and samples. Provide resume to be kept on file for future assignments. No originals returned to artist at job's completion.

THE PRODUCERS, 4131 N. 36th St., Phoenix AZ 85018. (602)956-0100. Contact: Nick Pellegrino, producer. Audiovisuals/TV/film producer. Estab. 1975. Clients: Industrial and corporate. Produces filmstrips, multimedia kits, slide sets and videotapes. Assigns 100 jobs and buys 50 illustrations/year; local artists only. Arrange interview to show portfolio. Reports in 1-2 weeks.
Needs: Uses artists for slide and ad illustrations and retouching. Pays $35/job, layout.

PRUITT, HUMPHRESS, POWERS ADVERTISING AGENCY, INC., 516 N. Adams St., Tallahassee FL 32301. (904)222-1212. Ad agency. Clients: industrial, financial. Media used includes: billboards, consumer and trade magazines, direct mail, newspapers, P-O-P displays, radio, and TV.
Needs: Uses artists for direct mail, television, brochures/flyers, trade magazines and newspapers. "Freelancers used in every aspect of business and given as much freedom as their skill warrants."
First Contact & Terms: Write and request personal interview to show portfolio (including tearsheets) or send resume and portfolio for review. Provide brochures, flyers, business cards, resumes and tearsheets to be kept on file for future assignments. Negotiates payment based on client's budget and amount of creativity required from artist. Pays set fee/job.
Portfolio Tips: "Submit examples of past agency work in clean, orderly, businesslike fashion including written explanations of each work. 10 illustrations or less.

PUBLIC COMMUNICATIONS, INC., 35 E. Wacker Dr., Chicago IL 60601. (312)558-1770. PR firm.

Needs: There are several account executives here. Each account executive probably uses 10-12 illustrators/year. Uses artists for annual reports, brochures, newsletters and exhibits.
First Contact & Terms: Call one of the account executives for appointment to show portfolio. Negotiates pay based on client's budget.

PUBLIC RELATIONS MANAGEMENT CO., Box 23902, San Jose CA 95153. (408)984-8987. Contact: Larry McCook, president. Advertising/public relations firm. Estab. 1971. Clients: Sportswear manufacturers. Annual billing: $2,000,000+. Buys 1,200-1,400 illustrations/year. Query with samples. SASE. Reports in 2 weeks.
Needs: Uses artists for sales and direct mail brochures and 4-color national ad layouts. Pays $1,000 min./job.

PUCK PRODUCTIONS, 676 N. LaSalle St., Chicago IL 60610. Producer: Hank Puckhaber. "We produce in all media." Submit resume.
Needs: Uses artists for animation, slides, industrial films and graphic design.

PUNCH FILMS INC., Box Q, New York NY 10011. Contact: Ms. F. Davis. Produces language arts sound filmstrips and motion pictures. Submit resume.
Needs: Uses artists for stop-motion animation.

PUOPOLO PRODUCTIONS INC., 381 Park Ave. S., New York NY 10016. Contact: Tana Marcuse. Motion Picture Producer. Clients: advertising agencies. Produces TV commercials.
Needs: Works with 2-3 illustrators and 12-15 designers/year. Uses artists for animation, design and illustration.
First Contact & Terms: Send samples. Provide resume and/or brochure to be kept on file for future assignments.

R.C.H. GRAPHIC ENTERPRISES, 726-B N. Glendale Ave., Glendale CA 91206. (213)240-2261. President: Rod Hallenberg. Ad/graphics firm. Clients: hospitals, financial, industrial and retail. Annual billing: $200,000.
Needs: Assigns 20-30 jobs/year. Uses artists for all types of artwork.
First Contact & Terms: Query with samples or arrange interview to show portfolio. SASE. Reports in 3 weeks. Pays $25/hour.

STAN RADLER/ASSOCIATES INC., Pine Hill, Framingham MA 01701. (617)875-1007. Contact: Stan Radler. PR/Ad agency. Annual billing: $500,000. Clients: electronics, computer equipment, food services and industrial equipment and services firms.
First Contact & Terms: Local artists only. Call for interview. Provide brochures/flyers and business card to be kept on file for future assignments. No originals returned to artist at job's completion.
Needs: Works with 1-2 designers/month. Uses artists for filmstrips, TV, brochures/flyers and trade magazines. Also uses artists for layout, illustration, technical art, type spec, paste-up and retouching for newspapers, trade magazines, direct mail and collateral material.

RAFSHOON ADVERTISING INC., 2 Northside 75, Atlanta GA 30318. (404)351-8212. Contact: Bill Selman. Clients: Tourism, industry, building materials, realty, electronics, sports equipment, financial, manufacturers, pest control, men's clothing, automotive replacement parts and retailers. Annual billing: $9,000,000. Mail samples or call.
Needs: Layout, illustration, paste-up, retouching and lettering for newspapers, TV, magazines, billboards, collateral and direct mail. Pays $100-250 minimum, layout; $20 minimum/hour, paste-up.

JOANNE RALSTON & ASSOCIATES, INC., 3003 N. Central, Phoenix AZ 85012. (602)264-2930. Vice President: Melissa Moore. Account Executive: Penny Pfaelzer. PR firm. Annual billing: $325,000. Clients: financial institution, real estate developers/homebuilders, industrial electronics manufacturing firms, political campaigns, architectural, major sports events (Phoenix Open PGA tourney, etc.)
Needs: Works with 2 illustrators and 1 designer/month. Uses artists for brochures/flyers and trade magazines.
First Contact & Terms: Write and request personal interview to show portfolio and/or send resume. Selects freelancers based on needs, cost, quality, and ability to meet deadlines. Provide flyers/brochures and ads to be kept on file for future assignments. No originals returned to artist at job's completion. Negotiates payment based on client's budget, amount of creativity required from artist, where work will appear, artist's previous experience/reputation, and ability to meet deadlines.

L.W. RAMSEY ADVERTISING AGENCY, 111 E. 3rd St., Davenport IA 52801. (319)326-0157. Art Director: James E. Kelley. Clients: consumer and industrial. Pays "going rate."
Needs: Uses artists for illustration and retouching.

RANCK-ROSS-MOORE, INC., 36 Steele St., Denver CO 80206. (303)320-3901. Art Director: Inge Christensen. Ad agency. Clients: financial, recreational, and food.
Needs: Has worked with 1 freelance illustrator one time and paste-up 10 times.
First Contact & Terms: Call for personal appointment to show portfolio. Negotiates payment based on hourly rate of artist. "I know approximately my price and I pick someone who has experience and fee per hour to fit the job."
Portfolio Tips: Wants to have variety in portfolio but should be what artist is strongest in. Likes to work with person who has experience.

THE RATH ORGANIZATION, Hills Building, Syracuse NY 13202. PR Firm. Contact: Thomas Burke. Annual billing: $250,000. Clients: industrial, business systems, graphics, markets, photographic markets, mail handling, filing, office environment and EDP. Media used includes direct mail, brochures/flyers and A/V.
Needs: Works with 1-2 freelance designers/month.
First Contact & Terms: Send resume. SASE. Negotiates payment based on client's budget, artist's daily or hourly fee and estimate based on area of work.
Portfolio Tips: "Because of our location we may ask only for representative samples related to our area of interest. We will note type of work submitted in our files."

RAUL DA SILVA & OTHER FILMMAKERS, 1400 East Ave., Rochester NY 14610. (716)442-1373. Creative Director: Raul da Silva. TV/film/animation/AV producer and limited publishing firm. Clients: business, industrial, institutional, educational and entertainment.
Needs: Works with 3-4 illustrators and 1 designer/month. "Seeking several artists with experience in slide/multimedia production, layout and materials. Also seeking designers." Uses artists for filmstrips, motion pictures, record jackets, multimedia kits, storyboards and titles.
First Contact & Terms: Send resume including references with phone numbers and addresses. SASE. Returns only solicited work. File kept on freelancers for future assignments. Payment for illustrations and layout "depends completely on end use." Storyboards, $15-50/frame and continuity design, $300 and up/program.

READ-POLAND INC., 411 Adolphus Tower, Dallas TX 75202. (214)742-9238. General Manager: David Dunnigan. Ad/PR/public affairs firm. Clients: corporate and political.
Needs: Assigns 6 jobs/year. Uses artists for support projects such as conventions, seminars and product promotion.
First Contact & Terms: Local artists only. Arrange interview to show portfolio. SASE. Reports in 2 weeks. Negotiates pay.

REEVES COMMUNICATIONS CORP., (formerly Reeves Teletape Corp.), 708 3rd Ave., New York NY 10017. (212)573-8600. Art Director: Michael B. Rolston. Produces TV, AV, multimedia presentations, slides and collateral material.
Needs: Uses artists for storyboards, layout, models, multimedia, paste-up, technical charts/illustrations and display.
First Contact & Terms: New York artists only. Call for interview. "After interview" provide original art in any form to be kept on file for future assignments. Material copyrighted. Pays $20 max./hour, design; $15 max./hour, paste-up.

RESCO, 99 Draper Ave., Meriden CT 06450. (203)666-6911, ext. 5828 or (203)238-4709. Producer: Ronald F. LaVoie. AV/PR/graphic arts producer. Clients: schools, associations, corporations and individuals.
Needs: Works with 1-2 illustrators/month. Also works with genegraphics animators. Uses artists for filmstrips, storyboards, charts/graphs, overhead transparencies, print ads and general graphics/art.
First Contact & Terms: Send brochure/flyer or call. Prefers "some kind of non-returnable brief." Works on assignment only. Returns only requested samples. Reports back on future assignment possibilities. Payment determined by "pricing guidelines of the Graphic Artists Guild; negotiation, per hour basis; and client and artist." Also considers client's budget "when no other type of determination can be made."

RESPONSE GROUP INC., Box 1173, North Miami Beach FL 33160. (305)652-4610. Contact: Joy Warech.

Needs: Uses artists for direct mail promotion, design, catalog illustrations/covers, paste-up, calligraphy, convention exhibits, decorative spots, lettering, posters, technical illustration, theater programs, trademarks, envelopes, booklets and forms.
First Contact & Terms: Local artists only. Prior direct response advertising experience necessary. Query with resume. Contacts artists as needs arise. Pays $200, direct mail brochure design; $25, spot illustration.

RESPONSE INDUSTRIES INC., 1414 Ave. of the Americas, New York NY 10017. President: D. Savage. Direct mail firm. Clients: publishers, clocks and records. Annual billing: $2,000,000. Pay determined by job.
Needs: Uses local artists for layout, technical art, paste-up and retouching for newspapers, consumer magazines and direct mail.

DOMINGO NICK REYES & ASSOCIATES, Box 15096, Alexandria VA 22309. (703)780-6783 or 768-3776, answering service. Contact: Talent Director or Art Director. Multimedia producers/communications counselors. AV producer. Produces audiovisual materials for government and industry, specializing in marketing products of every type to the federal government and the development of bilingual bicultural (English-Spanish) for the emerging $180 billion Hispanic market in the US.
Needs: Works with 2 illustrators/month. Uses illustrators for album covers, books, catalogs and filmstrips. Also uses artists for design and illustration of a series of booklets, VIVA series, which is converted to films, graphics and filmstrips. "We look for specialists in bilingual, bicultural materials. Greatest need is for nonverbal graphics communicators."
First Contact & Terms: Query with samples. "Our program people travel widely and often make it a point to call on artists and talent outside of DC. We often urge freelancers to send us a brochure or resume and when in their locale, will come by. We assign jobs out of town frequently. All work performed in accord with a written contract." SASE. Reports in 3 weeks. Provide resume and tearsheets to be kept on file for future assignments. Originals returned to artist at job's completion. Pays $17.50/hour minimum; negotiable.

RFM ASSOCIATES INC., 35 Atkins Ave., Trenton NJ 08610. President: Rodney F. Mortillaro. Annual billing: $1 million. Clients: industrial, food, home furnishing, travel, real estate, record manufacturer and fashion. Buys 135-150 illustrations/year.
Needs: Works with 5 illustrators and 7 designers/month. Uses artists for billboards, P-O-P displays, consumer and trade magazines, stationery design, multimedia kits, direct mail, brochures/flyers, album covers and newspapers. Also uses artists for illustrations, color separations, layout, paste-up and retouching for billboards, catalogs, magazines, letterheads, newspapers, posters and trademarks.
First Contact & Terms: Local artists only. Mail tearsheets or photocopies. No samples or originals returned at job's completion. Reports in 1 week. Pays $5-12/hour for lettering, illustrations and color separations. No payment for unused assigned illustrations. "Be familiar with printing and press procedures."

RICHARD-LEWIS CORP., 455 Central Park Ave., Scarsdale NY 10583. President: R. Byer. Estab. 1948. Clients: Machinery, tool, publishers, office supplies, chemical, detergent, film and printing supplies. Query with resume or arrange interview to show portfolio; local artists only. SASE. Reports in 2-3 weeks.
Needs: Uses artists for illustrations, retouching and some ad layout and mechanicals. Negotiates pay.

RICHARDSON, MYERS AND DONOFRIO, 10 E. Baltimore St., Baltimore MD 21202. Senior Art Directors: John Burk, David Curtis and Joe Herrick. Ad agency. Clients: consumer, agricultural, commercial and industrial.
Needs: Works with 4-6 illustrators and 1-2 designers/month. Uses artists for billboards, P-O-P displays, consumer and trade magazines, stationery design, multimedia kits, direct mail, TV, slide sets, brochures/flyers and newspapers.
First Contact & Terms: Provide brochures/flyers to be kept on file for future assignments. No originals returned to artist at job's completion.

RICHLAND ADVERTISING/CREATIVE HOUSE INC., 21 E. 40th St., New York NY 10016. (212)532-5250. Art/Creative Director: Michael Nowack. Ad/PR firm. Annual billing: $1 million. Clients: men's, children's and women's fashion manufacturers and retailers.
Needs: Assigns 50-75 jobs and buys 400-450 illustrations/year. Uses male, female and children's wear art for catalogs, TV storyboards and magazine ads, color separations, paste-up and mechanicals and retouching.

First Contact & Terms: Pays $10-30/hour for mechanicals and layout.

RICHTER McBRIDE PRODUCTIONS INC., 150 E. 52nd St., New York NY 10022. President: Robert Richter. Clients: government, organizations, industries, schools and TV. Produces motion pictures.
Needs: Buys 5-10/year. Uses artists for motion picture work.
First Contact & Terms: Local artists only. Query with 16mm sample reel. SASE. Reports in 2 weeks. Buys all rights. Originals returned to artist at job's completion. Pays $1,500-3,000/minute, animation; $75-1,500, titles.

RICKS EHRIG & ASSOCIATES, 4th and Vine Bldg., Seattle WA 98121. (206)623-6666. Creative Directors: Vicki Brems, Bruce Howard. Art Directors: Stan Hudson, Susan Cummings, Barbara Andrews and Renae Lovre. Clients: banks, dairy association and wood products firms. Buys 20-50 illustrations/year.
Needs: Works with 10-20 illustrators/month. Uses artists for billboard, P-O-P displays, filmstrips, consumer and trade magazines, stationery design, TV, slide sets and brochures/flyers. Also uses artists for layout, lettering, paste-up, retouching and animation.
First Contact & Terms: Query with samples or arrange interview. SASE. No file kept on artists. Originals returned to artist at job's completion. Pays promised fee for unused assigned illustrations.

RIVES, SMITH BALDWIN & CARLBERG, Division of Young & Rubicam, 6363 Richmond Ave., Houston TX 77057 or Box 27359, Houston TX 77027. (713)783-7640. Art Director: Bill Pinkston. Ad agency. Clients: oil-related industrial and some consumer.
Needs: Works with 2 freelance illustrators/month. Uses freelancers for direct mail, brochures/flyers, newspapers, TV and trade magazines.
First Contact & Terms: Call for appointment to show portfolio. Selection based on portfolio review. Negotiates payment based on particular job requirements, i.e., time involved, etc.
Portfolio Tips: Wants to see features which show individual style and past work used by ad agencies and tear sheets of published art. "Illustrators are hard to come by in Houston."

RIVIERA PRODUCTIONS, 6610 Selma Ave., Hollywood CA 90028. Contact: Will Zens. Produces films.
Needs: Works with about one freelance artist/year.
First Contact & Terms: Query with resume.

RMI MEDIA PRODUCTIONS INC., 120 W. 72nd St., Kansas City MO 64114. (816)523-4004. President: David L. Little. AV producer. Clients: schools, libraries, business and industry. Produces educational filmstrips, motion pictures, multimedia kits, slide sets, sound-slide sets and videotapes. Assigns 3-5 jobs/year.
Needs: Works with 1 illustrator/month for filmstrip art.
First Contact & Terms: Query. SASE. Reports in 2 weeks. Provide photocopied samples to be kept on file for future assignments. No originals returned to artist at job's completion. Buys one-time rights. Pays on production. Negotiates pay. Free catalog.

JOHN ROBERT PRODUCTIONS, 186 Francisco St., San Francisco CA 94133. Executive Producer: Henrietta Matta. TV/film producer.
Needs: Uses artists for audiovisual projects. Pays flat fee.

ROBERTS KETCHUM INTERNATIONAL LTD., 234 Eglinton Ave. E., Toronto, Ontario Canada M4P 1K7. (416)489-4222. Art Director: John Grant. Ad agency. Clients: all types.
Needs: Works with 4 illustrators and 4 designers/month. Uses artists for all media.
First Contact & Terms: Call for appointment to show portfolio and be persistent only if you can show exceptional work—"no rank amateur stuff." Pays standard rates.

ROBINSON-GERARD/McKINNEY, 3723 Westheimer Rd., Houston TX 77027. (713)627-2200. Contact: Dick Schnell. Ad agency. Clients: industrial.
Needs: Works with 2 freelance illustrators/month, occasionally uses designers. Uses talents of designer for billboards, consumer magazines, brochures/flyers, and occasionally trade magazines.
First Contact & Terms: Call for personal appointment to show portfolio. Selects freelancers on basis of portfolios and also does a lot of work with people they already know. Negotiates payment based on client's budget.
Portfolio Tips: Wants to see industrial illustrations. Would like designers to include previous

work done on brochures and magazine ads.

ROD/COM ADVERTISING/MARKETING, 520 N. Michigan, Suite 1504, Chicago IL 60611. (312)337-2992. President: R.J. Burnstein. Executive Vice President: L.E. Comitor. Estab. 1969. Annual billing: $1,500,000. Assigns 150 jobs and buys 10-20 illustrations/year. Query with samples or arrange interview to show portfolio. Usually prefers local artists. Reports in 2-3 weeks.

RICHARD H. ROFFMAN ASSOCIATES, 697 West End Ave., Suite 6A, New York NY 10025. (212)749-3647. Art/Creative Director: Malvina Cohn. PR firm. Annual billing: $200,000. Clients: all types. Media used includes consumer and trade magazines, direct mail, newspapers, radio, and TV.
Needs: Works with artists infrequently. Uses artists for all types of assignments.
First Contact & Terms: Send resume with SASE. Keeps no artist's file. Send no materials to be returned. Negotiates payment based on client's budget. Pays $25/job "taking 90 minutes."

GERALD A. ROGOVIN-PUBLIC RELATIONS INC., 51 Shornecliffe Rd., Newton MA 02158. (617)969-9699. President: Gerald A. Rogovin. PR firm. Clients: industrial, financial, real estate, and nonprofit agency.
Needs: Works with 1-2 illustrators and 1-2 designers/month. Uses artists for brochures/flyers, letterheads, direct mail, slide sets, ad designs, illustrations, graphs and charts for annual reports.
First Contact & Terms: Send resume, SASE. "We maintain file of information on those who solicit our interest." Provide business card, resume and/or flyers to be kept on file for future assignments. Negotiates payment based on freelancer's rates, client's budget and amount of creativity required from artist. No originals returned to artist at job's completion.

RONAN, HOWARD, ASSOCIATES, INC., 11 Buena Vista Ave., Spring Valley NY 10977. (914)356-6668. Ad firm. Clients: mostly manufacturers. Assigns 50-100 jobs/year.
First Contact & Terms: Query. "Samples and/or other material will not be returned. Please do not send unordered material with a demand for return. It is an unwarranted burden on our shipping department." SASE. Reports immediately. Pays $10 minimum for illustrations, layout, lettering, paste-up, retouching and mechanicals for newspapers, magazines, catalogs and POP displays. Pays promised fee for unused assigned illustrations.

PETER ROSEN PRODUCTIONS INC., 19 E. 62nd St., New York NY 10021. (212)751-7788. President: Peter Rosen. Estab. 1970. Produces motion picture films for government and TV. Buys 1 design/year; local artists only. Query with resume. SASE. Buys all rights.
Needs: Uses artists for animation. Pays $5,000/job or $200 minimum, animation shooting.

ALBERT JAY ROSENTHAL & CO., 400 N. Michigan, Chicago IL 60611. (312)337-8070. Creative Coordinator: Genese West. Ad agency. Clients: fashion, consumer foods, kitchen utensils, automotive repair and cosmetics.
Needs: Works entirely with freelance illustrators. Needs vary. Uses freelancers for billboards, consumer and trade magazines, brochures/flyers, P-O-P displays and TV.
First Contact & Terms: Call for appointment to show portfolio. Payment: 30 day/2%; 60 day/no discount.
Portfolio Tips: Wants to see features which demonstrate freelancer's ability to organize and implement concepts.

ALBERT JAY ROSENTHAL & CO., 545 Madison Ave., New York NY 10022. (212)826-6610. Executive Art Director: Jack McKie. Clients: "all kinds from packaged goods to automotive transmissions." Annual billing: $21,000,000.
First Contact & Terms: Local artists only. Query with samples and explain interests or call for an appointment. SASE. Provide business card, flyers, brochures and tearsheets. No originals returned to artist at job's completion. Pays $10/hour, paste-up; $15/hour, layout. Payment for illustration depends on type.
Needs: Works with 2 illustrators, 1 designer/month. Uses artists for advertising layout and design; illustration; lettering; and storyboards.

WAYNE H. ROSS, CO. INC., 406 W. 34th, V.F.W., Kansas City MO 64111. (816)531-6300. Contact: Wayne H. Ross. Ad agency. Annual billing: $500,000. Clients: industrial and general.
Needs: Works with 4 illustrators/month. Uses illustrators for brochures/flyers, trade magazines and newspapers. Also uses artists for illustration and design for trade papers and reports. Negotiates pay. "All work is estimated by the artist prior to our order."

First Contact & Terms: Query with resume by mail or phone. Contacts artists as needs arise.

ROSS-GAFFNEY INC., 21 W. 46th St., New York NY 10036. (212)582-3744. President: J. Gaffney. Estab. 1955. TV/film producer. Clients: CBS-TV, NBC-TV, Time-Life, Volkswagen and U.S. Information Agency. Produces motion pictures. Assigns 20 jobs/year; local artists only. Query with resume. SASE. Buys all rights. Pays on acceptance.
Needs: Uses artists for animation, charts/graphs and all services. Pay varies.

PETER ROTHHOLZ ASSOCIATES INC., 380 Lexington Ave., New York NY 10017. (212)687-6565. President: Peter Rothholz. PR firm. Clients: government (tourism and industrial development), publishing, pharmaceuticals (health and beauty products).
Needs: Works with 2 illustrators, 2 designers/month.
First Contact & Terms: Call for appointment to show portfolio. Provide resume to be kept on file for future assignments. No originals returned to artist at job's completion. Pays $25 min./job, design and layout; $15 min./job, illustration and lettering. Negotiates payment based on client's budget.
Tips: Assignments made based on freelancer's experience, cost, style and whether he/she is local.

ROTSINGER TENNEY RICHARD INC., 3450 W. Central, Suite 336, Toledo OH 43606. President: A.H. Rotsinger. Clients: Industrial and consumers.
Needs: Uses graphic artists for direct mail brochures, annual reports, billboards, public service TV spots, capability brochures and house organs.
First Contact & Terms: Mail samples. Minimum payment: $22.50/hour, keylining; $27.50/hour, illustration.

ROSS ROY OF CANADA LTD., 2 Carlton St., Toronto 2, Ontario Canada. (416)977-2270. Contact: Doug Bedard. Ad agency. Clients: consumer products.
Needs: Works with several illustrators and designers/month. Uses artists for all print media.
First Contact & Terms: Call Doug Bedard for appointment to show portfolio. Negotiates pay based on client's budget, amount of creativity required from artist/photographer and where the work will appear.

RPG AND ASSOCIATES, (formerly Persuasive Communications), 6677 N. Lincoln Ave., Lincolnwood IL 60645. Art/Creative Director: Mark Gruen. Estab. 1976. Clients: Consumer products firms and specialized industrial markets. Annual billing: $1,000,000. Call or write for appointment; local artists only.
Needs: Uses artists for layout, paste-up, illustration, type spec and retouching for newspapers, magazines, direct mail and collateral. Pays $20/hour, paste-up.

RUBEN, MONTGOMERY & ASSOC., 1812 N. Meridian, Indianapolis IN 46202. (317)924-6271. Creative Director: Allan Godshall. Ad agency. Clients: industrial, consumer and retail.
Needs: Works with 10-20 freelance illustrators/month. Uses freelancers for billboards, consumer and trade magazines, direct mail, brochures/flyers, newspapers, P-O-P displays and stationery design.
First Contact & Terms: Send letter with examples of work. Negotiates payment based on client's budget and freelancer's fee.
Portfolio Tips: Wants to see individual's specialty rather than a wide variety.

HORACE SADOWSKY & ASSOCIATES, 20 Jerusalem Ave., Hicksville, Long Island NY 11801. (516)681-6550. President/Creative Director: Horace Sadowsky. Clients: industrial machinery and hard goods firms.
Needs: Works with 1 illustrator and 1 designer/2 months. Uses designers for brochures/flyers and trade magazines. No originals returned to artist at job's completion. Uses artists for layout, illustration, technical art, paste-up and retouching for magazines, direct mail, brochures, annual reports and corporate promotions.
First Contact & Terms: Local artists only. Arrange interview. Provide brochures, flyers, tearsheets, business card or resume to be kept on file for future assignments. No originals returned to artist at job's completion.

SAMPSON & CRANOR ADVERTISING CO., INC., 165 W. 46th St., New York NY 10036. (212)354-8198. Contact: Bill Sampson or Foster Wright Cranor. Ad agency. Clients: motion picture companies and movie theaters. Annual billing: $750,000.
Needs: Works with 3-4 illustrators/month. Uses artists for movie posters and ads. Especially

needs full-color realistic renderings for movie posters. Pays promised fee for unused assigned illustrations.
First Contact & Terms: Local artists only. Query with samples (original art and copies) for files. Reports in 1 week. Provide brochures, flyers, business card, resume and tearsheets to be kept on file for future assignments. No originals returned to artist at job's completion. Pays $50-1,000/job, posters; $4-8/hour, paste-up.

GILBERT SANDLER & ASSOCIATES, INC., 501 St. Paul Pl., Baltimore MD 21202. (301)837-7100. Art Director: Jim Maslovsky. Ad agency. Clients: Institutional advertising (financial, industrial).
First Contact & Terms: Call for personal appointment to show portfolio. Negotiates payment based on client's budget and particular job. "Prefer to get an estimate from the freelancer and negotiate payment based on the budget."
Portfolio Needs: Wants to see a little bit of all freelancer can do but especially specific style and best work. Uses many types of art and prefers to see artist's speciality.

JIM SANT'ANREA INC., 320 W. 57th, New York NY 10019. (212)974-5400. Senior Vice President: Richard Portner. Multimedia producer. Clients: "top companies." Produces motion pictures, multimedia kits, sound-slide sets and videotapes.
Needs: Assigns approximately 20 jobs/year. Uses artists for design, storyboards, and comprehensive stage renderings.
First Contact & Terms: Prefers local artists. Call and make an appointment to show samples. Provide resume to be kept on file for future assignments. "Payment varies depending on the complexity. An 80-frame storyboard would pay around $500-600. We pay by the job."

JIM SANT'ANREA MIDWEST INC., 875 N. Michigan Ave., Chicago IL 60611. (312)787-2156. Contact: Howard Hirsch, production manager. AV producer. Estab. 1970. Clients: insurance and agricultural concerns. Producers filmstrips, motion pictures, multimedia kits, slide sets, sound-slide sets and videotapes. Assigns 30 jobs/year; local artists only. Arrange interview to show portfolio. SASE. Reports in 2 weeks.
Needs: Uses artists for proposal sketches, slides, filmstrips, storyboards, illustrations for slides, films, animation and video, and collateral print materials. Pays $50-150, sketches; $8-12/frame; $50-1,000, illustrations.

SAXTON COMMUNICATIONS GROUP, LTD., 605 Third Ave., New York NY 10158. (212)953-1300. Art Directors: Al Battista and Don Grodt. AV/film producer and advertising promotion. Clients: industrial corporations.
Needs: Works with 5 illustrators/month. Uses artists for audiovisuals, storyboards, charts/graphics and retouching.
First Contact & Terms: Call for appointment to show portfolio. Works on assignment only. Provide resume and/or tearsheet to be kept on file for future assignments. Negotiates pay based on client's budget, amount of creativity required, where work is to appear and artist's previous experience/reputation.

THE SCHRAM ADVERTISING CO., 170 W. Washington, Chicago IL 60602. (312)346-8585. President: Ira P. Weinstein. Ad agency.
Needs: Works with 2-3 illustrators/month and uses freelance designers. Uses artists and designers for collateral material and ads.
First Contact & Terms: Call for appointment to show portfolio. Negotiates payment with freelancer.

SCHWANBERG-BOLSTA-BROWN ASSOCIATES, INC., Box 1513, St. Cloud MN 56301. (612)251-2170. Art/Creative Director: Jan Nohner. Estab. 1973. Clients: Boat manufacturers, photo album manufacturers, granite products, wire products, balers, tool and die companies, freezer manufacturers, eyeglasses and egg producers. Annual billing: $500,000. Buys 10 illustrations/year; mostly local artists. SASE. Reports in 2 weeks.
Needs: Pays $10-20/hour, catalogs; $100-125/job, special illustrations. Pays promised fee for unused assigned work.

GERALD SCHWARTZ AGENCY, 420 Lincoln Road Bldg. Miami Beach FL 33139. (305)531-1174. Executive Vice President: Felice P. Schwartz. Ad/PR/fund-raising firm. Clients: banks, savings and loan associations, Miami Beach Redevelopment Project, hospitals, universities, philanthropic agencies, political party campaigns and nursing homes. Annual billing: $1,000,000. Assigns 100 jobs and buys 25 illustrations/year.

Needs: Works with 2 illustrators/month. Uses billboards, filmstrips, slide sets, brochures/flyers and newspapers.
First Contact & Terms: Query with samples (photocopies). SASE. Reports in 2 weeks. No file kept on artists. Originals returned to artist at job's completion. Payment by job: $15-250, annual reports; $12-750, catalogs; $20-50, letterheads; $12-500, newspapers; $25-75, trademarks; $8-50, layout and lettering. Pays promised fee for unused assigned work.

LIZ SCOTT ASSOCIATES, 121 University Place, Pittsburgh PA 15213. (412)682-5429. Manager: Liz Scott. Ad/PR firm. Clients: social service agencies, small businesses and individuals.
Needs: Assigns 3-5 jobs/year. Uses artists for illustration and mechanicals for annual reports, ads and brochures.
First Contact & Terms: Local artists only. "Send letter, follow up with call and arrange interview to show work." SASE. Reports in 2-3 weeks. Provide "any small samples" to be kept on file for future assignments. No originals returned to artist at job's completion. Negotiates pay; $15 min./hour.
Tips: "Don't label yourself as 'fashion' or 'graphic'; this makes you look limited to us." Experience in commercial work preferred.

SEIDELMAN/NICE PRESENTS INC., & VANNET PRODUCTIONS INC., (formerly L.S.V. Productions, Ltd.), 723 7th Ave., New York NY 10019. Contact: Arthur Allan Seidelman. Motion picture producer.
Needs: Works with 3-4 illustrators and designers/year. Uses artists for advertising art/design/layout, film titles, fine art, lettering, posters and theater programs/posters.
First Contact & Terms: Submit ink or line and wash samples. Buys all rights.

SELZ, SEABOLT & ASSOCIATES, INC., 221 N. LaSalle, Chicago IL 60601. (312)372-7090. Contact: Paul Fullmer. PR firm.
Needs: Works with 5 designers/month. Uses artists in literature area such as brochures.
First Contact & Terms: Call for appointment to show portfolio. Reviews local portfolios only.
Tips: Wants to see a "potpourri of things done, and things done recently" from designers and photographers. Every subject is of interest because of the broad range of clients. Negotiates pay based on client's budget, prevailing rates and what time is involved.

SERIOUS BUSINESS COMPANY, 1145 Mandana Blvd., Oakland CA 94610. (415)832-5600. Contact: Ms. Freude Bartlett. AV producer/distributor. Clients: educational institutions. Audience: kindergarten through graduate school. Produces shorts.
Needs: Works with 2 designers/year. Buys 6 designs/year. Uses artists for catalogs and brochures/flyers. Also uses artists for paste-up.
First Contact & Terms: Prefers local artists. Query. SASE. Reports in 1 week. Usually buys one-time rights. Sample catalog $2. Pays $25-350.

SHAILER DAVIDOFF ROGERS INC., Heritage Square, Fairfield CT 06430. (203)255-3425. Contact: Hal Rogers, executive vice president. Estab. 1966. Clients: Financial, package goods, food products, condominiums, insurance and retailers. Annual billing: $6,500,000. Arrange interview to show portfolio; local artists only. SASE. Reports in 2-3 weeks.
Needs: Uses artists for layout, technical art, and illustration of ads, direct mail, booklets and folders. Negotiates pay. "We deal with each artist and each job individually."

SHECTER & LEVIN ADVERTISING/PUBLIC RELATIONS, 1800 N. Charles St., Baltimore MD 21201. (301)752-4088. Production Executives: S. Sybert or David J. Levin. Ad/PR firm. Clients: manufacturers, contractors, builders, institutions, organizations and retail store chains.
Needs: Works with 3-4 illustrators/month. Uses designers for billboards, consumer magazines, stationery design, direct mail, television, brochures/flyers, trade magazines and newspapers. Also uses artists for layouts and mechanicals for brochures, newspaper and magazine ads.
First Contact & Terms: Query or arrange interview to show portfolio. SASE "but prefer no samples be sent unless arranged." No file kept on artists. No originals returned to artist at job's completion. Negotiates pay.

SHIPLEY ASSOCIATES INC., 3844 Kennett Pike, Suite 214, Powder Mill Square, Greenville DE 19807. (802)652-3051. Art Director: Kevin McLaughlin. Ad/PR firm. Clients: retail. Annual billing: $1,300,000.
Needs: Works with 2 illustrators and 1 designer/month. Assigns 9 jobs/year. Uses artists for annual report illustrations, mechanicals, brochure and sign design.
First Contact & Terms: Query with previously published work. No originals returned to artist at

job's completion. Negotiates pay. Especially needs spot illustrations.

SHOREY & WALTER INC., 1617 E. North St., Greenville SC 29607. (803)242-5407. Sr. Art Director: M.G. Coyle. Ad agency. Clients: industrial and financial. Annual billing: $3,000,000.
Needs: Works with 1 illustrator and 2 designers/month. Uses artists for consumer magazines, brochures/flyers and trade magazines.
First Contact & Terms: Query with samples or call. Provide materials to be kept on file for future assignments. No originals returned to artist at job's completion. Pays $60+ /job.

SHOTWELL AND PARTNERS INCORPORATED, 1400 Harding Pl., Charlotte NC 28204. (704)372-8880. Art Director: Murray Craven. Ad agency. Clients: general.
First Contact & Terms: Call for personal appointment to show portfolio. Negotiates payment based on client's budget, amount of creativity required from artist, where work will appear, and artist's previous experience/reputation. "Prefer artist to set fee—consider to buy out for unlimited use. Would be preference to buy the work for unlimited use but that doesn't mean we don't pay per use."

SEIBER & McINTYRE, INC. 625 N. Michigan Ave., Chicago IL 60611. (312)266-9200. Contact: art director. Ad agency. Clients: pharmaceutical and medical devices manufacturers.
Needs: Works with about 2 freelance illustrators/month. Uses freelancers for medical trade magazines, brochures/flyers and direct mail to physicians.
First Contact & Terms: Call for appointment to show portfolio. Negotiates payment based on client's budget and where work will appear.
Portfolio Tips: Prefers to see original "terrific work" rather than reproductions but will review past work used by other ad agencies. Needs good medical illustrators but is looking for illustrators that can accomplish quality executions other than medical.

PETER SIMMONS PRODUCTIONS, 17 Diamond Rd., Lexington MA 02173. President: Peter Simmons. AV/film producer. Clients: corporations.
Needs: Works with 2 illustrators/month. Uses artists for filmstrips, motion pictures and storyboards.
First Contact & Terms: Write for interview to show portfolio or send resume or brochure/flyer. SASE. Works on assignment only. Provide resume, business card, flyers, and/or brochures to be kept on file for future assignments. Pays $5-20/hour for art and graphics. Negotiates pay based on amount of creativity required and artist's previous experience/reputation.

SIMMONS PUBLIC RELATIONS, 1750 Chichester Ave., Louisville KY 40205. Contact: Raymond L. Simmons. Uses local artists for technical bulletins.

SIX PICTURES CO. INC., 715 Park Ave., New York NY 10021. President: E. P. Eisenstein. TV/film producer. Audience: broadcast, cable and satellite TV.
Needs: Assigns 6 jobs/year. Uses artists for album covers, filmstrips and motion pictures. Also uses artists for filmstrip animation, catalog design and advertising.
First Contact & Terms: Local artists only. Query with resume and samples. SASE. Reports in 2 weeks. Provide resume, brochures/flyers and tearsheets to be kept on file for future assignments. Pays $1,500-2,500/job.

A.L. SKAAR & COMPANY, (formerly Elgee & Skarr Advertising), South 104 Freya, Suite 209, Spokane WA 99202. (509)535-9702. Creative Director: Al Skaar. Ad agency. Clients: boat manufacturers, retailers and distributors. Annual billing: $1,250,000.
Needs: Works with 2 illustrators and 2 designers/month. Assigns 150 jobs and buys 50 illustrations/year. Uses artist for consumer magazines, stationery design, direct mail, television, brochures/flyers, trade magazines and newspapers. Also uses artists for poster design and illustration, spot illustrations and mechanicals.
First Contact & Terms: Local artists only. Query with resume and previously published work; "follow-up with phone call." SASE. Reports in 2 weeks. Fees negotiated.

SKYLINE FILMS INC., 160 E. 38th St., New York NY 10016. (212)490-1668. Contact: Office. Audiovisuals and TV/film producers. Clients: educational, industrial, corporate and TV. Produces filmstrips, motion pictures, slide sets, sound-slide sets and videotapes.
Needs: Works with about 10 freelance illustrators and 5 designers/year. Uses artists for filmstrip animation, slide illustration and graphics for films and videotapes.
First Contact & Terms: Query with resume and samples. SASE. Reports in 3 weeks. Provide resume and tearsheets to be kept on file for future assignments. Negotiates pay.

SLEEPING GIANT FILMS INC., 3019 Dixwell Ave., Hamden CT 06518. Contact: Anthony Guarino Jr. AV/TV/Film producer. Produces slides, filmstrips, film loops, motion pictures and multimedia kits.
Needs: Works with 4-5 illustrators and designers/year. Uses artists for audiovisuals.
First Contact & Terms: Provide resume to be kept on file for future assignments.

SLIM BARNARD ENTERPRISES, 1543-B N. Serrano Ave., Hollywood CA 90027. (213)465-9111. General Manager: David C. Eisenlohr. TV/film producer. Produces motion pictures.
Needs: Assigns 20 jobs/year. Also uses artists for animation, catalog covers/illustrations, magazine ads and models.
First Contact & Terms: Local artists only. Query with samples. SASE. Reports in 1 week. Pays $100-500, layout.

SMITH & DOUGLAS ADVERTISING, INC., 6033 Berkshire Lane, Dallas TX 75225. Art/Creative Director: Howard N. Smith. Clients: Food, mail order, recruitment, store fixture, investigations and electronic supply firms. Call for interview; local artists only.
Needs: Layout, illustration, technical art, type spec, paste-up and retouching for newspapers, trade magazines, TV, radio, billboards and direct mail.

MARC SMITH CO., Box A, Severna Park MD 21146. (301)647-2606. Art/Creative Director: Marc Smith. Clients: consumer and industrial products, sales services and public relations firms.
Needs: Uses artists for layout, illustration, lettering, technical art, type spec, paste-up and retouching for newspapers, magazines, TV, billboards and direct mail.
First Contact & Terms: Local artists only. Mail samples or call for interview.

SMITH, DORIAN & BURMAN, INC., 589 New Park Ave., Hartford CT 06110. Production Manager: Edwin F. Snelgrove. Industrial clients. Annual billing: $3,800,000. Call for interview; local artists only.
Needs: Uses artists for layout, illustration and retouching for trade magazines, collateral, direct mail and POP display.

JOE SNYDER & COMPANY LIMITED, 155 W. 68th St., New York NY 10023. (212)595-5925. Contact: Joe H. Snyder. Clients: industrial and bank.
First Contact & Terms: Send resume and/or portfolio for review. Works on assignment only. Has "a very extensive file; I like a brief statement–to one page." Accepts resume or brochure. Negotiates payment based on client's budget.
Needs: Works with 2-3 illustrators/month. All work open to freelancers. Uses artists for boards, consumer magazines, direct mail, brochures/flyers, TV and trade magazines.

KEN SNYDER ENTERPRISES, 2032 Alameda Padre Serra, Santa Barbara CA 93103. (805)962-8171. Project Director: Tish Gainey. Production Manager: Duane Busick. AV/TV producer. Produces multimedia kits, films, presentations, videotapes, package designs, radio/TV advertising, public relations, exhibitions and theme parks. Buys 200 designs/year.
Needs: Works with 3 illustrators, 2 designers/month. Uses artists for animation, calligraphy, catalog covers/illustrations, dioramas, direct mail brochures, filmstrips, games, layout, magazine ads, models, multimedia kits, paste-up, posters, study prints, technical charts/illustrations and type spec.
First Contact & Terms: Needs artists who "can come into our office, sometimes frequently." Query or arrange interview. SASE. Reports in 2 weeks. Provide resume and photocopies of work to be kept on file for future assignments. No originals returned to artist at job's completion. Buys all rights. Minimum payment: $5/foot, 35mm animation; $150, posters.

SODERBERG ADVERTISING AGENCY, 221 1st Ave. W., Seattle WA 98119. Creative Director: P. Stanley Soderberg. Ad agency. Clients: banks, industrial, fast food, auto dealers and restaurants
Needs: Works with 5-10 illustrators, 10-15 designers/month. Uses artists for layout, illustration, type spec, paste-up, retouching and lettering for newspapers, magazines, radio, TV, billboards, P-O-P displays, filmstrips and direct mail.
First Contact & Terms: Mail samples. Provide business card and flyers to be kept on file for future assignments. Originals returned to artist at job's completion.

THE SOFTNESS GROUP INC., 3 E. 54th St., New York NY 10022. Executive Vice President: Carol Blades. PR firm. Clients: corporations and manufacturers.

Needs: Works with 3 illustrators, 1 designer/month. Uses artists to work with filmstrips, consumer magazines, stationery design, multimedia kits, slide sets, brochures/flyers, trade magazines and newspapers.
First Contact & Terms: Query with resume and samples. SASE. Reports in 2 weeks. Provide brochures and flyers to be kept on file for future assignments. No originals returned to artist at job's completion. Negotiates pay.

SOLID SOUL & BOLD SOUL, 3282 E. 119th St., Cleveland OH 44120. (216)231-0772 or (216)752-1904. Vice President: Anthony Luke. Publicity/concert promotion firm. Clients: soul, Latin and pop groups.
Needs: Works with 1 illustrator and designer/month. Uses artists for television, brochures/flyers, album covers and newspapers.
First Contact & Terms: Local illustrators/designers only. Mail query, include resume and samples. SASE. Reports in 1 month. No originals returned to artist at job's completion. Pays 5% royalty.

ROBERT SOLOMON & ASSOCIATES ADVERTISING, INC., 3500 Book Bldg., Detroit MI 48226. Executive Art Director: Dean Adams. Clients: Food chains, theaters, remodeling, furniture and travel firms. Mail samples; local artists only.
Needs: Uses artists for layout, illustration, paste-up, retouching and lettering for newspapers, consumer magazines, radio, TV, billboards, direct mail, public relations and business cards.

SORGEL-LEE-RIORDAN INC., 205 W. Highland Ave., Milwaukee WI 53203. (414)224-9600. Graphics Arts Director: Dave Sorgel. AV/TV/film producer. Clients: Business, corporate, performing arts groups, libraries and museums. Produces filmstrips, motion pictures, slide sets, sound-slide sets, videotapes and multi-image features. Assigns 5 jobs/year.
Needs: Works with 1 illustrator/month. Uses artists for stylized illustrations, human figures and animation.
First Contact & Terms: Local artists only. Query with resume and samples (slides). SASE. Reports in 3 weeks. Provide resume and brochures/flyers to be kept on file for future assignments. No originals returned to artist at job's completion. Negotiates pay.

SOUNDLAB INC., 4130 Aurora St., Coral Gables FL 33146. President: Eduardo More. AV/motion picture/TV producer. Audience: TV and non-theatrical. Produces animation, slides, industrial films and documentaries.
Needs: Works with 3 illustrators and 1 designer/month. Uses artists for filmstrips and motion pictures. Also uses artists for animated cartoons and slide illustrations. Negotiates pay.
First Contact & Terms: Prefers local artists with professional experience and demos. Contact by mail only. Provides resume and brochures to be kept on file for future assignments. No originals returned to artist at job's completion.

SOUTHWARD & ASSOCIATES, INC., 20 N. Wacker Dr., Chicago IL 60606. Art/Creative Director: Don Kassel. Clients: Financial, data processing and resort/hotel. Call for interview.
Needs: Uses artists for layout and illustration for newspapers, trade magazines, billboards and direct mail. Pays $35-250/b&w illustration. Payment depends on complexity of illustration, subject and number of illustrations in one assignment. "Jobs are usually rush."

J.J. SPECTOR & ASSOCIATES, 2900 NE 30th St., Ft. Lauderdale FL 33306. (305)563-4093. Contact: J.J. Spector. Direct mail marketing consultants/ad agency. Annual billing: $1,500,000. Clients: Publishers, manufacturers, insurance companies, banks, commercial/industrial firms and others who use direct mail heavily. Buys 10-15 illustrations/year.
Needs: Color separations, layout, lettering, paste-up, retouching and type spec for ads, annual reports, catalogs, letterheads, packages and direct mail package components.
First Contact & Terms: Query. SASE. Reports in 1 week. Provides brochures, flyers, business card, resume and tearsheets. Originals returned to artist at job's completion. Pays $200-350, package design; $50-175, paste-up/mechanicals; $20-50/page, catalog layout. Pays original fee as agreed for unused assigned illustrations.
Tips: "Collect direct mail packages received at home and redesign them more forcefully into alternative dummies for submission as samples."

SPEER, YOUNG & HOLLANDER INC., 3055 Wilshire Blvd., Los Angeles CA 90010. (213)487-2363. Art Director: Bill Owen. Ad agency. Estab. 1949. Clients: Industrial, financial and retail. Annual billing: $1,000,000. Assigns 50 jobs/year; local artists only. Arrange interview to show portfolio.

NEAL SPELCE ASSOCIATES/MANNING SELVAGE & LEE, 1500 Austin Bank Tower, Austin TX 78701. (512)476-4644. Creative Director: Hank Smith. Ad agency. Annual billing: $4.5 million. Clients: travel, financial, trade associations, real estate and professional firms.
Needs: Works with 3 illustrators and 4 designers/month. Uses artists for consumer and trade magazines, direct mail, newspapers, P-O-P displays, brochures/flyers and TV.
First Contact & Terms: Write requesting interview to show portfolio (illustrations and printed pieces incorporating the illustrations), send resume or make contact through artist's rep. Provide resume, brochure or promotional materials showing work and/or samples to be kept on file for future assignments. Works on assignment only. Negotiates pay based on client's budget, amount of creativity required and artist's previous experience/reputation.

SPENCER, BENNETT, NOWAK, INC., 70 Harborside Dr., Providence RI 02905. (401)785-2350. Creative Director: Glenn M. Spencer. Ad agency. Annual billing: $3,500,000. Clients: 90% industrial. Media used include trade magazines, direct mail, P-O-P displays, and editorial (industrial).
First Contact & Terms: Call for personal appointment to show portfolio. Negotiates payment based on client's budget and amount of creativity required from artist. Hourly fee: $20-50.
Portfolio Tips: "Should be directed at 1 or 2 styles, 10 to 12 items, layout (30%), and some tear sheets." Selects artist according to concept, comprehensive layout ability (presentation), and technical illustration.

SPITZ ADVERTISING AGENCY, 530 Oak St., Syracuse NY 13203. Contact: William Spitz or Nick Bibko. Clients: educational, institutional, retail, hotel, motel, bank and industrial.
Needs: Uses artists for illustration, design, animated cartoons, technical art layout and retouching for catalogs, direct mail, graphics, trademarks, letterheads, newspapers, trade magazines, radio, TV and billboards.
First Contact & Terms: Mail samples. Payment varies with job.

EDGAR S. SPIZEL ADVERTISING INC., 1782 Pacific Ave., San Francisco CA 94109. (415)474-5735. Contact: Edgar S. Spizel. AV producer. Clients: "Consumer-oriented from jeans to symphony orchestras to supermarkets to personalities." Works a great deal with major sports stars and TV personalities.
Needs: Uses artists for posters, ad illustrations, brochures and mechanicals.
First Contact & Terms: Query with samples (tearsheets). SASE. Reports in 3 weeks. Provide materials to be kept on file for future assignments. No originals returned to artist at job's completion. Negotiates pay.

J. SPONZA & ASSOCIATES INC. ADVERTISING, 3 Belden Ave., Norwalk CT 06850. (203)847-4509. Vice President/Creative Director: Doris Anderson. Clients: manufacturing and services. Assigns 52+ jobs/year.
Needs: Works with 1 illustrator, 1 designer/month. Uses artists for brochures/flyers. Also uses artists for design and mechanicals for newspaper ads, catalogs and brochures. Negotiates pay.
First Contact & Terms: Query or arrange interview to show portfolio. SASE. Reports in 1-2 weeks. Provide business card, tearsheets and resume to be kept on file for future assignments. No originals returned to artist at job's completion.

SPOONER & CO., 309 Bloomfield Ave., Verona NJ 07044 (201)857-0053. President: William B. Spooner III. Ad agency. Clients: mills, mixers, vacuum pumps, metals and ores, plastic blow molding machines and conveyor belts.
Needs: Works with 2 illustrators and 2 designers/month. Uses artists for stationery design, slide sets, brochures/flyers and trade magazines. Also uses artists for layout, illustration, technical art, type spec, paste-up, retouching and lettering for newspapers, trade magazines, direct mail, technical literature and trade shows.
First Contact & Terms: Mail samples or call. Provide brochures, flyers, business card and resume. No originals returned to artist at job's completion. Payment negotiated.

SPOTLIGHT PRESENTS, INC., 20 E. 46th St., New York NY 10017. (212)986-5520. Producer: Trebbe Johnson. AV firm. Clients: corporations, associations, government agencies.
Needs: Works with 1-2 illustrators and 1 animator/month. Also needs board artists. Uses artists for filmstrips, motion pictures, multimedia kits, storyboards, charts/graphs, overhead transparencies and exhibitions.
First Contact & Terms: Write for interview to show portfolio of published work, AV work, examples of slide animation and board work or send resume and letter of inquiry to be kept on file for future assignments. Works on assignment only. Samples returned by SASE; reports back on

future assignment possibilities. "We look for versatile people who can do board work, art prep for slides, stats and color keys. Familiarity with AV is preferable." Minimum pay $10-13/hour based on amount of creativity required and artist's previous experience/reputation.

SSC & B INC., (formerly Erwin Wasey), 5455 Wilshire Blvd., Los Angeles CA 90036. (213)931-1211. Senior Art Directors: Jerry Voss and Asa Duff. Ad agency. Clients: Consumer package goods firms. Annual billing: $30,000,000.
Needs: Since this firm is in a period of transition since SSC & B took them over, the needs for freelance illustrators have increased. Before transition, rarely used freelance designers; now need a few of them. Expects this trend to continue but is hard to give figures on their need because of the situation. Uses illustration, design, mechanicals and paste-up. Call to arrange interview; local artists only. Originals returned to artist after publication.

AL STAHL ANIMATED, (formerly Animated Productions Inc), 1600 Broadway, New York NY 10019. Contact: Al Stahl. AV/motion picture producer. Converts slide shows into motion pictures. Clients: photographers, film producers, ad agencies and artists. Arrange interview to show samples.
Needs: Works with 2 illustrators and 2 animators/month. Uses artists for filmstrips, motion pictures, slide shows, animation and graphic design.

STANART STUDIOS, 45 W. 45th St., New York NY 10036. Contact: Stan Popko. Specializes in creative animation for industrial films, including slides and graphic design. Query.

LEODA STEINHEIMER ADVERTISING, 4949 Wise Ave., St. Louis MO 63110. Art/Creative Director: Leoda Steinheimer. Clients: Retail fashion chain, home sewing products, misses and junior sleep/loungewear and orthodontic appliance firms. Call for interview; local artists only.
Needs: Uses artists for layout, fashion illustration, paste-up and lettering for newspapers, magazines, direct mail, catalogs, packaging and displays.

STERN-WALTERS/EARLE LUDGIN, 9911 Pico Blvd., Los Angeles CA 90035. (213)277-7550. Art Director: Stewart Mills. Ad agency.
First Contact & Terms: Call or write, including resume, and request personal appointment to show portfolio. Negotiates payment based on "whatever the going rate is for a particular job."
Portfolio Tips: "No more than 25-30 examples, after that it's boring. Send along anything of quality that shows what the individual can do."

STONE & ADLER, INCORPORATED, Division of Young & Rubicam, Inc. 150 N. Wacker Dr., Chicago IL 60606. (312)346-6100. Art Director: Robert Specht. Ad agency. Clients: industrial, financial and entertainment.
Needs: Works with 2-3 freelance illustrators/month. Uses freelancers for billboards, consumer and trade magazines, brochures/flyers, newspapers, P-O-P displays, stationery design, TV and especially direct mail.
First Contact & Terms: Call for appointment to show portfolio. Selection based on portfolio review. Negotiates payment based on client's budget and particular job.
Portfolio Tips: Wants to see anything which indicates individual's style (original and printed samples). Uses all styles of work.

THE ROBERT STORY CO., 1620 Vista Del Mar, Hollywood CA 90028. Contact: Cynthia Smith. Animation/live action. Clients: TV producers and ad agencies.
Needs: Works with approximately 3 illustrators, approximately 2 designers/month. Uses artists for filmstrips, motion pictures and animation.
First Contact & Terms: Query with resume. Provide brochures/flyers, resume and tearsheets to be kept on file for future assignments. No originals returned to artist at job's completion.

MARTY STOUFFER PRODUCTIONS, 300 S. Spring St., Aspen CO 81611. (303)925-5536. Contact: Marty Stouffer. Audiovisuals and TV/film producer. Clients: educational and TV. Produces motion pictures. Assigns "several" jobs/year.
Needs: Number of freelancers used "depends on the project we're working on. Sometimes we use a good many freelance illustrators." Uses artists for animation for natural history motion pictures.
First Contact & Terms: Query with samples. Provide resume and tearsheets to be kept on file for future assignments. Negotiates pay.

STUDIO CENTER CORPORATION, 200 W. 22nd St., Norfolk VA 23517. (804)622-2111. Executive Producer: Fred Donour. Creative Director: Vince Ahern. AV producer/print and

exhibit design. Clients: ad agency, government, corporation.
Needs: Works with 2-4 illustrators/month. Uses artists for filmstrips, multimedia kits, storyboards, charts/graphs, packaging, print ads and convention exhibit designs.
First Contact & Terms: Call (only) for appointment to show portfolio. "Live appointments only." Reports back on future assignment possibilities. Provide resume and letter of inquiry to be kept on file for future assignments. Negotiates pay based on client's budget, amount of creativity required and where work is to appear. "Every project is different but we work on a fixed fee basis and not by the hour."

STUDIOS KAMINSKI PHOTOGRAPHY LTD., 1040 Matley Lane, Reno NV 89502. (702)786-2615. President: P.J. Kaminski. AV/TV/Film producer. Clients: educational, industrial and corporate. Produces filmstrips, motion pictures, multimedia kits, overhead transparencies, slide sets, sound-slide sets and videotapes.
Needs: Works with about 1 illustrator/year. Has need of illustrators to paint portraits from photos once in a while. Uses artists for slide illustration and retouching, catalog design and ad illustration.
First Contact & Terms: Local artists only. Arrange interview to show portfolio. Reports in 2 weeks. Provide samples and general information to be kept on file for future assignment. Pays $20+/hour.

SUDLER & HENNESSEY INCORPORATED/CHICAGO, Chicago office of Sudler & Hennessey, 1 E. Wacker Dr., Chicago IL 60601. (312)836-1888. Executive Art Director/Chicago: Dennis Frank. Ad agency. Clients: medical and pharmaceutical.
Needs: This office has not been in operation long enough to project number of freelance illustrators needed. Anticipates using freelancers for medical journals, direct mail and brochures.
First Contact & Terms: Call or write requesting appointment to show portfolio. Selection based on portfolio review and contact with reps. Negotiates payment based on going rate. Clients have good budgets.
Portfolio Tips: Interested in all areas; could possibly even use humor in future. Will review samples of past work used by other agencies and tear sheets of published art.

SUN CREATIVE GROUP, 1341 S. Claudina St., Anaheim CA 92805. (714)635-9504. Art/Creative Director: Oscar Wright. Clients: Electronics and video.
Needs: Works with 2 designers/month on brochures/flyers and trade magazines. Payment by hour: $9-25, catalogs; $3-25, layout; $3-10, paste-up; $3-15, mechanicals.
First Contact & Terms: Uses mostly local artists. Query with resume and follow up by phone. SASE. Reports in 3 weeks. Provide samples (tearsheets). No originals returned to artist at job's completion.

THOMAS R. SUNDHEIM INC., The Benson East, Jenkintown PA 19046. Creative Director: John F. Tucker, Jr. Clients: industrial and technical.
Needs: Works with 2 illustrators, 3 designers/year. Uses artists for illustration, technical art and retouching for trade magazines, stationery design, direct mail and collateral; also work on P-O-P displays, stationery design and newspapers.
First Contact & Terms: Prefers local artists. Call for interview. No originals returned to artist at job's completion. Provide ad reprints, brochures, technical literature and direct mail to be kept on file for future assignments.

SUNFLOWER FILMS INC., 15 W. 46th St., New York NY 10036. (212)869-0123. Contact: Ray Seti, president. AV/TV/film producer. Clients: ad agencies, medical agencies and business film producers.
Needs: Works with 3 illustrators, 1 designer/month. Assigns 200 jobs and buys 2,000 illustrations/year. Also uses artists for animation, tightly rendered storyboard frames and ad illustrations.
First Contact & Terms: Local artists only. Arrange interview to show portfolio. Negotiates pay.

CHARLES SWEENEY & ASSOCIATES, 1625 W. Olympic Blvd., Los Angeles CA 90015. (213)386-5050. Art Director: Steve Sugarman. Ad agency. Clients: jewelry, food, camera and toy companies. Annual billing: $2,400,000.
Needs: Works with 2 illustrators and 1 designer/month. Uses artists for billboards, P-O-P displays, consumer magazines, TV, brochures/flyers, trade magazines and newspapers.
First Contact & Terms: Call (Tues. mornings between 9 and 12) to arrange interview. Provide materials to be kept on file for future assignments.

SYNERGISTIC ASSOCIATES INTERNATIONAL, INC., 900 Dudley Ave., Cherry Hill NJ 08002. (609)665-8833. Contact: Irwin Lowen. Marketing consultant.
Needs: Works with 2 illustrators and 3 designers. Uses artists for consumer magazines, direct mail, brochures/flyers and newspapers.
First Contact & Terms: Local artists only. Call for interview. Artists must have experience in designing mailings and/or ads for major consumer direct mail business, preferably in insurance, financial services, etc. Provide brochures, flyers, business card, resume and tearsheets, etc. No originals returned to artist at job's completion. "We generally work on a per job basis not an hourly one, and we find that we are paying the generally accepted fees in this area of the country."

TALCO PRODUCTIONS, 279 E. 44th St., New York NY 10017. President: Alan Lawrence. TV/film producer. Clients: nonprofit organizations, industry, associations and public relations firms. Produces motion pictures, videotapes and some filmstrips and sound-slide sets.
Needs: Assigns 4-10 jobs/year. Works with an average of 1 illustrator/month for filmstrips, motion pictures, animation and charts/graphs.
First Contact & Terms: Prefers local artists with professional experience. Query with resume. SASE. Reports in 3 weeks. Provide resume to be kept on file for future assignments. On some jobs returns originals to artist after completion. Buys all rights. Pays on production.

THE TARRAGANO COMPANY, 444 Madison Ave., New York NY 10022. (212) 758-1885. President: Morris Tarragano. Ad agency and PR firm. Clients: manufacturers of products of all types. Media used include consumer and trade magazines, direct mail and newspapers.
First Contact & Terms: Write and request personal interview to show portfolio and/or send resume. Selection based on review of portfolio and references. Negotiates payment based on amount of creativity required from artist and previous experience/reputation.

TATHAM-LAIRD & KUDNER, INC., 625 N. Michigan Ave., Chicago IL 60611. Executive Creative Director: Dave Fairman.

TELEMATED MOTION PICTURES, 51 E. 42nd St., New York NY 10017. (212)682-3434. Producer/Director: Saul Taffet. AV/TV/film producer. Clients: industry, ad agencies, film producers and business. Produces filmstrips, motion pictures, slide sets and sound-slide sets.
First Contact & Terms: Local artists only. Call to arrange interview. Do not submit art. Buys all rights. Pays on production. Pays $5-10 min./hour for animation, charts/graphs, storyboards, lettering, illustrations, retouching and technical art.

TELESOUND INC., 1088 Howard St., San Francisco CA 94103. (415)863-4880. Creative Division Manager: Karl Sjodahl. AV/TV/film producer. Clients: TV stations, program producers and networks. Produces motion pictures, videotapes and film animation.
Needs: Uses artists for animation, motion pictures, logo design, illustration, layout and storyboards.
First Contact & Terms: Local artists preferred. Query with resume and samples. SASE. Reports in 2-4 weeks. Provide materials to be kept on file for future assignments. Negotiates pay.

J. WALTER THOMPSON COMPANY, 1 Maritime Plaza, Golden Gateway Center, San Francisco CA 94111. (415)421-3510. Contact: Art Director. Ad agency. Clients: variety, including an oil company and a spa.
Needs: Works with 3 freelancer illustrators/month. Uses talents for work with consumer/trade magazines, direct mail, brochures/flyers, newspapers, and TV.
First Contact & Terms: Call art director for appointment to show portfolio. Selects illustrators through portfolios.
Portfolio Tips: Wants to see samples of produced work.

J. WALTER THOMPSON COMPANY, 1156 15th St. NW, Washington DC 20005. (202)861-8500. Art Director: John Ambrose. Ad agency. Clients: NEA, banks, holding company.
Needs: Works with a varied number of freelance illustrators. Uses talents for work with billboards, consumer/trade magazines, direct mail, brochures/flyers, newspapers, P-O-P displays, stationery design, and TV.
First Contact & Terms: Call for appointment to show portfolio through artist's rep. Negotiated payment.
Portfolio Tips: Wants to see style and a broad spectrum. Usually uses artist's reps.

J. WALTER THOMPSON COMPANY, 2828 Tower Pl., 3340 Peachtree Rd. NE, Atlanta GA 30326. (404)266-2828. Senior Art Director: Dan Grieco. Ad agency. Clients: mainly financial and

industrial. This office does creative work for the following branch offices: Richmond, Birmingham, Charlotte, Louisville, New Orleans, and Memphis.
Needs: Works with 4-5 freelance illustrators and 1 designer/month. Uses designers when handling large projects. Uses artists for billboards, P-O-P displays, consumer magazines, stationery design, slide sets, brochures/flyers, trade magazines and newspapers.
First Contact & Terms: Call for appointment to show portfolio. Provide brochures, flyers, business cards and tearsheets to be kept on file for future assignments. No originals returned to artist at job's completion. Payment based on job's budget.
Portfolio Tips: Wants to see samples of work done for different clients and clear idea of style. Likes to see work done in different mediums. Likes variety and versatility.

J. WALTER THOMPSON COMPANY, 1700 Executive Plaza, Dearborn MI 48126. (313)336-6900. Secretary to Art Directors: Maryann Inson. Ad agency. Clients: industrial, recreational, banking, media accounts and automotive accounts.
Needs: This office consists of two sections: one section works exclusively with auto accounts; the other with aftermarket, service and recreational accounts.
First Contact & Terms: Call for appointment to arrange a show for all interested art directors. A viewing room (equipped for slides, etc.) is available for just this purpose. This firm has an open door policy. Usually negotiates payment.
Portfolio Tips: Interested in seeing wide variety of good pieces representative of freelancer's individual style.

J. WALTER THOMPSON COMPANY, LTD., 300 Oceanic Plaza, 1066 W. Hastings St., Vancouver, B.C. Canada V6E 3Y1. (604)683-4466. Vice President/Creative Director: Phil La Borie. Ad agency. Clients: packaged goods.
Needs: Works with 6 illustrators and 2-3 designers/year. Uses artists for print media.
First Contact & Terms: Call Mr. La Borie for appointment to show portfolio. Negotiates pay based on client's budget.

J. WALTER THOMPSON COMPANY, LTD., 102 Bloor St. W., Toronto 5, Ontario Canada. (416)924-9171. Ad agency. Clients: packaged goods, automotive, liquor, beer and soft drinks.
Needs: Works with 1 illustrator and 1 designer/month. Uses artists for billboards, consumer and trade magazines, TV, brochures/flyers and newspapers.
First Contact & Terms: Contact art director for appointment to show portfolio. Negotiates pay based on client's budget, amount of creativity required from artists/photographer and where the work will appear.
Tips: Portfolio should be up-to-date with current styles and trends.

ROGER TILTON FILMS INC., 241 W. G St., San Diego CA 92101. (724)233-6513. Production Manager: Robert Hitchcox. Film producer. Clients: industrial and corporate. Produces filmstrips, motion pictures and videotapes.
Needs: Uses artists for filmstrip animation, retouching, catalog design, slide illustration and advertising.
First Contact & Terms: Query with resume and samples or arrange interview to show portfolio. Provide resume to be kept on file for future assignments. Originals become client's property. Negotiates pay.

TRANSMEDIA INC., (formerly Film Associates Inc.), 4600 S. Dixie Hwy., Dayton OH 45439. (513)298-1189. President: Charles McDaniel. Art studio, AV/motion picture/TV producer. Produces motion picture services. Buys up to 5 designs/year.
Needs: Works with 4 illustrators and designers/year.
First Contact & Terms: Query with samples. SASE. Reports in 2 weeks. Provide resume and/or portfolio to be kept on file for future assignments. Pays $10-20/hour for animation.

TRAVIS-WALZ AND ASSOCIATES, INC., 5201 Johnson Dr., Suite 350, Mission KS 66205. Contact: Gary Otteson. Ad agency. Clients: electronics, food, finance, retailers, home maintenance and media.
Needs: Works with 4-8 illustrators/month. Uses illustrators for billboards, P-O-P displays, consumer magazines, direct mail, brochures/flyers, trade magazines and newspapers. Also uses artists for retouching.
First Contact & Terms: Mail samples (tearsheets and photocopies). No file kept on artists. No originals returned to artist at job's completion.

DON TREVOR ASSOCIATES INC., 20 E. 9th St., New York NY 10003. (212)260-2984. Producer/Director: Don Trevor. Produces documentaries, commercials and sales training/industrial films.
Needs: Uses artists for animation and set design.
First Contact & Terms: Query with resume.

TRI-SON INC., Box 177, Wild Horse CO 80862. (303)962-3543. Contact: Loudilla Johnson, president. Publicity firm. Clients: country, country-gospel, country-rock and middle-of-the-road record manufacturers.
Needs: Buys 1-2 illustrations/year. Uses artists for ad illustrations, brochure/letterhead design, billboards and other printed materials.
First Contact & Terms: Query with resume and samples. SASE. Reports in 2 weeks. Provide ads/catalogues, etc. to be kept on file for future assignments. No originals returned to artist at job's completion. Pays flat fee.

TRI-STATE ADVERTISING, 307 S. Buffalo, Warsaw IN 46580. Contact: Tweed Robinson. Estab. 1948. Clients: Industrial manufacturers of raw materials, steel, plastics, equipment and construction machinery. Annual billing: $2,000,000. Assigns 10-20 jobs and buys 1-2 illustrations/year. Query with samples or arrange interview. SASE. Reports in 1 week.
Needs: Payment by hour: $10-20, layout; $5-15, paste-up; $10-30, retouching.
To Break In: "Learn something about the graphic arts; make up a hypothetical assignment and do it for a portfolio, instead of carrying schoolwork."

TROLL ASSOCIATES, 320 Rte. 17, Mahwah NJ 07430. Vice President, Production: Marian Schecter. AV producer/book publisher. Audience: children. Produces books, records, filmstrips and multimedia.
Needs: Buys approximately 200 designs/year. Uses artists for catalog covers/illustrations, direct mail brochures, multimedia kits, record album designs and book illustrations.
First Contact & Terms: Local artists only. Query or write for interview. SASE. Reports in 3 weeks. Provide material to be kept on file for future assignments. No originals returned to artist at job's completion. Buys all rights.

TUCKER WAYNE & CO., 230 Peachtree St. NW, Suite 2700, Atlanta GA 30303. (404)522-2383. Contact: Creative Secretary. Ad agency. Clients: financial, industrial, software, textile, food and tobacco.
Needs: A total of 6 art directors work with about 6 freelance illustrators/month. Uses freelancers for consumer and trade magazines, newspapers and TV.
First Contact & Terms: Call creative secretary for appointment. Selection based on portfolio review. Negotiates payment based on budget, where work will appear, travel expenses, etc.
Portfolio Tips: Each art director has individual preference.

TPC COMMUNICATIONS,INC., (formerly television production center), Production Plaza, Pittsburgh PA 15143.(412)771-4700. Contact: Lee Knepshield. TV producer. Clients: commercial and industrial. Produces commercial, institutional and industrial videotapes.
Needs: Works with 2-5 illustrators and 2-5 designers/month. Uses artists for televison production.
First Contact & Terms: Query with resume. Provide brochures and resume to be kept on file for future assignments. No originals returned to artist at job's completion. Payment based on experience.

UNDERCOVER GRAPHICS, 1169 Howard St., Suite A, San Francisco CA 94103. (415)626-0500. Creative Director: L.A. Paul. AV producer. Clients: musical groups, producers, record companies and book publishers. Annual billing: $300,000.
Needs: Works with 2-3 illustrators and 2-3 designers/month. Uses artists for billboards, P-O-P displays, stationery design, multimedia kits, direct mail, TV, brochures/flyers, album covers and books.
First Contact & Terms: Query with samples. SASE. Reports in 4 weeks. Provide brochures, tearsheets, slides, business card and/or resume to be kept on file for future assignments. Originals returned to artist at job's completion. Pays $250-5,000, comprehensive layout and production; $10-25/hour, creative services; $25-500, illustrations. Pays original fee as agreed for unused assigned illustrations.

UNIFILM, 419 Park Ave. S., New York NY 10016. (212)686-9890. Promotional Director: Gary Crowdus. Film distributor. Clients: schools, universities and movie theaters.
Needs: Works with 1 illustrator/month. Uses artists for print ads, brochures and posters.

First Contact & Terms: Write or call for appointment to show portfolio or send brochure/flyer of published work. SASE. Provide resume and/or brochure/flyer to be kept on file for future assignments. Works on assignment only. Samples returned by SASE. Negotiates pay based on client's budget and amount of creativity required.

UNITED STATES CHAMBER OF COMMERCE, 1615 H St. NW, Washington DC 20062. (202)659-6239. Contact: Bob Adams, broadcast center manager. Audiovisuals and TV/film producer. Clients: Industrial, corporate, educational, broadcast and cable TV stations. Produces filmstrips, multimedia kits, overhead transparencies, slide sets, sound-slide sets and videotapes. Assigns 3 jobs/year; local artists only. Query with previously used work. Reports in 2 weeks.
Needs: Uses artists for "a wide variety of artwork which includes layer slide projects, cartooning, and logo or box cover design." Negotiates pay.

UNIVERSAL PICTURES CO., 100 Universal City Plaza, Universal City CA 91608. Arrange interview. Buys all rights.
Needs: Interested in graphic designs, illustrations and complete concepts for motion picture advertising.

UNIVERSAL TRAINING SYSTEMS CO., 3201 Old Glenview Rd., Wilmette IL 60091. (312)251-8700. Art Director: Bob Glassman. AV training program developers. Clients: associations, manufacturers, retailers, service firms, publishers, bankers and financial institutions. Buys 500 illustrations/year; local artists only.
Needs: Works with 1 illustrator and 1 designer/month. Uses designers for work on direct mail and books. Also uses artists for layout and paste-up for workbooks, training manuals, flipcharts, overhead transparencies, slide films and posters.
First Contact & Terms: Query. SASE. Provide brochures, flyers, business cards, resumes, tearsheets, etc. to be kept on file for future assignments. No originals returned to artist at job's completion.

V.I.P. PRODUCTIONS INC., 750 W. Algonquin Rd., Arlington Heights IL 60005. (312)439-9250. Art Director/Vice President: Richard Wilson. Estab. 1968. Audiovisual/TV/film producer. Clients: Corporate offices, manufacturing divisions and distributors. Produces filmstrips, motion pictures, multimedia kits, slide sets and sound-slide sets. Assigns 20 jobs/year; local artists only. Query with resume and sample, and arrange interview. SASE. Reports in 2 weeks. Buys all rights. Pays on production.
Needs: Minimum payment by hour: $10-15, animation; $7-10, charts/graphs and direct mail brochures; $10, lettering and technical art; $15, illustrations; $20, retouching. Pays $20-35 min./frame for cartoons.

VALENTINE-RADFORD INC., Box 13407, Kansas City MO 64199. Creative Director: Joe Stockwell. Clients: Agricultural, industrial and consumer. Assigns 200 jobs/year; local artists preferred. Query with 4-5 samples for files. Contacts artists as needs arise.
Needs: Illustrations of all types, cartooning, retouching, technical, straight advertising illustration of products, etc. No design work. Payment determined by job.

VICTOR VAN DER LINDE CO., INC., 25 W. 43rd St., New York NY 10036. (212)921-4555. Art/Creative Director: Peter Hutchins. Ad agency. Clients: over-the-counter drugs and insurance.
Needs: Works with 4 illustrators and 1-2 designers/year. Uses artists for lettering for newspapers, magazines, TV and direct mail.
First Contact & Terms: Prefers local artists. Query. SASE. Reports in 1 week. Originals returned at job's completion.

VARIS ASSOCIATES, 66 Bethpage Rd., Hicksville NY 11801. Contact: Mel Eisenberg. Produces educational materials. Arrange interview and/or do a 1-picture test; prefers New York City area artists.

VIDEO FILMS INC., 2211 E. Jefferson Ave., Detroit MI 48207. (313)393-0800. Contact: Production Manager. AV/MP/TV Producers. Produces slide programs, filmstrips, motion pictures and videotapes.
Needs: Works with 2-3 illustrators/year. Uses artists for animation.
First Contact & Terms: Query. Provide information to be kept on file for future assignments. Pays by job.

VIDEOCOM INC., 502 Sprague St., Dedham MA 02192. Vice President of Production and Creative Services: Lucien A. Lessard. TV/AV/film producer. Clients: industry and ad agencies. Produces motion pictures, slide and slide film presentations and videotapes.
Needs: Works with 2 illustrators and 1 designer/month. Uses artists for TV graphics, filmstrips, motion pictures, print design and studio design.
First Contact & Terms: Experienced local artists only. Query. Reports in 2-3 weeks. Provide representative sample to be kept on file for future assignments. Originals returned to artist at job's completion. Negotiates pay.

JEANNE VINER ASSOCIATES, 2113 S St. NW, Washington DC 20008. (202)462-5200. Contact: Jeanne Viner. PR firm. Annual billing: $210,000. Clients: financial, real estate, cultural, associations, hotels, authors and nonprofit organizations.
Needs: Works with 2 freelance illustrators/month for an average of 30 hours of work per artist and 3 designers. Uses designers for consumer magazines, stationery design, direct mail, brochures/flyers, trade magazines, album covers, newspapers and books.
First Contact & Terms: Local artists only. Call for appointment to show portfolio. Artists are initially chosen according to the expertise exhibited in their portfolios and are hired for specific projects according to their style and area of specialty (e.g., logo, ads, illustration, brochure layout). Provide business cards to be kept on file for future assignments. No originals returned to artist at job's completion. Negotiates payment based on client's budget, amount of creativity required, and artist's experience/reputation.
Portfolio Tips: "Portfolio should include full variety of the kinds of projects the artist has completed, with emphasis on the kind of work he/she most desires."

WILL VINTON PRODUCTIONS, 3436 NW Thurman, Portland OR 97210. (503)225-1130. Production Manager: Rick Cooper. Film producer. Clients: film distributors and ad agencies (commercial films). Produces motion pictures. Assigns 2-3 jobs/year.
Needs: Works with 2 illustrators and 2 designers/month. Uses artists for clay and cel animation, storyboards, special book projects, motion pictures and poster design.
First Contact & Terms: Local artists only. Query with resume. SASE. Reports in 2 weeks. Provide resumes and samples if available (pictures, photocopies and slides) to be kept on file for future assignments. No originals returned to artist at job's completion. Pays $5-20/hour.

VINYARD & LEE & WILLIAMS, INC., 7701 Clayton Rd., St. Louis MO 63117. (314)725-2277. Executive Art Director: Steve Morris. Ad Agency. Clients: general, "from packaged goods to industrial."
First Contact & Terms: Call for personal appointment to show portfolio. Negotiates payment based on client's budget, amount of creativity required from artist, where the work will appear, and artist's previous experience/reputation. When there aren't set budgets on jobs like layouts, price is set per hour.
Portfolio Tips: "Many times we prefer to see a wide variety of styles that the person is capable of doing." When a person shows only 1 style and it's not needed at that time, then sometimes there will be the tendency to forget about him.

VISUAL HORIZONS, 208 Westfall Rd., Rochester NY 14620. President: Stanley Feingold. AV producer. Clients: industrial and corporate. Produces filmstrips, multimedia kits, overhead transparencies, slide sets, sound-slide sets and videotapes.
Needs: Works with 1-2 illustrators and 1-2 designers/year. Uses artists for slide illustration and catalog design.
First Contact & Terms: Query with resume and photocopied samples. SASE. Reports in 2 weeks. Provide tearsheets to be kept on file for future assignments. No originals returned to artist at job's completion. Negotiates pay.

VISUALSCOPE PRODUCTIONS DIVISION OF REEVES TELETAPE CORP., 708 3rd Ave., New York NY 10017. (212)573-8600. Contact: Leonard Talan, creative producer. Animation/audiovisuals/TV/film producer. Estab. 1938. Clients: Corporate, commercial and industrial. Produces motion pictures, multimedia kits, videotapes and shows. Query with resume and samples or arrange interview to show portfolio.
Needs: Uses artists for filmstrip animation, retouching, catalog design, slide illustration and ads. Negotiates pay.

VITAMIN INFORMATION BUREAU INC., 664 N. Michigan Ave., Chicago IL 60611. (312)751-2223. President: Caryl Wright. AV producer. Clients: educational and medical. Produces wall charts, booklets, filmstrips and multimedia kits. Buys 1-2 designs/year.

Needs: Works with 1 illustrator and 1 designer/month. Uses illustrators for books, filmstrips and ads. Also uses artists for filmstrip frames, direct mail brochures, multimedia kits and technical charts/illustrations.
First Contact & Terms: Chicago artists only. Query, mail samples or write for interview. SASE. Reports in 1-2 weeks. Buys all rights. Provide brochures/flyers, resumes and tearsheets to be kept on file for future assignments. Free catalog. Pays $1,500-3,000 for 50-frame filmstrips.

VOCATIONAL EDUCATION PRODUCTIONS, California Polytechnic State University, San Luis Obispo CA 93407. Art Director: Gordon Hayduk. Estab. 1951. Clients: High school and junior college vocational agriculture departments. Produces filmstrips, multimedia kits, slide sets and sound-slide sets. Assigns 10 jobs/year. Query with slides and resume. SASE. Reports in 1-4 weeks. Buys all rights. Pays on acceptance. Free catalog.
Needs: Pays $15-50/frame for animation. Payment by job: $400 minimum, catalogs; $100-200, advertising; $100-300, direct mail brochures; $10-75, book illustrations. Type spec and mechanicals included in payment.
To Break In: "Be aware that audiovisual artwork must be simple in content, while maintaining the author's intent of any particular 'frame' within a filmstrip script. Also, it is necessary to realize that when this type of artwork is photographically copied, the camera 'sees' even the slightest defects. Attention to line quality and use of color which reproduces well are major considerations in designing and producing artwork of this type."

VOMACK ADVERTISING INC., 215 W. Broadway, Inwood NY 11696. (516)371-2600. Art Director: Ray Wallace. Clients: manufacturers of jewelry, cosmetics, hair and skin products, other beauty aids for black people.
Needs: Assigns 4 jobs/year. Uses artists for illustrations of jewelry and clothing for direct mail pieces.
First Contact & Terms: Local artists only. Beginners welcome. Query with resume and submit "line or wash drawing of jewelry or woman's figure." SASE. Reports in 3 months. Pays $30-50, illustrations; $8/hour, mechanicals.

WADLER-MAYO, 175 W. 73rd St., New York NY 10023. (212)724-0014. Contact: S.L. Wadler, manager. Advertising/public relations/exhibit/display firm. Estab. 1950. Clients: Drugs, food, publisher and museum. Arrange interview to show portfolio. SASE. Reports in 3 weeks.
Needs: Uses artists for illustrations of food. Pays $10-100.

WAHLSTROM & COMPANY, 207 Atlantic St., Stamford CT 06901. (203)348-7347. Ad agency. Clients: Yellow Pages, insurance, industrial.
Needs: Works with 1 freelance illustrator/month. Uses talents for work with ads for Yellow Pages and brochures/flyers.
First Contact & Terms: Send resume. Negotiates payment based on client's budget.

WARING & LAROSA, INC., 555 Madison Ave., New York NY 10022. (212)755-0700. Contact: art director. Ad agency. Clients: fashion, food, business machines and liquor.
Needs: Works with approximately 1 illustrator/month. Uses artists for billboards, P-O-P displays, consumer magazines, TV and newspapers.
First Contact & Terms: Contact art director for appointment to show portfolio. Negotiates pay based on client's budget.

HERBERT S. WARMFLASH & ASSOCIATES, INC., 26 Washington St., East Orange NJ 07017. Art Director: B. Martin Grubman. Specializes in industrial accounts: conveyor systems, towline, switchcart and order picking systems.
Needs: Uses artists familiar with mechanicals, illustration for trade magazines, direct mail, POP displays, transit, brochures, filmstrips and collateral.
First Contact & Terms: Prefers local artists with a minimum of two years' experience with mechanicals. Write. Provide "anything available" to be kept on file for future assignments. No originals returned to artist at job's completion. Pays $8-10.

ROBERT WARNER PRODUCTIONS, 7 E. 78th St., New York NY 10021. Contact: Robert Warner. TV producer. Clients: national advertisers.
Needs: Uses artists for animation and commercials.
First Contact & Terms: Query with resume. No file kept on artists for future assignments.

WARREN, MULLER, DOLOBOWSKY, INC., 747 3rd Ave., New York NY 10017. (212)754-1600. Contact: Harvey Kimmelman. Ad Agency. Estab. 1963. Clients: Drug products

firms and manufacturers. Annual billing: $25,000,000. Buys 12 illustrations/year. Call for interview or mail photocopy.
Needs: Illustrations, lettering, layout, paste-up, retouching and costume/set/jewelry design for ads, billboards, catalogs, packaging, POP displays, posters, TV and trademarks. Pays $1,000-5,000, 4-color magazine ad campaign or TV animation design; $250-1,000, b&w magazine ad campaign. Pays percentage of promised fee for unused work.

WATIER PUBLICITE LTEE., 2055 Peel St., Montreal, Quebec CN H3A 1V4. (514)288-2511. Contact: Mr. El Hage. Ad agency. Annual billing: $40,000,000. Clients: general advertising.
Needs: Works with 2-3 illustrators and 5-7+ designers/month. Uses artists for all media. Especially needs illustrators who work with air brush (not touch-up).
First Contact & Terms: Call Mr. El Hage for appointment to show portfolio. Negotiates pay based on client's budget.
Tips: Submit best work and those things that best represent your own style.

WATKINS & ASSOCIATES, INC., (formerly Advertising Associates, Inc.), 2030 Northern Bank Bldg., Little Rock AR 72201. Creative Director: Larry Stone. Estab. 1975. Clients: Financial. Annual billing: $2,000,000. Buys 25-50 illustrations/year. Mail art. SASE. Reports in 1 week.
Needs: Uses artists for illustration, layout, lettering, paste-up and retouching for annual reports, trademarks, brochures, billboards, print ads, letterheads, POP displays, posters and TV. Pays $30-200, b&w newspaper illustration.

MORTON DENNIS WAX & ASSOCIATES, 200 W. 51st St., New York NY 10019. (212)247-2159. Public relations firm. Clients: entertainment, industrial, health. Media used include consumer and trade magazines, newspapers, and P-O-P displays.
First Contact & Terms: Write and request personal interview to show portfolio. "We select and use freelancers on a per project basis, based on specific requirements of clients. Each project is unique." Negotiates payment based on client's budget, amount of creativity required from artist and artist's previous experience/reputation.

WEEKLEY & PENNY, INC., 3322 Richmond Ave., Houston TX 77098. (713)529-4861. Art Director: Ellie Malavis. Ad agency. Clients: industrial, real estate, and some consumer.
Needs: Limited outside art needs. Uses illustrators for direct mail, brochures/flyers and newspapers.
First Contact & Terms: Call for personal appointment to show portfolio, send printed samples of work with SASE (preferable), or send portfolio for review. Provide brochures, flyers, business cards and tearsheets to be kept on file for future assignments. No originals returned to artist at job's completion. Negotiates payment based on client's budget, amount of creativity required from artist, where work will appear, and artist's previous experience/reputation.
Portfolio Tips: "We do a lot of real estate and industrial work. We consider how adaptable work is to our needs." Especially interested in type of work freelancer does.

GORDON J. WEISBECK, INC., 5555 Main St., Buffalo NY 14221. Art Director: Frank Mazerowski. Ad agency. Clients: electronics, precious metals, solid waste disposal, machinery, plant and building design, sealing devices, industrial property development valves and controls, cryogenics, expansion joints and construction engineering.
Needs: Works with 4-5 illustrators/month. Uses artists for stationery design, direct mail, brochures/flyers, trade magazines and album covers. Also uses artists for layout, illustration, technical art, type spec, paste-up, retouching, charts and presentations.
First Contact & Terms: Local artists only. Call for interview. Provide brochures and resumes, including experience in actual reproduction, to be kept on file for future assignments. No originals returned to artist at job's completion. "Payment dependent upon ability and experience. Would rather pay $30-40 per hour to a person who knows his business than 5 or 10 or 15 or 20 to one who doesn't. Prefer to work on flat fee estimate based upon layout."

BERNARD WEISS & ASSOCIATES, 833 Summer St., Suite 2-A, Stamford CT 06901. (203)348-3719. President: Bernard Weiss. Clients: health care industry and professions. Produces multimedia materials.
Needs: Works with 1+ illustrators and 1+ designers/month. Uses artists for catalog covers/illustrations, direct mail brochures, layout, multimedia kits, paste-up, anatomical drawings and type spec.
First Contact & Terms: Query or arrange interview. SASE. Reports in 1 week. Buys one-time and reprint rights. Provide name, address, phone number on 3x5 card to be kept on file for future assignments. Originals returned to artist at job's completion. Pays $500-1,200, brochure layout,

design, type spec and paste-up; $50-500, anatomical illustrations.

WENTLING MULTI MEDIA CENTER, 1673 Willow Pass Rd., Concord CA 94520. Contact: Ben Wentling. Audiovisuals producer. Estab. 1975. Clients: Industrial, educational, governmental, public relations and "safety and training." Produces filmstrips, multimedia kits, slide sets, sound-slide sets and flat artwork. Assigns 5-10 jobs and buys 30-50 illustrations/year. Query with resume and samples. SASE. Reports in 1 week.
Needs: Uses artists for slide and graphic illustrations. Pays $30-50 for single 11x14; $10-15 for sets of 7 or more.

WEST GRAPHICS, 2722 3rd Ave. N., Box 1049, Billings MT 59101. (406)252-2273. Vice President Creative Services: Bill Gibson. Estab. 1978. In house ad agency. Annual billing: $150,000.
Needs: Works with 1 illustrator/month. Uses illustrators for consumer magazines, television, trade magazines and newspapers.
First Contact & Terms: Query. Provide materials to be kept on file for future assignments. No originals returned to artist at job's completion.

WESTIN & ASSOCIATES, 272 Mantoloking Rd., Brick Town NJ 08723. (201)477-6600. Contact: David Hunziker, president. Advertising/public relations firm. Estab. 1962. Clients: Retail drug, hardware, clothing, real estate, food display, institutional auto display, restaurants, mail order and marine. Annual billing: $600,000. Assigns 50 jobs and buys 30 illustrations/year. Query with resume or arrange interview to show portfolio. Reports in 2 weeks.
Needs: Uses artists for design and graphics for annual reports, direct mail, brochures, press releases, press kits, billboards, menus and logos. Pays $10-20/hour. Negotiates pay.

THE WESTPORT COMMUNICATIONS GROUP INC., 155 Post Rd. E., Westport CT 06880. (203)226-3525. Art Director: H. Lindsay. AV producer. Clients: educational and corporate. Produces filmstrips, multimedia kits, slide sets, sound-slide sets and booklets.
Needs: Works with 15-20 illustrators/year. Uses artists for filmstrip, slide, booklet, brochure and trade magazine illustrations.
First Contact & Terms: Query or arrange interview to show portfolio. Reports in 1 month. Provide tearsheets to be kept on file for future assignments. Pays $20+/filmstrip frame; negotiates pay on other assignments.

RUTH WHITE FILMS, Box 34485, Los Angeles CA 90034. Contact: Ruth White. Produces multimedia educational materials.
Needs: Uses artists for animation, slide films and graphic/book design.
First Contact & Terms: Query with resume. Buys all rights.

WILK & BRICHTA ADVERTISING, 875 N. Michigan, Chicago IL 60611. (312)280-2807. Art Director: Carl Hofmann. Ad agency. Clients: automotive, food service, dental and finance.
Needs: Works with 8 illustrators and 4 designers/month. Uses artists for billboards, direct mail, brochures/flyers, trade magazines and newspapers.
First Contact & Terms: Call for appointment to show portfolio. Negotiates pay based on client's budget.
Tips: Especially likes 4-color work.

STUART WILLIAMS ASSOCIATES, 40 Signal Rd., Stamford CT 06902. (203)348-2621. Vice President/Executive Art Director: Noel E. Weber. Clients: Pharmaceutical. Mail samples or call for interview.
Needs: Uses artists for layout, illustration, technical art and mechanicals.

H. WILSON CO., 555 Taft Dr., South Holland IL 60473. (312)339-5111. Advertising Manager: B.J. Bond. Assigns 20 jobs/year.
Needs: Works with 2 illustrators and 2 designers/month. Uses artists for sales and marketing presentations, catalogs, direct mail, convention exhibits and promotion.
First Contact & Terms: Query with resume and samples (ads, brochures, etc.) then arrange interview to show portfolio. SASE. Reports in 2 weeks. No originals returned to artist at job's completion. Provide resume, calling card and brochure to be kept on file for future assignments. Pays "for creative work on a job basis, final art on an hourly basis."

THOMAS C. WILSON ADVERTISING AGENCY, Box 1011, Reno NV 89504. (702)329-3173. Contact: Thomas C. Wilson. Ad agency. Clients: financial, industrial and utility.
Needs: Works with 4 illustrators and 2 designers/month. Uses artists for billboards, P-O-P

displays, consumer magazines, direct mail, brochures/flyers and newspapers.
First Contact & Terms: Query with samples and fees or arrange interview to show portfolio. SASE. Samples "not returnable unless so specified in our request. We keep file for use internally and often with clients." Reports in 2 weeks. Provide brochures to be kept on file for future assignments. Rarely returns originals to artist at job's completion. Pays $20 min./hour for mechanicals, design, roughs and comps for brochures, newspapers, billboards and magazines. Pays up to $1000 for illustration. Often allows 4 to 6 months to meet deadline.

WINARD ADVERTISING AGENCY, INC., 343 Pecks Rd., Pittsfield MA 01201. (413)445-5657. Art/Creative Director: Edward Treitler. Estab. 1955. Clients: Banking, abrasives, paper machinery, truck manufacturing, paper, plastics, publishing, nuclear components, electronics, nonwoven machinery manufacturers, surveying, coffee makers, physical fitness institution, transformers, florists and wallpaper. Annual billing: $500,000. Assigns approximately 500 jobs and buys approximately 75 illustrations/year. Query with resume and samples, or arrange interview. SASE. Reports in 2 weeks.
Needs: Payment by hour: $10-25, animation, packaging, billboards, trade magazines, letterheads, newspapers and retouching; $20-30, annual reports, POP displays and color separations; $15-30, catalogs and trademarks; $15-25, layout and lettering; $7.50-12.50, paste-up and mechanicals; $10-20, type spec. Pays promised fee for unused assigned illustrations.

WINIUS-BRANDON/TEXAS, INC., 4710 Bellaire Blvd., Suite 310, Bellaire TX 77401. (713)666-1765. Art/Creative Director: Ed Kennard. Ad/PR firm. Clients: airlines, fast foods, package goods, home and office furnishings, auto dealers, restaurants, hotels, industrial equipment, banks, wholesale appliance distributors, TV and radio stations, jewelry, men's and women's fashions stores and paper products manufacturers. Annual billing: $12,000,000.
Needs: Works with 50 illustrators/month. Uses artists for billboards, P-O-P displays, consumer magazines, direct mail, television, slide sets, brochures/flyers, trade magazines and newspapers. Buys 100-200 illustrations/year.
First Contact & Terms: Uses mostly local artists. Arrange interview. SASE. Reports in 2 weeks. Payment by job: $100-1,000, billboards and consumer magazines; $100 minimum, letterheads and newspapers. Payment by hour: $20 minimum, type spec, mechanicals and paste-up; $20 minimum, layout. Pays promised fee for unused assigned illustrations.

WINTERS, FRANCESCHI & CALLAHAN, 100 W. Clarendon, Suite 2206, Phoenix AZ 85103. (602)274-8775. Creative Director: Gil Franceschi. Ad agency. Estab. 1980. Clients: construction, financial, retail, communications, book and record publisher.
Needs: Works with 2-3 freelance illustrators/month. Uses freelancers for billboards, consumer and trade magazines, brochures/flyers, newspapers, P-O-P displays and TV storyboards and animation.
First Contact & Terms: Call for appointment to show portfolio or make contact through artist's rep. Selection based on portfolio review. Negotiates payment based on bids from artist and how often work used.
Portfolio Tips: Wants to see originality and individual techniques.

WITI-TV 6, 9001 N. Green Bay Rd., Milwaukee WI 53209. Contact: Dick Eyrise. Clients: mostly local–car dealers, furniture, etc.
Needs: Works with 1 designer/month. Uses artists for illustrator and designer collateral, courtroom sketching, keylines, mechanicals, animation and graphic/set design.
First Contact & Terms: Query with resume. Provide resume to be kept on file for future assignments. No originals returned to artist at job's completion. Pays $10 minimum; $15/hour minimum for pastel or opaque watercolor TV slides.

WMZI/TED JOHNSON PRODUCTIONS, 150 Riverside Ave., Jacksonville FL 32502. (904)354-7000. Vice President: Lou Digiusto. TV/film/animation/AV producer. Clients: business, industrial, governmental and educational.
Needs: Works with freelance artists on filmstrips, motion pictures, multimedia kits, storyboards, charts/graphs and print ads. Send resume or brochure/flyer to be kept on file for future assignments. SASE. Works on assignment only. Negotiates pay based on client's budget and scope of work.

WOIKAS ADVERTISING INC., 8 Wade Rd., Latham NY 12110. (518)783-5151. Creative Director: Stewart Sacklow. Clients: retail and heavy industrial. Annual billing: $2,000,000.
Needs: Works with 4 illustrators and 3 designers/month. All jobs are freelance and buys 50-60 illustrations/year. Uses artists for billboards, P-O-P displays, consumer magazines, stationery

design, direct mail, television and newspapers.
First Contact & Terms: Query with samples (photocopies and/or tearsheets) or arrange interview to show portfolio. Reports in 2 weeks. Provide brochures, flyers and resumes to be kept on file for future assignments. No originals returned to artist at job's completion. Negotiates pay.

WREN ASSOCIATES INC., 145 Witherspoon St., Princeton NJ 08540. (609)924-8085. Contact: Joanne Colley or Ira Beckoff. Animation/AV/TV/film producer. Produces filmstrips, motion pictures, multimedia kits, overhead transparencies, slide shows and videotapes.
Needs: Works with 4 illustrators and 2 designers/month. Uses artists for paste-up, type spec, illustration and animation.
First Contact & Terms: Local artists only. Write or call with samples. Provide brochures/flyers, resumes, tearsheets and samples of slide and AV work to be kept on file for future assignments. No originals returned to artist at job's completion.

WRTV, McGraw-Hill Broadcasting Co., Inc., 1330 N. Meridian St., Indianapolis IN 46202. (317)635-9788. Art Director: Pam Helms. TV producer. Produces graphics, advertising, direct mail and set design.
Needs: Works with 2 illustrators/month. Assigns 50-75 jobs/year. Uses artists for charts/graphs, advertising, direct mail brochures, mechanicals, courtroom art, lettering, illustration and retouching.
First Contact & Terms: Mainly local artists. Query with samples and resume for files, and arrange interview. Reports as needs arise. Provide resume and example of work to be kept on file for future assignments. Buys all rights. Payment by hour: $5-10, charts/graphs, advertising, direct mail brochures and mechanicals. Payment by job: $25-50, courtroom art; $10-50, lettering; $10-200, illustrations; $10 minimum, retouching. Pays on production.

YOUNG & RUBICAM INC., 285 Madison Ave., New York NY 10017. Senior Vice President/ Group Creative Director: Don Egensteiner.
Needs: Works with 5-10 illustrators/month. Uses artists for work with billboards, consumer magazines, television, trade magazines and newspapers.
First Contact & Terms: Provide small 3x5 or 4x5 cards to be kept on file for future assignments. No originals returned to artist at job's completion.

YOUNG & RUBICAM LTD., 60 Bloor St. W., Toronto, Ontario Canada M4W 1J2. (416)961-5111. Ad agency. Clients: packaged goods.
Needs: Freelance needs vary. Uses artists for billboards, P-O-P displays, consumer and trade magazines, stationery design, direct mail, TV, brochures/flyers and newspapers.
First Contact & Terms: Call art director for appointment to show portfolio or make contact through artist's rep. Negotiates pay.

YOUNG & RUBICAM LTD., 1155 Dorchester Blvd. W., Montreal, Quebec Canada H3B 3I2. (514)866-8941. Creative Director: Mr. Simard. Ad agency. Clients: packaged goods and services.
Needs: Works with 4 illustrators/month. Uses artists for all media.
First Contact & Terms: Call Mr. Simard for appointment to show portfolio. Negotiates pay based on client's budget, amount of creativity required from artist/photographer and where the work will appear.
Tips: Submit no more than 12 illustrations. Some of this number should be product-related and ½ of this number should be experimental.

YOUNG & RUBICAM WEST/LOS ANGELES, 3435 Wilshire Blvd., Los Angeles CA 90010. (213)736-7400. Contact: Kit Zeldman. Ad agency. Clients: food and beverage, financial.
Needs: Works with about 3 freelance illustrators/month. Uses freelancers primarily for TV storyboards and comps to clients.
First Contact & Terms: Call for appointment to show portfolio. Selection based on portfolio review. Negotiates payment based on amount of creativity required from artist.
Portfolio Tips: Wants to see versatility, new concepts and most importantly, indication that storyboards can be executed quickly while maintaining quality.

YOUNG & RUBICAM WEST/SAN DIEGO, 530 B St., Suite 2222, San Diego CA 92101. (714)232-7491. Art Director: Tom Frost. Ad agency. Clients: industrial and entertainment.
Needs: Works with about 5 freelance illustrators/month. Uses freelancers for consumer and trade magazines, direct mail, brochures/flyers, newspapers, P-O-P displays and TV.
First Contact & Terms: Call for appointment to show portfolio. Selection based on portfolio review. Negotiates payment based on client's budget.

Portfolio Tips: Include tear sheets of previously published art and work used by other ad agencies.

JAMES BARTON ZABIN INC., 6229 N. Charles St., Baltimore MD 21212. (301)377-4313. Contact: J. Zabin. Ad/PR firm.
Needs: Uses artists for layouts, finished art and mechanicals.
First Contact & Terms: Query with samples and arrange interview to show portfolio. SASE. Reports in 2-3 weeks. Originals returned to artist at job's completion. Provide resume, calling card, brochure and some idea as to pricing to be kept on file for future assignments. Negotiates pay.

ZIGMAN-JOSEPH-SKEEN, 700 North Water St., Milwaukee WI 53202. (414)273-4680. PR firm. Clients: consumer, finance, investor, medical, health care, marketing and opinion research.
Needs: Freelance needs vary. Uses artists for annual reports, brochures, catalogs, posters, exhibits, layout, paste-up, newsletters and trade magazines. Negotiates pay based on client's budget.
First Contact & Terms: Call an account executive for appointment to show portfolio, send resume or samples.

GLORIA ZIGNER & ASSOCIATES INC., 328 N. Newport Blvd., Newport Beach CA 92663. (714)645-6300. Contact: Gloria Zigner. PR firm. Clients: hotels, insurance companies, hospitals, restaurants, financial institutions, manufacturers, builders and developers. Buys 12-24 illustrations/year.
Needs: Works with 2-4 illustrators and 2-4 designers/month. Uses artists for billboards, P-O-P displays, consumer magazines, stationery design, multimedia kits, direct mail, brochures/flyers, trade magazines and newspapers. Also uses artists for design, color separations, layout, lettering, paste-up and type spec.
First Contact & Terms: Local artists only. Write for interview. SASE. Reports in 2 weeks. Provide brochures, flyers, business cards, resumes and tearsheets to be kept on file for future assignments. No originals returned to artist at job's completion. Pays promised fee for unused assigned work.

ZIMMER-McCLOSKEY-LEWIS INC., 1469 S. 4th, Louisville KY 40208. (502)636-0441. Art Director: Todd Hoon. Ad agency. Clients: packaged goods, industrial, service accounts and race track.
Needs: Freelance needs vary. Uses artists for billboards, P-O-P displays, consumer and trade magazines, stationery design, direct mail, TV, brochures/flyers and newspapers.
First Contact & Terms: Call for appointment to show portfolio or make contact through artist's rep. Negotiates pay.

Architectural, Interior and Landscape Design

Contrary to popular belief, this section is not limited to technical specialists. While there are a few listings that specify they want experts with special architectural skills, these are the exception rather than the rule.

You'll find work here for architectural renderings, interior design, graphic design, signage art, model making, murals, sculpture, landscape design, charts and graphs and even stained glass work. One of the most demanding areas might be architectural renderings. It is not an area necessitating the work of a specialist, though. All you need is talent and a good sense of perspective.

Work for architectural firms is almost exclusively by assignment. To get an assignment, most companies request a resume of other information that can be kept on file for future assignments. When work requires the talents of a freelancer, they will contact someone based on the material in their files.

One of the most effective ways to establish and maintain contact with these firms is a self-promoting brochure. The brochure is the staple of the architecture/design industry. Not only do many firms maintain files of freelance brochures, they often have their own brochures, for their clients. The brochure is frequently the only tidy and convenient method of keeping records of talent. And even though an assignment is rarely based on examples shown in a brochure alone, more rare is an assignment made without first viewing brochures or small samples.

The American Society of Landscape Architects publishes a book titled *Developing Your Brochure: A Comprehensive Guide for the Landscape Architect*. Though primarily intended for firms, the booklet includes information valuable to anyone designing a brochure. Some of the best magazine reading in the Architectural field can be found in the *American Institute of Architects Journal*; *Contract* (Grall Publications), and *Interiors* (Billboard Publications).

ABEND SINGLETON ASSOCIATES, 1016 Baltimore, Kansas City MO 64105. (816)221-5011. Contact: Steve Abend. Clients: Corporate, government, institutional, financial and residential. Services: architectural, interior design, engineering, planning and landscape architecture.
Needs: Works with 8 architectural renderings; 1, interior design; 2, graphic design; 2, model making; 1, landscape design; and 1, stained glass.

FRANK ADLER ARCHITECT, 54 Rte. 17, Paramus NJ 07652. (201)843-5248. Contact: Frank Adler. Estab. 1963. Architecture/interior design/landscape firm. Clients: Residential, commercial and industrial. Assigns 5 jobs/year; local artists only. Query or call for interview. Contacts artists as needs arise.
Needs: Uses artists for architectural art and full-color renderings, graphic and interior design, and model buildings. Pays $250-500, renderings; $275-750, models.

ALL-ART VISUAL MEDIA ASSOCIATES, 1525 Hi Point St., Los Angeles CA 90035. (213)479-3521. Contact: Stevin L´ Day. Estab. 1973. Visual artists group. Clients: Architectural and interior design firms. Assigns 6 design jobs/year. Query and submit photos of actual installations, if possible. SASE. Reports in 4 weeks.
Needs: Uses artists for commercial, residential and corporate art projects utilizing graphics, sculpture, multimedia and paintings. Pays 60/40% split, or negotiable.

ALTMAN-SAICHEK-ADAMS LTD., 300 W. Washington, Chicago IL 60606. Contact: S. Altman.
Needs: Uses artists for architectural renderings.
First Contact & Terms: Prefers local artists. Send resume and art, tearsheets or photocopies of published work. Buys all rights. Pays on acceptance.

ARCHITECTS UNLIMITED, 9433 Montgomery Rd., Cincinnati OH 45243. Contact: Donald Pansiera.
Needs: Uses 2 artists/year for architectural renderings. Also uses artists for building interiors and interior design.
First Contact & Terms: Send resume and samples (photos) and arrange interview. Works on assignment only. Samples returned. Only reports when assignment is available. Pay determined by job.

ARCHITECTURAL CONCEPTS, INC., 5104 Grand Ave. NE, Albuquerque NM 87108. (505)268-5240. Contact: John C. Bland. Clients: commercial. Assigns 3-5 jobs/year.
Needs: Works with 1 artist for architectural renderings, interior design, model making, landscape design and stained glass. Also uses artists for furniture design, murals, sculpture and wall art.
First Contact & Terms: Local artists only. Query with resume and samples. SASE. Reports in 1 week. Works on assignment only. No samples returned. Reports back on assignments. Provide resume and brochure to be kept on file for future assignments.

ART-IN-ARCHITECTURE PROGRAM, U.S. General Services Administration, 18th and F Sts. NW, Washington DC 20405. (202)566-0950. Director: Donald Thalacker. Clients: federal agencies.
Needs: Works with 10 artists for murals; 10, wall hangings; 10, sculpture; and 2, stained glass. Uses artists to create works as an integral part of federal architecture. Recent commissions include exterior sculpture by Stephen Antonakos, oil on canvas mural by Blue Sky, and water sculpture by Ned Smyth.
First Contact & Terms: Mail nonreturnable 35 mm slides of existing work only and resume. Reports in 4 weeks. Provide resume and 35 mm color slides in plastic sheet to be kept on file for future assignments. Pays $750-250,000 for original art.
Tips: "Getting exposure is usually the key to getting more exposure. Even if you're not selected for a commission, your work has at least been seen and studied. And once your work has been seen, somebody may remember it. If one panelist thinks your work is excellent and another says he's heard of you, your chances of being selected are improved. Don't waste time and money creating a design to submit to the panel. Send slides of completed work. And send quality slides. Even if your work is great, a poor slide won't sell it. Though many commissioned works have been done by big names like Louise Nevelson and George Segal, there is plenty of room for locally and regionally-known artists. Of the approximately 20 artists accepted annually from about 1,000 applications, there are as many local and regional artists as there are nationally-known people."

ASHWORTH DESIGN INC.,, 10255 N. 32nd St., Phoenix AZ 85028. (602)992-6560. Contact: Dean Ashworth. Architecture/commercial/apartments/golf course/landscape/interior design firm. Clients: commercial, industrial and residential.
First Contact & Terms: Mail designs. SASE. Reports in 3 weeks. Pays $8-14/hour or $400-1,000+/job.
Needs: Assigns 40 jobs/year. Uses artists for architectural renderings, art renderings, interior design, architectural models, murals, ceramics, fiber arts and stained glass.

WILLIAM BALDWIN & ASSOCIATES, LTD., 1100 Jorie Blvd., Suite 272, Oak Brook IL 60521. (312)323-9710. President: William Baldwin. Clients: residential and commercial.
Needs: Works with artists for architectural renderings, interior design, graphic design, sinage design and landscape design.
First Contact & Terms: Query with resume and samples. SASE. Reports in 2 weeks. Works on assignment only. Samples returned by SASE; and reports back on future possibilities. Provide calling card and brochure to be kept on file for future assignments. Negotiates pay.

BANGKOK INDUSTRIES INC., Gillingham and Worth St., Philadelphia PA 19124. (215)537-5800. Director of National Sales: Richard Miller. Manufactures interior design products. Clients: commercial.
Needs: Assigns 10-20 jobs/year. Uses artists for art renderings ($200-800); graphic design ($300-500); furniture design ($100-300); room sketches ($100-200).
First Contact & Terms: Prefers artists who have worked with other firms of this type. Query. SASE. Reports in 2 weeks. Pays by job.

BARBITTA, JAMES & ASSOCIATES INC., 576 Diagonal Rd., Akron OH 44320. Arrange interview or mail photos or transparencies.
Needs: Uses artists for architectural renderings. Pays by job.

A BARREL N' CRATE INC., 200 Crandon Blvd., Key Biscayne FL 33149. (305)361-2098. Contact: Helyn L. Boyajian. Interior design/landscape firm. Estab. 1963. Clients: Commercial. Query with photos. SASE. Reports in 1 week.
Needs: Uses artists for architectural renderings, building interiors, calligraphy, full-color renderings, graphic, interior, industrial and landscape design, murals, paintings, room sketches, sculpture and signs. Pays $100 minimum, renderings.

MARVIN M. BECK, AIA, ARCHITECT & ASSOCIATES, 9050 Santa Monica Blvd., Los Angeles CA 90069. (213)275-8898. Contact: Marvin M. Beck. Architecture firm. Clients: residential and commercial. Assigns 1 job and buys 2 renderings/year.
Needs: Works with 2 artists for architectural renderings; 2, interior design; 2, graphic design; 1, wall hanging; and 1, photo art.
First Contact & Terms: Local artists only. Arrange interview to show portfolio. Reports in 3-4 weeks. Works on assignment only. Samples returned by SASE; and reports back on future assignment possibilities. Provide calling card to be kept on file for future assignments.

CHARLIE L. BELLAH, ARCHITECTS, ENGINEERS, PLANNERS, 1020 Lansdowns, Corpus Christi TX 79412. (512)855-3335. Architecture, landscape and interior design firm. Contact: Charlie L. Bellah. Estab. 1969. Clients: Commercial and residential. Assigns 5-20 jobs/year. Query with resume and samples. No work returned. Reports in 2 weeks.
Needs: Payment by job: $75-500, architectural renderings; $35-600, art renderings; $75-600, calligraphy; $25-500, graphic design; $150-3,000, murals; $75-1,500, paintings; $50-300, room sketches; $100-1,000, scale models; $50-2,500, sculpture; $45-700, signs; $75-800, site plans; $500-10,000, urban planning projects; $35-500, wall art. Pays $15-25/hour, interior design.

BARRY BENEPE, 130 E. 16th St., New York NY 10003. (212)477-3220. Contact: Barry Benepe. Architecture/planning firm. Clients: nonprofit and public.
Needs: Assigns 1-4 jobs/year. Uses artists for architectural and full-color renderings, graphic design and urban planning. Especially needs completed and installed signs.
First Contact & Terms: Query with photos, transparencies or published samples. Contacts artists as needs arise. Pays $200-500, renderings; $50-200, graphics; $40-500, signs (if installed).

DWIGHT E. BENNETT & ASSOCIATES, 3929 Long Beach Blvd., Long Beach CA 90807. (213)595-1691. Contact: Dwight Bennett. Architecture firm. Clients: industrial, residential and commercial. Local artists only. Query with brochure or samples. Reports in 1 week. Pays $100-1,000.
Needs: Assign 4 jobs/year. Uses artists for architectural renderings.

NATHAN BERNSTEIN ASSOCIATES, 1991 Lee Rd., Cleveland OH 44118. Contact: Nathan Bernstein. Architecture/engineering firm. Clients: Commercial and industrial. Assigns 20 jobs/year; local artists only. Call for interview. Reports in 1 week.
Needs: Uses artists for architectural and art renderings, building interiors, landscape design, room sketches and signs. Negotiates pay.

RICHARD L. BOWEN, AIA AND ASSOCIATES, 13124 Shaker Square, Cleveland OH 44120. Clients: developers, municipal, industrial, institutional, residential multi-family and private projects.
First Contact & Terms: Query with resume or mail samples. Reports in 10 days.
Needs: Works with 2-3 artists for architectural renderings; 1, interior design; 1, graphic design; 1, advertising art; 2, model making; and 1, landscape design.

BROWN, BROWN & ASSOCIATES, AIA, 13333 N. Central Expressway, Dallas TX 75243. (214)235-8379. Contact: John Hall Brown. Architecture firm. Clients: churches, industrial, residential and commercial.
First Contact & Terms: Local artists only. Prefers artists who have worked with other firms of this type or have had work published. Arrange interview to show portfolio. SASE. Reports in 1 week. Pays $300-700/job.
Needs: Assigns 12 jobs/year. Uses artists for architectural renderings, interior design and illustrations.

ROBERT V. BUCK AND ASSOCIATES, 704 N. GPM Tower, San Antonio TX 78216. (512)344-8367. Contact: Robert Buck. Architecture/interior design firm. Estab. 1962. Clients: Industrial, residential and commercial. Assigns 20-30 jobs and 5-12 renderings/year. Query with samples. SASE. Reports in 1-2 months.

Needs: Uses artists for architectural renderings, site plans, models and interior design. Pays $2,000.

CADMAN DROSTE & THOMAS, 405 Broadway, Troy NY 12180. (518)274-2105. Contact: B.M. Cadman. Estab. 1962. Clients: Commercial and public. Mail designs or query with samples. SASE. Reports in 1 week.
Needs: Pays $1,500 max./job, architectural renderings and scale models; $6,000 max./job, sculpture. Negotiates payment for graphic design, room sketches, signs and site plans.

S. FRED CARBONE, ARCHITECT, 505 S. Lenola Rd., Moorestown NJ 08057. Clients: Commercial. Mail samples.
Needs: Uses artists for architectural renderings and building interior/landscape design. Pays $350 for 2x3' tempera rendering.

CARMICHAEL-KEMP, ARCHITECTS, 2870 Los Feliz Place, Los Angeles CA 90039. (213)666-1265. Contact: Richard J. Kemp. Architecture firm. Clients: institutional. Assigns 2-10 jobs/year.
Needs: Uses 1 artist/year for architectural renderings and 1 artist/year for landscape design. Also uses model buildings, statuary, sculpture, graphic design, murals, mosaics and stained glass.
First Contact & Terms: Call for interview to show portfolio, brochure and samples. SASE. Contacts artists as needs arise. Works on assignment only. Samples returned. Provide resume and brochure to be kept on file for future assignments. Pays $100-1,000, architectural renderings; $300-2,500, model buildings; $25-60/square foot, installed stained glass; $15-45, installed mosaic work.

CARRIAGE HOUSE INTERIORS, 5800 State, Saginaw MI 48603. (517)799-1110. Contact: A. Van Vlaenderen. Estab. 1953. Interior design firm. Clients: Residential, commercial and industrial. Assigns 12-15 jobs/year. Mail photos. Reports in 3 weeks.
Needs: Uses artists for interior design, graphics, paintings, room sketches, sculpture, signs and wall art. Pay varies.

THOMAS PAUL CASTRONOVO, ARCHITECT, 1175 Main St., Akron OH 44310. Clients: Residential and commercial. Mail slides or b&w photos. Reports in 10 days.
Needs: Uses artists for architectural and art renderings, interior/landscape design, building interiors and model-building. Pays by job.

JIM CHARLTON, ARCHITECT, 2825 S. King St., #1101, Honolulu HI 96826. (808)946-6655. Architecture firm. Estab. 1967. Clients: Commercial and residential. Query. SASE. Reports in 1 week.

WILLIAM A. CIOTTI & ASSOCIATES/ARCHITECTS, 309 S. 13th St., Phildelphia PA 19107. Contact: William A. Ciotti. Architecture firm. Clients: industrial.
First Contact & Terms: Call or visit. Reports immediately. Negotiates pay.
Needs: Uses artists for architectural renderings.

FREDERICK P. CLARK ASSOCIATES, 29 Locust Ave., Rye NY 10580. (914)967-6540. Contact: David J. Portman.
Needs: Uses artists for architectural renderings, landscape design, urban planning materials, charts and maps.
First Contact & Terms: Mail photos or transparencies.

DAVID FRANCIS COSTA JR. & ASSOCIATES, 210 S. Ellsworth St., Albany OR 97321. (503)926-2263. Contact: David Francis Costa Jr. Estab. 1958. Architecture firm. Commercial clients. Assigns 2 jobs min./year; out-of-town artists only. Query. SASE. Reports in 7 days.
Needs: Uses artists for full-color renderings, graphic/landscape design, model buildings, paintings and sculpture. Pays $275-600, renderings; $100 minimum, original art; $1,000 minimum, sculpture.

RUFUS COULTER ASLA, (formerly Coulter Associates), Box 588, 111 Corcoran St., Durham NC 27702. (919)688-2182. Contact: Rufus Coulter. Landscape firm. Clients: commercial. Assigns 3 jobs/year.
First Contact & Terms: Provide brochure to be kept on file for future assignments. Mostly out-of-town artists. Query with samples. SASE. Reports in 3 weeks. Pays $100-300/job, architectural renderings; $100-500/job, graphic design.
Needs: Works with 1 artist for architectural renderings; 1, graphic design; 1, signage; and 1 artist/year model making.

MAURICE COURLAND & SON, 2112 Broadway, New York NY 10023. (212)362-7018. Contact: R.H. Courland or N.M. Courland. Architecture/engineering/space planning/design firm. Clients: industrial, residential, commercial, financial institutions, government, public and semi-public, institutional and educational.
First Contact & Terms: Query with brochure. SASE. Reports in "weeks." Negotiates pay.
Needs: Buys 2-6 renderings of new buildings/year. Uses artists for architectural and interior renderings, murals/graphics and scale models.

CROVATTO MOSAICS INC., 1085 Yonkers Ave., Yonkers NY 10704. (914)237-6210. Contact: Costante Crovatto. Executes all types of mosaic murals for public buildings, churches and synagogues. Clients: various government, schools, banks, religious institutions, architects, artist and private residences.
Needs: Uses 2 artists/year for murals (experts in mosaic). Also uses artists for cartoons.
First Contact & Terms: Query with art or design ideas. "We generally recommend the artist to our client in need of a mosaic mural. Our firm, for ethical reasons, does not submit color renderings." Provide brochure to be kept on file for future assignments. Pay is 10-20% of the total cost of the project.

JERRY CUMMINGS ASSOCIATES INC., 758 E. Pico Blvd., Los Angeles CA 90021. (213)748-0468. Contact: Jerry Cummings. Landscape architect firm. Clients: commercial and residential. Assigns 20-30 freelance renderings/year.
Needs: Works with artists for architectural and landscape renderings.
First Contact & Terms: Query and arrange interview. SASE. Reports in 2 weeks. Works on assignment only. Samples returned by SASE; and reports back on future possibilities. Provide resume, calling card, brochure, flyer and tearsheet to be kept on file for future assignments. Pays $20/hour.

CURTIS-RASMUSSEN & ASSOCIATES, AIA, 122 Broad Blvd., Cuyahoga Falls OH 44224; or Quaker Square, 120 E. Mill St., Suite 408, Akron OH 44308. Contact: Ted Curtis.
First Contact & Terms: Query or submit photos or transparencies. Reports in 30 days. Provide calling card, brochure and price lists if appropriate to be kept on file for future assignments..
Needs: Works with 3-5 artists for architectural renderings; 2-3, interior design; 2, graphic design; 1, signage design; 1, model making; 1, sculpture; and 2, landscape design.

DAT CONSULTANTS LTD., 118 W. 16th, New York NY 10011. (212)777-7282. Architect: S. Fernandez. Architecture/interior design firm. Clients: industrial, residential and commercial.
First Contact & Terms: Local artists only. Query with resume or arrange interview to show portfolio. Reports in 1 week. Pays $200-400/job or $15-25/hour.
Needs: Assigns 10 jobs and buys 10 renderings/year. Uses artists for renderings, interior design, sculptures, graphics and scale models.

A. DEWITT DAY & ASSOCIATES, 4566 Office Park Dr., Jackson MS 39206. Contact: A. Dewitt Day. "We do all types of landscape architecture and land planning; commercial, industrial, recreational, institutional, subdivisions, multi-family housing, single-family housing, historic preservation and restoration, land and water reclamation and conservation, community planning, etc."
Needs: Works with 2-3 artists for architectural renderings; 2-3, interior design; 3-4, signage design; 0-3, model making; 1-2, murals; 6-7, wall hangings (must withstand the weather); 1-2, sculpture; and 1-2, stained glass.
First Contact & Terms: Mail transparencies or photos of work. Works on assignment only. Samples returned by SASE; and reports back on future assignment possibilities. Provide resume, calling card, brochure and flyer to be kept on file for future assignments. "We allow the artists to work directly with our clients. We approve space, size, color, etc. only. Clients also pay directly to the artist–we add nothing to the cost of the artist's work itself."

DEL CAMPO ASSOCIATES, 507 Howard St., San Francisco CA 94105. (415)777-4025. Contact: Martin Del Campo. Architecture firm. Clients: residential, commercial and institutional. Assigns 6 jobs/year.
First Contact & Terms: Local artists only. Query with resume. Reports in 2 weeks. Works on assignment only. Samples returned by SASE; and reports back on future assignment possibilities. Provide resume and flyer to be kept on file for future assignments. Pays $300-350, "sometimes up to $1000."
Needs: Works with 1 artist for architectural renderings; 1, advertising art; 1, wall hangings; and 1, landscape design. Uses artists for architectural renderings.

Tips: "We don't like drawings that are 'stiff' or commercial-looking."

DERR & CORNACHIONE, ARCHITECTS, 2830 Copley Rd., Akron OH 44321. Contact: Paul Lorentzen. Clients: Commercial, industrial and religious. Arrange interview.
Needs: Uses artists for architectural renderings and building interiors; tempera or opaque medium. Pay determined by job.

DESIGN AND LIGHT INC., 225 Madison Ave., Morristown NJ 07960. (201)377-6656. Contact: David C. Washington. Estab. 1965. Clients: Residential.
Needs: Uses artists for room sketches, full-color renderings, wall art and murals.

DESIGN CONSORTIUM, 3784 Watuga, Walled Lake MI 48088. (313)363-1144. Architectural Designer: Michael G. Walsh. Clients: residential, industrial, churches and commercial. Assigns 0-50 jobs/year. Prefers "architectural artists" experienced in logo, design, layout, drawings, specs, color coordination, etc. Query and arrange interview. SASE. Reports in 3 weeks.
Needs: Works with artists for interior design, graphic design, murals, wall hangings and landscape design. Payment by job: $200 minimum, display design and technical charts/illustrations; $100-200 minimum, print media ads; $225 minimum, scale models. Pays $6.50/hour, display backdrops.

DESIGN GROUP 3, 1349 Larkin St., San Francisco CA 94109. (415)673-8995. Contact: Betty Blomberg. Interior design firm. Clients: residential and commercial. Assigns 50 jobs/year.
First Contact & Terms: Query with samples or arrange interview to show portfolio. SASE. Provide slides to be kept on file for future assignments. Pays $200-2,000.
Needs: Works with 3 artists for architectural renderings; 5, model making; 4-5, murals; 4-5, wall hangings; 2, sculpture; and 2-3, stained glass.

DMI FURNITURE INC., State Rd. 64, Box 129, Huntingburg IN 47542. (812)683-2123. Contact: Kip Miller. Manufacturer of home furnishing products. Clients: Residential. Assigns 50 jobs/year. Query with samples. SASE. Reports in 4 weeks.
Needs: Pays $60 min./job, art renderings and graphic design; $16 min./job, room sketches. Negotiates payment by job for interior and furniture design.

WILLIAM DORSKY ASSOCIATES, 23200 Chagrin Blvd., Cleveland OH 44122. (216)464-8600. Contact: Curt Johnson. Architecture firm. Clients: commercial.
First Contact & Terms: Call for interview to show photos or transparencies. Works on assignment only. Samples returned by SASE; and reports back on future assignment possibilities. Provide resume and brochure to be kept on file for future assignments.
Needs: Works with 3-4 artists for architectural renderings; 2, interior design; 2, graphic design; 2, signage design; 1, model making; 2-3, sculpture; and 4-5 landscape design.

DURYEA AND WILHELMI PROFESSIONAL CORP., 1208 James St., Syracuse NY 13203. Contact: Henry P. Wilhelmi. Clients: government and institutions.
Needs: Works with 3-4 artists for architectural renderings; 1-2, graphic design; occasional, signage design; occasional, model making; 1-2, murals; and 1-2, sculpture.
First Contact & Terms: Local artists only. Mail photos or transparencies. SASE. Works on assignment only. Samples returned by SASE; and reports back on future possibilities. Provide resume, calling card, brochure, flyer and tearsheet or any combinations which will provide basic data to be kept on file for future assignments. Pays by job.

E/A DESIGN GROUP, 1625 K St. NW, #1100, Washington DC 20006. Contact: Jerrily Kress. Clients: commercial and governmental.
First Contact & Terms: Query with resume or arrange interview. Reports in 1 week. Works on assignment only. Samples returned by SASE; and reports back on future assignment possibilities. Provide resume, brochure and flyer to be kept on file for future assignments. Pays by job.
Needs: Works with artists for architectural renderings, graphic design, signage design, model making, wall hangings, sculpture and landscape design.

CHARLES M. EFFINGER, ARCHITECT, (formerly Thurman J. Peabody, Architect), Box 565, Norwalk OH 44857. Prefers artists with experience in architectural renderings. Send photos or transparencies. Reports in 10 days.
Needs: Uses artists for architectural renderings, interior design, art renderings and building interiors. Pays $15 min./hour, renderings.

RICHARD HENRY EISELT, 398 S. Grant Ave., Columbus OH 43215. (614)221-1013. Contact: Richard Henry Eiselt. Architecture/interior design firm. Clients: commercial.

Needs: Uses artists for architectural and full-color renderings, graphic and interior design, paintings, sculpture, signs and wall art.
First Contact & Terms: Mail photos or transparencies. Pay varies.

ELLERBE EAST, 2550 M St. NW, Washington DC 20037. (202)838-2500. Contact: Steve Grigg. Architectural/engineering firm. Clients: commercial, institutions and industrial.
First Contact & Terms: Query or write for interview. SASE. Reports in 2 weeks.
Needs: Assigns 4-5 jobs/year. Uses artists for architectural renderings, landscape design, signs and wall art. Pays $30-650, renderings.

ENVIRONMENTAL IMPACT PLANNING CORP., 319 11th St., San Francisco CA 94103. (415)626-9034. President: Russell Faure-Brac. Estab. 1967. Assigns 2-16 jobs/year; local artists only. Query. SASE. Reports in 4 weeks.
Needs: Payment by hour: $5-6, calligraphy; $5-7.50, graphic design; $5.50-6.50, paste-up.

GALERIA MARIA LUISA, 320 S. Mission Dr., San Gabriel CA 91776. (213)570-8456 or 289-3729. Contact: Maria Luisa Ramirez. Interior Design firm. Clients: Residential. Assigns 16 jobs/year. Mail photos. SASE. Reports in 3 weeks.
Needs: Interested in paintings, bronzes, porcelain, furniture and glass. "We need artists who paint in 'old world' style–'Renaissance-looking' paintings that blend with formal antique furniture." Also needs bronze statues.

GEOMEGA PLANNING SERVICES, 13437 Ventura Blvd., Suite 101, Sherman Oaks CA 91423. (213)788-3981. Contact: Julian Montrose. Environmental planning firm. Estab. 1974. Clients: Commercial, industrial, governmental and residential. Assigns 3-5 jobs/year. Query; local artists only. SASE. Reports in 2 weeks.
Needs: Uses artists for graphic design, mapping and urban planning exhibits. Pays $5/hour, mapping.

GLASER & MYERS AND ASSOCIATES INC., 2753 Erie Ave., Cincinnati OH 45208. President: Russell C. Myers. Clients: commercial, institutional and industrial.
First Contact & Terms: Query with resume and photos. Reports in 10 days. Pays $100-5,000.
Needs: Uses artists for architectural renderings, building interiors, interior/landscape design and urban planning graphics. Especially needs model builders. Prefers exterior renderings in tempera; interior renderings in tempera or watercolor.

GODWIN-BOHM-NBBJ, 505 S. High St., Columbus OH 43215. (614)224-7145. Project Manager–Graphics Communications: Linda Spohn. Clients: commercial and industrial.
First Contact & Terms: Local artists only. Arrange interview. Pay depends on job.
Needs: Uses artists for architectural renderings, graphic design, signs and mechanicals.

W.A. GOULD AND ASSOCIATES, 1404 E. 9th St., Cleveland OH 44114. Architects and city planners. Submit resume and fee schedule.
Needs: Uses artists for maps, presentations, architectural models, interior design, street furniture, street signs for new communities and brochures. Pay determined by job.

JON GREENBERG AND ASSOCIATES INC., 25100 Evergreen Rd., Southfield MI 48075. (313)354-8090. President: Jon Greenberg. Estab. 1972. Store interior design firm. Clients: Retailers. Nationally assigns 50 jobs/year. Query. SASE. Reports in 1 week.
Needs: Pays $10 min./hour, renderings and designs.

RICHARD S. GREER, AIA, 60 16th St. NW, Atlanta GA 30309. (404)483-5473. President: Richard S. Greer. Estab. 1975. Clients: Commercial. Assigns 1-4 jobs/year; local artists only. Query with resume. SASE. Reports in 1 week.
Needs: Pays $200 min./job, architectural renderings and scale models; $7 min./hour, site plans and urban planning projects.

HARLAND BARTHOLOMEW & ASSOCIATES, 201 E. Cary St., Suite 30, Richmond VA 23219. Architecture/landscape/planning firm. Query with resume and samples. SASE.
Needs: Uses artists for renderings, graphic design and scale models.

LAWRENCE C. HILTON/ARCHITECTS INC., 105 W 4th St., Cincinnati OH 45202.
Needs: Uses artists for architectural renderings, interior design, building interiors and landscape design.

First Contact & Terms: Arrange interview. Pays by job.

HOWARD, NEEDLES, TAMMEN & BERGENDOFF, 1805 Grand Ave., Kansas City MO 64108. Art Director: Don Stevens. Clients: commercial and industrial.
Needs: May use outside artists when excessive load on house's 3 artists. Assignment possibilities include interior design, architectural delineations and modelbuilding. Prefers renderings 30x40" in tempera and watercolor.
First Contact & Terms: Query with samples. Works on assignment only. No samples returned. Reports back on future assignment possibilities. Provide resume, calling card, brochure and flyer to be kept on file for future assignments. Pays $300-500.

IGLEBURGER HENDERSON NOWAK, 1612 Prosser Ave., Dayton OH 45409. (513)294-3394. Contact: Igleburger, Henderson or Nowak. Estab. 1963. Architecture/landscape firm. Clients: residential, commercial and industrial.
First Contact & Terms: Out-of-town artists only. Mail photos or art. Pays $175-300, color sketches.
Needs: Assigns 2-3 jobs/year. Uses artists for architectural renderings, building interiors, full-color renderings and landscape design.

IT'S A SMALL WORLD, 555 Lincoln Ave., Winnetka IL 60093. (312)446-8399. Contact: Mary Jane Graham. Interior design firm. Residential clients.
Needs: Works with 500+ artists for model making and 2, stained glass. Accessories and ceramics are scaled 1" to 1'. Interested in seeing miniature furniture, china and accessories.
First Contact & Terms: Mail photos or designs. SASE. Reports in 3 weeks. Works on assignment only. Samples returned by SASE; and reports back on future possibilities.

JAMES INTERIORS INC., 2733 Riverland Rd., Ft. Lauderdale FL 33312. (305)581-8028. Contact: James R. James or Robert C. Barnes. Interior design firm. Estab. 1956. Clients: Residential and commercial. Query or arrange interview. SASE. Reports in 1 week.
Needs: Uses artists for graphic design, murals, paintings, sculpture, signs and wall art. Pays $15-3,000, wall art.

JAMES M. JENNINGS ASSOCIATES, Box 21398 Columbus OH 43221. Contact: J.M. Jennings. Planning/development firm. Commercial and governmental clients.
First Contact & Terms: Local artists only. Query. SASE. Reports in 2 weeks. Works on assignment only. Material only returned if requested. No file kept on artists. Unsolicited material not returned.
Needs: Works with 1-2 artists for architectural renderings, graphic design, advertising art and charts/graphs. Also uses artists for graphic/landscape design, model buildings, site plans, urban planning materials, brochures and reports. Pays $200 minimum, illustrations.

GEROLD F. KESSLER & ASSOCIATES INC., 2101 S. Clermont, Denver CO 80222. (303)756-1536. Contact: Art Buyer. Architecture/landscape firm. Clients: residential and industrial.
First Contact & Terms: Query with photos or brochures; local artists only. SASE. Reports in 1 week. Works on assignment only. Samples returned by SASE; and reports back on future assignment possibilities. Pays $500-700, landscape and general site renderings; $600-1,000, subdivision land plan.
Needs: Works with 1 artist for architectural renderings; 1, graphic design; 1, model making; and 1, landscape design. Also uses artists for site plans and subdivision development layout.

LEWIS D. KLEIN, AIA, 1508 N. Main St., Dayton OH 45405. Clients: Residential, commercial, and industrial. Submit transparencies or b&w photos.
Needs: Uses artists for architectural/art renderings, building interiors and modelbuilding. Pays by job.

KOLBO, BOWMAN, SMALLWOOD & ASSOCIATES, AIA, 1090 N. Cole Rd., Boise ID 83704. (208)375-2800. Architecture/interior design firm. Estab. 1962. Clients: Commercial and industrial. Assigns 12 jobs/year; local artists only. Mail designs. SASE. Reports in 3 weeks.
Needs: Pays $12-800, architectural and art renderings; $12-6,000, graphic design; $12 minimum, interior design.

GEORGE J. KONTOGIANNIS & ASSOCIATES, 380 S. 5th St., Suite 1, Columbus OH 43215.
First Contact & Terms: Send photos or transparencies. Reports in 30 days. Works on assignment

only. Samples returned by SASE. Provide resume, brochure, flyer, tearsheet and price list to be kept on file for future assignments. Pay depends on job.
Needs: Works with 2 artists for architectural renderings; and 1, landscape design.

KORTE INTERIORS LTD., 36 W. Villard St., Dickinson ND 58601. (701)225-6317. Contact: Dick Korte. Estab. 1963. Clients: Residential and commercial.
Needs: Uses artists for room sketches and full-color renderings.

LAND DESIGN ASSOCIATES, 91 Green St., Huntington NY 11743. (516)549-4744. Contact: Robert Manniello. Architecture/landscape firm. Clients: commercial and industrial.
Needs: Works with 3 artists for architectural renderings; and 1, graphic design.
First Contact & Terms: Query with samples. SASE. Reports in 1 week. Works on assignment only. Samples returned by SASE; and reports back on future assignment possibilities. Provide brochure and flyer to be kept on file for future assignments. Pays $15/hour or $300/job for architectural renderings.

LAND DESIGN NORTH, 1709 S. Bragaw St., Suite J, Anchorage AK 99504. (907)277-7122. Contact: Kenneth E. Pendleton. Landscape firm. Estab. 1976. Clients: Commercial, residential and governmental. Assigns 4-6 jobs/year. Query or arrange interview. SASE. Reports in 1 week.
Needs: Pays $10-17/hour, architectural renderings.

LAND PLANNER & URBAN DESIGN CONSULTANTS, 20600 Leeward Lane, Miami FL 33189. Architecture/landscape firm. Estab. 1973. Clients: Commercial and residential. Assigns 10 jobs/year; local artists only. Mail designs, query with resume or arrange interview. SASE. Reports in 3 weeks.
Needs: Pays $10-20, art and architectural renderings; $15, urban planning projects; $10 min., ad illustration.

LAND SYSTEMS DESIGN, Box 322, Falls Church VA 22046. Contact: William Stanley. Architecture/landscape firm. Clients: private residence and small business.
First Contact & Terms: Query with resume. Reports in 10 days. Works on assignment only. Samples returned by SASE; and reports back on future assignment possibilities. Provide visual materials to be kept on file for future assignments. Pays up to $600 for completed plan.
Needs: Works with 2 artists/year for landscape design. Also uses artists for architectural renderings, landscape design, signs, graphic design, garden sculpture, site plans, engineering and structural elevations and scale models.

LEGENDRE-JOHNSON-MCNEIL-ARCHITECTS, (formerly Henri LeGendre & Associates/Architects) 96 Haarlem Ave., White Plains NY 10603. Contact: Henri LeGendre. Architecture/interior design firm. Clients: residential and commercial. Buys 6 renderings/year.
Needs: Works with 3 artists for architectural renderings; 1, model making; and 2, landscape design.
First Contact & Terms: Local artists only. Query with brochure or samples. SASE. Reports in 2 weeks. Provide flyer to be kept on file for future assignments. Pays $100/day or $20/hour.

LUCRETIA'S DECOR, 2393 S. Main St., Harrisonburg VA 22801. (703)434-9833. Interior design firm. Estab. 1973. Clients: Residential. Arrange interview; local artists only. SASE. Reports in 1 week.
Needs: Pays $20-175, graphic design; $25-100, interior design; $15-100, furniture design; $15 minimum, murals; $25 minimum, paintings, room sketches and sculpture; $25-125, scale models; $10 minimum, signs; $25-150, site plans.

PAUL R. McALLISTER, AIA, & ASSOCIATES, 915 W. Hedding St., San Jose CA 95126. (408)241-9272. Contact: P.R. McAllister. Architecture firm. Clients: industrial, residential and commercial. Buys 15-20 renderings/year.
Needs: Works with several artists for interior design and signage design.
First Contact & Terms: Local artists only. Query with brochure or samples and arrange interview to show portfolio. Reports in 1-2 weeks. Provide resume and examples of their work to be kept on file for future assignments.

JAMES A. MARTIS JR., ARCHITECTS, #250, 28790 Chagrin Blvd., Cleveland OH 44122. (216)247-3255. Contact: James A. Martis Jr. Architecture/interior design/construction management firm. Clients: commercial and residential.
Needs: Works with 2 artists for architectural rendering; 2, interior design; and 2, graphic design.

Also uses artists for graphic/interior/landscape design, model buildings, room sketches, signs and trademarks.
First Contact & Terms: Mail samples. SASE. Reports in 2 weeks. Works on assignment only. Samples returned by SASE; and reports back on future possibilities. Provide resume, brochure, flyer and tearsheet to be kept on file for future assignments. Pays $150-750 for renderings.

THE MARYLAND-NATIONAL CAPITAL PARK & PLANNING COMMISSION, 6600 Kenilworth Ave., Riverdale MD 20840. Chief Landscape Architect: Larry Hill.
Needs: Uses artists for landscape design, architectural renderings, urban walls, supergraphics and site plans.
First Contact & Terms: Mail photos or transparencies. Reports in 10 days. Pay determined by job.

DANIEL T. MEEHAN, ARCHITECT, 13 W. Sharon Rd., Cincinnati OH 45246.
Needs: Uses artists for architectural renderings, building interiors, model making and interior design.
First Contact & Terms: Submit photos or transparencies and/or resume. Provide resume and calling card to be kept on file for future assignments. Pay determined by job.

FRANK JON MESSINA AIA, 425 Harbor Blvd. Belmont CA 94002. (415)592-6667. Contact: Frank Jon Messina. Architecture/interior design firm. Clients: industrial, residential and commercial. Assigns 10-12 jobs/year.
Needs: Works with 1 artist for architectural renderings; 5, interior design; 1, mural; 1, wall hangings; and 10, landscape design.
First Contact & Terms: Query with samples. SASE. Reports in 1 week. Works on assignment only. Samples returned by SASE; and reports back on future assignment possibilities. Provide calling card and flyer to be kept on file for future assignments. Pays $200 min./job.

ELON MICKELS ASSOCIATES, 10641 W. McNichols, Detroit MI 48221. Urban planning and landscape design firm. Reports in 1 week.
Needs: Uses artists for design ideas for landscape and urban walls. Pays in stages of work.

JOHN M. MILES, ARCHITECT, Box 405, Snellville GA 30278. (404)972-5650. Contact: John M. Miles. Clients: commercial.
First Contact & Terms: Local artists only. Query. SASE. Reports in 2 weeks. Pays $200 minimum/job or $7.50 minimum/hour for drafting.
Needs: Assigns 4-5 jobs/year. Uses artists for architectural renderings and scale models.

MILLER WIHRY & LEE, Landward Court, 2147 Belcourt Ave, Nashville TN 37212. (615)298-5403. Contact: David O. Lose. Arrange interview. Uses artists for architectural renderings and garden sculpture.

WILTON FRANK MINCKLEY, AIA, AIP, ARCHITECT, URBAN PLANNER, 1421 Chandler Dr., Salt Lake City UT 84103. (801)531-0612. Contact: Wilton F. Minckley. Estab. 1961. Clients: Commercial, industrial, institutional and residential. Assigns up to 10 jobs/year. Mail designs. SASE. Reports in 2 weeks.
Needs: Pays $150-500/job, architectural renderings. Also uses artists for scale models and sculpture.

CLIFFORD MOLES ASSOCIATES, AIA, 405 Sansome St., San Francisco CA 94111. (415)981-2516. Contact: Anne Moles, secretary. Architecture firm. Estab. 1976. Clients: Industrial, residential and commercial. Assigns "a few" jobs/year; local artists only. Query with brochure or samples. SASE.
Needs: Uses artists for architectural renderings, models and murals.

J.G. MORAN & ASSOCIATES ARCHITECTS, 127 N. Marion on the Mall, Oak Park IL 60301. (312)383-3834 or 383-1131. President: John Moran. Architecture/interior design/space planning firm. Clients: commercial and residential.
First Contact & Terms: Mail designs, query with resume and samples, or arrange interview. SASE. Reports in 1 week. Artists should have had at least 2 professional assignments before submitting work. Works on assignment only. Samples returned by SASE; and reports back on future assignment possibilities. Provide resume, brochure and tearsheet to be kept on file for future assignments. Pays $75-600, architectural renderings; $15 minimum, interior design; $15-250, room sketches; $25 minimum, scale models; $10 min./hour, drafting.
Needs: Works with artists for architectural renderings, interior design, graphic design, signage design, model making, landscape design, charts/graphs and stained glass.

JAMES S. OLSAVSKY, AIA, ARCHITECT, (formerly Olsavsky & Ingledue, Architects), 312 N. Main St., Niles OH 44446. Mail photos or transparencies.
Needs: Uses artists for architectural and art renderings. Pay determined by job.

JAMES E. O'ROURKE ASSOCIATES, (formerly Planning Enterprises, Inc.) 5234 Jason Dr., Houston TX 77096. (713)665-7677. Contact: James E. O'Rourke. Architecture/landscape/engineering firm. Clients: commercial and industrial.
Needs: Works with 4 artists for architectural renderings; 3, graphic design; 2, signage design; 2, model making; 2, murals; 3, sculpture; 6, landscape design; and 2, stained glass.
First Contact & Terms: Query with returnable samples (simple sketches, slides or small reproductions) or arrange interview. SASE. Reports in 3 weeks. Works on assignment only. Samples returned by SASE; and reports back on future assignment possibilities. Provide resume, calling card and tearsheet to be kept on file for future assignments. Pays $50-100/hour or job rate that applies.

OSSIPOFF, SNYDER, ROWLAND & GOETZ, 1210 Ward, Honolulu HI 96814. Contact: Sidney E. Snyder, AIA. Clients: residential, governmental, medical and commercial.
Needs: Works with 2 artists for architectural renderings; 2, interior design; 3, graphic design; 3, signage design; 2, model making; and 3, landscape design.
First Contact & Terms: Call for interview. Reports in 10 days. Provide resume and brochure to be kept on file for future assignments. Pay determined by job.

PARKER ASSOCIATES: ARCHITECTURE/PLANNING, 17 Academy St., Newark NJ 07102. (201)624-8864. Contact: Terry Parker. Clients: commercial.
Needs: Works with 1 artist for architectural renderings; and 1, landscape design. Takes quotes for graphic design and scale models.
First Contact & Terms: Local artists only. Query. No work returned. Works on assignment only. Samples returned by SASE; and reports back on future assignment possibilities. Provide resume and brochure to be kept on file for future assignments. Pays $1000/job, architectural renderings.

PARKINS/ROGERS & ASSOCIATES INC., 925 Book Bldg., Detroit MI 48226. (313)961-9400. Architecture/landscape/urban design firm. Clients: Commercial, industrial, residential and governmental.
Needs: Works with 2 artists for architectural renderings and 2 for model-making/year.
First Contact & Terms: Local artists only. Should have experience in architectural renderings, brochure design and layouts. Arrange interview to show samples of work actually sold. SASE. Reports in 2 weeks. Works on assignment only. Samples returned by SASE; and reports back on future assignment possibilities. Provide resume and brochure..

PDT & COMPANY ARCHITECTS/LANNERS, 7434 Montgomery Rd., Cincinnati OH 45236. Contact: John Bammerlin.
Needs: Works with 2 artists for architectural renderings; 5, interior design; 1, model making; and 3, landscape design. Uses artists for architectural renderings.
First Contact & Terms: Mail samples (examples of finished work). Works on assignment only. Samples returned by SASE; and reports back on future possibilities. Provide calling card and brochure to be kept on file for future assignments. Pays by job.

PENCO STUDIOS, 1137 Bardstown Rd., Louisville KY 40204. (502)459-4027. Manufactures interior design products. General Manager: Julia M. Wirick. Clients: commercial, residential, churches and related liturgical.
Needs: Works with 2 artists for interior design; 3, graphic design; 2, sculpture; and 2, stained glass. Also uses artists for leaded glass design. Pays by job, based on square footage and size of work.
First Contact & Terms: Prefers artists with previous glass experience. Query with samples. SASE. Reports in 4 weeks. Works on assignment only. Samples returned by SASE; and reports back on future assignment possibilities. Provide resume and slides or photos to be kept on file for future assignments.

PEP INC., PROFESSIONAL ENGINEERS AND PLANNERS, 1612 Prosser Ave., Dayton OH 45409. (513)294-2422. Contact: Al Wahby. Prefers artists who have worked with other firms of this type. Mail samples.
Needs: Uses artists for architectural and art renderings, landscape design, urban planning materials, charts, maps, streetscaping and perspectives of house settings. Pays $100-500/job.

PFLUM, KLAUSMEIER & WAGNER CONSULTANTS, 424 E. 4th St., Cincinnati OH 45202. (513)721-4477. Contact: Peter Wagner. Architecture/landscape/planning firm. Clients: residential, commercial and industrial.
Needs: Assigns 12 jobs/year. Uses artists for architectural renderings, graphic design, landscape design, model buildings and urban planning materials.
First Contact & Terms: Local artists only. Query with photos. Reports in 3 weeks. Pays $750-2,500 graphic design.

ROLAND PIERSON, AIA, ARCHITECT, 1510 Oxley St., Suite I, South Pasadena CA 91030. (213)682-2621. Contact: Roland Pierson. Architecture/landscape/interior design firm. Estab. 1958. Clients: Industrial, residential and commercial. Assigns 1-3 jobs and buys 3-5 renderings/year; prefers local artists. "Artists must be able to produce on schedule; this does not rule out apprentices." Arrange interview to show portfolio. SASE. Reports in 3-4 weeks.
Needs: Uses artists for architectural renderings, murals, paintings, graphics and scale models. Pays $100-550, renderings; $50-8,000, designs; $200-750, models.

PPM DESIGN ASSOCIATES INC., 1865 Bernice Rd., Lansing IL 60438. (312)895-1905. Contact: Bill Purvis. Interior design firm. Clients: residential and commercial.
Needs: Uses artists for architectural and full-color renderings, building interiors, graphic design, model buildings, murals, original art, room sketches, paintings and signs.
First Contact & Terms: Local artists only. Query. SASE. Reports in 1 week. Pays $100-150 for renderings.

DAVID C. RACKER ASLA & ASSOCIATES, 57 W. South Temple, Suite 300, Salt Lake City UT 84101. (801)364-1718. Contact: Dave Racker. Architecture/landscape/land planning firm. Clients: commercial, residential and some industrial.
First Contact & Terms: Query. SASE. Reports in 2 weeks. Pays $50-500.
Needs: Assigns 20-30 jobs/year. Works with artists for architectural renderings, graphic design and scale models.

ROBERT RAIMIST, AIA, ARCHITECT, 11840 Gorham Ave., Los Angeles CA 90049. (213)820-4445. Contact: Robert Raimist. Architecture/landscape/interior design firm. Clients: industrial and commercial.
Needs: Works with 3 artists for architectural renderings; 2, interior design; 2, model making; 1, wall hangings; and 1, landscape design.
First Contact & Terms: Query with brochure. SASE. Reports in 2 weeks. Works on assignment only. Samples returned by SASE; and reports back on future assignment possibilities. Provide resume, calling card and brochure to be kept on file for future assignments.

JOHN CREWS RAINEY ASSOCIATES, 310 E. 55th St., New York NY 10022. Contact: Mary Jane Norcross Tougas. Architecture firm. Uses artists for architectural renderings, interior design and building interiors.

CHARLES H. RANDALL, AIA, ARCHITECT, 414 GPM South Tower, San Antonio TX 78216. (512)341-7139. Architecture/interior design firm. Estab. 1969. Clients: Industrial, residential and commercial. Assigns 3 jobs/year; local artists only. Query with brochure. Reports in 4 weeks.
Needs: Uses artists for architectural renderings and scale models. Pays $300, drawings; $15/hour.

NORMAN ROSENFELD, ARCHITECTS, 4 W. 62nd St., New York NY 10014. (212)489-6666. Contact: Marjorie Colt, designer. Architecture firm. Estab. 1970. Clients: Commercial. Query with samples or arrange interview to show portfolio. SASE. Reports in 1 week.
Needs: Uses artists for murals and paintings. Pays $100-200.

KENNETH H. ROSS ARCHITECT, 152 W. 42nd St., New York NY 10036. Contact: Kenneth Ross. Estab. 1967. Architecture firm. Clients: Residential, commercial and industrial. Assigns 6 jobs/year; or future assignments. Pays by job.
Needs: Uses artists for architectural and full-color renderings, interior design, building interiors, graphic design and model buildings. Pays $150, preliminary sketches.

ROSSI & NICKERSON INC., ENGINEERS & ARCHITECTS, 970 S. Byrne Rd., Toledo OH 43609. Contact: M.F. Nickerson III. Submit photos, transparencies or resume. Reports in 10 days.
Needs: Uses artists for architectural renderings. Pay determined by job.

SAGADENCKY & ASSOCIATES ARCHITECTS INC., 2239 Front St., Cuyahoga Falls, OH 44221. Contact: Trefon Sagadencky. Mail photos or transparencies.
Needs: Uses artists for architectural renderings and landscape design. Pays by job.

THE SCHEMMER ASSOCIATES INC., (formerly Gollehon Schemmer & Associates, Inc.), 3444 McCrory Place, Suite 250, Orlando FL 32803. Contact: L.W. Hughes. Architecture/landscape/engineering firm. Clients: commercial and industrial.
Needs: Works with 4 artists for architectural renderings and 2 for interior design.
First Contact & Terms: Query with photos. SASE. Reports in 1 week. Works on assignment only. Samples returned by SASE; and reports back on future assignment possibilities. Provide brochure and flyer to be kept on file for future assignments. Pays $150-550, renderings; $500-750, model buildings.

SCHENKER & SCHENKER, ARCHITECTS/PLANNERS, 35 Church St., Patterson NJ 07505. (201)271-7171. Contact: Sidney Schenker. Architecture/interior design firm. Clients: commercial, industrial and residential.
Needs: Works with 2 artists for architectural renderings; 1, model making; 1, murals; 1, wall hangings; 1, sculpture; 3, landscape design; 1, charts/graphs; and 1, stained glass.
First Contact & Terms: Artist must have professional experience working with similar type companies or have had work published. Query with resume. Reports in 2 weeks. Works on assignment only. Samples returned by SASE; and reports back on future assignment possibilities. Provide resume, brochure, flyer and tearsheet to be kept on file for future assignments. Pay varies.

SEIBERT WORLEY CADY KIRK PARTNERS INC., 2729 Prospect Ave., Cleveland OH 44115. (216)771-1845. Contact: Harold Van Niel. Architecture firm. Estab. 1948. Clients: Commercial. Assigns 3 jobs/year. Query; local artists only. SASE. Reports in 1-3 weeks.
Needs: Uses artists for architectural renderings, graphic/landscape design, murals, sculpture, signs and site plans. Pays $100-800, architectural renderings; $1,500-4,500, landscape design; $300-1,500, murals; $150-5,000, sculpture.

RICHARD SEIDEN INTERIORS, 238 N. Allen St., Albany NY 12206. (518)482-8600. President: Richard Seiden. Interior design firm. Clients: residential.
Needs: Works with 4 artists for graphic design; 3, signage design; 2, model making; 3, murals; 4, wall hangings; 3, landscape design; 2, charts/graphs; and 2, stained glass.
First Contact & Terms: Query with resume. SASE. Reports in 3 weeks. Works on assignment only. Samples returned by SASE; and reports back on future assignment possibilities. Provide materials to be kept on file for future assignments. Pays $150-1,800, original wall decor.

MARGOT SIEGEL, AIA, ARCHITECT INC., 8919 Harratt St., Los Angeles CA 90069. (213)276-5015. Architecture firm. Clients: residential and commercial. Buys 3 renderings/year.
Needs: Works with 3 artists for architectural renderings; 2, interior design; 3, graphic design; and 2, landscape design.
First Contact & Terms: Local artists only. Query with samples and arrange interview to show portfolio. SASE. Works on assignment only. Samples returned by SASE; and reports back on future assignment possibilities. Provide resume and calling card to be kept on file for future assignments.

THE SPINK CORP., 1311 I. St., Sacramento CA 91814. (916)444-8170. Chief Architect: Francis Koo. Clients: commercial, industrial and residential. Assigns 30 jobs/year.
Needs: Works with 3 artists for architectural renderings; 3, interior design; 1, graphic design; 1, advertising art; 2, signage design; 1, model making; 2, murals; 1, wall hangings; 2, landscape design; and 1, charts/graphs.
First Contact & Terms: Query. SASE. Reports in 1 week. Works on assignment only. Samples returned by SASE; and reports back on future assignment possibilities. Provide resume, calling card and brochure to be kept on file for future assignments. Maximum payment: $1,000, architectural renderings; $1,500, art renderings; $3,000, graphic design; $5,000, scale models; $10,000, signs; $40,000, murals and sculpture. Pays minimum $500. Negotiates payment for paintings and wall art.

STANLEY CONSULTANTS INC., Stanley Bldg., Muscatine IA 52761. Director of Public Relations and Publications: Deane N. Haerer. International engineering/architecture/planning/management consulting firm. Clients: *Fortune 500*, foreign governments, federal agencies, state, city and county governments. Query with resume and published samples.
Needs: Uses artists for direct mail brochures, interior designs and architectural renderings.

DUFFY B. STANLEY, ARCHITECTS, 308 Bassett Tower, El Paso TX 79901. Contact: Duffy Stanley. Submit photos or transparencies. Uses artists for renderings, urban planning materials, charts and maps. Pays by job.

GEORGE STATEN & ASSOCIATES INC., ARCHITECTS & PLANNERS, 4849 N. Mesa, Suite 1, El Paso TX 79912. (915)544-4444. Contact: George Staten Jr. Architecture/interior design firm. Clients: residential, institutional and commercial.
Needs: Works with 3 artists for architectural renderings; 1, interior design; 2, graphic design; 2, signage design; 1, model making; 2, sculpture; 2, landscape design; and 2, stained glass. Pays $200-2,500, architectural renderings; $50-1000, building interiors; $300-3,000, full-color renderings; $100 minimum, landscape design.
First Contact & Terms: Query or write for interview. SASE. Reports in 1 week. Works on assignment only. Samples returned by SASE; and reports back on future assignment possibilities. Provide resume, calling card and brochure to be kept on file for future assignments.

BRYAN H. THOMPSON, LANDSCAPE ARCHITECT, ASLA, 1415 Troup Rd., Tyler TX 75701. (214)595-0905. Contact: Bryan H. Thompson. Landscape firm. Estab. 1973. Clients: Commercial, residential and public institutional, including parks and recreation areas. Assigns 10 jobs/year. Query with resume or arrange interview. SASE. Reports in 2 weeks.
Needs: Minimum payment by hour: $10, architectural and art renderings, graphic design, signs, murals, paintings, room sketches and wall art; $12, scale models, and urban planning projects; $15, site plans and landscape lighting (interior and exterior). Pays $15 min./hour or $2,000 max./job, sculpture.

RONALD W. THURBER, AIA, 1523 Hays, Boise ID 83702. (208)345-4698. Contact: Ronald Thurber. Clients: commercial.
First Contact & Terms: Query. SASE. Reports in 1 week. Provide brochure to be kept on file for future assignments. Pays $100-300/job, renderings.
Needs: Works with 4 artists for architectural renderings; 2, interior design; 1, graphic design; 2, signage design; 3, landscape design; and 2, stained glass.

JOHANNES VAN TILBURG, AIA, ARCHITECTS & PLANNERS INC., 1211 Westwood Blvd., Los Angeles CA 90024. (213)477-4044. Contact: Johannes Van Tilburg. Architecture firm. Estab. 1972. Clients: Residential and commerical. Assigns 35 jobs/year; local artists only. "Phone the firm, introduce yourself and give credentials; then arrange interview to show portfolio." Reports in 2-3 weeks.
Needs: Uses artists for architectural renderings. Pays $500-1,000.

VITO J. TRICARICO, ARCHITECT, 3 E. 75th St., New York NY 10021. (212)421-9061. Mail samples or arrange interview. Reports in 30 days.
Needs: Uses artists for architectural renderings, interior design, building interiors and landscape design. Pay varies.

THE TWIGS INC., 44 Farnswich St., Boston MA 02210. (617)426-4069. Director: Arthur A. Athas. Manufactures interior design products. Clients: commercial and residential.
Needs: Uses artists for art renderings ($2,000 maximum); textile and wallpaper design ($150-500).
First Contact & Terms: Query. SASE. Reports in 1 week.

URBAN DESIGN ASSOCIATES, 258 Church St., New Haven CT 06510. Architect: George Conklin. Clients: commercial.
Needs: Works with 3 artists for architectural renderings; 1, interior design; 1, graphic design; 1, signage design; 1, model making; and 1, landscape design.
First Contact & Terms: Query with samples. SASE. Reports in 2 weeks. Works on assignment only. No samples returned. Reports back on future assignment possibilities. Provide resume and brochure to be kept on file for future assignments. Payment by job: $150 minimum, architectural renderings; $200 minimum, scale models; $50-250, graphic design; $40-300, signs.

WALTER DOUGLAS VOGEL ASSOCIATES, 1525 S. Mooney Blvd., Visalia CA 93277. (209)732-4793. Contact: Walter D. Vogel. Architecture/interior design firm. Estab. 1962. Clients: Industrial, residential and commercial. Arrange interview to show portfolio. SASE. Reports in 2 weeks.
Needs: Uses artists for murals and paintings.

WALLACE McHARG ROBERTS & TODD, 1737 Chestnut St., Philadelphia PA 19103. Contact: William Roberts or Thomas Todd. Architecture/planning/landscape firm. Mail samples or query with resume. Reports in 30 days.
Needs: Uses artists for architectural renderings, models and graphic design. Pays flat fee.

LORRIN L. WARD, ARCHITECT INC., 341 W. 4th St., Chico CA 95926. (916)342-4265. Contact: Lorrin Ward, president. Architecture firm. Clients: governmental, industrial and commercial. Buys 1-3 renderings/year.
Needs: Works with 2 artists for architectural renderings; 1, model making; and 1, landscape design.
First Contact & Terms: Prefers artists who have worked with other firms of this type. Query with brochure. SASE. Reports in 1-2 weeks. Provide resume, calling card and brochure to be kept on file for future assignments. Pays $50-500/job.

HELENE WEISSNER DESIGNS INC., 4330 NE 2nd Ave., Miami FL 33137. Contact: J. Weissner. Interior design firm. Clients: Residential and commercial.
Needs: Works with artists for architectural renderings, interior design, signage design, model making, murals, wall hangings, sculpture, landscape design and stained glass.
First Contact & Terms: Local artists only. Works on assignment only. No samples returned. Reports back on future assignment possibilities. Provide brochure to be kept on file for future assignments.

YUILL-THORNTON & LEVIKOW, 442 Post St., San Francisco CA 94102. Contact: John R. Levikow. Architecture firm. Clients: Institutional, educational, public and commercial. Submit resume and photos or transparencies. Reports in 10 days.
Needs: Uses artists for architectural renderings, interior design, model buildings, supergraphics and building interiors. Pays $250, sketches.

Art Studios

Few companies and advertising agencies could survive crunch periods of art demands without help from art studios. These groups specialize in providing a variety of art skills, including retouching, layout, paste-up, charts, graphs, technical art, illustrations, design work and even a cartoon or two. Similarily, the art studio's needs from freelancers fall within these areas of art.

Occasionally jobs for art studios can be done by mail, but most often work is done by an artist who is within commuting distance. Completed art usually becomes the property of the client for whom the art studio is working. For this reason, originals are rarely returned to the artist.

In addition to consulting the listings in this section, check the Yellow Pages for art studios in your locale.

ACCOLADE RETOUCHERS INC., 55 W. 42nd St., New York NY 10036. Art/Creative Director: Sal Terzo. Clients: Ad agencies, apparel and soft and hard goods manufacturers.
Needs: Uses artists for paste-up, retouching and package design for newspapers, magazines and direct mail.

AD SYSTEMS INC., 723 S. Wells St., Chicago IL 60607. (312)427-4025. Creative Director: Robert Tutskey. Art agency. Clients: manufacturers and retailers. Annual billing: $2,000,000.
Needs: Works with 1-2 illustrators/month. Uses artists for P-O-P displays, brochures/flyers and slide sets.
First Contact & Terms: Local artists only. Arrange interview to show portfolio. SASE. Provide material to be kept on file for future assignments. No originals returned. Pays $100-300, illustrations; $8-12/hour, mechanicals.

AMBROSI & ASSOCIATES INC., 75 E. Wacker Dr., Chicago IL 60601. (312)236-7262. Art/Creative Director: Garry Litton. Art Agency. Clients: retail, agency, financial and industrial.
Needs: Uses artists for layout, illustration, technical art and paste-up for print media.
First Contact & Terms: Local artists only. Submit samples (prefer original art, tearsheets or printed pieces) or call for interview. Provide brochures, flyers, business cards, resumes, tearsheets, etc. to be kept on file for future assignments. No originals returned to artist at job's completion.

AMERGRAPHICS & URBAN, INC., 25327 SW 142nd Ave., Princeton FL 33032. (305)248-5434. President/Creative Director: Alan Urban. Art agency. Clients: publishing, communications, financial, agency, manufacturing, performing arts, developers, travel industry, advertising and medical.
Needs: Works with 3-5 illustrators and 5 designers/month. Uses artists for billboards, consumer and trade magazines, direct mail, newspapers, P-O-P displays, stationery design and brochures/flyers.
First Contact & Terms: Provide portfolio with non-returnable samples to be kept on file for future assignments. "We like to have as much information as possible for our files. We will not start a file on an artist unless we are provided with non-returnable samples of work. We will look at any work of high quality and generally consider talent, creativity and professionalism more important than particular style or experience. Often we like illustrations that border on, or lapse into fine art. We are extremely critical about design and seldom consider more than 2-3 out of every 100 reviewed. Work is divided into distinct catagories: magazine, newspaper and advertising. We prefer experienced designers, but will review any quality, professional work." Especially interested in precise mechanical artists, 3-D work (cast paper, sculptures, ceramics, assemblages, etc), fresh styles and techniques for illustration and magazine and newspaper designers with talent and experience. Pays $25 minimum/spots; $8 minimum/hour for design/mechanicals and $75/day minimum for general assignment work. Considers client's budget, amount of creativity required, where work will appear and artist's previous experience/reputation.

LEE AMES & ZAK LTD., 6500 Jericho Turnpike, Commack NY 11725. Director: Lee J. Ames. Clients: Major book and educational publishers, toy manufacturers and children's and technical books. Query with samples; local artists only.
Needs: Uses artists for layout, illustration, technical art, paste-up and cartoons.

ANCO/BOSTON, 441 Stuart St., Boston MA 02116. (617)267-9700. Graphic Director: Matthew Fortado. Art agency. Clients: educational publishers, commercial and industrial.
Needs: Works with 10 illustrators and 1 designer/month. Uses artists for filmstrips, direct mail, slide sets, brochures/flyers and books. Also uses artists for charts, graphs, technical art and paste-up.
First Contact & Terms: Local artists only. Arrange interview. Provide business cards, resumes, tearsheets and brochure to be kept on file for future assignments. No originals returned to artist at job's completion.

ANDREN & ASSOCIATES INC., 6400 N. Keating Ave., Lincolnwood IL 60646. (312)267-8500. Contact: Kenneth E. Andren. Clients: beauty products, tools, clothing retailers, laboratories, banks, cameras and paper products.
Needs: Assigns 6-7 jobs/month. Uses artists for catalogs, direct mail brochures, flyers, packages, P-O-P displays and print media advertising.
First Contact & Terms: Local artists only. Query with samples or arrange interview. SASE. Reports in 1-2 weeks. Pays $10 min./hour for animation, design, illustrations, layout, lettering, mechanicals, paste-up, retouching and type spec.

BARLENMIR HOUSE OF GRAPHICS, 413 City Island Ave., City Island NY 10464. Creative Director: Barry L. Mirenburg. Clients: manufacturers and service companies.
Needs: Assigns 10 jobs/year. Uses artists for illustrations, paste-up, design and technical art for annual reports, posters, forms and trademarks.
First Contact & Terms: Query with small slides or prints. SASE. Reports in 2 weeks.

BARNHART ASSOCIATES INC., 27 Eisenhower Dr., York PA 17403. Mail tearsheets or photocopies. Reports in 10-20 days.
Needs: Uses artists for advertising, design, illustrations, industrial design, layouts, lettering and retouching. Especially needs "illustrations of an industrial or commercial situation."

BASIC/BEDELL ADVERTISING SELLING IMPROVEMENT CORP., 2042 Alameda Padre Serra, Santa Barbara CA 93103. President: C. Barrie Bedell. Clients: National and international newspapers, publishers, direct response marketers, retail stores, hard lines manufacturers and trade associations.
Needs: Uses artists for furniture and spot illustrations and cartoons. Especially needs layout. Pays $25, washes; $15, spots and cartoons.

JOHN BLAIR & CO., 717 5th Ave., New York NY 10022. Vice President, Communications: Josef B. Rosenberg. Vice President/Communications, Blair Graphics Division: Raymond Niziolek. Associate Promotion Manager: Nancy Reiersen. Promotion Manager: Dorothy Lancaster. Uses local artists for technical charts, annual reports, sales literature and exhibit designs.

CAMPAIGN COACHES, 80 Winifred Dr., Merrick NY 11566. Contact: Eliot Frank, president. Graphics/Exhibit/Display firm. Estab. 1968. Clients: Lighting, energy management, industrial and political.
Needs: Uses artists for finished artwork and mechanicals. Pays "according to budget."

THE CHESTNUT HOUSE GROUP INC., 535 N. Michigan Ave., Chicago IL 60611. (312)822-9090. Creative Directors: Norman Baugher and Miles Zimmerman. Estab. 1968. Clients: Major educational publishers and advertisers, and industry. Arrange interview.
Needs: Illustration, layout and assembly. Pays by job.

CROW-QUILL STUDIOS, 706 Sansome St., San Francisco CA 94111. Art/Creative Director: Jaren Dahlstrom. Graphic design firm. Clients: Publishers, paper companies, real estate developers, insurance companies, financial institutions and transportation firms.
Needs: Works with 2-3 illustrators/month. Uses artists for magazines, collateral, direct mail, annual reports, slide presentations and book design/illustration.
First Contact & Terms: Provide printed samples and/or tearsheets for files. Unsolicited samples cannot be returned.

CSOKA/BENATO/FLEURANT INC., 150 E. 35th St., New York NY 10016. (212)686-6741. President: Robert Fleurant. Estab. 1969. Clients: Insurance, national retail chains and communications. Assigns 10-20 jobs/year. Query with samples or arrange interview. No work returned.
Needs: Uses artists for record jacket covers and sales promotion posters. Pays $10-20/hour, layout; $6-12/hour, paste-up and mechanicals; $400 max./job, record jacket covers. Negotiates

payment by job for annual reports, catalogs, packaging, posters and POP displays.

CWI INC., 205 E. 42nd St., New York NY 10017. (212)682-1970. Contact: Geoffrey Chaite. Art agency. Clients: packaged goods, foods, tools, publishing, drugs, tobacco, banks and sports.
Needs: Works with up to 10 illustrators and 2-3 designers/month. Uses artists for P-O-P displays, stationery design, multimedia kits, direct mail, slide sets, brochures/flyers, trade magazines, newspapers, layout, technical art, type spec, paste-up, retouching and lettering.
First Contact & Terms: Minimum 3 years experience. Provide flyers, business card and tearsheets to be kept on file for future assignments. May return originals to artist at job's completion.

ALEX D'AMATO GRAPHIC DESIGN, 32 Bayberry St., Bronxville NY 10708. (914)774-6264. Creative Director: Alex D'Amato. Clients: publishers, audiovisual firms, manufacturers and trade advertisers.
Needs: Occasionally uses local artists for P-O-P displays, stationery designs, brochures/flyers, paste-up, realistic illustrations and retouching for books, book jackets, boxes and record albums.
First Contact & Terms: Original work not returned at job's completion. Pay determined by job.

DAVIS GRAPHIC, LTD., 468 Park Ave. S., New York NY 10010. (212)686-7128. Art Director: A.N. Qureshi. Estab. 1967. Clients: Publishers and businesses. Assigns 50 jobs/year. Query with samples. SASE. Reports in 4 weeks.
Needs: Uses artists for annual reports, catalogs, charts/graphs, direct mail brochures, flyers, print media advertising and book illustrations. Pay varies.

DEL GRAPHICS, 535 N. Michigan Ave., Chicago IL 60611. (312)337-3250. Contact: Arthur Cigoy, art director. Clients: Industrial and automotive. Annual billing: $250,000. Assigns 350-400 jobs/year; fully experienced local artists only. Arrange interview to show portfolio.
Needs: Uses artists for realistic and decorative illustrations, layout and comp designs, keyline and retouching. Pays by job.

THE DESIGN ELEMENT, 8624 Wonderland Ave., Los Angeles CA 90046. (213)656-3293. Creative Director: A. Marshall Licht. Clients: Publishers, industry and public relations firms. Query with samples or call for interview. SASE.
Needs: Uses artists for illustrations, cartoons and production.

DESIGNERS 3 INC., 555 5th Ave., New York NY 10017. Contact: Jack Golden. Art agency. Clients: Pharmaceutical, industrial, public relations, financial and printing.
Needs: Works with 2-3 illustrators/month. Uses New York City area artists for illustration and retouching for flyers/brochures, newspapers, magazines and direct mail.
Terms: Provide brochures, business card and flyers to be kept on file for future assignments. No originals returned to artist at job's completion.

DI FRANZA-WILLIAMSON INC., 1414 Avenue of the Americas, New York NY 10019. (212)832-2343. Contact: Jack Williamson. Estab. 1955. Clients: Businesses and advertising agencies. Annual billing: $1,250,000. Assigns 250 jobs/year; local artists only. Query with resume and request interview. No work returned.
Needs: Uses artists for layout, comps, illustration, cartoons, lettering and retouching for catalogs, direct mail brochures, flyers, packaging, POP displays and slides. Payment by hour: $12-20, design and layout; $15-30, illustrations; $10-15, mechanicals and paste-up; $12-15, type spec.

DIAMOND ART STUDIO LTD., 515 Madison Ave., New York NY 10022. (212)355-5444. Creative Director: Gary and Douglas Diamond. Art agency. Clients: advertising agencies, manufacturers and publishers. Assigns 24 jobs/year.
Needs: Works with 10 illustrators/month. Uses artists for cartoons, charts, graphs, illustrations, layout, lettering, logo design, paste-up, retouching, technical art and type spec.
First Contact & Terms: Write for interview. SASE. Provide resume and tear sheets to be kept on file for future assignments. Originals returned to artist at jobs completion. Pays $10 minimum.

DONATO & BERKLEY INC., 370 Lexington Ave., New York NY 10017. (212)532-3884. Contact: Sy Berkley. Art agency. Clients: ad agencies, public relations firms, direct mail response advertisers and publishers. Call for interview; local experienced artists only.
Needs: Works with 1-2 illustrators and 1-2 designers/month. Uses artists for filmstrips, consumer magazines, direct mail, brochures/flyers, newspapers, layout, technical art, type spec, paste-up, lettering and retouching.
First Contact & Terms: Local experienced artists only. Call for interview. Provide flyers, business

card, resume to be kept on file for future assignments. No originals returned to artist at job's completion.

THE DRAWING BOARD INC., 101 Park Ave., New York NY 10017. Contact: Stan Levy. Clients: Major corporations.
Needs: Uses artists for layout, illustration, paste-up, retouching and lettering for newspapers, magazines and direct mail.

MEL ERIKSON ART SERVICE, 200 13th Ave., Ronkonkoma NY 11779. (516)585-7775. Creative Director: Mel Erikson. Technical art studio. Clients: publishers and electronic, toy and plastic manufacturers.
Needs: Works with 5 illustrators and 2 designers/month. Uses artists for cartoons, illustrations, layout and paste-up work on books.
First Contact & Terms: Local artists only. Query with 8½x11 photocopies or call for appointment. No work returned. Reports in 2 weeks. Provide flyers and tearsheets to be kept on file for future assignments. No originals returned to artist at job's completion. Pays $50, mechanicals.

FINN STUDIO LIMITED, 154 E. 64th St., New York NY 10021. (212)838-1212. Creative Director: Finn. Estab. 1969. Clients: Theaters, boutiques and magazines. Assigns 500 jobs/year. Mail slides. SASE. Reports in 4 weeks.
Needs: Uses artists for illustrations, layout, lettering, logo design, paste-up and retouching. Pays $50-5,000, logo; $120-2,000, illustrations; $10-100, simple layout.

JOHN D. FIRESTONE & ASSOCIATES INC., 119 W. Waterloo St., Canal Winchester OH 43110. (614)837-4680. Creative Director: Lois A. Firestone. Art agency/AV producer/typesetter. Clients: primarily publishers.
Needs: Assigns 300 jobs/year. "We need many artists of all categories, media and techniques. Uses artists for cartoons, charts, graphs, illustrations, layout, design, paste-up, retouching, technical art and type spec. Media jobs include filmstrips, multimedia kits, slide sets and books.
First Contact & Terms: "We prefer Midwest or Southern artists." Query with 35mm slides. SASE. Reports in 2 weeks. Provide slides and tearsheets to be kept on file for future assignments. Originals seldom returned to client. Pays $25-55, 1-color; $35-80, 2-color; $55-175, full-color.

FLEX INC., (Free Lance Exchange, Inc.), 342 Madison Ave., New York NY 10017. (212)682-3042. Multi-service company. Clients: publications, TV, billboard and direct mail firms.
Needs: Uses artists for cartoons, charts, graphs, illustrations, layout, lettering, logo design and mechanicals.
First Contact & Terms: Mail resume and photocopied samples. "Say you saw the listing in *Artist's Market.*" SASE. Provide materials to be kept on file for future assignments. No originals returned to artist at job's completion.

L. HUNTER FRIEDMAN CO., 2618 W. Peterson Ave., Chicago IL 60659. (312)262-3300. Contact: Len Friedman. Art agency. Clients: manufacturers. Assigns 150 jobs/year.
Needs: Works with 2 illustrators and 3 designers/month. Uses designers for stationery design, direct mail, brochures/flyers and trade magazines.
First Contact & Terms: Query with resume or arrange interview. Provide flyers and business card to be kept on file for future assignments. No work returned.

GRAPHIC CONCERN INC., 10 E. 49th St., 7th Floor, New York NY 10017. (212)759-8248. President: Stanley R. Konopka. Contact Fran Newman for portfolio review, Joe Calabrese regarding boardwork. Clients: book publishers, primarily for school department.
Needs: Layout, illustration, technical art, cover, type spec and paste-up.
First Contact & Terms: Submit portfolio.

GRAPHIC DESIGN INC., 23800 Amber, Warren MI 48089. (313)758-0480. Art/Creative Director: Norah K. Gonyou. Clients: Automotive manufacturers, large ad agencies and printers. Arrange to show portfolio.
Needs: Uses artists for layout, illustration, technical art, paste-up, lettering and retouching for publications, direct mail and catalogs. Minimum payment: $40-100, comprehensive layout; $4-5/hour, paste-up.

GRAPHICS ARTS AGENCY, 12121 Wilshire Blvd., Suite 100, Los Angeles CA 90025. (213)820-3791. President: C. Holman. Clients: nationwide design firms, major corporations, motion picture studios, advertising agencies and book and magazine publishers.

Needs: Works with 50+ illustrators and 50+ designers/month. Uses artists for billboards, P-O-P displays, filmstrips, consumer and trade magazines, stationery design, multimedia kits, direct mail, TV, slide sets, brochures/flyers, album covers, newspapers and books.
First Contact & Terms: Query. SASE. Reports in 2 weeks. Provide slides (in plastic slide sheets; no glass mounts), resume and samples to be kept on file for future assignments. Usually pays $6-60/hour.

GRAPHICS INSTITUTE INC., 42 W. 39th St., New York NY 10018. Art Director: Wayne Peterson. Art agency. Clients: corporations, public relations firms and government health and welfare agencies.
Needs: Works with 1-2 illustrators/year. Uses artists for illustration for annual reports, booklets, brochures, slide shows and corporate identification campaigns.
First Contact & Terms: Mail samples (tearsheets) or arrange interview. Provide materials to be kept on file for future assignments. No originals returned to artist at job's completion.

GRIFFITH & CUSTER INC., 38 W. 21st St., New York NY 10010. Contact: Marcia Laredo. Arrange to show portfolio; prefers local artists.
Needs: Uses artists for layout, illustration, type spec, paste-up, lettering and retouching, especially for 4-color catalogs.

RICHARD M. GROSSMAN, 1918 W. Hood Ave., Chicago IL 60660. Contact: Dick Grossman. Publisher of a monthly auto newsletter. Clients: industrial. Assigns 10 jobs and buys 8 illustrations/year.
Needs: Uses cartoonist for political and philosophical automobile cartoons and some technical illustrations.
First Contact & Terms: Query with a letter and 2 or 3 photocopied samples of small (3x4 or 4x4) cartoons. Reports in 1 week. Provide photocopy of sample to be kept on file for future assignments. Original work returned upon request. Pays $25-50.

HARSH-FINEGOLD INC., 14 E. 60th St., New York NY 10022. (212)752-3720. Creative Director: Rupert Finegold. Art agency. Clients: manufacturers, magazines, newspapers, book publishers and service organizations. Assigns 30-75 jobs/year.
Needs: Works with 2-3 illustrators/month. Uses artists for direct mail, brochures/flyers, newspapers, cartoons, lettering, paste-up, retouching and technical art.
First Contact & Terms: Call for interview. Provide materials to be kept on file for future assignments. Originals returned to artist at jobs completion. Pays $25 minimum, spot illustration; $8-12/hour, mechanicals.

BARRON HOFFAR & CO., 185 N. Wabash, Chicago IL 60601. (312)782-1253. Contact: Barron Hoffar. Clients: restaurants, hospitals, insurance, banks, public relations firms and ad agencies.
Needs: Works with 1-4 illustrators/month for work on consumer magazines and brochures/flyers. Uses artists for lettering, logos, retouching photos and keyline.
First Contact & Terms: Arrange interview to show portfolio. Provide printed pieces with examples of work to be kept on file for future assignments. No originals returned to artist at job's completion. Pays $12.50 minimum/hour, keyline.

IMAGE STUDIO, Main St., Stockbridge MA 01262. (413)298-5500. Creative Director: Clemens Kalischer. Design/photo studio. Clients: institutions, colleges, small businesses, resorts and organizations.
Needs: Works with 2 illustrators and 2 designers/month. Uses artists for filmstrips, multimedia kits, direct mail, brochures/flyers, album covers, posters, exhibits, layout, lettering, logo design, paste-up and type spec.
First Contact & Terms: Query. SASE. Reports in 4 weeks. Provide samples of work and resume to be kept on file for future assignments. Originals returned to artist at jobs completion.

CATO JOHNSON INC., 225 E. 6th St., Cincinnati OH 45202. (513)241-6330. Contact: William C. Johnson, art director. Estab. 1958. Clients: Major US and foreign firms. Assigns 50-100 jobs/year. Query with samples or arrange interview to show portfolio; indicate fees. SASE. Reports in 2 weeks.
Needs: Uses artists for comp and finished illustrations for package graphics, lettering and retouching. Pays $10 min./hour.

JOHSON PEDERSEN HINRICHS & SHAKERY, 141 Lexington Ave., New York NY 10016. Estab. 1976. Clients: Corporations and publishers. Query; prefers local artists. SASE.

Needs: Uses artists for annual reports, publications, catalogs, and charts/graphs. Pays $10-15, mechanicals and paste-up. Negotiates pay for color separations, illustrations, lettering, retouching and technical art.

GEORGE JOSEPH & ASSOCIATES, 65 E. South Water, Chicago IL 60601. (312)346-4333. Contact: George J. Goldberg. Ad/promotional art agency. Clients: businesses, advertising agencies and industries. Annual billing: $650,000.
Needs: Works with 2-4 illustrators/month. Uses artists for designs, illustrations and cartoons for annual reports, billboards, bumper stickers, catalogs, charts/graphs, direct mail brochures, exhibits, flyers, packaging, POP displays, print media and TV.
First Contact & Terms: Query with samples or arrange interview. Professional artists with a minimum of 5 years experience only. SASE. Provide materials to be kept on file for future assignments. No originals returned to artist at job's completion. Negotiates payment.

KARZEN GRAPHICS, Division of Maxsan Enterprises, Suite 290, 2640 Golf Rd., Glenview IL 60025. (312)729-9760. Art/Creative Director: Max Karzen. Arrange interview.
Needs: Layout, illustration, technical art, paste-up, retouching and lettering for newspapers, magazines, billboards, direct mail and posters. Pays $10-25.

KDA INDUSTRIAL DESIGN CONSULTANTS INC., 1785-B Cortland Court, Addison IL 60101. (312)495-9466. Contact: John Howard. Estab. 1947. Clients: Manufacturers, businesses, schools, government agencies and hospitals. Annual billing: $250,000. Assigns 20-30 jobs and buys 5-10 illustrations/year. Query with resume or arrange interview. SASE. Reports in 2-4 weeks.
Needs: Uses artists for graphic design and packaging. Payment by hour: $15-20, design; $10-15, illustrations; $10 minimum, paste-up.

LARRY KERBS STUDIOS INC., 225 E. 57th St., New York NY 10022. (212)759-1040. Contact: Larry Kerbs or Jim Lincoln. Art agency. Clients: industrial, chemical, insurance and public relations.
Needs: Works with 3 illustrators and 1 designer/month. Uses artists for direct mail, layout, illustration, slide sets, technical art, paste-up and retouching for newspapers, trade magazines and direct mail.
First Contact & Terms: New York, New Jersey and Connecticut artists only. Mail samples or call for interview. Provide brochures, business card and resume to be kept on file for future assignments. No originals returned to artist at job's completion. Pays $10-15/hour, paste-up; $12-18, comprehensive layout.

KOOPMAN-NEUMER INC., 231 S. Green St., Chicago IL 60607. (312)726-3508. Contact: Bill Tuter, art director, or Jerry Kilarski. Clients: mail order houses (Sears, Wards), network radio/TV, manufacturers and agencies.
Needs: Freelance needs vary. Uses artists for P-O-P displays, direct mail, slide sets, brochures/flyers, trade magazines and newspapers.
First Contact & Terms: Local artists only. Query with samples (tearsheets, original art, photocopies) and arrange interview to show portfolio. SASE. Provide brochures, flyers, resume and tearsheets to be kept on file for future assignments. No originals returned to artist at job's completion. Pays $15-150/job.

LAKE END GRAPHICS, 225 Lafayette St., New York NY 10012. Art Director: Randall De Leeuw. Clients: Museums, art galleries, book publishers and corporations.
Needs: Uses artists for illustration, retouching and mechanicals.

LAWRENCE LEVY DESIGN/FILM, 1001 Maple Ave., Evanston IL 60202. Contact: Lawrence Levy. Clients: Publishers and film, filmstrip and multimedia firms. Mail samples.
Needs: Uses artists for editorial art for use in books, magazines and multimedia programs.

LITHOGRAPHICS, 303 N. 52nd St., Lincoln NE 68505. (402)467-3492. Contact: J.C. Lambert or Van Brown. Specializes in direct mail promotion. Query with resume to show portfolio, or mail samples. SASE. Reports in 3 weeks.
Needs: Uses artists for advertising, billboard design, catalog illustrations, direct mail brochures, letterheads, magazine layout, newspaper advertising layouts, package design and retail merchandise promotional art. Pays $4-30/hour, direct mail brochure design.

JACK LUCEY/ART & DESIGN, 84 Crestwood Dr., San Rafael CA 94901. (415)453-3172. Contact: Jack Lucey. Art agency. Clients: businesses, agencies and freelancers.
Needs: Works with 1 illustrator/month. Uses artists for illustration and lettering for newspaper work.
First Contact & Terms: Uses mostly local artists. Query. Provide brochures, business card and resume to be kept on file for future assignments. No originals returned to artist at job's completion.

DONYA MELANSON ASSOCIATES, 130 Oliver St., Boston MA 02110. Contact: Donya Melanson. Art agency. Clients: industries, associations, publishers, financial and government.
Needs: Most work is handled by staff, but may occasionally use illustrators and designers. Uses artists for stationery design, direct mail, brochures/flyers, books, annual reports, charts/graphs and book illustrations.
First Contact & Terms: Local artists only. Query with photocopies. Reports in 1-2 months. Provide materials (no originals) to be kept on file for future assignments. Originals only returned to artist when specified in advance. Pays $7-20/hour, cartoons, design, illustrations, lettering, retouching, technical art and logo design. Pays $3.50-12/hour, mechanicals.

THE MIND'S EYE STUDIO INC., Box 333, Lisle IL 60532. Contact: George Kotalik. Estab. 1974. Clients: Food, fashion, publishers, agencies and manufacturers. Assigns approximately 150 jobs/year. Query with samples. SASE. Reports in 1 week.
Needs: Uses artists for illustrations, TV storyboards, logos, layout, type spec and mechanicals. Pays $10 min./hour, mechanicals.

NIIMI DESIGN GROUP INC., 676 N. LaSalle, Chicago IL 60610. Contact: K.M. Niimi. Estab. 1964. Clients: Industrial and software manufacturers and services. Assigns 20-100 jobs/year. Query with samples or arrange interview; uses mostly local artists. SASE.
Needs: Uses artists for cartoons, design, illustrations, layout, lettering, paste-up, retouching and technical art for annual reports, catalogs, charts/graphs, direct mail brochures, exhibits, flyers, packaging, POP displays and print media advertising. Pay determined by job.

PENPOINT STUDIOS INC., 444 Park Ave. S., New York NY 10016. (212)685-2925. Contact: Ed Rotkoff. Art agency. Clients: magazine publishers, oil company, international industrial firms and insurance. Assigns 50-60 jobs and buys 30-35 illustrations/year.
Needs: Works with 2-3 illustrators/month. Uses artists for stationery design, direct mail, slide sets, brochures/flyers, newspapers, charts/graphs, exhibits and POP displays.
First Contact & Terms: Prefers local artists. Query with samples. SASE. Reports in 2-3 weeks. Provide resume and tearsheets to be kept on file for future assignments. No originals returned to artist at job's completion. Minimum payment by hour: $20, cartoons and lettering; $30, illustrations; $15, mechanicals, paste-up and retouching; $25, technical art.

HERBERT PINZKE DESIGN INC., 505 N. Lakeshore Dr., #1015, Chicago IL 60611. (312)644-7671. Contact: Herbert Pinzke, president. Estab. 1957. Clients: Publishers, corporations, professional associations, city commissions, industrial parks and nonprofit organizations. Annual billing: $150,000. Assigns 120-200 jobs/year. Query with samples or arrange interview. SASE. Reports in 1-2 weeks.
Needs: Uses artists for annual reports, catalogs, charts, graphs, direct mail brochures, exhibits, flyers, packaging, POP displays and print media ads. Pays $5-25/hour, design; $5-20/hour, layout, lettering, retouching and type spec; $25-500/job, illustrations; $5-15/hour, mechanicals and paste-up.

THE PRINTER'S DEVIL, 4501 N. 18th Ave., Phoenix AZ 85015. (602)264-1552. Creative Director: Edd Welsh. Clients: printers' suppliers, commercial artists and agencies. Assigns 4-6 jobs/year.
Needs: Works with 1 illustrator and 1 designer/month. Uses artists for illustration, brochures/flyers, trade magazines, books, technical art, charts and graphs.
First Contact & Terms: Local artists only. Query. Reports in 4 weeks. No file kept on artists. Originals returned to artist at jobs completion. Pays $15-75, technical art.

RAPECIS, 17 E. 45th St., New York NY 10017. (212)697-1760. Contact: Robert Bothell. Uses artists for medical advertising, editorial, promotion and technical illustrations.

S. ROSENTHAL & CO. INC., 9933 Alliance Rd., Cincinnati OH 45242. (513)984-0710. Creative Director: Claire Schwarberg. Clients: publishers, manufacturers, associations and schools.

Needs: Works with 1-3 artists/month for paste-up. Uses artists for layout and retouching for direct mail, magazines, catalogs and brochures.
First Contact & Terms: Local artists only. Query. No file kept on artists. No originals returned to artist at job's completion. Pay varies.

THE ANDREW ROSS STUDIO INC., 321 E. 48th St., New York NY 10017. (212)751-1975. Contact: Andrew Ross. Graphic design studio. Clients: magazines, AV, sales presentations and promotions and direct mail.
Needs: Works with 1 or 2 illustrators/month. Uses artists for direct mail, slide sets, brochure/flyers, trade magazines, illustration, paste-up, lettering and retouching.
First Contact & Terms: Local artists only. Call for interview. Provide brochures and tearsheets to be kept on file for future assignments. Originals returned to artist upon request. Pays $8-12 for pasteup done in studio.

JACK SCHECTERSON ASSOCIATES INC., 6 E. 39th St., New York NY 10016. (212)889-3950. Contact: Jack Schecterson. Art/ad agency. Clients: manufacturers of consumer/industrial products.
Needs: Uses artists for annual reports, catalogs, direct mail brochures, exhibits, flyers, industrial design, slide sets, album covers, corporate design, graphics, trademark, logotype design, sales promotion, audiovisuals, packaging, POP displays and print media advertising.
First Contact & Terms: Uses local artists. Query with resume and samples, or arrange interview. SASE. Call for appointment. Provide brochures, flyers and tearsheets to be kept on file for future assignments.

CARLA SCHROEDER, 40 Park Ave., New York NY 10016. Creative Director: Carla Schroeder. Estab. 1971. Clients: Manufacturers. Assigns 15-30 jobs/year. Call for interview; local artists only. Reports in 3-4 days.
Needs: Uses artists for graphs, logo design, paste-up and technical art. Pays $8-12/hour, paste-up.

SENSENBRENNER DESIGN ASSOCIATES, 1920 American Ct., Neenah WI 54956. (414)725-6351. Art agency. Clients: retail, industrial and packaging.
Needs: "Freelancers are generally used to augment our staff capabilities–generally in handling work overloads–and occasionally (in the case of illustrators) to offer a special talent or art style. The latter is only occasional, however." Uses artists for advertising, sales promotion and packaging, illustration, P-O-P displays, letterhead, direct mail, album covers, slide sets, print ads, retouching, layout, design and reproduction artwork.
First Contact & Terms: Local artists only. Query with resume. SASE. Reports in 2 weeks. Provide business card, resume to be kept on file for future assignments. No originals returned to artist at job's completion.

SIGNATURE GRAPHICS, 200 Administration Bldg., Rte. 3, Municipal Airport, Ames IA 50010. (515)232-5132. Contact: Art Harrison. Ad/PR firm. Clients: businesses.
Needs: Works with 1-2 illustrators and 1-2 designers/month. Uses artists for filmstrips, stationery design, direct mail, brochures/flyers,layout, lettering and paste-up.

SYNTHESIS, 100 E. Ohio St., Chicago IL 60611. (312)787-1201. Art Director: Michael Waitsman. Design studio. Clients: corporate. Annual billing: $40,000.
Needs: Works with 3 illustrators/month. Uses illustrators for brochures/flyers, album covers and books.
First Contact & Terms: Local artists only. Arrange interview to show portfolio. SASE. No file kept on artists. On some jobs, originals returned to artist at job's completion. Pays $10-20/hour, mechanicals.

THINK GROUP INC., 1140 Avenue of the Americas, New York NY 10036. (212)730-1919. Art Director: Tony Apilado. Clients: AT&T, New York Telephone, Charles of the Ritz International, American Dental Plan, Trifari, R.J. Reynolds, etc. Call for appointment. Artist must be available to come to office.
Needs: Illustrations, design, slides, and retouching for print, TV, radio and multimedia.

TRAFTON AND AUTRY PRINTERS, Box 9068, Amarillo TX 79105. (806)376-4347. Creative Director: Lorren Hallmark. Estab. 1973. Clients: Manufacturers and publishers. Assigns 20 jobs/year; local artists only. Call for interview. SASE. Reports in 2 weeks.
Needs: Uses artists for illustration, layout, lettering, logo design and retouching. Pays $15, layout and finished art.

VISUAL CONCEPTS, 212 E. 48th St., New York NY 10017. (212)935-9852. Contact: Barbara Patinkin. Clients: Publishers, manufacturers, direct mail firms, nonprofit organizations and other service companies.
Needs: Uses local artists for design, layout, illustration and mechanicals for promotion, catalogs, trade ad and direct mail. Pays $10/hour.

JEROME VLOEBERGHS, 251 Kearny St., Rm. 710, San Francisco CA 94108. (415)982-1287. Contact: Jerome Vloeberghs. Estab. 1950. Clients: Advertising agencies and photographers. Query with samples or arrange interview; prefers local artists.
Needs: Uses artists for retouching. Pays $25 min./hour.

DON ZUBALSKY AGENCY, 11284 Sunshine Terrace, Studio City CA 91604. Contact: Donald L. Zubalsky. Art agency.
Needs: Works with 2 illustrators/month. Uses artists for illustration, paste-up, retouching and lettering.
First Contact & Terms: Provide materials to be kept on file for future assignments. Originals may be returned to artist at job's completion.

Associations & Institutions

This section of *Artist's Market* is divided into two parts: associations and institutions of a general nature, and educational institutions. Their needs are for illustrations and designs to promote their causes and membership (enrollment).

Projects requiring artwork include brochures, posters, signs, ads, logos, POP displays, recruitment catalogs, annual reports, magazines and other promotional efforts.

For additional information on institutions and associations, consult the *Encyclopedia of Associations* (Gale Research Co.). Educational institutions are listed in *Barron's Profiles of American Colleges* (Barron's Educational Series, Inc.) and *Comparative Guide to American Colleges* (Harper & Row). All three reference books give descriptions of the institutions listed therein.

AMERICAN BAPTIST CHURCHES, USA, Division of Communication, 1st Ave., Valley Forge PA 19481. (215)768-2441. Director of Media Education & Development: Milton P. Ryder.
Needs: Works with 5 illustrators/year. Assigns 12 projects/year. Uses artists for posters, calendars, convention hand-outs and brochures.
First Contact & Terms: Query with samples (or sketches or thumbnails) or arrange interview to show portfolio. Works on assignment only. Samples returned by SASE; reports back on future assignment possibilities. Provide resume and samples. Pays about $50-100, illustration; has paid as high as $1,200 for graphic design of national offering campaign.

AMERICAN SOCIETY FOR THE PREVENTION OF CRUELTY TO ANIMALS, 441 E. 92nd St., New York NY 10028. (212)876-7700. Publications Editor: Alan Breznick. A non-profit humane society which cares for 200,000 animals annually. Its members are animal lovers and owners concerned about humane issues.
Needs: Often uses illustrators for posters, booklets and newspapers. "We usually prefer realism, though there is room for fantasy occasionally." Works with 3 artists/year for ad illustrations and 3/year for ad design.
First Contact & Terms: Write with samples. Samples returned by SASE. Reports back on future assignment possibilities. Provide resume, brochure/flyer and tear sheet samples to be kept on file for future assignments. Reports in 3 weeks. Pays $25/small illustration for a pamphlet; $25/minor layout work on newspapers. Pay for product design and illustration depends on job required and funds available.

AUGUSTANA HOSPITAL AND HEALTH CARE CENTER, 411 W. Dickens, Chicago IL 60614. Assistant Public Relations Director: Michael Kulczycki.
Needs: Works with 1 illustrator and 3 designers/year. Uses artists for advertising, annual reports, charts, direct mail brochures, magazines, newspapers, exhibits/displays, handbooks, posters and recruitment literature.
First Contact & Terms: Local artists only. Query with resume or samples. SASE. Reports in 1 month. Provide resume, calling card, brochure, flyer, tear sheet and photo slides of larger, bulky samples to be kept on file for future assignments. Periodicals: pays $20 min./page, design and illustration; $15 min./page, layout.

AUTOMOTIVE AFFILIATED REPRESENTATIVES, 10800 N. Military Trail, Suite 222, Palm Beach Gardens FL 33410. (305)626-8380. Executive Vice President: Mel Steinbrenner. Pay determined by project.
Needs: Uses artists for membership recruitment literature, public information brochures, annual reports, annual roster, trade show exhibits, convention and seminar literature and newsletters.
First Contact & Terms: Arrange interview to show ideas or sketches. Buys one-time rights.

BLACK RINER ACADEMY MUSEUM, Box 16, Ludlow VT 05149. (802)228-5050, 672-3842 or 228-2791. Director: Milton G. Moore. Historical Museum. Works with 1 artist/year for ad design. Write. SASE. Pays by agreement.

BORGESS HOSPITAL, 1521 Gull Rd., Kalamazoo MI 49001. (616)383-4878. Contact: R. Sue Smith, community relations manager.

Needs: Works with 5 illustrators and designers/year. Assigns 25-40 jobs/year. Uses artists for illustration of patient information publications, special displays, ads, recruitment folders, annual reports, and publications aimed at hospital employees, medical staff and external public communications. "My strongest need is for illustrators with the human touch."
First Contact & Terms: Query with samples (photocpies of ink drawings, sketches) and arrange interview to show portfolio; "I need and want freelance artwork and want to build up contacts with artists in this area." Reports in 2 weeks. Works on assignment only. Samples returned by SASE; reports back on future assignment possibilities. Provide resume, calling card and tear sheet to be kept on file for future assignments. Pays $12 minimum, cartoons; $35-50, pen and ink drawings.

CENTER FOR INTER-AMERICAN RELATIONS, 680 Park Ave., New York NY 10021. (212)249-8950. Contact: Edna Phillips, public information director. Provides "four basic programs to further better understanding in the U.S. of our neighbors--Canada, Central and South America and the Caribbean."
Needs: Works with 4-6 illustrators and designers/year. Uses artists for brochures and other publications. Style should relate to Canada/Latin America and Caribbean.
First Contact & Terms: Local artists only. Arrange interview to show portfolio. Reports in 2-3 weeks. Works on assignment only.

CHILD AND FAMILY SERVICES OF NEW HAMPSHIRE, 99 Hanover St., Manchester NH 03105. (603)668-1920. Public Relations Director: Everett Doe. "Our purposes are to reduce social problems, promote and conserve wholesome family life, serve children's needs and guard children's rights."
Needs: Works with 1 illustrator and designer/year; February-May only. Uses artists for annual reports, direct mail brochures, exhibits/displays, posters, publicity brochures and trademarks/logotypes. Especially needs illustrations of children and/or families.
First Contact & Terms: Query or arrange interview. Reports in 2 weeks. Works on assignment only. Samples returned by SASE; reports back on future assignment possibilities. Provide calling card and tear sheet to be kept on file for future assignments.

COMPUTER & BUSINESS EQUIPMENT MANUFACTURERS ASSOCIATION, 1828 L St. NW, Washington DC 20036. (202)466-2288. Communications Director: Timothy G. Donovan. Estab. 1916. Query with samples. SASE. Reports in 4 weeks. Buys all rights.
Needs: Uses artists for annual reports, lettering, publicity brochures, signage, technical charts/illustrations and publications. Pays $50, covers; $10, inside line art.

COUNCIL OF STATE GOVERNMENTS, Box 11910, Lexington KY 40578. (606)252-2291. Director of Communications: Jack Gardner. Provides services and research for the 50 state governments.
Needs: Assigns 6-8 jobs year. Uses artists for annual reports, direct mail brochures and trademarks/logos.
First Contact & Terms: Query. Reports in 2 weeks. Pays $25-200/job, illustration; $25-75/job, design.
Tips: "Give us illustrations on government issues without stereotypes or a cliche approach."

CZECH FINE ARTS ASSOCIATION, 1455 Parkview Dr., Marion IA 52302. Contact: Ronald L. Raim. Promotes arts related to Czech ethnic heritage.
Needs: Uses artists for direct mail brochures. Pays $30-200.

THE DAWES ARBORETUM, 7770 Jacksontown Rd. SE, Newark, OH 43055. (614)323-2355. Naturalist Educator: John V. Carrier. Provides programs, education and recreation in horticulture, history and nature. Works with artists for 5-10 illustrations/year. Also has "monthly art exhibits at which works may be sold."
First Contact & Terms: Write with samples. Works on assignment only. Samples returned by SASE. Reports back on future assignment possibilities. Provide brochure to be kept on file for future assignments. Pays illustrators $1/slide for general program use; $15/hour for map work. Product design and illustration paid by contract.

EDUCATIONAL FILM LIBRARY ASSOCIATION, INC., 43 W. 61st St., New York NY 10023. (212)246-4533. Executive Director: Nadine Covert. "The leading professional association concentrating on 16mm films and other non-print media for education and community use. Members include: film libraries, museums, community groups, film programmers, filmmakers, film teachers, etc.

Needs: Works with 1 artist/year for al illustrations; 1 for ad design. "Artists must work within strict guidelines."
First Contact & Terms: Query by mail or write with samples. Works on assignment only. Samples returned by SASE. Reports back on future assignment possibilities. Provide resume, calling card, brochure/flyer, tear sheet samples or "anything that gives a good idea of work experience" to be kept on file for future assignments. Pay is negotiable.

FEDERAL UNION INC., 1875 Connecticut Ave. NW, Washington DC 20009. (202)234-2211. Vice President: Patricia Chapman. Nonprofit, educational institution.
Needs: Works with 2 illustrators/year. Uses artists for charts, direct mail brochures, exhibits/displays, handbooks, posters, publicity brochures and recruitment literature. Especially needs "sophisticated interpretations of complex ideas into simple, humorous line drawings."
First Contact & Terms: "Art assignments depend on financial resources; it's hard to give a general figure." Query with samples. SASE. Reports in 4 weeks. Works on assignment only. Samples returned by SASE; reports back on future assignment possibilities. Proivde tear sheet to be kept on file for future assignments. Pays $25 max./job, illustration; $10-15/page, layout; $10 max./job, inside line art.

GIRL SCOUTS OF THE USA, 830 3rd Ave., New York NY 10022. Executive Art Director: Michael Chanwick. Submit published samples; New York City area artists only.
Needs: Uses artists for direct mail brochures, annual reports, promotions, publications, exhibits, catalogs and posters.

HEBREW REHABILITATION CENTER FOR AGED, 1200 Centre St., Roslindale MA 02131. (617)325-8000. Public Relations Director: Joseph Freedman.
Needs: Assigns 8-10 jobs/year. Uses artists for annual report, brochure, flyer, direct mail and letterhead design.
First Contact & Terms: Local artists only. "Artists can readily reach me by phone." Negotiates pay.

HUDSON COUNTY OFFICE FOR CULTURAL AND HERITAGE AFFAIRS, 595 Newark Ave., Jersey City NJ 07306. Director: Charles K. Robinson. Clearinghouse for services on culture and heritage.
Needs: Works with 2-5 illustrators and 3 designers/year. Assigns 25 jobs and buys 10 illustrations/year. Uses artists for bumper stickers, direct mail brochures, annual reports, flyers and posters.
First Contact & Terms: Mail art. SASE. Reports in 1 week. Works on assignment only. Samples returned by SASE; reports back on future assignment possibilities. Provide resume, brochure, flyer, tear sheet and slides of samples (portfolio) to be kept on file for future assignments. Pays $75-100, bumper stickers; $250-500, 60-page brochure cover and layout.

INTERNATIONAL ASSOCIATION OF INDEPENDENT PRODUCERS, Box 1933, Washington DC 20013. (202)638-5595.
Needs: Works with 15-25 illustrators and 3-4 designers/year. Uses graphic designers for art which pertains to motion pictures, TV, records, tapes, advertising and book/record cover illustrations. Specific needs include layouts, logos and column heads.
First Contact & Terms: Submit tearsheets, photocopies or transparencies. Usually buys all rights. Works on assignment only. Samples returned by SASE; reports back on future assignment possibilities. Provide resume, brochure and tear sheet to be kept on file for future assignments. Pays by job.

INTERNATIONAL FENCE INDUSTRY ASSOCIATION, Box 426, Mineral Wells TX 76067. Contact: Rodger D. Duke.
Needs: Uses artists for advertising art/design, animated cartoons, convention exhibits, direct mail brochures, graphic design, magazine covers, newspaper advertising layouts (software), newspaper editorial cartoons, sales promotion art and signs. Pays $100-500, advertising magazine layout; $400-1,200, brochures.

INTER-TRIBAL INDIAN CEREMONIAL ASSOCIATION INC., Box 1, Church Rock NM 87311. (505)863-3896. Program Director: Bill Ganong. Teaches Indian culture to nonIndians. Estab. 1922. Assigns 1 art job/year; Indian artists only. Mail art. SASE. Reports in 1 month.
Needs: Uses artists for direct mail brochures and posters. Pays $150 max./job, design.

JUNIOR ACHIEVEMENT INC., 550 Summer St., Stamford CT 06901. (203)359-2970. Art Director: Rich Gaipa. "National organization dedicated to instruct students about the business

world. Here at national headquarters we produce a large quantity of printed materials for our field operations."
Needs: Local artists only with previous experience. Works with 1 artist/year for illustrations on products. Also uses 3-4 paste-up artists and typesetters. Interested in charts and graphs, illustrations of students and line art.
First Contact & Terms: Write with resume and/or samples. Works on assignment only. Reports back on future assignment possibilities. Provide resume, calling card and tear sheet samples to be kept on file for future assignments. Pay is determined by job. "Being non-profit, we pay lower than other places. But it is a great place to have samples of art printed and distributed nationally."

MAINE STATE COMMISSION ON THE ARTS AND THE HUMANITIES, State House, State Rm 25, Augusta ME 04333. Executive Director: Alden C. Wilson.
Needs: Uses artists for direct mail brochures and posters.
First Contact & Terms: Send resume and samples. Works on assignment only. Samples returned by SASE; reports back on future assignment possibilities. Provide resume, brochures and flyer to be kept on file for future assignments.

MEMORIAL MEDICAL CENTER, 800 N. Rutledge, Springfield IL 62701. (217)708-3591. Public Relations/Development Director: Milton Niewsma. Estab. 1897. Assigns 4-6 jobs/year; local artists only. Arrange interview to show portfolio. Reports in 2 weeks.
Needs: Uses artists for brochures and magazines. Pays $10/hour.

MERCY CATHOLIC MEDICAL CENTER, Lansdowne Ave. and Baily Rd., Darby PA 19023. Public Relations Director: Robert L. Villier.
Needs: Works with 2-3 designers and 2-3 illustrators/year. Assigns 30 jobs/year. Uses artists for design of annual reports, brochures, direct mail pieces, programs, logos and letterheads.
First Contact & Terms: Query with resume or arrange interview to show portfolio. SASE. Reports in 3 weeks. Works on assignment only. Samples returned by SASE; reports back on future assignment possibilities. Provide resume, calling card and brochure to be kept on file for future assignments.

MIDDLESEX COUNTY ARTS COUNCIL, 37 Oakwood Ave., Edison NJ 08817. (201)549-4684. Director: Estelle Hasenberg.
Needs: Uses local artists for programs, posters and direct mail brochures.

NATIONAL-AMERICAN WHOLESALE GROCERS' ASSOCIATION (NAWGA), 51 Madison Ave., New York NY 10010. Editor: Ellen Lusk. Provides educational and representational services for members.
Needs: Works with 1 illustrator and 2 designers/year. Assigns 40 jobs/year. Uses artists for recruitment literature, publicity brochures, operations manuals, training guides, invitations, and educational meeting and convention announcements.
First Contact & Terms: Uses mostly local artists. Mail art, query with samples or call. SASE. Works on assignment only. Samples returned by SASE; reports back on future assignment possibilities. Proivde calling card, brochure, flyer and samples of work to be kept on file for future assignments. Pay varies for layout.

THE NATIONAL ASSOCIATION FOR CREATIVE CHILDREN & ADULTS, 8080 Springvalley Dr., Cincinnati OH 45236. Editor: Ann Isaacs.
Needs: Works with 1 artist/year for advertising design. Also uses artists for books and brochures.
First Contact & Terms: Write with samples. Samples returned by SASE. Reports back on future assignment possibilities. Provide calling card, brochure and/or tear sheet samples to be kept on file for future assignments. Reports in 3 months. Payment is in copies of publications.

NATIONAL ASSOCIATION OF PERSONNEL CONSULTANTS (formerly National Employment Association), 1012 14th St. NW, 15th Floor, Washington DC 20005. (202)138-1721. Contact: Nicholas Frabotta. Mail samples and fees. Buys one-time rights.
Needs: Uses artists for public information brochures, public service TV spots and trade show exhibits. Pays $30, TV spot graphics.

NATIONAL BICYCLE DEALERS ASSOCIATION INC., 435 N. Michigan Ave., Suite 1717, Chicago IL 60611. (312)644-0828. Executive Director: Glenn W. Bostrom.
Needs: Uses artists for membership recruitment literature, public information brochures, trade show exhibits and magazine graphics.
First Contact & Terms: Query. Pays $200-300/illustration on bicycle subjects.

NATIONAL BOWLING COUNCIL, 1919 Pennslyvania Ave. NW, Washington DC 20006. (202)659-9070. Director/Membership Services: Roland Schmitz. Trade association with 11 members to promote bowling.
Needs: Works with 3 artists/year for ad illustrations; 3 for ad design; 3 for product design and 3/year for product illustration. Also uses artists for brochures and slides.
First Contact & Terms: Greater DC area artists only. Write with samples. Works on assignment only. Samples returned by SASE. Provide calling card and tear sheet samples to be kept on file for future assignments. Pay depends on individual job.

NATIONAL COUNCIL ON ART IN JEWISH LIFE INC., 15 E. 84th St., New York NY 10028. (212)875-4500 or 833-1834. Executive Vice President: Julius Schatz. Provides education, exhibits and information.
Needs: Assigns 10-15 jobs/year. Uses artists for exhibits/displays, promotions and mailings.
First Contact & Terms: Mail art, or query with samples or previously used work. SASE. Reports in 2 weeks.

NATIONAL GALLERY OF ART DEPARTMENT OF EXTENSION PROGRAMS, National Gallery Plaza, Washington DC 20565. (202)737-4215. Curator: Ruth R. Perlin. Clients: Schools, museums and libraries.
Needs: Works with 3-4 designers/year. Uses artists for design of text brochures, programs, catalogs and posters.
First Contact & Terms: Local artists only. "Graphic designers must be on Government Services Administration schedule." Query with resume and samples (brochures, pamphlets, posters) and arrange interview to show portfolio. SASE. Works on assignment only. Samples returned by SASE; reports back on future assignment possibilities. Provide resume, calling card and brochure to be kept on file for future assignments.

NATIONAL INSTITUTE FOR AUTOMOTIVE SERVICE EXCELLENCE, 1825 K St. NW, Suite 515, Washington DC 20006. (202)833-9646. Contact: Barry McNulty.
Needs: Uses artists for magazine graphics, audiovisual materials, recruitment literature and public information brochures.
First Contact & Term: Call or write. Buys all rights. Minimum payment: $100, brochure design; $300, cartoon strip; $250, ad illustration line drawing.

NATIONAL MALE NURSE ASSOCIATION, 2309 State St., West Office, Saginaw MI 48602. (517)799-8208. Chairman: Dennis Martin. Promotes continuing education in nursing and encourages men to enter nursing as career.
Needs: Works with 74 illustrators and 20 designers/year. Uses artists for advertising, direct mail brochures, exhibits/displays, posters, publicity brochures and recruitment literature.
First Contact & Term: Local artists only. Mail art, or query with samples. SASE. Reports in 1 month. Provide resume and brochure to be kept on file for future assignments. Pays $30-200/job, design; $25-100/job, illustration; $10-20/hour, lettering; $75-200/job, layout; $200-550/job, production.

NATIONAL SCIENCE TEACHERS ASSOCIATION, 1742 Connecticut Ave. NW, Washington DC 20009. (202)265-4150.
Needs: Assigns 10-100 jobs/year. Uses artists for magazine illustration, direct mail brochures, design, illustration, lettering, layout and production, publicity brochures and recruitment literature.
First Contact & Terms: Query with samples, or arrange interview. SASE. Reports "as soon as possible."

PATIENTS' FAMILY SERVICES, INC., 8141 E. Outer Dr., Detroit MI 48213. (313)237-5810. Director: Fr. Russ Kohler. "We fund self employed artists to work for 15 weekly house calls to youth with cancer and long term illnesses."
Needs: Works with "artists as we need them upon referral of patients by physicians and medical social workers. We prefer artists who are shomewhat isolated in their medium and willing to enter the isolation of the child overly identified with his disease. Prefer a minimum of psychological and medical jargon; emphasis on the language of art and visual expression and experience."
First Contact & Terms: Write with resume to be kept on file for future assignments.

PARKWAY GENERAL HOSPITAL, 160 NW 170th St., North Miami Beach FL 33169. (305)651-1100. Contact: Saundra Atwood, public relations director. Estab. 1961. Assigns 15 jobs/year; local artists only. "Just call; I'm desperate for somebody in this area with some

creativity and imagination." Reports in 2 weeks.
Needs: Uses artists for design and illustration of brochures, campaigns, ads, newsletters, other publications and unusual projects. Negotiates pay.

PGA OF AMERICA, 804 Federal Highway, Lake Park 1 FL 33403. (305)844-5000. Advertising/Marketing Communications Manager: William A. Burbaum. Represents 13,000 golf club professionals and apprentices nationwide.
Needs: Works with 2 artists/year for ad illustrations and 2 for ad design; 3 for magazine illustrations. Artists "should know something about golf and golf tournaments." Interested in artistic essays for membership magazine and annual *Book of Golf*.
First Contact & Terms: Write with samples. Works on assignment most of the time. Samples returned by SASE. Reports back on future assignment possibilities. Provide tear sheet samples to be kept on file for future assignments. Reports in 2 weeks. Negotiates pay by prior agreement.

THE POLITICAL ACTION CAUCUS, 8314 Mary Ave. NW, Seattle WA 98117. (206)206-4688. Contact: Minister of Propaganda. Estab. 1977. "Militant anarcho-capitalist movement organized to abolish the state." Assigns 6 jobs/year. Query with samples. SASE. Reports in 1 month.
Needs: Maximum payment by job: $25, design; $15, illustration; $10, lettering; $35, layout. "Read *Romantic Manifesto* by Ayn Rand."

PONTIAC PUBLIC INFORMATION OFFICE, 450 Wide Track Dr. E., Pontiac MI 48058. (313)857-7777. Public Information Supervisor: Dean Hovey. Provides public relations for Pontiac. Assigns 1-10 jobs/year; local artists only. Query or arrange interview. Reports in 1 week.
Needs: Uses artists for charts, exhibits/displays and trademarks/logotypes. Especially needs thematic logo design for identity/promotion campaign. Pays $3-10/hour, production; $7-10/hour, design.

PORTLAND ADVENTIST MEDICAL CENTER, 10123 SE Market St., Portland OR 97216. (503)239-6162. Public Relations Director: Harold M. Wynne. Buys 6-8 illustrations/year.
Needs: Buys 8-10 illustrations/year. Publications include mostly staff-produced photographs and quality clipbook artwork augmented only rarely with illustrations produced by artists on assignment. Uses artists for medically-related advertising, annual reports, direct mail brochures, exhibits/displays, handbooks, posters, publicity brochures and medical staff recruitment literature. Typically pays $50-75/job, illustration; $250/job, on projects involving several illustrations and/or design and layout.
First Contact & Terms: Uses mostly local artists. Arrange interview.

PROVINCETOWN ART ASSOCIATION AND MUSEUM, 460 Commercial St., Provincetown MA 02657. (617)487-1750. Director: Annabelle Herbert.
Needs: Uses graphic artists for design and membership literature.
First Contact & Terms: Local artists only. Call and ask to speak with Annabelle Herbert (director), Ellen O'Donnell (assistant director).

J.K. RALSTON MUSEUM AND ART CENTER, Box 50, Sidney MT 59270. (406)482-3500. Art Director: Dave Torrence. Estab. 1972. Assigns 1 art job/year; local artists only. Query with resume. SASE. Reports in 6 weeks.
Needs: Uses artists for advertising, exhibits/displays, POP displays, posters, publicity brochures and trademarks/logos. Pays $2.30 min./hour or $25 max./job for design, illustration and lettering.

ROWAN COUNTY HISTORICAL SOCIETY, Rt. 6, Box 498, Morehead KY 40351. (606)784-9145. President: Lloyd Dean. "A society that studies the history of Rowan County and Morehead and collects, pictures, prints, histories, diaries and items of historical interest."
Needs: "We might need artists to draw pictures of historical places in Rowan County and Morehead."
First Contact & Terms: Query by mail or write with resume. SASE. Provide calling card, brochure and flyer to be kept on file for future assignments. Reports in 4-5 weeks.

SAN BERNARDINO COUNTY REGIONAL PARKS DEPARTMENT, 157 W. 5th St., 3rd Floor, San Bernardino CA 92415. (714)383-1912. Program Coordinator: Don V. Tucker. Estab. 1966. Promotes recreation and special programs in 10 regional parks. Assigns 20 plus jobs/year; local artists only. Query with samples or arrange interview. SASE. Reports in 2 weeks.
Needs: Uses artists for advertising, annual reports, direct mail brochures, posters and publicity brochures. Negotiates pay for design, illustration and lettering.

SANE INC., 514 C. St., Washington DC 20002. Executive Director: D. Cortright. Lobbying and educational organization created to reverse the arms race.
Needs: Buys 5-10 illustrations/year. Uses artists for flyers and other publications.
First Contact & Term: Query with samples. SASE. Reports in 2 weeks. Negotiates payment.

SWEDISH HOSPITAL MEDICAL CENTER, 747 Summit Ave., Seattle WA 98104. (206)292-2039. Public Relations Director: Dee Jones.
Needs: Works with 2 illustrators and 6 designers/year. Uses artists for brochures, reports and posters.
First Contact & Terms: Query with photocopies. SASE. Contacts artists as needs arise. Works on assignment only. Samples returned by SASE. Provide flyer to be kept on file for future assignments. Negotiates pay.

UNITED AUTO WORKERS, 8000 E. Jefferson, Detroit MI 48214. (313)926-5291. Managing Editor: David Elsila. "1.5 million member trade union representing US and Canadian workers in auto, aerospace, agricultural-implement and other industries."
Needs: Works with 4-6 artists/year for ad illustrations and 4-6 for ad design. Also uses artists for posters and magazine illustrations. Interested in graphic designs of publications, topical art for magazine covers with liberal-labor political slant.
First Contact & Terms: Prefers Detroit area artists. Query by mail, write with resume or samples. Provide resume, flyer and/or tear sheet samples to be kept on file for future assignments. Pays $75/small b&w spot illustration; $300+/designing small pamphlet. Payment for product design and illustration determined by size of project.

U.S. DEPARTMENT OF LABOR, Division of Audio-Visual Communication, Rm N6309, 200 Constitution Ave. NW, Washington DC 20210. Contact: Lionel F. White.
Needs: Works with 10 illustrators and 12 designers/year. Uses artists for information booklet design, illustrations, slides and other audiovisual materials, documentary films and displays.
First Contact & Term: Query. Provide resume to be kept on file for future assignments.

UNITED HOSPITALS AND ST. PAUL CHILDREN'S HOSPITAL, 345 N. Smith Ave., St. Paul MN 55102. (612)298-8666. Public Relations Director: George Ryan.
Needs: Works with 3 illustrators and designers/year. Uses artists for brochure and newsletter design, programs and general publications artwork.
First Contact & Terms: Local artists only. Query with resume. SASE. Reports in 2 weeks. Works on assignment only. Samples returned by SASE. Provides resume and calling card to be kept on file for future assignments. Pays by hour.

UNITED STATES SKI ASSOCIATION/EASTERN DIVISION, 22 High St., Brattleboro VT 05301. (802)254-6077. Media Coordinator: Mike Brophy. Estab. 1922. National amateur skiing organization which serves over 100,000 skiers' recreational and competitive needs. Assigns 30-40 jobs/year. Query with samples. SASE. Reports in 1 week.
Needs: Uses artists for advertising, magazines, newsletters, direct mail brochures, posters and publicity brochures. Buys mostly poster and brochure illustrations. Pays $15-100/job, illustration.

UNIVERSITY OF TENNESSEE CENTER FOR THE HEALTH SCIENCES, 1924 Alcoa Hwy., Knoxville TN 37920. (615)971-3535. Contact: Frank Limpus, public information director. Estab. 1956. Combined hospital, research center and medical school. Buys 20 illustrations/year; local artists only. Query with resume and samples. SASE. Reports in 3-4 weeks.
Needs: Uses artists for illustration of annual reports, internal publications, pamphlets, brochures and ads. Negotiates pay.

WISCONSIN INDIANHEAD VTAE DISTRICT, Box B, Shell Lake WI 54871. (715)468-2815. Public Relations Officer: James D. Bailey. An 11-county vocational, technical and adult education (VTAE) district with 4 technical institutes which develops programs to help its residents upgrade general living and work skills.
Needs: Works with 3-5 illustrators/year. Needs are seasonal: fall, winter, spring. Uses illustrators for advertising, annual reports, direct mail brochures, handbooks, posters, publicity brochures, recruitment literature, report covers and newsletters.
First Contact & Terms: Query with samples. SASE. Works on assignment only. Provide materials

---

to be kept on file for future assignments. Payment by job: $25-300, design, illustration, lettering, layout and production.

ZOOLOGICAL SOCIETY OF SAN DIEGO, Box 551, San Diego CA 92112. (714)231-1515.
Needs: Works with 1-2 illustrators and designers/year. Uses local artists only for publications.
First Contact & Terms: Query. SASE. Reports in 3-4 weeks. Provide calling card to be kept on file for future assignments. Negotiates pay.

Educational

ADELPHI UNIVERSITY, Garden City NY 11530. Director, University Relations: Ron Cannava.
Needs: Assigns 66-512 jobs/year. Uses artists for ads, annual reports, catalogs, magazines, newsletters, charts, brochures, exhibits, displays, handbooks, posters, recruitment literature and logos.
First Contact & Terms: Local artists only. Query with resume and sample. SASE. Reports in 1 month. Pays $100 maximum, illustration; $50, spot drawing; $200, ad layout.

BELOIT COLLEGE, Beloit WI 53511. (608)365-3391. Director/Information Services: Don Johnson.
Needs: Uses artists for illustrations for college magazine, brochures and mailers. Buys approximately 12 illustrations/year.
First Contact & Terms: Query with samples. SASE. Reports in 3 weeks. Pays $25/job.

BETHANY BIBLE COLLEGE, 800 Bethany Dr., Santa Cruz CA 95066. (408)438-3800. Director of College Relations: Wally Bennett. Estab. 1919. Coed Bible college affiliated with Assemblies of God. Assigns 15-30 jobs/year. Query with resume or arrange interview. SASE. Reports in 1 month.
Needs: Uses artists for advertising, catalogs, direct mail brochures, exhibits/displays, handbooks, posters, publicity brochures and recruitment literature. "We like to do business with Christian artists. Things that are acceptable even in a family newspaper are not necessarily acceptable in a conservative constituency such as the Assemblies of God." Pays $5-15/hour, design, illustration and layout.

BROWARD COMMUNITY COLLEGE, 225 E. Las Olas Blvd., Ft. Lauderdale FL 33301. (305)467-6700, ext. 250. Director of Cultural Affairs: Dr. Ellen Chandler. Assigns 2 jobs/year.
Needs: Works with 1 illustrator and 1 designer/year. Seasonal illustration needs during concert season: October-March. Uses artists for exhibits/displays.
First Contact & Terms: Mostly local artists. Query with samples (photographs) or call for interview. SASE. Reports in 1 month. Works on assignment only. Samples returned by SASE. Pay varies.

CALIFORNIA BAPTIST COLLEGE, 8432 Magnolia Ave., Riverside CA 92504. (714)689-5771. News Bureau Director: Carmen Sandoval Garcia. Estab. 1950. Assigns 3-5 jobs/year; local artists only. Query with samples. SASE. Reports in 3 weeks.
Needs: Uses artists for annual reports, catalog covers/layouts, direct mail/publicity brochures, displays, newspaper ad layouts, lettering, recruitment literature and company publications. Pays by hour.

CALIFORNIA INSTITUTE OF TECHNOLOGY, Ramo Auditorium, Office of Public Events (332-92), Pasadena CA 91125. Contact: Joe Farmer. Query with resume.
Needs: Buys designs for brochures from October-June. Art should be 10x14. Pays $10 min./hour.

THE CATHOLIC UNIVERSITY OF AMERICA, Office of Public Relations, Washington DC 20064. (202)635-5600. Editor: Peggy Spear. Estab. 1887. Founded as graduate school; 9 professional schools. Query with samples, particularly line art, or arrange interview. SASE. Reports in 1 week.
Needs: Uses artists for catalog covers/layouts, direct mail/publicity brochures, recruitment literature, student handbooks and college publications. Pays $25, illustrations; $10-15/page, tabloid layout and design.
To Break In: "Get a staff job in a publications office – become familiar with all stages in the development of a publication from initial planning through story development, layout and printing. Learn to expedite the production process."

CHAMPLAIN COLLEGE, 232 S. Willard St., Burlington VT 05401. (802)658-0800. Editor: Steve Harris. Estab. 1878. Private junior college. Query; local artists only. SASE. Reports in 3 weeks.

Needs: Uses artists for posters, publicity brochures and magazine. Recently assigned artist to illustrate article about one of the last rides on the Orient Express in Europe.

COLUMBIA COLLEGE, 10th and Rogers, Columbia MO 65201. (314)442-4921. Public Relations Director: Stan Dawgert. Estab. 1851. Assigns 20 jobs/year. Query with samples or arrange interview. SASE. Reports in 1 week.
Needs: Uses artists for advertising, annual reports, catalogs, direct mail brochures, exhibits/displays, handbooks, posters, publicity brochures and recruitment literature.

DREXEL UNIVERSITY, Dept. of Publications and Communications, 32nd and Chestnut Sts., Philadelphia PA 19104. (215)895-2613. Director: Philip Terranova. Assigns 20 jobs and buys 10 illustrations/year.
First Contact & Terms: Query with samples (b&w tearsheets; no slides) or arrange interview. SASE. Reports in 1 week. Provide resume, calling card and tearsheet to be kept on file for future assignments.
Needs: Works with 3 illustrators and 6 designers/year. Seasonal needs: September-June. Uses designers for pamphlets and posters; illustrators for covers, spot art, etc. Also uses artists for advertising, annual reports, charts, direct mail brochures, exhibits/displays, handbooks, publicity, recruitment literature, magazines, newsletters and trademarks/logos.

D'YOUVILLE COLLEGE, 320 Porter Ave., Buffalo NY 14201. Director of Information Services: Mary Ellen Telford.
Needs: Uses artists for posters and admissions department publications. Alumni department also uses artists.

EAST TEXAS BAPTIST COLLEGE, 1209 N. Grove, Marshall TX 75670. (214)938-7738. Public Relations Director: Vicki L. Dortch. Assigns 10-15 jobs/year.
Needs: Works with 1 illustrator and 4 designers/year. Uses artists for print advertising, catalogs, exhibits/displays, handbooks, publicity brochures, recruitment literature, and birthday/Christmas card designs.
First Contact & Terms: Query with previously used work, or arrange interview. SASE. Reports in 3 weeks. Works on assignment only. Samples returned by SASE; and reports back on future possibilities. Provide resume, calling card, brochure and samples (photocopied if possible) to be kept on file for future assignments. Pays $10-20/hour, design and layout; $50 min./job, illustration.

EMPIRE STATE COLLEGE, State University of New York, 2 Union Ave., Saratoga Springs NY 12866. (518)587-2100. Public Relations Director: Wesley Winn. Alternative institution without a campus. "The college operates through 33 locations around the state; there are no classes or courses; study is done independently."
Needs: Works with 4 illustrators and 4 designers/year. Uses artists for advertising, annual reports, catalogs, charts, direct mail brochures, exhibits/displays, handbooks, posters, publicity brochures, recruitment literature.
First Contact & Terms: Prefers local professionals. Reports in 2 weeks. Provide resume, brochure and flyer to be kept on file for future assignments. Pays $7.50 min./hour, design, illustration and lettering.

HANOVER COLLEGE, Office of Public Relations, Hanover IN 47243. (812)866-2151. Public Relations Director: David R. Langlais.
Needs: Assigns 5-10 jobs/year. Uses artists for logos, magazine and journal ads, brochure design, programs and etchings of buildings.
First Contact & Terms: Arrange interview to show portfolio. Reports in 3-4 weeks. Pays $40-50/etching.

HOME LEARNING CENTER, 605 Crapo St., Flint MI 48503. (313)762-1198. Coordinator: Michael Kelly. Estab. 1977. Provides adult and community education. Assigns 15 jobs/year. Query with previously used work. SASE. Reports in 2 weeks.
Needs: Uses artists for posters, brochures and newsletters.

HUNTINGDON COLLEGE, 1500 E. Fairview Ave., Montgomery AL 36106. Director of Public Relations: Mike Jones.
Needs: Works with 1 illustrator and 1 designer/month. Uses artists for catalogs, charts, publicity brochures and recruitment literature.
First Contact & Terms: Local artists only. Query with samples (catalog covers, etc.) or previously used work, or arrange interview. SASE. Reports in 1 month. Works on assignment only. Samples

returned by SASE; and reports back on future possibilities. No file kept on artists. Pays $25, design, layout and finished art.

JEFFERSON PARISH LIBRARY, Box 7490, Metairie LA 70010. (504)834-5850. Librarian: Maurice D. Walsh, Jr.
Needs: Works with 1 illustrator/year. Uses artist for posters.
First Contact & Terms: Query with resume. SASE. Reports in 2 weeks. Payment varies.

KNOX COLLEGE, Office of Public Information, Campus Box 160, Galesburg IL 61401. (309)343-0112. Publications Manager/Editor: James Rybels.
Needs: Works with 1-2 illustrators/year. Uses artists for direct mail brochure design.
First Contact & Terms: Query with samples. SASE. Reports in 2 weeks. Works on assignment only. Samples returned by SASE; and reports back on future possibilities. Provide brochure to be kept on file for future assignments. Negotiates pay.

LAFAYETTE COLLEGE, Publications Office, Easton PA 18042. Contact: R.A. Morrison, publications editor.
Needs: Works with 4 illustrators and 4 designers/year. Uses artists for cover art, illustrations, layout and design of college publications, posters, primarily recruitment and fundraising literature.
First Contact & Terms: Query with samples (college fundraising and student recruitment literature). Reports in 2-3 weeks. Works on assignment only. Samples returned by SASE; and reports back on future possibilities. Provide brochure and flyer to be kept on file for future assignments. Pays $100-700.

LAMAR UNIVERSITY, Box 10546, Beaumont TX 77710. (713)838-7612. Vice President, University Relations: W.S. Leonard. Estab. 1923. Assigns 40-60 jobs/year; local artists only. Query with samples. SASE. Reports in 2-4 weeks.
Needs: Uses artists for advertising, annual reports, catalogs, direct mail brochures, exhibits/displays, handbooks, posters, publicity brochures and recruitment literature. Pays $15 min./hour, design and illustration.

LANE COLLEGE, 545 Lane Ave., Jackson TN 38301. (901)424-4600, ext. 235. Public Relations Director: Mabel C. Clay. Predominantly black church-affiliated institution.
Needs: Assigns 5-10 jobs/year. Uses artists for advertising, exhibits/displays, publicity brochures, recruitment literature and trademarks/logos.
First Contact & Terms: Local artists only. Mail art, or query with samples. SASE. Reports in 2 weeks. Provide resume, calling card and brochure to be kept on file for future assignments. Payment by job: $10-75, design; $30-80, illustration; $40-100, layout; $40-80, production.

LE MOYNE COLLEGE, Le Moyne Heights, Syracuse NY 13214. (315)446-2882. Undergraduate liberal arts college.
Needs: Works with 2 illustrators and 4 designers/year. Uses artists for catalog covers, lettering, publicity brochures, student handbooks and college publications.
First Contact & Terms: Query with samples. SASE. Reports in 4 weeks. Provide resume, brochure and flyer to be kept on file for future assignments. Pays $25, cover art; $15, line drawings.

LONG BEACH STATE UNIVERSITY SPORTS INFORMATION BUREAU, 1250 Bellflower Blvd., Long Beach CA 90840. (213)498-4667. Sports Information Director: Terry Ross. Emphasizes sports publicity and publications for the men's and women's sports programs at Long Beach University.
Needs: Uses 2 local artists/year for product illustrations. "We don't have a huge art budget and we like them to be local."
First Contact & Terms: Write with samples. Provide calling card, brochure and tear sheets to be kept on file for future assignments. Works on assignment only. Samples returned by SASE. Reports back on future assignment possibilities.. Interest in sports drawings involving people. Pays $50 for cover design. Product design and illustration is negotiated with artist. Contact T. Ross for information regarding 1 year internship program.

MUNCIE PUBLIC LIBRARY, 301 E. Jackson St., Muncie IN 47305. Audiovisual Librarian and Director of Displays: Patricia Schaefer.
Needs: Uses local artists for posters and has collection of art reproductions and sculpture.

NASSON COLLEGE, Springvale ME 04083. (207)324-5340. Director of College Relations: Evelyne Neill. Assigns 4-5 jobs/year.
Needs: Uses artists for catalogs, direct mail brochures and recruitment literature.

First Contact & Terms: Query with samples for files, or arrange interview. Reports in 1 week. Pays $25-350/job, design; $25-100/job, illustration.

PACE UNIVERSITY, PLEASANTVILLE, (formerly The College of White Plains of Pace University) Bedford Rd., Pleasantville NY 10570. Assistant in University and Community Relations: Jean Marie Compe.
Needs: Works with 5 illustrators and 2 designers/year. Uses artists for advertising, catalogs, handbooks, posters, publicity brochures, recruitment literature and trademarks/logos.
First Contact & Terms: Mail art, query with samples or arrange interview. SASE. Reports in 2 weeks. Works on assignment only. Samples returned by SASE; and reports back on future possibilities. Provide resume, brochure, flyer, catalogs, handbooks and posters to be kept on file for future assignments. Pays $25/illustration.

FRANKLIN PIERCE COLLEGE, College Relations Office, Rindge NH 03461. Director/College Relations: Thomas C. Murphy. Local artists only.
Needs: Assigns 3 jobs/year. Works with 3 illustrators and 1 designer/year. Uses artists for cover illustrations for brochures and fundraising mailers, occasionally for brochure design.
First Contact & Terms: Query with previously published work. SASE. Reports in 3 weeks. Works on assignment only. Samples returned by SASE; and reports back on future possibilities. Provide resume and calling card to be kept on file for future assignments. Pays $100, design; $10+, sketch.

QUINIPIAC COLLEGE, Mt. Carmel Ave., Hamden CT 06518. Contact: Publications Manager.
Needs: Works with 2 designers/year; August-October and February-April only. Uses artists for program brochures, publications, catalog and viewbook design.
First Contact & Terms: Arrange interview. Works on assignment only. Samples returned by SASE. Provide resume, brochure and flyer to be kept on file for future assignments.

ROCKFORD COLLEGE, 5050 E. State St., Rockford IL 61101. (815)226-4149. Sports Information Director: Walter H. Wells, Jr. Query with resume and printed samples or call. Uses artists for direct mail brochures and posters related to campus sports activities.

ST. AUGUSTINE'S COLLEGE, Oakwood Ave., Raleigh NC 27611. Vice President/Development and Public Relations: Purdie Anders. Coed Episcopal school. Uses local artists for direct mail brochures, annual reports and posters.

ST. LAWRENCE UNIVERSITY, Canton NY 13617. Assistant Director of Public Relations: Neal S. Burdick.
Needs: Works with 1-2 illustrators and 1-2 designers/year. Uses artists for brochures and mailers.
First Contact & Terms: Local artists only. Send printed samples. Provide calling card to be kept on file for future assignments.

SAINT MARY'S COLLEGE, 109 Le Mans Hall, Notre Dame IN 46556. (219)284-4245. Contact: Richard Wilson, director/publications. Estab. 1844. Women's liberal arts school. Assigns 10-15 jobs and buys 30-50 illustrations/year. Query with previously published work, then arrange interview to show portfolio. SASE. Reports in 1-2 weeks.
Needs: Uses artists for illustrations for quarterly alumnae magazine, brochures, programs, annual report, newspaper ads and posters. Negotiates pay.

ST. VINCENT COLLEGE, Latrobe PA 15650. (412)539-9761. Director/Publications and Publicity: Don Orlando.
Needs: Assigns 25 jobs/year. Uses artists for advertising, annual reports, direct mail brochures, exhibits, flyers, graphics, posters and programs.
First Contact & Terms: Query with samples. SASE. Reports in 1 month. Pays $10 min./hour, design, illustration and layout.

SIENA COLLEGE, McGuire Hall, Loudonville NY 12211. Public Relations Director: Joseph P. Orzechowski. "We rely on freelance graphic artists exclusively. Last year we produced 90 college publications and 141 other jobs." Send samples or arrange interview; New York artists only.
Needs: Uses artists for direct mail brochures, alumni magazines/reports, billboards, airport displays, posters, admissions brochures and capital fund major publications. Pays $30/hour.

SOUTHEASTERN UNIVERSITY, 501 Eye St. SW, Washington DC 20024. (202)488-8162. Public Relations Director: Mary Ann Guyol.
First Contact & Terms: Local artists only. Query with samples. SASE. Reports in 1 week. Pays $8-25/hour for design, illustration, lettering, layout and production.
Needs: Works with 3 illustrators and 3 designers/year. Uses artists for advertising, direct mail brochures, posters and publicity brochures.

UNION OF INDEPENDENT COLLEGES OF ART, 4340 Oak St., Kansas City MO 64111. (816)753-6654. Executive Director: Dean Tollefson. Consortium of 9 visual arts colleges which promotes cooperative educational endeavors and provides information about the visual arts.
First Contact & Terms: Query. SASE. Reports in 1 day.
Needs: Works with 1 illustrator and 2 designers/year. Seasonal needs: fall. Uses designers for publication work.

U.S. MERCHANT MARINE ACADEMY, Steamboat Rd., Kings Point NY 11024. Public Relations Director: Martin Skrocki.
Needs: Works with 1 illustrator and 1 designer/year. Uses artists for direct mail brochures and publications. Alumni officer also uses artists; contact Frank Sinnott.
First Contact & Terms: Works on assignment only. No samples returned. Reports back on future assignment possibilities. Provide calling card and flyer to be kept on file for future assignments.

UNIVERSITY OF NEW HAVEN, West Haven CT 06516. (203)934-6321. Public Relations Director: Scott W. Tilden.
Needs: Works with 3-4 illustrators (but would like more) and 5 designers (for several jobs)/year. Uses artists for advertising, catalogs, magazines, newsletters, direct mail brochures, exhibits/displays, handbooks, publicity brochures and recruitment literature.
First Contact & Terms: Query with samples (brochures and other publications, especially those for educational or service organizations; cover designs; illustrations). SASE. Works on assignment only. No samples returned. Reports back on future assignment possibilities. Provide resume, calling card and samples of work to be kept on file for future assignments. Pays $25 min./job for design, illustration and layout; $2 min./word for lettering.

UNIVERSITY OF NORTHERN IOWA, Cedar Falls IA 50613. (319)273-2761. Director, University Publications: Susan Chilcott.
Needs: Works with 3-4 illustrators/year. Uses illustrators for annual reports, catalogs, direct mail brochures, posters, recruitment literature and internal publications such as student handbooks and activity calendars. Especially needs those good at "people" portrayal, collage, interpreting abstract ideas. Need both line and water color washes.
First Contact & Terms: Uses mostly local illustrators. Query with samples. SASE. Reports in 2 weeks. Works on assignment only. Samples returned by SASE; and reports back on future possibilities. Provide freelance illustration. Pays $150 minimum/job for illustration; $8 min./hour for keyline paste-up.

UNIVERSITY OF WISCONSIN-EXTENSION CENTER FOR CONSUMER AFFAIRS, 929 N. 6th St., Milwaukee WI 53203. (414)224-4177. Information Specialists: Kit McNally.
Needs: Works with 1-2 illustrators/year. Assigns 15 jobs/year. Uses artists for exhibits/displays, newsletters and publicity brochures.
First Contact & Terms: Local artists only. Query with samples. SASE. Reports in 2 weeks. Works on assignment only. Samples returned by SASE; and reports back on future possibilities. Provide brochure and flyer to be kept on file for future assignments. Pays $3.50-10, illustration.

UNIVERSITY OF WISCONSIN-WHITEWATER, 800 W. Main St., Whitewater WI 53190. University Relations Director: W.E. Zastrow. Uses local artists for direct mail brochures and alumni magazine.

WAYLAND ACADEMY, Beaver Dam WI 53916. (414)885-3373. Assigns up to 50 jobs/year; local artists only. Query with samples. SASE. Reports in 1-2 weeks. Buys all rights.
Needs: Uses artists for annual reports, catalog covers/layouts, direct mail/publicity brochures, displays, posters, recruitment literature, student handbooks, trademarks, logos and newspaper ad layouts. Pays $10-20/hour.

WEBER STATE COLLEGE, College Relations Office, 3750 Harrison Blvd., Ogden UT 84408. (801)626-6569. Publications Director: Mrs. Edie Hester. Offers liberal arts and vocational education.
Needs: Works with 2-3 illustrators and 3-4 designers/year. Uses artists for spot illustrations for booklets, reports and brochures; design and layout for brochures; and layout, design or illustration for programs.
First Contact & Terms: Query with resume, samples, fees and phone number "where you can be reached during business hours." Reports in 4-6 weeks. Works on assignment only. Samples returned by SASE; and reports back on future possibilities. Provide resume and sample of printed work to be kept on file for future assignments. Pays $50 min./job.

Book Publishers

Freelance art needs in the book publishing industry are increasing as firms reduce the size of their art staffs as a way to cut costs.

To help you get a feel for the amount of freelance help used, each listing in this section includes a line that tells: 1) the number of titles published each year; 2) the number of those titles that require the use of freelance designers; and 3) the number of books that require the work of freelance illustrators.

The specific types of work sought are found under subheads—which in themselves give an idea of what publishers need. These headings are Book Design, Jackets/Covers, Text Illustrations, Advertising and Production. Under each subhead is information on the type of art wanted, plus sample payments.

The nitty-gritty of how a book publisher should first be contacted is found under the First Contact & Terms subhead. Since most freelance work in publishing is assigned, you must first make the publisher aware of your talents. It's best—usually—to send a letter with samples or a request for an interview.

Some buyers may specify they work only with artists within commuting distance. That's bad news for freelancers who find a market appealing, but geographically off-limits. But, for many artists who are located outside major publishing centers, there are alternatives to in-person interviews if the publisher is open to working through the mail. One such option is to have a portfolio that can be mailed and to arrange phone interviews. But *only* send a portfolio *after* this alternative has been approved by the publisher.

In addition to specifying the method of first contact the book publisher prefers, the listings include information on the materials the publisher prefers to have in his file to refer to for future assignments. You'll find that most publishers like to receive a resume and perhaps a few samples and/or tearsheets for their files. In any case, the materials you send should be of a size that will be manageable in a file.

Other information you'll find in the listings in this section of *Artist's Market* includes the rights purchased, whether or not your original artwork is returned after the job is complete, and whether it is the artist's responsibility to supply color overlays for artwork. (Generally a publisher who buys all rights does not return the original artwork.)

Once you have contacted a publishing house, don't despair if you don't get a response immediately. Since most work is assigned, few art directors will report back unless they have a specific assignment for you. If after a couple of months you still don't hear from the publishing house, write again to express interest in a job and to keep your name current in their files.

Further reading in the publishing field should include *Publishers Weekly* (R.R. Bowker Co.) and *Literary Marketplace* (R.R. Bowker Co.).

A.D. BOOK CO., 10 E. 39th St., New York NY 10016. (212)354-0450. Art Director: Debra Schein. Publishes hardcover, and paperback originals on advertising design and photography. Publishes 12-15 titles/year; 4-5 of which require designers, 1-2 uses illustrators.

First Contact & Terms: Send letter of inquiry and arrange to show portfolio (4-10 tear sheets). Samples returned by SASE. Provide letter of inquiry to be kept on file for future assignments. Buys first rights. Originals returned to artist at job's completion. Free catalog.

Advertising Design: Must be contemporary. Pays $500 minimum/book design.

Jackets/Covers: Pays $200 minimum.

ACCENT BOOKS, Box 15337, Denver CO 80215. (303)988-5300. Art Director: Don Reiter. Publishes paperback originals on religious education ("such as songs, puppets, games, etc."), children's and general. Publishes 15 titles/year.

First Contact & Terms: Query with resume and samples. SASE. Reports in 4 weeks. Free artist's guidelines. Works on assignment only. Samples returned by SASE. Provide resume, brochures, flyers and samples of work that are put through copier on finished color art; artist must supply overlays to be kept on file for future assignments.
Jackets/Covers: Assigns 15 jobs/year. Pays $30, color comp; $180-380, finished color; $30-75, b&w line drawings and gray opaques.
Text Illustrations: Buys 200/year. Pays $30-75, b&w line drawings and gray opaques; $75 minimum, color washes and opaque watercolors.

ACROPOLIS BOOKS LTD., 2400 17th St. NW, Washington DC 20009. Production Manager: Lloyd Greene. Publishes how-to, self help, educational, political and Americana.
First Contact & Terms: Local artists only. Query with information on your background and specialities.
General Needs: Uses artists for jacket design and illustration and advertising layouts.

ADDISON-WESLEY, Reading MA 01867. Contact: Joseph F. Weiler. Publishes adult and juvenile trade books.
First Contact & Terms: Send tearsheets; photocopies or transparencies. Buys all rights. Original returned to artist at job's completion. Works on assignment only. No samples returned. Reports back on future assignment possibilities. Provide resume, business card and tear sheet to be kept on file for future assignments. Check for most recent titles in bookstores. Artist supplies overlays for cover artwork and inside illustrations.
Jackets/Covers: Pays $300-600.
Text Illustrations: Uses experienced artists for juvenile and adult trade art. "Most juvenile books are one color; some two-color, line or halftone art." Pays by contract or royalties for juvenile art.
Book Design: Pays $300-1200.

AERO PUBLISHERS INC., 329 W. Aviation Rd., Fallbrook CA 92028. (714)728-8456. Contact: E.J. Gentle, president, for editorial work; Tom Bowen, vice president/sales, for advertising work. Publishes hardcover and paperback originals on aviation and space. Produces 12-15 titles/year.
First Contact & Terms: Arrange interview to show portfolio. Samples should include "four-color creative art centering around aviation subjects." All work on assignment only. Provide resume, business card, inquiry letter and/or brochure to be kept on file for future assignments. Samples returned by SASE. Reports back to artist on future assignment possibilities. Reports in 3-4 weeks. Buys all rights; keeps originals. Artist should supply overlays for cover artwork (but not necessary). Free catalog.
Jackets/Covers: Assigns 3-5 jobs/year. Arts should pertain to aviation subjects. Pays $100-500. 4-color finished art.

ALBION PUBLISHING CO., 1736 Stockton St., San Francisco CA 94133. Publishes college textbooks. Query.
Needs: Uses artists for jacket designs and inside illustrations.

ALLYN AND BACON INC., College Division, 470 Atlantic Ave., Boston MA 02210. (617)482-9220. Cover Supervisor: Christy Rosso. Production Manager: Nancy Murphy. Publishes hardcover and paperback textbooks.
First Contact & Terms: Query.
Jackets/Covers: Pays $300-500, 2-color.
Text Illustrations: Pays $20 minimum, b&w.

ALLYN AND BACON INC., ELHI Division, 470 Atlantic Ave., Boston MA 02210. (617)482-9220. Design Director: Barry Wiedenkeller. Publishes hardcover and paperback educational text originals. Publishes 160-180 titles/year.
First Contact & Terms: Arrange interview. No advance. Provides tearsheets to be kept on file for future assignments. Buys all rights. Pays flat fee.
Text Illustrations: Buys b&w and full-color work.

ALLYN AND BACON INC., Longwood Division, 470 Atlantic Ave., Boston MA 02210. (617)482-9220. Design Director: Paula Carroll. Publishes hardcover and paperback professional books and college textbooks.
First Contact & Terms: Query. Provide business card and tear sheet to be kept on file for future assignments. Buys world rights. No originals returned to artist at job's completion. Artists must supply overlays for color inside illustrations.

Jackets/Covers: Uses artists for type only. Pays $200-300, 2-color.
Text Illustrations: Uses artists for technical illustrations. Pays $15-75, b&w.
Cartoons: Occasionally uses cartoonists. "Cartoons in our books have usually been supplied by the authors—they are apt to need revision. In other words, the cartoonist would be working with someone else's ideas."

AND/OR PRESS, INC., 909 Parker St., Berkeley CA 94710. Art Director: Carlene Schnabel. Publishes paperback originals on health and nutrition, travel, drugs and the mind futurism. Publishes 10 titles/year; local artists only.
First Contact & Terms: Query with samples; "not more than 20 works. Be sure to send nonreturnable, good quality photocopies of a range of subject matter and styles so we can see your capabilities and interests. Follow with a phone call one or two weeks after mailing." Buys first and reprint rights. Works on assignment only. No samples returned. Reports back on future assignment possibilities. Provide business card, brochure, flyer and "photocopies of line drawings showing the range of your style and technique" to be kept on file for future assignments. Check for most recent titles in bookstores. Artist sometimes supplies overlays for cover artwork.
Jackets/Covers: Assigns 6-8/year. Pays $250-950, airbrush, color washes, opaque watercolors, oils or acrylics. Offers advance.
Text Illustrations: Assigns 7-10 books/year (10-50 illustrations/book). Needs b&w line drawings. Negotiates pay. Offers advance.
Book Design: Assigns 3-6 jobs/year. Uses artists for layout. Negotiates pay.f4Production: Assigns 7-8 jobs/year. Pays $6.50 min./hour, paste-up.

ANDREWS AND McMEEL INC., 6700 Squibb Rd., Mission KS 66202. Contact: Tom Thornton. Publishes nonfiction books. Query with samples.
Needs: Uses artists for jackets, inside illustrations, advertising layouts and promotional brochures. Pays $150, jacket; $130, advertising layouts.

ANTHELION PRESS, Box 614, Corte Madera CA 94925. (415)924-5311. Editorial Director: William Whitney. Art Director: Chris Matthews. Estab. 1971. Publishes hardcover and paperback nonfiction originals. Publishes 30 titles/year. Query with resume. SASE. Reports in 4 weeks. Pays 2-5% royalty or flat fee. No advance. Pays 50% promised fee for unused assigned work. Buys all rights. Free catalog.
Book Design: Buys 6-8/year. Pays $3-10/hour, layout.
Jackets/Covers: Buys 8-12/year; line drawings, washes and color-separated work. Pays $25-200, b&w; $50-250, color.
Production: Assigns 10-12 jobs/year. Pays $10-50/job, color-separation and mechanicals.

ANTONSON PUBLISHING LTD., 12165 97th Ave., Surrey, B.C., Canada V3V 2C8. Editorial Director: Rick Atonson. Estab. 1973. Publishes Canadian outdoor and historical books; hardcover and paperback originals. Publishes 4-7 titles/year. Query with resume. SASE. Reports in 2 weeks. No advance. Pays promised fee for unused assigned work. Buys all rights. Free catalog.
Book Design: Assigns 6/year. Pays $10-15/hour, layout.
Jackets/Covers: Buys 3-4/year; b&w line drawings and washes, color washes and color-separated work. Minimum payment: $100, b&w; $200, color.
Text Illustrations: Buys 2-3 books/year; b&w line drawings. Pays $150+ maximum, book.
Advertising: Assigns 2 jobs/year. Pays $10/hour.

ARCO PUBLISHING INC., 219 Park Ave. S., New York NY 10003. Editorial Director: David Goodnough. Art Director: Wolfgang H. Reimann. Publishes hardcover and paperback trade and reference originals and reprints.
First Contact & Terms: Will keep on file submitted art samples. Will return samples submitted when required if return postage is provided. Provide resume to be kept on file for future assignments. On finished art, artist must supply overlays.
General Needs: Published 325 titles in 1979; will publish 340 in 1980. "We request that our authors supply all needed art work or photographs, and rarely use freelance illustrative materials."

ARES PUBLISHERS INC., 612 N. Michigan Ave., Suite 216, Chicago IL 60611. (312)642-7850. Vice President: A. Barozzi. Publishes ancient history, archaeology, history of ancient art, classics, Byzantium, Mediterranean studies and research books.
First Contact & Terms: Query.
General Needs: Uses artists for jacket design, inside illustrations, direct mail brochures, advertising, layouts, maps and plans of archaeological sites.

ARTISTS & WRITERS PUBLICATIONS, Drawer 668, San Rafael CA 94902. (415)456-1213. Publisher: Owen S. Haddock. Publishes "premium and gourmet consumer demand" books. Query with photocopies or transparencies. SASE.
Needs: Uses artists for jacket design, inside illustrations, direct mail brochures and advertising layout/art.

ART'S INC., 32 E. 58th St., New York NY 10022. Contact: B. Vanos.
First Contact & Terms: Local artists preferred. Query with minimum fee. Provide resume to be kept on file for future assignments. No originals returned to artist at job's completion. Artists supply overlays on all color art. Pays current market fees.
General Needs: Uses artists for text illustrations, book and jacket design, and layout.

ASHLEY BOOKS INC., 223 Main St., Port Washington NY 11050. (516)883-2221. President: Billie Young. Publishes hardcover originals; controversial, medical and timely. Publishes 30-35 titles/year.
First Contact & Terms: Arrange interview to show portfolio; local artists only. Buys first rights. Negotiates pay. Free catalog.
Book Design: Assigns 40 jobs/year. Uses artists for layout and paste-up.
Jackets/Covers: Assigns 35/year. Buys color washes.

ASI, 127 Madison Ave., New York NY 10016. Contact: Barbara Somerfield. Publishes astrology, healing and new age consciousness books.
First Contact & Terms: Query; send resume only. New York area artists only. Buys first rights. Original returned to artist at job's completion. Notes on assignment only. Provide resume and brochure to be kept on file for future assignments. Check for most recent titles in bookstores. Artist supplies overlays for cover artwork.
Jackets/Covers: Uses "cosmic and modern" themes. Pays $100.

ATHENEUM PUBLISHERS, 597 5th Ave., New York NY 10017. (212)486-2690. Vice President/Juvenile Books: Jean Karl. Publishes hardcover original trade juvenile books of all ages from 4-14. Publishes 60 titles/year; 60 of which require illustrators.
First Contact & Terms: Arrange to show portfolio (10-20 pieces, preferably printed but not absolutely necessary). Preferably realistic or completely fantasy and science fiction. Provide calling card and tear sheets to be kept on file for future assignments. Works on assignment only. Samples returned by SASE. Reports back on future assignment possibilities. Buys first rights. Originals returned to artist at job's completion.
Jackets/Covers: Realistic or fantasy including science fiction. Pays $200-350/b&w; $400-500/color.
Text Illustrations: Realistic or fantasy including science fiction. Pays $1,000-1,500/b&w.

THE ATHLETIC PRESS, Box 2314-D, Pasadena CA 91105. Contact: Donald Duke. Publishes sports training and conditioning books.
First Contact & Terms: Query.
Needs: "We are looking for line art of sport movements, anatomical drawings, etc."

AUGSBURG PUBLISHING HOUSE, 426 S. 5th St., Minneapolis MN 55415. (612)330-3300. Manager, Editorial/Design Services: James Lipscomb. Publishes paperback Protestant/Lutheran books. (40-45 titles/year); religious education materials; audiovisual resources; periodicals.
First Contact & Terms: Call, write, or send slides or photocopies. SASE. Reports in 3 weeks. Works on assignment only. Samples returned by SASE. Reports back on future assignment possibilities. Provide brochure, flyer, tear sheet, good photocopies and 35mm. transparencies to be kept on file for future assignments. Buys all rights on a work for hire basis, except for cartoons. May require artist to supply overlays on color work.
Jackets/Covers: Pays $200-400, b&w and color.
Text Illustrations: Negotiates pay, 1- and 2-color.
Cartoons: Buys 20 cartoons/year. Uses material on family, church situation and social commentary. Pays $10-15 minimum for one-time use.
Advertising: Uses artists for layout, design and illustrations. Negotiates pay, b&w and color.

AUTUMN PRESS INC., 1318 Beacon St., Brookline MA 02146. Art Director: Beverly Stiskin. Publishes paperbacks on "physical health, spiritual growth, social harmony and political justice." Publishes 7-10 titles/year.
First Contact & Terms: Query with resume and samples or arrange interview to show portfolio.

SASE. Reports in 1-3 months. Buys all rights. No originals returned to artist at job's completion. Works on assignment only. Provide resume, flyer and tear sheet to be kept on file for future assignments. Check for most recent titles in bookstores. Sometimes offers advance. Free catalog.
Jackets/Covers: Assigns 7-10 jobs/year. Pays $200-400, color washes and opaque watercolors; $100-250, gray opaques, woodblocks, etchings, b&w line drawings and washes.
Text Illustrations: Assigns 6 jobs/year. Pays $100-300, color washes and opaque watercolors; $100-250, gray opaques, b&w line drawings and washes.

AVE MARIA PRESS, Notre Dame IN 46556. Production Manager: Robert L. Mutchler. "We are Catholic publishers specializing in religious education, publishing books for the general Catholic market, with some crossover into other denominations, especially in the area of Charismatic Renewal books. We also publish a number of cassettes requiring jacket design. Most Catholic bookstores carry a representative range of our publications. Need for freelance art is minimal."
First Contact & Terms: "Artist should send photocopies or transparencies of work demonstrating style, subject matter and medium with which he or she is most comfortable." Buys one-time rights. No originals returned to artist at job's completion. Works on assignment only. No samples returned. Reports back on future assignment possibilities. Provide photocopies, transparencies or brochure to be kept on file for future assignments. Check for most recent titles in bookstores. Artist supplies all color overlays. "No specific type of experience needed, but it is most helpful if artist understands printing processes (the why and how of color separation, etc.)."
General Needs: Uses artists for jacket design and children's book illustrations, plus ink drawings for inside illustration. Also uses "general 'human situation' and/or scenics to enhance a religious textbook, books on prayer, the sacraments, etc. Usually b&w line, with or without wash (screened) overlay."Pays $10-20 for a simple illustration, to close to $3,000 for a complete series of paintings for use in both book and filmstrip.

AVON BOOKS, Art Department, 959 8th Ave., Rm. 403, New York NY 10019. Publisher: Walter Meade. Art Director: Barbara Bertoli. Publishes paperback originals and reprints. Publishes 300-350 titles/year. Query with samples. SASE. Reports in 3 weeks. Works on assignment only. Samples returned by SASE. Reports back on future assignment possibilities. No advance. Usually pays 1/3 promised fee for unused assigned work. Buys all reproduction rights.
Jackets/Covers: Buys 300/year; full-color renderings. Pays $350-3,000; lettering, $10 maximum/hour.
Text Illustrations: Occasionally uses children's illustrations; contact Children's Editor.
Production: Pays $100-500/job. Negotiates payment for color-separations and retouching.

AZTEX CORP., 1126 N. 6th Ave., Box 50046, Tucson AZ 85703. (602)882-4656. President: W. R. Haessner. Publishes hardcover and paperback originals on sports, mainstream and how-to. Publishes 9-12 titles/year.
First Contact & Terms: Query with samples. Reports in 6 weeks. Works on assignment only. Samples returned by SASE. Reports back on future assignment possibilities. Provide resume and/or brochure to be kept on file for future assignments. Buys reprint or all rights. No originals returned to artist at job's completion. Free catalog.
Jackets/Covers: Assigns 4 jobs/year. "We need technical drawings and cutaways." Pays $50-150, opaque watercolors and oils.

BAKER BOOK HOUSE, Box 6287, Grand Rapids MI 49506. Contact: Nick Goff, art director. Estab. 1939. Publishes religious paperback puzzle books and textbook reprints. Publishes 200 titles/year. Query with samples. SASE. Reports in 2 weeks. Buys all rights. Free catalog.
Book Design: Assigns 75 jobs/year. Uses artists for layout and type spec. Pays $125-175/job.
Jackets/Covers: Assigns 30 jobs/year. Buys b&w line drawings, washes, and color washes. Pays $125-150, color.

BALLANTINE BOOKS, 201 E. 50th St., New York NY 10022. (212)572-2251. Art Director: Ian. Publishes paperback fiction and nonfiction mass market books. Published 400 titles in 1976. Query with samples or write for interview. SASE. Buys all rights. Pays on acceptance. Pays promised fee for unused assigned work.
Jackets/Covers: Pays $600-1,500, full-color paintings.

BANTAM BOOKS INC., 666 5th Ave., New York NY 10019. Art Director: Leonard Leone. Publishes paperbacks.
First Contact & Terms: Drop off portfolio. Buys all rights. Original sometimes returned at job's completion. Works on assignment only. Provide brochure and tear sheet to be kept on file for future assignments. Check for most recent titles in bookstores.

General Needs: Uses artists for cover design and cartoons. Cartoons are "b&w sketches on chapter head pages or illustrations for how-to books."

BARLENMIR HOUSE OF GRAPHICS, 413 City Island Ave., New York NY 10064. Creative Director: Leonard Steffan. Publishes art, fiction, nonfiction, poetry, children's and humanities books.
First Contact & Terms: Send resume and photocopies. SASE.
General Needs: Uses artists for jacket design, inside book illustrations, direct mail brochures, advertising layouts/art, calligraphy, display/package design and posters.

WILLIAM L. BAUHAN, PUBLISHER, Dublin NH 03444. Art Director: W.L. Bauhan. Publishes hardbound and paperback books on New England. Publishes 6-8 titles/year.
First Contact & Terms: Written query. SASE. Reports in 4 weeks. Purchases outright. Works on assignment only. Returns samples only if originals. Reports back to artist on future assignment possibilities. Provide resume and sample or (samples) of work to be kept on file for future assignments. Check for most recent titles in bookstores.
General Needs: Uses artists for jackets, covers, text illustrations, advertising design and advertising illustrations. Uses line drawings and block prints, all b&w.

BELMONT TOWER & LEISURE BOOKS, 2 Park Ave., New York NY 10016. (212)679-7707. Art Director: Michael Copobianco. Publishes paperback originals and reprints for adult trade. Publishes 216 titles/year. Query with resume and samples or arrange interview to show portfolio. SASE. Reports in 1 week. Buys all rights.
Jackets/Covers: Assigns 200 jobs/year. Pays $400-900, oils or acrylics.

BERKLEY PUBLISHING CORP., 200 Madison Ave., New York NY 10016. Contact: Frank Kozelek. Uses artists for jacket designs for trade and mass market paperbacks. Send photocopies or transparencies.

THE BETABOOK CO., 10857 Valiente Ct., San Diego CA 92124. Vice President, Production: Gary W. Segraves. Publishes inspirational, self-help, science fiction and fiction paperback originals. "Only titles with strong moral standards in accordance with accepted biblical standards are accepted. We do not exclude secular books, however, which have a moral standard." Publishes 50-60 titles/year.
First Contact & Terms: Query with resume and arrange interview to show portfolio; local artists only. SASE. Reports in 8 weeks. Buys all rights. No originals returned to artist at job's completion. Works on assignment only. Samples returned by SASE. Reports back on future assignment possibilities. Provide resume, letter of inquiry and sample of work to be kept on file for future assignments. Check for most recent titles in bookstores. Free catalog.
Jackets/Covers: Assigns 50-60/year. Pays $60-200, color washes and opaque watercolors. Also buys b&w line drawings and washes.
Text Illustrations: Assigns 15-20/year. Pays $50-570, b&w line drawings. Also buys color washes and opaque watercolors.
Advertising: Uses artists for catalog design, brochures and ads.

BETHANY PRESS, Box 179, St. Louis MO 63166. Director of Design and Promotion: Guin Tuckett. Publishes paperback and cloth originals; juvenile, religious and secular. Publishes 10-15 books/year.
First Contact & Terms: Query with resume and samples. SASE. Reports in 6 weeks. Buys all rights. No originals returned to artist at job's completion. Works on assignment only. Samples returned by SASE. Reports back on future assignment possibilities. Provide resume and brochure to be kept on file for future assignments. Check for most recent titles in bookstores. Artist sometimes supplies overlays for cover artwork.
Jackets/Covers: Assigns 10-15/year. Pays $75-100, 2-color; $100 min., 4-color.
Text Illustrations: Assigns 50+/year. Pays $30-50, 2-color; $50-75, color.
Advertising: Uses artists for design and illustration of catalogs, letterheads, direct mail brochures and display pieces.
Cartoons: "In a teen-age monthly magazine we use about 8-10 cartoons/issue."

BOWLING GREEN UNIVERSITY POPULAR PRESS, Bowling Green University, Bowling Green OH 43403. (419)372-2981. Managing Editor: Pat Browne. Publishes hardcover and paperback originals on popular culture and folklore. Publishes 10-15 titles/year.
First Contact & Terms: Send previously published work. SASE. Reports in 2 weeks. Buys all rights. Free catalog.

Jackets/Covers: Assigns 20 jobs/year. Pays $50 minimum, color washes, opaque watercolors, gray opaques, b&w line drawings and washes.

BOWMAR/NOBLE PUBLISHERS INC., 4563 Colorado Blvd., Los Angeles CA 90039. Art Director: Glen Iwasaki. Publishes educational books. Uses artists for all aspects of book art and cartoons.
First Contact & Terms: Query. Do not send unsolicited samples. Provide brochure, flyer, tear sheet and photocopies of samples to be kept on file for future assignments. Originals may be returned to artist at job's completion.

BOXWOOD PRESS, 183 Ocean View Blvd., Pacific Grove CA 93950. (408)375-9110. Editorial Director: Ralph Buchsbaum. Estab. 1952. Publishes hardcover and paperback nonfiction, scientific and natural history originals. Publishes 6-8 titles/year. Query with samples. SASE. Reports in 2 weeks. Pays 2×-50% royalties or flat fee. No advance. Pays promised fee for unused assigned work. Buys book rights. Free catalog.
Jackets/Covers: Uses artists for jackets/covers. Fee negotiable.
Text Illustrations: Uses artists for line drawings and cartoons. Fee negotiable.
Advertising: Uses artists for illustrations. Fee negotiable.

BRASCH AND BRASCH, PUBLISHERS INC., 1707 S. Pleasant Ave., Ontario CA 91761. Editorial Director: Walter Brasch. Estab. 1977. Publishes hardcover and paperback historical fiction, nonfiction and children's originals. Publishes 10 titles/year. Query with samples. Uses local artists only. "I'm looking for artists who are professional in every sense. A track record isn't as important as ability." SASE. Reports in 3 weeks. Pays flat fee. No advance. Buys all rights, but may reassign rights to artist after publication. Free catalog and artist's guidelines.
Book Design: Assigns 1-10/year.
Jackets/Covers: Buys 5/year (dust jackets mostly). Pays $200-500 for full jacket design.

GEORGE BRAZILLER INC., 1 Park Ave., New York NY 10016. Contact: Art Director, for editorial work; Cindy Morgan, marketing manager, for advertising work. Estab. 1955. Publishes hardcover art, fiction and nonfiction books. Publishes 30 titles/year. Query with resume; local artists only. Reports in 3 weeks. Free catalog.
Jackets/Covers: Assigns 30 jobs/year. Pays $200-500, b&w.
Advertising: Assigns approximately 40 jobs/year. Uses artists for catalogs, ads and direct mail. Pays by job.

BROADMAN PRESS, 127 9th Ave. N., Nashville TN 37234. Contact: Supervisor, Art Section. Specializes in religious material.
Needs: Uses artists for text illustrations and jacket designs; music and recording covers. Pays $200, book jackets.

WILLIAM C. BROWN CO., PUBLISHERS, 2460 Kerper Blvd., Dubuque IA 52001. (319)588-1451. Production Development and Design Director: David Corona. Publishes hardbound and paperback college textbooks. Publishes 200 titles and buys 50 designs/year.
First Contact & Terms: Query with finished 11x14 or smaller (transparencies if larger) art samples or call for interview. SASE. Reports in 4 weeks. Works on assignment only. Samples returned by SASE. Reports back on future assignment possibilities. Provide resume, letter of inquiry, brochure, tear sheet or 8½x11 photocopies of samples to be kept on file for future assignments. Buys all rights. Pays half contract for unused assigned work.
Jackets/Covers: Pays $175-450, design.
Text Illustrations: Uses b&w and color work. Pays $35-200.
Advertising: Uses b&w and color work. Pays $35-200, promotional art.

JOHN W. CALER CORP., 7506 Clybourn Ave., Sun Valley CA 91352. Publishes aviation and general books.
First Contact & Terms: Submit photocopies or transparencies. SASE.
General Needs: Uses artists for jacket design, advertising/book layouts, inside illustrations and direct mail promotion brochures.

CATHOLIC HERITAGE PRESS, INC., Editorial Offices, Box 301, Sparkille NY 10976. Business office, Greenwich CT. (914)359-6916. Contact: Patricia Lowe. Estab. 1978. Clients: Religious and educational publishers and retailers. Buys 200 illustrations/year. Call for interview. Pays on publication.
Needs: Uses artists for jacket design and inside illustrations, retail, trade, space, advertising and

direct mail. Pays $150 minimum, 2-color cover; $15 minimum, b&w inside illustration.

CBI PUBLISHING CO., INC., 51 Sleeper St., Boston MA 02210. Design/Composition Director: Betsy Franklin. Advertising Manager: Fred Mullen. Publishes food service/hospitality and business management books, professional/reference.
First Contact & Terms: Query with resume. Also "like to see comprehensives of job and printed specimen." No phone calls; local artists only. Buys one-time rights. Original returned to artist at job's completion. Works on assignment only. Samples returned by SASE. Reports back on future assignment possibilities. Provide resume and business card to be kept on file for future assignments. Artist sometimes provides overlays for color artwork. Free catalog.
General Needs: Uses artists for jacket design (2-color) and production and design of direct mail and advertising brochures. Occasionally uses text illustrations (line art). Negotiates pay "within budget."
Cartoons: Buys 50 cartoons/year. "'Cartoons' are sometimes used in our training and self-improvement books—must therefore depict 'professionals' in a clean, 'mature' style."

CHAMPOEG PRESS, Box 92, Forest Grove OR 97116. (503)357-7192. Editor: Richard Abel. Publishes hardcover originals, reprints and limited editions on fly fishing, natural history, art and anthropology. Publishes 2 titles/year; sometimes uses freelance designers/illustrators.
First Contact & Terms: Send letter of inquiry, resume, samples and previously published work (illustrations, painting, line drawings, etc.). Samples returned by SASE. Reports back on future assignment possibilities. Provide resume and letter of inquiry to be kept on file for future assignments. Reports back in 4 weeks. Buys reprint rights. No originals returned to artist at job's completion. Artist supplies overlays for inside illustrations. Free catalog. Pays $100/minimum for book design, jacket/covers and test illustrations.

CHARLES RIVER BOOKS INC., 59 Commercial Wharf, Boston MA 02110. Editorial Director: Bruce P. Comjean. Art Director: Leslie Zhedthlin. Estab. 1969. Publishes hardcover and paperback originals and reprints. Publishes 70-110 titles/year. Submit art, query with resume or arrange interview. Local artists only. SASE. Reports in 4 weeks. Pays 1-10% royalty. Offers $100 advance. Pays promised fee for unused assigned work. Buys book, reprint or all rights. Free catalog.
Book Design: Assigns 15-20/year.
Jackets/Covers: Buys 50-70/year; b&w line drawings and washes and color. Pays $25 minimum.
Text Illustrations: Pays $50 minimum, b&w line drawings and washes, gray opaques, color washes and full-color renderings.
Advertising: Assigns 10 jobs/year. Pays $100 minimum/job, catalogs; direct mail brochures; $100-350/job, posters.

CHILTON BOOK CO., 201 King of Prussia Rd., Radnor PA 19089. (215)687-8200. Art Director: Edna H. Jones. Publishes hardbound and paperback arts and crafts, trade and automotive books. Buys 120 designs/year.
First Contact & Terms: Query. "I prefer to deal in person rather than through the mail." Reports in 3 weeks. Buys world rights. No originals returned to artist at job's completion. Works on assignment only. Samples returned by SASE. Provide resume, business card, flyer and tear sheet to be kept on file for future assignments. Check for most recent titles in bookstores. Artist sometimes supplies overlays for color work. Full payment for unused assigned work. Pays on acceptance.
Jackets/Covers: Pays $100-200, b&w; $200-400, color.
Text Illustrations: Pays $50-150, b&w.

CHRONICLE BOOKS, 870 Market St., San Francisco CA 94102. (415)777-7240. Senior Editor: Jane Vandenburgh. Publishes hardcover and paperback originals on fine art, California, how-to, fiction, architecture, lifestyle and photography, and guidebooks; some paperback reprints. Publishes 15-20 titles/year.
First Contact & Terms: Query with resume or arrange interview to show portfolio. SASE. Reports in 2 weeks. Buys various rights. Catalog $1.
Jackets/Covers: Assigns 40 jobs/year. Pays $200-500, b&w line drawings, washes and gray opaques; $400-600, color washes and opaque watercolors. Negotiates royalties. Offers advance.
Text Illustrations: Handled in association with jackets and covers.
Advertising: Uses artist for catalogs. Negotiates pay.
Book Design: Assigns 30 jobs/year. Pays $500-1,000, layout and type spec. Negotiates royalties. Offers advance.

DIXIE CLARK PRODUCTION, 47 Orient Ave., Melrose MA 02176. Produces hardcover and paperback text and trade book originals. Publishes 30-40 titles/year. Mail art or query with resume. SASE. Reports in 2 weeks.
Book Design: Pays $100-250.
Text Illustrations: Pays $7-25; $7-15, technical art; layout; $3.50-6/hour, mechanicals and paste-up.

CLIFFS NOTES INC., Box 80728, Lincoln NE 68501. Contact: Michele Spence. Publishes educational and trade (Centennial Press) books.
First Contact & Terms: Works on assignment only. Samples returned by SASE. Reports back on future assignment possibilities. Provide brochures, flyers and/or resume. No originals returned to artist at job's completion. Artist supplies overlays for color art.f4Jackets/Covers: Uses artists for covers and jackets.
Text Illustrations: Especially needs technical illustrators for precision drafting.

COFFEE BREAK PRESS, Box 103, Burley WA 98322. Art Director: D.M. Nicolai. Publishes approximately 6 titles/year on a variety of subjects. Current titles with heavy illustration: *Niddy Noddy the Noodle Maker*, children's picture book; *Cup of Sunshine*, poetry.
First Contact & Terms: Query with photocopies of samples and SASE. All work is assigned to freelance artists. Rights vary; usually buys first North American serial rights. Works on assignment only. No samples returned. Reports back on future assignment possibilities. Provide flyer and 3-6 photocopies of drawings to be kept on file for future assignments. Pays on acceptance.

COLORADO ASSOCIATED UNIVERSITY PRESS, University of Colorado, 1424 15th St., Boulder CO 80302. Publishes hardbound and paperback scholarly books. Query. SASE. Reports in 1 week. Pays on acceptance. No payment for unused assigned illustrations.
Jackets/Covers: Uses artists for color jacket design.

COLUMBIA PUBLISHING CO. INC., Frenchtown NJ 08825. (201)996-2769. President: Bernard Rabb. Publishes hardcover mainstream books. Also packages 20 titles/year.
First Contact & Terms: "We prefer a printed brochure showing samples of work which we can file for easy reference." SASE. Reports in 3 weeks. Works on assignment only. Samples returned by SASE. Provide brochure to be kept on file for future assignments. Artist provides overlays for color art. Buys first or reprint rights. No originals returned to artist at job's completion.
Jackets/Covers: Assigns 2-3/year. Material for cloth publications requires more sophistication than paper.
Text Illustrations: Assigns 5-10 projects/year.

COMPUTER SCIENCE PRESS INC., 9125 Fall River Lane, Potomac MD 20854. (301)251-9050. Publishes hardcover computer science textbooks. Publishes 7 titles/year.
First Contact & Terms: Call. Samples should include "an illustration or line drawing as well as an upper and lower case alphabet and some words in Leroy or Berol lettering. Xerox copy of work is OK. Buys all rights. No originals returned to artist at job's completion. Works on assignment only. Provide business card, letter of inquiry and sample of work to be kept on file for future assignments. Check for most recent titles in bookstores. Artist supplies overlays for cover artwork.
General Needs: Buys text illustrations (artist "reproduces our rough art"), jacket designs and cover designs.
To Break In: "We would like to develop a file of freelance technical draftsmen familiar with Leroy or Berol lettering. Local artists preferred. We provide rough art to copy."

CONSOLIDATED BOOK PUBLISHERS, 420 Lexington Ave., New York NY 10017. (212)867-2255. Executive Editor: Edward Finnegan. Hardbound and paperback cookbooks, dictionaries, and children's and medical books. Uses 6 artists/year. Arrange interview, or query with samples. Reviews all mailed materials. Reports only if interested; "I'll call the same day I get the samples." Pays $25 for unused assigned work. Buys all rights. Pays on publication.
Jackets/Covers: Uses artists for layout. Pays $75-150/semi-comp (between rough and finished) layout.
Text Illustrations: Pays $25 minimum, 2-color.

DAVID C. COOK PUBLISHING COMPANY, 850 N. Grove Ave., Elgin IL 60120. Art Director: Edmund G. Elsner Jr. Publishes children's lesson books (mainly) spanning ages nursery-adult. Publishes 40 titles/year.
First Contact & Terms: Query and send previously published work. SASE. Reports in 2 weeks. Buys all rights. No originals returned to artist at job's completion. Works on assignment only.

Samples returned by SASE; and reports back on future assignment possibilities. Provide "anything that can be kept or photocopied" to be kept on file for future assignments. Check for most recent titles in bookstores. Artist sometimes supplies overlays on inside illustrations.
Jackets/Covers: Contact: Bob Worcester. Assigns 20-35/year. Buys realistic illustrations. Uses layout and full-color art. Pays $100-350/job.
Text Illustrations: Uses line art.
Book Design: Contact: Bob Worcester. Assigns 20-35/year. Buys realistic illustrations. Uses layout and full-color art. Pays $100-350/job.
Cartoons: Buys 30 b&w cartoons/year. Minimum payment: $20.

R.D. CORTINA CO. INC., 136 W. 52nd St., New York NY 10019. Contact: Robert E. Livesey. Publishes language teaching materials.
First Contact & Terms: Send "outline of proposed project or photocopies only of table of contents and sample chapters." No originals returned to artist at job's completion. Works on assignment only. Samples returned by SASE; and reports back on future assignment possibilities. Provide resume and samples of style to be kept on file for future assignments. Artist supplies overlays for cover artwork.
Jackets/Covers: Uses artists for jacket design. Pays $200, jacket comps plus mechanicals.
Text Illustrations: Uses artists for text illustrations. Negotiates pay.
Advertising: Uses artists for direct mail promotion and advertising art.

CPI, 223 E. 48th St., New York NY 10017. (212)753-3800. Contact: Sherry Olan. Publishes hardcover originals for ages 4-7 (fiction) and ages 9-14 (nonfiction). Publishes 75 titles/year.
First Contact & Terms: Local artists only. Query with samples. Reports in 2 weeks. Works on assignment only. Samples returned by SASE; and reports back on future assignment possibilities. Provide flyer, tearsheet and photocopies of work will suffice to be kept on file for future assignments. No originals returned to artist at job's completion. Buys all rights. Free artist's guidelines.
Text Illustrations: "Submit color samples of action subjects. In general, realistic, representational art is required." Pays $50-100, opaque watercolors or any strong color medium. Also buys b&w line drawings.
General Needs: Also uses artists for instructional materials, workbooks and filmstrips.

CRESCENT PUBLICATIONS INC., 5410 Wilshire Blvd., Suite 400, Los Angeles CA 90036. Editor: Joseph Lawrence. Publishes general interest books.
First Contact & Terms: Query. Catalog available.
Needs: Uses artists for jacket design, text illustration, direct mail brochures and advertising layouts.

CRESTWOOD HOUSE INC., 515 N. Front St., Mankato MN 56001. (507)388-1616. Editorial/Art Director: K. Jacobsen. Publishes hardcover and paperback reading textbook originals. Publishes 20 titles/year.
First Contact & Terms: Prefers local artists. Query with resume and samples or arrange interview to show portfolio. SASE. Reports in 3 weeks. Works on assignment only. Samples returned by SASE; and reports back on future assignment possibilities. Provide resume and/or tearsheet to be kept on file for future assignments. Artist provides overlays for color art. No advance. Pays promised fee for unused assigned work. Buys all rights, but may reassign rights to artist after publication. Free catalog.
Book Design: Assigns 5/year. Pays $25-50/illustration, storyboards.
Text Illustrations: Buys 200-300/year; b&w line drawings and color washes. Pays $15-35, b&w; $25-50, color.
Advertising: Assigns 25 jobs/year. Pays $15 max./hour, catalogs, direct mail brochures, letterheads and magazines.

THE CROSSING PRESS, 17 W. Main St., Trumansburg NY 14886. (607)387-6217. Art Director: Mary Scott. Publishes hardcover and paperback cookbooks, how-to, mainstream and some poetry. Publishes 8-10 titles/year.
First Contact & Terms: Query. SASE. Reports in 4 weeks. Free catalog.
Jackets/Covers: Assigns 6/year. Pays $50-15, b&w line drawings and washes.
Text Illustrations: Assigns 3-4 jobs/year. Pays $5-25/illustration or $300-1,000/book for b&w line drawings and washes.

JONATHAN DAVID PUBLISHERS INC., 68-22 Eliot Ave., Middle Village NY 11379. Contact: Alfred J. Kolatch. Publishes mass-appeal nonfiction books.
First Contact & Terms: Prefers artists with at least two professional assignments. Pays $100

minimum, jacket design/mechanicals. Query.
Jackets/Covers: Uses artists for jacket design. "We are also interested in new, unpublished talent who can do spot illustrations, layout and paste-up."

DELACORTE PRESS, Division of Dell Publishing Co., 1 Dag Hammarskjold Plaza, New York NY 10017. Contact: Ann Spinelli. Publishes juvenile and adult books. Arrange interview to show photocopies or transparencies.
Needs: Uses artists for trade jacket design and inside illustrations.

DENLINGER'S PUBLISHERS LTD., Box 76, Fairfax VA 22030. (703)631-1501. Editorial/Art Director: W.W. Denlinger. Estab. 1926. Publishes hardcover and paperback historical fiction and canine originals and reprints. Publishes 10-20 titles/year. Query with samples. SASE. Reports in 1 week. No advance. Pays promised fee for unused assigned work. Buys all rights.
Book Design: Assigns 3-4/year. Pays $10-100, layout.
Jackets/Covers and Text Illustrations: Buys 3-4/year; b&w line drawings and color-separated work. Pays $10-100, b&w; $25-200, color.
Production: Assigns 3-4 jobs/year. Pays $25-200, color separations.
To Break In: "We are interested principally in artists capable of anatomical drawings of dogs."

DIMENSION BOOKS INC., Box 811, Denville NJ 07834. (201)627-4334. Editorial/Art Director: Thomas P. Coffey. Estab. 1962. Publishes hardcover and paperback Catholic and psychology originals and reprints. Publishes 35 titles/year.
First Contact & Terms: Query. SASE. Reports in 1 week. Works on assignment only. Samples returned by SASE; and reports back on future assignment possibilities. Provide resume to be kept on file for future assignments. Originals returned to artist at job's completion. Free catalog with SASE.
Needs: Uses artists for jacket design and advertising. Pays $100-300.

THE DONNING COMPANY/PUBLISHERS, 5041 Admiral Wright Rd., Virginia Beach VA 23462. (804)499-0589. Vice President: Stanley Hainer. Publishes hardcover and paperback originals on pictorial histories, illustrated cookbooks, general and regional. Publishes 20 titles/year; 3 of which require designers and 5 use illustrators.
First Contact & Terms: Send letter of inquiry to be kept on file for future assignments. Works on assignment only. Samples returned by SASE. Reports in 4 weeks. Buys first rights. Originals returned to artist at job's completion. Artist supplies overlays for cover artwork. Free catalog.

DORISON HOUSE PUBLISHERS, 69-12 223rd St., Bayside NY 11364. (212)224-0672. Editorial/Art Director: Trudy Settel. Publishes hardcover and paperback cookbook, decorating, baby care, gardening, sewing, crafts and driving originals and reprints. Publishes 30 titles/year.
First Contact & Terms: Query by mail; no samples until requested. Artists should have worked on a professional basis with other firms of our type. SASE. Reports in 3 weeks. Buys all rights. No advance. Pays promised fee for unused assigned work.
Book Design: Assigns 50/year. Pays $6 min./hour, layout and type spec.
Jackets/Covers: Buys 24/year. Pays $100-300, b&w; $250-500, color.
Text Illustrations: Uses artists for text illustrations and cartoons. Buys 250/year. Pays $10-30, b&w; $25-50, color.
Production: Assigns 25 jobs/year. Pays $5-10/hour, color-separations, lettering and mechanicals.
Advertising: Assigns 5 jobs/year. Pays $5-10/hour, catalogs and direct mail brochures.

DOUBLEDAY AND CO. INC., 245 Park Ave., New York NY 10017. Art Director: Alex Gotfryd. Publishes general adult, juvenile, western, science fiction, mystery, religious and special interest titles. Call for interview.
Needs: Uses artists for jackets, inside illustrations, advertising and sales promotion material.

DRAMA BOOK SPECIALISTS, 150 W. 52nd St., New York NY 10019. (212)582-1475. Editor-in-Chief: Ralph Pine. Contact: Judith Rudnicki. Publishes books on performing arts.
First Contact & Terms: Query or mail photocopies or transparencies. "Nonreturnable copies, no matter how primitive, preferred to returnable copies, no matter how slick." Local artists only. Buys various rights. Originals returned to artist at job's completion. Works on assignment only. Reports back to artist on future assignment possibilities. Provide samples of work to be kept on file for future assignments. Check for most recent titles in bookstores. Artist supplies overlays for cover artwork. Free catalog.
Needs: Uses artists for jacket design, inside illustration, direct mail brochures and advertising layouts.

EDITIONS QUINZE, 3465 Cote-Des-Neiges, Suite 50, Montreal, Quebec, Canada H3H 1T7. (514)937-6311. Editorial Director: Jacques Filion. Art Director: Mario Pelletier. Estab. 1976. Publishes hardcover and paperback poetry, novels, economics, politics, cooking and do-it-yourself originals and reprints. Publishes 50 titles/year. Submit art, query or arrange interview. Local artists only. "We are looking for artists who have already designed book covers." SASE. Reports in 2 weeks. Pays 10% royalty. No advance. No pay for unused assigned work. Buys all rights, but may reassign rights to artist after publication. Free catalog and artist's guidelines.
Jackets/Covers: Uses artists mainly for jacket design. Pays depends on work requested.
Text Illustrations: Uses artists for text illustrations and layout. Pay depends on work requested.
Production: Uses artists for layout. Pay depends on work requested.

EFFECTIVE LEARNING INC., Box 2212, Mount Vernon NY 10550. (914)664-7944. Art Director: Lawrence Tsuyuki. Estab. 1969. Publishes paperback educational materials. Publishes 10 titles/year. Send resume and samples; local artists only. SASE. Reports in 1 month. Buys all rights.
Book Design: Assigns 5-10 jobs/year. Uses artists for layout and type spec. Negotiates pay.
Jackets/Covers: Assigns 2 jobs/year. Buys color washes, opaque watercolors, gray opaques, b&w line drawings and washes. Negotiates pay.
Text Illustrations: Assigns 5 jobs/year. Buys opaque watercolors, color washes, gray opaques, b&w line drawings and washes. Negotiates pay.
Advertising: Uses artists for direct mail brochure illustration, catalog and letterhead design. Negotiates pay.

ELSEVIER/NELSON BOOKS, (formerly Thomas Nelson Inc.), 30 E. 42nd St., New York NY 10017. (212)697-5573. Editorial Director: Gloria Mosesson. Publishes juvenile and adult fiction and nonfiction hardcover originals. Publishes 50 titles/year.
First Contact & Terms: Query with samples or arrange interview. SASE. Reports in 2 weeks. Prefers to buy all rights. Catalog 75¢.
Jackets/Covers: Assigns 40-45 jobs/year. Pays $200 minimum, b&w or color.

F&W PUBLISHING, 9933 Alliance Rd., Cincinnati OH 45242. Art Coordinator: Carol Jacober. Publishes 8-10 hardcover books for writers annually. Query with samples, or request appointment. "Prefer that artist has had work published in area of assignment." SASE. Reports in 3 weeks.
Jackets/Covers: Buys 8-10/year. Pays $350-500 for concept through mechanical art.
Text Illustration: Uses artists for text illustration and cartoons. Pays $5 minimum.
Advertising: Assigns 25-50/year. Payment by job: $50-350, catalogs; $50 minimum, direct mail brochures; $25 minimum, magazines. Also uses artists for ad illustration and design.

FAIRCHILD BOOKS AND VISUALS, 7 E. 12th St., New York NY 10003. Promotion Director: Ken Handel. Publishes educational, commercial, careers and fashion books. Query.
Needs: Uses artists for book and cover design, text illustrations, direct mail brochures, advertising layouts and paste-up. Pays $20 minimum, b&w illustrrations.

FAR EASTERN RESEARCH & PUBLICATIONS CENTER, Box 3115, Washington DC 20031. Contact: Editor-in-Chief. Publishes reference books on Far Eastern subjects. Query.
Needs: Uses artists for jacket design and inside illustration.

FARRAR, STRAUS & GIROUX INC., 19 Union Square W., New York NY 10003. Contact: Dorris Janowitz. Publishes general fiction, nonfiction, biography and juveniles. Send samples.
Needs: Uses artists for jacket designs and inside illustrations. Pays $375, pre-separated 3-color jacket.

FAWCETT WORLD LIBRARY, 1515 Broadway, New York NY 10036. Art Director: Dale Phillips. Publishes Crest, Gold Medal and Premier Books. Call for appointment; usually held Tuesdays and Thursdays.
Needs: Uses artists for paperback cover illustrations.

FEARON/PITMAN PUBLISHING CO. INC., 6 Davis Dr., Belmont CA 94002. Art Director: Kauthar Hawkins. Publishes special education, teacher-aid, professional and management training books. Query.
Jackets/Covers and Text Illustrations: Uses artists for 1-, 2- and 4-color work. Also needs experienced book designers.

THE FEMINIST PRESS, Box 334, Old Westbury, NY 11568. (516)997-7660. Production Manager: Anita Steinberg. Publishes hardcover and paperback originals and reprints on educational non-sexist works, women's biographies and writings and children's stories. Publishes 18 titles/year; 4 of which require designers and 6 use illustrators.
First Contact & Terms: Send letter of inquiry, resume, samples and previously published work (photocopies of b&w (or color slides) dealing with women. Provide resume and samples to be kept on file for future assignment possibilities. Works on assignment only. Reports back on future assignment possibilities. Buys one-time rights. Originals returned to artist at job's completion. Interested in sexual and racial blends. Free catalog.
Book Design: Pays $100-200/job.
Jackets/Covers: Pays $150-250/b&w. Color negotiable.

FIESTA PUBLISHING CO., 6360 NE 4th Ct., Miami FL 33138. Contact: W. Allan Sandler. Publishes Spanish paperback sexy novels, mysteries, action books and magazines.
First Contact & Terms: Query or submit samples. Reports in 30 days. Buys 1-time rights. Pays on acceptance.
Text Illustration: Uses color and/or b&w "Wild West" action scenes. Pays $5-10 for b&w depending on size and detail of illustration. Will pay up to $50 for covers.

FILMS FOR THE HUMANITIES, Box 2053, Princeton NJ 08540. Contact: M. Mantell. Produces educational sound filmstrips, motion pictures, multimedia kits and slides. Material usually copyrighted. Catalog available.
Needs: Uses artists for book and advertising design.

FITZHENRY & WHITESIDE LTD., 150 Lesmill Rd., Don Mills, Ontario, Canada M3B 2T5. Editor-in-Chief: Robert W. Read. Publishes educational and some general trade hardcover and paperback books, study prints and filmstrips. Submit samples; prefers Canadian artists.
Needs: Uses artists for book, jacket and cover design; text illustration; filmstrips and graphic material for study prints; and promotion/advertising layout. Pays $3,000, total book designs; $100 maximum, 1- or 2-color illustrations; and $300 maximum, single 4-color illustration. Illustration contracts often given for complete books (100-200 illustrations).

FODOR'S MODERN GUIDES, 2 Park Ave., New York NY 10016. (212)340-9832. Editor: Robert C. Fisher. Associate Editor: Leslie Brown. Publishes hardcover and paperback travel guides. Published 47 titles and bought 200 designs in 1978. Query with samples. SASE. Full payment for unused assigned work. Buys all rights. Pays on acceptance.
Jacket Design: Pays $200 minimum, b&w; $250, color.
Inside Illustrations: Pays $20 minimum, b&w line drawings.
To Break In: "Avoid heavy black areas in drawings."

FORDHAM EQUIPMENT & PUBLISHING CO., 3308 Edson Ave., Bronx NY 10469. (212)379-7300. Contact: Al Robbins, president. Estab. 1951. Publishes children's books. Arrange interview to show portfolio. Reports in 3-4 weeks.
Needs: Uses artists for illustrations, posters and layout. Pays by job.

FOUR WINDS PRESS, 50 W. 44th St., New York NY 10036. (212)867-7700. Editorial Director: Judith Whipple. Art Director: Lucy Bitzer. Estab. 1968. Publishes hardcover juvenile originals. Publishes 30-40 titles/year. Arrange interview. SASE. Reports in 6-8 weeks. Pays royalties or flat fee. Offers advance. Pays promised fee for unused assigned work.
Book Design: Assigns 10/year. Pays $150.
Jacket Design: Buys 10/year. Minimum payment: $250, b&w; $275, color.
Inside Illustrations: Pays $75/page, b&w and color.

GARDEN WAY PUBLISHING, Ferry Rd., Charlotte VT 05445. Editorial Director: Roger Griffith. Design Director: David Robinson. Publishes quality paperback cooking, building, gardening, animal raising, energy conservation and how-to-do-it books. Publishes 12 titles/year.
First Contact & Terms: Query with samples of style only. SASE. Reports in 3 weeks. Buys one-time rights or purchase outright. No originals returned to artist at job's completion. No originals returned to artist at job's completion. Works on assignment only. samples returned by SASE. Reports back on future assignment possibilities. Provide resume, business card, letter of inquiry and tearsheet to be kept on file for future assignment. Check for most recent titles in bookstore. Artist supplies overlays for all color artwork. No advance. Buys all rights. Free artist's guidelines.
Inside Illustrations: Buys 300-400/year; uses b&w line drawings, washes and color-separated

work. Pays $10-40. "We probably don't work with more than 4 illustrators per year. More than half the books submitted to us have the illustrations taken care of by the author."
Advertising: For catalogs, POP displays and posters, contact Bob Bennett, special sales. Assigns 4-6 jobs/year. For fliers, inserts, POP displays and packaging, contact Bill Hanlon, marketing director. Assigns 20-30 jobs/year.

GENERAL HALL INC., 23-45 Corporal Kennedy St., Bayside NY 11360. Editor, for editorial and advertising work: Ravi Mehra. Publishes hardcover and paperback originals; college texts and supplementary materials. Publishes 3-5 titles/year.
First Contact & Terms: Local artists only. Query. SASE. Reports in 1-2 weeks. No originals returned to artist at job's completion. Works on assignment only. samples returned by SASE. Reports back on future assignment possibilities. Provide brochure/flyer to be kept on file for future assignment. Artists provides overlays for color artwork. Buys all rights. Free catalog and artist's guidelines.
Jackets/Covers: Assigns 3-5 jobs/year. Pays $50-100, b&w line drawings, washes, gray opaques and color washes.
Text Illustrations: Assigns 1-2 jobs/year. Pays $10-25, b&w line drawings, washes and gray opaques.
Advertising: Pays $50-100/job.

GERRY DE LA REE, 7 Cedarwood Lane, Saddle River NJ 07458. (201)327-6621. Editorial/Art Director: Gerry de la Ree. Publishes hardcover and paperback fiction, fantasy, science fiction or weird art originals and reprints. Publishes 3 titles/year.
First Contact & Terms: Submit art. "We want material only by previously published artists, not beginners." SASE. Reports in 1 week. Buys all rights, but may reassign rights to artist after publication. Offers advance. Pays promised fee for unused assigned work.
Text Illustrations: Negotiates pay for illustrations and paintings; science fiction, fantasy and weird art only.

GLOBE PEQUOT PRESS, Box Q, Old Chester Rd., Chester CT 06412. (203)526-9571. Contact: Linda Kennedy, publications director. Primarily publishes paperback originals on New England (travel, town histories, guides), cooking, biking and walking guides, how-to and crafts. Publishes 20 titles/year.
First Contact & Terms: Send resume and samples. SASE. Reports in 3 weeks. Buys all rights. No originals returned to artist at job's completion. No originals returned to artist at job's completion. Works on assignment only. samples returned by SASE. Reports back on future assignment possibilities. Provide resume, letter of inquiry, flyer and tearsheet. Check for most recent titles in bookstore. Artist occasionally supplies overlays for inside illustrations and advertising art. Free catalog and artist's guidelines.
Jackets/Covers: Assigns 20 jobs/year. Pays $200-300, b&w line drawings, washes and gray opaques; $200-350, 2-color washes and opaque watercolors.
Text Illustrations: Assigns 4 jobs/year. Buys b&w line drawings. "Payment usually included in billing for cover design or layout work."
Book Design: Assigns 20 jobs/year. Uses artists for layout and type spec. Pays $250-450/job.
To Break In: "Be familiar with our book selection; it's New England and has a quaint touch; we don't want anything psychedelic or 'artsy.' Proximity to our offices is a definite plus. Long-distance working relationships often are too time-consuming to pursue.

GOLDEN WEST BOOKS, Box 8136, San Marino CA 91108. Contact: Donald Duke. Publishes Americana railroad, steamship and transportation history books.
First Contact & Terms: Buys first rights. Catalog available.
Needs: Uses artists for jacket design. Pays $250 minimum.

GOODYEAR PUBLISHING CO. INC., 1640 5th St., Santa Monica CA 90401. (213)393-6731. Art & Design Director: Marvin R. Warshaw. Publishes hardcover and paperback business, professional and trade books, and college texts on business management, economics, education, mathematics, social science and vocational technology.
First Contact & Terms: Query with original and published art samples, or arrange interview. SASE. Buys all rights. No originals returned to artist at job's completion. Pays on acceptance.
Jackets/Covers: Pays $350 minimum, b&w and color.
Inside Illustrations: Buys b&w line drawings, halftones, washes and color-separated/full color work.
Cartoons: Buys 10 cartoons/year. Uses b&w cartoons for a variety of subjects pertaining to book being published. Pays $50 minimum.

Advertising: Uses artists for layout and illustration.

GOSPEL LIGHT PUBLICATIONS, REGAL BOOKS, 2300 Knoll Dr., Ventura CA 93003. Art Directors: Sissi Wilkins, Lee Kowell. Publishes hardcover and paperback books, christian, educational curriculum materials, posters, material for summer clubs, maps, *Family Life Today* magazine, and take-home papers for church use every Sunday. Submit portfolio. Reports in 2-4 weeks. Buys all rights. Pays within 4 weeks of acceptance.
Needs: Cover designs, line drawings, 4-color art and tone art. "Nearly all of the art we use contains people and children. We prepare roughs of what we want and buy the finished art from freelancers." Pays $25-100, spot drawings; $250-450, 4-color cover including paste-up.

GOVERNMENT INSTITUTES INC., 4733 Bethesda Ave. NW, Washington DC 20014. (301)656-1090. Contact: Martin L. Heavner, communications manager, for editorial and advertising work. Estab. 1973. Publishes books on conference proceedings and reference in the areas of energy, environment and toxic substances. Publishes 10 titles/year. Query with samples; local artists only. SASE. Reports in 2 weeks. Buys one-time rights. Free catalog.
Jackets/Covers: Assigns 2 jobs/year. Pays $20 maximum/hour, b&w line drawings and washes.
Advertising: Uses artists for catalogs, letterheads, direct mail brochures, logos and print ads. Pays $20 max./hour.

GREAT OUTDOORS PUBLISHING CO., 4747 28th St. N., St. Petersburg FL 33714. Contact: Joyce Allyn. Publishes books on Florida outdoor life: fishing, shells, reptiles, gardening and cooking. Query; prefers local artists. SASE.
Needs: Uses artists for jacket design and inside illustrations. Pays $10 minimum, b&w spot art; $150, 4-color cover.

THE GREEN TIGER PRESS, 7458 La Jolla Blvd., La Jolla CA 92037. (714)238-1001. Publishes hardcover and paperback books, calendars, and a large variety of stationery.
First Contact & Terms: Query with samples (prints or slides; not originals). SASE. Reports in 1 month. Buys various rights. Provide tearsheet to be kept on file for future assignments. Check for most recent titles in bookstores. Catalog $1.
Text Illustrations: Assigns 10/year. Buys b&w line drawings and watercolors. Pays 5-15% royalties. Offers advance.

THE STEPHEN GREENE PRESS, Box 1000, Brattleboro VT 05301. (802)257-7757. Managing Editor: Orion M. Barber. Publishes nonfiction hardcover and paperback books on Americana, (including New England), biography, self-help, sports (horse and individual outdoor), humor, technology, popular history, food, cooking, nature, environment, how-to and self-reliance.
First Contact & Terms: Query with samples. SASE. Buys only through specific commission as "work done for hire" under the meaning of the Copyright Act. Buys all rights, but will negotiate. No originals returned to artist at job's completion. Works on assignment only. Samples returned by SASE. Provide resume, tearsheet, brochure and photocopies to be kept on file for future assignments. Check for most recent titles in bookstores. Free catalog.
Jacket Design: Pays $150 minimum, flat color; $250 minimum, full-process color, both including type and finished mechanical.
Text: Pays $10-25, b&w.

MICKY HADES INTERNATIONAL, Box 476, Calgary, Alberta, Canada T2P 2J1. (403)285-6626. Editorial Director: Brian Hades. Art Director: Micky Hades. Publishes paperback magic (as entertainment) and related subject originals. Publishes 15-20 titles/year.
First Contact & Terms: Query with samples. SASE. Reports in 3 weeks. Buys all rights. No advance without agreement. Catalog $3.
Jackets/Covers: Assigns 15/year. Pays $25-150, b&w line drawings.
Inside Illustrations: Buys 150-200/year. Negotiates pay for b&w line drawings.

HARVARD UNIVERSITY PRESS, 79 Garden St., Cambridge MA 02138. Contact: Susan Hayes. Publishes scholarly works. Query with resume.
Needs: Uses artists for jacket design and direct mail brochures. Pays $125 minimum, jacket design.

HARVEST HOUSE LTD., 4795 St. Catherine St. W., Montreal, Quebec, Canada H3Z 2B9. Contact: Maynard Gertler. Publishes hardbound and paperback books. Submit previously published samples.
Needs: Uses artists for typography and jacket and book layout.

HARVEY HOUSE, PUBLISHERS, 20 Waterside Plaza, New York NY 10010. Art Director: L.F. Reeves. Publishes hardbound juvenile books. Query with samples or write for interview. SASE. Reports in 3 weeks. Buys all rights.
Needs: Uses artists for color jackets and b&w and color inside illustrations. Pays $150 minimum, 1-color jacket; $400-1,500 and "frequently royalties," inside art.

HAYDEN BOOK CO. INC., 50 Essex St., Rochelle Park NJ 07662. Contact: A. Victor Schwarz. Publishes English language, social studies, computer technology and theory, and electronics books.
First Contact & Terms: Prefers "mostly printed samples-a few original composite sketches." Buys all rights. No originals returned to artist at job's completion. Works on assignment only Samples returned by SASE; and reports back on future assignment possiblities. Provide business card to be kept on file for future assignments. Check for most recent titles in bookstores and "compare to competitive material."
General Needs: Buys jacket designs, inside illustrations, direct mail brochures and advertising layouts. Pays $150 minimum, cover design, plus mechanicals and art costs; $12/figure, electronics home study books (includes 75 figures).

D.C. HEATH AND CO., Division of Raytheon, 125 Spring St., Lexington MA 02173. (617)862-6650. Contact: School Division or College Division Art Depts. Publishes elementary, secondary and college textbooks.
First Contact & Terms: Submit samples. Prefers copies or tearsheets which can be kept on file. May show portfolio in person by appointment. Provide flyer, tearsheet and brochure to be kept on file for future assignments. Buys all rights. Doesn't usually return originals, "but can be arrange. Most artist don't seem to want routine textbook work back."
General Needs: Uses artists for inside illustrations and cover design. "Must be relevant to textbook subject and grade level."
Cartoons: "Recent major elhi series have used thousands of 4-color cartoon-type illustrations (spelling and math)."

T. EMMETT HENDERSON, PUBLISHER, 130 W. Main St., Middletown NY 10940. (914)343-3298. Contact: T. Emmett Henderson. Publishes hardcover and paperback local history, American Indian, archaeology, and genealogy originals and reprints. Publishes 2-3 titles/year.
First Contact & Terms: Query. No work returned. Reports in 4 weeks. Buys book rights. Originals returned to artist at job's completion. Works on assignment only. Provide resume to be kept on file for future assignments. Check for most recent titles in bookstores. Artist supplies overlays for cover artwork. No advance. No pay for unused assigned work.
Jackets/Covers: Buys 2-4/year. Uses representational art. Pays $20 minimum, b&w line drawings and color-separated work.
Inside Illustrations: Pays $10 minimum, b&w.
Advertising: Assigns 5 jobs/year. Pays $10 minimum.
Cartoons: Buys 5-15 cartoons/year. Uses cartoons as chapter headings. Pays $5-12 minimum, b&w.

LAWRENCE HERBST PUBLISHING CO., Box 1659, Beverly Hills CA 90213. (213)298-1084. Contact: Lawrence Herbst.
First Contact & Terms: Query with resume and samples. Reports in 3 weeks.
Jackets/Covers: Pays $25 minimum. Offers ¼-20% royalty.

HOLDEN-DAY INC., 500 Sansome St., San Francisco CA 94111. (415)433-0220. Contact: Barbara Gordon, production coordinator. Estab. 1959. Publishes hardcover and paperback college and graduate level textbooks in mathematics, computers, statistics, business management, chemistry and physics. Publishes 10-12 titles/year. Query with resume and previously published work or arrange interview to show portfolio. SASE. Reports in 2 weeks. Buys all rights. Free catalog.
Book Design: Assigns 8 jobs/year. Uses artists for type spec. Negotiates pay.
Jackets/Covers: Assigns 8 jobs/year. Buys opaque watercolors. Negotiates pay.
Text Illustrations: Assigns 8 jobs/year. Buys b&w line drawings. Negotiates pay.

HOLIDAY HOUSE, 18 E. 53rd St., New York NY 10022. (212)688-0085. Editor: Margery Cuyler. Publishes hardcover originals for juveniles; fiction, nature and picture books. Publishes 25 titles/year.
First Contact & Terms: Arrange interview to show portfolio. SASE. Buys all rights. Originals returned to artist at job's completion. Works on assignment only. Provide flyer and brochure to be kept on file for future assignments. Check for most recent titles in bookstores. Artist supplies

overlays for cover artwork and inside illustrations. Negotiates pay. Free catalog.
Jackets/Covers: Assigns 5-10 jobs/year. Uses mostly "young-adult-oriented themes (romance, humor and problems)." Buys color-separated work.
Text Illustrations: Assigns 5-10 jobs/year. Uses illustrations for non-fiction and picture books. Buys color-separated work and b&w line drawings. Offers advance.

HOUGHTON MIFFLIN/CLARION BOOKS, 52 Vanderbilt Ave., New York NY 10017. (212)972-1190. Art Director: Isabel Campbell. Publishes hardcover juvenile originals. Publishes 25 titles/year; 15 of which require designers and 15 use illustrators. Needs preseparated color illustrations.
First Contact & Terms: Send samples (tear sheets or photocopies) and arrange to show portfolio (originals, printed samples). SASE. Works on assignment only. Provide calling card, flyer, brochure and tear sheet to be kept on file for future assignments. Buys first rights and reprint rights on contract. Originals returned to artist at job's completion.
Book Design: Pays $150-250/job.
Jackets/Covers: Pays $300-450/color.
Text Illustrations: Pays 2%-6% royalty.

CARL HUNGNESS PUBLISHING, Box 24308, Speedway IN 46224. (317)244-4792. Editorial Director: Carl Hungness. Art Director: Cathy Schenk. Estab. 1970. Publishes hardcover automotive originals. Publishes 4-15 titles/year. Query with samples. SASE. Reports in 2 weeks. Offers $100 advance. Buys book, one-time or all rights. No pay for unused assigned work. Free catalog.
Jacket Design: Buys 12/year. Pays $25-75, b&w; $100-300, color.

IDEAL SCHOOL SUPPLY CO., 11000 S. Lavergne, Oak Lawn IL 60453. (312)425-0800. Art Director: Charles A. Koch. Graphic Designer: Lin Cleghorn. Publishes educational textbooks, workbooks and games.
First Contact & Terms: Query with resume, samples and prices, and arrange interview to show portfolio. SASE. Reports in 3 months.
Text Illustrations: Buys 100/year. "Artists must be able to illustrate children and objects." Pays $10-25, b&w work; $25-100, color; or $8-20/hour.

IDEAL WORLD PUBLISHING CO., Box 1237-EG, Melbourne FL 32935. (305)254-6003. Editor: Harold Pallatz. Publishes hardcover and paperback health, nutrition, vitamins, herbs, gold prospecting, treasure finding and ghost towns books. Query. SASE. Reports in 4 weeks. Buys all rights. Pays on acceptance. "No pay for unused assigned sketches or roughs; full pay for unused assigned illustrations backed by our written order."
Jacket Design and Inside Illustrations: Pays $5 minimum, b&w line drawings and halftones.
Advertising: Pays $5 minimum, layout and b&w illustration.

IMPACT PUBLISHERS INC., Box 1094, San Luis Obispo CA 93406. Marketing Manager: Tom Norwood. Publishes hardcover and paperback personal development and self-help books. Buys 2 designs/year.
First Contact & Terms: Mail art. SASE. Reports in 3 weeks. Buys all rights. No originals returned to artist at job's completion. Works on assignment only Samples returned by SASE; and reports back on future assignment possiblities. Provide resume and (nonreturnable) samples to be kept on file for future assignments. Check for most recent titles in bookstores. Artist supplies overlays for cover artwork and inside illustrations.Pays on publication. Negotiates pay for unused assigned work.Free catalog.
Jackets/Covers: Pays approximately $200, b&w and color.
Inside Illustrations and Advertising: Negotiates pay for b&w line drawings and color-separated work.
To Break In: "The biggest problem we have in dealing with freelance artists is their resistance to accommodating our requests and needs. We sincerely want originality and creativity, but we also know what our specific needs are. Many artists develop a design and then insist that it be used exactly as they designed it. The freelancer should be receptive to the specific requests of the publisher."

INSTITUTE FOR THE STUDY OF HUMAN ISSUES (ISHI PUBLICATIONS), 3401 Market St., Suite 252, Philadelphia PA 19104. (215)387-9002. Managing Editor: Douglas C. Gordon. Marketing Director: Edward A. Jutkowitz. Publishes hardcover and paperback political science, anthropology and history originals and hardcover reprints. Publishes 10-30 titles/year.
First Contact & Terms: Query with samples. SASE. Reports in 2 weeks. Buys all rights. No originals returned to artist at job's completion. Works on assignment only. Samples returned by

SASE. Provide letter of inquire to be kept on file for future assignments. Artist supplies overlays for cover artwork and advertising art. No advance. Pays promised fee for unused assigned work. Free catalog.
Book Design: Assigns 10/year. Pays $10 min./hour, layout; $150 min./job, type spec.
Jacket Design: Buys 12/year. Pays $200 minimum, b&w line drawings, gray opaques and b&w and 2-color washes.
Inside Illustrations: Buys 40/year, mostly technical drawings or maps. Pays $20 minimum, b&w line drawings.
Advertising: Assigns 10 jobs/year. Pays $10 min./hour, catalogs and direct mail brochures.

IOWA STATE UNIVERSITY PRESS, S. State Ave., Ames IA 50010. (515)294-5280. Production Manager: Robert Campbell. Publishes hardcover originals on agriculture, journalism, engineering, home economics, education, science, humanities, veterinary medicine and regional history. Publishes 35 titles/year.
First Contact & Terms: Query; local artists only. SASE. Reports in 2 weeks. Buys all rights.
Jackets/Covers: Assigns 2 jobs/year. Pays $50-100, b&w line drawings, washes and gray opaques.
Text Illustrations: Assigns 3 jobs/year. Pays $5-25, b&w line drawings.

JANUS BOOK PUBLISHERS, 3541 Investment Blvd., Suite 5, Hayward CA 94545. (415)785-9625. Production Manager: Carol Gee. Publishes remedial reading materials and softcover workbooks for high school and basic adult education. Publishes 10 titles/year.
First Contact & Terms: Send samples or arrange interview to show portfolio; local artists only. SASE. Reports in 3 weeks. Buys various rights. No originals returned to artist at job's completion. Works on assignment only Samples returned by SASE; and reports back on future assignment possiblities. Provide resume and "photocopies of samples" to be kept on file for future assignments. Artist supplies overlays for 2-color cover artwork; sometimes for adverstising art. Free catalog.
Jackets/Covers: Uses "2-color, very direct and very simple designs".
Text Illustrations: Assigns 8 jobs/year. "Primary concern is realism." Pays $10-50 for ¼- or ½-page spot drawings. Buys b&w line drawings and washes. Offers advance "upon completion of acceptable roughs."
Advertising: Uses artists for catalog design. Pays $15/hour.
Book Design: Assigns 10 jobs/year. Uses artists for layout. Pays $12-15/hour or $300-600/job. Offers advance "upon completion of acceptable roughs."
Cartoons: Uses a realistic type of cartoon. "Our 'cartoons' are used to illustrate meaning of words and phrases, are usually ½tone wash work. Artist is given specifications, and asked to supply rough, revised, rough and finished art." Pays $25, b&w.

JPR ASSOCIATES/PRODUCT DEVELOPERS, 143 Hudson Terrace, Piermont-on-Hudson, NY 10968. (914)359-6916. Contact: Bill Davenport. Exclusive agent for *The Catholic Heritage Press, Inc.* Publisher of spiritual titles for young people and their families. Clients: trade, religious and educational publishers, retailers (specialty and gift cards). Buys 200 illustrations/year.
First Contact & Terms: Call for interview. Works on assignment only Samples returned by SASE; and reports back on future assignment possiblities. Provide resume, business card, tearsheet, brochure and photocopies of work on actual samples to be kept on file for future assignments. Artist supplies color overlays on color covers. Pays on publication. Free catalog. Pays $150 minimum, 2-color cover; $15 minimum, b&w inside illustration.
General Needs: Uses artists for jacket design (fit for young people—ages 10-15—and their families), inside illustrations (line art), retail, trade, space advertising, direct mail.
Cartoons: Buys a minimum of 25 cartoons/year. Uses cartoons for spirit master worksheets and young peoples illustrated (line art) books.

JUDSON PRESS, Valley Forge PA 19481. (215)768-2155. Contact: Art Dept. Publishes American Baptist books. Published 40 titles in 1978. Submit photos or published samples.
Needs: Pays $200 for 5*x8* cover design.

KEATS PUBLISHING INC., 36 Grove St., New Canaan CT 06840. Contact: Nathan Keats. Publishes health, inspirational and business-sponsored books.
First Contact & Terms: Query with resume. Uses artists for book illustration and advertising layout.

B. KLEIN PUBLICATIONS INC., Box 8503, Coral Springs FL 33065. Editor: Bernard Klein. Publishes reference books, such as the *Guide to American Directories*.
Needs: Uses artists for jacket design and direct mail brochures. Submit resume and samples. Pays $50-300.

KNOWLEDGE TREE GROUP, INC., 360 Park Ave S., New York NY 10010. Editorial Director: Mark Zarowin. Estab. 1978. Produces educational books, kits, cassettes, records and filmstrips. Buys 500-700 designs/year; New York artists only.
First Contact & Terms: Query. SASE. Reports in 3 weeks. Buys all rights. Originals returned to artist at job's completion. Works on assignment only. Samples returned by SASE. Provide resume to be kept on file for future assignments. Artist supplies overlays for cover artwork and inside illustrations. Pays by job.
General Needs: Uses artists for layout, design, multimedia kits, paste-up, study prints, technical charts/illustrations, type spec and textbook illustrations and cartoons. Payment for book illustraton: $5-50, 1-color; $15-50, 2-color; $20, 4-color.

LA SOCIETE DE BELLES-LETTRES GUY MAHEUX INC., 7705 Boulevard De L´Acadie, Suite 10, Montreal, Quebec, Canada H3N 2W1. (514)272-3256. Editorial/Art Director: Guy Maheux. Estab. 1975. Publishes hardcover and paperback poetry, fiction and philosophy originals. Publishes 20-30 titles/year. Submit art or query. SASE. Reports in 2 weeks. Pays promised fee for unused assigned work. Buys all rights, but may reassign rights to artist after publication. Free catalog.
Jacket Design: Buys 20/year. Pays $75-300, color-separated work.

LAIDLAW BROTHERS PUBLISHERS, Thatcher and Madison, River Forest IL 60305. (312)366-5320. Art Director: Gloria Muczynski. Estab. 1919. Publishes hardcover elementary and high school textbooks on all subjects. Publishes 80 titles/year. Query with samples or arrange interview to show portfolio; "include slides, photostats or photocopies that can be kept on file." Reports in 2 weeks. Buys all rights.
Jackets/Covers: Assigns 25-50 jobs/year. Design and illustration. Pays $150-400, color washes and opaque watercolors; $75-125, gray opaques, b&w line drawings and washes.
Text Illustrations: Buys 10,000-15,000/year. Pays $40-125, color washes and opaque watercolors; $10-85, gray opaques, b&w line drawings and washes.
To Break In: "We use freelance artists exclusively. A disciplined, reliable freelancer has a good chance of working with us. Submit current samples appropriate to textbook work such as people-oriented illustrations with children actively involved. Realistic and stylized art as well as design art also used. No architectural renderings, landscapes or portraits."

LIBRARY-COLLEGE ASSOCIATES, Box 956, Norman OK 73070. (405)329-5120. Contact: Howard Clayton, editor. Estab. 1968. Publishes educational books and materials. Query with samples. SASE. Reports in 1 week.
Needs: Pays $15/hour for graphics.

LITTLE, BROWN AND COMPANY ADULT TRADE DIVISION, 34 Beacon St., Boston MA 02106. (617)227-0730. Art Director: Char Lappan. Estab. 1837. Publishes mainstream hardcover originals. Publishes 125 titles/year. Send samples or arrange interview to show portfolio. Reports in 2-3 weeks. Buys first or reprint rights. "We have no artist's guidelines but will gladly answer questions."
Jackets/Covers: Assigns 100 jobs/year. Buys color washes, opaque watercolors, gray opaques, b&w line drawings and washes. Negotiates pay.

LLEWELLYN PUBLICATIONS, Box 43383, St. Paul MN 55764. Art Editor: Bill Hamley. Publishes occult, astrology and witchcraft books. Reports in 8 weeks.
Covers: Pays $100, b&w; $200, color.

LOGOS INTERNATIONAL, 201 Church St., Plainfield NJ 07060. (201)754-0745. Art Director: David Tommasino. Publishes religious books.
First Contact & Terms: Buys one-time rights. No originals returned to artist at job's completion. Works on assignment only. Samples returned by SASE. Provide resume to be kept on file for future assignments. Check for most recent titles in bookstores. Artist sometimes supplies overlays for color artwork.
General Needs: Uses artists for jacket designs, inside illustrations, direct mail brochures and advertising layouts. Pays $250, full-color jackets.
Cartoons: Buys 10-25 cartoons/year. Interested in religious subjects. Pays $10-30, b&w.

McGRAW HILL PUBLISHING, College Division, 1221 6th Ave., New York NY 10020. Art Director, College and University Division: Merrill Haber. Submit samples. Reports in 3 weeks.
Needs: Uses artists for book and jacket design; technical, medical and biological illustrations; and cartography.

MacMILLAN PUBLISHING CORP., 866 3rd Ave., New York NY 10022. Design Director: Zlata Paces. Publishes hardcover and paperback originals and reprints for elementary and high schools. Publishes 300 titles/year; 30% of which require designers; 70% use illustrators.
First Contact & Terms: Send letter of inquiry, resume and arrange to show portfolio. SASE. Provide calling card, tear sheets and slides to be kept on file for future assignments. Works on assignment only. Samples returned by SASE. Buys one-time rights. Originals returned to artist at job's completion.
Inside Illustrations: Negotiates pay.

MACMILLAN PUBLISHING CO., INC., PROFESSIONAL BOOKS DIVISION, 866 3rd Ave., New York NY 10022. Contact: W. Weiss. Publishes college texts, professional, reference and trade nonfiction in social sciences, humanities, musicology, medicine, etc.
Needs: Pays $150+, interior and binding design; $200+, jacket or cover design/mechanicals.

MAJOR BOOKS, 21335 Roscoe Blvd., Canoga Park CA 91304. Contact: Art Director. Publishes western, gothic, mystery and educational books.
First Contact & Terms: Send photocopies or transparencies. Works on assignment only Samples returned by SASE; and reports back on future assignment possiblities. Provide brochure and/or tearsheets to be kept on file for future assignments. Buys all rights. No originals returned to artist at job's completion. Free catalog.
Jackets/Covers: Uses artists for realistic jacket designs.
Cartoons: Buys about 100 cartoons/year. Pays $15 minimum.

MANYLAND BOOKS INC., 84-39 90th St., Woodhaven NY 11421. Contact: Stepas Zobarskas. Send photocopies. SASE.
Needs: Pays $25 minimum, inside illustration; $85, jacket design.

MEMPHIS STATE UNIVERSITY PRESS, Memphis State University, Memphis TN 38152. (901)454-2752. Director: J. Ralph Randolph. Publishes regional studies, history and provides literary criticism.
First Contact & Terms: Mail samples. Works on assignment only. Provide resume, letter of inquiry and some kind of art that can be filed (jacket, brochure, etc.) to be kept on file for future assignments. Buys one-time rights or exclusive rights. Artist provides overlays on cover artwork, inside illustrations and advertising art.
Jackets/Covers: Uses "art that is supportive and not in conflict with the book design."

MERTON HOUSE PUBLISHING CO., 937 W. Liberty Dr., Wheaton IL 60187. (312)668-7410. Contact: Laurence Stevens, publisher. Estab. 1974. Publishes hardcover and paperback travel guides, textbooks, adult trade and nonfiction; originals. Publishes 5 titles/year. Query with resume. SASE. Reports in 1-4 months. Buys all rights. Free catalog with SASE.
Jackets/Covers: Assigns 2-3 jobs/year. Negotiates pay.

JULIAN MESSNER, Division of Simon & Schuster, 1230 Avenue of the Americas, New York NY 10020. Contact: Lee Hoffman or James Landis. Publishes nonfiction children's and teens' books. Query with resume.
Needs: Uses artists for jacket designs and inside b&w illustrations.

MILADY PUBLISHING CORP., 3839 White Plains Rd., Bronx, New York NY 10467. (212)881-3000. President: T. R. Severance. Publishes educational hardcover and paperback texts. Publishes 10 titles/year.
First Contact & Terms: Query. SASE. Works on assignment only. Samples returned by SASE; and reports back on future assignment possiblities. Provide materials to be kept on file for future assignments. On finished color inside illustrations, artist supplies overlay. Buys all rights. Catalog costs 50¢.
Inside Illustrations: Buys 300/year. Pays $5-100, technical and "fashion features and hairstyles" illustrations.

MODERN CURRICULUM PRESS, 13900 Prospect Rd., Cleveland OH 44136. (216)238-2222. Editorial Director: Tom Hatch. Art Director: Tom Sibila. Estab. 1957. Publishes elementary education workbooks; paperback originals. Publishes 15-30 titles/year. Query with samples. SASE. Reports in 2 weeks. Offers small advance. Buys all rights. Free catalog.
Book Design and Illustrations: Assigns 5-10/year. Pays $75-150/page, 4-color illustration, rough to final art.
Advertising: Assigns 20-30 jobs/year. Pays $500-2,500/job, catalogs; $50-1,000/job, direct mail brochures; $50-1,500/job, magazines.

MOJAVE BOOKS, 7040 Darby Ave., Reseda CA 91335. (213)342-3403. Editorial Director: Judith Bazol. Art Director: Zvi Erez. Publishes hardcover and paperback general, poetry and some juvenile originals. Publishes 35-40 titles/year.
First Contact & Terms: Query with resume and samples. SASE. Reports in 2 weeks. Buys all rights. No originals returned to artist at job's completion. Works on assignment only. Reports back to artist on future assignment possiblities. Provide resume and business card to be kept on file for future assignments. Artist supplies overlays for cover artwork. No advance. Pays promised fee for unused assigned work. Free catalog.
Jackets/Covers: Buys 10-15/year. Minimum payment: $100, b&w; $150, color.
Text Illustrations: Buys 6-10/year. Pays $25 minimum, b&w and color.

MOTT MEDIA, 1000 E. Huron, Milford MI 48042. Publishes hardcover and paperback Christian books and textbooks.
First Contact & Terms: Query with samples or tearsheets (originals not necessary) or contact by agent. Reports in 1 month. SASE. Buys all rights. No originals returned to artist at job's completion. Works on assignment only. Samples returned by SASE; and reports back on future assignment possiblities. Provide resume, flyer, tearsheet and letter of inquiry to be kept on file for future assignments. Artist supplies all color overlays. Pays ½ on acceptance of sketch and ½ on submission of finished art. Free catalog.
General Needs: Especially needs book design. Minimum payment: $150, jacket design; $400, 4-color cover art; $30, inside color illustrations; $25, inside b&w illustrations.

MUSEUM OF NEW MEXICO PRESS, Box 2087, Santa Fe NM 87503. (505)827-2352. Contact: James Mafchir, publisher. Publishes hardcover and paperback originals and reprints on history of the southwest, anthropology, archaeology, natural history, art, guidebooks and fiction with a regional and historical emphasis. Publishes 6-7 titles/year.
First Contact & Terms: Query with samples or arrange interview to see portfolio; local artists only. SASE. Reports in 4 weeks. Buys all rights. Negotiates pay. Free catalog.
Jackets/Covers: Assigns 2 jobs/year. Buys color washes, opaque watercolors, overlays, gray opaques, b&w line drawings and washes. Sometimes offers advance.
Text Illustrations: Assigns 2 jobs/year. Buys overlays, b&w line drawings and washes.
Book Design: Assigns 3 jobs/year. Uses artists for layout and type spec.

NATIONAL GALLERY OF CANADA, 75 Albert St., Room 330, Ottawa, Ontario, Canada K1A 0M8. (613)996-1434. Production Manager: Arnold Witty. Photo Editor: Colleen Evans. Publishes hardcoer and paperback originals on art, catalogs, monographs, journals and brochures. Publishes 25 titles/year; 20 of which require designers; 1-2 use illustrators.
First Contact & Terms: Send letter of inquiry and resume and samples (photographs, drawings, etc). Provide resume, calling card and fee schedule to be kept on file for future assignments. Works on assignment only. Samples returned by SASE. Reports back on future assignment possibilities. Buys first rights. No originals returned to artist at job's completion. Check for recent titales in bookstores. Free catalog (National Museums Corp., Esplanade LaMrier, West Tower, Ottawa). Hires on contract basis; best price and quality of work chosen.

NATUREGRAPH PUBLISHERS INC., Box 1075, Happy Camp CA 96039. (916)493-5353. Contact: David L. Moore, editor. Publishers of trade paperbacks on natural history and native Americans, gardening and New Age. Publishes 6 titles/year.
First Contact & Terms: Query with resume. SASE. Reports in 4-6 weeks. Buys one-time or all rights. Free catalog. Works on assignment only. Samples returned by SASE; and reports back on future assignment possiblities. Provide resume, flyer, letter of inquiry, brochure and sample to be kept on file for future assignments. Buys one-time for or all rights. Free catalog.
Jackets/Covers: Assigns 4 jobs/year. Pays $50-200 or 1-50% royalties, color washes.
Text Illustrations: Assigns 2 jobs/year. Scientific and general illustrations, some design graphics in text. Pays $50-200, b&w line drawings.
Cartoons: Buys a few cartoons, but not many.

NELLEN PUBLISHING CO., 386 Park Ave. S., New York NY 10016. Contact: M. Stanford or E.H. Nellen. Publishes trade and scholarly books.
First Contact & Terms: Prefer local artists with previous experience with book publishing firms. Telephone or send photocopies or transparencies. Works on assignment only. Samples returned by SASE; and reports back on future assignment possiblities. Provide flyer, letter of inquiry or brochure to be kept on file for future assignments. On finished color artwork, artist must supply overlays. Buys reproduction rights. Originals returned to artist at job's completion. Free catalog.
General Needs: Uses artists for jacket designs, text illustrations, direct mail brochures, catalogs

and advertising layouts. UDCM Division (publishes the scholarly books): Pays $75-100, jacket design; $150, catalog layout. Trade division: Pays $200-500, jacket design; $200-300, catalogs; $150 min., mail pieces.
Cartoons: Only buys cartoons "if we a book in which cartoons would be appropriate". Pays $25 minimum/cartoon.

NELSON-HALL INC., 111 N. Canal St., Chicago IL 60606. Vice President: Stephen A. Ferrara.
First Contact & Terms: Submit resume and photocopies. Buys all rights. Pays on acceptance. Catalog available.
General Needs: Uses artists for jacket designs and technical illustration. Pays $200, jacket design plus type.

THE NEW AMERICAN LIBRARY INC., 1301 Avenue of the Americas, New York NY 10019. Art Director: James Plumeri. Publishes paperback and hardcover books; paperback titles carry the Signet, Mentor and other trade names. Artist may leave portfolio for review. Query for details.

NEWBURY HOUSE PUBLISHERS, 54 Warehouse Lane, Rowley MA 01969. (617)948-2704. Editorial/Production Manager: Jacquelin Sanborn. Publishes language arts, sciences and English as second language texts; mostly paperback originals and reprints. Publishes 30-40 titles/year.
First Contact & Terms: Query with resume and samples. SASE. Reports in 4 weeks. No advance. Buys all rights. No originals returned to artist at job's completion. Provide resume, flyer, tearsheet, brochure and "inexpensive photocopies of artist's best work (in his/her opinion)" to be kept on file for future assignments. Write for free catalog, issued in September; usually not available between March and September.
Jackets/Covers: Buys 10-15/year. Pays $50 minimum, b&w line drawings, washes and color-separated work.
Text Illustrations: "Mostly charts." Pays $2.50 min./2x2", b&w line drawings, color-separated work and preliminary sketches.
Book Design: Assigns 15-20/year. Pays $50 min./job, layout.
Cartoons: Publishes cartoons "occasionally"; uses about 20 cartoons/year. Interested in "stick figure cartoons illustrating specific actions (usually to demonstrate verbs)."
Production: Assigns 20-25 jobs/year. Pays $35 min./job, paste-up. Negotiates payment for mechanicals and color-separations.

NORTHWOODS PRESS INC., Box 249, Stafford VA 22554. (703)952-2388. Art Director: R. Olmsted. Publishes hardcover and paperback books. Buys 3 designs/year.
First Contact & Terms: Query with samples. SASE. Reports in 4 weeks. Usually buys all rights. Pays on acceptance.
General Needs: Uses artists for b&w jacket designs and inside illustrations. Pays $5 minimum.

NOYES PRESS, 118 Mill Rd., Park Ridge NJ 07656. Contact: Robert Noyes. Publishes academic and technical books on chemistry, chemical engineering, food, environment, art, mental health, finance, archaeology and classical studies.
Needs: Uses artists for jacket design. Pays $250 minimum, 2-color camera-ready art.

OPEN COURT PUBLISHING CO., Box 599, LaSalle IL 61301. (815)223-2520. Art Director: Todd Sanders. Publishes kindergarten through sixth grade language arts and mathematics programs.
First Contact & Terms: Send samples and previously published work. Provide business card, brochure and tearsheet to be kept on file for future assignments. Works on assignment only. Samples returned by SASE. Reports back on future assignment possibilities. Buys reprint rights (international rights included). Originals returned to artist at job's completion. Artist sometimes supplies overlays for color artwork.
General Needs: Buys text illustrations directed to "K-6 age group; able to draw ethnics cartoon work generally not used. Tends toward realism but soft wash, etc." Pays $300-700/color for jackets/covers and $30-250/color for text illustrations.

ORCA SOUND PUBLICATIONS, Box 652, Station A, Vancouver, B.C., Canada. Editorial Director: Dona Sturmanis. Art Director: Marty Dolan. Estab. 1976. Publishes paperback poetry, art and general interest originals. Publishes 2-8 titles/year. Query with samples. SASE. Reports in 4 weeks. Pays royalties or flat fee. No advance. No pay for unused assigned work. Buys all rights. Free catalog and artist's guidelines.
Book Design: Assigns 3-4/year. Pays $3-4.50/hour, layout.
Jacket Design: Pays $5-25, b&w; $50-200, color.

Inside Illustrations: Pays $1-25, b&w line drawings and gray opaques.
Advertising: Pays $3-4.50/hour, letterheads and posters.
Production: Pays $3-4.50/hour, color separations, lettering, paste-up and retouching.

OUTDOOR EMPIRE PUBLISHING INC., 511 Eastlake Ave. E., Box C-19000, Seattle WA 98109. Publications Director: Fay Ainsworth. Publishes paperback outdoor and how-to books on all aspects of outdoor recreation. Published 8 new and 40 reprint titles and bought 16 designs in 1979.
First Contact & Terms: Arrange interview or mail art. SASE. Reports in 3 weeks. Buys all rights. No originals returned to artist at job's completion. Works on assignment only. Samples returned by SASE; and reports back on future assignment possiblities. Provide resume, flyer, business card, tearsheet, brochure and "photocopies of samples to show style" to be kept on file for future assignments. Artist sometimes supplies overlays for color artwork. Gives minimum payment for unused assigned work. Pays on publication.
Jackets/Covers: Pays $50 minimum, b&w and color.
Inside Illustrations: Minimum payment: $10, b&w; $15, color.
Advertising: Uses artists for layout and illustration. Minimum payment: $10-15, b&w; $15-20, color.
Cartoons: Occasionally uses cartoons. Buys 6 cartoons/year. Pays $10, b&w.

OXMOOR HOUSE, Box 2262, Birmingham AL 35202. Contact: John Logue, Editor-in-Chief. Advertising and Promotion Manager: Dianne Mooney. Publishes hardcover art books and paperback Family Guidebook series. Query.

PADRE PRODUCTIONS, Box 1275, San Luis Obispo CA 93406. Editor/Publisher: Lachlan P. MacDonald. Publishes county and area, especially California, guidebooks.
First Contact & Terms: Query. Answers queries in 10 days; book decisions, 2 months. Works on assignment only. Samples returned by SASE. Provide resume, flyer, tearsheet, brochure and book jacket samples to be kept on file for future assignments. Artist provides overlays for color art. "We typeset all text, but want the artist to be responsible for complete preparation of art." Usually buys all book rights. Originals returned to artist at job's completion. Pays $10-1,000.
General Needs: Uses artists for finished line drawings of western America. "We are interested in camera-ready books, collections of drawings by a single artist dealing with a single topic or area, or occasional freelance assignments for line drawings. We are also willing to look at general humor books that lend themselves to mass-market sales at drugstores, airports, gift shops, etc. They should be presented as a completed manuscript with sample line drawings."
Tips: "Artist who askes us what we mean by camera-ready are probably not sufficiently professional in graphic standards to meet our needs."

PALADIN PRESS, Box 1307, Boulder CO 80306. (303)443-7250. General Manager: Timothy J. Leifield. Publishes hardcover and paperback originals and reprints; military-related (weaponry, self-defense and survival) and titles of general interest. Publishes 20 titles/year.
First Contact & Terms: Query; local artists only. SASE. Reports in 1 month. Buys all rights. Works on assignment only. Samples returned by SASE; and reports back on future assignment possiblities. Provide resume, business card and letter of inquiry to be kept on file for future assignments. Artist supplies overlays for all color artwork. Free catalog for SASE.
Jackets/Covers: Assigns 10/year. Uses "full-color, some photo montage." Pays $100-400, b&w line drawings and washes; $300-800, color washes. "If artist develops original design, payment increases. If the artist is given a specific design to execute, payment is less."
Text Illustrations: Assigns 8/year. Uses "99% pen and ink, b&w. Often technical." Buys b&w line drawings and washes and color washes. Negotiates pay.
Cartoons: Buys 5 cartoons/year. Minimum payment; $25, b&w; $40, color.
Tips: "We prefer working with artists who have a strong background in mechanical and production skills (have they ever worked with a printer?)."

PARENTS' MAGAZINE PRESS, 52 Vanderbilt Ave., New York NY 10017. Art Director: Marc Gave. Publishes easy-to-read full-color picture books for ages 3-8.
First Contact & Terms: Write or call. Prefers full-color cartoon work-published or unpublished. "We are interested primarily in cartoonists who can produce lively, fun drawings with wide kid-appeal. Ability to work out a dummy for a given text is essential." Buys all rights. Originals returned to artist at job's completion. Works on assignment only. Samples returned by SASE; and reports back on future assignment possiblities. Provide resume, flyer, business card, tearsheet, letter of inquiry and brochure to be kept on file for future assignments. Write for free catalog to: Elsevier-Dutton, Dept.JH, 2 Park Ave, New York NY 10016.

General Needs: Buys full-color cartoons for jackets, covers and text illustrations.

PAULIST PRESS, 1865 Broadway, New York NY 10023. Contact: Michael Hunt. Publishes hardbound and paperback religious and educational books, both popular and scholarly.
First Contact & Terms: Query. Local artists only.
General Needs: Uses artists for jacket design, book illustrations, direct mail brochures and advertising layouts. Pays $10-20, inside page; $175, cover.

PAWNEE PUBLISHING CO. INC., Box 3435, Boulder CO 80303. (303)666-6594. President: Ernest W. Schafer. Estab. 1972. Publishes mathematics and science books and state history multimedia programs.
Needs: Uses artists for jacket design, inside illustrations, direct mail brochures and advertising. Pays $15, line drawing.

PEACOCK PRESS, Bantam Books, Rte. 212, Bearsville NY 12409. Contact: Betty Ballantine. Publishes 4-color art books. Query. Offers advance against royalties.

PELICAN PUBLISHING CO., 1101 Monroe St., Gretna LA 70053. (504)368-1175. Production Manager: Cathy Garber. Publishes hardcover and paperback originals and reprints. Publishes 30 titles/year.
First Contact & Terms: Send letter of inquiry and 3-4 samples. SASE. Works on assignment only. No samples returned. Reports back on future assignment possibilities. Provide resume, letter of inquiry, tear sheets, samples or slides to be kept on file for future assignments. No originals returned to artist at job's completion. Buys complete rights.

PENDULUM PRESS, Saw Mill Rd., West Haven CT 06516. (203)933-2551. Editorial Director: Linda Cadrain. Art Director: Karen Evonsion. Estab. 1969. Publishes hardcover and paperback illustrated classic originals. Publishes 90-180 titles/year. Query with resume and samples and arrange interview. SASE. Reports in 1 month. No advance. Pays 80-100% promised fee for unused assigned work. Buys all rights. Free brochure and artist's guidelines.
Jacket Design: Buys 24/year; realistic comic book style. Minimum payment: $50, b&w; $300, color.
Inside Illustrations: Buys 600-1,000/year. Pays $15-50, b&w line drawings.
Advertising: Assigns 5-25 jobs/year. Minimum payment by job: $300, catalogs and direct mail brochures; $25, letterheads; $75, packaging. Negotiates payment for POP displays and posters.
Production: Assigns 1-10 jobs/year. Pays by job, mechanicals and paste-up.

THE PERFECTION FORM CO., 8350 Hickman Rd., Des Moines IA 50322. Contact: Wayne F. DeMouth. Publishes educational workbooks, posters, filmstrips and books; originals and some reprints. Query or send samples; prefers local artists. "Write for our catalog."
Needs: Uses artists for inside book illustrations, posters and some covers.

PERGAMON PRESS INC., Fairview Park, Elmsford NY 10523. (914)592-7700. Art Department Manager: Elizabeth Trahim. Publishes scientific, technical, scholarly, educational, professional and business books.
First Contact & Terms: Call for interview. No originals returned to artist at job's completion. Works on assignment only. Check for most recent titles in bookstores.
General Needs: Uses artists for jacket designs, cover designs, text illustrations, advertising design, advertising illustrations and direct mail brochures; 1- and 2-color.

PJD PUBLICATIONS, Box 966, Westbury NY 11590. Contact: Art Director. Publishes hardcover and paperback college and biomedical texts and journals.
First Contact & Terms: Query with samples. Prefer artists with published work. Buys all rights. No originals returned to artist at job's completion. Works on assignment only. Provide resume, flyer, brochure, business card or tearsheet to be kept on file for future assignments. Artist supplies all color overlays.
General Needs: Uses artists for jackets, covers, text illustration, advertising design and b&w and color advertising illustrations. Pays $100 average, color-separated jacket design; $100-300, color-separated direct mail brochures.

PLAYMORE INC., PUBLISHERS, 1107 Broadway, New York NY 10010. (212)924-7447. Vice President: Robert Horwich. Publishes hardcover and paperback juvenile, adult and mass market originals and reprints. Published 50-150 titles/year.
First Contact & Terms: Query with samples. SASE. Reports in 2 weeks. Negotiates pay for design and illustration.

POCKET BOOKS, 1230 Avenue of the Americas, New York NY 10020. Vice President: Milton Charles. Publishes paperbacks.
First Contact & Terms: Deliver portfolio for review and later pick-up.
Needs: Uses artists for cover design.

POLARIS PRESS, 16540 Camellia Terrace, Los Gatos CA 95030. (408)356-7795. Editor: Edward W. Ludwig. Publishes hardcover originals primarily on non-fiction for young adults, historical and scientific for general audience, self help, possibly science fiction and science fantasy, ethnic and bilingual. Publishes 2-3 titles/year; all use illustrators.
First Contact & Terms: Send letter of inquiry, resume, samples (tear sheets or photocopies) and "inquire as to our current needs. Because our needs are small and varied, a query is essential. We are especially interested in hearing from minority artists: black, Chinese, Japanese, Amerindian, etc." Provide resume and letter of inquiry to be kept on file for future assignments possibilities. Works on assignment only. Samples returned by SASE. Reports back on future assignment possibilities. Reports in 2 months. Buys first rights. Originals returned to artist at job's completion. Check for most recent titles in bookstroes or "order 2 or 3 of our books directly." Artist supplies overlays for cover artwork if possible. Pays $50 minimum/b&w; $75 minimum/color for jackets/covers and $30 minimum/b&w text illustrations (one-time payments).

POPULAR LIBRARY BOOKS, CBS Publications, 1515 Broadway, New York NY 10036. Contact: Ed Rofheart and Don Puckey. Publishes fiction and nonfiction. Query or drop off portfolio. Local artists preferred. SASE.
Needs: Uses artists for jacket design. Pays $200, standard jacket design; $400, "realistic, 4-color painting for a mass market paperback."

CLARKSON N. POTTER INC., 1 Park Ave., New York NY 10016. (212)532-9200. Managing Editor: Michael Fragnito. Publishes hardbound and paperback books on Americana, fiction, fashion, interior decoration, satire, art, cooking and photography. Published 30 titles in 1979 and bought 100% of the designs.
First Contact & Terms: Query with photocopies or call for an appointment. SASE. Reports in 2 weeks "if we like samples." Buys all rights. Free sample catalog.
General Needs: Pays $300-400, jacket design; $50 minimum, full-page in side illustrations; $10-25, spot art.

PRAISE THE LORD PRESS, 2821 E. Ashman, Midland MI 48640. Editorial Director: Phil Silva. Art Director: Jacqueline Silva. Estab. 1976. Publishes paperback Christian poetry originals.Publishes 1-5 titles/year. Query with non-returnable samples. SASE. Reports in 4 weeks. No advance. No pay for unused assigned work. Pays up to $700 for full-color illustrations. Buys all rights. Catalog and artist's guidelines $1 each.
Jacket Design and Inside Illustrations: Buys 4/year. Pays $10 minimum, b&w line drawings.
Advertising: Assigns 4 jobs/year. Negotiates pay.

PRENTICE-HALL INC., Edgewood Cliffs NJ 07652. (201)592-2294. Art Director: Joseph Di Domenico Jr. Estab. 1913. Publishes college, elementary and high school texts and business, professional, trade, medical and nursing books; hardcover and paperback originals. Published approximately 700 titles in 1977 and in 1978. Query with resume and arrange interview. SASE. Reports in 2 weeks. No advance. Pays 50-100% promised fee for unused assigned work. Buys all rights.
Book Design: Assigns 2-6/year. Pays $1.50-4.50/page, layout; $300-600/job, type spec and design.
Jacket and Cover Design: Buys "hundreds"/year. Pays $300-400, b&w; $275-800, color.
Inside Illustrations: Buys "thousands"/year. Pays $10-250, b&w; $25-500, color.
Production: Pays 75¢-$1.50/page, mechanicals and paste-up; $5-250/job, retouching.

PRUETT PUBLISHING CO., 3235-F Prairie Ave., Boulder CO 80301. (303)449-4919. Contact: Editor. Publishes books on Americana, railroad histories and intermountain regional subjects.
First Contact & Terms: "We do not directly contract artwork. Authors of our titles supply their own art; however, we maintain a file of artists' brochures, query letters, etc., for the use of our authors in need of such services. No calls, please. Almost all of our freelance artwork is handled locally." Buys all rights. Works on assignment only. Provide business card and brochure to be kept on file for future assignments. Artist supplies overlays for cover artwork and advertising art. Free catalog.
General Needs: "We use freelance artists primarily for designing dust jacket covers, about 24 books/year.".

PULSE-FINGER PRESS, Box 16697, Philadelphia PA 19139. Contact: Orion Roche or Raphaello Farnese. Publishes hardbound and paperback fiction, poetry and drama. Publishes 7 titles/year.
First Contact & Terms: Query. "We can't use unsolicited material." SASE; "Inquiries without SASE will not be acknowledged." Prefers local artists. Reports in 4 weeks. Buys first serial and reprint rights. Pays on acceptance. Originals returned to artist at job's completion. Works on assignment only. Samples returned by SASE; and reports back on future assignment possiblities. Provide resume to be kept on file for future assignments. Artist supplies overlays for all color artwork.
Jackets/Covers: "Must be suitable to the book involved; artist must familiarize himself/herself with text. We tend to modernist/abstract designs. Try to keep it simple, emphasizing the thematic material of the book." Pays $25-100, b&w jackets.
Advertising Design: Uses artists for direct mail promos. Pays $25 minimum.
Advertising Illustrations: Pays $25 minimum.

G.P. PUTNAM'S SONS, Coward, McCann & Geoghegan, Inc., 200 Madison Ave., New York NY 10016. (212)576-8918. Art Director, Children's Books: Catherine Stock. Publishes hardcover juvenile books.
First Contact & Terms: Call Carolyn Craven for appointment or send several samples of work by mail. Buys all rights. Originals returned to artist at job's completion. Works on assignment only. Samples returned by SASE; and reports back on future assignment possiblities. Provide flyer, tearsheet, brochure and photocopy or stat sample to be kept on file for future assignments. Artist often supplies overlays for cover artwork and inside illustrations. Pays on acceptance. Small kill fee for unused assigned work. Free catalog.
Jackets/Covers: Uses "many styles; in particular naturalistic but distinctive portrait scenes for young adult novels." Pays $250-275. Pays $300-350 for jacket illustration.
Text Illustrations: Uses "many styles except very cartoony; in particular good naturalistic animal illustration."

QUICK FOX, MUSIC SALES INCORPORATED, 33 W. 60th St., New York NY 10032. Art Director: Barry L.S. Mirenburg. Estab. 1940. Publishes hardcover and paperback originals. Publishes books on "art, interior design, health, fine and applied art, design, crafts, how-to, psychology, sociology, photography, and music." Averages 218 titles/year. Uses both local and out-of-town freelance artists. Send resume, samples ("would appreciate holding samples on file"), and previously published work. SASE. Reports in 2 months. Copyrighted; all rights purchased.
Needs: Uses artists for photography, illustrations, design, and paste-up.
Jackets, Covers & Text Illustrations: Buys b&w line drawings, opaques, washes and color washes, and opaque watercolors. Interested in paintings and collages for jackets and covers.
To Break In: "We are looking for excellent creative design. Must have a good color and graphic sense. Illustrators should have a good command over the use of line and form. Quality and sophistication of these visual aspects is most important."

RANDOM HOUSE, Education Division, 201 E. 50th St., New York NY 10022. Contact: Stanley Wheatman. Publishes educational books. Send photocopies or transparencies.
Needs: Uses artists for jacket design, inside illustrations, direct mail brochures, advertising layout and book design. Pays $200-500, cover design; $200-500, book design.

RANDOM HOUSE, School Division, 201 E. 50th St., New York NY 10022. Art Director: Walter Norfleet. Publishes elementary through high school educational books.
First Contact & Terms: Send nonreturnable stats or photocopied samples. Provide resume, tearsheet and brochure to be kept on file for future assignments. Buys one-time reproduction rights. Originals returned to artist at job's completion. Artist supplies overlays for color art. Contracts assigned through the bidding process.
General Needs: Full service studios, capable of developing product from original manuscript through camera-ready mechanicals, including composition and illustration.

RESOURCE PUBLICATIONS, 7291 Coronado Dr., #3, San Jose CA 95129. Editorial Director: William Burns. Art Director: George F. Collopy. Publishes paperback religious originals. Publishes 1-5 titles/year.
First Contact & Terms: Query with samples. SASE. Reports in 4-6 weeks. No advance. Buys all rights. Free catalog.
Book Design: Assigns 1-4/year. Pays $5-25/hour, layout and type spec.
Jacket Design: Buys 1-4/year. Pays $45-125, b&w; $50-250, color.
Advertising: Assigns 4 jobs/year. Pays $4-25/hour, catalogs, direct mail brochures, letterheads and magazines.

Production: Assigns 12-16 jobs/year. Pays $3.50-10/hour, paste-up.

RICHARDS ROSEN PRESS INC., 29 E. 21st St., New York NY 10010. (212)777-3017. Editorial Director: Ruth C. Rosen. Art Director: Roger Forrester. Publishes hardcover young adult originals. Publishes 36 titles/year.
First Contact & Terms: Arrange interview. Reports in 1 week. No advance. Buys all rights. Originals returned to artist at job's completion. Works on assignment only. Provide resume and brochure to be kept on file for future assignments. Check for most recent titles in bookstores. Artist supplies overlays on cover art, inside illustrations and advertising art. Pays promised fee for unused assigned work.
Book Design: Assigns 10/year. Pays flat fee.
Inside Illustrations: Buys 50-100/year. Pays flat fee for b&w line drawings.

ROYAL PUBLISHING CO., Book Division of Recipes-of-the-Month Club, Box 5027, Beverly Hills CA 90212. (213)277-7220. Director: Mrs. Harold Klein. Publishes paperbacks on entertaining and cooking. Publishes 3 titles/year.
First Contact & Terms: Query with samples; local artists only. SASE. Reports in 4-6 weeks. Purchases outright. No originals returned to artist at job's completion. Works on assignment only. Samples returned by SASE; and reports back on future assignment possiblities. Provide brochure to be kept on file for future assignments. Check for most recent titles in bookstores. Negotiates pay.
Book Design: Assigns 3-4 jobs/year. Uses artists for layout and type spec.
Jackets/Covers: Assigns 3-4 jobs/year. Uses "4-color art; old-fashioned heirloom quality." Buys color washes, opaque watercolors and b&w line drawings.
Text Illustrations: Assigns 3-4 jobs/year. Buys b&w line drawings.
Advertising: Uses artists for brochures, ads, letterheads and business forms.

RUTGERS UNIVERSITY PRESS, 30 College Ave., New Brunswick NJ 08903. Marketing Manager: Phyllis Lanz. Managing Editor: Margaret L. Christ. Publishes scholarly and New Jersey regional books.
First Contact & Terms: Send resume with tearsheets. Prefers local artists. Buys various rights. Works on assignment only. No samples returned. Reports back on future assignment possiblities. Provide resume and tearsheet to be kept on file for future assignments. Artist supplies overlays for cover artwork.
Jackets/Covers: For jacket design must have previous experience. "Majority are 1- or 2-color typographic." Pays $175 minimum.
Text Illustrations: Previously published work not necessary but a plus.

WILLIAM H. SADLIER INC., 11 Park Place, New York NY 10007. (212)227-2120. Contact: Willi Kunz, design director, for editorial and advertising work. Estab. 1830. Publishes hardcover and paperback Catholic adult education, religious, mathematics, social studies and language arts books. Publishes 60 titles/year. Query with samples. SASE. Reports in 2 weeks. Buys all rights.
Book Design: Assigns 40 jobs/year. Uses artists for layout, type spec and mechanicals. Pays $8-12/hour.
Text Illustrations: Assigns 30 jobs/year. Pays $125-350, color washes and opaque watercolors; $75-150, gray opaques, b&w line drawings and washes.
Advertising: Uses artists for direct mail pieces and catalogs. Pays $10-12/hour or $175-250/job.

ST. MARTIN'S PRESS, 175 5th Ave., New York NY 10010. (212)674-5151. Art Director: Deborah Daly. Estab. 1952. Publishes hardcover general trade originals and reprints. Publishes 350-400 titles/year. Query with samples. SASE. Pays 25% of promised fee for unused assigned work. Buys all rights, but may reassign rights to artist after publication. Catalog available with 8½x11 SASE.
Book Design: Buys 40/year. Pays $100-150/job, type spec.
Jacket Design: Buys 150/year. Pays $150-300, b&w line drawings, washes and type; $250-600, color.

W.B. SAUNDERS CO., 210 W. Washington Square, Philadelphia PA 19105. Manager of Art Department: George W. Laurie. Book publisher/audiovisuals producer. Publishes hardcover and paperback books on medical and allied professional disciplines. Publishes 200 titles/year.
First Contact & Terms: Query with samples. Reports in 6 weeks. Buys all rights. Catalog available.
Text Illustrations: Assigns 25 jobs/year. Needs b&w line drawings and airbrush work. Pays $35-125/job pursuant to letter of agreement between artist and publisher.

Tips: "Common mistakes freelance artists make in working with us are failure to schedule, failure to ask questions regarding how much reduction artwork would take, and overcharging."

SCHOLASTIC BOOK SERVICES, 50 W. 44th St., New York NY 10036. Promotion Art Director, Trade and Book Club Promotion: Carol Gildar. Publishes book promotions for trade, consumer and school book clubs.
First Contact & Terms: Send samples of b&w or color line and tone illustrations, for files; no originals. Prefers local artists. Buys various rights. Originals not returned to artist at job's completion, unless requested. Works on assignment only. Provide business card, tearsheet and "samples of work" to be kept on file for future assignments. Check for most recent titles in bookstores. Artist sometimes supplies color overlays.
General Needs: Uses illustrators, designers, cartoonists and mechanicals artists for book publications, direct mail brochures, sales aids, advertising, layout and display. Also buys illustrations and photography for paperback book covers. Uses themes pertaining to children.

SCHOLIUM INTERNATIONAL INC., 130-30 31st Ave., Flushing NY 11354. (212)445-8700. President: A. L. Candido. Estab. 1970. Publishes scientific and technical books. Send photocopies or transparencies.
Needs: Uses artist for jacket design, direct mail brochures and advertising layouts/art.

SCOTT, FORESMAN AND CO., 1900 E. Lake Ave., Glenview IL 60025. Advertising Design Buyer: Joy Landgraf. Art Director: Hal Kearney. Publishes textbooks and instructional material.
First Contact & Terms: Write or call. Rights purchased vary; always buys exclusive textbook rights. Originals usually not returned to artist at job's completion. Works on assignment only. Samples returned by SASE; and reports back on future assignment possiblities. Provide resume, flyer, business card, tearsheet and brochure to be kept on file for future assignments.
Text Illustrations: Uses artists for all aspects of book illustration.
Advertising Design: Approximately 50% of advertising design is freelance.
Book Design: Approximately 15% of book design is freelance.
Cartoons: Cartoons published "but make up a small fraction of the whole." Negotiates pay.

CHARLES SCRIBNER'S SONS, 597 5th Ave., New York NY 10017. Contact: D. Hrisinko. Call for appointment.
Needs: Uses artists for jacket designs and inside illustrations. Pays $8-15/hour and $350/jacket illustration.

SERENDIPITY PRESS, Bld C, Suite 102, 3801 Kennett Pike, Wilmington DE 19807.
First Contact & Terms: Query with samples; local artists only. Buys various rights. Works on assignment only. Samples returned by SASE; and reports back on future assignment possiblities. Provide business card, tearsheet and brochure to be kept on file for future assignments. Artist supplies overlays for cover artwork, inside illustrations and advertising art.
General Needs: Uses artists for design of direct mail flyers, book interiors, posters, book end sheets, jackets and cartoons.

HAROLD SHAW PUBLISHERS, Box 567, 388 Gundersen Dr., Wheaton IL 60187. (312)665-6700. Production Editor: Ann Alexander for editorial work; Business Manager: John McDermott. Publishes original paperback Christian literature for adults and children, Bible study guide and literary criticism series.
First Contact & Terms: Query with samples and arrange interview to show portfolio; local artists only. SASE. Reports in 1-2 weeks. Buys all rights. Works on assignment only. Samples returned by SASE. Provide resume, brochure and "one or two samples or copies" to be kept on file for future assignments. Check for most recent titles in bookstores. Negotiate pay.
Jackets/Covers: Assigns 5-6 jobs/year. Buys color washes and opaque watercolors.
Text Illustrations: Assigns 2 jobs/year. Buys b&w line drawings.
Advertising Design: Uses artists for direct mail brochures, advertising and general design.
Book Design: Assigns 5-6 jobs/year. Uses artists for layout and type spec.
Cartoons: Buys 3-4 cartoons/year. Negotiates pay.

SIERRA CLUB BOOKS, 530 Bush St., San Francisco CA 94108. Contact: Jon Beckmann Daniel Moses or Eileen Max. Publishes books on natural history, science, ecology, alternate technology and conservation issues, and calendars and guides.
Needs: Uses artists for book illustration (maps, juvenille art) and jacket design.
First Contact & Terms: Query with resume.Provide resume, tearsheet and/or business card. Artist supplies overlays for all color art. Buys US world rights.

SILVER BURDETT CO., 250 James St., Morristown NJ 07960. Contact: Douglas R. Steinbauer. Publishes textbooks and educational materials. Submit samples.

SIMON & SCHUSTER INC., 1230 Avenue of the Americas, New York NY 10020. Director of Art & Design: Frank Metz. Publishes general adult fiction and nonfiction books. Leave portfolio for review and subsequent pick-up.
Needs: Uses artists for jackets and inside illustrations.

GEMINI SMITH INC., 5858 Desert View Dr., La Jolla CA 92037. (714)454-4321. Manager: Elisabeth Smith. Publishes oversize hardcover mainstream and visual books on art and history. Publishes 2 books/year.
First Contact & Terms: Send resume; "local artists only, although New York references preferred." SASE. Reports in 2 weeks.
Jackets/Covers: Assigns 2 jobs/year. Buys b&w line drawings. Negotiates pay.
Book Design: Assigns 3 jobs/year. Uses artists for layout, paste-up and type spec. Pays $100-3,000/job.
Tips: "Artists must have solid background in book design and production."

SINGER COMMUNICATIONS, INC., 3164 Tyler Ave., Anaheim CA 92801. (714)527-5650. Contact: Eldon Maynard. Publishes paperback originals and reprints; mass market, western, romance, doctor/nurse, mystery, science fiction and sex. Publishes 400 titles/year.
First Contact & Terms: Queary with samples. SASE. Reports in 2 weeks. Provide business card, tearsheet, brochures and samples of published work to be kept on file for future assignments. Buys first and reprint rights. Originals returned to artist at job's completion. Artist's guidelines $1.
Book Design: Assigns "many" jobs/year. Offers advance.
Jackets/Covers: Assigns 400 jobs/year. Popular styles include western, romance, mystery, science fiction, war and gothic. Pays $100-250, color. Offers advance.
Cartoons: Buys 3,000 cartoons/year to be internationally syndicated to newspaper and magazine publishers—also used for topical books. Pays minimum $10/b&w cartoon, $25/color.
Tips: "Look at published paperback covers and submit similar. "Check books in stores for popular styles and categories."

GEMINI SMITH INC., 5858 Desert View Dr., La Jolla CA 92037. (714)454-4321. Manager: Elisabeth Smith. Publishes oversize hardcover mainstream and visual books on art and history. Publishes 2 books/year.
First Contact & Terms: Send resume; "local artists only, although New York references preferred." SASE. Reports in 2 weeks.
Book Design: Assigns 2 jobs/year. Uses artists for layout, paste-up and type spec. Pays $100-3,000/job.
Jackets/Covers: Assigns 2 jobs/year. Buys b&w line drawings. Negotiates pay.
To Break In: "Artists must have solid background in book design and production."

SOUTHERN PUBLISHING ASSOCIATION, Box 59, Nashville TN 37202. Director of Book Design: Dean Tucker. Publishes inspirational biographies, nature stories and religious books.
First Contact & Terms: Send tear sheets or transparencies. Buys various rights. Works on assignment only. provide business card and samples to be kept on file for future assignments. Artist supplies overlays for cover artwork, inside illustrations and advertising art.
Jackets/Covers: Pays $300-600, full-color book cover painting.
Text Illustrations: Pays $40/full page for 1-color text illustration.
Advertising Design: Uses artists for advertising layouts.
Cartoons: Buys 15 cartoons/year. Pays $25, b&w; $50, color.

SOUTH-WESTERN PUBLISHING CO., 5101 Madison Rd., Cincinnati OH 45227. (513)271-8811. Art Director: E.H. Swillinger. Publishes hardcover and paperback business and economic textbooks. Buys 75%-90% of charts, graphs, etc. from freelancers. Arrange interview. Buys all rights. Pays $150-400, b&w cover; $250 minimum, color cover; $15-30.
Needs: Charts and graphs, average $25-50 each.

STANDARD PUBLISHING, 8121 Hamilton Ave., Cincinnati OH 45231. Advertising Manager: John Weidner. Art Director: Frank Sutton. Publishes religious, self-help and children's books.
Needs: Uses artists for design and illustrations for advertising, books, catalogs, convention exhibits, decorative spots, direct mail brochures, letterheads, magazines, packages and posters.
First Contact & Terms: Query with samples. Provide business card to be kept on file for future assignments. SASE. Reports in 2 weeks. Buys all rights. Free catalog.

CLAUDE STARK & COMPANY, PUBLISHERS, Box 43, W. Dennis, Cape Cod MA 02670. General Manager: J.J. Liebermann. Publishes "practical works of enduring beauty" including the God Series, Africana Series, New Age Series and a philosophy series. Query. Catalog available.
Needs: Uses artists for jacket design, book design, graphics and display ads; pen and inks, pastels, line drawings and prints.

STEIN AND DAY, Scarborough House, Briarcliff Manor NY 10510. Art Director: Robert McBroom. Jackets: Daphne Hougham. Publishes hardcover and paperback fiction and nonfiction. Published 105 titles in 1979.
First Contact & Terms: Prefers local artists with experience with other publishers. Query with samples. SASE. Reports in 4 weeks. Works on assignment only. Samples returned by SASE. Reports back on future assignment possibilities. Provide resume, brochure and/or flyer to be kept on file for future assignments. Artist provides overlays for color covers. Buys all rights. Negotiates pay for unused assigned work. Pays on publication. Free catalog.
Jacket Design: Uses artists for monstly straight-type covers (2-3 colors with WWII titles). Pays $175 minimum, color.
Text Illustrations: Uses artists for line work—how-to-do-it books. Rarely buys b&w line drawings.
Production: Uses artists for paste-up and dummying.

STONE WALL PRESS INC., 1241 30th St. NW, Washington DC 20007. Publisher: Henry Wheelwright. Publishes paperback and hardcover environmental, backpacking, fishing, cross-country skiing, beginning and advanced outdoor originals. Publishes 3-5 titles/year. Works on assignment only. Samples returned by SASE. Provide brochure to be kept on file for future assignments. Artist supplies overlays for cover artwork.
First Contact & Terms: Query with resume. SASE. Reports in 2 weeks. Buys one-time rights. No originals returned to artist at job's completion.
Text Illustrations: Buys b&w line drawings.
Cartoons: Buys cartoons "on a specific per project basis. Bought 4 cartoons at $50 each in 1979.

STRUCTURES PUBLISHING CO., Box 1002, Farmington MI 48024. (313)477-2600. Production Manager: Carey Jean Ferchland. Publishes reference and consumer construction books.
First Contact & Terms: Contact production manager by mail only, including resume and references. Buys one-time rights or purchases outright. Works on assignment only. Samples returned by SASE. Reports back on future assignment possibilities. Provide resume business card and other "applicable information" to be kept on file for future assignments. Check for most recent titles in bookstores. Artist sometimes supplies overlays for color work. Catalog 50¢.
Jackets/Covers: Uses color covers for how-to books: "vertical format; no people."
Text Illustrations: Uses b&w line art.
Cartoons: Occasionally uses cartoons. Interested in do-it-yourself themes.

SUHA PUBLICATIONS, 661 Main St., Malden MA 02148. (617)321-4295. Editorial Director: Yvette Grimes. Estab. 1977. Publishes poetry, anthologies, short stories and fiction; hardcover and paperback originals. Publishes 30-50 titles/year. Query with resume. SASE. Reports in 1 week. Offers advance. Pays promised fee for unused assigned work. Buys all rights, but may reassign rights to artist after publication. Free catalog and artist's guidelines.
Jacket Design: Buys 10/year. Minimum payment: $25, b&w; $35, color.
Inside Illustrations: Buys 30/year. Pays $5 minimum, b&w line drawings and washes.

SYCAMORE ISLAND BOOKS, Division of Paladin Enterprises, Inc., Box 1307, Boulder CO 80306. (303)443-7250. General Manager: Timothy J. Leifield. Publishes hardcover and paperback originals and reprints for general trade. Publishes 3-4 titles/year.
First Contact & Terms: Local artists only. Query. SASE. Reports in 1 month. Buys all rights. Free catalog for SASE.
Jackets/Covers: Assigns 3/year. Pays $100-400, b&w line drawings and washes; $300-800, color washes. "If artist develops original design, payment increases. If the artist is given a specific design to execute, payment is less."
Text Illustrations: Assigns 4/year. Buys b&w line drawings, washes and color washes.

SYRACUSE UNIVERSITY PRESS, 1011 E. Water St., Syracuse NY 13210. Manager, Design/Production: Sally Eddy. Publishes Adirondack series, Iroquois series, New York State Studies, special education series, contemporary issues in the Middle East series, foreign language bibliographies, history, geography, ecology and some technical books. Published 16 titles in 1979.
First Contact & Terms: Send original art, photocopies or transparencies. Works on assignment only. Samples returned by SASE. Provide resume flyer, tearsheet, brochure and anything which

shows artisticability to be kept on file for future assignments. Artist provides overlays for color cover art. Originals returned to artist upon request.
General Needs: Occasionally uses artists for jackets (2 color and varnish or lamination; good type style, with illustration or halftone–depending on suject matter of book) and/or paper covers, typography, rarely needs book illustrations (author's responsibility, but we occasionally offer suggestions) and direct mail brochures. Fees negotiated in advanced.

TAB BOOKS, Sylvester Court, East Norwalk CT 06855. (203)866-5450. Editorial Director: Dorothy M. Greenberg. Publishes hardcover and paperback originals on automotive and aviation subjects. Publishes about 25 titles/year.
First Contact & Terms: Query. Reports in 3 weeks. Buys first and reprint rights. Sample catalog and artist's guidelines available.

TAB BOOKS, INC., Blue Ridge Summit PA 17214. (717)794-2191. Editor (editorial work): Anthony R. Curtis. Vice President/advertising (advertising work): Bob Sites. Publishes hardcover and paperback originals on technical, hobby, electronics, how-to and craft subjects. Publishes 125 titles/year.
First Contact & Terms: Prefers professional experience with book publishing firms. Query with resume and samples or arrange interview to show portfolio. SASE. Reports in 2 weeks. Buys all rights. Free catalog.
Text Illustrations: Assigns 125 jobs/year. Buys b&w line drawing sand cartoons. Negotiates pay.
Book Design: Uses artists for layout and paste-up. Negotiates pay.
Tips: "Show us you can do quality technical illustrations and schematic diagrams."

TANDEM PRESS, Tannersville PA 18372. (717)629-2250. Contact: Judith Keith. Publishes hardcover and trade paperback books. Buys 3 designs/year. Query with resume. Contacts artists as needs arise. Pays on acceptance.
Needs: Pays $350 minimum, $600 average, for 4-color jacket design including mechanicals. Also uses artists for direct mail brochures.

TEACHERS COLLEGE PRESS, 1234 Amsterdam Ave., New York NY 10027. Design/Production Manager: Romeo M. Enriquez. Estab. 1908. Publishes educational books, classroom materials and teachers' guides; hardcover and paperback originals and reprints. Publishes 30-40 titles/year. Arrange interview. SASE. Reports in 1 week. No advance. Pays $50 kill fee for unused jackets and covers. Buys all rights. Free catalog.
Book Design: Assigns 20/year. Pays $200-250/job, layout.
Jacket Design: Buys 30/year. Pays $175-200, b&w; $250, color.
Inside Illustrations: Buys 100/year. Pays $25-50, b&w line drawings.

TEN SPEED PRESS, Box 7123, Berkeley CA 94707. (415)845-8414. Editorial Director: Phil Wood. Publishes hardcover and paperback cookbook, history, sports, gardening, career and life planning originals and reprints. Publishes 8-12 titles/year.
First Contact & Terms: Submit art or query. SASE. Reports in 1 week. Works on assignment only. Samples returned by SASE. Reports back on future assignment possibilities. Provide resume, flyer and/or sample art to be kept on file for future assignments. Originals returned to artist at job's completion. Buys all rights, but may reassign rights to artist after publication. Pays 3% royalty or flat fee. Offers advance. Pays promised fee for unused assigned work. Free catalog.
Jackets/Covers: Buys 10/year. Pays $100-500.
Inside Illustrations: Buys 100/year. Pay varies.
Advertising: Assigns 30 jobs/year. Pays $1,000 max./job, catalogs; $500 max./job, direct mail brochures.
Book Design: Assigns 10/year. Pays $500 minimum.
Cartoons: Needs fluctuate from year to year.
Production: Assigns 18 jobs/year. Pay varies.

TEXAS WESTERN PRESS, University of Texas at El Paso, El Paso TX 79968. Contact: Director. Publishes books on southwestern history.
First Contact & Terms: Query. Pays $100, jacket design.
General Needs: Uses artists for jacket design and inside illustrations.

TIME-LIFE BOOKS INC., 777 Duke St., Alexandria VA 22314. Art Director: Tom Suzuki. Assistant Art Director: Arnold C. Holeywell. Publishes hardcover books in series. Currently working on World War II, home repair, sea farers and epic of flight. Publishes 35-40 titles/year.
First Contact & Terms: Arrange interview to present portfolio. Do not mail original artwork.

SASE. Buys all reproduction rights, world wide. No originals returned to artist at job's completion. Works on assignment only. Samples returned by SASE. Reports back on future assignment possibilities. Provide flyer, tearsheet, brochure and photostats to be kept on file for future assignments. No advance. Negotiates pay for unused assigned work. Pays on acceptance.
Text Illustrations: Buys over 1,000/year. Art is scientific and technical. Pays $50-1,000, b&w; $80-1,500, color.

TIMES MIRROR MAGAZINES INC., BOOK DIVISION, 380 Madison Ave., New York NY 10017. (212)687-3000. Contact: Jeffrey Fitschen. Publishes hardcover originals on popular science, outdoor life, adult trade, home/shop/auto how-to, hunting, fishing and wilderness how-to subjects. Publishes 8-10 titles/year. Query or arrange interview to show portfolio. SASE. Reports in 1 month. Buys one-time rights. Free catalog.
Book Design: Assigns 3 jobs/year. Uses artists for layout and type spec. Pays $200-300/job.
Text Illustrations: Assigns 8 jobs/year. Buys b&w line drawings, technical line art, gray opaques, opaque watercolors and washes. Pays $30-100, b&w.

TRADO-MEDIC BOOKS, A Division of Conch Magazine Ltd., Publishers, 102 Normal Ave. (Symphony Circle) Buffalo NY 14213. (716)885-3686. Managing Editor: Lynda S. Anozie. Publishes hardcover and paperback originals on health, medicine and culture in the Third World, Africa in particular. Publishes 10 titles/year.
First Contact & Terms: Query with samples. Prefers "as wide a variety of samples as the artist has tearsheets preferred to originals." Artist should be professional, with a feel for African local color. SASE. Reports in 2 weeks. Buys all rights. No originals returned to artist at job's completion. Works on assignment only. Samples returned by SASE. Reports back on future assignment possibilities. Provide resume, flyer, tearsheet and brochure to be kept on file for future assignments. Artist supplies overlays for all color artwork. Free catalog if available.
Jackets/Covers: Assigns 4/year. Pays $25-50, b&w line drawings, gray opaques and 2-color designs.
Text Illustrations: Pays $25-50, b&w line drawings, gray opaques and 2-color designs. Buys over 1,000/year. Also uses cartoons.
Advertising: Uses artists for catalog, letterhead and envelope design and brochure illustrations. Themes include Africa, traditional medicine of all kinds, botany, etc. Pays $25-50/job, b&w or color.
Book Design: Assigns 4/year. Themes include Africa, traditional medicine of all kinds, botany, etc. Pays $25-50/job, layout.
Cartoons: Number cartoons bought/year varies. Themes include Africa, traditional medicine of all kinds, botany, etc. Minimum payment: b&w, $25.

TRANSACTION INC., Rutgers University, New Brunswick NJ 08903. Contact: Harry Moehring. Publishes social science books.
First Contact & Terms: Submit published samples. Reports in 4 months. Buys one-time rights. Pays on publication.
Cover Design: Pays $100.

TROUBADOR PRESS INC., 385 Fremont St., San Francisco CA 94105. (415)397-3716. Publisher: Malcolm K. Whyte. Production Manager: June Blackburn. Publishes hardcover and paperback project and activity, maze and puzzle, nonfiction and art originals. Publishes 10-15 titles/year.
First Contact & Terms: Query with copies of "b&w art outline of work." SASE. Reports in 4 weeks. Buys all rights. Originals returned to artist at job's completion. Provide resume and tearsheet to be kept on file for future assignments. Check for most recent tieles in bookstores. Pays 5-10% royalty. Offers advance. Pays promised fee for unused assigned work. Free catalog and artist's guidelines.
Needs: Uses artists for design and illustrations. Pays $25-100/illustration.

TYNDALE HOUSE PUBLISHERS, 336 Gundersen Dr., Carol Stream IL 60187. (312)668-8300. Contact: Tim Botts, art director. Publishes books and magazines on Christianity, the Christian life, family, the church and overseas missions for adult and juvenile trades. Publishes 100 titles/year.
First Contact & Terms: Query with samples. "We only want to see an illustrator's best work. So quality is more important than quantity." SASE. Reports in 3 weeks. Buys one-time rights. Provide samples of work to be kept on file for future assignments. Check for most recent titles in bookstores.Free catalog and artist's guidelines. Artist sometimes supplies overlays for cover artwork and inside illustrations.

Jackets/Covers: Assigns 20 jobs/year. Pays $100 minimum, b&w line drwings, washes and gray opaques; $200 minimum, color washes and opaque watercolors.
Text Illustrations: Assigns 60 jobs/year. Pays $50 minimum, b&w line drawings, washes and gray opaques; $75 minimum, color washes and opaque watercolors.
Cartoons: Buys 10 cartoons/year. Minimum payment: $35, b&w; $75, color.

UNION OF AMERICAN HEBREW CONGREGATIONS, 838 5th Ave., New York NY 10021. (212)249-0100. Director of Publications: Ralph Davis. Produces books, filmstrips and magazines for Jewish school children.
First Contact & Terms: Mail samples or write for interview. SASE. Reports in 3 weeks. Free catalog. Pays $50-200, illustrations.
General Needs: Buys book covers and illustrations.

UNITY PRESS, 235 Hoover Rd., Santa Cruz CA 95065. (408)427-2020. Art Director: Craig Caughlan. Publishes hardcover and paperback general trade books. Published 3 titles and bought 20 designs in 1977.
First Contact & Terms: Query "something that I can keep on file—photocopies, etc." SASE. Reports in 3 weeks. Buys one-time rights and all rights. Original returned to artist at job's completion, if requested. Works on assignment only. Samples returned by SASE. Reports back on future assignment possibilities. provide flyer, tearsheet and brochure to be kept on file for future assignments. Check for most recent titles in bookstores. Free catalog and artist's guidelines. Artist supplies overlap for inside illustrations and advertising art. Pays on acceptance.
Jacket Design: Pays $100-250, b&w; $200-400, color.
Inside Illustrations: Pays $20-50, b&w.
Advertising: Pays $25-75, b&w ad illustration; $50-150, b&w direct mail brochure; $100-250, color brochure.
Production: Pays $7.50/hour, mechanicals.

UNIVELT INC., Box 28130, San Diego CA 92128. (714)746-4005. Manager: H. Jacobs. Publishes hardcover and paperback originals on astronautics and related fields. Publishes 10 titles/year; all use illustrators.
First Contact & Terms: Prefers local artists. Send letter of inquiry. Provide resume, calling card, letter of inquiry and/or flyer to be kept on file for future assignments. Works on assignment only. Samples returned by SASE. Reports back on future assignmnt possibilities. Reports in 4 weeks on unsolicited submissions. Buys one-time rights. Originals returned to artist at job's completion. Artist supplies overlays for cover artwork. Free catalog. Pays $50-100/book design.

UNIVERSITY OF IOWA PRESS, Graphic Services Bldg., University of Iowa, Iowa City IA 52242. Director: John E. Simmons. Publishes scholarly works, poetry translations and short fiction series.
First Contact & Terms: Query with "two or three samples; originals not required." Works on assignment only. Samples returned by SASE. Reports back on future assignment possibilities. Check for most recent titles in bookstores.Free catalog and artist's guidelines. Free catalog.
General Needs: Pays $300 minimum, book design; $100, jacket.

UNIVERSITY OF NEBRASKA PRESS, 901 N. 17th St., Lincoln NE 68588. Art Director: Thomas E. Sheahan. Publishes hardcover and paperback books on western and literary history. Buys 10 designs/year.
First Contact & Terms: Query with samples (4-5 tearsheets). SASE. Reports in 3 weeks. Buys various rights. Originals returned to artist at job's completion. Works on assignment only. No samples returned. Reports back on future assignment possibilities. Provide tearsheet and brochure to be kept on file for future assignments. Check for most recent titles in bookstores. Negotiates pay for unused assigned work. Pays on acceptance.
Jackets/Covers: Pays $100-150, b&w; $150-200, color.
Inside Illustrations: Pays $30-60, b&w; $100-150, color.

UNIVERSITY OF NOTRE DAME PRESS, Notre Dame IN 46656. Editor: Ann Rice. Mail photocopies or transparencies. SASE.
Needs: Uses artists for jacket design, inside illustrations and direct mail brochures. "Our inside illustrations consist primarily of maps, graphs and charts. Jackets are 2- or 3-color." Pays $175-200, jacket design; $75, cover design of promotion piece.

UNIVERSITY OF PENNSYLVANIA PRESS, 3933 Walnut St., Philadelphia PA 19104. Editorial Director: Maurice English. Art Director: Tracy Baldwin. Publishes scholarly books and texts;

hardcover and paperback originals and reprints. Publishes 16-21 titles/year. Arrange interview; local artists only. SASE. Buys all rights. No advance. Negotiates payment for unused assigned work. Free catalog.
Book and Jacket Design: Buys 10-15 titles/year. Pays $200-250/job, layout; $50/job, type spec; $50-100, b&w line drawings and washes, gray opaques and color-separated work.
Advertising: Assigns 5 jobs/year. Minimum payment: $250, catalogs; $125, direct mail brochures.
Production: Assigns 15-20 jobs/year. Pays $5 max./hour, mechanicals and paste-up.

UNIVERSITY OF TREES PRESS, Box 644, Boulder Creek CA 95006. Advertising Director: Susan Welker. Publishes paperbacks on adult trade. Publishes 5 titles/year; all require designers.
First Contact & Terms: Send samples and previously published work. Reports in 1 month on unsolicited submissions. Provide resume, brochure and/or flyer to be kept on file for future assignments. Works on assignment only. Samples returned by SASE. Buys first rights. Artist supplies overlays for cover artwork, advertising art and inside illustrations. Check for most recent titles in bookstores. Pays $200-500/job for book design and jackets/covers.

THE UNIVERSITY OF WISCONSIN PRESS, 114 N. Murray St., Madison WI 53715. (608)262-4978. Production Manager: Gardner R. Wills. Publishes scholarly hardcover and paperback books. Publishes 25-35 titles/year.
First Contact & Terms: Query first. Reports in 2 weeks. Buys all rights. No originals returned to artist at job's completion. Works on assignment only. Samples returned by SASE. Reports back on future assignment possibilities. Provide letter of inquiry and samples as agreed upon to be kept on file for future assignments. Check for most recent titles in bookstores. Artist supplies overlays for cover artwork. No advance. Free catalog and artist's guidelines.
Jackets/Covers: Buys 20-25/year. Pays $150+, b&w line drawings, washes, halftones and color-separated work "only if part of the jacket/cover design package. We do not purchase individual items of art."
Book Design: Assigns 20-25/year. Pays $150+.

THE UNIVERSITY PRESS OF HAWAII, 2840 Kolowalu St., Honolulu HI 96822. (808)948-8275. Art Director: Janet Heavenridge. Publishes scholarly work in Pacific and Asian anthropology, art, linguistics and philosophy; hardcover and paperback originals and reprints. Publishes 60-75 titles/year.
First Contact & Terms: Query with resume and samples. Reports in 3 weeks. No advance. Pays promised fee for unused assigned work. Buys book rights.
Jacket Design: Buys 15-20/year. Pays $100 minimum, b&w; $200 minimum, color.
Advertising: Assigns 3-4 jobs/year. Pays $50 min./job, direct mail brochures; $100 min./job, catalogs.
Book Design: Assigns 10-12/year. Pays $5 min./hour, layout.

THE UNIVERSITY SOCIETY INC., 25 Cottage St., Midland Park NJ 07432. Editor-in-Chief: George W. Cooke. Estab. 1897. "We specialize in music books, specifically, high-quality anthologies and collections, some with full-color 9x12 cover illustrations. Our needs are specialized and extremely limited. Most of our work is supplied by local paste-up artists and illustrators."
Needs: Uses artists for jacket design, inside illustrations, direct mail brochures, and advertising layout/art. Pays $150, detailed schematic diagram; $1,000, cover painting.

VANGUARD PRESS INC., 424 Madison Ave., New York NY 10017. Contact: Thomas Woll or Evelyn Shrifte. Publishes general interest books. Mail art.
Needs: Uses artists for jacket design and inside illustrations.

VIRGO PRESS, 103 Church St., Suite 209, Toronto, Ontario, Canada M5C 2G3. (416)368-0073. Owner: Thad McIlroy. Publishes hardcover and paperback originals of a wide variety, but specializing in mysteries and true crime. Published about 5 titles in 1979.
First Contact & Terms: Send letter of inquiry and resume; local artists only. SASE. Reports in 4 weeks. Buys various rights. Original usually returned to artist at job's completion. Provide resume, tearsheet and letter of inquiry to be kept on file for future assignments. Check for most recent titles in bookstores. Free sample catalog with SASE.
Jackets/Covers: Assigns 5-8/year. Negotiates pay on b&w line drawings, gray opaques, b&w and color washes, and opaque watercolors; no royalties. Sometimes offers advance.
Text Illustrations: Assigns 3-4/year. Uses b&w line drawings, gray opaques, b&w and color washes and opaque watercolors. Sometimes pays a royalty and offers an advance if illustrations are a significant feature of the book.
Book Design: Assigns 5-8/year. Uses artists for layout. Negotiates pay; no royalties.

Cartoons: Number cartoons bought/year varies. Pays varying amounts.
Tips: "We are looking for experienced designers, particularly of mass-market paperbacks, who do not have an overly inflated view of their own talent and worth."

VISAGE PRESS INC., 108A South Columbus St., Alexandria VA 22314. (703)549-7694. Art Director: Sherry Icenhower. Publishes hardcover and paperback books. Publishes 5-10 titles (10-15 designs)/year.
First Contact & Terms: Query with samples. SASE. Reports in 1 month. Buys all rights. Pays on publication. Catalog and artist's guidelines with SASE.
Jacket Design: Pays $50 minimum, b&w and color.
Advertising: Uses artists for advertising and direct mail brochure layout and illustration. Pays $50 minimum, b&w and color.

WALKER & COMPANY, 720 5th Ave., New York NY 10019. (212)265-3632. Art Director: Robert Barto. Publishes hardcover originals and reprints on mysteries, regencey romance, children's science, adult trade, etc. Publishes 30 titles/year; 20 of which require designers, 4 use illustrators.
First Contact & Terms: Send resume, 20 samples of printed jacket designs and previously published work (eight samples of printed and bound book designs). Reports back in 6 months on unsolicited submissions. Works on assignment only. Samples returned by SASE. Reports back on future assignment possibilities. Provide resume, calling card and letter of inquiry to be kept on file for future assignments. Buys first rights. No originals returned to artist at job's completion. Artist supplies overlays for cover artwork and inside illustrations. Free catalog. Pays $200-500/job for book design; $150-250/b&w and color per job for jackets/covers and $20-40/b&w text illustration per job.

WARNER BOOKS INC., 75 Rockefeller Plaza, New York NY 10019. Art Director: Gene Light.
First Contact & Terms: Query or call. Buys first rights. Originals returned to artist at job's completion. Works on assignment only. Provide tear sheets to be kept on file for future assignments. Check for most recent titles in bookstores.
Jackets/Covers: Uses realistic jacket illustrations. Pays $400.

WILLIAM-FREDERICK PRESS, 308 E. 79th St., New York NY 10021. (212)628-1995. Contact: T. Reed. Custom-book-printing firm.
First Contact & Terms: Local artists should arrnge interview; out-of-towners should submit resume and photocopes. Pays $6/hour minimum.
General Needs: Uses artists for 6x9 or 8x11 jacket drawings and for spot art.

WILSHIRE BOOK CO., 12015 Sherman Rd., North Hollywood CA 91605. (213)875-1711 or 983-1105. President: Melvin Powers. Publishes paperback reprints on psychology, self-help, inspirational and other types of nonfiction. Publishes 25 title/year.
First Contact & Terms: Local artists only. Call. Buys first, reprint or one-time rights. Negotiates pay. Free catalog.
Jackets/Covers: Assigns 25 jobs/year. Buys b&w line drawings.

WINSTON PRESS, 430 Oak Grove, Minneapolis MN 55403. (612)871-7000. Contact: Kathe Wilcoxon, designer. Publishes curriculum and trade books. Publishes 20-30 titles/year; 2 of which require designers; 10 use illustrators. "Most illustration is purchased for curriculum."
First Contact & Terms: Send letter of inquiry and any samples available. Works on assignment only. Samples returned by SASE. Provide tear sheets to be kept on file for future assignments. Buys first rights. Originals sometimes returned at job's completion. Artist sometimes supplies overlays for inside illustrations. Pays $50-300 b&w/color for jackets/covers and $50-200/b&w; $50-300/color for text illustrations.

WISCONSIN TALES & TRAILS, INC., Box 5650, Madison WI 53705. (608)831-3363. Managing Editor: Jill Weber Dean. Publishes adult trade books; "only those that relate in some way to Wisconsin. 3 categories: Wisconsiana, guides, nature/environment. Publishes 2-3 titles/year; all of which require designers and illustrators. "Marketing department occasionally has need of artists and designers for brochures and other mailing pieces.
First Contact & Terms: Send letter of inquiry and samples to be kept on file for future assignments. Works on assignment only. Samples returned by SASE "if requested". Reports back on future assignment possibilities. Buys one-time rights. Return of original artwork "depends on individual contract or agreement negotiated." Artist supplies overlays for cover artwork. Check for most recent titles in bookstores or send for free guidelines. Pays by individual contract.

YE GALLEON PRESS, Box 25, Fairfield WA 99012. (509)283-2422. Editorial Director: Glen Adams. Publishes rare western history, Indian material, antiquarian shipwreck and old whaling accounts, and town and area histories; hardcover and paperback originals and reprints. Publishes 20-30 titles/year. Query with samples. SASE. No advance. Pays promised fee for unused assigned work. Buys book rights. Free catalog.
Text Illustrations: Buys b&w line drawings and some wood engravings, of a historical nature; prefers drawings of groups with facial expressions and some drawings of sailing and whaling vessels. Pays $5-35.

ZONDERVAN, 1415 Lake Drive SE, Grand Rapids, MI 49506. Contact: Art Jacobs. Publishes Christian fiction and nonfiction.
First Contact & Terms: Query with samples containing "type and illustration together", or portfolio with printed samples of past assigned work." Buys all rights. No originals returned to artist at job's completion. Works on assignment only. Samples returned by SASE. Reports back on future assignment possibilities. Provide samples of previously assigned jobs to be kept on file for future assignments. Check for most recent titles in bookstores.
General Needs: Uses artists for jacket design, some book illustration, music album covers, direct mail brochures and advertising. Pays $250 minimum, jacket design.

Businesses

Top selling products don't just happen. They're designed, manufactured and advertised. And, one important behind-the-scenes person in any product's development is the artist.

The markets listed below provide assignments for brochure design, posters, signs, print ads, logos, POP displays, annual reports, tie-in products and product design.

Each listing includes a description of the nature of each business after the name of the person who is to be contacted. Artists who are attracted by a particular listing, but feel they need more knowledge about the company's business can learn more about that industry by asking the local librarian to recommend a list of related trade publications.

ADVANCED R&D INC., Box 7600, Orlando FL 32804. Personnel Administrator: Ruth Byron.
Needs: Works with 4 artists/year for illustrators for use on products. For product designs, submit natural themes, such as technical illustrations, schematic, exploded views, aerospace, avionics equipment related also to product. Also needs technical art for catalog covers, publications, charts, graphs, manuals and isometrics (exploded and cutaway views and schematic).
First Contact & Terms: Provide resume to be kept on file for future assignments. Payment by the hour. Pays $7-8/day.

AFRICAN LION SAFARI, Box 326, Port Clinton OH 43452. (419)732-3606. Contact: Thurza Smith.
Needs: Uses artists for posters and signs.
First Contact & Terms: Query with resume and photos or tearsheets. Pays $10 minimum, signs.

ALBUQUERQUE CABLE TV, Box 3460, Albuquerque NM 87190. (505)293-3770. Public Relations/Marketing Manager: Roger Suppona. Estab. 1972. Distributes cable TV programs. Query; prefers local artists. SASE. Reports in 2 weeks.
Needs: Uses artists for advertising, direct mail brochures, handbooks, publicity brochures and signage.

THE ALLEN CO., Box 528, Broomfield CO 80020. Advertising Manager: George Cavanaugh. Manufactures gun cases, archery cases and accessories.
Needs: Uses artists for sales literature and annual catalogs.
First Contact & Terms: Query.

ALTON LITHO & GRAPHICS, 362 W. Garvey Ave., Monterey Park CA 91754. (213)288-8211. Estab. 1971. Typesetter and printer. Clients: Art studios, manufacturers and advertising agencies. Assigns 3-4 jobs/year; local artists only. Mail samples. SASE. Reports in 2 weeks.
Needs: Uses artists for illustrations, layout and logo design.

AMARILLO CHAMBER OF COMMERCE, 1000 Polk St., Amarillo TX 79101. (806)376-9083. Contact: Leslie Slak, media coordinator.
Needs: Works with 2 advertising designers/year. Uses artists for printed and video materials. Printed materials include magazines, brochures, pamphlets, directories, programs and posters.
First Contact & Terms: Local artists only. Query, "we need only to know who is available." SASE. Reports in 2-3 weeks. Provide calling card and tear sheet to be kept on file for future assignments. "Much of our work is donated to help the artist publicize. We use many student artists this way to help them build a portfolio."

AMERICAN AIR FILTER CO. INC., 215 Central Ave., Louisville KY 40277. (502)588-9501. Corporate Manager: Robert C. Braverman. Develops, manufactures and sells equipment and systems to improve and control air quality.
Needs: Uses artists for catalog covers/layouts, direct mail/publicity brochures, displays, exhibit designs, posters, technical charts/illustrations and company publications.
First Contact & Terms: Write for interview. Buys all rights. Works on assignment only. Samples returned by SASE; reports back on future assignment possibilities. Provide calling card, brochure and flyer to be kept on file for future assignments. Negotiates payment.

AMUSEMENT TECHNOLOGY INC., 1200 Memorial Dr., Asbury Park NJ 07712. (201)988-3100. Advertising Manager: M. Braverman. Estab. 1960. Manufactures amusement rides/devices and promotes and designs amusement parks. Assigns 60 jobs/year. Mail art, query with samples or arrange interview. SASE. Reports in 2 weeks.
Needs: Uses artists for advertising, brochures, logo designs and exhibits/displays. Pay varies.

ART ASSOCIATES, Box 4098, Waterville CT 06704. (203)574-3484 or 573-8293. Art Director: J. Semprini. Estab. 1976. Promotes artists' work. Assigns 50-100 jobs and buys 100 illustrations/year. Mail art, query with samples or arrange interview. SASE. Reports in 1 day.
Needs: Uses artists for advertising, charts, direct mail brochures, exhibits/displays, POP displays, posters and architecture. Payment by job: $10-500, design; $10-1,000, illustration; $10-100, lettering.

ATLANTA BRAVES BASEBALL CLUB, Box 4064, Atlanta GA 30302. (404)522-7630. Director of Publications: Bob Korch. Professional baseball club.
Needs: Works with 2 artists/year for ad illustrations; 2 for ad design and 3 artists/year for product illustrations. Also uses artists for magazine covers and promotional brochures.
First Contact & Terms: Write. Works on assignment only. Samples returned by SASE. Reports back on future assignment possibilities. Provide calling card to be kept on file for future assignments. Negotiates payment.

AVERY LABEL, 777 E. Foothill Blvd., Azusa CA 91702. (213)969-3311. Contact: Robert T. Cardinali. Manufactures pressure-sensitive labels and labeling equipment.
Needs: Works with 3 illustrations, 4 advertising design, 4 product design and 3 illustrations for use on products/year. Uses artists for catalog layout, packaging, simple literature, presentations (seminars, visuals, pages), short promotionals and label designs.
First Contact & Terms: Local artists only. Call for interview to establish working relationship. Currently working with graduating students. Will call when artist is needed; works on a 1-3 day turn around. Reports in 1-2 weeks. Works on assignment only. No samples returned. Reports back on future assignment possibilities. Provide calling card and flyer to be kept on file for future assignments. Pays $4.35/hour, average $10.

BARON PUTTERS INC., 156 W. Providencia, Burbank CA 91502. (213)846-9113. Manufactures golf putters. Arrange interview to show portfolio.
Needs: Uses artists for sales literature, catalog covers, displays and ads.

BEECH BEND PARK, Beech Bend Rd., Bowling Green KY 42101. (502)842-8101. Amusement park.
Needs: Uses artists for advertising work; especially need caricature artists.
First Contact & Terms: Query with resume and samples direct to Beech Bend Park. Pays $15-25.

BEROL USA, Berol Corp., Eagle Rd., Danbury CT 06810. (203)744-0000. Sales Promotion Manager: Marvin Zimmerman. Manufactures writing instruments.
Needs: Assigns 6 jobs/year. Uses artists for illustrations and layout for catalogs, ads, brochures, displays, packages and posters.
First Contact & Terms: Query with samples.

BEST WESTERN INC., Best Western Way, Box 10203, Phoenix AZ 85061. (602)957-5763. Director of Creative Services: Sal Casciaro. Motel inn/hotel resort chain.
Needs: Assigns 200 jobs/year.
First Contact & Terms: Query with samples.

BLONDER-TONGUE LABORATORIES INC., 1 Jake Brown Rd., Old Bridge NJ 08857. Director of Communications: George Bahue. Manufactures TV signal distribution equipment for schools, hotels, hospitals and communities.
Needs: Uses artists for catalog cover designs, spec sheet layouts, POP display designs and direct mail brochures.
First Contact & Terms: Submit resume. Reports in 2 weeks. Pays $10, line drawings; "up to several thousand dollars," catalog layout and POP display.

BLUE CROSS AND BLUE SHIELD OF MICHIGAN, 600 Lafayette E., Detroit MI 48226. Art/Production Manager: Robert H. Jones.
Needs: Uses 2 artists for product illustration/year. Also uses artists for designs for annual reports, brochures, posters, booklets, keylining, and figure illustrator.

First Contact & Terms: Local artists only. Query with printed samples. Artists must have 5-10 years in the field. Payment negotiated.

BLUEMONT SKI AREA, Box 5, Yorkshire NY 14173. (716)496-6041. Contact: Marketing director. Estab. 1970. Call; local artists only.
Needs: Uses artists for brochures, posters and ads. Negotiates pay.

BUSINESS CONSULTANTS OF AMERICA, Box 4098, Waterbury CT 06704. President: Greg Nolan. Uses artists for sales literature and catalog covers/illustrations. Negotiates payment. Sample payment: $25/hour.

CENEX, Box 43089, St. Paul MN 55164. (612)451-5490. Product Supervisor/Art Director: David Cummings. Regional farm supply cooperative.
Needs: Assigns 2-20 jobs/year. Direct mail brochures, employee handbooks, POP displays, slide presentations, posters, trade magazine ads and company publications.
First Contact & Terms: Local artists only. Query. SASE. Reports in 2 weeks. Buys one-time rights. Pays $20-35/hour, layout and design; $15-25/hour, keylining; $25-50/hour, illustrations.

CHAMPION BUILDING PRODUCTS, 1 Landmark Square, Stamford CT 06921. Contact: Mel Sperling. Manufactures and sells wood products.
Needs: Works with 5 ad illustrations and 5 advertising design/year. Specific projects include sales literature, catalog covers, exhibit designs, displays and employee handbooks.
First Contact & Terms: Prefers using local artists. Works on assignment only. Samples returned by SASE; reports back on future assignment possibilities. Provide calling card, brochure and tear sheet to be kept on file for future assignments.

CHARLOTTE MOTOR SPEEDWAY, Box 600, Harrisburg NC 28075. (704)455-2121. Public Relations Director: Joe Whitlock. Speedway for stock/sports cars and motorcycles. Assigns 6 jobs/year.
Needs: Uses artists for advertising, direct mail brochures, posters, publicity brochures, signage and souvenir program covers for races.
First Contact & Terms: Query with samples. SASE. Reports in 2 weeks. Pays $600 max./job, design/layout and illustration.

CHEERLEADER SUPPLY CO., 9150 Markville Rd., Dallas TX 75243. (214)231-8956. Vice President: Jim Hazlewood. Manufactures and retails cheerleader uniforms, shoes, pom poms, fund-raising items (printed ribbons, plastic buttons).
Needs: Uses artists for cartooning, full and part-time.

CONIMAR CORPORATION, Box 1509, Ocala FL 32670. (904)732-7235. Contact: Joan Heath. Manufacturers placemats, coasters, thermo mats and plant mats.
Needs: Buys 15-20 designs/year (6-12 of those are for placemats). Designs range from floral to abstract and childrens designs. Artist quotes price to be considered by Conimar. "Our designs are based alot on designs of dinnerware and glassware."
First Contact & Terms: Send letter, resume and samples of work. Reports in 1 week. Works on assignment only. Samples returned by SASE; reports back on future assignment possibilities. Provide resume and brochure to be kept on file for future assignments. Past payment has ranged from $100-250.

CUSTOM COMMUNICATIONS SERVICES INC., 30 Ruta Court S., Hackensack NJ 07606. (201)440-1020. Contact: Art Director.
Needs: "Greatest need is for artists with book design/layout skills; we produce books with almost 50-50 balance of pictures and text." Uses artists for direct mail brochures, dust jacket design, book design, promotional ad design, mechanical paste-up and advertising layouts/art.
First Contact & Terms: Prefers local artists with previous experience. Query with a resume or sample flyer. Resumes reviewed when assignments or projects arise. Send photocopies and transparencies.

CUSTOM STUDIOS, 1337 W. Devon Ave., Chicago IL 60626. (312)761-1150. President: Gary Wing. Custom T-shirt manufacturer. "We specialize in designing and screen printing of custom T-shirts for schools, business promotions, fundraising and for our own line of stock."
Needs: Works with 4 illustrators and 4 designers/month. Assigns 50 jobs/year. Uses artists for direct mail, brochures/flyers and designs for custom T-shirts and stock T-shirts.
First Contact & Terms: Query with samples, mail finished art or arrange interview. SASE.

Reports in 3-4 weeks. Provide resume and business card to be kept on file for future assignments. Originals returned upon request. Pays $35-150.

DAVENPORT HOTEL, W. 807 Sprague Ave., Spokane WA 99204. Public Relations Director: Jerry J. Shackette. Estab. 1914. Assigns 50 jobs/year. Query with previously used work. SASE. Reports in 1 week.
Needs: Uses artists for advertising, direct mail brochures, exhibits/displays, POP displays, posters and signage. Especially needs b&w advertising, brochures and menus. Minimum payment by hour: $20, design, illustration and production; $15, layout.

DENMAR ENGINEERING & CONTROL SYSTEMS INC., 2309 State St., Saginaw MI 48602. (517)799-8208. Contact: Chester A. Rettewski. Manufacturer of sheet metal, newspaper vending machines, etc.
Needs: Works with 6 artists for ad illustrations; 6 for ad design; 3 for product design; and 5 artists for product illustrations/year.
First Contact & Terms: Write with samples. Works on assignment only. Reports back on future assignment possibilities. Provide resume and tear sheets to be kept on file for future assignments. Pays $200 minimum for illustrations and $200 minimum for designers. Pay for product design and illustration determined by individual assignment.

DOW CHEMICAL USA, Audio-Visual Art Studio, 2030 Dow Center, Midland MI 48640. (517)636-2095. Manager, Art Studio: Gary Gustaf. "We function as a complete art facility for the entire company, specializing in product literature preparation."
Needs: Works with 20 artist for ad illustrations and 20 artist for product illustration/year. "We utilize art for projection (cartoon) and design, layout and art for product literature (printed media). Most assignments are realistic illustrations. We also assign brochure design. We design for 150 products—from commodity chemicals to consumer products—every product piece has a specific audience."
First Contact & Terms: Write with samples. Works on assignment only. Samples returned by SASE. Reports back on future assignment possibilities. Provide calling card and tear sheet samples to be kept on file for future assignments. Pay negotiated based on bids and budget. Contact G. Gustaf for information on 3-6 month internship program.

E.I. DUPONT DE NEMOURS & CO. INC., Advertising Department, Wilmington DE 19898. Contact: William D. Davis. Chemical company. AV division produces charts, motion pictures, multimedia kits, overhead transparencies, prerecorded tapes, cassettes and slides.
First Contact and Terms: Submit portfolio. Provide tearsheets and small brochure to be kept on file for future assignments.

DYNAMIC DISPLAYS, Box 3200, Detroit MI 48232. President: J. Thompson. Estab. 1961. Manufactures amusement park inflatable devices. Assigns 100 jobs/year. Query. SASE. Reports in 1 week.
Needs: Uses artists for illustration, layout, design and paste-up for advertising, animation, direct mail brochures, exhibits/displays, publicity brochures and trademarks/logos. Pays $10-25/sketch, graphic arts.

EDUCATIONAL PRODUCTS CO., Box 295, Hope NJ 07844. (201)459-4220. General Manager: H.R. Maier. Operates Land of Make Believe children's theme park and manufactures plastic cookie cutters.
Needs: Uses artists for illustration of direct mail pieces, catalogs and brochures.
First Contact & Terms: Local artists only. Query with previously published work and arrange interview to show portfolio. SASE. Reports in 2-3 weeks. Negotiates pay.

EMERSON ELECTRIC CO. ELECTRONICS & SPACE DIV., Station 3232, 8100 W. Florissant, St. Louis MO 63136. (314)553-3232. Manager/PR and Advertising: Bart C. Cusick. Manufacturer for domestic and international government, military, industry/aerospace.
Needs: Works with 1 illustrator and 1 designer/month. Uses artists for brochures/flyers and trade magazines. "Trade show oriented and mail give away art suitable for printing."
First Contact & Terms: Prefers personal letter with photocopied work samples (military/aviation oriented; copies of published or publicly used materials; quality of repro not important) to be kept on file for future assignments. Works on assignment only. Will call for better copies when needed. Negotiates pay based on client's budget, artist's previous experience/reputation and what's being offered in competition.

ENTELEK, Ward-Whidden House/The Hill, Box 1303, Portsmouth NH 03801. Editorial Director: Albert E. Hickey. Publishes paperback educational originals; specializing in computer books and software. Published 4 titles in 1979.
Needs: Works with 1 ad illustrations, 1 advertising design and 1 illustrations for use on products/year.
First Contact & Terms: Query with samples. SASE. Reports in 1 week. Free catalog. Works on assignment only. Samples returned by SASE; reports back on future assignment possibilities. Provide brochure, flyer and tear sheet to be kept on file for future assignments. Pays $300, catalogs and direct mail brochures.

FINESTONE CORPORATION, 12416 Cloverdale, Detroit MI 48204. (313)984-0880. Marketing Manager: Jim Gow. Manufactures architectural surfacing, composite panels, and racquetball court walls and ceilings.
Needs: Assigns 6 jobs/year. Uses artists for brochures, labels and magazine ads.
First Contact & Terms: Local artists only. Query with samples (past work of labels, brochures or advertising work). SASE. Reports in 2-3 weeks. Pays $250/brochure, $30/label and $50/magazine ad. A construction materials background is helpful.

FOX VENICE THEATER, 620 Lincoln Blvd., Venice CA 50291. (213)396-4543. Contact: Michael Donnelly, programmer. Estab. 1972. Produces motion pictures, multimedia kits and graphics. Assigns 20 jobs/year. Query or arrange interview to show portfolio; local artists only. SASE. Reports in 2 weeks.
Needs: Uses artists for ads. Negotiates pay.

GADSDEN COUNTY CHAMBER OF COMMERCE, Box 389, Quincy FL 32351. (904)627-9231. Executive Director: Jack P. Strickland.
Needs: Assigns 10 jobs/year. Uses artists for direct mail/publicity brochures, newspaper ad layouts, trade magazine ads and publications.
First Contact & Terms: Arrange interview or mail art. SASE. Reports in 1 month. Negotiates payment.

THE GARBER CO., 600 N. Union St., Ashland OH 44805. Contact: D.R. Foster.
Needs: Uses artists for advertising, catalog illustrations/covers, direct mail packages, folding carton design, premiums and direct response.
First Contact & Terms: Write for interview. SASE. Reports in 2 weeks.

GATE CITY STEEL CORP., Box 14022, Omaha NE 68114. (402)399-1750. Contact: P.N. Weaver, communications specialist. Estab. 1963. Query with resume and samples. SASE. Reports in 4 weeks.
Needs: Uses artists for 4-color covers and 2-color section dividers for reference books and handbooks. Negotiates pay.

GEAUGA LAKE AMUSEMENT, PARK ART SHOPPE, 1541 Bell Rd., Chagrin Falls OH 44022. (216)338-3015. Contact: Richard Kaman. Interested in artists for quick portrait sketches.
First Contact & Terms: Query with resume and arrange interview to show portfolio. Season runs from May til Labor Day. Will train in April and May. All work is around Cleveland, Ohio and Pittsburgh Pennsylvania area. Pay averages $2,500 per season/40 hour work week.

GENERAL MOTORS CORP., 3044 W. Grand Blvd., Detroit MI 48202. (313)556-2017. Contact: Art Director, public relations staff. Estab. 1908. Manufactures cars and trucks. Call for interview or send fees and samples for files; local artists only. SASE. Buys all rights.
Needs: Uses artists for annual reports, employee/student handbooks, technical charts/illustrations and company publications. Pay varies.

GEORGIA-PACIFIC CORP., 900 SW 5th Ave., Portland OR 97204. Manager, Graphics Production: Ted Haines. Manufactures building products, pulp, paper and chemicals.
Needs: Works with 5-10 ad illustrations, 15-20 advertising design, 3 product design and 4-5 illustrations for use on products. Direct mail brochures, annual reports, billboards, interior design, posters, catalogs, spec sheets and print collateral.
First Contact & Terms: Prefers local artists. Query with resume and printed samples. Provide resume, calling card, brochure and flyer to be kept on file for future assignments. Pays $30-35/hour, design; $20-25/hour, finish. Fees on large projects are estimated by artist—"generally runs at $30-35/hour."

GOLIAD COUNTY CHAMBER OF COMMERCE, Box 606, Goliad TX 77963. (512)645-3563. Contact: Directors. Query. SASE. Reports in 2 weeks.
Needs: Uses artists for magazine ads, direct mail brochures, newspaper layout ads, posters, publicity brochures, signage, trademarks, logos and publications. Pay determined by job.

GRAND RAPIDS AREA CHAMBER OF COMMERCE, 17 Fountain St. NW, Grand Rapids MI 49503. (616)459-7221. Contact: Toni J. Morris. Submit attractive portfolio, query with samples or arrange interview. SASE. Reports in 1 month.
Needs: Uses artists for annual reports, charts, direct mail brochures, posters, publicity brochures and signage. Pays $25 maximum, design, lettering and keying; $10 maximum, layout and production.

GREATER COLUMBIA CHAMBER OF COMMERCE, Box 1360, Columbia SC 29202. Contact: Mike Gibson. Arrange interview to show portfolio; local artists only.
Needs: Brochures, annual reports, slide film presentations and public service TV spots.

GREATER HARTFORD CHAMBER OF COMMERCE, 250 Constitution Plaza, Hartford CT 06103. Director of Communications: Grace S. Martin.
Needs: Works with 2 advertising design/year. Uses artists occasionally for direct mail brochures, annual reports and 3-screen slide presentations.
First Contact & Terms: Area artists only. Works on assignment only. Sample returned by SASE; reports back on future assignment possibilities. Provide resume, calling card and brochure to be kept on file for future assignments. Fee to be determined.

GUILFORD PUBLICATIONS INC., 200 Park Ave. S., New York NY 10003. (212)674-1900. Vice President: Robert Matloff. Produces professional, educational and industrial audiovisuals and books.
Needs: Assigns 20 jobs/year. Uses artists for catalog design and ads.
First Contact & Terms: Local artists only. Query. SASE. Reports in 4 weeks. Pays by job.

GUTHRIE SHOWS INC., November-April: 2362 Kingsgate Ct., Dunwoody GA 30338. April-October: Box 349C, Hollywood Rd., Middleboro KY. (404)457-4513. Contact: Pat Guthrie. Produces carnivals.
Needs: Works with 1-5 illustrators/year for equipment design. Assigns 100 jobs/year. Uses artists for scenery for carnival rides, ticket booths, trucks, signs, brochures and ads.
First Contact & Terms: Call or contact show on location; query with samples (clowns, merry-go-round horses, etc) or arrange interview to show portfolio. Provide calling card, brochure and flyer to be kept on file for future assignments. Pays by job. Example: paid $700 for scenery for one amusement ride.

H.I. EXPRESS, 1211 Marinette Ave., Marientte WI 54143. (715)735-9786 or 735-9438. Contact: Terry L. Hecket or Greg Ilse. "We produce custom designed silk screened garments which are retailed as Art Shirt. We promote various firms and organizations via custom designed silk screened T-shirts."
Needs: "In both instances we are looking for artists who can supply various designs which could be used in either of the two ways mentioned above."

HACHAR DEPARTMENT STORE INC., 11119 Farragut St., Box 1579, Laredo TX 78040. (512)723-9141. President: George L. Hachar.
Needs: Works with 1 ad illustrator and 1 ad designer/year. Assigns 25 jobs/year. Uses artists for newspaper ads and some direct mail.
First Contact & Terms: Query with resume. Reports in 2 weeks. Negotiates pay.

HALLS, RETAIL DIVISION FOR HALLMARK CARDS, 200 E. 25th St., Kansas City MO 64108 and 211 Nichols Rd., Kansas City MO 64112. (816)274-8145. Contact: Sharon Murray, art director. Estab. 1910. Two specialty gift shops with catalog division; Sells designer clothes, decorative accessories, silver, china and crystal. Assigns 15-50 jobs/year.

HELENOR TRADING CORP., 60 Marbledale Rd., Tuckahoe NY 10707. (914)337-7373. Contact: Norm Ament. Specializes in sewing notions and writing instruments.
Needs: Uses artists for sales promotion/advertising, layouts, package design and direct mail brochures.
First Contact & Terms: Arrange interview to show portfolio.

HOLLY'S, INC., 255 Colrain SW, Grand Rapids MI 49509. Marketing Vice President: Richard Webster. Specializes in theme and family restaurants. In-house agency "Adfare" handles family restaurant media and promotional advertising.
Needs: Assigns at least 12 jobs/year. Uses artists for ad layout and paste-up for newspaper, magazine and outdoor media presentation. Illustrations and layouts for internal organs, i.e. annual reports, employee handbooks, etc.
First Contact & Terms: Local artists only. Query and arrange interview to show portfolio. SASE. Reports in 3 weeks. Pays $20, b&w spot; $50, b&w page.

HOLLYWOOD PRESBYTERIAN MEDICAL CENTER, 1300 N. Vermont, Los Angeles CA 90027. Contact: Jeff Merkow.
Needs: Works with 1 ad illustrator and 5 publicity designer/year. Uses artists for catalogs, layouts, lettering and public relations art.
First Contact & Terms: Prefers local artists. Query with resume. Pays on acceptance.

IDAHO MOUNTAIN GRAPHICS, (formerly The Paper Mill), Box 494 Council ID 83612. (208)253-4551. Contact: Julie Peurasaari. Pays on acceptance.
Needs: Works with about 24 ad illustrators; 24 ad designers; 24 production designers; and 24 illustrators for work on products/year. Uses artists for art and design work for brochures, posters, logos and other printing jobs.
First Contact & Terms: Query with samples (photocopy of art work—preferably something published) for file of available artists. "From this file we will be sending out assignments." SASE. Pays $5 min., spot illustration. "We could pay on a percentage basis of a complete job, such as a promotion campaign."

IDEAL SCHOOL SUPPLY CO., 11000 S. Lavergne, Oak Lawn IL 60453. Art Director: Charles A. Coch. Designer: Lin Cleghorn. Manufactures educational materials.
Needs: Assigns 75-100 jobs and buys 25 illustrations/year. Uses artists for catalogs, direct mail brochures, magazine ads, packaging, multimedia kits, book illustrations and game designs (cartoon style). Especially needs illustrations, keyline and production.
First Contact & Terms: Mostly uses local artists. Send resume or letter. Follow up with samples and prices. SASE. Reports in 1 month. Prefers artists with work published. Pays $10 min./hour, graphic art.

INDIANA BEACH INC., 306 Indiana Beach Dr., Monticello IN 47960. Contact: T.E. Spackman. Submit samples.
Needs: Uses artists for direct mail brochures, newspaper releases, costume design, exhibits, displays, signs and public relations.

INTER-AMERICAN FOUNDATION, 1515 Wilson Blvd., Rosslyn VA 22209. Contact: Mel Asterken. Call or write.
Needs: Artists with both writing and design backgrounds for booklet design and illustrations for other printed materials.

INTERNATIONAL FINALS RODEO, Box 615, Pauls Valley OK 73075. (405)238-6488. President: Bob Ink. Office Manager: Dianna Beason. "This is the World Series of rodeo for the top 15 contestants in the 7 International Rodeo Association championship events." Submit photos or tearsheets.
Needs: Uses artists for direct mail brochures, posters, programs, advertising, costume design, exhibits, displays, signs, bumper stickers, and tie-in products such as T-shirts, toys, posters, ashtrays, lighters, glasses and buttons.

JAY PEAK INC., Jay VT 05859. (802)988-2611. Public Relations Director: Al Cahill. Ski area. Estab. 1955. Assigns 20 jobs/year. Query with samples. Reports in 2 weeks.
Needs: Uses artists for newspaper ads, brochure designs and programs. Negotiates pay.

HOWARD JOHNSON CO., 222 Forbes, Braintree MA 02184. Graphics/Design Director: Robert C. Downing. Services/Products: Food and lodging and speciality restaurant concepts, grocery products, ice cream and frozen foods and candy products.
Needs: Works with 6-8 illustrations, advertising design agency, product design internal and 2-3 freelance and 2-3 illustrations for use on products/year. Also uses artists for sales promotion literature, menu design, children's menu (entertainment) design, annual reports, catalog covers/illustrations, exhibit designs and displays.
First Contact & Terms: Prefers local artists. Must have professional experience in food and/or

lodging industry. Query with samples. "Illustrators should submit samples which will be returned. Would especially like to see food illustration all styles, color and/or black and white." Provide resume, brochure and flyer to be kept on file for future assignments. "All copyrights on purchased material will be assigned to Howard Johnson's with original artist retaining the right to use designs for self-promotion only."

JOULE TECHNICAL CORP., Rte. 22 W., Union NJ 07083. Contact: E.N. Logothetis. Engineering firm.
Needs: Uses artists for advertising gimmicks, graphic sales promotion, audiovisual presentations and exhibit equipment.
First Contact & Terms: Works on assignment only. Sample returned by SASE; reports back on future assignment possibilities. Provide calling card and brochure to be kept on file for future assignments. Pays $300 average for camera-ready art.

KFYE-Y 94, Fresno Towne House .535, Fresno CA 93721. (209)486-5294.Contact: Creative Services Director. Call for an interview to show samples.
Needs: Uses artists for posters, billboards, newspaper ad layouts, sales sheets and transit signage.

KOPPEL COLOR, 153 Central Ave., Hawthorne NJ 07507. (201)427-3151. Sales and Creative Director: Wesley Glass. Printer serving photographers, artists, hotels, motels and small businesses.
Needs: Works with 2-3 advertising design and 2-3 illustrations for use on products/year. Uses artists for animation, cartoons, illustration, design, layout, lettering, technical art, mechanicals and retouching for catalogs, direct mail brochures, flyers and postcards.
First Contact & Terms: Local artists only. Query with resume. SASE. Reports in 2 weeks. Works on assignment only. No samples returned. Reports back on future assignment possibilities. Provide resume and copies of samples, reduced to fit a standard file to be kept on file for future assignments.

KRON TV, NBC, 1001 Van Ness Ave., San Francisco CA 94119. (415)441-4444. Assistant Art Director: David Patton. Director of Creative Services: Dennis Fitch. TV/film producer. Produces videotapes and still photos.
First Contact & Terms: Local artists only. Query. Provide resume and calling card to be kept on file for future assignments.
Needs: Works with 1-2 ad illustrations, 1-2 advertising design and 1-5 product design/year. Uses artists for design and production of all types of print advertising, direct mail brochures, promotion and sales pieces.
Tips: "We're looking for experienced designers with heavy production knowledge that would enable them to handle a job from design concept through printing."

KUSP, Box 423, Santa Cruz CA 95061. Contact: Bruce N. Larsen. Prefers phone interview.
Needs: Uses artists for program promotion folders, posters and newspaper ad layouts. Pays $50, poster design; $75, promotional package design.

KVCR, TV/FM RADIO, 701 S. Mount Vernon Ave., San Bernardino CA 92403. Program Director: Lew Warren. Specializes in public and educational radio/TV.
Needs: Works with 1 ad illustrations and 2 illustrations for use on products/year. Assigns 1-10 jobs/year. Uses artists for graphic/set design, set design painters and camera-ready cards.
First Contact & Terms: Query and mail photos or slides. SASE. Reports in 2 weeks. Works on assignment only. Sample returned by SASE; reports back on future assignment possibilities. Pays $15-25, camera-ready cards.

LAKEVIEW PARK, Rte. 16, Mendon MA 01756. Contact: Ed Rouleau. Submit photos or tearsheets.
Needs: Uses artists for newspaper ads and posters.

LEISURE AND RECREATION CONCEPTS INC., 1949 Stemmons Freeway, Dallas TX 75207. (214)698-1911. President: Michael Jenkins. Designs and builds amusement and theme parks.
Needs: Assigns 200 jobs/year. Uses artists for exhibits/displays and sketches of park building sections and bird's eye views of facilities.
First Contact & Terms: Query with samples or previously used work, or arrange interview. SASE. Reports in 1 week. Pay determined by job.

LEISURE LEARNING PRODUCTS INC., 50 Greenwich Ave., Greenwich CT 06830. (203)661-2777. Advertising/Sales Promotion Manager: R. Bendett. Manufactures children's games, activities, books and educational products.
Needs: Uses artists for illustration and design for sales literature, in-house publications, recruitment literature, catalogs, exhibits and displays. Also needs cartoon type color illustrations similar to the style of of Walt Disney type illustrations, Peanuts and Nancy strips. Must appeal to the 3-8 year old range.
First Contact & Terms: Query with photocopies or art. Pays $10-25 minimum, product illustration.

LONGHORN WORLD CHAMPIONSHIP RODEO INC., Box 8160, Nashville TN 37207. (615)876-1016. President: W. Bruce Lehrke. Produces and promotes major league rodeos/rodeo publications.
Needs: Assigns 24 jobs/year. Uses artists for catalog covers/layouts, magazine ads, direct mail/publicity brochures, displays, exhibit designs, newspaper ad layouts, lettering, packaging, POP displays, posters, signage, trademarks, logos and company publications.
First Contact & Terms: Query with samples. SASE. Reports in 4 weeks. Provide resume and brochure to be kept on file for future assignments. Pays $100-250, rodeo program covers.

LOON MOUNTAIN RECREATION CORP., Kancamagus Hwy., Lincoln NH 03251. (603)745-8111. Marketing Director: Rick Owen. Ski resort with inn, restaurants and lounges.
Needs: Works with 2 advertising design/year. Assigns 6 jobs and buys 2 illustrations/year. Uses artists for design and illustration of brochures, signs, displays, mailings and other promotional materials.
First Contact & Terms: Arrange interview. SASE. Reports in 2 weeks. Negotiates pay.

LOS ANGELES MEMORIAL COLISEUM AND SPORTS ARENA, 3939 S. Figueroa, Los Angeles CA 90037. Public Relations Director: Glenn E. Mon.
Needs: Works with 2 ad illustrations and 1 advertising design. Uses artists from January-June at arena, August-December at coliseum.
First Contact & Terms: Arrange interview. Provide brochure to be kept on file for future assignments.

LUBBOCK ARTS COUNCIL, Box 561, Lubbock TX 79408. (806)763-4666. Contact: Executive Director.
Needs: Uses artists for illustrations and direct mail brochure design.
First Contact & Terms: Query with samples. SASE. Reports in 1 week. Pays $15/hour.

McALLEN CHAMBER OF COMMERCE, Box 790, McAllen TX 78501. (512)682-2871. Publicity Director: Jack McNally. Estab. 1935. Promotes conventions, tourism, community programs, industry and legislation for McAllen. Assigns 8-15 jobs and buys 12 illustrations/year. Query with samples. SASE. Reports in 1 week.
Needs: Uses artists for advertising, magazines, newsletters, publicity brochures, exhibits/displays and trademarks/logos. Pays $10-20/hour for illustration.

ERIC McMILLAN INC., 366 Adelaide St. E., Toronto, Ontario, Canada M5A 3X9. (416)366-0585. Director: Rosemarie Duell. Estab. 1974. Plans and designs playgrounds, recreational facilities, theme parks, museums and educational exhibits and shows. Assigns 5-6 jobs and buys 5-50 illustrations/year. Query with previously used work. SASE. Reports in 2 weeks.
Needs: Uses artists for ads, exhibits, displays and publicity brochures. Pays $5-15/hour for illustrations and layout.

MAPLE CITY RUBBER CO., 55 Newton St., Norwalk OH 44857. Contact: M.B. Switzer. Toy balloon manufacturer. Send tearsheets, photocopies or transparencies. Reports in 30 days.
Needs: Designs for advertising balloons.

MARIN CENTER AUDITORIUM/EXHIBIT HALL/FAIRGROUNDS, Civic Center Dr., San Rafael CA 94903. (415)479-4493. Events Manager: James Farley.
Needs: Uses artists for advertising, direct mail brochures, posters and publicity brochures.
First Contact & Terms: "We prefer to work with someone local, partly because we need our work done quickly." Query with samples. Maintain file of resumes. "We will get in contact with the artist if his or her work fits a particular project." Payment depends on job, roughly in the area of $50-200.

METROMEDIA, (formerly Metro TV Sales), 485 Lexington Ave., New York NY 10017. Vice President of Creative Services: Mort Slakoff. Metromedia company and broadcast time sales representative.
Needs: Works with 3 ad illustrators, 3 ad designers and 6 product designers/year. Uses artists for sales literature, in-house publications, annual reports, catalog covers/illustration, displays and technical charts.

METROPOLITAN EVANSVILLE CHAMBER OF COMMERCE, 329 Main St., Evansville IN 47708. (812)425-8147. Executive Vice President: James T. Dittoe. Estab. 1887. Assigns approximately 12 jobs/year; local artists only. Query. SASE. Reports in 1 week.
Needs: Direct mail/publicity brochures, displays, newspaper layouts ads, lettering, signage, trademarks, logos and company publications.

MILLER PRESS, 1430 Prudential Dr., Jacksonville FL 32207. Contact: Alfred Miller, Jr. Commercial printing. Specializes in advertising printing.
Needs: Works with 2-3 illustrators and 2-3 designers/year. Uses artists for direct mail and brochures/flyers. Also uses artists for layout, illustration, type spec, technical art and retouching.
First Contact & Terms: Mail samples. No originals returned for refused work.

WARREN MILLER PRODUCTIONS, 505 Pier Ave., Hermosa CA 90254. (213)376-2494. Produces sports documentaries.
Needs: Works with 1 ad illustrations and 1 advertising design/year. Direct mail brochures and magazine ads.
First Contact & Terms: Query with samples (original sports illustration—skiing) or write for interview. SASE. Reports in 2 weeks. Buys nonexclusive rights. Works on assignment only. Sample returned by SASE; reports back on future assignment possibilities. Provide resume to be kept on file for future assignments. Pays $100-200.

MITTEN DESIGNER LETTERS, 85 5th Ave., New York NY 10003. (212)741-1000. Manufactures display letters. Estab. 1934. Query by phone; local artists only.
Needs: Uses artists for design and layout of brochures and ads. Negotiates pay.

MURRAY HILL PRESS, 55 W. 42nd St., New York NY 10036. (212)563-0364. President: Ralph Ceisler. Estab. 1952. Printer. Assigns 12 jobs/year; uses mostly local artists. Query with samples. SASE. Reports in 2 weeks.
Needs: Uses artists for catalogs, direct mail brochures, flyers and POP displays.

J. CASIMIR NADOLNY CO., 79 Pleasant Ave., East Bridgewater MA 02333. Contact: Joseph C. Nadolny.
Needs: Uses artists for direct mail brochures, annual reports, billboards, posters, public service TV spots and interior designs.
First Contact & Terms: Query with samples.

O'DONNELL-USEN FISHERIES, 1 Fish Pier, Boston MA 02210. (617)542-2700. Executive Vice President: Arnold S. Wolf. Processes frozen seafoods.
Needs: Assigns 20-30 jobs and buys 15 illustrations/year. Uses artists for packaging, point of sale material and letter header, etc.
First Contact & Terms: Query with samples (rough sketches). SASE. Reports in 3 weeks. Provide resume to be kept on file for future assignments. Pays agreed upon fee.

PENNSYLVANIA MANUFACTURERS ASSOCIATION INSURANCE CO., PMA Bldg., 925 Chestnut St., Philadelphia PA 19107. (215)629-5000. Contact: Constance Bille. Insurance firm.
Needs: Assigns 10-15 jobs/year. Uses artists for charts, handbooks, recruitment literature and audiovisuals.
First Contact & Terms: Local artists only. Query. SASE. Reports in 1 week. Payment by job: $100-200, design; $15-25, illustration and layout; $10-25, lettering.

PETERSEN HARNED VON MAUR, 131 W. 2nd St., Davenport IA 52801. Sales Promotion Director: Bob Behrends. Department store.
Needs: Works with 2 ad illustrators/year. Assigns 200 jobs/year. Uses artists for newspaper ads and direct mail.
First Contact & Terms: Local artists only. Query with samples and arrange interview to show portfolio. Reports in 2 weeks. Pays $10-25/figure or item.

PHILADELPHIA CONVENTION AND VISITORS BUREAU, 1525 John F. Kennedy Blvd., Philadelphia PA 19102. (215)864-1974. Public Relations Director: Samuel B. Rogers.
Needs: Assigns 10 jobs/year. Uses artists for exhibits/displays, posters, annual report, publicity brochures and recruitment literature.
First Contact & Terms: Local artists only. Query with samples. SASE. Reports in 2 weeks. Works on assignment only. Sample returned by SASE; reports back on future assignment possibilities. Provide brochure to be kept on file for future assignments. Pays $20 min./hour or $300 max./job for design and illustration.

PLEASANT VALLEY INVESTMENTS, 754 Boardwalk, Ocean City NJ 08226. (609)398-6059. Contact: Roger Jakubowski. Amusement pier including restaurants. Query with resume and arrange interview to show portfolio.
Needs: Uses artists for posters, exhibits, displays and portraits.

PROCON INTERNATIONAL INC., 50 UOP Plaza, Algonquin and Mt. Prospect Rds., Des Plaines IL 60016. Manager and Marketing: Glenn Scott. Engineering and construction firm.
Needs: Works with 6 ad illustrators and 6 ad designers/year. Uses artists for direct mail brochures, literature and publicity releases.
First Contact & Terms: Local artists only. Query with resume and samples of industrial illustration.

PROFESSIONAL TRAINING AIDS, 38 W. Bethune, Detroit MI 48202. Contact: H. Hook. Produces direct mail sales and motivation programs for businesses.
Needs: Works with 1 ad illustrations, 1 advertising design and 1 illustrations for use on products/year. Uses artists for line art, cartoons, posters, etc. Interested in line drawings and poster style.
First Contact & Terms: Submit tearsheets or photocopies. Reports in 10 days. Provide brochure, tearsheet and photocopy of samples to be kept on file for future assignments. Pays $25, spot drawings.

RED BARN SYSTEM, 6845 Elm St., McLean VA 22101. (703)893-2111. Vice President, Marketing: Sherry More. Estab. 1961. Fast food restaurants. Assigns "dozens" of jobs/year. Query.
Needs: Uses artists for catalog covers/layouts, direct mail/publicity brochures, displays, employee handbooks, exhibit designs, newspaper ad layouts, packaging, POP displays, recruitment literature, signage, student handbooks, technical charts/illustrations and company publications.

REDGRAVE PUBLISHING CO., 430 Manville Rd., Pleasantville NY 10570. (914)769-3629. Publisher: S. Wolf. Publishes academic journals and educational workbooks. Query.
Needs: Pays $100 minimum, brochure; $3.50-6/hour, paste-up.

RKO RADIO, 6255 Sunset Blvd., Los Angeles CA 90028. (213)462-6255. Vice President: Harvey Mednick. Owns and operates 12 radio stations.
Needs: Works with 6 artists for ad illustrations; 3 for ad design; 5 for product design and 10 for product illustrations/year. Also uses artists for logo design, brochures, posters, calendars, cards, etc.
First Contact & Terms: Query by mail. Works on assignment only. Samples returned by SASE. Reports back on future assignment possibilities. Provide resume, brochure and flyer to be kept on file for future assignments. Pays $50 minimum for thumb-nail sketch for ad; $100 minimum for design clean-up or up-date. Product design and and illustration pay determined by mutual agreement between client and artists.

ROCKING HORSE, Box 306, Highland NY 12528. Contact: "Bucky" Turk. Convention center.
Needs: Works with 2 ad illustrators, 2 ad designers, 2 or 3 product designers and 2 illustrators for use on products/year. Uses artists for descriptive brochures, exhibits, signs and meeting room decorations.
First Contact & Terms: Send published samples (resort ads around a western scene).

ROCKY POINT PARK, Warwick RI 02889. President/General Manager: Conrad Feria.
Needs: Uses artists for direct mail brochures, programs, trade magazine ads and bumper stickers.
First Contact & Terms: Submit photos or tearsheets of published work.

RPM RADIO PROGRAMMING AND MANAGEMENT INC., 25140 Lanser Rd., Suite 232, Southfield MI 48075. (313)358-1040. President: Thomas M. Krikorian. Provides radio music programming.
Needs: Assigns 5-10 jobs/year. Uses artists for advertising design/layout, billboards, bumper

stickers, direct mail brochures and trade magazine ads.
First Contact & Terms: Mail photos or tearsheets. SASE. Contacts artists as needs arise. Pays $50-100, trade ads; $20-100, logo design.

ST. BONIFACE CHAMBER OF COMMERCE, (La Chambre de Commerce de St. Boniface), Box 37, Norwood Grove Post Office, St. Boniface, Manitoba, Canada R2H 3B8.
Needs: Works with 3 ad illustrations and 4 advertising design/year. Uses local artists for assignments in Winnipeg area.
First Contact & Terms: Provide resume and calling card to be kept on file for future assignments.

SANTA FE PARK SPEEDWAY, 9100 S. Wolf Rd., Hinsdale IL 60521. (312)839-1050. Public Relations Assistant: Mary Lou Tiedt. Stock car racetrack.
Needs: Works with 2 artists/year for advertising design. Uses artists for advertising, direct mail brochures, posters, publicity brochures, yearly programs, bumper stickers and road signs. "We are looking for new original layouts and designs for racing. Stock cars and motorcycles in the past have all been repeats of former designs."
First Contact & Terms: Mail art. SASE. Reports in 2-4 weeks. Provide calling card to be kept on file for future assignments. Negotiates pay.

SAWYER'S INC., 1 Mill St., Dover NH 03820. Contact: Advertising Manager. Discount department store. Estab. 1956. Assigns 24-36 jobs/year. Query with samples or arrange interview to show portfolio. "We welcome the opportunity to look at new artists." SASE. Reports in 1 week.
Needs: Uses artists for line drawings of fashions, hardgoods, brown goods and appliances in newspaper ads and pre-prints. Pays $6-12/job.

SHREVEPORT-BOSSIER CONVENTION-TOURIST BUREAU, Box 1761, Shreveport LA 71166. (318)222-9391.
Needs: Works with 4 ad illustrators, 4 ad designers, 7 product designers and 3 illustrators for use on products/year. Uses artists for catalog covers/layouts, consumer magazine ads, direct mail/publicity brochures, newspaper ad layouts, lettering and posters.
First Contact & Terms: Local artists only. Call for interview. SASE. Reports in 1 week. Negotiates payment.

THE SOUTHLAND CORP., 2828 N. Haskell Ave., Box 719, Dallas TX 75221. Director Corporate Design: Hans A. Streich. "Originator of the convenience store concept, dairy products processor, fast food manufacturer."
Needs: Works with 5 product design and 3 illustrations for use on products/year. Uses artists for direct mail brochures, annual reports, package design, store interior design, trademarks, etc.
First Contact & Terms: Prefers local artists. Query with resume and previously published samples (any printed sample and portfolios, corporate I.D., logo design, illustration). Works on assignment only. Sample returned by SASE; reports back on future assignment possibilities. Provide calling card to be kept on file for future assignments.

SPENCER GIFTS, INC., 1050 Black Horse Pike, Atlantic City NJ 08411. (609)645-3300; ext. 286. Contact: James Stevenson, art director. Retail gift chain located in approximately 400 malls in 43 states; gifts range from posters and jewelry to personalized glassware. Estab. 1965. Assigns 40-60 jobs/year. Query with samples, previously published work or arrange interview to show portfolio. With samples, enclose phone number where you can reached during business hours. Prefers artists with professional experience in their field of advertising art. Reports in 2 weeks.
Needs: Uses artists for package design illustration, hard line art, fashion illustration, newspaper ads and toy, poster, package and product design. Negotiates pay.

TRI-COMMUNITY AREA CHAMBER OF COMMERCE, 111 Main St., Southbridge MA 01550. Contact: John S. Frykenberg. The tri-community area consists of Southbridge, a primarily industrial community; Sturbridge, a restored historical village and tourist mecca; and Charlton, an agricultural community.
Needs: Works with 3 ad illustrations and 2 advertising design/year. Uses artists for ad illustrations.
First Contact & Terms: Prefers local artists. Call for interview to show portfolio. Works on assignment only. Sample returned by SASE; reports back on future assignment possibilities. Provide brochure to be kept on file for future assignments. Pays $500, brochure design.

UNITED ARTS FUND, 334 Westminster Mall, Providence RI 02903. (401)351-2540. Executive Director: Jane G. Phelps. Conducts annual United Arts Fund corporate drive. Works with graphic designers.

U.S. POSTAL SERVICE, Write to nearest U.S. Postal Region for Bidder's Mailing List Application. Contracts and Supply Management Branch: New York NY 10098; Philadelphia PA 19101; Memphis TN 38166; Chicago IL 60694; San Bruno CA 94099. Indicate service or commodity of interest and geographical marketing area preferences. Applicants placed on mailing list to receive appropriate solicitations for bids, proposals or quotations. The Small Business Administration (SBA) publication *U.S. Government Purchasing and Sales Directory*, a guide to selling or buying in the government market, is available from the Superintendent of Documents and may be examined at SBA offices.
Needs: Some included are exhibits/display designs, sales promotion, advertising/training films and instructional material.

UTA FRENCH AIRLINES, Tishman Airport Center, 9841 Airport Blvd., Rm. 1000, Los Angeles CA 90045. Public Relations Manager: Maria L. Cigliano.
Needs: Uses artists for sales literature, catalog covers/illustrations, public service newspaper ads and multimedia slide presentations.

VENICE AMUSEMENT CORP., Casino Pier, Seaside Heights NJ 08751. Contact: Kenneth Wynne. Seashore resort/amusement park. Submit photos or tearsheets.
Needs: Direct mail brochures, ads, exhibits, displays, signs, bumper stickers and painting rides.

WEBB TEXTILES INC./WEBB DESIGN PRODUCTS, 1115 N. Johnson Ave., El Cajon CA 92022. (714)442-0391. Sales Manager: Charlotte Webb. President: Bob Webb. Manufactures drapery fabrics, upholstery, wallcoverings and woven wood window shades.
Needs: Uses artists for textile and product design as well as brochure and package design.
First Contact & Terms: Query with samples or arrange interview to show portfolio. Reports in 2-3 weeks. Negotiates pay.

WHITE SEWING MACHINE CO., 11750 Berea Rd., Cleveland OH 44111. Advertising Manager: B. Gold. Estab. 1876. Manufactures sewing machines. Arrange interview; prefers local artists.
Needs: Uses artists for sales promotion/ad layouts.

THE WILD SIDE INC., 7300 SW 42nd St., Miami FL 33155. (305)264-7320 or (800)327-3588. Contact: Chris Fowler. T-shirt company. Assigns 50+ jobs/year.
Needs: Needs artists for T-shirt design. "Doesn't matter if artist calls himself an illustrator or designer."
First Contact & Terms: Query with resume and samples. Reports in 1 week. No original art returned at job's completion. Pays $100 minimum, design and illustration of T-shirts, buttons, posters, ads and commercials.

H. WILSON CO., 555 Taft Dr., South Holland IL 60473. (312)339-5111. Contact: B.J. Bond, advertising manager. Estab. 1959. Assigns 12 jobs/year. Query with resume and samples, then arrange interview to show portfolio. SASE. Reports in 2 weeks.
Needs: Uses artists for sales and marketing presentations, catalogs, direct mail, convention exhibits and promotion. Pays "for creative work on a job basis, final art on an hourly basis."

WINDHAM MOUNTAIN CLUB, Windham NY 12496. (518)734-4300. Contact: Gene McMasters, general manager. Estab. 1967. Member-owned ski facility. Query with previously published work and fees for files. SASE. Reports in 2-3 weeks.
Needs: Uses artists for illustration of brochures, real estate sales promotional materials and ads. Negotiates pay.

WORLD ATTRACTIONS INC., Box 907, Gibsonton FL 33534. (813)677-9480. President: C.M. Christ. Produces shows for fairs, carnivals and theatre.
Needs: Works with 2 ad illustrations, 1 advertising design and 3 illustrations for use on products/year. Assigns 9 jobs/year. Uses artists for advertising, animation, exhibits/displays, posters, publicity brochures, signage, show fronts, circus side show banners, theatrical scenery and costumes.
First Contact & Terms: Query with samples. SASE. Reports in 2 weeks. Works on assignment only. Sample returned by SASE; reports back on future assignment possibilities. Provide brochure to be kept on file for future assignments. Payment by job: $150-1500, lettering and layout; $500-5,000, show fronts.

WYANDOTTE GENERAL HOSPITAL, 2333 Biddle Ave., Wyandotte MI 48192. (313)282-2400. Community Relations Director: Stephen C. Lada.
Needs: Assigns 40-100 jobs/year. Uses artists for annual reports, direct mail brochures, displays, employee handbooks, newspaper ad layouts, posters and company publications.
First Contact & Terms: Query or arrange interview to show portfolio. "Portfolio should include samples of human response, persons reacting to situations and events." SASE. Reports in 2 weeks. Pays $25-100, illustrations for publications and brochures.

YUMA CIVIC CONVENTION CENTER, Box 5653, Yuma AZ 85364. (602)344-3800. Director: Paul Whitehead.
Needs: Works with 2-3 ad illustrations and 2-3 advertising design/year. Assigns 20 jobs/year. Uses artists for illustration, design, layout, lettering and production for ads, direct mail brochures, posters, publicity brochures and trademarks/logo.
First Contact & Terms: Mostly local artists. Mail art or query of advertising art with samples (¼ page in magazine). SASE. Reports in 2 weeks. Works on assignment only. No samples returned. Reports back on future assignment possibilities. Provide calling card and brochure to be kept on file for future assignments.

Exhibit, Display & Sign Firms

Exhibits, displays and signage advertising are easily recognized as forms of advertising, but not always thought of by artists as they compile lists of freelance opportunities. Actually, there are good opportunities here for the artist—lettering, design, trademarks, illustrations, etc.

This type of advertising must snag the customer's eye as he rushes by rows of booths at a convention, through aisles of a supermarket or drives along the highway. Both design and color are vital to achieving this goal.

Firms listed in this section include department stores, store fixture manufacturers and props, exhibit design companies and sign firms. Additional markets can be found by consulting the Yellow Pages and by reading *Signs of the Times* and *Visual Merchandising* magazines.

ADVERTISING METAL DISPLAY CO., 4620 W. 19th St., Chicago IL 60650. (312)863-8900. Design Director: Ray Baluk. Clients: automotive, cosmetic, hardware, electronics and sign firms.
Needs: Works with 1-2 artists/year for P-O-P design.
First Contact & Terms: Local artists only. Query. SASE. Reports in 1 week. Samples should include original renderings, if requested. Works on assignment only. Samples returned by SASE. Provide resume to be kept on file for future assignments. Pays $15-30/hour, P-O-P displays.

ALBEE SIGN CO., 561 E. 3rd St., Mt. Vernon NY 10553. (914)668-0201. Vice President: William Lieberman. Produces interior and exterior signs and graphics. Clients are commercial accounts, banks and realestate companies.
Needs: Works with 6 artists for sign design, 6 for display fixture design, 6 for P-O-P design and 6 for custom sign sign illustration. Pays by job.
First Contact & Terms: Local artists only. Query with samples (pictures of completed work). Previous experience with other firms preferred. SASE. Reports in 2-3 weeks. Works on assignment only. No samples returned. Reports back as assignment occurs. Provide resume, calling card and pictures of work to be kept on file for future assignments.

ALFORD ADVERTISING INC., 800 Graves St., Chillicothe MO 64601. (816)646-3653. President: William E. Alford. Clients: banks, restaurants, motels and retailers.
First Contact & Terms: Query with samples. SASE. Reports in 1 week. Works on assignment only. Samples returned by SASE; and reports back on future possibilities. Provide resume, calling card and samples of work to be kept on file for future assignments. Pays $8-15, billboards and neon signage; $8-10, sign redesign.
Needs: Works with 4 artists for sign design, 1 for exhibit design and 2 for custom sign illustration. Assigns 20-40 jobs/year.

ANNIS-WAY SIGNS LTD., 595 West St. S., Orillia, Ontario, Canada. Contact: Lloyd H. Annis.
Needs: Uses artists for exhibit, trademark and display design, sign redesign and lettering.
First Contact & Terms: Send resume.

APPLETON NEON SIGN CO. INC., Box 1152, Appleton WI 54910. Contact: Harold F. Hartzheim. Mail samples or arrange interview.
Needs: Uses artists for advertising, sign redesign, lettering and trademark design.

BULLETIN & DIRECTORY BOARD MFG. CO., 2317 W. Pico, Los Angeles CA 90006. Manager: John Curtis. Exhibit/sign firm. Assigns 30 jobs/year.
Needs: Works with 3-6 artists for sign design, 3-6 for exhibit design, 10 print advertising and custom sign illustration.
First Contact & Terms: Query or send samples. Reports in 1 week. Works on assignment only. Samples returned by SASE; and reports back on future possibilities. Provide brochure, flyer and sample of print work if possible to be kept on file for future assignments. Pays $10/hour minimum.

CARIBBEAN EXHIBITS INC., Box 6806, Loiza Station, Santurce, Puerto Rico 00914. (809)726-4630. Design Director: Franklin Sotomayor. Estab. 1971. Exhibit/display/sign firm. Assigns 15-25 jobs/year. Arrange interview; especially needs artists September-June. SASE. Reports in 2 weeks
Needs: Uses artists for calligraphy, fine art, murals, neon signage and scale models. Pays $50-300, decoration rendering; $75-400, scenery; $50-500, exhibits.

CENIT LETTERS, 7436 Varna Ave., North Hollywood CA 91605. (213)983-1234 or (213)875-0880. Contact: Don Kurtz. Sign firm producing custom cutout letters. Clients: building managers and their tenants (high rise), designers and architects. Assigns 25 jobs/year.
Needs: Works with 2 artists for sign design, 1 for exhibit design, 1 for display fixture, 1 for costume design, 1 for model-making, 1 for P-O-P design, 1 for print advertising and 2 for custom sign illustration. Also uses artists for layout and gold leaf works.
First Contact & Terms: Local artists only. Query or call. SASE. Reports in 1 week. Works on assignment only. Samples returned by SASE; and reports back on future possibilities. Provide resume to be kept on file for future assignments. Pays $100 minimum, gold leaf.

COLLINS-LACROSSE SIGN CORP., 222 Pine St., LaCrosse WI 54601. (608)784-8200. President/Manager: Charles C. Collins. Outdoor advertising sign firm. Clients: food maufacturers and beer bottlers.
Needs: Works with 2 artists for sign design and 2 for custom sign illustration. Also uses artists for billboards, displays, neon signs and sign redesign.
First Contact & Terms: Mail photos or color sketches. Reports in 3 days. Works on assignment only. Samples returned by SASE; and reports back on future possibilities. Provide resume, brochure and flyer to be kept on file for future assignments. Pays $7-30, sketches.

COMMUNA-K SIGN CO. INC., 1964 Wisconsin Ave., Grafton WI 53024. (414)377-8920. Vice President: Richard Reimer. Annual billing: $2,000,000.
Needs: Works with 3 artists for sign design and 3 for P-O-P design. Also uses artists for custom sign faces, brochure and ad design.
First Contact & Terms: Local artists only. Arrange interview to show portfolio. Works on assignment only. Samples returned by SASE; and reports back on future possibilities. Provide resume, calling card and brochure to be kept on file for future assignments.

CONSOLIDATED MOUNTING & FINISHING, 50-10 Kneeland St., Elmhurst NY 11373. Chief Designer: C. Sutnar. Display firm. Assigns 60-100 jobs/year.
Needs: Works with 2 artists for exhibit design, 1 for display fixture design, 2 for model-making, 3 for P-O-P design and 2 for print advertising.
First Contact & Terms: Query with samples (cardboard, corrugated board, plastics and wood) or write for interview. SASE. Reports in 3 weeks. Works on assignment only. Provide resume, calling card and flyer to be kept on file for future assignments. Pays $5-9/hour, scale models.

CORONET ADVERTISING PRODUCTS INC., Box 56000 N, Miami FL 33156. Contact: W. R. Gersch. Manufactures signs and displays. Clients: brewery, packaged liquor, cosmetics, watch and electronic.
Needs: Works with 2 artists for sign design, 3 for display fixture design, 3 for model-making and 3 for P-O-P design. Specifically needs designs for "small back bar illuminated signs for the beer and liquor industries, as well as window and wall signs with and without color motion. We also need designs for signs in the same categories which are not illuminated."
First Contact & Terms: Mail tearsheets, photocopies or transparencies. Works on assignment only. Samples returned by SASE; and reports back on future possibilities. Provide brochure to be kept on file for future assignments.

DE NOVA ASSOCIATES LTD., 2820 Duchesne St., Ville St. Laurent, Montreal, Quebec, Canada H4R 1J4. (514)336-3444. Contact: Terry Lapointe. Uses artists for exhibit and display design. "We prefer an artist to live in the radius of 75 miles from Montreal."

DISCOVERIES INC., 235 W. 1st St., Bayonne NJ 07002. Contact: Frank Latino. Submit tearsheets. Reports in 2-3 weeks.
Needs: Buys ideas for department store window and interior display props. Pays 10% of sales ($40-10,000) for display sold to individual store; 5% of sales ($1,000-100,000) for display purchased by chain. Pays when idea is sold.

THE DISPLAY HOUSE INC., 1101 S. 20th St., Philadelphia PA 19146. (215)735-4448. Contact: B. Lewy. Estab. 1932. Exhibit/display firm. Query or call for interview in January-June or

September-November; local artists only. SASE.
Needs: Uses artists for brochures, display design, murals, POP displays and trade show and museum exhibits. Pays $75-1,000.

DISPLAY SALES INC., 5555 Fair Lane, Cincinnati OH 45227. Contact: Fred C. Pottschmidt.
Needs: Uses artists for advertising, exhibit design, scale models and murals.
First Contact & Terms: Arrange interview.

DISPLAYCRAFT, 457 W. 45th St., New York NY 10036. (212)586-6820. Estab. 1959. Clients: Travel, institutional and museums. Assigns 40 design jobs/year; local artists only. Query with resume. SASE. Reports in 2 weeks.
Needs: Pays $50 min./job, display, exhibit and POP display design.

DOTHAN OUTDOOR ADVERTISING, Box 1849, Dothan AL 36302. (205)794-5404. Manager: Lee Hale. Estab. 1958. Clients: Retail. Assigns 15-20 jobs/year. Query with samples. SASE. Reports in 2 weeks.
Needs: Pays $5/hour or $100/job, billboards, neon signage and sign redesign.

DUKE'S CUSTOM SIGN CO., 601 2nd St. NE, Canton OH 44702. (216)456-2729. Art Director: Walter Shallenberger Clients: banks, merchants, architects, hospitals, schools and construction firms. Annual billing: $200,000. Assigns 5-10 jobs/year.
Needs: Works with 5-10 artists/year for sign design.
First Contact & Terms: Local artists preferred. Query with resume or call. SASE. Reports in 2 weeks. Works on assignment only. Samples returned by SASE; and reports back on future possibilities. Provide resume and samples (photographic, etc.) to be kept on file for future assignments. Pays $12-15/hour.

DYECO STORE FIXTURE & DISPLAY MFG. CO., 1 Pines Plaza, Oregon IL 61061. (815)732-2411. Contact: D. Dean Dye. Estab. 1961. Exhibit/display firm. Assigns 12 jobs/year. Send resume and sketches. SASE. Reports in 2 weeks.
Needs: Uses artists for catalog layouts, direct mail brochures and sketches of store fixtures, elevations and store interiors. Pays $20, sketch.

EMBOSOGRAPH DISPLAY MFG. CO., 1430 W. Wrightwood, Chicago IL 60632. Research and Development: Lee Frizane. Specializes in "complete creative art services and manufacturing in litho, silk screen, plastic molding of all kinds, spray, hot stamping, embossing, die cutting, metal work and assembly." Clients: brewery, beverage, food, automotive, hardware, cosmetics, service stations, appliances and clocks.
Needs: Assigns 50-100 jobs/year. Works with 15 artists for sign design, 15 for display fixture design, 15 for costume design, 15 for model-making, 15 for P-O-P design, 15 for print advertising and 15 for custom sign illustration.
First Contact & Terms: Query with resume or call. SASE. Reports in 2 weeks. Works on assignment only. Samples returned by SASE; and reports back on future possibilities. provide resume and brochure to be kept on file for future assignments. Pays $10-25/hour.

EXHIBIT ASSOCIATES, 1732 Campbell, Kansas City MO 64108. (816)221-8855. Design Director: Darrell McCluhan. Estab. 1978. Clients: Medical, sporting goods, electronic and government. Assigns 12 jobs/year; local artists only. Query with samples or call. SASE. Reports in 1 week.
Needs: Uses artists for display backdrops, display design, exhibit design, scale models, trademark design, store decor and museum designs. Pays by job. Prefers artists who have worked on a professional basis with other firms.

EXHIBIT BUILDERS INC., Box 226, Hwy. 17 N., Deland FL 32720. (904)734-3196. Contact: J. C. Burkhalter. Produces custom exhibits, displays, scale models, dioramas, sales centers and character costumes. Clients: primarily manufacturers, ad agencies and tourist attractions.
Needs: Uses artists for exhibit/display design and scale models.
First Contact & Terms: Works on assignment only. Samples returned by SASE; and reports back on future possibilities. Provide resume, calling card and brochure to be kept on file for future assignments.

EXHIBITS OF CALIFORNIA INC., 1877 Bay Rd., Palo Alto CA 94303. (415)323-7778. Design Director: Ken Hata. Exhibit firm. Specializing in the design and the fabrication of exhibits, interiors, P-O-Ps and graphics. Clients: electronics, food, energy industries, sporting goods and others. Assigns 15-25 jobs/year.

Needs: Works with 3 artists for sign design, 4 for exhibit design, 3 for display fixture design, 3 for model-making 3 for P-O-P design, 2 for print advertising and 3 for custom sign illustration.
First Contact & Terms: Local experienced artists only. Query with photos or transparencies or call to make an appointment to go over portfolio. Works on assignment only. Samples returned by SASE; and reports back on future possibilities. Samples returned by SASE; and reports back on future possibilities. Pays $5-50.

GEORGE E. FERN CO., 1100 Gest St., Cincinnati OH 45203. (513)621-6111. General Manager: George J. Budig. Exposition service contractor/display firm.
First Contact & Terms: Query by phone. SASE. Reports in 1 week. Works on assignment only. Samples returned by SASE; and reports back on future possibilities. Pays $50-300, sketch of exhibit.
Needs: Very limited art needs; "almost zero." Sometimes uses artists for backdrop displays, trade show exhibit/design, convention entrances and special room decorations.

GEORGIA OUTDOOR ADVERTISING, Box 5562, Rome GA 30161. (404)291-7740. General Manager: Jerry P. Cram. Estab. 1965. Assigns 25 jobs/year; local artists only. Query with resume and samples. SASE. Reports in 2 weeks.
Needs: Pays $5/hour or $20/job for billboards.

GEORGIA OUTDOOR ADVERTISING INC., 1960 Winterville Rd., Athens GA 30605. Vice President: Stan Henderson. Estab. 1966. Clients: Banks, retailers, manufacturers, automobile dealers and government agencies. Assigns 200 jobs/year. Query with samples. SASE. Reports in 2 weeks.
Needs: Pays $15-25 for billboard art.

INTERNATIONAL DESIGN CORP., 3441 W. Grand Ave., Chicago IL 60651. Contact: A. Stone. Display and exhibit company.
Needs: Works with 1 artist for sign design, 4 for exhibit design, 2 for display and 2 for P-O-P design. Also uses artists for convention exhibits, industrial design, window displays and sculpture.
First Contact & Terms: Query with samples. Reports in 3 months. Works on assignment only. Samples returned by SASE; and reports back on future possibilities. Provide resume and brochure to be kept on file for future assignments. Pays flat fee or 5% royalty.

KREBS MERCHANDISING DISPLAYS CORP., 635 W. 23rd St., New York NY 10011. (212)741-1780. Contact: J.C. Clients: hardware, housewares, cosmetics and consumer-oriented products.
Needs: Assigns 50 jobs/year.
First Contact & Terms: Local artists only. Query with resume or call. SASE. Reports in 1 week. Pays $25-100/sketch for display design, fixture design and POP displays.

MARKETECHS INC., Rte. 5, York PA 17402. Contact: Otis Morse. Exhibits firm.
Needs: Uses artists for advertising, exhibits, display design and scale models.
First Contact & Terms: Arrange interview. Pays up to $300 for 15' exhibit.

MAYHEW PRODUCTS CORP., 2809 E. Hwy. 30, Grand Island NE 68801. (308)382-7529. Contact: Raymond Mayhew, vice president. Electric sign manufacturer. Estab. 1945. Annual billing: $1,200,000. Query with samples.
Needs: Uses artists for sign design and some brochure work. Pays by job, sign design; $15, line drawings; $25-100, color illustrations.

MISSOURI NEON & PLASTIC ADVERTISING INC., 3160 W. Kearney, Springfield MO 65803. (417)862-1778. Contact: Vernon M. Boyle, president. Estab. 1936. Clients: Banks, motels, restaurants, grocery stores, resorts and "just about every type of business." Arrange interview to show portfolio.
Needs: Uses artists for sign design. Negotiates pay.

MODERN DESIGNS OF MIAMI INC., 5900 Flagler St., Box 3805, Hollywood FL 33023. (305)961-1362. President: Charles G. Lynn. Estab. 1964. Assigns 8-10 jobs/year; local artists only. Query with samples. SASE. Reports in 2 weeks.
Needs: Uses artists for brochures, display backdrops, display design, exhibit design, fixture design, store fixture design, residential renderings and designs and POP displays. Negotiates pay.

NEBRASKA NEON SIGN CO., 1140 N. 21st St., Lincoln NE 68503. Contact: Bob Norris. Handles design, contraction and service of signs. Clients: all types (many financial institutions).

Needs: Works with 2 artists/year on sign design.
First Contact & Terms: Mail photos or transparencies.

NORTON ADVERTISING, 5280 Kennedy Ave., Cincinnati OH 45213. (513)631-4864. Contact: Tom Norton. Sign firm.
Needs: Assigns 30-60 jobs/year. Uses artists for billboards.
First Contact & Terms: Local artists only. Call for interview. Pays $20 minimum, roughs; $75-100, finished sketch.

P.O.P. DISPLAYS, INC., (formerly Phase Four Products, Inc.) 11-12 30 Drive Astoria, New York NY 11102. Creative Director: Mr. Small. Display/POP firm. Clients: distillers, cosmetic firms and various others.
First Contact & Terms: Query with samples. SASE. Reports in 1 week. Works on assignment only. Samples returned by SASE; and reports back on future possibilities. Provide resume and brochure to be kept on file for future assignments. Pays $12/hour.
Needs: Assigns 400-500 jobs/year. Works with six artists for P-O-P design.

THE RAVENWARE CO. INC., 360 Scholes St., Brooklyn NY 11206. (212)497-1232. Vice President: Richard G. Galef. Fixture manufacturer/display firm specializing in P-O-P displays. Clients: national advertisers. Assigns 200 jobs/year.
First Contact & Terms: Local artists only. Query. Reports in 1 week. Works on assignment only. Samples returned by SASE; and reports back on future possibilities. Provide resume and calling card to be kept on file for future assignments. Pays $40-150.
Needs: Works with 10 artists for display fixture design, 5 for model-making, 10 for P-O-P design and 5 for custom sign illustration. Also uses artists for display/POP/fixture design, scale models and trade show exhibits.

REISLER STORE EQUIPMENT CO., 1727-1737 S. Michigan Ave., Chicago IL 60616. (312)427-1900. Contact: Mr. G. Reisler. Estab. 1956. Assigns 50 jobs/year; local artists only. Query with samples or mail art. SASE. Reports in 3 weeks.
Needs: Uses artists for fixture design.

BOB ROBINSON MARKETING INC., 366 N. Broadway, Jericho NY 11753. (516)931-5900. President: Bob Robinson.
Needs: Assigns 100 jobs/year. Uses artists for display/POP design and scale models.
First Contact & Terms: Arrange interview to show portfolio. SASE. Reports in 2 weeks. Pays $25-75/sketch or $200-300/job for design of permanent displays,

ROGERS DISPLAY STUDIOS INC., 1000 Wayside Rd., Cleveland OH 44110. Director of Design: Bernard Digman. Submit samples.
Needs: Uses designers and artists for trade show exhibits and graphics. Also will pay "fee" to artists for exhibits work and point-of-purchase work referred to Rogers. Pays $25-40.

SELEXOR DISPLAYS, 1916 Park Ave., New York NY 10037. (212)368-7791. Vice President: C.M. Kingsley. Estab. 1935. Exhibit/display/sign firm. Query with sketches, or arrange interview; local artists only. SASE. Reports in 1 week.
Needs: Uses artists for display backdrops, design, POP displays, scale models, sign redesign, technical charts/illustrations and trade show exhibits. Pays $100-300, exhibits; $100-250, POP displays; $150-500, scale models.

SERVILIO ASSOCIATES INC., 2 Prince St., Brooklyn NY 11201. Contact: Richard Stern. Mail photos or arrange interview.
Needs: Uses artists for exhibit/display design, scale models, concepts, props, drawings and painting. Negotiates pay.

SITKA STORE FIXTURES, Box 392, Kansas City MO 64141. (816)221-4520. President: Earl A. Hogan. Manufacturer of wood store fixtures and merchandisers. Clients: pharmacies, hardware, paint and wallpaper stores, bakers and jewelers.
Needs: Works with 5-10 artists/year for fixture design.
First Contact & Terms: Query. SASE. Reports in 3 weeks. Works on assignment only. Samples returned by SASE; and reports back on future possibilities. Provide resume to be kept on file for future assignments. Pay determined by job.

W.H.B. SPANGENBERG STUDIOS, 1010 Central Ave., Metairie LA 70001. Contact: Walker Spangenberg. Specializes in trade show exhibitis and stage settings.

Needs: Works with 2 artists for sign design, 2 for exhibit design, 1 for costume design, 1 for P-O-P design and 1 for custom sign illustration.
First Contact & Terms: Mail photos or transparencies. Provide portfolio and/or resume to be kept on file for future assignments.

T-K INDUSTRIES, 38 W. Mall, Plainview NY 11803. President: George Finegold. Estab. 1975. Clients: Department stores, display distributors, mass merchandisers and industry. Assigns 25-30 jobs/year. Query with samples. SASE. Reports in 2 weeks.
Needs: Payment by job: $25 minimum, display design and sign redesign; $50 minimum, fixture design, POP displays and print media ads; $75 minimum, brochures; $100 minimum, display backdrops and scale models.

TURNROTH SIGN CO., Box 456, Sterling IL 61081. (815)625-1155. Contact: R. Neil Turn-roth. Clients: banks, business, retail and industry.
Needs: Works with artists for billboards ($25-50), neon signage ($20-75), sign redesign ($20-100). Assigns 15-20 jobs/year.
First Contact & Terms: Mostly out-of-town artists. Query with samples. SASE. Reports in 1 week. Payment by job.

UNICUBE CORP., 1290 Oak Point Ave., Bronx NY 10474. Contact: Robert J. Burg. Mail photos or transparencies.
Needs: Uses artists for advertising and exhibit/display/store fixture design.

VANADCO SIGN INC., US. 31 E. 16th Rd., Argos IN 46501. (219)892-5000. President: Bruce Van Der Weele. Sign firm. Clients: retailers, manufacturers (P-O-P and off-premise displays).
Needs: Works with 2+ artists for sign design.
First Contact & Terms: Out-of-town artists only. Query. Reports in 1 week. Works on assignment only. No samples returned. Reports back to artist n possible assignments. "Pay determined when query is made."

WESCO ASSOCIATES INC., 1600 Broadway, New York NY 10019. Art Director/General Manager: Jack Kamhi.Clients: liquor, beer, tobacco, candy and gum. Assigns 200 jobs/year.
Needs: Works with 3 artists for model-making and 6 for P-O-P design.
First Contact & Terms: Local artists only. SASE. Works on assignment only. Samples returned by SASE. Provide calling card and brochure to be kept on file for future assignments. Pays $300 min./job, brochures; $75-150/job, display design.

DONALD WIEDEMAN INC., Box 186, Riverside NJ 08075. Contact: Don R. Wiedeman. Estab. 1971. Clients: Industry. Assigns 10-12 jobs/year. Query with resume; local artists preferred. SASE. Reports in 2 weeks.
Needs: Uses artists for design, sales presentations and promotion. Pays by job.

Fashion Firms

There are three basic types of fashion markets listed in this section: 1) manufacturers that are buying clothing design 2) companies needing textile design and 3) department and specialty stores assigning fashion illustration for advertising.

While the majority of the fashion design markets are located in the New York City area, fashion illustration for stores, is a much wider market with most in-house advertising departments requiring at least some freelance help.

Whether an assignment comes from a manufacturer, or the advertising department of a store, each company has its own image. One house may specialize in exotic fashions, another in conservative styles. A store's ads should also be studied to see what types of layouts and illustrations are used.

Most of the listings in this section specify that initial contact be made by sending samples though the mail. Some will return these examples of your work if a self-addressed stamped envelope is enclosed. Others will keep material on file to refer to when an assignment develops.

Often times the work in the fashion industry is seasonal. Where this is true, we have provided that information in the listing.

Since most fashion designs are completed almost a year before they appear on the market, it is important that you keep abreast of upcoming trends. Both *Woman's Wear Daily* (Fairchild Publications, Inc.) and *California Apparel News* (California Fashion Publications, Inc.) are leading trade newspapers that signal up-and-coming designs.

ACT YOUNG IMPORTS INC., 49 W. 37th St., New York NY 10018. (212)354-8894. Executive Vice President: Joe Hafif. Estab. 1965. Manufactures infants' and children's clothes; polyester and cotton; Act Young Fashions label. Buys 200-400 designs/year; local artists only. Query with samples. SASE. Reports in 2 weeks.
Needs: Uses artists for fashion design.

AFRICAN FABRIC PRINTS/AFRICAN GARMENTS INC., 303 W. 42nd St., New York NY 10036. Contact: Vince Jordan.
Needs: Uses artists for fashion and textile design and ready-to-wear patterns.
First Contact & Terms: Mail tearsheets, original art or design ideas. Reports in 5-6 weeks. Pays $50 minimum.

LILLIAN ALBUS SHOPS INC., 139 Kings Hwy. E., Haddonfield NJ 08033. (609)429-1875. Contact: Mr. S. Ross, general manager. Women's retail specialty chain. Sells better ready-to-wear, sportswear and gifts.
Needs: Works with 1 freelance illustrator or designer/year.
First Contact & Terms: Local artists only. Arrange interview to show portfolio. SASE. Reports in 1 week. Works on assignment only. Samples returned by SASE; and reports back on future assignment possibilities. Pays $15-25/job, newspaper ad illustrations.

AMBE DIVISION OF CHARTER OAK INDUSTRIES, 1407 Park St., Hartford CT 06106. (203)249-5205. Vice President: Larry Bell. Manufactures women's and men's coats; leather and wool under the Ambe, Ambe Sport, Leather Factory and Hartford Gear labels. Also have new men'swear line under supervision of Richard J. Bell, vice president. Buys 30 illustrations/year.
Needs: Works with 1+ designer and 2+ illustrator/designer per year. Uses artists for newspaper illustrations.
First Contact & Terms: Prefers artists with experience in leather accessories, handbags or items that have required attention to detail. Prefers illustrators with a new approach. Query. SASE. Reports in 2 weeks. Works on assignment only. Samples returned by SASE; and reports back on future assignment possibilities. Provide resume and samples of work to be kept on file for future assignment possibilities.

ANGELIQUE JEWELRY, 7263 Engineer Rd., Suite B, San Diego CA 92111. (714)292-8300. Art Director: Jeff Elden. Estab. 1969. Specializes in porcelain, floral and feather jewelry for Casual

Corner, Macy's and Bloomingdale's; Angelique label. Buys 100-200 designs/year. Query with color drawings. SASE. Reports in 2 weeks.
Needs: Uses artists for product design and illustration. Pays $5-25, pendant designs.
To Break In: "Prepare a series based on one theme. Look for fashion trends and develop an original offshoot. Feb./March submissions should relate to the following fall. June/July submissions should relate to the following spring."

ARKAY OUTERWEAR, Division of Arkay Pants Co., Box 588, Fall River MA 02722. Director: H.G. Katzman. Estab. 1934. Manufactures children's outerwear; nylon, wool and corduroy; McGregor label. Assigns 3-5 design jobs and buys 10 illustrations/year. Mail designs or query with samples. SASE. Reports in 2 weeks.
Needs: Uses artists for fashion design and hang tags.

AVON GLOVE CORP., 10 E. 38th, New York NY 10016. Contact: Mr. D. Schwartz. Specializes in gloves, mittens and headwear. Arrange interview; prefers New York City artists.
Needs: Uses artists for sales promotion/advertising layouts and direct mail brochures.

BAIMS, 408 Main, Pine Bluff AR 71601. (501)534-0121. Contact: David A. Shapiro. Retailer. Carries Haggar, Van Heusen and other labels. Assigns 25-100 jobs/year.
Needs: Works with 2-3 illustrators/designers/year. Uses artists for ad illustrations.
First Contact & Terms: Query with resume and samples and arrange interview to show portfolio. SASE. Reports in 2 weeks. Provide resume, calling card and samples to be kept on file for future assignments. Pays $5-20/job.

BATIK IMPORTS, A.R. Lawrence & Associates, Box 4096, Fullerton CA 92634. (714)525-7069. Contact: A. Robert Lawrence. Specializes in original and hand-printed batik fabrics. Call for interview or mail 8x10 samples.
Needs: Uses artists for fashion design of men's sport shirts, women's blouses, sales promotion layouts, direct mail brochures, tags and inserts. Negotiates payment.

BENO'S, 1515 Santee St., Los Angeles CA 90015. (213)748-2222. Contact: Barbara Strauss, advertising manager. Estab. 1938. Department and family apparel chain in California, Oregon and Washington. "We buy a lot of freelance artwork." Arrange interview to show portfolio; local artists only. SASE. Reports in 1-2 weeks.
Needs: Uses artists for illustrations of men's, women's and children's fashions for newspaper ads and direct mail coupon books. Pays $20-35, small line drawing.

LARRY BERMAN, 8004 Bustleton Ave., Philadelphia PA 19152. Contact: Lorraine Berman. Retail apparel shop. Uses artists for men's fashion design, package design, shopping bag art and window displays.

SAM BOBMAN DEPARTMENT STORE, 2877 Kensington Ave., Philadelphia PA 19134. Contact: Sam Bobman. Arrange interview to show portfolio.
Needs: Uses artists for newspaper advertising layout in strong b&w or reverse design, billboard advertising, bags and window display.

BREAD & BUTTER, 1 Pennsylvania Plaza, New York NY 10001. Contact: Carolyn Jones. Fabric design studio.
Needs: Uses illustrators for children's designs appropriate for sleepwear, playwear, T-shirts, etc. Buys "color roughs–we'll send instructions." Send resume and 2 photocopies of work. Reports in 1 week. Pays $126 minimum/design. "Artist is paid when design is sold. Designs are kept on file for presentations. We will send artists a booklet explaining our market, how artwork should be prepared, etc."

THE BROADWAY, 625 SW Broadway, Portland OR 97205. (503)221-1901. Contact: Cynthia Van Vechten, advertising coordinator. Estab. 1975. Retailer. Buys 36 illustrations/year; local artists only. Arrange interview to show portfolio. SASE. Reports in 1 week.
Needs: Uses artists for fashion illustrations for newspaper and direct mail ads. Pays $25-40/figure.

BROZMAN'S INC., 349 Pine St., Williamsport PA 17701. (717)323-7155. Contact: Michael Verdini, advertising director. Chain of 6 women's fashion stores. Assigns 30 jobs/year.
Needs: Works with 6 designers and 6 illustrators/designers/year. Uses artists for fashion illustrations, some graphic design work for semiannual 2-color brochure.
First Contact & Terms: Prefers artists with published work. Arrange interview to show portfolio "with pieces applicable to women's fashion ads." Reports in 2 weeks or less. Works on assignment

only. Samples returned by SASE; and reports back on future assignment possibilities. Provide tearsheet to be kept on file for future assignments. Pays $10, rough; $15-25, finished illustration.

THE BUGATTI, 222 3rd St., Cambridge MA 02142. Contact: Terry Scheller. Send samples.
Needs: Uses artists for fashion design of leather handbags, luggage and sales promotion layouts. Pays $25 minimum, fashion design. Send samples.

CHATTANOOGA CHOO-CHOO, 2354 Hunters Woods Plaza, Reston VA 22091. Contact: Reza. Retail store. Uses artists for art renderings, building interiors, fashion design, newspaper advertising layouts, sales promotion art, shopping bags and window displays.

DUNN AND McCARTHY INC., 41 Washington St., Auburn NY 13021. Advertising Manager: Walter F. Schoonmaker. Manufactures women's shoes, leather and urethane under the Emma Jetticks, Hill and Dale and Station Wagons labels.
Needs: Assigns 10-15 design jobs and buys 5-6 illustrations/year. Uses artists for catalog illustrations.
First Contact & Terms: Query. SASE. Report in one week. Pays $30, inside; $50-100, cover.

DUOFOLD INC., Drawer A, Mohawk NY 13407. (315)866-4000. Contact: Douglas J. Pirnie. Manufactures tennis and golf shirts, tennis shorts and underwear. Query with samples.

J. M. DYER CO., Box 620, Corsicana TX 75110. Contact: Bob Cathey. Department store. Uses artists for art renderings, building interiors, fashion design, graphic design, newspaper advertising layouts, posters and window displays.

ELDER MANUFACTURING CO., Box 273, St. Louis MO 63166. Contact: Mick Zoll. Manufactures sportswear and men's and boys' wear. Prefers artists with some professional experience. Arrange interview; prefers local artists.
Needs: Uses artists for sales promotion/ad layouts and direct mail brochures. Pays $30-75/illustration.

FARIS BROTHERS INC., 13122 Saticoy St., North Hollywood CA 91605. (213)764-7778. Vice President: Joseph Faris. Estab. 1946. Manufactures ladies' lingerie and loungewear; nylon tricot and satin; Treasure of California label. Assigns 25 design jobs/season; local designers only. Arrange interview. SASE. Reports in 3 weeks.
Needs: Uses artists for fashion design.

FIFTH AVENUE ROBES, 105 Madison Ave., New York NY 10016. Contact: Mort Winkel, president. Manufactures loungewear and robes; Fifth Avenue label. Sold at specialty and department stores. Query with resume or arrange interview.

FIGURE FAIR, Box 13147, St. Petersburg FL 33733. President: David B. Fyvolent. Estab. 1925. Retailer of bras, girdles, lingerie and leisurewear. Assigns 20-30 design jobs/year. Mail designs. SASE. Reports in 3 weeks.
Needs: Uses artists for newspaper advertising. Negotiates pay.

FLAH'S INC., 878 Albany-Shaker Rd., Latham NY 12110. (518)785-3294. Contact: Art Director. Sells men's and women's clothing and accessories, giftware and cosmetics. Buys 350-450 illustrations/year.
Needs: Uses artists for newspaper ad illustrations and direct mail pieces.
First Contact & Terms: Local artists only. Arrange interview to show resume and portfolio. Works on assignment only. Samples returned by SASE; and reports back on future assignment possibilities. Provide resume, flyer and samples to be kept on file for future assignments. "Pay comparable with experience."
Tips: "We are a very progressive fashion store. Stylized art preferred. Experience in newspaper illustration helpful."

GANTOS INC., 4025 Broadmoor SE, Grand Rapids MI 49508. (616)949-7000. Advertising Director: Rebecca Estabrook. Chain of 30 women's specialty stores.
Needs: Buys 125 illustrations/year. Uses artists for layout and illustration of fashion newspaper ads.
First Contact & Terms: Arrange interview to show references and portfolio. SASE. Reports in 1 month. Pays $50-90/figure.

I. GOLDBERG ARMY-NAVY, 902 Chestnut St., Philadelphia PA 19107. (215)925-2418. Contact: Advertising Director. Retail store. Sells outerwear, underwear, footwear, sweatclothes, military surplus, fashion clothing and camping clothes and gear including the Sebago, BVD, Oshkosh, Levi, Lee, Wrangler and Timerland labels.
Needs: Works with 5 freelancer illustrators/designers/year. Uses artists for advertising, catalog covers, direct mail brochures and fashion illustration.
First Contact & Terms: Local artists only. Call or send sketches. No work returned. Contacts artists as needs arise. Provide resume and tearsheet to be kept on file for future assignments. Pays $8-15, spot illustration; $6-25, newspaper ad; $175-200, catalog cover; $25-50, bag ad design.

CAROL GOUN MANUFACTURING INC., 208 S. Jefferson St., Chicago IL 60606. (312)263-5977. Contact: Walter D. Nager, president. Estab. 1946. Manufactures young women's clothing. Query; local artists only.

HAPHAZARD DESIGNS INC., 1177 Clare Ave., West Palm Beach FL 33461. (305)832-1774. President: Suzanne Thayer. Manufactures young women's clothing.
Needs: Works with 5 designers/year. Uses artists for fabric, clothing and screen print design.
First Contact & Terms: Prefers local artists. Query with resume and samples "Please be specific in stating what you specialize in—detailed drawings suitable for screen printing, smaller designs for textiles, etc." Reports in 2 weeks. Provide resume and brochure to be kept on file for future assignments. Pays $40 min./job.

HARUKO, 875 Waimanu St., Suite 535, Honolulu HI 96813. (808)538-1314. Contact: Haruko Moberg. Estab. 1972. Manufactures young women's clothing; cotton and cotten blends; Haruko and Faiva labels. Assigns 20 minimum jobs/year. Arrange interview to show portfolio. Reports in 2 weeks.
Needs: Uses artists for clothing and fabric design. Pays by job.

ITALIA LTD., Box 1145, Pawtucket RI 02860. (401)723-2322. President: Paul DeFruscio. Estab. 1976. Manufactures 14 and 18 kt. gold jewelry. Mail designs. SASE. Reports in 2-3 weeks.
Needs: Uses artists for design and ad layout. Pays $50+.

JAYVEE BRAND INC., Box 409, Lake Oswego OR 97034. (503)636-9691. Vice President: Walter Emery. Estab. 1946. Manufactures infants', children's and juniors' sleepwear; children's playwear and infants' accessories; Kiddie Kover, Kitten Kudlers and Betsy Clark labels. Assigns 1-5 design jobs and buys 5-15 illustrations/year; mostly local artists. Query with samples. SASE. Reports in 3 weeks.
Needs: Uses artists for fabric design, fashion design, hang tags, inserts and package design. Pays by job.

JOSEPH & FEISS, 1290 Avenue of the Americas, New York NY 10019. Contact: Susan Smyth. Produces men's wear; Cricketeer label. Prefers New York area artists.
Needs: Uses artists for design of men's suits, sports coats and slacks and ad illustration. Pays $100 minimum, illustrations.

JUST ACCESSORIES INC., 112 W. 34th St., Room 710, New York NY 10001. (212)564-5168. President: Richard N. Bloch. Estab. 1961. Manufactures children's clothing and accessories; Miss Boutique label. Assigns 200+ design jobs and buys 150 illustrations/year. Mail designs. SASE. Reports in 1 week.
Needs: Uses artists for fashion accessory design, package design, inserts, direct mail brochures and T-shirt art. Negotiates pay by job.

KAYSER ROTH HOSIERY CO. INC., 1221 Avenue of the Americas, New York NY 10021. (212)764-4335. Regional Sales Manager: Robert M. Lieberman. Estab. 1958. Produces socks; cotton, nylon and orlon; Fruit of the Loom, Esquire and Perma-Pair labels; for department stores, supermarkets and mass merchandisers. Buyers are "everyone with feet!" Send resume, sketches or call for interview. Reports in 1 week.
Needs: Uses artists for advertising/catalog layouts, direct mail brochures, inserts, package design and window display.

KLOPMAN MILLS, 7 Link Dr., Rockleigh NJ 07647. (201)564-7000, ext. 563. Contact: Stan Cohen. Produces textile and fabric designs.
Needs: Prefers using local artists for fashion design, sales promotion/ad layouts, direct mail brochures, window display, hang tags and inserts.

LAMOUREUX, 191 NW 71st St., Miami FL 33150. Contact: E. Lamoureux. Estab. 1969. Manufactures men's, women's and children's apparel. Query.
Needs: Designs suitable for screen printing. Negotiates pay.

LEE CO., Division of Lee Byron Corp., Empire State Bldg., Suite 4619, New York NY 10001. Contact: Dan L. Lieberfarb. Produces accessories and boys' wear. Mail samples or call for interview; prefers New York City artists.
Needs: Uses artists for fashion design of men's and boys' belts, sales promotion/ad layouts, package design and direct mail brochures.

LIBERTY ORGANIZATION INC., 4116 La Crescenta Ave., La Crescent CA 91214. (213)248-0618. Marketing/Advertising Manager: Ian J. Skone-Rees. Estab. 1952. Manufactures recreational warm-up suits; Liberty Action label. Assigns 20 design jobs and buys 10 illustrations/year; mostly local artists. Mail designs. SASE. Reports in 2 weeks.
Needs: Pays $100-200, catalog covers and layouts; $10-40/job, package design; $8-15/job, advertising layouts; $6-10/job, direct mail brochures.

MADEMOISELLE PROMOTIONS LTD., 350 7th Ave., New York NY 10001. Contact: Sharon Fenster. Prefers local artists. Buys all rights. Pays on acceptance.
Needs: Uses line illustrations made from photos of women's sportswear and corporate logos made into textile patterns. Pays $10 min./figure, line illustration.

MEI JAN OF HAWAII, Box 25536, Honolulu HI 96825. (808)949-3306. Contact: Linda or Calvin Lee. Manufactures mens' 2nd women's sports and resort wear in cotton and polyester under the Mei Jan of Hawaii and Lori Lee labels. Assigns 6 jobs and buys 24 illustrations/year.
Needs: Works with 3 designers/year. Uses artists for fabric and clothing design and ad illustrations.
First Contact & Terms: Arrange interview to show portfolio. SASE. Reports in 3 weeks. Works on assignment only. Samples returned by SASE; and reports back on future assignment possibilities. Provide resume to be kept on file for future assignments. Negotiates pay.

MISS BOUTIQUE, 112 W. 34th St., New York NY 10001. (212)564-5168. President: Richard N. Bloch. Estab. 1973. Manufactures children's clothing and accessories; Miss Boutique label. Assigns 200+ design jobs/year. Mail designs or query with samples. SASE. Reports in 1 week.
Needs: Pays $100 min./job for fashion and item design. Also uses artists for cartoons.

MOBIL SOX CORP., 366 5th Ave., New York NY 10001. Contact: Stanley Kreinik. Specializes in anklets and knee-hi socks for all ages.
Needs: Uses artists for sales promotion/ad layouts, package design and direct mail brochures. "We're also interested in screen prints (i.e. comics) on socks."

NATIONAL ASSOCIATION OF HOSIERY MANUFACTURERS, Box 4098, Charlotte NC 28204. President: S.M. Berry. Estab. 1905. Members produce hosiery. Send resume.
Needs: Uses artists for fashion design, advertising/catalog layouts and direct mail brochures. Negotiates payment.

NATIONAL DOLLAR STORES, 929 Market St., San Francisco CA 94103. (415)392-1371. Contact: Harold Sun, advertising director. Estab. 1903. Buys 300-400 illustrations/year; local artists only. Query with samples. SASE. Reports in 2-3 weeks.
Needs: Uses artists for illustrations of figures for clothing ads, mostly for men, women and children. Pays $200.

NAZARETH/CENTURY MILLS, 350 5th Ave., New York NY 10001. (212)868-0200. Designer: Michele Lesser. Manufactures children's sleepwear, men's, boys', girls' and ladies' sportswear and underwear; cotton and polyester/cotton; Nazareth Mills, Bojangles, Savage and Acorn labels.
Needs: Buys 50-100 illustrations/year.
First Contact & Terms: Local artists only. Query with samples. SASE. Reports in 4 weeks. Works on assignment only. Samples returned by SASE; and reports back on future assignment possibilities. Provide flyer to be kept on file for future assignments. Pays $50-100/job, artwork for screen printing.

PALM BEACH CO., 1290 Avenue of the Americas, New York NY 10019. Advertising Director: Ceci Murphy. Specializes in men's tailored clothing and sportswear.
Needs: Uses artists for sales promotion/ad layouts and fashion illustration.

First Contact & Terms: Prefers New York City artists. Call for interview.

THE PARIS, 618 Felix St., St. Joseph MO 64501. (816)232-8446. Contact: Paul Yanuck, general manager. Women's and junior clothing store. Estab. 1931. Assigns 150+ jobs/year. Query with samples. Reports in 1 week.
Needs: Pays $10-25, newspaper ad illustrations.

PENN OUTERWEAR CO., 625 Broadway, New York NY 10012. Contact: M.B. Friedman. Specializes in boys' wear, sportswear and outerwear.
Needs: Uses artists for fashion design of apparel and direct mail brochures. Pays $30/hour maximum.

PINEHURST TEXTILES INC., Box 1628, Asheboro NC 27203. (919)625-2153. Contact: Lloyd E. Milks Jr. Manufactures ladies' lingerie, sleepwear and leisurewear; nylon tricot, woven polyester/cotton, brushed tricot and fleece; Pinehurst Lingerie label.
Needs: Works with 2 illustrators/year. Seasonal needs: Spring and summer due September 1; fall and winter due March 1.

PLAYTIME HEADWEAR INC., 3651 Farm Ranch Rd., Bethpage NY 11714. President: Richard Miller. Estab. 1945. Manufactures women's and girls' headwear. Assigns 4 design jobs/year; local artists only. Arrange interview. SASE. Reports in 2 weeks.
Needs: Uses artists for direct mail brochures, hang tags and iron-ons.

MAYA ROMANOFF TEXTILES, 4722 N. Malden, Chicago IL 60640. President: Maya Romanoff. Manufactures interior design products: handpainted batik and wall paper fabrics. Clients: commercial and residential.
Needs: Works with artists for fabric, tapestry and rug designs.
First Contact & Terms: Firm is just beginning to request freelance design work. Mail designs, or query with resume and samples. SASE. Reports in 3-4 weeks. Provide resume, brochure, flyer and tearsheet to be kept on file for future assignments. Pays by job.

ROSSELLA & JOSEPH OF ROME, 7 Green St., Huntington NY 11763. (516)427-9355. Contact: Rossella Koopmann, president. Estab. 1969. Manufactures women's evening gowns. Buys 3 illustrations/year. Prefers artists with previous experience in fashion. Query with resume and samples or send roughs; local artists only. Reports in 3 weeks.
Needs: Uses artists for fabric and clothing design and ads. Pays $30-150.

SEIBEL & STERN, 112 W. 34th St., New York NY 10001. (212)563-0326. Executive Vice President: L.S. Davis. Estab. 1921. Manufactures children's clothes; Kim Originals, Little Star and Yves St. Laurent (for girls) labels. Assigns 3-6 design jobs/year; local artists only. Write or call.
Needs: Negotiates pay for styling.

SHORELINE SPORTSWEAR INC., Box 2548, Santa Barbara CA 93120. Art Director: Ernest P. Garcia. Manufactures screen printed T-shirts, sweatshirts, nylon jackets and tank tops. Primarily aimed at the college market. Assigns 40 design jobs/year.
Needs: Works with 5-6 illustrators/designers/year. Uses artists for sports, beer, liquor and recreational fashion designs, also for a series of college-oriented design concepts.
First Contact & Terms: Professional caliber artists only. Query with samples. "Photocopies of designs are fine for intro; but I like to see samples or portfolio when (and only then) we get more interested." SASE. Reports in 30 days. Buys copyright and all rights. Terms of purchase are negotiable. Works on assignment only. Samples returned by SASE; and reports back on future assignment possibilities. Provide 8½×11 brochure or flyer to be kept on file for future assignments. Pays $50-300.
To Break In: "I'm looking for artists who are more than just 'picture makers'—artists who can capture the feeling of the subject."

SILVIL CORP., 34 W. 33rd St., New York NY 10001. Contact: Sy Silverberg. Produces boys' robes and pajamas. Mail samples.
Needs: Uses artists to design screen prints for pajamas.

SMART STYLE INDUSTRIES, 350 5th Ave., New York NY 10001. (212)564-0760. Contact: Howard Feigelman. Specializes in boys' wear. Send samples of work from inception to completion; prefers local artists.
Needs: Uses artists for direct mail brochures.

STRETCH & SEW INC., Box 185, Eugene OR 97401. (503)686-9961. Contact: Joan Plahm. Sells knit fabrics, patterns, notions and teaches sewing methods.
First Contact & Terms: Artists with fashion illustration experience and technical art inking experience. Query with samples. SASE. Reports in 2 weeks. Pays $30-65, fashion illustration.
Needs: Assigns 200 jobs/year. Uses artists for pattern envelopes/instructions, catalog covers/layouts, direct mail/publicity brochures, newspaper ad layouts, packaging, posters and company publications.

TAMI, 235 2nd St., San Francisco CA 94105. (415)982-4677, ext. 40 or 66. Contact: Billie Sher, merchandiser. Estab. 1963. Manufactures young women's clothing; Tami label. Assigns 10 jobs/year. Arrange interview to show portfolio. Reports in 2 weeks.
Needs: Uses artists for advertising illustrations, catalog design, fabric design, clothing design and print designs. Negotiates pay.
To Break In: "A good portfolio, new ideas and creative thinking and input will help the artist break into our firm."

ANN TAYLOR INC., 50 W. 40th St., New York NY 10018. (212)354-9191. Vice President: Mimi Liebeskind. Contemporary women's sportswear shop. Estab. 1953. Sells natural fabric and some leather products; Perry Ellis, Willi Smith, Maurice Sasson, Bern Conrad, Regina Kravitz and St. Tropez West labels. Query with resume and samples; local artists only. Reports in 2 weeks.
Needs: Uses artists for advertising illustration.
To Break In: "Be Familar with Ann Taylor and Ann Taylor concept. Read *Women's Wear Daily* for news on trends."

E.J. TOWLE CO., 406 Dexter Ave. N., Seattle WA 98109. (206)624-0013. President: W.G. Lefort. Produces jewelry oriented to the West Coast of the US, including Hawaii and Alaska, for gift and jewelry stores. Products include airline jewelry, earrings, emblematics, money clips, pendants, rings, tie bars and tie tacs. Buys 10-20 designs/year.
Needs: Works with 6-8 designers and 1-2 illustrators/designers/year. Uses artists for jewelry designer graphics, wax models and originals in metal.
First Contact & Terms: Query. Reports in 2 weeks. Works on assignment only. Samples returned by SASE; and reports back on future assignment possibilities. Provide resume, calling card, brochure, flyer, portfolio, slides and photographs to be kept on file for future assignments. Pays $25-450.

TRIBORO QUILT MFG. CORP., 172 S. Broadway, White Plains NY 10605. (914)428-7551. Sales Manager: Alvin Kaplan. Produces infants' wear under the Triboro label; for chain stores.
Needs: Works with 3 designers, 3 textile designers and 3 illustrator/designers/year. Uses artists for advertising/catalog layouts, direct mail brochures, fabric and fashion design, hang tags, inserts, iron-ons and package design.
First Contact & Terms: Call for interview. SASE. Reports in 1 week. Works on assignment only. Samples returned by SASE; and reports back on future assignment possibilities. Provide resume, calling card and brochure to be kept on file for future assignments.

JOE WEBB, 460 Bryant St., San Francisco CA 94107. (415)957-9322. Contact: Joe Webb. Estab. 1975. Manufactures junior sportswear blouses; primarily cotton knits; Joe Webb label. Query with resume and samples or garment roughs. Reports in 2 weeks.
Needs: Uses artists for clothing design. "We usually pay a set rate agreed upon in terms of sales of a garment; for example, 50¢ per garment shipped to retailers."

WESTERN ART MFG. CO. INC., 38 E. 5th Ave., Denver CO 80203. President: Robert Hilb. Specializes in children's wear, juniorwear and men's wear.
Needs: Works with 2-3 designers/year. Uses artists for T-shirt and sweatshirt art and children's wear. Especially interested in cartoons and styled art for T-shirts.
First Contact & Terms: Mail samples (slides or sketches showing artist's ability). Works on assignment only. Samples returned by SASE; and reports back on future assignment possibilities. Provide resume, brochure and flyer to be kept on file for future assignments.

Greeting Cards

The greeting card and paper product (plates, napkins, party favors, calendars, etc.) market has a number of characteristics that make it a popular freelance market—a very large percentage of the work is done by mail, designs can be submitted without an assignment, quite a few new products are produced annually, and the market isn't affected by the economic climate.

Most of the top greeting card companies are included since our only requirement is that they buy art from freelancers. One big name you won't find, though, is Hallmark. Although this firm claims about 50% of the market, it relies almost exclusively on in-house artists.

When designing for the companies in this section, remember that most of these firms, particularly calendar businesses, work as much as two years in advance. Where the timing of submissions is important, this information is given in the listing.

Trends in today's greeting card market are toward realistic, sentimental cards, but new and interesting graphic ideas are also catching on.

Cartoonists and caricature artists also have a market in the paper products and greeting card industry with studio cards remaining popular. In addition to cartoon sketches for studio cards, these illustrations are sought for party plates and gift wrapping.

More information on trends and outlets for your artwork can be found in *Greetings Magazine* (Mackay Publishing Corp.). Also ask about *Greetings* annual directory of greeting card companies and related firms. Another helpful annual publication is the *Artists & Writers Market List*, published by the National Association of Greeting Card Publishers. The latter publication is free to artists who send a self-addressed, stamped # 10 envelope to the association at 600 Pennsylvania Ave. SE, # 300, Washington, DC 20003.

AA SALES INC., 9600 Stone Ave. N., Seattle WA 98103. Art Director: Gail Gastfield. Publishes posters. Artist's guidelines available. Query; then submit sketch or photo of art. SASE. Reports in 2 weeks.

ACME GREETING CARD CO. INC., 201 3rd Ave. SW, Cedar Rapids IA 52406. (319)364-0233. Art Director: S. Richardson. Estab. 1928. Publishes funeral director paper specialties. Query with samples. SASE. Reports in 1 week. Previously published, photocopied and simultaneous submissions OK. Buys all rights.
Needs: Uses artists for product design and illustration. Pays $30 minimum, 1-color.

AFRICA CARD CO. INC., 303 W. 42nd St., New York NY 10036. (212)582-2930. President: Vince Jordan. Estab. 1967. Publishes greeting cards and posters. Mail art, or arrange interview. SASE. Reports in 6 weeks. Buys all rights.
Needs: Buys 25 designs/year. Pays $50 minimum, greeting cards and posters.

AMBASSADOR CARDS, Division of Hallmark, 2501 McGee, Kansas City MO 64141. (816)221-9555. Director of Creative Recruiting: Arch Unruh. Firm has sufficient art staff and outside contacts to handle present needs.

AMBERLEY GREETING CARD CO., 1738 Tennessee Ave., Cincinnati OH 45229. Contact: Ned Stern. Publishes studio and humorous greeting cards, plaques and humorous postcards.
Needs: Assigns 200 jobs/year. For consideration for publication of a line of cards, submit 5 humorous cards.
First Contact & Terms: Prefers local artists. Query with samples. SASE. Reports in 3 weeks. Buys all rights. No original work returned at job's completion. Pays $60, color illustrations; on acceptance.
Tips: Write for artists guidelines and visit staionery shop to get a better idea of the types of cards published by Amberly.

AMERICAN GREETINGS CORP., 10500 American Rd., Cleveland OH 44144. Director of Recruitment/Creative: Tony Byrd. Publishes humorous, studio and conventional greeting cards, calendars and giftwrapping. Manufactures candles and ceramic figurines.
First Contact & Terms: Query with resume; then mail ideas, samples or portfolio. Buys all rights. Pays on acceptance.

ANTIOCH BOOKPLATE CO., 888 Dayton St., Box 28, Yellow Springs OH 45387. Creative Director: Ann S. Harris. Publishes calendars, bookmarks and bookplates; some book-oriented, humorous, religious and inspirational. Prefers "full color work we can keep in reference file, or slides or prints we can file. Send enough to show variety of styles you are comfortable with." Buys various rights.
Needs: Uses artists for illustrations. Buys 100-150 designs/year. Pays $50-150, art; $25, bookmark ideas.

BARKER GREETING CARD CO., Division of Rust Craft Greeting Cards, Inc., Rust Craft Park, Dedham MA 02026. Humor Director: Bill Bridgeman. Works on assignment only. Seasonal Christmas, Easter, Father's Day, Hanukkah, St. Patrick's Day, Mother's Day, Thanksgiving, Valentine's Day and Halloween deadlines outlined in artist's guidelines. Publishes studio greeting cards.
First Contact & Terms: Query with color line drawings or washes. SASE. Reports in 4 weeks. Buys all rights. No originals returned to artists at job's completion. All work done on assignment. Pays $70 minimum for complete job (design, blackline key with lettering and hand-separated color overlays).
Tips: Visit stationery shop and/or request artist's guidelines.

BARNARD, ROBERTS & CO., INC., 6655 Amberton Dr., Baltimore MD 21227. Contact: Charles S. Roberts. Publishes greeting cards, certificates and stationery primarily for the Catholic religious field.
First Contact & Terms: Submit seasonal (Christmas) and occasional ideas 1 year in advance. SASE. Reports in 2-3 weeks. Buys all rights. Previously published work OK "only if exclusive in our field." No original work returned at job's completion. Write for artist's guidelines. Pays $75, design idea; $100, color transparency; $150, full-color art.

BARTON-COTTON INC., 1405 Parker Rd., Baltimore MD 21227. (301)247-4800. Art Director: A. Robert Nohe. Produces religious and wildlife calendars and greeting cards. Free catalog. Submit seasonal work "any time of year." Interested in any kind of samples. Previously published work and simultaneous submissions OK. SASE. No originals returned to artist at job's completion. Reports in 4 weeks.
Illustrations: Buys 50 illustrations/year. Pays $100-350, color washes, opaque watercolors, pastels, oils and acrylics; on acceptance. Query with resume and samples or send roughs.

BAUMGARTEN'S, 1190-A N. Highland Ave. NE, Atlanta GA 30306. President: H.J. Baumgarten. Publishes rice paper napkins to complement fine china.
First Contact & Terms: Mail art or query with samples. SASE. Reports in 2 weeks. Previously published and simultaneous submissions OK. Buys copyright for design. Pays on acceptance. Free catalog.
Needs: Assigns 6 jobs/year. Pays $25-50, full-color renderings.

BEACH PRODUCTS, 2001 Fulford St., Kalamazoo MI 49001. (616)349-2626. Art Director: Sue Turner. Publishes paper tableware products; general, birthday, special occasion and seasonal.
First Contact & Terms: Mail color art; plates, cups, tablecovers, placemats, luncheon napkins, beverage and dinner napkins, plastic glasses, coasters, tallies, etc. Submit seasonal (general wedding, showers, birthdays, Christmas, New Year's, Easter, etc.) art in September, everyday material in June. SASE. Reports in 6-8 weeks. Previously published work OK. Buys all rights. No original work returned to artist at job's completion. Pays $50 minimum, color sketch.
Needs: Buys 75-100 designs/year. Uses artists for product design and illustration. Submit at least 10 examples on a single theme to be considered for "line" publication.

BRILLIANT ENTERPRISES, 117 W. Valerio St., Santa Barbara CA 93101. Art Director: Ashleigh Brilliant. Publishes postcards.
First Contact & Terms: Submit 5½x3½ horizontal b&w line drawings. SASE. Reports in 1 week. Buys all rights. "Since our approach is very offbeat, it is essential that freelancers first study our line. We supply a catalog and sample set of cards for $1." Pays $30 minimum, camera-ready word-and-picture design.

Needs: Buys up to 200 designs/year. Uses artists for word-and-picture postcards, illustrated with line drawings.

SIDNEY J. BURGOYNE & SONS INC., 2120 W. Allegheny Ave., Philadelphia PA 19132. Art Director: Jon Harding. Publishes greeting cards; religious and Christmas. Mail art; September-March only. Prefers samples of unpublished original art. Simultaneous submissions OK.SASE. Reports in 2 weeks. No originals returned to artists at job's completion. Buys all rights.
Needs: Buys 40-50 designs/year. Uses artists for product design and illustration. "We do very little work on an assignment basis. Artists submit designs and if we like the designs we purchase them."

BUTTERNUT CARDS INC., 103 Hillside Rd., Montague MA 01351. (413)863-2556. Art Director: Claudia Di Peri. Produces stationery, notecards and postcards; country and outdoor themes. Artists guidelines available. Submit seasonal work 6 months in advance. SASE. Reports in 4 weeks. Buys all rights.
Illustrations: Buys 20 illustrations/year. Query with resume and samples. Needs designs for silkscreen note cards and greeting cards with 3-4 color-separated overlays. "The best procedure for the artist to follow with these would be to send copies of samples which exhibit the artist's style and skill." Pays 2% royalty.

CAPE SHORE PAPER PRODUCTS INC., 57 High St., South Portland ME 04106. (207)799-5906. President: Fred Palmer.Publishes greeting cards, stationery and note paper; traditional, nautical, landscape and floral.
Needs: Assigns 60 design jobs/year for cards, notes and stationery. Buys 30 illustrations/year; needs oils and pencil sketches. Special need for note paper measuring 3 11/16x5 1/4. Also interested in receiving batches of illustrations to consider for use as a line.
First Contact & Terms: Query with resume and samples. Submit seasonal work 1 year in advance. SASE. Reports in 1 month. Original work returned to artist at job's completion. Pays on acceptance. Write for free catalog.

CARD MASTERS, 2990 Griffin Rd., Ft. Lauderdale FL 33312. (305)989-8877. Executive vice president: Lawrence Horowitz. Produces greeting cards and giftwrapping.
First Contact & Terms: Submit seasonal material (Christmas, Passover, Mother's Day, Easter, Father's Day, Valentine's Day and Hanukkah) in advance of holiday. Interested in 5x7 everyday, masculine, floral, sympathy and baby designs. SASE. Reports in 1 week. No originals returned at job's completion. Pays on acceptance. Free artist's guidelines.
Design: Uses artists for greeting cards. Query with resume and samples.

CELEBRATION CARDS, Box 2052, Falls Church VA 22042. (703)931-5100. Art Director: Linda Spivak. Estab. 1975. Publishes calendars, greeting cards and stationery; humorous and sensitive. Mail art or query with samples; submit seasonal art 6 months in advance. SASE. Reports in 3 weeks. Buys all rights. Pays on acceptance.
Illustrations: Buys 40 illustrations/year. Pays $30 minimum, b&w line drawings; $50 minimum, color-separated work.

CPS INDUSTRIES, Columbia Hwy., Franklin TN 37064. Art Director: Ruby Knauss. Publishes giftwrapping: Christmas, wedding, shower, baby, floral, masculine, abstract, juvenile and birthday. Artist's guidelines available. Submit seasonal work 9 months in advance. "Will review seasonal work at any time, however." No originals returned to artist at job's completion.
Needs: Uses artists for giftwrapping design and printed dimensional package decorations. "We prefer a comprehensive sketch at least partially complete, with a layout of the repeat pattern." Repeats must be even division of 18" such as 9", 6", 4" or 3" for Christmas only.

CREATIVE PAPERS BY C.R. GIBSON, The C.R. Gibson Co., Knight St., Norwalk CT 06856. (203)847-4543. Manager of Social Stationery: Steven P. Mack. Publishes stationery, note paper, invitations and gift wrap. Interested in material for lines of products. "Two to three designs are sufficient to get across a concept. We are interested in series of 4 notes on any subject from animals to scenics. We don't use too many regional designs. Stationery themes are up-to-date, fashion oriented. Designs should be somewhat sophisticated without being limiting. Classic designs do well. Current material from the giftware business." Prefers 4-6 samples (slides or chromes of work or originals), published or unpublished. Previously published, photocopied and simultaneous submissions OK, if they have not been published as cards and the artist has previous publishers permissions. SASE. Reports in 6 weeks. Usually buys all rights; sometimes buys limited rights.
Design: Buys 200-300/year.

To Break In: "Almost all of the artists that we work with or have worked with are professional in that they have a background of other professional assignments and exhibits as well as a good art education. We have been fortunate to make a few 'discoveries,' but even these people have been at it for a number of years and have a very distinctive style with complete understanding and control of what they are doing."

CROCKETT COLLECTIONS, Box 1428, Rt. 7, Manchester Center VT 05255. (802)362-2913. Contact: James Anderson, president. Publishes traditional greeting cards, postcards and note cards. Free artist's guidelines. Submit seasonal work 1 year in advance. Interested in material for lines of cards, napkins, placemats and gift wrap. Submit "unpublished samples only. Art should be in relative finished form." SASE. Reports in 4 weeks. No originals returned to artist at job's completion. Buys all rights.
Needs: Uses artists for greeting cards. Assigns 150 jobs/year. Pays $50-150; negotiates pay. Pays on acceptance.

THE DRAWING BOARD, 256 Regal Row, Dallas TX 75247. (214)637-0390. Design Director: Richard Hunt. Produces greeting cards, calendars, giftwrapping, paper tableware products and stationery. Submit seasonal work 6 months-1 year in advance. Interested in 10-20 of any kind of samples of style. SASE. Reports in 1 week. Buys all rights.
Illustrations: Number bought/year varies. Uses gray opaques, b&w and color washes, opaque watercolors and oil or acrylics. Pays $125 minimum for color; on acceptance.
Tips: "Have prior greeting card experience and an unusual style or technique."

EUREKA, Box 160, Dunmore PA 18512. Marketing Manager: John A. Yourishen. Manufactures decorations and school and stationery supplies. Send samples. Reports in 30 days. Pays on acceptance. Uses artists for party decorations, package design, greeting cards and lettering.

FANTUS PAPER PRODUCTS, 2727 W. Chicago Ave., Chicago IL 60622. Contact: Jeffrey Polon, art director. Estab. 1953. Publishes greeting and note cards; everyday and Christmas. Submit seasonal work 1 year in advance. SASE. Reports in 4 weeks. Simultaneous submissions and previously published work OK. Buys first or reprint rights. Pays on acceptance.
Design: "Just beginning to use freelance work." Plans to use artists for greeting and note cards. Query with previously published work or arrange interview to show portfolio.

D. FORER & CO., 511 E. 72nd St., New York NY 10021. Contact: Art Director. Publishes greeting cards; Christmas and everyday. Send samples. Reports in 4 weeks. No originals returned to artist at job's completion. Buys all rights.
Needs: Uses artists for design of 6x9 and 4½x6 Christmas cards, and 4¾x6½ everyday cards.

FRAN MAR GREETING CARDS LTD., Box 1057, Mt. Vernon NY 10550. (914)664-5060. President: Stan Cohen. Publishes plaques, invitations, stationery, pads and novelty products; cute, erotic and humorous.
First Contact & Terms: Query with samples. SASE. Reports in 2 weeks. Buys all rights. Pays on the 10th of the month following acceptance. Free catalog for SASE. No originals art returned to artist at job's completion. Pays $45-300.
Needs: Buys 150-200 designs/year. Art style should be mostly graphic, but can be whimsical. Current needs: 4x6 novelty pads, 6x8 novelty stationery, 4x6 invitations and thank yous printed on one side, 2x3½ humourous friendship or business cards. Submit 6-20 illustrations/batch to be considered for publication of a "line".
Tips: Visit stationery shops, write with SASE for samples and/or request artist's guidelines to get a better idea of the type of work published by Fran Mar.

FRAVESSI-LAMONT INC., 11 Edison Place, Springfield NJ 07081. Contact: Helen M. Monahan, art director. Publishes greeting cards; general, cute and some humorous. Send samples of work. Submit seasonal work 5-6 months in advance. SASE. Reports in 2 weeks. Not copyrighted. Pays on acceptance. Free artist's guidelines.
Needs: Uses artists for calligraphy, and greeting card design and illustration. Pays $50 minimum. Query with previously published work.

FREEDOM GREETING CARD CO. INC., 409½ Canal's End Rd., Box 715, Bristol PA 19007. (215)785-4042. President: Jerome Wolk. Publishes greeting cards and stationery; black ethnic. Free catalog. Artist's guidelines available. Submit seasonal art 18 months in advance. Prefers original art or photos of art. SASE. Reports in 1 week. No originals returned to artist at job's completion. Buys all rights.

Illustrations: Buys 20-25 illustrations/year. Pays $75-125, full-color renderings; on acceptance.

GALLERIE RABINDRA; THE ART EXPERIENCE, 2720 S. LaCienega Blvd., Los Angeles CA 90034. (213)837-1205. Art Director: Larry Morgan. Publishes notecards, greeting cards, posters and art prints. Arrange interview or submit slides or photos of work. Interested in material for lines of products; submit 6 or more illustrations. SASE. Reports in 3 weeks. Originals returned to artist at job's completion.
Needs: New and innovative artwork and concepts for studio and greeting cards and related stationery and gift products. Pays 5% royalty.

THE C.R. GIBSON CO., 32 Knight St., Norwalk CT 06856. Art Director: Gary E. Carpenter. Publishes stationery, jigsaw puzzles, albums and gift products. SASE. Reports in 4 weeks. No finished art, paid for, is returned. Buys all rights.
Needs: Buys 200 designs/year. Uses artists for product design, illustrations and calligraphy. Assigns specific art needs for individual projects. Does not buy unsolicited finished art. Query with samples. Pays $100-150, full-color notes.

GRAND RAPIDS CALENDAR CO., 906 S. Division Ave., Grand Rapids MI 49507. (616)243-1732. Art Director: Rob Van Sledright. Publishes calendars; pharmacy, medical and family themes.
Needs: Buys approximately 15 designs/year. Uses artists for advertising art and line drawings.
First Contact & Terms: Query with b&w drawings. SASE. Reports in 1 week. Previously published, photocopied and simultaneous submissions OK. Pays $10 minimum.

GRAPHIC ADVENTURES, Box 52937, Houston TX 77052. (713)789-4280. Manager: Penny Rogers. Estab. 1970. Publishes posters, greeting cards and postcards; advertising, package and trademark design. Mail art or query with resume and samples. SASE. Reports in 1 month. Pays on publication.
Needs: Buys 200 illustrations/year. Pays $75 min./job, graphic art; $100 min./job, package and trademark design; $250 min./job, product design.

THE GRAPHIC ARTISAN, LTD., 8 Roosevelt Ave., Spring Valley NY 10977. (914)352-3113. Art Director: Peter A. Aron. Estab. 1966. Publishes stationery, greeting cards, invitations, calendars, posters, diplomas and certificates; general, romantic and biblical. Mail samples or arrange interview; submit Christmas and Jewish New Year's designs 9 months in advance. SASE. Reports in 2 weeks. Previously published and simultaneous submissions OK. Buys all rights.
Needs: Buys 50-100 designs/year. Pays $10-100, illustrations. Present needs are predominantly in realistic/cartoon pen and ink sketches of people "in action"—playing games, sports, partying, etc. Also needs animal sketches—single, cartoon type.

VIVIAN GREENE INC., 15240 NW 60th Ave., Miami Lakes FL 33014. (305)558-1810. Assistant to the President: Janet E. Ritenbaugh. Publishes greeting cards, books, cartoon strips and gifts. Artist's guidelines $5. Submit seasonal work 1 year in advance. Interested in material for lines of cards, stationery and activity books; "humor, energy conservation and naughty but nice sexy themes." Submit cover letter along with samples of work. SASE. Reports in 6 weeks. No originals returned to artist at job's completion. Buys all rights.
Needs: "We are looking for talent, not experience, however we expect things to be submitted in a professional manner. We do not want any submissions over 8x10 in size and everything must have SASE enclosed. We strongly urge all people to familiarize themselves with the Kisses comic strip, animation, or greeting cards now on the market." Pays $10-100, illustrations and cartoon strips; multipanel. Pays on publication.

GREENTREE PUBLISHERS INC., 14-16 Greenbaum St., Boston MA 02127. (617)426-0707. Contact: Martin H. Slobodkin. Publishes Christmas cards. Mail full-color watercolors. Reports in 2 days.

HAPPINESS INC., 300 Happiness Lane, Kingman KS 67068. Toll free: (800)835-2232. Contact: Joanne Thomas. Estab. 1965. Publishes greeting cards, plaques, postcards and stationery; contemporary and traditional. Query with samples. SASE. Reports in 4 weeks. Buys all rights. Pays 30 days after acceptance.
Illustrations: Buys 150 designs/year. Pays $50-75 for complete greeting card art including lettering.

HELLO STUDIO INC., Brush Ridge Rd., Fleischmanns NY 12430. (914)254-4666. Estab. 1974. Publishes calendars, greeting cards, giftwrapping, paper tableware products, posters and statio-

nery; humorous. Submit seasonal work 1 year in advance. SASE. Reports in 2-3 weeks. Buys all rights. Pays on publication.
Design: Contact Shelli Lipton, president. Uses artists for paper products. Negotiates pay. Query with resume and samples.
Illustrations: Contact Nick Verni, art director. Needs b&w line drawings, washes, gray opaques, color washes and opaque watercolors. Negotiates pay. Contact in any method.

IMINAC INC., 4003 S. Hwy. 288, Angleton TX 77515. (713)849-4306. Contact: B.G. Harper, president. Estab. 1972. Publishes calendars, stationery, notebooks and fashion albums; nature-oriented. Submit seasonal work 6 months in advance. SASE. Reports in 2 weeks. Previously published work OK. Not copyrighted. Pays on acceptance.
Illustrations: Buys 12-30/year. Needs b&w line drawings, and b&w or color washes. Query with resume and samples.

INDIVIDUALITY POSTERS, 575 3rd St., Brooklyn NY 11215. (212)499-2127. Contact: Franklin Greenwald, president. Estab. 1974. Publishes greeting cards, posters and transfers; self-help, spiritual and psychological. Submit seasonal work 3 months in advance. SASE. Reports in 4 weeks. Simultaneous submissions and previously published work OK. Buys first rights. Pays on acceptance. Free artist's guidelines.
Illustrations: Buys 20+/year. Pays $35 minimum, b&w line drawings. Query with resume and samples.

INTERCONTINENTAL GREETINGS LTD., 29-46 Northern Blvd., L. I. C. NY 11101. (212)784-2323. Art Assistant: Ann Godwin. Publishes calendars, greeting cards, postcards, puzzles and stationery. Annual sales: $1,500,000-2,000,000.Interested in material for lines of cards, stationery and all paper products. Prefers samples of "published greeting cards or paper products." Simultaneous submissions OK. No originals returned to artist at job's completion. SASE. Reports in 4 weeks. Buys complete international publication rights.
Needs: Assigns 3-500 jobs and 1,000 illustrations/year. Mail artwork or query with samples. Pays on acceptance with royalty contract.

KUSTOM QUALITY, Box 3459, 2416 Montana, El Paso TX 79903. (915)532-3233. Art Director: Kerry Harding. Estab. 1972. Publishes calendars, greeting cards, posters, stationery, postcards, prints and coloring books; western, tourist-oriented with historic and educational themes. Submit seasonal work 9 months in advance. Reports in 4-6 weeks. Simultaneous submissions OK. Buys various rights. Pays on publication.
Needs: Uses artists for greeting card, stationery and calendar concepts. Send concepts with preliminary samples.

LAFF MASTERS STUDIOS INC., Box T, Merrick NY 11566. Creative Art Director: Sylvia Hacker. Publishes greeting cards: humorous, sophisticated, conventional and youth-oriented. Publishes seasonal cards. Submit published samples only. "Never send unsolicited unpublished material." SASE. Reports in 1 week. No originals returned to artist at job's completion. Buys all rights.
Illustrations: Buys 150-250/year. Pays $40 minimum, full-color renderings; on acceptance.

THE STEPHEN LAWRENCE CO., Box 2324, 150 Louis St., So. Hackenshack, NJ 07606. (201)641-4611. Art Director: Sheldon Babyatsky. Produces Christmas and everyday giftwrapping and other paper products. Free artist's guidelines. Submit seasonal work 18 months in advance. Prefers "sketches or basic ideas." Simultaneous submissions OK. SASE. Reports in 2 weeks. Originals returned to artist at job's completion. Buys "all stationery rights."
Design: Uses artists for gift cards, tags, giftwrapping and invitations. Negotiates pay.
Tips: "We are very interested in typography."

WHITNEY McDERMUT FINE ART GREETING CARDS, 35 Market St., Box 385, Elmwood Park, NJ 07407. (201)791-8866. President: Whitney McDermut. Publishes greeting cards, notes and stationery; general and religious Christmas. Artist's guidelines available. Publishes seasonal cards for Christmas only; submit seasonal art 10 months in advance.Previously published work OK. SASE. Reports in 1 week. No originals returned to artist at job's completion. Buys card reproduction rights.
Illustrations: Assigns 7-10 jobs and buys 25-30 illustrations/year.Pays $40 minimum, b&w line drawings and washes; $80 minimum, color washes and full-color renderings; on acceptance.

ALFRED MAINZER INC., 27-08 40th Ave., Long Island City NY 11101. (212)392-4200. Art Director: Arwed H. Baenisch. Publishes calendars, greeting cards and postcards; religious, tradi-

tional and ethnic European. Submit seasonal work 12 months in advance.Previously published work OK. SASE. Reports in 2 weeks. Originals returned to artist at job's completion. Purchases outright.
Illustrations: Buys 500-1,000 illustrations/year. Pays $25-250, color; on acceptance.

MARK I INC., 1733-55 W. Irving Park Rd., Chicago IL 60613. (312)281-1111. Vice President/ Creative Director: Alex H. Cohen. Estab. 1969. Publishes greeting cards, posters and plaques; cartoony, sensitive, floral, scenic and couples. Query with samples. SASE. Reports in 2 weeks. Buys all rights. Pays on acceptance.
Needs: Buys 250 illustrations/year. Pays $50-150/job, cartoons and illustrations; $10/hour, lettering.

MASTERPIECE STUDIOS, 5400 W. 35th St., Chicago IL 60650. (312)656-4000. Art Director: George Major. Publishes Christmas cards only. Free artist's guidelines. Sumbit seasonal work "any time." Intereted in material for lines of cards and stationery. Prefers samples of unpublished Christmas cards and stationery. SASE. Reports in 3-4 weeks. No originals returned to artist at job's completion. Buys all rights.
Needs: "We are interested in reviewing any Christmas art on spec, regardless of experience." Pays on acceptance.

MECHANICAL MIRROR WORKS INC., 661 Edgecombe Ave., New York NY 10032. (212)795-2100. Art Director: J. Bezzy. Estab. 1942. Publishes greeting cards, posters and mirror graphics. Mail art if no larger than 8½x11; submit art in transparent plastic sheets for mirror graphics. SASE. Reports in 3-4 weeks. Previously published, photocopied and simultaneous submissions OK. Buys all rights.
Needs: Buys 50-100 designs/year. Minimum payment: $30, product design; $200, full-color illustrations. B&w line drawings, color washes and separations OK.

MERRY THOUGHTS INC., Bedford Hills NY 10507. Specializes in stationery decoration and paperware design. Sumbit seasonal work "as soon as possible" in advance. Prefers transparencies or photocopies. SASE.

MESSENGER CORP., 318 E. 7th St., Auburn IN 46706. Creative/Art Director: Fred Simon. Estab. 1913. Publishes calendars, greeting cards, plaques, posters and stationery; funeral. Query. SASE. Reports in 2 weeks. Pays on acceptance.
Needs: Buys 50 illustrations/year. Buys b&w and color illustrations.

MICHEL & CO., 2919 S. La Cienega Blvd., Culver City CA 90230. (213)836-6737. Art Director: M. Bernstein. Publishes greeting cards, giftwrapping, posters and stationery; juvenile and sophisticated. Submit seasonal work 1 year in advance. Interested in material for lines of products; submit 3 samples. Prefers "finished samples of artist's work; if photography, transparancies all right." SASE. Reports in 2 weeks. No originals returned to artist at job's completion. Buys all rights.
Illustrations: Buys 2 illustrations as needed. Query with samples, slides, roughs or finished art, or arrange interview to show portfolio. "Any artwork received will not be returned unless SASE accompanies sample." Negotiates pay; pays on acceptance.

MILLEN CARDS INC., 230-03 Linden Blvd., Jamaica NY 11411. (212)525-9100. Contact: Mr. Millner, president. Estab. 1949. Produces traditional greeting cards. Submit seasonal work 6 months in advance. SASE. Reports in 3-4 weeks. Simultaneous submissions OK. Buys first rights. Pays on acceptance. Free artist's guidelines.
Design: Assigns over 50/year. All artwork is freelanced. Negotiates pay. Query with samples of previously published work.

MR. B GREETING CARD CO., 3305 NW 37th St., Miami FL 33142. (305)638-8808. President: Harry Gee. Publishes calendars, greeting cards, giftwrapping, stationery, boutique notes, invitations, thank you notes, studio cards.
Needs: Works with artists for greeting cards, gift wrapping, posters, calendars, stationery and games. Submit 24 cards in a batch to be considered for publication of a "line.
Illustration Needs: Submit seasonal work (Christmas, Passover, Mother's Day, Easter, Rosh Hashanah, Thanksgiving, Yom Kippur, Father's Day, Valentine's Day and Hanukkah) 6-8 months in advance. Query with resume and samples or arrange interview to show portfolio. SASE. Reports in 4-6 weeks. Simultaneous submissions OK. Buys first or reprint rights. No originals returned to artist at job's completion. Pays on acceptance.

NASCO INC., 27 N. Main St., Springfield TN 37172. (615)384-7511. Art Director: William B. Robinson. Publishes calendars, greeting cards, paper tableware, posters and stationery; "products that appeal to the whole family." Artist's guidelines available. Submit seasonal work 6 months-1 year in advance. Prefers 1 printed sample. Previously published work OK. SASE. Reports in 4 weeks. No originals returned to artist at job's completion. Buys reproduction rights.
Design: Buys designs for greeting and note cards, posters and place mats. Negotiates pay; on acceptance.
Illustration: Buys 20 illustrations/year. Pays $100-300, color washes and opaque watercolors; on acceptance.
Advertising: Assigns 200 jobs/year. Uses artists for catalogs, direct mail, brochures and trade magazines. Negotiates hourly rate.
Tips: "We are looking for new design approaches for all of our sales literature and products. Material must be dramatic, bold, creative, attract attention and do a selling job."

NATIONAL CHIROPRACTIC PUBLICATIONS INC., Box 125, Union Springs AL 36089. (205)738-3211. Publisher: W.H. Garner. Estab. 1957. Publishes greeting cards, stationery and chiropractic tracts. Annual sales: $100,000. Artist's guidelines available. Free brochures. Submit seasonal work 5-6 months in advance. SASE. Reports in 2 weeks. No originals returned to artist at job's completion. Buys exclusive rights.
Illustrations: Assigns 30-35/year. Pays $50-150, color-separated work, full-color renderings and color overlays or transparencies; on acceptance.
Production: Assigns 20-25 jobs/year. Pays $100-150/job, color separations; $40-65/job, mechanicals; on acceptance.

NICHOLAS PRESS, 132 Nassau St., New York NY 10038. Art Director: Mr. A. Goldson. Publishes stationery, black greeting cards and posters. Query with samples. SASE. Reports in 4 weeks. Previously published samples OK. Buys all rights.
Needs: Uses artists for calligraphy and studio card ideas and illustrations; 4x9 and 5x7 line art and color washes. Pays $25, ideas; $50-75, finished art.

NORCROSS INC., 950 Airport Rd., West Chester PA 19380. (215)436-8000. Contact: Nancy Lee Fuller. Publishes calendars, stationery, giftwrapping and greeting cards. Artist's guidelines available. See artist's guidelines for seasonal production schedule. Interested in material for lines of greeting cards, stationery and gift wrap. Prefers "full-color samples"; published or unpublished greeting cards. SASE. Reports in 3 weeks. No originals returned to artist at job's completion. Buys all rights.
Needs: Uses artists for product design and illustrations. Pays $100 minimum, greeting card design.

NU-ART INC., 6247 W. 74th St., Chicago IL 60638. Art Director, Christmas Cards: Gil Gaw. Art Director, Wedding Invitations: Leo J. LaVela. Publishes personalized cards sold in multiples of 25 from books or albums in better gift, stationery and department stores.
Needs: Works with artists for Christmas gift wrap and wedding stationery.
First Contact & Terms: Submit seasonal (Christmas) material at least 6 months before holiday. Send 5⅝x7–5x7⅞, or 4x8¼ cards by mail. Reports in 1-6 weeks. Buys exclusive rights. No originals returned to artist at job's completion. Pays $20-30, roughs of ideas; $30-45, finished dummies or comps; $45-100, final art.

PAKWELL PAPER PRODUCTS, Box 800, Wilsonville OR 97070. (503)638-9833. Art Director: Anna Bijan. Publishes gift boxes, giftwrapping and paper bags.
Needs: Buys 100 designs/year. Uses artists for product design and illustration. "For use in department stores as courtesy wrap or used for prewrapped box coverings."
First Contact & Terms: Mail 8x11 line art. SASE. Reports in 2 weeks. Buys all rights. No originals returned to artist at job's completion. Pays $50 minimum, giftwrapping design.
Tips: To get an idea of the type of work sought, take notice of department store packaging. "Traditional Christmas motifs still very popular with us—in traditional reds, greens and golds."

PAPERCRAFT CORP., Papercraft Park, Pittsburgh PA 15238. (412)362-8000. Art Director: Ralph E. Marmo, Jr. Estab. 1945. Publishes greeting cards and giftwrapping; traditional Christmas subjects. Mail art. SASE. Reports in 2-3 weeks. Buys all rights.
Needs: Buys 150 designs/year. Uses artists for greeting card and giftwrapping illustrations. Price must accompany all submissions.

PAPER M'SHEA, 4640 SW 75th Ave., Miami FL 33155. Art Director: Robert Shea. Estab. 1975. Publishes greeting cards, notes and invitations; whimsical, short verse for everyday, juvenile,

seasonal, and sophisticated (for notes and invitations). Query with samples; submit seasonal ideas 6 months in advance. SASE. Reports in 4 weeks. Buys all rights.
Needs: Uses artists for product design and illustration. Pays $10-25.

THE PARAMOUNT LINE INC., 400 Pine St., Pawtucket RI 02863. Art Director: Walter A. Jones. Publishes greeting cards: general, religious, floral, cutes and "studio" humor. Sumbit seasonal work 1 year in advance. Prefers "published or original art for greeting cards only." SASE. Reports in 2-3 weeks. No originals returned to artist at job's completion. Buys all rights, world wide.
Needs: Uses artists for design and illustrations. Pays $75-125, cover illustration.

PECK INC., 516 Lafayette Rd., St. Paul MN 55101. (612)222-1731. Art Director: Richard Wells. Estab. 1947. Publishes Christmas tags and holiday cutouts; juveniles greeting card type art. Query with samples. SASE. Reports in 8 weeks.
Needs: Buys 12 tags and 32 packages annually. Uses artists for product design and illustrations. Pays $30-75, tags; $50-500, cutouts.

PERMA-GREETINGS INC., 2470 Schuetz Rd., Maryland Heights MO 63043. Creative Coordinator: Kathy Ludditt. Estab. 1976. Publishes greeting cards; sentimental, mood, humorous, religious and seasonal. Submit seasonal work 1 year in advance. SASE. Reports in 1 month. Previously published work OK. Not copyrighted. Pays on acceptance. Free artist's guidelines.
Design: Contact JoAnne Vaughan, vice president/creative productions. Uses artists for greeting cards. Negotiates pay. Query with resume and samples.

PIONEER PRODUCTS INC., Box 279, Ocala FL 32670. (904)622-3134. Senior Art Director: Kenneth Heller. Publishes greeting cards and paper tableware products. Annual sales $10,000,000.
Needs: Buys 10-20 designs/year. Works with party papers primarily birthdays, party games and books; and in conjunction with candy birthday cake decorations.
First Contact & Terms: Query with published samples. Submit seasonal art 12 months in advance. SASE. Buys first rights. No originals returned to artist at job's completion. Pays $25-75, b&w; $75-250, color. Pays on acceptance.

PLUS +MARK INC., (formerly RJR Archer Inc.), Box 3306, Greeneville TN 37743. (615)639-2161. Art Director: Robert T. Casteel. Estab. 1966. Manufactures giftwrapping, gift boxes, cards, tags, seals, candles, ribbons and bows. Mail 10x10 color art in February-May. SASE. Reports in 2 weeks. Photocopied and simultaneous submissions OK.
Needs: Buys 23-30 designs/year. Uses artists for product design and illustration. Pays $100-200, designs.

PLYMOUTH INC., Box 308, Bellmawr NJ 08031. (609)931-8700 or (800)257-7845. President: Norman Weisbord. Produces stationery, school supplies and novelty pads. Free artist's guidelines. Submit seasonal material 10 months in advance. Reports in 2 weeks. Previously published work OK.
Design: Assigns 40 jobs/year. Negotiates pay; Pays on acceptance.Query with resume and previously published work.
Illustrations: Buys 30 illustrations/year. Query with resume and samples, send roughs or finished art. Negotiates pay; pays on acceptance.
Advertising: Assigns 10 jobs/year. Uses artists for package design and catalog illustrations. Negotiates pay. Pays on acceptance.

RECYCLED PAPER PRODUCTS INC., 3325 N. Lincoln Ave., Chicago IL 60657. Art Director: Audrey Christie. Publishes greeting cards and related products; unique subjects. Annual sales: $10,000,000. Artist's guidelines available. Submit seasonal material 1 year in advance; 18 months for Christmas. Interested in material for lines of cards. Prefers 2 or 3 samples of any kind. SASE. Reports in 6 weeks. Original artwork sometimes returned to artist at job's completion. Usually buys all rights; negotiates pay.
Illustrations: Buys 1,500 illustrations/year. Pays $100 minimum, b&w line drawings and color; on acceptance of finished art.

REED STARLINE CARD CO., 3331 Sunset Blvd., Los Angeles CA 90026. Publishes everyday and seasonal greeting cards; regular and studio.

REPRODUCTA CO. INC., 11 E. 26th St., New York NY 10010. Art Director: Thomas B. Schulhof. Publishes stationery, postcards and greeting cards; religious and general.

Needs: Buys 750 designs/year. Works with all occasions—religious plus floral, wildlife and "cutes."
First Contact & Terms: Mail art. SASE. Seasonal: Christmas, Mother's Day, Easter and Father's Day themes. No originals returned to artist at job's completion. Request artist's guidelines. Buys all rights. Pays $50-200.

ROTH INTERNATIONAL, 31368 Via Colinas, Suite 110, Westlake Village CA 91361. Contact: Charles Roth. Uses artists for full-color studio and "cute" everyday greeting cards. "We supply gags and copy, and we're only interested in hearing from experienced artists." Buys all rights.

ROUSANA CARDS, 28 Sager Place, Hillside NJ 07205. (201)373-1000. Art Director: June Ulrich. Publishes traditional greeting cards. Artist's guidelines available. Submit seasonal work 1 year in advance. Interested in material for lines of cards; submit 6 illustrations. Prefers "published or original samples, but in vertical greeting card format." Send samples registered mail. No originals returned to artist at job's completion. Buys all rights.
Needs: Pays $100, color finishes.
Tips: Artists should have greeting card experience.

THE ROYAL COMPANIES, (formerly Royal Stationery Co.), 13000 County Rd. 6 at Hwy. 55, Minneapolis Industrial Park, Minneapolis MN 55441. (612)559-3671. Art Director: Randi L. Van Brocklin. Produces calendars, stationery, post cards, note cards, mugs, key chains and soaps; floral, scenic, animal, children and novelty. Interested in material for lines of products. Submit 4-5 illustrations. Prefers unpublished samples. SASE. Reports in 4 weeks. No originals returned to artist at job's completion. Buys all rights.
Needs: Buys 50 designs/year. Uses artists for product design and b&w and color illustrations. Pays $25 minimum, camera-ready designs.

RUST CRAFT GREETING CARDS INC., Rust Craft Rd., Dedham MA 02026. Vice President/Creative: Theodore R. Musto. Publishes a full line of conventional, humorous, studio, juvenile cards, special promotions and other gift-product lines.
Needs: Uses artists for greeting cards, giftwrapping, paper tableware products, calendars and stationery. Also interested in batches of about 6 designs to be used for "lines" for the same products as mentioned above.
First Contact & Terms: Submit seasonal (Christmas, Passover, Mother's Day, Sweetest Day, Easter, Rosh Hashanah, Thanksgiving, Yom Kippur, Father's Day, St. Patrick's Day, Hanukkah and Halloween) material 18 months in advance. Query with resume and samples. Buys exclusive rights. No originals returned to artist at job's completion. Visit stationery stores to study examples of Rust Craft Greeting Cards.

ST. CLAIR MFG. CORP., 120 25th Ave., Bellwood IL 60104. (312)547-7500. Design Art Director: Elaine Brochocki. Publishes gift boxes, giftwrapping and graphic packaging. Query. SASE. Reports in 3 weeks. Buys all rights.
Needs: Buys 50-150 designs/year. Uses artists for calligraphy, logos and design.

SANGAMON CO., Rte. 48 W., Taylorville IL 62568. Art Director: Gary DeCourcy. Publishes calendars, stationery, greeting cards and giftwrapping; religious, juvenile, floral, landscape and humorous.
Needs: Uses artists for design and illustration of giftwrapping, stationery and color greeting cards. Watercolors only. Negotiates pay.
First Contact & Terms: Submit seasonal (Christmas, Mother's Day, Sweetest Day, Easter, Thanksgiving, Father's Day, St. Patrick's Day, Valentine's Day, Halloween, Grandparent's Day and Graduation) material 1 month in advance. Query with samples. SASE. Reports in 2 weeks. Buys all rights. No originals returned to artist at job's completion. Visit stationery shops for an idea of the types of products produced by Sangamon.

SMALL WORLD GREETINGS, Box 787, El Segundo CA 90245. Art Director: W.J. Shaw. Estab. 1969. Publishes calendars, stationery and greeting cards; "charming little animals, flowers and children." Mail printed samples or color photos for files. Reports in 2 weeks. SASE. Buys exclusive rights.
Needs: Buys 150-200 designs/year. Uses artists for product design and illustration. Pay varies.

SPRINGFIELD PHOTO MOUNT CO., 475 Canal St., Holyoke MA 01040. (413)534-3371. Treasurer: R.G. Quimper. Estab. 1917. Publishes calendars, gift boxes, greeting books, plaques, stationery, photo albums and scrapbooks. Query. SASE. Reports in 3 weeks. Previously published

work OK. Buys all rights. Pays on acceptance. Free catalog.
Needs: Assigns 20 jobs and buys 100 illustrations/year. Buys b&w line drawings and color-separated work.

STAR CITY INC., 16134 Valerio St., Van Nuys CA 91406. (213)782-0500. Art Director: Hal Tupler. Estab. 1960. Publishes humorous posters and scrolls. Query with samples. SASE. Reports in 2 weeks. Previously published and simultaneous submissions OK. Buys all rights.
Needs: Uses artists for product design and illustration. Pays $25 minimum, b&w and color.

STEVENS LINEN ASSOCIATES INC., Box 220, Webster MA 01570. (617)943-0600. Contact: John Flack. Produces textile screen prints, calendars, linen towels, pot holders, place mats, napkins, wall hangings and aprons; scenics, humorous, florals, still life and anything home- and kitchen-oriented.
Needs: Assigns 25/year. Buys pattern design for linen calendar towels, kitchen towels and related products; also color separating of designs.
First Contact & Terms: Time allowed for seasonal work varies with assignment. Submit slides for consideration. Reports in 1-4 weeks. Buys exclusive rights on calendars. Previously published work OK. If purchased No-If rights pruchased only-Yes. Pays $15-500 on acceptance. Free artist's guidelines. Also visit kitchen shops–domestic departments–for an idea of the types of product produced by Stevens.

STRAND ENTERPRISES, 1809 N. Orangethorpe Park, Anaheim CA 92801. (714)871-4744. Art Director: S.S. Waltzman. Estab. 1967. Publishes stationery, greeting cards, posters, note cards and memo board novelties; scenic, inspirational, humorous, nature and animal. Query with samples. SASE. Reports in 2 weeks. Buys all rights.
Needs: Buys 50-100 designs/year. Uses artists for prints, calligraphy, design and illustration. Pays $25 minimum, prints and note cards.

STUART HALL CO, INC., Box 1381, Kansas City MO 64141. (816)221-8480. Art Director: Ann Havlicek. Produces home office supplies, school supplies, boxed stationery, social writing tablets and envelopes. "We use floral and children subjects a lot." Free artist's guidelines. Publishes no seasonal cards. Interested in material for lines of stationery. Prefers resume and samples. Simultaneous submissions OK. SASE. Reports in 2 weeks. No originals returned to artist at job's completion. Exclusive reproduction rights.
Illustrations: Buys 200 illustrations/year. Interested in color washes, opaque, watercolors and oils. Negotiates pay; pays on acceptance.
Design: Assigns 300 jobs/year; all work is freelanced. Interested in design for stationery, box notes, social writing tablets and envelopes. Negotiates pay; pays on acceptance.

SUNRISE PUBLICATIONS INC., Box 2699, Bloomington IN 47402. (812)336-9900. Art Director: Jeffrey Willsey. Publishes greeting cards, posters and art prints. Submit seasonal work 18 months in advance. SASE. Reports in 30-60 days. Originals returned to artist at job's completion. Interested in material for lines of note cards; "strong fantasy; (romantic) unicorns, elves, wizards, etc." "We prefer slides or samples of previous greeting card work. Published or un-published. Please do not send original work. SASE is a must!" Previously published work OK. Buys non-exclusvie world-wide rights.
Needs: Carefully executed full-color illustrations, scaled to 5x7. Design quality work and conception; attention to detail; warm color; animals, fantasy, nature; also humor in good taste, using color with strong tie between image and work for development of a line of color." Excellent remuneration."

SUNSHINE ART STUDIOS INC., 45 Warwick St., Springfield MA 01101. Art Director: L. Wright. Publishes calendars, stationery, post cards and greeting cards; religious and humorous. Mail 5x7 color art; submit Christmas designs in May. SASE. Reports in 1 week. Buys exclusive rights.
Needs: Buys 300 designs/year. Uses artists for calligraphy, product design and illustration. Pays $75-175, illustrations.

TAYLOR & NG, Box 200, Brisbane CA 94005. Contact: Personnel. Estab. 1958. Publishes gift boxes, greeting cards, paper tableware products, postcards, stationery and cookware. Query with resume. Reports in 4 weeks.
Needs: Uses artists for illustrations and advertising. Pays by job.

TIME GREETING CARD CO., 3901 Hampton Blvd., Norfolk VA 23508. (804)489-3956. Estab. 1967. Produces religious and everyday greeting cards. Submit seasonal work 3 months in advance.

Reports in 2 weeks. Copyrighted. Buys first or reprint rights. Pays on publication. Free artist's guidelines.
Design: Contact: Lawrence Shao, design director. Assigns 58 jobs/year, greeting cards only. Query with resume and samples.
Illustrations: Contact: Robert Rogers, product director. Pays 20-30% royalties for opaque watercolors. Offers advance. Query with resume and samples.
Advertising: Contact: Gordon Shao, president and publisher. Assigns 25 jobs/year for catalog illustrations and print media advertising illustrations. Query with resume and samples.

TUTTLE PRESS CO., Box 759, Appleton WI 54912. Art Coordinator: Robert Jensen. Publishes paper tableware products and giftwrapping; juvenile, floral, geometric and Christmas.
Needs: Works with artists for b&w line drawings, color-separated work and full-color renderings.
First Contact & Terms: Mail art. Submit seasonal art 6 months in advance. Reports in 3 weeks. Previously published and simultaneous submissions OK. Pays on acceptance.

VAGABOND CREATIONS, 2560 Lance Dr., Dayton OH 45409. (513)298-1124. Art Director: George F. Stanley, Jr. Publishes stationery, post cards, greeting cards, posters and spiral notebook covers; contemporary humor. 99% of artwork used in the line is provided by staff artists working with the company.
Needs: Buys 750 designs/year. Uses artists for product design and illustration; line drawings, washes and color-separations should fit in standard envelope.
First Contact & Terms: Query. SASE. Reports in 2 weeks. Submit (Christmas, Mother's Day, Father's Day and Valentine's Day) material at any time. Originals only returned upon request. Pays $10-25.
Tips: Visit stationery shops and request for artist's guidelines.

VESTA CHRISTMAS COLLECTION, Box 1426, Corning NY 14830. (607)962-2800. Art Director: Peter Burke. Produces Christmas ornaments decorated with 4-color art reproductions. Free artist's guidelines. Interested in material for lines of Christmas ornaments. SASE. Reports in 2 weeks. No originals returned to artist at job's completion. Buys all rights.
Illustrations: Buys 25 illustrations/year on wintry, Christmas or realistic wildlife themes. Query with resume and samples or roughs. Pays $250 minimum, watercolor, acrylics, pastels, oils, colored pencil; on publication.
Tips: "No cartoons or purely whimsical art, although photographice realism, while often acceptable, isn't necessary. Artists don't usually realize the amount of reduction necessary when we reproduce their work. Art reproduced is approximately 2⅝x4⅝ inches. Opportunities are excellent. We are a new firm needing art."

WESTVACO, C.A. REED DIVISION, 99 Chestnut St., Williamsport PA 17701. Art Director: Bob Crain. Publishes paper tableware products; birthday, everyday, seasonal and holiday.
Needs: Buys 150-200 designs/year. Uses artists for product design and illustration. Interested in material for lines of greeting cards, gift wrap and paper tableware.
First Contact & Terms: Query with samples. SASE. Reports in 3 weeks. Photocopied and simultaneous submissions OK. "Buys all rights within our field of publication." No originals returned for refused work. Pays $50-100, product design.
Tips: Artist should visit stationery shops and/or request for artist's guidelines.

WILLIAMHOUSE-REGENCY INC., & CENTURY GREETINGS, (formerly Regency Greetings), 1500 W. Monroe St., Chicago IL 60607. (312)666-8686. Art Director: David Cuthbertson. Publishes Christmas cards; traditional and some religious Christmas.
Illustrations: Buys 200 illustrations and designs/year. Pays $50 minimum, b&w; $75, color; $75-120, design.
First Contact & Terms: Query with samples. Submit seasonal art 18 months in advance. Reports in 4 weeks. Previously published work OK. Buys exclusively Christmas card reproduction rights. Originals returned to artist at job's completion. Pays on acceptance.
Tips: Artist should visit stationery shops and request for artist's guidelines in familiarizing with our products. "Traditional stills sells best in more expensive lines."

Performing Arts

The last fifteen years has been a growth period for the performing arts field. According to the National Endowment for the Arts, the number of dance companies has increased from 37 to 200; professional symphony orchestras have grown from 58 to 144; theaters from 22 to 270 and professional opera companies increased to 65 from 26. Likewise, the markets for freelancers interested in animation art; set, light and costume design; direct mail brochures; and advertising have increased.

Promotional art is an area most talented illustrators and designers can move into comfortably. Artists interested in working on lighting, costume and set design, though, will find themselves faced with a need for a more technical knowledge.

Developing a portfolio for stage, costume and lighting design is also a little more complicated than for promotional art. For stage and set design, illustrations or photos of past work are recommended. But, for lighting design, you'll need to have photos of sets you've worked on, or a scale (light plot) of lights.

A list of references and an outline of past experience should also be included when you seek work as a lighting, costume or set designer.

To stay current on the performing arts, consult these publications: *Dance Magazine* (Danad Publishing Company, Inc.), *The Artist's Directory* (Sar-Les Music, Inc.) and *Musical America, International Directory of the Performing Arts* (ABC Leisure Magazines Inc.).

AKRON SYMPHONY ORCHESTRA, E.J. Thomas Performing Arts Hall, Center and Hill Sts., Akron OH 44325. (216)535-8131. General Manager: Robert L. Henke. Estab. 1951. Classical, pop and young people's educational programs. Assigns 1 job/year; local artists only. Query with samples.
Needs: Uses artists for advertising. Negotiates pay.

ALBANY SYMPHONY ORCHESTRA INC., 19 Clinton Ave., Albany NY 12207. (518)465-4755. Manager: Fred Leise. Estab. 1929. Some pop and dance programs. Assigns 5 jobs/year. Query with samples. SASE. Reports in 2 weeks.
Needs: Uses artists for advertising, direct mail brochures, flyers and posters. Payment by job: $25-150, design and lettering; $25-200, layout.

REYNALDO ALEJANDRO DANCE THEATER, 160 Bleecker St., Suite 5-G W., New York NY 10012. (212)674-0673. Artistic Director: Ron Alejandro. Modern dance troupe inspired by Philippine traditions.
First Contact & Terms: Query with samples. SASE. Reports in 1 month. Works on assignment only. No samples returned. Reports back on future assignment possibilities. Provide calling card and/or brochure to be kept on file for future assignments. Pays $30-50/job for illustration, design and lettering.
Needs: Works with 10 illustrators/year. Uses artists for advertising, costumes, direct mail brochures, flyers, posters and programs.

FRANCES ALENIKOFF DANCE THEATRE INC., 537 Broadway, New York NY 10012. Artistic Director: Frances Alenikoff. Estab. 1968. Contemporary dance troupe. Assigns 4 jobs/year; local artists only. Query with samples. SASE.
Needs: Uses artists for advertising, direct mail brochures, flyers, graphics, posters, sets and theatrical lighting.

ALLNATIONS DANCE COMPANY, 500 Riverside Dr., New York NY 10027. Contact: Herman Rottenberg. Ethnic dance company.
First Contact & Terms: Submit photos or tearsheets.
Needs: Uses artists for direct mail brochures, trade magazine ads, programs, posters and bumper stickers.

AMERICAN DANCE CENTER, 203 Union Ave., Saratoga Springs NY 12866. (518)584-8733. Contact: Judy Atchinson, secretary. Estab. 1970. Studio at which professional dancers train. Assigns 4 jobs/year. Query with samples; local artists only for scenery design. SASE. Reports in 3 weeks.
Needs: Uses artists for brochures, logos, programs, T-shirts, stationery, ads, other promotional items and scenery. Negotiates pay.
To Break In: "We are looking for someone who has had at least five years experience in set design with a professional company, or has served an apprenticeship under someone who has had that particular experience."

ATLANTA BALLET, 1404 Spring St. NE, Atlanta GA 30309. (404)873-5811. Contact: B.J. Dubois, promotional liason. Estab. 1929. Assigns 12 jobs/year; local artists only. Query with resume and arrange interview to show work. SASE. Reports in 4 weeks.
Needs: Uses artists for brochures, ads and mailing pieces.

ATLANTA CONTEMPORARY DANCE CO., Box 54039, Atlanta GA 30308. (404)658-2549. General Manager: Susan Hunter.
First Contact & Terms: Works on assignment only. Samples returned by SASE; and reports back on future assignment possibilities. Query with samples of work done for other clients or arrange interview. SASE. Reports in 1 month. Provide resume, brochure, flyer, tearsheet and samples. Pays $50-500/job for design; $5 min./job for layout.
Needs: Works with 3 designers/year; summer and early fall only. Uses artists for costumes, direct mail brochures, exhibits, flyers, graphics, posters, sets/stages, theatrical lighting and concert announcements.

BACH SOCIETY OF ST. LOUIS, 7317 Cornell, St. Louis MO 63130. Contact: L. Compton, executive director. Estab. 1941. Presents Baroque orchestral and choral concerts. Assigns 10 jobs/year; local artists only. Query with samples. SASE. Reports in 2 months.
Needs: Uses artists for promotional brochures, concert progam booklets, letterheads and posters. Pays $15-35/hour or $50-200/job.

BALLET FOLK OF MOSCOW INC., University of Idaho, Ridenbaugh Hall, Moscow ID 83843. Contact: Joan Muneta. Send samples. Uses artists for poster and program designs.

BALLET ODYSSEY, 2025 Cheremoya Ave., Suite 203, Hollywood CA 90068. (213)465-1894. Contact: Carolena Nicassio, director. Estab. 1976. Query with samples. SASE. Reports in 2-3 weeks.
Needs: Uses artists for posters, ads, brochures and lettering. Pays by job.

ZINA BETHUNE & COMPANY, 3096 Lake Hollywood Dr., Hollywood CA 90068. Contact: Lois Scotts. Specializes in contemporary, classical, dramatic and multimedia dance.
First Contact & Terms: Send photos or tearsheets. Works on assignment only. Samples returned by SASE; and reports back on future assignment possibilities. Provide resume, tearsheet and anything the artists feels represents his abilities.
Needs: Uses artists for direct mail brochures, posters, programs, trade magazine ads, and painting and drawing for scenery and film.

BIGFORK SUMMER PLAYHOUSE, Box 456, Bigfork MT 59911. (406)837-4886. Producer: Donald Thomson. Estab. 1960. Musical comedy. Repertory theatre. Assigns 5 jobs/year. Arrange to show portfolio. Apply immediately after January 1; company is established by mid-March. SASE. Reports in 3 weeks.
Needs: Uses artists for designer-in-residence, set design painters and costume/set/stage/graphic/theatrical lighting design. Pays $150-250, set design; $150-250, costume design.

BLOSSOM MUSIC CENTER, 1145 W. Steels Corners Rd., Cuyahoga Falls OH 44223. (216)929-3048. Director of Communications: Gary S. Oppito. Estab. 1968. Summer home of Cleveland Orchestra; center performances include classical, contemporary, soft rock, jazz and folk music. Assigns 1-2 jobs/year; primarily December-May. Query with resume. SASE. Reports in 2 weeks.
Needs: Uses artists for advertising, direct mail brochures, posters and season brochures. Pays $30 min./hour for design and illustration.

THE BODY POLITIC THEATRE, 2261 N. Lincoln, Chicago IL 60614. (312)525-1052. Public Relations Director: Mary Kelsey. Estab. 1965. Assigns 12 jobs/year; local artists only. Arrange interview. SASE. Reports in 1 week.

Needs: Uses artists for advertising, direct mail brochures, exhibits, flyers, graphics, posters and programs. Pays up to $150/job, illustration; $4-10/hour, layout and typesetting.

BROOKLYN CENTER FOR THE PERFORMING ARTS AT BROOKLYN COLLEGE (BCBC), Nostrand and Flatbush Aves., Brooklyn NY 11210. (212)780-5291. Assistant Program Coordinator: Ella Weiss. Estab. 1954. Two auditoriums used for music, dance and theater. Assigns 50 jobs/year; local artists only. Query with samples. No work returned. Reports in 1 month.
Needs: Uses artists for illustration, design, layout and production for advertising, direct mail brochures, flyers and graphics. Pay determined by job.

CASA MANANA MUSICALS INC., Box 9054, Ft. Worth TX 76107. (817)332-9319. General Manager/Producer: Bud Franks. Director of Playhouse/Assistant Manager: Michael Cook. Dance troupe performing summer stock, children's theater and classics.
First Contact & Terms: Query with resume. SASE. Reports in 2 weeks. Pay varies.
Needs: Assigns 8 jobs/year. Uses artists for costumes, promotional materials, sets and theatrical lighting.

CECILWOOD THEATRE, Box 56, Fishkill NY 12524. (212)866-4238. Producer: James Glass. Estab. 1948. Summer theater. Assigns 4 jobs/year. Query with resume or arrange interview. SASE. Reports in 2 weeks.
Needs: Uses artists for costumes, designer-in-residence, sets and theatrical lighting. Employs designer and/or costumer plus 16 apprentices during summer season. Pays $200 min./week, design of stages and scenery.

CELEBRATION MIME THEATRE, RFD #, Box 44, South Paris ME 04281. (207)743-8452. Managing Director: Alan Day. Estab. 1972. Mime troupe which performs and teaches at universities and community art centers. Assigns 3 jobs and buys 2 illustrations/year. Call or query with samples. SASE. Reports in 2 weeks.
Needs: Uses artists for advertising, costumes, cartoons, designer-in-residence, direct mail brochures, flyers, graphics, posters, programs, sets or stages and technical art. Maximum payment by job: $1,000, design; $200, illustration; $50, lettering.

CHICAGO CONTEMPORARY DANCE THEATRE, 2261 N. Lincoln Ave., Chicago IL 60614. (312)871-5386. Director: Maggie Kast. Specializes in modern dance. Assigns 6-10 jobs/year.
First Contact & Terms: Local artists only. Query. SASE. Reports in 2 weeks. Works on assignment only. Samples returned only upon request. Reports back on future assignment possibilities. Provide resume to be kept on file for future assignments. Pays by job.
Needs: Works with 2 illustrations and 6 designers/year. "We usually have a spring concert in April or May and a fall concert in October or November. So our time of need would be 2 months before each concert season." Uses artists for costume design, advertising design/layout, direct mail brochures, flyers, graphic design, newspaper ads, paste-up, posters, programs, technical charts/illustrations and theatrical lighting design. Pays by job.

CIRCLE REPERTORY COMPANY, 111 8th Ave., New York NY 10011. (212)691-3210. Artistic Director: Marshall W. Mason. Contact: Richard Frankle. Season runs September-August. Call for interview to show portfolio.
Needs: Uses artists for graphics and graphic design. Pays minimum fee for poster/program design and/or newspaper ad layout. Gives program credits.

THE CLEVELAND INSTITUTE OF MUSIC, 11021 East Blvd., Cleveland OH 44106. (216)791-5165. Public Relations Director: Jean Caldwell. Performing arts center and conservatory of music.
First Contact & Terms: Local artists only. Mail art, query with samples or arrange interview. SASE. Reports in 1 day.
Needs: Assigns 15 jobs and buys 20 illustrations/year. Uses artists for illustration, layout and graphics for advertising, annual reports, bumper stickers, costumes, direct mail brochures, exhibits, flyers, graphics, posters, programs, stages, record jackets and catalogs.

CLEVELAND MODERN DANCE ASSOCIATION, 11125 Magnolia Dr., 3rd Floor, Cleveland OH 44106. "Nonprofit organization which sponsors dance and dance therapy workshops, several major concerts and master classes." Assigns 1-2 jobs/year.
First Contact & Terms: "Query to obtain current mailing material, and offer valid plan for improvement for the next one." SASE. "Reports as soon as possible, immediately if not needed."

Works on assignment only. Samples returned by SASE; and reports back on future assignment possibilities. Provide resume, calling card, brochure, flyer and tearsheet to be kept on file for future assignments. "Pays standard union scale."
Needs: Works with 2-3 illustrators and 2-3 designers/year. Uses artists for brochures, logos and ads. "Pays standard union scale."

CLEVELAND STATE UNIVERSITY MODERN DANCE COMPANY, 2451 Euclid Ave., Cleveland OH 44115. (216)687-4883. Director: Linda Fischer-Pachales. Assigns 3 jobs/year.
First Contact & Terms: Local artists only. Query or mail art. SASE. Reports in 2 weeks. Works on assignment only. Samples returned by SASE; and reports back on future assignment possibilities. Provide brochure to be kept on file for future assignments. Pays $3-10/hr.
Needs: Works with 1 illustrator and 1 designer/year; early December, early March and early May only. Uses artists for direct mail brochures, flyers, graphic design, posters, programs and set/theatrical lighting design. Pays $2.30-6/hour.

THE COCKPIT IN COURT SUMMER THEATRE IN RESIDENCE, Essex Community College, 7201 Rossville Blvd., Baltimore County MD 21237. (301)682-6202. Managing Director: F. Scott Black. Performing arts center; presents musicals, cabaret plays, open-air Shakespearean plays and seminars. "Cockpit is in residence at Essex Community College. This is on 8 consecutive seasons. We try to use the services of the school graphics department as much as possible but sometimes must use freelance artists because the staff at the school is too overloaded or they are unable to give us what we want."
First Contact & Terms: Local artists only. Query with samples or arrange interview. SASE. Reports in 2 weeks. Works on assignment only. Samples returned by SASE; and reports back on future assignment possibilities. Provide resume, calling card, brochure, flyer and tearsheet to be kept on file for future assignments.
Needs: Works with 2 illustrators and 2 designers/year. "Our brochure is our most important tool for publicity as it creates an image for our theatre. Work on the brochure begins in early fall for the following summer season." Uses artists for advertising, billboards, designer-in-residence, direct mail brochures, flyers, graphics, posters, sets and technical art.

JEAN COCTEAU REPERTORY, 330 Bowery, New York NY 10012. (212)677-0060. Artistic Director: Eve Adamson. Estab. 1971. Theatrical troupe performing the classics. Assigns 2-6 jobs/year; local artists only. Query with resume. SASE. Reports in 2 weeks.
Needs: Uses artists for costumes, designer-in-residence, stages and theatrical lighting. Pay is minimal.

ELINOR COLEMAN DANCE ENSEMBLE, 394 Elizabeth St., San Francisco CA 94114. (415)648-0936. Artistic Director: Elinor Coleman. Estab. 1977. Modern and jazz dance troupe and music ensemble. Query with samples or arrange interview; local artists only. SASE. Reports in 1 day.
Needs: Uses artists for illustration, design, layout, lettering and production for advertising, costumes, direct mail brochures, flyers, graphics, posters, sets and theatrical lighting.

CONCENTUS MUSICUS, 905 4th Ave. S., Minneapolis MN 55404. (612)332-1511. Administrator: Ann Maud. Renaissance resource center; offers Renaissance music and dance ensembles, workshops and lectures.
First Contact & Terms: Local artists only. Query with samples or arrange interview. SASE. Reports in 1 month. Works on assignment only. Samples returned by SASE; and reports back on future assignment possibilities. Provide resume, calling card, brochure, flyer and tearsheet to be kept on file for future assignments. Pays $40-80, posters. Negotiates pay for costumes.
Needs: Works with 1 illustrator and 2 designers/year; July-October only. Uses artists for costumes, calligraphy, exhibits, posters, sets and theatrical lighting.

CONCERT DANCE CO., 23 Main St., Watertown MA 02172. (617)923-1709. Contact: Company Manager. Query with samples or arrange interview. Works on assignmnet only. Negotiates pay.
Needs: Works with 1 designer/year. Uses artists for brochures and posters.

CONCORD COMMUNITY ARTS, 1950 Parkside Dr., Concord CA 94519. (415)671-3065. Contact: Jim Jester. Produces musicals, comedy, drama and ballet, September-May. Assigns 3-10 jobs/year.
First Contact & Terms: Query, then mail slides or photos. No work returned. Works on assignment only. Samples returned by SASE; and reports back on future assignment possibilities. Provide resume to be kept on file for future assignments.

Needs: Works with up to 4 illustrators and 4 designers/year. Uses artists for costume design, flyers, graphic/set design, posters, programs and theatrical lighting.

CONCORD PAVILION, Box 6166, Concord CA 94524. (415)671-3270. Public Relations Director: Jay Bedecarre. Performing arts center; presents dance, rock, pop music, jazz, symphonies, sports and boat shows. Assigns 3-5 jobs/year.
First Contact & Terms: Prefers local artists. Send photos, tearsheets or portfolio. SASE. Reports in 4 weeks. Works on assignment only. Samples returned by SASE. Provide resume, brochure and flyer to be kept on file for future assignments. Pays $150-500, poster design/paste-up; $50-200, newspaper ads.
Needs: Works with 1-2 illustrators and 1-2 designers/year; spring and summer only. Uses artists for advertising design/layout, billboards, bumper stickers, direct mail brochures, flyers, graphic design, posters, programs, set design, set/stage design painters, technical charts/illustrations and theatrical lighting design.

CORTLAND REPERTORY THEATRE INC., Box 783, Cortland NY 13045. Managing Director: Deborah Frame. Performing arts center which produces 5 shows in summer. Assigns 5 jobs/summer.
First Contact & Terms: Query with resume in late winter. SASE. Works on assignment only. Samples returned by SASE; and reports back on future assignment possibilities. Provide resume to be kept on file for future assignments. Pays $1,000-1,700 for 2* months work.
Needs: Works with 5 designers/year; summers only. Uses designers for properties, sets, costume and lighting.

CUESTA COLLEGE DANCE THEATRE, Cuesta College, Evening Division, San Luis Obispo CA 93401. (805)544-4487. Contact: Director. Estab. 1976. Presents dance performances, lecture demonstrations and workshops. Assigns 8 jobs/year; local artists only. Query with resume. No work returned. Reports in 1 month.
Needs: Uses artists for advertising, costumes, exhibits, flyers, graphics, posters and programs.

DALHOUSIE ARTS CENTRE, 6101 University Ave., Halifax, Nova Scotia, Canada B3H 3J5. (902)424-2276. Public Relations Officer: Dorothy Read-Horne. Performing arts center.
First Contact & Terms: Query with samples. SASE. Reports in 2 weeks. Works on assignment only. Samples returned by SASE; and reports back on future assignment possibilities. Provide resume, brochure and flyer to be kept on file for future assignments. Pays $10 min./hour for design.
Needs: Uses 10 illustrators and 5 designers/year. "We would like to be using freelance artists with a greater degree of regularity." Seasonal needs: August, November and May–preparation of seasonal brochures; September and May–advertising illustrations for various shows. Uses brochure preparation.

DANCE ALLIANCE, Box H, Westville Station CT 06515. (203)776-7358. Contact: Larry Rapoport, manager. Estab. 1965. Assigns 2-3 jobs/year; local artists only. Call or mail samples; local artists with experience in drawing bodies only. SASE. Reports in 2 weeks.
Needs: Uses artists for direct mail brochures, posters, stationery and publicity brochures. Pays $5-15/hour.
To Break In: "Come and take dance classes–I'm serious!"

DANCE EDUCATION SERVICES OF LONG ISLAND INC., (formerly Posey Dance Education Services Inc.) 21 Marions Lane, Northport NY 11768. (516)757-2700. President: Elsa Posey Novak. Nonprofit organization which promotes, sponsors and coordinates educational and theatrical dance.
First Contact & Terms: Local artists only. Query with samples. SASE. Reports in 1 week. Works on assignment only. Samples returned by SASE; and reports back on future assignment possibilities. Provide resume and samples to be kept on file for future assignments. Pay varies.
Needs: Works with 1 designer and 1 illustrator/year. Uses artists for advertising, costumes, direct mail brochures, exhibits, flyers, posters, programs, sets, and theatrical lighting. Pay varies.

DANCE GALLERY, 242 E. 14th St., New York NY 10003. (212)685-5972. Administrative Director: J. Antony Siciliano. Dance troupe and theater.
First Contact & Terms: Query with resume or arrange interview to show portfolio. SASE. Reports in 2 weeks. Works on assignment only. Samples returned by SASE; and reports back on future assignment possibilities. Provide resume and brochure to be kept on file for future assignments. Negotiates pay.

Needs: Works with 2 illustrators and 2 designers/year. Uses artists for direct mail brochures, posters, programs, flyers and newspaper ads.

DANCE THEATRE OF THE SOUTHWEST, Box 1294, Denton TX 76201. (817)387-8072. Manager: Timothy T. Sline. Estab. 1973. Assigns 3-4 jobs/year. Query with resume. SASE. Reports in 2 weeks.
Needs: Uses artists for advertising, billboards, bumper stickers, brochures, costumes, flyers, graphics, posters, programs, sculpture, stages, technical art and theatrical lighting. Pays $25-100/job; $700 minimum, costumes, sets and sculpture.

DELL'ARTE INC., Box 816, Blue Lake CA 95525. Administrative Director: Joan Schirle. Professional theater, school and touring company performing traditional and modern mime and comedy. Assign 6-10 jobs/year.
First Contact & Terms: Query with samples. SASE. Provide calling card, brochure and flyer to be kept on file for future assignments. Pays $25-125/job for design and illustration; $50-200/job for layout.
Needs: Works with 2 illustrators/year. Uses artists for advertising, direct mail brochures, flyers, posters and programs.

DENVER SYMPHONY, 1615 California St., Denver CO 80202. (303)292-1580. Contact: Jeff Bell, public relations director. Assigns "a few" jobs/year; local artists only. Query with samples; "a freelancer's work is what sells me first—the interesting and unusual sample that I see will usually get a personal interview; a cold query via the phone might catch me at the wrong time and never get any further." SASE. Reports "as soon as possible."
Needs: Uses artists for brochures, posters and direct mail pieces. Pays by job.

FLINT BALLET THEATRE, 6255 Torrey Rd., Flint MI 48507. (313)655-4960. Director: Lena Pelio. Estab. 1960. Classical ballet. Query with samples; local artists only. SASE.
Needs: Uses artists for costumes, flyers, stationery, posters, programs and sets or stages.

FLINT INSTITUTE OF MUSIC, 1025 E. Kearsley, Flint MI 48503. (313)238-9651. Public Relations Director: Trish Williamson. Includes dance troupe and orchestra. Assigns 20+ jobs/year.
First Contact & Terms: Query with samples (sample brochures produced preferabley) or arrange interview to show portfolio. SASE. Reports in 1-2 months. Works on assignment only. Samples returned by SASE; and reports back on future assignment possibilities. Provide brochure flyer and tearsheet to be kept on file for future assignments. Pays $300-3,500/job.
Needs: Works with 1 designer/year. Uses artists for poster, flyer, program design and total concept promotion brochure and flyers.
Tips: "It helps to have worked with arts organizations, preferably music organizations, on promotional ideas and marketing concepts."

FLORIDA PHILHARMONIC, 105 SE 2nd Ave., Suite 1010, Miami FL 33131. (305)358-3500. General Manager: Azim L. Mayadas. Estab. 1926. Orchestra; offers traditional pop, family and youth concerts. Assigns 12 jobs/year. Arrange interview. SASE.
Needs: Uses artists for advertising animation, annual reports, billboards, bumper stickers, direct mail brochures, flyers, graphics, posters, programs and magazine covers. Pays $50-200, design.

FUSION DANCE COMPANY INC., 4542 SW 75th Ave., Miami FL 33155. Contact: William Lord. Performs modern, ballet and theatrical dance.
First Contact & Terms: Mostly local. Submit samples of creative ideas about products and performance posters. Provide tearsheet and samples of work to be kept on file for future assignments. Minimum payment: $50, ads; $150, programs.
Needs: Works with 1 illustrator and 2 designers/month. Uses artists for trade magazine/newspaper ads, posters, direct mail brochures and programs. Also has needs for lighting and costume design.

GEVA THEATRE, 168 Clinton Ave. S., Rochester NY 14604. (716)232-1366. Public Relations Director: Jayne M. Hustead. Professional theater. Assigns approximately 4 jobs/year. Query with samples. SASE. Reports in 1 week.
Needs: Works with 1 illustrator (September-April) and 1 designer (April-September)/year. Uses artists for direct mail brochures, exhibits, flyers, graphics, posters and program covers. Also displays the work of local artists in the theatre lobby from time to time.

GLOBE OF THE GREAT SOUTHWEST, 2308 Shakespeare Rd., Odessa TX 79761. (915)332-1586. Business Manager: David Weaver. Replica of Shakespearean Globe Theatre; houses Summer Shakespeare Festival.
First Contact & Terms: Query with resume. SASE. Works on assignment only. Samples returned by SASE; and reports back on future assignment possibilities. Provide resume and brochure to be kept on file for future assignments. Pays $150-200/week.
Needs: Works with 4 illustrators and 6 designers/year; during fall and spring only. Uses artists for costumes, theatrical lighting, technical art and designer-in-residence.

GOODSPEED OPERA HOUSE, Box A, East Haddam CT 06423. Contact: Kay McGrath. Send samples; local artists only.
Needs: Uses artists for programs, posters, direct mail and set/stage design.

GRAND RAPIDS SYMPHONY ORCHESTRA, 1st Floor, Exhibitors Bldg., Grand Rapids MI 49503. Manager: Gwynne MacIntyre. Send published samples.
Needs: Uses artists for direct mail brochures, posters, newspaper ads, bumper stickers and programs.

THE GREEN MOUNTAIN GUILD INC., White River Junction VT 05001. (802)295-7016. Managing Director: Marjorie O'Neill-Butler. Touring repertory theatrical company which performs children's theater, summer theatre, musicals, plays and workshops.
First Contact & Terms: Query with resume and photos. SASE. Reports in 2 weeks. Pays $25-50/job, scenic design; $25-100/job, costumes; $3-4/hour, layout.
Needs: Assigns 8 jobs/year. Uses artists for advertising, costumes, designer-in-residence, direct mail brochures, flyers, graphics, posters, programs and sets.

HELIUM MIME SHOW, c/o Modern Theatre, 523 Washington St., Boston MA 02111. (617)426-8445. Contact: Carolann Biederman, business manager. Mime and music trio. Estab. 1975. Assigns 4 jobs/year. Prefers local artists. Query with resume and samples or arrange interview to show portfolio. SASE. Reports in 2 weeks.
Needs: Uses artists for direct mail brochure and program design, newspaper ads, large signs, letterheads, business cards, props and scenery. Pays $15 min./job.

FRANK HOLDER DANCE CO. INC., 314 S. Greene St., Greensboro NC 27401. (919)275-8573. General Manager: Louis Hrabovsky.
First Contact & Terms: Local artists only. Query with resume and arrange interview. SASE. Reports in 2 weeks. Pays by job.
Needs: Assigns 5 jobs/year. Uses artists for programs, brochures and newspaper ads.

HONOLULU SYMPHONY AND HAWAII OPERA THEATRE, 1000 Bishop St., Suite 901, Honolulu HI 96813. (808)537-6171. Public Relations Director: Jan Stark.
First Contact & Terms: Local artists only. Query with previously published work. SASE. Reports in 2 weeks. "Pay is negotiable but usually low."
Needs: Assigns 30 jobs/year. Uses artists for direct mail, brochures, posters, programs, annual reports, newspaper ads and season promotions.

HOUSTON GRAND OPERA, 615 Louisiana, Houston TX 77002. Contact: James F. Beecher.
First Contact & Terms: Send samples (designer: printed samples; illustrator: portfolio plus samples). Works on assignment only. Samples returned by SASE; and reports back on future assignment possibilities. Provide resume, calling card, brochure, flyer, tearsheet and representative samples if possible to be kept on file for future assignments.
Needs: Works with 4-8 illustrators and 3-4 designers/year. Seasonal needs: August-October and January-May. Uses brochures, flyers, posters and newspapers.

HUDSON STREET STUDIO INC., 1 Hudson St., New York NY 10013. (212)349-4251. Director: Jim Moore. Produces theatrical performances and teaches classes in mime, clowning, puppetry, magic and related arts. Assigns 5 jobs and buys 2 illustrations/year.
Needs: Works with 3 illustrators/year. Uses artists for advertising materials, brochures for classes and illustrations for shows.
First Contact & Terms: Local artists only. Query with photocopied samples; "avoid being overly persistent; we may not need the work at the moment and don't like to be bothered constantly." Reports in 1 week. Works on assignment only. Samples returned by SASE. Reports back on future assignment possibilities. Provide calling card, brochure and tearsheet to be kept on file for future assignments. Pays $50-500, illustrations.

VALERIE HUSTON DANCE THEATRE, 1836 Cliff Dr., Santa Barbara CA 93109. Technical Director: Jim Cook. Estab. 1977. Modern dance and ballet troupe. Assigns 3-12 jobs/year. Mail art or query with samples. SASE. Reports in 1 month.
Needs: Uses artists for advertising, costumes, direct mail brochures, flyers, graphics, posters, programs and sets. Pays $50 min./job for design.

INDIANA REPERTORY THEATRE, 140 W. Washington St., Indianapolis IN 46204. (317)635-5277. Contact: Ed Cimbala, public relations director. Nonprofit theater troupe.
Needs: Uses designers for posters, program covers, ads, brochure and total marketing campaigns; illustrators for program covers and posters.
First Contact & Terms: Query with previously published work. Prefers local artists. SASE. Reports in 2 weeks. Provide resume and tearsheet to be kept on file for future assignments. Pays $50-900/job.

THE INNER CITY CULTURAL CENTER, 1308 S. New Hampshire Ave., Los Angeles CA 90006. (213)387-1161. Executive Director: C. Bernard Jackson. Arts organization specializing in theater, dance activities, music and educational programming.
Needs: Uses artists for advertising design/layout, billboards, bumper stickers, costume design, direct mail brochures, exhibit/graphic design, flyers, paste-up, posters, programs, set design painters, stage/set design, technical charts/illustrations and theatrical lighting design.
First Contact & Terms: Works on assignment only. Samples returned by SASE. Reports back on future assignment possibilities. Provide resume to be kept on file for future assignments. Mail samples with resume and photo; October-June best. SASE. Reports in 4 weeks. Pay varies.

INTERNATIONAL ARTS RELATIONS INC., Box 788, Times Square Station, New York NY 10030. (212)247-6776. Estab. 1966. Produces theatrical performances and workshops. Assigns 20-25 jobs and buys 5-6 illustrations/year; local artists only. Query with samples. SASE.
Needs: Uses artists for costumes, flyers, posters, programs, sets and lighting design. Pays $50-200.
To Break In: "We prefer designers of Hispanic background or empathy with our culture, but it's not a prerequisite."

THE INVISIBLE THEATRE CO., 1400 N. 1st Ave., Tucson AZ 85719. (602)882-9721. Manager/Publicity: Vera Marie Badertscher. Theatrical troupe and performing arts center. Assigns 8 jobs/year.
Needs: Works with 4 illustrators and 4-8 designers/year; pre-Christmas and summer Shakespeare. Uses artists for set, costume, lighting, sound, posters, flyers, brochures and mailers.
First Contact & Terms: Local artists only. Query with resume and samples. SASE. Reports in 1-6 months. Works on assignment only. Provide resume and tearsheet to be kept on file for future assignments. Pays $25-200/job, design.

JACKSON SYMPHONY ASSOCIATION, Box 3098, Jackson TN 38301. Music Director/Conductor: James Petty. Send samples.
Needs: Uses artists for direct mail brochures, posters, newspaper ads, bumper stickers and programs.

JACOBS LADDER DANCE COMPANY, 39 A Gramercy Park N., New York NY 10010. (212)254-4397. Contact: Judith Jacobs, director. Estab. 1972. Assigns 2 jobs/year. Query with resume. SASE. Reports in 2 weeks.
Needs: Pays $25-75 for logos, stationery and press kits.

JOHNSTOWN SYMPHONY ORCHESTRA, 230 Walnut St., Johnstown PA 15901. General Manager: Patricia Minot. Assigns 3-5 jobs/year.
Needs: Works with 1-2 illustrators/year in February. Needs design work in December and February. Uses artists for bumper stickers, direct mail brochures, flyers, graphics, posters, programs and record jackets. Pays $25-200/job for design.
First Contact & Terms: Mail art or query with samples and resume. SASE. Reports in 1 week. Provide resume, brohure and flyer to be kept on file for future assignments.

SHEILA KAMINSKY AND COMPANY, 317 E. 18th St., New York NY 10003. Contact: Lukie Kornbluth, public relations director. Estab. 1975. Modern dance company. Query with resume. SASE. Reports in 2 weeks.
Needs: Uses artists for flyers, posters and lighting design.

KLS MANAGEMENT, LTD., 76 Pearl St., New York NY 10004. (212)741-0368. Contact: Carole Dickey, vice president. Estab. 1976. Manages dance and theater troupes. Assigns 12 jobs and buys

20 illustrations/year; local artists only. Query with resume and arrange interview to show portfolio. SASE. Reports in 2-3 weeks.
Needs: Uses artists for publicity brochures, posters and newspaper and trade ads. Pays $177 minimum, magazine ad design; $225 minimum, poster design.

PHYLLIS LAMHUT DANCE CO., 225 W. 71st St., New York NY 10023. (212)799-9048. Contact: 1970. Modern dance troupe. Assigns 2-3 jobs/year.
Needs: Works with 1 illustrator and 1 designer/year; in the spring. Uses artists for advertising, costumes, direct mail brochures, flyers, posters and programs. Negotiates pay.
First Contact & Terms: local artists only. Call for interview. SASE. Reports in 1 week. Works on assignment only. Samples returned by SASE. Reports back on future assignment possibilities. Provide brochure to be kept on file for future assignments.

LEXINGTON PHILHARMONIC ORCHESTRA, Box 838, Lexington KY 40587. Managing Director: George Benson. Submit photos or tearsheets.
Needs: Uses artists for direct mail brochures, newspaper ads, posters and bumper stickers.

LINEA DANCE COMPANY, 350 W. 15th St., Suite 2, New York NY 10011. (212)929-7332. Contact: Yvonne D. Hicks, artistic director. Assigns 2-3 jobs/year.
Needs: Works with 1-2 illustrators and 2-4 designers/year. Uses artists for costume designing, desigining of posters, flyers and advertising in general.
First Contact & Terms: Local artists only. Query with resume. SASE. Reports in 1-2 weeks. Works on assignment only. Samples returned by SASE. Reports back on future assignment possibilities. Provide resume, calling card, brochure and flyer to be kept on file for future assignments. Negotiates pay.

LOS ANGELES MOZART ORCHESTRA ASSOCIATION INC., 444 S. Kingsley Dr., Suite 355, Los Angeles CA 90020. Director of Development: Ginni Keith. Estab. 1974. Chamber orchestra. Assigns 2-6 jobs/year. Mail art. SASE. Reports in 2 weeks.
Needs: Uses artists for advertising, direct mail brochures, flyers, posters, programs and fundraising promotional materials. Pays $25-150/job for design; $25-100/job for layout; $50-200/job for fundraising materials.

LOVELACE THEATRE, 5888½ Ellsworth Ave., Pittsburgh PA 15232. (412)361-4835. General Manager: Dave Weiss. Puppet and mask theater troupe. Assigns 2-10 jobs/year.
Needs: Works with 2 illustrators and 4 designers/year; designers needed in October and April; illustrators needed in September and February. Uses artists for programs, newsletters and porters.
First Contact & Terms: Query with resume and samples (brochure and flyers). SASE. Reports in 2 weeks. Works on assignment only. Samples returned by SASE. Reports back on future assignment possibilities. Provide resume, brochure and flyer to be kept on file for future assignments. Pays $25 min./job for design, illustration and layout.

LYRIC OPERA COMPANY OF LONG ISLAND INC., Box 848, Bayport, Long Island NY 11705. Artistic Director: Michael Signorelli. Estab. 1970. Assigns about 4 jobs/year "when active." Send resume.
Needs: Uses artists for costume design. Submit estimated costs.

MAGIC THEATRE, Building 314, Fort Mason, San Francisco CA 94123. Production Manager: Suresa Dundes. Estab. 1968. Contemporary theatrical troupe. Assigns 2-3 jobs/year; local artists only. Query with resume. SASE. Reports in 1 month.
Needs: Uses artists for costumes, direct mail brochures, flyers, graphics, posters, programs, stages and theatrical lighting. Pays $50-500/job for design.

MANGROVE, 499 Alabama, #120, San Francisco CA 94110. (415)552-4190. Publicist: Bob Rease. Dance troupe. Assigns 10 jobs/year.
Needs: Works with 3 illustrators/year for brochures and posters.
First Contact & Terms: Local artists only. Query. SASE. Reports in 2 weeks. Works on assignment only. Samples returned by SASE. Reports back on future assignment possibilities. No file kept on artists. Pays $5/hour.

MARYLAND BALLET, 2510 St. Paul St., Baltimore MD 21218. (301)366-5800. Publicity Director: Shelly R. Rudick. Estab. 1960. Ballet company. Assigns 5 jobs/year; local artists only. Query. SASE. Reports in 1 week.
Needs: Uses artists for advertising, annual reports, bumper stickers, direct mail brochures, flyers, posters and programs. Pays $150-500/job for design and paste-up.

MEADOW BROOK MUSIC FESTIVAL, Oakland University, Rochester MI 48063. Contact: Stuart Hyke.
Needs: Works with 3-5 illustrators and 3-5 designers/year; spring and summer.
First Contact & Terms: Send photos or tearsheets. Provide resume, calling card and tearsheet to be kept on file for future assignments.

METROPOLITAN CIVIC BALLET CENTER, 23 Main St., Watertown MA 02172. (617)923-0076. Contact: Marjorie E. Medland, director. Estab. 1974. Ballet troupe and school. Query with samples. SASE. Reports "as soon as possible."
Needs: "The school/company needs a logo for its posters, stationery, etc.," says Medland. Negotiates pay.

MICHIGAN OPERA THEATRE, 350 Madison Ave., Detroit MI 48226. (313)963-3717. Director, Public Relations/Marketing: Blanche M. Robinson. Assigns 7-8 jobs/year.
Needs: Works with 2 illustrators and 2 designers/year; fall and spring. Uses artists for ads, billboards, bumper stickers, direct mail pieces, renewal brochures, flyers, posters, program books, costumes, set and theatrical lighting.
First Contact & Terms: Local artists only. Query with samples or portfolio. SASE. Reports in 1 month. Works on assignment only. Samples returned by SASE. Reports back on future assignment possibilities. Provide resume and brochure to be kept on file for future assignments.

MICHIGAN STAR THEATRES INC., Box , Hartford OH 44424. (313)239-1464. Contact: Frank Kenley. Submit resume.
Needs: Scenic artist for staff position June-August. Pays $400/week.

MIDDLETOWN SYMPHONY ORCHESTRA, 1040 Knoll Lane, Middletown OH 45042. (513)422-0859. Contact: Ginny Dagenbach Turvey, business manager. Estab. 1943. Performs 1 pop, 1 children's and 4 regular concerts. Assigns 1 job/year. Arrange interview. SASE.
Needs: Uses artists for direct mail brochures, flyers, programs and lighting.

MILLBROOK PLAYHOUSE, Mill Hall PA 17751. (717)748-8083. President: John W. Akeley. Estab. 1962. Summer stock theater. Assigns 4 jobs/year.
Needs: Works with 1 illustrator and 2 designers/year; June-August only. Uses artists for advertising, costumes, direct mail brochures, flyers, graphics, posters, programs, stages and theatrical lighting.
First Contact & Terms: Query with resume. SASE. Reports in 2 weeks. Provide resume to be kept on file for future assignments. Pays room, board and spending money for design.

MILWAUKEE FLORENTINE OPERA CO., 750 N. Lincoln Memorial Dr., Milwaukee WI 53202. Contact: Robert L. Caulfield. Uses artists for direct mail brochures, posters, bumper stickers, programs and newspaper/trade magazine ads.

MILWAUKEE SYMPHONY ORCHESTRA, Performing Arts Center, 929 N. Water St., Milwaukee WI 53202. (414)273-7121. Development/Promotion Director: D. Andrew Moquin. Estab. 1959. Query or arrange interview; local artists only. SASE. Reports in 2 weeks.
Needs: Uses artists for advertising, flyers, graphics and posters.

MINNESOTA DANCE THEATRE AND SCHOOL, 528 Hennepin Ave., Minneapolis MN 55403. (612)339-9150. General Manager: Beverly Simone. Estab. 1962. Classical ballet and contemporary dance company and school. Assigns 25 jobs/year; local artists primarily. Query with samples. SASE. Reports in 2 weeks.
Needs: Uses artists for advertising, direct mail brochures, flyers, graphics and posters. Pays $50 min./job for design and illustration; $50 min./job for layout.

MJT DANCE CO., Box 108, Watertown MA 02172. (617)482-0351. Director: Margie J. Topf. Modern dance troupe.
Needs: Assigns 2-10 jobs/year. Uses artists for advertising, bumper stickers, direct mail brochures, flyers, graphics, posters, programs, tickets, exhibits and lighting.
First Contact & Terms: Local artists only. Query with resume or arrange interview. SASE. Reports in 2 weeks. Pays $5-10/hour.

MOZART FESTIVAL, 33 Greenwich Ave., New York NY 10014. (212)675-9127. Contact: Baird Hastings, conductor. Estab. 1960. Chamber orchestra. Query with previously used work; local artists only. SASE. Reports in 1 week.
Needs: Uses artists for direct mail brochures and flyers.

JENNIFER MULLER & THE WORKS, Affiliate of the Lost and Foundation for the Arts, Inc., 131 W. 24th St., New York NY 10011. (212)691-3803. Artistic Director: Jennifer Muller. Executive Director: John Philip Luckacovic. Contemporary dance company using song and dialog as well as movement. Assigns 10-30 jobs/year.
Needs: Works with 1-3 illustrators and 1-3 designers/year. Uses artists for posters, flyers, brochures, costumes and sets. Also, uses artists for advertising, graphics and theatrical lighting.
First Contact & Terms: Query with resume and samples, or arrange interview. SASE. Reports in 2 weeks. Works on assignment only. Samples returned by SASE. Reports back on future assignment possibilities. Provide resume, brochure and flyer to be kept on file for future assignments. Pay determined by job and experience.

MUSICAL MIME INC., 272 W. 84th St., New York NY 10024. (212)724-2853. Contact: R. Ruggieri, director. Estab. 1969. Dance troupe. Assigns 150 jobs/year. Arrange interview to show portfolio. Reports in 3 weeks.
Needs: Uses artists for design of direct mail brochures, programs and newspaper ads. Negotiates pay.

NEW ENGLAND DINOSAUR, 507 Ward St., Newton, MA 02159. (617)527-5227. Contact: Joel Press, manager. Estab. 1968. Dance troupe. Assigns 20 jobs and buys 5 illustrations/year. Send resume, samples and published work; "follow up with call after 2 weeks and call again after another 2 weeks." SASE. Reports in 2 weeks.
Needs: Uses artists for technical work, posters and brochures. Pays $50-250.

NEW JERSEY SHAKESPEARE FESTIVAL, Drew University, Madison NJ 07940. Artistic Director: Paul Barry. Contemporary and classical theatrical troupe. Assigns 3-6 jobs/year.
Needs: Works with 1 or 2 illustrators and 3 designers/year. Design work for costumes, sets, prop and lighting is seasonal, May-November/December. Uses artists for advertising, costumes, designer-in-residence, direct mail brochures, exhibits, flyers, graphics, posters, programs, sets and theatrical lighting.
First Contact & Terms: Query with resume or arrange interview to show portfolio. SASE. Reports in 1 week. Interviews for designers are held in March and April. Provide resume to be kept on file for future assignments. Pays $600/play for design.

NEW ORLEANS PHILHARMONIC-SYMPHONY ORCHESTRA, 203 Carondelet St., Suite 903, New Orleans LA 70130. (504)524-0404. Public Relations/Advertising Director: Bette Moore.
Needs: Assigns 5 jobs/year. Uses artists for advertising, billboards, bumper stickers, direct mail brochures, exhibits, flyers, graphics, posters and programs.
First Contact & Terms: Local artists only. Query with samples. SASE. Reports in 2 weeks. Pay to be negotiated.

NEW YORK BAROQUE DANCE CO., 280 Riverside Dr., Apt. 5-H, New York NY 10025. Contact: Ann Jacoby, co-director. Estab. 1976. Dance troupe specializing in performances of 18th century French theater dance. Query with samples; local artists only. SASE. Reports in 1-2 weeks.
Needs: Uses artists for brochure design, programs, newspaper ads and flyers. Pays $4/hour.

THE NEW YORK HARP ENSEMBLE, 140 W. End Ave., New York NY 10023. Director: Aristid von Wurtzler. Concert group which tours the U.S., Europe, Africa, South America, Australia and the Near and Far East.
Needs: Works with 1 designer/year, summer only. Uses artists for direct mail brochures, posters, programs and record cover layouts.
First Contact & Terms: Local artists only. Submit samples (brochures, posters and record covers). Works on assignment only. Samples returned by SASE. Reports back on future assignment possibilities. Provide flyer to be kept on file for future assignments.

NEW YORK MIME AND DRAMA CO., 245 E. 11th St., New York NY 10003. (212)477-3896. Artistic Director: Gabriel Oshen. Estab. 1976. Repertory mime company. Assigns 3-5 jobs and buys 1-2 illustrations/year; local artists only. Query with resume and previously used work. SASE. Reports in 1 week.
Needs: Uses artists for advertising, costumes, direct mail brochures, flyers, graphics, posters, programs and sets. Pay determined by budget.

NORTH CAROLINA SYMPHONY, Box 28026, Memorial Auditorium, Raleigh NC 27611. (919)733-2750. Public Relations Director: James R. Van Laan. Estab. 1932. Query with samples. SASE. Reports in 1-3 months.

Needs: Uses artists for advertising, annual reports, billboards, bumper stickers, direct mail brochures, exhibits, flyers, graphics, posters and programs. Pays $30 max./hour, lettering and layout; $35 max./hour, illustration; $40 max./hour, production; $50 max./hour, design.

THE ODYSSEY THEATRE ENSEMBLE, 12111 Ohio Ave., West Los Angeles CA 90025. (213)879-5221. Publicity: Shelly Parsons. Estab. 1968. Experimental theater troupe. Assigns 10 jobs/year. Query. SASE. Reports in 1 month.
Needs: Uses artists for advertising, billboards, costumes, flyers, graphics, posters, programs and sets. Pays $25-300.

OGUNQUIT PLAYHOUSE, Ogunquit ME 03907. Contact: John Lane. Season runs June-September. Query with resume. Uses artists for set/stage designers and painters.

OHIO UNIVERSITY ARTIST SERIES, Memorial Auditorium, Athens OH 45701. (614)594-6231. Director: Richard F. Stevens. Performing arts center.
Needs: Uses artists for direct mail brochures, flyers, graphics, programs and sets.
First Contact & Terms: Query with resume and samples. SASE. Reports in 1 week.

OLATUNJI CENTER OF AFRICAN CULTURE INC., 43 E. 125th St., New York NY 10035. (212)427-5757. Contact: M.B. Olatunji, director. Estab. 1954. Ethnic dance troupe. Query with resume and samples or arrange interview. SASE. Reporting time determined by "if we are in the city or on tour."
Needs: Uses artists for ads, direct mail brochures, flyers, posters, programs, sets and lighting. Negotiates pay; "our funds are extremely limited."

OPERA/OMAHA, 1200 City National Bank Bldg., Omaha NE 68102. General Manager: Martha Elsberry. Arrange interview to show portfolio or samples; local artists only.
Needs: Uses artists for direct mail brochures; also, occasionally for ad illustrations and billboard and program cover design. Pays $65-400.
To Break In: "We would prefer artists with some professional experience marketing arts organizations, but would consider beginning artists with only a few assignments, provided we could agree on advertising concepts."

OPERA THEATRE OF NEW YORK INC., 344 W. 89th St., New York NY 10024. (212)877-7507. Director: Richard Barri. Estab. 1963. Assigns 3-4 jobs/year. Query with resume. SASE. Reports in 3 weeks.
Needs: Uses artists for ads, direct mail pieces, brochure design, flyers, posters, programs, costumes and sets. Pays $25-200, ads and promotional art; $1,500, 30 costumes.

OPERA THEATRE OF SYRACUSE INC., Civic Center, Suite 60, Syracuse NY 13202. Contact: Robert B. Driver Jr.
Needs: Uses artists for direct mail brochures, posters, newspaper/trade magazine ads, bumper stickers and programs.

OPUS I CHAMBER ORCHESTRA, 15700 Detroit Ave., Lakewood OH 44107. (216)221-3442. Contact: Elliot Higgins, manager. Estab. 1973. Performs 10 concerts/season plus 15 concerts for clients. Assigns 5 jobs/year. Query.
Needs: Uses artists for brochure design, programs, newspaper ads and posters.

PACIFIC NORTHWEST DANCE BALLET COMPANY, 4649 Sunnyside Ave. N., Seattle WA 98103. Artistic Director: Kent Stowell. Assigns 10-15 jobs/year.
Needs: Works with 10-15 illustrators and 10-15 designers/year; September-May only. Uses artists for advertising, billboards, costumes, posters, programs and sets.
First Contact & Terms: Query with samples. SASE. Works on assignment only. Samples returned by SASE. Reports back on future assignment possibilities. Provide resume, calling card, brochure and flyer to be kept on file for future assignments. Pays "going rates."

PARADISE SYMPHONY ORCHESTRA, 6686 Brook Way, Paradise CA 95969. (916)877-8360. Contact: Thomas E. Wilson, conductor. Estab. 1958. Query with resume; prefers local artists. SASE. Reports in 1 month.
Needs: Uses artists for logos and direct mail brochures.

PARK SQUARE THEATRE, 400 Sibley St., St. Paul MN 55101. (612)291-7005. Managing Director: Paul Mathey. Classical theater.

Needs: Assigns 2-3 jobs/year. Uses artists for bumper stickers, flyers, posters and programs.
First Contact & Terms: Local artists only. Query with tearsheets. SASE. Reports in 3 weeks. Pays $20-25, posters; $15-25, flyer brochures.

PENDLETON FESTIVAL SYMPHONY "SUMMERFEST", 421 E. State St., Pendleton IN 46064. (317)778-3009. Artistic Director: George Daugherty Jr. Annual summer festival presenting orchestral, ballet, opera and theatrical performances. Assigns 5-10 jobs/year.
Needs: Works with 2 illustrators and 2 designers/year; spring and summer only. Uses artists for costumes, graphics, sets, technical art and theatrical lighting.
First Contact & Terms: Mail art, or query with samples (sets, costumes, programs and posters) and arrange interview. SASE. Reports in 2 weeks. Works on assignment only. Samples returned by SASE. Reports back on future assignment possibilities. Provide resume and/or brochure to be kept on file for future assignments. Negotiates pay.

PENTACLE MANAGEMENT, 200 W. 72nd St., Suite 20, New York NY 10023. Director: Ivan Sygoda. "We provide booking, touring and fiscal management to touring dance companies." Assigns 1 job/year.
Needs: Works with 5 illustrators/year. Promotional brochure/newsletters are developed in spring/ dance concert phots completed at various times. Uses artists for annual direct mail brochure design, newspaper ads, concert programs, posters and flyers.
First Contact & Terms: Local artists only. Query with samples. SASE. Reports in 3 weeks. Works on assignment only. Samples returned by SASE. Provide resume, flyer and tearsheet to be kept on file for future assignments. Pays $4/hour.
Tips: "Timing is important. For fall promotional campaigns, make submissions in late spring. Only intriguing samples will make us look twice; otherwise, our clients will stick with known quantities—graphic artists they have worked with in the past."

PERFORMANCE COMMUNITY INC., 1225 W. Belmont, Chicago IL 60657. (312)929-7367. Performing arts center and contemporary theater troupe. Assigns 30 design jobs/year.
Needs: Works with 3-4 illustrators and 3-4 designers/year. Uses artists for newspaper advertising, billboards, costumes, direct mail brochures, flyers, graphics, posters, programs, sets and theatrical lighting. Also needs fine art to display in theater lobby.
First Contact & Terms: Local artists only. Query with resume and samples. SASE. Reports in 1 month. Works on assignment only. Pays $25-250.

STANZE PETERSON DANCE THEATRE INC., Box 14380, Houston TX 77021. (713)748-2574. Director: Stanze Peterson. Dance troupe.
Needs: Uses artists for direct mail brochures, programs and newspaper ads.
First Contact & Terms: Local artists only. Query and arrange interview to show portfolio. SASE. Pays by job.

PHILADELPHIA DANCE CO., 6249 Market St., Philadelphia PA 19139. (215)472-5015. General Manager: Sanda Stovall. Estab. 1971. Ballet, modern and ethnic dance troupe. Assigns 6 jobs/year; local artists only. Query with resume. No work returned. Reports in 1 week.
Needs: Uses artists for advertising, costumes, flyers, posters, programs and brochures. Maximum payment by job: $300, design, illustration and layout; $100, lettering; $600, production.

PHILHARMONIC SOCIETY OF NORTHEASTERN PENNSYLVANIA, Box 7, Avoca PA 18641. General Manager: Sally Preate. Query with resume.
Needs: Uses graphic artists for direct mail brochures, programs, posters and public service TV spots.

PICCOLO OPERA COMPANY, 18662 Fairfield Ave., Detroit MI 48221. (313)861-6930. Contact: Lee Jon, personnel. Estab. 1961. Query. SASE. Reports in 3-4 weeks.
Needs: Uses artists for design of flyers. Negotiates pay.
To Break In: Prefers artists with layout experience.

PURDUE CONVOCATIONS, Room 417, ENAD, Purdue University, West Lafayette IN 47907. (317)749-2562. Publicity Director: Annette C. Goben. Concert bureau offering music, theater and dance programs. Assigns 5-10 jobs/year.
Needs: Works with 4 illustrators/year. Uses artists for advertising, direct mail brochures, flyers, posters, programs and season brochures.
First Contact & Terms: Query with samples, or arrange interview if artist is local. SASE. Reports in 2 weeks. Works on assignment only. Samples returned by SASE. Reports back on future

assignment possibilities. Provide calling card and tearsheet to be kept on file for future assignments. Pays $20-45/job for poster design; $200-600/job, sets, and theatrical lighting. Pay varies.

QWINDO'S WINDOW, Box 6333, Washington DC 20015. Contact: Anne Dunkin, co-director. Estab. 1970. Creates and produces live and film presentations for children. Query with resume and fees. SASE. Reports in 2-4 weeks.
Needs: Uses artists for posters, brochures, costume design, drawings to illustrate productions for sales meetings, and mask and specialty productions. Pays $20-120/job.

RAM ISLAND DANCE CENTER, 103 Exchange St., Portland ME 04111. (207)773-2562. Managing Director: Victoria Nolan. Estab. 1974. Modern dance company and school. Assigns 2-3 jobs/year. Query. SASE. Reports in 2 weeks.
Needs: Uses artists for advertising, costumes, direct mail brochures, flyers, graphics, posters, programs and theatrical lighting. Pays $100 max./job for design; $200 max./job for costume design.

THE RENAISSANCE DANCE COMPANY OF DETROIT, 19977 Snowden, Detroit MI 48235. (313)967-4030 or 864-9067. Artistic Director: Harriet Berg. Performs 16th century dance in costume.
Needs: Assigns 4 jobs/year. Uses artists for flyers, programs, announcements and ads.
First Contact & Terms: Query. SASE. Negotiates pay.

RHODE ISLAND PHILHARMONIC ORCHESTRA, 334 Westminster Mall, Providence RI 02903. (401)831-3123. Manager: Mrs. Stevens. Estab. 1944. Assigns 2-5 jobs/year; local artists only. Query. SASE. Reports in 2 weeks.
Needs: Uses artists for advertising, direct mail brochures, graphics, posters, programs and fund-raising literature. Pays $1,000/year.

RITES AND REASON, Box 1148, Brown University, Providence RI 02912. (401)863-4177. Managing Director: Craig Watson. Estab. 1970. Black visual and performing arts organization. Assigns up to 12 jobs/season. Query with resume. SASE. "We prefer working with artists directly, but certain services can be adapted through the mail easily." Reports in 2 weeks.
Needs: Uses artists for all aspects of theater, music and dance productions; plus multimedia and visual exhibitions. Negotiates pay.
To Break In: "We are the university/community arts component of the Afro-American studies program at Brown University. Our original productions of drama, music and dance primarily concern the the interpretation of black people's experiences in the New World. A multidisciplinary approach to research and performance is used by artists and scholars who work together in creation of new productions. An effort is made, through the performing arts, to bring members of the community to a forum where they are given the opportunity to confront scholars and artists, and to critique their work. The dialogues with the community direct subsequent scholarly research that often becomes the basis for other new productions."

RIVERSIDE OPERA ASSOCIATION, Box 2353, Riverside CA 92501. (714)686-4175. General Director: Frances Calkins. Estab. 1932. Assigns 2 jobs/year. Query with samples. SASE. Reports in 1 month.
Needs: Uses artists for advertising, costumes, designer-in-residence, flyers, posters, programs and sets. Pays $300 max./job for set design.

SALT LAKE SYMPHONIC CHOIR, Box 45, Salt Lake City UT 84110. (801)466-8701. President/Manager: R.M. Taggart. Assigns 5 jobs/year.
Needs: Works with 5 illustrators and 2 designers/year; fall only. Uses artists for advertising, billboards, costumes, direct mail brochures, flyers, posters, programs, theatrical lighting and record jackets.
First Contact & Terms: Mail art. SASE. Works on assignment. Provides resume, brochure and flyer to be kept on file for future assignments. Pay determined by bid.

SAN DIEGO BALLET ASSOCIATION, 526 Market St., San Diego CA 92101. Company Manager: M. Woodworth. Classical and modern ballet.
Needs: Assigns 3-6 jobs/year. Uses artists for advertising, costumes, subscriptions, flyers, posters, programs, sets and direct mail brochures.
First Contact & Terms: Local artists only. Resumes not returned. Reports in 2 weeks. Salaries negotiable.

SAN FRANCISCO CONSERVATORY OF MUSIC, 1201 Ortega St., San Francisco CA 94112. (415)564-8086. Contact: Diana Cohen, public relations director. Estab. 1917. College of music including chamber, full ochestra and opera company. Buys 6-10 illustrations/year; prefers local artists. Query with samples. SASE. Reports in 2 weeks.
Needs: Uses artists for posters and programs. Negotiates pay.

SAN FRANCISCO'S BALLET CELESTE-INTERNATIONAL, 1929 Irving St., San Francisco CA 94122. (415)731-7755. Director: Merriem Lanova. Touring amateur dance company.
First Contact & Terms: Query with samples. SASE. Reports in 2 weeks. Negotiates pay.

SAN JOSE SYMPHONY, 170 Park Center Plaza, Suite 100, San Jose CA 95113. (408)287-7383. Contact: Public Relations Manager.
Needs: Assigns 10-15 jobs/year. Uses artists for advertising, billboards, direct mail/developmental brochures, ticket sales material, flyers, posters, programs and educational materials.
First Contact & Terms: Local artists only. Query with resume and samples. SASE. Reports in 1 month. Negotiates pay.

SCORPIO REPERTORY THEATRE, 426 N. Hoover St., Los Angeles CA 90004. Artistic Director: Louise Newmark.
Needs: Works with 2 illustrators/year. Uses artists for set, costume, program, lighting, and graphic design.
First Contact & Terms: Write. Negotiates pay.

SEATTLE SYMPHONY ORCHESTRA, 305 Harrison St., Seattle WA 98109. (206)447-4782. Public Relations Director: Marianne Lewis. Assigns approximately 8 jobs/year.
Needs: Works with 4 illustrators/year; September-April, only. Uses artists for advertising, direct mail brochures, flyers, graphics and posters.
First Contact & Terms: Local artists only. Query with samples. SASE. Reports in 2 weeks. Works on assignment only. No samples returned. Reports back on future assignment possibilities. Provide resume, brochure and flyer to be kept on file for future assignments. Pays $25-100/job for design and illustration; $10-100/job for lettering.

SENECA THEATRE CENTRE, 1750 Finch Ave. E., Willowdale, Ontario, Canada. Contact: Kathleen Young. Submit slides or published samples.
Needs: Uses artists for direct mail brochures, posters and newspaper ads.

ARTHUR SHAFMAN INTERNATIONAL LTD., 1560 Broadway, New York NY 10036. Contact: Arthur Shafman, president. Estab. 1968. Produces and manages dance, theater and music concerts. Assigns 10-15 jobs/year. Query with samples; "if there is interest in artist's work, we will send samples of what we are looking for to artist." SASE. Reports in 2 weeks.
Needs: Uses artists for brochure design, posters and newspaper ads. Pays $200/job.

SINGING BOYS OF PENNSYLVANIA, (formerly Pocono Boy Sigers), Box 110, State College, East Stroudsburg PA 18301, or Box 206, Wind Gap PA 18091. (717)421-6137 (business office); (215)863-5717 (rehearsal hall). Director: K. Bernard Schade.
Needs: Uses artists for direct mail brochures, flyers, posters and record jackets.
First Contact & Terms: Local artists only. Query.

MICHAEL SOKOLOFF DANCE ENSEMBLE, Box 6110, San Francisco CA 94101. (415)661-0809. Director: Michael Sokoloff. Estab. 1975. Modern dance troupe. Assigns 50 jobs/year. Query with samples. SASE. Reports in 2 weeks.
Needs: Uses artists for advertising, costumes, direct mail brochures, flyers, graphics, posters, programs, sets and theatrical lighting.

SOUTH BEND SYMPHONY ORCHESTRA, 215 W. North Shore Dr., South Bend IN 46617. (219)232-6343. Business Manager: Mrs. B.D. Cullity.
Needs: Works with 1 designer/year; July and August. Uses artists for brochures, programs and posters.
First Contact & Terms: Query with samples. SASE. Reports in 1 month. Works on assignment only. Pays $100-350/job, design.

STAGE SOUTH, South Carolina Arts Commission, 829 Richland St., Columbia SC 29201. (803)758-3442. Director of Audience Development: Dennis Moore. Estab. 1973. Theatrical

troupe; presents 2 annual tours. Assigns 2-4 jobs/year. Query with samples. SASE. Reports in 1 week.
Needs: Uses artists for bumper stickers, costumes, direct mail brochures, exhibits, flyers, graphics, posters, programs, sets and theatrical lighting. Pays $100 min./job, design, illustration and layout; $1,000 max./job, production.

STATE UNIVERSITY AT ALBANY PERFORMING ARTS CENTER, Albany NY 12222. (518)457-8608. Specializes in educational programming. Assigns 1 job/year. Send resume. SASE. Contacts artists as needs arise.
Needs: Costume design, flyers, set/stage design, set design painters and theatrical lighting design. Pays $100-250/week.

"STRIKE AT THE WIND!" OUTDOOR DRAMA, Box 1059, Pembroke NC 28372. (919)521-2401. General Manager: Rock Kershaw. Outdoor drama. Assigns 6-12 jobs/year.
Needs: Works with 4-6 illustrators and 4-6 designers/year; winter and spring (January-April). Uses artists for billboards, bumperstickers, poster, animated TV spots, souvenir program cover, brochure illustration, poster illustrations and inside ads and editorials. Needs art that is "dramatic, historically accurate, entertainment-oriented with concepts illustrating Civil War era characters, places and things in southeastern North Carolina."
First Contact & Terms: Mail art or query with samples. SASE. Reports in 2 weeks. Works on assignment only. Samples returned by SASE. Reports back on future assignment possibilities. Provide resume, calling card, brochure, flyer and tearsheet to be kept on file for future assignments. Pays $25-200/job for design and lettering; $25-250/job for illustration.

THEATRE ARTS CORP., Box 5856, Santa Fe NM 87501. (505)982-0252. Art Director: Bob Tzudiker. Estab. 1963. Contemporary theatrical troupe. Assigns 10 jobs/year; mostly local artists. Query. SASE. Reports in 2 months.
Needs: Uses artists for advertising, posters and sets. Pays $50-200/job, set design; $25-75/job, poster design.

THEATRE AT MONMOUTH, THE SHAKESPEAREAN THEATRE OF MAINE, Drawer 3047, Lewiston ME 04240. (207)782-9784. Managing Director: Glen Cooper. Estab. 1970. Classical repertory theater. Assigns 2-3 jobs/year; mostly out-of-town artists. Query with resume and arrange interview. SASE. Reports in 1 month.
Needs: Uses artists for theatrical lighting, sets, costumes, advertising, billboards, bumper stickers, direct mail brochures, exhibits, flyers, posters and programs. Pays $250-2,200/job, design; $100 max./job, illustration and lettering; $10-15/hour, layout. Also offers apprentice design positions at $10/week and room and board during summer.

THEATRE BALLET OF SAN FRANCISCO, 1929 Irving St., San Francisco CA 94122. (415)731-7755. Director: Merriem Lawson. Touring professional dance company that presents a "lavish poduction of *The Nutcracker*."
Needs: Uses artists for scenery designs and occasional costumes.
First Contact & Terms: Query with resume and samples. SASE. Reports in 2 weeks. Negotiates pay.

THEATRE EXPRESS, 4615 Baum Blvd., Pittsburgh PA 15213. (412)621-5454. General Manager: Caren Harder. Resident repertory theatrical company.
Needs: Assigns 5-6 jobs/year. Uses artists for advertising, costumes, direct mail brochures, flyers, posters, programs, sets and lighting.
First Contact & Terms: Query with resume and samples. SASE. Reports in 2 weeks. Pays $25 max./job, design; $400 max./job, lighting and costumes.

THEATRE OF THE RIVERSIDE, 490 Riverside Dr., New York NY 10027. (212)864-2929. Managing Director: David Manion. Estab. 1965. Assigns 5 jobs and buys 1 illustration/year. Query with resume and samples. SASE. Reports in 2 weeks.
Needs: Uses artists for costumes, designer-in-residence, sets and theatrical lighting. Pay varies.

THEATRE OF YOUTH CO. INC., 681 Main St., Buffalo NY 14203. (716)839-3390. Artistic Director: Rosalind Cramer. Theater in the schools providing workshops and productions. Assigns 3-4 jobs/year; local artists only. Write. SASE.
Needs: Uses artists for costumes, direct mail brochures, flyers, graphics, posters, programs and sets. Pays $300-500, costume and set design.

THEATRE-BY-THE-SEA, Moonstone Beach, Matunuk RI 02879. (401)789-0692. Contact: Tommy Brent, producer. Estab. 1933. Summer theater. Assigns 8 jobs/year. Query with resume. SASE. Reports in 2 weeks.
Needs: "We have openings for scenic, lighting and costume designers and assistants in each department. We pay weekly salaries. Designers must execute their own work with a staff under them."

UNIVERSAL MOVEMENT THEATRE REPERTORY, Box 774, Times Square Station, New York NY 10036. Contact: Mark Hall Amitih. Submit published samples.
Needs: Uses artists for direct mail brochures, posters, programs and trade magazine ads.

UNIVERSITY OF UTAH LECTURES AND CONCERTS, Kingsbury Hall 210, Salt Lake City UT 84112. Contact: Paul Cracroft. Booking and promoting office for performing arts. Mail resume, published samples or slides.
Needs: Uses artists for direct mail brochures, posters and newspaper ads. Pays $50-85, posters; $60-120, direct mail brochures design.

MARUJA VARGAS AND COMPANIA DEL ORO, 509 W. 15th St., Tempe AZ 85281. (602)966-5995. Artistic Director: Vargas. Estab. 1975. Specializes in Spanish classical dance. Assigns 3 jobs/year. Query. SASE. Reports in 2 weeks.
Needs: Uses artists for flyers, graphic design, paste-up, posters and theatrical lighting design. Pays $300, master design.

WASHINGTON PERFORMING ARTS SOCIETY, 425 13th St. NW, Suite 712, Washington DC 20004. (202)393-3600. Associate Manager: Jan Kendall. Estab. 1966. Presents modern dance, folk dance, orchestra, solos and chamber music. Assigns 4 jobs/year; local artists only. Mail art, query with samples, or arrange interview. SASE.
Needs: Uses artists for direct mail brochures. Pays up to $1,000.

WATERLOO-CEDAR FALLS SYMPHONY ORCHESTRA, Box 864, Waterloo IA 50705. (319)235-6331. Contact: Joseph Giunta, director. Assigns 1 job/year.
Needs: Works with 2 illustrators and 2 designers/year; fall and spring. Uses artists for program design.
First Contact & Terms: Query with resume. SASE. Reports in 1 week. Provide materials to be kept on file for future assignments. Negotiates pay.

DENNIS WAYNE'S DANCERS LTD., 450 Avenue of the Americas, New York NY 10011. (212)260-0453. Contact: Taffy Wendelken, managing director. Estab. 1977. Assigns 2 jobs/year. Query with samples or previously published work. SASE. Reports in 3-4 weeks.
Needs: Uses artists for posters, flyers, solicitation campaigns, programs and newspaper ads. Negotiates pay.

WISCONSIN ARTS QUINTET, University of Wisconsin, Stevens Point WI 54481. Contact: Julius Erlenbach. Woodwind quintet.
Needs: Uses artists for newspaper ads, programs, posters and direct mail brochures.
First Contact & Terms: Submit photos or tearsheets.

WISCONSIN CHAMBER ORCHESTRA, 731 State St., Madison WI 53703. (608)257-6307. Contact: Egons Plavnieks, general manager.
Needs: Works with 2 illustrators and 4 designers/year. Uses artists for posters, brochures, concert programs and flyers.
First Contact & Terms: Local artists only. Query with samples (brochures and commercial advertising pieces). SASE. Reports in 2-4 weeks. Works on assignment only. Samples returned by SASE. Reports back on future assignment possibilities. Provide calling card to be kept on file for future assignments. Pays $100 min./job.

WISDOM BRIDGE THEATRE, 1559 W. Howard St., Chicago IL 60626. (312)743-6442. Executive Director: Jeffrey Ortmann. Public Relations Director: Peter Syvertsen. Assigns 28-62 jobs/year.
Needs: Works with 3 illustrators and 15 designers/year. Uses artists for advertising, billboards, bumper stickers, costumes, direct mail brochures, exhibits, flyers, graphics, posters, programs, sets, technical art and lighting. Pays $100-300/job, design of sets, lights and costumes. Pays $25-400/job, brochure design.
First Contact & Terms: Arrange interview or query with resume and samples. SASE. Works on

assignment only. Samples returned by SASE. Reports back on future assignment possibilities. Provide resume, brochure, flyer, tearsheet and sketches to be kept on file for future assignments.

WORCESTER COMMUNITY CONCERT ASSOCIATION, Box 1141, Worcester MA 01613. Vice President/Publicity: Joseph O. Lupien. Performing arts organization. Assigns 1-10 jobs/year.
Needs: Works with 2-3 illustrators and 2-3 designers/year; April-May only. Uses artists for advertising, bumper stickers, direct mail brochures, exhibits, flyers, graphics, posters and programs.
First Contact & Terms: Query with samples. SASE. Reports in 1 week. Works on assignment only. Samples returned by SASE. Reports back on future assignment possibilities. Provide brochure, flyer to be kept on file for future assignments. Payment varies.

THE ANNA WYMAN DANCE THEATRE, 656 15th St., West Vancouver, B.C., Canada V7T 2S7. Manager: Richard Brownsey. Query with published samples.
Needs: Uses dance-related graphics for brochures, programs, and advertising.

Periodicals

This is a section that should bring smiles to the faces of artists who want to sell their work, but don't want to wait for assignments. Not only is this the largest section in *Artist's Market*, but it is one in which unsolicited submissions are generally welcome.

Another appealing factor of publications markets is they rarely require past experience or in-person appointments, and rarely do they ask to see portfolios. Usually, all you need to do is read sample copies of the publication, study the style used, and then check out the submission requirements listed in this book. If these guidelines are followed, the talented freelance artist who has never sold a cartoon or illustration has as much chance of getting work accepted as the artist who sells work regularly.

Work submitted to publications should include a typewritten cover letter and SASE. Some smaller publications prefer that you include your fee request in your initial letter, while larger publishers determine payment. When in doubt, omit the price and allow the publication to bring up the subject. The Cartoonist Guild, Inc. (156 W. 72nd St., New York NY 10023) and the Graphic Artists Guild's *Pricing & Ethical Guidelines* (30 E. 20th St., New York NY 10003) are both sources for pricing guidelines.

The listings below frequently include payment along with the type of art used. The basic structure of a listing begins with the address, name of the person to contact and a brief paragraph about the publication.

Subsequent paragraphs in the listings in the Periodicals section are subheads describing the type of work purchased. Subheads include Cartoons, Illustrations, General Needs and Advertising. For each type of artwork purchased, there is information as to the amount used per issue, how many of those come from freelancers and how many submissions are received weekly from freelancers. This gives you a feel for the opportunity with each listing. For instance, if a publication runs 10 illustrations per issue, of which only one comes from a freelancer and yet receives 1,000 submissions a week, you know the chances of breaking in to that publication are rather slim.

Other information provided in the subheads includes specifics on the manner in which the work should be presented and whether color or black and white is purchased, payment rates, reporting time on submissions, how soon the publication reports whether an artist's work interests them, and what rights are purchased.

The Periodicals section of *Artist's Market* is broken into two parts—magazines and newspapers. You can also find the names and addresses of additional publications by consulting *Editor & Publisher Year Book, Ayer Directory of Publications*, and *Gebbie House Magazine Directory.*

Magazines

AB BOOKMAN PUBLICATIONS MAGAZINE, Box AB, Clifton NJ 07015. Contact: Jacob L. Chernofsky. For book dealers. Offset. Query with resume.
Needs: Buys cartoons on bookselling, books, libraries and book collecting. Also uses artists for ad layout and paste-up.

ABC AMERICAN ROOFER AND BUILDING IMPROVEMENT CONTRACTOR, Shelter Publications, Inc., 2051 Ogden Ave., Downers Grove IL 60515. (312)964-6200. Editor-in-Chief: J.C. Gudas. For owners of roofing businesses. Monthly; 8½x11; 32 pages. Offset. Estab. 1911.

Circ. 29,220. Query. SASE. Reports in 1 week. "We want only that which is pertinent to our field, which is roofing and exterior improvements, not general construction or interior home improvement. Usually, we get a lot of material that is totally irrelevant." Buys all rights. Pays on publication. Free sample copy.
Cartoons: Buys 2-3/year on roofing; single panel. Pays $5-50, line drawings.
Illustrations: Buys 15/year on the industry. Cover and inside: Pays $5, b&w.

ACCENT, 1720 Washington Blvd., Box 2315, Ogden UT 84404. (801)394-9446. Editor: Dick Harris. Concerns travel. Circ. 600,000. Monthly.
Cartoons: Buys 10-12/year on business, sports and everyday life, "in good taste." Prefers roughs. SASE. Reports in 3 weeks. Pays $15, b&w; $20, color; on acceptance.

ACCENT ON LIVING, Box 700, Bloomington IL 61701. Editor: Ray Cheever. Emphasis on success and ideas for better living for the physically handicapped. Original artwork returned after publication, if requested. Sample copy $1.25.
Cartoons: Uses 18-20/issue; buys all from freelancers. Receives 5 submissions/week from freelancers. Interested in people with disabilities in differnt situations. Prefers finished cartoons. SASE. Reports in 2 weeks. Buys all rights. Pays on acceptance.
Illustrations: Uses 3-5 illustrations/issue. Interested in illustrations that depict articles/topics we run. Works on assignment only. Samples returned by SASE. Reports back on future assignment possiblities.Providesample of style to be kept on file for future assignments. SASE. Reports in two weeks. Buys all rights on awork-for-hire basis. Pays on acceptance.

ACCENT ON YOUTH, 201 8th Ave. S., Nashville TN 37202. Editor: Margaret L. Barnhart. "Leisure reading for ages 12-14 in the United Methodist Church." Quarterly. Previously published work OK.
Needs: Uses artists for 2- and 3-color illustrations, full-color cover illustrations, cartoons and cover design. Query with resume. Buys all rights; reprint rights on cartoons. Sample payment: $75, 4-color cover; on acceptance.

ACROSS THE BOARD, 845 3rd Ave., New York NY 10022. (212)759-0900, ext. 356. Editor-in-Chief: Lewis Bergman. Art Director: Josef Kozlakowski. For corporate executive officers. Monthly. Circ. 47,000. Will consider photocopied submissions. Buys first rights on acceptance.
Cartoons: Number cartoons bought/issue varies. Interested in current events and business-related topics; single panel. Query with roughs. SASE. Reports in 2 weeks. Buys first rights. Pays $75-175, b&w; $100-175, color; on acceptance.
Illustrations: Number illustrations bought/issue varies. Interested in current events, education, environment, politics, editorial and business-related topics. Works on assighment only. Provide post-card-size calling card containing illustration or sample to be kept on file for future assignments. SASE. Reports in 2 weeks. Buys first rights. Cover: Pays $200-325, color. Inside: Pays $75-175, b&w; $75-200, color; on acceptance.

ADAM, 8060 Melrose Ave., Los Angeles CA 90046. Concerns "human sexuality in contemporary society." Monthly.
Cartoons: Buys 8-12 cartoons/issue. Interested in sexual and erotic themes. Send roughs. SASE. Reports in 2-3 weeks. Pays $20, b&w; $35-100, color.
Illustrations: Buys 1-2 illustrations/issue on assigned themes. Arrange interview to show portfolio. SASE. Reports in 2-3 weeks. Pays $25-100, b&w; $35-150, color.

ADAM FILM WORLD, 8060 Melrose, Los Angeles CA 90046. Editor-in-Chief: Edward S. Sullivan. Editorial Assistant: Freddie Fischer. For fans of X- and R-rated movies. Bimonthly. Circ. 250,000. SASE. Will consider previously published work. Pays on publication. Sample copy $2.25; free artist's guidelines.
Cartoons: Buys 4-6/issue on erotica and cinema; include gag line.Mail roughs or finished art. Buys various rights. Pays $15, b&w spot; $35, full-page b&w; $25, color spot; $75, full-page color; on publication.
Illustrations: Buys erotic film themes. Query with resume and samples. Reports in 2 weeks. Inside: Pays $20-100, b&w; $25-125, color.

AFFAIR, Editorial Enterprises, Inc., 313 W. 53rd St., New York NY 10019. (212)265-3400. Editor: Jack Tabatch. Art Director: Hank Mason. Male entertainment publication. Monthly; 8x11; 100 pages. Offset. Estab. 1974. Circ. 100,000. Query with resume of samples or arrange interview to show portfolio. SASE. Reports in 2-3 weeks. Buys all rights. Pays 30-60 days after publication.

Illustrations: Buys 2-3/issue on assigned fiction themes. Inside: Pays $125-500, b&w line drawings, washes and gray opaques.

AFTER DARK, 1180 Avenue of the Americas, New York NY 10036. Editor-in-Chief: Charles Kriebel. Concerns entertainment, including theater, films, TV, dance, opera, music, happenings and travel. Monthly. Original artwork returned after publication. Sample copy $2.50.
Illustrations: Uses 1-3 illustrations/issue. Works on assignment only. Samples returned. Does not report back on future assignment possiblities. Provide brochure and tearsheet to be kept on file for future assignments. Prefers portfolio. Reports in 1 week. Buys all rights on a work-for-hire basis. Pays on publication.

AGENCY SALES, Manufacturers' Agents National Association, Box 16878, Irvine CA 92713. Contact: Dan Bayless. For independent, commissioned industrial salesmen. Monthly. Previously published work OK.
Needs: Query with resume. Reports in 30-60 days. Buys first or all rights. Pays $70 for camera-ready art in black plus another color (with white paper as background); $10-15 for spot drawings; $15 for cartoons about business, marketing and industry, on publication.

AGRI FINANCE, 5520-G Touhy Ave., Skokie IL 60077. (312)676-4060. Production Director: Bruce Herz. Concerns financial management for "ag-bankers and agricultural-related professions." Published 9 times/year. Circ. 23,000. Simultaneous submissions and previously published work OK. Sample copy $2.75.
Illustrations: Buys 2/issue on assigned themes. Cover: Buys color and b&w work. Inside: Buys b&w line drawings, washes and gray opaques. Arrange interview to show portfolio. SASE. Reports in 3 weeks. Negotiates pay, pays on publication.

AGRI MARKETING, 5520-G Touhy Ave., Skokie IL 60077. (312)676-4060. Publication Manger: Lyle E. Oenig. For professionals selling to the farm market. Published 13 times/year; Simultaneous submissions and previously published work OK. Sample copy $2.50.
Illustrations: Buys 2/issue on assigned themes. Cover: Buys color washes, opaque watercolors and b&w line drawings. Inside: Buys gray opaques, b&w line drawings and washes. Arrange interview to show portfolio. SASE. Reports in 3 weeks. Negotiates pay; pays on publication.

AIM, Box 20554, Chicago IL 60620. (312)874-6184. Editor-in-Chief: Ruth Apilado. Managing Editor: Dr. Myron Apilado. Art Director: Bill Jackson. Readers are those "wanting to eliminate bigotry and desiring a world without inequalities in education, housing, etc." Quarterly. Circ. 16,000. Sample copy $1.50; artist's guidelines for SASE. Reports in 3 weeks. Previously published, photocopied and simultaneous submissions OK.
Cartoons: Uses 4 cartoons/issue; all from freelancers. Interested in education, environment, family life, humor through youth, politics and retirement; single panel with gag line. Mail finished art. SASE. Reports in 3 weeks. Buys all rights on a work-for-hire basis. Pays $5-15, b&w line drawings; on publication.
Illustrations: Uses 6 illustrations/issue; half from freelancers. Interested in current events, education, environment, humor through youth, politics and retirement. Provide brochure to be kept on file for future assignments. No samples returned. Reports in 4 weeks. Format: b&w for cover and inside art. Buys all rights on a work-for-hire basis. Pays $5-15, b&w line drawings; on publication.

AIR LINE PILOT, 1625 Massachusetts Ave. NW, Washington DC 20036. Editor: C.V. Glines. Original artwork not returned after publication.
Cartoons: Uses 1 cartoon/issue; buys from freelancer. Interested in themes truly representative of the airline pilot and his working world. Prefers roughs. SASE. Reports in 2 weeks. Buys all rights. Pays $25, with gag line; on publication.
Illustrations: Rarely uses freelance illustrations. Uses illustrations to support feature articles. Works on assignment only. Samples returned by SASE. Reports back on future assignment possibilities. Reports in 2 weeks. Buys all rights on a work-for-hire basis.

ALFRED HITCHCOCK MYSTERY MAGAZINE, Davis Publications, 229 Park Ave. S., New York NY 10003. Contact: Irving Bernstein. Reports in 1 week. Pays on acceptance. Buys first rights.
Needs: Minimum payment: $20, line drawings; $400, full-color cover; on acceptance.

ALIVE!, Christian Board of Publication, Box 179, St. Louis MO 63166. Editor: Jerry O'Malley. For junior high students. Monthly.
Cartoons: Buys 8 cartoons/issue on life and teenage problems. Prefers finished cartoons. SASE.

Reports in 2 weeks. Buys one-time rights. Pays $8.
Illustrations: Illustrations should appeal to junior high. Interested in inks, line drawings and washes. Provide business card, brochure and/or tearsheets to be kept on file for future assignments. Samples returned with SASE. Prefers finished art and samples of style. SASE. Reports in 2 weeks. Buys first North American serial rights. Pays $30-50; on acceptance.

ALOHA-THE MAGAZINE OF HAWAII, Box 3260, Honolulu HI 96801. Editor: Rita Witherwax. Concerns Hawaii's history, ethnic groups and famous and out-of-the-way areas. Bimontly. Circ. 80,000.
Illustrations: Buys b&w and color. Reports in 6 weeks. Pays on publication.

AMAZING GRACE, 3822 Campus Dr., Suite 213, Newport Beach CA 92660. (714)549-4060. Art Editor: Laurel Watson. Readers are Born Again Christians in the US. Bimonthly. Circ. 125,000. Estab. 1980.
Illustrations: Uses 14 illustrations/issue; buys all from freelancers. Selection based on previous contact and by portfolio review. "Open to good people who can work by phone and mail." Interested in illustrations to accompany articles on the Christian experience. Arrange personal appointment to show portfolio or send samples of style. SASE. Reports in 2 weeks. Prefers b&w line drawings for inside and cover. Buys on a work-for-hire basis. Pays up to $400 for b&w and color cover/inside; on publication.

AMERICAN ART ENTERPRISES INC., 12011 Sherman Rd., North Hollywood CA 91605. (213)982-4000. Art Director/Manager: Jerome Pecoraro. Publishes paperback books under imprint: Carousel Books.
Illustrations: Interested in romance, western, science fiction, adventure, mystery, historical romance, occult and fantasy. Original artwork not returned after publication. Works on assignment only. Does not report back on future assignment possiblities. Provide samples of style to be kept on file for future assignments. Query with previously published work. SASE. Reports on delivery. Buys all rights on a work-for-hire basis. Paperback cover illustrations pay $150-300 color. B&W line illustrations pay $75-100.

AMERICAN ART REVIEW, Box 689, Old Lyme CT 06371. (203)434-8183. Contact: Tom Kellaway. Concerns American art history; for libraries, museums, art historians, artists and collectors. Estab. 1973. Circ. 14,000. Bimonthly. SASE. Reports in 1 month. Pays on publication.
Illustrations: Buys themes from Colonial-1950. Negotiates pay. Call.

AMERICAN ARTIST, 1515 Broadway, New York NY 10036. (212)764-7300. Emphasizes the American artist–realistic, naturalistic and fine art for artists, students and teachers. Monthly. Circ. 140,000. Sample copy $1.50; art guidelines for SASE.
Needs: Does not assign or use freelancers. If an artist wants to be the subject of a feature article, he should contact the editor. Wants to see slides of b&w glossies of artist's work for possible feature articles.

THE AMERICAN ATHEIST, Box 2117, Austin TX 78768. (512)458-1244. Editor: Madalyn M. O'Hair. For atheists, agnostics, materialists and realists. Monthly. Circ. 30,000.Previously published and simultaneous submissions OK. Free sample copy.
Needs: Buys b&w drawings, cover designs and cartoons. Especially needs 4- seasons art for covers and greeting cards. Send photocopies. "All illustrations must have bite from the atheist point of view and hit hard." Pays $5-25; on publication.

THE AMERICAN BAPTIST MAGAZINE, 1st Ave., Valley Forge PA 19481. (215)768-2441. Director, Media Education & Development: Milton P. Ryder. National Protestant denomination magazine.
Cartoons: Uses 1 cartoon/issue, all from freelancers. Interested in "seasonal (religious)" themes. Prefers roughs. SASE. Reports in 2 weeks.
Illustrations: Uses 5-10 illustrations/issue, all from freelancers. Interested in "seasonal (religious)" themes and current issues. Works on assignment only. Samples returned by SASE. Reports back on future assignment possibilities. Provide resume to be kept on file for future assignments. Prefers roughs and portfolio. SASE. Reports in 1 week.
Needs: Uses artists for article illustration, 1-, 2-, and 4-color separated covers, posters, slide show and video art, convention handouts and brochures. "We have paid as little as $10 for a b&w illustration and as much as $1,200 for graphic design of a national offering campaign."
Tips: "Be accessible, be able to 'sense' our need, listen, produce on time and with accuracy, and don't sacrific artistic integrity."

AMERICAN BAR ASSOCIATION JOURNAL, American Bar Association, 77 S. Wacker Dr., Chicago IL 60606. (312)621-9200. Editor-in-Chief: Richard B. Allen. Director of Graphics: David Jendras. For lawyers, judges and law teachers and students. "The magazine is not limited to law, but also handles social problems that have legal implications." Monthly. Circ. 249,000. Original artwork not returned after publication, except by prearrangement. Free sample copy and artist's guidelines.
Cartoons: Uses 3 cartoons/issue; buys 2/issue from freelancers. Receives 40 submissions/week from freelancers. Interested in "legal theme, lawyer in office, courtroom, homelife." Prefers roughs. SASE. Reports in 2 weeks. Buys all rights on a work-for-hire basis. Single and multipanel with gag lines. Pays $25-100, b&w line drawings and washes on acceptance.
Illustrations: Uses 3 illustrations/issue; buys 2/issue from freelancers. Interested in the legal profession. Works on assignment only. Samples returned by SASE. Reports back on future assignment possibilities. Provide brochure, flyer or tearsheet to be kept on file for future assignments. Prefers portfolio and samples of style. SASE. Reports in 1 week. Buys all rights on a work-for-hire basis. Cover: Pays $600 maximum, full-color. Inside: Pays $100-175, b&w line drawings and washes; $300 maximum, full-color; on acceptance.

AMERICAN BOOKSELLER, Booksellers Publishing Inc., 122 E. 42nd St., Suite 1410, New York NY 10017. (212)867-9060. Editor-in-Chief: Ann S. Haslam. Production Manager: Amy G. Bogert. For booksellers interested in trends, merchandising, recommendations, laws and industry news. Monthly. Circ. 8,000. Original artwork returned after publication. Sample copy.
Cartoons: Uses 1 cartoon/issue; buys 1/issue from freelancers. Receives 10 submissions/week from freelancers. Interested in bookselling, authors and publishing; single panel with gag line. Send finished cartoons. SASE. Reports in 2 weeks. Buys first North American serial rights.
Illustrations: Uses 6 illustrations/issue; buys 6/issue from freelancers. Receives 10 submissions/week from freelancers. Interested in books, inventory or material for specific assignments. Works on assignment only. Samples returned by SASE. Reports back on future assignment possibilities. Provide calling card, flyer and tearsheet to be kept on file for future assignments. Prefers finished art samples of style or portfolio. SASE. Reports in 2 days. Buys first North American serial rights. Pays $25 minimum for b&w line drawings, washes and gray opaques; on acceptance.
Other Needs: Photos (by assignment only).

AMERICAN DANE, Box 31748, Omaha NE 68131. (402)341-5049. Editor-in-Chief: Robert E. Coffey. Concerns Danish heritage and traditions. Monthly. Circ. 11,000. Original artwork returned after publication. Pays on publication.
Illustrations: Buys 1/issue on nature, people and scenes from Denmark. Provide resume to be kept on file for future assignments. Query with samples. Prefers rough. SASE. Reports in 4 weeks. Buys first North American serial rights. Pays $15-25, b&w; on publication.

AMERICAN DEMOGRAPHICS, Box 68, Ithaca NY 14850. (607)273-6343. Managing Editor: F. Jill Charboneau. Emphasizes demographics and population trends. Readers are business decision makers, advertising agencies, market researchers, newspapers, banks and professional demographers and business analysts. Monthly. Circ. 5,500+ Original artwork returned after publication. Sample copy $4.
Cartoons: Uses 1-5 cartoons/issue, all from freelancers. Receives 10-20 submissions/week from freelancers. Interested in population trends including moving, aging, families, birth rate, the census, surveys, changing neighborhoods, women working, data (use, computers, etc.), market research, business forecasting and demographers. Format: single panel b&w line drawings and b&w washes with gag line. Prefers finished cartoons. SASE. Reports in 2 weeks. Buys one-time rights. Pays $75-100 on publication.
Illustrations: Uses 2 illustrations/issue; on assignment only. Interested in demographic themes. Needs "styles that reproduce best in b&w. Spare statements with a light approach to the subject. Samples returned by SASE. Reports back on future assignment possibilities. Provide photocopies of work to be kept on file for future assignments. Prefers portfolio. Contact F. Jill Chaboneau. SASE. Reports in 1 month. Buys all rights on a work-for-hire basis. Inside: pays $35, under ½ page; $50, ½ page; $100-200, full page. Cover: pay is negotiable ($100-300).

AMERICAN FAMILY PHYSICIAN, 1740 W. 92nd St., Kansas City MO 64114. Publisher: Walter H. Kemp. Submit art. Reports in 2 weeks. Buys all rights. Pays on acceptance.
Cartoons: Uses 2 cartoons/issue, all from freelancers. Receives 30 submissions/week from freelancers. Original artwork not returned after publication. Interested in medical and hospital themes. Prefers furnished cartoons. SASE. Reports in 1 week. Buys all rights on a work-for-hire basis. Pays $25; on acceptance.
Illustrations: Uses 6-8 illustration/issue, all from freelancers to be kept on file for future assign-

ments. Buys 12-24/year on everything from scientific to legislative information of interest to doctors. Works on assignment only. Samples returned by SASE. Reports back on future assignment possibilities. Provide letter of inquiry to be kept on file for future assignments. Reports in 1 week. Buys all rights on a work-for-hire basis. Pays $25.

AMERICAN HAIRDRESSER/SALON OWNER, 100 Park Ave., Suite 1000, New York NY 10017. Art Director: Richard Schemm. Executive Editor: Gaith Garrett. Concerns the art of cosmetology and related fashion; for beauty salons. Monthly. Circ. 158,000. Offset. Simultaneous submissions OK "if trade exclusive."
Cartoons: Buys women's and men's hairsyling themes; single panel with gag line. Query with samples or mail roughs or finished art. Negotiates pay, b&w line drawings and washes; on publication.
Illustrations: Editor: Louise Cotter. Buys themes on hairstyling. Inside: Negotiates pay, b&w line drawings and photos. Query with resume and samples or arrange interview to show portfolio. SASE. Reports in 3-4 weeks. Buys all rights.

AMERICAN HERITAGE, 10 Rockefeller Plaza, New York NY 10020. (212)399-8478. Art Director: Murray Belsky. Concerns American history. Bimonthly. Circ. 150,000. Bimonthly.
Illustrations: Assigns work for 1-2 articles/issue. Arrange interview to show portfolio.

AMERICAN HISTORY ILLUSTRATED, Box 1831, Harrisburg PA 17105. (717)234-5091. Art Director: Frederic Ray. For the general public with an interest in well-researched historical articles. Circ. 160,000. Monthly except March and September.
Illustrations: Buys American history (1492-Korean War) themes. Query with samples. SASE. Reports in 2 weeks. Pays $10-100, b&w or color; on acceptance or publication.

THE AMERICAN HUNTER, National Rifle Association, 1600 Rhode Island Ave. NW, Washington DC 20036. (202)828-6230. Editor: Earl A. Shelsby Jr. For hunters. Monthly. Circ. 200,000. Photocopied submissions OK. Free sample copy.
Illustrations: Buys 18 illustrations/year. Interested in hunting. Submit art. SASE. Reports in 2 weeks. Buys first rights. Inside: Pays $100 minimum, b&w line drawings and washes; on acceptance.

AMERICAN JEWISH TIMES-OUTLOOK, 1400 W. Independence Blvd., Charlotte NC 28234. (704)372-3296. Editor-in-Chief: Ron Unger. For Jewish readers interested in world affairs, politics, sports, entertainment and literature. Circ. 5,000. Previously published and simultaneous submissions OK. Free sample copy.
Illustrations: Buys 2 illustrations/year. Interested in Judaism. Cover: Pays $35 minimum, color; $15-25, b&w. Inside: Pays $15-20, b&w line drawings; on publication. Mail art. SASE. Reports in 4 weeks. Buys all rights; on publication.

AMERICAN JOURNAL OF NURSING, 10 Columbus Circle, New York NY 10019. (212)582-8820. Editor-in-Chief: Thelma Schorr. Managing Editor: Gretchen Gerds. Art Director: Forbes Linkhorn. For nursing professionals. Monthly. Circ. 350,000.
Cartoons: Buy 36 cartoons/year. Interested in nursing. "Please keep cartoons tasteful; no nudes, buxom nurses or sexual connotations. Do not show nurses as receptionists." Mail art. SASE. Reports in 4 weeks. Buys all rights. Pays $20-50 on acceptance, line drawings, halftones and washes; on acceptence.
Illustrations: Buys 300 illustrations/year on assigned themes. Arrange interview. Reports in 4 weeks. Buys all rights. Pays $75-300 b&w line drawings, duotones, washes and full cover, any media; on publication. Arrange interview.
To Break In: "Visit hospitals to study nurses in their natural habitat. Try to get inside humor, not just nurses vs. doctors, or nurses as receptionists, etc."

THE AMERICAN LEGION, Box 1055, Indianapolis IN 46205. Contact: Cartoon Editor. Original artwork not returned after publication.
Cartoons: Uses 6 cartoons/issue, all from freelancers. Receive 150 submissions/week from freelancers. "Generally interested in cartoons with a broad, mass appeal. Prefer action in the drawing, rather than the illustrated joke-type gag. Those which have a beguiling character or ludicrous situation that attract the reader and lead him to read the caption rate the highest attention. Require 1 column 2-inch cartoon in addition to usual 2 column 4-inch cartoon. No-caption gags purchased only occasionally. Because of the tight space problem, we're not in the market for the spread-type or multipanel cartoon. Themes should be home life, business, sports and everyday Americana. Cartoons which pertain only to one branch of the service are too

restricted for this magazine. The service-type gag should be recognized and appreciated by any ex-serviceman or woman. Cartoons in bad taste, off-color or which may offend the reader not accepted. Liquor, sex, religion and racial differences are taboo. Ink roughs not necessary, but are desirable. Finish should be line, Ben-Day." Prefers roughs. Reports immeadiatly. Buys first rights "pays on receipt of Ben-Day acceptence." Pays $75-125.

AMERICAN LIBRARIES, American Library Association, 50 E. Huron St., Chicago IL 60611. (312)944-6780. Editor-in-Chief: Arthur Plotnik. Art Director: Edith McCormick. For professional librarians, library employees and individuals in business-related fields. Published 11 times/year. Circ. 40,000. Sample copy $1.50. Free artist's guidelines.
Cartoons: Buys 4-10/year on libraries and library-patron interaction; single panel with gag line. Query with samples or with resume and portfolio. SASE. Reports in 3 weeks. Buys first North American serial rights. Pays $20-75, b&w line drawings and washes.
Illustrations: Buys 4-8/year on libraries, library-patron interaction and assigned themes. Query with samples or with resume and portfolio. SASE. Reports in 3 weeks. Buys first North American serial rights. Cover: Pays $50-200, b&w; $300 maximum, color. Inside: Pays $15-200, color and b&w; on acceptance.

AMERICAN MIZRACHI WOMAN, 817 Broadway NY 10003. (212)477-4720. Exceutive Editor: Avi Feinglass. Readers are members of the major religious women's Zionist organization in the US having above-average education and committed to Jewish tradition. Published 8 times/year. Circ. 50,000. Original artwork returned after publication. Free sample copy.
Illustrations: Uses 1-2 illustrations/issue; buys 1-2 from freelancers. "Editor finds artwork in standard publications and asks personal contacts." Illustrations should pertain to Jewish holidays, ritual objects, religious observances, and daily Orthodox Jewish living; Israeli themes.Format: b&w line drawings for inside. Provide resume, letter of inquiry, or tearsheet to be kept on file for future assignments. Arrange personal appointment to show portfolio or send samples of style or finished art. SASE.Reports in 1 month. Buys all rights on a work-for-hire basis. Pays $20 minimum on publication.
Other Needs: Greeting cards, promotional literature for fund raising, posters, brochures, flyers and calendars.

AMERICAN MOTORCYCLIST, (formerly *AMA News*), American Motorcyclist Association, Box 141, Westerville OH 43081. (614)891-2425. Editor-in-Chief: Bill Amick. Art Director: Greg Harrison. Monthly: Circ. 130,000. Free sample copy.
Cartoons: Uses 2-3 cartoons/issue; all from freelancers. Receives 5-10 submissions/week from freelancers. Interested in motorcycling; "single panel gags." Prefers finished cartoons. SASE. Reports in 2 weeks. Buys all rights on a work-for-hire basis. Pays $15 minimum, b&w washes; on publication.
Illustrations: Uses 1-2 illustrations/issue, all from feelancers. Receives 3-5 submissions/week from freelancers. Interested in motorcycling. Works on assignment only. Samples returned by SASE. Reports back on future assignment possiblities. Provide resumes and tearsheet to be kept on file for future assignments. Prefers samples of style and resume. SASE. Reports in 2 weeks. Buys first North American serial rights. Cover: Pays $75 minimum, color. Inside: $30-100; b&w and color; on publication.

AMERICAN OPINION, 395 Concord Ave., Belmont MA 02178. (617)489-0600. Editor: Scott Stanley Jr. "Conservative, anti-Communist journal of political affairs." Monthly except August. Estab. 1958. Circ. 50,000. SASE. Reports in 2 weeks. Pays on acceptance.
Cartoons: Buys 4/issue on general and conservative political themes. Pays $25, b&w. Send finished artwork.

AMERICAN PAINTING CONTRACTOR, American Paint Journal Co., 2911 Washington Ave., St. Louis MO 63103. (314)534-0301. Editor-in-Chief: John L. Cleveland. For painting contractors interested in quality professional painting and industry developments. Monthly; 6x8; 90 pages. Offset. Estab. 1924. Circ. 34,000. Previously published and simultaneous submissions OK. Original artwork returned after publication. Free sample copy and artist's guidelines.
Cartoons: Uses 3 cartoons/issue, all from freelancers. Receives 5 submissions/week from freelancers. Interested in paint; single panel with gag line. Prefers finished cartoons. SASE. Reports in 2 weeks. Buys all rights on a work-for-hire basis. Pays $2.50-5, b&w line drawings and gray opaques; on publication.
Illustrations: Uses 4 illustration/issue, all from freelancers. Themes vary. Works on assignment only. Samples returned by SASE. Provide calling card to be kept on file for future assignments. Prefers finished art. SASE. Reports in 2 weeks. Buys all rights on a work-for-hire basis. Cover:

Pays $100-200, full-color; $75-150, b&w. Inside: Pays $25-75, b&w line drawings and gray opaques; $75-150, color; on publication.

AMERICAN PRINTER AND LITHOGRAPHER, (formerly *Inland Printer/American Lithographer*), 300 W. Adams St., Chicago IL 60606. (312)726-2802. Editor: Michael Chazin. Printing, publishing and graphic arts industry magazine.
Cartoons: Uses 1-2 cartoon/issue, all from freelancers. Interested in printing industry; especially needs general cartoon characters. Prefers finished cartoons. SASE. Reports immediately. Buys all rights on a work-for-hire basis. Pays $10.
Illustrations: Uses 2-3 illustrations/issue, all from freelancers. Interested in "any style-some general, some specific to the industry." Works on assignment only. Samples returned with SASE and request. Reports back on future assignment possiblities. Provide resume, calling card or letter of inquiry to be kept on file for future assignments. Prefers resume, portfolio and samples of style. SASE. Reports in 30-60 days. Buys all rights on a work-for-hire basis. Pays $50-250, sometimes higher.

THE AMERICAN RIFLEMAN, 1600 Rhode Island Ave. NW, Washington DC 20036. (202)783-6505. Editor: William F. Paekerson III. For National Rifle Association members with interests in hunting, competitive shooting, conservation, legislation, hunter safety, gunsmithing and anything technical pertaining to firearms. Monthly. Circ. 1,000,000. Free sample copy.
Illustrations: Buys 8-9/year on shooting sports. Query. SASE. Reports in 2 weeks. Buys first North American serial rights. Inside: Pays $50 minimum, b&w line drawings and washes; on acceptance.

THE AMERICAN SPECTATOR, Box 1969, Bloomington IN 47402. Contact Erich Eichman, managing editor. Concerns politics and literature. Monthly. Circ. 25,000. Original artwork returned after publication. Sample copy $1.
Illustrations: Uses 2-3 illustrations/issue, all from freelancers. Interested in "caricatures of political figures (or portraits with a point of view)." Works on assignment only. Samples returned by SASE. Reports back on future assignment possiblities. Provide resume, brochure and tearsheet to be kept on file for future assignments. Prefers portfolio and samples of style. SASE. Reports in 2 weeks. Buys first North American serial rights. Cover: Pays $100 minimum, b&w line drawings. Inside: Pays $20 minimum, b&w line drawings; on publication.

AMERICAN SQUAREDANCE, Box 488, Huron OH 44839. Editors: Stan and Cathie Burdick. For squaredancers. Monthly. Photocopies OK. Original artwork returned after publication, if requested. Free sample copy.
Cartoons: Uses 1 cartoon/issue; buys 6/year from freelancers. Interested in dance theme; single panel. Prefers finished cartoons. SASE. Reports in 1 week. Buys all rights on a work-for-hire basis. Pays $5-15, halftones and washes; on publication.
Illustrations: Uses 5 illustrations/issue; buys 1/issue from freelancers. Interested in dance. Prefers finished art. SASE. Reports in 1 week. Buys all rights on a work-for-hire basis. Cover: Pays $10-25, b&w line drawings, washes and color-separated art. Inside: Pays $5-15, b&w line drawings and washes; on publication.

AMERICAN TEACHER, 11 Dupont Circle NW, Washington DC 20036. (202)797-4400. Editor: Linda Chavez. For members of American Federation of Teachers and other education personnel.Monthly except June, July and August, with combined Dec./Jan. issue. Circ. 500,000. Original artwork returned after publication, if requested.
Cartoons: Uses 1-2 cartoons/issue; buys 1-2/issue from freelancers. Interested in education, school children and labor. "No anti-teacher or anti-labor stuff." Prefers finished cartoons. SASE. Reports in 3 weeks. Buys all rights on a work-for-hire basis. Pays $25, b&w.
Illustrations: Uses 2-3 illustration/issue; buys 2-3/issue from freelancers. Interested in illustrations "that easily illustrate points of view and abstract themes. Works on assignment only. Samples returned. Does not report back on future assignment possiblities. Prefers portfolio (finished art). SASE. Reports in 3 weeks. Buys all rights on a work-for-hire basis. Negotiates pay, b&w line drawings.

AMERICAN TOOL, DIE & STAMPING NEWS, Box 81, Brighton MI 48116. (313)474-8439. Editor-in-Chief: Art Brown. Art Director: Carol Brown. Bimonthly. Circ. 21,000. Photocopied submissions OK. Pays 60 days after acceptance.
Cartoons: Buys 30/year on current events, the tool, die and stamping industry, and the environment; single panel with gag line. Mail art. SASE. Reports in 1 week. Buys all rights. Pays $15, b&w line drawings; pays 60 days after acceptance. Should be ¼-page: 3⅓x4⅞.

THE AMERICAN ZIONIST, 4 E. 34th St., New York NY 10016. (212)481-1480. Journal of contemporary Jewish affairs. Bimonthly. Circ. 45,000.
Cartoons: Uses 1-3 cartoons/issue; buys all from freelancers. Receives 1-2 submissions/week from freelancers. Interested in Middle East, pro-Israel, depicting political mood of U.S., world. Prefers finished cartoons. SASE. Reports in 3-4 weeks. Buys first rights. Pays on publication.
Illustrations: Uses 2-5 illustrations/issue; buys all from freelancers. Receives 1-2 submissions/week. Interested in Jewish-oriented themes dealing with Israel, Jewish life in U.S. Provide calling card and sample to be kept on file for future assignments. Prefers finished art. SASE. Reports in 3-4 weeks. Buys first North American serial rights. Cover and Inside: Pays $15-25, b&w line drawings; on publication.

AMERICAS, Organization of American States, Washington DC 20006. (202)789-6201. Assistant Editor: Veronica Stoddart. Emphasizes inter-American affairs. Readers are persons interested in inter-American relations and history, culture, geography, and development of Latin American countries. Monthly. Circ. 100,000. Original artwork returned after publication.Free sample copy.
Illustrations: Uses 2-3 illustrations/issue; buys 1/issue from freelancer. "Major need is for illustrations for fiction (short stories). Themes and styles vary according to topic and style of story." Works on assignment only. Samples returned by SASE. Reports back on future assignment possiblities. Provide letter of inquiry, resume and tearsheet to be kept on file for future assignments. Prefers portfolio and samples of style. SASE. Reports in 2 weeks. Buys first worldwide serial rights. Pays $35-75 on publication for inside b&w or color; on publication.
Other Needs: "Occasional need for technical illustrations."

ANIMAL KINGDOM, New York Zoological Park, Bronx NY 10460. (212)220-5121. Contact: Eugene J. Walter Jr. For members of zoological societies and individuals interested in wildlife, zoos and aquariums. Bimonthly. Circ. 100,000.
Illustrations: Uses up to 6 illustrations/issue. Receives 10 submissions/week from freelancers. Interested in wildlife (usually with habitat); occasionally, people. Works on assignment only. Samples returned by SASE. Reports back on future assignment possibilities. Provide brochure, tearsheet and copies of samples to be kept on file for future assignments. Prefers samples of style (photocopies). SASE. Reports in 2 weeks. Buys first North American serial righs. Pays $150 minimum; on acceptance.
Other Needs: "Paintings and b&w drawings. No cartoons."
Tips: "Aside from producing an attractive picture, the most important thing is biological accuracy."

ANIMALS, 350 S. Huntington Ave., Boston MA 02130. Editor-in-Chief: Susan Burns. Art Director: Malcolm Mansfield. For members of 3 affiliated humane organizations in the Northeast. Bimonthly; 8¼x11; 40 pages. Offset. Estab. 1868. Circ. 30,000. Query with samples. SASE. Reports in 2 weeks. Simultaneous submissions OK. Buys one-time or all rights. Sample copy for $1.25 and SASE. Artist's guidelines with SASE.
Illustrations: Buys 2-3/issue on animals. Cover: Pays $50-100, full-color. Inside: Pays $15-40, b&w line drawings; $25-80, color washes and full-color renderings.

THE ANNALS OF ST. ANNE DE BEAUPRE, Box 1000, Ste-Anne De Beaupre, Quebec, Canada G0A 3C0. (418)827-4538. Editor-in-Chief: E. Lefebre. Art Director: F.J. Plourde. For Catholics. Monthly. Circ. 70,000. Free sample copy and artist's guidelines.
Cartoons: Interested in education, family life, humor through youth and religion; single panel with gag line. Query with resume. SASE. Reports in 3 weeks. Buys first North American serial rights. Pays $5 minimum, b&w line drawings.
Illustrations: Interested in education, family life, humor through youth and religion; single panel with gag line. Query with resume. SASE. Reports in 3 weeks. Buys first North American serial rights. Pays $5 minimum, b&w line drawings; on acceptance.

THE ANTIQUARIAN, Box 798, Huntington NY 11743. (516)271-8990. Editor: Marguerite Cantine and Elizabeth Kilpatrick. Concerns antiques, arts, shows and news of the market; for dealers and collectors. Monthly. Circ. 10,000.
Illustrations: "We are one magazine that hates the use of photography but it's more available to us than good illustrations. We recently ran a complete history of the teddy bear issue and would have used all drawings if we could have found an illustrator. Instead we had to use photos." Buys b&w line drawings and washes. Query with resume and samples. SASE. Reports in 4-8 weeks. Buys all rights. Pay "depends on the size of the article. We commission the entire article or issue if possible to one artist." Pays $10 maximum, b&w; on acceptance.
Tips: "Our covers are us. They are children's illusrations from fine, usually German, books circa

1850-1875. If an artist can get the feel of what we're trying to convey with our covers, the rest is easy."

THE ANTIQUES DEALER, 1115 Clifton Ave., Clifton NJ 07013. (201)779-1600 or (212)947-9270. Editor: Kathy Moor O'Brien. For antiques dealers. Monthly. Circ. 7,000. Photocopies OK.
Cartoons: Buys 2-3/year on antiques; single panel. Query or mail art. SASE. Reports in 4 weeks. Buys all rights. Pays $5, b&w line drawings, washes and half tones.
Illustrations: Buys 2-3/year on antiques. Query or mail art. SASE. Reports in 4 weeks. Buys all rights. Cover: Pays $5-10, b&w. Inside: Pays $5, b&w.

APARTMENT LIFE, 1716 Locust, Des Moines IA 50336. (515)284-2119. Art Director: Robert C. Furstenau. For apartment dwellers. Monthly. Circ. 850,000.
Illustrations: Assigns 6-10/issue on lifestyle; humorous or serious. "Illustrators should be highly conceptual in their execution of ideas." Query with samples or arrange interview to show portfolio. SASE. Assignment work only.

APPALACHIA BULLETIN, 5 Joy St., Boston MA 02108. Contact: Managing Editor. Published by "oldest mountaineering/conservation group in U.S." Monthly. "We offer superb exposure to East Coast business and academic markets."

APPALOOSA NEWS, Box 8403, Moscow ID 83843. (208)882-5578. Contact: Editor. For Appaloosa owners, breeders and those interested in horses. Estab. 1950. Circ. 29,000. Monthly. SASE. Reports in 6 weeks. Pays on acceptance.
Cartoons: Buys 8-12/issue on horse shows, tack, Appaloosas and current issues in the Appaloosa industry. Pays $5, b&w. Send finished art.
Illustrations: Buys assigned themes. Pays $10-30, b&w. Query with samples.

APPLEWOOD JOURNAL, Box 1781, San Francisco CA 94101. (415)668-6691. Emphasizes 1980's independent lifestyles. "Reaches a nationwide audience of people that want independence, who are interested in gardening, holistic health, alternative energy, shelter, environment, self-employment, rural living, nature and getting out of the ratrace." Bimonthly. Circ. 35,000. Sample copy $1.50; art guidelines for SASE.
Cartoon Needs: Uses 2-4 cartoons/issue, all from freelancers. Receives 6-8 from freelancers/week. "Cartoons should have nature, rural themes, upbeat approach to 1980's West Coast life-styles, dealing with music, shelter, life-styles, food, alternative energy, new news, technology and high technology, parodies, Jerry Brown type of political cartoons, Zenness, humor, 1980 California-Marin County-hot-tub-est-organic-healthy-self-sufficient-me- generation (parodies)–smart, sharp stuff. And that includes New England Bert & I type of dry witticism, rural and country humor that parodies or reveals life." Format: single or multi-panel, b&w line drawings or b&w washes with gag line. Send finished cartoons and/or if in Bay area arrange for interview with Mr. Kim Huegel, editor. SASE. Reports in 2 weeks. Buys first North American serial rights. Pays $5-25 on publication.
Illustration Needs: Uses 6-8 illustrations/issue, 4-6 from freelancers. Receives 10 from freelancers/week. "We accept unsolicited illustrations all the time . . . quality and theme are what we look for. Given the right situation we will assign an artist spot illustration, covers and other illustration work. And, we like to develop relationships with artists where we work together on a regular basis. We are flexible and also welcome unusual, Ralph Steadman type of work. We'll be careful with your art. Illustrations should preferably be b&w line drawings, washes, airbrush that visualize the following themes–nature, rural scenes, animals, plants, people, technology & high technology, music & musicians, shelter, food, alternatives, life, personalities in the news, humor, hot tub-est-organic-healthy-self sufficient, ala American gothic, civilization gone amok-joys of independence and doing what you like. Fantastic material always welcome! We need more illustrators. We *will* reprint previously published material. Indicate where published and when." Send finished art, and/or if in Bay area, phone Mr. Kim Huegel, editor for appointment. SASE. Reports in 2 weeks. Buys first North American serial rights. Pays $75-300 on publication for b&w cover, $15-150 for inside b&w.

APPLIANCE SERVICE NEWS, 110 W. St. Charles Rd., Lombard IL 60148. Editor/Publisher: William Wingstedt. For owners/managers of service firms, service divisions of sales organizations, electric/gas appliance service shops, and repairmen of home appliances.
Cartoons: Buys 25-30/year. Submit roughs. SASE. Reports in 30 days. Buys all rights. Pays $15-25; on acceptance.

ARARAT, 628 2nd Ave., New York NY 10016. (212)684-7530. Contact: Leo Hamalian. For those interested in Armenian life and culture, for Americans of Armenian descent, and Armenian immigrants. Quarterly. Circ. 2,000.
Illustrations: SASE. Pays on publication.

ARCHERY RETAILER, 225 E. Michigan, Milwaukee WI 53202. (414)276-6600. Editor-in-Chief: Glenn Helgeland. Art Director: Al Jacobs. For archery equipment retailers. Published 5 times/year. Circ. 13,600. Free sample copy.
Cartoons: Buys 7-8/year on archery retailing; single panel. Query with samples or mail roughs. SASE. Reports in 3 weeks. Buys one-time rights. Pays $15-25, b&w line drawings; on publication.

ARES, 257 Park Ave. S, New York NY 10010. (212)673-4103. Contact: Redmond Simonsen. Science fiction, fantasy simulation games for fans and simulation gamers. Bimonthly. Sample copy $3.
Illustrations: Uses about 12 illustrations/issue. Works on assignment. Arrange personal appointment to show portfolio or send samples (tear sheets that need not be returned). Reports back on future assignment possibilities. Prefers b&w line drawings. Buys all rights. Pays $100 minimum b&w/inside, $300 color/cover and $20-30 spot art/page.

ARMY, 2425 Wilson Blvd., Arlington VA 22201. Contact: Managing Editor. "Professional journal devoted to the advancement of the military arts and sciences." Monthly. Circ. 123,779.
Needs: Send samples. Reports in 6 weeks. Pays $25 and up for inside b&w drawings; on acceptance.

ARTIST'S MARKET, 9933 Alliance Rd., Cincinnati Oh 45242. (513)984-0717. Contact: Editor. Annual directory of freelance markets for commercial artists listing places to sell their artwork. Estab. 1975. Send b&w original art; photos or veloxes OK. SASE. Reports in 4-6 weeks. Buys one-time rights.
Needs: Buys 50-100/year. "I need examples of art that have been sold to one of the listings in *Artist's Market*. Thumb through the book to see the type of art I'm seeking. The art must have been freelanced; it cannot have been done as staff work for one of the firms listed herein. Include the name of the listing which purchased the work, what the art was used for, the rights purchased, the person with whom you worked at the firm or organization, and the payment you received." Pays $5 on acceptance; free copy of *Artist's Market* when published.

ASSEMBLY ENGINEERING, Hitchcock Publishing Co., Hitchcock Bldg., Wheaton IL 60137. Editor-in-chief: Robert T. Kelly. Managing Editor: Richard D. Holtz. For design and manufacturing engineers and managers. Monthly; 8¼x11¼; 88 pages. Offset. Estab. 1958. Circ. 73,000. Mail art. SASE. Reports in 3 weeks. Photocopies OK "but original required if accepted." Buys all rights, but may reassign rights to artist after publication. Pays on acceptance. Free sample copy.
Cartoons: Buys 15/year on product assembly, design and conversion to metrics; single panel. Metric conversion is increasingly important in our field; we need cartoons on that subject. Send roughs of suggested cartoon series. Such cartoons should refer to the humorous side of conversion, not the difficulties. Fine detail may be lost in printing, artwork should thus be relatively simple." Pays $15 minimum, line drawings.
Tips: "If you don't have an engineering or manufacturing background, bounce your ideas off some engineers you know, and then send us samples."

ASSOCIATION AND SOCIETY MANAGER, Brentwood Publishing Corp., 825 S. Barrington Ave., Los Angeles CA 90049. Contact: Kathy Kubik.
Needs: Submit published samples. SASE. Reports in 30 days. Buys all rights. Pays $45, spot art; $225, full-color cover; on acceptance.

ATLANTA SKIER, 1430 W. Peachtree St. NW, Atlanta GA 30309. (404)892-1286. Emphasizes skiing and outdoor recreation for Atlanta and southern residents who are active in skiing and other outdoor sports. Published 5xyear. Circ. 4,000. Free sample copy.
Cartoons: Uses 0-1 cartoon/issue; buys all from freelancers. Interested in humorous skiing situations aimed particularly at Southerners.Prefers single panel cartoons with gag line. Send finished cartoons to Peggy Nieman, editor to be kept on file. Buys one-time rights. Pays $10/b&w on publication.

THE ATLANTIC ADVOCATE, P.O. Box 3370, Fredericton, New Brunswick, Canada E3B 5A2. Editor: H.P. Wood. For professional men and women interested in matters concerning the Atlantic provinces. Monthly. Sample copy $1.00. Mail art. Buys first North American serial rights. Pays on publication.

ATLANTIC MONTHLY, 8 Arlington St., Boston MA 02116. (617)536-9500. Art Director: Stephen Snider. For a professional, academic audience. Circ. 325,000. Original artwork returned after publication.
Illustrations: Uses 7-10 illustrations/issue; buys 7/issue from freelancers. Receives 7-10 submissions/week from freelancers. Interested in "illustrations for fictional short stories, book reviews; illustrations for political reports, foreign and domestic—portraits and conceptualizations of more abstract political themes." Works on assignment only. Samples returned by SASE. Reports back on future assignment possibilities. Provide resume, calling card, letter of inquiry, brochure or tearsheet to be kept on file for future assignments. Prefers portfolio or samples of style. SASE. Reports in 2 weeks. Buys one-time reproduction rights. Pays "standard fee".

AUSTIN MAGAZINE, 307 E. 2nd St., Austin TX 78701. (512)476-8654. Art Director: Barbara Jezek. City magazine. Monthly. Circ. 8,500. Original artwork returned after publication.
Illustrations: Contact Paul Beutel. Uses 4 illustrations/issue; buys all from freelancers. Varied themes, business through lighter themes; all styles; b&w mostly, some color. Works on assignment only. Samples returned by SASE. Reports back on future assignment possiblities. Provide brochure to be kept on file for future assignments. Arrange interview to show portfolio or send samples of style. SASE. Reports in 1 week. Buys one-time rights. Pays $15-75, b&w; $25-125, color; on publication.
Cartoons: Uses 3 cartoons/year; buys all from freelancers. Interested in political; panel to illustrate situation. Prefers finished cartoons. SASE. Reports in 1 week. Pays on publication.

AUTO & FLAT GLASS JOURNAL, 2844 Westchester Ave., Bronx NY 10461. (212)863-1800. Editor: Eric Cosentino. For auto glass and flat glass replacement specialists. Monthly. Circ. 2,800.
Cartoons: Uses less than 1 cartoon/issue, all from freelancers. Receives approximately 2 submission/month from freelancers. Interested in cartoons showing automobiles, focusing on auto glass, and illustrating service shops for auto glass, business management and retail salesmanship. Mail art. SASE. Reports in 60 days. Buys one-time rights. Pays $15-30, spot drawing; on acceptance.

AUTO TRIM NEWS, 1623 Grand Ave., Baldwin NY 11510. Contact: Nat Danas. Query. Reports in 30 days. Pays on publication.
Illustrations: Pays $5, spot drawings; $25-50, cover design. Needs pen and ink, step-by-step technical illustrations.

AUTOMATIC MACHINING MAGAZINE, 65 Broad St., Rochester NY 14614. Tel. (716)454-3763. Editorial Director: Wayne Wood. Emphasizes metalworking. Readers are management and engineering personnel. Monthly. Circ. 16,000. Original artwork not returned after publication. Sample copy $1.50.
Cartoons: Uses 3-4 cartoons/issue, all from freelancers. Receives 5 submissions/week from freelancers. Interested in engineering and metalworking. Formats: single panel b&w line drawings with gag lines. Prefers finished cartoons. SASE. Reports in 1 week. Buys one-time rights. Pays $5-10; on acceptance.

AUTOMOBILE QUARTERLY, 221 Nassau St., Princeton NJ 08540. (609)924-7555. Art Director: Theodore R.F. Hall. Concerns autos and auto history, primarily through photographic means.Circ. 40,000. Quarterly. Original artwork returned after publication, by arrangement.
Cartoons: Uses less than 1 cartoon/issue. Interested in antique and classic cars. Prefers roughs. SASE. Reports in 2 weeks. Buys various rights. Negotiates pay; pays on publication.
Illustrations: Uses 8 illustrations/issue, all from freelancers. Interested in antique, classic cars and cutaway technical illustrations. Works on assignment only. Samples returned by SASE. Reports back on future assignment possiblities. Provide "sample of rendering" to be kept on file for future assignments. Prefers samples of style. SASE. Reports in 2 weeks. Buys various rights. Negotiates pay (part of payment may be posters of work); pays on publication.

AUTOMOTIVE AGE, 6931 Van Nuys Blvd., Van Nuys CA 91405. (213)873-1320. Editor: Chris Hosford. Managing Editor: Mo Mehlsak. Art Director: David Folkman. For college-educated owners and management personnel of new car dealerships. Emphasizes the dealership owner as a successful businessman and an individual with a private nonbusiness life. Monthly. Circ. 44,000. Simultaneous submissions OK if accompanied by list of other publications receiving same or very similar material. Original artwork not returned after publication. Free sample copy.
Cartoons: Uses 1 cartoon/issue; buys 1/issue from freelancers. Receives 10 submissions/week from freelancers. Interested in themes on retail auto sales and management; single and double panel. Prefers roughs. SASE. Reports in 2-4 weeks. Buys all rights on a work-for-hire basis, but

may reassign upon request. Pays $10 minimum, b&w; $20 minimum, color; on publication.
Illustrations: Uses 1 illustration/issue, all from freelancers. Receives 2 submissions/week from freelancers. Works on assignment only. Provide brochure and flyers to be kept on file for future assignments. Prefers portfolio. SASE. Reports in 2-4 weeks. Buys all rights on a work-for-hire basis, but may reassign upon request. Pays on publication.

AVIATION QUARTERLY, Box 606, Plano TX 75074. (214)423-8516. Managing Editor: Glenn Bierman. Concerns aviation, classic planes, aviation history and personalities. Mail large aviation-related drawings, paintings, etc. SASE. Reports in 2-4 weeks. Negotiates payment.

AVIATION TRAVEL, Box 606, Plano TX 75074. (214)423-8516. Editor: Glenn Bierman.
Cartoons: Buys themes related to private and business travel via small planes. Primarily interested in material that the average private pilot can relate to. SASE. Reports in 2-4 weeks. Pays $10-20 for cartoons. Negotiates pay for illustrations.

B.C. BUSINESS, 601-510 West Hastings St., Vancouver, B.C., Canada V6B 1L8. (604)689-2021. Editor-in-Chief: J.R. Martin. For business and professional men and women. Monthly Circ. 21,000. Previously published, photocopied and simultaneous submissions OK. Free sample copy.
Illustrations: Buys 6/year on assigned themes. Query; Canadian artists only. SASE. Reports in 3 weeks. Buys first rights. Cover: Pays $200-400, color. Inside: Pays $10-50, b&w.

B.C. OUTDOORS, 202-1132 Hamilton St., Vancouver, British Columbia, Canada V6B 2S2. (604)687-1581. Editor: Donald Stainsby. Readers are interested in the outdoors. Monthly Circ. 36,000. Original artwork returned after publication, unless bought outright. Free sample copy.
Cartoons: Uses 3-4 cartoons/issue; buys all from freelancers. Cartoons should pertain to the outdoors "including fishing, but seldom hunting. All outdoors recreation, but not competitive sports. No macho put-downs of women, please, they're fine campers/outdoors people in this neck of the woods." Format: single panel b&w line drawings with or without gag line. Prefers finished cartoons. SASE. Pays $7.50 on acceptance. Reports in 2 weeks. Buys one-time rights.
Illustrations: Uses 6 illustrations/year. Interested in outdoors, creatures and activities as stories require. Freelancers selected "generally because I've seen their work." Format: b&w line drawings for inside, rarely for cover; b&w washes for inside; and color washes for inside and cover. Works on assignment only. Samples returned by SASE. Reports back on future assignment possibilities. Arrange personal appointment to show portfolio or send samples of style. SASE. Reports in 2 weeks. Buys first North American serial rights or all rights on a work-for-hire basis. Payment negotiable, depending on nature of assignment. Pays on acceptance.
Other Needs: Maps on assignment.

BABY CARE, 52 Vanderbilt Ave., New York NY 10017. Concerns baby care from birth through the first year. Circ. 500,000. Quarterly. SASE. Pays on acceptance.
Illustrations: Contact Ruth Kitaif. Buys 1/issue on "life with baby." Pays $100-200, b&w; $200-300, color. Arrange interview to show portfolio.

BACKPACKER INCLUDING WILDERNESS CAMPING, 65 Adams St., Bedford Hills NY 10507. Editor: Dawn de Boer. Concerns backpacking and the outdoors. Bimonthly. Circ. 150,000. Sample copy $2.75; free artist's guidelines.
Cartoons: Buys 12/year on backpacking or camping; single panel with gag line. Query with samples. Pays $25-50, b&w line drawings; on acceptance.
Illustrations: Buys 20/year on the environment, backpacking, camping and nature. Query with previously published work. SASE. Reports in 6-8 weeks. Buys reprint or all rights. Inside: Pays $10-75, b&w line drawings; on acceptance.
Tips: "Spot illustrations are always needed."

BAJA CALIFORNIA BULLETIN, Apdo. Postal 127, La Paz, Baja California Sur, Mexico. Phone: LA PAZ 2-57-14. Contact Luisa Porter. Emphasizes tourism in Baja California. Estab. 1972. Circ. 10,000. Bimonthly. Exchange coupons necessary for return of submissions. Reports in 2 weeks. Pays on acceptance.
Cartoons: Contact Luisa Porter. Buys very few/issue; Mexican-oriented humorous material. Pays $5-20, b&w. Query and send samples.
Illustrations: Very seldom used. Negotiates pay, b&w. Query with samples.

BARTER COMMUNIQUE, Box 2527, Sarasota FL 33578. (813)349-2242. Art Director: Robert J. Murley. Concerns bartering; for radio, TV stations, newspapers, magazines, travel and ad agencies. Published every 6 months. Circ. 30,000. Pays on publication.

Cartoons: Buys 5/issue on barter situations. Send roughs. Pays $5, b&w; on publication.
Illustrations: Query with sample. SASE. Reports in 2 weeks. Pays $5, b&w; on publication.

BE BEAUTIFUL, Redbook Publishing Co., 230 Park Ave., New York NY 10017. (212)983-3138. Editor: Kay Sullivan. For young women interested in self-improvement, with emphasis on beauty, fashion, diet and exercise. Biannual. Circ. 400,000.
Illustrations: Uses 20-50/year on beauty and fashion themes. Mail art, query with samples, or arrange interview to show portfolio. SASE. Reports in 3 weeks. Buys all rights. Inside: Pays $50-75, b&w line drawings and washes; $100, color washes; and $1000, special sections; on acceptance.

BEAVER, 235 Park Ave. S., New York NY 10003. Editor-in-Chief: Jayson Rollands. Art Director: Ben Harvey. For ages 18-40 with high school education, interested in pretty women and sex. Bimonthly; 8½x11; 80 pages. Offset. Estab. 1976. Circ. 200,000. Mail art. SASE. Reports in 4 weeks. Photocopies OK. Buys first North American serial rights. Pays on acceptance. Sample copy $2.
Cartoons: Buys 180/year on erotic themes. Pays $50, b&w line drawings, halftones and washes.
Illustrations: Buys 24/year on assigned themes. Pays $50-400, b&w.

THE BEEHIVE, 201 8th Ave. S., Nashville TN 37203. Editor-in-Chief: Martha Wagner. Cartoon Editor: Dave Dawson. For ages 9-11 in church school. Weekly. Circ. 250,000. Free sample copy.
Cartoons: Uses 1 cartoon/issue; buys 1/issue from freelancers. Receives 25 submissions/week from freelancers. "Cartoons for children, not about them." No "swearing, off-color, smoking/drinking, adult-type" themes. Uses line drawings, halftones and washes. Prefers finished cartoons. SASE. Reports in 1 month. Buys one-time rights. Minimum payment: $7.50, b&w; $35, color; on acceptance.
Illustrations: Uses 8 illustrations/issue, all from freelancers. Interested in illustrations for specific stories. "Knowledge of human figure is important." Works on assignment only. Samples returned by SASE. Reports back on future assignment possibilities. Provide brochure, flyer and tear sheet to be kept on file for future assignments. Prefers finished art. SASE. Reports in 2 weeks. Buys all rights on a work-for-hire basis. Pays on acceptance.

BEHAVIORAL MEDICINE, Magazines for Medicine Inc., 475 5th Ave., New York NY 10017. (212)889-1050. Art Director: Paul Nemesure. For physicians in family practice and psychiatry interested in patient management. Monthly. Circ. 100,000. Simultaneous submissions and previously published work OK. Sample copy $2.
Cartoons: Buys 2 cartoons/issue from freelancers. Receives 10 submissions/week from freelancers. Interested in medical and psychiatric themes; single, double or multipanel with gag line. Query with samples. SASE. Reports in 4 weeks. Buys various rights. Pays $50 maximum, b&w line drawings, washes and gray opaques; on publication.
Tips: "We prefer strong, simple ideas to emphasize a point."

BEND OF THE RIVER, Box 239, Perrysburg OH 43551. Editors-in-Chief: Chris Alexander and Lee Raizk. For local history enthusiasts. Monthly Circ. 1,500. Previously published and photocopied submissions OK. Original artwork returned after publication. Sample copy 50¢.
Cartoons: Buys 1 cartoon/issue from freelancers. Interested in nostalgia; single panel with gag line. Prefers resume. SASE. Buys first North American serial rights or all rights on a work-for-hire basis. Pays $5, b&w line drawings.
Illustrations: Buys 20 illustrations/year. Interested in "historic buildings for ads." Works on assignment only. No samples returned. Reports back on future assignment possibilities. Prefers roughs. SASE. Reports in 1 week. Buys first North American serial rights or all rights on a work-for-hire basis. Inside: Pays $5, b&w line drawings.
Other Needs: Advertising.

BEST WISHES, Box 8, Station C, Toronto, Ontario, Canada M6J 3M8. Contact: Mrs. K. Applegate. For new mothers. Quarterly. Mail art. Reports in 1 month. Previously published work OK. Pays on acceptance.
Needs: Buys spot drawings, cartoons and illustrations relating to parenting infants and toddlers. Fees negotiable.

BETTER HOMES & GARDENS, Meredith Corp., 1716 Locust, Des Moines IA 50321. Contact: Cartoon Editor. For readers who want to "do something" for the family and home. Monthly. Circ. 8,000,000. Original artwork not returned after publication. Free artist's guidelines.
Cartoons: Uses 2 cartoons/issue; buys all from freelancers. Receives 50-75 submissions/week

from freelancers. Interested in current events, education, environment, family life, humor through youth, politics, religion, retirement, hobbies, sports and businessmen; single panel with gag line. Prefers finished cartoons. SASE. Reports in 2- weeks. Buys all rights. Pays $200 minimum, b&w line drawings; on acceptance.

BEYOND REALITY, 303 W. 42nd St., New York NY 10036. Contact: Harry Belil. For those interested in the occult, UFOs, psychic and strange.
Illustrations: Mail art. Reports in 30 days. Buys all rights. Pays $15-20, 8½x11 spot drawings; $35-50, half-page editorial illustration. Cover: 4-color art; $100-150. Pays on acceptance.

BIG FARMER, 131 Lincoln Hwy., Frankfort IL 60423. (815)469-2163. Editor: Rich Fee. "For farmers with 400 or more cropland acres; topics covered are money management, purchasing decisions, crop production techniques and marketing wisdom." Monthly. Circ. (except July) 325,000. Free sample copy and artist's guidelines.
Cartoons: Submit to editorial department. Buys 9/year on farm-related topics; single panel with gag line. Query with samples. Pays $20 minimum, b&w line drawings; on publication. SASE. Reports in 6 weeks. Buys all rights.
Illustrations: Submit to editorial department. Buys current events and farming topics. Buys cover opaque watercolors and inside b&w line drawings, washes and opaque watercolors. Query with resume and samples. Inside: Pays $35 minimum, b&w; on publication. SASE. Reports in 6 weeks. Buys all rights.
Other Needs: Design. Contact Andrew Miller, production manager. Uses artists for covers and layout. Arrange interview to show portfolio. SASE. Reports in 6 weeks. Buys all rights.

BIKE WORLD, Box 366, Mt. View CA 94040. Managing Editor: Kevin Shafer. For participant bike tourists and racers of high level of sophistication. Monthly. Submit art. Reports in 1 week. Buys all rights. Pays on publication. Will send sample copy to artists.
Illustrations: Pays $5, spot art; $50-100, 8½x11 minimum, color-separated cover designs.

BILLIARDS DIGEST, 875 N. Michigan, Chicago IL 60611. Tel. (312)266-7179. Editor: Dennis Bergendorf. Emphasizes pool and billiards. Readers are accomplished players and hardcore fans. Bimonthly Circ. 7,000. Estab. 1978. Original artwork returned after publication. Sample copy $2; art guidelines for SASE.
Cartoons: Uses 2 cartoons/issue, both supplied by freelance artists. Receives 1 submission/week from freelancers. "We are anxious to use good art, so we would probably buy more if available. The only restriction is it must pertain to pool/billiards. We commission specific themes from time to time." Formats: single panel b&w washes with gag line. Prefers roughs, finished cartoons, or samples of style. SASE. Reports in 2 weeks. Buys first North American serial rights. Pays $15 and up/b&w cartoon on publication; negotiable payment/color cartoon.
Illustrations: Use 1-2 illustrations/issue, all supplied by freelance artists. Receives 1 submission/week from freelancers."Most illustrations are commissioned because of specific story needs. As for specific needs, "we have no set style, but usually run one humorous or reminiscent piece that can use 'light' approach. Open to new concepts. We haven't put wash on cover but would consider." Uses b&w line drawings and washes for inside. Provide letter of inquiry, flyer or tear sheet to be kept on file for future assignments. Send resume, finished art, roughs, samples of style, or arrange for personal appointment to show portfolio. SASE. Reports in 2 weeks. Buys first North American serial rights.

BLACK AMERICAN LITERATURE FORUM, Parsons Hall 237, Indiana State University, Terre Haute IN 47809. (812)232-6311, ext 2760. Editor-in-Chief: Joe Weixlmann. Concerns black American writers and their work. Quarterly. Circ. 950. Simultaneous submissions OK. Sample copy $1; free artist's guidelines.
Illustrations: Buys 8/issue on black life. Mail art. SASE. Reports in 2 weeks. Buys all rights, but may reassign rights to artist after publication. Cover and inside: Pays $15 maximum, b&w line drawings; on acceptance.

THE BLACK COLLEGIAN, 3217 Martin Luther King, Jr. Blvd., New Orleans LA 70125. Editor: Kalama ya Salaam. For black college students. Bimonthly during academic year. Query: "We will tell them what articles we need illustrated and they can submit material to meet our needs." Previously published work OK. Buys serial and first serial rights. Pays on publication. Sample copy available.
Cartoons: Pays $5.
Illustrations: Cover: Pays $75, color. Inside: Pays $25, spot drawing; $30-50, full-color. Issue themes: Careers in health, September; black history, November; work, study, travel and engi-

neering, January; jobs and science, March; women and entertainment, May.

BLACK FORUM MAGAZINE, Box 1090, Bronx NY 10451. Art Directors: Freddy Richardson and Barry Dye. For unpublished artists and writers interested in literary subjects. Estab. 1975. Circ. 2,000. Semiannual. SASE. Reports in 2-3 months. Pays on publication.
Cartoons: Pays $15 maximum. Query or mail roughs.
Illustrations: Assigns themes. Pays $15 maximum. Query with samples.

THE BLACK WARRIOR REVIEW, University of Alabama, Box 2936, University AL 35486. (205)348-5526. Editor: Marne Prange. For general literary audience. Published semiannually. Circ. 1,000. Sample copy $2.50.
Illustrations: Buys assigned themes or for artistic value. Submit art or query with samples. SASE. Reports in 4 weeks. Buys all rights, but may reassign rights to artist after publication. Cover: Pays $25, b&w; on publication.

THE BLADE SUNDAY MAGAZINE, 541 Superior St., Toledo OH 43660. Editor: Tom Gearhart. Weekly. Circ. 210,000. Query. Previously published and simultaneous submissions OK. Free sample copy.
Illustrations: Buys 6-12/year on local or regional themes. "Most of our original art is done by staff artists or Toledo-area people. We currently use very little outside freelance illustration since it is hard to illustrate a Toledo story with work from a New York artist." Query. SASE. Reports in 3 weeks. Buys one-time rights. Cover: Pays $30-75, color. Inside: Pays $35-50, color; $20-30, b&w; on publication.

BLUEGRASS UNLIMITED, Box 111, Broad Run VA 22014. Contact: Peter V. Kuykendall.
Illustrations: Pen and ink cartoons and spot drawings on old-time, traditional or bluegrass country music. Buys all rights, but sometimes reassigns rights to artist after publication. Pays $15-25 plus; on publication.

BLUENOSE MAGAZINE, Box 580, Port Maitland, Nova Scotia, Canada BOW 2VO. (902)649-2789. Art Director: Bill Crowell. "For and about our 'maritime' way of living—history, nostalgia, environment, etc." Estab. 1976. Circ. 3,000. Quarterly. SASE. Reports in 6-8 weeks. Pays on acceptance.
Illustrations: Buys 5/issue on assigned themes. Pays $5, b&w. Query with samples.

BODY FASHIONS/INTIMATE APPAREL, 757 3rd Ave., New York NY 10017. (212)888-4364. Editor: Jill Jacobson. Information for merchandise managers, buyers, manufacturers and suppliers about men's and women's hosiery and underwear and women's intimate apparel and leisurewear. Monthly. Circ. 13,500.
Illustrations: Interested in fashion illustrations of intimate apparel. Do not mail artwork. Arrange interview to show portfolio. Works on assignment only. Keeps file consisting of editor's comments on portfolio review, and samples of work. Reports in 4 weeks. Pays on publication.

BON APPETIT, 5900 Wilshire Blvd., Los Angeles CA 90036. Art Director: Bernard Rotondo. For affluent young men and women interested in food, cooking, wine and "the good things of life." Circ. 1,000,000. Monthly. SASE. Pays on publication.
Illustrations: Buys 1-6/issue. Pays $75-150, b&w; $300-500, color. Query with samples or arrange interview to show portfolio.

THE BOOK MART, Box 481, Pinellas Park FL 33565. Editor: David G. MacLean. Concerns book collecting and the used-book trade. Monthly. Circ. 1,500. Original artwork not returned after publication.
Cartoons: Uses 1 cartoon/issue, all from freelancers. Receives 0-10 submissions/week from freelancers. Interested in book collecting, antiquarian book selling and used-book stores. Prefers roughs or finished cartoons. SASE. Reports in 3-4 weeks. Buys first North American serial rights. Pays $5, b&w; on publication.
Illustrations: Uses 1-4 illustrations/issue; number bought from freelancers varies. Receives few submissions/week from freelancers. Interested in pen-and-ink portraits. Provide letter of inquiry to be kept on file for future assignments. Prefers samples of style. SASE. Reports in 2 weeks. Buys first North American serial rights. Pays $5-10, b&w; on publication.

BOWHUNTER, 3808 S. Calhoun St., Fort Wayne IN 46807. (219)432-5772. Editor-in-Chief: M.R. James. Concerns hunting with bows and arrows. Bimonthly. Circ. 120,000.
Cartoons: Uses few cartoons; buys 1/issue from freelancer. Interested in "bowhunting and

wildlife. No unsafe hunting conditions; single panel." Prefers roughs. SASE. Reports in 4 weeks. Buys all rights on a work-for-hire basis; will reassign rights. Pays $15-25, line drawings; on acceptance.
Illustrations: Uses 1-2 illustrations/issue, all from freelancers. Receives few submissions/week from freelancers. Interested in "wildlife-bowhunting scenes." Works on assignment only. Samples returned by SASE. Reports back on future assignment possibilities. Provide brochure or flyer to be kept on file for future assignments. Prefers roughs or sample of style. SASE. Reports in 4 weeks. Buys all rights on a work-for-hire basis; will reassign rights. Cover: Pays $50-250, color. Inside: Pays $25-150, b&w; on acceptance.

BOWLERS JOURNAL, 875 N. Michigan Ave., Suite 3734, John Hancock Center, Chicago IL 60611. (312)266-7171. Managing Editor: Jim Dressel. Monthly Circ. 19,000. Simultaneous submissions and previously published work OK. Sample copy.
Cartoons: Buys 1/issue on bowling; single panel. Query with samples or mail finished art. SASE. Reports in 2 months. Buys one-time rights. Pays $5-25, b&w line drawings; $75, feature; on acceptance.
Other Needs: Design. Query with previously published work.

BOY'S LIFE, North Brunswick NJ 08902. Cartoon Editor: Jon Halter. For boys ages 8-14. Monthly. Estab. 1911. Circ. 2,000,000. Query. Reports in 2 weeks. Buys first North American serial rights. Pays on acceptance.
Cartoons: Buys 4-6/issue on sports or general interest. "No cute stuff." Pays $75.
Illustrations: Assigns b&w line drawings, line and wash, and full-color illustrations.

BRANCHING OUT, CANADIAN MAGAZINE FOR WOMEN, New Women's Magazine Society, Box 4098, Edmonton, Alberta, Canada T6E 4S8. (403)433-4021. Editor-in-Chief: Sharon Batt. Art Director: Barbara Hartmann. For Canadian women interested in creative work and feminist issues. Quarterly.Circ. 4,000. Original artwork returned after publication.
Needs: Prefers portfolio; unsolicited work from Canadian women only. SASE. Reports in 4 weeks. Buys first North American serial rights. Pays on publication. Sample copy $1.75. Pays $5-15, cover designs, cartoons and illustrations; on publication.

BREAD, Nazarene Publishing House, 6401 The Paseo, Kansas City MO 64131. (816)333-7000. Editor-in-Chief: Debbie Salter. For ages 12-17 with denominational interests. Monthly. Circ. 40,000. Previously published and simultaneous submissions OK. Original artwork returned after publication. Free sample copy and artist's guidelines.
Cartoons: Buys 6 cartoons/year; buys all from freelancers. Receives 10 submissions/week from freelancers. Interested in humor through youth—teen, school, religious dating; single panel with gag line. Prefers finished cartoons. Reports in 4-6 weeks. Buys all rights, but may reassign rights to artist after publication. Pays $6-10, b&w line drawings; on acceptance.
Illustrations: Uses 6 illustrations/year; buys all from freelancers. Interested in teen, education and religion. Works on assignment only. Samples returned by SASE. Reports back on future assignment possibilities. Provide tear sheet to be kept on file for future assignments. Prefers portfolio. SASE. Reports in 4-6 weeks. Buys all rights on a work-for-hire basis; will reassign rights. Cover: Pays $25-75, color. Inside: Pays $6-20, b&w; on acceptance.

BRIGADE LEADER, Box 150, Wheaton IL 60187. (312)665-0630. For Christian laymen and adult male leaders of boys enrolled in the Brigade man-boy program. Circ. 16,500. Published 4 times/year. Simultaneous submissions and previously published work OK. Original artwork not returned after publication. Sample copy $1; free artist's guidelines.
Cartoons: Editor: Michael Chiapperino. Uses 1 cartoon/issue, all from freelancers. Receives 10 submissions/week from freelancers. Interested in sports, nature and youth; single panel with gag line. "Keep it clean." Prefers roughs. SASE. Buys all rights on a work-for-hire basis; will reassign rights. Pays $10 minimum, b&w line drawings; on publication.
Illustrations: Contact: Lawrence Libby. Uses 2 illustrations/issue. Interested in man and boy subjects, sports, camping—out of doors, family. Works on assignment only. Samples returned by SASE. Reports back on future assignment possiblities. Provide resume and flyer to kept on file for future assignments. Prefers portfolio and samples of style. Reports in 1 week. Buys all rights on a work-for-hire basis; will reassign rights. Cover: Pays $80-100, b&w line drawings and washes. Inside: Pays $50-85, b&w line drawings and washes.

BRONZE THRILLS, 1220 Harding St., Box 2257, Ft. Worth TX 76113. For middle and lower income blacks. Monthly. For sample copy send 50¢ for postage.
Cartoons: Buys 100/year; 5x7; no over-used sex. Reports in 90 days. Buys all rights. Pays $7.50; on acceptance.

BROTHERHOOD OF MAINTENANCE OF WAY EMPLOYES JOURNAL, 12050 Woodward Ave., Detroit MI 48203. Associate Editor: R.J. Williamson. For members of international railroad maintenance workers' union, who build, repair and maintain tracks, buildings and bridges. Monthly. Circ. 150,000. Previously published, photocopied and simultaneous submissions OK. Original artwork returned after publication. Free sample copy.
Cartoons: Uses 3 cartoons/issue; buys less than 1/issue from freelancers. Receives less than 1 submission/week from freelancers. Interested in railroad themes; single panel. Prefers finished cartoons. SASE. Reports in 2 weeks. Buys simultaneous rights. Pays $5-15, line drawings; on publication.

BROWARD LIFE, 3081 E. Commercial Blvd., Ft. Lauderdale FL 33308. (305)491-6350. Editor: W.D. Luening. Emphasizes leisure activities in Broward County. "We are a regional magazine of general interest. Content emphasizes life style improvement for government entertainment fashion." Monthly. Circ. 20,000.
Illustrations: Buys 2-5/issue for existing stories. Interested only in themes of local interest. Arrange interview to show portfolio. SASE. Reports in 3 weeks. Pays $50-500; on publication.

BULLETIN OF THE ATOMIC SCIENTISTS, Educational Foundation for Nuclear Science, 1020 E. 58th St., Kent Hall, Room 105, Chicago IL 60637. Contact: Susan Cullen. For scientists, technologists, legislators, government people and the energy industry; emphasis on disarmament and nuclear weaponry, nuclear power, energy, environment and scientists. Monthly (except July and August). Circ. 25,000. Sample copy $2.
Cartoons: Buys 100/year on environment, politics, science, technology, energy (especially nuclear), developing countries, weapons and disarmament; single panel with gag line. Mail art or query with samples. SASE. Reports in 1 week. Buys first rights. Pays $20 minimum, b&w line drawings, washes and gray opaques; on acceptance.

BUSINESS & COMMERCIAL AVIATION, Hangar C, Westchester City Airport, White Plains NY 10604. Art Director: Elaine Jones. Technical publication for corporate pilots. Monthly; 8¼x11+; 120 pages. Offset. Estab. 1958. Circ. 55,000. Query with samples. SASE. Reports in 4 weeks. Photocopies OK. Buys all rights, but may reassign rights to artist after publication. Pays on acceptance. Free sample copy.
Illustrations: Buys 15-20/year on aviation. "We generally only use artists with a fairly realistic style. This is a serious business publication—graphically conservative." Cover: Pays $350-1,100, color. Inside: Pays $100-500, color; $50-300, b&w. Pays $5/hour minimum, paste-up/mechanicals; local artists only. Pays $100 minimum, portraits of editors for monthly columns, printed size 2+x3".

BUSINESS INSURANCE, 740 N. Rush, Chicago IL 60611. (312)649-5286. Editor: Kathryn J. McIntyre. Emphasizes commercial insurance. Weekly. Circ. 36,000. Sample copy $1; free art guidelines.
Cartoons: Uses 2 cartoons/issue; buys all from freelancers. Receives 2 submissions/week from freelancers. Interested in business related cartoons only. Prefers single or multi panel b&w line drawings. Send resume and/or samples of style. Reports in 2 weeks. Works on assisnment only. Samples returned by SASE. Buys first North American serial and all rights. Pays $10-50 for b&w; on publication.
Illustrations: Uses 2 illustrations/issue; buys 1/issue from freelancers. Receives 1 submission/week from freelancers. Interested in "business oriented management. No travelling salesmen." Works on assignment primarily but will consider unsolicited material. Prefers b&w line drawings for inside. Send resume and/or samples of style. SASE. Reprts in 2 weeks. Buys all rights. Pays $10-50 for inside b&w; on publication.

BUSINESS TODAY, Aaron Burr Hall, Princeton NJ 08540. (609)921-1111. Editor: Alan G. Thomas. For college undergraduates interested in business, politics and careers in those fields. Published 3 times/academic year; 8+x10⅞; 52 pages. Offset. Estab. 1968. Circ. 205,000. Query with resume or samples, or mail art. SASE. Previous work as magazine illustrator preferred. Reports in 1-2 months. Previously published, photocopied and simultaneous submissions OK. Buys one-time, reprint or simultaneous rights. Pays on publication. Free sample copy and artist's guidelines.
Cartoons: Buys 2-6/issue on current events, education, environment, politics, college life and careers; prefers single panel. "Keep the student readership in mind; no typical scenes with executives and secretaries." Pays $10 minimum, b&w line drawings and washes; $20 minimum, color.
Illustrations: Buys 10-20/issue on current events, education, environment, politics, college life

and careers. "We like the style of *The New Yorker.*" Cover: Pays $50 minimum, color; $25 minimum, b&w. Inside: Pays $20 minimum, color; $10 minimum, b&w.

BUSINESS WEEK, 1221 Avenue of the Americas, New York NY 10020. Art Director: John R. Vogler. Original artwork returned after publication.
Cartoons: Uses 6-10 cartoons/issue; buys all from freelancers. Interested in op ed style. Prefers tearsheets. SASE. Reports on request only.
Illustrations: Uses 6-12 illustrations/issue; buys all from freelancers. "Most art is commissioned but we welcome samples from artists who are in easy reach of New York City." Themes vary; mostly op ed. Works on assignment only. Samples returned by SASE, on request only. Provide tearsheet to be kept on file for future assignments. Prefers samples of style, or tearsheets (non-returnable). SASE. No report unless requested. Pays $100 per column, spot illustrations; $750 for covers.

BUSINESS WORLD MAGAZINE, Box 24, Waterloo, Ontario Canada. (519)578-2580. Emphasize general and community business for small- to medium-sized businesses. Monthly. Circ. 32,000. Free art guidelines.
Cartoons: Uses 1-2 cartoons/issue; buys all from freelancers. Receives 2 submissions/week from freelancers. Interested in general business. Prefers single panel b&w line drawings with gag line. Send resume, roughs, samples of style or finished cartoons to Ron Mason. SASE. Reports in 2 weeks. Buys first North American serial rights. Pays $15-20 for b&w on publication.
Illustrations: Uses 1-2 illustrations/issue; buys all from freelancers. Receives 2 submissions/week from freelancers. Interested in editorial themes for individual business articles. Keeps file of samples for future assignments. Send resume, roughs, samples of style or finished art to R. Mason. SASE. Reports in 2 weeks. Prefers b&w line drawings for inside and cover. Buys first North American serial rights. Pay negotiable on publication.

BUTTER FAT MAGAZINE, Box 9110, B.C., Ontario Canada V6B 4G4. (604)420-6611. Readers are dairy farmers. Bimonthly. Circ. 3,000. Free sample copy.
Cartoons: Uses 3 cartoons/issue; buys all from freelancers. Receives 20 submissions/week from freelancers. Interested in agriculture, dairy farming and Canadian marketing systems. Prefers single or multi panel b&w line drawings or washes with gag line. Send finished cartoons to C.A. Paulson, editor. SASE. Reports in 1 week. Buys no rights. Pays $10 for b&w on acceptance.
Illustrations: Local B.C. area artists only. Uses 3 illustrations/issue; buys all from freelancers. Currently receives no submissions from freelancers. Interested in making assignments for specific issues—variable technical, food. Prefers b&w line drawings and washes for inside. Arrange personal appointment to show portfolio. Reports in 1 week. Buys no rights. Pays $10 minimum for b&w inside.

C.S.P. WORLD NEWS, Box 2608, Station D, Ottawa, Ontario, Canada K1P 5W7.Contact: Guy F. Claude Hamel. Concerns book reviews and poetry. Monthly. Circ. 200,000.
Cartoons and Illustrations: Buys 24/year. Needs b&w. Query on cartoons; send samples for illustrations. Reports in 1 week. Negotiates pay; pays on acceptance.

CALIFORNIA OPTOMETRY, California Optometric Association, Box 2591, Sacramento CA 95812. (916)441-3990. Editor-in-chief: Byron Y. Newman. Managing Editor: Andree Zetterbaum. Monthly. Circ. 3,500. Sample copy $1.50; free artist's guidelines.
Cartoons: Buys 15/year on themes "applicable to not only optometrists, but their spouses, office assistants and patients. And, remember that not all optometrists are male and not all office assistants are female. Make sure you know the difference between optician, optometrist and ophthalmologist; cartoons suitable to one group are not humorous to the others"; single panel with gag line. Mail finished cartoons. SASE. Reports in 4 weeks. Pays $10 minimum, b&w line drawings; on acceptance.
Illustrations: Buys 3-5 covers/year, all from freelancers, on assigned themes. Works on assignment only. Samples returned by SASE. Reports back on future assignment possibilities. Provide tearsheet or photocopy of sample line art, to be kept on file for future assignments. Query in person with samples of style. Reports instantly. Pays $100-200, b&w line drawings and color-separated work; on acceptance. Buys line art to illustrate copy (Sacramento artists only). Pays $15/illustration; on acceptance.

CALIFORNIA QUARTERLY, 100 Sproul Hall, University of California, Davis CA 95616. Managing Editor: Dianne McDougal. Fiction and poetry journal. Quarterly. Circ. 500. Original artwork returned after publication. Sample copy $1.50.
Illustrations: Uses 6-10 illustrations/issue; buys all from freelancers. Receives 1-2 submissions/

week from freelancers. Prefers portfolio. SASE. Reports in 4-6 weeks. Buys first North American serial rights. "We don't buy illustrations so much as we buy pieces that are art in themselves. Sometimes we buy portfolios of drawings." Cover and inside: Pays $3/page, b&w line drawings, washes and gray opaques; on publication.

CALIFORNIA REAL ESTATE, California Association of Realtors, 505 Shatto Place, Los Angeles CA 90020. (213)380-7190. Editor-in-Chief: Keith Karpe. Monthly. Circ. 135,000. Query with samples for files or arrange interview. Buys all rights, but may reassign rights to artist after publication. Pays on acceptance. Free sample copy.
Illustrations: Buys very few outside illustrations. Works on assignment only. Reports back on future assignment possibilities. Provide samples plus such information as turn-around-time, fee, current phone number, etc. to be kept on file for future assignments. Cover: Pays $300-600, full-color. Inside: Pays $100-400, b&w line drawings.

CALIFORNIA TODAY, 750 Ridder Park Dr., San Jose CA 95190. (408)289-5602. Editor: John Parkyn. Art Director: Howard Shintaku. General interest magazine for subscribers of the *San Jose Mercury News*. Circ. 250,000. Weekly. Free sample copy.
Illustrations: Buys 2-3/issue on all themes except erotica. Query with resume and samples or previously published work, or arrange interview to show portfolio. Cover: Pays up to $400, opaque watercolors, oils, acrylics or mixed media. Inside: Pays $50-200, b&w line drawings, washes and gray opaques; $150-350, color washes, opaque watercolors, oils, acrylics or mixed media. Pays on acceptance.

CAMPGROUND MERCHANDISING, 401 N. Broad St., Philadelphia PA 19108. (215)925-9744. President: Scott Borowsky. Deals with operating campground stores and recreational vehicle centers. Quarterly. Circ. 14,000.
Illustrations: Buys 1-4 illustrations/issue on campground business. Query with resume and samples. SASE. Buys all rights. Cover and inside: Pays $50 minimum, b&w line drawings and gray opaques; on publication.
Other Needs: Uses artists for cover and layout. Query with resume and samples. Negotiates pay.

CAMPING INDUSTRY, 225 E. Michigan, Milwaukee WI 53202. (414)276-6600. Editor: Glenn Helgeland. For camping equipment manufacturers, distributors, wholesalers and retailers. Published 8 times/year. Circ. 16,500. Photocopied and simultaneous submissions (if exclusive in circulation area) OK. Free sample copy.
Cartoons: Buys 8 cartoons/year on environment, camping and retail sales; single panel. Query with samples. SASE. Reports in 3 weeks. Pays $10-30, b&w line drawings, halftones and washes; on publication.
Tips: "Only criterion is a good business-oriented cartoon."

CAMPUS LIFE, Box 712, Wheaton IL 60187. (312)260-6380. Editor: Gregg Lewis. Editor: Jim Long. For high school and college students. Monthly. Circ. 300,000. Submit portfolio. SASE. Reports in 3 weeks. Previously published, photocopied and simultaneous submissions OK.Original artwork returned after publication. No phone calls, please. Show us what you can do.
Cartoons: Uses 2-3 cartoons/issue; buys 2-3/issue from freelancers. Receives 10 submissions/week from freelancers. Buys 50/year on education, environment, family life, humor through youth, politics and religion; apply to 13-23 age groups; prefers single panel. Prefers finished cartoons and resume. Repoirts in 2 weeks. Pays $40 minimum, b&w; on acceptance.
Illustrations: Art Director: Joan Nickerson. Uses 2 illustratons/issue; buys 2/issue from freelancers. Interested in abstract designs. Receives 5 submissions/week from freelancers. Works on assignment only. Samples returned by SASE. Reports back on future assignment possibilities. Provide resume, letter of inquiry, brochure and tearsheet to be kept on file for future assignments. Prefers resume, portfolio and samples of style. SASE. Reporting time varies; at least 2 weeks. Buys first North American serial rights. Pays $150-250, color; $125-200, b&w; on acceptance.
Advertising: Pays $100 minimum.

CANADA WEST, Box 3399, Langley, B.C., Canada V3A 4R7. Contact: G. Basque. Concerns pioneer history, primarily of Alberta, British Columbia and the Yukon. Quarterly. Circ. 5,000. Original artwork returned after publication, with SASE.
Illustrations: Buys 4 covers/year on Canadian historical scenes. Prefers finished art, roughs, portfolio or sample of style. SASE. Reports in 2 weeks. Buys all rights on a work-for-hire basis. Pays $100 maximum, preferably oils. Query with samples.

CANADIAN AUTHOR AND BOOKMAN, 24 Ryerson Avenue. Toronto. Ontario. Canada M5T 2P3. (416)868-6916. Editor: D.S. Pollock. For writers of all ages and all levels of experience. Circ. 4,500. Quarterly.
Cartoons: Buys 1/issue on the writing life. Send roughs or finished art. Pays $5 min., b&w; on publication.

CANADIAN CONSUMER, 200 1st Ave., Ottawa, Ontario, Canada K1S 5J3. (613)233-9383. "Concerns consumer information for very broad readership." Estab. 1963. Circ. 145,000. Bimonthly. SASE. Reports in 1 month. Pays on publication.
Cartoons: Pays $25, b&w. Query or send roughs.
Illustrations: Buys 2/issue. Pays $150, b&w or color. Arrange interview to show portfolio.

CANADIAN DATASYSTEMS, 481 University Ave., Toronto, Ontario, Canada M5W 1A7. (416)595-1811. Contact: Tom Weissmann. For data processing managers, computer systems managers, systems analysts, computer programmers, corporate managers and similar people concerned with the use of computers in business, industry, government and education. Monthly. Circ. 30,000. Original artwork not returned after publication.
Cartoons: Uses 1 cartoon/issue, all from freelancers. Receives 10 submissions/week from freelancers. Prefers roughs. SASE. Reports in 1 week. Buys first North American serial rights.

CANADIAN DRIVER/OWNER, 481 University Ave., Toronto, Ontario, Canada M5W 1A7. (416)595-1811. Contact: Editor. For owner/operators of heavy-duty trucks in Canada. Bimonthly. Circ. 27,000.
Cartoons: Uses 0-2 cartoons/issue; buys all from freelancers. Receives 5 submissions/week from freelancers. Interested in trucks and truck operations; trucker as anti-hero. Prefers finished cartoons. Reports in 2 weeks. Pays $20-40, b&w; on acceptance. Query or send roughs.

CANADIAN EQUESTRIAN, 212-20216 Fraser Hwy., Langley, British Columbia, Canada V3A 4E6. (604)687-6233. Editor: Raymond R. Brickell. Monthly. Estab. 1978. Circ. 3,600. SASE. Previously published and simultaneous submissions OK. Original artwork returned after publication. Free sample copy.
Cartoons: Uses 1-2 cartoons/issue. Buys themes on the environment, humor through youth and horses; single panel. Prefers roughs; SASE. Reports in 2 weeks. Buys first North American serial rights. Pays $10; on publication.

THE CANADIAN FICTION MAGAZINE, Box 946, Station F, Toronto, Ontario, Canada M4Y 2N9. Editor: Geoffrey Hancock. Anthology devoted exclusively to contemporary Canadian fiction. Quarterly. Canadian artists or residents only. Sample copy $4.00.
Illustrations: Uses 16 pages of art/issue; also cover art. SASE. Reports in 4-6 weeks. Pays $10/page; $25, cover. Uses b&w line drawings, photographs.

THE CANADIAN FORUM, 70 The Espalande, 3rd Floor, Toronto, Ontario, Canada M5E 1R2. Editor: Sam Solecki. Publishes Canadian nonfiction, political and literary commentary, experimental and mainstream fiction, poetry and verse. Monthly. Circ. 10,000. Original artwork returned after publication. Reports in 2 months. Buys one-time rights. Sample copy $1.50.
Cartoons: Uses 10 cartoons/issue, all from freelancers. Receives 20 submissions/week from freelancers. Interested in political themes. Prefers finished cartoons. SASE. Reports in 2 weeks. Buys all rights on a work-for-hire basis.
Illustrations: Uses 4 illustrations/issue, all from freelancers. Receives 10 submissions/week from freelancers. Needs b&w line drawings and cover designs. Provide calling card and letter of inquiry to be kept on file for future assignments. Prefers finished art. SASE. Reports in 2 weeks. Buys all rights on a work-for-hire basis.

CANADIAN FUNERAL DIRECTOR, 1658 Victoria Park Ave., Suite 5, Scarboro, Ontario, Canada M1R 1P7. (416)755-7050. Art Director: Peter Perry. For those concerned with funeral home operations. Monthly. Circ. 1,700.
Cartoons: Buys 2/issue on the funeral industry. Send roughs or finished art. SASE. Reports in 1 month. Pays $20, b&w; on publication.
Illustrations: Buys 1/issue on the funeral industry. Send roughs. SASE. Reports in 1 month. Pays $20, b&w; on publication.

CANADIAN PHARMACEUTICAL JOURNAL, 1815 Alta Vista Dr., Ottawa, Ontario, Canada K1G 3Y6. (613)523-7877. Contact: Editor. For pharmacists. Monthly. Circ. 8,700.
Cartoons: Rarely buys cartoons. Interested in health-related subjects. Prefers finished cartoons.

SASE. Reports in 2 weeks. Pays $5 minimum, b&w; on publication.
Illustrations: Rarely buys illustrations. Interested in health-related subjects. Provide resume to be kept on file for future assignments. Prefers resume. SASE. Reports in 2 weeks. Pays $10 minimum., b&w; on publication.

CANADIAN PLASTICS, 1450 Don Mills Rd., Don Mills, Ontario, Canada M3B 2X7. (416)445-6641. Contact: Victor Von Buchstab or Jacques Pineault. For management and technical people in the plastics industry. Monthly. Circ. 8,000
Cartoons: Buys 1-2/issue with a positive attitude, especially towards plastics. Send finished art. SASE. Reports in 6 weeks. Pays $5, b&w; on publication. Send finished art.

CANADIAN PRINTER & PUBLISHER, Maclean-Hunter Publications, 481 University Ave., Toronto, Ontario, Canada M5W 1A7. Publisher: John Galbraith. Editor: Jack Homer. Executive Editor: Wm. B. Forbes. Original artwork not returned after publication. Previously published work OK.
Cartoons: Uses 1 cartoon/issue; buys all from freelancers. Receives 5 submissions/week from freelancers. Interested in printing and publishing. Prefers finished cartoons. SASE. Reports in 2 weeks. Buys all rights. Pays $25, spot art; $25-35, cartoons; on acceptance.
Illustrations: Uses 1-4 illustrations/issue. Interested in pen and ink, line drawings and washes. Works on assignment only. Mail art. SASE. Reports in 2 weeks. Buys all rights on a work-for-hire basis.

CANADIAN SKATER, 333 River Rd., Ottawa, Ontario, Canada K1L 8B9. (613)746-5953. Editor: Teresa C. Moore. Emphasizes figure skating. "Readers are upper-middle class girls (mainly) 15 years plus university education. Interested in quality goods." Quarterly. Circ. 8,000. Original artwork returned after publication. Free sample copy; art guidelines for SASE.
Illustrations: Uses 1 illustraton/issue; buys from freelancer. Format: b&w line drawings for cover and inside. Works on assignment only. Samples returned by SASE. Reports back on future assignment possibilities. Provide calling card to be kept on file for future assignments. Arrange appointment to show portfolio. SASE. Reports in 1 week. Buys all rights on a work-for-hire basis. Pays $200 maximum for inside b&w, $400 maximum for color cover; on publication.

CANOE, Voyager Publications Inc., 131 E. Murray St., Fort Wayne IN 46803. Editor: John Viehman. Art Director: Jim Bonfitto. "Readers are lifestyle canoeists and kayakers; they're interested in camping, fishing, hiking, sailing, racing and whitewater river running." Bimonthly. Circ. 45,000. Previously published work OK (if published in unrelated or noncompeting magazine). Original artwork not returned after publication. Buys first, one-time or reprint rights. Pays on acceptance or publication. Free sample copy and artist's guidelines with 9x12 SASE.
Cartoons: Uses 2-3 cartoons/issue, all from freelancers. Interested in the environment, family canoe life, humor through youth, canoeing, camping, kayaking, fishing and outfitters/retailers; single panel with gag line. Prefers finished cartoons. SASE. Reports in 4-5 weeks. Pays $25 minimum, b&w line drawings and washes; on acceptance or publication.
Illustrations: Uses 6 illustrations/issue; buys 2-3/issue from freelancers. Interested in canoeing, kayaking and camping "as fits the subject." Provide resume, tearsheet and samples to be kept on file for future assignments. Prefers finished art. SASE. Reports in 3-5 weeks. Buys various rights. Cover: Pays $25 minimum, b&w; $50, color. Inside: Pays $25 minimum, b&w line drawings and gray opaques; on acceptance.

CAR AND DRIVER, Ziff-Davis, 2002 Hogback Rd., Ann Arbor MI 48104. (313)994-0055. Editor-in-Chief: David E. Davis Jr. Art Director: Anthony J. Nelson. For auto enthusiasts. Monthly. Circ. 700,000+. Offset. SASE. Reports in 2 months. Buys first rights. Pays on acceptance.
Cartoons: Uses 6 cartoons/year, all from freelancers. Receives about 5-6 submissions/month from freelancers. SASE. Reports in 2 months. Buys first rights. Pays on acceptance.
Illustrations: Uses 3 illustrations/issue, all from freelancers. Receives 3 submissions/week from freelancers. Interested in autos. Works on assignment only. Samples returned by SASE. Reports back on future assignment possibilities. Provide business card and samples to be kept on file for future assignments. SASE. Reports in 2 months. Buys first rights. Cover: Pays $250 minimum, b&w; $360minimum, color; on acceptance.
Tips: "Show inventiveness in concept and media and provide more than a rendering of a subject; we never use art that is just a rendering of a photo."

CAR CRAFT, Petersen Publishing Co., 8490 Sunset Blvd., Los Angeles CA 90069. (213)657-5100. Editor-in-Chief: Jon Asher. Managing Editor: Pat Ryall. Art Director: Ken Hamilton. "We

feature articles on drag racing and on automotive modification. Monthly. Circ. 391,000. Original artwork not returned after publication. Free sample copy and artist's guidelines.
Illustrations: Uses 1 illustration/issue; buys 1/issue from freelancers. Interested in automotive oriented work. Works on assignment only. Samples returned by SASE. Reports back on future assignment possibilities. Provide calling card, letter of inquiry, brochure, flyer and tearsheet to be kept on file for future assignments. Prefers portfolio and samples of style. SASE. Reports in 6 weeks. Buys all rights on a work-for-hire basis. Inside: Pays $50-300, b&w line drawings and washes; $200-750, color washes and opaque watercolors; on publication.

CAR EXCHANGE, Krause Publications, 700 E. State St., Iola WI 54945. Editor/Art Director: R. Chris Halla. For 18-40 year-old postwar (1946-1973) automobile collectors and enthusiasts with average to above-average education. Monthly. Circ. 160,000.Estab. 1979. Free sample copy.
Cartoons: Uses 6 cartoons/issue, all from freelancers. Receives 50-100submissions/week from freelancers. "The theme and subject of cartoons would have to be geared toward people who collect and restore 1946-1980 automobiles. The heaviest emphasis is on the 50s and 60s. This should be of particular interest to an artist because there is a lot more character evident in the automobiles of the 50s era." Formats considered include single panel, multi-panel, b&w line drawings or line drawings with b&w washes; gag line a must. Prefers roughs, finished cartoons or resume. SASE. Reports in 1 month.Buys first North American serial rights. Payment negotiable with a $5 minimum; pays on acceptance.
Illustrations: Uses 6 illustrations/issue all from freelancers. Receives 10-25 submissions/week from freelancers. "I like first contact to be made from 4-5 samples of style accompanied by a short note telling a little about the artist. This is then kept in a file for later assignments. I may also make an assignment to a new person who comes along at the right time with the right thing, or if something is sent in unsolicited that happens to fill our immediate needs we may buy it. Needs are completely open within postwar era." Styles used range from photo realism to the highly bazaar. B&w line drawings and line drawings with washes in b&w only. Works on assignment only. Provide resume, calling card, letter of inquiry or brochure to be kept on file for future assignments. Prefers portfolio or samples of style. SASE. Reports in 1 month. Buys first North American serial rights. Payment is negotiable with a $10 minimum; pays on acceptance.

CARIBBEAN BUSINESS NEWS, 1255 Yonge St., Toronto, Ontario M4T 1W6 Canada. (416)925-1086. Managing Editor: Colin Rickards. Emphasizes business and finance relating to the Caribbean, mostly for readers in the business community in the Caribbean, and those outside it with Caribbean interests. Monthly. Circ. 32,000. Free sample copy.
Cartoons: Most cartoons are on an assignment basis. "Because of our special type of audience, we rarely accept freelance cartoons, such as we do use usually being commissioned to be in the events or copy, rather than purely as humor." Format: single panel b&w line drawings and washes with or without gag line. Prefers roughs and/or samples of style. SASE. Reports in 2 weeks. Buys one-time rights. Pays negotiable; pays on publication.
Illustration Needs: "Basically illustrations are used on assignment, usually for covers, and tied to copy/feature theme being used. Illustrations should relate to anything to do with Caribbean business if it ties in with copy." Uses b&w line drawings and color washes for cover. Prefers resume and samples of style. SASE. Reports in 2 weeks. Buys all rights on a work-for-hire basis. Negotiates pay; pays on publication.

CAROLINA COOPERATOR, 125 E. Davie St., Raleigh NC 27601. (919)828-4411. Editor-in-Chief: Robert J. Wachs. Managing Editor: Ken Ramey. For farm families in North and South Carolina. Monthly. Circ. 66,500. Previously published work OK. Free sample copy.
Cartoons: Rarely uses cartoons. Buys themes on farming, outdoor/current events, education and humor through youth; single panel. Query with samples. SASE. Reports in 2 weeks. Pays $5 minimum, line drawings; on acceptance.

CAROLINA COUNTRY, Box 27306, Raleigh NC 27611. Editor: Owen Bishop. Cartoon Editor: Patty Shelley. General interest, family magazine. Monthly.
Cartoons: Buys 1-2/issue. "We do not know from one month to the next what art we need, and when we do need it, the subject matter is specific and must be received promptly. We have a tight deadline." Submit published samples. Buys first rights. Pays $10; on acceptance.

CAROLINA SPORTSMAN, Wing Publications, Box 3, Columbia SC 29202. (803)796-9200. Editor in Chief: S.L. Wise. "We emphasize action accounts of outdoor sports such as hunting, fishing, skiing, dirt driving and skydiving." Bimonthly. Circ. 4,000. Mail art. Sample copy $1; free artist's guidelines.
Cartoons: Number cartoons bought/issue varies. Receives 5 submissions/week from freelancers.

Interested in outdoor sports; single panel with gag line. Buys all rights, but may reassign rights to artist after publication. Previously published work OK. SASE. Reports in 4 weeks. Pays $5 minimum, b&w line drawings; on publication.
Illustrations: Receives 15 submissions/week from freelancers. Interested in outdoor sports. Provide letter of inquiry to be kept on file for future assignments. Mail art. SASE. Reports in 4 weeks. Buys all rights, but may reassign rights to artist after publication. Cover: Pays $15-25, color-separated work; $5-25, b&w line drawings. Inside: Pays $5-10, b&w line drawings; on publication.
Other Needs: Uses mostly photographs.

CARTOONS, 8490 Sunset Blvd., Los Angeles CA 90069. Contact: Dennis Ellefson. For young males who like cars and bikes. Original artwork returned after publication if requested.
Cartoons: Buys 150 pages of cartoon stories and 60 single panel cartoons annually. Should be well-drawn, identifiable, detailed cars. Prefers roughs. SASE. Reports 2-4 weeks. Pays $75 min./page; $15/single panel; $15, spot drawings.

CASINO, Editorial Enterprises, Inc., 313 N. 53rd St., New York NY 10019. (212)265-3400. Editor: Jack Tabatch. Art Director: Wil Hulsey. Male entertainment publication. Monthly; 8x11; 100 pages. Offset. Estab. 1974. Circ. 100,000. Query with resume or samples or arrange interview to show portfolio. SASE. Reports in 2-3 weeks. Buys all rights. Pays 30-60 days after publication.
Illustrations: Buys 2-3/issue on assigned fiction themes. Inside: Pays $35-150, b&w line drawings, washes and gray opaques.

CAT FANCY, Fancy Publications Inc., Box 4030, San Clemente CA 92672. (714)498-1600. Editor: Linda W. Lewis. For cat owners, breeders and fanciers. Monthly. Circ. 60,000. Simultaneous submissions and previously published work OK. Sample copy $1.25; free artist's guidelines.
Cartoons: Buys 12/year; single, double and multipanel with gag line. "Central character should be a cat." SASE. Reports in 6 weeks. Buys first rights. Query with samples. Pays $25-50, b&w line drawings; on publication.
Illustrations: Buys 12/year of domestic and wild cats. Query with resume and samples or arrange interview to show portfolio. SASE. Reports in 6 weeeks. Buys first rights. Inside: Pays $50-125, b&w line drawings; on publication.

CATERPILLAR WORLD, 100 NE Adams AB1D, Peoria IL 61629. (309)675-4724. Contact: Editor. Concerns "anything of interest to Caterpillar people, plants or products." Estab. 1963. Circ. 100,000. Quarterly. Reports in 4 weeks. Pays on acceptance.
Cartoons: Buys "anything factory, equipment-oriented. Would like to see Caterpillar equipment, down assembly lines, at work, etc." Negotiates pay, b&w or color. Query or send roughs.
Illustrations: Buys 2-3/issue on factory, equipment themes. Negotiates pay, b&w or color. Query with samples.
Breaking In: "We need talented, experienced artists and high quality work."

CATS, Box 557, Washington PA 15301. Editor-in-Chief: Jean A. Laux. Co-editor: Linda J. Walton. "Half our readers are just general cat lovers; half are breeders and purebred-cat enthusiasts. We offer tips on care and feeding, plus coverage of national cat show scenes." Monthly. Circ. 75,000. "Send 5-6 photocopies of line art for my files. For spots, send the real thing because spot use isn't planned in advance." SASE. Free sample copy.
Cartoons: Buys 5 cartoons/year on cat owning, showing and breeding; single, double and multipanel with gag lines. SASE. Reports in 4 weeks. Buys first rights. Pays $15-30, b&w line drawings, washes and gray opaques; on publication.
Illustrations: Buys 2 illustrations/issue on cat owning, showing and breeding. SASE. Reports in 4 weeks. Buys first rights. Cover: Pays $100-125, full-color. Inside: Pays $5-50, b&w line drawings, washes and gray opaques; on publication.

THE CATTLEMAN, 410 E. Weatherford St., Fort Worth TX 76102. For southwestern cattle feeders and cattlemen. Monthly. Circ. 28,000. Monthly. Pays on acceptance. Sample copy $1.50.
Cartoons: Contact Susan Wagner. Uses 3 cartoons/issue. Receives 50 submissions/week from freelancers. Interested in beef cattle raising and the Old West; single panel with gag line. Prefers finished cartoons. SASE. Reports in 2 months. Buys first North American serial rights. Pays $10 minimum, b&w line drawings; on acceptance.
Illustrations: Contact Dale Segraves, editor-in-chief. Interested in beef cattle, raising cattle and horses, western art. Provide resume to be kept on file for future assignments. Query with resume and samples. SASE. Reports in 2 weeks. Buys first North American serial rights and buys all rights on a work-for-hire basis. Cover: Pays $100 minimum, color washes. Inside: Pays $15-25, color

washes and opaque watercolors; $15-20, b&w line drawings, washes and gray opaques; on acceptance.

CAVALIER, Dugent Publishing Corp., 316 Aragon Ave., Coral Gables FL 33134. Contact: Nye Willden. "For young men and college students interested in good fiction, articles and sex." Monthly. Circ. 250,000.Sample copy $1.50; free artist's guidelines.
Cartoons: Buys 5/issue on erotica; single panel with gag line. Query with samples. SASE. Reports in 2 weeks. Buys first rights. Pays $50-100, b&w line drawings and washes; 30 days after publication.
Illustrations: Buys 3/issue on erotica and assigned themes. Query with samples. SASE. Reports in 2 weeks. Buys first rights. Inside: Pays $150 minimum, b&w line drawings and washes; $250 minimum, color washes and full-color work; 30 days after publication.
To Break In: "We are an excellent market for unpublished but very talented artists and cartoonists. Many of the top people in both fields – Mort Druckner, Peter Max, Ed Arno, Sid Harris– started with us, and many of them still work for us."

CB MAGAZINE, Publishing Industries, Inc., 532 N. Ann Arbor, Oklahoma City OK 73127. (405)947-5731. Managing Editor: Gordon West. Art Director: Mike Redwine. For citizen band radio activists including technical buffs, CB club members and emergency team volunteers. Also dedicated to scanner-monitor listening, short wave receiving, radar detectors, long range television reception, radio technical topics and amateur radio preparation. Monthly. Free sample copy and artist's guidelines.
Cartoons: Uses 5 cartoons/issue, all from freelancers. Receives 15-20 submissions/week from freelancers. Interested in current events, environment, family life, humor through youth, politics and retirement in relation to CBs; single, double or multipanel with gag lines. SASE. Reports in 4 weeks. Buys all rights. Pays $25 minimum, b&w line drawings, washes and gray opaques; $50 minimum, color washes and full-color art. Pays on acceptance "if work is assigned."
Illustrations: Buys 2-3 illustrations/issue from freelancers, on assigned themes. Receives 2-3 illustrations/week from freelancers. Provide tearsheet to be kept on file for future assignments. SASE. Reports in 4 weeks. Buys all rights. Inside: Pays $50-200, b&w line drawings, washes and gray opaques; $100-250, color. Pays on acceptance "if work is assigned."

CHAIN STORE AGE SUPERMARKETS, 425 Park Ave., New York NY 10022. (212)371-9400. Emphasizes supermarkets. Readers are buyers, retail executives and store personnel. Monthly. Circ. 110,000.
Cartoon Needs: Uses 4 cartoons/issue; all from freelancers *by assignment only*. Send samples of style to Bonnie Meyer, art director. SASE. Keeps file on artists. Pays $50-150 on publication for b&w cartoon. Buys all rights on a work-for-hire-basis.
Illustration Needs: Uses 5 illustrations/issue, all from freelancers. We "keep samples on file; must be in NY area. Must see portfolio." Uses inside b&w line drawings and washes and cover color washes and pre-separated art. Send roughs, tear sheets, and samples of style and/or arrange personal appointment to show portfolio to Bonnie Meyer, art director. SASE. Reports in 1 week. Pays $50-150 on publication for inside b&w, $300-500 for color cover, $150-250 for inside color. Buys all rights.

CHANGING TIMES, 1729 H St. NW, Washington DC 20006. Editorial Director: Robert A. Marshall. Monthly. Original artwork returned after publication. Reports in 3 weeks. Pays on acceptance.
Cartoons: Uses 4 cartoons/issue; buys all from freelancers. Receives 300 submissions/week from freelancers. Interested in shopping, home budgeting, family cars, taxes, etc. Prefers roughs. SASE. Reports in 3 weeks. Pays $150, b&w line drawings with tone or color overlay.

CHARLOTTE MAGAZINE, Box 240843, Charlotte NC 28224. (704)588-2120. Emphasizes local people and local places. Bimonthly. Circ. 10,000. Original artwork returned after publication, if requested. Free sample copy, art guidelines.
Illustrations: Uses 7 illustrations/issue; buys from freelancers. Format: b&w line drawings, b&w and color washes for inside. Works on assignment only. Samples returned by SASE. Reports back on future assignment possibilities. Arrange appointment to show portfolio to Steve Thomas, art director. SASE. Reports in 2 weeks. Buys first rights. Pays $35-75 on publication for b&w; $150 for color.
Other Needs: Photography. Also, an advertiser will sometimes contact the art director for the name of an illustrator.

CHATELAINE, 481 University Ave., Toronto, Ontario, Canada M5W 1A7. Contact: Art Director. General interest magazine for Canadian women, age 20 up. Estab. 1928. Circ. 1 million. Monthly. SASE. Pays on publication.
Cartoons: Buys 1-5/issue on varied subjects. Pays $50, b&w; $50, color. Query.
Illustrations: Buys 2/issue on fiction themes. Arrange interview to show portfolio.

CHEMICAL PROCESSING, Putman Publishing Co., 430 N. Michigan Ave., Chicago IL 60611. Managing Editor: Margaret Malochleb. For management personnel in the chemical processing industry. Published 14 times/year. Circ. 80,000. Photocopied submissions OK. Original artwork not returned after publication. Buys first rights. Pays on acceptance. Free sample copy.
Cartoons: Buys 10-20 cartoons/year on current events, science and chemical processing industries; single panel with gag line. Prefers finished cartoons. SASE. Reports in 2-6 weeks. Pays $10 minimum, b&w line drawings and washes.

CHEMLINE, Borg-Warner Chemicals, International Center, Parkersburg WV 26101. (304)424-5661. Editor-in-Chief: Connie J. Groth. For employees. Bimonthly. Circ. 2,500. Query with previously published work or samples. Returns artwork only on request. Previously published work and simultaneous submissions OK. Free sample copy and artist's guidelines.
Cartoons: Buys 6 cartoons/year on assigned themes. Buys all rights or one-time rights. Pays $15 minimum for b&w line drawings, gray opaques and b&w washes. "I am interested in starting a cartoon strip (probably b&w)."
Illustrations: Buys 6/year on chemicals and varied topics. Buys all rights or one-time rights. Inside: Pays $15 minimum, b&w line drawings or washes and gray opaques. Cover: Pays $25 minimum, b&w line drawings or washes and gray opaques.
Design: "I would use a nearby designer for layout mockups. Publication redesign a future possibility. Will pay well—arrangements made before work is done."
Tips: "I have very specific jobs I need, so I don't want general submissions. I would like to get an idea of what an artist can do, then assign specific jobs. So often, when working with artists, I have to think up the idea totally—even down to drawing sketches. This is fine if I know exactly what I want, but I really appreciate it when an artist lends some of his/her creativity to the situation."

CHIC, Larry Flynt Publications, 2029 Century Park E., Suite 3800, Los Angeles CA 90067. (213)556-9200. Cartoon/Humor Editor: Dwane Tinsley. For men. Monthly. Mail samples. Reports in 3 weeks. Buys first rights. Pays on acceptance.

CHICAGO, 500 N. Michigan Ave., Chicago IL 60611. (312)751-7168. Editor-in-Chief: Allen H. Kelson. Art Director: Jack Lund. For active, well-educated, high-income residents of Chicago's metropolitan area concerned with qualify of life and seeking insight or guidance into diverse aspects of urban/suburban life. Monthly. Circ. 220,000. Original artwork returned after publication.
Cartoons: Uses 6 cartoons/issue, all from freelancers. Receives 24 submissions/week from freelancers. Interested in "social commentary, urban life, arts and dining." Single panel. Halftones and washes. Prefers finished cartoons. SASE. Reports in 2 weeks. Buys first North American serial rights. Minimum payment: $75, b&w.
Illustrations: Uses 8 illustrations/year, all from freelancers. Interested in "subjective approach often, but depends on subject matter." Works on assignment only. Samples returned by SASE. Reports back on future assignment possiblities. Provide resume, calling card, brochure, flyer or tearsheet to be kept on file for future assignments. Prefers resume, finished art, roughs, portfolio or samples of style. SASE. Reports in 2 weeks. Buys first North American serial rights. Cover: Pays $200 minimum, color-separated and reflective art. Inside: Pays $75 minimum, color; $35 minimum, b&w; on publication.
Advertising: Pays $50 minimum, advertisements, brochures and car card spots.

CHILD LIFE, Box 567B, Indianapolis IN 46206. (317)634-1100. Editor: John D. Craton. Art Director: Lawrence Simmons. Mystery and science-fiction magazine for children 9-14. Monthly except bimonthly June/July and August/September. Previously published work, photocopies and simultaneous submissions OK. Buys all rights.
Illustrations: Buys 120-180/year on assigned themes. Mail art or query with samples. SASE. Reports in 6 weeks. Buys all rights. Cover illustrations pay $135, color. Inside illustrations pay $20-50/illustration; on publication.

CHILDREN'S PLAYMATE, Box 567B, Indianapolis IN 46206. (317)634-1100. Editorial Director: Beth Wood Thomas. Art Director: Linda Simmons. For ages 5-8. Monthly. Previously published work OK. Sample copy sent if artist's work might be used.

Illustrations: Uses 25-35 illustrations/issue; buys 10-20 from freelancers. Receives 2-5 submissions/week from freelancers. Interested in "stylized, humorous, realistic themes; also nature and health." Works on assignment only. Samples returned by SASE. Reports back on future assignment possibilities. Provide brochure, flyer, tearsheet, stats or good photocopies of sample art to be kept on file for future assignments. Prefers portfolio and samples of style. SASE. Reports in 1 week. Buys all rights on a work-for-hire basis. Minimum payment: Cover: $135, color. Inside: $20-35/page, 2-color and b&w; $35-50/page, full-color.

THE CHRISTIAN CENTURY, 407 S. Dearborn St., Chicago IL 60605. (312)427-5380. Editor/Art Director: James M. Wall. For college-educated, ecumenically-minded, progressive church clergy and laymen. Circ. 30,000. Weekly. Free sample copy.
Cartoons: Uses 1 cartoon/issue; from freelancers. Receives 10-15 submissions/month from freelancers. Usually works on assignment basis but occasionally uses unsolicited material. Samples returned. Provide resume and samples (nonreturnable) to be kept on file for future assignments. SASE. Reports in 3-4 weeks. Buys all rights. Pays on publication.
Illustrations: Buys 20 illustrations/year, all from freelancers. Interested in current event, education, environment, politics and religious themes. Query with previously published work. Cover: pays $50. Inside: pays $15, b&w line drawings and washes.

THE CHRISTIAN MINISTRY, 407 S. Dearborn St., Chicago IL 60605. (312)427-5380. For the professional clergy (primarily liberal Protestant). Bimonthly. Circ. 12,000.
Cartoons: Buys 6 cartoons/issue on religious subjects. Send roughs or finished artwork. SASE. Reports in 1 week. Pays $15 minimum, b&w; on publication.

CHURCH MANAGEMENT-THE CLERGY JOURNAL, 4119 Terrace Lane, Hopkins MN 55343. (612)933-6712. Contact: Manfred Holck Jr. For professional clergy and church business administrators. Estab. 1924. Circ. 12,000. Original artwork returned after publication. Monthly (except June and December).
Cartoons: Uses 2 cartoons/issue on religious themes. Prefers cartoons. SASE. Reports in 2 months. Pays $10, b&w; on publication.

THE CHURCHMAN, 1074 23rd Ave. N., St. Petersburg FL 33704. (813)894-0097. Editor: Edna Ruth Johnson. Published 9 times/year. Circ. 10,000. Original artwork returned after publication. Sample copy available.
Cartoons: Uses 2-3 cartoons/issue. Interested in religious, political and social themes. Prefers finished cartoons. SASE. Reports in 1 week. Pays on acceptance.
Illustrations: Uses 2-3 illustrations/issue. Interested in themes with "social implications." Provide tearsheet to be kept on file for future assignments. Prefers finished art. SASE. Reports in 1 week. Pays $5, b&w spot drawings; on acceptance.

CINCINNATI ENQUIRER SUNDAY MAGAZINE, 617 Vine St., Cincinnati OH 45201. (513)721-2700. Editor: Graydon DeCamp. Art Director: Ron Huff. Weekly. Circ. 288,000.
Illustrations: Uses 1-2 illustrations/issue on assigned themes. "We rarely, if ever, use unsolicited freelance art. The usual procedure is for the artist to show a portfolio. If we like the work, we'll give the artist a manuscript to illustrate." Works on assignment only. Samples returned by SASE. Reports back on future assignment possibilities. Provide calling card to be kept on file for future assignments. Prefers portfolio. SASE. Reporting time varies. Buys all rights on a work-for-hire basis. Pays $50-200, b&w line drawings and washes.

CINCINNATI MAGAZINE, 120 W. 5th St., Cincinnati OH 45202. (513)721-3300. Editor: Laura Pulfer. Art Director: Kay Walker. For college-educated, ages 25+ with an excess of $25,000 incomes. Monthly. Circ. 25,534. Previously published and simultaneous submissions OK. Original artwork returned after publication. Buys all rights. Pays on acceptance.
Cartoons: Uses 2 cartoons/issue, all from freelancers. Receives 30 submissions/week from freelancers. Interested in current events, education and politics; single panel. Prefers finished cartoons. SASE. Reports in 2 weeks. Buys all rights on a work-for-hire basis. Pays $15-25, b&w washes; on acceptance.
Illustrations: Uses 3 illustrations/issue, all from freelancers. Buys cover art and article illustrations on assigned themes. Works on assignment only. Samples returned by SASE. Reports back on future assignment possibilities. Provide resume and brochure to be kept on file for future assignments. Prefers portfolio or samples of style. SASE. Reports in 2 weeks. Buys all rights on a work-for-hire basis.

CIRCLE K MAGAZINE, 101 E. Erie St., Chicago IL 60611. Production Editor: Betty Nakanishi. "Our readership consists almost entirely of college students interested in the concept of voluntary

service. They are politically and socially aware and have a wide range of interests." Published 5 times/year. Circ. 12,000.
Cartoons: Buys "minimal"/issue on campus, young lifestyle humor. Send finished artwork. SASE. Reports in 2 weeks. Negotiates pay; pays on acceptance.
Illustrations: Buys 1 illustration/issue; assigned according to feature needs. Query with samples. SASE. Reports in 2 weeks. Negotiates pay; pays on acceptance.

CIVIL ENGINEERING-ASCE, 345 E. 47th St., New York NY 10017. (212)644-7507. Readers are members of American Society of Civil Engineering. Monthly. Circ. 80,000. Free sample copy.
Cartoons & Illustrations: Occasionally uses cartoons relating to features. Send samples of style. SASE. Reports in 1 week. Buys one-time rights. Pays $225+ on acceptance.

CIVIL WAR TIMES ILLUSTRATED, Box 1831, Harrisburg PA 17105. (717)234-5091. Art Director: Frederic Ray. For the general public interested in well-researched historical articles. Monthly except March and September. Circ. 101,000.
Illustrations: Buys American history (1861-1865) themes. Query with samples. SASE. Reports in 2 weeks. Pays $10-100, b&w or color; on acceptance or publication.

THE CIVITAN LEADER, Box 2102, Birmingham AL 35201. (205)591-8910. Contact: Dorothy Wellborn, director of communications. For club and district officers of Civitan International, an association of local community-oriented service clubs. Quarterly. Circ. 5,000.
Illustrations: Uses 5 illustrations/issue on assigned themes. Works on assignment only. Samples returned by SASE. Reports back on future assignment possibilities. Provide resume and letter of inquiry to be kept on file for future assignments. Query. SASE. Reports in 2-3 weeks. Pays $20-50, "good b&w cover drawing."
Tips: "Artwork should tell a story independently of the accompanying article."

CLAVIER, 1418 Lake St., Evanston IL 60204. Editors: Christine A. Nagy and Lee Prater Yost. For teachers and students of keyboard instruments. Published 9 times/year. Buys all rights. Pays on acceptance. Sample copy available.
Cartoons: Buys 20/year on music, mostly keyboard music. Pays $6.

CLEANING MANAGEMENT, Harris Communications, 17915-B Sky Park Blvd., Irvine CA 92714. (714)979-9263. Editor-in-Chief/Art Director: R.D. Harris, Jr. For managers of in-plant cleaning maintenance crews. Monthly; 8¼x11; 48 pages. Offset. Estab. 1964. Circ. 30,000. Query with samples. SASE. Reports in 3 weeks. Simultaneous submissions OK. Buys first rights. Pays on publication. Free sample copy.
Cartoons: Buys 2-3/issue; single and multipanel with gag lines. Pays $10-15, b&w line drawings.
Illustrations: Just beginning to use illustrations on the custodial field. Pays $25-50, b&w; $20-100, color.

CLEVELAND MAGAZINE, 1621 Euclid Ave., Cleveland OH 44115. (216)771-2833. Art Director: Richard Woollacott. City magazine. Monthly. Circ. 58,000.
Cartoons: Buys 4-6 cartoons/issue, all from freelancers, on assigned themes. Receives 2-3 submissions/week from freelancers. SASE. Reports in 2 weeks. Pays $15-50, b&w; on publication. Query.
Illustrations: Buys 1-2 editorial or technical illustrations/issue on assigned themes. Call for appointment. Prefers resume. Art Director keeps file of his own notes with calling cards or flyers. SASE. Reports in 2 weeks. Pays $100/page, b&w; $150+/page, color; on publication.
Tips: "Artists used on the basis of talent; no experience criteria. We use many talented college graduates just starting out in the field."

CLIFTON MAGAZINE, 204 Tangeman University Center, University of Cincinnati, Cincinnati OH 45220. (513)475-6379. Editor-in-Chief: Chris O'Dell. General interest publication for the university community and neighborhood. Published 3 times/academic year. Circ. 1,200. SASE.
Illustrations: Contact Art Director. Illustrations and photography for feature stories; art photos published. Reports in 6-8 weeks. Buys all rights. Pays on publication.

CLUB LIVING, 250 Station Plaza, Hartsdale NY 10530. (914)472-9191. Art Director: Jane Ronayne. Concerns the lifestyle of private country club members in New York, New Jersey and Connecticut. Published 7 times/year. Original artwork returned after publication. Simultaneous submissions and previously published work OK. Sample copy $1.50 and postage; free artist's guidelines.
Cartoons: Uses 0-1 cartoons/issue; buys all from freelancers. Receives 1 submission/week from

freelancers. Interested in themes on golf, tennis, yachting, other club sports and country club life; single panel with gag line. Negotiates pay for b&w line drawings. Query with samples or arrange interview to show portfolio. Prefers finished cartoons. SASE. Reports in 2-4 weeks. Buys all rights. Pays on publication.
Illustrations: Uses 3 illustrations/issue; buys all from freelancers. Interested in country club life, sports (golf, tennis, yachting, squash, etc.). Cover: Buys color washes and opaque watercolors. Inside: Buys b&w line drawings, washes, color washes and opaque watercolors. Works on assignment only. Samples returned by SASE. Reports back on future assignment possibilities. Provide resume, calling card, flyer or tearsheet to be kept on file for future assignments. Query with resume and samples of previously published work, or arrange interview to show portfolio. Reports in 2-4 weeks. Buys first North American serial rights. Negotiates pay.
Design: *Club Living* commissions artists for 4-color and b&w designs and graphics. Query with resume and samples of previously published work, or arrange interview to show portfolio. Negotiates pay.

COACHING REVIEW, 333 River Rd., Ottawa, Ontario, Canada K1L 8B9. (613)746-0036. Emphasizes volunteer as well as paid sports coaching. Bimonthly. Circ. 12,000. Original artwork returned after publication. Free sample copy, art guidelines.
Cartoons: Uses 4 cartoons/issue, all from freelancers. Interested in coaching-related situations. Format: single panel b&w line drawings with or without gag lines. Prefers roughs and resume. SASE. Reports in 2 weeks. Buys all rights on a work-for-hire basis. Pays $25 on publication. Buys one-time rights.
Illustrations: Editor: Vic MacKenzie. Uses 6 illustrations/issue, all by freelancers. Illustrations should be in the style of "creative realism . . . [depicting] athletes in action." Format: color washes for cover and inside; b&w line drawings for inside. Provide resume and brochure to be kept on file for future assignments. Prefers portfolio and samples of style. SASE. Reports in 2 weeks. Buys all rights on a work-for-hire basis. Pays $250-500, color cover; $50-200, inside b&w; on publication.

COAST, Drawer 2448, Myrtle Beach SC 29577. (803)449-5415. Art Director: Steve Wilson. For tourists. Weekly. Circ. 17,500. Previously published work ("with release") and simultaneous submissions OK. Free sample copy.
Cartoons: Buys 30/year on all themes; single and double panel with gag lines. Query with samples. SASE. Reports in 2-3 months. Buys one-time rights. Pays $3-5, b&w line drawings; on publication.

COED, 50 W. 44th St., New York NY 10019. (212)867-7700. Editor: Kathy Gogick. For teenagers. Monthly. Circ. 1,000,000.
Needs: Arrange interview to show portfolio. Buys all rights. Pays $25 for b&w line drawings; on publication.

COFFEE BREAK, Box 103, Burley WA 98322. Editor/Art Director: D. M. Nicolai. For families. Quarterly. Circ. 6,000. Original artwork returned after publication. Sample copy $1; artist's guidelines with SASE.
Cartoons: Uses 4-6 cartoons/issue; buys all from freelancers. Receives about 100 submissions/week from freelancers. Interested in environment, humor through youth, retirement, hobbies, sports and family life; anything nonpolitical and suitable for a family publication; single panel with gag line. Prefers finished cartoons. SASE. Reports in 2-4 weeks. Buys first North American serial rights. Pays from $3, b&w line drawings; on publication.
Illustrations: Uses 6 illustrations/issue plus cover; buys all from freelancers. Receives 10 submissions/week from freelancers. Themes and styles vary with each issue, but prefers pen & ink line drawings. Provide photocopies of 3-6 drawings to be kept on file for future assignments. Prefers samples of style. SASE. Reports in 2 weeks. Buys first North American serial rights. Pays on publication. Pays from $3, b&w line drawings. All our artwork is done by freelance artists. Payment for each job is negotiated before work is accepted. We are not concerned with prior experience—only performance. New and experienced artists are treated equally.
Other Needs: Spots, cover design, calendars and brochure design.

COGENT COMMUNICATIONS CO., 517 15th Ave. S.E., Minneapolis MN 55414. Contact: James Reid.
Needs: Uses artists for greeting card design and illustration; only contemporary or unusual designs. Send resume. Pay determined by job.

COINS, 700 E. State St., Iola WI 54945. (715)445-2214. Emphasizes US and foreign coin and paper money for novice and experienced collectors and investors. Published monthly. Free sample copy.
Illustrations: Uses 2-3 illustrations/issue; buys all from freelancers. Needs artist to illustrate manuscripts and nonexisting coins. Prefers b&w line drawings for inside and color washes for inside and cover. Send broad range of nonreturnable samples, photo copies, tear cheeks OK, to Bob Lemke, assistant to publisher. Reports in 2 weeks. Buys all rights. Pays $10-25 and more—"negotiable to a few hundred dollars"—for inside b&w on acceptance.
Other Needs: Also has several other related publications for which freelancers provide work.

COLLEGE PRESS REVIEW, Dept. of Journalism, University of Mississippi, University MS 38677. Editor: John Windhauser. For journalism teachers, college publications advisers and general managers of student publications. Quarterly. Circ. 1,000. Sample copy $2.
Illustrations: All media OK. Mail art. SASE. Reports in 2-4 months. No payment.

COLLISION, Box M, Franklin MA 02038. Editor: J.A. Kruza. Art Director: P. Brog. Provides "technical tips and management guidelines for auto body repairmen and managers." Published every 6 weeks. Circ. 12,000. Previously published submissions OK. Sample copy $1; free artist's guidelines.
Illustrations: Buys 8/year on auto body repair, towing and recovery. Query with resume and samples. SASE. Reports in 2 weeks. Buys all rights. Inside: Pays $10-50, b&w line drawings and washes; on acceptance.
Advertising: Uses artists for special projects such as Christmas cards, logo designs and ads. Negotiates pay.

THE COLORADO EXPRESS, Box 18214, Capitol Hill Station, Denver CO 80218. "Emphasizes the outdoors, travel, food, consumer information, crafts, essential living and natural sciences for educated, well-informed people of all ages who *read* rather than skim." Semiannual.
Cartoons: Number of cartoons bought/issue varies. Reports in 8-12 weeks. Pays on publication.
Illustrations: Number bought per issue varies. Query with samples or arrange interview to show portfolio. Reports in 8-12 weeks. Pays $10-60, b&w; on publication.

COLUMBIA, Drawer 1670, New Haven CT 06507. (203)772-2130, ext. 263-64. Editor: Elmer Von Feldt. Fraternal magazine of the Knights of Columbus; themes include family life, social problems, education, current events and apostolic activities as seen from the Catholic viewpoint. Monthly. Circ. 1,263,000. Original artwork not returned after publication. Buys all rights. Sample copy available.
Cartoons: Uses 3 cartoons/issue; buys 3/issue from freelancers. Interested in pungent, captionless humor. Prefers finished cartoons. SASE. Reports in 2 weeks. Buys all rights on a work-for-hire basis. Pays $25; on acceptance.
Illustrations: Uses 2 illustrations/issue; buys 2/issue from freelancers. Provide tearsheet to be kept on file for future assignments. Prefers roughs. SASE. Reports in 4 weeks. Buys all rights on a work-for-hire basis. Pays $300, 2-color illustration; up to $750, full-color cover design; on acceptance.

COLUMBIA JOURNALISM REVIEW, 700 Journalism Bldg., Columbia University, New York NY 10027. Managing Editor: Gloria Cooper. Art Director: Christian von Rosenvinge. For professional journalists, government leaders and students. Bimonthly. Circ. 40,000. Query with resume and samples. Previously published work OK. Original artwork returned after publication.
Illustrations: Uses 1-6 illustrations/issue, all from freelancers. Interested in political and satirical themes and caricatures. Works on assignment only. Samples returned "only if necessary"; prefers "photocopies or other disposable material." Reports back on future assignment possibilities. Provide calling card, brochure, flyer, tearsheet or photocopies to be kept on file for future assignments. Prefers portfolio or samples of style. Reporting time varies. Buys one-time reproduction rights. Pays $300-500; 4-color. Inside: Pays $50-100, spot drawings; on publication.
Other Needs: New photography and symbolic photography.

COLUMBUS MONTHLY, Columbus Monthly Publishing Corp., 171 E. Livingston Ave., Columbus OH 43215. (614)464-4567. Editor: Max S. Brown. Design Director: Sanford Meisel. Regional/city publication. Circ. 38,000. Original artwork not returned after publication. Sample copy $1.50.
Illustrations: Uses 4-6 illustrations/year; buys 4-6/year from freelancers. Interested in contemporary editorial illustration. Works on assignment only. Samples returned. Does not report back on future assignment possibilities. Provide resume, calling card, letter of inquiry and brochure to be

kept on file for future assignments. Prefers portfolio (finished art). SASE. Reports in 6 weeks. Buys all rights on a work-for-hire basis. Cover: Pays $200-350, color washes and full-color art. Inside: Pays $35 minimum, b&w line drawings and washes; on publication.

COMMERCE, 130 S. Michigan Ave., Chicago IL 60603. (312)786-0111. Contact: Editor. For business and industrial leaders in greater Chicago area. Monthly. Circ. 12,000.
Cartoons: Buys themes on business, inflation, government spending, excessive government regulation (EPA, OSHA, etc.), "mess in Washington," banking, stock market and office situations. Send finished artwork. Pays $10, b&w; on acceptance. SASE. Reports in 2 weeks.

COMMODITIES, 219 Parkade, Cedar Falls IA 50613. Editor: Darrell Jobman. Concerns fundamental and technical aspects of trading commodity futures and options. Monthly. Query. Some previously published work OK. Buys all rights. Pays on publication. Sample copy available. Buys themes on agriculture and finance. "The artist should understand commodities, markets or options to know what sort of humor is appropriate to match our editorial comment." Pays $25-50, spot drawings; $15, cartoons (28x30 picas).

COMMONWEALTH, 1011 E. Main St., Suite 212, The Ironfronts, Richmond VA 23219. (804)780-1396. Emphasizes Virginia. Monthly. Circ. 8,000.
Illustrations: Uses 2-3 illustrations/issues; buys 2-3/issue from freelancers. Receives very few submissions/week from freelancers. "Illustrations used only in conjunction with stories." Works on assignment only. Samples returned by SASE. Reports back on future assignment possibilities. Provide resume and brochure or flyer to be kept on file for future assignments. Prefers resumes, roughs and samples of style. SASE. Reporting time varies (2 weeks at earliest). Buys first North American serial rights. Arrange interview to show portfolio. Pays $30-50, b&w; on publication.

COMMUNICATIONS WORLD, Davis Publications, 380 Lexington Ave., New York NY 10007. (212)557-9100. Contact: Irving Bernstein. Reports in 1 week. Buys first rights. Pays on acceptance.
Needs: Pays $20 minimum, line drawings; $400 maximum, full-color cover.

COMPETITIVEDGE, 405 Merchandise Mart, Chicago IL 60654. (312)836-0777. Contact: Mary Wynn. For top management of stores, specializing in all home furnishings products. Monthly. Circ. 15,000.
Illustrations: Buys 1-2/issue. Query with samples or arrange interview to show portfolio. Works on assignment only; assignments are usually for cover art. Provide printed samples and resume to be kept on file for future assignments. SASE. Samples returned. Negotiates pay (about $250, color). (Uses b&w and color.)
Other Needs: Uses mostly (90%) photography.

COMPUTER DECISIONS, 50 Essex St., Rochelle Park NJ 07662. Art Director: V. Kaps. For computer-involved managers in industry, finance, academia, etc.; well-educated, sophisticated and highly paid. Monthly. Circ. 110,000. Original artwork returned after publication.
Cartoons: Uses 3-4 cartoons/issue. Prefers roughs. SASE. Reports in 1 week. Buys first North American serial rights. Pays on acceptance.
Illustrations: Buys 4-5/issue. Assigned to illustrate articles; cover art also illustrates story line. Works on assignment only. Samples returned by SASE. Reports back on future assignment possibilities. Provide resume or brochure to be kept on file for future assignments. Prefers resume, portfolio, or samples of style. Reports in 1 week. Buys first North American serial rights. Negotiates pay.

COMPUTERWORLD, 375 Cochituate Rdl, Framingham MA 01701. (617)879-0700. Cartoon Editor: Steve M. Milmore. For management level computer users, chiefly in the business community, but also in government and education. Weekly. Circ. 97,000.
Cartoons: Uses 5-10 cartoons/issue, all from freelancers. Buys data processing subjects, "even if specific subject is primarily impact on people of a data processing system." Query. Prefers finished cartoons. SASE. Reports on publication. Buys first North American serial rights. Negotiates pay; pays on publication.
Illustrations: Uses 1-5 illustrations/issue from freelancers; ½ of those from freelancers. Receives no submissions from freelancers. Works on assignment only. No samples returned. Does not report back on future assignment possibilities. Provide resume, tearsheet and samples (photocopied) to be kept on file for future assignments. Buys first North American serial rights.

CONFRONTATION/CHANGE REVIEW, 1107 Lexington Ave., Dayton OH 45407. (513)275-8637. Editor-in-Chief: Frederick Finney. For college, university faculty and students,

2nd general audience. Quarterly. Circ. 2,000. Query with samples; particularly interested in black artists. SASE. Reports in 2-4 weeks. Previously published, photocopied and simultaneous submissions OK. Original artwork returned after publication. Sample copy with SASE.
Cartoons: Uses 4-6 cartoons/issue, all from freelancers. Interested in current events, education, politics, law and black history. "No satire unless supports editorially a current or historical line." Prefers finished cartoons. SASE. Reports in 1 week if not accepted; up to 8 weeks if accepted. Buys all rights on a work-for-hire basis. Pays $5-50, b&w line drawings; on publication.
Illustrations: Uses 12 illustrations/issue; buys 4/issue from freelancers. Interested in fiction, poetry, current events, politics, economics and black history. Prefers style of George L. Lee in "Interesting People (Vantage Press)." Provide resume, calling card, letter of inquiry or brochure to be kept on file for future assignments. Prefers portfolio and samples of style. SASE. Reports in 2 months. Buys all rights on a work-for-hire basis. Cover: Pays $10-50, b&w; $25-75, color. Inside: Pays $5-50, b&w line drawings; on publication.
Other Needs: "We have a need, on occasion for artwork to support ads."

THE CONGREGATIONALIST, 484 E. Grand Blvd., Detroit MI 48207. Editor: N.J. Manser. For members of the Congregational church. Estab. 1840. Circ. 7,500. Bimonthly; 8½x11; 28 pages. Offset. SASE. Reports in 2-3 months. Simultaneous submissions and previously published work OK. Not copyrighted. Pays on publication. Free sample copy and artist's guidelines.
Illustrations: Buys religious themes. Cover: Pays $15-30, b&w line drawings. Also buys b&w work for inside. Query with previously published work.
Tips: "We'll be publishing themes for upcoming issues on the inside of the front covers."

CONNECTICUT ARTISTS MAGAZINE, Box 131, New Haven CT 06501. (203)787-4106. Emphasizes the arts. Quarterly. Samples copy $2.
Cartoons: "We haven't used cartoons at this time but would consider any subject that would work within the areas of art covered; visual, performing, photographic and literary arts." Prefers b&w line drawings. Send finished cartoons to Salvatore Rascati, publisher. SASE. Reports in 1 month. Buys one-time rights. Pays $15 for b&w on publication.
Illustrations: Number of illustrations used varies with each issue. Selection based on "samples on file regarding assignments. Open submissions are selected also, if a tie in to a particular short story or poem is shown. We are open to any and all kinds of themes." Prefers b&w line drawings and b&w or color washes for inside. Send samples of style to S. Rascati. SASE. Reports in 6 weeks. Buys all rights and "open submission periodically."

CONSERVATIVE DIGEST, 7777 Leesburg Pike, Falls Church VA 22043. (703)893-1411. Editor-in-Chief: Brien Benson. Contact: Susan Fourt. Concerns activities and political issues for "new right conservatives." Circ. 80,000. Monthly. SASE. Simultaneous submissions and previously published work OK. Original artwork returned after publication. Buys one-time and reprint rights. Sample copy $1.50.
Cartoons: Uses 9 cartoons/issue; buys /issue from freelancers. Receives 80 submissions/weeks from freelancers. Interested in current events and politics (conservative view). Prefers finished cartoons or velox. SASE. Reports in 3 weeks. Buys reprint rights. Pays $15-100, b&w line drawings; on publication.
Illustrations: Uses 1 illustration/issue, all from freelancers. Receives 10 submissions/week from freelancers. Interested in political themes. Works on assignment only. Samples returned by SASE. Reports back on future assignment possibilities. Prefers finished art or samples of style. SASE. Reports in 3 weeks. Buys reprint rights. Cover: Pays $100 minimum, b&w line drawings; $200-400, color washes.

CONSTRUCTION DIMENSIONS, 1711 Connecticut NW, Washington DC 20009. (202)667-8400. Emphasizes interior construction for wall and ceiling contractors. Monthly. Circ. 9,500. Sample copy $1.50.
Cartoons: Uses 2 cartoons/issue; buys all from freelancers. "Will occasionally contract for cover art (prefer DC area artist). I script the theme, specifics, etc." Cartoons should be single panel b&w line drawings with gag line. Call Jim Van Loozen, editor. Reports in 2 weeks. Buys one-time rights and reserves reprint rights. Pays $5 for b&w upon receipt of invoice and acceptance.
Illustrations: Occasionally contracts for illustrations on same terms as cartoons. Call J. Van Loozen. Keeps file on freelancers for future assignments. Buys one-time rights and reserves reprint rights. Pays $50-100 for b&w cover upon receipt of invoice and acceptance.

CONSTRUCTION EQUIPMENT OPERATION AND MAINTENANCE, Construction Publications, Inc., Box 1689, Cedar Rapids IA 52406. (319)366-1597. Editor-in-Chief: C.K. Parks. Concerns heavy construction and industrial equipment for contractors, machine operators, me-

chanics and local government officials involved with construction. Bimonthly. Circ. 68,300. Simultaneous submissions OK. Original artwork not returned after publication. Free sample copy.
Cartoons: Uses 8-10 cartoons/issue, all from freelancers. Interested in themes "related to heavy constructions industry" or "cartoons that make contractors and their employees 'look good' and feel good about themselves;" multipanel. Perfers finished cartoons. SASE. Reports in 2 weeks. Buys all rights, but may reassign rights to artist after publication. Pays $7-10, b&w.
Illustrations: Uses 20+ illustrations/issue; "very few" are from freelancers. Pays $80-125; on acceptance.

CONSTRUCTIONEER, 1 Bond St., Chatham NJ 07928. (201)635-6450. Editor: Ken Hanan. Art Director: Richard E. Stevancsecz. For contractors, public officials, distributors and producers. Biweekly. Previously published work OK. Original artwork not returned after publication.
Cartoons: Buys 4-5 cartoons/year. Interested in heavy construction. Mail art. SASE. Reports in 2 weeks. Pays $5-10; on publication.

CONSUMERS DIGEST, 5705 N. Lincoln, Chicago IL 60659. (312)275-3590. Art Director: Larry Teeman. For consumers. Bimonthly. Circ. 650,000. Original artwork returned after publication. SASE. Reports in 3 weeks. Pays on publication.
Illustrations: Contact Walt Skibitski. Uses 10 illustrations/issue; buys all from freelancers. Assigned themes depending on article. Works on assignment only. Samples returned by SASE. Reports back on future assignment possibilities. Provide resume or tearsheet to be kept on file for future assignments. Prefers resume, portfolio or samples of style. SASE. Reports in 1 week. Buys all rights on a work-for-hire basis. Pays $150/page, b&w; $250/page, color; on publication.

CONSUMERS' RESEARCH MAGAZINE, Washington NJ 07882. Managing Editor: F.J. Schlink. Monthly.
Cartoons: Buys 10/year on themes of interest to consumers. Prefers finished cartoons. SASE. Reports in 1 week. Pays $10; on acceptance.

CONTACT, 302 Lake St., Box 650, Huntington IN 46750. (219)356-2312. Editor-in-Chief: Stanley Peters. Assistant Editor: Steve Dennie. For conservative, evangelical Christians. Weekly. Circ. 6,000. Previously published, photocopied and simultaneous submissions OK. Pays on acceptance. Sample copy and artist's guidelines with SASE.
Cartoons: Uses 1 cartoon/issue, all from freelancers. Receives 30 submissions/month from freelancers. Interested in current events, education, family life, religion and the ministry; single panel with gag line. Mail art. SASE. Reports in 4-6 weeks. Pays $2 minimum, b&w line drawings; on acceptance.

CONTACTS, Box 407, North Chatham NY 12132. Editor: Joseph Strack. For dental laboratories. Bimonthly. Circ. 1,000.
Cartoons: Buys 4-5/issue on the dental laboratory industry. Mail art. Reports in 1 week. Buys first serial rights. Pays $20; on acceptance.

CONTEMPORARY SURGERY, Bobit Publishing, 2500 Artesia Blvd., Redondo Beach CA 90278. (213)376-8788. For practicing surgeons. Monthly. Circ. 40,000. Original artwork returned after publication.
Illustrations: Occasionally uses medical illustrations for specific articles. "Medical illustrators only!" Accepts artwork only when requested. Buys first or reprint rights. Pays on publication.

CONTINENTAL, East-West Network, Inc., 5900 Wilshire Blvd., .300, Los Angeles CA 90036. (213)937-5810. Editor-in-Chief: Fred Smith. Monthly. Sample copy $1.50.
Illustrations: Buys assigned themes. Query with resume. Buys all rights. Pays $75 minimum, spot art; $450 maximum, full-page illustration; $600 maximum, full-color cover.

CONTRACT, Gralla Publications, 1515 Broadway, New York NY 10036. Editor: Len Corlin. Executive Editor: Anne Fallucchi. Provides "ideas for interior installations, product information, and news on developments in the commercial interior design industry." Monthly. Circ. 27,500.
Illustrations: Buys 2-4/year on interior design; all on assignment only. Mail art or samples, or arrange interview to show portfolio. SASE. Reports in 3 weeks. Buys one-time rights. Cover: Pays $300, full-color renderings; inside: Pays $150-250, b&w line drawings and washes; on publication.

CONVENIENCE STORES MAGAZINE, 708 3rd Ave., New York NY 10017. (212)490-1000. Contact: Mitch Shostak. For convenience store operators, managers, buyers and executives in the business. Circ. 35,000. Bimonthly.

Cartoons: Plans 2-3 cartoons/issue. Will hire freelancers for cartoon work.
Illustrations: Uses 2-8 illustrations/issue, all from freelancers, on assigned themes. Works on assignment only. Proide tearsheet or samples (no resumes) to be kept on file for future assignments. Pays 30 days after bills is submitted. Pays $75-100, spot b&w; $200-300, full page b&w; $200-400, color. Query with samples or arrange interview to show portfolio.

DAVID C. COOK PUBLISHING CO., 850 N. Grove, Elgin IL 60120. (312)741-2400. Publishers of *Looking Ahead, Bible Discoveries* and *Christian Living*. Magazines for "evangelical Christians, all age groups." Quarterly.
Cartoons: Submissions must be "top quality for different age groups. Ranging from Disney to *New Yorker* in style–depends on age. Most of our submissions come from a select group of artists we have been using for years, so it is rare that we buy material from other freelancers. However, if you feel that you have something that really fits our publications, we will consider it." Prefers single panel. Send roughs, finished cartoons or samples of style to Ed Elsner, art director. SASE. Pays on acceptance $15-up for b&w. Buys one-time rights.
Illustrations: Receives about 30 illustrations/week from freelancers. Prefers b&w line drawings and full color art for covers. Send samples of style, proofs or slides of work to E. Elsner. SASE. Reports in 1 week. Pays on acceptance $50 minimum for inside b&w; $150-300 for color cover and $100 minimum for inside color. Buys all rights.

CORE, 1916-38 Park Ave., New York NY 10037. (212)690-3679. Editor: Doris Innis. Monthly. Sample copy available.
Cartoons: Uses 3-4 cartoons/issue; buys 1-2/issue from freelancers. Receives 4 submissions/month from freelancers.
Illustrations: Uses 2 illustrations/issue, all from freelancers. Receives 4 submissions/week from freelancers. Provide resume and sample of work to be kept on file for future assignments.
Other Needs: 5x7 and 8x10 cover designs.

CORNHUSKER COUNTRY, 106 Navajo, Council Bluffs, IA 51501. Editor-in-Chief/Art Director: Robert Everhart. "For players and listeners of traditional and country music. We are a small, nonprofit publication and will use whatever is sent to us. A first time gratis use is the best way to establish communication." Monthly. Circ. 2,000. Simultaneous submissions and previously published work OK. Buys one-time rights. Free sample copy.
Cartoons: Buys 1/issue on country music; single panel with gag line. Mail roughs. Pays $5-15, b&w line drawings; on publication.
Illustrations: Buys 1/issue on country music. Query with resume and samples. SASE. Cover: Pays $5-15, b&w line drawings. Inside: Pays $5-15, b&w line drawings; on publication. Reports in 4 weeks.

COSMOPOLITAN, 224 W. 57th St., New York NY 10019. Cartoon Editor: Richard Amdur. Works only with extensive present list of cartoonists.

COUNTRY CLUB GOLFER, 2171 Campus Dr., Irvine CA 92715. (714)752-6474. Contact: E. Pazdur. For private country club members and club golfers; professional, affluent, college-educated. Circ. 70,000. Monthly.
Illustrations: Buys golf swing subjects for instruction articles. Query with samples by mail. Reports in 1 week. Negotiates pay; pays on publication.

THE COUNTRY GENTLEMAN, 1100 Waterway Blvd., Indianapolis IN 46202. Art Editor: Bruce Kinnaird. Readers interested in "the good life" in rural and suburban areas. Quarterly. Circ. 225,000. Original artwork returned after publication, except if all rights purchased.
Cartoons: Uses 8 cartoons/issue; buys all from freelancers. Receives 10-15 submissions/week from freelancers. Interested in rural themes. Prefers finished cartoons. SASE. Reports in 2 weeks. Buys all rights. Pays $50 for 8½x11½ finished art.
Illustrations: Uses 3 illustrations/issue; buys 1/issue from freelancers. Receives 10-15 submissions/week from freelancers. Interested in rural themes; line art relating to article. "We like illustrations in a representational vein, but we can use abstractions too." Works on assignment only. Samples returned by SASE. Reports back on future assignment possibilities. Provide resume or flyer to be kept on file for future assignments. Prefers resume or samples of style. Reports in 2 weeks. Buys all rights on a work-for-hire basis. Cover: Pays up to $500, finished. Inside: Pays $50, spot art; $100-200, full-color. Pays on publication.

COUNTRY GUIDE, 1760 Ellice Ave., Winnipeg, Manitoba, Canada R3H 0B6. (204)774-1861. Editor: Dave Wreford. For operating farmers. Monthly; 7x10; 80 pages. Offset. Estab. 1883. Circ.

252,000. Mail art. SASE. Reports in 2 weeks. Previously published and simultaneous submissions OK. Buys first rights. Pays on acceptance. Free sample copy.
Cartoons: Buys 40-60/year on politics and farming; single panel. "We like cartoons which depict politicans as con men, fools, etc." Pays $20, line drawings.

COUNTRY JOURNAL, 1600 E. Lincoln Ave., Suite 1, Decatur IL 62521. (217)422-9146. Contact: Mark Avery. For grain elevator operators and their farmer-customers in Illinois, Indiana, Iowa, Missouri, Ohio and Nebraska. Estab. 1972. Circ. 25,000. Monthly. SASE. Pays on publication.
Illustrations: Buys 1-2 editorial cartoons/issue on agricultural current economic issues. Pays $15, b&w. Query with samples.

COUNTY LIFE, 9B West Main St., Ephrata, PA 17522. (717)738-2438. Editor: Freida Syphard. Art Director: Carol Dale. Regional magazine for 4-6 county area. Monthly. Circ. 18,000. Original artwork returned after publication, if requested. Previously published, photocopied and simultaneous submissions OK. Sample copy $2; free artists' guidelines.
Illustrations: Uses 4-7 illustrations/issue; buys 1-3/issue from freelancers. Interested in regional and consumer illustrations; upbeat, contemporary; occasionally historical (local). Works on assignment only. Samples returned by SASE, if requested and SASE. Reports back on future assignment possibilities. Provide resume or calling card and tearsheet to be kept on file for future assignments. Query with previously published work or arrange interview to show portfolio. SASE. Reports in 4 weeks. 1 week on specific assignment. Buys all rights on a work-for-hire basis, usually.
How to Break In: We are looking for original and upbeat work.

COURIER, Saint Mary's Alumnae Association, Le Mans Hall, Saint Mary's College, Notre Dame IN 46556. (219)284-4245. Editor-in-Chief: Dr. Rita Cassidy. Art Director: Richard Wilson. For alumnae. Circ. 13,000. Quarterly; 8¼x11¼; 52 pages. Offset. SASE. Reports in 1 month. Not copyrighted. Pays on acceptance. Free sample copy and artist's guidelines.
Illustrations: Contact R. Wilson, illustration editor. Buys 25/year on general themes. Monochrome. Query with samples of previously published work.

COURT CRIER, National Association for Court Administration, 300 Newport Ave., Williamsburg VA 23185. Secretariat: Lee Powell. For association members. Estab. 1969. Circ. 600-800. Arrange interview. SASE. Reports in 1 month. Copyrighted. Pays on acceptance.
Needs: Negotiates pay, b&w and color cartoons and illustrations.

THE COVENANT COMPANION, 5101 N. Francisco Ave., Chicago IL 60625. (312)784-3000. Editor: James R. Hawkinson. For Christian-oriented readers. Twice monthly, except monthly in July and August. Circ. 28,000. Original artwork returned after publication, if requested. Sample copy available for 75¢.
Illustrations: B&w photos or drawings about Easter, Advent, Lent and Christmas. Works on assignment only. Samples returned by SASE. Write or submit art 10 weeks in advance of season. SASE. Reports immediately. Buys first North American serial rights. Pays on publication.

CRAFT HORIZONS, 22 W. 55th St., New York NY 10019. (212)397-0622. Art Director: Sydney Butchkes. For professional craftsmen, artists, teachers, architects, designers, decorators, collectors and consumers. Estab. 1941. Circ. 40,000. Bimonthly. SASE. Reports in 2-3 months. Pays on publication.
Illustrations: Pays $7.50, b&w. Arrange interview to show portfolio.

CRAFTS, PJS Publications Inc., Box 1790, Peoria IL 61656. Editor-in-Chief: Joyce Bennett. Art Director: Lucy Hartter. Provides how-to's and new ideas for craft consumers. Monthly. Estab. 1978. Original artwork returned after publication. Sample copy $1.
Illustrations: Uses 12 illustrations/issue on assigned themes. Interested in crafts; illustrations relating to articles. Works on assignment only. Samples returned with SASE. Query with samples. SASE. Reports in 2 weeks. Buys all rights. Inside: Pays $25-250, b&w line drawings and washes; on acceptance.

CREATIVE COMPUTING, Box 789-M, Morristown NJ 07960. (201)540-0445. Editor: Ted Nelson. Publisher: David Ahl. For educators, home computer hobbyists, small businessmen and other personal computer users interested in applications and software. "We have a nontechnical, down-to-earth approach." Monthly. Circ. 80,000. Sample copy $2.
Cartoons: Buys 8/issue on education, home computers, data processing, robots, calculators and

unusual applications of computers; single, double and multipanel with gag lines. Query with samples. SASE. Reports in 2 weeks. Previously published work OK. Buys all rights, but may reassign rights to artist after publication. Pays $5-20, b&w line drawings, washes and gray opaques; on acceptance.

Illustrations: Buys 50-60/year on home computers, data processing and assigned themes. Also buys schematic and technical diagrams. Query with samples. SASE. Reports in 2 weeks. Previously published work OK. Buys all rights, but may reassign rights to artist after publication. Cover: Pays $25-150, color. Inside: Pays $20-100, color; $5-75, b&w; $10-25, schematic and technical diagrams; on acceptance.

CREATIVE CRAFTS, Box 700, Fredon-Springdale Rd., Newton NJ 07860. (201)383-3355. Emphasizes how-to on all aspects of crafts and miniatures. Bimonthly. Circ. 100,000. Sample copy $1; free art guidelines for SASE.

Cartoons: Uses 0-1 cartoon/issue; buys all from freelancers. Receives 1 submission/week from freelancers. Interested in craft subjects and the human side of the hobbyist. Miniature subjects are also of interest. Prefer single panel b&w line drawings or washes with gag line. Send roughs and/or finished cartoons to Wendie R. Blanchard, managing editor. Reports in 2 weeks. Buys first North American serial rights. Pays $25-35 for b&w on publication.

Illustrations: Uses about 20/issue. Receives about 10 illustrations with mss./week and 5 without mss./week from freelancers. Interested in how-to craft techniques with clarity of illustration and hard lines with overlays. Prefers b&w line drawings and washes for inside. Send roughs, samples of style and cover letter outlining intent to W. Blanchard. Reports in 2 weeks. SASE. Buys first North American serial rights. Pays $50 minimum on publication.

CREATIVE LIVING, 515 Madison Ave., New York NY 10022. (212)752-4530. Art Director: Alice Degenhardt. Quarterly. Circ. 200,000.

Illustrations: Buys 5-7/issue, all from freelancers. Interested in "very conceptual—fine art quality on family, leadership, health and leisure activities." Works on assignment only. Samples sent through mail are not returned. Provide tearsheets to be kept on file for future assignments. SASE. Reports in 2-3 weeks. Pays $300-600, color; on publication.

CREATIVE WORLD, 1012 S. Robertson, Los Angeles CA 90035. Contact: Audree Coke. Write for sample copy.

Needs: Uses artists for jazz-related cover art. Reports in 15 days. Buys all rights.

CROPS & SOILS MAGAZINE, 677 Segoe Rd., Madison WI 53711. Editor: William R. Luellen. For farmers, seedgrowers, agri-business executives, salesmen, county agents, researchers and vocational-agriculture teachers. Published 9 times/year. Previously published work OK. Original artwork not returned after publication.

Cartoons: Uses 6-8 cartoons/issue, all from freelancers. Receives 30-50 submissions/week from freelancers. Prefers finished cartoons; 8½x11 or smaller, horizontal or square. SASE. Reports in 1 week. Buys one-time rights. Pays $7.50; on acceptance.

CRUSADER, Box 7244, Grand Rapids MI 49510. (616)241-5616. Editor: David J. Koetje. For boys ages 10-14. Published 7 times/year by the Calvinist Cadet Corps. Previously published work OK. Free sample copy.

Cartoons: Submit resume. Reports in 6 weeks. Minimum payment: $5, single panel; $10, double panel; $15, full page.

Illustrations: Uses b&w line drawings and washes. Illustrations of seasonal sports needed 4 months before publication date. Submit resume. Reports in 6 weeks.

CRUSADER, Baptist Brotherhood Commission, 1548 Poplar, Memphis TN 38104. (901)272-2461. Art Director: Herschel Wells. Christian-oriented mission magazine for boys ages 7-12. Monthly. Circ. 84,000. Photocopied and simultaneous submissions OK. Original artwork returned after publication, if requested. Buys reprint rights. Free sample copy and artist's guidelines.

Illustrations: Uses 10 illustrations/issue; buys 6/issue from freelancers. Interested in boys' youth and boys' activities. Works on assignment only. Samples returned by SASE. Reports back on future assignment possibilities. Provide tearsheet and "samples which may be returned or duplicated" to be kept on file for future assignments. Prefers roughs and samples of style. SASE. Reports in 3 weeks. Buys first North American serial rights. Cover: Pays $200-250, full color; $100-180, b&w line drawings, washes and gray opaques. Inside: Pays $45-120, b&w line drawings, washes and gray opaques.

CS GLOBE REPORTER, (formerly cs journal), Box 512A, Silver Spring MD 20907. (301)588-5709. Editor-in-Chief: R. Sublett Hawkins. For Christians and potential Christians. Monthly. Mail art. SASE. Reports in 4-6 weeks. Previously published work OK. Buys all rights, but will reassign rights to artist after publication upon request. Sample copy free w/SASE (50¢).
Cartoons: Themes on biblical background, biblical characters, serious humor, but wish to have a look at all cartoons on speculation.
Other Needs: The *CS GLOBE REPORTER* has changed its format and uses little freelance material; best opportunity, however, is in testimony area. Cartoons must have captions included for possible radio use. Our function is to present Christ as Saviour and Lord to unbelievers and present full coverage to our regional radio programs growing to become worldwide. Until some final plan is reached, payment is in contributor's copies and radio annnouncement of contributors and their work published in the *CS GLOBE REPORTER*. Great opportunity for getting work known to a vast public. Contributors who wish to receive a cassette or reel-to-reel tape of our program on which they or their work will be announced should send inquiries to: CSJ, Box 512AA, Silver Spring MD 20907.

CUISINE MAGAZINE, 500 N. Michigan Ave., Chicago IL 60611. (312)440-8400. Art Director: Diane Kavelaras. Focuses on food, travel and entertaining. Circ. 750,000. Published 10 times/year.
Illustrations: Number bought per issue varies. Query with samples or arrange interview to show portfolio. SASE. Reports in 2 months.

CURRENT HEALTH, 501 Lake Forest Ave., Highwood IL 60040. (312)432-2700. Executive Editor: Laura Ruekberg. Two editions: one for high school students, one for junior high. Published 9 times/year. Circ. 200,000. Previously published, photocopied and simultaneous submissions OK. Free sample copy.
Cartoons: Buys environment, family life, humor through youth and health themes. Query with samples. SASE. Reports in 4 weeks. Buys first, reprint and simultaneous rights. Pays $5 minimum, line drawings; on publication.
Illustrations: Buys assigned themes. Query with samples. SASE. Reports in 4 weeks. Buys first, reprint and simultaneous rights. Cover: Pays $25 minimum, full-color. Inside: Pays $10 minimum, b&w; on publication.

CYCLE GUIDE, 1440 W. Walnut, Compton CA 90220. Editor: Paul Dean. Send art. Reports immediately. Copyrighted. Pays on acceptance. Sample copy available.
Needs: Pays $25 for filler drawings of motorcycles.

CYCLE TIMES, 5242 Bolsa Ave., Unit 6, Huntington Beach, CA 92649. (714)891-4731. Publisher: Paul Hertzberg. Editor: Brad Zimmerman. For competitive dirt bike riders, who may own street bikes. Monthly. Circ. 40,000. Original artwork returned after publication. Free sample copy.
Cartoons: Buys 1-2/issue on motorcycling. Prefers finished cartoons. SASE. Reports in 3 weeks. Buys all rights, but may reassign rights to artist after publication. Pays $10 minimum, line drawings and halftones; on publication.

CYCLE WORLD, 1499 Monrovia Ave., Newport Beach CA 92663. (714)646-4451. For motorcycling enthusiasts. Monthly. Circ. 330,000. "Unless otherwise noted in query letter, we will keep spot drawings in our files for use as future fillers." Previously published work OK. Free sample copy and artist's guidelines.
Cartoons: Editor-in-chief: Allan Girdler. Uses 6 cartoons/year, all from freelancers. Receives 1 submission/week from freelancers. Interested in motorcycling; single or double panel with gag line. Send roughs or finished art or arrange interview. Buys all rights. Pays $30-100, b&w line drawings, washes and gray opaques; $45-150, color.
Illustrations: Art Director: Paul Zeek. Uses 7-8 illustration/issue, all from freelancers. Recieves 25-30 submissions/week from freelancers. Interested in motorcycling and assigned themes. Works on assignment only. Samples returned, if originals; kept if photocopies. Reports back on future assignment possibilities, to artists who phone. Does not report back to artists who contact through mail. Provide brochure, tearsheet, letter of inquiry and calling card to be kept on file for future assignments. Prefers resume and samples or portfolio. Buys all rights. Cover: Pays $250-375. Inside: Pays $25-100, b&w; $100-300, color; on publication.
To Break In: "We use a lot of spot drawings as fillers."

DAILY CAMERA FOCUS MAGAZINE, Box 591, Boulder CO 80306. (303)442-1202. Art Director: Barbara Baumgarten. For Boulder County residents. Weekly. Circ. 28,000.

Cartoons: Assigns themes. Mail finished art; include gag line. SASE. Reports in 6 weeks. Pays $10/up for b&w; on publication.
Illustrations: Buys 15/year. SASE. Reports in 6 weeks. Pays $10/up for b&w.

DAILY COMMERCIAL NEWS, 34 St. Patrick St., Toronto, Ontario, Canada M5T 1V2. Editor: T. McAuliffe. For architects, engineers, construction men, building officials, municipal and government officials. Buys first Canadian rights on cartoons. Pays on publication.

DAIRY GOAT JOURNAL, Box 1808, Scottsdale AZ 85252. (602)991-4628. Publisher: Kent Leach. For dairy goat breeders and raisers. Monthly. Circ. 14,000. Original artwork returned after publication.
Cartoons: Uses 1-3 cartoons/issue; buys 1-10 from freelancers on assigned themes. "Should not degrade the dairy goat or persons who raise them." Query or mail finished art. SASE. Reports in 2 weeks. Buys first North American serial rights. Pays $5, b&w; on publication.
Illustrations: Uses 6-20 illustrations/issue; buys 1-10 from freelancers on assigned themes. Works on assignment only. Samples returned by SASE. Reports back on future assignment possibilities. Provide resume or letter of inquiry to be kept on file for future assignments. Prefers finished art. Reports in 2 weeks. Buys first North American serial rights. Pays $10-20, b&w; on publication.

DAIRYMEN'S DIGEST, Southern Region Edition, Box 5040, Arlington TX 76011. (817)461-2674. Advertising Manager: Martha Wake. Company publication for dairy farmer members of Associated Milk Producers, Inc. Monthly. Circ. 7,850. Original artwork returned after publication. Free sample copy; art guidelines for SASE.
Cartoons: Uses 1 cartoon/issue; buys from freelancer. Receives about 10 submissions/week from freelancers. Interested in agricultural, preferably dairy-oriented cartoons. Format: b&w line drawings. Send finished cartoons to Phil Porter, editor. SASE. Reports in 2 weeks. Buys one-time rights. Pays $15 on publication.
Illustrations: Uses 1 illustration/issue; buys from freelancer. Receives 10 submissions/week. Interested in illustrations related to a particular article on dairying. Works on assignment only. Samples returned by SASE. Reports back on future assignment possibilities. Send samples of style to Phil Porter, editor. SASE. Reports in 2 weeks. Buys all rights on a work-for-hire basis. Pays on publication $75-150.

THE DALE CORP., 30500 Van Dyke, Suite 600, Warren MI 48093. (313)573-0200. Art Director: Gerald Turgeon. Publishes law enforcement, corrections, fire fighting, trucking and boating/marine publications. Estab. 1969. Circ. 240,000. Query with previously published work. SASE. Reports in 4 weeks. Buys all rights, but may reassign rights to artist after publication. Pays on acceptance. Free sample copies and artist's guidelines.
Illustrations: Buys 12/year. Cover: Pays $100-200, b&w line drawings; $200-400, color-separated work.

DANCE MAGAZINE, 1180 Ave. of the Americas, New York NY 10036. Editor-in-Chief: William Como. Monthly. Works on assignment only. Original artwork not returned after publication. Sample copy $2.
Illustrations: Uses 3-4 illustrations/issue; buys all from freelancers. Interested in dance-related themes (ballet, modern, ethnic, etc.). Provide resume to be kept on file for future assignments. Query. Prefers finished art or samples of style. SASE. Reports in 2 weeks. Buys all rights on a work-for-hire basis. Pays on publication.

DANCE SCOPE, American Dance Guild, 1133 Broadway, Rm 1427, New York NY 10010. Editor-in-Chief: H.B. Kronen. Art Director: Harriet Brickman. For dance professionals: performers, teachers, students and informed audiences. Quarterly. Circ. 7,000. Previously published and photocopied submissions OK. Sample copy $2.50.
Illustrations: Buys 10-20/year on education, dance and the arts. Query with resume or samples. SASE. Reports in 4 weeks. Buys one-time rights. Cover: Pays $20 minimum, b&w line drawings, washes and gray opaques. Inside: Pays $10 minimum, b&w line drawings, washes and opaques; on publication.

DAPPER, Editorial Enterprises, Inc., 313 N. 53rd St., New York NY 10019. (212)265-3400. Editor: Jack Tabatch. Art Director: Monty G. Locke. Male entertainment publication. Monthly; 8x11; 100 pages. Offset. Estab. 1974. Circ. 100,000. Query with resume or samples, or arrange interview to show portfolio. SASE. Reports in 2-3 weeks. Buys all rights. Pays 30-60 days after publication.
Illustrations: Buys 2-3/issue on assigned fiction themes. Inside: Pays $35-150, b&w line drawings, washes and gray opaques.

DARK TOWER, University Center 7, Cleveland State University, Cleveland OH 44115. Managing Editor: Linda Unger. For college students and local poets. Published annually; 6x9; 100-150 pages. Letterpress. Estab. 1972. Circ. 1,5000. Mail art. SASE. Reports in 4 weeks. Photocopied and simultaneous submissions OK. Buys first North American serial rights. Pays on publication. Sample copy $1.50.
Illustrations: Buys themes on "reflective people." Cover and inside: Pays $5 minimum, b&w.

DARKROOM PHOTOGRAPHY, 609 Mission St., San Francisco CA 94105. (415)543-8020. Editor-in-Chief: Susan R. Keller. Art Director: Jackie Jones. Deals with all aspects of darkroom photography techniques. Published 8 times/year. Estab. 1979. Circ. 100,000. Original artwork returned after publication. Sample copy: $1.50. Free editorial and photographic guidelines.
Illustrations: Uses 3 illustrations/year. Interested in technical drawings. Works on assignment only. Samples returned by SASE. Provide resume, calling card, brochure or tearsheet to be kept on file for future assignments. Buys first North American serial rights, or all rights on a work-for-hire basis. Pays on publication.

DART GAME RESEARCH, American Dart Association, 128 N. Main St., Ashley PA 18706. Editor: Edmund Carl Hady. Provides "research on old dart games and history, and where the games were first played." Quarterly. Circ. 8,000.
Illustrations: Buys 80% of art from freelancers. Needs drawings from "Columbus years, Roman days, cavemen times, old English pubs, towns, villages, Henry I times and Early American years." Mail art. SASE. Reports in 1 month. Pays $5 minimum, 8½x11 b&w drawings.

DASH, Box 150, Wheaton IL 60187. (312)665-0630. Editor: Michael Chiapperine. Art Director: Roy Green. For Christian boys ages 8-11 in the church's Brigade program. Published 8 times/year. Circ. 28,000. Simultaneous submissions and previously published work OK. Original artwork returned after publication.Sample copy $1. Free artist's guidelines with SASE.
Cartoons: Contact: Sharon Long, associate editor. Uses 1 cartoon/issue; buys from freelancer. Receives 15 submissions/week from freelancers. Interested in family life, humor through youth, nature, school, sports; single panel with gag line. "Keep it clean." Prefers finished cartoons. SASE. Reports in 4-8 weeks. Buys first time rights. Pays $10 minimum, b&w line drawings; on publication.
Illustrations: Contact Roy Green. Uses 3 illustrations/issue; buys 2/issue from freelancers. Interested in education, family life and camping; b&w only, clean/professional look. Works on assignment only. Samples returned by SASE. Reports back on future assignment possibilities. Provide calling card or photocopy of samples to be kept on file for future assignments. Prefers resume and samples. SASE. Reports in 2 weeks. Buys first time rights. Cover: Pays $80-100, b&w line drawings and washes. Inside: Pays $50-85, b&w line drawings and washes; on publication.

DC COMICS, 75 Rockefeller Plaza, New York NY 10019. Managing Editor: Joe Orlando. For comic book readers, average age 14. Published 35 times/month.
Cartoons: Assigns comic book art. "We generally use established characters owned and controlled by DC Comics, Inc. If you don't know what a superhero comic is like, you aren't likely to be qualified for work." Arrange interview. SASE. Buys all rights. Negotiates pay; pays on acceptance.
Illustrations: "We also buy artwork for science fiction and war stories. We work with artists who are recieving their first professional assignment from us, and artists who have been in the business for 30 years. Arrange interview. SASE. Buys all rights. Pays on acceptance. "Payment is per page of artwork, rates vary with experience."
Tips: "It's a hard market to break into."

THE DEAF CANADIAN MAGAZINE, Box 1291, Edmonton, Alberta, Canada T5J 2M8. Editor: Roger Carver. For teachers, professionals and the deaf. Monthly. Circ. 141,000. "Contributions cannot be acknowledged or returned. Although we're copyrighted, we don't buy any rights." Sample copy $1.
Cartoons: Buys 32 cartoons/year on the deaf; single panel. Query or mail art. SASE. Pays $30 minimum, line drawings; on publication.
Illustrations: Buys 30 illustrations/year on the deaf. Query or mail art. SASE. Cover: Pays $50 minimum, color washes. Inside: Pays $30 minimum, b&w line drawings; on publication.

DECOR, 408 Olive, St. Louis MO 63102. (314)421-5445. Asst. Editor: Sheila Flanagan. "Trade publication for retailers of art, picture framing and related wall decor. Subscribers include gallery owners/directors, custom and do-it-yourself picture framers, managers of related departments in department stores, art material store owners and owners of gift/accessory shops." Monthly. Circ.

16,000. Simultaneous submissions and previously published work OK. Original artwork not returned after publication. Sample copy $3.
Cartoons: Uses 1-2 cartoons/issue; buys all from freelancers. Receives 5-10 submissions/week from freelancers. Interested in galleries, frame shops, artists and small business problems; single panel with gag line. "We need cartoons as a way to 'lighten' our technical and retailing material. Cartoons showing gallery owners' problems with shows, artists and the buying public, inept framing employees, selling custom frames to the buying public and running a small business are most important to us." Prefers finished cartoons. SASE. Reports in 2 weeks. Buys various rights. Pays $15-20, b&w line drawings and washes; on acceptance.
Illustrations: Assigns illustration work to local artists.

DEFENSE ELECTRONICS, (INCLUDING ELECTRONIC WARFARE), EW Communications Inc., 1170 E. Meadow Dr., Palo Alto CA 94303. (415)494-2800. Editor-in-Chief: Richard V. Hartman. Art Director: Dolores McKendry. Provides industry reports and technical information for systems manufacturers and users in the defense electronics field. Monthly. Circ. 25,000. Sample copy $1.
Illustrations: Uses 7-10 illustrations/issue; buys less than 1/issue from freelancers. Interested in military hardware and technical subjects. "Art must be prepared after consultation with and under supervision of art director." Works on assignment only. Samples returned by SASE. Provide resume and printed sample related to electronics to be kept on file for future assignments. Prefers samples. SASE. Reports in 2 weeks. Buys all rights. Cover: Pays $200 minimum, full-color art. Inside: Pays $75 minimum, full-color art; $50 minimum, b&w line drawings and washes; on acceptance.

DELAWARE TODAY, 2401 Pennsylvania Ave., Wilmington DE 19806. (302)655-1571. Art Director: Steve Pinkston. Monthly. Circ. 13,500. Free sample copy.
Illustrations: Uses 2-3 illustrations/issue; buys all from freelancers. Interested in blackline, ink washes, spots on current events and environment. Works on assignment only. Samples returned by SASE. Provide calling card, brochure, flyer and tearsheet to be kept on file for future assignments. Cover: Pays $150, color. Inside: Pays $75-100, b&w; $100-150,color. Pays on publication. Query with resume and samples or arrange interview to show portfolio. SASE. Reports in 1 week. Buys first North American serial rights.
Breaking In: "Work must show knowledgeable use of technique. Artist must be able to convey a fresh perspective. No previous work necessary."

DELTA SKY, Halsey Publishing, 99 N.W. 183rd St., Miami FL 33169. Managing Editor: Donna Dupuy. Monthly. Sample copy $1.50.
Illustrations: Buys assigned themes. Query with resume. Reports in 4 weeks. Buys all rights. Pays $25 minimum, spot art; $400, full-color cover.

DELTIOLOGY, 3709 Gradyville Rd., Newtown Square PA 19073. (215)353-1689. Contact: James L. Lowe. For collectors of international antique picture postcards. Bimonthly.Circ. 2,600.
Cartoons: Buys postcard-collector themes. SASE. Reports in 3 weeks. Pays in copies only; on publication.

DESERT, Box 1318, Palm Desert CA 92261. (714)568-2781. Editor-in-Chief: Donald MacDonald. Art Editor: Tom Threinen. For desert buffs, backpackers, hikers and those who love the outdoors. Monthly. Circ. 75,000. Does not return original artwork after publication, except by negotiation. Unpublished work only. Free contributor's guide.
Illustrations: Uses 1-10 illustrations/issue; number bought/issue from freelancers varies. Interested in the desert. Assignments are usually to illustrate a specific article. Works on assignment only. Samples returned by SASE. Reports back on future assignment possibilities. Provide tearsheet and copies of samples to be kept on file for future assignments. Prefers samples of style. Reports in 2 weeks. Buys all rights on a work-for-hire basis; "will usually assign upon request." Cover: Pays $75-125, color. Inside: Pays $35-75, color; on acceptance.

DETROIT ENGINEER, 25875 Jefferson St., St. Clair Shores MI 48081. (313)774-8180. Contact: Editor. For members of the Engineering Society of Detroit. Readers are "engineers, architects and persons in related fields. The median age is about 45, mostly affluent, with wide-ranging interests." Monthly. Circ. 8,000.
Cartoons: Uses 1 cartoon/issue, all from freelancers. Receives less than 1 submission/week from freelancers. Interested in engineering or technical subjects, "but engineer must not be made fun of." Prefers finished cartoons. SASE. Reports in 4 weeks. Buys first North American serial rights.Pays $10, b&w; on acceptance.

Illustrations: Uses 4 illustrations/issue; buys 2/issue from freelancers. Receives less than 1 submission/week from freelancers. Interested in "those relating to issue themes: automotive, construction, steel, computes and management." Works on assignment only. Samples returned by SASE. Reports back on future assignment possibilities. Provide brochure or flyer to be kept on file for future assignments. Prefers samples of style. SASE. Reports in 4 weeks. Buys first North American serial rights. Pays $10, b&w; on acceptance.

DIRECTIONS LIVELY ARTS, 8301 SW 13th Terr., Miami FL 33144. Editor-in-Chief: Rhoda Gadol. Art Director: Allen Gadol. Concerns music, art, fiction, medicine, education, theatre, law, etc. and fashion. Bimonthly. Circ. 40,000. Simultaneous submissions and previously published work OK. Original artwork returned after publication, with SASE. Sample copy $3.75; includes postage; free artists guidelines.
Illustrations: Contact: Rhoda Gadol. Number illustrations/issue varies. Interested in current events, education, environment, family life, humor through youth, retirement, tennis and boating. Provide resume, brochure or flyer to be kept on file for future assignments. Prefers resume, finished art and samples of style. SASE. Reports in 2 weeks. Buys all rights on a work-for-hire basis. Receives cartoons on gratis basis. "Since we are a lively arts magazine, we offer a free promotion to artists, photographers and writers, a two-page write up about them and their work at no cost to them. However, a pre-paid envelope must be included with their write-ups as we cannot return their material until this has been done."
Other Needs: "Specifically layout artist, for paste-up, profile writers."

DIRT BIKE, 16200 Ventura Blvd., Encino CA 91436. Editor: Bruce Woods. Monthly; 8½x11. Circ. 150,000. Query with resume. Reports in 2 weeks. Buys all rights. Previously published work OK.
Illustrations: Buys b&w line drawings and washes.

THE DISCIPLE, Christian Board of Publication, Box 179, St. Louis MO 63166. Editor-in-Chief: James L. Merrell. For ministers and lay persons. Biweekly. Circ. 69,100. Photocopied and simultaneous submissions OK. Original artwork returned after publication, if requested. Sample copy 35¢; free artist's guidelines.
Cartoons: Uses 1 cartoon/issue, all from freelancers. Receives 5-10 submissions/week from freelancers. Interested in family life and religion; single panel. Church material only. Prefers finished cartoons. SASE. Reports in 4 weeks. Buys first North American serial rights. Pays $7.50 minimum, b&w line drawings and washes; on acceptance.
Illustrations: Uses 2 illustrations/issue; buys 1/issue from freelancers. Receives 5 submissions/week from freelancers. Interested in "seasonal and current religious events/issues." Provide resume to be kept on file for future assignments. Prefers resume, roughs and samples of style. SASE. Reports in 2 weeks. Buys first North American serial rights. Cover: Pays $50-100, b&w line drawings and washes; on acceptance.

DISCOVERIES, 6401 The Paseo, Kansas City MO 64131. (816)333-7000. Editor: Mark A. York. Sunday school paper for ages 8-12. Weekly. Circ. 75,000-100,00. Simultaneous submissions and previously published work OK. Original artwork returned after publication. Free sample copy and artist's guidelines.
Cartoons: Buys 1 cartoon/issue, all from freelancers. Interested in "humor that appeals to children: school, animals, children, religion, etc."; single, double or multipanel. Prefers finished cartoons. SASE. Reports in 3-4 weeks. Buys all or first rights. Pays $7-10, b&w line drawings; on acceptance.
Illustrations: Uses 2 illustrations/issue, all from freelancers, on assigned themes. "Illustrations must be realistic and appeal to children 8-12." Provide resume, letter of inquiry, brochure, flyer or tearsheet to be kept on file for future assignments. Prefers finished art and samples of style. SASE. Reports in 3-4 weeks. Buys all rights on a work-for-hire basis. Inside: pays $40, $35-40 maximum, b&w or color; on acceptance.

DISCOVERY, 999 College Ave., Winona Lake IN 46590. (219)267-7161. Contact: Vera Bethel. For ages 9-11. Estab. 1929. Circ. 29,000. Weekly. SASE. Reports in 1 month. Pays on acceptance.
Cartoons: Buys 1/issue on school, pets and family. Pays $25-35, b&w. Send finished artwork.

DISPENSING OPTICIAN, Opticians Association of America, 1250 Connecticut Ave. NW, Washington DC 20036. Editor: James H. McCormick. Published 11 times/year. Circ. 5,500. Query. Buys all rights, but may reassign to artist after publication. Pays on publication. Sample cpy sent "if initial query is close to target."
Cartoons: Buys themes on opticians. Pays $7-10.

Illustrations: Uses b&w drawings and full-color art. Cover: Negotiates pay. Inside: Pays $10-45 for spot drawings.

DIVER MAGAZINE, 1601 Granville St., Vancouver, B.C. Canada V6Z 2B3. (604)689-8688. Readers are sports divers. Published 8 times yearly. Circ. 25,000. Sample copy $1.50; art guidelines for SASE.
Cartoons: Uses 1-2 cartoons/issue; buys all from freelancers. Interested in diving related cartoons only. Prefers single panel b&w line drawings with gag line. Send samples of style to Neil McDaniel, editor. SASE. Reports in 2 weeks. Buys first North American serial rights. Pays $15 for b&w on publication.
Illustrations: Uses 1-5 illustrations/issue; buys all from freelancers. Interested in diving related illustrations only. Prefers b&w line drawings for inside and cover. Send samples of style to N. McDaniel. SASE. Reports in 2 weeks. Buys first North American serial rights. Pays $15 minimum for inside b&w; $60 minimum for color cover and $20 minimum for inside color.

DIXIE LOGGER AND LUMBERMAN, 210 N. Main St., Wadley GA 30477. (912)252-5237. Contact: Eileen Hutchins, assistant to the president. For management personnel in the forest products industry. Circ. 18,000. Monthly. Original artwork not returned after publication. Sample copy $1; free artist's guidelines.
Cartoons: Uses 1 cartoon/week, on field of forestry; single panel with gag line. Buys b&w line drawings. Prefers finished cartoons. SASE. Reports in 1 week. Buys all rights. Negotiates pay; pays on acceptance.
Illustrations: Uses 1 illustration/issue on "things pertaining to loggers, lumber, paper and related fields." Prefers finished art. SASE. Reports ASAP. Buys all rights. Pays on acceptance.

DOG FANCY, Box 4030, San Clemente CA 92672. (714)498-1600. Editor: Linda Lewis. For dog owners, breeders and fanciers. Bimonthly. Circ. 65,000. Simultaneous submissions and previously published work OK. Sample copy $1.25; free artist's guidelines.
Cartoons: Buys 12 cartoons/year; single, double or multipanel. "Central character should be a dog." Mail finished art.SASE. Reports in 6 weeks. Buys first rights. Pays $20-50, b&w line drawings; on publication.
Illustrations: Buys 12 illustrations/year on dogs. Query with resume and samples.SASE. Reports in 6 weeks. Buys first rights. Inside: Pays $50-125, b&w line drawings; on publication.

DOLL WORLD, Box 1952, Brooksville FL 33512. Editor: Barbara Hall Pedersen. Art Director: Carol Pedersen. For doll lovers. Bimonthly. Original artwork returned after publication, if requested. Sample copy with 9x12 and 66¢ postage.
Cartoons: Uses 3 cartoons/issue; buys 3/issue from freelancers. Recieves 10 submissions/week from freelancers. Interested in "dolls, but no mean and sick humor. This magazine is for adults. Gently kid doll collectors." Prefers finished cartoons; single panel. SASE. Reports in 2 weeks, if not accepted. "Hold much longer if it's something we can use." Buys all rights on a work-for-hire basis. Pays $15, line drawings; on acceptance.
Illustrations: Uses 2 illustrations/issue; buys 2/issue from freelancers. Interested in "crisp, realistic, b&w line art." Works on assignment only. Provide resume to be kept on file for future asstinments. Prefers resume and samples of style. SASE. Reports in 1 week. Buys all rights on a work-for-hire basis.

DOMESTIC ENGINEERING, 135 Addison St., Elmhurst IL 60126. Contact: Editor. For mechanical contractors in plumbing, heating and air conditioning.
Needs: Reports in 2 weeks. Buys all rights. Pays $10 minimum, drawings; on publication.

DOWN EAST, Box 679, Camden ME 04843. (207)594-9544. Art Director: F. Stephen Ward. Concerns Maine's people, places, events and heritage. Monthly. Circ. 72,000. Previously published work OK. Buys first North American serial rights. Sample copy $1.50.
Illustrations: Buys 50/year on current events, environment, family life and politics. Query with resume and samples or arrange interview to show portfolio. SASE. Reports in 2-3 weeks. Cover: Pays $50-200, color paintings in any medium; "must have a 'postery' feel and be unmistakably Maine." Inside: Pays $25-200, b&w or color; on publication.

DOWN RIVER, World Publications, Box 366, Mt. View CA 94040. Contact: Bob Anderson. "Our readers are participants and we try to use material that shows insight into the sports that we cover." Reports in 1 week. Buys reprint rights. Pays on publication.
Needs: Pays $10 for cover designs, spot drawings and cartoons.

THE DRAGON, Box 110, Lake Geneva WI 53147. Editor: Timothy Kask. For well-read and educated fans of all types of game playing, with the emphasis on strategy and simulation games, including role-playing games. Monthly; 8½x11; 56 pages. Offset. Estab. 1976. Circ. 10,000. Query with samples. SASE. Reports in 6 weeks. Buys all rights, but may reassign rights to artist after publication. Pays on publication. Sample copy $2.
Cartoons: Buys 24-72/year on war-gaming and game playing. Minimum payment: $5, b&w; $20, color.
Illustrations: Buys 120-150/year on fantasy, science fiction, sorcery and game playing. Minimum payment: Cover: $75, color; $50, b&w. Inside: $20, color; $5, b&w.

DRAMATIKA, 429 Hope St., Tarpon Springs FL 33589. (212)749-5629. Editor: J. Pyros. Published semiannually. Sample copy $1.
Illustrations: Prefers unpublished work. Query. SASE. Reports in 1 month. Cover: Pays $15, b&w. Inside: Pays $5, b&w line drawings; on acceptance.

THE DRILLING CONTRACTOR, International Association of Drilling Contractors, Box 4287, Houston TX 77210. Editor-in-Chief: Nixon Quintrelle. For oil well drilling contractor management. Monthly; 8¼x11¼; 120 pages. Offset. Estab. 1944. Circ. 16,000. Query with samples. SASE. Reports in 2 weeks. Buys first rights. Pays on acceptance.
Illustrations: Pays $25-50, b&w line drawings, washes and gray opaques; $250, cover.

DUDE, Dugent Publishing Corp., 316 Aragon Ave., Suite 209, Coral Gables FL 33134. (305)443-2378. Managing Editor: Nye Willden. "Readers look at our magazine mostly for pictures of sexy gals." Bimonthly. Circ. 150,000. Original artwork returned after publication, if requested. Sample copy $1.95.
Cartoons: Bruce Arthur, editor. Uses 6 cartoons/issue; buys 6/issue from freelancers. Receives 100 submissions/week from freelancers. Interested in erotic themes; single panel with gag line. Prefers finished cartoons; reports in 2 weeks. Pays $25, spot drawing; $35/page, B&w line drawings, washes, gray opaques and full-color; on publication.
Illustrations: Uses 4 illustrations/issue, all from freelancers. Interested in realistic illustrations with erotic themes. Works on assignment only. Samples returned by SASE. Reports back on future assignment possiblities. Provide tearsheet to be kept on file for future assignments. Prefers samples of styles and 35mm transparency. SASE. Reports in 1 week. Buys first North American serial rights. Inside: Uses b&w line drawings, washes and gray opaques. Pays $75/page; $100/spread; on publication.

DYNAMIC YEARS, 215 Long Beach Blvd., Long Beach CA 90802. For middle-aged people interested in pursuing an active life. Bimonthly. Circ. 230,000. Free sample copy and artist's guidelines.
Cartoons: Contact James Wiggins, executive editor. Uses 5-6 cartoons/issue; buys all from freelancers. Receives 100 submissions/week from freelancers. Interested in family life, retirement and situations pertaining to people in their middle years; single panel with gag line. Prefers finished cartoons. SASE. Reports in 1 week. Buys first North American serial rights. Pays $50 minimum, b&w line drawings; $100 minimum, color; on acceptance.
Illustrations: Uses 10-20 illustrations/issue; buys all from freelancers. Interested in family life, retirement, humor, medical, nutrition, office, economy, pension and situations pertaining to people in their middle years. Works on assignment only. Provide brochure, flyer or tearsheet to be kept on file for future assignments. Prefers roughs or samples of style. SASE. Reports in 1 week. Buys all rights on 1 work-for-hire basis. Cover: Pays $100 minimum, color. Inside: Pays $25 minimum, b&w line drawings; $50 minimum, color. Pays on acceptance.

EARNSHAW'S REVIEW, 393 7th Ave., New York NY 10001. (212)563-2742. Editor-in-Chief: Thomas Hudson. Executive Editor: Joyce Snyder. Art Director: Peter Chau. For designers, manufacturers, buyers and retailers in the children's fashion industry. Monthly. Circ. 10,000.
Illustrations: Buys 180/year on fashion (infants to pre-teenagers). Arrange interview. SASE. Reports in 1 week. Buys all rights. Cover: Pays $50-100, color; $50 minimum, b&w. Inside: Pays $30, color; $15-20, b&w.
Advertising: Pays $20-25/figure, b&w and color; on publication.
To Break In: "Artist must have at least 4 child fashion illustrations in his portfolio. He must work quickly and accurately and know the difference between the figures of a 3 and 6 year old."

EASTERN OUTDOORS, 24 Legendary Rd., East Lyme CT 06333. (203)739-9256. Editor-in-Chief: John Brett. Art Director: Lane Masur. Concerns hunting, fishing and camping. Monthly; 8¼x11; 60 pages. Offset. Estab. 1977. Circ. 100,000. Mail art. SASE. Reports in 4 weeks. Pre-

viously published and photocopied submissions OK. Buys all rights, but may reassign rights to artist after publication. Pays on publication. Sample copy 50¢; free artist's guidelines.
Cartoons: Buys 50/year on the environment, hunting and fishing; single panel with gag line. Pays $25-75, b&w line drawings and washes.
Illustrations: Buys 12/year on the environment, hunting and fishing. Cover: Pays $150, color. Inside: Pays $50, b&w.

EASTERN REVIEW, East-West Network, Inc., 5900 Wilshire Blvd., #300, Los Angeles CA 90036. (213)937-5810. Editor-in-Chief: Fred Smith. Monthly. Sample copy $1.50.
Illustrations: Buys assigned themes. Query with resume. Reports in 4 weeks. Buys all rights. Pays $50 minimum, spot art; $450, full-page color illustration.

EASYRIDERS, Box 52, Malibu CA 90265. Art Director: Denise Pierson. For adult bikers. Monthly. "Needs art cartoons, or scenes with choppers in them, sexy women – in other words, 'bikes, booze and broads,' or scenes depicting the good times derived from owning a Harley-Davidson (if a cycle is illustrated)."
Cartoons: SASE. Reports in 2 weeks. Buys all rights. Pays $35, small b&w gags; $100, full-page b&w; on application.
Illustrations: "We prefer to buy art related to our subject and hold it for possible use. We're only interested in finished art. Subject matter is more important than the medium. We use more b&w than color." SASE. Reports in 2 weeks. Buys all rights. Price depends on space and use. A spot drawing pays $25 minimum; a full-page b&w pays $100-200; full-color pays about $350.

EBONY JR!, Johnson Publishing Co., Inc., 820 S. Michigan, Chicago IL 60605. (312)322-9272. Managing Editor: Mary C. Lewis. Art Director: Herbert Temple. For black children ages 6-12. Published 10 times/year. Circ. 100,000. Original artwork returned after publication. Sample copy 75¢.
Cartoons: Uses 1 cartoon/issue; buys 1/month from freelancers. Receives 10 submissions/month from freelancers. Interested in education, family life, humor through youth, popular sports and hobbies, varied careers and black children involved in unusual activities; "all from a child's point of view, showing positive, no-sexist characterizations"; single, double and multipanel with gag lines. Prefers roughs, resume and photostated copies of art. SASE. reports in 3 weeks-3 months. Buys all rights. Pays $15-85, b&w line drawings; $25-125, color-separated work and full-color renderings; on acceptance.
Illustrations: Uses 15 illustrations/issue; buys 15/issue from freelancers. Receives 3 submissions/week from freelancers. Interested in humor, sports & hobbies, varied careers, adventure, mystery, wildlife, family life, crafts, recipes, black history, African or Caribbean folklore; all from a child's point of view, showing positive and non-sexist characterizations. Works on assignment only. No samples returned. Reports back on future assignment possibilities. Provide resume, letter of inquiry, tearsheet (only rough sketches or photostats should be sent.) to be kept on file for future assignments. Prefers roughs. SASE. Reports in 3 weeks-3 months. Buys all rights. Cover: Pays $250, color. Inside: Pays $15-85, b&w; $85-125, color.
Other Needs: "Games, especially hidden object games, and out-of-place object games. Freelancers should submit a sketch or photostat of finished art first."

THE EDGE, Nazarene Publishing House, 6401 The Paseo, Kansas City MO 64131. Editor: Melton Wienecke. Assistant Editor: Nina Beegle. For church school directors, council members, supervisors, teachers, pastors, superintendents and program directors. Quarterly. Circ. 42,000. Simultaneous submissions OK. Original artwork not returned after publication. Free sample copy.
Cartoons: Uses 1 cartoon/issue; buys less than 1/issue from freelancers. Interested in education, humor through youth, religion and Sunday school classroom activities. Prefers roughs, finished cartoons or resume. SASE. Reports in 6 weeks. Buys all rights. Buys first North American serial rights. Pays $10-20, b&w line drawings and washes; on acceptance.
Other Needs: Uses mostly photographs.

EDITOR AND PUBLISHER, 575 Lexington Ave., New York NY 10022. (212)752-7050. For the working journalist, the journalism student, the journalism professor and the journalistic layman. Circ. 26,000. Weekly.
Illustrations: Art Director: George Wilt. Query with samples. SASE. Pays on publication

EDITORIAL JOURNAL, 1629 K St. N.W., Washington DC 20006. Tel. (202)659-0668. Editor-in-Chief: George Mair. Emphasizes politics and public affairs issues. Readers are "op-ed page editors of every metropolitan daily newspaper plus editorial directors of every television station

and major radio station in the US." Quarterly. Circ. 7,000. Original artwork not returned after publication. Free sample copy.
Cartoons: Uses 1 cartoon/issue "none of which have been supplied by freelancers yet, but we are willing to look. Cartoons should be one of two themes: (1) about editorial writers themselves such as Jeff McNalty's 'Shoe' strip and (2) political, but non-partisan, or public affairs issues. We are apolitical and non-partisan, so cartoons should not reflect extreme partisan positions. Instead, satire about government goof-ups or foot-in-mouth statements by politicians such as Gerald Ford's freedom in East Europe, etc." Formats: single panel b&w line drawings with gag lines. Prefers finished cartoons. SASE. Reports in 1 week. Buys all rights. Pays $50 and up on acceptance.

EDUCATIONAL LEADERSHIP, Association for Supervision and Curriculum Development, 225 N. Washington St., Alexandria VA 22314. (703)549-9110. Editor-in-Chief: Ronald S. Brandt. Art Director: Amy Rupp. For superintendents, principals, professors and teachers. Published 8 times/year. Circ. 36,000. Arrange interview to show portfolio. SASE. Previously published work OK. Buys first and reprint rights. Free sample copy.
Cartoons: Uses 1 cartoon/issue. Intersted in education in primary and secondary schools; single, double and multipanel. Prefers portfolio (finished cartoons). SASE. Reports in 1 week. Buys all rights on a work-for-hire basis. Buys 5/year on education and humor through youth; single, double and multipanel. Negotiates pay for b&w line drawings; pays on publication.
Illustrations: Uses 1 illustration/issue. Interested in educational themes. Works on assignment only. Samples returned by SASE. Reports back on future assignment possibilities. Provide calling card to be kept on file for future assignments. Prefers portfolio (finished art). SASE. Reports in 1 week. Buys all rights on a work-for-hire basis. Cover: Pays $150-400 (negotiable), 2-color art. Inside: Pays $10-100, b&w line drawings and 2-color work; on publication.

EDUCATIONAL STUDIES: A JOURNAL IN THE FOUNDATIONS OF EDUCATION, 331 DeGarmo Hall, Illinois State University, Normal IL 61701. (309)436-5415, ext. 230. Art Director: Joan K. Smith. Emphasizes research, reviews and opinions in the foundations of education. Quarterly. Circ. 1,600. SASE.
Cartoons: Buys 0-3/issue on purposes of schools, learning situations and satires of school situations. Query or send roughs. Pays $10, b&w; on publication. SASE. Reports in 2-3 months.

EERIE COUNTRY, Box 35, Amherst Branch, Buffalo NY 14226. Editor-in-Chief: W. Paul Ganley. An irregular companion publication to *Weirdbook* for those interested in fantasy, adventure and horror. Semiannual. Estab. 1979. Circ. 300. Buys first or all rights. Sample copy $2.
Illustrations: Buys 20-40 illustrations/year. Interested in weird, macabre, supernatural and fantastic themes. "Illustrate scenes from famous weird writers like Bradbury, Lovecraft, Poe, etc." Mail art. Photocopies OK. Must be suited to photocopy. SASE. "Reports in a few weeks for submissions received in December, early January, May, June or July." Cover: Pays 5-25, b&w; Inside: Pays $1-5 b&w; on publication.

EL PALACIO, Box 2087, Santa Fe NM 87503. (505)827-2352. Editor: Richard Polese. Art Director: Glen Strock. Published by the Museum of New Mexico, magazine deals with fine art, folk art, regional anthropology, geography, natural history and history. Quarterly. Circ. 2,300. Original artwork returned after publication. Sample copy $2.
Illustrations: Uses 40 illustrations/issue; buys 1/issue from freelancers. Receives 2 submissions/week from freelancers. Interested in anthropology, archaeology, southwestern history and art to illustrate features. "We prefer to deal with artists and graphics people who live in this immediate area." Prefers finished art or samples of style. SASE. Reports in 3 weeks. Buys first North American serial rights, or all rights on a work for-hire-basis, depending on contract. Cover and inside: buys b&w line drawings, washes and gray opaques. "Pay determined by contract with the publisher."
Design: Contact Jim Mafchir, publisher. Uses artists for design, layout and paste-up. Negotiates pay. Query with resume and samples or previously published work, or arrange interview to show portfolio.

ELECTRIC COMPANY MAGAZINE, 1 Lincoln Plaza, New York NY 10023. (212)595-3456, ext. 573. Art Director: Paul Richer. For ages 6-11.
Illustrations: Buys 60/year. Query with photocopied samples. SASE. Reports in 2 weeks. Buys one-time rights. Pays $150 min./page, b&w; $200 max./page, color; on acceptance.

ELECTRICAL APPARATUS, Barks Publications, Inc., 400 N. Michigan, Chicago IL 60611. Contact: Elsie Dickson. Query with resume.

ELECTRICAL WORLD, McGraw-Hill Publishing Inc., 1221 Avenue of the Americas, New York NY 10020. (212)997-2440. Art Director: Kiyo Komoda. For electric utility management and engineers. Bimonthly. Original artwork returned after publication, on request.Pays on acceptance.
Cartoons: Uses 2 cartoons/issue; buys all from freelancers, on assignment only. Interested in industry-related situation cartoon, usually related to editorial articles. Prefers resume. SASE. Reports in 1 week. Buys one-time and reprint rights. Pays on acceptance.
Illustrations: Uses 20 illustrations/issue, buys all from freelancers. Interested in energy systems; 90% are mechanical line drawings, maps, flow designs, graphs and charts. Works on assignment only. Samples returned by SASE. Provide resume or calling card to be kept on file for future assignments. Prefers portfolio or finished art. SASE. Reports in 1 week. Buys one-time and reprint rights. Cover: Pays $150-350, color. Inside: Pays $30-300, color; $10-200, b&w line drawings. Pays on acceptance.
To Break In: "We prefer artists with clean and crisp line works. They should know about color separation and use of zippertones. Young artists welcomed."

ELECTROMECHANICAL BENCH REFERENCE, Barks Publications, Inc., 400 N. Michigan, Chicago IL 60611. Contact: Elsie Dickson. Query with resume.

ELECTRONICS, McGraw-Hill Publishing Co., 1221 Avenue of the Americas, New York NY 10020. (212)997-2430. Art Director: Fred Sklenar. For college graduates, electronics engineers, marketing people and executives. Biweekly. Circ. 100,000. Original artwork returned after publication. Photocopied and simultaneous submissions OK.
Illustrations: Uses 60 illustrations/issue; buys all from freelancers. Buys 26 covers/year on assigned themes. Works on assignment only. Samples returned by SASE. Provide tearsheet and sample art to be kept on file for future assignments. Prefers finished art, portfolio, samples of style, or tearsheets. SASE. Reports when applicable to needs. Buys all first-time world rights. Cover: Pays $300 minimum, color. Inside: Pays $30-300; on acceptance.

ELECTRONICS HOBBYIST, Davis Publications, 380 Lexington Ave., New York NY 10017. (212)557-9100. Contact: Irving Bernstein. Reports in 1 week. Buys first rights. Pays on acceptance.
Needs: Pays $20 minimum, line drawings; $400 maximum, full-color cover.

ELECTRONICS JOURNAL, Elexpro Enterprises, Inc., 213 Fernwood Dr., Aurora IL 60538. (312)897-4000. Editor-in-Chief: William C. Sands Jr. Art Director: Art McAllister. Concerns industrial electronics in the Midwest. Monthly. Circ. 5,000. Simultaneous submissions OK. Free sample copy; artist's guidelines $5.
Cartoons: Buys 1-2 cartoons/issue from freelancers. Interested in field of industry; single panel. "Material must be pertinent to the field and must be well done." Prefers samples. SASE. Reports in 6-8 weeks. Buys first rights. Pays $30-100, b&w line drawings.
Illustrations: Works on assignment only. Provide letter of inquiry and samples to be kept on file for future assignments. Prefers samples. SASE. Reports in 6-8 weeks. Buys first rights. Pays $30-100; b&w line drawings; on publication.
To Break In: Send for free copy of the Editorial Calendar, which indicates the specific needs of this publication.

ELEMENTARY ELECTRONICS, Davis Publications, 380 Lexington Ave., New York NY 10017. (212)557-9100. Contact: Irving Bernstein. Reports in 1 week. Buys first rights. Pays on acceptance.
Needs: Pays $20 minimum, line drawings; $400 maximum, full-color cover; on acceptance.

ELITE, 234 Eglinton Ave. E., Suite 401, Toronto, Ontario, Canada M4P 1K5. Editor-in-Chief: David Wells. For men ages 18-33, interested in modern lifestyles. Monthly. Circ. 300,000. Photocopies OK. Original artwork returned after publication.
Cartoons: Editor: Chris Curl. Uses 12 cartoons/issue, all from freelancers. Receives 150 submissions/week from freelancers. Interested in erotica; single panel. Prefers finished cartoons. SASE. Reports in 2 weeks. Buys all rights on a work-for-hire basis. Pays $20-25 b&w; color $40-50; on publication. Buys 200/year on current events and erotica; single panel.
Illustrations: Art Director: Rick Bookman. Uses 8 illustrations/issue; buys 4/issue from freelancers. Themes "open to article being illustrated." Works on assignment only. Samples returned by SASE. Reports back on future assignment possibilities. Provide resume, calling card, letter of inquiry, brochure, flyer or tearsheet to be kept on file for future assignments. Prefers portfolio and samples of style. SASE. Reports in 2 weeks. Buys all rights on a work-for-hire basis. Inside: Pays $10 minimum, b&w; $200+, color; on publication.

THE ELKS MAGAZINE, 425 W. Diversey Pkwy., Chicago IL 60614. Managing Editor: Donald Stahl. For members of the Elks. Monthly. Circ. 1,600,000. Original artwork not returned after publication. Buys first and North American serial rights. Pays on acceptance. Free sample copy.
Cartoons: Uses 1 cartoon/issue, all from freelancers. Receives 50 submissions/week from freelancers. Buys 12-36/year; single panel. "Must have family appeal." Interested in general interest cartoons. Prefers finished cartoons. Reports in 2 weeks. Buys first and North American serial rights. Buys 12-36/year; single panel. "Must have family appeal." Pays $50 minimum, line drawings; on acceptance.

ELLERY QUEEN'S MYSTERY MAGAZINE, Davis Publications, 380 Lexington Ave., New York NY 10017. (212)557-9100. Contact: Irving Bernstein. Reports in 1 week. Buys first rights. Pays on acceptance.
Needs: Pays $20 minimum, line drawings; $400 maximum, full-color cover.

EMERGENCY, (formerly *Emergency Product News*), Box 159, Carlsbad CA 92008. (714)438-3457. Managing Editor: Richard Minerd. For emergency medical technicians, paramedics, doctors, nurses and rescue squads. Monthly. Circ. 35,000. Original artwork returned after publication. Free sample copy.
Cartoons: Uses 2 cartoons/issue, all from freelancers. Receives 5 submissions/week from freelancers. Interested in emergency technicians in situations. Prefers roughs or finished cartoons. Reports in 2 weeks. Buys first North American serial rights. Pays $25 minimum, b&w line drawings, halftones and washes; $35, color; on publication.
Illustrations: Uses 2 illustrations/issue, all from freelancers, on assigned themes. Receives 5 submissions/week from freelancers. Provide resume and flyer to be kept on file for future assignments. Prefers resume and samples of style. SASE. Reports in 2 weeks. Buys first North American serial rights. Minimum payment: Cover: $100, color. Inside: $35-50, color; $25, b&w; on publication.

EMPIRE MAGAZINE, c/o *Denver Post*, Box 1709, Denver CO 80202. (303)820-1687. Editor-in-Chief: Carl Skiff. Art Director: Jack Flemming. Weekly. Circ. 375,000. Original artwork not returned after publication.
Cartoons: Number cartoons/issue varies. Interested in "family-oriented humor"; single panel. Prefers finished cartoons-"line or line and wash." SASE. Reports immediately. Buys first rights. Pays $15 minimum, b&w halftones and washes; on acceptance.

ENERGY EFFICIENT HOMES, Box 640, Jarvis, Ontario, Canada N0A 1J0. Editor: Wendy Priesnitz. Quarterly. Circ. 5,000. Estab. 1980. Emphasizes renewable energy technologies relating to home building, retrofitting-home design. Interested in energy efficient homes, log construction, solar systems, wood heated, owner-built wind systems, underground homes and passive solar in b&w or color. Pays $10-150 on acceptance.

THE ENERGY PEOPLE, Public Service Electric and Gas Co., 80 Park Place, Newark NJ 07101. (201)430-5989. Contact: Eugene Murphy, employee information. For 13,000 employees and 5,000 retirees; includes company news and some New Jersey-oriented stories. Quarterly.
Cartoons: Buys 2/issue on environment and utilities; single panel with gag line. Query with samples. SASE. Reports in 2 weeks. Pays $5-25, b&w line drawings; on acceptance.
Illustrations: Occasionally buys artwork on assigned themes. SASE. Reports in 2 weeks. Pays on acceptance.

ENGINEERING AND CONTRACT RECORD, 1450 Don Mills Rd., Don Mills, Ontario, Canada M3B 2X7. Editor: Nick Hancock. Previously published work in non-Canadian magazines OK.
Cartoons: "We use 3-4 cartoons/issue relating to heavy construction themes: equipment, labor, safety, roadbuilding, sewer construction, general business management; we prefer winter settings in winter months. Send any construction theme applicable except house building." Send art or photocopies. Buys first and second Canadian rights. Pays $10 minimum; on publication.

THE ENTHUSIAST, Harley-Davidson Motor Co. Inc., 3700 W. Juneau, Milwaukee WI 53201. Editor: Robert H. Klein. For "motorcycle riders of all ages, education and professions." Quarterly. Estab. 1916. Circ. 150,000. Mail art. Reports in 2 months. Previously published work OK. Not copyrighted. Pays on publication. Sample copy available.
Needs: Buys finished cartoons and b&w line drawings of Harley-Davidson motorcycles. Pays $15.

ENTREPRENEUR MAGAZINE, 2311 Pontius Ave., Los Angeles CA 90064. Tel. (213)478-0437. Creative Director: William Nirenberg. Emphasizes small business opportunities. Monthly. Circ.

60,000. Original artwork returned after publication. Art guidelines for SASE.
Cartoons: Managing Editor: John Hiatt. Uses 12 cartoons/issue, all from freelancers. Receives 3-4 submissions/week from freelancers. We use small business themes, financial themes, bizarre strange inventions and obscure franchise ideas;" single panel, b&w line drawings and washes with gag line. Prefers resume with samples of style or finished cartoons. SASE. Reports in 4 weeks. Buys all rights. Pays $25-35, b&w cartoons; on acceptance.
Illustrations: Creative Director: William Nirenberg. Uses 1 illustration/issue, bought from freelancer. "We use small business, financial and realism themes." Prefers resume and samples of style or arrange personal appointment to show portfolio. SASE. Reports in 2 weeks. Buys all rights on a work-for-hire basis. Pays $100-150 for b&w cover, $30-50 for inside b&w, $200-300 for color cover, $50-100 for inside color; on acceptance.
Other Needs: "We periodically use all types of freelance artists from paste-up to illustration—all samples are filed respectfully in their category."

ENVIRONMENT, 4000 Albermarle St., Washington DC 20016. Tel. (202)362-6445. Associate Editor: Joy O'Rourke. Emphasizes energy, conservation, pollution, ecology and environmental issues. Readers are "college undergrads to scientists and business and government executives." Monthly. Circ. 17,000. Original artwork returned after publication.
Cartoons: Uses less than 1 cartoon/issue; buys 1/issue from freelancers. Receives 2 submissions/ week from freelancers. Interested in single panel b&w line drawings or b&w washes with or without gag line. Send finished cartoons. SASE. Reports in 2 weeks. Buys first North American serial rights. Pays $35, b&w cartoon; on acceptance.

ENVIRONMENT NEWS DIGEST, 1025 Connecticut Ave. NW, Washington DC 20036. Editor-in-Chief: Charles W. Felix. Primarily concerns proper safeguard procedures in restaurants; also covers solid wastes and litter disposal and public health. Bimonthly. Circ. 10,000. Simultaneous submissions and previously published work OK. Free sample copy.
Cartoons: Buys 8/year on environment, food service and inspection, solid wastes, litter, paper cups and plates; single panel with gag line. SASE. Reports in 3 weeks. Buys reprint rights. Prefers roughs. Pays $15 minimum, b&w line drawings; on acceptance.

EQUUS, Equine Health Publications Co., 656 Quince Orchard Rd., Gaithersburg MD 20760. Editor-in-Chief: Ami Shinitzky. Art Director: Carl Miller. "Concerns the health, care and wonders of the horse." Monthly. Circ. 171,000. Previously published, photocopied and simultaneous submissions OK. Sample copy $2.25.
Illustrations: Buys 12-18/year on horses and veterinary medicine. Submit art or query with samples. SASE. Reports in 4 weeks. Buys first, reprint, one-time or all rights. Cover: Pays $300 average, color. Inside: Pays $200 minimum, b&w; $250, color, per assignment; 30 days after publication.

ERBE PUBLISHERS, 220 Tyrone Circle, Baltimore MD 21212. Contact: Theodore H. Erbe. Publishes philatelic magazine. Query.
Needs: Uses artists for covers, illustrations and layout. "It helps if you are a stamp collector." Pays by job.

ESCAPADE, 210 E. 35th St., New York NY 10016. Contact; Art Director. Readers are 18-40, high school educated and interested in sexual entertainment.Monthly. Circ. 150,000.
Cartoons: Uses 5-6 cartoons/issue; buys all from freelancers. Receives 25-50 submissions/week from freelancers. Interested in titillating sex themes. Pays $15, b&w. Prefers finished cartoons. SASE. Reports in 2 weeks. Pays on publication.
Illustrations: Uses 1-2 illustrations/issue; buys all from freelancers. Interested in sexually titallating themes. Works on assignment only. No samples returned. Reports back on future assignment possibilities. Provide resume, brochure, or tearsheet to be kept on file for future assignments. Prefers portfolio or roughs. SASE. Reports in 1 week. Buys first North American serial rights. Pays $50-100, b&w; on publication.

ESQUIRE, 488 Madison Ave., New York NY 10022. Art Director: Michael Gross. Arrange interview to show portfolio.
Needs: Pays $100-150/page, b&w; $200-250/page, full-color.

EUROPE, MAGAZINE OF THE EUROPEAN COMMUNITY, 2100 M St., NW, #707, Washington, DC 20037. (202)862-9500. Emphasizes European affairs, US-European relations—particularly economics, trade and politics. Readers are businessmen, professionals, academics, government officials and consumers. Bimonthly. Circ. 45,000. Free sample copy.

Cartoons: Assistant Editor: Candace Denning. Uses 8-10 cartoons/issue, mostly from a cartoon service. "We are strictly a European-oriented magazine on topics such as economics, trade, business, industry, politics, energy, inflation, etc. Current news topics as well as European-US relations";single panel b&w line drawings or b&w washes with or without gag line. Send resume plus finished cartoons and/or samples. SASE. Reports in 3-4 weeks. Buys one-time rights. Pays $25; on publication.
Illustrations: Assistant Editor: Candace Denning. Uses 3-5 illustrations/issue. "At present we work exclusively through our designer and set up charts and graphs to fit our needs. We would be open to commissioning artwork should the need and opportunity arise. We look for economic graphs, tables, charts and story-related statistical artwork"; b&w line drawings and washes for inside. Send resume and samples of style. SASE. Reports in 3-4 weeks. Buys all rights on a work-for-hire basis. Pays from $25; on publication.

EVANGEL, 999 College Ave., Winona Lake IN 46590. (219)267-7161. Contact: Vera Bethel. Readers are 65% female, 35% male; 25-to 31-year-old, married, city-dwelling, mostly nonprofessional high school graduates. Estab. 1897. Circ. 35,000. Weekly. SASE. Reports in 1 month. Pays on acceptance.
Cartoons: Buys 1-2/issue on family subjects. Pays $5, b&w. Mail finished art.
Illustrations: Buys 2/issue on assigned themes. Pays $35, 2-color. Query with samples.

EVENT, Box 2503, New Westminster, B.C., Canada V3L 5B2. (604)588-4411. Published semiannual. Circ. 800. Original artwork returned after publication. Sample copy $2.50.
Illustrations: Editor: Ken Hughes. Uses 16-20 illustrations/issue, buys 16-20/issue from freelancers. Interested in experimental drawings and prints. Mail finished art. SASE. Reporting time varies; at least 2 weeks. Buys first North American serial rights. Cover and inside: Pays $5 minimum, b&w line drawings, photographs and lithographs; on publication. Payment includes free copies.
Other Needs: Photography.

EXCAVATING CONTRACTOR, 3221 W. Big Beaver Rd., Suite 204, Troy MI 48084. (313)362-4650. Readers are small earthmoving contractors. Monthly. Circ. 33,000. Free sample copy; art guidelines for SASE.
Cartoons: Receives 1 submission/week from freelancers. Interested in anything having to do with earthmoving or construction. Prefers single panel b&w line drawings with gag line. Send finished cartoons to Drew Winter, editor. SASE. Reports in 2 weeks. Buys no rights. Pays $5-10 for b&w on publication.
Illustrations: Uses some illustrations for covers. Works on assignment only. Prefers b&w line drawings for inside and cover. Send resume or arrange personal appointment to show portfolio. SASE. Reports in 1 week. Buys all rights. Pays $75 minimum for covers on acceptance.

EXECUTIVE REVIEW PUBLISHERS, 224 S. Michigan Ave., Chicago IL 60604. Contact: Editor. Monthly. Previously published work OK. Sample copy available.
Cartoons: Uses 2 cartoons/issue; buys most from freelancers. Interested in any theme as long as it is "tasteful." SASE. Reports in 1 week. Buys one-time rights. Pays on publication.
Illustrations: Works on assignment only. Interested in business, office and plant. Provide resume, brochure, or flyer to be kept on file for future assignments. Prefers samples of style. SASE. Reports in 1 week. Buys all rights on a work-for-hire basis. Pays on publication.

EXPECTING, 52 Vanderbilt Ave., New York NY 10017. For expectant mothers. Circ. 1,000,000. Quarterly. SASE. Pays on acceptance.
Illustrations: Contact Ruth Kitaif. Buys 1/issue on pregnancy. Pays $100-200, b&w; $200-300, color. Arrange interview to show portfolio.

EXPORT, 386 Park Ave.S., New York NY 10016. (212)689-0120. Editor: Robert Weingarten. For importers and distributors in 167 countries who handle hardware, air conditioning and refrigeration equipment and related consumer hardlines. Bimonthly. Circ. 38,500.
Cartoons: Buys 2-3/issue on consumer durables-hardware, housewares, lawn and garden equipment, sporting goods and other leisure items, with an international touch if possible. SASE. Reports in 4 weeks. Pays $50 for b&w; on acceptance.
Illustrations: Buys 1/issue. Inside: "We like collage-type treatments of whole areas of the consumer hardgoods world. These can be relatively abstract." Cover: "Cover illustrations should be amusing or dramatic pictures which convey the idea of export." Query with samples. SASE. Reports in 4 weeks. Pays $150, color cover illustrations; on acceptance.

FACE-TO-FACE, 201 8th Ave. S., Nashville TN 37202. (615)749-6225. Contact: Dave Dawson. For United Methodist youth, ages 15-18. Quarterly. Circ. 30,000. Original artwork not returned after publication.
Illustrations: Uses 12 illustrations/issue; assigns themes. Works on assignment only. Samples returned by SASE. Reports back on future assignment possibilities. Provide tearsheet to be kept on file for future assignments. Prefers furnished art and samples of style. SASE. Reports in 1 week. Buys all rights on a work-for-hire basis. Pays $50, 1-color; $55, 2-color; $60, 3-color; $75, full-color; on acceptance.

FAMILY CIRCLE, 488 Madison Ave., New York NY 10022. Art Director: John Bradford. Circ. 8,200,000. Supermarket-distributed publication for women/homemakers. Submit portfolio on "portfolio days," every other Wednesday. All art is commissioned for specific magazine articles. Will look at mailed submissions if preceded by letter of inquiry detailing experience.
Cartoons: Contact: Managing Editor.
Illustrations: Uses 20 illustrations/issue, all from freelancers. Works on assignment only. Samples returned by SASE. Reports back on future assignment possibilities. Provide resume, calling card, brochure, flyer or tearsheet to be kept on file for future assignments. Prefers portfolio (finished art). SASE. Reports in 1 week. Buys all rights on a work-for-hire basis.
Other Needs: "Extensive photgraphy assignments."

THE FAMILY FOOD GARDEN, 1999 Shepard Rd., St. Paul MN 55116 (612)647-7478. Editor: Sharon M. Ross. For home gardeners and fruit growers. Published 9 times/year. Circ. 300,000.Sample copy $l.
Cartoons: Uses 2-3 cartoons/issue, all from freelancers. Receives 2 submissions/week from freelancers. Interested in vegetable gardening; single panel. Mail brochure or samples with SASE. Reports in 4 weeks. Buys all rights. Pays $20 minimum, pen and ink; on acceptance.
Illustrations: Uses 5 illustrations/issue; buys 0-2/issue from freelancers. Works on assignment only. Samples returned if requested. Provide tearsheet or brochure (no resumes) to be kept on file for future assignments. Mail brochure or samples with SASE. Reports in 4 weeks. Buys all rights. Pays on acceptance.

FAMILY PET, Box 22964, Tampa FL 33622. Editor-in-Chief: M. Linda Sabella. For Florida pet owners, including those who show their pets in competitions. Quarterly. Circ. 3,200. Original artwork not returned after publication. Free sample copy and artist's guidelines.
Cartoons: Uses 1-2 cartoons/issue on pets; single panel with gag line. Prefers finished cartoons. SASE. Reports in 1-2 months. Pays $3-5, b&w line drawings; on publication.
Illustrations: Buys 3-4/year on pets. Prefers finished art. SASE. Reports in 1-2 months. Buys one-time rights. Cover: Pays $5-20, b&w line drawings. Inside: Pays $3-10, b&w line drawings; on publication.

FANTASTIC STORIES, 69-62 230th St., Bayside, Queens NY 11364. Contact: Sol Cohen. For science fiction buffs. Submit published samples. Reports in 60 days. Buys first or reprint rights. Pays on acceptance.
Illustrations: Cover: Pays $50, full-color. Inside: Pays $10, line drawings.

FARM SUPPLIER, Watt Publishing Co., Mount Morris IL 61054. Editor: Ray Bates. Monthly.
Cartoons: Buys 1-2cartoons/issue. Interested in situations in retail farm supply stores or related to outside sales and services by representatives of such local firms. SASE. Buys all rights. Pays $8; on acceptance.

FARMSTEAD MAGAZINE, Box 111, Freedom ME 04941. (207)382-6200. Publisher: George Frangoulis. Focuses on home gardening and small farming. Published eight times a year. Circ. 100,000. Original artwork returned after publication when requested. Free sample copy and artist's guidelines.
Illustrations: Buys 25 illustrations/issue; buys 10/issue from freelancers. Receives 5 submissions/week from freelancers. Interested in farming, gardening, plants, wildlife, etc., (pen & ink, wood block, etching). Works on assignment only. Samples returned by SASE. Reports back on future assignment possibilities. Provide resume, calling card, letter of inquiry, brochure, flyer, or tearsheet to be kept on file for future assignments. Prefers query with resume and samples or arrange interview to show portfolio, finished art, roughs. SASE. Reports in 4 weeks. Buys all rights on a work-for-hire basis. Pays $25-100, b&w inside; on publication.

THE FAULT, 33513 6th St., Union City CA 94587. (415)489-8561. Editor: Terrence McMahon. For small press aficionados. Semiannual. Circ. 500. Previously published and photocopied submissions OK. Sample copy $2.25.

Cartoons: Buys 40/year. Interested in surrrealistic and Dada themes. Prefers query with 5x7 photo of art. SASE. Reports in 2 weeks. Pays $5-10, washes; on receipt of grant (usually 1 year after publication).
Illustrations: Buys 40/year. "I select work from portfolios, rather than have artists conceive for a publication. Their work is placed alongside parallel themes from writers." SASE. Reports in 2 weeks. Pays $5-10, b&w line drawings, washes and litho prints; on receipt of grant (usually 1 year after publication).

50 PLUS, 850 3rd Ave., New York NY 10022. Editor: Jess Gorkin. Art Director: Jan Foster. For active pre-retirees and retirees, with news and features on financial planning, health care, consumerism, housing, living environments, hobbies, crafts, travel, personality profiles and leisure. Sample copy $1.25 plus postage.
Cartoons: Uses 2-4 cartoons/issue, all from freelancers. Interested in "topical, human interest" themes. Prefers finished cartoons. SASE. Reports in 2 weeks. Buys first North American serial rights. Pays $35-75, b&w drawing; on acceptance.
Illustrations: Uses 1-2 illustrations/issue; buys 1-2/issue from freelancers. Works on assignment only. No samples returned. Reports back on future assignment possibilities. Interested in "strong line illustrations." Uses b&w and full-color drawings. Prefers samples of style. SASE. Reports in 30-60 days. Buys all rights on a work-for-hire basis.

THE FIGHTER'S HOME, 202 Lucerne Ave., Lake Worth FL 33460. Contact: Daniel Gorham. Query. Reports in 3 months. Not copyrighted.
Needs: Uses b&w line drawings, line and wash, cover designs, full-color illustrations with color separations and cartoons. "We prefer that the artist set his own rates with us so we can be fair, and also see if we can afford him."

FIGHTING STARS, 1845 W. Empire Ave., Burbank CA 91504. Editor: Pamela Finke. Features personality pieces on media stars involved with martial arts. Bimonthly. Previously published work OK. Sample copy available.
Illustrations: Mail art. Buys all rights. Pays $100 average, 4-color cover; on publication.

FIGHTING WOMAN NEWS, Box 5416, Grand Central Station, New York NY 10017. Art Director: Muskat Buckby. Concerns martial arts, self-defense and combative sports; "Our readers are active female practitioners, 1/3 of whom have black belts." Quarterly. Circ. 5,000. Previously published work OK. Sample copy $1.75.
Cartoons: Uses 1-2 cartoons/issue, all from freelancers. Interested in women's martial arts. Prefers finished cartoons and tearsheets. SASE. Reports ASAP. Buys first rights or one-time rights.
Illustrations: Uses 1-2 illustrations/issue, all from freelancers. Interested in women's marital arts. "We use cartoons, sketches, graphics and whatever else we can get. What the science-fiction group calls fan art is welcome here. For inside work, we pay in copies, T-shirts, ads, etc." Provide tearsheet or samples to be kept on file for future assignments. SASE. Reports ASAP. Buys first rights or one-time rights. Cover: Pays $10. Buys 1/issue.
To Break In: "Technical accuracy is paramount in material illustrating the martial arts. Sergio Aragones doesn't know marial arts at all and used our file photos as reference for some details—Japanese fencing armor for example—but the thrust of his stuff was not illustration but comment. So it didn't matter that he showed a woman working the speed bag wearing boxing gloves instead of hand wraps because the focus was on the coach holding two small kids. Study us and the male-oriented martial arts periodicals as well as the mainstream coverage of women's sports in general. Our reason for being is to supply what they don't."

FINANCE, 25 W. 39th St., New York NY 10018. (212)221-7900. Publisher: James C. Burke. For senior executives and decision makers in business and finance. Bimonthly. Circ. 35,000.
Cartoons: Buys banking and business themes. Write. SASE. Reports in 4 weeks. Pays $25, b&w; on publication.
Illustrations: Buys assigned themes. Write and send samples. SASE. Reports in 4 weeks. Pays $25-50; on publication.

FIND MAGAZINE, 353 Lexington Ave., New York NY 10016. (212)685-4900. Readers are Jewish families in NY, NJ, and Eastern PA. Monthly. Circ. 250,000. Estab. 1980. Free sample copy.
Illustrations: Uses 5 illustrations/issue. Interested in artwork to illustrate lifestyle articles and topical issue stories of interest to the affluent Jew. Prefers b&w line drawing and washes; color washes for inside. Arrange personal appointment to show portfolio or send samples of style that

need not be returned to be kept on file for future assignments. Works on assignment only. Reports back on future assignment possibilities. Buys all rights. Negotiates pay by the job and "standard editorial rates". Payment made 30 days after invoice.

FIRELANDS REVIEW, Firelands College, Huron OH 44839. (419)433-5560. Executive editor: Joel Rudinger.
Illustrations: Uses 15-20 illustrations/issue. Interested in watercolors with obvious contrast, still life, charcoal renderings, nudes, pen & ink and serious art. "We do not try to match illustrations with features. We can determine from slides if we can use illustrations and are always looking for new and original talent." Buys first North American serial rights. Pays in copies on publication.

FISHING WORLD, 51 Atlantic Ave., New York NY 11001. (516)352-9700. Editor: Keith Gardner. Emphasizes angling. Readers are adult male US sport fishermen. Bimonthly. Circ. 235,000. Original artwork returned after publication. Free sample copy.
Illustrations: Uses one illustration/issue, buys from freelancers. Interested in realistic illustrations. Uses inside color washes. Works on assignment only. No samples returned. Provide brochure, flyer and tear sheets to be kept on file for future assignments. SASE. Reports in 2 weeks. Buys first North American serial rights. Pays $150 for inside color; on acceptance.

FLEA MARKET QUARTERLY, Box 243, Bend OR 97701. Contact: Kenneth Asher. "In addition to flea market coverage, we also feature items on changing lifestyles, ecology, money-making ideas and money-saving tips." Reports in 6 weeks. Buys all rights. Pays on acceptance.
Needs: Pays $5, drawing; $30, cover.

FLING, 1485 Bayshore Blvd., San Francisco CA 94124. Bimonthly. Query. Reports in 3 weeks. Buys first rights. Pays on acceptance. Sample copy (with editorial guidelines) $2.
Cartoons: Buys 10/issue with sophisticated male slant; double-page spreads and multipanel gags. Will buy idea for cartoon spreads; roughs to be farmed out to regulars. Pays $20-50; $50-100, spreads.

FLORIDA BANKER, Florida Bankers Association, Box 6847, Orlando FL 32853. Editor: William P. Seaparke, CAE. Provides educational and legislative material relevant to Florida bankers. Published 11 times/year. Circ. 5,300. Original artwork not returned after publication. Prefers artists who have had work published.
Cartoons: Buys very few cartoons/issue. Interested in banking; single, double and multipanel with gag lines. Prefers roughs. Reports in 8 weeks. "Don't telephone editor. " Buys all rights. "Loans rights back to artists on occasions." Pays $20-50, b&w line drawings and washes; on publication.
Illustrations: Buys 1 illustration/issue on business or banking. Uses 10-15 illustrations/issue. Interested in business or banking. Works on assignment only. No samples returned. Reports back on future assignment possibilities. "Assignments made only after query. Do not send art before requested to do so." Provide letter of inquiry to be kept on file for future assignments. Reports in 8 weeks. "Don't telephone editor." Buys all rights on a work-for-hire basis. "Loans rights back to artists on occasions." Cover and inside: Pays $50-100, b&w line drawings, b&w or color washes and full-color art; on publication.

FLORIDA SINGLES MAGAZINE & DATE BOOK, Box 83, Palm Beach FL 33480. (305)833-8507. Editor: Harold Alan. Emphasizes singles lifestyle for single, divorced, widowed or separated people who comprise over 40% of the adult population over 18. Bimonthly. Circ. 10,000. Estab. 1978. Free sample copy.
Cartoons: "We want to meet cartoonists who can draw our ideas and deliver quickly. Must live in South Florida." Interested in couples and dating situations but "nothing off-color." Prefers single panel with gag line. Send finished cartoons, samples of style or arrange interview. SASE. Reports in 1 week when assignment is available. Buys rights for Florida, Washington and Philadelphia single magazines. Pays $25-50 within 30 days of publication.
Illustrations: Uses 2-3 illustrations/issue; buys all from freelancers. Illustrators must live in South Florida and be able to deliver assignments quickly. Interested in drawings of couples in happy situations. Prefers b&w line drawings for inside. Send samples of style for assignment. SASE. Reports in 1 week or when assignment is available. Buys all rights. Pays $25-50 for b&w cover.

THE FLORIDIAN, Box 1211, St. Petersburg FL 33731. (813)893-8372. Editor: Judy Sedgeman. For middle-income readers with a contemporary outlook. Weekly. Circ. 270,000. Original artwork returned after publication.

Illustrations: Uses 10+ illustrations/issue; buys 5+/issue from freelancers. Receives 20+ submissions/week from freelancers. Interested in Florida life style issues, events and people. Provide resume, calling card, letter of inquiry and tearsheet to be kept on file for future assignments. Prefers resume and samples of style. SASE. Reports in 2 weeks. Buys first North American serial rights. Pays $25-50, b&w; $25-150, color; on publication.

FLORIST, Florists Transworld Delivery Association, Box 2227, Southfield MI 48037. (313)355-9300. Editor-in-Chief: William Golden. Production Manager: Jo Garder. For florists and floriculturists. Monthly. Circ. 24,000. Reports in 4 weeks. Previously published and simultaneous submissions OK.
Cartoons: Uses 4 cartoons/issue, all from freelancers. Interested in retail florists and floriculture; single, double and multipanel with gag lines. Mail art. SASE. Buys one-time rights. Pays $10-50, b&w line drawings; on acceptance.

FLOWER AND GARDEN, 4251 Pennsylvania, Kansas City MO 64111. (816)531-5730. Emphasizes "gardening for avid home gardeners." Monthly. Circ. 500,000. Sample copy $1.
Cartoons: Editor: Rachel Snyder. Uses 1 cartoon/issue. Receives about 10 submissions/week. Needs cartoons related to "indoor or outdoor home gardening." Format: single panel b&w line drawings or washes with gag line. Prefers finished cartoons. SASE. Reports in 4 weeks. Buys one-time rights.Pays $25, b&w cartoon; on acceptance.

FLOWERS &, (formerly Teleflorists), Box 6034, Inglewood CA 90312. (213)973-2501. Editor: Barbara Cady. Art Director: M.J. Cody. For flower shop management. Monthly. Circ. 20,000. Original artwork returned after publication.
Cartoons: Uses 1 cartoons/issue, all from freelancers. Receives 5 submissions/week from freelancers. Prefers finished cartoons. SASE. Reports in 2 weeks. Buys all rights on a work-for-hire basis.
Illustrations: Uses 10 illustrations/issue, all from freelancers. Interested in business, floral and flower industry related themes. Works on assignment only. No samples returned. Reports back on future assignment possibilities. Provide calling card, brochure and flyer to be kept on file for future assignment. Prefers finished art, portfolio or samples of style. SASE. Reports in 1 week. Buys all rights on a work-for-hire basis. Inside: Pays $15-30, b&w and color; $15-75, full page of spot illustrations; on acceptance.
Other Needs: Uses artists for layout, advertising and brochures. Pays $15 minimum; on acceptance.

FLY FISHERMAN, Editorial Offices, Dorset VT 05251. (802)867-5951. Art Director: James H. Sulham. Emphasizes fly fishing. Readers "devote an average of 35 days a year to fly fishing. They are 99% male; 79% are college graduates; 79% are married. The average household income is $34,500 and 55% are professionals or managers. 85% keep their copies for future reference." Bimonthly. Circ. 130,000. Original artwork returned after publication. Sample copy $1.95; art guidelines for SASE.
Illustrations: Uses 6 illustrations/issue; buys 5/issue from freelancers. Receives about 5 submissions/week from freelancers. Interested in "saltwater and freshwater fly-fishing or stream-scene in all areas of the country. Scenics including insects, fish—preferably not dead or braces of—and related subjects." Format: b&w line drawings, b&w washes and color washes for inside magazine. Freelancers are selected from "samples and spot—filler—work kept on file. Assignments are also made." Provide letter of inquiry or a sample of work preferably in the fly-fishing or stream area to be kept on file for future assignments. Prefers samples of style or arrange personal appointment to show portfolio. SASE. Reports in 4-6 weeks. Buys one-time North American magazine rights. Pays $25-100 for b&w "depending on size and use inside the magazine"; color payment negotiated; on publication.

THE FLYFISHER, 390 Bella Vista, San Francisco CA 94127. (415)586-8332. Editor-in-Chief: Michael Fong. Art Director: Ed Ow. For members of the Federation of Fly Fishermen; concerns fly-fishing and conservation. Quarterly. Circ. 7,000. Buys first North American serial rights. Sample copy $1.50 from Federation of Fly Fishermen main office, 519 Main St., El Segundo CA 90245; free artist's guidelines with SASE.
Illustrations: Interested in fly-fishing themes. Works on assignment only. Samples returned by SASE. Reports back on future assignment possibilities. Query with resume and samples. SASE. Reports in 4 weeks. Buys first North American serial rights. Inside: Pays $10-25, b&w line drawings and washes; on acceptance.

FOOD PROCESSING, Putman Publishing Co., 430 N. Michigan, Chicago IL 60611. Editorial/Publishing Director: Roy Hlavacek. For executives and managers in food processing industries.

Monthly. Circ. 56,000. Photocopied submissions OK. Original artwork not returned after publication. Free sample copy and artist's guidelines.
Cartoons: Uses 1 cartoon/issue, all from freelancers. Receives 15-20 submissions/week from freelancers. Interested in "situations in and around the food plant (e.g. mixing, handling, transporting, weighing, analyzing, government inspection, etc.)"; single panel with gag line. Prefers finished cartoons. SASE. Reports in 1 week. Buys all rights. Pays $20 minimum, b&w line drawings.

FOOTWEAR FOCUS, 200 Madison Ave., New York NY 10016. (212)686-7520. Readers are shoe retailers. Quarterly. Circ. 20 million. Free sample copy.
Illustrations: Uses 8 illustrations/issue; buys all from freelancers. Currently receives no submissions from freelancers. Works on assignment only. Interested in fashion illustrations—ready-to-wear and shoes. Prefers b&w line drawings and b&w or color washes. Arrange personal appointment to show portfolio or send samples of style to Diane Sambora, managing editor. SASE. Reports in 2 weeks. Buys all rights. Pays $35 maximum for inside b&w and $75 for color inside; on acceptance.

FORD TIMES, Ford Motor Co., Box 1509-B, Dearborn MI 48121. (313)322-9262. Contact: Editor-in-Chief or Art Director. General interest publication with emphasis on travel in the US. Monthly. Circ. 1,800,000. Original artwork not returned after publication. Free sample copy and artist's guidelines.
Illustrations: Buys 20/issue on assigned themes. Uses 20 illustrations/issue, all from freelancers, on assignment themes. Receives no submissions/week from freelancers. Works on assignment only. Samples returned by SASE. Reports back on future assignment possibilities. Provide resume and tearsheet to be kept on file for future assignments. Prefers portfolio. SASE. Reports in 1 week. Buys all rights on a work-for-hire basis. Pays $65, b&w spots; $225, color work; $400, color cover; on acceptance.

FORE, Southern California Golf Association, 3740 Cahuenga Blvd., North Hollywood CA 91604. Editor: Charles H. Bobo. Quarterly.

FORECAST FOR HOME ECONOMICS, 50 W. 44th St., New York NY 10036. (212)867-7700, ext. 436. Art Director: Elena Beck. Uses as a teaching guide for *Co-Ed* magazine. Estab. 1954. Circ. 78,000. Monthly (September-June). SASE. Pays on publication.
Cartoons: Buys 5-8/issue on people engaged in home activities and food. Pays $25, b&w; $50, color. Call for appointment to show portfolio.
Illustrations: Buys 1-3/issue on assigned themes. Pays $50-100, b&w; $50-200, color; varies according to size. Arrange interview to show portfolio.

THE FOREMAN'S LETTER, National Foremen's Institute, 24 Rope Ferry Rd., Waterford CT 06386. Editor: Pamela Akins. Sample copy 75¢.
Cartoons: Usually uses 1 cartoon/issue; may buy up to 2/issue from freelancers. Receives 20 submissions/week from freelancers. Interested in "supervisor-worker relations; avoid sexism and other discriminatory situations"; single panel. Prefers finished cartoons. SASE. Reports in 1 week. Buys all rights. Pays $10; on acceptance.

FORET ET PAPIER, 625 President Kennedy Ave., Montreal, Quebec, Canada H3A 1K5. (514)845-5141. Editor-in-Chief: Paul Saint-Pierre. For engineers and foremen in paper mills and woodlands operations. Published six times/year. Circ. 5,500. Free sample copy.
Illustrations: Buys 4/year on paper mills, paper-making machines, men at work and tree harvesting. Query with samples. SASE. Reports in 2 weeks. Buys all rights, but may reassign rights to artist after publication. Pays $125-175, 4-color art; on acceptance.

FORM, National Business Forms Association, 433 E. Monroe Ave., Alexandria VA 22301. Managing Editor: E.C. Raleigh. Query with resume.
Needs: Magazine cover ideas appropriate to business forms design and construction and illustrations of interior construction of business forms. Also uses artists for advertising art/design, cartoons, decorative spots, direct mail brochures, editorial and technical illustrations. Pays $20-50, illustraions; $50-100, covers. "We usually provide artist with copy and rough sketch of what we want to illustrate. We expect artist to refine and revise into best possible artistic and graphic presentation."

FORMS, THE REVIEW OF ANTHROPOS THEOPHOROS, Box 3379, San Francisco CA 94119. Editor-in-Chief: Emily McCormick. Art Editor: Raymond Hoche-Mong. Concerns art in

all forms. Quarterly. Circ. 400. Previously published, photocopied and simultaneous submissions OK. Original artwork returned after publication. Sample copy $1; "strongly suggest seeing copy before submitting."
Other Needs: Publishes 4-6 pages of art/issue. "Regular feature of 4-7 pages. Photographs of sculpture and large works also considered." Preferably b&w drawings or photographs; occasional color. Do not send slides." Submit art or query with samples. SASE. Reports in 2 weeks. Buys first rights. Pays on publication. Subject open but requires written articulation of artist's art, but not explanation or apologia."

FREE ENTERPRISE, 1212 Avenue of the Americas, New York NY 10036. (212)354-4100. Art Director: Ezra Shapiro. "Includes stories about fascinating people, articles about making money, and undiscovered new places." Bimonthly; 8x11; 112-128 pages. Offset. Estab. 1971. Circ. 425,000. Query with samples or arrange interview to show portfolio. SASE. Buys one-time rights. Sample copy $1.50.
Illustrations: Buys 20/issue on assigned themes. Cover: Pays $400 minimum, full-color. Inside: Pays $50 minimum, b&w; $100 minimum, color.

FRIDAY, 226 S. 16th St., Philadelphia PA 19102. (215)893-5745. Editor-in-Chief: Jane Biberman. Literary supplement to *Jewish Exponent*. Monthly. Circ. 75,000. Original artwork returned after publication. Free sample copy and artist's guidelines.
Illustrations: Uses 2 illustrations/issue. Works on assignment only. Samples returned by SASE. Reports back on future assignment possibilities. Provide tearsheet to be kept on file for future assignments. Prefers porfolio; SASE. Reports in 3 weeks. Buys all rights on a work-for-hire basis. Pays on publication.

THE FRIEND, 50 E. North Temple, Salt Lake City UT 84150. Art Director: Richard D. Brown. Children's publication of the Church of Jesus Christ of Latter-day Saints. Original artwork returned after publication, usually after about 1 year.
Illustrations: Uses 30-35 illustrations/issue. Buys about 15/issue from freelancers. Interested in themes mostly specific to individual art assignments from our concepts (child-related, dealing with ages 1-12); excellent, competitive quality. Covers often emphasize seasons and holidays; wide spectrum of styles and ideas. Works with freelancers on assignment basis only except for activity related things. Samples returned if artist requests. Provide printed samples to be kept on file for future assignments. Prefers roughs of ideas for finishing, portfolio or samples of style. SASE. Report depends on specific art assignment. Need to retain art for a year or two. Pays $150-350, b&w, 2-color and full-color; on acceptance.
Other Needs: Well-written, simple and interesting photo stories, b&w or color for children age 1-12.

FROLICS, Frolics Publications, Inc., Box 412, Ithaca NY 14850. Publisher: Jack Tate. Editor: Erika Tate. Concerns adult eroticism and sexuality. Quarterly. Circ. 5,000. Previously published, photocopied and simultaneous submissions OK. Original artwork returned after publication. Sample copy $2; artist's guidelines with SASE.
Cartoons: Uses 3-5 cartoons/issue; buys 2-4/issue from freelancers. Interested in current events, erotica, family life pertaining to sexuality and morals; and politics; single, double and multipanel. Prefers finished cartoons. SASE. Reports in 2 weeks. Pays $5-25, b&w; on acceptance.
Illustrations: Uses 6-8 illustrations/issue; buys 1-2/issue from freelancers. Interested in current events, erotica, family life and politics. Works on assignment only. Samples returned by SASE. Reports back on future assignment possibilities. Provide brochure, flyer or tearsheet to be kept on file for future assignments. Prefers finished art or samples of style. SASE. Reports in 2 weeks. Buys all rights on a work-for-hire basis. Cover: $10-35, b&w. Inside: $5-25, b&w.
Other Needs: Anything pertaining to erotic art. Would like to give exposure to artists who enjoy working on subject matter allowing public to purchase works.

FRONT LINE, Merck Sharp & Dohme, West Point PA 19486. (215)699-5311. Editor: William P. Pearre. For Merck Sharp & Dohme field representatives. Quarterly. Circ. 1,500. Free sample copy.
Cartoons: Buys 24/year on medicine or selling to the medical/pharmacy professions; single panel. "Prefer not to see cartoons that poke fun at patients."Mail art. SASE. Reports in 2 weeks. Buys first rights. Pays $100, b&w washes; on publication.

FRONT PAGE DETECTIVE, RGH Publications, 235 Park Ave. S., New York NY 10003. Editor: Diana Lurvey. For mature adults — law enforcement officials, professional investigators, criminology buffs and interested laymen. Monthly.

Cartoons: Must have crime theme.. Submit finished art. Reports in 10 days. Buys all rights. Pays $25; on acceptance.

FRONTIER TIMES, Western Publications, Inc., Box 3338, Austin TX 78764. Publisher: Joe Austell Small. Editor: Pat Wagner. For those interested in 1840-1910 western Americana nonfiction. Submit 4x5 transparency. Reports in 2-3 weeks. Previously published work OK "depending on where it appeared." Buys one-time rights. Pays on acceptance. Sample copy 75¢.
Illustrations: Buys cover art in 4-color oils. "We prefer a color snapshot or transparency for evaluation of the artist's style. Transparency is returned after publication. We also prefer vertical paintings because the use of bands above and below a horizontal gives issues a look of sameness. We also have to pass up good paintings at times because our titles would cover some vital element or because the painting has no space left for story titles. We like to leave the artist's work as uncluttered as possible, but a certain amount of type is required. Often, the artist doesn't take this into account." Pays $100.

FUGUE, 49 Avenue Rd., Toronto, Ontario, Canada M5R 2G3. (416)960-5889. Editor-in-Chief: Diane Watts. Concerns classical music. Published 12 times/year. Circ. 25,000, Canada and U.S.; 17,000, U.K.Previously published work OK. Free sample copy and artist's guidelines.
Cartoons: Uses 2-3 cartoons/issue; buys all from freelancers. Receives 10-20 submissions/week from freelancers. Interested in classical music themes and personalities; single, double or multi-panel with gag line. "We are anxious to have cartoons and look forward to hearing from as many cartoonists as possible." Prefers roughs. SASE. Reports in 2-3 weeks. Buys all rights. Pays $25 minimum, b&w line drawings, washes and gray opaques; 30 days after acceptance.
Illustrations: Uses 1-2 illustrations/issue; buys all from freelancers. Interested in classical music composers, living personalities or illustrating the theme of a particular article; strong graphic quality. Uses line drawings mostly but some color wash type. Works on assignment only. Samples returned by SASE. Reports back on future assignment possibilities. Provide letter of inquiry or photocopy of an illustration to be kept on file for future assignments. Prefers samples of style. SASE. Reports in 2-3 weeks. Buys first North American serial rights. Inside: Pays $50-100, b&w; $50-150, color; 30 days after acceptance.

FUR-FISH-GAME, A.R. Harding Publishing Co., 2878 E. Main St., Columbus OH 43209. (614)231-9585. Editor-in-Chief/Art Director: A.R. Harding. For practical, rural outdoorsmen. Monthly. Circ. 190,000. Previously published work OK in some cases. Sample copy 75¢. Free artist's guidelines.
Illustrations: Uses 12 illustrations/issue; uses 1/issue from freelancers. Receives 1 submission/week from freelancers. Interested in game animals, gamebirds, gamefish, furbearers. Prefers color photograph of art. SASE. Reports in 4 weeks. Buys 12/year on hunting, fishing and trapping. Pays $50-75, full-color cover renderings; on acceptance.

GALILEO, 339 Newbury, Boston MA 02115. (617)266-7834. Emphasizes science and science fiction. Readers average age 29, are male, college educated, and are homeowners. Bimonthly. Circ. 100,000. Original artwork returned after publication. Sample copy $1.95; art guidelines for SASE.
Cartoons: Uses 3 cartoons/issue; buys all from freelancers. Interested in science or science fiction and humor. Format: single panel b&w line drawings with gag line. Send finished cartoons to attention of the editor. SASE. Reports in 4-6 weeks. Buys first world rights with non-exclusive option for reprint. Pays $15-25 on publication.
Illustrations: Uses 7 illustrations/issue; buys all from freelancers. Interested in dramatic-action illustrations, strong on characterization and detail. Oil or acrylic art used for both cover and inside. Works on assignment only. Samples returned by SASE. Sometimes reports back to artist whether he/she might expect future assignments. Provide letter of inquiry, brochure, flyer, tearsheet, photocopies or slides to be kept on file for future assignments. Contact art director by phone or letter to request a personal appointment to show portfolio or send samples of style for review. SASE. Reports in 4 weeks. Buys first world rights plus non-exclusive option for anthology reprint. Pays $50-75 for inside b&w; $300-500 for color cover; $100-150 for inside color; on publication.

GALLIMAUFRY, Box 32364, Washington DC 20007. Editor: Mary MacArthur. Published semi-annually. Send samples; prefers local artists. SASE. Reports in 3 months. Buys one-time rights. Sample copy $1.25.
Needs: Uses 1 freelance artist/issue. Pays $25, 1-color cover.

THE GAMBLING SCENE, Box 4483, Stanford CA 94305. (415)964-5740. Editor: Michael Wiesenberg. Emphasizes gambling and gaming for mostly beginning gamblers. Many play cards

in legal cardrooms on West Coast. Monthly. Circ. 10,000. Estab. 1979. Sample copy $1; art guidelines for SASE.
Cartoons: Editor: Michael Wiesenberg. Uses less than 1 cartoon/issue; all by freelancers. Receives less than 1 submission/week from freelancers. Cartoons should pertain to playing cardgames, upgrade card playing image, gambling on sports, professional fighting, horse racing, casinos, cardrooms; single panel b&w line drawings with gag line. Send finished cartoons and samples of style. SASE. Reports in 2 weeks. Pays $5-10; for b&w; on publication. Buys all rights.
Illustrations: Editor: Michael Wiesenberg. Uses 10-20 illustrations/issue; all from freelancers. Receives more than 20 submissions/week from freelancers. "We want local artists from San Francisco area; will make assignments from submissions in standard, drop-in artwork—gambling related." Illustrations should pertain to all types of gambling. "We will assign art to accompany articles." Format: b&w line drawings. Works on assignment only. Samples returned by SASE. Reports back on future assignment possibilities. Provide resume, letter of inquiry, tearsheet or samples to be kept on file for future assignments. Prefers finished art or samples of style. SASE. Reports in week. Buys all rights on a work-for-hire basis. Pays on publication.
Other Needs: "Photos-usually only accompanying manuscripts. Also uses freelancers for subscription solicitation materials. Also needs gambling-related article; with or whitout accompanying photos or art. Send for guidelines. SASE.

GAMBLING TIMES, 1018 N. Cole Ave., Hollywood CA 90038. (213)463-4833. Editor-in-Chief: Len Miller. Cartoon Editor: Richard Stone. For gamblers. Monthly. Circ. 100,000. Original artwork returned after publication. Sample copy $1; free artist's guidelines.
Cartoons: Buys approximately 20/year on topic directly related to gambling. Prefers finished cartoon, full-page, single panel; b&w line drawings.SASE. Reports in 2 weeks. Buys all rights. Pays $10-35; on publication.
Illustrations: Uses 6-7 illustrations/issue; buys 5/issue from freelancers. Interested in simple and clean b&w line drawings; satrirical or humorous visuals used occasionally. Works on assignment only. Samples returned by SASE. Provide calling card or tearsheet to be kept on file for future assignments. Prefers portfolio. (Note: Generally use only Los Angeles area illustrators.) SASE. Reports in 1 week. Buys all rights on a work-for-hire basis. Pays on publication.

GAMES, 515 Madison Ave., New York NY 10022. (212)421-5984. Emphasizes games, puzzles, mazes, brain teasers, etc. for teachers, students, computer analysts and mathematicians interested in paper and pencil games. Bimonthly. Circ. 550,000. Free sample copy.
Illustration Needs: Uses 40 illustrations/issue; 39 supplied by freelancers. "I see a style I like, then ask the artist to execute an idea I have to illustrate a puzzle." Illustrations should be light hearted but not childish drawings. Anything from Renaissance to cartoons. Format: b&w line drawings and color washes for inside and cover. Contact Lillian Nahmias, art director, to arrange personal appointment to show portfolio and/or photocopies of samples with cover letter including experience and turn-around time. Drop off on Wednesday and pick up Thursday. Reports in two weeks or whenever an assignment is available. Pays on publication $100-350 b&w/inside; $350-500 color/inside. Buys all rights on a work-for-hire basis.

THE GARLINGHOUSE CO., Box 299, Topeka KS 66601. (913)267-2490. President: Whitney B. Garlinghouse. Publishes magazines and newspapers.
Other Needs: Uses artists for advertising and production. Query with samples. SASE. Reports in 4 weeks. Pays promised fee for unused assigned work.
Production: Pays $5-25/hour, layout, paste-up, retouching, type spec and mechanicals.
Advertising: Pays $10-25/hour, consumer magazines; $7.50-15/job, newspapers.

GAS DIGEST, Box 35819, Houston TX 77035. Editor: Ken Kridner. For those in the gas industry. Monthly. Circ. 9,200. Sample copy with SASE.
Cartoons: Buys themes on the gas industry only; single panel. Query. SASE. Reports in 1 week. Buys all rights, but may reassign rights to artist after publication. Pays $10 minimum, b&w line drawings; on acceptance.

GENERAL DENTISTRY, Academy of General Dentistry, 211 Chicago Ave., Chicago IL 60611. (312)449-4300. Editor-in-Chief: William W. Howard. Director of Communications: Leslie Joan Millenson. Bimonthly. Circ. 40,000. Original artwork returned after publication. Free sample copy.
Cartoons: Uses 2 cartoons/issue. Interested in dentist- or health-care-related themes. Prefers roughs. SASE. Reports in 6 months. Buys all rights.
Illustrations: Uses 1 illustration/issue. Interested in dentistry. "Art must be related to specific needs and be prepared under the supervision of the art director." Works on assignment only.

Samples returned by SASE. Reports back on future assignment possibilities. Provide resume, calling card, letter of inquiry, brochure and tearsheet to be kept on file for future assignments. Prefers portfolio (roughs). Reports in 3 months. Buys all rights. Maximum payment: Cover: $400, color-separated and full-color art; $250, b&w line drawings. Inside: $300, color-separated and full-color art; $100, b&w line drawings; on publication.

GENESIS, 770 Lexington Ave., New York NY 10021. (212)486-8430. Monthly. Circ. 600,000. Original artwork returned after publication.
Cartoons: Contact Paula Schwartz. Uses 2-8 cartoons/issue, all from freelancers. Interested in erotic themes. Prefers finished cartoons. SASE. Reports in 2 weeks. Buys first North American serial rights. Pays $75-150, b&w or color; on publication.
Illustrations: Art Director: Pat Garling. Buys 10 illustrations/issue on assigned thems. Styles vary. Works on assignment only. No samples returned. Reports back on future assignment possibilities. Provide resume and tearsheet to be kept on file for future assignments. Prefers portfolio and samples of style. SASE. Reports "when needed." Buys first North American serial rights. Pays $25-135, b&w; $50-800, color; on publication.

GENIE CONSTRUCTION, 310 Victoria Ave., Suite 201, Westmount, Quebec, Canada H3Z 2M9. (514)487-2302. Readers are in the construction industry. Monthly. Circ. 6,000.
Cartoons: Uses 1 cartoon/issue; buys all from freelancers. Interested in humoristic construction or management themes. Prefers single panel. Send finished cartoons to Judith Hebert, assistant editor. SASE. Reports in 2 weeks. Buys first North American serial rights. Pays $40 for b&w on acceptance.
Illustrations: Uses 1 illustration/issue; buys all from freelancers. Interested in construction and forestry themes. Works on assignment only. Prefers b&w line drawings for inside. Send finished art to J. Hebret. SASE. Reports in 2 weeks. Buys first North American serial rights. Pays on acceptance.

GENT, Dugent Publishing Co., 316 Aragon Ave., Coral Gables FL 33134. Publisher: Douglas Allen. Editor: John Fox. Managing Editor: Nye Willden. For men.
Cartoons: Buys "funny, somewhat 'sick' humor and sexual themes." Mail cartoons. Submit illustration samples for files. Buys first rights. Pays $35, b&w spot drawing; $50/page.
Illustrations: Buys 3-4/issue on assigned themes. Mail cartoons. Submit illustration samples for files. Buys first rights. Pays $75-100.

GENTLEMANS QUARTERLY, 350 Madison Ave., New York NY 10017. (212)880-7902. Emphasizes "mens fashions and grooming for middle to upper income professional males ranging in age 20 to 35." Monthly. Circ. 400,000. Free sample copy and art guidelines.
Cartoon Needs: Uses about 30 cartoons/issue, all supplied by freelancers. Format: b&w line drawings. Send samples of style or present portfolio for review to Guy Augri, art assistant. SASE. Reports in 1 week. Pays either on acceptance or publication. Buys all rights.
Illustration Needs: Uses about 30 illustrations/issue, all supplied by freelancers. Selection based on review of portfolios and by reviewing files maintained on freelancers. Format: B&w line drawings. Send finished art to G. Augri, art assistant. SASE. Reports in 1 week. Pays 30 days after work is completed. Buys all rights on a work-for-hire basis.

GEORGIA STRAIGHT, Georgia Straight Publishing Ltd., 2110 W. 4th Ave., Vancouver, B.C., Canada V6K 1N6. Contact: Dan McLeod. Alternative press. Submit photocopies or photos. SASE. Reports in 2 weeks. Buys one-time rights. Pays on acceptance.
Needs: Pays $4, spot drawing; $25-50, 7x7 color cover.

GLAMOUR, 350 Madison Ave., New York NY 10017. Art Director: George Hartman. Women's fashion magazine. Query with resume and arrange interview to show portfolio.
Needs: "All work done here is freelance." Pays $225/page.

GLASS DIGEST, 110 E. 42nd St., New York NY 10017. Editor: Oscar S. Glasberg. For management in the distribution, merchandising, and installation phases of the flat glass, architectural metal, and allied products industry (including stained, art glass and mirrors). Original artwork not returned after publication. Free sample copy.
Cartoons: Uses 0-3 cartoons/issue; buys about 2/issue from freelancers. Receives 5 submissions/week from freelancers. Interested in storefront and curtain wall construction and automotive glass industry. Prefers finished cartoons. SASE. Reports in 1 week. Pays $7.50; on acceptance.
Illustrations: Works on assignment only. Samples returned by SASE. Reports back on future assignment possibilities. Prefers roughs. SASE. Reports in 1 week. Buys first North American serial rights. Pays on acceptance.

GLIMPSES OF MICRONESIA & THE WESTERN PACIFIC, Box 3191, Agana, Guam 96910. 477-7606. "A regional publication for Micronesia lovers, travel buffs, and readers interested in the U.S.'s last frontier. Our audience covers all age levels and is best described as well educated and fascinated by our part of the world." Quarterly. Circ. 15,000. Original artwork returned after publication. Sample copy $2; art guidelines for SASE.
Cartoons: "Use very little, but willing to look at Pacific related themes."
Illustrations: "We are interested in story illustration. Both color and b&w. We will assign story." Works on assignment only. Samples returned. Provide tearsheet to be kept on file for future assignments. Send samples of style to Sue Couch, art director. SASE. Reports in 2 weeks. Buys all rights on a work-for-hire basis, or first North American rights if work was not solicited by us. Pays $100 for full-page b&w; $200 for full-page color; on publication.

GOLF, Times Mirror Magazines, 380 Madison Ave., New York NY 10017. (212)687-3000. Editor: George Peper. Art Director: Daryl Herrmann. For golf enthusiasts. Monthly. Circ. 725,000. Query with samples. SASE. Reports in 4 weeks. Buys all rights. Pays on acceptance. Free sample copy and artist's guidelines.
Cartoons: Uses 3 cartoons/week, all from freelancers. Receives 2 submissions/week from freelancers. SASE. Interested in golf; single and double panel with gag lines. SASE. Reports in 4 weeks. Pays $75 minimum, b&w line drawings; on acceptance; on acceptance.
Illustrations: Buys 6 illustrations/issue from freelancers. Recieves 6 submissions/month from freelancers. Works on assignment only. Samples returned by SASE. Reports back on future assignment possibilities. Provide 8½x11, 4-color tearsheet to be kept on file for future assignments. Prefers samples. SASE. Reports in 4 weeks. Buys all rights. Minimum payment: Inside: $200 and up, drawings; $300 and up, full-color; on acceptance.

GOLF DIGEST, 495 Westport Ave., Norwalk CT 06856. Art Director: Pete Libby.
Needs: Buys golf themes. Query with resume. Reports in 2 weeks. Buys first rights. Pays $250/page, full-color illustrations; $150/page, b&w; on acceptance.

GOLF JOURNAL, Golf House, Far Hills NJ 07931. (201)234-2300. Managing Editor: George Eberl. Readers are "literate, professional, knowledgeable on the subject of golf." Monthly. Circ. 100,000. Original artwork not returned after publication. Free sample copy.
Cartoons: Uses 2 cartoons/issue, all from freelancers. Receives 50 submission/week from freelancers. "The subject is golf. Golf must be central to the cartoon. Drawings should be professional, and captions sharp, bright and literate, on a par with our generally sophisticated readership." Formats: single or multi-panel, b&w line drawings with gag line. Prefers finished cartoons. SASE. Reports in 1 month. Buys one-time rights. Pays $25, b&w cartoons; on acceptance.
Illustrations: Uses 2 illustrations/issue, all from freelancers. "We maintain a file of samples from illustrators. Our needs for illustrations–and we do need talent with an artistic light touch–are based almost solely on assignments, illustrations to accompany specific stories. We would assign a job to an illustrator who is able to capture the feel and mood of a story. Most frequently, it is light-touch golf stories which beg illustrations. A sense of humor is a useful quality in the illustrator; but this sense shouldn't lapse into absurdity." Uses color washes. Provide samples of style to be kept on file for future assignments. SASE. Reports in 2 weeks. Buys all rights on a work-for-hire basis. Pays on acceptance.

GOLF SHOP OPERATIONS, 495 Westport Ave., Norwalk CT 06856. (203)847-5811. Editor: Nick Romano. Art Director: Carol Petro. For golf professionals. Published 6 times/year. Circ. 13,000. Original artwork not returned after publication. Free sample copy.
Illustrations: Uses 4 illustrations/issue; buys 1/issue from freelancer. Soft goods oriented. Illustrations often used for conceptual pieces. Works on assignment only. Samples returned by SASE. Reports back on future assignment possibilities. Prefers finished art, roughs, portfolio, or samples of style; color or b&w. SASE. Reports in 2 weeks. Buys all rights on a work-for-hire basis. Pays $50-100; on publication.

GOOD HOUSEKEEPING, Hearst Corp., 959 8th Ave., New York NY 10019. Editor-in-Chief: John Mack Carter. Art Director: Herb Bleiweiss. For women. Monthly. Circ. 5,000,000. Free sample copy.
Cartoons: Contact: Patricia McBride, editor. Buys 150/year on family life, animals and humor through youth; single panel. Arrange interview to show portfolio. Reports in 3 weeks. Buys all [illegible]roduction rights. Pays $150 maximum, b&w line drawings and washes; on acceptance.
[illegible]tions: Buys 15/issue on romantic themes. Arrange interview to show portfolio. Reports in [illegible]uys all reproduction rights. Inside: Pays $100-300, b&w line drawings and washes; [illegible]0, color washes and full-color renderings; on acceptance.

GOOD NEWS BROADCASTER, Box 82808, Lincoln NE 68501. Managing Editor: Thomas Piper. Organizational religious magazine. Monthly. Circ. 200,000. Query with resume or send samples. Previously published work OK. Original artwork returned after publication. Free sample copy.
Illustrations: Uses 2 illustrations/issue. Interested in themes that are "serious, related to the subjects of the articles about the Christian life." Works on assignment only. Samples returned by SASE. Provide resume, calling card, letter of inquiry, brochure, flyer, tearsheet or "whatever is available to be kept on file for future assignments. Helps to know if person is a Christian too, but not necessary." Prefers resume. SASE. Reporting time varies. Buys first North American serial rights. Pays on acceptance.
Needs: Buys "b&w photos (for use inside) when they accompany an article and color transparencies (for covers) when they relate to the theme of a particular issue."

GOOD READING MAGAZINE, Litchfield IL 62056. (217)324-2322. Editor: Diane M. Dudley. "Nonfiction magazine which emphasizes travel, business, human interest and novel occupations." Monthly. Circ. 12,000. Original artwork returned after publication, only if requested.
Cartoons: Uses 1 cartoon/issue, all from freelancers. Receives 20 submissions/week from freelancers. Interested in "business, children, animals and wholesome humor." Prefers finished cartoons. SASE. Reports in 2 weeks. Buys first North American serial rights. Pays $15, b&w; on acceptance.

GRADUATE WOMAN, 2401 Virginia Ave. NW, Wasington DC 20037. (202)785-7727. Editor: Patricia Jenkins. Magazine of the American Association of University Women. For women of all ages who are interested in and involved with humanity, their communities and the world. Published 6 times/year. Circ. 190,000. Original artwork not returned after publication.
Cartoons: Uses 1-2/issue; buys all from freelancers. Interested in women's issues, current affairs and family. "Nothing demeaning to any human beings." Prefers finished cartoons. SASE. Reports in 1-5 weeks. Pays $25, b&w.

GRAFICA, 5300 Santa Monica Blvd., Los Angeles CA 90029. Contact: Armando del Moral. For the Hispanic family. Bimonthly. Original artwork returned after publication.
Cartoons: Interested in Hispanic-slanted themes. Prefers resume. Reports in 1 week. Buys first North American serial rights. Pays on acceptance.
Illustrations: Buys spot drawings on the problems and progress of target audience. Prefers roughs. Reports in 1 week. Buys first North American serial rights. Pays $4; on acceptance.

GRAIN & FEED REVIEW, 320 Shops Bldg., Des Moines IA 50309. (515)283-0431. Editor-in-Chief: Randy S. Allman. For agribusiness owners and managers in Iowa and Missouri. Published 10 times/year. Simultaneous submissions and previously published work OK. Free sample copy and artist's guidelines.
Cartoons: Buys 12 cartoons/year on current events, politics and agribusiness; single panel with gag line. SASE. Reports in 2 weeks. Send finished art. Pays $20 minimum, b&w line drawings; on publication.
Illustrations: Buys 60 illustrations/year on current events, politics and agribusiness. Query with samples. SASE. Reports in 2 weeks. Minimum payment: Cover: $75, color; $50, b&w. Inside: $40, color; $30, b&w line drawings and washes; on publication.

GRAND RAPIDS MAGAZINE, Grand Rapids Area Chamber of Commerce, 17 Fountain St. NW, Grand Rapids MI 49503. (616)459-4545. Managing Editor: John Brosky. Art Director: Jan Ensing-Keelean. For greater Grand Rapids residents. Circ. 10,000. Original artwork returned after publication.
Cartoons: Uses 4 cartoons/issue; buys 4/issue from freelancers. Interested in "Wester Michigan or Michigan, Lake Michigan, business or consumer/household themes." Prefers finished cartoons (or samples) and cover letter. SASE. Reports within 1 month. Buys all rights. Pays 15 days after publication.

GRAPHIC ARTS MONTHLY, 666 5th Ave., New York NY 10019. (212)489-2503. Editor: Bertram D. Chapman. Managing Editor: Lynn Nicholson. For management and production personnel in commercial and specialty printing plants and allied crafts. Monthly. Circ. 77,000. Sample copy $5.
Cartoons: Buys 15/year on printing, layout, paste-up, typesetting and proofreading; single panel. Mail art. SASE. Reports in 3 weeks. Buys first rights. Pays on acceptance.

GRAY'S SPORTING JOURNAL, 1330 Beacon St., Brookline MA 02146. (617)731-8691. Editor-in-Chief: Ted Williams. Art Director: DeCourcy Taylor. Concerns the outdoors, hunting and

fishing. Published 7 times/year. Circ. 50,000. Sample copy $1; free artist's guidelines.
Illustrations: Buys 28/year on hunting and fishing. Query with samples or previously published work. SASE. Reports in 4 weeks. Buys one-time rights. Inside: Pays $100-300, full-color art; $50-100, b&w line drawings.

GREEN REVOLUTION, Box 3233, York PA 17402. (717)755-1561. Editor Emeritus: Mildred J. Loomis. Editor: Rarihokwats. For those interested in "back to the land." Monthly. Circ. 2,500. Previously published, photocopied and simultaneous submissions OK. Original artwork returned after publication. Free sample copy.
Cartoons: Rarely uses cartoons, but will consider any on current public issues. Prefers roughs. SASE. Reports in 2 weeks.
Illustrations: Buys up to 10 covers/year; all from freelancers. Interested in landscapes, agriculture, community and people; depends on "problem of living" being discussed. Prefers samples of style. SASE. Reports in 2 weeks. Pays $10 minimum, pen and inks.

THE GREENMASTER, 698 Weston Rd., Suite 32, Ontario, Canada M6N 3R3. (416)767-2550. Emphasizes golf course management and maintenance for golf course superintendents, nursery trade personnel and horticulturists across Canada. Published 8 times year. Circ. 2,400. Free sample copy and art guidelines.
Cartoons: Uses 1 cartoon/issue; hopes to use submissions from freelancers for future issues. Interested in anything pertaining to play golf or working on the course. Prefers single panel b&w line drawings with gag line. Send samples of style to David Gourlay, editor. SASE. Reports in 2 weeks. Pays on publication. Negotiates payment.
Illustrations: Send samples of style to D. Gourlay. SASE. Reports in 2 weeks. Buys all rights. Pays by agreement prior to acceptance.

GROCERY COMMUNICATIONS, Box 311, Barrington RI 02806. Editor: Brad McDowell. For executives, supervisors, buyers and management in the grocery industry as well as allied trades such as food brokers, wholesalers and manufacturers. Monthly.
Needs: Buys art and cartoons. Mail art. Reports immediately on rejections; on publication if used. Pays $10, 4x5.

GROUND WATER AGE, Scott Periodicals, 135 Addison Ave., Elmhurst IL 60126. (312)530-6160. Editorial Director: Gene Adams. Assistant Editor: Kathy Hagerty. For water well drilling contractors, water systems specialists and pump installers. Monthly. Circ. 16,000. Previously published, photocopied and simultaneous submissions OK. Submit art or query with samples. SASE. Reports in 2-3 weeks. Buys various rights. Free sample copy and artist's guidelines.
Cartoons: Uses 2-3 cartoons/issue; buys all from freelancers. Single, double and multipanel b&w line drawings and washes with gag lines. Send roughs or finished cartoons to Gene Adams, editorial director. SASE. Reports in 2 weeks. Buys first North American serial and all rights. Pays $10-12 for b&w; on acceptance.
Illustrations: Uses 4-5 illustrations/issue; buys all from freelancers. Selection based on samples kept on file for future assignments. Prefers b&w line drawings and washes. Send roughs and samples of style to G. Adams. SASE. Reports in 2 weeks. Buys first North American serial and all rights. Pays $10 minimum for b&w; on acceptance.

GRUB STREET, 2839 Valentine Ave., Bronx NY 10458. Editors: Alan Ball and Patricia Russell. Literary magazine. Published 2 times/year; 8½x5½; 48 pages. Offset. Estab. 1969. Circ. 750. Submit photocopies or samples. SASE. Reports in 4 weeks. Simultaneous submissions OK ("if we're aware"). Buys one-time rights. Pays on publication. Sample copy $1.50. Free artist's guidelines with SASE.
Cartoons: Buys 2-6/year on environment, politics and general social or literary themes; single, double and multipanel with or without gag lines. Pays $5 minimum, b&w or halftone.
Illustrations: Buys 6/year on politics and literary themes. Cover and inside: Pays $5 minimum.

GUIDEPOSTS, 747 3rd Ave., New York NY 10017. Design Director: Salvatore Lazzarotti. Interfaith publication. Monthly. Original artwork not returned after publication. Free sample copy.
Illustrations: Uses 2 illustrations/issue; buys 2/month from freelancers. Receives 10 submission/month from freelancers. Works on assignment only. Samples returned by SASE. Reports back on future assignment possibilities. Provide calling card, brochure, flyer and tearsheet to be kept on file for future assignments. Prefers finished art, portfolio and samples of style. SASE. Reports immediately. Buys all rights on a work-for-hire basis. Buys full-color illustrations, b&w line

drawings and washes. Inside: Pays $100-175, spot art; $600, full-color; on acceptance.

GUN WORLD, Box HH, Capistrano Beach CA 92624. Editorial Director: Jack Lewis. Managing Editor: Dean A. Grennell. For shooters and hunters. Monthly. Circ. 126,000. Mail art. SASE. Reports in 3 weeks. Buys all rights, but may reassign rights to artist after publication. Pays on acceptance. Free sample copy.
Cartoons: Buys 3-4/issue on shooting and hunting. Pays $7.50-12, halftones.
Illustrations: Buys assigned themes.

GYMNASTICS WORLD, World Publications, Box 366, Mt. View CA 94040. Contact: Bob Anderson. "Our readers are participants and we try to use material that shows insight into the sports that we cover." Reports in 1 week. Buys reprint rights. Pays on publication.
Needs: Pays $10 for cover designs, spot drawings and cartoons.

HADASSAH MAGAZINE, 50 W. 58th St., New York NY 10019. (212)355-7900. Editor-in-Chief: Jesse Zel Lurie. Art Director: Meyer Fecher. For American Jewish families; deals with social, economic and educational developments in Israel and Jewish communities in the U.S. and elsewhere. Monthly. Circ. 370,000. Sample copy $1. SASE. Reports in 6 weeks. Buys first rights. Pays on acceptance.

HAM RADIO, Greenville NH 03048. (603)878-1441. Editor-in-Chief: James Fisk. Art Director: Bill Scarborough. For licensed amateur radio operators. Monthly. Circ. 57,000. Original artwork not returned after publication. Free sample copy.
Cartoons: Buys 12-15/year on amateur radio communications (not CB); single panel. Prefers roughs. SASE. Reports in 2 weeks. Buys all rights. Pays $10-15, line drawings; on acceptance.
Illustrations: Buys 15-20/year on amateur radio and electronics. Provide calling card to be kept on file for future assignments. Prefers samples of style. SASE. Reports in 2 weeks. Buys all rights on a work-for-hire basis. Minimum payment: Cover: $100, color; $80, b&w. Inside: $25, b&w; on acceptance.
Advertising: Uses local artists for layouts and finished art. Negotiates payment.

HAM RADIO HORIZONS, Communications Technology, Inc., Main St., Greenville NH 03048. Editor-in-Chief: James R. Fisk. Art Director: Bill Scarborough. Concerns amateur ham radio. Monthly. Circ. 52,000. Original artwork not returned after publication. Previously published and photocopied submissions OK. Free sample copy and artist's guidelines.
Cartoons: Uses 2 cartoons/issue; buys all from freelancers. Interested in amateur radio, not CB. Prefers roughs. SASE. Reports in 2 weeks. Pays on publication.
Illustrations: Buys themes on amateur radio. Provide calling card to be kept on file for future assignments. Prefers samples of style. SASE. Reports in 2 weeks. Buys all rights on a work-for-hire basis. Cover: Pays $100, color; Inside: Pays $25, b&w line drawings; on publication.

HANDS O!, 4530 Wadsworth Rd., Dayton, OH 45144. (513)276-5201. Readers are interested in home or small workshop woodworking. Bimonthly. Art guidelines for SASE; ask for Editorial Forecast.
Cartoon Needs: Uses 0-3 cartoons/issue. Receives average of less than 1 cartoon from freelancers/month. Cartoons should pertain to people doing woodworking. Format: single panel b&w line drawings with or without gag line. Send finished cartoons or samples of style to Nick Engler. SASE. Reports in 2-4 weeks. Pays on acceptance $25-100 b&w. Buys first North American Serial rights.
Illustration Needs: Uses 2-3 illustrations/issue and wants to see increase in submissions by freelancers. Illustrations should include how-to themes of "people using shopsmith tools or other woodworking equipment. Step-by-step drawings and finished products." Freelancers "will also be considered for books and project plans artwork." Format: b&w line or stiple drawings for inside and cover. Arrange personal appointment to show portfolio or send samples of style and tear sheets to Nick Engler. Reports in 2-4 weeks. SASE. Pays on acceptance $25-100 inside b&w. Buys first North American serial rights.

HANG GLIDER, Box 1860-PROSTAFF, Santa Monica CA 90406. (213)393-7334. Publisher: Joe Faust. For hang gliding enthusiasts. Biweekly. Circ. 2,000. Two sample copies for $1.
Illustrations: Buys 150 illustrations/year. Mail art or query with resume. SASE. Reports in 1 week. Buys various rights. Pays $1-20/job; on acceptance.

HARDWARE AGE, Chilton Co., Chilton Way, Radnor PA 19003. Editor: Jay Holtzman. Managing Editor: Wendy Ampolsk. For retailers. Monthly. Circ. 56,000. Original artwork not returned

after publication. Simultaneous submissions OK.
Cartoons: Buys 1-2/issue; Receives 25 submissions/week from freelancers. Interested in hardware, economy and business; single panel with gag line. Prefers finished cartoons. SASE. Reports in 3-4 weeks. Buys first North American serial rights. Pays $10, b&w line drawings; on acceptance.

HARDWARE MERCHANDISING, 481 University Ave., Toronto, Ontario Canada M5W 1A7. (416)596-5797. Editor: Norm Rosen. Emphasizes Canadian hardware (retail level). Readers are Canadian hardware dealers. Monthly. Circ. 10,000.
Cartoon Needs: Uses 1-2 cartoons per issue, all from freelancers. Receives 5-10 cartoons from freelancers/week. Uses cartoons reflecting reality in hardware store. Format: b&w line drawings with gag line. Send samples of style to Norm Rosen, editor. SASE. Reports in 1 week. Pays $25 on acceptance. Buys first North American serial rights.

HARPER'S, 2 Park Ave., New York NY 10016. Contact: Sheila Berger. For well-educated, socially concerned men, women and college students active in community and political affairs. Monthly. Prefers portfolio be left at least half day or overnight for review.

HARROWSMITH, Camden House Publishing Ltd., Ontario, Canada K0K 1J0. (613)378-6661. Editor-in-Chief: James Lawrence. Concerns alternative lifestyles, energy sources and architecture, the environment, country living and gardening. Published 8 issues/year. Circ. 150,000. Free sample copy.
Cartoons: Uses 2-3 cartoons/issue, all from freelancers. Single panel with gag line. Prefers roughs, samples (not returned) and calling card. SASE. Reports in 1 week. Pays $50-150, b&w; $100-500, color; on acceptance.
Illustrations: Art Director: John Colville. Uses 12 illustrations/issue, all from freelancers. Interested in "high quality color, drawings and some fine art on country living theme." "Many have won awards." Works on assignment only. No samples returned. Reports back on future assignment possibilities. Provide calling card to be kept on file for future assignments. Prefers samples of style or samples for file. SASE. Reports in 1 week. Buys first North American serial rights. Cover: Pays $300-800, color. Inside: Pays $250-500, color; $150-300, b&w; on acceptance.

HARVEY FOR LOVING PEOPLE, 450 7th Ave., New York NY 10001. (212)564-0112. Creative Director: Bob Dominoe. Readers are loving human beings. "I bring very high standards to cartooning and expect the best." Circ. 150,000. Estab. 1979. Copies available on newsstands.
Cartoon Needs: Uses 20 cartoons/issue; all by freelancers. Receives 200 cartoons from freelancers/week. Cartoons should pertain to sex, topical cartoons, and modern living (couples, relationships). Format: single panel b&w and color. Send finished cartoons. SASE. Reports in 1 week. Pays $50-75 for b&w and $100-200 for color before publication. Buys first North American serial rights.
Illustration Needs: Uses 3-5 illustrations/issue; 1-5 are by freelancers. Illustrators are "referrals and people that we've worked with before." Illustrations should pertain to typical topical pictures, nudes and couples. Format: b&w line drawings and color washes for inside and cover. Send samples of style to Bob Dominoe, creative director. Reports in 1 week. Pays $75-150 for b&w cover and $150-250 for inside color either on acceptance or publication. Buys first North American serial rights.

HEALTHWAYS, 2200 Grand Ave., Des Moines IA 50312. Editor: Tracy Mullen. "For those interested in staying healthy in the most natural way, with minimal use of drugs, surgery, etc." Bimonthly. Circ. 96,000. Previously published and simultaneous submissions OK "if we are told." Original artwork not returned after publication. Free sample copy.
Cartoons: Uses 0-1 cartoons/issue; buys all from freelancers. Receives 10 submissions/week from freelancers. Interested in health-related themes. Prefers finished cartoons. SASE. Reports in 2 weeks. Pays on publication.
Illustrations: Uses 10 illustrations/issue; buys 4/issue from freelancers. Receives 10 submissions/week from freelancers. Interested in "healthy life style" themes. Usually works on assignment only. Samples returned by SASE. Reports back on future assignment possibilities. Provide letter of inquiry to be kept on file for future assignments. Prefers samples of style. SASE. Reports in 2 weeks. Buys first North American serial rights. Cover: Pays $15-25, b&w; $15-50, color. Inside: Pays $5 minimum, b&w; on publication. "The artists whose work we've used were contacted in visits to art shows, galleries or through seeing their work advertised."

HEAVY METAL, 635 Madison Ave., New York NY 10022. (212)688-4070. Editor: Ted White. Emphasizes science fiction and fantasy for adult readers of comic books. Monthly. Circ. 200,000. Art guidelines for SASE.

Cartoon Needs: Uses about 6 comic stories/issue; all supplied by freelancers. Receives many comic stories from freelancers/week. Themes of stories should be "suitable sequential material for adults in science fiction and fantasy. Mostly buying b&w from US and color from France." Format: b&w or color multi panel. Send finished comic stories to Ted White, editor. SASE. Reports in 1 week. Pays on publication $150/page, b&w story; $200/page, color story. Buys all rights.

THE HEFLEY PSYCHIC REPORT, Box 7242, Burbank CA 91510. (213)841-2733. Art Director: Linda L. Glut. Emphasizes psychic phenomena for a mass readership interested in the occult, psychic happenings, science, UFOs and witchcraft. Estab. 1977. Circ. 150,000. Bimonthly. SASE. Reports in 6 weeks. Pays on publication.
Illustrations: Buys 2-3/issue pertaining to psychic/occult subjects, ghosts, UFOs, New Age philosophies, etc. Pays $5-25, b&w. Arrange interview to show portfolio or write describing ideas.

HEIGHTS, Le Moyne College, Le Moyne Heights, Syracuse NY 13214. (315)446-2882. Contact: Manager Publications. Query with samples. SASE. Reports in 4 weeks.
Illustrations: Cover: Pays $25. Inside: Pays $15, line drawings.

HEIRS MAGAZINE INTERNATIONAL, 657 Mission St., San Francisco CA 94105. "Multicultural magazine in the vein of international art publications." Publishes articles in English, Spanish and Chinese. Original artwork returned after publication with SASE. Write for payment schedule and other guidelines. Sample copy $4.
Illustrations: Uses 4-6 illustrations/issue, all from freelancers. Subjects vary. Provide resume and tearsheet to be kept on file for future assignments. Prefers portfolio (finished art or roughs). SASE. Reports in 30-60 days. Buys all rights on a work-for-hire basis. Token payment within 30 days of publication.

HIGH COUNTRY, Box 494, Council ID 83612. (208)253-4551. Editor: Leo R. Peurasaari. Art Director: Jule Peurasaari. Rural regional magazine. Monthly; 10x13½; 36 pages. Offset. Estab. 1977. Circ. 5,000. Send samples (photocopies OK) for "the file we are building of available artists. From this file we will be sending out assignments." SASE. Reports in 4 weeks. Simultaneous submissions OK. Buys first or all rights. Pays on publication. Sample copy 78¢.
Cartoons: Buys 12/year on mining, logging, ranching and rural life; single panel with gag line or triple panel without gag line. "We accept cartoons over the transom. No query needed." Pays $5-20, b&w line drawings.
Illustrations: Cover and inside: Pays $5-30 for b&w line drawings, washes and gray opaques. Also uses artists for ads and promotion work. Buys illustrations only on assignment.

HIGH FIDELITY TRADE NEWS, 6 E. 43rd St., New York NY 10017. Editor: Mark Andrews. Buys all rights. Pays on acceptance.
Needs: "We're primarily looking for cartoonists and portrait artists who can do various views of people working from photos. Also looking for cover artists. All work by assignment." Pays $25-500.

HIGHLIGHTS FOR CHILDREN, 803 Church St., Honesdale PA 18431. Editor-in-Chief: Walter B. Barbe. Managing Editor: Kent L. Brown Jr. For ages 2-12. Monthly, bimonthly in June/July and August/September, biweekly in December. Circ. 1,300,000. Original artwork not returned after publication.
Cartoons: Uses 2 cartoons/issue; buys all from freelancers. Receives 20 submissions/week from freelancers. Interested in positive themes on family life and humor through youth; single panel. Prefers roughs or finished cartoons. SASE. Reports in 4-6 weeks. Buys all rights. Pays $20-25, line drawings; on acceptance. "One flaw in many submissions is that the concept or vocabulary is too adult, or that the experience necessary for its appreciation is beyond our readers. Frequently, a wordless self-explanatory cartoon is best."
Illustrations: Uses 30 illustrations/issue; buys 25 from freelancers. Works with freelancers on assignment only. "We are always looking for good hidden pictures. We require a picture that is interesting in itself and has the objects well hidden. Usually an artist submits pencil sketches. In no case do we pay for any preliminaries to the final art." Provide flyer to be kept on file for future assignments. Prefers samples of style. SASE. Reports in 4-6 weeks. Buys all rights on a work-for-hire basis. Pays on acceptance.

HISTORIC PRESERVATION, 1785 Mass. Ave. NW, Washington DC 20036. Editor: Thomas J. Colin. For members of the National Trust for Historic Preservation; concerns national and international preservation. Monthly. Circ. 160,000. Simultaneous submissions and previously published work OK. Artist's guidelines.

Illustrations: Buys 4/year on education, architecture, folk art and historical subjects. Query with previously published work. SASE. Reports in 2-4 weeks. Buys one-time rights. Inside: Pays $150 minimum, color washes; $75 minimum, b&w line drawings and washes; on publication.

HOBART WELDWORLD, 600 W. Main St., Troy OH 45373. (513)339-6011. Editor: Rob Doughty. Deals with welding as applied to Hobart welding systems. Published 3 times/year. Circ. 50,000. Simultaneous submissions and previously published work OK. Original artwork not returned after publication. Sample copy available. Free artist's guidelines.
Illustrations: Works on assignment only. Samples returned by SASE. Reports back on future assignment possibilities. Provide calling card and brochure to be kept on file for future assignments. Prefers resume and finished art. SASE. Reports in 2 weeks. Buys first North American serial rights. Pays on publication.

HOCKEY ILLUSTRATED, 333 Johnson Ave., Brooklyn NY 11206. Art Director: Steven Plunkett. Reports in 1 month. Buys first North American serial rights. Pays on publication. Sample copy available.
Needs: Buys b&w line drawings and spot illustrations from manuscripts. Prefers 8½x11. Pays $30-100.

HOME LIFE, 127 9th Ave. N., Nashville TN 37234. Editor: Reuben Herring. Monthly.
Cartoons: Buys 2/issue on family life situations; particularly interested in cartoons on marriage. No sex. Submit roughs. Reports in 45 days. Buys all rights. Pays $25+, line drawings and halftones; on acceptance.

HOME REPAIR, Davis Publications, 380 Lexington Ave., New York NY 10017. (212)557-9100. Contact: Irving Bernstein. Reports in 1 week. Buys first rights. Pays on acceptance.
Needs: Pays $20 minimum, line drawings; $400 maximum, full-color cover.

HOOSIER FARMER, Indiana Farm Bureau, Inc., 130 E. Washington St., Indianapolis IN 46204. Managing Editor: Clark Q. Lewis. Monthly. Original artwork returned after publication.
Cartoons: Uses 1-2 cartoons/issue, all from freelancers. Buys 2-3 submissions/week from freelancers. Interested in farming and agriculture related themes. Prefers roughs. SASE. Reports in 1 week. Buys first North American serial rights. Pays $5, pen and inks.
Illustrations: Uses 2-3 illustrations/issue; number bought from freelancers varies. Works on assignment only. Samples returned by SASE. Reports back on future assignment possibilities. Provide calling card and brochure to be kept on file for future assignments. Prefers roughs. SASE. Reports in 1 week. Buys first North American serial rights. Pays up to $150 for inside illustrations and cover designs; on acceptance.

HORSE LOVER'S NATIONAL MAGAZINE, Box 3003, Menlo Park CA 94025. (415)468-5414. Managing Editor: Nanette Meek. For competitive horsemen. Monthly. Circ. 96,000. Free sample copy.
Needs: Uses line drawings, b&w washes, color washes, pastels inside. Demand varies. Query with samples or mail art. SASE. Reports in 4 weeks. Buys first rights. Pays $10-40; on publication.

HORSE, OF COURSE, Temple NH 03084. Editor/Publisher: R.A. Greene. Sample copy $1.50.
Cartoons: Pays $4/panel.
Illustrations: Uses "simple line drawings, preferably realistic in style, depicting horses in action." Buys all rights. Pays $20 on the average, 5x7 minimum; on acceptance.

HORSE PLAY, 443 N. Frederick Ave., Gaithersburg MD 20760. (301)840-1866. Design Director: Robert McCaulley. Concerns horses and horse sports. Published 11 times/year. Circ. 43,000.
Cartoon Needs: Buys 1/issue on English riding. Send roughs or finished artwork. SASE. Reports in 2 months. Pays $7.50, b&w; on publication.
Illustrations: Buys 2-5/year on events, fox hunting and show jumping. Send roughs or finished artwork. Pays $15-20, b&w; on publication.

HORSES ALL, Box 550, Nanton, Alberta, Canada T0L 1R0. (403)486-2144. Editor: Jacki French. Readers are farmers and ranchers; owners of all breeds of horses. Monthly. Circ. 10,000. Free sample copy.
Cartoons: Uses 3-6 cartoons/issue; buys all from freelancers. Interested in themes relating to horses/farming/ranching. Prefers single or multi panel b&w line drawings, b&w or color washes, with or without gag line. Send finished cartoons or samples of style. SASE. Reports in 2 weeks. Buys one-time rights. Pays $5 for b&w or color; on publication.

Illustrations: Uses 20-50 illustrations/issue. Wants samples to be kept on file for future assignments. SASE. Interested in themes relating to horses/farming/ranching. Prefers b&w line drawings. Reports in 2 weeks. Buys all rights. Pay negotiated depending on complexity of job; on publication.

HORTICULTURE, 300 Massachusetts Ave., Boston MA 02115. (617)536-9280. Art Direction: Diane Schaefer/Designworks. Monthly. Circ. 160,000.
Illustrations: Buys 5/issue on plants (technical drawings), gardening methods (instructive, how-to drawings), garden implements and tools. Query with samples or arrange interview to show portfolio. SASE. Pays $100/page, b&w or color; on publication.

HOSPITAL FINANCIAL MANAGEMENT, 1900 Spring Rd., Suite 500, Oak Brook IL 60521. (312)787-3876. Editor: Timothy Murnane. For hospital financial managers. Monthly. Circ. 18,000. Previously published and simultaneous submissions OK.
Cartoons: Buys 12/year on economy and hospital financial/business offices; single panel with gag line. Submit art or query with samples. SASE. Reports in 2 weeks. Buys various rights. Pays $10 minimum, b&w and color; on publication.
Illustrations: Buys 4/year on hospital financial management, accounting and data processing. Submit art or query with samples. SASE. Reports in 2 weeks. Buys various rights. Minimum payment: Cover: $100, b&w; $150, color. Inside: $75, b&w line drawings; $100, color-separated work; on publication.

HOUSE & GARDEN, 350 Madison Ave., New York NY 10025. (212)880-8174. Readers are middle and upper income home owners or renters. Monthly. Circ. 1,136,000.
Cartoon Needs: Uses 3-4 cartoon/issue; all supplied by freelancers. "Cartoons are assigned, not bought at random. They are used to illustrate specific articles, not for humor or sports. Freelancers who want to submit samples can do so, but we rarely buy unassigned drawings." Format: b&w line drawings or washes without gag line. Send samples of style to Lloyd Ziff, art director. SASE. Reports "anywhere from immediately to 4 weeks." Payment on acceptance varies. Buys all rights.
Illustration Needs: Uses varying number of illustrations/issue; some of which are supplied by freelancers. Selection based on "previous work, samples on file, and from seeing work in other publications. Illustrations are almost always assigned to fit specific articles." Themes "vary with our current format and with article we want illustrated." Format: b&w line drawings or washes. Arrange personal appointment to show portfolio or send samples of style to Lloyd Ziff, art director. SASE. Reports "from immediately to 4 weeks." Payment on acceptance "varies depending on artist, size and type of illustration. Buys all rights.

HOUSE PLANTS & PORCH GARDENS, Scrambling Press, 1 Aldwyn Center, Villanova PA 19085. (215)527-5100. Editor: Peter Tobey. Photo/Art Editor: Ford R. Myers. For plant enthusiasts. Monthly. Circ. 200,000. Sample copy $1.75. Free artist's guidelines with SASE.
Cartoons: Uses 10 cartoons/issue, all from freelancers. Receives 5 submissions/week from freelancers. Interested in "plant themes-skills, humor, special interests." Prefers finished cartoons. SASE. Reports in 2 weeks. Buys all rights on a work-for-hire basis. Pays on publication.
Illustrations: Uses 15 illustrations/issue; buys 10/issue from freelancers. Receives 5 submissions/week from freelancers. Interested in "plants in interior settings." Provide calling card, tearsheet and "copies of illustrations" to be kept on file for future assignments. Prefers finished art. SASE. Reports in 2 weeks. Buys all rights on a work-for-hire basis. Inside: Pays $20 minimum, b&w line drawings and color-separated work; on publication.

HUGHES AIR WEST SUNDANCER, East-West Network, Inc., 5900 Wilshire Blvd., #300, Los Angeles CA 90036. (213)937-5810. Editor-in-Chief: James Clark. Monthly. Query with resume. Buys all rights. Sample copy $1.50.
Illustrations: Buys assigned themes. Pays $25 minimum, spot art; $400, full-color cover.

THE HUMANIST, 7 Harwood Dr., Amherst NY 14226. Editor: Lloyd Morain. Journal of humanist and ethical concerns. Published 6 times/year. Previously published work OK.
Illustrations: Send published samples. SASE. Reports in 1 month. Buys one-time rights. Cover: Pays $50, 2-color. Inside: Pays $15, spot art; on publication.

HUMPTY DUMPTY'S MAGAZINE, 52 Vanderbilt Ave., New York NY 10017. Art Editor: Duncan Morrison. Original artwork returned after publication. Local artists only.
Illustrations: Uses 30-35 illustrations/week, all from freelancers. Interested in line art illustrations; "no tints or washes." Works on assignment only. Provide flyer to be kept on file for future

assignments. Prefers samples of style. SASE. Reports "upon assignment."

HUNTING DOG MAGAZINE, Camargo Publications, 9714 Montgomery Rd., Cincinnati OH 45242. (513)891-0060. Editor-in-Chief: George R. Quigley. Art Director: Paul G. Oliver. For sporting dog enthusiasts. Monthly. Circ. 32,000. Previously published and photocopied submissions OK. Original artwork returned after publication. Sample copy $1.50.
Cartoons: Uses "0-1 maximum" cartoons/issue, all from freelancers. Interested in "sporting dog situations." Prefers finished cartoons. SASE. Reports in 8 weeks. Buys first North American serial righs ("usually return rights") or all rights on a work-for-hire basis.
Illustrations: Uses 4-5 illustrations/issue, all from freelancers. Receives 20 submissions/week from freelancers. Interested in "sporting dog and hunting situations." Provide calling card, tearsheet and photocopy of work to be kept on file for future assignments. Prefers finished art or samples of style. SASE. Reports in 8 weeks. Buys first North American serial rights ("usually return rights") or all rights on a work-for-hire basis. Inside: Pays $25 minimum, b&w line drawings and washes; on acceptance.

IDEALS, Box 1101, Milwaukee WI 53201. Managing Editor: Ralph Luedtke. Published 8 times/year. Five editions are Christmas, Easter, Thanksgiving, autumn and Mother's Day; other 3 issues devoted to inspirational and informative topics with emphasis on seasonal subjects.
Illustrations: Interested in pencil, pen and ink, line and wash, watercolor, designer's colors, pastels, acrylic and charcoal. "Most of our artwork is 1-color, but we do review 4-color artwork. For initial submissions we like to see a rough sketch showing enough detail for good impression. In the case of 4-color artwork, colors should be indicated on the sketch. We would prefer final artwork to be on flexible material since our artwork is now being separated by the scanning system." Works on assignment only. Samples returned by SASE. Reports back on future assignment possibilities. Provide calling card, tearsheet or photostats to be kept on file for future assignments. Prefers samples of style. SASE. Reports in 3 weeks. Buys all rights on a work-for-hire basis. Pays $25-300, 4-color; $50, 1-page vignette; $150-200, detailed double-page spread.

ILLINOIS, 320 S. Main, Benton IL 62812. (618)439-3893. Editor-in-Chief: Daniel Malkovich. Regional publication. Estab. 1962. Circ. 15,000. Monthly; 8½x11; 62 pages. Offset. SASE. Reports in 1 month. Buys all rights. Pays on publication. Sample copy 25¢.
Illustrations: Cover: Pays $50-100, color washes and opaque watercolors. Inside: Pays $10-20, b&w line drawings and washes. Query with samples or previously published work. "We will talk to anyone."

ILLINOIS BANKER, Illinois Bankers Association, 188 W. Randolph, Chicago IL 60601. (312)984-1500. Editor: Cindy L. Altman. Editorial Assistant: Kelly Cunningham. Monthly. Circ. 3,200. Sample copy $1.50; free artist's guidelines.
Cartoons: Buys 12-20/year on banking; single panel with gag line. Mail art. SASE. Reports in 2 weeks. Buys first rights. Pays $15 each, b&w line drawings; on acceptance.

IN A NUTSHELL, Box 22248, Sacramento CA 95822. Editor-in-Chief: Margaret Wensrich. For people who like to read and enjoy art. Quarterly. Circ. 5,000. Original artwork returned after publication, if artist requests. Sample copy $2.50.
Cartoons: Uses 2-4 cartoons/issue; buys all from freelancers. Interested in current events, education, environment, family life and humor through youth. Prefers finished cartoons. SASE. Reports in 2-3 weeks. Buys first rights. Pays $5 minimum; on acceptance.
Illustrations: Uses 2-4 illustrations/issue; buys all from freelancers. Interested in Theme illustrations, series of 3 pictures; past themes: "San Francisco," "Derelicts," and "Victoriana." Story Illustrations, pen and ink story illustrations. Works on assignment only. Samples returned by SASE. Reports back on future assignment possibilities. Provide resume and sample pen and ink illustrations to be kept on file for future assignments. Prefers resume and finished art or samples of style. SASE. Reports in 2 weeks. Buys first North American serial rights. Pays $15 minimum, series of 3 pictures illustrating a theme; $10 minimum, pen and ink story illustration; on acceptance.

IN TOUCH, Wesley Press, Box 2000, Marion IN 46952. Executive Editor: Keith W. Drury. Art Editor: Sandy Metz. Sunday school take-home paper for teens. Weekly. Circ. 35,000. Previously published, photocopied and simultaneous submissions OK. Free sample copy.
Cartoons: Uses 1 cartoon/issue. Interested in the environment, humor through youth and many sports and hobbies; single, double and multipanel with gag lines. Pays $7.50 minimum, b&w line drawings; on acceptance.
Illustrations: Uses 1 illustration/issue on assigned themes. Mail cartoons; query with samples of

illustrations. SASE. Reports in 6 weeks. Cover: Pays $10-35, b&w line drawings and washes; on acceptance.

INCENTIVE MARKETING/INCORPORATING INCENTIVE TRAVEL, 633 3rd Ave., New York NY 10017. (212)986-4800. Managing Editor: James Hogg. For buyers of merchandise and travel used in motivational sales promotions. Monthly. Circ. 37,000. Original artwork returned after publication.
Cartoons: Uses 1-2 cartoons/issue; buys all from freelancers. Receives 8-10 submissions/week from freelancers. Interested in our topic only, sales contests, bank premium programs, business travel and employee motivation, no general interest. Prefers finished cartoons. SASE. Reports in 2 weeks. Pays $50-75, b&w; on acceptance.

INCOME OPPORTUNITIES, Davis Publications, 380 Lexington Ave., New York NY 10017. (212)557-9100. Contact: Irving Bernstein. Reports in 1 week. Buys first rights. Pays on acceptance.
Needs: Pays $20 minimum, line drawings; $400 maximum, full-color cover.

INDIANAPOLIS MAGAZINE, 320 Meridian, Indianapolis IN 46204. (317)635-4747. City magazine. Readers have "high income and are highly educated." Monthly. Circ. 10,000. Sample copy $1.50.
Cartoon Needs: "We are just beginning to accept and publish cartoons. Will buy all from freelance artists." Needs cartoons related to the "consumer, tourist–business-related or city-related." Format: single panel b&w line drawings or b&w washes, with or without gag line. Send roughs or finished cartoons to Pegg Kennedy, editor. SASE. Reports in 2 weeks "but it depends on production schedule and amount of material we receive." Pays $10 on publication per b&w cartoon. Buys first North American serial rights.
Illustration Needs: Uses 2-5 illustrations per issue, 50% of which are supplied by freelancers. Works on spec or assignment basis. Needs illustrations that are "broad, general interest, or Indianapolis related." Format: b&w line drawings or b&w washes. Send finished art or roughs to Pegg Kennedy, editor. SASE. Reports in 2 weeks, "but depends on production schedule and influx of material." Pays $10 on publication per inside b&w or color illustration. Buys first North American serial rights.

INDUSTRIA AVICOLA, Mt. Morris IL 61054. (815)734-4171. For poultry producers (minimum 1,000 hens and/or 20,000 broilers annually and/or 1,000 turkeys annually) who have direct affiliation with the poultry industry in Latin America. Circ. 12,000.
Cartoons: Editor: Robert Tuten. Query or mail roughs. SASE. Reports in 4 weeks. Pays $7, b&w; on publication.

INDUSTRIAL DISTRIBUTOR NEWS, 1 W. Olney Ave., Philadelphia PA 19120. (215)224-7000. Managing Editor: Jerold Steinbrink. For industrial distributors, wholesalers of industrial equipment and supplies, business managers and industrial salesmen. Monthly. Circ. 33,000. Free sample copy and artist's guidelines.
Illustrations: Buys 3-4/issue on assigned industrial topics. Cover: Pays $165 minimum; prefers airbrush or strong color renderings. Arrange interview to show portfolio. SASE. Reports in 4 weeks. Buys all rights. Inside: Pays $45 minimum; b&w line drawings; on publication.

INDUSTRIAL LAUNDERER, 1730 M St. NW, Suite 613, Washington DC 20036. (202)296-6744. Editor: Jim Roberts. Monthly. Circ. 3,000. Submit resume. Reports as soon as possible. Buys first industry rights. Pays on publication.
Cartoons: Negotiates pay for b&w line drawings and washes.

INDUSTRIAL MACHINERY NEWS CORP., 29516 Southfield Rd., C.S. #5002, Southfield MI 48037. (313)557-0100. Contact: Ms. Lucky D. Slate. For those in the metal-working industry responsible for manufacturing, purchasing and engineering.
Cartoons: Interested in metalworking or personal relationships. Buys one-time rights. Pays $5 for line ink work; on publication.

INDUSTRIAL PROGRESS, Box 13208, Phoenix AZ 85002. (602)264-1579. Editor: Frederick H. Kling. Goodyear company publication. Readers include industrial research and development, production, maintenance supervisors and purchasing directors. Quarterly. Circ. 50,000. Art guidelines for SASE.
Cartoons: Uses 1 cartoon/issue supplied by freelancer. Receives 5 submissions/week from freelancers. Interested in "industrial subjects–shop, research, and management." Format: single panel b&w line drawings and b&w washes with or without gag lines. Prefers roughs or finished

cartoons. SASE. Reports in 3-4 weeks. Buys one-time rights. Pays $50-60 4 weeks after acceptance.

INDUSTRIAL SAFETY PRODUCT NEWS, 1 W. Olney Ave., Philadelphia PA 19120. (215)224-7000. Emphasizes industrial safety for safety directors, engineers and plant managers in charge of safety located in over 36,000 industrial plants. Monthly. Circ. 52,000. Free sample copy.
Illustrations: Uses 2-3 illustrations/issue; buys 1 from freelancers. Works on assignment only. "Freelancers are interviewed and their portfolios are reviewed." Interested in "straight forward illustrations that appeal to business personnel." Prefers b&w line drawings for inside. Arrange personal appointment to show portfolio. SASE. Reports in 1 week. Buys all rights. Pays $20-40 for inside b&w; $100-250 for color cover and $75-200 for inside color; on publication.
Other Needs: "Currently using freelance artist on a retainer basis to assist in design and layout of magazines and for promotional purposes for this Ames magazine and others. As the work expands we will consider adding other freelancers on an assignment basis."

INDUSTRY WEEK, 1111 Chester Ave., Cleveland OH 44114. (216)696-7000. Editor-in-Chief: Stanley J. Modic. Examines top- and middle-management problems in industry. Biweekly. Circ. 280,000. Simultaneous submissions and previously published work OK. Original artwork not returned after publication. Buys first and reprint rights. Sample copy $2.
Cartoons: News Editor: John Sheridan. Uses 2 cartoons/issue; buys 1/issue from freelancers. Receives 10 submissions/week from freelancers. Interested in management themes; single panel. Prefers roughs. SASE. Reports in 2 weeks. Buys various rights. Pays $35 minimum, b&w line drawings or washes; on acceptance.
Illustrations: Art Director: Nick Dankovich. Uses 5 illustrations/issue; buys 3/issue from freelancers. Provide resume, letter of inquiry, brochure and tearsheet to be kept on file for future assignments. Works on assignment only. Samples returned by SASE. Reports back on future assignment possibilities. Prefers resume and portfolio. SASE. Reports in 2 weeks. Buys various rights. Cover and inside: Buys b&w and color work, all media; on acceptance.

INFO: A WORLD OF SENSE, Box 123, Lyndhurst NJ 07071. (201)440-8400. Emphasizes consumer news and features. Monthly. Original artwork not returned after publication. Syndicated to newspapers. Sample copy 50¢; art guidelines for SASE.
Cartoons: Editor: Sylvia Helm. Uses 4 cartoons/issue, all from freelancers. Cartoons should pertain to consumer news. Format: single panel b&w line drawings with or without gag lines. Prefers finished cartoons. SASE. Reports in 1 week. Buys one-time rights. Pays $25; on publication.
Illustrations: Uses 14-20 illustrations/issue, all from freelancers. Interested in consumer-related themes. Works on assignment only. Samples returned by SASE. Prefers samples of style. Reports in 1 week.

INFO FRANCHISE NEWSLETTER, 736 Center St., Lewiston NY 14092. (716)754-4669. Art Director: Edward L. Dixon Jr. For franchisors. Monthly. Circ. 4,000.
Cartoons: Interested in cartoons dealing with business format franchising. Send roughs. SASE. Reports in 2 weeks. Pays $20, b&w; on acceptance.
Illustrations: Interested in b&w illustrations dealing with business format franchising. Query with samples. SASE. Reports in 2 weeks. Pays $20, b&w; on acceptance.

INLAND SHORES, 1135 Legion Dr., Elm Grove WI 53122. Publisher: Van B. Hooper. Midwest travel magazine. Quarterly. Previously published work OK. Sample copy $3.
Needs: "We feature area artists who have limited edition prints available and offer their prints for sale in our magazine; a different artist is featured in each issue." SASE. Reports in 2-3 months. Buys second serial or reprint rights. Pays on publication.

INSIDE DETECTIVE, RGH Publications, 235 Park Ave. S., New York NY 10003. Editor: Diana Lurvey. For mature adults–law enforcement officials, professional investigators, criminology buffs and interested laymen. Monthly.
Cartoons: Must have crime theme. Submit finished art. SASE. Reports in 10 days. Buys all rights. Pays $25; on acceptance.

INSIGHT, Box 7244, Grand Rapids MI 49510. Managing Editor: John Knight. For Christians ages 16-21. Monthly (except June, August). Circ. 22,000. Photocopied and simultaneous submissions OK. Free sample copy.
Cartoons: Buys 6 cartoons/year on current events, humor through youth and religion; single panel. "Our favorites are the ones that speak for themselves, no caption." Query. SASE. Reports

in 3 weeks. Buys first rights. Minimum payment: $15, b&w; $30, color; on publication.
Illustrations: Buys 3 illustrations/year on religious themes applied to current events. Query. SASE. Reports in 3 weeks. Buys first rights. Inside: Pays $25 minimum, b&w line drawings and washes, full color on assignment; on publication.

INSTRUCTOR PUBLICATIONS INC., 757 3rd Ave., New York NY 10017. Editor-in-Chief: Leanna Landsmann. Art Director: Cynthia Amrine. For elementary school teachers. Published 10 times/year. Original artwork returned after publication. Write for sample copy.
Cartoons: Uses 1-2 cartoons/issue; buys all from freelancers. Interested in themes on elementary school and children. Prefers finished cartoons. SASE. Reports in several weeks. Buys all rights. Pays on acceptance.
Illustrations: Interested in educational themes. Works on assignment only. Samples returned by SASE. Reports back on future assignment possibilities. Prefers portfolio. SASE. Reports in several weeks. Buys all rights on a work-for-hire basis. Pays on acceptance.

INSURANCE SALES, Rough Notes Publishing Co. Inc., Box 564, Indianapolis IN 46206. (317)634-1541. Editor: Roy Ragan. For life and health insurance agents; "emphasis on sales and marketing methods, and on the uses of life and health insurance to solve personal and business financial situations." Monthly. Circ. 40,000. Sample copy $1.
Cartoons: Uses 6-7 cartoons/year; all from freelancers. Interested in life insurance salesmanship, tax payer and IRS situations, inflation, recession, vagaries of bankers and stock market; single panel. "No cartoons which show salesman holding prospect on ground, twisting arm, knocking doors down, etc." Prefers finished cartoons. SASE. Reports in 1 week. Buys all rights. Pays $15, b&w line drawings; on acceptance.

INTERNATIONAL WILDLIFE, 225 E. Michigan St., Milwaukee WI 53202. Associate Editor: Nicoletta Barrie. For those concerned with the future of wildlife and the environment. Bimonthly. Circ. 550,000. Pays on acceptance.
Illustrations: Assigns art for one-two stories per issue. Works on assignment only. Provide flyer and tearsheet to be kept on file for future assignments. Prefers sample of style. SASE. Reports in 3 weeks. Previously published work OK. Usually buys all rights, but may reassign rights to artist after publication. Pays competitive rates; on acceptance.

INTERSEARCH, (formerly *Counterforce*), Box 26804, El Paso TX 79926. (915)592-5238. Editor-in-Chief: Frank W. Taggart. Managing Editor: Gavin de Becker. "Intelligence report on terrorism for executives, security directors, and other personnel in industry, business and government." Biweekly. Circ. 2,500. Previously published, photocopied and simultaneous submissions OK. Sample copy $1.50.
Cartoons and Illustrations: Buys 26/year on any aspect of terrorism; single panel. Query with samples. SASE. Reports in 2 weeks. Buys first rights. Pays $15, b&w; on acceptance.

IOWA MUNICIPALITIES, League of Iowa Municipalities, 900 Des Moines St., Suite 100, Des Moines IA 50316. Editor-in-Chief: Robert W. Harpster. Art Director: Linda Elliott. For city officials. Monthly. Circ. 10,400. Previously published, photocopied and simultaneous submissions OK. Original artwork returned after publication. Sample copy 75¢.
Cartoons: Buys 4 cartoons/year on current events and politics; single panel with gag line. Pays $20-30, b&w line drawings; on publication.

IOWA REVIEW, 308 EPB, University of Iowa, Iowa City IA 52242. (319)353-6048. Literary journal. Quarterly. Circ. 1,500.
Illustrations: Buys 1-2/issue. Needs line cuts, etchings and nature forms. Query with samples. SASE. Reports in 1-2 months. Pays $50, b&w; on publication.

IOWA RURAL ELECTRIC COOPERATIVES NEWS, 8525 Douglas, Suite 48, Urbandale, IA 50322. (515)276-5350. Editor: Thomas P. Graves. For rural electric consumers. Monthly. Circ. 140,000. Simultaneous submissions and previously published work OK.
Cartoons: Buys 3 cartoons/issue on current events, family life, politics and farming; single panel with gag line. Prefers roughs or finished cartoons. Pays $15 minimum, b&w line drawings; on publication.
Illustrations: Buys 2 illustrations/issue on current events, family life, politics and farming. Provide resume, brochure, flyer or tearsheet to be kept on file for future assignments. Prefers resume and samples. SASE. Reports in 2 weeks. Cover: Pays $30 minimum, b&w line drawings; $40 minimum, 2-color; on publication. Also buys inside b&w line drawings.

JACK AND JILL, 1100 Waterway Blvd., Indianapolis IN 46206. (317)634-1100. Editor-in-Chief: Beth Wood Thomas. Editor: William Wagner. Art Director: Edward F. Cortese. For ages 8-12. Published 10 times/year. Previously published, photocopied and simultaneous submissions OK. Original artwork not returned after publication. (Except in case where artist wishes to exhibit the art. Art must be available to us on request.) Buys all rights. Sample copy 50¢.
Illustrations: Uses 25-35 illustrations/issue; buys 10-15/issue from freelancers. Receives 2-5 submissions/week from freelancers. Interested in "stylized, realistic, humorous, mystery, adventure, science fiction, historical and also nature and health." Works on assignment only. Provide brochure, flyer, tearsheets, stats or good photocopies of artwork to be kept on file for future assignments. Prefers portfolio and samples of style. SASE. Reports in 1 week. Buys all rights on a work-for-hire basis. Cover: Pays $135, color. Inside: Pays $30-50, color; $25-35, b&w; on publication.

JACKSONVILLE, Box 329, Jacksonville FL 32201. For the business community. Bimonthly. Estab. 1963. Circ. 8,000-10,000. Local artists only. Buys one-time and all rights. Pays on publication.

JOBBER TOPICS, 7300 N. Cicero Ave., Lincolnwood IL 60646. News Editor: Gerry Dawson. Aimed at owners, managers and salesmen for automotive parts-and-supplies wholesalers. Monthly. Original artwork not returned after publication.
Cartoons: Uses 2-3 cartoons/issue. Interested in "dealing mainly with automotive parts stores, as well as some 'general'. No sex." Prefers finished cartoons. SASE. Reports in 1 week. Buys all rights on a work-for-hire basis. Pays $10; on acceptance.

"JOINT" CONFERENCE, Box 19332, Washington DC 20036. Editor-in-Chief: Kathryn E. King. For prison inmates and people interested in inmate writing. Published irregularly. Circ. 500-600. "I use material only from inmates in correctional institutions. I'd like to see some work from female inmates. I do not like to see drawings in pencil, or pornography." Photocopied and simultaneous submissions OK. Original artwork returned after publication, if requested. Free sample copy.
Cartoons: Uses 8-10 cartoons/issue, all from freelancers. Interested in current events, education, environment, family life, politics and prison life; single panel. Prefers finished cartoons. SASE. Reports in 8 weeks. Buys first North American serial rights. Will reassign rights to artist after publication. Pays $5-25, line drawings; on acceptance.
Illustrations: Uses 5-6 illustrations/issue, all from freelancers. Interested in prison life. Prefers finished art. SASE. Reports in 8 weeks. Buys first North American serial rights. Will reassign rights to artist after publication. Cover: Pays $10-25, b&w. Inside: Pays $5-25, b&w; on acceptance.

JOURNAL OF THE AMERICAN OPTOMETRIC ASSOCIATION, 243 N. Lindbergh Blvd., St. Louis MO 63141. (314)991-4100. Editor-in-Chief: Milton Eger. Art Director: Fred Jones. Monthly. Circ. 23,500. Query with previously published work. Work returned only if requested, prefers only samples not to be returned. Free sample copy.
Illustrations: Buys 10-20/year on optometry for inside illustrations. Works on assignment only. Prefers not to receive material that must be returned. Provide letter of inquiry, brochure, or tearsheet to be kept on file for future assignments. Prefers samples of style. SASE. Reports in 3-6 months. Buys all rights on a work-for-hire basis. Cover: Pays $50-200, b&w or color washes, b&w line drawings, color-separated and full-color art. Inside: Pays $50-100, color; $25-100, b&w. Pays on publication.

JOURNAL OF CARDIOVASCULAR AND PULMONARY TECHNIQUE, Brentwood Publishing Corp., 825 S. Barrington Ave., Los Angeles CA 90049. Contact: Martin Waldman. Submit published samples. SASE. Reports in 30 days. Buys all rights. Pays on acceptance.
Needs: Pays $30-up, spot art; $225-up, full-color cover.

JOURNAL OF COMMERCE, 2000 W. 12th Ave., B.C., Canada V6J 2G2. (604)731-1171. Emphasizes the construction industry, design professionals and manufacturers and suppliers. Audience is "Western Canada: B.C., Alberta, Saskatchewan, Manitoba and Western half of Ontario." Semiweekly. Circ. 10,000.
Cartoon Needs: Occasionally uses 1 cartoon/issue. Themes used: "humorous situations directly and specifically related to construction and its own peculiar problems and difficulties. Artist who has worked in the industry is most likely to understand humor possibilities." Format: single or multi-panel b&w line drawings with or without gag line. Send finished cartoons to Stefan Koehl, editor. SASE. Reports in 1 week. Pays $15 on acceptance. Buys one-time rights.

Illustration Needs: Uses freelancers on assignment only to illustrate specific on-going feature sections. Format: b&w line drawings and b&w washes for inside. Arrange appointment to show portfolio to Stefan Koehl, editor. SASE. Reports in 1 week. Pays $15-50 for inside illustration. Buys all rights on a work-for-hire basis.

JOURNAL OF FRESHWATER, Freshwater Foundation, 2500 Shadywood Rd., Box 90, Navarre MN 55392. (612)471-7467 or 8407. Coordinator of Information/Education: Karen Thompson. For people concerned about the quality of the freshwater environment. Annually. Query with samples or mail art. SASE. Reports in 4-6 weeks. Sample copy $5; free artist's and photographers' guidelines.
Cartoons: Uses less than 1 cartoon/issue. Receives less than 1 submission/week from freelancers. Interested in themes on the freshwater environment; single, double and multipanel. Prefers finished cartoons. Reports in 4 weeks. Buys all rights on a work-for-hire basis. Buys one-time rights. No doomsday philosophies or environmental cliches. May reassign rights to artist after publication. Pays $20 minimum, b&w line drawings; $35 minimum, color washes and full-color art; on acceptance.
Illustrations: Uses 2 illustrations/issue, all from freelancers. Interested in humorous themes on the freshwater environment. Receives 3 submissions/week from freelancers. Provide calling card, letter of inquiry and brochure to be kept on file for future assignments. Prefers samples of style. SASE. Reports in 3 weeks. Buys all rights or one-time rights. May reassign rights to artist after publication. Minimum payment: Cover: Pays $200, full-color art. Inside: Pays $50, color; $25, b&w line drawings; on acceptance.

JOURNAL OF NURSING CARE, 265 Post Rd., Westport CT 06880. (203)226-7203. Editor: Jerry C. Melson RN MA. For licensed practical and vocational nurses. Monthly. Circ. 70,000. Previously published, photocopied and simultaneous submissions OK. Free sample copy.
Cartoons: Buys medical themes; single panel. Prefers query or send samples. SASE. Reports in 2 weeks. Buys various rights. Pays $10-50, line drawings; on acceptance.
Illustrations: Buys 10-20/year on hospitals, nurses and health care. Prefers query or send samples. SASE. Reports in 2 weeks. Buys various rights. Cover: Pays $50-100, color; Inside: Pays $10-75, b&w line drawings; on acceptance.
Advertising: Pays $25-100.

JUDICATURE, 200 W. Monroe, Suite 1606, Chicago IL 60606. Contact: Martha Stevens. Journal of the American Judicature Society. Original artwork returned after publication.
Cartoons: Uses 2-3 cartoons/issue. Interested in "sophisticated humor revealing a familiarity with the courts and the administration of justice." Prefers finished cartoons. SASE. Reports in 2 weeks. Buys one-time rights. Negotiates payment; pays $25 for unsolicited cartoons.
Illustrations: Uses 2-4 illustrations/issue. Interested in styles from "realism to light cartoons." Provide resume, flyer, brochure, tearsheet and samples of style to be kept on file for future assignments. Prefers resume and samples of style ("tearsheets best"). SASE. Reports in 1 week. Buys one-time rights. Negotiates payment.
Needs: Assigns illustrations related to court organization, operations and personnel.

JUVENILE MERCHANDISING, 370 Lexington Ave., New York NY 10017. Editor: Lee Clarke Neumeyer. For juvenile products industry. Monthly. Mail art. Reports immediately. Previously published work OK. Sample copy available. Buys one-time rights. Pays on publication.

KARATE ILLUSTRATED, 1845 W. Empire Ave., Burbank CA 91504. Contact: Ben Kalb. Monthly. Query. Reports in 2 weeks. Pays on publication. Sample copy available.
Needs: Buys cover designs, inside illustrations and cartoons on the martial arts. Inside: b&w line drawings and washes OK.

KELLNER'S MONEYGRAM, 1768 Rockville Dr., Baldwin NY 11510. (516)868-3177. Contact: Art Director. For photographers, art directors, photo editors and anyone interested in buying and selling photos. Monthly. Circ. 2,000.
Cartoons: Buys 1 photo-related cartoon/issue. Query. SASE. Reports in 6 weeks. Pays $10 for b&w; on publication.

KEYBOARD WORLD, Box 4399, Downey CA 90241. (213)923-0331. Emphasizes organ and piano music. Monthly. Circ. 18,000 U.S. and Canada; 10,000 Australia.
Cartoons: Contact Bill Worrall. Number bought/issue varies. SASE. Reports in 2 weeks.
Illustrations: Contact Tony Ramos. Number bought/issue varies. Subjects include graphics of keyboards or music. Query with samples. SASE. Reports in 2 weeks.

KEYNOTER, Kiwanis International, 101 E. Erie St., Chicago IL 60611. (312)943-2300. Editor-in-Chief: David Dee. Art Director: Patrick Kane. Official publication of Key Club International, nonprofit high school service organization. Published 7 times/year. Circ. 95,000. Previously published, photocopied and simultaneous submissions OK. Original artwork returned after publication. Free sample copy and artist's guidelines.
Illustrations: Uses 3 illustrations/issue, all from freelancers. Works on assignment only. "We only want to work with illustrators in the Chicago area because otherwise it is too inconvenient. They should call our Production and Art Deptartment for interview." SASE. Reports in 2 weeks. Buys first rights. Pays on publication.

KILOBAUD MICROCOMPUTING, Peterborough NH 03458. (603)924-3873. Managing Editor: John Barry. Emphasizes microcomputers for owners, educators, and businessmen who use them. Monthly. Original artwork not returned after publication. Sample copy $3.50.
Cartoons: Uses 1 cartoon/issue; buys from freelancer. Receives 5 cartoons from freelancers/week. "Cartoons must pertain to computers, microcomputers, digital electronics, programming, and related areas. Should be funny—not trite. Offbeat approaches appreciated." Format: single panel b&w line drawings. Prefers finished cartoons. SASE. Reports in 2 weeks. Buys all rights. Pays $15-20; on acceptance.
Illustrations: "We are doing very little with freelance illustrators currently. Contemplating expanding amount of art in magazine. Interested illustrators should contact John Barry, managing editor.

THE KINDERGARTNER, 201 8th Ave. S., Nashville TN 37202. Contact: David Dawson. For children of kindergarten age. Monthly. Circ. 104,000.
Cartoons: Uses less than 1 cartoon/issue. Interested in family or child-to-child themes. Prefers finished cartoons. SASE. Reports as soon as possible. Buys all rights on a work-for-hire basis.
Illustrations: Uses 3 illustrations/issue. "Should be suited for Sunday school literature, primarily human involvement; children in classrooms, on playgrounds, with families etc. Ethnic and minority groups should be represented. Rendering to correct age group is important." Works on assignment only. Samples returned. Does not report back on future assignment possibilities. Provide resume and flyer to be kept on file for future assignments. Prefers resume and samples of style. SASE. Reports as soon as possible. Buys all rights on a work-for-hire basis. Pays $35, b&w; $35, 1-color; $40, 2-color; $45, 3-color; and $50, 4-color; on acceptance.

KITCHEN SINK ENTERPRISES, Division of Krupp Comic Works, Inc., Box 7, Princeton WI 54968. (414)295-3972. Editor-in-Chief: Denis Kitchen. Art Director: Steven Krupp. For ages 18-35 who enjoy historical, educational and "underground" comic books. Published 2 titles/month. Circ. 10,000-120,000. Previously published, photocopied and simultaneous submissions OK. Original artwork returned after publication. Sample copy $1.50.
Cartoons: Uses 36 pages of comics/issue; buys "several"/issue from freelancers. Receives 12 submissions/week from freelancers. Interested in autobiographical, insightful stories; historical themes; satire, parody, topical and fresh humor. We never buy single panel "gag" cartoons. We are strictly interested in comic book pages." Prefers rough or finished artwork. SASE. Reports in 2 weeks. Buys various rights. Pays $30, b&w page; $100, color cover, as royalties "for first printing only (10,000 copies). Additional royalties are paid for every subsequent printing." Pays on publication. Titles include: *Death Rattle, Corporate Crime, Snarf, Mr. Natural* and *Dope Comix*.
Illustrations: Uses 2-3 illustrations/issue; buys "few"/issue from freelancers. Receives several submissions/week from freelancers. Used for noncomic book magazines such as *Weird Trips*. Interested in "eccentric, fresh styles-good b&w drawings with superior technical quality." Provide calling card, letter of inquiry, brochure or tearsheet to be kept on file for future assignments. Prefers finished art, roughs or samples of style. SASE. Reports in 2 weeks. Buys various rights. Pays $10-50, b&w line drawings; $100 minimum, color.

KIWANIS, 101 E. Erie St., Chicago IL 60611. Editor: David B. Williams. Art/Design Coordinator: Patrick Kane. For business and professional men. Stresses civic and social betterment, business, education, religion and domestic affairs. Original artwork returned after publication. Published 10 times/year.
Cartoons: Uses 1-2 cartoons/issue, all from freelancers. Receives "dozens" of submissions/week from freelancers. Interested in "daily life at home or work. Nothing off-color, no silly wife stuff, no blue-collar situations." Prefers finished cartoons. SASE. Reports in 2 weeks. Pays $50; on acceptance.
Illustrations: Uses 6-8 illustrations/issue, all from freelancers. Interested in themes that correspond to themes of articles. Works on assignment only. Keeps material on file after in-person contact with artist. Prefers portfolio, "anything and everything." SASE. Reports in 2 weeks. Buys

first North American serial rights or negotiates. Cover: Pays $600-700, full-color. Inside: Pays $200-350, full-color; $50-75, spot drawings; on acceptance.

KREOLITE NEWS, Jennison-Wright Corp., Box 691, Toledo OH 43694. (419)382-3411. Vice President/Marketing: R.T. White. Concerns Kreolite products. Quarterly.
Cartoons: Buys 10-12/year on "anything that appeals to us"; single panel. Query with samples. SASE. Pays $5, b&w line drawings.

LAB WORLD, North American Publishing Co., 401 N. Broad St., Philadelphia PA 19108. (215)574-9600. Editor-in-Chief: A.E. Woolley, Ph.D. Cartoon Editor: Manley Witten. For clinical laboratory management. Monthly. Circ. 62,000. Photocopied submissions OK. Sample copy $2.50.
Cartoons: Buys 10 cartoons/year on medicine and medical laboratories; single panel with gag line. Query with previously published work. SASE. Reports in 2 weeks. Buys one-time rights. Pays $25-100, b&w; $50-150, color; on acceptance.

LADY'S CIRCLE, 23 W. 26th St., New York NY 10010. (212)689-3933. Editor-in-Chief: Adrian B. Lopez. Monthly; 8x11; 72 pages. Offset. Circ. 500,000. SASE. Buys all rights. Pays on publication.
Cartoons: Buys themes on family life and humor through youth; single and double panel. Pays $10 minimum, b&w.

LANDSCAPE ONTARIO/LANDSCAPE TRADES, 103-3034 Palstan Rd., Mississauga, Ontario, Canada. (416)276-6177. Managing Editor: Susan Lawrence. Readers are landscapers, nursery garden centers, grounds maintenance firms, suppliers of goods to the landscaping industry, parks and recreation officials, horticulturists and others. Monthly. Circ. 2,700. *Landscape Ontario* estab. 1973; *Landscape Trades* estab. 1979. Free sample copy.
Cartoons: Uses 1 cartoon/issue which should relate to the industry and have appeal to readers mentioned above. Prefers single- or multipanel b&w line drawings or washes with or without gag line but will also consider color cartoons. Send finished cartoons or samples of style. SASE. Reports in 1 month. Buys one-time rights. Pays $15/b&w on publication.
Illustrations: Uses 1 illustration/issue; buys 0-1 from freelancers. "I'd be happy to keep samples on file and request illustrations when a particular need or idea comes up." Prefers b&w line drawings or washes for inside. Send finished art or samples of style. SASE. Reports in 1 month. Pays $15 for inside b&w on publication.

LAWN CARE INDUSTRY, 9800 Detroit Ave., Cleveland OH 44102. (216)651-5500. Editor: Bob Earley. For lawn care businessmen. Monthly. Circ. 12,000.
Cartoons: Uses 1-2 cartoons/issue, all from freelancers. Receives 1 submission/week from freelancers. Interested in the problems of professional lawn/landscape care, dealing with customers, chemical and equipment salesmen, the government, the weather and employees. Query or send roughs. SASE. Reports in 2 weeks. Pays $10, b&w; on acceptance.

LE BUREAU, 625 President Kennedy Ave., Montreal, Quebec, Canada H3A 1K5. (514)845-5141. Editor-in-Chief: Paul Saint-Pierre. For office managers, electronic data processing experts and systems analysts. Bimonthly. Circ. 7,500. Free sample copy if artist sends samples.
Illustrations: Buys 12/year on calculators, small computers, in-plant printing and word processing. "We appreciate humor in good taste." Query with samples. SASE. Reports in 2 weeks. Buys all rights, but may reassign rights to artist after publication. Pays $125-200, color; on acceptance.

LEARNING, 530 University Ave., Palo Alto CA 94301. Contact: David Hale or Bob Bryant. For teachers of kindergarten-8th grade. Monthly during the school year. Send tearsheets or photocopies. Buys all rights. Pays on acceptance.
Illustrations: Pays $500 maximum, cover.

LEATHERNECK, Marine Corps Association, Box 1775, Quantico VA 22134. (703)640-3171. Editor: Ronald D. Lyons. Art Director: John DeGrasse. For active duty, retired and reserve Marines. Monthly. Circ. 45,000.
Cartoons: Buys 45 cartoons/year on Marines; single panel with gag line. SASE. Reports in 2 weeks. Buys all rights. Pays $25, b&w line drawings; on acceptance.

LEGAL ECONOMICS, Box 11418, Columbia SC 29211. (803)754-3563 or 359-9940. Managing Editor/Art Director: Delmar L. Roberts. Bimonthly. Circ. 17,000. Previously published work OK. Pays on publication.

Needs: Primarily interested in cartoons "depicting situations inherent in the operation and management of a law office, e.g., operating word processing equipment, interviewing, office meetings, and client/lawyer situations. We have rarely used cartoons, primarily because the calibre of the work we received was not suitable for our sophisticated audience. Cannot use material relating to trial law." Query with resume. Reports in 90 days. Usually buys all rights. Pays $15-20; on publication.
Illustrations: Uses illustrations and cover designs. Query with resume. Reports in 90 days. Usually buys all rights. Pays $50-75; on publication.

LEGION, 359 Kent St., Ottawa, Ontario, Canada K2P 0R6. (613)235-8741. Editor-in-Chief: Jane Dewar. Art Director: Dick Logan. For Royal Canadian Legion members. Monthly. Circ. 500,000. Original artwork not returned after publication. Free sample copy.
Illustrations: Uses 6-8 illustrations/issue, all from freelancers. Interested in "various techniques". Works on assignment only. Samples returned by SASE. Provide 35mm slides to be kept on file for future assignments. Prefers portfolio. SASE. Reports immediately. Buys various rights. Cover: Pays $450-1,500, color. Inside: Pays $40-1,200, b&w; $100-1,500, color; on acceptance.

LEISURE WHEELS, Box 7302, Station E, Calgary, Alberta, Canada T3C 3M2. (403)249-1755. Publisher: Murray Gimbel. Emphasizes recreational vehicles, travel and outdoors for upper income ages 30-65. Monthly. Circ. 15,000. Estab. 1979. Sample copy 50¢; free art guidelines.
Cartoons: Uses 4 cartoons/issue; buys all from freelancers. Receives 1 submission/week from freelancers. Subject matter should concern traveling and camping as it relates to trailering, motorhoming, fishing or hiking. Prefers b&w line drawings with gag line. Send samples of style. SASE. Reports in 2 weeks. "Prefer cartoons not appear in a similar magazine." Pays $25 for b&w.
Illustrations: Uses 4 illustrations/issue; buys all from freelancers. Receives 1 submission/week from freelancers. Usually works on assignment. Illustration needs identical to cartoons. Prefers b&w line drawings for inside. Send samples of style. SASE. Reports in 3 weeks. "Prefer illustrations not appear in a similar magazine." Pays $50-100 for inside b&w on publication.

THE LESBIAN TIDE, 1314 S. Tremaine Ave., Los Angeles CA 90019. (213)939-1200. Contact: Jeanne Cordova. For lesbians, feminists, women and gays. Bimonthly. Circ. 10,500. "Sorry, we don't accept work from men." Previously published, photocopied and simultaneous submissions OK. Original artwork returned after publication. Sample copy $1.50.
Cartoons: Uses 8 cartoons/issue; buys 4/issue from freelancers. Receives 8 submissions/week from freelancers. Interested in personal relationships; also gay, feminist, lesbian or political themes. Prefers finished cartoons. SASE. Reports within 1 month. Buys one-time rights. Pays $5, line drawings; on publication.
Illustrations: Uses 2 illustrations/issue; buys 2/issue from freelancers. Recieves 4 submissions/week from freelancers. Interested in personal relationships; also gay, feminist, lesbian or political themes. Samples returned. Does not report back on future assignment possibilities. Provide calling card and tearsheet to be kept on file for future assignments. Prefers samples of style. SASE. Reports within 1 month. Buys one-time rights. Pays $5, b&w line drawings; on publication.

LET'S LIVE, 444 N. Larchmont, Los Angeles CA 90004. (213)469-3901. Emphasizes nutrition, health and recreation. Monthly. Circ. 140,000. Sample copy $1.50; free art guidelines.
Illustrations: Managing Editor: William S. Koester. Uses 8-12 illustrations/issue; buys 2/issue from freelancers. Receives 2 illustrations from freelancers/week. Works on assignment only. "We like to check newspapers and magazines to find samples of the style we like to use or, we check the Creative Black Book for artists." Needs illustrations of inanimate objects: (e.g. salt shaker, vitamin bottles), sports action, charts, graphs, montages, spot illustrations, medical scenes (facilities, equipment), people, faces. "No mod or avant-garde styles, please." Format: color and b&w washes. Prefers samples, tearsheets and/or roughs. SASE. Reports in 2 weeks. Buys first North American serial rights. Pays $150-200 for color cover; $75-150 for inside color; $50-125 for inside b&w; on publication.
Other Needs: Department or column logos, promotional materials, displays (in-store, convention booths, etc.). "We initiate contact or view mail queries. Payment is on completion of assignment." Advance OK up to 15% of total job fee.

LI, 550 Stewart Ave., Garden City NY 11530. (516)222-5126. Editor-in-Chief: Stanley Green. Art Director: Miriam Smith. Published by *Newsday*, this magazine is for Long Islanders. Estab. 1972. Circ. 500,000. Weekly; 10x12¼; 48 pages. Rotogravure. SASE. Reports "on date of publication." Buys all rights. Pays on publication. Free sample copy and artist's guidelines.
Illustrations: Buys 2/issue on all themes. Cover: Pays $400, color washes; $200-300, b&w line drawings. Inside: Pays $200-300, color washes; $150-250, b&w line drawings. Arrange interview to show portfolio.

LIBERTY, 6840 Eastern Ave. NW, Washington DC 20012. (202)723-0800 ext. 745. Editor: R.R. Hegstad. Deals with subjects related to religious freedom and church-state separation, parochial aid, federal involvement in church activities and Sunday laws. Previously published work OK. Original artwork returned after publication, if requested. Sample copy and guidelines available.
Cartoons: Uses 2-3 cartoons/year. Interested in religious liberty. Prefers roughs or finished cartoons. SASE. Reports in 1-2 weeks. Buys one-time rights.
Illustrations: "Most of our illustrations-99%-come from our design studio." Prefers samples of style. SASE. Reports in 7-10 days. Buys one-time rights. Pays on acceptance; on publication if previously published. Minimum payment: $200, 4-color cover; $10-25, spot drawing.

LIBRARY JOURNAL, 1180 Avenue of the Americas, New York NY 10036. (212)764-5180. Art Director: Gilbert Fletcher. For librarians. Biweekly. Circ. 40,000.
Illustrations: Buys 20 illustrations/issue dealing with libraries (exterior and interior), new technology, card catalogs and book shelves. Query with samples or send finished work. Pays $15-20 for b&w; on publication.

LIGHT & LIFE, 999 College Ave., Winona Lake IN 46590. (219)267-7161. Art Director: Joyce LeMasters. "Emphasizes evangelical Christianity with Wesleyan slant for a cross-section readership." Readers are mostly of Free Methodist denomination. Monthly. Circ. 60,000. Original artwork returned after publication, if postage included. Sample copy 75¢.
Cartoons: "Might consider super cartoons." Interested in religious themes. Format: single panel b&w line drawings with or without gag line. Prefers finished cartoons. SASE. Reports in 2 weeks. Buys all rights. Pays $10 and up; on acceptance.
Illustration Needs: Uses 3 illustrations/issue, all from freelancers. Receives 0 submissions/week from freelancers. Interested in realistic art that illustrates themes of articles. Works on assignment only. Samples returned by SASE. Reports back on future assignment possibilities. Provide calling card, letter of inquiry and tearsheet to be kept on file for future assignments. Prefers portfolio, roughs and samples of style. SASE. Reports in 1 week. Buys all rights on a work-for-hire basis. Pays $10 and up, inside b&w; on publication.

LIGHTING DESIGN & APPLICATION MAGAZINE, 345 E. 4th St., New York NY 10017. (212)644-7922. Emphasizes lighting design and engineering. Readers are "lighting designers, engineers, architects, researchers, and scientists." Monthly. Circ. 13,000. Free sample copy.
Illustration Needs: Uses 10 illustrations per issue all done by freelancers. "Most are graphs, charts and line drawings. We have a regular contributor for most work. Special assignments occasionally require additional artists." Format: b&w line drawings. Freelancers should send samples of style to Robert England, editor. SASE. Reports in 1 month. Pays on acceptance. Buys first North American serial rights.

LIGUORIAN, Liguori Publications, 1 Liguori Dr., Liguori MO 63057. Editor-in-Chief: Father Norman Muckerman. Art Director: Jim Corbett. For Catholics. Monthly. Circ. 503,000. Original artwork not returned after publication. Free sample copy.
Cartoons: Uses 12/year; buys all from freelancers. Interested in current events, education, environment, family life, humor through youth, religion and retirement; single panel with gag line. Query with previously published work. SASE. Buys first and reprint rights. Pays $20 maximum, b&w line drawings; on publication.

LLEWELLYN PUBLICATIONS, Box 3383, St. Paul MN 55765. Art Editor: Nan Bruno. Publishes occult astrology and New Age magazines and books. Reports in 8 weeks. Previously published work OK.
Needs: Pays $5-20, b&w drawings.

LOGGING MANAGEMENT, 300 W. Adams, Chicago IL 60606. (312)977-7268. Managing Editor: Russ Gager. For management and operating executives involved in forest management, growing, felling, extraction, loading, shipping and exporting of timer. Bimonthly. Circ. 21,000.
Cartoons: Buys 1 cartoon/issue on humorous logging situations; b&w only. Negotiates pay. Send roughs. SASE. Pays on publication.
Illustrations: Buys 1-2 illustrations/issue on assigned themes. Query with samples or arrange interview to show portfolio. SASE. Negotiates pay; pays on publication.

LONG ISLAND MAGAZINE, 8 Bond St., Great Neck NY 11021. (516)482-6630. Publisher: Gordon Brown. Monthly. Regional magazine for upper income, college educated Long Island residents.
Illustrations: Interested in themes of the typical city magazine. Prefers b&w line drawings for

inside and cover. Send samples of style. Rights purchased vary. Negotiates payment.

THE LOOKOUT, 8121 Hamilton Ave., Cincinnati OH 45231. (513)931-4050. Editor-in-Chief: Mark A. Taylor. For Christian churches. Weekly. Circ. 160,000. Original artwork not returned after publication, unless requested. Free sample copy.
Cartoons: Uses 1 cartoon/issue; buys 0/issue from freelancers, "but we may buy some in the future." Interested in church, Sunday school and Christian family themes. Prefers roughs or finished cartoons. SASE. Reports in 2 weeks. Buys all rights, but will reassign.
Illustrations: Uses 3-4 illustrations/issue; receives 0 submissions/week from freelancers. Interested in "adults, families, interpersonal relationships; also, graphic treatment of titles." Works on assignment only. Samples returned by SASE. Reports back on future assignment possibilities. Provide letter of inquiry, brochure, flyer or tearsheet to be kept on file for future assignments. "We must see samples." Prefers samples of style. SASE. Reporting time varies. Buys all rights, but will reassign. Cover and inside: Pays $50-100, b&w line drawings; on acceptance.

LOPEZ PUBLICATIONS, 23 W. 26th St., New York NY 10010. Contact: Leonard Kabatsky. Publishes men's "girly" magazines.
Illustrations: Buys editorial illustrations for fiction. Query. Pays $80.

LOS ANGELES, 1888 Century Park E., Los Angeles CA 90067. (213)552-1021. Art Director: William Delorme. Concerns Los Angeles and the surrounding area. Monthly. Circ. 160,000. SASE. Reports in 2-3 weeks. Previously published work OK. Pays on publication. Sample copy $3.
Cartoons: Contact Geoff Miller, editor-in-chief. Buys 3-4/issue on current events, environment, family life, politics, social life and business; single, double or multipanel with gag line. Pays $15 minimum, b&w line drawings. Mail roughs.
Illustrations: Buys 4/issue on assigned themes. Inside: Pays $50 minimum, b&w line drawings. Query with resume and samples or submit portfolio for review.
To Break In: "Show work similar to that used in the magazine."

LOST TREASURE, 15115 S. 76th East Ave., Bixby OK 74008. (918)366-4441. Emphasizes treasure hunting for treasure hunters, coin shooters, bottle collectors, metal detector owners. Monthly. Circ. 50,000. Free sample copy.
Cartoon Needs: Uses 10-15 cartoons/issue; all from freelancers. Receives 1-2 cartoons from freelancers/week. Cartoons should pertain to treasure hunting, people using metal detectors, prospecting, etc. Format: Single panel b&w line drawings or b&w washes with gag line. Send finished cartoons to Michael Rieke, editor. SASE. Reports in 1 month or less. Pays $10 on publication. Buys first North American serial rights.
Illustrations: Specific subjects: stage coach robberies; miners in the Old West (gold mining); Indians with treasure; Spanish or Mexicans with pack trains; Spanish or Mexicans burying treasure; wooden sailing ships sinking on reefs or in open sea-storms; divers with sunken shipwreck or treasure chests; anything that illustrates lost treasures. Line drawings or dry brush OK. Pays $10 minimum, spot drawings; $25 minimum, half-page editorial illustrations; $100 4-color cover.

THE LUTHERAN, 2900 Queen Lane, Philadelphia PA 19129. (215)438-6580. Editor-in-Chief: Edgar R. Trexler. Associate Editor: Walter A. Kortrey. Biweekly; monthly in July and August. Circ. 590,000. Previously published work OK. Original artwork returned after publication. Free sample copy.
Cartoons: Mark Staples, editor. Uses 1 cartoon/issue; buys all from freelancers. Receives 30 submissions/week from freelancers. Interested in humorous or thought-provoking cartoons on religion or about issues of concern to Christians; single panel. Prefers roughs or finished cartoons. SASE. Reports usually within a week. Buys first rights. Pays $10-50, b&w line drawings and washes; on publication.
Illustrations: Bernhard Sperl, editor. Uses 2 illustrations/issue; buys all from freelancers. Interested in church related family scenes, Christmas, Advent, Baptism, Communion, Confirmation, church entering, leaving, interior, exterior, choirs, funerals, Easter and Lent. Works on assignment only. Samples returned by SASE. Reports back on future assignment possibilities. Provide resume or tearsheet to be kept on file for future assignments. Prefers portfolio or samples of style. SASE. Reports in 2 weeks. Buys all rights on a work-for-hire basis. Buys 30-40/year on assigned themes. Pays $10-50, b&w; on publication.

THE LUTHERAN JOURNAL, 7317 Cahill Rd., Edina MN 55435. Contact: J.W. Leykom. Previously published work OK. Free sample copy.

Illustrations: Seasonal 1, 2, or full-color covers. Mail art with price. Buys one-time rights. Pays on publication.

THE LUTHERAN STANDARD, 426 S. 5th St., Minneapolis MN 55415. (612)330-3300. Editor: Lowell G. Almen. Managing Editor: Donn S. McLellan. For members of the American Luthern Church. Biweekly. Circ. 577,000. Previously published, photocopied and simultaneous submissions OK. Original artwork returned after publication, if requested. Free sample copy.
Cartoons: Uses 1-2 cartoons/issue; buys all from freelancers. Receives 10 submissions/week from freelancers. Interested in current events, education, family life, humor through youth and religious themes. Prefers finished cartoons. SASE. Reports in 3-4 weeks. Buys first or simultaneous rights. Pays $7.50-10, b&w line drawings and washes; on acceptance.
Illustrations: Uses 4 illustrations/issue; buys all from freelancers. Works on assignment only. Samples returned by SASE if requested, and reports back on future assignment possibilities. Provide resume, calling card, brochure or tearsheet to be kept on file for future assignments. Prefers samples of style. SASE. Reports in 3-4 weeks. Buys first North American serial rights or buys all rights on a work-for-hire basis. Inside: Pays $10-20, b&w line drawings and washes; on acceptance.

McCALL'S, 230 Park Ave., New York NY 10017. Art Director: Alvin Grossman. Leave portfolio with art department for review.

McCALL'S WORKING MOTHER, 230 Park Ave., New York NY 10017. (212)551-9412. Art Director: Nina Scerbo. Emphasizes working mothers. Bimonthly. Circ. 275,000. Estab. 1978.
Cartoon Needs: Uses 1-2 cartoons/issue; all from freelancers.
Illustration Needs: Uses 5-10 illustrations/issue; all from freelancers. "I keep all samples from portfolios that I review on file; also refer frequently to books such as *The Black Book* and *American Showcase*, and the *Illustrators Annuals*. For editorial work I use artists on assignment only. However, I do buy b&w filler art from material that is submitted by artists. I look for artists who can handle children in an interesting and believable way; and also for unique handling of b&w art, which I use in every issue. For full-color art, I am particularly drawn to rich oil, charcoal and watercolor as opposed to commercial-looking airbrush. I prefer a fine-art style." Format: b&w line drawings and b&w washes; color washes. Arrange personal appointment to show portfolio or send samples of style to Nina Scerbo, art director. Reports immediately on commissioned work. SASE. Pays $150-250 on acceptance for inside b&w (spot illustration) and $350-800 for inside color. Buys all rights unless other agreement is negotiated.

MADE TO MEASURE, 300 W. Adams St., Chicago IL 60606. (312)263-6355. Publisher: William Halper. Published semiannually. Emphasizes uniforms, men's custom tailoring, formal wear rental and alterations for retailers, uniformed organizations, purchasing agents and others.
Cartoons: Uses 15 cartoons/issue relating to uniforms (policemen, firemen, letter carriers, military, men's custom tailoring, formal wear renting and men's clothing in general. Prefers single panel b&w line drawings with gag line. Send finished cartoons. SASE. Pays $15 minimum for b&w on acceptance.

MADEMOISELLE, 350 Madison Ave., New York NY 10017. Art Director: Susan Niles. For college-educated women, ages 18-25. Monthly. Bring portfolio on a Wednesday or query with resume.

MAGICAL BLEND, Box 11303, San Francisco CA 94101. Emphasizes the psychic, occult and spiritual. Publisher: Kathy Zunic. Quarterly. Circ. 10,000. Estab. 1979. Original artwork returned after publication. Sample copy $2; art guidelines for SASE.
Illustrations: Uses 60 illustrations/issue; buys 60/issue from freelancers. Receives 5 submissions/week from freelancers. Interested in fantasy and sorcery. "We both keep samples on file and work by assignment according to the artists and our time table and workability. We only accept b&w line drawings. We tend towards fantasy and new age styles. We again look for pieces with occult, psychic and spiritual subjects with positive, inspiring, uplifting feeling. No dark, bizarre, nor negative material will be considered." Provide letter of inquiry, brochure or flyer to be kept on file for future assignments. Prefers portfolio or samples of style. SASE. Reports in 2 weeks. Buys first North American serial rights. Rights revert to artist. Pays in copies.
Other Needs: "Comics and/or comixs about occult, sorcery, magic, psychic subjects with positive, uplifting endings."

MAKE IT WITH LEATHER, Box 1386, Fort Worth TX 76101. (817)335-4161. Editor-in-Chief: Earl F. Warren. For persons interested in leather crafts. 80% of articles are how-to-do-it, 20% are

profiles of people producing leatherwork. Bimonthly. Circ. 60,000. Previously published, photocopied and occasionally, simultaneous submissions OK. Free sample copy.
Illustrations: Buys leathercraft themes. "We are how-to-do-itoriented." Query. SASE. Reports in 6-8 weeks. Buys all rights. Pays $10-100, b&w line drawings, washes and reflective art; on publication.
Tips: "Most often we require a whole package, including an article and illustrations. Basically we are looking for journalists who can write a how-to-do-it or profile article who can also illustrate their piece, or for an artist who has teamed up with a writer to illustrate his/her submission. An example of this is that we recently bought an article on a bootmaker. The author submitted photos, but another alternative would have been if the author or an artist had submitted illustrations on how a boot is designed to fit a foot. A complete article/illustration package has the best chance here, but that's not to say we won't buy something that is appropriate."

MANAGEMENT ACCOUNTING, 919 3rd Ave., New York NY 10022. (212)754-9700. Editor: Erwin S. Koval. Cartoon Editor: Robert F. Randall. Monthly. Circ. 90,000. Original artwork not returned after publication.
Cartoons: Uses 1 cartoon/issue, all from freelancers. Receives 5 submissions/week from freelancers. Interested in corporate accounting and office themes; single panel. Prefers finished cartoons or roughs. SASE. Reports in 2 weeks. Pays $15-25, line drawings.

MANAGING THE LEISURE FACILITY, 1717 West End Ave., Nashville TN 37203. (615)329-3927. Editor-in-Chief: Paul Curran. For managers of leisure facilities including arenas, stadiums and amusement parks. Bimonthly. Circ. 17,000. Simultaneous submissions and previously published work OK. Free sample copy.
Cartoons: SASE. Reports in 2 weeks. Buys all rights. Pays $10 minimum, b&w line drawings; on publication.
Illustrations: Buys 5/year. Query with previously published work. SASE. Reports in 2 weeks. Buys all rights. Cover: Pays $250 minimum, color washes; $100 minimum, b&w line drawings. Inside: Pays $25 minimum, b&w line drawings.

MARATHON WORLD, Marathon Oil Co., 539 S. Main St., Findlay OH 45840. (419)422-2121. Editor-in-Chief: Robert Ostermann. For Marathon employees, shareholders, executives, customers and suppliers. Quarterly. 30 pages. Offset. Estab. 1964. Circ. 70,000. Query. SASE. Reports in 1 week. "We normally work through artists' agents. We're not a market for beginning artists. We usually use illustrators with a national reputation and/or a track record of work in publications like *Esquire*, *Time* and *Fortune*." Not copyrighted. Pays on acceptance. Free sample copy.
Illustrations: Stan Corfman, editor. Buys 10-15/issue on assigned themes. Inside: Pays $200-800, b&w; $400-1,000, color.

MARIAN HELPERS BULLETIN, Eden Hill, Stockbridge MA 01262. Art Director: Brother Frank Piorkowski. For members of the Association of Marian Helpers. Quarterly. Circ. 650,000. Free sample copy and artist's guidelines. SASE. Reports in 2-3 weeks. Buys first rights. Pays on acceptance.

MARRIAGE AND FAMILY LIVING, Abbey Press, St. Meinrad IN 47577. (812)357-8011. Editor: Ila M. Stabile. Art Director: Mark Laurenson. For married Christians. Monthly. Circ. 62,000. Buys one-time rights. Pays on publication. Sample copy, 25¢. Free artist's guidelines.
Illustrations: Buys 200/year.
Other Needs: Uses 200 photographs/year. Interested in education, family life and religion. Query with samples. SASE. Reports in 4 weeks. Cover: Pays $125, color slides; Inside: Pays $10-35, b&w 8x10 glossies.

MART MAGAZINE, Berkshire Common, Pittsfield MA 01201. (413)499-2550. For retailers of consumer electronics and major appliances. Estab. 1953. Circ. 45,000. Semimonthly. Pays on acceptance.

MARYLAND CONSERVATIONIST, Tawes State Office Building C-2, Annapolis MD 21401. (301)269-2235. Contact: Editor. "For outdoorsmen, between 10 and 100 years old." Estab. 1927. Circ. 8,000. Bimonthly. SASE. Reports in 3 weeks. Pays on publication.
Illustrations: Buys cover only. Pays $100/cover. Query with samples (slides) of work.

MASTER DETECTIVE, Reese Publishing Co., 235 Park Ave. S., New York NY 10003. Managing Editor: Walter Jackson. Monthly. Sample copy 60¢.

Cartoons: Buys 100/year; single panel. "Avoid overemphasizing cliche situations such as 2 convicts in cell. No horror. Cute, mild sex." Submit rough art. Reports in 2 weeks. Buys all rights. Pays $25; on acceptance.

MATURE CATHOLIC, 1100 W. Wells St., Milwaukee WI 53233. (414)271-8926. Contact: Carol Mitchell. Emphasizes the positive aspects of aging, current issues and trends in all aspects of life. Bimonthly. Circ. 6,000. Original artwork returned after publication.
Cartoons: Uses 1 cartoon/issue, all from freelancers. Receives 0 submissions/week from freelancers. Prefers finished cartoons. SASE. Reports in 2 weeks. Buys first North American serial rights. Pays $5, b&w; on publication.
Illustrations: Uses 2 illustrations/issue, all from freelancers. Receives 0 submissions/week from freelancers. Interested in themes to relate to article themes and designs for covers. Works on assignment only. Samples returned by SASE. Reports back on future assignment possibilities. Provide flyer to be kept on file for future assignments. Prefers finished art. SASE. Reports in 2 weeks. Buys first North American serial rights.

MATURE YEARS, United Methodist Publishing House, 201 8th Ave. S., Nashville TN 37202. Editor-in-Chief: Ewart Watts. Art Director: Dave Dawson. For ages 60+. Quarterly. Circ. 103,000. Free catalog and artist's guidelines.
Cartoons: Buys 4/year. Interested in current events, religion and retirement; single, double and multipanel. Query with samples. SASE. Reports in 4 weeks. Buys all rights. Pays $15 minimum, b&w; on publication.

MBA COMMUNICATIONS, 730 3rd Ave., New York NY 10017. (212)557-9240. Art Director: Cathy Cacchione. Publishes 4 bimonthly magazines for medical, law, business and engineering professions. Send tearsheets or photocopies. Reports in 30 days. Buys one-time rights. Pays on publication.
Illustrations: Needs cover and inside art. Pays $50-400.

MEDIA WEST, 601-510 W. Hastings St., Vancouver, B.C., Canada V6B 1L8. (604)689-2021. Associate Publisher: Gabrielle Minot. Biweekly. Circ. 4,000. Estab. 1980.
Cartoons: Uses 1 cartoon/issue which must relate to the advertising industry. Prefers single panel. Previously published, photocopied and simultaneous submissions OK. SASE. Reports in 3 weeks. Buys first rights. Pays $10-15 for b&w washes on acceptance.

MEDICAL ECONOMICS, Litton Publications, 680 Kinderkamack Rd., Oradell NJ 07649. Concerns the business side of medicine, home life of physicians, and general areas of everyday life. Biweekly. Sample copy $2. Guidelines available.
Cartoons: Send cartoons. Reports in 4-5 weeks. Buys all rights. Pays $80 minimum; on acceptance.

MEDICAL TIMES, 80 Shore Rd., Port Washington NY 11050. Contact: James McCarthy. Monthly.
Needs: "We are interested in medical scenes—doctors, nurses, patients, hospitals." Send art or samples. Reports in 1 month. Buys all rights. Pays $20, cartoons; $25-100, spot art; negotiates pay for finished color covers; on acceptance.

MEN'S HAIRSTYLIST, 100 Park Ave., New York NY 10017. (212)532-5588. Editor: Jody Byrne d'Honau. Emphasizes men's grooming services. Read in professional hairstyling salons. Monthly. Circ. 45,000. Sample copy $1.
Cartoons: Interested in men's hairstylists; single or multi-panel b&w line drawings with gag lines. Send roughs. SASE. Reports only on acceptance. Buys first North American serial rights. Pays $10; on publication.
Illustrations: Buys only assigned freelance work. Uses line drawings for how-to articles; b&w line drawings for cover and inside. Send resume, samples or roughs, or arrange appointment to show portfolio. SASE. Reports only on acceptance. Buys all rights on a work-for-hire basis. Pay is negotiable; pays on publication.
Other Needs: Mechanical artists, $8/hour.

MERLIN PAPERS, Box 5602, San Jose CA 95150. Editor-in-Chief: Jennifer McDowell. Managing Editor: Milton Lowenthal. Intellectual, cultural publication. Annually. Circ. 1,000. Photocopied and simultaneous submissions OK. Sample copy 50¢.
Illustrations: Editor: Daniel Marlin. Buys cultural and nature themes. "We are interested in any work that accurately renders the relationship between the individual and society." Mail art.

SASE. Reports in 2 months. Buys all rights, but may reassign rights to artist after publication. Cover: Pays $50, b&w line drawings; on publication.

MESSAGE MAGAZINE, Box 59, Nashville TN 37202. (615)889-8000. Emphasizes religious subject matter. Readers are people of African heritage. Bimonthly. Circ. 120,000. Original artwork not returned after publication. Free sample copy; art guidelines for SASE.
Illustrations: Uses 2 illustrations per issue; buys 1 or 2 from freelancers. Interested in illustrations for "articles covering current events: social problems such as divorce, drugs, family, marriage, abortions, etc." Illustration styles can be pencil renderings or overlays for 2 color work. "Rendering should be fairly tight but stylized illustration is acceptable as well." Uses inside b&w line drawings with b&w washes and color washes inside, and tight rendering required for 4 color cover. Works on assignment only. Samples returned by SASE. Reports back on future assignment possibilities. Provide resume or letter of inquiry to be kept on file for future assignments. Prefers samples of style and/or personal appointment to show portfolio to Robert Wright, designer. SASE. Reports in 2 weeks. Buys all rights on a work-for-hire basis. Pays $30-75 for inside b&w, $100-350 for color cover and $75-200 for inside color; on acceptance.

METLFAX, 5821 Harper Rd., Solon OH 44139. (216)248-1125. Editor-in-Chief: Thomas H. Dreher. Concerns the metalworking field. Monthly. Circ. 102,000. Mail art. SASE. Reports in 2 weeks. Buys all rights. Pays on acceptance. Free sample copy.
Cartoons: Buys 18/year on the metalworking industry; single panel. Pays $15 maximum, line drawings.

METRO, THE MAGAZINE OF SOUTHEASTERN VIRGINIA, Box 1995, Norfolk VA 23501. Publisher: Paul G. Katabian. Editor-in-Chief: William H. Candler. Regional publication. Monthly. Circ. 20,000. Previously published work OK. Sample copy available.
Cartoons: "We use cartoons on an assignment/spot illustrator basis. Seldon use freelance cartoons. Prefers resume. "Need to know whether cartoonist is accessible for assigned work." SASE. Reports in 2 weeks. Buys all rights on a work-for-hire basis. Pays $5-15; on publication.
Illustrations: Pays $20, spot drawing; $100, full-color; $50-100, advertising assignment. Requires color separations.

MICHIANA, Colfax and Lafayette, South Bend IN 46626. (219)233-6161. Editor: Bill Sonneborn. Sunday magazine of the *South Bend Tribune*. Estab. 1953. Circ. 130,000. Weekly; 11-5/8x14; 24 pages. Letterpress. SASE. Reports in 2 weeks. Simultaneous submissions and previously published work OK. Buys first or simultaneous rights. Pays on publication.
Cartoons: Buys 50/year on education, family life and humor through youth; single panel with gag line. Pays $7.50 minimum, b&w line drawings. Mail finished art.
Illustrations: Buys 10/year on education, family life and humor through youth. Inside: Pays $10-40, b&w line drawings, washes and gray opaques. Query with resume and samples.

MICHIGAN OUT OF DOORS, Box 30235, Lansing MI 48909. Contact: Kenneth S. Lowe. "Following the various hunting and fishing seasons we have a need for illustration material; we consider submissions 6-8 months in advance." Reports as soon as possible. Sample copy 50¢.
Needs: Pays $10 for pen and ink illustrations in a vertical treatment; pays on publication.

MICHIGAN SPORTSMAN, Michigan Sportsman Publications, Box 2483, Oshkosh WI 54901. Editor-in-Chief: Thomas C. Petrie. Art Director: John Johanek. Contains practical information on Michigan outdoors. Bimonthly. 56-60 pages. Offset. Estab. 1976. Circ. 30,000. Mail art or query with samples or previously published work. SASE. Reports in 3 weeks. Photocopied submissions OK. Buys all rights, but may reassign rights to artist after publication. Pays on publication. Free sample copy.
Cartoons: Buys 20/year on the environment, hunting and fishing; single, double and multipanel with gag lines. Pays $30 minimum, b&w and color.
Illustrations: Buys 15-20/year on the environment, hunting, fishing, the outdoors and wildlife. "No Disney-type animals. Must be geographically correct. No palm trees, snow-capped mountains, etc." Cover: Pays $150 minimum, color. Inside: Pays $15 minimum, b&w; $25, color.

MICROFORM REVIEW, 520 Riverside Ave., Westport CT 06880. Contact: Alan Meckler. Buys cartoons dealing with microforms in the library (microfilm, microfiche). Pays $5 minimum for all rights. Sample copy available.

THE MIDWEST MOTORIST, 201 Progress Pkwy., Maryland Heights MO 63043. (314)576-7350. Associate Editors: Carolyn Callison or Tim Sitek. For members of the Auto Club

of Missouri. Features articles on travel and driving safety. Bimonthly. Circ. 280,000. Original artwork returned after publication, if requested.
Cartoons: Receives 2 submissions/week from freelancers. Interested in automoblile and travel related themes. Prefers finished cartoons and resume. SASE. Reports in 2-3 weeks. Negotiates pay; on publication.
Illustrations: Uses 1 illustration/issue, all from freelancers. Interested in illustrations to accompany articles. Works on assignment only. Samples returned by SASE. Reports back on future assignment possibilities. Provide resume and brochure to be kept on file for future assignments. Prefers portfolio or samples of style. SASE. Reports in 1 week. Negotiates pay; on publication.

MILITARY COLLECTORS NEWS, Box 7582, Tulsa OK 74105. Editor-in-Chief: Jack Britton. For collectors of military items. Monthly; 8½x7; 30 pages. Offset. Estab. 1967. Circ. 10,000. Original artwork not returned after publication.
Cartoons: Buys 12-24/year on medals, badges, uniforms and insignia; single panel. Uses 1-2 cartoons/issue, all from freelancers. Interested in military themes; single panel. Prefers finished cartoons. SASE. Reports in 30 days. Buys all rights on a work-for-hire basis. Pays $1-5, line drawings; on publication.
Illustrations: Uses 5-6 illustrations/issue; buys 1-2/issue from freelancers. Interested in military themes. Works on assignment only. No samples returned. Reports back on future assignment possibilities. Provide letter of inquiry to be kept on file for future assignments. Prefers finished art. SASE. Reports in 30 days. Buys all rights on a work-for-hire basis. Cover: Pays $1-15, b&w line drawings. Inside: Pays $1-10; on publication.

MILITARY ELECTRONICS/COUNTER MEASURES, 2065 Martin Ave., Suite 104, Santa Clara CA 95050. (408)727-3330. Art Director: Dale Bates. For people interested in military electronics systems for military and industry engineers and program managers in electronics. Monthly. Circ. 31,000.
Illustrations: Buys 3-5 illustrations/issue; mostly b&w. Query with samples. SASE. Reports in months. Pays on publication.

THE MILITARY ENGINEER, Society of American Military Engineers, Suite 905, 740 15th St. NW, Washington DC 20005. (202)638-4010. Editor: John J. Kern. Bimonthly. Circ. 22,000. Sample copy $4.
Cartoons: Buys 15-20 cartoons/year on military and civil engineering, construction, biography and history; single panel with gag line. Mail art. SASE. Reports in 1 week. Buys all rights. Pays $15-25, b&w line drawings; on acceptance.

MILITARY JOURNAL, 218 Beech St., Bennington VT 05201. (802)447-0313. Publisher/Editor: Ray Merriam. For historians, hobbyists, veterans and enthusiasts of military history, especially 1900-present. Bimonthly. Circ. 3,000. Simultaneous submissions and previously published work OK. Sample copy $2; free guidelines.
Illustrations: Uses 10-30 illustrations/issue. Most supplied by authors. Interested in military subjects, especially weapons (aircraft, ships and vehicles), combat scenes, etc; also multi-view illustrations (plan views) in detail and in scale. Samples returned by SASE and reports back on future assignment possibilities. Provide resume, letter of inquiry or tearsheet to be kept on file for future assignments. Prefers roughs, portfolio and samples of style. SASE. Reports in 4 weeks. Buys first North American serial rights. Pays $25 minimum/cover (b&w line drawings, washes and gray opaques). Inside: Pays $2 minimum (b&w line drawings); on publication.

MILITARY MEDIA REVIEW, Public Affairs Office, Defense Information School, Ft. Benjamin Harrison IN 46216. Editor: Mary Rothgeb. For and about information people. Concerns information techniques, including articles, fillers, artwork, photos and cartoons on the following: print and broadcast journalism, oral communication, public relations, internal information programs and problems, media relationships and new directions in communicative arts–especially with application to military information and public affairs. Quarterly. Query. Indicate if material should be returned; SASE not required. Guarantees wide exposure to all service information offices and many federal agencies, as well as to commanders in the field and several schools of journalism.
Needs: Finished b&w line drawings, washes and gray opaques. Pays contributor's copies.

MIND MAGAZINE, Box 9482, Catonsville MD 21228. (301)788-6208. Emphasizes new age and psychic articles for readers who are intellectually curious, interested in new discoveries about themselves, self growth, and bettering their lives; male and female of all ages. Circ. 2,000. Estab. 1979. Free sample copy; art guidelines for SASE.

Illustration Needs: Uses 6 illustrations/issue; all by freelancers. Receives 1 illustration from freelancers/week. "We regularly work with 3 freelance artists." Illustrations should pertain to people in daily living situations, self-improvement classes, and science illustrations (such as the brain). Format: b&w line drawings and collages for inside. Send tearsheets and resume to Michael Cain, managing editor. Reports in 1 month. SASE. Pays $25-150 on acceptance. Buys all rights on a work-for-hire basis.
Other Needs: Promotional.

THE MINIATURE MAGAZINE, Box 700, Fredon-Springdale Rd., Newton NJ 07860. (201)383-3355. Emphasizes how-to on all aspects of crafts and miniatures. Bimonthly. Circ. 100,000. Sample copy $1; free art guidelines for SASE.
Cartoons: Uses 0-1 cartoon/issue; buys all from freelancers. Receives 1 submission/week from freelancers. Interested in craft subjects and the human side of the hobbyist. Miniature subjects are also of interest. Prefers single panel b&w line drawings or washes with gag line. Send roughs and/or finished cartoons to Wendie R. Blanchard, managing editor. Reports in 2 weeks. Buys first North American serial rights. Pays $25-35 for b&w on publication.
Illustrations: Uses about 20/issue. Receives about 10 illustrations with mss./week and 5 without mss./week from freelancers. Interested in how-to craft techniques with clarity of illustration and hard lines with overlays. Prefers b&w line drawings and washes for inside. Send roughs, samples of style and cover letter outlining intent to W. Blanchard. Reports in 2 weeks. SASE. Buys first North American serial rights. Pays $50 minimum on publication.

MINIATURES DEALER, Clifton House, Clifton VA 22024. (703)830-1000. Readers are "retailers in the dollhouse/miniatures trade who are generally independent small store owners who don't have time to read anything that doesn't pertain specifically to their own problems." Monthly. Estab. 1978. Sample copy $1; art guidelines for SASE.
Cartoon Needs: Uses 1 cartoon/issue which is supplied by freelancers. Format: single panel b&w line drawings with gag line. Send finished cartoons to Marla Young, editor. SASE. Pays on publication.

MINNESOTA MOTORIST, 7 Travelers Trail, Burnsville MN 55337. For Minnesota AAA members. Estab. 1914. Circ. 270,000. Bimonthly; 32-40 pages. Offset. SASE. Reports in 3 weeks. Buys first North American rights. Pays on acceptance. Free sample copy.
Illustrations: Buys 8/year on historical and outdoor sports themes. Inside: Pays $50 minimum, b&w line drawings; $75 minimum, color.

MINNESOTA SPORTSMAN, Minnesota Sportsman Publications, Box 3003, Oshkosh WI 54901. Editor-in-Chief: Thomas C. Petrie. Art Director: John J. Johanek. Contains practical information on outdoors Minnesota. Bimonthly. 56 pages. Offset. Estab. 1977. Circ. 15,000. Mail art or query with samples or previously published work. SASE. Reports in 3 weeks. Photocopied submissions OK. Buys all rights, but may reassign rights to artist after publication. Pays on publication. Free sample copy.
Cartoons: Buys 20/year on the environment, hunting and fishing; single, double and multipanel with gag lines. Pays $30 minimum, b&w and color.
Illustrations: Buys 15-20/year on the environment, wildlife and outdoors. "No Disney-type animals. Must be geographically correct. No palm trees, snow-capped mountains." Cover: Pays $150 minimum, color. Inside: Pays $15 minimum, b&w; $25, color.

MISSOURI LIFE, 216 E. McCarty, Jefferson City MO 65101. (314)635-7921. Editor: John M. Hall. Four color magazine about Missouri. Readers are people interested in the beauty and fascination of Missouri places and faces. Bimonthly. Circ. 25,000. Original artwork returned after publication. Sample copy $2.50; art guidelines for SASE.
Cartoons: Used "only to illustrate feature on cartoonist. Write with article proposed."
Illustrations: Uses original artwork depicting Missouri places or people. Format: b&w, color cover washes, inside and cover color washes and original art that will reproduce for offset printing/web. Works on assignment only. Samples returned by SASE. Reports back on future assignment possibilities. Provide letter of inquiry, tearsheet, proposal and sample of work to be kept on file for future assignments. "Prefer slides of freelancer's original work, then I negotiate with the artist." SASE, "but I do not encourage use of mails for slides without prior discussion of shipping." Reports in 2 weeks. Buys first North American serial rights. Pays $50-100 for b&w, cover; on publication. Depending on amount used, payment ranges from $50-300.

MODEL RETAILER, Clifton House, Clifton VA 22024. (703)830-1000. Editor-in-Chief: Douglas R. Pratt. For hobby store owners. Monthly. Circ. 5,000. Previously published and

simultaneous submissions ("must be notified") OK. Original artwork not returned after publication. Sample copy $1.50.
Cartoons: Uses 1-2 cartoons/issue, all from freelancers. Receives 4-5 submissions/month from freelancers. Interested in themes pertaining to hobbies, hobby stores or small businesses; double panel. Prefers finished cartoons. SASE. Reports in 3-4 weeks. Buys "all rights in our field." Pays $10 minimum, line drawings; on publication.

MODERN BRIDE, Ziff-Davis Publishing Co., 1 Park Ave., New York NY 10016. Contact: Meredith Bohm. Bimonthly. SASE. Reports in "months." Pays on publication.
Cartoons and Illustrations: Buys 4-5/issue on beauty and table settings. Pays $25-75, b&w. Query with samples.

MODERN BULK TRANSPORTER, 4801 Montgomery Lane, Washington DC 20014. Editor-in-Chief: John L. Conley. For tank truck industry executives in petroleum, gases, chemicals and milk and bulk foods. Monthly. 40 pages. Offset. Estab. 1937. Circ. 10,000. Query with samples. SASE. Reports in 2 weeks. Buys first rights. Pays on acceptance. Free sample copy.
Cartoons: Buys 5/year on tank truck operation; single panel. "Must be favorable to company management operating trucks." Pays $7 minimum, line drawings.

MODERN CARTOONING, 48 Belle Air Dr., North Kingstown RI 02852. Editor-in-Chief: Joyce A. Covington. Art Director: Shannon Lea. For working cartoonists and gag writers. Monthly. Previously published, photocopied and simultaneous submissions OK. Original artwork not returned after publication. Sample copy $3. Free artist's guidelines.
Cartoons: Uses 6-10 cartoons/issue; buys 6-10/issue from freelancers. Slanted towards the rejection or acceptance theme. Of humorous interest to cartoonists and gag writers. Single panel, with gag line or captionless. Prefers finished cartoons. SASE. Reports in 1-2 weeks. Pays $7.50-10, b&w line drawings; on acceptance.

MODERN DRUMMER, 1000 Clifton Ave., Clifton NJ 07013. (201)778-1700. Editor-in-Chief: Ronald Spagnardi. For drummers, all ages and levels of playing ability with varied interests within the field of drumming. Bimonthly. Circ. 35,000. Previously published work OK. Original artwork returned after publication. Sample copy $1.75.
Cartoons: Buys 12-20/year. Uses 2-3 cartoons/issue. Interested in drumming; single and double panel. "We want strictly drummer-oriented gags." Prefers finished cartoons or roughs. SASE. Reports in 2 weeks. Buys first North American serial rights. Pays $5-15, halftones; on publication.
Illustrations: Buys 10-15 illustrations/year. Uses 2 illustrations/issue. Interested in drummers. Cover: Pays $35-75, b&w; $50-125, color. Inside: Pays $10-30, color; $10-25, b&w; on publication.

MODERN LITURGY, Box 444, Saratoga CA 95070. Editor-in-Chief: William Burns. Art Editor: George Collopy. For religious artists, musicians and planners of worship services for Catholic and Protestant liturgical traditions. Published 8 times/year. Circ. 16,000. Sample copy $2.50.
Cartoons: Buys 8 cartoons/year from freelancers. Interested in "situations depicting humorous or other aspects of contemporary religious celebrations." Prefers query with samples. SASE. Reports in 4-6 weeks. Buys all rights, but may reassign rights to artist after publication. Pays $10-25, halftones; on publication.
Illustrations: Buys 4 illustrations/year from freelancers on assigned themes. Prefers query with samples. SASE. Reports in 4-6 weeks. Buys all rights but may reassign rights to artist after publication. Pays $25-50, color-separated art.

MODERN MATURITY, 215 Long Beach Blvd., Long Beach CA 90801. Editor: Hubert C. Pryor. For members of American Association of Retired Persons. Bimonthly. Mail art. Previously published work OK. Original artwork returned after publication. Sample copy available.
Cartoons: Uses 4 cartoons/issue; buys 2/issue from freelancers. Receives 50 submissions/week from freelancers. Interested in general interest themes. Prefers finished cartoons. SASE. Reports in 2 weeks. Buys all rights on a work-for-hire basis. Pays $50, 8x10 finished cartoons.

MODERN MEDICINE, 757 3rd Ave., New York NY 10017. (212)888-2632. Editorial Assistant: Dax Wexper. Published 21 times/year. Circ. 170,000. Emphasizes practical update in diagnoses and management of common illnesses for general and family practice physicians.
Cartoons: Uses 3 cartoons/issue. Receives 4-5/week from freelancers. Themes must apply to medical situations. Prefers single and double panel; b&w line drawings with gag line. Send finished cartoons. SASE. Reports in 1 week. Buys one-time rights. Pays $35 for b&w on acceptance.

MODERN TIRE DEALER, 77 N. Miller Rd., Akron OH 44313. (216)867-4401. Editorial Director: Charles Staybaugh. Circ. 33,000. For owners-operators of independent retail/wholesale tire shops. Buys all rights. Pays on publication.
Cartoons: Buys themes relating to automotive and tire services. Send actual cartoons; include gag line. SASE. "When a cartoonist sends cartoons that are already complete and asks us to consider them, chances are good we will use them. If we don't, after a few months we return them." Pays $50, pen and ink, approximately 8x10 to be shot down to about 3x5; on publication.
Illustrations: Buys automotive services and tire-related themes, using line drawings of men performing services on tires, brakes, shocks and mufflers. Assignments given based on samples. Query with samples of artistic style. SASE. Reports in 1 week. Cover: Pays $100-200, color. Inside: Pays $20-50, drawings; on publication.

MOMENT, 462 Boylston St., Suite 301, Boston MA 02116. (617)536-6252. Editor-in-Chief: Leonard Fein. Art Director: Frank Glickman. "Primarily Jewish audience; includes fiction, poetry, politics, psychology, human interest, community concerns and pleasures." Published 10 times/year. Circ. 25,000. Sample copy $2; free artist's guidelines.
Cartoons: Buys themes on current events, education, environment, family life, humor through youth, politics and religion; "almost anything if it can be broadly defined as of Jewish interest;" single panel. "No old nostalgic Jewish joke types; we are contemporary." Query or mail art. SASE. Reports in 4 weeks. Buys first North American serial rights. Pays $25 minimum, b&w line drawings; on publication.
Illustrations: Buys 30/year on current events, education, environment, family life, humor through youth, politics, religion and "anything of Jewish interest." Query or mail art. SASE. Reports in 4 weeks. Buys first North American serial rights. Cover: Pays $100 minimum, color. Inside: Pays $50 minimum, b&w line drawings; on publication.

MOODY MONTHLY, 2101 W. Howard, Chicago IL 60645. (312)274-2535. Emphasizes Christian family life for Protestant evangelical readers. Monthly. Circ. 335,000. Free sample copy.
Illustration Needs: Uses about 5 illustrations/issue; all supplied by freelancers. Assigns illustrations to accompany articles. Themes should include people in daily living and children's stories. Also interested in other peripheral material. Format: b&w line drawings and washes for inside and color washes and chalk for cover. Send samples of style and tear sheets to Dick Bohrer, senior editor. Reports "when we have an assignment." Payment on acceptance is negotiable. Buys first North American serial rights.

MOTHERS' MANUAL, 176 Cleveland Dr., Croton-on-Hudson NY 10520. (914)271-8415 or 271-8926. Editor-in-Chief: Beth Waterfall. Art Editor: Kenneth McMullen. Bimonthly; 8½x11; 52 pages. Offset. Estab. 1965. Circ. 900,000. Mail art; prefers local artists. SASE. Reports in 4 weeks. Buys one-time rights. Pays on publication. Sample copy 75¢.
Cartoons: Buys family life themes; "especially interested in pregnancy and parenting through age 6. Would like to see truly funny cartoons in good taste reflecting the joys and sorrows of child-rearing." Pays $40, b&w halftones and washes.
Illustrations: Buys themes on family life with children under age 6. Pays $35 minimum, b&w line drawings and washes.
To Break In: "We're always interested in good cartoonists. We don't like to see stereotypes. Mothers, fathers and children should be presented as intelligent, likeable people. A drawing depicting people as stupid, ugly, mean, inferior or superior is an automatic reject—no matter how 'amusing.' We're looking for quality humor drawn from real life."

MOTOCROSS ACTION, 16200 Ventura Blvd., Encino CA 91436. (213)981-2317. For men and women, ages 12-30. Monthly. Circ. 100,000. SASE.
Cartoons: Buys 1/issue on motocross racing. Send roughs or finished art. Pays $25, b&w; on publication.
Illustrations: Buys 1/issue on motocross racing and bikes. Query with samples. Pays $25 minimum, b&w; on publication.

MOTOR NORTH, 904 W. Broadway, Minneapolis MN 55411. (612)529-9659. Editor-in-Chief: Gary Jacobson. Art Director: Stephanie Yant. For the automotive parts and service industry. Monthly. Circ. 7,500. Simultaneous submissions and previously published work OK. Sample copy $5.
Cartoons: Buys 60/year. Send reproducible finished art. SASE. Reports in 2 weeks. Buys simultaneous rights. Pays $6 minimum, b&w line drawings; on publication.
Illustrations: Buys 6/year on automotive themes. Query with resume and samples. SASE. Reports in 2 weeks. Buys simultaneous rights. Cover: Pays $25 minimum, b&w; $50 minimum, color; on publication.

MOTORBOATING & SAILING, 224 W. 57th St., New York NY 10019. (212)262-8768. Emphasizes powerboats and large sailboats for those who own boats and participate in boating activities. Monthly. Circ. 133,000.
Cartoon Needs: Uses an average of less than 1 cartoon/issue which is supplied by freelancers but "would like to use more." Cartoons should pertain to humorous aspects of owning and operating powerboats and sailboats. Format: Single panel. Send finished cartoons to Oliver S. Moore III, editor. Reports in 1 month. SASE. Payment is negotiable when work confirmed for publication. Buys one-time rights.
Illustration Needs: Uses varying number of illustrations/month. Makes assignments based on samples on file. Illustrations should pertain to maintenance how-to, or powerboats and large sailboats in motion. Format: b&w line drawings. Send samples of style that can be kept on file to Oliver S. Moore III, editor. Reports in 1 month "or when assignment is available." SASE. Payment is negotiable when work confirmed for publication. Buys first North American serial rights.

MOTORCYCLIST, Petersen Publishing Co., 8490 Sunset Blvd., Los Angeles CA 90069. (213)657-5100. Editor-in-Chief: Dale Boller. Art Director: Nancy Lenn. For motorcycle riders and enthusiasts. Monthly. Circ. 200,000. Free sample copy and artist's guidelines.
Cartoons: Uses 1 cartoon/issue. Receives 3 submissions/week from freelancers. Interested in motorcycling themes. Prefers finished cartoons, or arrange interview to show portfolio. SASE. Reports in 1 week. Pays $25 minimum, b&w; Inside: $150 minimum, color; on publication.
Illustrations: Uses 1 illustration/issue. Buys 1/issue from freelancers. Receives 1-2 submissions/week from freelancers. Interested in all styles. Often need illustrations as lead art for stories. Reports back on future assignment possibilities. Provide resume, calling card, tearsheet to be kept on file for future assignments. Prefers finished art. SASE. Reports in 1 week. Buys all rights on a work-for-hire basis, or can be negotiated. Pays $25 minimum (b&w inside); $150 minimum (color); on publication.

MOTORLAND, California State Automobile Association, 150 Van Ness Ave., San Francisco CA 94101. (415)565-2451. Editor-in-Chief: William C. Ellis. Art Director: Al Davidson. For association members in northern California and Nevada. Bimonthly. Circ. 1,200,000. Free catalog and artist's guidelines.
Illustrations: Uses 2-3 illustrations/issue, all from freelancers. Interested in western history, attractions, recreation and travel. Works on assignment only. Reports back to artist on future assignment possibilities. Provide samples, reproductions or photos of work to be kept on file for future assignments.

MPLS. ST. PAUL MAGAZINE, 512 Nicollet Mall, Suite 615, Minneapolis MN 55402. (612)339-7571. Contact: Maureen Ryan. City/regional magazine. Monthly. Circ. 30,000. Original artwork returned after publication.
Cartoons: Uses 3 cartoons/issue; buys 3/issue from freelancers. Receives 10 submissions/week from freelancers. Interested in general humor and local politics. Prefers query, roughs, finished cartoons or photocopies of finished cartoons. SASE. Reports in 2 weeks. Pays on acceptance.
Illustrations: Uses 4 illustrations/issue. Works on assignment only. Samples returned by SASE. Reports back on future assignment possibilities. Provide calling card, flyer or tearsheet to be kept on file for future assignments. Prefers samples or arrange interview to show portfolio. SASE. Reports in 2 weeks. Buys first North American serial rights, and all rights on a work-for-hire basis. Pays $75-200, b&w; $350 maximum/full-page, color; on acceptance.

MR. LONGEARS MAGAZINE, 100 Church St., Amsterdam NY 12010. (518)842-2660. Contact: Tom Constantino. For people that own donkeys or are interested in equines and history and role of animals. Estab. 1971. Circ. 1,500. Quarterly. Reports in 3-4 weeks.
Cartoons: Buys 1/issue on human interest subjects relative to animals, preferably donkeys and mules. Pays $20, b&w. Send roughs.

MUSCLE MAG INTERNATIONAL, Unit 1, 270 Rutherford Rd. S., Brampton, Ontario, Canada L6W 3K7. (416)457-3030. Editor-in-Chief: Robert Kennedy. Published 6 times/year. Circ. 210,000. Previously published work OK. Original artwork not returned after publication. Sample copy $3.
Cartoons: Uses 6 cartoons/issue, all from freelancers. Receives 20 submissions/week from freelancers. Interested in weight lifting and body building; single panel; "well-drawn work—professional." Prefers finished cartoons. SASE. Send $2 for return postage. Reports in 2 weeks. Buys all rights on a work-for-hire basis. Pays $15-25, color; $10-20, b&w; on acceptance.
Illustrations: Uses 2 illustrations/issue; buys 1/issue from freelancers. Receives 20 submissions/week from freelancers. Interested in "professionally drawn exercise art of body builders training

with apparatus." Prefers finished art. SASE. Send $2 for return postage. Reports in 2 weeks. Buys all rights on a work-for-hire basis. Cover: $50, color. Inside: $80, color; $50, b&w; on acceptance. "Pay can be triple for really professional or outstanding artwork."

MUSIC EDUCATORS JOURNAL, 1902 Association Dr., Reston VA 22091. (703)860-4000. Editor-in-Chief: Malcolm E Bessom. Managing Editor: Duke Johns. Production Manager: Barbara Sweeney. Monthly. Circ. 60,000.
Illustrations: Uses 5 illustrations/issue; buys 3/issue from freelancers. Interested in "collages, figure drawings, abstract design—anything that works." Works on assignment only. Samples returned by SASE. Provide brochure, flyer or tearsheet to be kept on file for future assignments. Prefers portfolio. SASE. Reports in "up to 6 months." Buys all rights on a work-for-hire basis. Cover: Pays $400 maximum, full-color art. Inside: Pays $25-100 per item: b&w line drawings, washes, gray opaques and color-separated work; on acceptance.

NARD JOURNAL, 1750 K St. NW, Suite 1200, Washington DC 20006. (202)347-7495. Editor: Harris A. Erstein. For independent community pharmacists who own either one pharmacy or a small chain. Monthly. Circ. 21,500.
Illustrations: Occasionally buys cover art on assigned drug-related subjects. Query or arrange interview to show portfolio. SASE. Reports in 2-4 weeks. Negotiates pay; pays on publication.

NATIONAL DEFENSE, 819 Union First Bldg., Washington DC 20005. (202)347-7250. Contact: Editor. For members of industry and U.S. Armed Forces. Estab. 1920. Circ. 34,000. Bimonthly. Pays on publication.
Cartoons: Negotiates subjects and pay.
Illustrations: Negotiates subjects and pay. Query with samples.

NATIONAL FIRE PROTECTION ASSOCIATION, 470 Atlantic Ave., Boston MA 02210. Contact: Lee Liberman. Publishes comic books and other material teaching fire prevention. Send art or samples; Boston and New York City artists only. Reports in 1 month. Buys all rights. Pays on acceptance.
Needs: Buys illustrations, comic book art and graphic design.

NATIONAL 4H NEWS, 7100 Connecticut Ave., Washington DC 20015. Editor: Suzanne C. Harting.
Illustrations: Provide tearsheet or photocopies to be kept on file for future assignments. May be any type b&w technique, watercolor, charcoal sketch, scratchboard, pen and ink or woodcuts. "Art should suggest rather than show literal detail." SASE. Reports in 1 month. Buys one-time rights. Pays $10-50; on acceptance.

THE NATIONAL FUTURE FARMER, Box 15130, Alexandria VA 22309. (703)360-3600. Editor: Wilson Carnes. For ages 14-21. Bimonthly. Estab. 1952. Circ. 500,000. Reports in 2 weeks. Buys all rights. Pays on acceptance. Sample copy available.
Cartoons: Buys cartoons on Future Farmers of America or assigned themes. Pays $10, cartoons; negotiable. Uses some illustration also.

NATIONAL GEOGRAPHIC, 17th and M Sts. NW, Washington DC 20036. (202)857-7000. Editor: Gilbert M. Grosvenor. Art Director: Howard E. Paine. Monthly. Circ. 10,000,000. Original artwork returned after publication, in some cases.
Illustrations: Number illustrations/issue varies. Interested in "Full color, representational renderings of historical events. Nothing that can be photographed is illustrated by artwork." Works on assignment only. Samples returned by SASE. Reports back on future assignment possibilities. Provide brochure, flyer or tearsheet to be kept on file for future assignments. Prefers portfolio and samples of style. "The artist should be familiar with the type of painting we use." SASE. Reports in 2 weeks. Buys all rights on a work-for-hire basis. Minimum payment: Inside: $1,000, color; $200, b&w; on acceptance.

NATIONAL GLASS BUDGET, Box 7138, Pittsburgh PA 15213. (412)682-5136. Manager: Liz Scott. Emphasizes glass manufacturing and industry news for glass manufacturers, dealers, and others involved in making, buying, and selling glass items and products. Semimonthly. Circ. 1,500. Free sample copy.
Cartoons: Uses 1 cartoon/issue. Receives an average of 1 submission/week from freelancers. Cartoons should pertain to glass manufacturing (flat glass, fiberglass, bottles and containers. No mirrors). Format: single and multi-panel b&w line drawings with gag line. Prefers roughs or finished cartoons. SASE. Reports in 1 month. Buys all rights. Pays $25; on acceptance.

NATIONAL GUARD, 1 Massachusetts Ave. NW, Washington DC 20001. "We have recenty reorganized and redirected our magazine." Original artwork not returned after publication. Mail art for files. SASE.
Illustrations: Assigns themes for spot drawings.

NATIONAL JEWISH MONTHLY, B'nai B'rith, 1640 Rhode Island Ave. NW, Washington DC 20036. (202)857-6645. Art Director: Carolyn Yalkut. For the Jewish family. Readers are "middle class, middle brow, mostly middle age and male." Monthly. Circ. 200,000. Original artwork returned after publication. Free sample copy.
Cartoons: Uses 1 cartoon/issue; buys 1/issue from freelancer. Receives 3 cartoons/week from freelancers. Interested in politics, current events, and culture related to Jewish interests. Prefers finished cartoons; b&w line drawings and b&w washes. SASE. Reports in about 1 month. Buys first North American serial rights. Pays $20-50; after publication.
Illustrations: Uses 3 illustrations/issue. Buys 1/issue from freelancers. Interested in a wide range of themes, but especially those related to current Jewish affairs. Works on assignment only. Samples returned by SASE. Reports back on future assignment possibilities. Provide letter of inquiry, brochure or flyer to be kept on file for future assignments. Prefers finished art (b&w Line drawings and washes for inside and cover); samples of style. SASE. Reports in about 1 month. Buys first North American serial rights. Pays $50-100 after publication for b&w cover and $20-75 for inside b&w.
Other Needs: "Design, lettering, calligraphy on assignment. We call or write the artist, pay after publication."

NATIONAL MALL MONITOR WEEKLY, Suite 500, 1321 US 19 S., Clearwater FL 33526. (813)531-5893. Editor: Terry Dunham. Emphasizes shopping center industry methods and activities. Readers are shopping center developers, managers, promotion directors, leasing agents and retailers. Weekly. Also publishes bimonthly National Mall Monitor. Circ. 22,000. Original artwork returned after publication, if requested. Sample copy $4; art guidelines for SASE.
Cartoons: Can use 1 cartoon/issue by freelancer. "Cartoons will be sold to this market primarily on basis of contents. Remember NMM is not a consumer magazine; we're seeking cartoons that would amuse our developers, mall managers, and other readers, not shoppers." Formats: single or multi-panel with gag line. Prefers roughs and/or finished cartoons. SASE. Reports in 4 weeks. Buys all rights. Pays $25 for b&w cartoons; on publication.

NATIONAL PARKS & CONSERVATION, National Parks & Conservation Association, 1701 18th St. NW, Washington DC 20009. Editor: Eugenia Horstman Connally. For well-educated and environmentally-conscious readership. Monthly; 8½x11; 32 pages. Offset. Estab. 1919. Circ. 43,000. Submit art by mail or query with samples. SASE. Reports in 4 weeks. Previously published work OK. Buys all rights on assigned work; one-time rights on spot art. Sample copy $2. Free artist's guidelines.
Cartoons: Buys 3-4/year on the environment; single panel with gag line. Pays $15 minimum, b&w line drawings.
Illustrations: Buys 1-2/issue on the environment, wildlife and habitat, especially endangered species. Cover: Pays $75-150, full-color renderings. Inside: Pays $15-75, b&w line drawings.

NATIONAL REVIEW, 150 E. 35th St., New York NY 10016. Contact: Anna Lieber. Original artwork returned after publication.
Cartoons: Uses 10-15 cartoons/issue; buys 10-12/issue from freelancers. Receives "100 or more" submissions/week from freelancers. Interested in "political, social commentary." Prefers finished cartoons or roughs. SASE. Reports in 2 weeks. Buys first North American serial rights or all rights on a work-for-hire basis. Pays on acceptance.
Illustrations: Uses 15 illustrations/issue, all from freelancers. Receives 30 submissions/week from freelancers. Works on assignment only. No samples returned. Reports back on future assignment possibilities. Provide resume, calling card, letter of inquiry, brochure, flyer and tearsheet to be kept on file for future assignments. Prefers finished art, porftolio, samples of style or "published tearsheets." SASE. "Immediate purchase or assignment." Buys first North American serial rights or all rights on a work-for-hire basis. Pays $15, spot drawings; $35, editorial art; on acceptance.

NATIONAL RURAL LETTER CARRIER, Suite 1204, 1750 Pennsylvania Ave. NW, Washington DC 20006. (202)393-5840. Editor: Olin Armentrout. Managing Editor: RuthAnn Saenger. For rural letter carriers and family-oriented, middle-Americans; many are part-time teachers and businessmen. Weekly. Circ. 60,000. Mail art. SASE. Reports in 4 weeks. Original artwork returned after publication. Previously published, photocopied and simultaneous submissions OK. Buys first rights. Sample copy 24¢.

Illustrations: Buys 12 covers/year on rural scenes, views of rural mailboxes and rural people. Uses 1 illustration/issue; buys 1/issue from freelancers. Receives 1 submission/week from freelancers. Interested in pen and ink or pencil, on rural, seasonal and postal matter. Works on assignment only. Samples returned by SASE. Reports back on future assignment possibilities. Provide resume, samples of work and tearsheet to be kept on file for future assignments. Prefers resume, finished art, roughs or samples of style. SASE. Reports in 1 week, if accepted; 1 month if not accepted. Buys all rights on a work-for-hire basis. Pays $50, b&w; on publication. Also needs art for convention issue of Wichita, Kansas and covers depicting Christ for Easter and Christmas issues.

NATIONAL SAFETY NEWS, National Safety Council, 444 N. Michigan Ave., Chicago IL 60611. (312)527-4800. For those responsible for developing and administering occupational safety and health programs. Monthly. Circ. 56,000. Original artwork returned after publication. Free sample copy and artist's guidelines.
Cartoons: Contact Susan Shemerdiak. Uses 4-6 cartoons/issue, all from freelancers. Interested in occupational safety and health; single, double or multipanel with gag line. Prefers roughs. SASE. Reports in 2 weeks. Buys first North American serial rights or all rights on a work-for-hire basis. Pays $10 minimum, b&w line drawings.
Other Needs: Periodicals and Technical Publications Director: Robert Meyer. Uses artists for 4-color cover design, publication redesign and layout mock-ups.

NATIONAL SOCIETY OF PUBLIC ACCOUNTANTS, 1717 Pennsylvania Ave. NW, Suite 1200, Washington DC 20006. Managing Editor: Elsie Weigel. Send samples.
Illustrations: Buys assigned themes on accounting, business, finances, taxes and economics. Pays $25 minimum, line drawings.

NATIONAL WILDLIFE, 225 E. Michigan St., Milwaukee WI 53202. Associate Editor: Nicoletta Barrie. For those concerned with the future of wildlife and the environment. Bimonthly. Circ. 880,000. Previously published work OK.
Illustrations: Assigns art on 1-2 stories/issue. Works on assignment only. Provide flyer and tearsheet to be kept on file for future assignments. Prefers samples of style. SASE. Reports in 3 weeks. Usually buys all rights, but may reassign rights to artist after publication. Pays competitive rates; on acceptance.

NATURAL HISTORY, American Museum of Natural History, Central Park W. and 79th St., New York NY 10024. (212)873-1300. Editor-in-Chief: Alan Ternes. Art Director: Tom Page. For well-educated professionals interested in the natural sciences. Monthly. Circ. 500,000. Previously published work OK.
Illustrations: Buys 10-15 illustrations/year. Interested in current events and environment. Works on assignment only. Samples returned by SASE. Provide "any pertinent information" to be kept on file for future assignments. Query with samples. SASE. Reports in 1 week. Buys one-time rights. Inside: Pays $100, b&w line drawings and washes; on publication.

NATURAL LIFE, Box 640, Jarvis, Ontario, Canada N0A 1J0. Editor: Wendy Priesnitz. Concerns "a wholistic approach to living for rural and urban readers interested in natural foods, alternate energy, do-it-yourself projects and self-sufficiency." Bimonthly. Circ. 70,000. Original artwork returned after publication, if requested.
Cartoons: Uses 2-3 cartoons/issue; buys 2-3/issue from freelancers. Receives 2-3 cartoons/week from freelancers. Interested in alternate energy and agri-business politics. Pays $20-75, b&w; on acceptance. Send finished artwork.
Illustrations: Works on assignment only. Samples returned by SASE. Reports back on future assignment possibilities. Provide resume and letter of inquiry to be kept on file for future assignments. Send samples of style. SASE. Reports in 2 weeks. Pays on acceptance. Buys all rights on a work-for-hire basis.

NEAR EAST BUSINESS, 386 Park Ave., New York NY 10016. (212)689-0120. Emphasizes "business in Middle East for businessmen, diplomats and government officials, official residents in the Arab world, Turkey, Iran and Cyprus." Monthly. Circ. 20,000. Free sample copy; art guidelines for SASE.
Cartoon Needs: Uses 3-7 cartoons per issue, all supplied by freelancers. Likes "humorous cartoons of interest to businessmen living and working in the Middle East; specific themes include oil, agriculture, irrigation, travel, communications (and difficulties encountered with), economics, development, trade, import-export, shipping." Format: single panel b&w line drawings with gag line. Freelancers should send roughs to Charles Glass, editor. SASE. Reports immediately. Pays

$25-30 on acceptance for b&w and $50-60 for color cartoons (more for cover). Buys one-time rights; "distribution is in Middle East only."
Illustration Needs: Uses 1-5 illustrations per issue which are all from freelancers. "At present, we use commissioned illustrations only. The illustrations are used for specific articles. We would like to keep samples on file in order to have a wider range of illustrators to choose from for commissioning illustrations. We like variety in our use of illustrations, so there are no specific guidelines. We sometimes need humorous illustrations to accompany articles; we occasionally need good graphic illustrations to display statistics. The needs vary from month to month." We buy all types of art. Freelancers should send resume and samples of style to Charles Glass, editor. SASE. Reports back immediately. Pays on acceptance. Buys first British serial rights.

NEBRASKALAND, Box 30370, Lincoln NE 68503. (402)464-0641. Editor-in-Chief: Lowell Johnson. For hunters, anglers, campers, hikers and history buffs. Monthly. Circ. 60,000. Previously published, photocopied and simultaneous submissions OK. Free sample copy.
Cartoons: Buys 30 cartoons/year on environment, hunting, fishing, camping and outdoor recreational themes; single panel. Mail art. SASE. Reports in 2 weeks. Pays $5 minimum, halftones.

NEW COVENANT, Servant Publications, Box 8617, Ann Arbor MI 48107. Editor-in-Chief: Bert Ghezzi. Art Director: Mike Andaloro. For college-educated Christians, interested in furthering Christian growth. Monthly; 8½x11; 36 pages. Offset. Estab. 1971. Circ. 75,000. Query with samples. SASE. Reports in 3 weeks. Previously published, photocopied and simultaneous submissions OK. Buys all rights, but may reassign rights to artist after publication. Pays on publication. Free sample copy and artist's guidelines.
Cartoons: Buys 10-12/year on religion; double panel. Pays $20-100, b&w.
Illustrations: Buys 50-60/year on religion. Cover: Pays $100-250, b&w. Inside: Pays $20-150, b&w.

NEW EARTH REVIEW, Box 483, Murfreesboro NC 27855. (919)398-3341. Editor-in-Chief: Robert Mulder. Art Editor: Anne K. Hunt. For poetry lovers, mostly older women. Quarterly. Circ. 2,000. Previously published and photocopied work OK. Sample copy $2.
Cartoons: Buys 10/year on writing, current events, education, family life, humor through youth and religion; double panel. Mail art. SASE. Reports in 2 weeks. Pays $5-10, line drawings; on acceptance.
Illustrations: Buys 30/year for poems. Mail art. SASE. Reports in 2 weeks. Pays $5-10, b&w line spot drawings; on acceptance.

THE NEW ENGLAND GUIDE, 2 Steam Mill Ct., Box 1108, Concord NH 03301. Emphasizes travel of all kinds. Readers are "those planning on going on vacation trips, weekend jaunts, mini-holidays, day trips, conventions, combination business/pleasure trips. For North American & overseas visitors to New England." Annual. Circ. 200,000. Sample copy $2.25; art guidelines for SASE.
Illustrations: Uses 10 or more illustrations/issue, all done by freelancers on assignment only. Interested in "illustrations of episodes; humor; some scenics; in all, depends on articles used." Format: inside b&w line drawings and washes. Freelancers should "send letter with background and samples (clips are OK), or drop in, if in area." SASE. Reports in 1 week. Buys one-time rights. Pays $50-150 on publication for inside b&w, depending on assignment.

NEW ENGLAND OFFSHORE, Offshore Publications, Inc., 66 Central St., Wellesley MA 02181. (617)235-8484. Editor-in-Chief: Herbert Gliick. For local boating enthusiasts and waterfront lovers. Monthly oversize magazine. Circ. 12,000. Previously published, photocopied and simultaneous submissions OK. Free sample copy and artist's guidelines available after querying with samples or art.
Cartoons: Buys 20/year on boating and waterfront; single, double and multipanel with gag lines. Submit art or query with samples. SASE. Reports in 1 week. Pays $10-18, b&w line drawings; on acceptance. Buys various rights.
Illustrations: Buys 12/year on boating and waterfront. Submit art or query with samples. SASE. Reports in 1 week. Cover: Pays $20-50, b&w line drawings; $35-65, 2-color. Inside: Pays $10-18, b&w line drawings; on acceptance. Buys various rights.

THE NEW ERA, 50 E. North Temple, Salt Lake City UT 84150. (801)531-2951. Editor: Brian K. Kelly. For ages 12-18 of the Church of Jesus Christ of Latter-day Saints. Monthly. Circ. 180,000.
Cartoons: Mail samples. SASE. Reports in 30-60 days. Buys all rights. Pays $25-30.
Illustrations: Mail samples. SASE. Reports in 30-60 days. Buys all rights. Pays $60-140 for spot drawings; $100-250 for full-color illustrations; $150-400 for full-color cover design.

NEW GUARD, Woodland Rd., Sterling VA 22170. (703)450-5162. Editor: Richard F. LaMountain. "Magazine of Young Americans for Freedom, which is a conservative political organization promoting the principles of limited government, individual freedom, capitalism and a strong national defense." Original artwork returned after publication, if requested.
Cartoons: Uses 4-5 cartoons/issue; buys 1/issue from freelancers. Receives 2 submissions/week from freelancers. Interested in politics and world affairs. Prefers finished cartoons. SASE. Reports in 2 weeks. Buys various rights. Pays $15 minimum; on publication.
Illustrations: Uses 2 illustrations/issue, all from freelancers. Interested in politics and world affairs. Provide brochure to be kept on file for future assignments. Prefers finished art. SASE. Reports in 2 weeks. Buys various rights. Pays $15 minimum; on publication.
Other Needs: "Occasionally buys freelance photos."

NEW HAMPSHIRE PROFILES, 2 Steam Mill Ct., Concord NH 03301. (603)224-9934. For state residents. Bimonthly. Circ. 20,000. SASE. Reports in 6-8 weeks. Simultaneous submissions OK. Original artwork not returned after publication, unless requested. Buys first North American rights. Pays on publication. Sample copy $2; free artist's guidelines.
Cartoons: Editor: Brenda Joziatis. Seldom uses cartoons, but willing to see samples with New Hampshire themes.
Illustrations: Editor: Brenda Joziatis. Uses 2 illustrations/issue; buys 2/issue from freelancers. Receives 0-1 submissions/week from freelancers. Interested in humorous characters (generally used with historic article). Works on assignment only. Samples returned by SASE. Reports back on future assignment possibilities. Provide resume and tearsheet to be kept on file for future assignments. Prefers resume and samples of style. SASE. Reports in 1 week; 6-8 weeks on unsolicited material. Buys all rights on a work-for-hire basis. Inside: Pays $25-100, b&w line drawings and washes.
Other Needs: Photographs; b&w and color of New Hampshire people and places.

NEW INFINITY REVIEW, Box 804, Ironton OH 45638. Editor: James R. Pack. Art Director: Ariyan. For independent thinkers interested in new perspectives, the mysterious and the unknown. Quarterly. Circ. 500. Sample copy and artist's guidelines: $1.
Illustrations: Buys 3 illustrations/year on abstract, surrealistic, experimental and imaginative themes. Submit art or query with samples. SASE. Reports in 4 weeks. Buys first North American serial or all rights. Cover: Pays $10, b&w line drawings. Inside: Pays $5, b&w line drawings; on publication.

NEW JERSEY MONTHLY, 1101-I State Rd., Princeton NJ 08540. (609)921-7576. Art Director: Lawrence Barth. Interested in general interest themes. Monthly. Circ. 100,000.
Illustrations: Buys 8 illustrations/issue on assigned themes. Arrange interview to show portfolio. SASE. Reports in 6 weeks. Pays $150/spot, $300/full page, b&w; $300-600, color; on publication.

NEW LETTERS, 5346 Charlotte, Kansas City MO 64110. Contact: Judy Ray. Sample copy $2.
Needs: Buys camera-ready spot drawings, cartoons and cover designs. Submit art. Reports in 2-8 weeks. Buys all rights. Pays $5-10, pen and inks, line drawings and washes, b&w photographs.

NEW OREGON REVIEW, 537 NE Lincoln St., Hillsboro OR 97123. Editor: Steven Dimeo, Ph.D. For college students, professors and those interested in the humanities. Published semiannually. Circ. 300. Sample copy $1 (mention *Artist's Market*).
Cartoons: Buys 2/issue; "We are looking for witty, intelligent, satirical editorial cartoons that show the timelessness of human folly." Buys current event, education, politics, religious, writing, publishing and "fads" themes; single panel OK. Query with samples and 3-5 sentence biographical statement. SASE. Reports in 2-3 months. Buys all rights. Pays $5, line drawings; on publication.
Illustrations: Buys 2-5/year. Primarily purchases photos. "We like drawings that deal uncommonly with the common, surrealistic landscapes of the mind featuring nudes, portraits or nature." Query with samples and 3-5 sentence biographical statement. SASE. Reports in 2-3 months. Buys all rights. Pays $10, b&w line drawings and washes; $25, commissioned work; on publication.

NEW ORLEANS, Flambeaux Publishing Co., 6666 Morrison Rd., New Orleans LA 70126. (504)246-2700. Managing Editor: Jean Stewart. Art Director: John Maher. For readers with high income and education. Monthly. Circ. 200,000. Previously published and photocopied submissions OK. Sample copy $2.50.
Illustrations: Query with samples. SASE. Reports in 1 week. Buys 36/year on current events, education and politics. Pays $40-100, spot drawings; $200, full-color illustrations/cover designs; on publication. Buys first rights.

NEW ORLEANS REVIEW, Box 195, Loyola University, New Orleans LA 70118. (504)865-2294. Editor: John Biguenet. Journal of literature and culture. Published 3 times/year. Sample copy $2.50; free artist's guidelines.
Illustrations: Buys 5-10/issue on environment and human interest. Cover: Pays $75 minimum, color washes and opaque watercolors. Query with resume and samples. SASE. Reports in 2-3 weeks. Buys all rights. Inside: Pays $10 minimum, b&w line drawings, washes and gray opaques; on publication.

THE NEW PHYSICIAN, 14650 Lee Rd., Box 131, Chantilly VA 22021. Art Director: Jim Bubb. For physicians-in-training; concerns primary medical care, political and social issues relating to medicine. Monthly. Circ. 70,000. SASE. Reports in 6 weeks. Simultaneous submissions OK. Original artwork returned after publication. Buys one-time rights. Pays on publication. Free sample copy and artist's guidelines.
Cartoons: Uses cartoons rarely. Interested in medical education. Send finished artwork. Reports in 2 weeks.
Illustrations: Uses 5 illustrations/issue. Buys infrequently from freelancers. Interested in "whimsical line work that reproduces well in b&w." Works on assignment only. Samples returned by SASE. Provide resume, letter of inquiry, brochure and flyer to be kept on file for future assignments. Submit resume and samples of style. Reports in 2 weeks. Buys one-time rights.
Design: Uses artists for 4-color cover design, illustration and layout mock-ups. Negotiates pay. Query with resume and samples.

NEW REALITIES, 680 Beach St., Suite 408, San Francisco CA 94109. Editor-in-Chief: James Bolen. Art Director: Ron Rutter. Concerns "holistic health and human potential." Estab. 1969. Bimonthly; 8x10½. Offset. Reports immediately. Previously published work OK. Pays 30 days after acceptance.
Cartoons: Buys 3-5/issue on current events, education, environment and consciousness-raising. Pays $35 minimum, b&w; $50 minimum, color. Send roughs.
Illustrations: Buys 4-7/issue on environment and assigned themes. Minimum payment: Cover: $150, 4-color. Inside: $75, b&w and color. Arrange interview to show portfolio.

NEW YORK AFFAIRS, New York University, 419 Park Avenue South, New York NY 10016. (212)689-1240. Editor-in-Chief: Dick Netzer. Art Director: Rose DeNeve. "For people—politicians, administrators, planners, architects, concerned citizens—interested in urban problems, planning and policy, and in reading sophisticated, often technical, studies." Quarterly. Circ. 3,000.Simultaneous submissions OK. Sample copy $3.
Cartoons: Uses less than 1 cartoon/issue. Buys about half of all cartoons from freelancers. SASE. Reports in 3 weeks. Buys all rights, but may reassign rights to artist after publication. Pays on publication.
Illustrations: Uses 2-3 illustrations/issue; buys 1-2/issue from freelancers. Interested in urban problems relating to issues' themes. Works on assignment only. Samples returned by SASE. Provide samples of past work on urban subjects to be kept on file for future assignments. SASE. Reports in 3 weeks. Buys all rights, but may reassign rights to artist after publication. Cover: Pays $300 minimum, b&w line drawings. Inside: Pays $50 minimum, b&w line drawings; on publication.

NEW YORK MAGAZINE, 755 2nd Ave., New York NY 10017. Contact: Tom Tarnowsky or Nina Subin. Circ. 355,000. Arrange interview or leave portfolio overnight, prefers artists with professional experience.
Illustrations: Assigns themes.

NEW YORK TIMES BOOK REVIEW, 229 W. 43rd St., New York NY 10036. Art Director: Steven Heller. Sunday newspaper supplement.
Illustrations: Uses 8 illustrations/issue, all from freelancers. Receives 8 submissions/week from freelancers. Interested in "satiric, political and conceptual" themes. Works on assignment only. No samples returned. Reports back on future assignment possibilities. Provide tearsheet to be kept on file for future assignments. Prefers roughs. SASE. Reports "that day." Buys first North American serial rights. Pays $75-125; on publication.

THE NEW YORKER, 25 W. 43rd St., New York NY 10036. Contact: Cartoon Editor. Mail art or deliver sketches on Wednesdays. SASE.
Needs: Buys cartoons, spots and cover designs. Strict standards regarding style, technique, plausibility of drawing. Pays $350 minimum, cartoons; top rates for spots and cover designs.

NEWFOUNDLAND HERALD TV WEEK, Box 2015, St. John's, Newfoundland, Canada A1C 5R7. (709)579-5015. Editor-in-Chief: Gary Anstey. Entertainment magazine which carries TV guide for the province. Estab. 1977. Circ. 60,000. Weekly; 7½x11; 64 pages. Offset. SASE. Simultaneous submissions and previously published work OK. Not copyrighted. Pays on publication. Free sample copy.
Cartoons: Buys TV-oriented themes. Send roughs.

THE NEWS CIRCLE, Box 74637, Los Angeles CA 90004. (213)469-7004. Contact: Laila Haiek. For Arab-Americans. Monthly. Circ. 3,000.
Cartoons: Buys 5-8 cartoons/issue. Needs b&w. Send roughs. Reports in 3 weeks. Negotiates pay; pays on publication.
Illustrations: Buys b&w Arabic and arabesque designs. Query with samples. Reports in 3 weeks. Negotiates pay; pays on publication.

NITTY-GRITTY, 331 W. Bonneville, Pasco WA 99301. (509)547-5525. Editor-in-Chief: W.R. "Bill" Wilkins. Quarterly; 8½x11; 150 pages. Offset. Estab. 1976. Circ. 3,000. Mail art; 7x9 maximum. SASE. Reports in 8 weeks. Photocopies OK. Buys all rights, but may reassign rights to artist after publication. Pays on acceptance.
Cartoons: Buys 6/issue on current events, erotica, humor through youth and politics related to the issue's "tool-theme." Pays $2-25, line drawings.
Illustrations: Buys 20/issue on the issue's "tool-theme." Cover: Pays $25-50, color. Inside: Pays $2-10, b&w line drawings.

NJEA REVIEW, 180 W. State St., Box 1211, Trenton NJ 08607. Editor-in-Chief: George M. Adams. For New Jersey teachers and administrators. Monthly. Circ. 110,000. Previously published work OK. Original artwork not returned after publication. Free sample copy.
Cartoons: Number cartoons/issue varies; buys 3-4/issue from freelancers. Receives 20-30 submissions/week from freelancers. Interested in cartoons with an "education theme-do not make fun of teachers or children"; single panel. Prefers finished cartoons. Buys all rights on a work-for-hire basis. Pays on acceptance.
Illustrations: Uses 1-2 illustrations/issue, all from freelancers. Receives 10-15 submissions/week from freelancers. Provide resume and tearsheet to be kept on file for future assignments. Prefers samples of style. SASE. Reports as soon as possible. Buys all rights on a work-for-hire basis. Inside: Pays $5-100, b&w; on acceptance.

NORTH AMERICAN MENTOR, Drawer 69, Fennimore WI 53809. (608)822-6237. Editor-in-Chief: John Westburg. Managing Editor: Mildred Westburg. Send art submissions to Martial R. Westburg, art editor, North American Mentor, Box 558, Old Chelsen Station, New York NY 10011. For professional people, half of whom are age 60. Quarterly. Circ. 400. Previously published, photocopied and simultaneous submissions OK. Original artwork not returned after publication. Sample copy $1.25.
Illustrations: Buys 1 (cover) illustration/issue. Receives less than 10 submissions/year from freelancers. Interested in "b&w fine drawings only." Provide resume, brochure, flyer and tearsheet to be kept on file for future assignments. Prefers samples of style (non-returnable). SASE. Reports in "6 months or more." Buys all rights. Pays $25 minimum, b&w line drawings; on publication.

NORTH SHORE, Essex County Newspapers, Whittemore St., Gloucester MA 01930. Editor: Tom Meade. For state residents on the North Shore. Estab. 1964. Circ. 38,700. Weekly; 9½x13½; 32 pages. Offset. SASE. Reports in 3 weeks. Buys all rights. Pays on publication. Free sample copy with SASE.
Illustrations: Buys 30-40/year on assigned themes. Cover: Pays $30-70, opaque watercolors; $25-50, b&w line drawings and gray opaques. Inside: Pays $10-30, b&w line drawings and gray opaques. Query with resume and samples or previously published work.

NORTHEAST OUTDOORS, Box 2180, Waterbury CT 06722. (203)755-0158. Art Director: John Florian. For camping families in the northeastern states. Monthly. Circ. 20,000. Original artwork returned after publication, if requested. Pays on acceptance (cartoons only).
Cartoons: Buys 1/issue on camping and recreational vehicle situations. Mail finished art. SASE. Reports in 2 weeks. Pays $10, b&w; on acceptance.

THE NORTHERN LOGGER & TIMBER PROCESSOR, Northeastern Loggers Association Inc., Box 69, Old Forge NY 13420. (315)369-3078. Editor: George D. Fowler. "For loggers, timberland managers and processors of primary forest products." Monthly. Circ. 8,370. Free sample copy.

Cartoons: Uses 1 cartoon/issue, all from freelancers. Receives 1 submission/week from freelancers. Interested in "any cartoons involving forest industry situations." Prefers finished cartoons. SASE. Reports in 1 week. Pays $10 minimum, b&w line drawings; on publication.

NORTHERN VIRGINIAN, Box 334, Vienna VA 22180. "Typical regional magazine." Bimonthly. Previously published work OK. Buys various rights. Sample copy available.
Illustrations: Uses 2 illustrations/issue, all from freelancers. "The regional nature of our market should not discourage artists from other parts of the country. We do publish topical and issue pieces which are not specific to Northern Virginia. Also, article illustrations, if assigned far enough in advance, often can be done anywhere. This is a good publication for young artists looking to develop a portfolio." Works on assignment only. No samples returned. Reports back on future assignment possibilities. Prefers samples of style. SASE. Reports in 6 weeks. Buys all rights on a work-for-hire basis. Pays $5 minimum, b&w line drawings; on publication.
To Break In: "Team up with a writer and illustrate an article for submission; the art supports the copy and vice versa."

NORTHWEST REVIEW, 369 PLC, University of Oregon, Eugene OR 97403. (503)686-3957. Editor: John Witte. Original artwork returned after publication. Published 3 times/year. Arrange interview or mail slides. SASE. Reports immediately. Buys one-time rights. Pays on publication.
Needs: B&w line drawings and cover designs. "We run a regular art feature of the work of one artist, printed in b&w, 133-line screen on quality coated paper. A statement by the artist accompanies the feature." Sample copy $2.

NORTHWOODS JOURNAL, Box 249, Stafford VA 22554. (703)952-2388. Art Director: R. Olmsted. Literary journal. Quarterly. Circ. 300.
Illustrations: Buys 2/issue on all subjects. Query with samples. SASE. Reports in 3-5 weeks. Pays $2 minimum, b&w; on acceptance.

NOTRE DAME, University of Notre Dame, 415 Main Bldg., Box M, Notre Dame IN 46556. (219)283-1234. Editor: Ronald R. Parent. Art Director: Don Nelson. For university alumni. Published 5 times/year. Circ. 80,000. Submit samples or brochure; professional artists only. "We don't have time to send sample copies or reply to submissions." Previously published and simultaneous submissions OK. Original artwork usually returned after publication.
Illustrations: Uses 5-10 illustrations/issue, all from freelancers. Interested in "current events, religious topics and social community" themes. Works on assignment only. Samples returned by SASE. Reports back on future assignment possibilities. Provide calling card, brochure or slides to be kept on file for future assignments. Prefers portfolio and samples of style. SASE. Reports in 2 weeks. Buys first North American serial rights. Cover: Pays $800-1000, color. Inside: Pays $150-200, b&w; on acceptance.

NPN, 1221 Avenue of the Americas, New York NY 10020. (212)997-2361. Editor-in-Chief: William Olcott. Concerns petroleum marketing. Monthly. Circ. 20,000. Previously published work OK. Sample copy available.
Needs: Reports immediately. Buys all rights. Pays $10, spot drawings; on acceptance.

NRTA JOURNAL, National Retired Teachers Association, 215 Long Beach Blvd., Long Beach CA 90801. Editor: Hubert C. Pryor. Bimonthly. Sample copy available.
Cartoons: Uses 0-1 cartoons/issue; buy 0-1/issue from freelancers. Buys b&w spot drawings and 8x10 finished cartoons. SASE. Reports in 2 weeks. Buys all rights on a work-for-hire basis. Pays $50; on acceptance.

NUGGET, Dugent Publishing Co., 316 Aragon Ave., Coral Gables FL 33134. Editor: John Fox. Managing Editor: Nye Willden. For men and women with fetish interests.
Cartoons: Uses 10 cartoons/issue, all from freelancers. Receives 100 submissions/week from freelancers. Interested in "funny, somewhat 'sick' humor and sexual themes." B&w only for spots, b&w and color for page. Prefers finished cartoons. SASE. Reports in 2 weeks. Buys first North American serial rights. Pays $25, spot drawings; $35, page.
Illustrations: Uses 4 illustrations/issue, all from freelancers. Interested in "erotica, cartoon style, etc." Works on assignment only. No samples returned. Reports back on future assignment possibilities. Provide brochure or flyer to be kept on file for future assignments. Prefers samples of style. Buys first North American serial rights. Pays $75-100, b&w.

NUTRITION ACTION, 1755 S St. NW, Washington DC 20009. Editor: Tom Monk. Concerns food issues such as nutrient value, effects of agribusiness and multinational corporations, govern-

ment regulation, and the politics of food; for health professionals and laymen. Monthly. Circ. 12,000. SASE. Reports in 1 month. Simultaneous submissions and previously published work OK. Original artwork not returned after publication. Buys one-time rights. Pays on publication. Free sample copy.
Cartoons: Number cartoons used/issue varies. Interested in "cartoons that depict our political–food and nutrition–point of view. Send for free sample of magazine." Prefers roughs, finished cartoons or resume. SASE. Reports within 6 weeks. Buys all rights on a work-for-hire basis. Pays $15 minimum, b&w line drawings; on publication.
Illustrations: Uses 3 illustrations/issue, all from freelancers. Interested in illustrations on nutrition, good food, etc., "that depict our political–food and nutrition–point of view. Send for free sample of magazine." Reports back on future assignment possibilities. Prefers finished art, roughs or samples of style. SASE. Reports within 6 weeks. Buys all rights on a work-for-hire basis. Cover: Pays $30-75, b&w line drawings. Inside: Pays $10-25, b&w line drawings; on publication.
Other Needs: "Photographs: check with us first."

O AND A MARKETING NEWS, Box 765, LaCanada CA 91011. (213)790-6554. Editor: Don McAnally. For service station dealers, garagemen, TBA (tires, batteries, accessories) people in oil company marketing management. Bimonthly. Circ. 15,000. Original artwork not returned after publication.
Cartoons: Uses 3 cartoons/issue, all from freelancers. Receives 3 submissions/week from freelancers. Prefers finished cartoons. SASE. Reports in 1 week. Pays $7.50, b&w. Query.

OCEANS, Oceanic Society, 315 Fort Mason, San Francisco CA 94123. (415)567-3597. Editor-in-Chief: Keith Howell. Art Director: Dugald Stermer. "For those interested in the beauty, science, adventure and conservation of the oceans and the life forms which live therein." Bimonthly. Circ. 50,000. Original artwork returned after publication.
Cartoons: Uses 1 cartoon/issue, all from freelancers. Receives 10 submissions/week from freelancers. Interested in sea-oriented themes. Prefers roughs. SASE. Reports in 1 week. Buys First North American Serial rights. Pays $25 minimum, b&w and 2-tone; on publication.
Illustrations: Uses 4 illustrations/issue. Interested in the environment, ocean dwellers and subjects pertaining to oceans. Works on assignment only. Samples returned by SASE. Reports back on future assignment possibilities. Provide tearsheet to be kept on file for future assignments. Prefers samples of style. SASE. Reports in 1 week. Buys First North American Serial rights. Cover: Pays $150, full-color. Inside: Pays $30-100, b&w and color (including diagrammatic illustrations).

OEA COMMUNIQUE, 1120 Morse Rd., Columbus OH 43229. (614)888-5776. Editor: Jody Olson. For members of Office Education Association. Estab. 1976. Circ. 75,000. Quarterly during academic year; 24 pages. Offset. SASE. Reports in 2 weeks. Simultaneous submissions and previously published work OK. Not copyrighted. Pays on acceptance. Free sample copy.
Cartoons: Buys 4/year on education, humor through youth and business occupations; single, double or multipanel. Pays $15-50, b&w; $75-200, color. Query with samples.
Illustrations: Buys 8/year on education, business and office careers and assigned themes. Cover: Pays $100-250, color washes; $75-150, b&w. Inside: Pays $25-75, color; $15-50, b&w. Query with resume and samples.
To Break In: "Be flexible. Meet specifications and be willing to submit up to 3 drawings."

OFFICE PRODUCTS DEALER, Hitchcock Bldg., Wheaton IL 60187. (312)665-1000. Emphasizes office products and procedures for independent dealers of office supplies, machines, furnishings and systems. Monthly. Circ. 26,000. Free sample copy.
Cartoon Needs: Uses about 1 cartoon/issue; all are supplied by freelancers. Receives "a few" cartoons from freelancers/week. Cartoons should pertain to "anything related to office procedures. We look for humor, graphic competence and good taste." Format: single panel b&w line drawings and washes with gag line. Send finished cartoons to R. Mueller, editor. SASE. Reports in 2 weeks. Pays on publication $10-20 b&w cartoon. Buys first North American serial rights.
Illustration Needs: Uses fewer than 1 illustration/issue; all are supplied by freelancers. Arrange personal appointment to show portfolio. SASE. Reports in 2 weeks. Payment on publication "varies–most illustrations are assigned and negotiated." Buys all rights on a work-for-hire basis.

OFFICIAL DETECTIVE STORIES, 235 Park Ave. S., New York NY 10003. Editor: Albert P. Govoni. For readers of factual crime stories. Monthly.
Cartoons: Buys crime genre themes. "Avoid cliche situations such as 2 convicts conversing in cell; cute, mild sex." Submit roughs. Reports in 2 weeks. Buys all rights. Pays $25; on acceptance.

THE OHIO FARMER, Harvest Publishing Co., 1350 W. 5th Ave., Columbus OH 43212. (614)486-9637. Editor: Andrew L. Stevens. For farmers interested in applying scientific findings and agricultural business to their farms. Biweekly. Circ. 102,000.
Cartoons: Buys 20-30/year. Query. SASE. Buys first rights. Pays $3, finished art.

OHIO MAGAZINE, Ohio Magazine, Inc., 40 S. Third St., Columbus OH 43215. (614)461-5083. Publisher: Melvin E. Tharp. Editor-in-Chief: Robert B. Smith. Design Director: J. Porter. Managing Editor: J. Porter. For Ohioans. Monthly. Estab. 1978. Circ. 100,000. Query with samples or arrange interview to show portfolio. Previously published work OK. Original artwork returned after publication. Free sample copy and artist's guidelines.
Cartoons: Uses 6 cartons/issue; buys 4-5/issue from freelancers. Interested in cartoons in general, especially those "with an Ohio angle or orientation." Prefers finished artwork. Reports in 2 weeks.
Illustrations: Uses 35-40/issue; buys 20-25/issue from freelancers. Interested in current events, education, environment, family life, politics and religion in Ohio. Works on assignment only. Samples returned by SASE. Reports back on future assignment possibilities. Provide resume, brochure and tearsheet to be kept on file for future assignments. Query with finished artwork or arrange interview. SASE. Reports in 2 weeks. Cover: Pays $200-400, color. Inside: Pays $100-200, b&w; $150-350, color; on acceptance. Buys one-time publication rights.

OKLAHOMA LP GAS ASSOCIATION, 2910 N. Walnut, Suite 114A, Oklahoma City OK 73105. Contact: John E. Orr. Monthly. Send samples. Reports in 2 weeks. Pays $5 minimum.

OLD BOTTLE, Box 243, Bend OR 97701. Contact: Kenneth Asher. Send art. Reports in 6 weeks. Buys all rights. Pays on acceptance.

ON LOCATION, SEDCO Inc. 1901 N. Akard, Dallas TX 75201. Editor: Larie Engles. For employees. Circ. 5,000. Offset. Contacts artists as needs arise. Simultaneous submissions and previously published work OK. Free sample copy and artist's guidelines.
Illustrations: Buys 5/year on current events and oil and gas drilling. Query with previously published work. Buys one-time rights. Inside: Pays $50-200, b&w line drawings and washes; on publication.
Design: Uses artists for publication redesign and design of one-time communications pieces. Arrange interview to show portfolio. Buys one-time rights. Negotiates pay; pays on publication.

1001 TRUCK AND VAN IDEAS, 12301 Wilshire Blvd., Los Angeles CA 90025. (213)820-3601. Editor: Peter DuPre. Emphasizes use of trucks, RVs, vans and mini-trucks for drivers who use, modify, customize and "go fun truckin" with these vehicles. Estab. 1975. Circ. 200,000. Monthly. SASE. Reports in 2 months.
Cartoons: Buys 1-2/issue on vans, trucks, custom vans, "van-ins" and trucking. Pays $10, b&w. Query or send finished artwork.

ONTARIO OUT OF DOORS, 11 King St. W., Toronto, Ontario, Canada M5H 1A3. (416)361-0434. Art Director: Ralph Tibbles. For fishermen, hunters and campers. Published 10 times/year. Circ. 55,000. Previously published work OK. Original artwork not returned after publication. Free sample copy and artist's guidelines.
Cartoons: Editor-in-Chief: Burton Myers. Uses 2 cartoons/issue, all from freelancers. Original artwork returned after publication. Interested in fishing, hunting and camping themes; single panel. Prefers roughs. SASE. Reports within 6 weeks. Buys all rights. Pays $15-25, b&w line drawings; 4 weeks after acceptance.
Illustrations: Editor-in-Chief: Burton Myers. Uses 1 illustration/issue, all from freelancers. Interested in wildlife and fish themes. Provide business card to be kept on file for future use. Prefers roughs. SASE. Reports in 6 weeks. Buys all rights. Cover: Pays $100-200, color; 4 weeks after acceptance.

OPERATIONS FORESTIERES ET DE SC., 310 Victoria Ave., Suite 201, Westmount, Quebec, Canada H3Z 2M9. (514)487-2302. Readers are in the forestry industry. Monthly. Circ. 4,400.
Cartoons: Uses 1 cartoon/issue; buys all from freelancers. Interested in humoristic forestry or management themes. Prefers single panel. Send finished cartoons to Judith Hebert, assistant editor. SASE. Reports in 2 weeks. Buys first North American serial rights. Pays $40 for b&w on acceptance.
Illustrations: Uses 1 illustration/issue; buys all from freelancers. Interested in forestry themes. Works on assignment only. Prefers b&w line drawings for inside. Send finished art to J. Hebert. SASE. Reports in 2 weeks. Buys first North American serial rights. Pays on acceptance.

OPINION, Box 1885, Rockford IL 61110. Contact: J. Kurtz. "We are a philosophical, sociological and theological journal." Buys one-time rights. Buys b&w line drawings.

ORAL IMPLANTOLOGY, 469 Washington St., Abington MA 02351. Editor-in-Chief: Dr. Isaih Lew. For dentists. Quarterly; 6x9; 160 pages. Offset. Estab. 1970. Circ. 2,000. Query with samples. SASE. Reports in 6 months. Previously published work OK. Pays on publication. Free sample copy.
Cartoons: Buys themes on dentistry; single panel. Negotiates payment for line drawings, halftones and washes.
Illustrations: Cover and inside: Buys b&w line drawings, washes, color-separated and reflective art. Also uses artists to touch-up poor artwork and to do new layouts and ad designs.

OREGON VOTER DIGEST, Who's Who Publications Inc., 108 NW 9th St., Portland OR 97209. Editorial Director: Victor Graf. Concerns public affairs, business and industry. Monthly; 5½x8½; 24-32 pages. Offset. Estab. 1915. Circ. 2,500. Mail art. SASE. Reports in 2 weeks. Photocopied and simultaneous submissions OK. Not copyrighted. Pays on publication. Free sample copy.
Cartoons: Buys 6-12/year on current events, elections and politics; single panel with gag line. Pays $5-10, b&w line drawings.

ORGANIC GARDENING, 33 E. Minor St., Emmaus PA 18049. (215)967-5171. Art Director: Robert E. Ayers. Emphasizes organic gardening and self-sufficiency. Monthly. Circ. 1,400,000. Free sample copy; author's handbook for SASE.
Cartoons: Interested in gardening, health, wood stove and alternative energy subjects; single panel b&w line drawings and b&w washes. Send resume and samples of style. SASE. Reports in 1 month. Buys all rights. Pays $35-50; on publication.
Illustrations: Uses 20 illustrations/issue. Interested in gardening, insects, flowers and vegetables and energy themes. Works on assignment only. Prefers b&w line drawings and washes for inside. Send resume and calling card with samples of style and/or arrange appointment to show portfolio. SASE. Reports in 1 month. Buys all rights. Pays $35, spot illustrations; larger illustrations priced per job and style; on publication.

THE OTHER SIDE, Box 12236, Philadelphia PA 19144. (215)849-2178. Editors: John Alexander, Philip Harden, Alfred Krass and Mark Olson. "We are read by Christians with a radical commitment to social justice and a deep allegiance to Biblical faith. We try to help readers put their faith into action." Monthly; 5½x8½; 64 pages. Offset. Estab. 1965. Circ. 12,000. Query with samples or previously published work. SASE. Reports in 6 weeks. Photocopied and simultaneous submissions OK. Pays "within 4 weeks of acceptance." Sample copy $1.
Cartoons: Buys 2/issue on current events, environment, economics, politics and religion; single and multipanel. Pays $10-25, b&w line drawings. "Looking for cartoons with a radical political perspective." Cover: Pays $35-50, color-separated work; $25-50, b&w line drawings. Inside: Pays $10-30, b&w line drawings.

OTTAWA CITYLIFE MAGAZINE, Box 3560, Station C, Ottawa, Ontario, Canada K1Y 4J7. (613)722-2867. Art Director: Crys Blundell. Emphasizes lifestyles for sophisticated, middle & upper income, above average education professionals. Heavy readers are women. Monthly. Circ. 50,000. Estab. 1978. Sample copy $1.
Illustrations: Uses 8-12 illustrations/issue; buys 5-10 from freelancers. Receives 2-3 submissions/week from freelancers. "Illustrations are geared to editorial copy and run from cartoon sketches to *Esquire*, *New York* and *Psychology Today* styles. Subjects range from fast-food franchising to how civil servants cope with stress. Art usually produced by local artists because of time and communication problems." Prefers b&w line drawings and b&w and color washes for inside and cover. Also uses photographic treatments. Arrange personal appointment to show portfolio or send samples of style. "Do not send original artwork." No samples returned. Reports in 1 month. Buys all rights or by arrangement with artist. Pays $20-100 for inside b&w; $100-250 for color cover and $50-150 for inside color on publication.

OUI, Playboy Enterprises, 8560 Sunset Blvd., Los Angeles CA 90069. Editor-in-Chief: Richard Cramer. Art Director: Michael Brock. "For the man of the world." Monthly. Original artwork returned after publication. Circ. 850,000. Query with samples or arrange interview to show portfolio. SASE. Pays on publication. Free sample copy and artist's guidelines.
Illustrations: Uses 10/issue and buys 10/issue from freelancers. Interested in all subjects. Works on assignment only. Samples returned by SASE. Reports back on future assignment possibilities. Provide business card, tearsheet and transparencies to be kept on file for future assignments. Query with samples or arrange interviews to show portfolio. Prefers finished art, portfolio or

samples. Reports in 2 weeks. Buys all rights. Inside: Pays $50-150, b&w line drawings and washes; $100-900, full-color renderings; on publication.
Cartoons: Contact Michele Urry, 747 3rd Ave., Playboy Enterprises, NYC.

OUR FAMILY, Oblate Fathers of St. Mary's Province, Box 249, Battleford, Saskatchewan, Canada S0M 0E0. (306)937-2131 or 937-7344. Editor-in-Chief: Albert Lalonde. Inspirational, educational magazine. Monthly. Circ. 14,744. Previously published, photocopied and simultaneous submissions OK. Original artwork returned after publication. Sample copy $1 to cover cost of magazine and postage.
Cartoons: Buys 5/issue on family situations, especially parent-children relationships; single panel with gag line. Query with finished cartoons. SASE. Reports in 2-4 weeks. Pays $5-15, b&w line drawings and washes; on acceptance.
Illustrations: Uses 1 illustration/issue; buys 1 illustration/issue from freelancers. Receives several submissions/month from freelancers. Subject "depends on the article we want illustrated. We usually commission this work to a specific artist." Works on assignment only. Samples returned by SASE. Reports back on future assignment possibilities. Provide brochure and tearsheet to be kept on file for future assignments. SASE. Reports in 2-4 weeks. Buys first North American serial rights. Inside: Pays $10-100, b&w.

OUTDOOR LIFE, Times Mirror Magazines, 380 Madison Ave., New York NY 10017. Art Director: Gary Gretter. Concerns hunting, fishing and the outdoors. Circ. 1,750,000. Monthly; 190 pages. Offset. SASE. Buys first rights. Pays on acceptance.
Illustrations: Buys b&w and color work for inside. Query with resume and samples or arrange interview to show portfolio.
Design: Uses artists for design of annual publications. Pays $6/hour. Query with resume and samples or arrange interview to show portfolio.

OUTDOORS TODAY, Box 6852, St. Louis MO 63144. (314)727-2722. Contact: Editor. For outdoorsmen: hunters, fishermen, campers and boaters. Deals with issues and events concerning the outdoors. Estab. 1970. Circ. 90,000. Weekly. SASE. Reports in 2 weeks. Pays on publication.
Cartoons: Assigns themes. Query or mail roughs or finished art.
Illustrations: Assigns themes. Query with samples or arrange interview to show portfolio.

OUTSIDE, (formerly Mariah/Outside), 3401 W. Division St., Chicago IL 60651. (312)342-7777. Managing Editor: John Rasmus. Art Director: John Askwith. Concerns enjoyment and participation in the great outdoors. Bimonthly. Circ. 200,000. Previously published work OK. Free sample copy.
Illustrations: Uses 12 illustrations/year; buys 9/year from freelancers. Receives 2-3 submissions/week from freelancers. Interested in wilderness art and sketchbooks. "We are also interested in seeing any contemporary still for assignment purposes." Works on assignment only. Provide samples or tearsheet to be kept on file for future assignments. Prefers samples. SASE. Reports in 2 weeks. Buys one-time rights. Inside: Pays $100-250, b&w line drawings, washes and full-color renderings; on publication.

OVERSEAS LIFE, Str. 9, 6382 Friedrichsdorf 2, West Germany. Managing Editor: James Kitfield. For young males in the U.S. military based in Europe. "Though primarily a travel magazine, *Overseas Life* is also a music, photo, sports and general entertainment magazine." Monthly.
Cartoons: Uses single panel b&w cartoons. Interested in subjects familiar to American military personnel stationed in Europe. Mild sex tones and mild pokes at the military are acceptable. Particularly seeks cartoons addressing funny situations encountered by GIs as they travel around Europe. Query. SASE and International Reply coupons. Buys rights to military communities in Europe. Negotiates pay for cartoons.
Illustrations: Buys 2-3 illustrations/issue. "Europe-based illustrators should contact us for possible assignments." SASE and International Reply coupons. Buys rights to military communities in Europe. Cover: Pays $150 (used only occasionally). Inside: Pays $25-50, full-page b&w; $75, full-page color; and $200, 2-page color.

OZARK FLIGHTIME, East-West Network, Inc., 5900 Wilshire Blvd., #300, Los Angeles CA 90036. (213)937-5810. Editor-in-Chief: James Clark. Monthly. Sample copy $1.50.
Illustrations: Query with resume. Reports in 4 weeks. Buys all rights.Pays $75 minimum, spot art; $450, full-page illustration; and $600, full-color cover.

PACIFIC BOATING ALMANAC, Box Q, Ventura CA 92001. Publisher/Editor: Bill Berssen. Published annually in three separate regional editions for West Coast boat owners. Circ. 30,000.

Original artwork returned after publication. "We only buy specially commissioned art."
Illustrations: Uses 25 illustrations/issue; all from freelancers. Interested in marine and boating. Works on assignment only. Samples returned by SASE. Reports back on future assignment possibilities. Provide resume and printed samples to be kept on file for future assignments. Prefers resume and samples of style. SASE. Reports in 3 weeks. Buys all rights on a work-for-hire basis.
Other Needs: Vignettes and 4-color cover illustrations.

PACIFIC SKIPPER, 300 N. Newport Blvd., Suite G, Newport Beach CA 92663. Art Director: Blossom Siegel. For those interested in family cruising, sail and power. Monthly; 8⅓x10⅓. Mail art. Previously published work in noncompeting publications OK. Buys all rights. Pays on publication.
Needs: Boating scenes with people (close-up) on light paper or tissue ready to paste down—no illustration board. Cover: Pays $100. Inside: Pays $20, color; $25, full-page b&w drawing; $12.50, half-page; $10, spot drawing.

PAINT HORSE JOURNAL, Box 18519, Fort Worth TX 76118. (817)439-3400. Editor: Byron Travis. Official publication of breed registry for paint horses. Monthly. Circ. 10,000. Previously published work OK. Original artwork not returned after publication. Free sample copy and artist's guidelines.
Cartoons: Buys 5 cartoons/issue, all from freelancers. Interested in horses; single panel with gag line. Prefers finished cartoons. SASE. Reports in 2 weeks. Negotiates rights. Pays $5 minimum, b&w line drawings; on acceptance.
Illustrations: Uses 2 -3 illustrations/issue; buys few/issue from freelancer. Receives few submissions/week from freelancer. Interested in horses. Works on assignment only. Samples returned by SASE. Reports back on future assignment possibilities. Provide letter of inquiry and tearsheet to be kept on file for future assignments. Prefers portfolio. SASE. Reports in 2 weeks. Negotiates rights. Inside: Pays $5-25, b&w line drawings. Cover: Pays $50, paintings; on acceptance.

PAINTBRUSH, English Dept., Northeastern University, Boston MA 02115. Contact: Editor. Literary journal. Published every 6 months. Circ. 500.
Illustrations: Buys b&w art. All new artwork by assignment only. Query with samples. SASE. Reports in 2-4 weeks. Negotiates pay; pays on publication.

PALM BEACH LIFE, 265 Royal Poinciana Way, Palm Beach FL 33480. (305)655-5755. Art Director: Anne Wholf. General interest publication. Readers are affluent, educated. Monthly. Circ. 18,000. Sample copy $2.33; art guidelines for SASE.
Illustration Needs: Uses 3-4 illustrations/issue; all from freelancers. Only assigned work. Uses line drawings to illustrate regular columns on gardening, health and wine, as well as features. Format: color washes for inside and cover; b&w washes and line drawings for inside. "Any technique that can be reproduced is acceptable." Send samples and/or arrange appointment to show portfolio. SASE. Reports in 2-3 weeks. Buys all rights on a work-for-hire basis or first North American serial rights. Pays $150-300 on acceptance for color cover; $50-150 for inside color; $20-100 for inside b&w. Top price on covers only paid to established artists.

PAMPHLETEER MONTHLY, 308 E. 79th St., New York NY 10021. (212)628-1995. Contact: T. Reed. For library trade; buying guide for public school, college, university and special libraries; book review source. Monthly. Circ. 6,000.
Cartoons and Illustrations: Works on assignment only. Query. SASE. Reports in 2 weeks. Pays some $6/hour; on publication.

PANORAMA, 850 3rd Ave., New York NY 10022. (212)759-8100. Emphasizes television. Audience is "the selective television viewer. This is the person who watches less television than the average and more public television documentaries and quality prime time material." Estab. 1980.
Cartoon Needs: Uses 1 cartoon/issue. Cartoons should pertain to anything television related. Format: single and multi-panel b&w line drawings with gag line. Send roughs and samples of style to Norman Hotz, art director. SASE. Reports in 1 week. Pays on acceptance. Buys first North American serial rights.

PANORAMA, Greer Bldg., Morgantown WV 26505. Editor: Sarah Stevenson. For southwestern Pennsylvania and northern West Virginia residents with emphasis on the arts, history and life style of Appalachians. Weekly. Query. Reports in 2 weeks. Pays on publication. Sample copy available.
Needs: Buys assigned themes. Pays $5, spot drawing; $15, full-color illustration.

Illustration Needs: Uses 30 illustrations/issue; all from freelancers. "We maintain extensive files of artists' samples. We use a wide variety of illustrations and styles" pertaining to television related subjects. Format: b&w line drawings for inside and color washes for cover. Send samples of style and tearsheets to Norman Hotz, art director. SASE. Reports in 1 week. Pays on acceptance. Buys first North American serial rights.

PARABOLA, 150 5th Ave., New York NY 10011. (212)924-0004. Art Director: Suzanne Haldane. Concerns "exploration of the wisdom and truth transmitted through myth and the great religious traditions." Quarterly. Circ. 14,000. Original artwork returned after publication.
Illustrations: Buys b&w work. Provide resume, business card and brochure to be kept on file for future assignments. Prefers resume and portfolio. SASE. Reports in 1 week. Buys first North American serial rights. Pays on publication.

PARENT'S CHOICE, Box 185, Waban MA 02168. (617)332-1298. Editor: Diana Huss Green. Emphasizes review of children's media. Designed to alert parents to trends and events in books, TV, records, movies, music, toys. Quarterly. Estab. 1978. Original artwork returned after publication. Sample copy $1.50; art guidelines for SASE.
Illustration Needs: Uses 10 illustrations/issue, 6 from freelancers. Uses drawings of children and parents with children. Format: b&w line drawings for inside and cover. Works on assignment only. Samples returned. Prefers portfolio. SASE. Reports in 2 weeks. Buys first North American serial rights. Send sample or arrange appointment to show portfolio. Pays $50-100 on publication for cover; $15-25 for inside.

PARKING, 1101 17th St. NW, Washington DC 20036. (202)296-4336. Editor-in-Chief: Kevin Leary. For members of National Parking Association–trade organization of the commercial off-street parking industry–architects, engineers, traffic planners and city officials. Quarterly. Previously published and simultaneous submissions OK. Original artwork returned after publication. Free sample copy.
Cartoons: Uses less than 1 cartoon/issue, all from freelancers. Receives 1 submission/week from freelancers. Interested in environment, parking, engineering, construction and transportation. Prefers finished cartoons. Reports in 2 weeks. Buys one-time rights. Pays $5 minimum, halftones and washes; on acceptance.
Illustrations: Uses 8 illustrations/issue, all from freelancers. Receives 8 submissions/week from freelancers. Buys parking themes; "would especially like to see a particularly dramatic rendering of attractive parking garage or lot." Prefers roughs. SASE. Reports in 2 weeks. Buys one-time rights. Minimum payment: Cover: $35, color; $20, b&w. Inside: $10, b&w; on acceptance.

PARTS PUPS, 2999 Circle 75 Parkway, Atlanta GA 30339. Editor: Don Kite. For automotive repairmen. Circ. 210,000. Monthly. Free sample copy and artist's guidelines.
Cartoons: Buys 144/year on "girlie" themes, auto repairmen, current events, education, environment, family life, humor through youth, politics and retirement; single panel with gag line. Mail finished artwork. SASE. Reports in 6-8 weeks. Pays $20, b&w line drawings and washes; on acceptance.

PASSENGER AND INFLIGHT SERVICE, International Publishing, 665 LaVilla Dr., Miami Springs FL 33166. (305)887-1701. Readers are flight attendants and reservations personnel. Bimonthly. Circ. 25,100. Free sample copy and art guidelines.
Cartoons: Uses 2-4 cartoons/issue, all from freelancers. Interested in "cartoons showing insight into common, unusual occurrences in airline public contact personnel's profession depicted in a humorous way. Cartoons should reflect flight attendants, reservationists, ticket or sales agents (generally good attitude) in dealing with the common hassles of their chosen profession. In portraying this group, one should keep in mind that they are young, attractive and well-groomed. A common offense is exaggerating their sexual attributes." Send finished cartoons to Mary Thompson, assistant editor. SASE. "No correspondence unless cartoon is accepted." Buys one-time rights. Pays $10 for b&w on publication.
Illustrations: "We prefer to keep a telephone number for artist on file with samples of their work. When a story needs illustration we will contact them and explain what we're looking for. Artist sometimes works with writer or editor to illustrate stories–often exaggerated character profiles in a humorous vein." Prefers b&w line drawings for inside. Send samples of style and telephone number to Pat Morrissey, editor or Mary Thompson, assistant editor. Works on assignment only. No samples returned. Reports back on future assignment possibilities. Buys all rights on a work-for-hire basis. Pays $10 for inside b&w on publication.
Other Needs: "Design work, paste-up, advertising (designing ads). Send resume, samples of work for freelance contact only."

PATIENT AID DIGEST, 2009 Morris Ave., Union NJ 07083. (201)687-8282. For pharmacists with home health care departments. Bimonthly. Circ. 11,000.
Cartoons: Contact Laurie Cassak. Mail roughs. Pays on publication.

PENNSYLVANIA ILLUSTRATED, Box 657, 17 S. 19th St., Camp Hill PA 17011. (717)761-6605. Editor-in-Chief: Albert Holliday. Art Editor: Robert Hillegas. For college-educated readers, ages 35-50, interested in self-improvement, history, and civic and state affairs. Bimonthly; 8x11; 68 pages. Offset. Estab. 1976. Circ. 105,000. Query with samples. SASE. Reports in 3 weeks. Previously published, photocopied and simultaneous submissions OK. Buys first North American serial rights. Pays on publication. Sample copy $1.50.
Cartoons: Buys 6/year on history; single panel. Minimum payment: $15, b&w; $25, color.
Illustrations: Buys 12/year on history-related themes. Minimum payment: Cover: $70, color; $45, b&w. Inside: $55, color; $30, b&w.

PEOPLE ON PARADE, 1720 Washington Blvd., Box 2315, Ogden UT 84404. (801)394-9446. Editor: Dick Harris. Emphasizes profiles of interesting business and industrial people. Monthly. Circ. 200,000.
Cartoons: Buys 1-2/issue. Pays $15, b&w; $20, color; on acceptance. Send roughs. SASE. Reports in 3 weeks.

PERSONAL COMPUTING, 1050 Commonwealth Ave., Boston MA 02215. Managing Editor: Don Wood. For people interested in computers for their own personal use, whether at home, school or business. Monthly. Circ. 50,000. Photocopies OK. Originals not returned after publication. Buys all rights. Pays on publication.
Cartoons: Uses 1-5 cartoons/issue; buys 1-5/issue from freelancer. Receives 10-20 submissions/week from freelancers. Interested in humorous themes that apply to computers and the people using them. Send finished artwork. Reports in 1 week. Minimum payment: $15, b&w; $35, color.
Illustrations: Uses 15-20 illustrations/issue; tailored to specific articles. Works on assignment only. Samples returned by SASE. Reports back on future assignment possibilities. Provide resume and letter of inquiry to be kept on file for future assignments. Query with samples, resume or portfolio. SASE. Reports in 1 week. Cover: Pays $300, color. Inside: Pays $50-250, color; $25-150, b&w. Buys all rights on a work-for-hire basis.

PERSONNEL CONSULTANT, National Association of Personnel Consultants, 1012 14th St. NW, Washington DC 20005. (202)638-1721. Contact: Patricia A. Sciarra.
Cartoons: Uses 1 cartoon /issue; buys most from freelancers. Receives 0 submissions/week from freelancers. Interested in single panel cartoons. Mail samples and fees. SASE. Buys one-time rights.

PERSPECTIVE, 501 N. Calvert St., Baltimore MD 21203. Editor: Richard O'Mara. Emphasizes current affairs, national and international politics. Estab. 1968. Circ. 300,000. Weekly. SASE. Reports in 4 weeks. Pays on publication.
Illustrations: Buys 1/issue on assigned themes. Pays $50, b&w.

PETERSENS HUNTING MAGAZINE, Petersen Publishing Co., 8490 Sunset Blvd., Los Angeles CA 90069. (213)657-5100. Editor: Basil Bradbury. Art Director: Dianne Ortman. For hunting enthusiasts. Monthly. Circ. 250,000. Sometimes returns originals after publication. Arrange interview to show portfolio. SASE. Reports in 4 weeks. Buys all rights, but may reassign rights to artist after publication. Pays on publication. Sample copy $1.50.
Cartoons: Uses 1-2 cartoons/year from freelancers on hunting scenes and wildlife. Prefers finished cartoons; original artwork not accepted. Reports in 1 week.
Illustrations: Buys 8-10 illustrations/year on "very realistic wildlife themes and action hunting scenes"; some "how-to" drawings. Works on assignment only. Samples returned by SASE. Reports back on future assignment possibilities. Provide resume, business card, letter of inquiry; also brochure or fyler containing examples of work to be kept on file for future assignments. Prefers finished art, roughs, portfolio, samples of style or previously published work. Arrange interview to show portfolio. Buys various rights. Inside: Pays $75-150, b&w line drawings.
Other Needs: We occasionally use production paste-up artists on an hourly wage.

PHARMACEUTICAL TECHNOLOGY, 101 N. La Brea St., Suite 205, Inglewood CA 90301. (213)671-8075. Editor: Michael Thacher. Art Director: Rita Stanley. For quality-control and production/research/development management personnel at pharmaceutical, clinical diagnostic and cosmetic manufacturing firms. Monthly. Circ. 19,000. Free sample copy and artist's guidelines.

Illustrations: Uses 4 illustrations/issue, all from freelancers. Receives 1 submission/week from freelancers. Interested in pharmaceutical manufacturers. Works on assignment only. Samples not returned. Provide resume and nonreturnable samples to be kept on file for future assignments. Query with samples or previously published work, or arrange interview to show portfolio. SASE. Reports in 3 weeks. Buys all rights, but may reassign rights to artist after publication. Cover: Pays $300-350, color. Inside: Pays $75-200 color; $50-200, b&w; on acceptance.

PHI DELTA KAPPAN, Box 789, Bloomington IN 47402. Editor-in-Chief: Stanley M. Elam. Design Director: Carol Bucheri. For members of the educational organization Phi Delta Kappa. Published 10 times/year. Circ. 125,000. Considers unpublished artists on a speculative basis. SASE. Reports in 4 weeks. Previously published work OK ("specify where item appeared"). "we return cartoons after publication; we do not return assigned illustrations unless agreed at time of assignment." Sample copy $1.25.
Cartoons: Uses 10 cartoons/issue, all from freelancers. Receives 40 submissions/week from freelancers. Interested in themes that "relate to education–check our journal and news reports for current topics to use as themes. Considers drawing quality (i.e. line) of vital importance"; single panel with gag line. Prefers finished cartoons. SASE. Reporting time varies. "I usually return cartoons during the first weeks of each month–so best to submit towards the end of the month for an early return." Buys one-time rights.Pays $10-25, b&w line drawings and washes.
Illustrations: Uses 2 illustrations/issue, all from freelancers. interested in education. "Quality of drawing most important aspect-i.e., the kind of line, the graphic use of the space. Next is ability to depict appropriate image from editor and create a certain tension or humanistic quality between figures. Most illustrations depict student/teacher relationships. (Use some caricatures and some political media. Cartoons assigned.)" Works on assignment only. Samples returned by SASE. Reports back on future assignment possibilities. Provide calling card, tear sheet and "copies of line drawings to be kept on file for future assignments. Prefers resume, samples of style and list of publications. SASE. Reports during "first two weeks of each month." Buys all rights on a work-for-hire basis. Cover: Pays $25-100, color-separated work and full-color renderings. Inside: Pays $10-25, b&w line drawings and washes.
Other Needs: "We also need small spot drawings, 1 column by various heights, to fill out columns. Any subject, but especially education related. Should be b&w line. We pay $7.50 for all rights."

PHOTO MARKETING MAGAZINE, 603 Lansing Ave., Jackson MI 49202. (517)783-2809. Emphasizes the photographic industry. Readers are camera store dealers, photofinishers, manufacturers and distributors of photographic equipment. Monthly. Circ. 15,000. Free sample copy; art guidelines for SASE.
Cartoon Needs: Needs vary each issue. Freelancers are selected for particular subject matter or story topic. Format: b&w line drawings without gag line. Freelancer should send samples of style and resume to Pamela Wright, managing editor. SASE. Reports in 1 week. Pays on publication. Buys first North American serial rights.
Illustration Needs: Runs 2-4 illustrations/issue, all from freelancers. "Selection is made from freelancers on file, per assignment basis only." Uses inside b&w line drawings and color washes. Freelancers should send resume and samples of style or arrange for a personal appointment to show portfolio to Pamela Wright, managing editor. SASE. Reports in 1 week. Pays on publication. Buys first North American serial rights.

PIG IRON, Box 237, Youngstown OH 44501. (216)744-2258. Editor-in-Chief: Jim Villani. For upwardly mobile adults. Semiannual. Circ. 1,000. Previously published and photocopied work OK. Original artwork returned after publication. Sample copy $2.50.
Cartoons: Uses 1-15 cartoons/issue, all from freelancers. Receives 1-3 submissions/week from freelancers. Interested in "the arts, political, science fiction, fantasy, alternative lifestyles"; multipanel. Especially needs fine art cartoons. Prefers finished cartoons. SASE. Reports in 1 month. Buys first North American serial rights. Pays $2 minimum, b&w halftones and washes; on acceptance.
Illustrations: Uses 15-30 illustrations/issue, all from freelancers. Receives 1-3 submissions/week from freelancers. Interested in "any media: pen and ink washes, lithographs, silk screen, charcoal, etc. College themes: fine art illustrations–any subject matter." Especially needs artwork for 'Fascia,' a fast-paced, broad-based editorial that advocates social and cultural change. Prefers finished art. Reports in 1 month. Buys first North American serial rights. Minimum payment: Cover: $4, b&w. Inside: $2; on acceptance.
Other needs: Photographs.

PILLOW TALK, 215 Lexington Ave., New York NY 10016. Editor-in-Chief: I. Catherine Duff. "For people interested in all areas of human relationships: meeting, dating, arguing, making up,

sex (in all aspects)." Monthly. Circ. 120,000. Simultaneous submissions and previously published work OK. Original artwork returned after publication. Buys all rights. Sample copy $1.75; free artist's guidelines with SASE.
Cartoons: "Uses 5-8 cartoons/issue; buys 5-8 cartoons/issue from freelancers. Receives 200 submissions/week from freelancers. Interested in health, sex, problems and news items;" single panel with gag line. Prefers finished cartoons. SASE. Reports in 2 weeks. Pays $25-35, b&w line drawings, gray opaques, washes and opaque watercolors; on publication. Mail roughs or finished art. No pornography.
Illustrations: Most illustrations are assigned for specific articles. Works on assignment only. Samples returned by SASE. Reports back on future assignment possibilities. Provide resume and flyers to be kept on file for future assignments. Reports in 2 weeks. Buys first North American serial rights. Inside: Pays $25-150, b&w; on publication.

PITTSBURGH MAGAZINE, 4802 5th Ave., Pittsburgh PA 15213. (413)622-1358. Editor: Tim Whitaker. City magazine. Monthly. Circ. 70,000. Sample copy $1.50.
Cartoons: Buys 3 cartoons/issue from freelancers. Intested in political, social and satirical themes. Format: single panel and b&w line drawings. Prefers roughs. SASE. Reports in 2 weeks. Buys one-time rights. Pays $75-350 on publication.
Illustrations: Runs 15 illustrations/issue, all from freelancers. Uses "the kinds of illustrations that are able to stand up on their own." Uses inside and cover b&w line drawings and inside b&w washes. Works on assignment only. Prefers roughs. SASE. Reports in 2 weeks. Buys all rights on a work-for-hire basis. Pays on publication.

PLAN AND PRINT, International Reprographic Blueprint Association, 10116 Franklin Ave., Franklin Park IL 60131. Editor: James C. Vebeck. For commercial reproduction company owners and managers and dealers in architects', engineers' and draftsmen's supplies and equipment, in-plant reproduction department supervisors, in-plant design and drafting specialists and architects. Monthly. Circ. 23,000. Originals not returned after publication. Free sample copy and artist's guidelines.
Cartoons: Uses 1-2 cartoons/issue; buys 1 cartoon/issue from freelancers. Interested in themes "related to reproduction or design/drafting"; multipanel. Prefers finished cartoons. SASE. Reports in 1 week. Buys all rights on a work-for-hire basis.
Illustrations: Buys 1 illustration/issue. Interested in reproduction and design/drafting. Works on assignment only. Samples returned by SASE. Reports back on future assignment possibilities. Keeps files of information on artists for future assignment possibilities. Prefers samples of style. SASE. Reports in 1 week. Buys all rights on a work-for-hire basis. Pays $7.50 minimum, b&w line drawings.

PLANNING, American Planning Association, 1313 E. 60th St., Chicago IL 60637. (312)947-2108. Editor-in-Chief: Sylvia Lewis. Art Director: Richard Sessions. For urban and regional planners interested in land use, housing, transportation and the environment. Monthly. Circ. 25,000. Previously published work OK. Original artwork returned after publication, upon request. Free sample copy and artist's guidelines.
Cartoons: Buys 6 cartoons/year on the environment, city/regional planning, energy, garbage, transportation, housing, power plants, agriculture and land use; single, double and multipanel with gag lines ("provide outside of cartoon body if possible"). SASE. Reports in 2 weeks. Buys all rights. Pays $25 minimum, b&w line drawings; on publication.
Illustrations: Buys 8/year on the environment, city/regional planning, energy, garbage, transportation, housing, power plants, agriculture and land use. Prefers roughs and samples of style. SASE. Reports in 2 weeks. Buys all rights. Cover: Pays $125 minimum, 4-color drawings. Inside: Pays $25 minimum, b&w line drawings; on publication.

PLANTS ALIVE, 2603 3rd Ave., Seattle WA 98121. (206)623-9364. Editor/Publisher: Ted Marston. Deals with indoor, greenhouse and outdoor gardening. Bimonthly. Circ. 175,000. Original artwork not returned after publication. Free sample copy and artist's guidelines.
Illustrations: Buys 35 illustrations/issue, all from freelancers. Interested in plant and garden themes. Works on assignment only. Samples returned by SASE. Reports back on future assignment possibilities. Provide resume, letter of inquiry, brochure, flyer, tearsheet or something showing style. Prefers portfolio. SASE. Reports in 2 weeks. Buys first North American serial rights. Inside: Pays $50 minimum, color washes and opaque watercolors; $15 minimum, b&w line drawings and washes; on publication.

PLAY GIRL, 3420 Ocean Park Blvd., Santa Monica CA 90405. (213)450-0900. Emphasizes entertainment for 18-40 year old women. Monthly. Circ. 850,000.

Cartoon Needs: Uses 0-10 cartoons/issue; all by freelancers. Receives 10 cartoons from freelancers/week. Cartoons should be "slanted towards women's problems, intellectual humor, and topical issues." Format: Single and multi-panel b&w line drawings and color washes with gag line. Prefers finished cartoons or send samples of style to Mr. J.T. Steiny, art department. SASE. Reports in 30 days. Pays on publication; $100 for b&w and $250 for color. Buys first North American serial rights.
Illustration Needs: Uses 2-3 illustrations/issue; all by freelancers. Receives 5 illustrations from freelancers/week. Artists are selected from "walk-ins" doing editorial artwork to illustrate fiction. Format: b&w line drawings and color washes for inside. Arrange personal appointment to show portfolio and/or send samples of style and tearsheets. SASE. Reports in 30 days. Pays on publication. Buys first North American serial rights.

PLAY METER MAGAZINE, Box 24170, New Orleans LA 70184. (504)282-0261. Contact: Ralph Lally. Trade publication for owners/operators of coin-operated amusement machine companies (pinball, video games, etc). Monthly. Circ. 5,400.
Cartoons: Uses 1-2 cartoons/issue, all from freelancers. Receives 2 submissions/week from freelancers. Themes: "Violence gags in relation to coin-operated games are over-done. Sexuality, or the sight gag based on "over-sexed" individuals, ditto. Coin operated amusement games have become extremely innovative. Your cartoon involving a "space war" type game should not revolve around a 1950 era gag theme such as a henpecked Dagwood or Fonzie playing pinball—more like an astronaut getting lost in the video game, that would be our fare." Prefers finished cartoons. SASE. Reports in 2 weeks. Buys first serial rights. Pays $20, b&w; $50, color; on publication.
Illustrations: Uses 2-4 illustrations/issue; buys 1-2/issue from freelancers. Receives 1-2 submissions/week from freelancers. Interested in "line art of amusement machine locations. Study the magazine before submitting." Works on assignment only. Samples returned by SASE. Reports back on future assignment possibilities. Provide letter of inquiry and tearsheet to be kept on file for future assignments. Prefers resume, roughs and samples of style. Reports in 1 week. Buys first serial rights. Negotiates pay for b&w and color. Query with samples.
Other Needs: "logos for departments—music, technical, etc. (change periodically)."

PLAYBILL, 100 Aveune of the Americas, New York NY 10013. (212)751-9550. Editor-in-Chief: Joan Alleman Rubin. Concerns theater in New York City. Monthly. Circ. 1,040,000. Free sample copy and artist's guidelines.
Cartoons: Buys b&w line drawings on New York City theater. SASE. Reports in 4 weeks. Buys all rights. Pays on acceptance.
Illustrations: Assigns work on New York City theater. SASE. Reports in 4 weeks. Buys all rights. Pays on acceptance.

PLAYBOY, 919 Michigan Ave., Chicago IL 60611. Art Director: Arthur Paul. All work generally done on assignment. Reports in 2-4 weeks.
Cartoons: Submit roughs with one finished drawing to Michelle Urry, 747 3rd Ave., New York City 10017. Buys 35/month on satirical, sophisticated, "girly" and other situations; must deal with sex and be slanted toward young, urban male market. "Style and technique very important." Pays $350, b&w; $600, full-page color.
Illustrations: Submit samples to Kerig Pope. Pays $800/page or $1,200/spread; $200-250, spot drawings.

PLAYERS, 8060 Melrose Ave., Los Angeles CA 90046. Editor: Ray Locke. Black men's magazine. Original artwork not returned after publication.
Cartoons: Uses 6-8 cartoons/issue; buys all from freelancers. Receives 5 submissions/week from freelancers. Interested in black themes. Prefers finished cartoons. SASE. Reports immediately on non-acceptance. Buys all rights. Pays $35-75, b&w; $25-125, full-color; half-rates on previously published work. Pays on publication.
Illustrations: Uses 4 illustrations/issue; buys all from freelancers. Local artists only. Interested in movement. Works on assignment only. Samples returned by SASE. Reports back on future assignment possibilities. Provide resume, calling card or brochure to be kept on file for future assignments. Prefers samples of finished art and roughs. SASE. Reports in 1 week. Buys first North American serial rights. Pays $35-75, b&w; $25-125, full-color; half-rates on previously published work. Pays on publication.

PLYWOOD & PANEL MAGAZINE, Box 567B, Indianapolis IN 46206. (317)634-1100. Editor: Donald Phelan. Trade magazine which emphasizes manufacture of veneer and wood-based

panels. Monthly. Circ. 16,000. Original artwork not returned after publication. Free sample copy; art guidelines for SASE.
Cartoons: Uses 1-2 cartoons/issue on wood products. Uses single & multi-panel, b&w line drawings and washes with gag line. Send finished cartoons or query with ideas to Joan Pauls, production manager. SASE. Reports in 1-2 months. Pays up to $25 on publication for b&w cartoons. Buys first North American serial rights.
Illustrations: Uses 0-1 illustration/issue. Interested in industrial theme, especially wood products, usually to illustrate a particular story or issue. Uses inside b&w line drawings and washes for cover & inside color washes. Works on assignment only. No samples returned. Reports back on future assignment possibilities. Provide resume, brochure, flyer and tearsheet to be kept on file for future assignments. Send resume and nonreturnable printed samples of work to Steve Miller, art director. Buys first North American serial rights. Negotiates payment; pays on publication.

POLICE PRODUCT NEWS, 6200 Yarrow Dr., Carlsbad CA 92008. (714)438-3286. Editor: Denny Fallon. Emphasizes law enforcement. Readers are "line" or "beat" officers. Monthly. Circ. 50,000. Free sample copy; art guidelines for SASE.
Cartoons: Uses 4 cartoons/issue. Receives 12-25 submissions/week from freelancers. Interested in humorous cartoons concerning law enforcement officers; b&w line drawings with gag line. Prefers finished cartoons. SASE. Reports in 1 week. Buys one-time rights. Pays $15-35 for b&w cartoons on publication.
Illustrations: Uses 1-2 illustrations/issue, mostly on assignment. "We will review samples of an illustrator's work and then contact the illustrator if we have an assignment that we feel he or she might be able to help us on. We look for illustrations to accompany humorous fiction pieces." Uses inside b&w line drawings and inside color washes. Prefers samples of style and/or finished artwork. SASE. Reports in 1 week. Buys one-time rights only. Pays $125-175 for inside b&w and $150-200 for inside color; on publication.

POOL & SPA NEWS, 3923 W. 6th St., Los Angeles CA 90020. Contact: J. Field.
Cartoons: Buys themes on swimming pools, spas, hot tubs and the swimming pool industry. Send art. Reports immediately. Buys all or reprint rights. Pays $10; on acceptance.

POOR FARM COMICS & STORIES, Starvation Studios, 103 Myrtle St., Methuen MA 01844. (617)664-4744 or 682-5802. "This is a proving ground for untried and otherwise unacceptable experiments." Published semiannually; 8½x11; 48 pages. Offset. Estab. 1974. Circ. 7,000. Query with samples. SASE. Reports in 1-3 weeks. Previously published, photocopied and simultaneous submissions OK. Buys first rights. Pays on acceptance. Sample copy $1; free artist's guidelines.
Cartoons: Contact Eric Standway, editor. Buys 20/year on current events, politics, fantasy and science fiction; multipanel. "No Blondie & Dagwood, Snoopy type pap." Pays $5-10, b&w line drawings.
Illustrations: Contact Joe Tyburczy, editor. Buys 20/year on current events, politics, fantasy and science fiction. Cover: Pays $10-20, color. Inside: Pays $2-10, b&w line drawings and washes.

POPULAR ELECTRONICS, 1 Park Ave., New York NY 10016. Contact: Ed Buxbaum. Call or send resume. Reports in 2 weeks. Buys first rights plus reprints. Pays on acceptance.
Cartoons and Illustrations: Buys themes on electronics, test instruments, experimenters, hi-fi, TV service and CB/ham radios; usually uses pen and ink or line and wash. Pays $50-150, art; $15-30, cartoons.

POPULAR HANDICRAFT HOBBIES, Tower Press, Inc., Box 428, Seabrook NH 03874. Editor-in-Chief: Karen P. Sherrer. For amateur hobbyists and crafters, mostly women. "Our readers are interested in easy-to-do crafts, which require a minimum of expensive materials and tools." Bimonthly; 8x11; 72 pages. Offset. Estab. 1964. Circ. 140,000. Mail art. SASE. Reports in 6-8 weeks. Buys all rights. Pays on acceptance. Free artist's guidelines for SASE.
Cartoons: Buys 12/year on crafts or hobbies; single panel. "Show women in a favorable light; we're very square, no sick humor." Pays $20 minimum, b&w washes.

POPULAR SCIENCE, Times Mirror Magazines, Inc., 380 Madison Ave., New York NY 10017. Art Director: David Houser. Original artwork returned after publication.
Illustrations: Uses 30-40 illustrations/issue; buys 30/issue from freelancer. Interested in technical 4-color art and 2-color line art dealing with automotive or architectural subjects. Works on assignment only. Samples returned by SASE. Reports back on future assignment possibilities. Provide tearsheet to be kept on file for future assignments. "After seeing portfolios, I photocopy or photostat those samples I feel are indicative of the art we might use." Send portfolio. Reports whenever appropriate job is available. Buys first publishing rights.

POTATO GROWER OF IDAHO, Harris Publishing Inc., Box 98, Idaho Falls ID 83401. Editor-in-Chief: Darryl Harris. Art Director: Don Taylor. Monthly; 8x11; 40 pages. Offset. Estab. 1972. Circ. 17,000. Mail art. SASE. Reports in 1 week. Photocopied and simultaneous submissions OK. Buys one-time rights. Pays on publication. Free sample copy.
Cartoons: Buys 2-3/issue on farming and agriculture; single panel with gag line. Pays $15 maximum, b&w line drawings.

POULTRY PROCESSING AND MARKETING, (formerly *Broiler Business*), Watt Publishing Co., Mount Morris IL 61054. Editor: Bernard E. Heffernan. For businessmen engaged in the processing and marketing of broilers, turkeys and fowl. Monthly. Mail art. Buys all rights. Pays on acceptance.
Cartoons: Buys 2-3/issue on broilers and turkeys. Pays $15-25.

POWER, McGraw-Hill Publishing, Inc., 1221 Avenue of the Americas, New York NY 10020. (212)997-2440. Art Director: Kiyo Komoda. For power generation and plant energy systems. Monthly plus 2 annuals. Original artwork returned after publication, on request only.
Illustrations: Uses 30 illustrations/issue on energy systems. Buys 10/issue from freelancers; most are graphs, charts and mechanical line drawings. Works on assignment only. Samples returned by SASE. Reports back on future assignment possibilities. Provide resume and calling card to be kept on file for future assignments. Arrange interview to show portfolio. SASE. Reports in 1 week. Buys one-time and reprint rights. Cover: Pays $150-350, color. Inside: Pays $30-300, color; $10-200, b&w line drawings; on acceptance.
To Break In: "We prefer artists with clean and crisp line works. They should know about color separation and the use of zipper tones. Young artists welcomed."
Cartoons: Uses 1 cartoon/issue; buys 1 cartoon/issue from freelancers. Receives 1 submission/month from freelancers. Interested in situations in industry; cartoons usually go with editorials. Send resume. Reports in 1 week.

POWER TRANSMISSION DESIGN, 614 Superior Ave. W, Cleveland, OH 44113. (216)696-0300. Assistant Editor: Alex Krislov. Readers are designers, users and maintainers of industrial power transmission equipment. Monthly. Circ. 50,500. Free sample copy.
Cartoons: Uses 1 cartoon/issue; buys 50% from freelancers. Themes "should relate to design, manufacture, use, maintenance or government regulation of such power transmission components as bearings, controls, drives or motors." Prefers single panel b&w line drawings with gag line. Send finished cartoons. SASE. Reports in 2 weeks. Buys one-time rights. Pays $25 for b&w on publication.

PRAIRIE SUN, Box 876, Peoria IL 61652. (309)673-6624. Contact: Bill Knight, editor. For music listeners also interested in films, books and entertainment. Weekly. Circ. 35,000. Weekly. Original artwork returned after publication.
Cartoons: Uses 5 cartoons/issue. Prefers roughs. Reports in 2 weeks.
Illustrations: Uses 2 illustrations/issue. Buys 1/issue from freelancers. Interested in music, politics and personality caricatures. Samples returned with SASE; reports back on future assignment possiblities. Provide letter of inquiry to be kept on file for future assignments. Prefers roughs. Reports in 2 weeks. Buys first North American serial rights. Pays $15-25; on publication. Pays $15-25, b&w. Query with samples.

PREMIERE, (formerly *Writers Premiere*), 1211 E. 7th St., St. Paul MN 55106. (612)774-5708. Emphasizes short stories, poetry and quality illustrations for children, students, middle age and senior citizens. Quarterly. Estab. 1978. Sample copy $1; art guidelines for SASE.
Illustration Needs: Uses 4 illustrations/issue; all supplied by freelancers. Illustrations of short stories and poems should pertain to family living, slice of life and nature. Format: b&w line drawings for inside. Send finished art or samples of style to Gerald Fechner, editor. Reports in 4-6 weeks. Pays $10-15 for b&w inside.

THE PRESBYTERIAN RECORD, 50 Wynford Dr., Don Mills, Ontario, Canada M3C 1J7. (416)441-1111. Art Director: Mary Visser. Deals with family-oriented religious themes. Circ. 85,600. Original artwork returned after publication. Simultaneous submissions and previously published work OK. Free sample copy and artist's guidelines.
Cartoons: Uses 1 cartoon/issue; buys from freelancers. Interested in some theme or connection to religion. Prefers roughs. SASE. Reports in 2 weeks. Pays on publication.
Illustrations: Buys 10/year on religion. "We generally do not use freelance material, but we are interested in excellent color artwork for cover." Any line style acceptable– should reproduce well on newsprint. Works on assignment only. Samples returned by SASE. Reports back on future

assignment possibilities. Provide calling card to be kept on file for future assignments. Prefers roughs. Reports in 2 weeks. Buys all rights on a work-for-hire basis. Cover: Pays $35, color washes and opaque watercolors; inside: pays $5-12, b&w line drawings; on publication. Query with resume and samples.

PRESBYTERIAN SURVEY, 341 Ponce de Leon Ave. NE, Atlanta GA 30308. (404)873-1531. Editor: William P. Lamkin. Monthly. Circ. 120,000. Sample copy available.
Illustrations: Buys several/issue on religious themes. Buys one-time rights. Pays $25-100, spot art; $50-250, cover design.

PRESENT TENSE, c/o CBS, 51 W. 52nd St., Rm. 2719, New York NY 10019. Contact: Ira Teichberg. Quarterly magazine of journalism and writing concerning Jewish affairs. Query. Reports in 4-6 weeks. Buys all rights. Pays on publication. Sample copy $2.50.
Needs: Pays $25-75, b&w line drawings, washes and graphic art.

PRESERVATION NEWS, 1785 Massachusetts Ave. NW, Washington DC 20036. (202)673-4000. Editor: Carleton Knight III. Readers are members of the National Trust for Historic Preservation. Monthly. Circ. 175,000. Free sample copy; art guidelines for SASE.
Cartoons: Uses 1-2 cartoons/issue; buys 1/issue from freelancers. "Since our newspaper is limited to the preservation of historic sites and buildings, cartoons should be on that subject. This subject is broad, however, and can range from architecture (old and new) to history." Uses single or multi-panel b&w line drawings and washes with or without gag lines. Prefers samples. SASE. Reports in 4 weeks. Buys one-time rights. Pays $25-50, b&w cartoons; on acceptance.
Illustrations: Uses 10-15 illustrations/issue; buys 1-2/issue from freelancers. "We sometimes commission special illustrations (from samples and persons whose work we know) for the newspaper. Most of our art, however, is photographs. As we are usually in a hurry, we tend to use local artists on deadline." We look for "drawing of historic structures. Occasionally, we will have a special piece of art that relates to a general subject such as neighborhood conservation. Line art is best because it shows the detail." Uses b&w line drawings and washes for cover and inside. Send samples of style and/or arrange personal appointment to show portfolio. SASE. Reports in 1 week. Buys all rights on a work-for-hire basis. Cover: Pays $25-100, b&w. Inside: Pays $25-100, b&w; on acceptance.

PRISM INTERNATIONAL, Creative Writing Dept., University of British Columbia, Vancouver, B.C., Canada V6T 1W5. Editor-in-Chief: John Simmons. Managing Editor: Francois Bonneville. For a literary audience interested in poetry, short fiction, drama and literature in translation. Semiannually. Circ. 1,000. Original artwork not returned after publication. Sample copy $4.
Illustrations: Buys 1-15/year of graphics, photos. Excellence only criterion. Works on assignment only. Samples returned by SASE. Reports back on future assignment possibilities. Prefers samples of style. SASE. reports in 6 weeks. Buys all rights on a work-for-hire basis. Negotiates pay. Pays on publication.

PRIVATE PILOT, Box 4030, San Clemente CA 92672. (714)498-1600. Contact: Editor. For owners/pilots of private aircraft, student pilots and others aspiring to attain additional ratings and experience. Circ. 100,000. Monthly.
Cartoons: Buys a varied amount/issue on flying. Send finished artwork. SASE. Reports in 3 months. Pays $15-50, b&w; on publication.
Illustrations: Pays $25-75, b&w; $75-100, color. Query with samples. SASE. Reports in 3 months.

PRIVATE PRACTICE, 3400 N.W. Expressway, Suite 206, Oklahoma City OK 73112. (405)943-2318. Art Director & Design Director: Hal Smith. Editorial features "maintenance of freedom in all fields of medical practice and the effects of socioeconomic factors on the physician." Monthly. Circ. 200,000. Previously published work OK. Free sample copy and artist's guidelines.
Illustrations: Buys 1-4/issue on politics, medicine and physicians' leisure activities. Query and arrange interview to show portfolio. SASE. Reports in 2-3 weeks. Buys first and reprint rights. Cover: Pays $200-500, color washes and opaque watercolors. Inside: Pays $60-110, color washes and opaque watercolors; $40-100, b&w line drawings and washes; on acceptance.
Design: Uses artists for 4-color cover design. Query with resume and samples or arrange interview to show portfolio. SASE. Reports in 2-3 weeks. Negotiates pay; pays on acceptance.

PROBE, Baptist Brotherhood Commission, 1548 Poplar, Memphis TN 38104. (901)272-2461. Art Director: Herschel Wells. Christian-oriented mission magazine for boys ages 7-12. Monthly.

Original artwork returned after publication, if requested. Circ. 50,000. Previously published, photocopied and simultaneous submissions OK. Free sample copy and artist's guidelines.
Illustrations: Uses 3 illustrations/issue; buys 1/issue from freelancers. Interested in family life with emphasis on boys and their interests. "Our freelance needs are usually directed toward a specific story; we very seldom use art submitted on spec." Samples returned by SASE and reports back on future assignment possibilities. Provide resume or brochure to be kept on file for future assignments. Prefers samples of style or roughs. SASE. Reports in 3 weeks. Buys first North American serial rights. Cover: Pays $200-250, full color; $100-180, b&w line drawings, washes and gray opaques. Inside: Pays $45-120, b&w line drawings, washes and gray opaques. Pays on acceptance.

PROFESSIONAL AGENT, 400 N. Washington St., Alexandria VA 22314. (703)836-9340. Editor-in-Chief: Edward F. Campbell. For independent insurance agents and other affiliated members of the American Agency System. Monthly. Circ. 27,500. Original artwork not returned after publication. Free sample copy.
Illustrations: Contact Arya Safa-Nunn, assistant editor. Uses 32 illustrations/issue; buys 3/issue from freelancers. Provide resume and tearsheet to be kept on file for future assignments. Prefers samples of style or roughs. SASE. Reports in 2 weeks. Buys all rights. Cover: Pays $250, 4-color and other media; on acceptance.
To Break In: "Our issues are topic-oriented, such as 'Legislative Issues' or 'Getting Ahead in the Business.' We need a creative, conceptual approach instead of a stilted, cliched illustration."

PROFESSIONAL DECORATING & COATING, 7223 Lee Hwy., Falls Church VA 22046. (703)534-1201. Editor/Manager: H. K. Darby. Contains technical, business and new product information for professional painters. Monthly. Circ. 15,500. Free sample copy.
Cartoons: Uses less than 1 cartoon/issue, all from freelancers. Would like to receive more submissions from freelancers. Interested in painters; single panel with gag line. SASE. Reports in 3 weeks. Pays $10, b&w line drawings; on acceptance.

PROFESSIONAL MEDICAL ASSISTANT, 1 E. Wacker Dr., Chicago IL 60601. (312)944-2722. Editor: Susan S. Croy. For office employees of physicians. "The editorial goal is to communicate with medical assistants stressing their importance in helping the doctor respond successfully to the demands for medical services. Articles deal with responsibilities and offer education to increase professionalism." Bimonthly. Circ. 21,000. SASE. Reports in 3 weeks.
Cartoons: Buys 2 cartoons/issue dealing with the medical assistant's role in the physician's office. Send finished artwork or roughs. SASE. Reports in 3 weeks. Pays $8.50; on acceptance.

THE PROFESSIONAL PHOTOGRAPHER, 1090 Executive Way, Des Plaines IL 60018 (312)298-4680. Editor: Gordon F. Bieberle. Emphasizes professional photography. Readers are "mostly members of the Professional Photographers of American, Inc., a trade association of portrait, commercial and industrial photographers." Monthly. Circ. 28,500. Sample copy $2.50.
Cartoons: Uses 2-3 cartoons/year. Receives 1 cartoon from freelancers/week. Cartoons "must be humorous and relate to some aspect of professional photography." Format: b&w line drawings with gag line. Prefers finished cartoons. SASE. Reports in 1 month. Buys first North American serial rights. Pays $10 for b&w cartoon; on publication.

PROFESSIONAL REMODELING, 111 E. Wacker Dr., Chicago IL 60601. (312)938-2323. Editor: Norman C. Remich, Jr. Emphasizes professional remodeling. Readers are mostly remodeling contractors. Monthly. Circ. 30,000. Estab. 1978. Free sample copy; art guidelines for SASE.
Illustrations: Uses 3 illustrations/issue. Interested in home improvement. Uses b&w line drawings with b&w washes inside, and color washes for cover. Works on assignment only. Samples returned by SASE. Reports back on future assignment possibilities. Provide resume or letter of inquiry to be kept on file for future assignments. Prefers samples of style or portfolio. SASE. Reports in 2 weeks. Buys all rights on a work-for-hire basis. Pays $100 for inside b&w, $200 for color cover, and $100 for inside color; on publication.

PROFESSIONAL SAFETY, American Society of Safety Engineers, 850 Busse Highway, Park Ridge IL 60068. (312)692-4121. Editorial Director: Ed Schwenn. For the safety profession. Monthly. Circ. 16,500. Simultaneous submissions and previously published work OK. Sample copy $2.
Illustrations: Buys 3 illustrations/year on environment, safety and health. Query with resume and samples or arrange interview to show portfolio. SASE. Reports in 4 weeks. Buys all rights, but may reassign rights to artist after publication. Cover: Pays $150, color washes and opaque watercolors; on publication.

PROFITABLE CRAFT MERCHANDISING, PJS Publications Inc., Box 1790, Peoria IL 61656. Editor: Geoff Wheeler. Art Director: Diane Cashen. For crafts wholesalers and retailers. Monthly. Circ. 25,000. Sample copy $1.
Cartoons: Buys 25 cartoons/year. Interested in selling and teaching crafts; single panel with gag line. Prefers letter and samples. SASE. Reports in 2 weeks. Buys all rights. Pays $10-15, b&w line drawings and washes; on acceptance.
Illustrations: Buys 8-10 illustrations/year. Assigned themes. Prefers letter with samples. SASE. Reports in 2 weeks. Buys all rights. Cover: Pays $150-350, full-color; Inside: Pays $25-150, b&w line drawings and washes; on acceptance.

THE PROGRESSIVE, 408 W. Gorham St., Madison WI 53703. (608)257-4626. Editor-in-Chief: Erwin Knoll. Associate Editor/Art Director: Sam Day. Monthly. Circ. 35,000. SASE. Reports in 1 week. Buys first rights. Pays on publication. Free sample copy and artist's guidelines.
Cartoons: Uses 6 cartoons/issue; buys 1/issue from freelancers. Receives 1-2 submissions/week from freelancers. Subjects are "political, taking a progressive viewpoint on issues in energy, the military, feminism, events, environment, consumer rights." Prefers finished cartoons. Reports in 2 weeks. Pays $25 minimum, b&w drawings.
Illustrations: Uses 18 illustrations/issue; buys 18/issue from freelancers. Subjects: same as in "cartoons" section. Works on assignment only. Samples returned by SASE. Reports back on future assignment possibilities. Provide letter of inquiry and tearsheet to be kept on file for future assignments. Prefers samples. Reports in 1 week. Buys first North American serial rights. Inside: pays $25 minimum, b&w line drawings.

THE PROGRESSIVE FARMER, 820 Shades Creek Pkwy., Birmingham AL 35202. Art Director: Al Ellis. Concerns agricultural interests of the South and Southwest. Submit roughs. Reports in 1 week. Buys all rights. Pays on acceptance.
Cartoons: Buys 75/year. "Would like to see more cartoons about actual farming operations, use of farm machinery and cattle. We use quite a few around-the-home, family, recreation, school and church activities gags; also hunting and fishing gags." Pays $40 minimum.

PROGRESSIVE GROCER MAGAZINE, 708 3rd Ave., New York NY 10017. (212)490-1000. Contact: Mitch Shostak. For supermarket operators, managers, buyers and executives in the grocery business. Monthly. Circ. 90,000.
Illustrations: Buys 2-8 illustrations/issue on assigned themes. Query with samples or arrange interview to show portfolio. Pays $75-100/spot, $200-300/full page, b&w; $200-400, color. Pays 30 days after bill is submitted.

PROPERTY MANAGEMENT JOURNAL, 10933 E. Valley Blvd., El Monte CA 91731. Publisher: Ben Hegel. For real estate people, owners of rental property, resident managers and property management companies in California. Monthly; 11x14; 12-16 pages. Offset. Estab. 1971. Circ. 7,000. Query with samples. SASE. Reports in 4 weeks. Previously published and simultaneous submissions OK. Pays on acceptance. Sample copy $1.
Cartoons: Buys 12/year on problems or topics common to landlord/tenant/manager relationships. Pays $10-15, b&w line drawings.

PSA, East-West Network, Inc., 5900 Wilshire Blvd., #300, Los Angeles CA 90036. (213)937-5810. Editor: John Johns. Creative Director: Mika Kyprianides. Monthly. Original artwork not returned after publication. Sample copy $1.50.
Illustrations: Uses 10 illustrations/issue; buys 6/issue from freelancers. Works on assignment only. Query with resume. Reports in 4 weeks. Buys all rights. Pays $25 minimum, spot art; $400, full-color cover.

PSYCHOLOGY TODAY, 1 Park Ave., New York NY 10016. (212)725-7530. Editor: Jack Nessel. Art Director: Carveth Kramer. For laymen interested in social science and the human condition. Monthly. Circ. 1,100,000.
Illustrations: Buys 120 illustrations/year on assigned themes. Arrange interview, mail art or deliver portfolio. SASE. Buys first, all or one-time rights. Inside: Pays $650 minimum, color; $100-300, b&w; on acceptance.

PUBLISHERS WEEKLY, R.R. Bowker Co., 1180 Avenue of the Americas, New York NY 10036. Art/Production: Ann Green. For the book publishing industry. Weekly. Circ. 36,000. Original artwork returned after publication. Free artist's guidelines.
Illustrations: Buys approximately 2-3 illustrations/year on subjects relating to the book trade. Works on assignment only. Samples returned by SASE. Reports back on future assignment

possibilities. Provide resume, calling card, letter of inquiry, brochure, flyer or tearsheet to be kept on file for future assignments. Prefers portfolio or samples of style. SASE. Reporting time varies. Buys first North American serial rights. Cover: Pays $500 maximum, color washes, oils and opaque watercolors. Inside: Pays $300 maximum, b&w line drawings and washes; on publication.
Design/Production: Uses artists for dummying layouts. Pays $10/hour. Query with resume and samples or arrange interview to show portfolio.

PULP & PAPER CANADA, Southam Business Publications, 310 Victoria Ave., Westmount, Quebec, Canada H3Z 2M9. (514)487-2302. Editor: W. Schabas. For woods and mills employees of the pulp and paper industry. Monthly. Circ. 12,000. Original artwork returned after publication. Free sample copy.
Cartoons: Uses 1 cartoon/issue; rarely buys cartoons from freelancers. Interested in wood harvesting, forest management and pulp and paper making; single panel with gag line. Prefers roughs. SASE. Reports in 1 week. Buys first North American serial rights. Pays $30 minimum, b&w line drawings; on acceptance.
Illustrations: Uses 1 illustration/issue. Works on assignment only. Samples returned by SASE. Reports back on future assignment possibilities. Provide brochure to be kept on file for future assignments. Prefers samples of style (roughs). SASE. Reports in 1 week. Buys first North American serial rights.

THE QUARTER HORSE OF THE PACIFIC COAST, Box 254822, Sacramento CA 95825. Editor-in-Chief: Jill Scopinich. For horse breeders, trainers and owners interested in performance, racing and showing of quarter horses. Monthly. Circ. 7,800. Previously published and simultaneous submissions OK "if we are notified."
Cartoons: Buys 12 cartoons/year on horses; single panel. Query with samples. SASE. Reports in 4 weeks. Buys first, reprint, all or simultaneous rights. Pays $10-20, washes; on acceptance.

THE QUILL, 35 E. Wacker Dr., Chicago IL 60601. Contact: Charles Long. "For journalists about the practice of journalism—newspapers, radio/TV news, magazines, journalism education and the campus press."
Illustrations: Buys assigned themes. Query with tearsheets or art. Cover and inside: Pays $25, ink drawings; on publication.

QUILT WORLD, Box 1952, Brooksville FL 33512. Editor: Barbara Hall Pedersen. Art Director: Carol Pedersen. Concerns patchwork and quilting. Bimonthly. Circ. 100,000. SASE. Reports in 2 weeks. Previously published work OK. Original artwork not returned after publication. Sample copy with 9x12 SASE, 66¢.
Cartoons: Uses 2 cartoons/issue, all from freelancers. Receives 25 submissions/week from freelancers. Uses themes "poking gentle fun at quilters." Prefers finished cartoons. Reports in 1 week if not accepted. "I hold cartoons I can use until there is space." Buys all rights. Pays on acceptance.

RACQUETBALL ILLUSTRATED, 7011 Sunset Blvd., Hollywood CA 90028. (212)467-1300. Editor: Ben Kalb. Emphasizes racquetball for beginner and advanced racquetball players. Most are members of clubs. Monthly. Circ. 105,000. Estab. 1978. Original artwork returned after publication. Sample copy for $1.50.
Cartoons: Uses 1-3 cartoons/issue. Receives 5-10 submissions/week from freelancers. Cartoons should pertain to racquetball games, equipment, courts, clubs, personalities, and audience. Format: single and multi-panel b&w line drawings with gag line. Prefers finished cartoons. SASE. Reports in 2 weeks. Buys first North American serial rights. Pays $10-20 after acceptance for b&w cartoons.

R-A-D-A-R, 8121 Hamilton Ave., Cincinnati OH 45231. Editor: Dana Eynon. For ages 8-12. Original artwork not returned after publication.
Cartoons: Buys 1 cartoon/month on animals, school and sports. Prefers finished cartoons. Reports in 2-4 weeks. Pays $10-15; on acceptance.
Illustrations: Uses 5 or more illustrations/issue. "Art that accompanies nature or handcraft articles may be purchased, but most everything is assigned." Works on assignment only. Samples returned by SASE. Reports back on future assignment possibilities. Provide tearsheet to be kept on file for future assignments. Prefers samples of style. SASE. Reports in 2-4 weeks. Buys all rights on a work-for-hire basis. Cover: Pays $50, line drawing. Inside: Pays $10-30, spot art; on acceptance.

RADIO-ELECTRONICS, 200 Park Ave. S., New York NY 10003. (212)777-6400. Managing Editor: Arthur Kleiman. Monthly. Circ. 185,000. Previously published work OK. Free sample copy.
Cartoons: Buys 3/issue on electronics, service, hi-fi, computers and TV games; single panel. Mail art. SASE. Reports in 1 week. Buys first or all rights. Pays $15 minimum, b&w washes; on acceptance.

RAILROAD MODEL CRAFTSMAN, Box 700, Newton NJ 07860. (201)383-3355. Editor: Tony Koester. Monthly. Buys all rights.
Needs: Uses line drawings of railroad equipment and model railroad layouts requiring extensive knowledge of real/scale model railroading; 5x7 minimum. Write for payment rates.

THE RANGEFINDER, Rangefinder Publishing Co., Box 1703, Santa Monica CA 90406. Contact: Charlene Marmer Solomon. Trade magazine for professional photographers. Readership includes commercial, editorial, advertising, industrial, portrait, scientific and freelance photographers. Monthly. Previously published work OK. Sample copy $1.50.
Cartoons: Buys photography themes. Query. Reports in 2 weeks. Buys first serial rights. Pays $5-7.50 for b&w line drawings for one-column format.

RANGER RICK'S NATURE MAGAZINE, 1412 16th St. NW, Washington DC 20036. Editor-in-Chief: Trudy Farrand. Art Director: Donna Miller. For children ages 4-12. Monthly. Circ. 850,000. Pays on acceptance.
Illustrations: Buys 4-6/issue on children involved with wildlife. "We're looking for light, humorous animal illustrations." Query with previously published work. SASE. Reports in 1 month. Buys all rights. Inside: Pays $200 min./page, color washes and opaque watercolors; $100 min./page, b&w line drawings, washes and gray opaques; on acceptance.

RAPIDFIRE REVIEW, Box 779, Glendora CA 91740. Editor-in-Chief/Art Director: Jim Bianchi. For collectors of rapidfire weapons. Bimonthly; 46 pages. Estab. 1977. Submit art or query. SASE. Reports in 1 week. Previously published and simultaneous submissions OK. Buys all rights, but may reassign rights to artist after publication. Pays on publication. Free sample copy and guidelines.
Cartoons: Buys themes on rapidfire weapon collecting. Pays $5 minimum, b&w line drawings.
Illustrations: Buys themes on rapidfire weapon collecting. Inside: Pays $5 minimum, b&w line drawings and washes.

READERS NUTSHELL, PO Drawer 189, Palm Beach FL 33480. Concerns insurance and safety. Bimonthly.
Cartoons: Buys 3-4/issue on family, office and general themes. Send finished art. SASE. Reports in 2 weeks. Pays $5, b&w; on publication.

RECREATIONAL VEHICLE RETAILER, Trailer Life Publishing Co., Inc., 29901 Agoura Rd., Agoura CA 91301. Editorial Director: Alice M. Robison. For recreational vehicle dealers, manufacturers and suppliers. Monthly. Circ. 25,000. Free sample copy.
Illustrations: Art Director: Mirante Almazan. Buys 1/issue on recreational vehicles. Query with samples or arrange interview to show portfolio. SASE. Reports in 3 weeks. Buys all rights. Pays on publication.

REDBOOK, 230 Park Ave., New York NY 10017. Assigns illustrations.

REDWOOD RANCHER, 756 Kansas St., San Francisco CA 94107. (415)824-1563. Editor: Sally Taylor. For grapegrowers and other California north coast ranchers. Monthly. Circ. 7,000.
Cartoons: Uses 1 cartoon/issue; buys 1/issue from freelancers on ranching. Query. SASE. Reports in 2 weeks. Pays $5-100, b&w; on publication.

REFEREE, Box 161, Franksville WI 53126. (414)632-8855. Editor-in-Chief: Barry Mano. Art Director: Scott Krahn. For sports officials. Monthly. Circ. 42,000. Free sample copy and artist's guidelines, for 9x12 SASE and 28¢ postage.
Cartoons and Illustrations: Buys 40 cartoons and 25 illustrations/year on sports officiating. Query with samples. SASE. Reports in 4 weeks. Previously published work OK. Buys all rights, but may reassign rights to artist after publication. Pays on publication. Inside: Pays $15-50, b&w line drawings and washes; $25-100, color washes and full-color renderings; $15-25 b&w cartoons; on publication.

REFLECTION, Box 788, Wheaton IL 60187. (312)293-1600. Editor: Laura Alden. "For junior and senior high girls; objective is to present Christ and make Scriptures relevant to daily living and to develop maturity and interpersonal skills." Bimonthly. Circ. 10,000. Simultaneous submissions and previously published work OK. Sample copy and photography guidelines; $1.50.
Cartoons: Buys 6 cartoons/year. Interested in current events, education, environment, family life, humor through youth, politics and sports; single or double panel with gag line. Prefers samples, roughs, or finished art. SASE. Reports in 4-8 weeks. Buys first, reprint, one-time or simultaneous rights. Pays $5-20, b&w line drawings; on acceptance.
Illustrations: Buys 1-2 illustrations/year. Interested in current events, education, family life, politics and humor through youth. Prefers resume and samples or previously published work. SASE. Reports in 4-8 weeks. Buys first, reprint, one-time or simultaneous rights. Cover: Pays $20-35, b&w line drawings; Inside: Pays $10-25, b&w line drawings; on acceptance.

RENTAL EQUIPMENT REGISTER, 2048 Cotner, Los Angeles, CA 90025. (213)477-1033. Readers are small and large independent owners of rental centers including firms engaged in rental of tools, trucks, trailers, contractor equipment, sickroom and party goods. Monthly. Circ. 10,000. Free sample copy for SASE.
Cartoons: Uses 6-10 cartoons/issue; buys all from freelancers. Interested in cartoons with slant to the rental center owner. Prefers single panel b&w line drawings or b&w washes. Send finished cartoons to Richard Cerilli or Tim Novoselski, editors. SASE. Reports in 2 weeks. Buys all rights. Pays $10-15 for b&w; on acceptance.
Illustrations: Prefers b&w line drawings for inside and color washes for cover. Send finished art or samples of style to Tim Novoselski, editor. SASE. Reports in 2 weeks. Buys all rights. Pays $25-35 for inside b&w and $50-150 for color cover; on acceptance.

RESIDENT AND STAFF PHYSICIAN, 80 Shore Rd., Port Washington NY 11050. Cartoon Editor: James F. McCarthy. For hospital physicians. Monthly.
Cartoons: Buys 4-6 cartoons/issue. Interested in "inside" medical themes. Submit art. SASE. Reports in 2 weeks. Buys all rights. Pays $20; on acceptance. Also buys spots; pays $10-50; on acceptance.

RESPIRATORY THERAPY, Brentwood Publishing Corp., 825 S. Barrington Ave., Los Angeles CA 90049. Art Director: Kathy Kubik.
Needs: Submit published samples. Reports in 30 days. Buys all rights. Pays $45, spot art; $225, full-color cover; on acceptance.

RESPONSE, 173 Boston Post Rd., Milford CT 06460. Art Director: Amy Gaskin. Concerns sexual matters, from erotica to medical problems. Montly. Circ. 200,000. Simultaneous submissions OK. Original artwork returned after publication. Buys first or all rights. Sample copy 50¢; free artist's guidelines.
Cartoons: Uses 4 cartoons/issue, all from freelancers. Interested in "sex and political" cartoons; single panel. Prefers finished cartoons. Buys all rights on a work-for-hire basis. Pays $25 minimum, b&w; on publication.
Illustrations: Uses 12 illustrations/issue, all from freelancers. Receives 2 submissions/week from freelancers. Interested in "erotica and medicine." Works on assignment only. Samples returned by SASE. Reports back on future assignment possibilities. Provide brochure and tearsheet to be kept on file for future assignments. Prefers finished art or roughs. SASE. Reports in 2 weeks. Buys all rights on a work-for-hire basis. Inside: Pays $25 minimum, b&w; on publication.
Design: Uses artists for layout mock-ups and publication redesign. Negotiates pay. Query with resume and samples. Also uses "all types (of art) for consumer publications."

RETAILER AND MARKETING NEWS, Box 57194, Dallas TX 75207. (214)528-5910. Circulated to retail dealers and wholesalers in appliances, televisions, furniture, consumer electronics, records, air conditioning, housewares, hardware and all related businesses. Monthly. Circ. 10,000.
Cartoons: Buys 1/issue on business, TV repair and selling. Mail roughs or finished art. SASE. Reports in 1 month. Pays $5, b&w; on publication.

THE RETIRED OFFICER, 201 N. Washington St., Alexandria VA 22314. (703)549-2311. Art Director: Rene S. San Miguel. "For retired officers of the seven uniformed services; concerns history, humor, culture, second career opportunities and current events." Monthly. Circ. 260,000. Simultaneous submissions and previously published work OK.
Illustrations: Buys 12 illustrations/year on assigned themes. Query with resume and samples. SASE. Reports in 4 weeks. Buys first or all rights. Inside: Pays $20-40, b&w line drawings and washes; on publication.

REVIEW, East-West Network Inc., 5900 Wilshire Blvd., Suite 300, Los Angeles CA 90036. (213)937-5810. Editor-in-Chief: Fred R. Smith. "In-flight Eastern Airlines publication; features fiction and nonfiction articles on art, sports, travel, the media, business, self-improvement and health." Monthly. Simultaneous submissions and previously published work OK. Free sample copy and artist's guidelines.
Illustrations: Buys 1-4/issue on current events, sports, travel, the media and self-improvement. Query with resume and samples or arrange interview to show portfolio. SASE. Reports in 2-4 weeks. Buys various rights. Inside: Pays $450, color; $50-350, b&w; on publication.

THE REVIEW OF THE NEWS, 345 Concord Ave., Belmont MA 02178. (617)489-0600. Editor: Scott Stanley. "News magazine with a conservative and freemarket orientation for people interested in conservative oriented news in capsulated form." Weekly. Circ. 60,000. Free sample copy (mention *Artist's Market*).
Cartoons: Uses 3+ cartoons/issue, all by freelancers. Receives 1,000 submissions/week from freelancers. Interested in general humor for a conservative family audience. Format; single panel b&w line drawings with gag line. Sizes must be 2x2' or 4x2¼'. Prefers finished cartoons. SASE. Reports in 2 weeks. Will send tearsheets. Buys all rights. Pays $25; on acceptance.

RICHMOND LIFE STYLE MAGAZINE, 701 E. Franklin, Suite 1100, Richmond VA 23219. (804)644-1800. Art Director: John MacLellan. City magazine. Estab. 1979. Circ. 16,000. Monthly.
Illustrations: Buys 3 illustrations/issue. Query with samples. SASE. Pays $15-100, b&w; on publication.

RN MAGAZINE, 680 Kinderkamack Rd., Oradell NJ 07649. (201)282-3030. Readers are registered nurses. Monthly. Circ. 330,000. Sample copy $1.
Cartoons: "We are not currently buying cartoons but plan to in the future. They should deal with nursing and health care in a manner sympathetic to nurses." Prefers single panel b&w line drawings or washes with or without gag line. Send samples of style to Charlotte Isler, clinical editor. SASE. Reports in 2 weeks. Buys first North American serial rights. Pays $50 for b&w; on publication.
Illustrations: Uses 10 illustrations/issue; buys all from freelancers. Works on assignment only. Provide roughs to be kept on file for future assignments. Samples returned by SASE. Prefers b&w line drawings and washes for inside and color washes, oils, acrylics, etc. for cover. Arrange personal appointment to show portfolio to Hector Marrero, art director. Buys first North American serial rights, reprints and promotional rights. Pays $50-300 for inside b&w, $300-800 for color cover and $200-500 for inside color; on publication.

ROAD KING MAGAZINE, 233 E. Erie Ave., Chicago IL 60611. (312)664-2959. Editor: George Friend. Readers are over-the-road truckers. Quarterly. Circ. 200,000. Sample copy 50¢.
Cartoons: Uses 4 cartoons/issue; buys all from freelancers. Receives 1-2 submissions/week from freelancers. Interested in over-the-road trucking experiences. Prefers single panel b&w line drawings with gag line. Send finished cartoons. SASE. Reports in 2 months. Buys first North American serial rights. Pays $25-50 for b&w; on acceptance.

ROAD RIDER, Box 678, South Laguna CA 92677. Editor/Publisher: Roger Hull. Managing Editor: R.L. Carpenter. For cross-section of touring motorcyclists. Monthly; 8½x11; 96 pages. Offset. Estab. 1969. Circ. 35,000. Query with samples. SASE. Reports in 3 weeks. Buys all rights, but may reassign rights to artist after publication. Pays on publication. Free sample copy.
Cartoons: Contact Dave Peterson, editorial assistant. Buys 12-16/year on street-touring motorcycling; single panel. "Our audience is sophisticated, hence our cartoons must represent motorcycling insights which are virtually impossible to achieve without riding knowledge." Pays $15 minimum, line drawings.
Illustrations: Buys assigned themes only.
To Break In: Must be knowledgeable, active motorcyclists. "To date, only one cartoonist who was not also a rider has been successful here. It should be added that she now owns and rides a bike as a result of our relationship through the magazine."

ROSICRUCIAN DIGEST, Rosicrucian Park, San Jose CA 95191. Editor: Robin M. Thompson. Philosophical journal which features articles on mysticism, science and the arts. Original artwork returned after publication.
Illustrations: Buys "rarely more than 1" illustration/issue from freelancers. "We mostly use staff artists. Interested in philosophical themes. Works on assignment only. Samples returned by SASE. Reports back on future assignment possibilities. Provide resume and brochure to be kept on file for future assignments. Prefers resume and brochure. SASE. Reports in 2 weeks. Buys

various rights. "Payment is negotiated at time of purchase." Pays on acceptance.

THE ROTARIAN, 1600 Ridge Ave., Evanston IL 60201. Editor: Willmon L. White. For business and professional men. Monthly. Sample copy and artist's guidelines available.
Cartoons: Buys 4-5 cartoons/issue. Interested in general themes. "Avoid sex, national origin, politics." Query. Reports in 2-4 weeks. Buys all rights. Pays $50; on acceptance.
Illustrations: Buys assigned themes. All editorial illustrations are commissioned. Query. Reports in 2-4 weeks. Buys all rights. Pays on acceptance.
Other Needs: Also uses artists for cover design. Query. Reports in 2-4 weeks. Buys all rights. Pays on acceptance.

ROUGH NOTES, 1200 N. Meridian, Indianapolis IN 46204. Editorial Assistant: Linda J. Collins. Monthly. Pays on acceptance.
Cartoons: Buys 2-3 cartoons/issue on property and casualty insurance, some life insurance and general humor. No risque material. Submit art the first week of the month. Reports in 1 month. Buys all rights. Prefers 5x8 or 8x10 finished art. Pays $10, line drawings and halftones; on acceptance.

THE ROYAL NEIGHBOR, Royal Neighbors of America, 230 16th St., Rock Island IL 61201. Editor: Priscilla Ann Curtis. Fraternal, benefit insurance society publication. Mail art. Previously published work OK. Buys one-time rights. Sample copy available.

RUNESTONE, 1776 East Ave., Turlock CA 95380. (209)634-6500. Emphasizes religion for "readers who are primarily people who follow the pagan religion of the Vikings and related peoples, or who are interested in neo-Paganism generally." Quarterly. Circ. 200+. Free sample copy.
Illustration Needs: Is interested in submissions from freelancers. Illustrations should pertain to "the Vikings, deities of Northern heathendom, scenes from the sagas and Eddas, etc. Battle scenes are all right, but we don't want to get in a rut in this regard. Style: realistic to fantastic. Also usable—borders and decorative designs done in the old Scandinavian interlacing (similar to the better-known Celtic artwork."

RUNNER'S WORLD, World Publications, Box 366, Mt. View CA 94040. Contact: Lew Karchin. "Our readers are participants and we try to use material that shows insight into the sports we cover." Original artwork returned after publication.
Cartoons: Uses 3 cartoons/issue. Prefers finished cartoons. SASE. Reports in 1 week. Buys all rights on a work-for-hire basis. Pays $25-500; on publication.
Illustrations: Uses 3 illustrations/issue. Interested in all subjects. Works on assignment only. Samples returned by SASE. Reports back on future assignment possibilities. Provide brochures, flyer or tearsheet to be kept on file for future assignments. Prefers portfolio (finished art). SASE. Reports in 1 week. Buys all rights on a work-for-hire basis. Pays $25-500; on publication.
Other Needs: Cover design.

RUNNING TIMES, 12808 Occoquan, Woodbridge VA 22192. (703)550-7799. Emphasizes running and jogging. Readers are runners, joggers, and racers; people interested in fitness. Monthly. Sample copy $1.75.
Cartoons: Uses 1 cartoon/issue, all from freelancers. Receives 2 submissions/week from freelancers. Interested in running, jogging, and races. Format: single and multi-panel b&w line drawings preferably with gag line. Prefers finished cartoons. "Style has a lot to do with selection." SASE. Reports in 4 weeks. Buys all rights on a work-for-hire basis. Pays $10-40; on publication.
Illustrations: Uses 3-5 illustrations/issue, all from freelancers. Format: b&w line drawings and b&w washes for inside and color washes for cover. Reports back to artist on future assignment possibilities. Provide tearsheet to be kept on file for future assignments. Prefers finished art, portfolio or sample of style. SASE. Reports in 4 weeks. Buys all rights on a work-for-hire basis. Pays $15-50 for inside and $100 minimum for cover; on publication. Buys first North American serial rights.

SAGA, Gambi Publications, 333 Johnson Ave., Brooklyn NY 11206. (212)456-8600. Editor-in-Chief: David Elrich. Art Director: Michael Aldinger. Monthly. Circ. 300,000. Original artwork not returned after publication.
Cartoons: Buys 5 cartoons/year. Receives 25 submissions/week from freelancers. Interested in current events, environment, family life and politics; single panel. Prefers roughs. Reports in 2 weeks. Buys first North American serial rights. Pays $25-50; b&w; $35, 2-color; on acceptance.
Illustrations: Uses 1 illustration/issue, all from freelancers. Works on assignment only. Samples

returned by SASE. Reports back on future assignment possibilities. Provide calling card and tearsheet to be kept on file for future assignments. Prefers portfolio. SASE. Reports in 2 weeks. Buys first North American serial rights. Minimum payment: Cover: $250, color. Inside: $200, color; on acceptance.

SAIL, 38 Commercial Wharf, Boston MA 02110. (617)227-4700. Editor-in-Chief: Keith Taylor. Managing Editor: Patience Wales. Senior Designer: William Gotha. Monthly. Circ. 175,000. Original artwork returned after publication. Photocopies OK. Free sample copy.
Illustrations: Uses 3 illustrations/issue; rarely buys from freelancers. Assigned sailing themes. Works on assignment only. Samples by SASE. Reports back on future assignment possibilities. Provide resume or letter of inquiry to be kept on file for future assignments. Prefers resume and samples of style. SASE. Reports in 4 weeks. Buys first North American serial rights. Pays $100-250/page, b&w; $200-350/page, color. Prefers to pay on publication. Free sample copy.

SAILING, 125 E. Main St., Port Washington WI 53074. (414)284-2626. Editor: William F. Schanen III. Monthly. Circ. 45,000. Original artwork returned after publication. Previously published work OK. Sample copy $2.
Illustrations: Uses very few illustrations/year. Interested in action sailing only. Works on assignment only. Samples returned by SASE, if requested. Provide letter of inquiry to be kept on file for future assignments. Prefers resume, finished art, or samples of style. Reports in 2-3 weeks. Buys one-time rights. Pays $50 minimum, color cover.

THE ST. LOUIS JOURNALISM REVIEW, 928 N. McKnight, St. Louis MO 63132. (314)991-1699. Contact: Charles L. Klotler. Features critiques of St. Louis media-print and broadcasting. Bimonthly. Circ. 6,000.
Cartoons: "We have never bought a cartoon, but will consider." Subject should pertain to the news media; preferably local. Query. SASE. Report in 4-7 weeks. Pays on publication.
Illustrations: Query with samples. SASE. Reports in 4-6 weeks. Pays $10-15 (negotiable) for b&w and color illustrations pertaining to the news media (preferably local); on publication.

SALES AND MARKETING MANAGEMENT, 633 3rd Ave., New York NY 10017. (212)986-4800. Art Editor: Tom Loria. For sales managers. Biweekly. Circ. 45,000. Simultaneous submissions OK. Pays on acceptance.
Cartoons: Buys 36 cartoons/year. Interested in sales management and selling; single panel. Prefers art. SASE. Reports in 1 week. Buys all rights, but may reassign rights to artist after publication. Pays $30-45, b&w; on acceptance.
Illustrations: Buys 2 illustrations/issue. SASE. Reports in 1 week. Buys all rights, but may reassign rights to artist after publication. Pays $20-40, b&w spot line drawings; on acceptance.

SALESMAN'S OPPORTUNITY, 6 North Michigan Ave., Chicago IL 60602. Managing Editor: Jack Weissman. For independent salesmen, agents, jobbers, distributors, sales managers, franchise seekers, route salesmen, wagon jobbers, and people seeking an opportunity to make money full- or part-time. Monthly. Original artwork not returned after publication.
Cartoons: Uses 2-3 cartoons/issue; buys all from freelancers. Interested in themes dealing with humorous sales situations affecting salespeople. Prefers finished cartoons. SASE. Reports in 4 weeks. Buys all rights. Pays $5 on publication.

SALT WATER SPORTSMAN, 10 High St., Boston MA 02110. (617)426-4074. Editor-in-Chief/Art Director: Frank Woolner. For saltwater fishermen. Monthly. Circ. 113,000. Original artwork returned after publication. Free sample copy and artist's guidelines.
Illustrations: Uses 1 illustration/issue; buys from freelancer. Receives 1 submission/week from freelancers. Interested in all phases of salt water sport fishing—mood, how-to, etc. Works on assignment only. Samples returned by SASE. Reports back on future assignment possibilities. Provide letter of inquiry or brochure to be kept on file for future assignments. Prefer finished art or photos of art. SASE. Reports in 4 weeks. Buys first North American serial rights. Buys themes on saltwater fishing. Cover: Pays $200 minimum, color; Inside: Buys b&w line drawings and washes and color washes; on acceptance.

SAN GABRIEL VALLEY MAGAZINE, 2908 W. Valley Blvd., Alhambra CA 91803. (213)284-7607. Editor: Joseph Miller. Emphasizes local news and entertainment. Readers of our magazine are mainly upper-middle class people who enjoy dining out often. Our readers' interests are about places in the San Gabriel Valley and Southern California to go for sports, recreation and dining. We carry features on successful personalities of the valley and articles on success in all fields. Bimonthly. Circ. 3,500. Sample copy $1.

Cartoon Needs: Uses 2 cartoons/issue; buys 1/issue frm freelancers. Cartoons should pertain to taxes and politics. Format: b&w line drawings. Send finished cartoons. SASE. Reports in 2 weeks. Buys one-time rights. Pays $25 on acceptance.
Illustration Needs: Uses 4 illustrations/issue. Illustrations should pertain to California life and early California. Format: b&w line drawings for inside and cover. Provide brochure to be kept on file for future assignments. Send finished art and samples of style. SASE. Reports in 2 weeks. Pays $40 on acceptance for cover; $25 for inside.

SAN JOSE STUDIES, San Jose State University, San Jose CA 95192. (408)277-3460. Editor: Arlene N. Okerlund. Emphasizes the arts, humanities, business, science, social science; scholarly. Published 3 times/year. Circ. 500. Original artwork returned after publication. Sample copy $3.50.
Cartoons: Number of cartoons/issue varies. Interested in "anything that would appeal to the active intellect." Format: single panel b&w line drawings. Prefers roughs. SASE. Reports in 2 weeks. Buys first North American serial rights. Pays in 2 copies of publication, plus entry in $100 annual contest.
Illustrations: Number of illustrations/issue varies. Format: b&w line drawings. Prefers roughs. SASE. Reports in 2 weeks. Buys first North American serial rights. Pays in 2 copies of publication, plus entry in $100 annual contest.
Other Needs: Photographic essays.

SANDAL PRINTS, The Province of St. Joseph of the Capuchin Order, 1820 Mt. Elliott Ave., Detroit MI 48207. Editor-in-Chief: William M. La Forte. Art Director: Carol Wyatt. Concerns the work of the Capuchins in the U.S. and their missions. Bimonthly; 16 pages. Offset. Estab. 1950. Circ. 8,000. Query. SASE. Reports in 1 week. Not copyrighted. Pays on acceptance. Free sample copy.
Illustrations: Buys assigned themes. Pays $25/issue, b&w line drawings.

SATURDAY EVENING POST, Curtis Publishing Co., 1100 Waterway Blvd., Indianapolis IN 46206. (317)634-1100. Family magazine. Published 9 times/year. Circ. 600,000. Simultaneous submissions OK. Sample copy $1.
Cartoons: Cartoon Editor: Bruce Kinnaird. Buys 24 cartoons/issue; single and double panel with gag lines. SASE. Reports in 4 weeks. Buys all rights, "generally." Pays $125, b&w line drawings and washes; on publication.
Illustrations: Art Director: Don Moldroski. Uses 3 illustrations/issue; buys 80% from freelancers. Works on assignment only. Samples returned by SASE. Provide "slides or past-printed material." Original artwork returned after publication. Material on file will absolutely not be returned. SASE. Reports in 4 weeks. Buys all rights, "generally."

SATURDAY REVIEW, 1290 Avenue of the Americas, New York NY 10019. Magazine on international affairs, the arts, science, education and literary matters. Bimonthly. Original artwork returned after publication.
Cartoons: Editor: Clarence Brown. Uses 6-10 cartoons/issue. Interested in all subjects; single panel. Send finished cartoons. SASE. Reports in 2 weeks. Buys first rights. Pays $150, line drawings and halftones; on acceptance.
Illustrations: Contact: Bryan Canniff. Buys first rights. Inside: Pays $150-300, illustration; $75, spot drawing; on acceptance.

SAVER, Box 4444, Chicago IL 60680. Associate Editor: Chester Myszkowski. Consumer publication focusing on the savings and loan industry in Chicago. Quarterly. Circ. 250,000+. Original artwork returned after publication.
Illustrations: Uses 3-4 illustrations/issue; buys all from freelancers. Works on assignment only. Samples returned by SASE. Reports back on future assignment possibilities. Provide resume or samples to be kept on file for future assignments. Prefers portfolio. SASE. Reports in 6-8 weeks unless assigned, then as soon as possible. Buys first North American serial rights. Pays $250-500, b&w; $350-750, color; on acceptance.

SAVVY, 111 8th Ave., New York NY 10011. (212)255-0990. Art Director: Carol Devine Carson. For the executive woman; highly educated with high professional jobs and high incomes. Monthly. Estab. 1980.
Illustrations: Uses 20-25 illustrations/issue, all from freelancers. "Our art director contacts people he has worked with before and sees work in other publications. Subjects are assigned based on article topics." Format: b&w line drawings. Prefers samples of style. "Send us something we can keep on file. We will contact artist when we have a specific assignment." Buys first North

American serial rights. Pays $125 minimum for b&w cover; on publication.

SCANDINAVIAN REVIEW, 127 E. 73rd St., New York NY 10021. Editor-in-Chief: Nadia Christensen. For people of Scandinavian descent or interested in contemporary Scandinavia. Quarterly. Circ. 7,000. Photocopied and simultaneous submissions OK. Original artwork returned after publication.
Cartoons: Rarely uses cartoons. Should relate to contemporary Scandinavian life, history or literature. Negotiates payment for halftones.
Illustrations: Uses 50 illustrations/issue; buys 3/issue from freelancers. Cover: Color-separated art OK. Inside: B&w line drawings and color-separated art OK. Provide brochure to be kept on file for future assignments. Prefers finished artwork. SASE. Reports in several weeks. Negotiates rights purchased. Negotiates payment; pays on publication.
Other Needs: "Mood photographs or photographs about Scandinavia."

SCHOLASTIC EDITOR, 720 Washington Ave. SE, Suite 205, University of Minnesota, Minneapolis MN 55414. Art Director: Jon Kavanaugh. Editor: Tom Rolmicki. Contains "how-to articles for student staffs and faculty advisers of high school and college student publications (yearbooks, newspapers and magazines)." Free sample copy.
Illustrations: Buys b&w spot drawings, cover designs, and line or halftone illustrations on assigned themes. Artist receives credit line. Pays 5 contributor's copies. "Successful completion of cartoons or spot illustration may qualify the artist for a larger assignment and/or cover work. Students and developing artists are at an advantage here as the editorial content reflects student efforts; beginning or unknown artists have better opportunity to get published quickly and consistently." Query. Reports in 3 weeks. Buys all rights, but will reassign rights to artist after publication.

SCHOOL ARTS, 50 Portland St., Worcester MA 01608. (617)754-7201. Editor: David Baker. Emphasizes art education for art teachers and supervisors and university teacher training programs, museum education and craft teachers. Monthly except June and August. Circ. 28,000. Free sample copy.
Cartoons: Interested in art education and children involved in the making of art. Prefers single and multi panel b&w line drawings. Send roughs. SASE. Reports in 4 weeks. Buys first North American serial rights. Pays on publication.
Illustrations: Uses 20 illustrations/issue. Selection of freelancers based on editorial need and appropriateness of illustration. Interested in material dealing with art education. Prefers b&w line drawings for inside and cover and color washes for cover. Send roughs. SASE. Reports in 4 weeks. Buys first North American serial rights. "Payment would depend upon illustration."

SCHOOL SHOP, Box 8623, Ann Arbor MI 48107. Managing Editor: Howard Kahn. For industrial and technical education personnel. Published 10 times/year. Circ. 45,000. Original artwork not returned after publication. Free artist's guidelines.
Cartoons: Uses 1+ cartoons/issue; buys all from freelancers. Interested in vocational/industrial education; single, double or multipanel. Prefers finished cartoons. SASE. Reports in 6 weeks. Buys all rights. Pays $15, b&w line drawings; on publication.

SCIENCE, 801515 Massachusetts Ave., Washington DC 20005. (202)467-5200.
Cartoon Needs: Uses 2 cartoons/issue; all by freelancers. Receives 2 cartoons from freelancers/week. Buys cartoons with science theme. Format: single and multi-panel b&w line drawings with gag line. Send roughs and/or samples of style to Rodney Williams, art editor. SASE. Reports in 2 weeks. Pays on publication. Buys first North American serial rights.
Illustration Needs: Uses 15-20 illustrations/issue; all by freelancers. Receives illustrations from 4-5 freelancers/week. Selects freelancers from "listings, seeing work in other illustrations, and through reps." Illustrations should be "science related, contemporary themes. Illustrators "must have patience to research subject and offer several sketches." Format: b&w line drawings and color washes for inside. Query about sending portfolio and send samples of style. SASE. Reports in 2 weeks. Pays $400-500 for inside color. Buys all rights on a work-for-hire basis.
Other Needs: Spot art for departments and possibly promotion. On assignment.

SCIENCE AND CHILDREN, National Science Teachers Association, 1742 Connecticut Ave. NW, Washington DC 20009. (202)265-4150. Editor-in-Chief: Phyllis Marcuccio. For elementary school science teachers, educators, administrators and personnel. Published 8 times/year. Circ. 17,000. Original artwork not returned after publication. Free sample copy.
Cartoons: Uses 1 cartoon/issue; buys all from freelancers. Interested in science-technology and environment; multipanel with gag lines. Prefers finished cartoons. SASE. Reports in 2 weeks.

Buys all rights. Pays $10-20, b&w line drawings and washes; on publication.
Illustrations: Uses 10-15 illustrations/issue; buys all from freelancers. Interested in education and environment; light, stylized, realistic science illustrations (no stock illustrations). Works on assignment only. Samples returned by SASE. Reports back on future assignment possibilities. Provide resume, brochure, flyer, or photocopy of work to be kept on file for future assignments. Prefers portfolio with samples of style. SASE. Reports in 2 weeks. Buys all rights on a work-for-hire basis. Cover: Pays $50-150, b&w line drawings, washes and color; Inside: Pays $10-100, b&w line drawings and washes; on publication.

SCIENCE DIGEST, 224 W. 57th St., 7th Flr., New York NY 10019. (212)262-4161. Editor: Daniel E. Button. Managing Editor: Joan Lippert. Monthly. Circ. 156,000. For people with a scientific interest. Buys all rights. SASE. Simultaneous submissions and previously published work OK.
Cartoons: Buys 25 cartoons/year on science; single, double, and multi-panel with gag line. Send package of cartoons along with a letter. Reports in 4 weeks. Pays $25-35 minimum, b&w line drawings.

THE SCIENCE TEACHER, 1742 Connecticut Ave. NW, Washington DC 20009. Editor-in-Chief: Rosemary Amidei. Assistant Editor/Art Director: Molly B.C. Ruzicka. For junior and senior high school science teachers. Published 9 times/year. Circ. 21,000. Buys all rights. Sample copy $3.25.
Cartoons: Buys 3-5/year on classroom science education and the environment; single and double panel with gag line. Send finished art. SASE. Reports in 3-4 weeks. Pays $10 minimum, b&w line drawings; on publication.
Illustrations: Buys 2/issue on education, animals, environmental issues and science students. Send roughs. SASE. Reports in 3-4 weeks. Buys all rights. Cover: Pays $100 minimum, color and b&w; Inside: Pays $15 minimum, b&w line drawings and washes.

SEA, CBS Publishing, 1499 Monrovia, Newport Beach CA 92663. (714)646-4451. Editor-in-Chief: Harry Monahan. Art Director: Tony Dempsey. Concerns conventional boating. Monthly. Circ. 200,000. Original artwork not returned after publication. Free sample copy and artist's guidelines.
Illustrations: Uses 10-12 illustrations/issue; buys10-12/issue from freelancers, on boating. Works on assignment only. Samples returned by SASE. Reports back on future assignment possibilities. Provide samples of style, concept, medium, to be kept on file for future assignments. Send portfolio ("if long distance, send slides"). SASE. Reports in 1 week. Buys all rights on a work-for-hire basis. Inside: Pays $25 minimum, b&w line drawings and washes; $200-1,200, color; on acceptance.
Other Needs: "Photographs of power boats for covers."

SEARCH & RESCUE, Box 641, Lompoc CA 93438. Managing Editor: Renee Havens. For adventurers of all ages. Quarterly. Circ. 31,000. Previously published, photocopied and simultaneous submissions OK. Sample copy $3.50.
Cartoons: Buys 8 cartoons/year. Interested in current events, environment and safety outdoors themes; single panel. Prefers samples. SASE. Reports in 4 weeks. Buys one-time rights. Minimum payment: $5, b&w; $10, color; on publication.
Illustrations: Buys 16 illustrations/year. Interested in survival, search and rescue. SASE. Reports in 4 weeks. Buys one-time rights. Minimum payment: Cover: $20; Inside: $5; on publication.

SEATTLE BUSINESS MAGAZINE, Seattle Chamber of Commerce, 215 Columbia St., Seattle WA 98104. (206)447-7214. Editor-in-Chief: Ed Sullivan. Art Director: Kerry Leimer. For Seattle-area business people. Monthly. Circ. 6,300. Free sample copy.
Illustrations: Buys 12/year on assigned themes. Query with samples. SASE. Reports in 3 weeks. Buys all rights. Cover: Pays $75-100, b&w line drawings; on publication.

SECURITY MANAGEMENT, 2000 K St. NW, Suite 65, Washington DC 20006. (202)331-7887. Editor-in-Chief: Shari Mendelson. For security managers who protect assets, personnel and information of organizations. Monthly. Circ. 15,000. Previously published and simultaneous submissions "to other markets OK. Want exclusive in Security Market. Please state where else work has been submitted." Original artwork not returned after publication. Sample copy $3.
Cartoons: Uses 1-2 cartoons/issue, all from freelancers. Receives "dozens" submissions/week from freelancers. Interested in "management and protection–avoid emphasizing 'dumb-guard' aspect–our readers are fighting that image and don't appreciate it." Prefers roughs. SASE.

Reports as soon as possible. Buys all rights "to our field. May reassign for noncompetitive use." Pays $5 minimum, b&w halftones and washes.
Illustrations: Number illustrations/issue used "fluctuates considerably." Interested in "fairly conservative, generally b&w or 2 colors (art provided pre-separates) management illustrations or all kinds of topics." Works on assignment only. Samples returned by SASE. Reports back on future assignment possibilities. Provide resume, calling card, letter of inquiry, brochure, flyer tearsheet and references to be kept on file for future assignments. Prefers resume, roughs and samples of style. SASE. Reports as soon as possible. Buys all rights "to our field. May reassign for noncompetitive use." Minimum payment: Cover: Pays $50, b&w; $75, color. Inside: $20, b&w; $50, color. Pays $25, workshop brochures.

SEEK, 8121 Hamilton, Cincinnati OH 45231. (513)931-4050, Ext. 165. Emphasizes religion/faith. Readers are church people; young and middle adults. Quarterly in weekly issues. Circ. 60,000. Free sample copy.
Cartoons: Editor: R.W. Baynes. Uses 2-3 cartoons/quarter. Buys "church or Bible themes–contemporary situations of applied Christianity." Formats: single panel b&w line drawings with gag line. Prefers finished cartoons. SASE. Reports in 2 weeks. Buys first North American serial rights. Pays $10 on acceptance.
Illustrations: Art Director: Frank Sutton. Uses 1-2 illustrations/issue. Uses cover & inside b&w line drawings and washes. Works on assignment only. Arrange appointment to show portfolio. Reports in 1 week. Pays $50, cover or full page art–$20-30, inside pieces; on acceptance. Buys first North American serial rights.

SELF, 350 Madison Ave., New York NY 10017. (212)880-8830. Art Director: Ellen Bernie. Emphasizes self improvement of mental and physical well-being mostly for women, ages 25 and up. Monthly. Circ. 750,000. Estab. 1979. Free art guidelines.
Illustrations: Uses 6-8 illustrations/issue; buys all from freelancers. Works on assignment only. Provide samples and tear sheets to be kept on file for future assignments. Samples returned by SASE. Interested in artwork to accompany articles on psychological and physical self-improvement. Prefers b&w line drawings and color washes for inside. Arrange personal appointment to show portfolio. Reports in 1 month. Buys all rights. Pays $350/page; on publication.

SELF-DEFENSE WORLD, World Publications, Box 366, Mt. View CA 94040. Contact: Bob Anderson. "Our readers are participants and we try to use material that shows insight into the sports that we cover." Reports in 1 week. Buys reprint rights. Pays on publication.
Needs: Pays $10 for cover designs, spot drawings and cartoons.

SELLING SPORTING GOODS, 717 N. Michigan Ave., Chicago IL 60611. (312)944-0205. Emphasizes sporting goods for retailers in specialty shops and general merchandise stores. Geared toward bringing manufacturer and retailer together. Monthly. Free sample copy and art guidelines.
Cartoon Needs: Uses fewer than 1 cartoon/issue "but would like to use more"; all are supplied by freelancers. Cartoons should pertain to sporting goods retailers–window displays, security, salespeople, inventory, etc. Format: single panel with gag line. Send finished cartoons or samples of style to Bob O'Quin, editor. SASE. Reports in 1 week. Payment on acceptance varies. Buys first North American serial rights.
Illustration Needs: Uses 1-2 illustrations/issue; all supplied by freelancers. Interested in illustrations to accompany articles on retail sporting goods operations. Format: b&w line drawings for inside. Send finished art to Bob O'Quin, editor. SASE. Reports in 1 week. Payment on acceptance varies. Buys first North American serial rights.

SELLING TODAY, 444 N. Michigan Ave., Chicago IL 60611. Contact: Editor. For people in the automotive service industry. Bimonthly. Circ. 10,000.
Cartoons: Buys 2-3/issue on selling in the automotive aftermarket. Send roughs. SASE. Pays $10 for b&w, on publication.

THE SENSIBLE SOUND, 403 Darwin Dr., Snyder NY 14226. Art Director: John A. Horan. Quarterly. Circ. 4,450. SASE. Reports in 2 weeks. Previously published work OK. Original artwork returned after publication. Free sample copy and artist's guidelines.
Cartoons: Uses 1 cartoon/issue. Interested in high fidelity music; single panel with gag line. Prefers roughs, finished cartoons or resume. SASE. Buys all rights. Pays $3-10, gray opaques, b&w line drawings and washes; on acceptance.
Illustrations: Uses 1 illustration/issue on high fidelity music. Query with resume and samples. SASE. Buys all rights. Cover: Pays $6-20, 2-color, gray opaques, b&w line drawings and washes; on acceptance.

SERGEANTS, Air Force Sergeants Association, 4235 28th Ave., Marlow Heights MD 20031. Art Director: Karen E. Thuermer. For Air Force, Air National Guard, Air Force Reserves and retired enlisted personnel. Monthly. Circ. 130,000.
Cartoons: Uses 1-2 cartoons/issue; buys all from freelancers. Receives 2 submissions/week from freelancers. Interested in Air Force related themes, particularly toward the retired. Prefers resume and finished cartoons. SASE. Reports in 1 week. Pay negotiable; on publication.
Illustrations: Uses 5 illustrations/issue; buys 1/issue from freelancers. Receives 1 submission/ week from freelancers. Interested in realistic artwork depicting the Air Force—airplanes, people, places; artwork which is political, i.e., illustrations of Congressmen, Washington, D.C., presidential elections; artwork depicting aspects of health care and social security. Works on assignment only. Samples returned by SASE. Reports back on future assignment possibilities. Provide resume, calling card, or photocopies of artwork to be kept on file for future assignments. Prefers portfolio or samples of style. SASE. Reports in 2 weeks. Buys all rights on a work-for-hire basis. Pay negotiable; on publication.
Other Needs: Graphic design; unusual photography.

THE SERTOMAN, 1912 East Meyer Blvd., Kansas City MO 64132. (816)333-8300. Director, Public Relations: Patrick Burke. Readers are "members of Sertoma. Civic minded people. Motto: Service to Mankind. Business and professional men and their families. Bimonthly. Free sample copy; art guidelines.
Cartoons: Wants to use 2-3 cartoons/issue which should be "family oriented, nothing risque." Especially interested in those that would be similar in style/slant to those you might see in the *Saturday Evening Post*. Format: single panel. Send samples of style. Reports in 2 weeks. Pays $10 on acceptance. Buys one-time rights.
Illustrations: "I have no particular need for illustrations at this time. However, I would like to have the opportunity to have sources for illustrations, i.e., for the cover or to accompany a story that might better utilize line drawing as opposed to a photograph." Format: b&w line drawings for cover. Send resume and tearsheets and/or samples of style to Patrick Burke, public relations. SASE. Reports in 2 weeks. Pays $10-25 on acceptance for b&w cover and inside. Buys first North American serial rights.

SERVICE SHOP, 2708 W. Berry St., Ft. Worth TX 76109. (817)921-9062. Editor-in-Chief: W.S. (Bob) Harrison. For owners, technicians and managers of consumer electronics sales and service firms. Monthly. Circ. 9,000. Free sample copy.
Cartoons: Buys themes on electronics sales/service, association management, conventions and directors' meetings; single panel with gag line. Submit art. SASE. Reports in 2 weeks. Buys first rights. Pays $10 maximum, b&w line drawings; on acceptance.
Illustrations: Buys assigned themes. Submit art. SASE. Reports in 2 weeks. Buys first rights. Cover: Pays $30-60, b&w line drawings. Inside: Pays $10-15, b&w line drawings; on acceptance.

SESAME STREET, 1 Lincoln Plaza, New York NY 10023. (212)595-3456. Art Director: Paul Richer. Emphasizes education for preschool age children. Monthly. Circ. 600,000.
Illustration Needs: Uses 12-15 illustrations/issue; all supplied by freelancers. Receives 2 illustrations from freelancers/week. Selection based on file samples which the art director selects and photocopies from portfolios. Artists are assigned two-page spreads. Any child oriented theme, such as thc Muppets, is considered. Format: any color medium for inside. Drop off portfolio on Wednesday and pick up later the same day. Reports immediately. Pays $200/page after close of issue. Buys one-time rights.

73 MAGAZINE, Peterborough NH 03458. Publisher: Wayne Green. For amateur radio operators and experimenters. Sample copy $2.
Illustrations: Uses 15 illustrations/issue; buys 0/issue from freelancers on amateur radio or electronic themes. Works on assignment only. Does not return samples. Does not report back on possible future assignments. Provide resume and letter of inquiry to be kept on file for future assignments. Prefers resume, finished art and samples of art. SASE. Reports in 2 weeks. Buys all rights on a work-for-hire basis. Submit rough line drawings for assignment as oil, watercolor or pastel covers. Pays $5-20, spot art; $75/page, finished art; on acceptance.

SEXOLOGY, 173 Boston Post Rd., Milford CT 06460. Art Director: Pat Diorio. Concerns sexual matters, from erotica to medical problems. Monthly; 100 pages. Offset. Estab. 1972. Circ. 200,000. SASE. Query with resume and samples. Reports in 3 weeks. Simultaneous submissions OK. Buys first or all rights. Pays on publication. Sample copy 50¢; free artist's guidelines.
Cartoons: Buys 30/issue on current events, education, erotica, humor through youth, sports and business; single panel. Pays $25 minimum, b&w. Query with samples or mail roughs.

Illustrations: Buys 10/issue on environment, erotica, sports and assigned themes. Inside: Pays $25 minimum, b&w. Query with resume and samples.
Design: Uses artists for layout mock-ups and publication redesign. Negotiates pay. Query with resume and samples.

SEXOLOGY TODAY, 313 W. 53rd St., New York NY 10019. Contact: Jan Poretz.
Illustrations: "We look for well-drawn illustrations of all sexual subjects—not pornographic—in all styles with a contemporary look. Subjects include love-making, nudes, prostitution, homosexuality and sexual variations." Send published samples. Reports in 2 weeks. Buys all rights. Pays $50/page, b&w 5x8 roughs; on acceptance.

SHASTA FORUM, Box 1106, Mt. Shasta CA 96069. Readers are individuals interested in growth awareness. Quarterly. Circ. 15,000. Estab. 1979. Sample copy $1.
Illustration Needs: Uses 5-6 illustrations/issue; 2-4 supplied by freelancers. Receives 10-20 illustrations from freelancers/week. Selection based on "resumes and samples. Assignments only." Illustrations should pertain to "growth awareness and human potential movement." Format: b&w line drawings for inside and cover. Send resume and samples of style to Richard Pinkerton, photo and art editor. SASE. Reports in 4-6 weeks. Pays on publication $25-50 b&w cover; $5-20 b&w inside. Buys first North American serial rights.

THE SHOOTING INDUSTRY, 291 Camino de la Reina, San Diego CA 92108. (714)297-5352. Art Director: Syd Barker. For manufacturers, dealers and sales representatives of archery and shooting equipment. Monthly. Circ. 24,000.
Illustrations: Buys gun shop and gun show themes. Query with samples. SASE. Reports in 2 weeks. Pays $20-50, b&w; on publication.
PJS Publications Inc., Box 1790, Peoria IL 61656. Editor-in-Chief: Alex Bartimo. Art Director: Randy Cook. For hunters, reloaders and gun buffs. Monthly; 80-120 pages. Offset. Circ. 175,000. Query with samples. SASE. Reports in 2 weeks. Buys all rights. Pays on acceptance. Sample copy $2.
Cartoons: Buys 10/year on guns, equipment, accuracy, reloading and ammunition; single panel with gag line. Pays $10-15, b&w line drawings and washes.

SIERRA-THE SIERRA CLUB BULLETIN, 530 Bush St., San Francisco CA 94108. (415)981-8634. Production Coordinator: Jerry Klein. Emphasizes conservation and environmental politics for young adults on up who are well educated, activists, outdoor oriented and politically well informed with a dedication to conservation. Bimonthly. Circ. 180,000. SASE. Reports in 2 weeks.
Cartoons: "Have not run any cartoons in the last year," but may resume running them. Prefers finished cartoons. SASE. Reports in 2 weeks. Buys one-time rights. Pays $75, b&w; on publication.
Illustrations: Uses 1-2 illustrations/issue, all from freelancers. Interested in "pencil, pen/ink, etc.—should show people, usually in outdoor activities (hiking, skiing, etc.)." Works on assignment only. Provide calling card, tearsheet and copies of illustrations to be kept on file for future assignments. Prefers resume, portfolio and samples of style. SASE. Reports in 2 weeks. Buys one-time rights. Pays $75, spot; up to $250, spread; on publication.

SIGN, Monastery Place, Union City NJ 07087. (201)867-6400. Art Director: Michael Milo. For Catholics. Published 10 times/year. Circ. 150,000.
Cartoons: Contact Patrick McDonough. Uses 3-5 cartoons/issue, all from freelancers. Receives 108 submissions/week from freelancers. Interested in "need not be specifically religious; funny life situations." Prefers finished cartoons. SASE. Reports in 2 weeks. Buys all rights on a work-for-hire basis. Pays $50 minimum, b&w line drawings. Mail finished art.

SIGNATURE, 880 3rd Ave., New York NY 10022. (212)888-9450. Executive Editor: Peter Andrews. Art Director: Stan Braverman. For Diners Club members: urban, affluent, traveled businessmen. Monthly. Query with resume and arrange interview to show portfolio; prefers New York area artists. Reports in 2 weeks. Pays on acceptance. Sample copy available.
Needs: Pays $50-100, spot drawings; $400-700, full-color illustrations.

SIMMENTAL SCENE, Suite 120, 310 9th Ave. SW, Calgary, Alberta, Canada T2P 1K5. Editor-in-Chief: Sandy Sharp. Art Editor: Keith J. Wilson. For cattle producers and farmers; education limited in older readers; younger readers usually agricultural college graduates. Monthly; 60-72 pages. Offset. Estab. 1973. Circ. 6,000. Query with samples. SASE. Reports in 4 weeks. Not copyrighted. Pays on publication. Free sample copy.

Illustrations: Buys "rural and cattle scenes to accompany animal health and research articles." Cover: Pays $100-150, b&w; $150-250, color. Inside: Pays $10-100, b&w.

SKI, 380 Madison Ave., New York NY 10017. Editor: Richard Needham. For new and expert skiers. Published 7 times/year. Previously published work OK "if we're notified."
Cartoons: Mail art. SASE. Reports immediately. Buys first serial rights. Pays $50, b&w skiing themes; on publication.
Illustrations: Mail art. SASE. Reports immediately. Buys one-time rights. Pays $100-300, full-color art; on acceptance.

SKIER, 22 High St., Brattleboro VT 05301. Contact: Editor. For members of the Eastern Ski Association. Published 8 times/year. Reports in 2 weeks. Buys first rights. Pays on publication. Sample copy available.
Cartoons: Buys skiing themes. Avoid injuries as subject. Pays up to $15, 2x5 minimum.

SKIER'S WORLD, World Publications, Box 366, Mt. View CA 94040. Contact: Bob Anderson. For downhill and cross-country skiers.
Illustrations: Assigns themes. Reports in 2-4 weeks. Buys reprint rights. Pays $100-250 for illustrations; on publication.

SKIING, 1 Park Ave., New York NY 10016. Editor-in-Chief: Alfred Greenberg. Published 7 times/year; 200-250 pages. Letterpress. Circ. 475,000. Arrange interview. Reports in 1-4 weeks. Buys all rights. Pays on acceptance.
Cartoons: Contact Rick Fiala, editor. Buys 35/year on skiing; single panel. Halftones and washes OK.
Illustrations: Buys 3-4/issue on skiing. Pays $50-350, b&w line drawings and washes.

SKIN DIVER, 8490 Sunset Blvd., Los Angeles CA 90069. Art Director: Art Smith. Monthly. Circ. 175,000. Mail art. Reports in 1-4 weeks. Pays on publication.
Needs: Buys drawings, sketches, charts, maps, paintings and cartoons related to skin diving, equipment and personalities.

SKY AND TELESCOPE, 49 Bay State Rd., Cambridge MA 02138. Editor-in-Chief: L.J. Robinson. Art Director: J. Kelly Beatty. Concerns astronomy, building telescopes and space exploration for laymen and professionals. Monthly; 8½x11; 96-112 pages. Offset. Estab. 1941. Circ. 75,000. Buys one-time rights. Pays on publication. Free sample copy.
Cartoons: Buys 4/year on astronomy, telescopes and space exploration; single panel preferred. Pays $10-25, b&w line drawings, washes and gray opaques. Query with samples.
Illustrations: Buys assigned themes. Pays $75 minimum, color cover; $50 minimum, inside color. Query with previously published work.

SLO PITCH MAGAZINE, 15250 Ventura Blvd., Sherman Oaks CA 91403. (213)995-7973. Publisher/Art Director: Ron Rubenstein. Emphasizes slo pitch softball. Readers are men, women and youth slo pitch softball players, managers, fans, sponsors. Bimonthly. Circ. 50,000. Estab. 1978. Sample copy $1.50 plus postage.
Cartoons: Uses 2-3 cartoons/issue, all from freelancers. Interested in anything pertaining to slo pitch softball. Format: single panel b&w line drawings with gag line. Prefers finished cartoons. SASE. Reports in 2 weeks. Buys outright. Pays $35-50; on publication.
Illustrations: Uses 1 illustration/issue working mostly on consignment. Interested in illustrations that are slo pitch softball oriented or player likenesses and/or caricatures. Format: b&w line drawings and washes. Send samples of style and/or arrange personal appointment to show portfolio. SASE. Reports in 2 weeks, depending on timing or assignment. Buys all rights on a work-for-hire basis. Pays $15-25, spots; $50-100, feature illustrations; on publication.

THE SMALL BOAT JOURNAL, 21 Elm St., Camden ME 04843. (207)236-4342. Editor: James P. Brown. Readers are owners of boats under 30 feet, enthusiasts, some designers and builders. Monthly. Circ. 30,000. Estab. 1979. Free sample copy.
Cartoons: Uses 1 cartoon/issue; buys all from freelancers. Interested in small boat activities, maintenance, purchase and owners. "Would like to find a cartoonist familiar with boats." Prefers single panel with gag line. Send finished cartoons and/or samples of style. Reports in 2 weeks. Buys first North American serial rights. Pay negotiable; on acceptance.
Illustrations: Uses 20 illustrations/issue; buys 10/issue from freelancers. Selection based on experience or ability in marine illustration. Interested in action on the water, maintenance, repairs and boatbuilding. Prefers b&w line drawings. Send samples of style. SASE. Reports in 2 weeks.

Rights purchased vary. Pay negotiable; on acceptance.

THE SMALL POND MAGAZINE, Box 664, Stratford CT 06497. Emphasizes poetry and short prose. Readers are people who enjoy literature—college and college grads mostly. Published 3 times/year. Circ. 300. Sample copy $2; art guidelines for SASE.
Illustrations: Editor: Napoleon St. Cyr. Uses 1-3 illustrations/issue. Receives 6-10 illustrations/year. Uses "line drawings (inside and on cover) which generally relate to natural settings, but have used abstract work completely unrelated." Send finished art or photocopies. SASE. Reports in 2 weeks. Pays 2 copies of issue in which work appears on publication. Buys copyright in convention countries.
Other Needs: "Need cover art work, but inquire first, or send for sample copy."

SMALL WORLD, Volkswagen of America, Englewood Cliffs NJ 07632. (201)894-6314. Editor: Burton Unger. For Volkswagen owners. Quarterly. Circ. 400,000. Previously published and photocopied submissions OK. Free sample copy.
Cartoons: Buys 10/year on Volkswagens and their owners. Query with samples. SASE. Reports in 6 weeks. Buys all rights. Pays $15 minimum, halftones and washes; on acceptance.
Illustrations: Buys 120/year on assigned themes. Query with samples. SASE. Reports in 6 weeks. Buys all rights. Cover: Pays $250 minimum, color. Inside: Pays $15 minimum, b&w and color; on acceptance.

SNOWMOBILE NEWS,(formerly Chicagoland Snowmobiler), 222 W. Adams, Chicago IL 60606. (312)236-5550. Editor-in-Chief: Paul Hertzberg. Managing Editor: Al Robinson. Published 6 times/year, September-February. Circ. 70,000. Query with samples. SASE. Reports in 3 weeks. Simultaneous submissions OK. Buys all rights, but may reassign rights to artist after publication. Free sample copy.
Cartoons: Buys 1-2/issue, all from freelancers. Receives 5 submissions/week from freelancers. Interested in snowmobiling. Samples returned with SASE. Provide tearsheets or samples to be kept on file for future assignments. Pays $10 minimum, line drawings and halftones.

SOARING, Soaring Society of America, Box 6607, Los Angeles CA 90066. Editor: Doug Lamont. "We are a low-budget magazine and depend on society members for art, but I'd like to have the names of some artists to whom I could send a manuscript and description of what we need and figure on getting the work back in time for the next month's issue." Monthly. Circ. 18,000. Send published samples. Reports immediately. Buys one-time rights. Pays on publication. Original artwork returned after publication, if requested. Sample copy $1.10.
Cartoons: Uses less than 1 cartoon/issue. Prefers finished cartoons. Reports in 1 month. Buys one-time rights. Pays on publication.
Illustrations: Uses less than 1 illustration/issue. Interested in cutaway 3-dimension technical illustrations and illustrations for realism in flight stories. Provide brochure and tearsheet to be kept on file for future assignments. Prefers samples of style. SASE. Reports in 1 week. Buys one-time rights. Cover: Pays $40. Inside: Negotiates payment for line drawings, pen and ink, and washes.
Needs: "Readership is nuts-and-bolts oriented. We are leery of nonrepresentational art, though not adamant. We receive many flight stories which call for illustration. Occasional articles offer opportunity for quick sketch or cartoon-type treatment. Technical cutaway drawing for display of aircraft very desirable."

SOCCER AMERICA, Box 23704, Oakland CA 94623. Publisher: Clay Berling. Editor-in-Chief: Lynn Berling. For soccer fans of all ages including players, coaches, managers and referees. Weekly. Circ. 5,000. Free sample copy.
Cartoons: Uses 1-2 cartoons/issue; buys cartoons rarely from freelancers. Receives 2-3 submissions/week from freelancers, on soccer. Prefers finished cartoons and resume. Reports in 4 weeks. Buys first North American serial rights. Pays $5-15, b&w halftones and washes; on publication.
Illustrations: Uses 1 illustration/issue; buys occasionally from freelancers. Receives 1-2 submissions/week from freelancers. Needs art for issues on: pro-season preview, April; camp directories, March; gifts and equipment, October; and the holidays, December. Provide resume, calling card, letter of inquiry and tearsheet to be kept on file for future assignments. Prefers finished art. SASE. Reports in 4 weeks. Buys first North American serial rights. Cover: Pays $15 minimum, b&w. Inside: Pays $5 minimum, b&w; on publication.

SOCCER CORNER, 2150 N. Lincoln St. Burbank CA 91504. (213)849-2350. Art Director: Larry Brown. For all levels of soccer players and fans from professional, collegiate and olympic to youth

soccer organizations. Monthly. Circ. 60,000. Photocopies OK. Original artwork returned after publication. Free sample copy.
Cartoons: Uses 1-2 cartoons/issue; buys 1-2/issue from freelancers. Receives 2-3 submissions/ week from freelancers. Interested in soccer humor; double panel. Prefers roughs or finished cartoons. Reports in 3 weeks. Buys first North American serial rights. Pays $20, b&w; on publication.
Illustrations: Uses less than 1 illustration/issue; buys less than 1/issue from freelancers. Subjects include aspects of soccer; by assignment. Works on assignment only. Samples returned by SASE. Reports back on future assignment possiblities. Provide resume, calling card, brochure, flyer and/or tearsheet to be kept on file for future assignments. Prefers finished art, portfolio, roughs or samples of style. SASE. Reports in 3 weeks. Buys first North American serial rights. Pays $25 min., b&w and color; on publication.

SOCCER WORLD, World Publications, Box 366, Mt. View CA 94040. Contact: Kevin Shafer. "Our readers are participants and we try to use material that shows insight into the sports that we cover." Reports in 1 week. Buys reprint rights. Pays on publication.
Needs: Pays $10 for cover designs, spot drawings and cartoons.

SOLDIERS, Department of the Army, Cameron Station, Alexandria VA 22314. (202)274-6671. Editor-in-Chief: Lt. Col. Gordon Taylor Bratz. Art Director: Tony Zidek. For soldiers and Army civil service personnel. Monthly. Circ. 207,000. Previously published and simultaneous submissions OK. Pays on acceptance. Free sample copy and artist's guidelines.
Cartoons: Buys approximately 42 cartoons/year on the military; single panel with gag line. Submit art. SASE. Reports in 2 weeks. Buys all rights. Pays $15 minimum, b&w line drawings; on acceptance.

SOONER LPG TIMES, 2910 N. Walnut, Suite 114-A, Oklahoma City OK 73105. (405)525-9386. Contact: John E. Orr. For dealers and suppliers of LP-gas and their employees. Monthly. Circ. 2,000.
Cartoons: Buys 1/issue on industry-related subjects and safety, but will consider anything. Mail roughs. SASE. Reports in 4 weeks. Pays $5, b&w.

SORCERER'S APPRENTICE, Flying Buffalo Inc., Box 1467, Scottsdale AZ 85252. Emphasizes science fiction and fantasy wargaming for interested readers, especially those who play Tunnels and Trolls. Quarterly. Free sample copy. Mention *Artist's Market*.
Cartoon Needs: Uses about 1 cartoon/issue; all supplied by freelancers. Interested in submissions from freelancers. Cartoons should pertain to science fiction, fantasy, and fantasy gaming. Format: single or multi panel b&w line drawings with or without gag line. Send finished cartoons or samples of style to Elizabeth Danforth, production editor. SASE. Reports in 4-6 weeks. Pays on publication $7-25 b&w cartoon. Buys one-time rights.
Illustration Needs: Uses about 20 illustrations/issue; 15 supplied by freelancers. Selection based partially on ability to work on short deadline. Likes to use variety of illustrators and styles. Most work done on assignment. Format: b&w line drawings for inside; full color for covers. Arrange personal appointment to show portfolio or send samples of style and tear sheets to Elizabeth Danforth, production editor. SASE. Reports in 2-4 weeks. Pays on publication $5-15 inside b&w; $35-50 cover color; $35 layout. Buys one-time rights plus advertising rights.
Other Needs: Also interested in one-time projects such as calendars, solitaire dungeon adventures connected with Tunnels and Trolls and game booklets.

THE SOUTH, Box 2350, Tampa FL 33601. (813)247-5411. Art Director: Jean Thomas. Emphasizes southern business community and climate. Estab. 1974. Circ. 50,000. Monthly. Pays on publication.
Cartoons: Buys 1-2/issue on politics, business, finance and assigned themes. Pays $40-50, b&w. Query.
Illustrations: Buys 2-4/issue on assigned themes. Pays $50 minimum, b&w; $250 maximum, color. Query with samples.

SOUTH CAROLINA WILDLIFE, Box 167, Columbia SC 29202. Editor: John Davis. Art Director: Kay Howie. Deals with wildlife, outdoor recreation, natural history and environmental concerns. Bimonthly. Previously published work OK. Copyrighted. Sample copy available.
Illustrations: Uses 10-20 illustrations/issue; buys 6-10/issue from freelancers. Interested in wildlife art; all media; b&w line drawings, washes, full-color illustrations. "They must be technically accurate." Provide resume, brochure, or flyer to be kept on file for future assignments. Prefers finished art, portfolio, samples of style, slides, or transparencies. SASE. Reports in 2-8 weeks.

Rights negotiable. Pays $25, ¼-page b&w illustration; $200, 17x11 full spread 4-color illustration; on acceptance.
Other Needs: B&w photography, 4-color transparencies.

SOUTHEASTERN DAIRY REVIEW, Box 7775, Orlando FL 32854. (305)647-8899. Editor: Melissa Reeves. Concerns Florida dairy industry. Estab. 1960. Circ. 1,700. Monthly; 8½x11; 4 pages. Offset. SASE. Simultaneous submissions and previously published work OK. Not copyrighted. Pays on publication. Free sample copy.

SOUTHERN ANGLER'S GUIDE, Box 2188, Hot Springs AR 71901. (501)623-8437. Editor: Don J. Fuelsch. Covers hunting and fishing in southern states. Estab. 1961. Circ. 125,000. Annual. SASE. Reports in 4 weeks. Pays on acceptance.
Cartoons: Buys 25/issue on fishing and hunting. Mail roughs or finished art.
Illustrations: Buys 300/issue on fish and game. Prefers pen and inks or scratchboards. Query with samples.

SOUTHERN BOATING, 615 SW 2nd Ave., Miami FL 33130. Editor-in-Chief: Skip Allen. Art Director: June Finch. Concerns boating, sport fishing, navigation and other marine themes. Estab. 1972. Circ. 18,000. Monthly; 8½x11. Offset. SASE. Reports in 3 weeks. Previously published work OK. Buys various rights. Pays on publication. Free sample copy and artist's guidelines.
Cartoons: Buys 6/year on boating and sport fishing; single, double or multipanel. Pays $10-25, b&w or color. Send finished work with price.
Illustrations: Buys 6/year on boating and sport fishing. Cover: Pays $25-50, color. Inside: Pays $25-50, color; $15-25, b&w line drawings and washes. Query with samples.

SOUTHERN HUNTER'S GUIDE, Box 2188, Hot Springs AR 71901. (501)623-8437. Editor: Don J. Fuelsch. Complete coverage of the southern scene on hunting and fishing. Estab. 1961. Circ. 125,000. Annual. SASE. Reports in 4 weeks. Pays on acceptance.
Cartoons: Buys 25/issue on fishing and hunting. Mail roughs or finished art.
Illustrations: Buys 300/issue on wildlife (fish and game). Prefers pen and inks or scratchboards. Query with samples.

SOUTHERN MOTOR CARGO, Box 4169, Memphis TN 38104. Contact: Mike Pennington. For trucking management and maintenance personnel of private, contract and for-hire carriers in 16 southern states (Alabama, Arkansas, Delaware, Florida, Georgia, Kentucky, Louisiana, Maryland, Mississippi, North Carolina, Oklahoma, South Carolina, Tennessee, Texas, Virginia and West Virginia) and the District of Columbia. Monthly. Circ. 50,000.
Cartoons: Buys 1-2 cartoons/issue on truck management situations. "Stay away from stereotyped 'truckin' on' theme." Mail roughs. Pays $10, b&w; on publication. SASE. Reports in 6 weeks.

SOUTHERN PRINTER, 75 3rd St. NW, Atlanta GA 30308. Editor and Assistant General Manager: Roy Conradi. For commercial printing plant management in 14 Southern states. Monthly. Circ. 6,000. Previously published work OK. Sample copy $1.25.
Cartoons: Buys 6 cartoons/year on printing industry; single panel with gag line. Mail finished art. SASE. Reports in 4 weeks. Pays $5-10, b&w line drawings; on publication.
Illustrations: Buys 6 cartoons/year on printing industry. Query with previously published work. SASE. Reports in 4 weeks. Cover and inside: Pays $10 minimum, color and b&w; on publication.
Other Needs: 4-color cover design. Query with previously published work. Pays $50 minimum; on publication.

SOUTHWEST HOMEFURNISHING NEWS, 4313 N. Central Expressway, Dallas TX 75206. (214)526-7757. Art Director: Julia McNair. For retail home furnishing business people, home furnishings manufacturers and others in related fields. Quarterly. Circ. 12,000. Reports in 2 weeks.
Cartoons: Buys 4-6/issue on any subject related to homes, furniture and/or stores of same; homefurnishings in general. Query. Negotiates pay; pays on publication.

SOUTHWEST SPORTS, (formerly *New Mexico Sports*), Albuquerque NM 87106. Editorial Coordinator: Richard H. Rogers. For those interested in team or individual sports and outdoor activities.
Needs: Buys illustrations and cartoons. Pays $8-20, fairly simple work; $21-100, more elaborate work.

SOUTHWESTERN MUSICIAN, Box 9908, Houston TX 77013. Editor: J.F. Lenzo. For music educators in Texas. Monthly, August-May. Mail art. Reports in 30 days. Buys all rights. Pays on acceptance.
Cartoons: Buys music themes. Pays $5-10 for finished b&w art with captions.
Illustrations: Cover: Pays $50, b&w and color. Inside: Pays $5, b&w and color.

SOYBEAN DIGEST, Box 27300, 777 Craig Rd., St. Louis MO 63141. (314)432-1600. Editor: Grant Mangold. Concerns agricultural and ag-business, specifically soybean production and marketing. Audience: high-acreage soybean growers. Monthly. Circ. 110,000. Previously published work OK. Original artwork returned after publication. Sample copy 50¢.
Cartoons and Illustrations: Buys maximum 12 cartoons/year and 6 illustrations/year on agriculture, soybean production and marketing. Submit art or query. SASE. Reports in 2-3 weeks. Buys all rights, but may reassign rights to artist after publication. Inside: Pays $5 minimum, b&w; $15 minimum, color; on acceptance.

SPARKS, Society of Wireless Pioneers, Box 530, Santa Rosa CA 95402. Editor: William A. Breniman. For radio-telegraph men who handle(d) communications with ships and at shore stations; included are military, commercial, aeronautical and governmental communications personnel. "Since many have earned their living aboard ships as 'Sparks,' we like to bring a nautical flavor to our pages."
Needs: Buys reprint rights. Pays $5, drawings; rates open, cartoons; pays on acceptance.

SPECIALTY SALESMAN AND BUSINESS OPPORTUNITIES, (formerly *Specialty Salesman and Business Opportunities*), 6285 Barfield Rd., Atlanta GA 30328. (404)256-9800. Editor: Leslie King. "For independent businessmen and women who sell door-to-door by the party-plan method, through direct mail or phone solicitation; products or services are bought directly from manufacturers and sold by our readers." Monthly. Circ. 500,000. Free sample copy and artist's guidelines.
Cartoons: Uses 2 cartoons/issue, all from freelancers. Receives 5 submissions/week from freelancers. Interested in current events, direct selling, salespeople not employed by retailers and self-employed entrepreneurs without employes; single panel. "Cartoons should illustrate the typical door-to-door or office-to-office salesperson, women who sell party-plan, or phone solicitors." SASE. Reports in 3-4 weeks. Buys first rights. Pays $5 minimum, b&w line drawings; on publication.
Illustrations: Provide samples, calling card, complete mailing information and social security number to be kept on file for future assignments. SASE. Reports in 3-4 weeks. Buys first rights.

SPERRY NEW HOLLAND NEWS, Sperry New Holland Division, Sperry Corp., New Holland PA 17557. Editor: Michael A. Balas. For dairy and beef farmers and others interested in grassland farming. Published 8 times/year.
Cartoons: "Situations must not be cynical or touch on farmer's problems or differences from his city cousin." Pen and ink. Query. Reports in 2 weeks. Pays on publication.

"SPIRIT OF 375", Joseph E. Seagram & Sons, Inc., 800 3rd Ave., New York NY 10022. Editor: Irving Babbitt. For employees. Quarterly. Not copyrighted. Pays on acceptance. Sample copy available.
Cartoons: Buys 4/year on office themes. Pays $10.

SPORTING GOODS TRADE, 380 Wellington St. W, Toronto, Canada M5V 1E3. (416)366-4608. Emphasizes sporting goods for retailers, wholesalers and manufacturers. Bi-monthly. Circ. 9,500. Sample copy $2.
Cartoons: Uses 1 cartoon/issue; buys all from freelancers. Interested in themes relating to retailing sporting goods. Prefers single panel b&w line drawings with gag line. Send samples of style. SASE. Reports in 2 weeks. Buys first North American serial rights. Pays $30 for b&w; on publication.
Illustrations: Uses illustrations only for b&w and color cover art. Send samples of style to Graham Campbell, publisher. SASE. Reports in 2 weeks. Buys all rights. Pays $200 maximum/cover; on publication.

SPORTS CAR NEWS, 15 Mardin Ln., New York NY 10038. (212)732-4445. Emphasizes amateur motor sports for owners and others interested in sports cars. Monthly. Circ. 5,000. Free sample copy.
Cartoon Needs: Uses 1 cartoon/issue which is from freelancer. Receives 1 cartoon from freelancers/week. Cartoons should pertain to "racing, rallying, safety, and current issues of the

car industry." Format: single and multi panel b&w line drawings with gag line. Send finished cartoons and/or samples of style to Cathy Jeffers, editor. SASE. Reports in 2 weeks. Pays $5-15 on publication. Buys first North American serial rights.

Illustration Needs: Uses 1 illustration/issue which is by freelancer. Receives 1 illustration from freelancers/week. Illustrators are chosen "by submission and samples of work." Illustrations should pertain to racers, rallies, people, pit work, fancy cars, custom interiors, vintage cars, how-to mechanical, and race driving tips. Format: b&w line drawings for inside and cover. Send resume and samples of style or arrange personal appointment to show portfolio. SASE. Reports in 2 weeks. Pays $20 for cover and $5-15 for inside on publication. Buys first North American serial rights.

Other Needs: "Send samples of design layout and advertising."

SPOTLIGHT, Box 45497, Los Angeles CA 90045. Publisher: Richard Deal. For competitors, parents, coaches, administrators and others involved in swimming, diving and water polo. Monthly. Submit cartoons; query on illustrations. Reports in 30 days. Buys all rights. Pays on publication. Sample copy available.

Cartoons: Buys 12/year on diet, body conditioning, medicine as it applies to competitive swimming, nutrition, stroke and diving techniques, and developments in pool purification. Pays $6 maximum.

SPOTLIGHT, 8060 Melrose Ave., Los Angeles CA 90046. Editor-in-Chief: Sean Martin. For "swingers and would-be swingers." Bimonthly. Circ. 150,000. Previously published work OK. Sample copy $1; free artist's guidelines.

Cartoons: Buys 6-7 cartoons/issue. Interested in erotica with emphasis on couples and groups; single, double or multipanel with gag line. SASE. Reports in 2 weeks. Buys first North American or all rights. Prefers samples. Pays $15-35, b&w washes; on publication.

THE STAMP WHOLESALER, Box 706, Albany OR 97321. Publisher: Jim Magruder. Pays on acceptance. Original artwork not returned after publication. Sample copy available.

Cartoons: Uses 2 cartoons/issue; buys 2/issue from freelancers. Receives 2 submissions/week from freelancers, on stamp dealers. Prefers finished cartoons. SASE. Reports in 6 weeks. Buys all rights on a work-for-hire basis; buys all rights on speculative submissions. Pays $10 minimum; on acceptance.

Illustrations: Uses 7 illustrations/issue; buys 0/issue from freelancers. Receives 0 submissions/week from freelancers. Interested in business, stamp dealers, mail order for the inside. All subjects for the cover. Returns samples by SASE and reports back on future assignment possibilities. Provide letter of inquiry, brochure or tearsheet to be kept on file for future assignments. Prefers finished art, portfolio or samples of style. SASE. Reports in 4 weeks. Buys all rights on a work-for-hire basis; buys all rights on speculative submissions. Pays $10 minimum; on acceptance.

Special Needs: "Cover art for books. We plan to publish about 2-4 books each year. Never contacted by illustrators—would like to hear from some."

STARWIND, Box 3346, Columbus OH 43210. Editor: Laura Reutter. Emphasizes science fiction and fantasy. Semiannual. Circ. 1,500. Sample copy $2; art guidelines for SASE.

Cartoons: Uses 2 cartoons/issue, buys both from freelancers. Receives 1 submission/week from freelancer. Interested in science fiction and fantasy, "but we're less than enthusiastic about swords and sorcery." Format: single and multipanel b&w line drawings. Prefers finished cartoons or resume. SASE. Reports in 2 weeks. Buys first North American serial rights. Pays $15 on publication.

Illustrations: Uses 21 illustrations/issue; buys 2-5/issue from freelancers. Receives 1 submission/week from freelancers. "We judge (illustrators) work as they send it to us and then hire them to illustrate a story." Starwind is primarily a magaazine which publishes the work of artists who are working on getting started in the field. We have 5 staff artists who do a fair amount of the work needed each issue; but, we are committed to providing opening positions for talented artists who can fulfill our needs. We honestly prefer to be the first or second publisher of any freelancer. Works on assignment only. Samples returned by SASE. Reports back on future assignment possibilities. Provide resume or brochure to be kept on file for future assignments. Prefers resume and samples of style. Works with science fiction and fantasy subjects. Illustrates stories rather extensively (normally an 8x11" and an interior illustration. Format: b&w line drawings for inside and covers. SASE. Reports in 2 weeks. Buys first North American serial rights.Pays for cover; on publication.

THE STATE, Box 2169, Raleigh NC 27602. Editor: W.B. Wright. Regional publication about North Carolina. Subjects include travel, history, nostalgia and humor. Estab. 1933. Circ. 22,000.

Monthly. SASE. Reports in 4 weeks. Pay on acceptance.
Cartoons: Varied subjects. Mail roughs.
Illustrations: Assigns themes. Pays $20, b&w. Query with samples.

STEERING WHEEL, Government Employees Insurance Co. (GEICO), GEICO Plaza, 5260 Western Ave., Chevy Chase MD 20076. (301)986-2262. Art Director: Jim Van Meer. For employees. Quarterly. Circ. 8,000. Simultaneous submissions and previously published work OK. Free sample copy and artist's guidelines.
Illustrations: Buys 2-3 illustrations/year from freelancers. Interested in insurance and assigned themes. Works on assignment only. Provide resume, copies of samples and rates to be kept on file for future assignments. Prefers phone call to arrange appointment. Reports in 6-8 weeks. Buys all rights. Cover and inside: Pays $10-25, b&w; $80-200, b&w; on acceptance.
Design: Uses artists for cover and publication design. Pays $8-10/hour, layout and paste-up.

STEREO REVIEW, 1 Park Ave., New York NY 10016. (212)725-3500. Emphasizes stereo equipment, classical and popular music for music enthusiasts. Monthly. Circ. 500,000.
Illustration Needs: Uses about 6 illustrations/issue; 3 supplied by freelancers. Illustrators "must be local and fast. Our lead time is very short. We are always looking for new talent." Especially interested in artwork to accompany articles on classical and popular music celebrities. Format: b&w line drawings and color washes for inside. Send samples of style and photocopies to Wm. Anderson, editor. Reports in 1 week or when assignment is needed. Payment on acceptance is negotiated. Buys one-time rights plus promotional use.

STITCH 'N SEW, Box 1952, Brooksville FL 33512. Editor-in-Chief: Barbara Hall Pedersen. Managing Editor: Edward Kutlowski. For women who like to sew. Circ. 158,900. Original artwork returned after publication, if requested. SASE. Reports in 2 weeks. Buys all rights. Pays on acceptance. Sample copy, 9x12 SASE with 66⅜ postage.
Cartoons: Uses 1 cartoon/issue. Interested in needle work; single panel. Prefers finished cartoons. SASE. Reports in 2 weeks if not accepted. "May hold several months" if accepted. Buys all rights on a work-for-hire basis. Pays $15-20, line drawings; on acceptance.
Illustrations: Editor: Carol Pedersen. Illustrations are rarely used. Interested n b&w line drawings. Works on assignment only. No samples returned. Does not report back on future assignment possibilities. Provide resume to be kept on file for future assignments. Prefers samples of style. SASE. Reports in 2 weeks. Buys all rights on a work-for-hire basis. Inside: Pays $5 minimum, b&w line drawings; on acceptance.

STOCK CAR RACING MAGAZINE, 67 Peach Orchard, Burlington MA 01803. (617)272-7635. Editor: Dick Berggren. Readers are from the racing community. Monthly. Circ. 120,000. Sample copy $2.
Cartoon Needs: Uses 4 cartoons/issue; all from freelancers. Receives 4 cartoons from freelancers/week. Interested in cartoons pertainng to racing. Format: single or multi panel b&w line drawings with gag line. Prefers samples of style or finished cartoons. SASE. Reports in 2 weeks. Buys all rights. Pays $15-20 on publication.
Illustration Needs: Number of illustrations/issues varies. Freelancers are used "on assignment—we are looking for caricature artists." Format: b&w line drawings. Prefers rough or finished art. SASE. Reports in 2 weeks. Buys all rights. Payment varies considerably; pays on publication.

STONE COUNTRY, 20 Lorraine Rd., Madison NJ 07940. Editor-in-Chief: Judith Neeld. Art Editor: Pat McCormick. For serious poets and poetry supporters. Published 3 times/year. Circ. 700. Previously published work OK. Sample copy $1.75.
Illustrations: Uses 3 covers/year and 5-6 illustrations/issue; buys 3-4 issues from freelancers. Must be camera-ready. Cover design can be 8½x5½ or wrap-around 8½x11; inside drawings no larger than 3x4. Interested in b&w drawings only, any style or theme; size is important; not washes or pencil shading; to achieve shading, use fine b&w lines. "We are interested in abstract as well as representational work. Art students welcome." Provide letter of inquiry, brochure, flyer or tearsheet to be kept on file for future assignments. Prefers finished art. SASE. Reports in 6-8 weeks. Buys first North American serial rights. Cover: Pays $10, b&w; on publication. Inside: Pays 1 contributor's copy, b&w.

STONE IN AMERICA, 6902 N. High St., Worthington OH 43085. (614)885-2713. Managing Editor: Catherine White. Journal of the American Monument Association; deals with production, marketing and sales of memorial stones. Estab. 1889. Circ. 2,600. Monthly. Reports in 4 weeks. Simultaneous submissions and previously published work OK. Buys first rights. Pays on publication. Free sample copy and artist's guidelines.

Cartoons: Buys 10/year on family life and memorial stone manufacturing; single panel with gag line. Pays $5-20, b&w line drawings. Mail roughs.

STORE CHAT, Strawbridge & Clothier, 801 Market St., Philadelphia PA 19105. For department store employees. Bimonthly. Circ. 10,000. Simultaneous submissions and previously published work OK. Free sample copy.
Cartoons: Uses 2-3 cartoons/issue; buys 2-3/month from freelancers. Interested in department stores, customers, employees, bowling, golf, skiing, softball, travel, safety, holidays, and other business topics; single panel with gag line. Prefers finished cartoons. SASE. Reports in 2 weeks. Pays $7.50-10, b&w line drawings; on acceptance.
Tips: "We want professional looking renderings with a message, whether serious or humorous, gags, gentle jabs. No ugly humor, sarcasm, etc."

STREET CRIES, 33 Edi Ave., Plainview NY 11803. Editors: Robbie Woliver and Pat Velazquez. Literary and art magazine. Published 2-3 times/year. Circ. 5,000. Query. Previously published work OK. Pays on publication.
Needs: Buys b&w drawings and cover designs usually passed over by more traditional magazines.

THE SUGAR BEET, The Amalgamated Sugar Co., Box 1520, Ogden UT 84402. (801)399-3431. Contact: Dale Hicks. For beet growers in Idaho, Oregon and Utah. "Also goes to research personnel, agricultural companies, local bankers, equipment dealers, etc. and other beet sugar companies." Estab. 1937. Circ. 4,500. Published quarterly.
Cartoons: Buys agricultural subjects. Negotiates pay. Query.

THE SUGAR PRODUCER, Harris Publishing Inc., Box 98, Idaho Falls ID 83401. Editor-in-Chief: Darryl Harris. Art Director: Brian Crane. For sugarbeet growers. Published 7 times/year; 8x11; 32 pages. Offset. Estab. 1973. Circ. 20,000. Mail art. SASE. Reports in 1 week. Photocopied and simultaneous submissions OK. Buys one-time rights. Pays on publication. Free sample copy.
Cartoons: Buys 1-2/issue on the sugarbeet industry and agriculture in general; single panel with gag line. Pays $15 maximum, b&w line drawings.

SUNDAY DIGEST, 850 N. Grove Ave., Elgin IL 60120. (312)741-2400. Emphasizes Christian faith for protestant readers in U.S., Canada, and several foreign countries. Quarterly; in weekly sections. Circ. 100,000. Free sample copy and art guidelines.
Illustration Needs: Uses 4 illustrations/issue; all by freelancers. "We keep samples of artists work on file and make assignments accordingly. All illustrations must relate directly to editorial content. I buy both b&w line art as well as full-color art and look for originality of style and quality of execution. Price is determined according to page size. All work on assignment." Format: b&w line drawings and color washes for cover and inside. Send samples of style to William G. Patton, designer. SASE. Reports in 1 week. Pays on acceptance $75-150 for b&w cover; $25-100 for b&w inside; $125-250 for color cover; $50-150 for inside color. Buys all rights on a work-for-hire basis.

SUPER-8 FILMAKER, 609 Mission St., San Francisco CA 94105. (415)543-8020. Editor-in-Chief: Richard J. Jantz. Art Director: Brian Dessin Day. Deals with all aspects of Super-8 film. Published 8 times/year. Circ. 45,000. Sample copy $2.50; free artist's guidelines.
Illustrations: Buys 4/issue on film-making. Arrange interview to show portfolio. SASE. Reports in 1 week. Buys all rights. Cover: Buys color washes, opaque watercolors and b&w line drawings. Inside: Buys color washes and opaque watercolors. Negotiates pay; pays on publication.

SUPERMARKET BUSINESS, 1515 Broadway, New York NY 10036. (212)869-1300. Editor: Bruce Buckley. Concerns merchandising methods, industry news, convention coverage and surveys of the supermarket industry. Monthly. Circ. 80,000.
Cartoons: Buys 12-15 cartoons/year on the grocery business; single, double or multipanel. "Cartoons are best if artist works with us to develop an idea." Query with samples. SASE. Reports in 1 month. Pays $25 minimum, gray opaques, b&w line drawings and washes; on acceptance.
Illustrations: Buys 12-15/year on the grocery business. Query with resume and samples or arrange interview to show portfolio. SASE. Reports in 1 month. Cover: Pays $30 minimum, color washes and opaque watercolors. Inside: Pays $25 minimum, gray opaques, b&w line drawings and washes; on acceptance.

SURGICAL BUSINESS, 2009 Morris Ave., Union NJ 07083. Contact: Sid Frier. For manufacturers, distributors and dealers in medical-surgical products. Sample copy available.
Needs: Submit art. Pays $100-150, 2-color cover; $10, cartoons.

TALK, 485 Madison Ave., New York NY 10022. Contact: Tina Davis, art director. For young women in their 20s and 30s. Original artwork not returned after publication.
Cartoons: Uses 1 cartoon/issue; buys 1/issue from freelancers, on "women's problems–work and in the home." Prefers finished cartoons. SASE. Reports when material is used. Buys all rights on a work-for-hire basis. Pays $25; on publication.
Illustrations: Uses 2-5 illustrations/issue; buys 2-5/issue from freelancers. Interested in all subjects. Works on assignment only. No samples returned. Does not report back on future assignment possibilities. Provide calling card, flyer and tearsheet to be kept on file for future assignments. Provide portfolio. SASE. Reports in 1 week. Buys all rights on a work-for-hire basis. Pays $25; on publication.

'TEEN, Petersen Publishing Co., 8490 Sunset Blvd., Los Angeles CA. (213)657-5100. Art Director: Janice Billings. Deals with self-development for girls 12-19. Monthly. Circ. 150,000. Free artist's guidelines.
Cartoons: Contact Sarah Lancaster. Buys 1-2 cartoons/issue on humor through youth; single panel with gag line. Prefers roughs. SASE. Reports in 2 weeks. Buys all rights. Pays $15-20, b&w line drawings and washes; on acceptance.
Illustrations: Contact Janice Billings. Buys 1-4 illustrations/issue for fiction, fashion and beauty sections. Works mostly on assignment basis. Prefers resume and photocopies. SASE. Reports in 2 weeks. Buys all rights. Inside: Pays $25 minimum, b&w line drawings, washes, gray opaques and color; on acceptance.

TEENS TODAY, 6401 The Paseo, Kansas City MO 64131. (816)333-7000. Managing Editor: John L. Denney. For high school students who attend Church of the Nazarene. Weekly. Circ. 35,000. Original artwork not returned after publication. Free sample copy.
Cartoons: Uses 1-2 cartoons/issue; buys 1-2/issue from freelancers. Receives 30 submissions/week from freelancers. Interested in teen issues. Prefers finished cartoons. Reports in 4-6 weeks. Buys all rights. Pays $7.50-12.50, b&w halftones and washes; on acceptance.
Illustrations: Uses 1-2 illustrations/issue; buys 1-2/issue from freelancers; all illustrations go with stories. Works on assignment only. Samples returned by SASE. Reports back on future assignment possibilities. Provide resume, flyer and tearsheet to be kept on file for future assignment. Prefers resume and samples of style. SASE. Reports in 4-6 weeks. Buys all rights on a work-for-hire basis. Pays $35, 1-color overlays; on acceptance.

TENNIS, 495 Westport Ave., Norwalk CT 06856. (203)847-5811. Editor: Shepherd Campbell. Managing Editor: Jeffrey N. Bairstow. For young, affluent tennis players. Monthly. Circ. 440,000. Original artwork not returned after publication.
Cartoons: Uses 3 cartoons/issue; buys 3/issue from freelancers. Receives 6 submissions/week from freelancers on tennis. Prefers finished cartoons, single paneled. Reports in 2 weeks. Pays $50 minimum, line drawings.
Illustrations: Uses 10 illustrations/issue; buys 8/issue from freelancers. Works on assignment only. Samples returned by SASE. Reports back on future assignment possibilities. Provide brochure to be kept on file for future assignment. Prefers portfolio. SASE. Reports in 2 weeks. Buys all rights on a work-for-hire basis. Pays on acceptance.

TENNIS CHAMPIONSHIP, 156 Broad St., Lynn MA 01901. (617)598-9230. Art Director: Helen Zimman. For audience at tennis matches. Estab. 1952. Circ. 900,000. Published for scheduled events; 8⅞x11¾; 64 pages. Offset. Simultaneous submissions OK. Not copyrighted. Pays on publication. Sample copy $2; free artist's guidelines.
Illustrations: Contact Michael Lefkowitz, editor-in-chief. Buys 10/year on tennis. Cover: Pays $250 minimum, color washes and opaque watercolors. Inside: Pays $100 minimum, color washes and opaque watercolors; $50 minimum, b&w line drawings and gray opaques. Query with previously published work.

TENNIS USA, Chilton Co., Chilton Way, Radnor PA 19089. (215)687-8200. For members of the United States Tennis Association and tennis enthusiasts. Estab. 1937. Circ. 100,000. Monthly. SASE. Reports in 3-4 weeks. Buys all rights. Pays on publication. Free sample copy and artist's guidelines.
Cartoons: Contact Alex McNab. Buys 2/issue on tennis; single panel with gag line. Pays $20-50, b&w line drawings. Mail roughs.
Illustrations: Contact Edwin Dahl. Buys 10-20/year on tennis. Cover: Pays $400-500, 4-color. Query with resume and samples.

TENNIS WEEK, 120 E. 56th St., New York NY 10022. (212)355-3611. Readers are tennis

fanatics. Weekly. Circ. 30,000. Sample copy 50¢.
Cartoons: Editor: Linda Pentz. Uses 1 cartoon/issue all from freelancers. We consider cartoons geared to a "tennis audience, droll, if you please." Format: b&w line drawings with gag line. Prefers finished cartoons.SASE. Reports in 2 weeks. Buys first North American serial rights. Pays $10 on publication.
Illustrations: Publisher: E.L. Scott. Uses 1-2 illustrations/issue. Selects freelancers by "query and accuracy and editor's sense of relevance." Looking for "caricatures of pros portraying personalities." Format: inside b&w line drawings and cover color washes. Prefers finished art. SASE. Reports in 2 weeks. Buys first North American serial rights. Pays $10-25, for b&w cover; on publication.

TEXAS FARMER-STOCKMAN, Box 31368, Dallas TX 75231. Concerned with helping rural families grow better crops and improve their livestock. Reports in 1 week. Buys all rights. Pays on acceptance. Sample copy available.
Cartoons: Buys 25/year on farm and ranch situations. Pays $10.

TEXAS GIRL, Box 1185, Bellaire TX 77401. (713)784-5520. Editor: Earl Hollbrook. Emphasizes Texas style entertainment for Texas men. Monthly. Circ. 100,000. Estab. 1979. Free sample copy.
Cartoons: Uses 20 cartoons/issue. Interested in anything funny, sexy or stimulating to a Texas male. Prefers single panel b&w line drawings and b&w or color washes with gag line. Send roughs or finished cartoons or samples of style. SASE. Reports in 2 weeks. Buys first North American serial rights. Pays $25 for b&w; $50 for color; on publication.
Illustrations: Uses 2-3 illustrations/issue. Interested in full page humorous illustrations pertinent to Texas entertainment. Will consider all types illustrations. Works on assignment only. Provide resume and samples to be kept on file for future assignments or send finished art. SASE. Buys all rights. Full page color illustrations assigned by editor. Pays $25 minimum for b&w inside and $200 for inside color; on publication.

TEXAS HUNTERS DIRECTORY, 1647 S. Alameda, Corpus Christi TX 78404. (512)882-2953. Editor: Heidi Jensen. Emphasizes hunting and wildlife management in Texas for outdoors people and hunters in and out of Texas. Annually. Circ. 25,000. Free sample copy.
Cartoons: Uses 1-2 cartoons/issue; buys all from freelancers. Interested in tall tales, hunter ridiculousness, outdoor survival, camping, safari, taxiderming, bow hunting and trapping. Prefers single panel b&w line drawings with gag line. Send finished cartoons and/or samples of style. SASE. Reports in 1 week. Buys first North American serial rights. Pays $15 for b&w; on publication.
Illustrations: Uses 3-5 illustrations/issue; buys all from freelancers. Receives 1-2 submissions/week from freelancers. Interested in hunting, exotic hunting, outdoor survival and camping, taxidermy, trapping, gun safety and wildlife management. Prefers b&w line drawings for inside. Send rough and samples of style to be kept on file for future assignments. Samples returned by SASE. Reports in 1 week. Buys all rights. Pays $25 for b&w; on publication.

THE TEXAS MUSIC EDUCATOR, Box 9908, Houston TX 77013. For music educators in Texas. Monthly, August-May. Query. Reports in 30 days. Buys all rights. Pays on acceptance.
Cartoons: Buys music themes; with gag line. Pays $5-10, finished b&w.
Illustrations: Cover: Pays $50, b&w and color. Inside: Pays $5, spot drawings.

TEXAS OUTDOOR GUIDE, Smith Publishing Co., Inc., Box 55573, Houston TX 77055. (713)525-1026. Editor-in-Chief: Stan Slaten. Art Director: Marti Collier. Concerns outdoor sports and recreation. Bimonthly. Circ. 100,000. Submit art or query with samples. SASE. Reports in 4 weeks. Buys all rights. Pays on publication. Free sample copy and artist's guidelines.
Illustrations: Buys 60/year on environment and outdoor sports. Inside: Pays $25-100, b&w and color.

TEXAS SPORTS, Box 402086, Dallas TX 75240. (214)385-8040. Emphasizes sports in Texas, of interest to and about Texans. Audience is young, 90% male. Monthly. Free sample copy; art guidelines for SASE.
Cartoons: Uses 6 cartoons/issue, all from freelancers. Themes should be sports related including professional, collegiate, amateur, leisure, and outdoor sports. Format: single panel b&w line drawings. Send finished cartoons, samples of style, call or write. SASE. Reports in 2-4 weeks. Buys all rights but may reassign. Pays $10-25.
Illustrations: Creative Director: Paul Black. Uses 1-2 major and 5-10 smaller illustrations/issue, all from freelancers. "See 4-5 freelancers monthly. Artists should feel free to contact us. We will be depending heavily on freelancers." Selects freelancers from samples on file and seeing work in

other publications. Illustrations should pertain to sports. Format: color washes for cover and inside. Prefers samples of style or arrange personal appointment to show portfolio. SASE. Reports in 2-4 weeks. Buys various rights. Pay is negotiable. Pays $50-700; on acceptance.
Other Needs: Uses promotional material.

TEXAS TOWN AND CITY, 1020 Southwest Tower, Austin TX 78701. Contact: Erin Morrison. For municipal government officials. Send published samples. Buys all rights. Pays on publication. Sample copy available.
Needs: "Our needs in artwork are usually directed toward topics such as law enforcement, workmen's compensation, the legislature, etc." Pays $10, spot drawing; $35 minimum, black plus 2 other colors cover design.

THESE TIMES, Box 59, Nashville TN 37202. Art Director: Gail R. Hunt. Interdenominational journal published by Seventh-day Adventist Church. "The goal is to bring Christianity to the reader in a believable, readable and usable way." Send published samples. SASE. Buys all or one-time rights. Pays on publication. Guidelines and sample copy available.
Illustrations: Does not publish 'say-nothing' artwork such as portraits, still lifes of Bibles, candles and the like, pretty vacation-like scenics, clip-art style or anything similar. "We cover subject matter involved with current issues (drugs, crime, ecology), the Bible, health, family and home topics, science and nature, church history and current events in the world of religion." Cover: Pays $100-350, full-color. Inside: Pays $75-200/full-color page; $30-75, b&w line drawings and 2-color.

THIRD EYE, 250 Mill St., Williamsville NY 14221. (716)634-2735. Editor-in-Chief: Patrick Lally. Art Editor: Nancy Wall. For poetry-oriented, very literate audience. Quarterly. Circ. 300. Mail art. SASE. Reports in 4 weeks. Simultaneous submissions OK. Buys reprint rights. Pays on publication. Free sample copy.
Illustrations: Buys 12/year on poetic themes. Cover: Pays $5 and contributor's copies. Inside: Pays $4 and contributor's copies. Buys b&w line drawings and washes.

THIS, 3 Church St., Suite 40, Toronto, Ontario, Canada M5E 1M2. (416)364-2431. Art Director: Lorraine Filyer. Emphasizes Candian education, culture and politics for teachers, professors, students, radicals, union leaders and community workers. Circ. 6,000. Bimonthly. SASE. Reports in 2 months. Buys first rights. Pays on publication. Free sample copy and artist's guidelines.
Cartoons: Buys 3/issue on current events, education, environment and politics; single, double or multipanel. Pays $20-40, b&w line drawings. Query with samples.
Illustrations: Buys 3/issue on current events, education, environment and politics. Cover and inside: Pays $80-100, b&w line drawings. Query with resume and samples.

TIC, Box 407, North Chatham NY 12132. Editor: Joseph Strack. For dentists.
Cartoons: "Remember, it's for dentists, not patients—so no pain gags, please." Reports in 10 days. Buys exclusive dental publication rights; will release reprint rights. Pays $20 for washes, pen and inks and line drawings; on acceptance.

TIGER BEAT MAGAZINE, 7060 Hollywood Blvd. #800, Hollywood CA 90028. (213)467-3111. Editor: Kathy Kirkland. For teenage girls and subteens. (Median age: 15.) Monthly. Circ. 700,000. Original artwork not returned after publication.
Cartoons: Uses 1-3 cartoons/issue, all from freelancers. Receives 0 submissions/week from freelancers. Interested in "teen or star-oriented" themes. Prefers roughs of finished cartoons. SASE. Reports in 2 weeks. Buys all rights on an assigned basis or first North American serial rights. Pays $20-150, b&w; on acceptance.
Illustrations: Uses 1-3 illustrations/issue. Buys "none yet" from freelancers. Interested in "teen or star-oriented" themes. Provide calling card and "some kind of sample" to be kept on file for future assignment. Prefers roughs or samples of style. SASE. Reports in 2 weeks. Buys all rights on an assigned basis or first North American serial rights. Pays $20-150, b&w; on acceptance.

TODAY'S ANIMAL HEALTH, 1905 Sunnycrest Dr., Fullerton CA 92635. Editor-in-Chief: Richard Glassberg. For animal owners. Bimonthly. Circ. 35,000. Previously published, photocopied and simultaneous submissions OK. Sample copy $1. "Since our magazine is published by the nonprofit, charitable Animal Health Foundation, we like donations. Therefore, the best way to get into our magazine is to donate material. We only buy material when we can't get good material donated."
Cartoons: Buys 2-16/year on animal health-related themes; single panel. Mail art. SASE. Reports in 2 months. Buys all rights. Pays $5-25, line drawings and color; on acceptance.

Illustrations: Buys up to 5/year on animals. Mail art. SASE. Reports in 2 months. Buys all rights. Cover: Pays $25-50, color; $5-25, b&w. Inside: Pays $5-25, color; $5-15, b&w; on acceptance.

TODAY'S CHRISTIAN PARENT, 8121 Hamilton Ave., Cincinnati OH 45231. Editor: Mildred Mast. Original artwork not returned after publication. Sample copy available.
Cartoons: Uses 1 cartoon/issue; from freelancers. Number of submissions/week received from freelancers varies. Interested in family, animal and seasonal themes. Prefers finished cartoons. SASE. Reports in 6 months. Buys all rights on a work-for-hire basis, but negotiable. Negotiates pay; pays on acceptance.
Illustrations: Uses 3-4 illustrations/issue, all from freelancers. Number of submissions/week received from freelancers varies. Interested in "various aspects of family life." provide brochure and tearsheet to be kept on file for future assignment. Prefers finished art and samples of style. SASE. Reports in 6 months. Buys all rights on a work-for-hire basis, but negotiable. Negotiates pay; pays on acceptance.

TODAY'S POLICEMAN, Box 594, Kansas City MO 64141. (816)221-7075. Contact: Editor. For persons employed in and interested in police services. Quarterly. Circ. 10,000.
Cartoons: Buys 6 cartoons/issue dealing with law enforcement and politics. Send finished art. SASE. Pays $2.50 for b&w.

TODAY'S SECRETARY, McGraw-Hill, Inc., 1221 Avenue of the Americas, New York NY 10020. (212)997-4157. Editor-in-Chief: Nhora Cortes-Comerer. Art Director: Barbara Groenteman. For secretarial students. Published 8 times/year. Circ. 60,000. Original artwork not returned after publication.
Illustrations: Uses 4 illustrations/issue; buys 4/issue from freelancers. prefers portfolios and samples of style. Buys exclusive rights.Cover: Pays $100-200, b&w; $100-150, color. Inside: Pays $30-70, b&w; $40-85, color.

TOO, Box 8316, Los Angeles CA 90008. (213)296-8565. Editor-in-Chief: Lawrence Walker. Art Director: Lana Bingham. "Promotes togetherness of black men and women." Monthly. Estab. 1978. Query with resume or samples or arrange interview to show portfolio. SASE. Reports in 6 weeks. Buys all rights, but may reassign rights to artist after publication. Pays on publication. Free sample copy; artist's guidelines for SASE.
Cartoons: Buys 20/issue on current events, education, politics and black men's and women's relationships and professional aspirations; single panel with gag line. Pays $100-200, b&w line drawings; $150-250, full-color.
Illustrations: Buys 15/issue on current events, education, politics and black men's and women's relationships and professional aspirations. "No lewd sexual relationships." Cover: Pays $700-1,500, full-color. Inside: Pays $100, full-color; $75, b&w line drawings.

TORCHBEARER MAGAZINE, Life Insurance Company of Virginia, Box 27601, Richmond VA 23261. (804)281-6569. Editor: Matthew W. Beha. For employees; features articles on how to sell, recognition of sales achievements, company news, industry developments and finance. Monthly. Circ. 3,500. Reports in 3 weeks. Previously published work OK. Free sample copy and artist's guidelines.
Illustrations: Uses 10 illustrations/issue; buys 2/issue from freelancers. Receives 3-4 submissions/week from freelancers. Uses assigned themes. Works on assignment only Samples returned by SASE. Provide samples of published work and information on other fields of artistic talent to be kept on file for future assignment. Reports in 3 weeks. Inside: Pays $25-50, b&w line drawings. Query with resume and samples.
Other Needs: Uses artists for 2-color cover design and special projects. Pays $50-100. Is considering using cartoons in the near future.
To Break In: "We're looking for a clean, up-to-date style."

TOURIST ATTRACTIONS AND PARKS, 401 N. Broad St., Suite 904, Philadelphia PA 19108. (215)925-9744. Deals with arenas, attractions, fairgrounds, stadiums, concerts and theme and amusement parks. quarterly. Circ. 20,000.
Illustrations: Buys 1-4/issue. Prefers resume and samples. SASE. Buys all rights. Cover: Pays $50 minimum, gray opaques; on publication. Inside: Buys gray opaques.
Design: Contact Scott Boroughsby, president. Uses artists for cover and layout. Query with resume and samples. Negotiates pay.

TOW-AGE, Box M, Franklin MA 02038. Contact: J. Kruza. For readers who run their own service business. Estab. 1978. Circ. 15,000. Published every 6 weeks.
Cartoons: "Temporarily overloaded."

Illustrations: Buys 5/issue on assigned themes. Query with samples. SASE. Reports in 3 weeks-1 month. Pays $10-40, b&w; on acceptance.

TOWN & COUNTRY, 717 5th Ave., New York NY 10022. Editor-in-Chief: Frank Zachary. Managing Editor: Jean Cook Barkhorn. Art Director: Melissa Tardiff. For high-income, well-educated adults interested in sophisticated travel, fashion, food, beauty and society. Monthly. Circ. 200,000. Query with portfolio. Previously published work OK. Original artwork returned after publication. Pays on acceptance.
Cartoons: Uses 1 cartoon/issue; buys 1/issue from freelancer, on financial themes. Buys one-time reproduction rights. Pays on acceptance.
Illustrations: Uses 1 illustration/issue; buys from freelancer. "We use only very sophisticated artwork, preferably b&w line." Works on assignment only. Samples returned by SASE. Reports back on future assignment possibilities. Provide calling card, flyer and tearsheet to be kept on file for future assignment. Prefers portfolio. SASE. Reports in 1 week. Buys first North American serial rights. Pays $100-150 minimum/page; on acceptance.

TRAILS, Box 788, Wheaton IL 60187. (312)293-1600. Editor: Laura Alden. Christian publication for girls ages 7-12. Bimonthly. Circ. 20,000. Simultaneous submissions and previously published work OK. Pays on acceptance. Sample copy and artists guidelines $1.50.
Cartoons: Buys 6 cartoons/year. Interested in education, environment, family life, humor through youth, children's sports and animals; single or double panel with gag line. SASE. Reports in 4-8 weeks. Buys first, one-time, reprint or simultaneous rights. Pays $5-20, b&w line drawings; on acceptance. Prefers samples, or mail roughs or finished art.
Illustrations: Buys 1-2 illustrations/year. Interested in education, environment, family life, humor through youth, children's sports and animals. Prefers resume and samples. SASE. Reports in 4-8 weeks. Buys first, one-time, reprint or simultaneous rights. Cover: Pays $20-35, b&w line drawings and washes. Inside: Pays $10-25, b&w line drawings; on acceptance.

TRANSAMERICA, Transamerica Corp., 600 Montgomery St., San Francisco CA 94111. (415)983-4088. Editor: Delphine Hirasuna. For employees. Quarterly. Circ. 38,000. SASE. Reports in 6 weeks. Previously published work OK. Pays on acceptance.
Cartoons: Buys 4-5/year on assigned themes. Uses b&w line drawings. Query with samples. Negotiates pay.
Illustrations: Buys 1/year on assigned themes. Cover: Uses b&w line drawings. Query with previously published work or arrange interview to show portfolio. Negotiates pay.
To Break In: "We look for artists who have experience in corporate artwork. We buy mostly cartoon-type drawings to illustrate stories that don't lend themselves to photographs."

TRAVEL & LEISURE, 1350 6th Ave., New York NY 10019. (212)399-2500. Emphasizes travel and leisure. Monthly. Circ. 925,000. Original artwork returned after publication. Art guidelines for SASE.
Cartoons: Associate Art Director: Giovanna Mantorani. Rarely uses cartoons. Interested in travel or leisure related themes. Format: b&w line drawings and b&w and color washes without gag lines. Prefers roughs. SASE. Reports in 1 week. Buys first North American serial rights. Pays $200-800, b&w; on publication.
Illustrations: Associate Art Director: Giovanna Mantorani. Art Director: Adrian Taylor. Uses 1-15 illustrations/issue, all from freelancers. Interested in travel and leisure related themes. "Illustrators are selected by excellence and relevance to the subject." Works on assignment only. Samples returned by SASE. Provide calling card to be kept on file for future assignment. Prefers samples of style. SASE. Reports in 1 week. Buys first North American serial rights. Pays a minimum of $150 inside b&w and $800-900 maximum, inside color; on acceptance.

TRAVELSCENE, R.H. Donnelley Travel Media, 888 7th Ave., 29th Floor, New York NY 10019. (212)977-8300. Editor-in-Chief: Martin B. Deutsch. Art Director: Leslie Heffernan. Trade magazine for travel agents, airline employees and business travelers. Monthly. Circ. 109,000. Query with samples or previously published work, or arrange interview. SASE. Contacts artists as needs arise. Buys all rights, but may reassign rights to artist after publication. Pays on acceptance. Free sample copy.
Cartoons: Buys 2/issue on travel and travelers; single panel with gag line. Pays $40 maximum, b&w line drawings.
Illustrations: Buys 4/issue on assigned themes. Minimum payment: Cover: Pays $200, color. Inside: Pays $100, color; $50, b&w.

TRIQUARTERLY, 1735 Benson Ave., Northwestern University, Evanston IL 60201. (312)492-3490. Art Director: Cynthia Anderson. Publishes fiction and criticism. Circ. 5,000.

Published 3 times/year. Sample copy $5.95; free artist's guidelines.
Illustrations: Buys 3 illustrations/year. "We need artwork to accompany fiction or self-contained portfolios of drawings." Interested in b&w line drawings, washes and gray opaques. Prefers resume and samples. SASE. Reports in 4-6 weeks. Buys all rights. Pays $100 minimum, negotiates on a per-issue basis. Pays on publication.

TROPIC, 1 Herald Plaza, Miami FL 33101. Editor: Lary Bloom. *Miami Herald* Sunday magazine.
Illustrations: Reports in 4-6 weeks. Buys first rights. Inside: Pays $50-200; on publication.

TRUCK CANADA, 27 Centrale St., LaSalle, Quebec, Canada H8R 2J1. (514)363-1481. Editor-in-Cheif: Keith Fredricks. Deals with Canadian heavy trucking industry. Monthly. Circ. 18,500. Simultaneous submissions OK. Original artwork not returned after publication. Buys one-time rights. Free sample copy and artist's guidelines. Query with previously published work and rough samples.
Cartoons: Uses 3-4 cartoons/issue; all from freelancers. Receives 12 submissions/month from freelancers. Interested in heavy trucking themes; single panel with gag line. Prefers finished cartoons. SASE. Reports in 2 weeks. Pays $5-10, b&w line drawings; on publication. Buys all rights on a work-for-hire basis.
Illustrations: Uses 3-4 illustrations/issue; all from freelancers. Works on assignment only. Samples returned by SASE. Reports back on future assignment possibilities. Provide resume, brochure, flyer and tearsheet to be kept on file for future assignments. Prefers roughs, portfolio or samples of style. SASE. Reports in 2 weeks. Buys all rights on a work-for-hire basis. Negotiates pay; pays on publication.

TRUCK TRACKS, Box 1575, Lake Grove Station, Lake Oswego OR 97034. (503)635-4391. Editor-in-Chief: Virginia Gray. For professional truck drivers and owners interested in equipment, accessories, laws, regulations, service facilities, trucking people and companies. Monthly. Circ. 15,000. Original artwork not returned after publication. Free sample copy.
Cartoons: Uses 4-6 cartoons/issue, all from freelancers. Interested in trucking themes; single panel. Prefers finished cartoons. SASE. Reports in 4 weeks. Buys first rights, but may reassign rights to artist after publication. Pays $5 maximum, b&w line drawings; on publication.

TRUE DETECTIVE, 235 Park Ave. S., New York NY 10003. Managing Editor: Walter Jackson. For middle-aged fact crime readers. Monthly.
Cartoons: Buys 100/year on crime themes; single panel. "Avoid cliche situations such as 2 convicts conversing in cell. No horror. Slant toward male audience. Cute, mild sex. Police image must be good." Reports in 1 week. Buys all rights. Pays $25, line drawings and halftones; on acceptance.

TRUE WEST, Western Publications, Inc., Box 3338, Austin TX 78764. Publisher: Joe Austell Small. Editor: Pat Wagner. For those interested in western Americana nonfiction, 1840-1910. Submit 4x5 transparency. Reports in 2-3 weeks. Previously published work OK "depending on where it appeared." Buys one-time rights. Pays on acceptance. Sample copy 75¢.
Illustrations: Pays $100 for cover in 4-color oils. "We prefer a color snapshot or transparency for evaluation of the artist's style. Transparency is returned after publication. We also prefer vertical paintings because the use of bands above and below a horizontal gives issues a look of sameness. We also have to pass up good paintings at times because our titles would cover some vital element or because the painting has no space left for story titles. We like to leave the artist's work as uncluttered as possible, but a certain amount of type is required. Often, the artist doesn't take this into account."

TRUTH ON FIRE!, Box 223, Postal Station A, Vancouver, B.C., Canada V6C 2M3. Editor: Wesley H. Wakefield, evangelist. Publication of the Bible Holiness Movement. Bimonthly; 60 pages. Estab. 1949. Circ. 5,000. Query. Reports in 4 weeks. Previously published work OK. Buys all or one-time rights. Sample copy available.
Illustrations: Buys cover designs and b&w drawings "with a message on racism, worship, education, war-peace, labor, drug addiction or alcoholism." Cover: Pays $5-50, 1-color.

TULSA, Box 1620, Tulsa OK 74101. (918)582-6000. Editor: Ellen Sue Blakey. Monthly. Circ. 5,100. Original artwork returned after publication. Sample copy $1.
Illustrations: Uses 6-10 illustrations/issue; buys 1-2/issue from freelancers. Works on assignment only. Samples returned by SASE. Reports back on future assignment possibilities. Provide resume, calling card and tearsheet to be kept on file for future assignments. Prefers finished art and

samples of style. SASE. Reports in 2 weeks. Buys all rights on a work-for-hire basis. Cover: Pays $75-100, full-color. Inside: Pays $50-75, spot drawing.

TURF AND SPORT DIGEST, 511-513 Oakland Ave., Baltimore MD 21212. Publisher: Allen L. Mitzel Jr.
Cartoons: Interseted in horse racing themes. Pays $10; on publication.

TURKEY CALL, Box 467, Edgefield SC 29824. (803)637-3106. Emphasizes wild turkey conservation and restoration and the sport of calling and hunting them. Bimonthly. Circ. 30,000. Sample copy 50¢.
Cartoons: "We are not a good cartoon or art market; but we *will* consider submissions, of course." Format: single panel b&w line drawings and b&w washes with gag line. SASE. Reports in 3 weeks. Buys one-time rights. Pays $10/panel on publication.
Illustrations: Editor: Gene Smith. Uses 1 illustration/issue; buys 1/issue from freelancers. Interested in the wild turkey and/or its habitat, hunting, etc. B&w line drawings and washes for inside and cover. Send samples. SASE.Reports in 3 weeks. Buys one-time rights. Pay is negotiable on publication.

TV GUIDE, Radnor PA 19088. Cartoon Editor: Harold B. Clemenko. Art Director: Jerry Alten. Weekly. Query. Reports in 2 weeks. Buys all rights. Pays on acceptance.
Cartoons: Buys TV themes. Pays $125, single cartoon; $400, 3 cartoons used as full-page feature. Also uses cartoons for editorial features. Line drawings and halftones.

TV NEWS, 425 Park Ave. S., New York NY 10016. (212)532-4000. Publisher: Allan Horwitz. For TV viewers. Weekly; 7x10⅞; 28-40 pages. Offset. Copyrighted. Pays on acceptance. Buys entertainment and consumer news themes and retail artwork (ad layout and illustrations). Pays $4-5/hour. Must have advertising experience.

TWA AMBASSADOR, Webb Co., 1999 Shepard Rd., St. Paul MN 55116. Executive Art Director: Jerald Johnson. For 26 publications. Biweeklies, monthlies and quarterlies. Circ. 35,000-1,000,000.
Illustrations: Uses 1 illustration/issue; from freelancer. Receives 1 submission/week from freelancers. Interested in themes for 10 agriculture magazines, 1 horticulture magazine, 1 home magazine, 1 snow mobile magazine and 13 consumer magazines. Buys business and general interest themes. Works on assignment only. Samples returned by SASE. Provide brochure, flyer, tearsheet and slides to be kept on file for future assignments. Prefers portfolio and samples of style. SASE. Reports in 2 weeks. Buys all rights on a work-for-hire basis. Pays $50-800, b&w color; on acceptance.

UFO REPORT, Gambi Publications, 333 Johnson Ave., Brooklyn NY 11206. Contact: Michael Aldinger. Query. SASE. Reports in 1 month. Buys first North American serial rights. Pays on publication. Sample copy available.
Needs: Buys b&w line drawings and washes with 2-color overlays. Prefers 11x6. Pays $200, 2-color art.

UNEARTH-THE MAGAZINE OF SCIENCE FICTION DISCOVERIES, Box 779, Cambridge MA 02139. Editor-in-Chief: Jonathan Ostrowsky. Art Director: Wayne Dewhirst. Contains science fiction by new writers and columns by established science fiction figures. Quarterly; 5¼x7l 128 pages. Offset. Estab. 1976. Circ. 5,500. Query with samples or previously published work. SASE. Reports in 3 weeks. Buys first North American serial rights. Pays on publication. Sample copy $1.50.
Illustrations: Buys 6/issue on assigned themes. Cover: Pays $70 max./page, color. Inside: Pays $10 min./page, b&w.
To Break In: "We like to see illustrations that treat the underlying mood or theme of a story, rather than ones which merely depict a scene."

UNITED MAINLINER, East-West Network, Inc., 5900 Wilshire Blvd., #300, Los Angeles CA 90036. (213)937-5810. Editor: James Clark. Monthly.
Illustrations: Query with resume. Reports in 4 weeks. Buys all rights. Pays $75 minimum, spot art; $750, cover; $450 full-page illustration.

THE UNSPEAKABLE VISIONS OF THE INDIVIDUAL, Box 439, California PA 15419. Editors-in-Chief: Arthur and Kit Knight. For people with a better-than-average education interested in "beat" literature. Annually. Circ. 2,000. Sample copy $2.

Illustrations: Uses 3-6 illustrations/issue. Number illustrations/issue bought from freelancers varies. Receives 1 submission/month from freelancers. Interested in beat related themes, such as writers Jack Kerouac, William S. Burroughs, Allen Ginsberg, Gary Snyder and Diane di Prima. Prefers finished art. SASE. "Work without SASE will be destroyed." Reports in 2 weeks-2 months. Buys first North American serial rights. Cover and inside: Pays 2 contributor's copies, minimum; $10 maximum; on publication.

USA TODAY, (formerly *Intellect*), 1860 Broadway, New York NY 10023. (212)265-6680. Editor-in-Chief: Stanley Lehrer. Managing Editor: Bob Rothenberg. For intellectual college graduates. Monthly. Circ. 10,000. Free sample copy.
Illustrations: Buys 70-80 illustrations/year on assigned themes. Query with samples. SASE. Reports in 1 week. Buys all rights. Cover: Pays $100, color. Inside: Pays $15-50, b&w line drawings; on publication.

VAN, PICKUP AND OFF-ROAD INDUSTRY NEWS, Box 7130, Newport Beach CA 92660. (714)751-1265. Editor-in-Chief: Bill Bagnall. For new car dealers selling vans, pickups or off-road vehicles.Monthly. Circ. 24,000. Previously published work OK. Free sample copy and artist's guidelines.
Illustrations: Buys 4-10/year on vans, pickups and off-road vehicles. Send roughs. SASE. Reports in 2 weeks. Buys first rights. Cover: Pays $100-250, color. Inside: Pays $25-100, b&w line drawings; on publication.

VAN WORLD, 16200 Ventura Blvd., Encino CA 91436. Editor: Chris Hosford. For custom van owners. Monthly. Circ. 80,000. Query with resume. Reports in 2 weeks. Buys all rights. Editorial guidelines available. Sample copy $1.50
Needs: Buys line drawings and washes.

VEGETARIAN TIMES, 124 N. Austin Blvd., Oak Park IL 60302. (312)848-8120. Editor-in-Chief: Paul Obis Jr. Published 8 times/year. Circ. 50,000. Previously published and simultaneous submissions OK. Original artwork returned after publication. Buys first and reprint rights. Pays on publication. Sample copy $2.
Cartoons: Uses 4 cartoons/issue; buys 4/issue from freelancers, on "organic, health, vegetarianism. Nothing portraying women as stupid"; single panel. Prefers finished cartoons. SASE. Reports in 2 weeks. Buys first North American serial rights. Pays $15 minimum, b&w; on publication.
Illustrations: Uses 6 illustrations/issue; buys few or none from freelancers. Does not report back on future assignment possibilities. Does not keep file. Buys first North American serial rights. Pays $150,color cover; on publication.

VENTURE, Christian Service Brigade, Box 150, Wheaton IL 60187. (312)665-0630. For boys 12-18. "We seek to promote consciousness, acceptance of and personal commitment to Jesus Christ." Monthly. Circ. 22,500. Simultaneous submissions and previously published work OK. Original artwork returned after publication. Sample copy $1; artist's guidelines with SASE.
Cartoons: Associate Editor, Sharon Long. Uses 1 cartoon/issue; buys 1 cartoon/issue from freelancers. Receives 15 submissions/week from freelancers, on nature, sports, school, camping, hiking; single panel with gag line. Prefers finished cartoon. SASE. Reports in 4-8 weeks. Buys first-time rights. Pays $10 minimum, b&w line drawings; on acceptance.
Illustrations: Art Director: Roy Green. Uses 3 illustrations/issue; buys 2/issue from freelancers, on education, family life and camping. B&w only. Works on assignment only. Samples returned by SASE. Reports back on future assignment possibilities. Provide calling card, tearsheet and photocopies of samples to be kept on file for future assignments. Prefers samples of SASE. Reports in 2 weeks. Buys first-time rights. Cover: Pays $80-100, b&w line drawings and washes. Inside: Pays $50-80, b&w line drawings and washes; on publication.

VICTIMOLOGY: AN INTERNATIONAL JOURNAL, Box 39045, Washington DC 20016. (703)549-7694. Editor-in-Chief: Emilio Viano. For professionals, lawyers, criminologists, medical personnel and others helping child/spouse abuse programs, hotlines, rape crisis centers and other victim programs. "By 'victim,' we mean not only those victimized by crime, but by earthquakes, the evironment, accidents, pollution and the state." Quaterly; 200 pages. Offset. Estab. 1976. Circ. 2,500. Query with samples. SASE. Reports in 4 weeks. Buys all rights. Pays on publication. Sample copy $5. Write to be put on mailing list to receive periodical announcements.
Illustrations: Buys 6/year on victimization. "We like to see illustrations on what is done in behalf of the victim." Mimimum payment: Cover: Pays $100 color; $50, b&w. Inside: Pays $30, b&w. Brochure: Pays $50.

THE VINE, 201 8th Ave. S., Nashville TN 37202. Editor: Betty M. Buerki. Story paper for ages 8-9 in United Methodist and United Presbyterian churches. Weekly. Sample copy available.
Needs: "Our magazine has the potential for 4-color art on all pages. Occasionally we use 2-or 3-color artist-separated drawings but the majority of drawings are not art-separated. Buys cartoons, full-color illustrations and some color-separated, b&w drawings and cover designs. Mail art. Reports in 1 month. Buys one-time or first serial rights. Pays $50 for full-color illustration and cover design; on acceptance.

VIRGINIA WILDLIFE, Virginia Commission of Game and Inland Fisheries, Box 11104, Richmond VA 23230. (804)786-4974. Editor-in-Chief/Art Director: Harry L. Gillam. Concerns conservation and native wildlife. Monthly. Circ. 60,000. Previously published and photocopied submissions OK. Free sample copy and artist's guidelines.
Illustrations: Uses 3-5 illustrations/issue; buys 1-2/issue from freelancers. Receives 2 submissions/week from freelancers. Interested in "outdoor themes, fishing, hunting, wildgame, people in the outdoors, endangered species, conservation, camping, boating, etc." Provide resume and calling card to be kept on file for future assignments. Prefers portfolio (finished art). SASE. Reports in 45 days. Buys "rights to publish and reprint." Cover: Pays $100, color-separated work and full-color renderings. Inside: Pays $15-25, b&w line drawings and washes; $10-50, color washes; on acceptance.

VISTA, The Wesley Press, Box 2000, Marion IN 46952. Monthly in weekly parts. Mail art or samples. Reports in 30 days. Previously published work OK. Not copyrighted. Pays on acceptance.
Illustrations: Buys assigned themes. Minimum payment: Cover: $25-30, 2-color. Inside: $15, spot drawings. Line and wash OK.

VISUAL MERCHANDISING, 407 Gilbert Ave., Cincinnati OH 45202. (513)421-2050. Emphasizes store design and display. Monthly. Circ. 10,000.
Cartoons: Editor: Pamela Gramke. Cartoons should pertain to retailing. Query. SASE. Reports in 3 weeks. Pays on publication.
Illustrations: Art Director: Ruth Schulte. "Query art director for editorial schedule." Arrange interview to show portfolio. Reports in 3 weeks. Pays on publication.

VIVA NEW MEXICO, 4131 Montgomery Blvd., Albuquerque NM 87109. (505)883-1001. Editor: Lanny Tonning. Bimonthly.
Cartoons: Uses 1-2 cartoons/issue; buys all from freelancers and would buy more if submitted. Interested in New Mexico related themes including desert life, high technology industries, energy, environment and highly seasoned foods. Prefers single panel b&w line drawings with gag line. Send finished cartoons. SASE. Buys all rights. Pays $25 for b&w; on publication.

VOGUE, 350 Madison Ave., New York NY 10017. Art Director: Roger Schoening. Write and send resume; will then review portfolio; works primarily with New York area artists. Leave photocopies for referral.

WAGNER MAGAZINE, Wagner College, 631 Howard Ave., Staten Island NY 10301. (212)390-3124. Editor: Russ Johnson. For college alumni. Estab. 1883. Circ. 14,000. Query with samples. SASE. Reports in 1 week. Previously published submissions OK. Not copyrighted.
Illustrations: Buys 6/year. Pays $25-75, b&w.

WALLACES FARMER, Wallace Homestead Co., Box 1317, Des Moines IA 50305. Editor-in-Chief: Monte N. Sesker. Contact: Cartoon Editor. For farmers. Bimonthly. Circ. 144,000. Free sample copy.
Cartoons: Buys 10-15 cartoons/issue on current events, education, environment, family life on the farm, humor through youth and farm animals; single panel. Mail art. SASE. Reports in 4 weeks. Buys one-time rights. Pays $10, b&w line drawings; on acceptance.

WALLS & CEILINGS, 14006 Ventura Blvd., Sherman Oaks CA 91423. Editor: Robert F. Welch. Monthly. Send roughs. Reports in 30 days. Not copyrighted. Pays on publication.
Cartoons: Buys 25/year on plastering and drywall. Pays $3-5.

WASHINGTON DOSSIER, 3301 New Mexico Ave., Washington DC 20016. (202)362-5894. Editor-in-Chief: Sonia Adler. "For Washington's society." Monthly. Circ. 40,000. Photocopied and simultaneous submissions OK.
Cartoons: Buys current event and political themes; single panel. Mail art. No work returned.

Reports in 4 weeks. Buys all rights. Pays $25-100, line drawings; on publication.
Illustrations: Editor: Liane Uyada. Mail art. No work returned. Reports in 4 weeks. Buys all rights. Cover: Pays $25-250; on publication.

THE WASHINGTON MONTHLY, 2712 Ontario Rd., Washington DC 20009. (202)659-4866. Editor-in-Chief: Charles Peters. Art Director: Chuck Myers. For journalists, government officials, teachers and general public. "We examine government's failures and suggest solutions." Monthly. Circ. 30,000. Previously published and photocopied submissions OK. Free sample copy and artist's guidelines.
Cartoons: Buys 10-20 cartoons/year on education, politics and government; single panel. Query with samples or arrange interview to show portfolio; local artists preferred. SASE. Reports in 2 weeks. Buys one-time rights. Pays $35 minimum, b&w line drawings; on publication.
Illustrations: Buys 20-30 illustrations/year on education, environment, politics and government. Query with samples or arrange interview to show portfolio; local artists preferred. SASE. Reports in 2 weeks. Buys one-time rights. Inside: Pays $35-80, b&w line drawings and washes. Cover: Pays $80-140, color-separated work; $50 minimum, b&w; on publication.

THE WASHINGTONIAN MAGAZINE, 1828 L St. NW, Washington DC 20036. (202)296-3600. About Washington, for Washingtonians. Monthly. Circ. 95,000. Simultaneous submissions and previously published work OK. Original artwork returned after publication. Sample copy and artist's guidelines.
Cartoons: Cartoon Editor: Howard Means. Uses 5 cartoons/issue; buys 5/issue from freelancers, on "sophisticated topics, urban life"; single and double panel with gag line. Uses b&w line drawings, gray opaques, b&w washes, color washes and opaque watercolors. Prefers finished cartoons. Reports in 4-6 weeks. Buys one-time rights. Pays $50, b&w; on publication.
Illustrations: Illustration Editor: Linda Otto. Uses 5 illustrations/issue; buys 5/issue from freelancers, on a variety of subjects. Uses b&w line drawings, gray opaques, b&w washes, color washes and opaque watercolor. Also accepts color photography for covers. Works on assignment only. Returns samples if requested. Does not report back on future assignment possibilities. Provide resume, calling card and tearsheet to be kept on file for future assignments. Prefers portfolio and samples of style. SASE. Reports in 1 week. Buys one-time rights. Pay is negotiable; on publication.
Other Needs: Freelance pasteup artists.

THE WATER SKIER, Box 191, Winter Haven FL 33880. Editor: Tom C. Hardman. Aims to encourage the safe enjoyment of water skiing as a primary means of family recreation. Published 7 times/year. Sample copy available.
Cartoons: Buys 6/year on water skiing. Mail roughs. SASE. Reports in 10 days. Buys North American serial rights. Pays $15; on acceptance.

WAY, 109 Golden Gate Ave., San Francisco CA 94102. Editor-in-Chief: Simon Scanlon. Art Director: Ron Sugiyama. For middle-age readers. Published 10 times/year. Circ. 10,000. Query with samples. SASE. Reports in 4 weeks. Previously published work OK. Buys first North American serial rights. Pays on publication. Free sample copy.
Cartoons: Buys themes on current events, education, environment, family life, politics and religion; single panel. Pays $10 minimum, line drawings.
Illustrations: Buys 4/issue on "social landscapes." Cover and inside: Pays $10 minimum, b&w line drawings.

WEIGHT WATCHERS, 149 5th Ave., New York NY 10010. Editor-in-Chief: Bernadette Carr. Art Editor: Arthur Welthas. For those interested in weight-control, proper nutrition and self-improvement. Monthly. Circ. 800,000. Query with samples. SASE. Reports in 1-4 weeks. Photocopies OK. Buys all rights. Pays on acceptance. Sample copy $1. Needs mechanical artists during deadline; must be fast and accurate with minimum of 2 years experience. Pays $8/hour.
Cartoons: Buys 5-10/year on positive, weight-related themes; single and double panel. Pays $35-50, line drawings and halftones.
Illustrations: Buys 1-5/issue with "sympathetic treatment of someone on a weight-loss program"; b&w line drawings, washes and color-separated art.

WEIRD TRIPS, Krupp Comic Works, Box 7, Princeton WI 54968. (414)295-3972. Art Directors: Denis Kitchen and Leonard Rifas. For underground comics fans; concerns "experiences which extend or reshape the boundaries of the credible." Circ. 10,000. Published irregularly. Simultaneous submissions and previously published work OK. Original artwork returned after publication. Sample copy $1.25.

Cartoons: Uses 6 pages of cartoons/issue; buys "most" from freelancers. Interested in "no gag cartoons, no one panel cartoons; want comic book pages." Prefers finished cartoons. SASE. Reports in 2 weeks. Buys first North American serial rights. Pays $30/page, b&w; $200, color cover. Pays royalty figures per 10,000 sales; on publication.
Illustrations: Uses 6-8 illustrations/issue; buys 2-3/issue from freelancers. Interested in "bizarre styles, sometimes surrealistic, eccentric techniques" to be kept on file for future assignments. Prefers finished art and samples of style. Reports in 2 weeks. Buys first North American serial rights. Pays $30/page, b&w; $200, color cover. Pays royalty figures per 10,000 sales; on publication.
Other Needs: "Full comic book stories; "underground" approach: (autobiographical, topical and honest)."

WELL-BEING, Box 1829, Santa Cruz CA 95061. Editor-in-Chief: Barbara Salat. Concerns natural health care, do-it-yourself approaches, diet, exercise, gardening, alternative energy, recycling, massage, leisure activities, sports and family-oriented activities. Monthly. SASE. Reports in 1 month. Simultaneous submissions and previously published work OK. Buys all rights. Pays on publication. Sample copy $1; free artist's guidelines.
Cartoons: Buys 3/issue on education, environment, humor through youth, running, gardening and "health nut" activities; single panel with gag line. Pays $10-25, b&w. Query with samples or mail roughs.
Illustrations: Buys 4/issue on environment, herb plants, kitchen scenes and food. "Good plant illustrators are especially needed." Inside: Pays $10-25, b&w. Query with resume and samples.

WEST COAST REVIEW OF BOOKS, 6311 Yucca St., Hollywood CA 90028. Editor-in-Chief: D. David Dreis. Managing Editor: Crane Jackson. For book customers. Bimonthly. Circ. 76,000. Query with samples. SASE. Reports in 4 weeks. Buys all rights. Pays on publication. Sample copy $1.25.
Cartoons: Contact Henry Zorich, editor. Buys 36/year on bestseller book reading; single panel. Minimum payment: $50/3 b&w cartoons; $75/3 color cartoons.
Illustrations: Contact Bonita Montano, editor. Buys 24/year on assigned themes. Minimum payment: Cover: $100, color. Inside: $75, color; $50, 3 b&w.

WESTCHESTER MAGAZINE, 437 Ward Ave., Mamaroneck NY 10543. (914)698-8203. Contact: Evelyn Mertens. Emphasizes general interests in Westchester. Original artwork returned after publication.
Cartoons: "None at the moment but would be interested." Cartoons should pertain to life in Westchester County. Prefers finished cartoons and resume. SASE. Reports in 2-6 weeks.
Illustrations: Uses 4 illustrations/issue; buys 1/issue from freelancers. Interested in "humor-thematic." Works on assignment only. No samples returned. Reports back on future assignment possibilities. Provide resume, calling card, letter of inquiry and tearsheet to be kept on file for future assignments. Prefers finished art and samples of style. SASE. Reports in 2-6 weeks. Buys all rights on a work-for-hire basis. Pays $15-35, b&w; $25-50, color.

THE WESTERN HORSEMAN, Box 7980, Colorado Springs CO 80933. (303)633-5524. Editor: Chan Bergen. For professional horsemen, pleasure riders, ranchers and cowboys. Monthly. Circ. 180,000. Sample copy $1.25.
Illustrations: Buys art with manuscripts only. Prefers articles of 1,500 words with strong horse angle. Buys one-time rights. Pays $85-100 for package; on acceptance.

WESTERN HUMANITIES REVIEW, University of Utah, Salt Lake City UT 84112. (801)581-7438. Literary magazine. Readers are "highly educated and interested in all aspects of the humanities. Most of our subscribers are libraries." Quarterly. Circ. 1,100. Original artwork returned after publication. Sample copy $2.
Cartoons: Uses 4 cartoons/issue; buys 4/issue from freelancers. Receives 4 submissions/week from freelancers. Format: b&w line drawings with a touch of wit preferred. Single panel without gag line. "Artists should look at some of the recent issues." Send finished cartoons to Jack Garlington, editor. SASE. Reports in 1 week if "uninterested; longer if interested." Pays $50 on acceptance. Buys first North American serial rights.
Illustrations: Uses 4 illustrations/issue; buys 4/issue from freelancers. Receives 4 submissions/week from freelancers. Prefers finished art. SASE. Reports in 1 week if "uninterested; longer if interested." Buys first North American serial rights. Pays on acceptance.
Other Needs: "We also need covers, for which we pay $150 each. Artists should look at past issues to see the sort of things we use."

THE WESTERN PRODUCER, Box 2500, Saskatoon, Saskatchewan, Canada S7K 2C4. (306)665-3500. For farm families in western Canada. Weekly. Circ. 140,000.
Illustrations: Buys 10/year on rural life in western Canada. Send resume and samples of work to be kept on file for future assignments. SASE. Reports in 2 weeks. Buys first North American serial rights. Inside: Pays $10-100, b&w line drawings; on acceptance.

WESTERN SPORTSMAN, Nimrod Publications Ltd., Box 737, Regina, Saskatchewan, Canada S4P 3A8. (306)352-8384. Editor-in-Chief: Red Wilkinson. For fishermen, hunters, campers and outdoorsmen. Quarterly. Circ. 18,500. Previously published and simultaneous submissions OK ("as long as they're not in our market area of Alberta and Saskatchewan"). Original artwork not returned after publication. Sample copy $1.50; free artist's guidelines.
Cartoons: Buys 40 cartoons/year on the outdoors; single, double and multipanel with gag lines. Mail art or query with samples. SASE. Reports in 3 weeks. Buys first, reprint, simultaneous or first North American serial rights. Pays $5-10, b&w line drawings; on acceptance.
Illustrations: Buys 8 illustrations/year on the outdoors. Mail art or query with samples. SASE. Reports in 3 weeks. Buys first, reprint, simultaneous or first North American serial rights. Inside: Pays $10-175, b&w line drawings; on acceptance.

WESTERN WEAR AND EQUIPMENT, 2403 Champa, Denver CO 80205. (303)572-1777. Managing Editor: Jessica Severn. Circ. 14,000. Monthly. Previously published work and simultaneous submissions OK "if not submitted to a competing magazine." Original artwork returned after publication, if requested. Free sample copy and artist's guidelines.
Illustrations: Uses 1-3 illustrations/issue; buys 1/issue from freelancers. Receives 4 submissions/week from freelancers, on rodeo, western wear retailing and ranching. Cowboy themes. Works on assignment only. Samples returned by SASE. Reports back on future assignment possibilities. Provide letter of inquiry and tearsheet or samples to be kept on file for future assignments. Prefers samples of style. SASE. Reports in 2-4 weeks. Cover: Pays $25-150, color washes and opaque watercolors. Inside: Negotiates pay, b&w line drawings and gray opaques; on publication.
Other Needs: Buys b&w photos/photo essays. Pays $15-50. Color slides. Query with samples first. All work returned if requested with SASE.

WESTERN'S WORLD, 141 El Camino, Beverly Hills CA 90212. (213)273-1990. Art Director: Tom Medsger. For Western Airlines passengers. Published 6 times/year. Circ. 250,000.
Cartoons: Uses 1-2 cartoons/issue, all from freelancers. Receives 25-30 submissions/week from freelancers. Interested in travel. Prefers finished cartoons. SASE. Reports in 1 week. Buys all rights on a work-for-hire basis. Pays $35 minimum, b&w; on publication.
Illustrations: Uses 1-2 illustrations/issue, all from freelancers. Works on assignment only. Sometimes reports back on future assignment possibilities. Provide "anything with a name, phone number, address and samples" to be kept on file for future assignments. Prefers portfolio, finished art and samples of art. SASE. Reports in 1 week. Buys all rights on a work-for-hire basis. Pays $60/spot and $200/page, b&w; $250/page, color.

WESTWAYS, Box 2890 Terminal Annex, Los Angeles CA 90051. (213)741-4760. Editor: Frances Ring. Art Director: Elin Waite. Monthly. Circ. 465,000. Old copies available.
Illustrations: Buys assigned themes on travel, history, and arts in the West. Send resume and arrange interview. Buys all rights or partial, based on decision of the artist. Cover: Pays $500. Inside: Pays $150, drawings; $300, 4-color illustrations; on acceptance.

WESTWORLD, Box 6680, Vancouver, B.C., Canada V6V 4L4. (604)732-1371. Editor: Bill Mayrs. Concentrates on travel, leisure and living in western Canada. Bimonthly. Circ. 225,000. Original artwork returned after publication. Sample copy available.
Cartoons: Uses 2-3 cartoons/issue, all from freelancers. Receives 5-10 submissions/week from freelancers. Interested in "general themes (no girlie)." Prefers finished cartoons. Reports in 3-4 weeks. Buys all rights on a work-for-hire basis. Pays $15, b&w line drawings and washes; on publication.
Illustrations: Uses 2-3 illustrations/issue, all from freelancers. Works on assignment only. Provide brochure and flyer to be kept on file for future assignments. Prefers samples of style. SASE. Reports in 1 week. Buys all rights on a work-for-hire basis. Cover: Pays $125-150, full-color. Inside: Pays $35, spot drawings; $75-100, full-color.

WHISPERS, Box 1492-W, Browns Mills NJ 08015. Editor-in-Chief/Art Director: Stuart David Schiff. For college-educated adults interested in literate fantasy, horror art and fiction. Published 2-3 times/year. Circ. 3,000. Original artwork returned after publication. Sample copy $1.25.
Illustrations: Uses 10-20 illustrations/issue; buys 2-3/issue from freelancers. Receives 5-10

submissions/week from freelancers. Interested in fantasy and horror. Provide flyer and tearsheet to be kept on file for future assignments. Prefers finished art (photocopied samples). SASE. Reports in 30-60 days. Buys first North American serial rights. Cover: Pays $25-50, b&w. Inside: Pays $10-25, b&w. Pays $10-35 extra to retain artwork after use.

WHITMAN COMICS, (formerly Gold Key Comics), 850 3rd Ave., New York NY 10022. Art Director: Frank Taggart. Comic books for children 6-15. Monthly. Free sample copy.
Needs: "Get copies of our comics and become familiar with them. Send in samples. If general samples of adventure art, draw them in comic format. We look for professional quality drawing and ink technique, story-telling ability, action and vitality. If samples of animated art, draw a page in comic format plus model sheets of the main characters. Model sheets should consist of several heads in different positions with different expressions, and full-length figures in different poses from different angles. Drawings of characters must be exact and correct; close isn't good enough." SASE. Reports in 4 weeks. Buys all rights. Pays on acceptance.

THE WHOLESALER, 135 Addison Ave., Elmhurst IL 60126. (312)530-6160. For plumbing, heating and air conditioning and refrigeration wholesalers. Monthly. Circ. 25,000.
Cartoons: Buys themes on the industry, especially for use in calendar in December issue. Buys first serial rights. Pays $10/cartoon; $7.50 each if more than 5 bought; on acceptance.

WILSON LIBRARY BULLETIN, 950 University Ave., Bronx NY 10452. (212)588-8400. Editor: Milo Nelson. For librarians. Published 10 times/year. Circ. 30,000. Free sample copy.
Cartoons: Buys 5-6 cartoons/year on education and librarianship; single panel with gag line. Mail finished art. SASE. Reports in 1 week. Buys first North American serial rights. Pays $50, b&w line drawings and washes.
Illustrations: Uses 5 illustrations/issue; buys 5/issue from freelancers. Receives 10-15 submissions/week from freelancers. Interested in education and librarianship. Provide flyer to be kept on file for future assignments. Prefers finished art. SASE. Reports in 1 week. Buys first North American serial rights. Cover: Pays $100, color washes. Inside: Pays $100-250, b&w line drawings and washes; $20, spot drawings; on publication.
Design: Uses artists for cover design and publication redesign. Negotiates pay. Arrange interview to show portfolio.

WIND, The Wesleyan Church, Box 2000, Marion IN 46933. (317)674-3301. Editor: StanHoover. Religious magazine for teens. Monthly. Circ. 6,000. Submit art or query with samples. SASE. Reports in 2 weeks. Previously published, photocopied and simultaneous submissions OK. Not copyrighted. Pays on publication. Free sample copy.
Cartoons: Buys 20/year on education, humor through youth, military and religion; include gag line. Pays $15, b&w line drawings.
Illustrations: Buys 3/issue on education, humor through youth, military and religion. Cover: Pays $10-20, b&w; Inside: Pays $5-15, b&w.

WIND POWER DIGEST, Box 539, Harrisburg PA 17108. (717)233-3996. Editor: Paul Gipe. Emphasizes windmills. Quarterly. Circ. 10,000. Free sample copy.
Cartoons: Uses 2 cartoons/issue, all from freelancers. Receives 2 submissions/week from freelancers. Interested in public issues—political cartoons, related to alternative energy or windmills. Format: single panel b&w line drawings and washes. Send samples of style or call for an appointment to Paul Gipe, editor. SASE. Reports in 2-4 weeks depending on time of receipt. Pays $25-40; on acceptance. Buys first North American serial rights.
Illustrations: Uses 2 illustrations/issue, all from freelancers. Receives 2 submissions/week from freelancers. "Open for freelancer-initiated suggestions, some assignments. Looks for alternative energy and windmill themes. Uses inside b&w line drawings and washes. Send samples of style and/or call or write with ideas. SASE. Reports in 2-4 weeks. Pays $25-50; on acceptance. Buys first North American serial rights.

WINDSOR THIS MONTH MAGAZINE, Box 1029, Station A, Windsor, Ontario, Canada N9A 6P4. (519)256-2323. Managing Editor: J.S. Woloschuk. Features Windsor-oriented issues, interviews, opinion, answers. Published 12 times/year. Circ. 22,000.
Illustrations: Buys 3/issue on assigned themes. Query with samples. SASE. Reports in 1 week. Buys first North American serial rights. Negotiates pay, b&w only; on publication.

WINNING, Box 412, Station F, Toronto, Ontario, Canada. (416)366-9701. Editor-in-Chief: Don Valliere. For racing fans, casino gamblers and those who enjoy social gambling. Bimonthly. Circ. 35,000. Query with samples. SASE. Reports in 1 week. Previously published work OK. Buys all

rights. Pays on publication. Free sample copy.
Cartoons: Buys 1-2/issue on gambling. Minimum payment: $20, b&w; $25, color.
Illustrations: Buys gambling themes. Negotiates payment.

WISCONSIN RESTAURATEURS, 122 W. Wash, Madison WI 53703. (608)251-3663. Editor: Jan LaRue. Readers are "restaurantuers, hospitals, schools, institutions, cafeterias, food service students, chefs, etc." Monthly. Circ. 3,000. Original artwork returned after publication. Free sample copy; art guidelines for SASE.
Cartoons: Uses 1 cartoon/issue; buys 1/issue from freelancer. Receives 5 cartoons/week from freelancers. "Uses much material pretaining to conventions, food shows, etc. Sanitation issue good. Cartoons about employees. No off-color material." Format: b&w line drawings with gag lines. Send finished cartoons. SASE. Reports in 2 weeks. Buys first North American serial rights. Pays $8 on publication.
Illustrations: Uses 5 illustrations/issue; buys 1/issue from freelancer. Freelancers chosen "at random, depending on theme and articles featured for the month." Looks for "the unusual, pertaining to the food service industry. No offbeat or questionable material." Format: b&w line drawings and washes for covers. Send samples of style to to be kept on file for future assignments. Buys first North American serial rights. Pays $10-50 on acceptance for b&w cover and $5-20 for inside b&w.
Other Needs: Cover material.

WISCONSIN SPORTSMAN, Box 1307, Oshkosh WI 54901. Editor-in-Chief: Thomas C. Petrie. Art Director: Janet Wissin. "Our readers want practical information on Wisconsin outdoors; they are tired of reading about bass fishing in Georgia, deer hunting in Texas or camping in Maine." Bimonthly. Circ. 55,000. Photocopied submissions OK. Original artwork returned after publication. Free sample copy.
Cartoons: Uses 2-3 cartoons/issue. Receives 10 submissions/week from freelancers. Interested in "sophisticated outdoors humor"; single, double and multipanel with gag lines. Prefers finished cartoons. SASE. Reports in 2 weeks. Buys all rights on a work-for-hire basis. Pays $30-100, b&w and color; on publication.
Illustrations: Buys 20-35 illustrations/year on outdoor and wildlife themes. "No Disney-type animals. All elements must be technically correct; Wisconsin has no palm trees or snow-capped mountains." Interested in airbrush, pencil, pen and ink drawings. Provide b&w photcopied samples, "particularly published work" to be kept on file for future assignments. Prefers samples of style ("transparencies if color"). SASE. Reports in 2 weeks. Buys all rights on a work-for-hire basis. Minimum payment: Cover: Pays $200, color. Inside: Pays $25-150, color; $15-100, b&w; on publication.

WISCONSIN TRAILS, Box 5650, Madison WI 53705. (608)831-3363. Managing Editor: Jill Weber Dean. Concerns travel, recreation, history, industry and personalities in Wisconsin. Quarterly. Circ. 25,000. Previously published and photocopied submissions OK. Free sample copy and artist's guidelines.
Illustrations: Uses 6 illustrations/issue, all from freelancers. Receives less than 1 submission/week from freelancers. "Ad work is done on assignment, to illustrate specific articles. All articles deal with Wisconsin. We allow artists considerable stylistic latitude." Provide "samples (photocopies OK) of style; indication of artists favorite topics; name, address and phone number" to be kept on file for future assignments. Prefers samples of style. SASE. Reporting time varies. Buys all rights on a work-for-hire basis. Inside: Pays $25, b&w line drawings and washes; $50, color washes and color-separated work; on publication.
Other Needs: Marketing Manager: Jim Hornik. Uses artists for design/layout of sales pages, ads and brochures. Send samples of graphic design and layout. Pays by job.

THE WITTENBURG DOOR, 1224 Greenfield Dr., El Cajon CA 92021. (714)440-2333. Contact Wayne Rice. For men and women, usually connected with the church. Bimonthly. Circ. 12,000. Reports in 2 months.
Cartoons: Buys 2-4 cartoons/issue on assignment. Uses satire/humor on religious themes. Mail finished art or roughs. SASE. Reports in 2 months. Pays $20-150, b&w; on publication.
Illustrations: Number bought varies. Assigns themes. Arrange interview to show portfolio. Reports in 2 months. Negotiates pay; pays on publication.

WOMAN BEAUTIFUL, Drawer 189, Palm Beach FL 33480. (305)833-4593. Editor: Susan Gregg. For students at beauty schools and people who patronize beauty salons. Bimonthly. Circ. 12,000.
Cartoons: Buys 2 cartoons/issue on any subject. Send finished art. SASE. Reports in 2 months. Pays $5 for b&w; on publication.

WOMEN IN BUSINESS, Box 8728, Kansas City MO 64114. (816)361-6621. Art Director: Isabel Deaver. For businesswomen, all levels in all fields. Published 9 times/year. Circ. 110,000. Free sample copy.
Cartoons: Buys 1-2 cartoons/year on businesswomen; single panel. Query with samples. SASE. Reports in 4 weeks. Buys all rights, but may reassign rights to artist after publication. Pays $25, halftones; on acceptance.
Illustrations: Uses 3-4 illustrations/issue. Buys 50% of all illustrations from freelancers. Assigns themes. Returns samples if requested. Provide copies of samples and resumes to be kept on file for future assignments. SASE. Reports in 4 weeks. Buys all rights, but may reassign rights to artist after publication. Cover: Pays $75, color; $50, b&w. Inside: Pays $25, b&w and color. Negotiates pay.

WOMEN TODAY, 261 5th Ave., New York NY 10016. Editor-in-Chief: Diana Johnson. Monthly. Circ. 200,000. Mail art or query with samples. SASE. Reports in 1 week. Previously published, photocopied and simultaneous submissions ("let us know") OK. Buys first, reprint or all rights. Pays on publication. Sample copy $1.
Cartoons: Buys 20/issue on women. Pays $15-20, b&w.

WOMEN'S CIRCLE HOME COOKING, Box 1952, Brooksville FL 33512. Editor: Barbara Hall Pedersen. For women and men who enjoy cooking. Monthly. Circ. 225,000. Mail art; submit seasonal work 6-7 months in advance. Reports in 2-8 weeks. Buys all rights. Previously published work OK. Original artwork not returned after publication. Sample copy for SASE and 40¢ postage.
Cartoons: Uses 3 cartoons/issue, all from freelancers. Receives 30 submissions/week from freelancers. Themes should not be "demeaning to cooks, especially women cooks." Prefers finished cartoons. SASE. Reports in 2 weeks. Buys all rights on a work-for-hire basis. Pays $20.
Illustrations: Uses 6 illustrations/issue. Provide resume and samples of style to be kept on file for future assignments. SASE. Reports in 1 week. Buys all rights on a work-for-hire basis. Pays $5-10, b&w spot drawings.
Other Needs: "Line art drawings of food."

WOMEN'S RIGHTS LAW REPORTER, 180 University Ave., Newark NJ 07102. (201)648-5320. Contact: Business Manager. For lawyers, students and feminists; concerns law and feminism. Estab. 1971. Circ. 1,500. Quarterly. Reports in 6 weeks. Pays on publication.
Cartoons: Buys 1-2/issue on women's roles and social commentary. Pays $30, b&w. Query.

WOOD AND WOOD PRODUCTS, 300 W. Adams St., Chicago Il 60606. (312)977-7268. Managing Editor: Russ Gager. For owners and managers of furniture and woodworking companies, plywood mills, particleboard mills and wood products such as laminated panels or millwork. Monthly. Circ. 30,000.
Cartoons: Buys 1 cartoon/issue on assigned themes. Send roughs. SASE. Negotiates pay; pays on publication.
Illustrations: Buys 1-2 illustrations/issue on assigned themes. Query with samples or arrange interview to show portfolio. SASE. Negotiates pay; pays on publication.

WOODALL'S TRAILER & RV TRAVEL, 500 Hyacinth Place, Highland Park IL 60035. (312)433-4550. Editor-in-Chief: Kirk Landers. Art Editor: Paul Casper. For those involved with recreational vehicles and camping. Monthly. Circ. 280,000. "We are looking for both new talent and proven professionals."
Cartoons: Buys 30 cartoons/year on recreational vehicles and camping; single and multipanel. Query. SASE. Reports in 2 weeks. Buys first rights. Pays $20-45, b&w halftones and washes; on acceptance.
Illustrations: Buys 50 illustrations/year. Interested in all themes. Query. SASE. Reports in 2 weeks. Buys first rights. Cover: Pays $300-500, color. Inside: Pays $100-500, color; $25-300, b&w; on acceptance.

WOODENBOAT, Box 78, Brooklin ME 04616. Editor-in-Chief: Jonathan A. Wilson. Managing Editor: Jane Day. Concerns building, repairing and maintaining wooden boats. Bimonthly. Circ. 35,000. Query with samples. SASE. Reports in 1-2 months. Previously published work OK. Buys first North American serial rights. Pays on publication. Sample copy $2.50.
Illustrations: Buys 48/year on wooden boats or related items. Cover: Pays $50 minimum, color washes. Inside: Pays $10, b&w; $15, color. "We are always in need of high quality technical drawings. Most are redrawn from roughs." Also needs advertising art. Pays $10 minimum.

WOODMEN OF THE WORLD, 1700 Farnam St., Omaha NE 68102. (402)342-1890. Editor-in-Chief: Leland A. Larson. For family readers. Monthly. Circ. 456,000. Previously published work OK. Original artwork returned after publication, if arrangements are made. Free sample copy.
Cartoons: Uses 1-6 cartoons/issue; buys 1-6/issue from freelancers. Receives 10-50 submissions/week from freelancers. Interested in general interest subjects; single panel. Send finished cartoons. SASE. Reports in 2 weeks. Buys various rights. Pays $10, b&w line drawings, washes and halftones; on acceptance.
Illustrations: Uses 5-10 illustrations/year; buys 3-4/year from freelancers. Interested in lodge activities, seasonal, humorous and human interest themes. Works on assignment only. Does not report back on future assignment possibilities. Provide brochure or flyers to be kept on file for future assignments. Prefers finished art. SASE. Reports in 2 weeks. Buys various rights. Cover: Pays $60-150, color; $50-150, b&w. Inside: Pays $40-100, color; $20-80, b&w; on acceptance.

WORK BOAT THE, Box 217, Mandeville LA 70448. (504)626-3151. Editor: H.L. Peace. Monthly. Circ. 13,600.
Illustrations: Suitable subjects are tow boats, pushboats, tug boats, offshore crew/supply boats, dredges; photos for cover. "Must evoke feeling of working in our industry. Action required. Must be effective when cropped square for cover use. Allow 3 months lead for seasonal covers." Query with samples. Prefers color prints, but will accept slides. SASE. Reports in 4 weeks. Pays on acceptance.

WORKBENCH, Modern Handcraft, Inc., 4251 Pennsylvania, Kansas City MO 64111. Editor-in-Chief: Jay W. Hedden. For woodworkers and do-it-yourself persons. Bimonthly. Circ. 600,000. "Art accepted only as part of a package of copy, photos and drawings." Free sample copy and artist's guidelines.
Cartoons: Buys 15 cartoons/year. Interested in woodworking and do-it-yourself themes; single panel with gag line. Submit art. SASE. Reports in 1 week. Buys all rights, but may reassign rights to artist after publication. Pays on acceptance. Pays $20 minimum, b&w line drawings.

WORKING WOMAN MAGAZINE/HAL PUBLICATIONS INC., 600 Madison Ave., New York NY 10022. (212)750-0020. Emphasizes work. Readers are working woman. Monthly. Circ. 400,000.
Illustration Needs: Uses 2-5, sometimes more, illustrations/issue. "Assignment only, we do keep a file of work. We always like to see portfolios. If work is suitable for our publication, we'll keep the illustator in mind for future assignments." Buys "editorial illustrations, occasionally of food and clothing. We prefer loose work to slick." Format: b&w line drawings and color washes for inside. Drop off portfolio any day to Susan Niles, art director. SASE. Payment varies. Generally buys one-time rights.

THE WORLD OF RODEO AND WESTERN HERITAGE, Box 660, Billings MT 59103. (406)245-2313. Editor: Jack Tanner. A Rodeo Construction Agency publication. Readers are "rodeo fans, rodeo contestants, historians and individuals interested in rodeo and/or western history, sports fans and general magazine audience." Monthly. Circ. 18,100. Original artwork returned after publication. Sample copy $1; art guidelines for SASE.
Illustrations: Uses 3-5 illustrations/issue, buys 3-5/issue from freelancers. "Illustrations are selected on 2 criteria: quality and relevance to articles. Illustrations are used in conjunction with articles almost totally." Looks for rodeo and western history/heritage art. Format: b&w line drawings, b&w color washes, and original oils for covers and inside. Provide resume, brochure and tearsheet to be kept on file for future assignments. Prefers finished art, rough or samples of style. SASE. Reports in 2 weeks. Pays $25-100 for b&w cover, $10-100 for inside b&w, $50-200 for color cover, $10-100 for inside color and $5-25 for line illustrations; on publication.Buys various rights.
Other Needs: "Original art (color) suitable for a cover. Some advertising design work."

WORLD OVER, 426 W. 58th St., New York NY 10019. (212)245-8200. Art Director: Stephen Schaffzin. Concerns Jewish life and history; for ages 8-13. Circ. 50,000. Published 8 times/academic year.
Illustrations: Buys 3/issue. Query with samples. SASE. Reports in 3 weeks. Pays $50-150; b&w; on acceptance.

WORLD RESEARCH INK, 11722 Sorrento Valley Rd., San Diego CA 92121. (714)276-9620. Emphasizes the free market system for students, professionals and business people. Purpose: Educational institute which produces material to provoke thought and discussion on the freemarket system. Quarterly. Circ. 50,000. Estab. 1979. Free sample copy; art guidelines for SASE.

Cartoon Needs: Uses 2-4 cartoons/issue; all supplied by freelancers. Cartoons should pertain to current issues in economics and personal freedom. "Themes will be assigned to freelancers whose style fits." Format: single and multi panel with or without gag line. Send only samples of style that can be kept on file to Chris Leffler, art director. Pays within 30 days after publication $50-100 b&w. Buys one-time rights.
Illustration Needs: Uses about 3 illustrations/issue; all supplied by freelancers. Interested in artwork to accompany articles on current issues in the free market system, individual freedom, education and government regulation. Format: b&w line drawings or color washes for inside. Send resume and samples of style we can keep on file or arrange personal appointment to show porfolio to Chris Leffler, art director. Pays within 30 days of publication $75-100 b&w inside: $200-250 color inside. Buys all rights on a work-for-hire basis.

WORLD TRAVELING, 30943 Club House Lane, Farmington Hills MI. Art Director: David Keranidas. Concerns travel. Estab. 1978. Bimonthly. Simultaneous submissions OK. Sample copy $2.
Cartoons: "Would like to buy cartoons on travel"; include gag line. Mail roughs or finished art. SASE. Reports in several months. Buys one-time rights. Pays on publication. Pays $20 maximum, b&w line drawings.

XANADU, Long Island Poetry Collective, Box 773, Huntington NY 11743. Art Editor: Coco Gordon. For poetry enthusiasts. Published semiannually or biannually. Circ. 1,000. Sample copy $2. Free artist's guidelines with SASE.
Illustrations: Buys up to 8/issue. Prefers finished art, slides or b&w photos. SASE. Reports in 2 weeks. "Xanadu is copyrighted by LI Poetry Collective, Inc. Rights revert to artist upon request." Cover: Pays $25 minimum, b&w line drawings and washes and photos of art, sculpture or other. Inside: Pays $5 minimum, b&w line drawings and washes.
Other Needs: "Serious professional fine art (reproduced by photos if necessary) selected for applicability to theme of poetry volume."

YACHTING, 1 Park Ave., New York NY 10016. (212)725-7800. Editorial Director: Richard L. Rath. Managing Editor: Marcia Wiley. For top-level participants in boating in all its forms, power and sail. Monthly. Circ. 150,000.
Illustrations: Buys 100 illustrations/year. Interested in boating. Query. SASE. Reports in 2-3 weeks. Buys first North American serial rights. Cover: Pays $350, color. Inside: Pays $50-200, color; $25-150, b&w.

YANKEE MAGAZINE'S GUIDE TO NEW ENGLAND, Main St., Dublin NH 03444. (603)563-8123. Emphasizes travel and recreation in New England. Semiannual. Circ. 150,000. Sample copy $1.50; art guidelines for SASE.
Illustrations: Art Director: Robert Orlando. Uses 4-6 illustrations/issue. Freelancers are "selected from samples kept on file—artists hired according to specific needs." Needs illustrations pertaining to food and architecture. Arrange for personal appointment to show portfolio. Reports "immediately." Buys one time North American rights. Pays $25 average for inside b&w spot to $150, for 1-page b&w; on acceptance.

YOUNG AMBASSADOR, Box 82808, Lincoln NE 68501. (402)474 4567. Art Director: Win Mumma. "Our purpose is to help Christian teens live consistently for Christ, and to help them grow in their knowledge of the Bible and its principles for living." Monthly. Circ. 80,000. Original artwork not returned after publication. Free sample copy.
Cartoons: Managing Editor: James D. Wallace. Uses 3-4 cartoons/issue; buys 3-4/issue from freelancers. Receives 10 submissions/week from freelancers. Interested in wholesome humor for terms; single panel. Prefers finished cartoons. Reports in 2 weeks. Buys all rights on a work-for-hire basis.
Illustrations: Uses 3-4 illustrations/issue. Uses no illustrations from freelancers. but possibly will do so in future. Works on assignment only. Samples returned by SASE. Reports back on future assignment possibilities. Provide resume, letter of inquiry and tearsheet to be kept on file for future assignments. Prefers resume and samples of style. SASE. Reports in 2 weeks. Buys all rights on a work-for-hire basis.

YOUNG JUDAEAN, Hadassah Zionist Youth Commission, 50 W. 58th St., New York NY 10019. Editor: Barbara Gingold. For members of Young Judaeans, ages 8-13. Monthly, November-June. Send samples. Reports in 1-3 months. Previously published work OK. Buys first rights. Pays on publication. Sample copy 35¢.

Needs: Buys spot line drawings, cover designs and cartoons. Pays $2, spot drawings; $10, b&w cover.

YOUNG MISS, 52 Vanderbilt Ave., New York NY 10017. Contact: Barbara Taff. For girls ages 10-14. Prefers local artists. Sample copy $1.
Cartoons: Uses 1 cartoon/issue, all from freelancers. Interested in themes of general interest to young women. Prefers roughs. Prefers personal interview; no mail. SASE. Reports in 1 week. Buys first rights.
Illustrations: Uses 20 illustrations/issue, all from freelancers. Receives 3-5 submissions/week from freelancers. "I look for fine quality-clean lines, crisp looking, all mediums and styles." Works on assignment only. Provide calling card and tearsheet to be kept on file for future assignments. Prefers portfolio. SASE. Reports in 1 week. Buys first North American serial rights. Pays $35-300.

YOUNG MUSICIANS, 127 9th Ave. N., Nashville TN 37234. (615)215-2359. Art Director: Shirley Johnson. For Southern Baptist children's choirs and choir directors. Estab. 1963. Monthly. SASE. Pays on acceptance.
Illustrations: Buys 20/issue on assigned themes. Pays $50-100, color. Arrange interview to show portfolio.

YOUR HOME, Box 2315, Ogden UT 84403. (801)394-9446. Editor: Helen S. Crane. For young couples who are interested in improving their homes. Monthly. Circ. 650,000.
Illustrations: Buys 10 illustrations/issue on "ideas for improving lifestyles inside and outside the home." Query with samples. SASE. Reports in 2 weeks. Pays $20, b&w; $25 minimum, color; on acceptance.

YOUTH IN ACTION, Free Methodist Headquarters, Dept. of Christian Education, 901 College Ave., Winona Lake IN 46590. (219)267-7656. For church youth. Published 6 times/year. Circ. 5,000. Query with samples. SASE. Reports in 4 weeks. Previously published, photocopies and simultaneous submissions OK. Not copyrighted. Pays on publication. Free sample copy.
Cartoons: Buys 18-20/year on current events, education, environment, family life and humor through youth; single, double and multipanel with gag lines. Pays $10 minimum, b&w line drawings.
Illustrations: Buys 27-30/year on assigned themes. Cover: Pays $20 minimum, b&w; $25 minimum, color. Inside: Pays $15 minimum, b&w line drawings and washes.

ZIP MAGAZINE, 401 N. Broad St., Philadelphia PA 19108. (215)574-9600. Art Director: Frank Moore. Features how-to articles on new developments, methods, systems and regulations for mail-oriented professionals, mass mailers and mail-order companies. Estab. 1978. Circ. 37,500. Published 9 times/year.
Cartoons: Buys 1 cartoon/issue on mail subjects, computers, post offices and lists of various types. Send roughs. SASE. Reports in 2 weeks. Pays $25, b&w; on acceptance.
Illustrations: Buys 2-3 illustrations/issue on assigned themes. Query with samples or arrange interview to show portfolio. SASE. Reports in 2 weeks.Pays $100, b&w; $200, color; on acceptance.

Newspapers and Newsletters

ACTION IN KENTUCKY, 200 W. Chestnut St., Louisville KY 40202. (502)587-0769. Editor-in-Chief: C. Daniel Huck. For conservative businessmen in Kentucky and the Southeast. Biweekly newspaper; 11½x17; 8 pages. Offset. Estab. 1959. Circ. 5,000. Query. SASE. Reports in 2 weeks. Previously published and photocopied submissions OK. Not copyrighted. Pays on publication. Free sample copy.
Cartoons: Buys 12/year on business and industry; single panel. Pays $5 minimum, line drawings.

THE ADVOCATES, New Mass Media, Inc., Box 85, Amherst MA 01002. Contact: Linda Matys. Publishes 3 alternative-style weeklies serving western Massachusetts and Connecticut. Includes seasonal, entertainment, travel and outdoor sections. Send published samples or art. SASE. Reports in 1-2 months. Previously published work OK. Buys all rights, but may reassign rights to artist on request. Pays on publication.
Needs: Pays $20 for b&w spot drawings.

ALFA OWNER, Box 331, Northbrook IL 60662. Editor-in-Chief: Evan Wilson. For Alfa Romeo owners. Monthly newsletter; 8½x11; 12 pages. Offset. Estab. 1958. Circ. 4,000. Query with samples. SASE. Reports in 2 weeks. Buys first rights. Pays on acceptance.
Illustrations: Minimum payment: Cover: $15, color; $10, b&w. Inside: $8, color; $5, b&w.

ALLIED INDUSTRIAL WORKER, International Union, Allied Industrial Workers of America, AFL-CIO, 3520 W. Oklahoma Ave., Milwaukee WI 53215. (414)645-9500. For 100,000 members of the AIW labor union. Monthly tabloid. Circ. 100,000. Original artwork returned after publication, if requested. Free sample copy.
Cartoons: Contact Ken Germanson. Buys 2 cartoons/issue, all from freelancers. Interested in economy, politics, retirement, factory work and union activity; single or multipanel with gag line. Pays $25 minimum, b&w line drawings or washes; on acceptance. Prefers finished cartoons. SASE. Reports in 2-4 weeks. Buys one-time rights.
To Break In: "Understand today's labor movement; have a good idea about contemporary factory life, health and occupational safety conditions; and avoid stereotypes, i.e., majority of factory workers are no longer white middle-aged males."

AMERICAN COLLECTOR, Crain Consumer Group, 740 Rush St., Chicago IL 60611. Antiques and collector tabloid. Query or mail art.
Needs: Pays $10, spot drawings and cartoons; half-page maximum size.

AMERICAN GOLD NEWS, 263 Church St., Box 457, Ione CA 95640. Editor-in-Chief: Cecil Helms. "Our readers are interested in anything related to gold, silver and uranium—from mine to money. *AGN* reports on gold in economics, laws, legislation, mines, exploration companies, stocks, coins and related information." Monthly newspaper. Circ. 3,500. Previously published work OK. Original artwork not returned after publication. Free sample copy and artist's guidelines.
Cartoons: Uses 1-2 cartoons/issue; buys 1-2/issue from freelancers. Interested in politics, gold, silver and uranium mining, milling, money, coins and "taking government down a peg by showing their over-control of land, money and business"; single, double and multipanel with gag lines (if needed). Prefers finished cartoons. SASE. Reports in 2-4 weeks. Buys first North American serial rights. Pays $2.50-25, b&w line drawings; on acceptance.
To Break In: "Research the subject, particularly what the government is doing to the people under the guise of 'human rights' and 'environmental protection.' "

AMERICAN MEDICAL NEWS, 535 N. Dearborn St., Chicago IL 60610. (312)751-6633. Editor-in-Chief: Larry Boston. Senior Editor: Barbara Bolsen. For physicians. Weekly newspaper. Circ. 270,000. Photocopied and simultaneous submissions OK. Original artwork not returned after publication. Free sample copy.
Cartoons: Uses 1 cartoon/issue, all from freelancers. Receives "hundreds" of submissions/week from freelancers. Interested in medical, current events and education; single panel. Prefers finished cartoons. SASE. Reports in 3 weeks. Usually buys first North American rights. Pays up to $100, b&w; on acceptance.
Illustrations: Art Director: Jim Kolar. Number illustrations used/issue varies; number bought/issue from freelancers varies. Works on assignment only. Samples returned by SASE. Reports back on future assignment possibilities. Provide resume, letter of inquiry, brochure and flyer to be kept on file for future assignments. Prefers portfolio. Usually buys first North American rights. Inside: Pays $50-150, b&w; on acceptance.

APA MONITOR, American Psychological Association, 1200 17th St. NW, Washington DC 20036. (202)833-7635. Editor: Pamela Moore. Managing Editor: Karen Schaar. For psychologists and other behavioral scientists. Published monthly, except combined July/August. Circ. 63,000. Original artwork returned after publication, if requested. Free sample copy.
Illustrations: Uses 4 illustrations/issue; buys 4/issue from freelancers. Interested in current events in behavioral sciences/mental health area. Works on assignment only. Samples returned by SASE. Reports back on future assignment possibilities. Provide letter of inquiry and tearsheet to be kept on file for future assignments. Prefers portfolio or samples of style. SASE. Reports in 2 weeks. Buys first North American serial rights. Pays $40-200/b&w; on publication.

ART & ARCHAEOLOGY NEWSLETTER, 243 E. 39th St., New York NY 10016. Editor: Otto F. Reiss. Concerns Old World archaeology and ancient mythology. Quarterly. Circ. 2,000. Sample copy $1.50 in 15¢ stamps.
Cartoons: "A cartoonist who is steeped in Graeco-Roman lore could come up with usable cartoons. He should have an excellent background in mythology and classical history." No

archaeologists wearing pith helmets. Buys one-time rights.

THE ASIA MAIL, Potomac-Asia Communications, Inc., Box 1044, Alexandria VA 22313. (703)548-2881. Managing Editor: Donna Gays. For those who do business, travel, read about or have an interest in the Pacific or Orient. Monthly. Circ. 30,000. Previously published and photocopied submissions OK (if *Asia Mail* is advised of such). Original artwork returned after publication. Free sample copy.
Cartoons: Uses 1-3 cartoons/issue; buys 1-2/issue from freelancers. Interested in Asia; single panel. Prefers roughs or finished cartoons. SASE. Reports in 8 weeks. Buys first North American serial rights. Pays $15 minimum, b&w line drawings; on publication.
Illustrations: Uses 1-3 illustrations/issue; buys 1-2/issue from freelancers. Interested in Asia. Provide letter of inquiry and tearsheet to be kept on file for future assignments. Prefers finished art or roughs. SASE. Reports in 8 weeks. Buys first North American serial rights. Cover: Pays $15 minimum, b&w line drawings and washes. Inside: Pays $10 minimum, b&w line drawings; on publication.

ATTLEGRAM, Texas Instruments Inc., 34 Forest St., Attleboro MA 02703. (617)222-2800. Contact: Lise Gramolini, editor/communications specialist. For employes and retirees. Estab. 1968. Circ. 7,500. Monthly newspaper; 11x17; 16 pages. Offset. SASE. Simultaneous submissions and previously published work OK. Reports in 2-3 weeks.
Cartoons: Buys industrial and electronic themes. Uses b&w line drawings. Negotiates pay.
Illustrations: Buys current event and safety in industry themes. Negotiates pay.

BAY AND DELTA YACHTSMAN, Recreation Publications, 2019 Clement Ave., Alameda CA 94501. (415)865-7500. Editor-in-Chief: Glenda Ganny Carroll. Art Director: Pat O'Daniels. Concerns boating and boat owners in northern California. Monthly newspaper. Circ. 19,000. Previously published and simultaneous submissions (if not published in northern California) OK. Original artwork returned after publication, if requested. Sample copy $1.
Cartoons: Buys 4-5/year on boating. Prefers roughs. SASE. Reports in 2 weeks. Buys all rights on a work-for-hire basis. Pays $5 minimum, b&w line drawings; on publication.
Illustrations: Uses 2-3 charts and technical drawings/issue on boating. Provide letter of inquiry and resume to be kept on file for future assignments. Prefers roughs. SASE. Reports in 2 weeks. Buys all rights on a work-for-hire basis. Pays $5 minimum, b&w line drawings; on publication.

BERKELEY BARB, Box 1247, Berkeley CA 94701. Editor: Rob Howe. For those interested in leftist politics, avante-garde artists and the counterculture. Weekly newspaper. Circ. 7,000. Free sample copy.
Illustrations: Reports in 6 weeks. Pays $15-40/drawing.

THE BREAD RAPPER, 2104 S. Colfax, Evanston IL 60201. Editor-in-Chief: Laurie Lawlor. Concerns banking services and involvement of bank with community; received with checking account statement. Photocopied submissions OK. Sample copy and artist's guidelines with SASE.
Cartoons: Buys 1 cartoon/issue on banking; single panel with gag line. Mail art. SASE. Reports in 8 weeks. Buys all rights. Pays $20 minimum, b&w line drawings and washes; on publication.

BUSH PILOTS INTERNACIONAL NEWSLETTER, Drawer 310, Escondido CA 92027. Editor-in-Chief: Arnold Senterfitt. Bimonthly newsletter. "We don't mind looking over materials from someone just starting but please don't expect critiques. Only by doing things fast and leaving out rejection slips can we get the one week turnaround." Previously published work OK.
Cartoons: Buys 10-30 cartoons/year on aviation and small planes; single panel. "We like simple drawings without large masses of ink, humorous in a whimsical way, about general aviation, or what some call 'little airplaines.' Cartoons should not poke fun *at* pilots but certainly can laugh along with him." Query with samples; no portfolios. SASE. Reports in 1 week. Buys all rights, but may reassign rights to artist after publication. Pays $10-25, b&w; on acceptance.
Illustrations: Buys themes on Latin American scenes and aviation. Query with samples; no portfolios. SASE. Reports in 1 week. Buys all rights, but may reassign rights to artist after publication. Pays $5-10, b&w line drawings; on acceptance.

BUSINESS INSURANCE, 740 N. Rush, Chicago IL 606ll. (312)649-5278. Editor: Susan Alt. Emphasizes commercial insurance. Weekly. Circ. 36,000. Sample copy $1; free art guidelines.
Cartoons: Uses 2 cartoons/issue; buys all from freelancers. Receives 2 submissions/week from freelancers. Interested in business related cartoons only. Prefers single or multi panel b&w line drawings. Send resume and/or samples of style. Reports in 2 weeks. Works on assignment only. Samples returned by SASE. Buys first North American serial and all rights. Pays $10-50 for B&W; on publication.

Illustrations: Uses 2 illustrations/issue; buys 1/issue from freelancers. Receives 1 submission/week from freelancers. Interested in "business oriented management. No travelling salesmen." Works on assignment primarily but will consider unsolicited material. Prefers b&w line drawings for inside. Send resume and/or samples of style. SASE. Reports in 2 weeks. Buys all rights. Pays $10-50 for inside b&w; on publication.

CAPPER'S WEEKLY, 616 Jefferson, Topeka KS 66607. Editor: Dorothy Harvey. Human interest and news weekly for families in small towns and rural areas. Original artwork not returned after publication. Sample copy 35¢.
Cartoons: Uses 2-3 cartoons/issue; buys 1/issue from freelancers. Receives 20 submissions/week from freelancers. Interested in family, garden and rural themes. Prefers finished cartoons. SASE. Reports in 2 weeks if accepted, 3-4 weeks if not accepted. Buys one-time and first serial rights. Pays $5; on acceptance.

CHARLOTTE OBSERVER & CHARLOTTE NEWS, Box 32188, Charlotte NC 28232.
Advertising: Contact: Sam Morgan.Uses artists for newspaper ad layouts and sales promotion art. Query with resume.

CHICAGO READER, Box 11101, Chicago IL 60611. (312)828-0350. Editor-in-Chief: Robert A. Roth. Cartoon/Illustration Editor: Bob McCamant. For young adults in lakefront neighborhoods interested in things to do in Chicago and feature stories on city life. Weekly. Circ. 103,000. Previously published, photocopied and simultaneous submissions OK. Sample copy $1.
Cartoons: Buys 5 cartoons/issue on anything; single, double and multipanel. "At present, we carry five regular cartoon features. We will consider others, but no one-time cartoons. Please submit at least eight samples in one series for consideration." Send photocopies or arrange interview to show portfolio. SASE. Buys one-time rights. Pays on publication.
Illustrations: Buys 3 illustrations/issue on assigned themes. Send photocopies or arrange interview to show portfolio. SASE. Buys one-time rights. Pays on publication. Cover and inside: Pays $60-125, b&w line drawings and washes.

THE CHRISTIAN SCIENCE MONITOR, 1 Norway St., Boston MA 02115. Daily newspaper. Send art or published samples. SASE. Reports in 2 weeks. Buys all rights. Pays on acceptance.
Cartoons: Buys family themes. Pays $50, line drawings, pen and inks and washes.

COLLAGE, Box 965, Los Gatos CA 95030. (408)264-5504. Editor-in-Chief: Timothy Seidler. For general audience. Monthly. Circ. 180,000. Original artwork returned after publication. Free sample copy.
Cartoons: Uses 3 cartoons/issue; buys 3/issue from freelancers. Receives 10 submissions/week from freelancers. Interested in "anything that's funny to 18-40-year olds." Single, double and multipanel. Also interested in continuing comic strips. Prefers finished cartoons. SASE. Reports in 4 weeks. Buys first North American serial rights. Pays $5 minimum, b&w line drawings and washes; on acceptance.
Illustrations: Uses 2 illustrations/issue; buys 1/issue from freelancers; for features, fiction and poetry. Works on assignment only. Samples returned by SASE. Reports back on future assignment possibilities. Provide calling card, flyer and tearsheet to be kept on file for future assignments. Prefers resume, finished art and samples of style. SASE. Reports in 4 weeks. Buys first North American serial rights. Cover: Pays $25 minimum, b&w line drawings and washes. Inside: Pays $10 minimum, b&w line drawings and washes; on acceptance.

COLLEGE STORE EXECUTIVE, Box 1500, Westbury NY 11590. (516)887-1800. Editor: Holly Klokis. For bookstore managers, publishers' representatives and merchandising people affiliated with the college bookstore industry. Published 10 times/year. Circ. 9,500. Original artwork returned after publication, if requested. Free sample copy and artist's guidelines.
Cartoons: Buys 10/year on education, humor through youth, retailing, merchandising and the college store industry; single panel with gag line (4⅞" square). Pays $5-7.50, b&w; on acceptance.
Illustrations: Number illustrations/issue varies. Interested in themes relating to bookstore or publishing. Works on assignment only. Samples returned by SASE. Reports back on future assignment possibilities. Provide letter of inquiry to be kept on file for future assignments. Prefers samples of style. SASE. Reports in 2 weeks. Buys all rights on a work-for-hire basis.Inside: Pays $10, b&w; $25, color; on acceptance.

THE COLORADO ALUMNUS, Koenig Alumni Center, University of Colorado, Boulder CO 80309. (303)492-8484. Editor: Ronald A. James. For university administrators, alumni, librarians and legislators. Published eight times/year. Circ. 78,000. Previously published work and simulta-

neous submissions OK. Original artwork not returned after publication. Free sample copy.
Cartoons: Uses 1 cartoons/issue, all from freelancers. Receives 5-6 submissions/week from freelancers. Interested in sports, humor through youth, environment, campus and problems in higher education. Prefers finished cartoons. SASE. Reports in 2 weeks. "Work becomes the property of the Universtiy of Colorado." Pays $15 minimum, line drawings and halftones; on acceptance.
Illustrations: Uses 1 illustration/issue, all from freelancers. Receives 1-2 submissions/week from freelancers. Interested in sports, campus and higher education. Provide calling card to be kept on file for future assignments. Prefers finished art. SASE. Reports in 2 weeks. "Work becomes the property of the University of Colorado." Cover and inside: Pays $15 minimum, b&w line drawings; on acceptance.

COMMUNICATIONS NEWS, 124 S. 1st St., Geneva IL 60134. (312)232-1400. Editor: Don Wiley. For managers of communication systems–including telephone companies, broadcasting stations and large communication systems. Monthly tabloid. Previously published work OK. Sample copy $1.
Needs: Buys communications management themes. Mail art. Reports in 3 weeks. Buys all rights. Pays $10, spot drawings and cartoons; on publication.

COMMUNITY WOMAN, Box 8234, Holiday Station, Anaheim CA 92802. (714)778-3708. Art Director: Melody Brunsting. Deals with women in the home and the community. Monthly newspaper. Circ. 15,000. Simultaneous submissions and previously published work OK. Free sample copy and artist's guidelines for SASE.
Cartoons: Buys 12-24 cartoons/year. Interested in topics related to today's woman; single panel with gag line. Query with roughs or finished art. SASE. Reports in 4 weeks. Pays $2-25, b&w line drawings and washes; on publication.
Illustrations: Contact W. C. Huber. Buys 25-50 illustrations/year on assigned topics. Query with previously published work. SASE. Reports in 4 weeks. Cover: Pays $25-200, full color; on publication.

COMPUTER CAREER NEWS, 708 3rd Ave., New York NY 10017. (212)697-5580. Editor: Steve Enright. Emphasizes career and job opportunities for data processing professions, programmers and systems analysts. Biweekly. Circ. 40,000. Estab. 1980. Free sample copy.
Cartoons: Uses 1-2 cartoons/issue "when we receive submissions from freelancers." Interested in data processing themes. Prefers single panel b&w line drawings with gag line. Send finished 3 3/4 wide x 4-5 high cartoons. SASE. Reports in 1 week. Buys first North American serial rights. Pays $25 for b&w; on acceptance.

THE CONSTANTIAN, 123 Orr Rd., Pittsburgh PA 15241. (412)831-8750. Editor: Randall J. Dicks. "We (Constantian Society) are monarchists and royalists, interested in monarchy as a political system and royalty as persons and personalities." Bimonthly newsletter. Circ. 400. Previously published work OK. Sample copy for SASE; free artist's guidelines.
Cartoons: "We have used a cartoon only once, but would certainly consider using them. It is best to write us about the idea first and send samples." SASE. Reports in 1 week. Buys various rights. Pays $5-10, b&w line drawings; on acceptance or publication.
Illustrations: "We use a lot of decorative drawings and work which relates to our subject matter (heraldic items of different nationalities, coats of arms, monograms, etc.)." SASE. Reports in 1 week. Buys various rights. Pays $5 minimum, b&w line drawings; on acceptance or publication.

CONSTRUCTION FOREMAN'S & SUPERVISOR'S LETTER, 24 Rope Ferry Rd., Waterford CT 06386. (203)442-4365. Editor: DeLoris Lidestri. Emphasizes construction supervision. Readers are construction supervisors who work with their crews. This covers bricklayers, carpenters, electricians, painters, plasterers, plumbers and building laborers. Semimonthly. Circ. 3,700. Original artwork not returned after publication. Free sample copy.
Cartoons: Uses 1 cartoon/issue which is done by a freelancer. Receives 5-7 submissions/week from freelancers. Uses "situations that deal with supervision in construction. Cartoons that depict both men and women as workers and/or supervisors needed. No sexist material, please." Format: single panel, b&w line drawings with gag line. Prefers finished cartoons.SASE. Reports in 2 weeks. Buys all rights. Pays $10 on acceptance.

COUNTRY JOURNAL, 1600 E. Lincoln, Decatur IL 62521. (217)422-9146. Editor-in-Chief: Mark Avery. For elevator operators and farmers. Estab. 1972. Circ. 25,000. Monthly newspaper; 11x14; 24 pages. Offset.
Cartoons: Pays $15 minimum, b&w line drawings. Query with samples.

Needs: "We have not used freelance art yet but are interested. The best way to break in is by direct mail or phone contact and by submitting work. We are interested in political cartoon dealing with current economic and political events."

COUNTRY STYLE, 11058 W. Addison, Franklin IL 60131. Editor-in-Chief: Vince Sorren. Biweekly; 10x12; 48 pages. Offset. Estab. 1976. Circ. 450,000. Mail art or query with samples. SASE. Reports in 3 weeks. Previously published and photocopied work OK. Buys all rights, but may reassign rights to artist after publication. Pays on acceptance. Sample copy $1.
Cartoons: Contact Ray Bachar, managing editor. Buys themes on country lifestyle/music. Pays $15-50, b&w; $30-100, color.
Illustrations: Contact Mike Ryan, layout editor. Cover: Pays $200, color. Inside: Pays $20, b&w; $40, color.

CRAIN'S CLEVELAND BUSINESS, 140 Public Square, Cleveland OH 44114. (216)522-1383. Editor: Frederick Freeman. Emphasizes business in the Cleveland, Akron, Lorain area for upper income executives, professionals and entrepreuners. Biweekly. Circ. 25,000. Estab. 1980.
Cartoons: Uses 1-2 cartoons/issue. Interested in business related subjects especially pertaining to the industries of northeastern Ohio. Prefers single panel b&w line drawings with gag line. Send finished cartoons. SASE. Reports in 2 weeks. Buys first North American serial rights. Pays $10-15 for b&w; on publication.
Illustrations: Uses 3-4 illustrations/issue. Assigns spot art and larger illustrations based on samples reviewed. Prefers artists to be located near or in city where overnight mail service is available. Interested in business themes related to northeastern Ohio industries. Prefers b&w line drawings for inside. Send resume and/or samples of style. SASE. Reports back on future assignment possibilities. Buys all rights. Pays $15 for inside b&w; on publication.

THE CRANSTON MIRROR, 250 Auburn St., Cranston RI 02910. Contact: Malcolm L. Daniels. Weekly newspaper. Original artwork returned after publication.prefers local artists.
Cartoons: Uses 2 cartoons/issue; buys 1 or none/issue from freelancers. Receives 3-4 submissions/week from freelancers. Interested in local editorial subjects. Call for interview to show portfolio (except July and August). Prefers finished catoons. SASE. Reports in 1 week.
Illustrations: Uses 2-4 illustrations/issue; buys 1-2/issue from freelancers. Call for interview to show portfolio (except July and August). Provide resume to be kept on file for future assignments. Prefers resume. SASE. Reports in 1 week.
Needs: Layout, illustration, technical art, paste-up, lettering and retouching. Pays $175, booklet; $15-75, illustrations.

CROSS COUNTRY NEWS, Meacham Field, Forth Worth TX 76106. (817)624-3600. Editor-in-Chief: Tony Page. For pilots who own planes. Newspaper published every 3 weeks. Circ. approx. 12,000. Free sample copy.
Cartoons: Uses 3 cartoons/issue, all from freelancers. Interested inaviation/UFOs; single panel. "Be sure the art has some cheesecake." Mail art. SASE. Reports in 1 week. Pays $10 minimum, line drawings; on acceptance.

CYCLE NEWS, 2201 Cherry Ave., Long Beach CA 90801. Editor: Charles Morey. For the motorcycle enthusiast/racer. Weekly newspaper. Circ. 100,000. Previously published work OK. Free sample copy.
Needs: Mail art. SASE. Buys all rights. Pays $5-15, spot drawings/cartoons; $50, cover; on publication.

CYCLE NEWS, EAST, Box 805, Tucker GA 30084. (404)934-7850. Editor-in-Chief: Jack Mangus. For motorcycle competition enthusiasts. Weekly newspaper. Circ. 45,000.
Cartoons: Buys 25/year on motorcycle-related current events, education, environment and politics, and on the hobby and profession of motorcycling. Reports "as soon as requested if SASE enclosed." Buys all rights, but may reassign rights to artist after publication. Pays $10-100, b&w line drawings, halftones and washes; on publication.
Illustrations: Buys 25/year on motorcycles. Reports "as soon as requested if SASE enclosed." Buys all rights, but may reassign rights to artist after publication. Pays $10-100, b&w line drawings; on publication.

DRUG SURVIVAL NEWS, Box 5115, Phoenix AZ 85010. (602)257-0797. Editor: Dario McDarby. Published by Do It Now Foundation/Institute for Chemical Survival, publication concerns drug and alcohol abuse. Circ. 10,000. Bimonthly newspaper. Previously published work and simultaneous submissions OK; however, "let us know." Free sample copy.

Cartoons: Uses 0-1 cartoons/issue, all from freelancers. Receives 0-10 submissions/week from freelancers. Interested in "substance abuse, alcoholism and domestic violence." Single, double or multipanel with gag line. Prefers roughs or finished cartoons. SASE. Reports in 1 week-1 month. Buys all rights; will "glady reassign aal rights upon request." Pays $5-25, gray opaques, b&w line drawings and washes; on publication.
Illustrations: Uses 0-1 illustrations/issue, all from freelancers. Receives 0-10 submissions/week from freelancers. Works on assignment only. Samples returned by SASE. Reports back on future assignment possibilities. Provide resume and samples to be kept on file for future assignments. Prefers resume, roughs and samples. SASE. Reports in 1 week-1 month. Buys all rights; will "gladly reassign all rights upon request." Cover and inside: Pays $5-25, gray opaques, b&w line drawings and washes; on publication.

THE DRUMMER PLANET, 250 W. Girard Ave., Philadelphia PA 19123. (215)627-1700. Contact: Robert Cherry. Weekly alternative newspaper. For educated Philadelphians, ages 18-45, interested in politics, arts, manifestation of current reality and progressive social change. Submit art or published samples. Reports in 2-3 weeks. Previously published work OK. Pays on publication.
Needs: Buys political themes. Pays $10.

DRYCLEANERS NEWS, Box 2180, Waterbury CT 06722. (203)755-0158. Contact: John Florian. For drycleaners in the Northeast. Monthly. Original artwork returned after publication, if requested. Free sample copy.
Cartoons: Buys 1 cartoon/issue on drycleaning plant owners or their business. Prefers finished cartoons. SASE. Pays $10; on publication; on acceptance.

THE EDGE, 25 Huntington Ave., Boston MA 82116. (617)353-1506. Readers are 18-24 years old. Weekly. Free sample copy.
25 Huntington Ave., Boston MA 82116. (617)353-1506. Readers are 18-24 years old. Weekly. Free sample copy.
Cartoon Needs: Uses 2-3 cartoons/issue from freelancers. Receives 0-1 cartoon from freelancers/week. Cartoons should pertain to "anything for 18-24 year old students and young professionals." Format: single and multi panel with gag line. Send finished cartoons or samples of style to Karen Riley, managing editor. Reports in 2 weeks. SASE.

ENGINEWS, 1910 S. 53rd St., Milwaukee WI 53219. (414)259-1339. Editor: Ray I. Scroggins. For customers, distributors and prospects of Teledyne Wisconsin Motor. Monthly newsletter. Circ. 15,000+. Simultaneous submissions and previously published work OK. Original artwork not returned after publication. Free sample copy.
Cartoons: Uses 1 cartoon/issue, all from freelancers. Interested in mechanics (or any field using small engines), turf care, construction, and plant maintenance; single or double panel with gag line. Prefers roughs. SASE. Reports in 6-8 weeks. Pays $10, b&w line drawing; on acceptance.

EXECUTIVE DIGEST, FOR TOURIST ATTRACTIONS AND PARKS, 401 N. Broad St., Philadelphia PA 19108. (215)925-9744. President: Scott Borowsby. Concerns amusement and theme parks, museums, zoos, landmarks, caves and attractions. Estab. 1978. Bimonthly newsletter. Circ. 20,000.
Cartoons: SASE. Reports in 3-4 weeks. Buys all rights.Pays $50 minimum, gray opaques; on publication.
Illustrations: Buys 1 illustration/issue; "must be tied to reader business." SASE. Reports in 3-4 weeks. Buys all rights.Cover: Pays $50 minimum, b&w; on publication. Query with resume and samples.
Design: Uses artists for cover. Query with resume and samples. SASE.

FAMILY FOOD GARDEN, 1999 Shepard Rd, St. Paul MN 55116. (612)647-7478. Managing Editor: Sharon Ross. For home gardeners and fruit growers. Published 10 times/year. Circ. 250,000. Sample copy $1.
Cartoons: Uses 2-3 cartoons/issue- all from freelancers. Receives 1 submission/week from freelancers. Interested in vegetable gardening; single panel. Mail brochure or samples with SASE. Reports in 5 weeks. Buys all rights for cartoons. Pays $15 minimum, pen and ink; on acceptance.

THE FIRE FIGHTERS DIGEST, Triple-One Publications, 9014 Birchleaf Ave., Downey CA 90241. Editor-in-Chief/Art Director: Steve W. Deeble. For paramedics and fire personnel. Monthly newsletter; tabloid; 72 pages. Offset. Estab. 1978. Circ. 5,000. Query. SASE. Reports in 3 weeks. Previously published and simultaneous submissions OK. Buys simultaneous or all rights,

but may reassign rights to artist after publication. Pays on publication. Sample copy $2. Artist's guidelines $1.
Cartoons: Buys 3/issue on paramedics and firefighting. Pays $5 for b&w cartoons.
Illustrations: Buys 12/year on current events, education, family life, firefighting and saving lives; 10¼x6, 3x3 and 6½x4½ only. Cover: Pays $5-150, b&w line drawings and washes. Inside: Pays $2-20, b&w line drawings and washes.

FISHING AND HUNTING NEWS, Box C-19000, Seattle WA 98109. Executive Editor: Stan Jones. Managing Editor: Vence Malernee. Weekly; 11½x17½; 28 pages. Offset. Circ. 135,000. All methods of contact OK. Reports in 3 weeks. Previously published, photocopied and simultaneous submissions OK. Buys one-time or all rights. Pays on publication. Sample copy for 9x12 SASE.
Cartoons: Buys less than 20/year on fishing, hunting, boating, camping and outdoor activities. "No sexist, racist or slob hunter stereotypes. No young Disney-like animals, or scenes showing overkill or hunting of protected species. Include common sense safety concerns." Pays $15-50, color; $5-10, b&w.
Illustrations: Buys up to 24/year on outdoor recreation, how-to diagrams, technical illustrations of boats and recreational vehicles and maps. "Subject should portray the excitement of the hunt, the nobility of the elusive wildlife or a fighting fish that just might 'get away.'" Minimum payment: Cover: $25, color; $10, b&w. Inside: $25, color; $5, b&w.
Advertising: Pays $5-10 minimum, b&w spot illustration for advertising, promotional material and brochures.

FREE FOR ALL, Box 962, Madison WI 53701. (608)255-2798. Art Director: Mark Saunders. Concerns socialist and feminist politics. Biweekly newspaper. Circ. 11,000. Simultaneous submissions and previously published work OK. Sample copy and artist's guidelines obtained for 50¢.
Cartoons: Contact Michael Kaufman, business manager. Buys 6/year on current events, education, environment, family life and politics; multipanel.Mail finished art. SASE. Reports in 1 month. Pays $10, b&w line drawings; on publication.
Illustrations: Contact Don Palmer, editor-in-chief. Buys 4/year "with socialist or feminist perspective" on current events, education, environment, family life, politics and retirement. SASE. Reports in 1 month.Cover: Pays $10, b&w line drawings; on publication.
To Break In: "Send a sample for us to use free, or if the artist lives nearby, stop by our office at 306 N. Brooks."

FREELANCE ART MONTHLY, Box 332-B, Wheeling IL 60090. (312)541-0614. Editor and Publisher: Paul Casper. Art Director: Kathleen Zawacki. For art directors and freelance commercial artists and photographers. Monthly newsletter. Reports in 3-4 weeks. Simultaneous submissions and previously published work OK. Buys first rights. Pays on publication. Free sample copy and artist's guidelines.
Cartoons: Buys 2 cartoons/year; single panel with gag line. Interested in graphics and commercial art. Prefers finished cartoons. SASE. Reports in 1 week. Pays $10 minimum, b&w line drawings and washes.
Illustrations: Uses 6 illustrations/issue. Receives 10 submissions/week from freelancers. Interested in "all types" of illustrations. Provide tearsheet to be kept on file for future assignments. Prefers tearsheet. SASE. Reports in 2 weeks. Cover: Pays $100 minimum, b&w line drawings and washes. Inside: Pays $75 minimum, b&w line drawings and washes.
Other Needs: Uses artists for special projects and issues of publication, ads and promotional pieces. Query with resume and samples. Pays according to piece.

FROM THE KENNELS, Specialty Publications, Box 1369, Vancouver WA 98666. (206)696-2971. Editor-in-Chief: J. C. Perkins. Concerns purebred dogs and shows. Biweekly tabloid; 20 pages. Offset. Estab. 1970. Circ. 15,000 plus. Query. SASE. Reports in 4 weeks. Previously published, photocopied and simultaneous submissions OK. Not copyrighted. Pays on publication. Sample copy $1.
Cartoons: Buys 5-6/year on dog shows; single panel with gag line. Negotiates pay for b&w line drawings.

GARDEN CENTER NEWS, 9800 Detroit Ave., Cleveland OH 44102. (216)651-5500. Editor: Bob Earley. Readers are retail garden center operators. Monthly. Estab. 1979. Free sample copy.
Cartoons: Uses 2 cartoons/issue; buys all from freelancers. Interested in humorous situations dealing with plants, employees and the business of garden centers. Prefers single panel b&w line drawings with gag line. Send finished cartoons. Reports in 2 weeks. Buys first North American serial rights. Pays $10-15 for b&w; on acceptance.

GAY SUNSHINE, A JOURNAL OF GAY LIBERATION, Box 40397, San Francisco CA 94140. (415)824-3184. Contact: W. Leyland. For gay people interested in the political and literary aspects of the gay liberation movement. Quarterly. Circ. 10,000.
Illustrations: Buys gay themes, b&w line drawings. Query with samples. SASE. Reports in 4 weeks. Negotiates pay; pays on publication.

GENERAL AVIATION NEWS, Box 1094, Snyder TX 79549. Editor: M. Gene Dow. For aircraft owners. Biweekly newspaper. Estab. 1945. Circ. 34,000. Query with resume. Reports in several days. Previously published work OK. Pays on acceptance. Sample copy $1.
Cartoons: Pays $5, b&w line drawings and washes. "We cover only general aviation—no military or airline."
Illustrations: Buys assigned themes. Pays $10, b&w line drawings and washes.

GLENDALE NEWS-PRESS, 111 N. Isabel, Glendale CA 91206. Art Director: Frank Rietta. Arrange interview to show samples of ad/promotional art, illustrations and other freelance work.

GOLD NEWSLETTER, National Committee for Monetary Reform, 8422 Oak St., New Orleans LA 70118. (504)865-9919. Editor: Jim Blanchard. Concerns gold as an investment. Monthly.Circ. 14,500. Free sample copy and artist's guidelines.
Cartoons: Buys 36 cartoons/year. Interested in inflation, government spending, the gold market and rising price of gold; single panel with gag line. Mail finished art. SASE. Reports in 1 month. Buys all rights. Pays $30-50, b&w; on publication.
Illustrations: Buys 15-25/year. Needs pen and ink drawings of gold coins, stacks of gold bars and gold ingots. Query with resume and samples. SASE. Reports in 1 month. Buys all rights. Pays $20-100; on publication.
Advertising: Assigns 70-80 jobs/year. Uses artists for ads, brochures, catalogs, charts, posters and recruitment literature.

GROUP, Thom Schultz Publications, Inc., Box 481, Loveland CO 80537. (303)669-3836. Editor-in-Chief: Thom Schultz. For high school members of Christian youth groups. Published 8 times/year. Circ. 40,000. Previously published, photocopied and simultaneous submissions OK. Original artwork returned after publication, if requested. Sample copy $1.
Cartoons: Uses 2 cartoons/issue; buys 2/issue from freelancers. Interested in humor through youth and religion. Send finished artwork. Reports in 1 week. Buys first, reprint or all rights, but may reassign rights to artist after publication. Pays on publication.
Illustrations: Uses 8 illustrations/issue; buys 8/issue from freelancers. Provide flyer and/or tearsheet to be kept on file for future assignments. Query with finished art or roughs. Reports in 1 week. Cover: Pays $50-100, color. Inside: Pays $5-50, b&w line drawings and washes. Buys all rights on a work-for-hire basis.

THE GUILD REPORTER, 1125 15th St. NW, Washington DC 20005. Contact: James M. Cesnik. "Our interests are almost exclusively in areas related directly to activities of the Newspaper Guild." Semimonthly (monthly in July and December). Query with resume; Newspaper Guild members only. Reports in 2 weeks. Previously published work OK. Pays on acceptance.
Needs: Pays $25 minimum, spot drawings and newspaper-related cartoons.

HORSEMEN'S YANKEE PEDLAR, 25 Harvard St., Worcester MA 01609. Publisher: Christine S. Dillard. Circ. 12,500. Monthly newspaper. Sample copy $1.
Cartoons: Senior Assistant Editor: Joann Griffin. Single panel with gag line. Mail finished art. SASE. Reports in 8-10 weeks. Buys all rights. Pays $10 minimum, b&w line drawings; on publication.

HOSPITAL SUPERVISOR'S BULLETIN, 24 Rope Ferry Rd., Waterford CT 06386. (203)442-4365. Pat Ryan. Emphasizes management methods for hospital supervisors of nonmedical departments. Biweekly newsletter. Circ. 7,000. Original artwork not returned after publication. Free sample copy and artist's guidelines.
Cartoons: Buys 2/issue on any aspect of hospital environment; single panel with gag line. "We prefer cartoons that emphasize the natural humor in life, life's foibles, rather than humor at the expense of others." Pays $10, b&w line drawings. Mail roughs. SASE. Reports in 2 weeks. Pays on acceptance. Buys all rights.

HOUSTON BUSINESS JOURNAL, 5314 Bingle, Houston TX 77092. (713)688-8811. Editor: Mike Weingart. Managing Editor: Bill Schadewald. For highly-educated business executives, average age 40. Weekly. Circ. 15,000. Previously published work OK. Original artwork not returned after publication.

Cartoons: Uses 1 cartoons/issue, all from freelancers. Receives 3 submissions/week from freelancers. Interested in business; single panel. Prefers finished cartoons. SASE. Reports in 2 weeks. Buys all rights on a work-for-hire basis. Pays $7.50 minimum, line drawings; on acceptance.
Illustrations: Uses 2 illustrations/issue; buys 1/issue from freelancers. Interested in business. Works on assignment only. Samples returned by SASE. Prefers conference. Reports "as needed." Buys all rights on a work-for-hire basis. Pays on acceptance.

ILLINOIS WILDLIFE, Illinois Wildlife Federation, Box 116, Blue Island IL 60406. (312)388-3995. Editor-in-Chief: Ace Extrom. For sportsmen and conservationists. Monthly. Circ. 35,000. Previously published work OK. Sample copy 50¢.
Cartoons: Buys 6/year on hunting, fishing, trapping and conservation; single panel with gag line. Submit art. SASE. Reports in 2 weeks. Pays $5-10, b&w; on publication. Buys one-time rights.

IOWA DEVELOPMENT COMMISSION DIGEST, 250 Jewett Bldg., Des Moines IA 50309. (515)281-3098. Editor-in-Chief: Megan Manning. "For those interested in Iowa and how it's being promoted." Estab. 1972. Circ. 13,000. Monthly newsletter; 8¼x11; 12 pages. Offset. SASE. Reports in 2 weeks. Previously published work OK. Not copyrighted. Pays on publication. Free sample copy and artist's guidelines.
Illustrations: Buys themes relating to Iowa, its attractions and events. Cover and inside: Pays $75 maximum, b&w line drawings. Arrange interview to show portfolio.
Design: Uses artists for layout mock-ups and publication redesign. Pays approximately $20/hour. Arrange interview to show portfolio.

JEWISH CURRENT EVENTS, 430 Keller Ave., Elmont NY 11003. Editor-in-Chief: Samuel Deutsch. Art Director: S. Askenazi. For Jewish audience. Biweekly. Previously published and simultaneous submissions OK.
Cartoons: Buys camera-ready art with Jewish content or flavor or adaptable for such; single, double and multipanel. Submit art. SASE. Reports in 1 week. Pays $15-50 plus, b&w line drawings; on publication.

THE JOURNAL, 33 Russell St., Toronto, Ontario, Canada M5S 2S1. (416)595-6053. Editor: Anne MacLennan. Concerns drug and alcohol research, treatment and education. Monthly. Circ. 16,000. Previously published work OK. Original artwork returned after publication. Free sample copy.
Cartoons: Uses 2-3 cartoons/issue; buys 1/issue from freelancers. Receives 1 submission/month from freelancers. Interested in "themes relating to alcohol and other drug use. Prefers finished cartoons. "We confirm receipt immediately." Pays $25, 3x5 minimum cartoons; on publication.

KEY, Voice Publications, Goreville IL 62939. (618)995-2027. Editor-in-Chief: Bernard Lyons. For direct marketing/mail order people and firms which use national classified media. Monthly newsletter. Sample copies two for $3.
Cartoons: Buys 1 cartoon/issue on direct marketing/mail order themes—especially from the business point of view, e.g., selling by mail; single panel. "We seldom use cartoons because we can't get what we want." Mail art. SASE. Reports in 2 weeks. Buys all rights. Pays $10-25, b&w line drawings; on acceptance.

LONG TIME COMING, Box 128, Station G, Montreal, Quebec, Canada H2W 2M9. (416)842-4781. Editor-in-Chief: J. Manthorne. Art Editor: Judith Carison. For lesbians and feminists. Bimonthly; 8x11½; 35 pages. Mimeograph. Estab. 1973. Circ. 2,000. Mail art. SASE. Reports in 3 weeks. Previously published, photocopied and simultaneous submissions OK. Pays on acceptance. Free sample copy.
Cartoons: Buys themes on lesbians and feminists; single panel. Pays $2-5, halftones.
Illustrations: Inside: Pays $2-5, b&w.

LOS ANGELES FREE PRESS, 5850 Hollywood Blvd., Los Angeles CA 90028. Editors: Ron Ridenour and Jeff Nightbyrd. Weekly. Circ. 50,000. Write. Inside: Pays $2-20, b&w line drawings and washes. Pays on publication.
Needs: Pays $25 for spot drawings.

THE MANITOBA TEACHER, 191 Harcourt St., Winnipeg, Manitoba, Canada R3J 3H2. (204)888-7961. Editor: Mrs. Miep van Raalte. Emphasizes education for teachers and others in Manitoba. Monthly except July and August. Circ. 17,500. Free sample copy and art guidelines.
Cartoons: Uses 1-3 cartoons/year relating to education in Manitoba. Prefers single panel b&w line drawings with gag line. Send roughs and samples of style. SASE. Reports in 1 month.

Illustrations: Interested in b&w line drawings for inside. Send roughs and samples of style. SASE. Reports in 1 month.

MARIN CENTER NEWSLETTER, Civic Center Dr., San Rafael CA 94903. (415)479-4493. Editor-in-Chief: Jim Farley. Provides schedule of events and news of the Marin County performing arts center. Monthly newsletter. Circ. 11,000. Previously published work OK. Free sample copy.
Illustrations: Buys 2-5 illustrations/year on assigned themes. Query or arrange interview to show portfolio; mostly local artists. SASE. Reports in 1 week. Cover and inside: Pay varies for b&w line drawings.

MASSACHUSETTS LAWYERS WEEKLY, 30 Court Square, Boston MA 02108. Editorial Department: (617)227-6034. Advertising Department: (617)367-8616. Editor-in-Chief: Sam Spencer. Art Director: Jeff Bryan. Provides digested court opinions, calendar items and lawyers news. Weekly. Circ. 7,350. Previously published, photocopied and simultaneous submissions OK. Sample copy $2; free artist's guidelines.
Illustrations: Uses 5-15 illustrations/issue; buys 3-5 from freelancers. Interested in politics and legal themes. Provide resume to be kept on file for future assignments. Prefers samples and resume. SASE. Reports in 2 weeks. Buys first rights. Cover and inside: Pays $75-150, b&w line drawings and color-separated work; on publication.

MFC NEWS, Box 449, Jackson MS 39205. Editor: Jim Cleveland. "Our publication is distributed to nearly 59,000 farm homes each month with news of importance to the farmer, with articles of special interest to the farm wife. We are often in the market for farm pictures or illustrations sutied to mid-south agriculture and rural life, as well as cartoons." Prefers samples. Previously published work OK. Sample copy available.
Illustrations: Buys cover designs, line drawings, washes and layout. Negotiates pay; pays "upon receipt."

MILWAUKEE JOURNAL, Newspapers, Inc., 333 W. State, Milwaukee WI 53201. Managing Editor: Joe Shoquist. Daily. Circ. 330,000.
Cartoons: Asst. Managing Editor: George Lockwood. Buys themes acceptable to family readership; single panel. Query with samples. SASE. Reports in 2 weeks. Buys all rights. Pays $15 minimum, washes.
Illustrations: Art Director: Vincent Catteruccia. Buys themes acceptable to family readership. Query with samples. SASE. Reports in 2 weeks. Buys all rights. Inside: Pays $10 minimum.

NATIONAL ENQUIRER, Lantana FL 33464. Executive Editor: Thomas Kuncl. Weekly tabloid. Circ. 6,000,000. Previously published work and photocopies OK. Free sample copy.
Cartoons: Buys 540/year on "all subjects the family reader can relate to. We like cartoons with lots of visual impact." Especially needs Christmas cartoon spread (submit 2 months in advance). Mail art. SASE. Reports in 1 week. Buys first rights. Pays $210 maximum, b&w single panel; $25 every panel thereafter. Pays on acceptance.

NATIONAL JOGGING ASSOCIATION, 2420 K St., NW, Washington DC 20037. (202)965-3430. Managing Director: Liz Eliott. Concerns healthful jogging.
Cartoons: Uses 2-3 cartoons/issue, all from freelancers. Mail art or query with samples. SASE. Reports in 2 weeks. Pays $5-30/cartoon.
Illustrations: Uses 2-5 illustrations/issue; buys 1 or 2/issue from freelancers. Usually works on assignment basis. Samples returned by SASE. Provide tearsheet, samples, artist's rates and expectation to be kept on file for future assignment possibilities. Mail art or query with samples. SASE. Reports in 2 weeks. Pays $5-50, sometime $100.

NBDA NEWS, (formerly Bicycle Dealers), National Bicycle Dealers Association Inc., 435 N. Michigan Ave., Suite 1717, Chicago IL 60611. (312)644-0828. Executive Director: Glen W. Bostrom. For retail servicing dealers. Bimonthly newsletter. Not copyrighted. Submit rough art.
Cartoons & Illustrations: Needs b&w and color cartoons and spot drawings on bicycle themes. Pays $200-300/illustration.

THE NEVADAN, Box 70, Las Vegas NV 89101. Editor: A. D. Hopkins. Deals with history, outdoor and small-town life in Nevada. Weekly newspaper. Circ. 90,000. Previously published work OK. Free sample copy.
Illustrations: Buys art *only* with accompanying mss. Query with resume and samples. SASE. Reports in 3 weeks. Pays $6, b&w line drawings and gray opaques; on publication.

NEW ENGLAND SENIOR CITIZEN/SENIOR AMERICAN NEWS, Prime National Publishing Corp., 470 Boston Post Rd., Weston MA 02193. Editor-in-Chief/Art Director: Ira Alterman. Monthly newspaper; tabloid; 32-36 pages. Offset. Estab. 1970. Circ. 60,000. Query or mail samples. SASE. Reports in 4 weeks. Previously published work OK. Pays on publication. Sample copy 50¢.
Illustrations: Buys 1-5/issue. Cover: Pays $10-50, b&w.

NEW YORK ANTIQUE ALMANAC, Box 335, Lawrence NY 11559. (516)371-3300. Editor-in-Chief: Carol Nadel. Managing Editor: Lola Richter. For art, antiques and nostalgia collectors/investors. Monthly newspaper. Circ. 35,000. Reports in 4 weeks. Previously published work OK. Original artwork returned after publication, if requested. Free sample copy.
Cartoons: Uses 1 cartoon/issue; buys 1/issue from freelancers. Receives 1 submissions/week from freelancers. Interested in antiques, nostalgia and money. Prefers finished cartoons. SASE. Reports in 4 weeks. Buys all rights, but may reassign rights to artist after publication. Pays $5-20, b&w; on publication.
Illustrations: Buys 24/year on collecting and investing. Buys all rights, but may reassign rights to artist after publication. Pays $5 minimum, b&w; on publication.

NEW YORK ARTS JOURNAL, Manhattan Arts Review, Inc., 560 Riverside Dr., New York NY 10027. (212)663-2245. Editor-in-Chief: Richard Burgin. Art Director: Mike Feldman. Provides a critical and creative study of the arts. Bimonthly newspaper; tabloid. Circ. 25,000. SASE. Previously published, photocopied and simultaneous submissions OK. Sample copy $1.
Illustrations: Buys 5/issue. Submit art or query with samples. Buys first rights. Pays $10-25, b&w line drawings, washes, reflective art and veloxes; pays on publication.

THE NEW YORK CULTURE REVIEW, 128 E. 4th St., New York NY 10003. Editor-in-Chief: Daniel M. J. Stokes. For poets and New York City residents interested in literature, art, dance and publishing. Monthly newsletter; 8½x11; 14 pages. Offset. Estab. 1974. Circ. 2,000. Submit art. SASE. Reports in 1 week. Photocopied submissions OK. Buys first rights. Pays on publication.
Cartoons: Buys 1-4/issue on education, environment, politics, writing and publishing; single panel with gag line. Pays $5-25, b&w line drawings.
Illustrations: Buys 12/year on education, politics, writing and publishing. Cover and inside: Pays $5-25, b&w line drawings.

NORTHEAST OUTDOORS, Box 2180, Waterbury CT 06722. (203)755-0158. Editor/Art Director: John Florian. For campers living in the northeastern states. Monthly. Circ. 23,000. Free sample copy and artist's guidelines.
Cartoons: Uses 1 cartoon/issue. Interested in family, camping and recreational vehicles, all in northeastern states setting; single panel with gag line. Prefers finished cartoons. SASE. Reports in 2 weeks. Buys first rights. Pays $10 minimum, b&w line drawings; on acceptance.

NURSERY DAYS, United Methodist Publishing House, 201 8th Ave. S., Nashville TN 37202. Editor: Doris Willis. Art Director: Dave Dawson. For home use to correlate with church school for ages 2-4. Weekly storypaper; 8½x11; 4 pages. Estab. 1964. Circ. 85,000. Query with samples. SASE. Reports in 4 weeks. Previously published work OK. Pays on acceptance. Free sample copy.
Illustrations: Buys 3-4/issue on education, environment, family life and religion. Pays $45, full-color illustrations; $40, 3-color art. Also buys b&w line drawings.

NURSERY PRODUCT NEWS, 9800 Detroit Ave., Cleveland OH 44102. (216)651-5500. Editor: Bob Earley. Readers are nurserymen and wholesale plant growers. Monthly. Estab. 1979. Free sample copy.
Cartoons: Uses 2 cartoons/issue; buys all from freelancers. Interested in humorous situations dealing with growing plants, nursery employees, weather or business of selling plants wholesale. Prefers single panel with gag line. Send finished cartoons. Reports in 2 weeks. Buys first North American serail rights. Pays $10-15 for b&W; on acceptance.

NURSING JOB NEWS, 470 Boston Post Road, Weston MA 02193. (617)899-2702. Editor: Ira Alterman. Readers are "experienced and student nurses interested in seeking employment, these nurses are interested in trends in nursing employment, relocation or area hiring trends in nursing." Monthly. Circ. 40,000. Sample copy $2.
Cartoons: Uses 1-3 cartoons/issue; buys 3-5/issue from freelancers. Receives 25 submissions/month from freelancers. Interested in hospital or nursing themes. Prefers b&w line drawing with gag line. Send finished cartoons. SASE. Reports in 2 weeks. Buys one-time rights. Pays $5-10 for b&w; on publication.

Illustrations: Uses 3 illustrations/issue; buys 13/issue from freelancer. Receives 10 submissions/month from freelancer. Interested in general illustrations that go along with editorial; usually people or nature. Works on assignment. "Freelancers call, send us samples, and we make a decision at that time if their style fits our paper. If it does, we keep their names on file, then contact them for assignments. Send roughs. SASE. Reports in 2 weeks. Prefers b&w line drawings. Buys all rights on a work-for-hire basis. Pays $50-100 for b&w or color cover. $50 for inside b&w. Pays on publication.

NUTRITION HEALTH REVIEW, Box 20, Haverford PA 19041. Editor-in-Chief: F.R. Rifkin. Quarterly. Circ. 125,000. Previously published work OK "if we're told." Sample copy $1.00.
Cartoons: Buys 40-50/year on medicine, doctors, nutrition, food purveyors and restaurants; single panel. Mail art. SASE. Reports in 4 weeks. Buys first rights. Pays $10 minimum, line drawings.
Illustrations: Buys 40-50/year on nutrition, health and food. Mail art. SASE. Reports in 4 weeks. Buys first rights. Cover: Pays $50 minimum, b&w line drawings.

OFFROAD EAST, 6637 Superior Ave., Sarasota FL 33581. (813)921-5687. Editor: George J. Haborak. Offroad and 4-wheel drive newspaper pertaining to offroading, 4x4 racing and trucks; automotive publication. Serves readers in 32 states east of Colorado. Circ. 40,000. Monthly tabloid; 68-72 pages offset. SASE. Reports in 3 weeks. Pays on publication.
Cartoons and Illustrations: Buys approximately 10 offroad theme cartoons/illustrations per year. Needs b&w work. Negotiates pay. Send samples of work, along with your drawing fee.

OIL, CHEMICAL AND ATOMIC UNION NEWS, Box 2812, Denver CO 80201. (303)893-0811. Editor: Jerry Archuleta. For union members. Circ. 185,000. Monthly newspaper. Free sample copy and artist's guidelines.
Cartoons: Buys 75/year on current events, politics and union members; single panel with gag line. Mail finished art. SASE. Reports in 2 weeks. Pays $12-15, b&w line drawings. Mail finished art; on acceptance.
Illustrations: Buys 2/year on assigned themes. Query with resume and samples. SASE. Reports in 2 weeks. Cover: Pays $50-100, color. Inside: Pays $25-75, b&w; on acceptance.

OLD CARS, 700 E. State St., Iola WI 54945. (715)445-2214. Editor: LeRoi Smith. Deals with antique and special interest automobiles. Weekly newspaper. Circ. 99,000. Free sample copy.
Cartoons: Uses 25 cartoons/year; all from freelancers. Receives 3-4 cartoon packages/week. Interested in old car themes. Submit b&w single panel with gag line or line with b&w wash. SASE. Reports in 1 week. Buys all rights or buys first North American serial rights. Pays $5 minimum.

THE PATRIOT, 243 W. Main St., Kutztown PA 19530. (215)683-7343. Editor-in-Chief: A. R. Floreen. For general audience. Weekly newspaper. Circ. 5,000. Originals returned to artist after publication.
Illustrations: Buys newspaper ad layouts and sales promotion art. Works on assignment only. Samples returned by SASE; and reports back on future assignment possibilities. Provide calling card to be kept on file for future assignments. Prefers portfolio (roughs). Pays $5-10/sketch.

PERSONNEL ADVISORY BULLETIN, Bureau of Business Practice, 24 Rope Ferry Rd., Waterford CT 06386. Supervisory Editor: Barbara Kelsey. For personnel managers in all tyes and sizes of companies–white collar and industrial. Features interviewing and hiring, training, benefits, career developments, promotion practices, counseling, record keeping, etc. Biweekly newsletter. Original artwork not returned after publication. Free sample copy and artist's guidelines.
Cartoons: Uses 1 cartoon/issue; buys 1/issue from freelancers. Receives 15 submissions/week from freelancers. Buys 30/year on "personal oriented situations. Please spare me sexist suggestions and male boss/dumb female secretary jokes." Double panel. Pays $10 for b&w line drawings. Mail finished art. SASE. Reports in 2 weeks. Buys all rights. Pays on acceptance.

PET BUSINESS, (formerly *Aquarium Industry*), Toadtown, Magalia CA 95954. (916)872-1200. Editor-in-Chief: Robert Behme. For those in the pet trade: manufacturers, wholesalers, and livestock breeders and farmers. Monthly newspaper. Circ. 15,000. Free sample copy.
Cartoons: Buys 1 cartoon/issue on pet-related themes; single panel. Query. SASE. Reports in 3 weeks. Pays $15-25, b&w line drawings and halftones; on acceptance.
Illustrations: Buys 20 illustrations/year on assigned themes. Query. SASE. Reports in 3 weeks. Cover: Pays $40, color; $25-40, b&w; on acceptance.
Other Needs: Also uses artists for layout and book art.

PHOTO INSIGHT, Suite 2, 169-15 Jamaica Ave., Jamaica NY 11432. Editor-in-Chief: Conrad Lovelo, Jr. Art Director: Jacqueline Wright. Provides photo contest and exhibition information. Bimonthly. Circ. 1,500. Simultaneous submissions OK. Originals returned to artist after publication. Sample copy $2.
Cartoons: Uses 2 cartoons/issue, all from freelancers. Receives 5 submissions/week from freelancers. Interested in cartoons about photography; single panel with gag line. prefers finished cartoons. SASE. Reports in 2 weeks. Buys one-time rights. Pays $5 minimum, b&w line drawings; on acceptance.

POWER LINES, Box 14042, St. Petersburg FL 33733. Editor-in-Chief: Margaret Shaleuly. For employees and retirees of Florida Power Corp. Biweekly newspaper. Circ. 5,000. Simultaneous submissions and previously published work OK. Free sample copy and artist's guidelines.
Cartoons: Buys 10 cartoons/year on environment, family life, retirement, sports, utilities and solar or nuclear energy; single panel. Query with samples or mail finished art. SASE. Reports in 2 weeks. Pays $5-15, b&w line drawings; on publication.
Illustrations: Buys 25 illustrations/year on current events, environment, family life, retirement, sports and utilities. Query with resume and samples. SASE. Reports in 2 weeks. Cover and inside: Pays $5-20, b&w line drawings and color washes; on publication.
Other Needs: Design: Uses artists for cover design and layout mock-ups. Query with resume and samples. Pays $15-150.

PRESERVATION NEWS, 1785 Massachusetts Ave. NW, Washington DC 20036. (202)673-4000. Readers are members of the National Trust for Historic Preservation. Monthly. Circ. 175,000. Free sample copy; art guidelines for SASE.
Cartoon Needs: Uses 1-2 cartoons/issue, 1 of which is by freelancer. "Since our newspaper is limited to the preservation of historic sites and buildings, cartoons should be on that subject. This subject is broad, however, and can range from architecture (old and new) to history." Uses single or multi-panel b&w line drawings and washes with or without gag lines. Freelancers should send samples of style to Carleton Knight, III, editor. SASE. Reports in 4 weeks. Pays $25-50 on acceptance for b&w cartoons. Buys one-time rights.
Illustration Needs: Uses 10-15 illustrations/issue, 1-2 bought from freelancers. "We sometimes commission special illustrations (from samples and persons whose work we know) for the newspaper. Most of our art, however, is photographs. As we are usually in a hurry, we tend to use local artists on deadline." We look for "drawings of historic structures. Occasionally, we will have a special piece of art that relates to a general subject such as neighborhood conservation. Line art is best because it shows the detail." Uses b&w line drawings and washes for cover and inside. Freelancers should send samples of style and/or arrange personal appointment to show portfolio to Carleton Knight, III, editor. SASE. Reports in 1 week. Pays $25-100 on acceptance for b&w cover and $25-100 for inside b&w. Buys all rights on a work-for-hire basis.

PSE&G NEWS, 80 Park Place, Newark NJ 07101. (201)430-6017. Editor: Frank Hummler. For employees and retirees of Public Service Electric and Gas Company. Biweekly newspaper. Simultaneous submissions and previously published work OK.
Cartoons: Buys cartoons sporadically on environment and utilities; double panel wth gag line. Query with samples. SASE. Reports in 2 weeks. Pays $5-25, b&w line drawings; on acceptance.

PULP, 720 Greenwich St., New York NY 10014. Editor-in-Chief: Howard Sage. Concerns poetry and fiction. Quarterly newspaper. Circ. 2,000. Original artwork returned after publication. Mail art. SASE. Reports in 4 weeks. Buys first rights. Sample copy $1 cash.
Illustrations: Uses 7-8 illustrations/issue, all from freelancers. Interested in electric themes Reports back on future assignments. Provide resume and tearsheet to be kept on file for future assignments. Prefers finished art. SASE. Reports in 1 week. Buys first North American serial rights. Cover and inside: Pays $2, b&w; on publication.

QUALITY CONTROL SUPERVISOR'S BULLETIN, 24 Rope Ferry Rd., Waterford CT 06386. (203)442-4365. Contact: Editor. Emphasizes quality control and quality assurance for front-line supervisors in the quality function. Semimonthly. Estab. 1978. Free sample copy.
Cartoons: Uses 1 cartoon/issue; buys all from freelancers. Interested in nonsexist material which pokes fun at aspects of supervising the quality function. Prefers single panel b&w line drawings with gag line. Send roughs. SASE. Reports in 2 weeks. Buys all rights. Pays $10 for b&w; on acceptance.

REVIEW PRINTING CO., Box 010589, Miami FL 33101. Contact: Lee Ruwitch. Estab. 1926. Publishes legal, business and financial newspapers. Mail art or make personal visit.

Needs: Buys business and legal cartoons and illustrations. Pays $1-2.50, cartoons.

ROLLING STONE, 745 5th Ave., New York NY 10022. Art Director: Mary Shanahan. Coverage includes music, film, social issues, investigative reporting, books and new life styles. Biweekly tabloid. Original artwork returned after publication.
Cartoons: Uses 1 regular cartoon/issue; buys none/issue from freelancers.
Illustrations: Buys 5-6 illustrations/issue; spot drawings and illustrations on assigned themes, usually of an additional nature. Works on assignment only. Samples returned by SASE. Reports back on future assignment possibilities. Provide calling card to be kept on file for future assignments. Submit samples of style or portfolio. Reports in 1 week. Buys one-time publication rights.

SALINAS CALIFORNIAN, Box 109, Salinas CA 93901. Advertising Director: Jack Rogers. Previously published work OK.
Needs: Advertising. Buys architectural renderings, furniture design, layouts, and especially fashion design; b&w halftones, washes and color. Mail art. Reports in 10 days. Buys all rights. Pays $15 minimum; on acceptance.

SAN FRANCISCO BAY GUARDIAN, 2700 19th St., San Francisco CA 94110. (415)824-7660. Art Director: Louis Dunn. For "a young liberal to radical well-educated audience." Estab. 1966. Circ. 35,000. Weekly newspaper. SASE. Pays on publication.
Cartoons: "Almost all cartoons are assigned; we are, however, always looking for strips that have a Bay area theme. We pay, on the average, $25/strip, which can be a one-shot deal or continuing." Query.
Illustrations: Buys assigned themes. Pays $65+. Arrange interview to show portfolio.

SCREW, 116 W. 14th St., New York NY 10011. Contact: Frank Bruno. Tabloid newspaper. Emphasizes sex.
Illustrations: "We like the artist's imagination and creativity to run wild. Sexual cliches are of no interest to us." Send rough drawings or published samples. SASE. Buys one-time rights. Cover: Pays $125, color. Inside: Pays $50-100, b&w; on publication.

SEATTLE TIMES, Box 70, Seattle WA 98111. (206)464-2283. Editor: Larry Anderson. For readers with above-average income and education. Weekly; tabloid; 16 pages. Letterpress. Circ. 310,000. Query with samples. SASE. Reports in 1 week. Previously published work OK. Buys first rights. Pays on publication. Free sample copy.
Illustrations: Buys 20-30/year (mainly covers) on Pacific Northwest subjects. Cover: Pays $125, color. Inside: Pays $20-30, b&w.

SHUTTERBUG ADS, Box F, 407 S. Washington Ave., Titusville FL 32780. Contact: Roger Wolf. Photography and computer newspapers. Previously published work OK. Original artwork not returned after publication.
Cartoons: Uses 1 cartoon/issue, all from freelancers. Interested in "photography related and computer related themes." Prefers finished cartoons. SASE. Reports "when cartoons are published." Pays $15, spot drawing; on publication.

SKYDIVING, Box 189, Deltona FA 32725. (904)789-4212. Editor: Michael Truffer. Monthly. Circ. 5,000. Estab. 1979.
Cartoons: Uses 1-2 cartoons/issue; buys 0-1 from freelancers. Receives 1-2 submissions/week from freelancers. Interested in themes relating to skydiving or aviation. Prefers single panel b&w line drawings with gag line. Send finished cartoons or samples of style. SASE. Reports in 1 week. Buys one-time rights. Pays $10 minimum for b&w; on publication.

SMILE & CHUCKLE INC., 108 S. Iris St., Alexandria VA 22304. (703)370-2085. Publisher: Dan Boger. Emphasizes humor. Readers are "residents in a zip code area." Monthly. Circ. 10,000. Free sample copy (mention *Artist's Market*; art guidelines for SASE.
Cartoons: Uses 10-12 cartoons/issue, all from freelancers. Cartoons should pertain to family, daily and suburban living. No sex, violence, politics and controversial issues. Format: single panel b&w line drawings with gag line. Prefers finished cartoons. SASE. Reports in 2 weeks. Buys one-year rights. Pays $10-20 on publication.
Illustrations: Uses 25 illustrations/issue, all from freelancers. Provide tearsheet to be kept on file for future assignments. Prefers samples of style. SASE. Reports in 2 weeks. Buys one-year rights.

SOUL America's Most Soulful Newsmagazine, 6331 Hollywood Blvd., Suite 1103, Hollywood CA 90028. (213)460-6889. Audience is 18-30-year-olds interested in all areas of black entertainment.

Monthly. Circ. 175,000. Original artwork returned after publication. Free sample copy.
Cartoon Needs: Currently uses no cartoons but "would like to include 1 cartoon per issue of entertainment related material." Format: single or multi panel b&w line drawings with gag line. Send roughs, finished cartoons, or samples of style to Lois Green, art director. SASE. Reports in 30 days. Pays $10-25 on publication. Buys one-time rights.
Illustration Needs: Uses 1 illustrations/issue. Works with illustrators "on assignment after seeing samples of their work. We keep samples on file. On occasion an illustration of a famous Black entertainer has been submitted and accepted." Uses themes illustrating a story. Format: b&w line drawings for inside. Send roughs, samples of style and/or arrange personal appointment to show portfolio. SASE. Reports in 30 days. Pays $25-100 on publication for inside b&w. Buys first rights.
Other Needs: Uses artists for layout, advertising, brochures, logos, symbols and stationery. Pays $25 minimum.

SOUTHERN JEWISH WEEKLY, Box 3297, Jacksonville FL 32206. (904)355-3459. Editor: I. Moscovitz. "The only Jewish newspaper covering all of Florida and the Southeast." Weekly.Circ. 28,500.
Illustrations: Buys 2 illustrations/year on Jewish themes that pertain to newspaper's articles. Pays $10 minimum, b&w; on acceptance. Query with samples. Seasonal themes must arrive 3-4 weeks in advance of holiday. SASE. Reports in 2 weeks.

SUNSHINE SERVICE NEWS, Box 529100, Miami FL 33152. (305)552-3891. Editor: Jay Osborne. Emphasis on employees and retirees of Florida Power and Light. Monthly. Circ. 12,000. Free sample copy.
Cartoons: Buys no cartoons now but "willing to use cartoons, if they are related to the industry—linemen, office workers, plant personnel—electricity oriented." Format: single or multi panel b&w line drawings with gag line. Prefers samples of style. SASE. Reports in 2 weeks.Buys one-time rights. Pays on publication.
Illustrations: Uses 2 illustrations/issue both by freelancers. Illustrations "must be imaginative as they can, sometimes deal with technical matter." Uses illustrations relating to fuels, energy, power plants and electricity. Prefers samples of style. SASE. Reports in 2 weeks. Buys all rights on a work-for-hire basis. Pays $100-400 for b&w cover; $50-350 for inside b&w; on publication.

SUPERVISOR'S BULLETIN, 24 Rope Ferry Rd., Waterford CT 06386. (203)442-4365. Contact: Editor. Emphasizes "manufacturing supervision for front-line supervision in the shop. Not office and non-union." Semimonthly. Free sample copy.
Cartoons: Uses 1-2 cartoons/issue; buys all from freelancers. Interested in nonsexist material which pokes fun at aspects of shop supervision: safety, productivity, motivation, discipline, etc. Prefers single panel b&w line drawings with or without gag line. Send roughs. SASE. Reports in 2 weeks. Buys all rights. Pays $10 for b&w; on acceptance.

TELEBRIEFS, Illinois Bell Telephone Co., 225 W. Randolph, Chicago IL 60606. Editor-in-Chief: Dan Bilardello. For telephone customers. Monthly newsletter.Circ. 3,500,000. Mail art. SASE. Reports in 2 weeks. Photocopies OK. Original artwork not returned after publication. Free sample copy.
Cartoons: Uses 1 cartoon/issue, all from freelancers. Receives 8 submissions/week from freelancers. Cartoons "must be telephone, telephone company of communications related." Single panel. "No ethnic humor. We reduce cartoons to 1¾x1¾ so we need few elements and drawn very boldly. Prefer strong visual with captions of 10 or fewer words." Prefers finished cartoons. SASE. Reports in 2 weeks. Buys all rights on a work-for-hire basis. Pays $40, line drawings with shading; on acceptance.
Illustrations: Uses 1 illustration/issue, all from freelancers. Works on assignment only. Samples returned by SASE. Reports back on future assignment possibilities. Provide resume and calling card to be kept on file for future assignments. Prefers samples of style. SASE. Reports in 2 weeks. Buys all rights on a work-for-hire basis. Pays on acceptance.

TIE LINES, Michigan Bell Telephone Co., 1365 Cass Ave., Rm. 1812, Detroit MI 48226. (313)223-7250. Editor-in-Chief: Rick Wilbind. For telephone company employes and retirees. Biweekly. Circ. 38,000. Previously published, photocopied and simultaneous submissions OK. Free sample copy.
Cartoons: Uses 1 cartoon/issue (use them as fillers), all from freelancers; uses unsolicited cartoons. Interested in telephones. Call for imformation. Reports in 4 weeks. Pays $20-50, b&w line drawings; on acceptance.
Illustrations: Uses 2 illustrations/issue, all from freelancers. Interested in telephones. Works on assignment basis only. Prefers telephone call to make appointment to show work. Pays $50-200, b&w line drawings.

TODD NEWS, Todd Pacific Shipyards Corp., 1801 16th SW, Seattle WA 98124. (206)623-1635. Editor: D.V. Corsilles. For employees, customers and editors of local industrial publications. Bimonthly newspaper. Circ. 4,000.
Cartoons: Buys safety themes; include gag line. Needs b&w line drawings. Query with samples. Pays on publication.

THE TREFOIL, The Fidelity Bank, Broad and Walnut Sts., Philadelphia PA 19109. (215)985-7228. Contact: J. Barford, director of employee communications. For employees. Monthly newspaper. Circ. 4,000. Simultaneous submissions and previously published work OK. Original artwork returned after publication.Free sample copy.
Cartoons: Uses less than 1 cartoon/issue, all from freelancers. Prefers finished cartoons. SASE. Reports in 2 weeks. Pays $10, b&w line drawings; on acceptance. Interested in banking themes; single panel with gag line.

TRI-STATE TRADER, Box 90, Knightstown IN 46148. Managing Editor: Kevin Tanzillo. Concerns antiques, collectibles, local history and genealogy. Weekly newspaper; tabloid. Circ. 30,000. Estab. 1968. Reports in 1-2 weeks. Previously published work (in noncompeting publications) OK. Not copyrighted. Pays on publication.
Needs: Always interested in seasonal material that expresses the appropriate greetings in an antique-related manner. Submit 2-4 months in advance.

UTILITY SUPERVISION, 24 Rope Ferry Rd., Waterford CT 06386. (203)442-4365. Contact: Editor. Emphasizes utility system installation, maintenance and repair for front-line supervisors in the field (not plant or office). Semimonthly. Circ. 4,000. Free sample copy.
Cartoons: Uses 1 cartoon/issue; buys all from freelancers. Interested in non-sexist material which pokes fun at some of the problems of utility supervision and/or utility field work. Prefers single panel b&w line drawings with or without gag line. Send roughs. SASE. Reports in 2 weeks. Buys all rights. Pays $10 for b&w on acceptance.

WAREHOUSING SUPERVISOR'S BULLETIN, 24 Rope Ferry Rd., Waterford CT 06386. (203)442-4365. Contact: Editor. Emphasizes warehouse, shipping, traffic, material handling for front-line supervision. Semimonthly. Circ. 4,000. Free sample copy.
Cartoons: Uses 1 cartoon/issue; buys all from freelancers. Interested in non-sexist material which pokes fun at aspects of warehouse operations and supervision. Prefers single panel b&w line drawings with or without gag line. Send roughs. SASE. Reports in 2 weeks. Buys all rights. Pays $10 for b&w on acceptance.

WDS FORUM, 9933 Alliance Rd., Cincinnati OH 45242. (513)984-0717. Editor: Ms. Kirk Polking. Emphasizes writing techniques and marketing for Writer's Digest School students. Bimonthly. Circ. 3,000.
Cartoons: Needs work on "the joys and griefs of freelancing, that first check/rejection slip, trying to find time to write, postal problems, editor/author relations, etc." Send roughs. SASE. Reports in 3 weeks. Pays $10, b&w.
Illustrations: "We might buy a few spot drawings, as fillers, of writer-related subject matter." SASE. Reports in 3 weeks. Query with samples. Pays $2-5, each drawing; on acceptance.

WEEKLY BIBLE READER, 8121 Hamilton Ave., Cincinnati OH 45231. Editor: Barbara Cottrell. Sunday School take home paper for ages 6-7. Quarterly in weekly parts; 4 pages. Estab. 1965. Circ. 72,000. Reports in 1 month. Buys first or one-time rights. Pays on acceptance. Free sample copy, writer's guidelines and syllabus.
Cartoons: Attemps to include 1 cartoon or puzzle/issue; single panel reduced to ¼ of a page. Pays $7.50, b&w. Send actual cartoons. Include SASE for return.
Illustrations: Usually assigned to relate to Bible stories and poems. (Each issue contains a Bible story and a story correlating with that Bible theme.) Send samples, requesting syllabus and assignmnt consideration. Pays $5-35/spot drawing, b&w.
Puzzles: "Most of our need is for puzzles (dot to dot or simple) and cartoons. We like to include at least one of either of these per issue, but don't always have one."

WESTERN CANADA OUTDOORS, Box 430, North Battleford, Saskatchewan, Canada S9A 2Y5. (306)445-4401. General Manager: E.E. Gould. For hunting, fishing and outdoor families. Bimonthly newspaper. Circ. 40,000. Previously published work OK. Free sample copy.
Cartoons: Uses 3 cartoons/issue, all by freelancers. Receives 0-1 submission/week from freelancer. Interested in "an outdoor, conserving enviroment theme"; single panel. Prefers finished cartoons. SASE. Reports in 1 month. Buys "once-rental" rights. Pays $5-10, halftones; on acceptance.

Illustrations: Uses 0-1 illustrations/issue, all from freelancer. Receivres no submissions/week from freelancers. Interested in wildlife. Prefers finished art. SASE. Reports in 1 month. Buys "once-rental" rights. Pays on acceptance.

WOMEN ARTISTS NEWS, Box 3304, Grand Central Station, New York NY 10017. (212)666-6990. Executive Editor: Cynthia Navaretta. For women in the arts with focus on the visual arts fields. Monthly newsletter. Circ. 4,500. SASE. Reports in 2 weeks. Previously published work and photocopied submissions OK. Original artwork returned after publication. Buys all rights. Pays on publication. SASE for sample copy.
Cartoons: Uses 0-2 cartoons/issue. Receives 1 submission/week from freelancers. Contact feature editor. Accepts cartoons on art and artists; double panel. Send finished art. Reports in 2 weeks. Pays $0-5, b&w washes.
Illustrations: Uses 20 illustrations/issue; buys 4/issue from freelancers. Receives 10 submissions/week from freelancers. Provide samples (roughs) or published work to be kept on file for future assignments. Reports in 2 weeks. Buys all rights on a work-for-hire basis.
Other Needs: Uses artists for layout and brochures. Also needs photographs.

WORCESTER, 25 West St., Worcester MA 01609. (617)799-0511. Art Director: Deborah Norton. Concerns central Massachusetts. Weekly newspaper. Circ. 30,000. Simultaneous submissions and previously published work OK. Sample copy $1; free artist's guidelines with SASE.
Illustrations: Buys 5/issue on assigned themes. Query with resume and samples or arrange interview to show portfolio. SASE. Reports in 4 weeks. Buys all rights. Cover: Pays $50-100, gray opaques, b&w line drawings and washes. Inside: Pays $10-50, gray opaques, b&w line drawings and washes; on acceptance.

Record Companies

Though records are made from a petroleum by-product, and their sales are off, there's no shortage of demand from record companies for well-designed jackets and covers. These wise businessmen know their important role in selling an album. In addition to commissioning cover and jacket designs, promotional art is also sought.

Payment for record designs is in the form of royalties, advances and/or flat fees.

Work is done mostly on assignment, since besides selling the record, the cover must illustrate the music or performer's message. Submit samples for the company's files for future commissions.

Additional names and addresses of record firms can be found in *Songwriter's Market* (Writer's Digest Books) or Peter Glenn's *Madison Avenue Handbook*.

ABC RECORDS INC., 8255 Beverly Blvd., Los Angeles CA 90048. (213)651-5530. Creative Director: Stuart Kusher. Produces rock-and-roll, disco, soul, rhythm-and-blues, classical and country records. Assigns 200 jobs and buys 25-30 illustrations/year; local artists only. Arrange interview to show portfolio. SASE. Reports in 2-3 weeks.
Needs: Uses artists for record covers, ads, posters and other merchandising aids. Pays $300-1,000.
Tips: "Show us references and published works from other local record companies."

ACTION TICKET AGENCY & PROMOTION, 2609 NW 36th St., Oklahoma City OK 73112. (405)942-0462. Contact: Bobby Boyd. Record company.
Needs: Works with 2 illustrators/month. Uses artists for album covers.
First Contact & Terms: Send query with previously published work (copies that do not have to be returned).

ADELPHI RECORDS INC., Send mail to: Box 288, Silver Spring MD 20907; United Parcel Service to 6401 Chillum Place NW, Washington DC 20012. (202)723-6958. President: Gene Rosenthal. Vice President: Gayle Moore. Produces "virtually everything except classical, opera, spoken word and instruction." Recent releases: "Jacks and Kings," by The Nighthawks; "5 O'Clock Bells," by Lenny Breau and "Eye Witness Blues, by Catfish Hodge.
Needs: Produces 5-10 records/year; all of which use freelance designers and illustrators.
First Contact & Terms: Professionals only. Query with resume and samples (other album art or original art). SASE. Reports in 6-8 weeks. Provide resume, letter of inquiry and brochure to be kept on file for future assignments. Originals returned to artists at job's completion. Pays $100-500; "anything other than flat fee is negotiable under special circumstances."
Tips: "Submit ideas (for specific projects) which indicate some familiarity with the recording artist in question."

AQUILA RECORD CO./ALDOO RECORD CO., Box 600516, N. Miami Beach FL 33160. (305)945-3738. Executive Director: J. "Gil" Girday. Produces country, jazz, folk, pop and gospel. Recent releases: "A Little Bit More," by Tony Messina, "Jest Jazz;," by Phil Brown and "A Father's Prayer," by Don C. Davis.
Needs: Produces 20 records/year; 15 of which have cover/jackets designed and illustrated by freelance artists. Interested in action and locations shots.
First Contact & Terms: Send query and samples. SASE. Reports in 2 weeks. Pays $300-850 set fee/job.

ARTEMIS RECORDS LTD., Box 110, 157-52 96th St., Howard Beach, NY 11414. (212)738-4806. President: Mr. John P. Giamundo. Produces rock-and-roll, soul, disco and new wave. Recent release: "Reverie," by New York Disco Orchestra.
Needs: Produces 5 records/year; some of which have cover/jackets designed and illustrated by freelance artists. Interested in cosmic futuristic and sensuous art for designs of albums, record labels, 45 RPM sleeves and print advertising illustrations.
First Contact & Terms: Send brochure or materials that can be kept on file for future reference. SASE. Reports back on future assignment possibilities. Negotiates pay based on assignment.

AURVID/VIDEO PRODUCTIONS, Box 11860, Philadelphia PA 19128. Executive Producer: F.O. Pease. Produces educational/news materials and jazz records. Query. SASE. Reports in 4 weeks. Buys all rights. Pays $100 minimum.
Needs: Buys 3-5 designs/year. Uses artists for catalog covers/illustrations, direct mail brochures, magazine ads and album design.

BEAVERWOOD STUDIOS, 133 Walton Ferry, Hendersonville TN 37075. (615)824-2820. Contact: Clyde Beavers. Produces educational, country, folk, pop, R&B and gospel.
Needs: Produces 100 records/year; some of which have cover/jackets designed and illustrated by freelance artists.
First Contact & Terms: Send query and samples. No samples returned. Reports back on future assignment possibilities.

BLIND PIG RECORDS, 208 S. 1st St., Ann Arbor MI 48103. Contact: Jerry Del Giudice. Produces mostly blues and rhythm-and-blues; some swing, rock-and-roll and jazz. Recent releases: "It's All Rock & Roll," by Steve Nardella and "Comin' Your Way," by John Mooney.
Needs: Produces 6 records/year; all of which have cover/jackets designed and illustrated by freelance artists. Assigns 6-12 jobs/year;Uses artists for album illustration, brochure design and illustrations.
First Contact & Terms: Local artists only. Query with "a few published samples or photos of original work." SASE. Reports in 2 months. Works on assignment only. No samples returned. Reports back on future assignment possibilities. No file kept on artists. Negotiates pay; $5/hour average.

BOUQUET-ORCHID ENTERPRISES, Box 4220, Shreveport LA 71104. (318)686-7362. Contact: Bill Bohannon, president. Produces country, pop and middle-of-the-road records.
Needs: Produces 10 records/year; 5 of which have cover/jackets designed and illustrated by freelance artists. Uses artists for record album and brochure design.
First Contact & Terms: Query with resume and samples. "I prefer a brief but concise overview of an artists' background and works showing the range of their talents." SASE. Reports in 2 weeks. Provide resume, letter of inquiry and brochure to be kept on file for future assignments. Negotiates pay.

BOYD RECORDS, 2609 NW 36th St., Oklahoma City OK 73112. (405)942-0462. Produces soul records. Estab. 1960. Buys 20 illustrations/year; out-of-town artists only.

BRIARMEADE RECORDS, Box 1830, New Orleans LA 70053. President: Ken Keene. Estab. 1970. Produces country, rock, middle-of-the-road and soul records. Buys 10-25 freelance designs/year. Mail color slides, glossy color photos or original art. SASE. Reports in 4 weeks. Buys all rights.
Needs: Payment by job: $50 minimum, direct mail brochures; $150 minimum, magazine ads; $150-500, record album.

BUDDAH RECORDS INC., 1350 Avenue of the Americas, New York NY 10019. (212)582-6900. Vice President-Creative Services: Milton Sincoff. Estab. 1966. Arrange interview. Reports in 2 weeks.
Needs: Uses designers and illustrators for graphics, posters, album cover designs, and merchandising and marketing.

CHAPMAN RECORDING STUDIOS, 228 W. 5th St., Kansas City MO 64105. (816)842-6854. Contact: Chuck Chapman. Produces rock-and-roll, soul, country, jazz, folk, pop and R&B. Recent releases: "Titan Sampler," by Assorted artists and "The Roads We Travel," by John Biggs.
Needs: Produces 25 records/year; 15 of which have cover/jackets designed and illustrated by freelance artists. Interested in record album design.
First Contact & Terms: Send brochure or material that can be kept on file for future reference. SASE. Reports in 2 weeks. Negotiates pay based on set fee/job.

CHELSEA HOUSE FOLKLORE CENTER, Box 1057, Brattleboro VT 05301. (802)257-1482. Director: Carol Levin. Folklore center featuring traditional folk music, dance and arts.
Needs: Uses artists for advertising, direct mail brochures, exhibits, flyers, posters, programs and record jackets.
First Contact & Terms: Assigns most work to local artists. Query or arrange interview. SASE. Reports in 2 weeks. Pays by job.

CHIMNEYVILLE RECORDS, Malaco Records, Box 9287, Jackson MS 39206. Contact: Tommy Couch. Submit resume and samples. Uses artists for album cover designs.

CLARUS MUSIC LTD., 340 Bellevue Ave., Yonkers NY 10703. (914)375-0864. Contact: Selma Fass, president. Music publisher and children's record company. Assigns 2-3 jobs/year.
Needs: Produces 2-3 records year; all of which have cover/jackets designed and illustrated by freelance artists. Uses artists for record covers, lettering and catalog design.
First Contact & Terms: Query with resume and samples. SASE. Reports in 2-4 weeks. Works on assignment only. Samples returned by SASE. Reports back on future assignment possibilities. Provide resume, letter of inquiry, brochure, flyer and tear sheet to be kept on file for future assignments. Pays $250-450.

CLAY PIGEON INTERNATIONAL RECORDS, Box 20346, Chicago IL 60620. (312)778-8760. Contact: Vito Beleska or Rudy Markus. Produces rock-and-roll, pop, new wave and avant-garde.
Needs: Produces 5 records/year; 3 of which have cover/jackets designed and illustrated by freelance artists. Uses artists for design and illustrations for LP jackets, brochures, 45 RPM picture sleeves and advertising. Interested in "belt tightening—stuff that looks good wihout the expensive frills. More b&w."
First Contact & Terms: Send query and resume or send brochure or materials that can be kept on file for future reference. Reports in 1 month or when assignment is available. Negotiates pay based on amount of creativity required and artist's previous experience/reputation.

CURTISS UNIVERSAL RECORD MASTERS, Box 4740, Nashville TN 37216. (615)859-0355. Manager: S.D. Neal. Produces soul, country, jazz, folk, pop, rock-and-roll and R&B. Recent release: "Dixie Dee & The Rhythm Rockers."
Needs: Produces 10 records/year; some of which have cover/jackets designed and illustrated by freelance artists. Uses artists for LP's and advertisements.
First Contact & Terms: Send query and samples or send brochure or materials that can be kept on file for future reference. SASE. Reports in 3 weeks. Negotiates pay based on artist involved.

DANCE-A-THON RECORDS, 1957 Kilburn Dr., Atlanta GA 30324. (404)872-6000. Director of Creative Services: Melanie Phillips. Produces rock, disco, bluegrass, country, and spoken-word comedy records.
Needs: Buys 5 illustrations/year. Uses artists for designing album jackets and accompanying advertising logos for labels and artists.
First Contact & Terms: Prefers artists with previous experience in the advertising/record medium. Query with resume and samples or previously published work. SASE. Reports in 6-8 weeks. Pays $45-225.

DAWN PRODUCTIONS, Cloud 40, Paradise PA 17562. President: Joey Welz. Produces rock and pop music albums.
Needs: Buys 1-3 illustrations/year. Uses artists for flyers, sketches for poetry on song books and record jackets.
First Contact & Terms: Mail art or query with samples. SASE. Reports in 1 month. Negotiates royalties.

DELMARK RECORDS, 4243 N. Lincoln, Chicago IL 60618. (312)528-8834. Contact: Steve Tomashefsky, art director. Produces blues and jazz records. Recent releases include "To Many Roads," by Otis Rush; "Johnson's Whack," by Jimmy Johnson and "Reality," by Frank Walton.
Needs: Chicago area artists only. Produces 5-10 records/year; all of which have cover/jackets designed and illustrated by freelance artists. "Our records do not sell like hits, but remain in our catalog and active on the market for many years. We are therefore more interested in clean designs that do not date than in flashy covers. Most of the artists who work for us are interested in the music we issue: jazz and blues. We are especially interested in artists who can arrive at interesting multicolor designs based on black and white photographs."
First Contact & Terms: Arrange interview to show portfolio (mixture of original and printed art). Reports in 2 weeks. Works on assignment only. Samples returned by SASE. Reports back on future assignment possibilities. Provide resume, tear sheet and samples to be kept on file for future assignments. Pays $50-250.

DIT DOT RECORDING STUDIO, 155 NW 28th Ave., Pompano Beach FL 33060. (305)972-0812. Contact: Willie A. Brown, president. Estab. 1964. Produces all types of records. Buys 5 illustrations/year. Query with resume and samples. SASE. Reports in 6 weeks.
Needs: Pays $200-300, album and jacket design.

DIVINE RECORDS, 140-11 Benchley Place, Bronx NY 10475. (212)671-4042. Vice President: Gilbert Northern. Estab. 1975. Produces black jazz records and posters. Buys 2 designs/year. Mail scale samples. SASE. Reports in 3 weeks. Buys all rights.
Needs: Uses artists for layout, magazine ads, paste-up and album design. Pays $200-400, album design; $50-120, layout.

SPENCER M. DRATE, 119 W. 80th St., Apt. 10, New York NY 10024. (212)751-2031. Creative Director: Spencer Drate. Produces graphics for record albums and promotional graphics for all phases of the record industry. "We have been doing graphics for 'New Wave' groups such as Ramones and Talking Heads and for blues, rock and jazz artists."
Needs: Produces 10-15 album covers and 45 jacket covers/year; 3-5 of which have cover/jackets designed and illustrated by freelance artists. Also assigns 5-10 covers to photographers. Uses artists for illustration of record albums, trade and children's book jackets, posters and logos.
First Contact & Terms: Query with resume and samples or arrange interview to show portfolio. SASE. Contacts artists as needs arise. Provide business card to be kept on file for future assignments.

DREAMPOWER, 8101 Melrose Ave., Suite 202, Hollywood CA 90046. (213)653-1380. Contact: Steven Doctrow, president. Estab. 1977. Produces rock, disco and contemporary records. Assigns 10 jobs/year; local artists only. Query with resume and samples. SASE. Reports in 4 weeks.
Needs: Uses artists for ad illustrations, promotional brochures and record album design. Pays $500-2,500.

EDUCATOR RECORDS INC., 1023 Filbert St., Philadelphia PA 19107. (215)923-1886. President: Bart Arntz. Produces educational records.
Needs: Local artists only. Produces 3-4 records/year; all of which have cover/jackets designed and illustrated by freelance artists. Uses artists for record album and jacket design, album and print advertising illustrations and brochure design.
First Contact & Terms: Send query and samples. SASE. Reports in 3 weeks. Or send brochure or materials that can be kept on file for future reference. Reports when assignment is available. Negotiates pay.

E.L.J. RECORD CO., 1344 Waldron, St. Louis MO 63130. (314)863-3605. President: Eddie Johnson. Produces R&B, rock-and-roll, jazz and pop music.
Needs: Produces 12 records/year; all of which have cover/jackets designed by freelance artists.
First Contact & Terms: Send query and samples. SASE. Reports in 6 weeks. Negotiates pay based on amount of creativity required.

PHIL GABER RECORD PRODUCTION AND PERSONNEL MANAGEMENT, 7141 Rutland St., Philadelphia PA 19149. (215)728-1699. Contact: Phil Gaber. Estab. 1963. Produces "anything I feel is saleable except hard or punk rock." Query with resume and samples; follow up with personal contact or call. SASE. Reports in 2 months.
Needs: "I've used some freelance art in the past and may again in the future." Uses artists for design of albums, jackets, brochures and labels. Pays 1-2% royalties.

MARC GORDON PRODUCTIONS, 1022 N. Palm Ave., Los Angeles CA 90069. (213)659-6034. Contact: Rudyard Butler, media director. Estab. 1962. Produces soul and pop records. Assigns 2 jobs and buys 1 illustration/year; local artists only. Query with resume and samples. SASE. Reports in 3 weeks. Negotiates pay.

GUSTO RECORDS, 220 Boscobel, Nashville TN 37213. Contact: Brenda McClearen, art director. Estab. 1971. Produces bluegrass, country, contemporary country, gospel and pop. Assigns 10 jobs/year. Query with resume and samples. Contacts artists as needs arise.
Needs: Uses artists for album design and illustration. Pays by job.

THE HERALD ASSOCIATION, INC., Box 218, Wellman Hts., Johnsonville SC 29555. (803)386-2600. Director: Erv Lewis. Produces religious music only. Recent releases: "Life Giving Song," by Sandy Bond; "Long Winding Road," by Erv Lewis and "You Can't Hide From God," by The Singing Echoes.
Needs: Local artists only. Produces 9 records/year; 2 of which have cover/jackets designed and illustrated by freelance artists. Interested in religious themes only.
First Contact & Terms: Send brochure or material that can be kept on file for futre reference. SASE. Reports in 2 months. Negotiates pay and royalties based on amount of creativity required.

LAWRENCE HERBST RECORDS, Box 1659, Beverly Hills CA 90213. Contact: Lawrence Herbst. Produces all types of records.
Needs: Uses artists for album design and illustration, jacket design, ad illustrations and brochure design.
First Contact & Terms: Query with resume and samples. Reports in 3 weeks. Pays $25 minimum; offers 14-20% royalties and advance.

JEM RECORDS/PASSPORT RECORDS, 3619 Kennedy Rd., South Plainfield NJ 07080. (201)753-6100. Art Director: Murray Brenman. Produces rock-and-roll and pop music. Recent releases: "Games," by Synergy; "Bullshot," by Link Wray; "Sides," by Anthony Phillips, "Product," by Brand X and "Surveillance," by FM. Buys 10-25 designs/year.
Needs: Produces 20 records/year; 6 of which have cover/jackets designed and illustrated by freelance artists. Uses artists for album jacket and inner sleeve design and possible poster design.
First Contact & Terms: Send query and samples. SASE. Reports only when an assignment is available. Negotiates pay based on amount of creativity required.

KEN KEENE INTERNATIONAL, Box 24561, Nashville TN 37202. President: Ken Keene. Produces country, rock, middle-of-the-road and soul records. Recent releases: "Frankie Ford," by Frankie Ford; "The Memphis Sessions," by Billy Joe Duniven and "Saxy Country Soul," by Johnny Pennino.
Needs: Produces 20 records/year; 10-20 of which have cover/jackets designed and illustrated by freelance artists.
First Contact & Terms: Mail color slides/photos or art. SASE. Reports in 4 weeks. Buys all rights. Works on assignment only. Samples returned by SASE. Reports back on future assignment possibilities. Provide resume, business card, brochure, flyer, tear sheet—"2-3 copies (not originals) of what artist feels is his/her best work"—to be kept on file for future assignments. Pays $25 minimum, direct mail brochures; $150 minimum, magazine ads; $150-500, album design.

KICKING MULE RECORDS, Box 3233, Berkeley CA 94703. Manager: Ed Denson. Estab. 1973. Produces guitar and banjo records. Buys 10-20 designs/year. Query with full-size covers or layouts; local artists only. SASE. Reports in 2 weeks. Buys all rights. Catalog 25¢.
Needs: Pays $2.50/page, layout of tab books; $75-250, album cover design; $25-75, album liner design.

SID KLEINER MUSIC ENTERPRISES, 3701 25th Ave. SW, Naples FL 33999. Managing Director: Sid Kleiner. Estab. 1949. Produces folk, rock and country recordings, and nutritional, organic gardening and health audiovisuals. Query. SASE. Reports in 4 weeks. Material copyrighted.
Needs: Uses artists for album design, type spec and audiovisuals. Pays $50 min./job.

L & R PRODUCTIONS, 16 E. Broad St., Mt. Vernon NY 10552. (914)668-4488. President: Richard Rashbaum. Produces rhythm-and-blues and disco records. Assigns 3 jobs/year.
Needs: Produces 2 records/year; both have cover/jackets designed and illustrated by freelance artists. Uses artists primarily for record album design, also for jacket design, and album and ad illustrations.
First Contact & Terms: Local artists only. Query with resume and samples. SASE. Reports in 2 weeks. Works on assignment only. Samples returned by SASE. Reports back on future assignment possibilities. Provide resume, brochure and flyer to be kept on file for future assignments.

LA VAL RECORDS, 1327 Cobb St., Kalamazoo MI 49006. Contact: Vic La Val.
Needs: Uses artists for album cover designs.
First Contact & Terms: Submit resume and samples. Reports in 30 days. Buys all rights.

LE MANS RECORD CO., Box 24, Belle Mead NJ 08502. (201)359-5520. Contact: Bernard Goydish. Produces polka albums.
Needs: Assigns "happy" themes for album cover design.
First Contact & Terms: Query. Reports in 5 days. Pays $10-25, album designs; $75-150, finished art.

LEMON SQUARE PRODUCTIONS, Box 31819, Dallas TX 75231. (214)690-4155. A&R Director: Mike Anthony. Estab. 1980. Produces country and gospel music. Recent release: "Airborne Four."
Needs: Plans on having cover/jackets designed and illustrated by freelance artists. Will use artists

for record album, jacket and brochure design, album and print ad illustrations, etc.
First Contact & Terms: Send brochure or materials that can be kept on file for future reference. SASE. Reports only when assignment is available. Negotiates pay based on amoun of creativity required.

LONDON RECORDS INC., POP PRODUCTS DIVISION, 539 W. 25th St., New York NY 10001. (212)675-6060. Pop Product Administrator: Anne Adams. Produces artists such as Moody Blues, Savoy Brown, early Rolling Stones and early Thin Lizzie. Assigns 50 jobs/year. Call to arrange interview to show portfolio; leave sample (color photocopy, slide or printed piece) for files. Reports in 1-2 weeks.
Needs: Uses artists for cover illustrations and logo designs. Pays $200-800.

DANNY LUCIANO PRODUCTIONS, 2655 Philmont Ave., Suite 206, Huntingdon Valley PA 19006. (215)947-7743 or 947-7778. President: Danny Luciano. Executive Vice President: Ray Royal. Talent Coordinator: Bill Mathias. Producer, Direcor: Guy Galante. Produces disco, soul and top 40 records.
Needs: Uses artists for albums, ads, brochures and TV buffers.
First Contact & Terms: Query with resume and samples. SASE. Reports in 1 month. Negotiates pay.

LUCIFER RECORDS INC., Box 263, Hasbrouck Heights NJ 07604. (201)288-8935. Contact: Ron Luciano, president. Produces top 40, disco, rock-and-roll and country records.
Needs: Uses artists for album, jacket and brochure design and ads.
First Contact & Terms: Query with resume and samples. SASE. Reports in 6-8 weeks. Negotiates pay.

LEE MAGID MUSIC INC., Box 532, Malibu CA 90265. (213)858-7282. Contact: Lee Magid. Produces jazz, rock, disco, country, blues, gospel and salsa records. Assigns 15 jobs/year.
Needs: Produces 12 records/year; all of which have cover/jackets designed and illustrated by freelance artists.
First Contact & Terms: local artists only. Write or call with resume and samples. SASE. Reports in 2 weeks. Provide resume, brochure and flyer to be kept on file for future assignments. Negotiates pay.

MAJEGA RECORDS/PRODUCTIONS, 240 E. Radcliffe Dr., Claremont CA 91711. (714)624-0677. Contact: Gary K. Buckley, president. Produces gospel, country and pop records, audio-visual presentations; i.e., filmstrips, slide/sound sync and multimedia programs. Recent releases: "Country Love," by Jerry Roach; "Steppin Out," by The Gospelones and "Sending a Copy Home," by Jody Barry.
Needs: Produces about 6 records/year; 4 of which have cover/jackets designed and illustrated by freelance artists. Uses artists for album covers, ad illustrations, logo designs, cartoons, charts & graphs and other promotional materials.
First Contact & Terms: Query with resume, letter of inquiry, brochure, flyer and samples (2-3 tear sheets of varied styles if possible) to be kept on file for future assignments. Works on assignment only. Samples returned by SASE. Reports back on future assignment possibilities. Negotiates pay.

MALACO RECORDS, Box 9287, Jackson MS 39206. Contact: Tommy Couch. Submit resume and samples. Uses artists for album cover designs.

MARK RECORDS, 10815 Bodine Rd., Clarence NY 14031. (716)759-2600. Art Director: Bruce Marsh. Produces classical, choral and all types of records and advertising. Mail samples. Buys all rights.
Needs: Pays $150, color comps for album covers.

MIDSONG INTERNATIONAL RECORDS, 1650 Broadway, New York NY 10019. (212)541-5100. Contact: Harry Spero. Estab. 1974. Produces pop, disco and rhythm-and-blues records. Assigns 15 jobs/year. Query with resume and samples or arrange interview to show portfolio. Reports in 2 weeks.
Needs: Pays $100-1,000, jackets and ads.

MIRROR RECORDS INC; HOUSE OF GUITARS BLVD., 645 Titus Ave., Rochester NY 14617. (716)544-3500. Art Director: Armand Schaubroeck. Produces rock-and-roll, MOR and new wave music. Recent releases: "Over the Rainbow," by Don Potter.
Needs: Produces 4 records/year; all of which have cover/jackets designed and illustrated by

freelance artists. Uses artists for catalogs, album covers, inner sleeves and advertising designs. "Always looking for new talent."
First Contact & Terms: Send query and samples. SASE. Reports in 1 month. Or send brochure or materials that can be kept on file for future reference. Negotiates pay based on amount of creativity required, artist's previous experience, amount of time and artist expense.

MITCHELL RECORDING AND MUSIC PUBLISHING CO. INC., Rt. 7, Box 67, Ridge Rd., Columbus MS 39701. Contact: Vimla C. Mitchell, art director. Estab. 1973. Produces pop, soul, disco, blues and country records. Assigns 2 jobs/year; out-of-town artists only. Query. SASE. Reports in 2 weeks.
Needs: Uses artists for album and promotional design. Negotiates pay.

MONUMENT RECORD CORP., 21 Music Sq. E., Nashville TN 37203. (615)244-6565. Art Director: Ken Kim. Estab. 1962. Produces pop records. Assigns 12 jobs/year. Call. Reports in 1 week.
Needs: Uses artists for album covers. Negotiates pay.

W.R. MORRIS ENTERPRISES, Box 737, Lexington TN 38351. (901)968-9323. Manager: Cathy Meadows. Produces country, folk and gospel music. Recent releases: "Walking Tall Sheriff Buford Pusser Talks With W.R. Morris," by Eddie Bond.
Needs: Produces 35 records/year; all of which has cover/jackets designed by freelance artists. Interested in record album, jacket and brochure design, album and print ad illustrations, etc.
First Contact & Terms: Send query and samples. SASE. Reports in 3 weeks. Negotiates payment.

MUSIC MINUS ONE/CLASSIC JAZZ, INNER CITY/GUITAR WORLD, 43 W. 61st, New York NY 10023. Contact: Irv Kratka. Mail resume, samples, jacket layouts or typical work showing artist's style and concepts for drawing and typesetting. Reports in 5 days. "We work quickly and need work within two weeks of order. We buy all rights."
Needs: Buys album cover designs.

MYSTIC MUSIC CENTER INC., Mystic Records-Mystic Sound Studios, 6277 Selma Ave., Hollywood CA 90028. (213)464-9667. President: Doug Moody. Estab. 1968. Produces TV and film music and records. Buys approximately 20 designs/year.
Needs: Pay varies for album design.

NASHVILLE INTERNATIONAL, 20 Music Square W., Nashville TN 37203. (615)256-2885. Production Manager: Peggy Churchwell. Produces album jackets.
Needs: Uses local artists for layout, illustration, type spec, paste-up and lettering.

NATURAL GROOVE RECORDS INC., 3588 Big Tree Cove, Memphis TN 38105. Contact: Professional Manager. Estab. 1972. Produces modern and jazz records. Assigns 5 jobs and buys 10 illustrations/year. Mail art. SASE. Reports in 1 week.
Needs: Uses artists for advertising, bumper stickers, posters and record jackets. Pays $50-200/job, production; $75-150/job, design; $7-15/hour, lettering.

NEW DIMENSION RECORDING CORP., 9120 Livernois, Detroit MI 48204. Contact: Mtesa Tirharka, Artist and Repertoire. Estab. 1970. Produces soul records. Assigns 50 jobs/year; local artists only. Query with resume and samples. SASE. Reports in 2 months.
Needs: Uses artists for design and illustration of albums, jackets and promotional materials. Negotiates pay.

NEW ENGLAND ("HANK THE DRIFTER") HITS, Drawer 250, Stafford TX 77477. Produces country and western cassettes, albums, 45s and 8-track tapes.
Needs: Uses artists for record album and jacket design.

NEW WORLD RECORDS, 2309 N. 36th St., Milwaukee WI 53201. (414)445-4872. President: Marvell Love II. Produces soul, pop and R&B music.
Needs: Produces 4 records/year; all of which have cover/jackets designed and illustrated by freelance artists. Interested in album design.
First Contact & Terms: Send brochure or materials that can be kept on file for future reference. SASE. Reports only when assignment is available. Pays set fee/job based on amount of creativity required.

NIC-LYN MUSIC CO., 1033 Little East Neck Rd., West Babylon NY 11704. Artist and Development Department: Gary Amos. Produces soul, country, rock-all-roll, pop and R&B music.

Needs: Produces 6 records/year; all of which have cover/jackets designed and illustrated by freelance artists. Interested in record album and brochure design and print ad illustrations.
First Contact & Terms: Send query and resume. SASE. Send brochure or materials that can be kept on file for future reference. Reports in 3-5 weeks. Negotiates pay based on "provisions and needs of both parties."

NORTH COUNTRY FAIRE RECORD CO., INC., 314 Clemons Ave., Ottawa Ontario Canada K1S 2B8. (613)234-6992 or (613)225-5959. President: Peter Hern. Produces rock-and-roll, classical, educational, country, jazz, folk and pop.
Needs: produces 10 records/year; all of which have cover/jacket designed by freelance designer or illustator. Uses artists for record album design, jacket design and album illustrations. Interested in "a clear, concise communication piece that graphically relates to the style of music represented in the package (cover)."
First Contact & Terms: Send query and samples, call for appointment, call for an interview to show portfolio or send brochure or materials that can be kept on file for future reference. SASE. Reports in 2 weeks. Negotiates fee based on the amount of creativity required

TROD NOSSEL ARTISTS, 10 George St., Box 9, Wallingford CT 06492. Art Director: Robert Orsi. Produces rock-and-roll records and tapes. Recent releases: "Rescue" by The Scratch Band and "Idiot Optimism" by Van Duren. Assigns 15-20 jobs/year.
Needs: Produces 10 records/year; 8 of which have cover/jackets designed and illustrated by freelance artists. Uses artist for design and illustration of record albums and cassettes, posters, promotional flyers, labels, merchandising aids and recording artists and personnel.
First Contact & Terms: Send resume and samples of work. SASE. Reports in 3-4 weeks. Provide resume and samples of work to be kept on file for future assignments. "Samples can be in the form of photos, color slides and the number depends upon the artist. If 1-2 samples convey his talents, that's fine." Pays $25-500.

OLD HAT RECORDS AND ROYAL T MUSIC, Box 54, Man's Field TX 76063. (817)477-2897. President: James M. Taylor. Produces country and rock-and-roll. Recently released: "Texas Rain," by TX H2O.
Needs: Produces 2 records/year; both have cover/jackets designed by freelance artists. Interested in record album, jacket and brochure designs, album and print ad illustrations, logos and sheet music design/illustration.
First Contact & Terms: Send query and samples or call for interview to show portfolio. SASE. Send brochure or materials that can be kept on file for future reference. "Usually my reply will be immediate." Negotiates pay based on "use value."

OLYMPIC RECORD CORP., 200 W. 57th St., Suite 802, New York NY 10019. Office Manager: Sharon Becker. Produces classical, pop, ethnic, children's and other types of records.
Needs: Assigns 20+ jobs/year. Uses artists for album and typeface design and illustration. "We are interested in concepts for 'series' releases, especially for classical and pop lines."
First Contact & Terms: Arrange interview to show portfolio. Reports in 2-3 weeks. Pays $250/record; may be less for series, minimum 3 records.

ORIGINAL CAST RECORDS; BROADWAY/HOLLYWOOD VIDEO PRODUCTIONS, Box 1314, Englewood Cliffs NJ 07632. (201)224-5811 after 10:30 am. Executive Producer: Doris Yeko. Produces educations and original cast musicals, children's shows, operettas, video tapes and movies. Recent releases: "Piano Bar," with Kelly Bishop, "Nefertiti Christy," by Various Artists.
Needs: Produces 10 records/year; all of which have cover/jackets designed and illustrated by freelance artists. Interested in musical poster art style, realistic styles, graphics designs, etc. Looking for artists with costume design, set design experience. Uses artists for record album design, insert designs, album illustrations and graphics, brochure design, video production design, some print ad design and illustrations.
First Contact & Terms: Call for appointment or interview to show portfolio. Send brochure or materials that can be kept on file for future reference. SASE. Reports in 1 month or when assignment becomes available. Negotiates pay based on amount of creativity required and artist's previous experience/reputation "and also set fee/job of $1-75 for cover design and execution including paste-up; up to $150 for album cover front and back." Contact D. Yeko for information regarding internship of 6+ weeks.

OVATION, INC., 1249 Waukegan Rd., Glenview IL 60025. (312)729-7300. President: Dick Scholry. Publicity Director: Cary Baker. Produces soul, country, jazz, pop, rock-and-roll and R&B music.

Needs: Produces 40 records/year; some of which have cover/jackets designed and illustrated by freelance artists. Interested in contemporary concepts.
First Contact & Terms: Send query and samples. SASE. Reports only when assignment becomes available. Negotiates pay based on amount of creativity required and artist's previous experience/reputation.

PARK RECORDS, 100 Park Place, Newark NJ 07102. (201)622-8453. Contact: J. 1953. Produces all types of records.
Needs: Produces 2 records/year; both have cover/jackets designed and illustrated by freelance artists. Uses artists for album and jacket design.
First Contact & Terms: Query with resume and samples. Reports in 2 weeks. Negotiates pay.

PHAROAH CAPITAL, 1260 E. Main, Meriden CT 06450. (203)728-5639. President. B.L. Loyh. Produces classical, country, jazz and folk music. Recently released: "Starting All Over Again," by Daviliska.
Needs: Produces 20 records/year; all of which have cover/jackets designed and illustrated by freelance artists. Interested in nudes in country settings. Uses artists for record album and jacket design.
First Contact & Terms: Send query and samples. SASE. Reports in 4 weeks. Negotiates pay based on amount of creativity required. Send resume and photo for information on 6 month internship program.

REAL TO REEL CUSTOM SERVICES, 98 Benz St., Ansonia CT 06401. (203)735-5883. Chairman of the Board: Martin G. Kugell. Record/tape duplicator company. Produces middle-of-the-road, disco, top 40/pop, rock and easy listening records.
Needs: Buys 20 illustrations/year. Uses artists for record album design, jacket design, album illustrations, advertising illustrations and brochure design.
First Contact & Terms: Query with resume and samples. SASE. Reports in 1 month. Pay varies.

REBEL RECORDING CO. INC., Rte. 12, Ashbury WV 24916. (304)645-6650. President: Charles R. Freeland. Estab. 1959. Produces bluegrass records and tapes. Query. SASE. Reports in 3 weeks. Buys all rights. Free catalog.
Needs: Uses artists for layout, magazine ads and album design. Pays $100 minimum.

REQUEST RECORDS, 3800 S. Ocean Ave., Hollywood FL 33019. (305)456-0847. General Manager: Ruth Gamba. Produces ethnic, classical, disco, country, pop and contemporary records. Recent releases: "Aloha, Hawaii," by Black Diamond Trio and 6 different of Haydn Symphonies. Assigns 24 jobs and buys 30 illustrations/year.
Needs: Produces 12-18 records/year; all of which have cover/jackets designed and illustrated by freelance artists. Interest primarily in scenic art. Uses artists for album design, ad illustrations and logos. Negotiates pay.
First Contact & Terms: Call or query with previously published work or arrange interview to show portfolio. Reports in 2 weeks. Works on assignment only. Samples returned by SASE. Reports back on future assignment possibilities. Provide resume, business card and brochure to be kept on file for future assignments.

RHYTHMS PRODUCTIONS, Whitney Bldg., Box 34485, Los Angeles CA 90034. (213)836-4678. President: R.S. White. Produces educational records, books and multimedia materials.
Needs: California artists only. Produces 5-6 records/year; all of which have cover/jackets designed and illustrated by freelance artists. Uses artists for catalog covers/illustrations, direct mail brochures, layout, magazine ads, multimedia kits, paste-up and album design.
First Contact & Terms: Buys 3-4 designs/year. Query with samples. SASE. Reports in 3 weeks. Buys all rights.

ROB-LEE MUSIC, Box 1385, Merchantville NJ 08109. (609)663-4540. Executive Vice President: R.L. Russon. Produces rock-and-roll, soul, country, pop and R&B music.
Needs: Produces 6 records/year; 4 of which have cover/jackets designed and illustrated by freelance artists. Uses artists for records, brochures, flyers, etc.
First Contact & Terms: Send query and samples. Send brochure or materials that can be kept on file for future reference. SASE. Reports in 2 weeks. Pays set fee/job.

ROUNDER RECORDS, 186 Willow Ave., Somerville MA 02144. (617)396-8400. Contact: Bill Nowlin. Estab. 1970. Produces American folk records. Buys 35 designs/year. Arrange interview;

local artists only. Material copyrighted. Free catalog.
Needs: Uses artists for catalog covers/illustrations and album design. Pays $100-125, album design.

SKOKIE RECORDS, 5230 W. Howard St., Skokie IL 60077. (312)675-4285. Contact: Edward Mravik, president. Produces bluegrass, classical and country and western records. Assigns 10 jobs/year; out-of-town artists only. Query with resume and samples. SASE. Reports in 1 month.
Needs: Uses artists for album and jacket design. Pays royalties.

SONRISE RECORDS, Box 607, Malibu CA. President: Bob Cotterell. Produces contemporary Christian music. Recent releases by Love Song Strings, Bob and Cindy Kilpatrick and Mountain Ansci Band.
Needs: Produces 5 records/year; all of which have cover/jackets designed and illustrated by freelance artists. Uses artists for record album design.
First Contact & Terms: Send query and samples. SASE. Reports in 2 weeks. Negotiates pay based on amount of creativity required and artist's previous experience/reputation.

STARCREST PRODUCTIONS, 2516 S. Washington St., Grand Forks ND 58201. (701)772-6831. President: George Hastings. Produces country, pop and gospel music. Recently released: Country gospel by Mary Joyce.
Needs: Produces 5 records/year; all of which have cover/jackets designed and illustrated by freelance artists. Uses artists for jacket and brochure design and print ad illustrations.
First Contact & Terms: Send query and samples. SASE. Reports in 2 months. Negotiates pay based on amount of creativity required.

STEADY RECORDS, 846 7th Ave., New York NY 10019. Contact: Art Department. Estab. 1968. Produces pop and rock records. Query with samples. SASE. Reports in 2 weeks.
Needs: Uses artists for flyers, posters and record jackets. Pays by job.

T.R. RECORDS, 747 10th Ave., New York NY 10019. (212)582-5600. Contact: S.J. Cohen, president. Estab. 1965. Produces pop and Latin records. Buys 5 illustrations/year; local artists only. Query with resume and samples. SASE. Reports in 3 weeks.
Needs: Uses artists for design and illustration of albums, jackets, ads and brochures. Pays $250-1,000.

TELARC RECORDS, 23293 Commerce Rd., Cleveland OH 44122. (216)464-2313. Producer: Robert Woods. Estab. 1961. Produces classical records. Buys 25-30 designs/year. Query with samples. SASE. Reports in 4-6 weeks. Buys all rights.
Needs: Uses artists for catalog covers/illustrations, direct mail brochures, layout, magazine ads and album design. Pays $200-450, color record jacket.

THIRD PHASE MARKETING INDUSTRIES CORP., 39 W. 55th St., New York NY 10019. (212)586-3350. Artist Representative: Nathaniel Adams. Production Manager: J.R. Lucas. Produces soul, pop and R&B music. Recently released artists: Al Johnson, Lloyd Price and Joyce Thorne.
Needs: Produces 6 records/year; 4 of which have cover/jackets designed and illustrated by freelance artists. Uses artists for record album, jacket stationery and brochure design, album and print ad illustrations and press releases.
First Contact & Terms: Send query and resume. Send brochure or material that can be kept on file for future reference. SASE. Reports back only on future assignment possibilities. Negotitates pay based on amount of creativity required and artist's previous experience/reputation.

TOTAL SOUND RECORDS, Box 1659, Beverly Hills CA 90213. Contact: Lawrence Herbst. Produces all types of records.
Needs: Uses artists for album design and illustration, jacket design, ad illustrations and brochure design.
First Contact & Terms: Query with resume and samples. Reports in 3 weeks. Pays $25 minimum; 14-20% royalty and advance.

TREND RECORDS, Box 201, Smyrna GA 30081. (404)432-2454. President: Tom Hodges. Produces soul, country, pop, R&B and MOR music. Recent release: "Feet," by Jim Single.
Needs: Freelance artists design and illustrate 1 cover/jacket per year. Uses artists for album design.
First Contact & Terms: Send query and samples. Send brochure or materials that can be kept on

file for future reference. SASE. Reports in 1-3 weeks. Negotiates pay based on amount of creativity required.

WAYLON RECORDS, 1216 Granby St., Norfolk VA 23510. (804)625-0534. Contact: Don Burlage, president. Produces rock and country-rock records.
First Contact & Terms: Query with resume and samples. Reports in 2 weeks.

WILDWOOD ENTERTAINMENT, 114 W. Maiden Ln., Monroe CT 06468. (518)273-7660. President: Vincent E. Meyer, Jr. Vice President: Erich C. Borden. Produces rock-and-roll, pop, top 40, educational, country, jazz and folk music.
Needs: Produces 8 records/year; 4 of which have cover/jackets designed and illustrated by freelance artists. Uses artists for jackets, album illustrations and artist promotional material.
First Contact & Terms: Send query and resume. Send brochure or materials that can be kept on file for future reference. SASE. Reports in 6 weeks or only when assignment becomes available. Negotiates pay based on amount of creativity required.

WORLD RECORDS, 484 Waterloo Court, Oshawa, Ontario, Canada L1H 3X1. (416)576-0250. General Manager: Bob Stone. Estab. 1969. Produces spoken word, classical, instructional foreign language and folk records, and charts and print folios for record and educational markets. Buys 35 designs/year. Query. SASE. Reports in 2 weeks. Buys all rights. Free catalog.
Needs: Uses artists for animation, catalog covers/illustrations, layout, magazine ads, models, multimedia kits, album design and technical charts/illustrations. Pays $200 minimum, albums.

ZONDERVAN CORP., 1415 Lake Dr. SE, Grand Rapids MI 49506. (616)698-6900. Contact: Art Jacobs, art director. Produces religious records.
Needs: Produces 20 records/year; all of which have cover/jackets designed and illustrated by freelance artists.Uses artists for design and illustration of albums and jackets.
First Contact & Terms: Query. SASE. Reports in 2 weeks. Works on assignment only. Samples returned by SASE. Reports back on future assignment possibilities. Provide photocopied samples of previous art to be kept on file for future assignments. Reports in 2 weeks. Negotiates pay.

Syndicates & Clip Art Firms

The cartoonists who achieve the most fame are generally syndicated. Because of this, syndicates are the cartoonist's "glamour" markets, with more than 35,000 strips submitted to national syndicates annually.

Syndicates and clip art firms both serve as middleman between the artist and publisher. The difference between them is that syndicates buy continuing material, usually cartoons or strips, and clip art firms usually purchase "one-shot" cartoons, spot drawings or decorative art. Also, syndicates usually require exclusive representation while clip art firms do not.

Clip art firms generally want to see photocopies or original art that can easily be filed. Syndicates, on the other hand, require much more thought be put into the submissions of materials.

Follow these guidelines when submitting a strip to a syndicate:

- Create the artwork two to three times larger than it will be reproduced, taking care not to change the proportional scale. Photocopies of the artwork are sufficient.
- Submit two or three weeks of finished work so the editor gets a feel for the major characters, their world and the direction in which they're moving.
- Make certain your ruling and lettering are of the same professional quality as that of published strips.

The Cartoonist Guild strongly recommends that you copyright strips and major characters prior to submitting them.

The Cartoonist Guild (156 W. 72nd St., New York NY 10023) publishes a useful guide for dealing with syndicates titled *Syndicate Survival Kit*. Other syndicate names and addresses are available in *Editor & Publisher Annual Directory of Syndicated Services.*

Syndicates

ALA, LATIN AMERICAN FEATURE SYNDICATE, 2355 Salzedo St., Suite 203, Coral Gables FL 33134. (305)442-2462. Editor: Arturo Villar. Syndicates to 120 regional magazines and newspapers.
Needs: Cartoon strips about Latino situations and illustrations for editorial material on the same theme; single panel. Also buys one-shot material.
First Contact & Terms: Submit work. SASE. Reports in 3 weeks. Buys first Latin American rights. Pays on acceptance. Originals returned to artist. Negotiates payment.

DANNEY BALL PRODUCTIONS, 1105 E. Florida Ave., Hemet CA 92343. (714)652-4459. Senior Editor: Robert Righetti. Syndicates to 72 weekly newspapers; features include *Bad Libs*, *For Pete's Sake*, *Noodles* and *Milo*.
Needs: "Until recently all material was produced by our staff, but we are presently looking for material that can be marketable on a syndication level. Cartoons and spot drawings should be camera-ready, reducible at least by 50% and be presentable to all ages; single, double and multipanel."
First Contact & Terms: Submit artwork. SASE. Reports in 2 weeks. Original artwork returned to artist. Buys first rights. Pays 50% commission.

CHICAGO TRIBUNE-NEW YORK NEWS SYNDICATE INC., 220 E. 42nd St., New York NY 10017. Editor: Don Michel. Syndicates to newspapers.
Needs: Considers comic strips and continuing panel themes.
First Contact & Terms: Submit photocopies. SASE. Buys all rights.

COMMUNITY AND SUBURBAN PRESS SERVICE, Box 639, Frankfort KY 40602. (502)223-1736. Editor: Kennison Keene. Syndicates to 500 weekly newspapers.
First Contact & Terms: Send reports in 10 days. No originals returned to artist at job's completion. Pays $15, cartoons.

COMMUNITY FEATURES, 870 Market St., San Francisco CA 94102. Art Editor: B. Miller. Syndicates to 400 weekly newspapers, shoppers, some college papers and alternative press. Mails brochure of syndicated offerings to 1500 newspapers several times a year. Guidelines 50¢ and SASE.
Needs: Interested in cartoon strips, illustrations, spot drawings, line art, square single panel, double panel and multipanel cartoons.
First Contact & Terms: Send samples (published and unpublished, tear sheets best—at least 5) with previously published work. SASE. Reports in 4-8 weeks. Buys various rights. Purchase one-shot. Will consider line-art on all topics listed in our guidelines. $10 minimum. Pays flat rate or 50% commission. Pays on publication.

CONTEMPORARY FEATURES SYNDICATE INC., Box 1258, Jackson TN 38391. Editor: Lloyd Russell. Syndicates to newspapers and magazines.
Needs: Considers single panel cartoons and line drawings.
First Contact & Terms: Mail b&w originals. SASE. Reports in 4-6 weeks. Buys various rights. Pays $5 minimum flat fee or takes 50% commission. Pays on publication.

DICKSON FEATURE SERVICE, 17700 Western, #69, Gardena CA 90248. Associate Director: Naida Dickson. "We work in a cooperative partnership with R-Gabs Comic Features Syndicate of St. Joseph, MO." Syndicate to about 10 newspapers; features include "the work of about 35 artists, which we are offering for sale."
Needs: Considers general interest, politically conservative, family and humorous cartoons and spot drawings; strips or single panels. We also distribute puzzles, children's features and columns both humorous and informative. "Moral values are in with us. We will not use racy, radical, bawdy or ultra-liberal material."
First Contact & Terms: "We accept artists' work on a consignment basis, and submit copies and descriptions of artwork to newspapers or magazines who answer our advertising. We do not employ salesmen to sell artwork in person, so it can be a long time between sales when an artist is still unknown. We ask for a commitment of at least one year for testing our ability to market an artist's work, an arrangement terminable only on 90 days' notice." Submit material for consideration. SASE. Reports in 3 weeks. Negotiates rights purchased. Pays 50% commission for all rights; less for reprint rights only. No originals returned unless requested with SASE at time of submission.
Tips: "Send samples. We are a small organization, seeking recognition in the field. An artist must be willing to accept very little pay for his talents, perhaps for a long time. We distribute samples among editors we solicit. Unless they like the artist's work, he will get nothing even though we may like it very much. If we find that any work we recieve has charm or appeal we will try to sell it for the artist."

FEATURE ASSOCIATES, 3334 Kerner Blvd., San Rafael CA 44901. (415)457-1947. Comic Strip Editor: Peter Menkin. Currently has 11 cartoonists under contract for weekly comic strips.
Needs: Interested in honest, original, well-drawn themes; multi-panel only.
First Contact & Terms: Send 5 samples of style "that need not be returned." Reports in 4 weeks. Buys all rights, or may negotiate. Pays a percentage of what the strip sells for. Payment is made quarterly.

FIELD NEWSPAPER SYNDICATE, 1703 Kaiser Ave., Irvine CA 92714. President/CEO: Richard Sherry. Syndicates to 2,500 newspapers. Titles include "Andy Capp," "Mary Worth" and "Dennis the Menace."
Needs: Considers cartoon strips; single, double and multipanel; must have strong main characters and theme.
First Contact & Terms: Submit work (6-12 unpublished items) with cover letter. SASE. Reports in 2 months. Buys various rights. Original returned to artist at job's completion. Pays royalties on publication. Free artist's guidelines.

FOUR STAR FEATURES, Box 8643, Philadelphia PA 19101. General Manager: John Prinkey. Syndicates to 37 newspapers and magazines.
Needs: Considers cancer related art, articles, photos and clippings.
First Contact & Terms: Mail photocopies. SASE. Reports in 3 weeks. Originals returned to artist at job's completion. Buys various rights. Pays $35 minimum, b&w; on publication.

HARRIS & ASSOCIATES PUBLISHING DIVISION, 247 S. 800 E., Logan UT 84321. (801)753-3587. Contact: Dick Harris. Syndicates to 200 newspapers.
Needs: Buys 10-12 cartoons/year on golf, tennis and families.

First Contact & Terms: Query with photocopies or roughs. SASE. Reports in 2 weeks. Buys all rights. Pays $5-25, b&w; on acceptance.

HUMORAMA INC., 100 N. Village Ave., Rockville Centre NY 11570. Editor: Ernest N. Devver. Humorama includes *Popular Jokes, Joker, Fun House, Cartoon Fun & Comedy* and *Popular Cartoons.*
Needs: Considers erotic but tasteful cartoons for adults; topical, risque and visually identifiable. No porno or blatant obscenity. Wants parody on any popular subject.
First Contact & Terms: Query. SASE. Buys all rights. Pays $12, 4-panel pen and inks. Pays 15 days after acceptance.

JOURNAL PRESS SYNDICATE, 250 Park Ave., New York NY 10017. Editor: Eugene R. Smith. Syndicates to newspapers.
Needs: Buys 3 pieces/year. Needs comic strips, panels and editorial cartoons.
First Contact & Terms: Query or submit photocopies (no originals) of material for consideration. SASE. Reports in 6 weeks. Original returned to artist. Buys all rights. Negotiates pay.

KING FEATURES SYNDICATE, 235 E. 45th St., New York NY 10017. Comics Editor: Hal Smith. Buys 300 cartoons/year for syndicated panel feature laff-a-pay.
First Contact & Terms: Submit roughs. SASE. Reports in 2 weeks. Buys all rights. Pays $35, cartoon panels, on acceptance.

KNOWLEDGE NEWS & FEATURES SYNDICATE, Kenilworth IL 60043. Executive Editor: Dr. Whitt N. Schultz. Syndicates to daily, weekly and monthly publications.
Needs: Considers humorous, business, communications, family and political cartoons.
First Contact & Terms: Query with photocopies. Always SASE. Reports in 2 weeks. Buys exclusive rights. Pays $5 minimum on publication.

LOS ANGELES TIMES SYNDICATE, Box 39, Los Angeles CA 90053. (213)972-7900 or toll-free (800)421-8603. Editor: Tom Dorkin. Syndicates to 1,500 newspapers, magazines and tablvids.
Needs: Considers humorous cartoon strips and contemporary graphics; single, double and multi-panel.
First Contact & Terms: Submit work. SASE. Reports in 4 weeks. Buys all rights. Pays 50% commision.

McNAUGHT SYNDICATE, 60 E. 42nd St., New York NY 10017. Contact: Cartoon Editor. Submit square, single panels, drawn in line, no Ben-Day. Reports in 2 weeks. Buys all rights. Pays on acceptance.
Needs: Buys about 10 cartoons/week for newspaper feature, "This Funny World." Pays $25.

MAGNUM WEST, Box 722, Corte Madera CA 94928. Editor: William Whitney. Emphasizes gorwth movement publications for a general readership. Weekly. Circ. 800. Estab. 1978.
Illustrations: Uses 6-10 illustrations/issue; buys all from freelancers. Receives 20-30 illustrations/week from freelancers. Themes or style is "open." Prefers b&w line drawings and b&w washes for inside and cover. Send resume and samples of style. SASE. Reports in 4-6 weeks. Purchase rights and payment are negotiated. Pays on publication.

MINORITY FEATURE SYNDICATE, Box 421, Farrell PA 16121. (412)981-2019. President: Bill Murray. Syndicates to 80 newspapers and magazines. Buys 300 pieces/year.
Needs: Humor through youth and family themes for single panel, strips and multipanel cartoons. Also needs writers for "All In The Family," and "Black Giants." Needs ideas for anagrams, editorial cartoons and puzzles.
First Contact & Terms: Query. SASE. Reports in 4-6 weeks. No originals returned to artist. Buys all rights. Pays 40% commission on acceptance.

NC NEWS SERVICE, 1312 Massachusetts Ave. NW, Washington DC 20005. Director/Editor-in-Chief: Richard W. Daw. Syndicates to Catholic religious press. Query. Reports in 2 weeks. Buys first or second rights. Pays on acceptance.
Needs: Religious or moral commentary 8x10 b&w ink drawings/cartoons. Pays $15-18, original illustration for religious education series; $5-10, cartoons.

NEW YORK TIMES SYNDICATION SALES CORP., 200 Park Ave., New York NY 10017. Executive Vice President: Jesse E. Levine. Syndicates to newspapers and periodicals worldwide.
Needs: Cartoons. Pays 50% commission.

NEWS WORLD SYNDICATE, 401 5th Ave., New York NY 10028. (212)532-8300. Editor: Julie Phillips. Estab. 1978. Query with work. SASE. Reports in 4-8 weeks. Buys all rights. Pays on publication.
Needs: Especially interested in multipart series with b&w illustrations and photos. Pays 50% commission.

NEWSPAPER ENTERPRISE ASSOCIATION INC., 230 Park Ave., New York NY 10017. (212)679-3600. Editorial Director: Robert Cochnar. Syndicates to 750 newspapers and periodicals.
Needs: Comic strip ideas, editorial cartoons and comic panels. If used in NEA Daily Service, pays flat fee. If used in Enterprise Features syndicate division, 50% commission.

OCEANIC PRESS SERVICE, Box 4158, North Hollywood CA 91607 or 4717 Laurel Canyon Blvd., North Hollywood CA 91607. (213)980-6600. Manager: John R. West. Syndicates to 300 magazines, newspapers and subscribers in 30 countries.
Needs: Buys several hundred pieces/year. Considers cartoon strips (single, double and multipanel) and illustrations. Themes include published sex cartoons, family cartoons, inflation, juvenile activities and jacket covers for paperbacks (color transparencies). Especially needs juvenile themes.
First Contact & Terms: Query with work. Accepts tearsheets and clippings. SASE. Reports in 4 weeks. Buys all rights. Pays on publication. Originals returned to artist, or put on auction. Free artist's guidelines with SASE.
Trends: "The trend is definitely toward women's market: money saving topics, service features—how to do home repair—anything to fight inflation."

PRESS ASSOCIATES INC., 806 15th St. NW, 632, Washington DC 20005. Contact: Art Editor. Syndicates to 300 newspapers and magazines, predominantly trade union.
Needs: Buys 125 spot drawings and cartoons/year. Working (blue collar and white collar alike) people-oriented cartoon strips (single panel) and spot b&w line drawings; trade union, work, job, health, safety, retirement and supervisors themes. Prefers captionless but not required.
First Contact & Terms: Submit work. SASE. Reports in 2 weeks. Material is not copyrighted. Pays $10-15/piece, on acceptance.

PUBLICATIONS COMPANY CLIP ART, 1220 Maple Ave., Los Angeles CA 90015. (213)747-6541. Manager: John Raydell. Syndicates clip art to small newsletters. Buys 80 pages/year.
Needs: Buys full pages of 9-20 bits of art 4½x7½ on the same subject, e.g., sports, office scenes, dancing, related objects, animals, cars, cowboys. Original can be on 8½x11 paper with 6x10 image area.
First Contact & Terms: Mail art. SASE. Reports in 3 weeks. Originals only returned to artist upon request. Pays $25-30/page.

THE REGISTER AND TRIBUNE SYNDICATE INC., Box 4994, Des Moines IA 50306. President: Dennis R. Allen. Estab. 1932. Syndicates to 1,700 newspapers. Buys several regular comic strips or panels/year. Submit work. SASE. Reports in 8 weeks. Buys all rights. Pays on publication.
Needs: Cartoon strips (single and multipanel); contemporary themes.

R-GABS COMIC FEATURES, 1324½ N. 3rd St., St. Joseph MO 64501. (816)279-9315. President: Gerald Bennett. Syndicates to 200 daily and weekly newspapers; strips include *Moms Boarding House* and *Marty*. Also associated with Dickson Features.
First Contact & Terms: "Write to Comic Art Editor, send one sample of work and ask for type of work needed." Submit camera-ready (reduced to correct size—strips 2¼x7; single panel 3½x3½). First showing can be mimo-graphic copy. SASE. Reports in 6 weeks. Originals only returned upon request. Pays 50% commission. Artist's guidelines for price of postage.
Needs: Considers cartoons and spot drawings; single panel and strips. "Strip can be of the continued story form type because we syndicate to weekly and daily newspapers."
Trends: "Many weekly papers are now begining to want cartoons and puzzles. This market in previous years due to space and the unavailable features was thought too costly for weekly newspapers. Now many weekly editors realize they must give readers the same material as the larger daily markets do."

SINGER COMMUNICATIONS,INC., 3164 Tyler Ave., Anaheim CA 92801. (714)527-5650. Vice President: Eldon Maynard. Syndicates to 300 magazines, newspapers, book publishers and

poster firms; strips include *Airhawk*, *7 Errors* and *Fun & Games*.
Needs: Buys several thousand pieces/year. Considers cartoon strips; single, double and multi-panel; family, children, sex, juvenile activities and games themes.
First Contact & Terms: Send clips. SASE. Reports in 2-3 weeks. Returns originals to artist at job's completion if requested at time of submission with SASE. Buys reprint or all rights. Pays 50% commission. Artist's guidelines $1.
Tips: "Send us cartoons on subjects like inflation, taxes or Christmas; we get thousands on sex."

SOCCER COMMUNICATIONS, 166 Madison Ave., New York NY 10016. (212)686-6850. Editor: Ray Thompson.Syndicates to 12 magazines and newspapers.
Needs: Buys cartoons, illustrations and spot drawings; single panel and strips.
First Contact & Terms: Query with previously published work or submit artwork. SASE. Reports in 3 weeks. Buys all rights. Negotiates pay. Pays on publication.

TEENAGE CORNER INC., 70-540 Gardenia Court, Rancho Mirage CA 92270. President: David J. Lavin. Syndicates to 63 daily newspapers.
Needs: Spot drawings and illustrations.
First Contact & Terms: Query. SASE. Reports in 1 week. Buys one-time and reprint rights. Negotiates commission. Pays on publication.

UNIVERSAL PRESS SYNDICATE, 6700 Squibb Rd., Mission KS 66202. Editor: James F. Andrews.
Needs: Cartoon panels, text features and strips.
First Contact & Terms: Reports in 4 weeks. Buys syndication rights.

WILLIAMS NEWSPAPER FEATURES SYNDICATE INC., Box 8005, Charlottesville VA 22906. (804)293-4706. President: G. Walton Lindsay. Syndicates to 1,200 newspapers.
Needs: Religious illustrations. No cartoons.
First Contact & Terms: Query or write for interview. SASE. Reports in 3 weeks. Buys all rights. Pays $60-75, b&w, on acceptance.

WILSON FEATURES SYNDICATE, Box 369, Marysville OH 43040. Contact: Cheryl Wilson, editor. Estab. 1974. Syndicates to 100 newspapers and similar publications; strips include *Figleaves* by Greg Curfman and *Doc Doodle* by Ross E. Bunch. Buys 2-3 strips and 25-50 illustrations/year. "Mail your ideas with a cover letter, typed if possible, and explain your feature; be clear on your intentions and strong on why your feature will sell." SASE. Reports in 3-4 weeks. Buys reprint or all rights. Free artist's guidelines.
Needs: Buys cartoons and illustrations; single panel and strips. Pays 50% commission. Also looking for crossword puzzles and similar "games."

WORLD NEWS SYNDICATE, LTD., 6223 Selma Ave., Hollywood CA 90028. Executive Editor: Bill Lane. Query or submit ideas or samples. Pays 50% commission.

Clip Art Firms

CARICATURE CLIP ART, Box 8643, Philadelphia PA 19101. General Manager: John Prinkey. Estab. 1970. Distributes to 37 newspapers and magazines. Mail photocopies. SASE. Reports in 3 weeks. Buys various rights. Pays on publication.
Needs: Political single-panel and caricature cartoons. Pays $35 minimum, b&w.

CELEBRATION: A CREATIVE WORSHIP SERVICE, Box 281, Kansas City MO 64141. (816)531-0538. Editor: Bill Freburger. Clients: Churches, clergy and worship committees.
Needs: Assigns 60/year. Uses artists for spot and line drawings on religious themes.
First Contact & Terms: Query; out-of-town artists only. Reports in 1 week. No originals returned to artist at job's completion. Pays $25/illustration.

COLLEGE PRESS SERVICE, 1140 Delaware #3, Denver CO 80204. (303)825-7501. Graphics Coordinator: Ed Stein. Distributes to 350 college papers, libraries and other educational institutions.
Needs: Considers spot drawings for college and contemporary young audiences, editorial and college cartoons and graphics.
First Contact & Terms: Query with art. SASE. Reports in 3 weeks. Buys reprint rights of pre-

viously published art. Originals only returned upon request. Pays $2-15, line drawings, on publication.

CREATIVE CARTOON SERVICE, 3109 W. Schubert Ave., Chicago IL 60647. Contact: Peter Vaszilson. Query. SASE. Buys cartoons.

CUSTOM CARTOONING, Box 8643, Philadelphia PA 19101. (215)338-0325. Contact: John Prinkey, managing editor. Estab. 1967. Syndicates to 25 magazines and newspapers; strips include *Bee Smart* and *Zodiyaks*. Buys 60 pieces/year. Query with previously published work. SASE. Reports in 1 month. Buys all rights. Pays on publication.
Needs: Buys cartoons; single, double or multipanel. Also buys one-shot illustrations. Pays flat rate.

DYNAMIC GRAPHICS INC., 6707 N. Sheridan Rd., Peoria IL 61614. (309)691-0428. Art Director: Frank Antal. Distributes to thousands of magazines, newspapers, agencies, industries and educational institutions.
Needs: Works with 15-20 artists/year. Illustrations, graphic design and elements; primarily b&w, but will consider some 2- and full-color.
First Contact & Terms: Submit portfolio. SASE. Reports in 1 month. Buys all rights. Pays on acceptance. Negotiates payment.

FILLERS FOR PUBLICATIONS, 1220 Maple Ave., Los Angeles CA 90015. Editor-in-Chief: John Raydell. Managing Editor: Dean Bowie. Distributes to magazines and newspapers.
Needs: Buys 72 pieces/year. Considers single panel current event, education, family life, retirement and office themes.
First Contact & Terms: Mail art. SASE. Reports in 2 weeks. Previously published and simultaneous submissions OK. Buys all rights, but may reassign rights to artist after publication. Originals only returned upon request. Pays $5-10, line drawings, on acceptance.

FIRMSBANKER & BRISEBOIS CO., 3300 Book Tower, Detroit MI 48226. Contact: Harry Gilmore. Send samples or clips.
Needs: Uses artists for illustrations of furniture for newspaper ad layouts. Artist must be skilled in perspective drawing from photos.

FORWARD GRAPHICS, 7031 University Ave., Des Moines IA 50311. (515)274-4621. Contact: Myron Warm, art director. Estab. 1970. Distributes to schools, publishers, businesses and printers. Buys 100 pieces/year. Submit artwork. SASE. Reports in 1 week. Buys all rights. Free artist's guidelines.
Needs: Buys spot drawings and illustrations. Pays $25 minimum.

PUBLICATIONS CO., 1220 Maple Ave., Los Angeles CA 90015. Contact: George Dubow. Distributes to in-house publications.
Needs: Buys 8-10/month on general and political themes.
First Contact & Terms: Send art. Reports in 2 weeks. Previously published work OK. Buys all rights. Originals returned to artist only upon request. Pays $5-10, on acceptance.
Illustrations: Considers line drawings and pen and inks.

REPORTER, YOUR EDITORIAL ASSISTANT, 1220 Maple Ave., Los Angeles CA 90015. (213)747-6542. Editor: George Dubow. Syndicates to newspapers and magazines from secondary level schools and colleges.
Needs: Considers single panel cartoons on teenage themes.
First Contact & Terms: Mail art. SASE. Reports in 2 weeks. Buys all rights. Originals returned to artist only upon request. Pays $5-10.

SAWYER PRESS, Box 46-578, Los Angeles CA 90046. President: Eric Matlen. Estab. 1967. Distributes to 100 magazines. Buys 250 pieces/year. Submit work. SASE. Reports in 3 weeks. Buys all rights. Pays on acceptance.
Needs: Spot drawings, illustrations and cartoons; single, double and multipanel. Also buys material with kinky, adult themes. Pays $10 minimum.

Art Publishers

The listings in this section are interested in buying serigraphs, oil paintings, watercolors, woodcuts, etchings, lithographs, drawings and other reproducible art.

Unsolicited submissions are welcomed by most art publishers, though it is wise to be selective in what you send. Publishers, like other businessmen, are intent on making a profit, and will choose only artwork they believe will sell well. In return, they pay artists by royalties, a fixed fee for rights to a limited edition or a combination of royalties and a fixed fee.

Additional print publishers and distributors for artwork can be found by reading the ads in *Art Dealer & Framer* and *Decor*, publications for the framing industry.

AARDVARK ART, 1100 Bryn Mawr, Bensenville IL 60106. (312)766-0400. President: Gerald McGlothlin. Produces limited and unlimited edition offset and collotype reproductions for galleries. Publishes 10 artists/year. Negotiates ownership of original art. Send letter of inquiry and photos of art. SASE.
Acceptable Work: Considers drawings, paintings, pastels, sculpture, watercolors, and anything with mass appeal; sunsets, scenics, boats, ships, wildlife, photography, earth-tone abstracts, any rich earth-tone subjects, and oriental art. Maximum size: proportional to 12x16 and 18x24.

AARON ASHLEY INC., 230 5th Ave., New York NY 10001. (212)532-9227. (Also 174 Buena Vista Ave., Yonkers NY 10702. (914)969-2782. President: Ashley L. Leavitt. Vice President: Philip D. Ginsburg. Produces unlimited edition fine quality offset and hand colored reproductions for distributors, manufacturers, jobbers, museums, schools and galleries. Publishes 10-40 artist/year. Pays 2½% royalties or $150-500. Offers advance. Buys all rights. Requires exclusive representation. Provides insurance while work is at publisher, shipping from publisher and written contract. Query, arrange interview or submit slides or photos. SASE. Reports immediately.
Acceptable Work: Unframed realistic and impressionistic paintings; individual works and pairs.

AARON BROTHERS CO./AARON ART PUBLISHING, 960 N. La Brea Ave., Los Angeles CA 90038. (213)874-8700 or 874-2423. Director of Publishing: Michael Aaron. Produces unlimited edition offset reproductions for art shops, framers, department stores and craft and gift stores. Pays 10% royalty or flat fee. No advance. Requires exclusive representation. Provides insurance while work is at publisher, shipping and written contract. Negotiates ownership of original art. Mail slides or photos or arrange interview. SASE. Reports in 4 weeks.
Acceptable Work: Unframed still life, wildlife, floral, landscapes, seascape and children subjects.
Tips: "A background in commercial art is helpful; the artist should at least be familiar with the general trend in the print and poster market; be aware of trends which affect customer needs—furnishings, fabrics and social trends."

ALVA MUSEUM REPLICAS INC., 140 Greenwich Ave., Greenwich CT 06830. (203)661-2400. Contact: Karen Kulish. Publisher and distributor. Clients: Museum shops, department stores, libraries and universities. Mail slides or photos stating size, medium and showing all views. SASE. Reports in 4 weeks.
Acceptable Work: Sculpture.

AMBASSADOR GRAPHICS & WILDLIFE, (formerly *Ambassador Art Galleries Inc.*), Box 1625, Summerville SC 29483. (803)556-9162. Contact: James R. Chapman, president. Publishes limited and unlimited offset reproductions for collectors, galleries and decorator firms. Publishes 3-5 artists/year. Send slides or photos or arrange interview. SASE. Reports immediately. Provides promotion, shipping, written contract, "articles written for magazines, color photography and some travel expenses."
Acceptable Work: Realistic oils, watercolors, acrylics, some b&w for printing and hand color by artist; southeastern coast, marsh, old barns, buildings and some florals; individuals, pairs or

series. Maximum size: 48x36x36. Negotiates royalties and advance, takes 33⅓% commission, or buys outright for $1,000-3,500.

AMERICAN MASTERS FOUNDATIONS INC., 10688 Haddington, Houston TX 77043. President: Randy Best. Clients: Dealers, galleries and framers. Send slides or photos. Reports in 2-4 weeks. SASE.
Acceptable Work: Landscape, wildlife, floral and other representational paintings and prints.

AMERICANA GRAPHICS INC., 312 Gallatin Rd. S., Madison TN 37115. (615)868-5510. President: V. Ann Royse. Produces limited and unlimited edition offset reproductions for framers and gift shops. Publishes 5-10 artists/year. Pays 10% royalty; or charges 50% commission on marketing of original graphics. Requires exclusive representation. Provides promotion and written contract. Artist owns original art. Submit slides or photos; then arrange interview. SASE. Reports in 2 weeks.
Acceptable Work: Unframed realistic individual works; 26x20" maximum.

APPLE ARTS, LTD., Rt. 33 E. Industrial Complex, Freehold NJ 07728. (201)462-8686. President: M. Lav. Produces limited edition hand-pulled originals and aluminum plate lithographs for own publishing and distribution and custom work for the trade. Publishes 40-80 artists/year. Pays flat fee. Offers advance. Buys all rights. Provides promotion and shipping. Publisher owns original art. Arrange interview. SASE. Reports in 2 weeks.
Acceptable Work: Unframed woodcuts, etchings and lithographs.

ART CONNECTION INC., 8407 Melrose Place, Los Angeles CA 90069. (213)651-0655. President: Cindy Adams. Distributes limited edition hand-pulled originals for galleries, interior designers, architects and corporations. Publishes 40-45 artists/year. Full editions purchased. Prefers exclusive representation. Submit slides or photos or arrange interview. SASE. Reports in 1 day.
Acceptable Work: Unframed landscapes, florals, geometrics, nautical images and impressionism.

ART DIMENSIONS INC., 6899 Peachtree Industrial Blvd., Suite J, Norcross GA 30092. (404)447-9331. Contact: B. Norman Bingham, president. Estab. 1978. Publishes limited hand-pulled originals for galleries, frame shops and designers. Query or arrange interview. Reports in 1 week. Provides insurance while work is at publisher, promotion, shipping from publisher and written contract.
Acceptable Work: "Ninety percent of our line is contemporary etchings." Also considers paintings and watercolors; individuals.

ART IMAGE INC., Box 4763, North Hollywood CA 91607. (213)788-3888. President: Allan Fierstein. Produces limited editions, hand-colored originals and offset reproductions for galleries, framed picture manufacturers and auctioneers. Publishes 4-6 artists/year. Negotiates payment; dependent on exclusivity. Provides promotion. Negotiates ownership of original art. Query to arrange interview or send photos. SASE. Reports in 1 week.
Acceptable Work: Unframed scenics, animals and decorative girls from oils, watercolors and pencil drawings; pairs or series.

ARTAFAX SYSTEMS LTD. INC., Box 568, N. Commercial St., Manchester NH 03105. (603)669-3162. Contact: H.R. Ostresh, vice president. Contract art publisher. Publishes limited editions and hand-pulled originals for architects, interior designers and specifiers for the contract furnishings market. Query with slides or photos of art; prefers out-of-town artists. Reports in weeks. Provides promotion, shipping from publisher and written agreement.
Acceptable Work: Drawings and photos, primarily nature-oriented. "Our present line is primarily hard-edge geometric in nature (hand-painted by our own people in various sizes as specified by the purchaser). We plan to increase our screen printing department to include other 'themes' and styles as required by the contract art market." Negotiates pay.

ALICE ATWOOD PRODUCTIONS INC., Box 96, Boston MA 02129. (617)628-1495. Art Director/President: Alice A. Mahoney. Produces limited edition (1,000) offset reproductions for own retail sales and mail order. Publishes 5-6 or more artists/year.
First Contact & Terms: Send letter of inquiry, slides, photos, or arrange interview. SASE. Reports in 1 month. No originals returned to artist at job's completion. Buys outright or works under contract. Flat fee paid by written contract.
Work: Considers pastels, watercolors, and illustration types; mostly pen and ink illustrations of an idea. Prefers individual works of art. Maximum size: 25x38.

JOHN BARTON ASSOCIATES INC., 915 Broadway, New York NY 10010. President: John Barton. Publishes limited edition hand-pulled originals and unlimited edition offset reproductions for galleries, frame shops, department stores, furniture stores, architects, designers and chain stores. Publishes 100 artists/year. Send slides or photos of art or arrange interview. SASE. Reports in 1 month. Provides promotion and individual purchase order.
Acceptable Work: Paintings and watercolors on any subject matter. Maximum size: 24 wide x 30 high. Buys all rights. Pays flat fee. Offers advance.

BERMOND ART LTD., 3000 Marcus Ave., Lake Success NY 11040. (516)328-3550. President: Raymond Kay. Secretary: Bernice Weiss. Publishes and distributes limited edition hand-pulled originals at wholesale only. Submit proofs with details and arrange interview. SASE. Reports in 2 weeks.
Acceptable Work: Unframed contemporary etchings, lithographs and serigraphs.

BLUE SKY, 211 W. 28th St., New York NY 10001. (212)564-2137. Contact: E. Kidder. Produces limited edition hand-pulled originals. Artist retains original art. Query and submit slides or photos. SASE.
Acceptable Work: Considers etchings and mixed media.

THE BRADFORD EXCHANGE, 9333 N. Milwaukee Ave., Niles IL 60648. (312)966-2770. Contact: Tom Foster. Produces limited edition collectors' plates. Pays flat fee and/or advance against royalties. Provides heavy media and mail promotion. Submit slides or photos. SASE. Responds to unaccepted artists immediately.
Acceptable Work: Acrylics, airbrush, oils, sculpture and watercolors.

CANADIAN NATIVE PRINTS LTD., 775 Homer St., Vancouver, British Columbia, Canada V6B 2W1. (604)681-3485. President: J.H. Krieger. Publishes limited edition hand-pulled originals and offset reproductions for galleries, card and gift shops, department stores, framers and museum shops.
First Contact & Terms: Send slides or photos. Reports in 3 weeks. Provides promotion, shipping from publisher and written contract. Pays advance against 10-50% royalties or takes 40% commission.
Needs: Publishes 40-50 artists/year. Considers paintings, pastels, watercolors and serigraphs by Canadian artists; series.

CIRCLE FINE ARTS CORP., 58 E. Walton St., Chicago IL 60611. Director of Artists Relations: David Oates. Produces limited edition hand-pulled originals and offset posters for galleries and interior designers. Published 50+ editions in 1979. Requires exclusive representation. Provides promotion. Query and submit slides or photos. SASE. Reports in 3 weeks. Buys various rights.
Acceptable Work: Unframed paintings, serigraphs and lithographs.

CIRRUS EDITIONS, 542 S. Alameda St., Los Angeles CA 90013. President: Jean R. Milant. Produces limited edition hand-pulled originals for museums, galleries and private collectors. Publishes 3-4 artists/year.

COLBERT GALLERY, 8271 Melrose Ave., Los Angeles CA 90046. (213)655-0460. Contact: Anca Colbert. Produces limited edition hand-pulled originals for galleries, designers and decorators. Publishes 3 artists/year. Pays flat fee or charges 40% commission. Offers advance. Requires exclusive representation. Provides insurance while work is at publisher, promotion (including catalog and mailings) and written contract, if desired. Artist owns original art. Submit color slides. SASE. Reports in 2 weeks.
Acceptable Work: Unframed landscape, romantic, surrealistic, naive and whimsical work; prefers aquaints; pairs and series; 30x40" maximum.

COLLECTIVE IMPRESSIONS LTD., 796 A-Fairmount Ave., Towson Plaza, Towson MD 21204. (301)296-2117. President: D.H. Isennock. Produces limited edition hand-pulled originals and unlimited edition letterpress reproductions for graphics retailers and investors. Publishes 2-5 artists/year. Provides insurance, promotion, shipping and written contract. Artist owns original art (subject to purchase by publisher). Query and submit slides or photos. SASE. Reports in 2 weeks.
Acceptable Work: Unframed abstract and impressionistic paintings and etchings; individual works.

H. S. CROCKER CO., 1000 San Mateo Ave., San Bruno CA 94066. Contact: Al Trice. Publishes posters, fine art prints, post cards, catalogs and fine art books for restaurants, distributors and fund raisers. Negotiates rates; pays flat fee or up to 20% royalties. Send resume and slides.

CUSTOM ART DISTRIBUTORS, 426 South St., Philadelphia PA 19147. (215)WA2-5708. Owner: John T. deVechis Jr. Publisher, dealer and gallery. Publishes limited edition hand-pulled originals for galleries and department stores. Publishes 6 artists/year. Send query. SASE. Reports in 2-3 weeks. Provides promotion and written contract. Buys all rights.
Acceptable Work: Impressionistic, realistic and contemporary drawings, paintings and pastels; individuals. Maximum size: 36x24.

DONALD ART CO. INC., 90 S. Ridge St., Port Chester NY 10573. (914)937-2700. President: Randolph Bonnist. Produces unlimited edition offset reproductions for wholesale picture frame manufacturers, and manufacturers using art in their end products, for premiums and promotions.
First Contact & Terms: Send photos or slides. Reports in 1 week. Provides in-transit insurance, insurance while work is at publisher, promotion and written contract. Pays advance (sometimes) against 5-10% royalties.
Acceptable Work: Publishes 50 artists/year. Considers contemporary paintings, oils, pastels and watercolors; series of at least 4 related pieces in size and theme. No traditional styles, abstracts, "cute" stuff or "message" material. Maximum size: 22x28.

EDITIONS PRESS, 915 Bryant St., San Francisco CA 94103. Contact: Walter Malbaum. Publishes lithographs from hand-inked stones and plants.

ELDON OFFICE PRODUCTS, 1130 E. 230th St., Carson CA 90749. (213)518-1600. Product Manager: Albert A. Kovac. Produces limited and unlimited edition prints for office supply firms and furniture dealers. Buys reproduction rights. Query with samples. SASE. Reports in 3 weeks. Free catalog.
Acceptable Work: Realistic themes, including landscapes and seascapes.

FABULOUS FORGERIES LTD., 230 Central Park S., New York NY 10019. Contact: Ted Marshall. "Our technique utilizes both lithography and photography combining either with an acrylic to form a true mixed media; finished product usually on canvas or wood. Some consider this a new art form." Pays 10% royalties. Submit resume and slides or transparencies.
Acceptable Work: Traditional, contemporary and realistic.

FAIRFAX PRINTS LTD., Box 230, E. Lansing MI 48823. President: Gary Fairfax. Publishes limited and unlimited edition offset reproductions for bookstores, record stores, galleries and department stores. Publishes 1-2 artists/year. Send slides. SASE. Reports in 2-4 weeks. Provides insurance while work is at publisher, promotion, shipping from publisher and written contract. Buys poster rights only; sometimes negotiates rights.
Acceptable Work: Realistic paintings and sculpture on fantasy/science fiction themes (though work can be quite stylized); series. Maximum size: 24x2x36. Pays advance against 5-10% royalties.

FELICIE, 141 E. 56th St., New York NY 10022. (212)752-7567. Director: Judith Cohen. Produces limited edition hand-pulled originals for galleries, decorators, architects and consultants. Publishes 8-9 artists/year. Pays flat fee. Offers advance. Requires exclusive representation. Provides promotion and written contract. Artist owns original art. Submit slides or photos. SASE. Reports in 1 month.
Acceptable Work: Unframed paintings; individual works.

FORUM DEL SOL, 344 E. Foothills Pky., Suite 8E, Ft. Collins CO 80525. (303)226-2818. Contact: Nancy Halliwell, president. Produces hand-pulled originals and offset reproductions for galleries. Publishes 12 artists/year. Query with slides or photos or arrange interview. Reports in 2 weeks. Provides insurance, promotion, shipping from publisher and written contract.
Acceptable Work: Realistic drawings, paintings, pastels, watercolors and sculpture. Negotiates pay.

FOXFIRE FINE ARTS INC., 2730 N. Graham St., Charlotte NC 28206. (704)377-0024. President: Jerome O'Boyle. Produces hand-pulled originals and offset reproductions for galleries and framers. Publishes 6-9 artists/year. Pays 10% royalty or charges 40% commission. Buys all rights. Requires exclusive representation. Provides insurance while work is at publisher, promotion, shipping from publisher and written contract. Artist owns original art. Call or submit slides or photos. Reports in 1 week.
Acceptable Work: Unframed realistic paintings; individual works and series; 3x2' maximum.

GALLERIE RABINDRA, 2720 LaCienega Blvd., Los Angeles CA 90034. (213)837-1205. Art Director: Larry Morgan. Produces limited and unlimited offset reproductions. Pays 10% royalty. Buys all rights. Artist keeps original art. Arrange interview or submit slides or photos. SASE. Reports in 3 weeks.
Acceptable Work: All media and subjects.

GOES LITHOGRAPHING CO., 42 W. 61st St., Chicago IL 60621. Contact: Walter J. Goes. Estab. 1878. Pays flat fee. Mail samples. SASE.
Acceptable Work: Landscape and wildlife.

GRAPHICS EDITIONS, 2842 Pierce St., San Francisco CA 94123. Contact: Mr. R. Strauss. Publishes hand-printed limited edition originals. Send resume and educational background. SASE.

GREEN-FIELD GALLERY PUBLISHING, 1131 E. Yandell Dr., El Paso TX 79902. (915)533-5690. Managing Director: Edgar Schnadig. Produces limited and unlimited edition letterpress and offset reproductions for galleries. Negotiates pay. Query. SASE. Reports in 2 weeks.
Acceptable Work: Unframed work in all media.

H. S. GRAPHICS LTD., Box 243, Keasbey NJ 08832. Director: Vivian Bullaudy. Clients: Galleries. Pays $500-1,000 flat fee. Query or send slides. SASE. Reports in 1 week.
Acceptable Work: Wood and stone etchings and lithographs.

HADDAD'S FINE ARTS INC., Box 3016 C, Anaheim CA 92803. President: James Haddad. Produces limited and unlimited edition originals and offset reproductions for galleries, art stores, schools and libraries. Publishes 40-70 artists/year. Buys reproduction rights. Provides insurance while work is at publisher, shipping from publisher and written contract. Submit slides. SASE. Reports in 60 days.
Acceptable Work: Unframed individual works and pairs; all media.

HEDGEROW HOUSE PUBLISHING CO. INC., 230 5th Ave., New York NY 10001. (212)679-2532. President: Robert A. Hill. Publisher and distributor. Clients: Framers, jobbers, dealers, galleries and department stores. Pays flat fee or royalties. Buys reproduction rights. Requires exclusive area representation. Arrange interview. SASE. Reports in 2 weeks.
Acceptable Work: Impressionistic and realistic landscape and floral acrylics, watercolors and graphics for lithography and etchings.

INTERNATIONAL ART CO., 1640 NE 123rd St., North Miami FL 33181. (305)891-4182. Contact: Sidney Litwin. Publisher and distributor. Clients: Galleries, framers, department stores and gift shops. Pays royalties. Mail photos or slides. SASE. Reports in 3 weeks.
Acceptable Work: Oils and watercolors for serigraphy and lithography.

JAMIN EDITIONS INC., 16140 Valerio St., Van Nuys CA 91406. (213)882-8901. President: K. Benjamin. Produces limited edition hand-pulled originals and letterpress and offset reproductions for department stores, galleries and card shops. Pays royalties or $100 minimum flat fee. Provides insurance while work is at publisher, promotion, shipping from publisher and written contract. Publisher keeps original art. Submit slides or photos or call. SASE. Reports in 1 month.
Acceptable Work: Unframed work in all media.

ARTHUR A. KAPLAN CO. INC., FINE ART REPRODUCTIONS, 28 W. 25th St., New York NY 10010. (212)691-4030. President: Arthur A. Kaplan. Produces unlimited edition offset reproductions of artwork and photography for framers and other manufacturers. Publishes about 100 artists/year. Submit slides or photos. SASE. Reports in 2 weeks. Provides insurance while work is at publisher, promotion, shipping from publisher and written contract. Originals returned to artists at job's completion. Buys reproduction rights. Pays 10% royalty or $50-500 flat fee.
Work: Considers unframed florals, landscapes, wildlife and people; oils, acrylics, watercolors and pastels; series. Maximum size: 4×3'.

MURRAY KLEIN ASSOCIATES INC., Box 741, 1983 Ladenburg Dr., Westbury NY 11590. (516)333-0516. President: Murray Klein. Publishes unlimited edition offset reproductions for art galleries, museums, colleges, and book and department stores. Publishes 4 artists/year. Query or arrange interview. Reports in 2-3 weeks. Provides promotion, shipping to publisher and written contract.

Acceptable Work: Impressionistic drawings, cartoons, paintings and watercolors including wildlife and flowers; series. Maximum size: 22x28. Pays $200 mimimum against 5-15% royalties. Also will work on consignment with commission arrangement. Offers advance.

LAMBERT STUDIOS INC., 9263 W. 3rd St., Suite 115, Beverly Hills CA 90210. (213)275-8056. Vice President: Stefon Marin. Publishes lithographs printed directly on textured artist's canvas for mail order firms, colleges, department stores, card/gift shops and bookstores. Publishes 25 artists/year. Send slides or photos of art. Reports in 2 weeks. Provides promotion and shipping from publisher.
Acceptable Work: Realistic and impressionistic paintings on several themes; individuals. Maximum size: 18x24. Buys outright.

MARTIN LAWRENCE LIMITED EDITIONS, 7011 Hayvenhurst Ave., Van Nuys CA 91406. (213)988-0630. President: Larry Ross. Produces limited and unlimited edition hand-pulled originals for galleries, distributors and wholesalers. Publishes 20-25 artists/year. Pays flat fee. Offers advance. Buys all rights. Requires exclusive representation. Provides insurance while work is at publisher, promotion and written contract. Publisher owns original art. Submit slides or photos. SASE. Reports in 2 weeks.
Acceptable Work: Unframed abstracts and contemporary graphics in paintings, etchings and sculpture; series.

LONDON ARTS INC., 321 Fisher Bldg., Detroit MI 48202. (313)871-3606. Director: Gary Turla. Produces limited edition hand-pulled originals for galleries. Published 20 artists in 1977 and 1978. Negotiates flat fee. Offers advance. Buys all rights. Provides insurance, promotion, shipping and written contract. Publisher keeps original art. Submit slides or photos. SASE. Reports in 1 month.
Acceptable Work: Unframed individual works; all media.

LOS ANGELES ART PROJECTS INC., 3360 Livonia Ave., Los Angeles CA 90034. (213)204-2870. Vice President: Janet Ames. Publisher and dealer. Publishes limited edition and unlimited edition hand-pulled originals and offset reproductions for galleries, card shops, department stores, dealers and decorators. Publishes 8/year. Contact by any method. SASE. Reports asap. Provision terms subject to negotiation.
Acceptable Work: Drawings, paintings, pastels, sculpture and watercolors; individuals, pairs or series. Negotiates pay.

PHYLLIS LUCAS GALLERY/CAMILLA LUCAS INC. PUBLISHING, 981 2nd Ave., New York NY 10022. Contact: Phyllis Lucas. "We specialize in original signed graphics. We publish exclusive Dali signed graphics.

MITCH MORSE GALLERY INC., 305 E. 63rd St., New York NY 10021. (212)593-1812. Vice President: Carri Stone. Produces limited edition hand-pulled originals for framers, galleries, interior designers and architects. Publishes 15 artists/year. Negotiates payment. Offers advance. Publisher owns original art. Arrange interview or submit slides or photos. SASE. Reports in 1 week.
Acceptable Work: Unframed realistic, impressionistic and romantic paintings, lithographs and etchings; individual works; 4x4' maximum.

NATURE HOUSE INC., Box 222, Griggsville IL 62340. Contact: Art Director. Send resume and slides or 8x10 glossies.
Acceptable Work: Specializes in detailed watercolor landscapes featuring animals or birds; 22x28".

NEW YORK GRAPHIC SOCIETY, LTD., 140 Greenwich Ave., Greenwich CT 06830. (203)661-2400. Assistant to President: Titina Liverakos. Publishes unlimited reproduction and editions, hand-pulled originals, graphic work of offset, gravure and colotype reproductions for stores, galleries, interior designers and libraries. Publishes 50 artists/year. Pays 1.2% royalty. Offers $300 nonrefundable advance. Purchases complete graphic editions at negotiated price. Provides insurance, promotion, shipping from publisher and written contract. Artist retains original art. Submit slides or photos. SASE. Reports in 3 weeks.
Acceptable Work: Paintings, graphics and sculpture; some abstracts; individual works; 4x2½x3' maximum.

OPEN STUDIO, 520 King St. W., Toronto, Ontario Canada M5V 1L7. (416)368-8238. Contact: Jini L. Stolk, coordinator. "We offer rental of facilities for etching, screen printing amd lithography to artists; we also offer classes and sell some artists' work to galleries, dealers and private collectors. Rental is $40/month. Artists may work independently on their own editions or may work in collaboration with our master printers and have their work custom printed." Publishes 12 artists/year. "We do not accept submissions but invite artists whom we wish to publish." Query.

ORIGINAL PRINT COLLECTORS GROUP, LTD., 120 E. 56th St., New York NY 10022. Contact: Marjorie Katzenstein or Bruce Whyte. Publishes hand-signed and numbered, limited edition originals. "Artist must have printmaking expertise. It is preferred, although not required, that artists pull their own prints." Send resume and slides.
Acceptable Work: Representational and semi-abstract art for etchings, lithography and screen prints.

PACE EDITIONS INC., 32 E. 57th St., New York NY 10011. (212)421-3237. Director: Karen McCready. Clients: Individuals, designers and corporations. Arrange interview to show prints. SASE. Reports in 1 week.
Acceptable Work: Screen prints, lithographs, etchings, intaglio prints and relief engravings.

PARASOL PRESS, LTD., 289 Church St., New York NY 10013. (212)431-9387. Director: Carol Androccio. Produces limited edition hand-pulled originals for dealers and museums. Publishes 6-8 artists/year. Pays 50% royalty. Offers advance. Buys rights for plates to be cancelled. Requires exclusive representation. Provides insurance, promotion, shipping to publisher and written contract. Publisher owns original art. Arrange interview. No work returned.
Acceptable Work: All media.

PHOENIX STUDIOS INC., Box 2963, Fayetteville OK 72701. Contact: Michael R. Balot, president. Estab. 1974. Publishes limited edition relief sculpture in natural marble, glass and gemstones for galleries, gift shops, museum shops, interior decorators and commercial designers. Publishes 4-6 artist/year, "would like to solicit many more." Query with slides or photos of art. SASE. Reports in 2 weeks. Provides in-transit insurance, promotion, shipping from publisher and written contract.
Acceptable Work: B&W artwork, pen and ink line drawing, graphic illustrations, and woodcut designs; individual works, pairs series. Will consider all subjects in realism, but also geometrics, impressionism and abstract. Pays royalty of 5% minimum (negotiable) or $50 minimum flat fee.

PORTAL PUBLICATIONS, LTD., 21 Tamas Vista Blvd., Corte Madera CA 94925. (415)924-5652. Art Director: Pamela Prince. Produces unlimited edition reproductions and photo-lithographs for retail outlets, department stores, galleries, card shops, bookstores and framers. Publishes 20 artists/year. Provides insurance while work is at publisher, promotion, distribution, shipping and written contract. Query or arrange interview. SASE.

THE PRINTMAKERS, 3373 Wrightwood Dr., Studio City CA 91604. (213)656-1797. President: Marcia Isaacs. Publishes fine art. Hand-pulled originals for galleries, designers and architects. Publishes 20-30 artists/year. Send slides or photos. SASE. Reports in 1-2 weeks. Provides promotion, shipping from publisher and written contract.
Acceptable Work: Emphasizes on realistic etchings, lithographs and serigraphs; individuals, pairs and series. Preferred sizes: 12x24, 22x30. Pays royalty or purchases editions.

RAE ROY & CO., Box 656, McAllen TX 78501. (512)682-0593. Contact: Rae Roy Anderson. Estab. 1958. Produces unlimited edition offset reproductions for department stores, wholesale framers and chain stores. Publishes 1,000 artists/year. Pays 5% royalty. Provides insurance, shipping and written contract. Artist keeps original art. Submit slides or photos. SASE. Reports in 2 months.
Acceptable Work: All media except abstracts; unframed work in pairs and series. Maximum size: 4x3'.

RED BARON ART PUBLISHING INC., Box 789, Chatsworth CA 91311. President: S.P. Schmidt. Produces limited and unlimited edition offset reproductions for distributors, manufacturers and other dealers. Publishes 12-20 artists/year. Pays 5-10% royalty or $250 minimum flat fee. Buys all rights. Sometimes requires exclusive representation. Provides promotion, shipping from publisher and written contract. Submit slides or color photos. SASE. Reports in 10 weeks.
Acceptable Work: Unframed paintings in series. Maximum size: 3x4'.

ROSEART INC., 5181 NE 12th Ave., Ft. Lauderdale FL 33334. (305)772-1531. Contact: Howard Rosenbaum, president. Produces limited edition hand-pulled originals for galleries, dealers,

department stores, commercial interior design firms, museums and corporations. Publishes 15-30 artists/year. Send slides or photos. SASE. Reports in 2 weeks. Provides insurance, promotion and written contract.
Acceptable Work: Drawings, paintings, pastels and watercolors; all styles and subjects; series. Maximum size: 30x40. Pays flat rate.

ARTHUR ROTHMANN FINE ARTS, Box 1124, Deerfield Beach FL 33441. Editor: Arthur Rothmann. Clients: Galleries and museums. Pays flat fee: $100-1,000. Query with 8x10 or 24x36 samples or write for interview. SASE. Reports in 2 weeks.
Acceptable Work: Figurative and representational graphics, etchings, drawings, engravings and woodcuts.

SCAFA-TORNABENE ART PUBLISHING CO. INC., 100 Snake Hill Rd., West Nyack NY 10994. (914)358-7600. Executive Vice President: Frank Tornabene. Produces unlimited edition offset reproductions for framers, galleries, museums, commercial art trade and manufacturers. Publishes 50-100 artists/year. Pays $100-250 flat fee. Published artists (successful ones) can advance to royalty arrangements with advance against royalty. Buys reproduction rights. Requires exclusive representation. Provides insurance, shipping from publisher and written contract. Artist owns original art. Query first; submit slides or photos and then arrange interview. SASE. Reports in 2 weeks.
Acceptable Work: Unframed decorative paintings and drawings; pairs and series.

SHIP LORE LTD., 470 Park Ave., New York NY 10022. (212)759-1175. Publishes limited and unlimited edition prints for framers, galleries and specialty stores.

NATHAN SILBERBERG FINE ARTS, 16 E. 79th St., New York NY 10021. (212)861-6192. Clients: galleries and art dealers. Arrange interview.
Acceptable Work: Twentieth century and "School of Paris" silkscreens and paintings.

SOLO PRESS, 461 Park Ave. S., New York NY 10016. (212)683-4412. Master Printer: Judith Solodkin. Produces limited edition hand-pulled originals for museums, galleries and artists. Publishes 2 artists/year.Provides written contract. Publisher owns original art. Query or submit slides. SASE. Reports in 2 weeks.
Acceptable Work: Unframed works; series. Maximum size: 53x32".

JOHN SZOKE GRAPHICS, 144 E. 57th St., New York NY 10022. (212)759-9405. Director: John Szoke. Produces limited edition hand-pulled originals for galleries, museums and private collectors. Publishes 10-25 artists/year. Charges commission or negotiates royalties. Offers advance. Requires exclusive representation. Provides promotion and written contract. Publisher owns original art. Arrange interview or submit slides. SASE. Reports in 1 week.
Acceptable Work: Unframed landscapes, representational and abstracts.

TRANSWORLD ART INC., 20 W. 57th St., New York NY 10019. (212)757-2700. President: Alex Rosenberg. Produces limited editions for galleries, museums and collectors. Publishes 8 artists/year.
First Contact & Terms: Submit photos with letter and resume. SASE. Reports in 2 weeks. Provides insurance, promotion, exhibitions, shipping and written contract. Requires exclusive representation. No originals returned to artist at jobs completion. Buys all rights. Pays flat fee or royalty. May offer advance; 33⅓% of agreed price.
Work: Consider framed representational and some abstract paintings, drawings and original prints; series.

VANGUARD STUDIOS INC., Subsidiary of Kirsch Co., 5775 N. Lindero Canyon Rd., Westlake Village CA 91361. Design Director: Joann Alesch. Produces paintings, reproductions, limited edition prints, posters and decorative mirrors. Negotiates royalties. Buys exclusive reproduction rights. Publisher owns original art. Arrange interview or send slides.
Acceptable Work: Considers sports posters in all medias.

EDWARD WESTON GRAPHICS INC., 149 Mercer St., New York NY 10012. (212)226-4141. Contact: Frances Thompson, director. Main Showroom and warehouse located at 19355 Business Center Dr., Northridge CA 91324. (213)885-1044. Contact: Ann Weston. Produces limited and unlimited edition hand-pulled originals and posters for galleries and wholesalers. Publishes 10 artists/year. Query with slides or photos or arrange interview. SASE. Reports in 2 weeks. Provides insurance, promotion, shipping and written contract. The division Edward Weston Editions (same address) buys image rights for limited edition plates for the plate collector market.

Acceptable Work: Drawings, paintings, pastels and watercolors; individual pieces. Negotiates pay.

WORKSHOP INC., 3145 Newark St. NW, Washington DC 20008. (202)966-4202. President: Lou Stovall. Produces limited edition hand-pulled originals for galleries and artists. Publishes 10-12 artists/year. Negotiates pay. Artist owns original art. Submit slides, photos or art. SASE. Reports in 3 weeks.
Acceptable Work: Landscape and abstract paintings and drawings; individual works. Maximum size: 40x30.

YAMET ARTS INC., 1097 Madison Ave., New York NY 10028. (212)249-2355. Contact: I. or R. Yamet. Produces limited edition hand-pulled originals for galleries. Publishes 25 artists/year. Pays $1,000 minimum flat fee. Provides promotion and written contract. Publisher owns original art. Arrange interview. SASE. Reports in 1 week.
Acceptable Work: Paintings, woodcuts, etchings, original lithographs and sculpture.

YANEFF GALLERY, 119 Isabella St., Toronto, Ontario, Canada M4Y 1P2. (416)924-6677. Contact: Chris Yaneff. Produces limited and unlimited edition hand-pulled originals and letterpress and offset reproductions for galleries. Publishes 3-10 artists/year. 33⅓% commission. Requires exclusive area representation. Provides insurance and promotion. Publisher owns original art. Query or submit slides. SASE. Reports in 3 weeks.
Acceptable Work: Unframed landscapes and impressionistic themes in all media.

Contests and Awards

Entering contests can be worthwhile in many ways. There's always the excitement of competing—and possibly winning—with others in your field. Compiling and viewing your best work to submit can bring a great deal of satisfaction and perhaps give you a new perspective of your work. A winning entry not only brings you an award, but also looks very good on your resume. Often, part of the prize is publication and this can help in the future, too.

For entry blanks, complete rules and deadlines write or call the individual competitions. Check with clubs, businesses, schools and community groups for local competitions.

Art festivals, fairs and shows also provide good local markets for freelance sales and they sometimes give awards. Consult the Shows & Fairs section of *Craftworker's Market* (Writer's Digest Books) for such events and *Gadney's Book of Contests* for additional competitions.

AMERICAN FILM FESTIVAL, Educational Film Library Association, 43 W. 61st St., New York NY 10023. (212)246-4533. Festival Director: Nadine Covert. Annual. $40-110 entry fee; no fee for Film as Art program. Entry deadline: mid-January.
Acceptable Work: Animated or live-action 16mm optical track flat prints released within the last 2 years; must be available for general distribution in the U.S.
Awards: Emily Award, for film which receives highest score; John Grierson Award ($500), for new filmmaker who shows outstanding talent in social documentary field; Blue Ribbon and Red Ribbon Awards, for highest rated films in each category.

AMERICAN GRAPHICS GALLERY, INC., Box 448 A, Village Station, New York NY 10014. Contact: Catryna Ten Eyck. Mail order print club. Price range: $50-250. Jury. Artist sets retail price. Art must be offered for sale; 50% commission. Provides promotion in quarterly journal for members and written contract. Send 9x12 SASE (54¢ postage) for entry information and sample copy of *American Graphics*.
Acceptable Work: Prints; 200" square minimum; unframed.

THE ART ANNUAL, Communication Arts Magazine, Box 10300, 410 Sherman Ave., Palo Alto CA 94303. Executive Editor: Jean Coyne. Annual Awards of Excellence. Purpose: To give recognition to photographers, illustrators and the art directors who commissioned the best of the media arts. Entry fee: $6, single entry; $12, series. Entry deadline: March 21.
Acceptable Work: Photography, prints, 3-dimensional work, collage, illustration, or any media art that was commissioned for publication.
Awards: Award of Excellence certificates. Winning entries reproduced in July/August issue of *Communication Arts.*

AWARDS FOR THEATRICAL DESIGN EXCELLENCE, American College Theatre Festival, John F. Kennedy Center for the Peforming Arts, Washington DC 20566. (202)254-3437. Contact: David Young, producing director. Estab. 1978. Annual awards. Entry deadline: October.
Acceptable Work: Costume and set design used in a regular ACTF or university production. Open to students enrolled in ACTF-member schools.
Awards: "Two designers in professional theatre will select a winner in Costume Design and one in Scene Design. . . . Each national winner will receive a $300 cash award and an expense paid trip to New York City for 7 days. Winners will visit the studios of distinguished designers, film and TV studios, and professional costume and scene shops."

BEST ILLUSTRATED CHILDREN'S BOOKS, *The New York Times, 229 W. 43rd St., New York NY 10036. (212)556-7156. Contact: George A. Woods, children's book editor. Annual. Purpose: "To recognize outstanding examples of art for young students and to encourage better art for the young in their books." No entry fee. Entry deadline: early October.*
Acceptable Work: Must be contained in a children's book published or to be published in the year of the contest. May be sent in advance of publication date. Galleys and/or folded and gathered sheets OK.
Awards: "The prize is purely honorary. One of the artist's winning illustrations is reproduced in

The New York Times' special fall children's books issue." Hopes to award plaques to winning illustrators and their publishing house editors in the future.

IRMA SIMONTON BLACK AWARD, Publications/Communications Division, Bank Street College of Education, 610 W. 112th St., New York NY 10025. (212)663-7200. Chairman: William H. Hooks. Annual. Purpose: To honor the author and illustrator of an outstanding young children's book. "Entries are judged for a blend of excellence in story line, language and illustration." No entry fee. Entry deadline: "Publishers submit books between Nov. 15 and Jan. 1."
Acceptable Work: Published, illustrated children's books.
Awards: "A scroll presented in May and Maurice Sendak's honor Medallion on books."

CA 80, Communication Arts Magazine, Box 10300, 410 Sherman Ave., Palo Alto CA 94303. Executive Editor: Jean A. Coyne. Annual awards. Purpose: to give international recognition to outstanding designers, art directors and copywriters. Entry fee: $6/single units; $12, print series; $12, single broadcast commercial; $18, broadcast commercial series. Entry deadline: July.
Acceptable Work: Any advertising or design work that was produced or published between July 1, 1979, and June 30, 1980. Categories include Consumer Magazine Advertising, Consumer Newspaper Advertising, Trade/Business Advertising, Poster, Record Jacket, Packaging/Labeling, Trademark, Letterhead, Company Literature, Self-Promotion, Book, Editorial, TV Advertising, Radio Advertising and Miscellaneous (greeting cards, display, signage, interiors, calendars, menus, anything not covered in other categories).
Awards: Winning entries reproduced in the *CA Annual*, a 260-page special issue of *Communication Arts* published in December. Winners also given "Award of Excellence" certificate.

CERTIFICATE OF DISTINCTION, Art Direction Magazine, 10 East 39th St., New York NY 10016. (212)354-0450. Creativity Show Manager: Ray Morrison. Entry fee: $4. Application deadline: June.
Acceptable Work: Open to advertising artists, illustrators and designers.

DUCK STAMP CONTEST, U.S. Fish and Wildlife Service, Audiovisual Office, Dept. of the Interior, 18th and C Sts. NW, Washington DC 20240. (202)343-5611. Contact: Bob Hines. Annual award. Purpose: to select the design for the following year's duck stamp. No entry fee. "Contest closes October 15."
Acceptable Work: Illustrations of any living species of North American ducks or geese. Correct color, anatomy, action and habitat required. Work cannot be copied from previously published art or photos. Open to illustrators, graphic designers, painters and wildlife artists. Any medium okay; 5x7 with 8x10 mat.
Award: One sheet of 30 stamps of the artist's design; face value is $225. Award is for 1st place only.

JIM MERRELL RELIGIOUS LIBERTY MEMORIAL, Merrell Enterprises, 1500 Massachusetts Ave. NW, Washington DC 20005. Contact: Jesse H. Merrell, president. Annual. Purpose: To honor newspaper work which "best defends, promotes and advances the cause of religious liberty as guaranteed by the First Amendment." No entry fee or limit to number of entries. Entry deadline: March 30.
Acceptable Work: Editorial cartoons, news stories, editorials and columns published in the previous calendar year.
Awards: $1,000 for best editorial cartoon; $1,000 for best news story, column or editorial.

NATIONAL COUNCIL OF COLLEGE PUBLICATIONS ADVISERS (NCCPA), Box 11429, Columbia SC 29211. (803)777-6802. Contact: Reid Montgomery. Annual contest for cartoons in college publications. No entry fee. Entry deadline: June. Submit entries on sheets of paper or light cardboard no larger than 8½x11".
Acceptable Work: Cartoons must have appeared in college publications since July 1, 1978. There are two categories to be judged: editorial cartoons and comic strip cartoons. Any student publication in the U.S. may submit no more than 3 cartoons from any one student in each of the divisions.
Awards: First, second and third places will be named in each of the two divisions, with possible honorable mentions. Announcement of the winners will be made at the national convention of college publications advisers. Winning cartons will be published in national journalism magazines.

THE NATIONAL FOUNDATION FOR HIGHWAY SAFETY CONTEST, Box 3043 Westville Station, New Haven CT 06515. President: W.H. Veale. Annual contest. Editorial cartoonists eligible. No entry fee. "Entry blanks not required. We will acknowledge receipt of entries when received." Entry deadline: January 31st.

Acceptable Work: Must depict any phase of "Driving Carries a Moral Responsibility": depicting drinking driving, speedsters, tailgaters, bright-lighters, thoughtless and careless operation of a car." Send three clip sheets and glossy prints of cartoons.
Awards: $100 U.S. Savings Bond. The National Foundation for Highway Safety may reproduce entries without profit in the interests of highway safety, certifying the sources.

JAMES D. PHELAN AWARDS IN ART, San Francisco Foundation Awards Office, 425 California St., Suite 1602, San Francisco CA 94104. Awards Coordinator: Susan Kelly. Annual competition conducted by a San Francisco foundation. Purpose: to honor outstanding California-born artists age 20 through 40. No entry fee. Entry deadline: undetermined.
Acceptable Work: Medium undetermined for 1981 contest.
Awards: First prize: $1,500. Runner-up receives $1,000. A showing of the work is held.

PRINT COMPETITION, American Graphics Gallery Inc., Box 448A, Village Station, New York NY 10014. (212)924-3362. President: Catryna Ten Eyck. Monthly award. Juried. Purpose: to provide recognition for little-known American printmakers. No entry fee. No entry deadline.
Acceptable Work: Fine art original prints, at least 200 square inches in size, in limited editions not exceeding 100 numbered copies.
Awards: Winning entries are published in quarterly journal sent to print club members and offered for sale to members. Send 9x12 SASE (54¢ postage) for entry information and sample copy of *American Graphics.*

SOCIETY OF ILLUSTRATORS SCHOLASTIC COMPETITION, 128 E. 63rd St., New York NY 10021. Instructors should write: Chairman. Annual award. Purpose: to encourage and assist talented college-level art students. Charges entry fee. Entry deadline: February.
Acceptable Work: Open to college-level art students.
Awards: Over $10,000 in cash grants.

WORLD PRINT, Box 26010, San Francisco CA 94126. Contact: Trisha Garlock, director. (Sponsored by World Print Council, exhibition held at San Francisco Museum of Modern Art, traveling exhibition through Smithsonian Institution Traveling Exhibition Service.) Triennial show (which also offers awards). No entry fee. Return fee. Write for prospectus.
Acceptable Work: Prints.

Organizations of Interest

The following national and regional organizations are related to the art field and of interest and benefit to the fine art and commercial artist. We have included their purpose and activities to inform you better how they might serve you.

Association with professional groups can help build your professional image. In fact, inclusion in a membership directory increases your visibility and might lead to assignments.

If you are interested in a more complete list of associations, arranged by state, consult the "Artist's Associations in the U.S.A." (available for $4 plus tax and postage from The Boston Visual Artists Union, Inc., 77 N. Washington, Boston MA 02114).

ALLIED ARTISTS OF AMERICA INC., 15 Gramercy Park S., New York NY 10003. President: William D. Gorman.
Purpose: To further the cause of the contemporary American artist through our annual exhibition each fall in New York City, and through our educational programs of demonstrations.
Eligibility: Applicants must be sculptors or painters. Active membership in Allied Artists of America is by invitation. The society also has an associate membership category. Write for details.

AMERICAN INSTITUTE OF LANDSCAPE ARCHITECTS, 602 East San Juan Ave., Suite 1, Phoenix AZ 85012. (606)277-0096. President: Robert R. Cardoza.
Purpose: The advancement of education and skill in the art of landscape architecture as an instrument of service in the public welfare and to promote good professional practice.
Eligibility: Applicants must be landscape architects or other people engaged in the commercial or educational aspects of landscaping.

THE ART DIRECTORS CLUB INC., 488 Madison Ave., New York NY 10022. (212)838-8140. President: William Taubin.
Purpose: To promote and elevate the profession of art directing.
Offerings: An annual exhibition and publishes an annual on the materials exhibited.
Eligibility: Applicants must be art directors of advertising firms or magazine or book publishing firms. Associate and junior members are animators, illustrators, photographers, graphic designers, educators, journalists, etc.

ARTISTS EQUITY ASSOCIATION, 3726 Albemarle NW, Wasington DC 20016. (202)244-0209. President: Michael C. Gast.
Purpose: A collective action organization for professionals in the visual arts dedicated to economic and social change. Publications include *Artists Equity News*; a series of "action kits" on topics of concern to visual artists; model contracts. Offers major medical, hospital indemnity and life insurance (available at group rates); group legal services.
Eligibility: Applicants must be working professionally in the visual arts. Associate membership open to all who support AEA principles.

ARTISTS RIGHTS TODAY, INC., 250 W. 57th St., Room 615, New York NY 10019. (212)581-5335. President: Rubin L. Gorewitz. Executive Director: Carolyn N. DeLisser.
Purpose: To provide new rights for artists by legislation and other legal procedures and correcting inequities in existing laws.
Eligibility: "All artists and people interested in the arts are eligible for membership."

BOARD REPORT, Box 1561, Harrisburg PA 17105. (717)774-5413. Publisher: Drew Allen Miller.
Purpose: To promote the profession of graphic design and visual communications. Publishes *Board Report Newsletter*, *Designer's Compendium* and *Trademark Trends*.

CALIFORNIA WOMEN'S ART GUILD, Box 496, Forestville CA 95436. (707)887-2173. President: Michelle Lunsford. Estab. 1978.
Purpose: "To promote women's art through shows and through the media. We also catalog women's art through slide registry, and keep resource files on women's shows and art-related

projects." Shows include The Northern California Women's Art Festival & Crafts Exhibition held in Santa Rosa, California; and one membership-only show/year.
Eligibility: Open to all California women artists in any media. Membership dues are $10/year.

CARTOONISTS GUILD, 156 W. 72nd St., New York NY 10023. (212)873-4023. President: Michael C. Witte (through 12/31/81). Executive Director: Ron Wolin.
Purpose: To safeguard and promote the interests of freelance cartoonists; raise the basic rate of payment for cartoons; effect the assignment of all secondary rights, both foreign and domestic, to the cartoonist; introduce and secure acceptance by publications of "The Cartoonists and Media Joint Code of Professional Practices and Ethics"; create new market areas for cartoons and cartoonists; provide a forum for exchange of information and discussion of problems relating to cartooning; and increase public appreciation of cartooning as an art form.
Committees: Market Promotion, Media Relations. Publications: *CG Newsletter*, bimonthly; has also published cartoon collections, including *Animals Animals Animals* (Harper & Row) and *The Art in Cartooning--75 Years of American Magazine Cartoons* (Scribners), both in hard and paperback editions; the *Syndicate Survival Kit*, a study of major syndicates' contracts, with Guild comments and recommendations; and *An Introduction for Cartoonists to the New Copyright Law*. The latter two publications are available from the Cartoonists Guild for $6.00 and $4.75, respectively, including postage and handling charges.
Eligibility: "Any individual actively and professionally engaged as a practicing cartoonist in any of the various fields of cartooning, such as magazine cartooning, book illustration, comic strips and panels, advertising, animation, TV, public relations and sales promotion is eligible." Offers both a full and apprentice membership.

FEDERAL DESIGN COUNCIL, Box 7537, Washington DC 20044. President: Elaine S. Hamilton. Estab. 1970. Purpose: The Federal Design Council is a professional society of government designers engaged in the management, direction or production of visual communications programs.
Eligibility: Applicants must be animators, illustrators, cartoonists, photographers, graphic or interior designers, sculptors or painters.

FOUNDATION FOR THE COMMUNITY OF ARTISTS, 280 Broadway, Suite 412, New York NY 10007. (212)227-3770. President: Elliott Barowitz. Estab. 1971. Purpose: A national organization for research and reporting on artists' problems and advocacy of the rights of artists. Activities include the *Artworkers News, Health Hazards*, an art hazards resource center, a printing facility, a health insurance program for artists and an internship program.
Eligibility: "Anyone who pays the $15 membership fee is eligible for membership."

GRAPHIC ARTISTS GUILD, 30 E. 20th St., New York NY 10003. (212)982-9298. President: Gerald McConnell. National organization with area chapters in L.A., San Francisco, Atlanta, Boston and Detroit.
Purpose: The G.A.G. is a guild of professional artists from every area of the graphic arts field committed to promoting their professional and economic interests. Offers group insurance plans, publications and talent directories. Also offers seminars on various topics: marketing, business practices; National and local newsletters.
Eligibility: Applicants must be animators, illustrators, cartoonists, photographers, graphic designers, book designers, textile designers, technical illustrators, children's book designers, audiovisual designers, letterers, retouchers, mechanical and keyline, and fashion, general, scientific medical and advertising illustrators.

GRAPHIC ARTS AGENCY, 12121 Wilshire Blvd., Suite 100, Los Angeles CA 90025. (213)820-3791. President: C. Holman.
Purpose: A national employment and search firm representing over 300 employers for permanent and freelance jobs. Clients: nationwide design firms, major corporations, advertising agencies, motion picture studios, and book and magazine publishers. The employers pay all fees; there is never a charge to the independent contractor (artist). Mail resume and 20 nonreturnable 35mm slides in a plastic slide sheet; no glass mounts. Also offers speaker/conducts workshops regarding putting together portfolios, interviews, the job market in the West, Midwest and the East, etc.
Eligibility: Specializes in the placement of graphic designers, packaging designers, annual report designers, collateral designers, exhibit designers, commercial interior designers, space planners, advertising agency art directors, advertising agency creative directors, marketing executives, industrial and product designers, illustrators and production staff.

MUSEUM OF CARTOON ART, Comly Ave., Port Chester NY 10573. (914)939-0234. President: Mort Walker.

Purpose: "We serve as a central location where cartoons are protected for posterity, studied, discussed and appreciated." The museum has over 50,000 original cartoons. The archives and library are available on an appointment basis.
Offerings: The permanent exhibit features work by about 1,000 different cartoonists and informative displays on the history of cartoons, how cartoons are made, and the different ways cartoons are used. The museum also offers courses in cartoon production and appreciation. Members are entitled to a yearly subscription to the quarterly magazine *Cartoonist Profiles*, free admission to the museum, and a 20% discount on specialy selected artwork, books and other cartoon-related items available to members only.
Eligibility: Applicants are cartoon enthusiasts. Membership dues are $20/individual or $30/family.

NATIONAL CARTOONISTS SOCIETY, 9 Ebony Ct., Brooklyn NY 11229. (212)743-6510.
Purpose: To advance the ideals and standards of the profession of cartooning and to stimulate interest in the art of cartooning.
Eligibility: Applicants must be professional cartoonists earning the major portion of their living as cartoonists.

NATIONAL SCULPTURE SOCIETY, 15 East 26th St., New York NY 10010. (212)889-6960. President: Granville W. Carter.
Purpose: Encouragement of creation of American sculpture; clearinghouse for all information about American sculpture. Publishes *National Sculpture Review*, a quarterly magazine, as well as annual illustrated exhibition catalogs.
Eligibility: Applicants must be sculptors, patrons, architects or art historians.

SCULPTORS' SOCIETY OF CANADA, 1750-B Avenue Rd., Toronto, Ontario, Canada M5M 3Y9. President: Irene Blogg. Estab. 1928. Purpose: To promote the art of sculpture and assist sculptors as professionals.
Eligibility: Applicants must be sculptors.

THE SOCIETY OF AMERICAN GRAPHIC ARTISTS INC., 32 Union Square, New York NY 10003. (212)260-5706. President: Gerson Leiber.
Purpose: Upgrading and preserving quality and standards of fine printmaking by exhibitions, demonstrations, competitions, lectures, etc.
Eligibility: "Fine printmakers or artists who make prints meeting our standards are eligible for membership."

SOCIETY OF CHILDREN'S BOOK WRITERS, Box 296, Los Angeles CA 90066. President: Stephen Mooser.
Purpose: To assist those in the children's book field, in particular writers and illustrators.
Eligibility: Anyone with an interest in children's literature is eligible for membership.

SOCIETY OF ILLUSTRATORS, 128 E. 63rd St., New York NY 10021. (212)838-2560. President: Warren Rogers.
Purpose: Professional and educational organization for illustrators.
Eligibility: Applicants must be illustrators.

VOLUNTEER LAWYERS FOR THE ARTS, 36 W. 44th St., New York NY 10036. (212)575-1150. Executive Director: Judith N. Stein, Esq.
Purpose: To provide free legal assistance and information to artists (with an income of $7,500 or less) and nonprofit art organizations. Publishes *Art and The Law* (subscription price, $15/year), quarterly journal; *Fear of Filing 1980; Tax Guide for Artists*; and other publications of interest to artists and art organizations.
Eligibility: All artists and organizations are eligible for membership. The $25 minimum membership fee includes a free subscription to *Art and The Law*.

Glossary

Acceptance (payment on). The artist is paid for his work as soon as the buyer decides to use or publish it.
Airbrush. Small pencil-shaped pressure gun used to spray ink, paint or dyes to obtain graduated tonal effects on art or for photo retouching.
Ben-day. An artificial process of shading line illustrations, named after its inventor.
Biennially. Once every two years.
Bimonthly. Once every two months.
Biweekly. Once every two weeks.
Calligraphy. The art of fine handwriting.
Camera-ready. Art that is completely prepared for copy camera plate making.
Cartography. The production of maps, including construction of projections, designs, compilation, drafting and reproduction.
Color separation. Process of preparing artwork for the printer by separating one color from another by using overlays of black or color negatives for each color.
Commission. A. Percentage of retail price taken by a sponsor/salesman on artwork sold. B. Assignment given to an artist.
Comprehensive. Complete sketch of layout showing how a finished illustration will look when printed. (Sometimes called comp.)
Direct mail package. Sales or promotional material that is distributed by mail. Usually, it consists of an outer envelope, a cover letter, a brochure or flyer, and a postpaid reply card or order form with business reply envelope.
Gag Line. The words printed, usually directly beneath, a cartoon. (Sometimes called caption.)
Graphic art. General term for the arts connected with engraving and printing.
Halftone. Reproduction of a continuous tone illustration with the image formed by dots produced by a camera lens screen.
International Postal Reply Coupon. Can be purchased at the post office and enclosed with artwork sent to a foreign buyer to cover his postage cost when replying.
Keyline. Identification, through signs and symbols, of the positions of illustrations and copy for the printer.
Kill fee. Portion of the agreed-on price the artist receives for a complete work that was assigned but which was subsequently canceled.
Layout. Arrangement of photographs, illustrations, text and headlines for printed material.
Line drawing. Illustration done with pencil or ink using no wash or other shading.
Logotype. Name or design of a company or product used as a trademark. (Sometimes called logo.)
Mechanicals. Paste-up or preparation of work for printing.
Mural. A picture, especially a large one, painted on a wall or ceiling.

Muslin. Made of muslin, a sample created to show how a final garment will appear.
Offset. Printing process in which a flat printing plate is treated to be ink-receptive in image areas and ink-repellent in non-image areas. Ink is transferred from the printing plate to a rubber plate, and then to the paper.
Overlay. Transparent cover over copy, where instructions, corrections or color location directions are given.
Panel. In cartooning, refers to the number of boxed-in illustrations, i.e. single panel, double panel or multipanel.
Paste-up. Procedure involving coating the backside of art, type, photostats, etc., with rubber cement or wax and adhering them to the proper positions on the mechanical board. The boards are then used as finished art by the printer.
Point-of-purchase. Display device or structure located with the product in or at the retail outlet; it advertises the product and is intended to increase sales of the product.
Publication (Payment on). The artist is paid for his work when it is published.
Query. Letter of inquiry to an editor or buyer eliciting his interest in a work you want to do or sell.
Royalty. An agreed percentage paid by the publisher to the artist for each copy of his work sold.
Second (reprint) rights. The artist (or owner of the art's rights) sells the right to reprint an already published artwork.
Semiannual. Once every six months.
Semimonthly. Once every two weeks.
Semiweekly. Twice a week.
Simultaneous rights. The artist sells the right to use his work simultaneously to more than one party.
Simultaneous submissions. Submission of the same artwork to more than one potential buyer at the same time.
Speculation. Creating artwork with no assurance that the buyer will purchase it or reimburse expenses in any way, as opposed to creating artwork on assignment.
Spot drawing. Small illustration used to decorate or enhance a page of type, or to serve as a column ending.
Storyboard. Series of panels which illustrates a progressive sequence of graphics and story copy for a TV commercial, film or filmstrip. Serves as a guide for the eventual finished product.
Tabloid. Newspaper that is about half the page size of an ordinary newspaper and which often contains news in condensed form and many photographs.
Tear Sheet. Published page containing an artist's illustration, cartoon, design or photograph of work.
Type spec. Determination of the size and style of type to be used in a layout.
Velox. Photoprint of a continuous tone subject that has been transformed into line art by means of a halftone screen.
Wash. Thin application of transparent color, or watercolor black, for a pastel or gray tone effect.

Index

A

B

C

D

E F

G

H I

M

N O

P

Q R

T

U V W